COMPUTER APPLICATIONS FOR HANDLING LEGAL EVIDENCE, POLICE INVESTIGATION AND CASE ARGUMENTATION

Law, Governance and Technology Series

VOLUME 5

Series Editors:

POMPEU CASANOVAS, *Institute of Law and Technology,
UAB, Spain*

GIOVANNI SARTOR, *University of Bologna (Faculty of Law-CIRSFID) and
European University Institute of Florence, Italy*

Scientific Advisory Board:

For further volumes:
http://www.springer.com/series/8808

COMPUTER APPLICATIONS FOR HANDLING LEGAL EVIDENCE, POLICE INVESTIGATION AND CASE ARGUMENTATION

Volume 2

by

Ephraim Nissan

Goldsmiths' College, University of London, UK

with a chapter
by the VIRTOPSY team;

a chapter by Richard Leary;

sections by Jonathan Yovel;
by John Zeleznikow with Andrew Stranieri and John
Yearwood, or with Richard Leary and Wim Vandenberghe;
by Louis Akin; and by Jeroen Keppens;

and sections co-authored
by S. Eyal Shimony and E. Nissan;
by Aldo Franco Dragoni and E. Nissan; and by
Carmelo Asaro, E. Nissan, and Antonio A. Martino.

Foreword by John Zeleznikow

 Springer

Dr. Ephraim Nissan
Department of Computing
Goldsmiths' College
University of London
London, SE14 6NW
England
ephraimnissan@hotmail.com

Printed in 2 volumes
ISBN 978-90-481-8989-2   ISBN 978-90-481-8990-8 (eBook)
DOI 10.1007/978-90-481-8990-8
Springer Dordrecht Heidelberg London New York

Library of Congress Control Number: 2011940957

Printed on acid-free paper

Springer is part of Springer Science+Business Media (www.springer.com)

This book is dedicated to the memory of Marco Somalvico (1941–2002). The thematic connection to the subject of this paper is provided by his encouragement – after a talk on ALIBI which as being his guest, I gave at my alma mater, the Technical University of Milan – to persist and further develop this direction of research, which on the evidence of the talk he considered very promising.[1] What I owe to Marco Somalvico is much more than that.[2]

---

[1] The next step in my actual induction into the discipline of AI & Law was the warm reception that Prof. Antonio Martino gave a talk of mine on ALIBI in Lisbon in 1989. I had originally been thinking of it mainly as an AI planning system for the generation of explanations; the latter also still is a thriving area of research in artificial intelligence.

[2] Cf. Nissan (2003i, 2007d); Colombetti, Gini, and Nissan (2007, 2008a, 2008b); Nissan, Gini, and Colombetti (2008 [2009], 2009a, 2009b).

Foreword

As a thirteen year old boy, the only articles I would read were the sporting columns of Melbourne daily newspapers. My mother was exasperated, how could she get her son to read books. Then she hit upon an excellent idea – *may be he would read novels by Sherlock Holmes.*

From that day in 1963, I became a voracious reader of stories about Sherlock Holmes – not only the countless short stories and four long stories, but also anything the author of the Holmes' stories, Sir Arthur Conan Doyle had written. And my interest included books about other detectives (such as Poirot and Maigret) and related movies.

But despite my interest in detective stories, for the next thirty-seven years I did not exhibit any interest in forensic science.[3] Then, in late 2000, Colin Aitken, then a reader in statistics at the University of Edinburgh, offered me the position as research director of a new centre for forensic statistics and legal reasoning. Having accepted the exciting position, I needed to explore the domain of forensic statistics and legal reasoning. And what an exciting trip it was.

When I arrived at the University of Edinburgh, I realised that Sir Arthur Conan Doyle had been a medical student there. One of his professors was Dr. Joseph Bell, a forensic pathologist. Bell was the man who inspired the character of Sherlock Holmes and shared many qualities with the famous detective. Thus we opened the Joseph Bell Centre for Forensic Statistics and Legal Reasoning. Its remit was to analyse, evaluate, interpret and present evidence using the skills in artificial intelligence, law and statistics from the University of Edinburgh, Glasgow Caledonian University and the Lothian and Borders Police Force Forensic Science Laboratory. Our goal was to develop software for the mathematically sound and legally permissible interpretation of scientific evidence. Then we needed to communicate and represent this knowledge to lawyers and juries at the trial stage. This requires interactions between different agencies – many police forces, forensic science laboratories, procurators fiscal, judges, advocates and juries.

The first areas of research at the Joseph Bell Centre for Forensic Statistics and legal reasoning were:

---

[3] As opposed to artificial intelligence for law (AI & Law).

- the definition and description of legal procedures for building a case based on evidence;
- the identification and application of mathematically acceptable techniques for interpreting and drawing conclusions from forensic evidence;
- the determination of the validity of conclusions drawn from analogous data or from a particular data sample;
- the investigation of the possibility of a common source for several samples of forensic significance;
- the identification and analysis of risk factors as part of the European anti-fraud initiative;
- the representation and implementation of all the above on a computer in an accessible format;
- the development of legal decision support systems.

The construction of such computer systems is a daunting task. Our initial approach has been to build small-scale knowledge-based systems in specific domains. Projects undertaken were:

(1) the value of trace evidence in linking a scene to a suspect, or a scene to a scene;
(2) the assessment of cross-transfer evidence;
(3) protocols for determination of sample size in criminal investigations;
(4) the reliability of eyewitness testimony;
(5) the examination of trends in European financial fraud;
(6) the role of statistical evidence in cases of suspected excess deaths in a medical context;
(7) the role of statistical evidence in cases of suspected credit card fraud; and
(8) the distinction between homicide, suicide and lawful deaths.

But the most daunting question was how could we integrate the vast multitude of knowledge required to undertake such a gigantic task. In his monumental book, *Computer Applications for Handling Legal Evidence, Police Investigation, and Case Argumentation,* Dr. Ephraim Nissan addresses this task. Rather than investigate biology, chemistry, law or statistics, Nissan focuses upon using computer techniques to organise the evidence and to enhance the analysis of forensic evidence. But even this is a major task, as can be seen by the size of his monograph.

Dr. Nissan's book of about one thousand three hundred pages investigates large areas of law, computer science, and some statistics, also addressing topics in the forensic disciplines, but mostly leaving the significant biological and forensic science topics to other treatises. See however the important Chapter 9 by the VIRTOPSY team in Bern. As Dr. Nissan states in his preface, his book provides an overview of computer techniques and tools for handling legal evidence, police intelligence, crime analysis or detection, and forensic testing, as well as investigating the modelling of argumentation and narratives. Whilst, over the past decade, there have been numerous publications discussing how computers can be used to evaluate legal evidence, Dr. Nissan's monograph is the first book to attempt this task. We are very grateful for the monumental book he has produced.

Dr. Nissan commences by investigating how one can reason with evidence. He looks at both logical and statistical models for modelling evidence and conducts an in depth investigation of his ALIBI system and Paul Thagard's work on the Claus von Bülow Trials, using ECHO, a Coherence Network, and Bayesian networks. He also informs readers about the Bayesian controversy among legal scholars. Becoming aware of the arguments put forth by Ron Allen is crucial, for readers entering the field covered by this book, whether one sides with the Bayesians, or accepts the critique. It is important to realise the reference-class problem, itself a source of disagreement among forensic statisticians.

Chapter 3 involves a detailed investigation of argumentation. Argumentation has been used in knowledge engineering in two distinct ways; with a focus on the use of argumentation to structure knowledge (i.e. non-dialectical emphasis) and with a focus on the use of argumentation to model discourse (i.e. dialectical emphasis). Dialectical approaches typically automate the construction of an argument and counter arguments normally with the use of a non-monotonic logic where operators are defined to implement discursive primitives such as *attack, rebut,* or *accept.*

In applications of argumentation to model dialectical reasoning, argumentation is used specifically to model discourse and only indirectly used to structure knowledge. The concepts of conflict and of argument preferences map directly onto a discursive situation where participants are engaged in dispute. In contrast, many uses of argumentation for knowledge engineering application do not model discourse. This corresponds more closely to a non-dialectical perspective. The analysis of argument advanced by Toulmin (1958) does not distinguish dialectical argumentation from non-dialectical argumentation. By illustrating that logic can be viewed as a kind of generalised jurisprudence rather than as a science, Toulmin (1958) advanced a structure of rhetoric that captures the layout of arguments. Jurisprudence focuses attention on procedures by which legal claims are advanced and attacked. Toulmin (1958) sought to identify procedures by which any claim is advanced. He identified a layout of arguments that was constant regardless of the content of the argument.

As well as the important argumentation theory of Toulmin, Dr. Nissan also devotes as much attention to the early work of analysis evidence of John Henry Wigmore. Wigmore developed a graphical method for evidence analysis. Wigmore's evidence rules are still used by many U.S. courts. His graphical method is used by some scholars, such as Dave Schum, Terence Anderson, and William Twining. Dr. Nissan also considers the argumentation schemes of Doug Walton, Katia Sycara (Persuader) and Tom Gordon (Carneades). Chapter 5 discusses in detail the related topic of narratives, considering what artificial intelligence offers for their treatment, as well as related legal scholarship.

Chapter 4 involves a lengthy examination of appropriate decision support systems (it concludes with a section about relevance and formalism, by Jonathan Yovel). As Oatley, Ewart and Zeleznikow (2006) say 'there exists very little literature about predictive models for police decision support'. Early work included the use of neural networks for the prediction of repeat victimisation (Oatley et al., 2002). This research predicted the occurrence of the next crime, and the expected time interval for this perpetration. The best neural network models trained on this data for predicting the next crime achieved an average performance, and it was impossible to find a neural network model for predicting the time interval without either obvious over-training, or extremely poor performance and it is unfortunate that in that earlier study there was no time to use a dataset where the time intervals were not left as single point values.

Until recently, very few computer systems have attempted to make decisions using evidence sources. Tillers and Schum (1998) and Schum (1994) discussed Wigmore's pioneering approach (Wigmore, 1913) to proof in litigation. Wigmore's method of diagramming the body of evidence in a case is the central method behind Walton's (2002) treatise on legal argumentation and evidence. Schum and Tillers (1991) examined marshalling legal evidence. Kadane and Schum (1996) used probability and Wigmore's diagrams of evidence to analyse the trial of the American anarchists Sacco and Vanzetti.[4] There is a controversy about Bayesianism in law. It should not be ignored. Some applications are less controversial; these are not about the judicial decision, or about strength claimed for the evidence in court, but rather for costs/benefits analysis, for the prosecutor to evaluate whether to prosecute, and for subservient tasks that do not affect the evaluation of the evidence (e.g., statistics inside tools for data mining is unlikely to be controversial among legal scholars). The real challenge for the application of artificial intelligence to legal evidence is to produce accounts of plausibility (ones that would take into account narrative coherence) that would not be the irritant that Bayesian accounts are within legal scholarship of evidence.

Various techniques have been used to construct criminal investigation decision support systems. Statistics has been used to analyse evidence (Aitken, 1995; Schum, 1994). Areas investigated include DNA testing, fingerprints, footwear and ballistics.

Chapter 6 involves a very thorough examination of crime data mining. In investigating the topic, Oatley, Ewart, and Zeleznikow stated (2006, p. 24):

> In 2003/2004, approximately 5.9 million crimes were notified to 43 Police Services in England and Wales. Property crimes such as theft and burglary account for 78% of recorded crimes and over 430,000 (14%) of these involve the burglary of a domestic dwelling.
>
> Once notified, the Police must investigate. Sometimes this will constitute only the recording of the details of the offence from the victim. More often, the investigation will comprise a detailed examination of the crime scene, the collection of forensic material and recording of witness and victim statements. This level of process is not just reserved for serious crimes, but is routine practice even for relatively minor ones.
>
> It is apparent that regardless of the level of investigation, a single recorded crime will generate a considerable amount and diversity of information. The challenge is not only to

---

[4] Combining Bayesianism and Wigmore Charts is also what is done in Dawid, Hepler, and Schum's (2011) "Inference Networks: Bayes and Wigmore". Also see Hepler et al. (2007).

store this information, but to use it to facilitate the investigative process. The features of one case at a particular point in time may have little value but the ability to retrospectively interrogate such a comprehensive crime database is a powerful investigative tool.

The value of this technological challenge is best understood through considering the task of the investigator. In general terms, it is worth noting that the detection of crime in many Police Services will involve not just Police Officers, but civilian crime analysts and scene of crimes officers (SOCOs). In respect of crime detection, Canter (2000) describes the nature of forensic decision making. It is how the investigators draw inferences and conclusions from the data they have available in order to embark upon the most appropriate way forward in order to identify and prosecute the culprit.

However, there is an established literature on the problems of information processing and inference that may beset human decision making. It should be evident that decision making with the forensic domain is problematic. This may be a contributory factor in the detection rate for a volume crime such as burglary is as low as 13% of recorded incidents.

Computer Science methodologies have the ability to select and display such information to the investigator. In this way, the salience of crime features is revealed. These are aspects of the crime which have most potential to assist the investigation in a number of ways, including the identification of crime patterns, linking offences and the identification of suspects.

Chapter 7, by Richard Leary, is about the FLINTS software for link analysis. That chapter enables a closer look at one of the kinds of tools that were discussed in Chapter 6. Chapter 8 looks at forensic techniques. Here and elsewhere in the book, one finds coverage of work by my former colleagues at the Joseph Bell Centre for Forensic Statistics and Legal Reasoning. Chapter 8 begins with coverage of research by Jeroen Keppens into the use of model based reasoning to evaluate possible scenarios at crime scenes, whilst a section inside Chapter 4 is concerned with Michael Bromby's ADVOKATE, a system developed to evaluate eye-witness identification. Chapter 8 also discusses the contexts of processing human faces, such as the generation of facial composites. A number of forensic disciplines are covered more concisely, before discussing fingerprint research more extensively. Controversies concerning both fingerprints and DNA are mentioned. Chapter 9 is about virtual autopsies by means of computer imaging, and was authored by a team in Bern.

Dr. Nissan's treatise offers a panoramic view of topics, techniques and tools. It is understandable to forensic scientists, statisticians and practitioners of Artificial Intelligence and Computer Science. Also legal scholars and practitioners will be interested. So will an audience within police science. Appropriate tools for legal professionals and law enforcement agencies are investigated in detail.

In order to deal with hypotheses, representations and tools for the organisation of arguments are useful; therefore research into argumentation is cited, and argumentation tools or methods that are useful for reasoning about the evidence are surveyed. The final part of the book is devoted to data mining and to a variety of forensic techniques. There is a useful glossary (a few of the entries are like brief sections providing additional discussion), and of course the bibliography is very large.

Dr. Nissan has compiled a monumental book. I strongly commend it as a book to be both read and referenced.

Melbourne, Victoria, Australia   John Zeleznikow

Acknowledgements

I am grateful to Ron Allen, Peter Tillers, and Bernard Jackson for specific comments on earlier drafts, to two extremely perceptive anonymous referees of the book the way it was submitted, as well as to an anonymous referee (of a related work) who provided a useful critique from the Bayesian camp (even though I have been trying to be neutral in the Bayesianism controversy among legal scholars or forensic statisticians). I am grateful to John Zeleznikow for sustained encouragement in this project, to Lars Ebert and his co-authors from the VIRTOPSY project in Bern, and to Richard Leary, to Jonathan Yovel, to John Zeleznikow, Andrew Stranieri, John Yearwood, and Wim Vanderberghe, to Louis Akin, and to Jeroen Keppens for their respective efforts in contributing to this volume the texts that appear under their names. Moreover, one of the sections in this book appears under Solomon Eyal Shimony's and my own names, the result of fruitful collaboration years ago. Another section is jointly authored by Aldo Franco Dragoni and myself, also based on a joint project of ours. The section on DAEDALUS, a tool developed by Carmelo Àsaro, is partly based on previous work I co-authored with him and Antonio Martino.

Charlie Frowd kindly provided an explanation about EvoFIT, as well as two screenshots reproduced in this book. Deirdre Hogan of Aprilage in Toronto kindly provided images generated by their age-progression software. Moreover, my gratitude goes to Laurance Donnelly and Alastair Ruffell, for enabling me to find out more about forensic geology. "Polo" Chau, his team leader Christos Faloutsos, and the latter's executive assistant Marilyn Walgora from Carnegie Mellon University generously enabled the reproduction of several images describing the team's NetProbe and Polonium systems. Louis Akin, a crime scene analyst from Austin, Texas, contributed a brief section, as well as several photographs. Richard Leary's chapter also comprises photographs from crime scene analysis, as well as many screenshots of the software he describes. From Milan, Mario Arrigoni Neri of Nova Semantics kindly drew a graph expressly for this book; it appears as Figure 6.1.7.3.2, and is intended in order to clarify a detail from a screenshot from software of his, appearing as 6.1.7.3.1 (for the permission to reproduce this, I also thank Marco Colombetti).

John Zeleznikow wrote the Foreword. Others provided encouraging comments on drafts. As to co-investigators, I am especially grateful to Aldo Franco Dragoni and Eyal Shimony: I present some of the results of joint research with each in turn, previously published as articles. The section about *Daedalus* is mostly based on Asaro, Martino, and Nissan (2001), and is indebted to Carmelo Àsaro's input to that article of ours, apart from *Daedalus* having been programmed by Judge Asaro himself, and all screen snapshots in that section having been made by him. Much reading went into the making of this book, but in particular, reading an excellent book by Jesús Mena (2003) gave me an idea not of replication, but of how to arrange the presentation in my chapter on data mining for criminal investigation or intelligence. Amina Memon's course handouts at her website helped me to better understand how to present the literature about eyewitness psychology.

Attending the workshop on Archaeology and Forensic Science, held at the British Academy in London on 27 February 2007, was very useful. Prof. Aron Vecht's explanations about the chemistry of a forensic application are gratefully acknowledged. Over the years, contacts with other scholars have helped me to improve specific parts of this book as it was taking shape. They include forensic geologists Laurance Donnelly and Alastair Ruffell, as well as Jeimy Cano, whose field of expertise is digital anti-forensics. I gratefully acknowledge extensive help from Mrs. Ann Aldridge, at the Inter-Library Loans Department of the Library at Goldsmiths' College of the University of London. Besides, I am grateful to Yaakov HaCohen-Kerner in Jerusalem for signalling to me a few articles.

Within my own family, this work would not have been possible without my mother's patience and abnegation. Words could not capture a "thank you" big enough. On one dramatic occasion in the early second century C.E., the renowned Rabbi Akiva, in fortuitous circumstances when coming home, introduced to his many pupils the lady to whom, rather than to him – he acknowledged – they owed what he had been able to teach them.[5]

On a very different plane, I acknowledge with gratitude the patience of Nachum Dershowitz, the joint editor with me of a jubilee volume, also published with Springer: that other project, also in its very final phases, had to queue as this one was getting its final touches. Eamonn Martin, a technician, recovered my file system in early 2011, when for weeks it wasn't clear whether the files of this and other projects were affected, which would have required reconstituting much of the work.

At Springer in Dordrecht in the Netherlands, my thanks go to Neil Olivier and Diana Nijenhuijzen. My contacts were initially especially with the former, and afterwards especially with the latter. Their role and patient support have been crucial in respectively the earlier phase and final phase of the process of getting this book accepted and then into shape. At Integra in Pondicherry in India, I thank Manoj

---

[5] There is no reason not to start giving proper citations already in the Acknowledgement section. Accounts of that episode were given in both the *Babylonian Talmud* (in two of its tractates: *Ketubbot* 62b; *Nedarim* 50a; cf. *Shabbat* 59a–b), and the *Jerusalem Talmud* (again, in two tractates: *Shabbat* 6:1, 7d; and *Sotah* 9:15, 24c), as well as in *Avot de-Rabbi Nathan* (in Version A, chapter 6, and in Version B, chapter 12). See however Tal Ilan's (2005) summary of current scholarly interpretations of that story.

Raju, Sangeetha Sathiamurthy, and Gandhimathi Ganesan, who in turn were assiduously in contact with me, during the quite demanding production process. There surely also were, among the typesetters, (to me) anonymous clever hands for whom I do not have a name by which to thank them.

Many persons have contributed to this book, and I had the benefit of advice from several scholars; I am responsible for any conceptual imperfections which remain in this work. Between the undertaking of this writing project, and the submission of the revised manuscript of over 1,500 pages in large type in late May, early June 2011, five years had elapsed. In January and February I was blocked by a computer crash, and it wasn't until February that I was relieved to hear that my file system could be recovered. Even after the recovery, large Word files with many figures belonging to my other writing projects, and which I was checking upon recovery, kept crashing at the press of the 'Save' button, and had to be recovered again from the burnt computer.

Miraculously I would say, the huge file of this book was recovered in good shape, and augmenting it (imagine the apprehension) did not result in the file being damaged by further crashes, even though separate small files had to be provided afterwards, especially footnotes. Needless to say, Since the recovery from the crash I was keeping backups of this book's main file on a very frequent basis. During the autumn of 2011, upon the instructions from the typesetters, I had to redraw many of the figures of this book, to ensure better reproduction. Then during the winter until the early spring, my task of correcting the proofs and providing index entries was very exacting, more exacting than any proof correction I had ever done in decades. It swallowed a huge amount of work in daylight and by night, on occasion into the little hours of the morning.

Come March, I only allowed the festival of Purim the half hour it took me to read aloud the Scroll of Esther in the original Hebrew with the traditional cantillation, as customarily required, and meanwhile, the huge reams of paper never left my kitchen table, except on Friday late afternoons for the entry of the Sabbath (in which case they remained stacked away until the end of the same). On the day after (the normatively joyful festival of) Purim, I was chagrined to find in an email that I was sternly given one more week with weekends at both ends to complete this project. Hardly the 'Thank you' I expected. Even though I tried to obtain a reprieve (a futile attempt), the correction process being curtailed means that typos or instances of misformatting from Chapter 6 to Chapter 9 and beyond (in the Glossary and Bibliography) could not be as thoroughly eliminated as from Chapters 1 to 5 and 10. I beg the benevolence and leniency of the reader for such typos and perhaps instances of misformatting that are left. At least, I hope I managed to catch broken cross-references. Meanwhile, a jubilee volume I had to complete for the Berlin offices of Springer had to wait one year, and I am thankful to my joint editor in that other project, to its many authors, and to the Jubilaris of that book for their patience.

Admittedly, the scope of the book you are now reading is very wide, so ideally there should have been more than one author; the participation of other authors for specific topics responds to this need. Even though the book is large, there still are various things that could be fleshed out. I have tried to take on board all the advice

I was given, within the timescales that this publication project required. Citations could be even more numerous, and the field keeps growing.

Along with the detailed, four-level table of contents, and with the cross-references in many of the entries of the Glossary, also this Subject Index is an important point of entry for accessing information in this book. Making it so detailed was indispensable. A thorough, detailed index is a crucial need for very long books with a broad scope such as this one. The rule of adequacy of the indexing is a linear function,[6] not a constant proportion: the longer the book, the more a thorough subject index becomes absolutely indispensable (obviously, also depending upon the kind of the book: a telephone directory needs no indexing. . .).[7]

The indexing of Chapters 2 to 5 is especially meticulous. Had I been allowed more time, I would have indexed as thoroughly – which was my intention to do - also Chapter 6 (the longest of this book: it takes about 200 pages), and Chapter 8. Hopefully also the indexing of Chapters 6 to 9 will be found to be adequate by the benevolent reader. Some sketchy indexing is also provided for the Glossary. Even just browsing the Subject Index will hopefully awaken the curiosity of those giving it a try. Try 'Forest spotted owlet', 'Walrus', and 'Whale'. Or then try and 'Footwear'. What do they do in an AI & Law book? Check in the index, to find out.

---

[6] The general formula $y = a + bx$ expresses a linear function. Let y be the percentage of a book length to be allocated to adequate indexing.

[7] The formula $y = 0 + 0x$ expresses the particular case of a phone directory.

Contents

Abstract

This book caters to a broad audience, and provides an overview of computer techniques and tools for handling legal evidence, police intelligence, crime analysis or detection, and forensic testing, with a chapter on the modelling of argumentation and its application to these, as well as with a chapter on how to handle narratives by computer. We also briefly address costs and benefits of obtaining more evidence while preparing a case, as a factor in deciding whether to prosecute or to litigate. Notwithstanding a few seminal precursors from the late 1980s, it is only with the new century that the modelling of reasoning on legal evidence has emerged as a significant area within the well-established field of AI & Law (active since the 1970s). An overview such as this one has never been attempted before between two covers. It offers a panoramic view of topics, techniques and tools. It is intended to clarify the broader picture for the specialist, as well as to introduce practitioners of AI or other computer scientists into this subject. For its newcomers, it is essential not to simplistically blunder into such design choices that would results in flaws making the tools unusable by legal professionals, so it is important to be aware of ongoing controversies. Other tools are appropriate for law enforcement, e.g., tools assisting in crime analysis. In order to deal with hypotheses, representations and tools for the organisation of arguments are useful; therefore, research into argumentation is cited, and argumentation tools or methods that are useful for reasoning about the evidence are surveyed. The final part of the book is devoted to data mining, and next, to a panoply of forensic techniques. For example, the book includes a chapter from the VIRTOPSY team in Bern, about how computer imaging can be used in order to plan autopsies by making them less invasive. The large bibliography is preceded by an extensive glossary, being a useful resource for many of the subjects covered in this book. Several of the entries afford an opportunity for further discussion of select topics.

Abstracts of the Chapters

Chapter 1 A Preliminary Historical Perspective

This introductory chapter makes considerations about the thematics, the organisation of the book, and (along very broad lines) the state of the art, the latter's historical development, and its publication forums. The book is organised around three poles: the modelling of reasoning, the modelling of argumentation and its application to narratives, and a cluster of data mining techniques and the specifics of forensic science disciplines. We mention the controversy, among legal scholars, among those willing to accept probabilistic models, and those who want instead a ranking of the relative plausibility of alternative accounts of a legal narratives, without committing to a Bayesian framework. Artificial intelligence is able to contribute to both camps, and has already done so. Bayesian networks are often applied to causality also in the legal domain, but those arguing against probabilistic quantification are at present vindicated by the rise of the plausibility ranking of legal narratives (Section 5.4) within argumentation research (Chapter 3). AI practitioners need to exercise care, lest methodological flaws vitiate their tools in the domain with some legal scholars, let alone opponents in litigation. There would be little point for computer scientists to develop tools for legal evidence, if legal scholars would find them vitiated ab initio. This is especially true of tools that would reason about the evidence in criminal cases, in view of fact-finding in the courtroom: whether to convict or not – this being different from the situation of the police, whose aim is to detect crime and to find suspects, without having the duty of proving their guilt beyond reasonable doubt, which is the task of the prosecutors. Tools helping the prosecutor to predict an outcome and choose whether to prosecute are not as central to the Bayesian controversy, as prescriptive models of judicial decision-making. This chapter also says something about the communities of users that may benefit from advances in AI & Law technology. In particular, we devote some discussion to computer assistance in policing.

Chapter 2 Models of Forming an Opinion

This chapter is concerned with models of reasoning about the evidence. We consider, in turn, "metre models" of the shifts of opinion in the adjudicators' mind as items of information come in, and a distributed belief revision model for such dynamics. We discuss the weight given jury research in North America. Then we consider some seminal computer tools modelling the reasoning about a charge and explanations: Thagard's ECHO (and its relation to Josephson's PEIRCE-IGTT), and Nissan's ALIBI, a planner seeking exoneration and producing explanations minimising liability. A quick survey of Bayesian approaches in law is followed with a discussion of the controversy concerning applications of Bayesianism to modelling juridical decision-making. We quickly sample some probabilistic applications (Poole's Independent Choice Logic and reasoning about accounts of a crime, and next, dynamic uncertain inference concerning criminal cases, and Snow and Belis's recursive multidimensional scoring). Finally, we consider Shimony and Nissan's application of the kappa calculus to grading evidential strength, and then argue for trying to model relative plausibility.

Chapter 3 Argumentation

We begin this chapter about argumentation, by considering types of arguments, and contrast Wigmore Charts to Toulmin's structure of argument. We develop two examples in detail, and then turn to Pollock's inference graphs and degrees of justification. We then discuss beliefs. From Walton's approach to commitment vs. belief and to argument schemes, we turn to Bench-Capon & Atkinson's approach to critical questions concerning a story of alleged crime. We consider arguments in PERSUADER, in *Carneades*, and in *Stevie*. We survey computer tools for argumentation, and computational models of argumentation, especially as far as they relate to legal argument. We distinguish between argumentation for dialectical situations, vs. for structuring knowledge non-dialectically: a section by Stranieri, Zeleznikow, and Yearwood discusses an integration of those two uses of argumentation in a legal context, in the Generic Actual Argument Model (GAAM), also considering a few applications of the latter.

Chapter 4 Computer Assistance for, or Insights into, Organisational Aspects

We first consider computer help for organising tasks relevant for managing the evidence. We consider the Lund procedure, as well as a few tools: *CaseNote, MarshalPlan*, and from Italy's judiciary, *Daedalus*. We develop in particular a discussion of the latter, which is a tool for the examining magistrate and then the prosecution. We then turn to criminal justice information systems, and discuss prosecutorial vs. judiciary discretion. We discuss facets of evaluating costs and benefits, beginning with the costs and benefits while preparing a case (discussing, in turn, the rules of evidence in terms of economic rationality, Alvin Goldman's concept of epistemic paternalism, the Litigation Risk Analysis method, and bargaining in relation to game theory). We then turn to evaluating the effects of obtaining or renouncing a piece of evidence, then to the benefits, costs, and dangers of argumentation, and finally to the costs and benefits of digital forensic investigations. Next, we discuss Bromby's ADVOKATE, for assessing eyewitness suitability and reliability (we also consider the Turnbull rules, and further elaborate on taxonomies of factors). In the section about policing, we consider organisational aspects of intelligence, and the handling of suspects, and deal in turn with organisational problems of police intelligence systems, with handling the suspects (equipment, techniques, and crucial problems), with polygraph tests and their controversial status, with the evidentiary value of self-incriminating confessions being culture-bound rather than universal in juridical cultures, and with computerised identity parades (lineups) and concerns about identity parades. This chapter concludes with a section (by Jonathan Yovel) on relevance, in relation to legal formalism as well as to logic formalism and artificial intelligence. A refutation is proposed, of the argument from the distinction between relevance and admissibility.

Chapter 5 The Narrative Dimension

We begin by discussing legal narratives, and overall narrative plausibility. We consider approaches from the New Evidence scholarship, discuss background generalisations, as well as the impact of modes of communication (the pragmatics of the delivery in court of a legal narrative), and then warn about pitfalls to avoid, in consideration of what controversy within legal scholarship implies about the need for the modelling of legal narratives with artificial intelligence techniques to meet with approval from legal scholars. We then undertake a long overview (in over twenty subsections) of artificial intelligence approaches to narratives. Historically, a legal context for narratives was involved in tools such as BORIS and STARE. Among the other things, we consider the JAMA model, and then conclude the overview with a project from quarters different from those traditionally associated with story-processing in the artificial intelligence research community: namely, Löwe, Pacuit and Saraf's application of mathematical logic to crime stories. We then explain episodic formulae, and develop an example: the controversy concerning a collection of stuffed birds amid allegations that items were stolen and restuffed. We finally consider Bex's approach to combining stories and arguments in sense-making software for crime investigation, and then Bex and Bench-Capon's undertaken project concerning persuasion stories vs. arguments.

Chapter 6 Accounting for Social, Spatial, and Textual Interconnections Link Analysis and Data Mining for Criminal Investigation

This is a chapter about what link analysis and data mining can do for criminal investigation. It is a long and complex chapter, in which a variety of techniques and topics are accommodated. It is divided in two parts, one about methods, and the other one about real-case studies. We begin by discussing social networks and their visualisation, as well as what unites them with or distinguishes them from link analysis (which itself historically arose from the disciplinary context of ergonomics). Having considered applications of link analysis to criminal investigation, we turn to crime risk assessment, to geographic information systems for mapping crimes, to detection, and then to multiagent architectures and their application to policing. We then turn to the challenge of handling a disparate mass of data, and introduce the reader to data warehousing, XML, ontologies, legal ontologies, and financial fraud ontology. A section about automated summarisation and its application to law is followed by a discussion of text mining and its application to law, and by a section on support vector machines for information retrieval, text classification, and matching. A section follows, about stylometrics, determining authorship, hand-writing identification and its automation, and questioned documents evidence. We next discuss classification, clustering, series analysis, and association in knowledge discovery from legal databases; then, inconsistent data; rule induction (including in law); using neural networks in the legal context; fuzzy logic; and genetic algorithms. Before turning to case studies of link analysis and data mining, we take a broad view of digital resources and uncovering perpetration: email mining, computer forensics, and intrusion detection. We consider the Enron email database; the discovery of social coalitions with the SIGHTS text mining system, and recursive data mining. We discuss digital forensics, digital steganography, and intrusion detection (the use of learning techniques, the detection of masquerading, and honeypots for trapping intruders). Case studies include, for example: investigating Internet auction fraud with *NetProbe*; graph mining for malware detection with *Polonium*; link analysis with *Coplink*; a project of the U.S. Federal Defense Financial Accounting Service; information extraction tools for integration with a link analysis tool; the Poznan ontology model for the link analysis of fuel fraud; and fiscal fraud detection with the Pisa SNIPER project.

Chapter 7 FLINTS, a Tool for Police Investigation and Intelligence Analysis
This chapter presents and discusses, in 28 sections, a link analysis tool for the British police, FLINTS. The chapter considers, in turn, the motivations and history of the project; the early beginning resulting in FLINTS 1; identifying "unknown" offend-ers, and systemising it; link detection; more about the first generation of FLINTS; integrations, linking and analysis tools; expanding FLINTS to other police areas; volume crimes and volume suspects; performance monitoring and system identifi-cation; a tour of FLINTS as the user sees it; the intellectual foundations; and what stands out in FLINTS. We turn to a case study in linked burglary. We then discuss forensic decision-making; second-generation FLINTS; access to the system (search-ing vs. surfing); asking questions about people and suspects; asking questions about crimes and events; displaying modified Wigmore Charts, and the graphical results in FLINTS; geographical analysis; temporal analysis; prolific (volume) offenders search; using geography to identify prolific offenders; hot spot searches; vehicle searching; and analytical audit trails.

Chapter 8 The Forensic Disciplines: Some Areas of Actual or Potential Application
We first begin with an artificial intelligence approach to crime scenario modelling once a dead body has been found. We then turn to a panoply of contexts and approaches to the processing of human faces: face recognition methods and tools for identification; foreseeing how aging would affect a face (e.g., of a child who went missing); facial expression recognition; digital image forensics (with doctored photographs); facial reconstruction from skeletal remains; and factors in portraiture analysed in the TIMUR episodic formulae model. Having begun with these two major areas (crime scenario modelling, and face processing), we take a broad view

of the forensic disciplines of expert opinion, and the sometimes controversial role of statistics in them. We then consider the contribution to forensic science of anthropology and archaeology, as well as software tools for human anatomy. Next, we turn to forensic geology and techniques from geophysics; scent-detection and electronic noses; forensic palynology and its databases; computing in environmental forensics; and forensic engineering. Two large sections, each internally subdivided into nine units, conclude this chapter: "Individual Identification", and "Bloodstain Pattern Analysis, and the Use of Software for Determining the Angle of Impact of Blood Drops". The former begins with a history of identification methods, and continues with DNA evidence, and a controversy among statisticians concerning this; we then discuss human fingerprints, and growing skepticism concerning reliability of identification by fingerprints. We then turn to computational techniques for fingerprint recognition, and having surveyed these, we proceed to describe in detail two such techniques.

Chapter 9 Virtopsy: The Virtual Autopsy

This chapter provides an overview of the Virtopsy procedure, a computerised approach to autopsy, lessening the need for invasive examination. Invasiveness results in the loss of evidence, and of the structural integrity of organs; it is also offensive to some worldviews. At the Institute of Forensic Medicine of the University of Bern, the Virtopsy project has unfolded during the 2000s, its aim being the application of high tech methods from the fields of measurement engineering, automation and medical imaging to create a complete, minimally invasive, reproducible and objective forensic assessment method. The data generated can be digitally stored or quickly sent to experts without a loss of quality. If new questions arise, the data can be revised even decades after the incident. This chapter describes technical aspects of the Virtopsy procedure, including imaging modalities and techniques (the Virtobot system, photogrammetry and surface scanning, post-mortem computer tomography, magnetic resonance imaging, post-mortem CT angiography, tissue/liquid sampling), then turning to the workflow of Virtopsy, and to a technical discussion of visualisation. Medical image data are for either radiologists and pathologists, or medical laypersons (such as in a courtroom situation). The final part of this chapter discusses Virtopsy in relation to the Swiss justice system.

Chapter 10 Concluding Remarks

This chapter briefly recapitulates which chapter discussed which topics. Then, in a few diagrams, an overarching view is taken of part of the broad set of domains we have been considering in this book. The themes in the book up to the conclusions chapters are supplemented with a Glossary following Chapter 10, and whose entries are often substantial and contain discussion. The bibliography is very large, as could be expected given the broad scope of the book, along with the latter often delving into details.

Call for Information

Future editions will hopefully appear in due course. I would appreciate it if readers will inform me about their research as it progresses, or their tools as they become available, and would provide me with copy of publications as they appear, in view of possible coverage in a future edition. I can be contacted by email (ephraimnissan@hotmail.com). Readers wishing to use the graphic files or the Latex code for the symbols of episodic formulae (see Section 5.3) are welcome to ask for them; I would be glad to provide copy of such files, and would like to learn about the applications.

List of Section Authors

Louis L. Akin Crime Scene Analyst, Austin, TX, USA, ai@akininc.com

Carmelo Asaro Tribunale della Libertà, Rome, Italy

Ursula Buck Center of Forensic Imaging and Virtopsy, Institute of Forensic Medicine, University of Bern, 3012 Bern, Switzerland

Aldo Franco Dragoni Dipartimento di Ingegneria Informatica, Gestionale e dell'Automazione, Università Politecnica delle Marche, Ancona, Italy

Lars C. Ebert Center of Forensic Imaging and Virtopsy, Institute of Forensic Medicine, University of Bern, 3012 Bern, Switzerland

Gary Hatch Center of Forensic Imaging and Virtopsy, Institute of Forensic Medicine, University of Bern, 3012 Bern, Switzerland

Jeroen Keppens King's College, London, England

Richard Leary Forensic Pathways Ltd.[8], Tamworth, Staffordshire, England, rleary@forensic-pathways.com

Antonio A. Martino Universidad del Salvador, Buenos Aires, Argentina, (emeritus of the University of Pisa, Pisa, Italy)

Ephraim Nissan Department of Computing, Goldsmiths' College, University of London, London, England, ephraimnissan@hotmail.com

Antoine Roggo Center of Forensic Imaging and Virtopsy, Institute of Forensic Medicine, University of Bern, 3012 Bern, Switzerland

Thomas Ruder Center of Forensic Imaging and Virtopsy, Institute of Forensic Medicine, University of Bern, 3012 Bern, Switzerland

Solomon E. Shimony Ben-Gurion University of the Negev, Beer-Sheva, Israel

Andrew Stranieri University of Ballarat, Ballarat, VIC, Australia

---

[8] See for example http://www.forensic-pathways.com/PDFs/FPL_Overview_of_Analytics.pdf

Michael Thali Center of Forensic Imaging and Virtopsy, Institute of Forensic Medicine, University of Bern, 3012 Bern, Switzerland

Wim Vandenberghe Dechert LLP, B-1050 Brussels, Belgium

John Yearwood University of Ballarat, Ballarat, VIC, Australia

Jonathan Yovel Law School, University of Haifa, Haifa, Israel; Yale Law School, Yale University, New Haven, CT, USA

John Zeleznikow Victoria University, Melbourne, VIC, Australia

David Zimmermann Center of Forensic Imaging and Virtopsy, Institute of Forensic Medicine, University of Bern, 3012 Bern, Switzerland

Stefan Zuber Center of Forensic Imaging and Virtopsy, Institute of Forensic Medicine, University of Bern, 3012 Bern, Switzerland

Chapter 6
Accounting for Social, Spatial, and Textual Interconnections

Link Analysis and Data Mining for Criminal Investigation

6.1 Methods

6.1.1 An Introduction

Already the second issue of the new journal *Wiley Interdisciplinary Reviews: Data Mining and Knowledge Discovery* (March/April 2011, vol. 1, no. 2) has featured 'Data Mining and Crime Analysis', an article by oatley and Ewart (2011). In fact, the pool of techniques that goes by the name *data mining* has found, among its many fields of application, also an important role in software for crime detection, crime analysis, and crime intelligence. "Data mining is the process of automated extraction of predictive information from large datasets" (Choudhary, Honbo, Kumar, Ozisikyilmaz, & Misra, 2011, p. 41). "Data mining is the analysis of (often large) observational data sets to find unsuspected relationships and to summarize the data in novel ways that are both understandable and useful to the data owner" (Hand, Mannila, & Smyth, 2001, p. 1).

Historically, there have been artificial intelligence tool prototypes (mainly expert system prototypes) originating in academia, and applied to detecting volume crimes, such as burglary (Lucas, 1986; Charles, 1998). Adderley and Musgrove (2003c, p. 26)[1] explain why such systems were not adopted in practice as operational systems:

---

[1] Richard Adderley is affiliated with the West Midlands Police, and P. B. Musgrove, with the University of Wolverhapton, in England. Their papers (Adderley & Musgrove, 2003a, 2003c) were incorporated into Mena's (2003) good textbook, as sections 1.15 and 6.12. That paper reported about an application of self-organising maps (SOM, i.e., neural networks with unsupervised learning) to linking crimes to perpetrators. The application reported about was clustering offender description for *bogus official burglaries* (also called *distraction burglaries*), i.e., burglaries where the offender gains access to premises by deception, by posturing to somebody innocent (typically, the victim, and typically, elderly) as though they want to gain access for some legitimate purpose, in some false capacity. A commercial data mining package was resorted to (Clementine, from SPSS), using its SOM option. The output was a five-row-by-seven-column table (a map), and the input was 105 offender descriptions, measured by 46 binary variables. The clustering is in the 35 cells of the table: "This allows for a potential of 35 different offenders each committing three crimes. If there were more than 35 offenders, it would force offenders with similar descriptions to be

E. Nissan, *Computer Applications for Handling Legal Evidence, Police Investigation and Case Argumentation*, Law, Governance and Technology Series 5, DOI 10.1007/978-90-481-8990-8_6, © Springer Science+Business Media Dordrecht 2012

While usually proving effective as prototypes for the specific problem being addressed, they have not made the transfer into practical working systems. This is because they have been stand-alone systems that do not integrate easily into existing police systems, thereby leading to high running costs. They tended to use a particular expert's line of reasoning, with which the detective using the system might disagree. Also they lacked robustness and could not adapt to changing environments. All this has led to wariness within the police force regarding the efficacy of AI techniques for policing.

It took the emergence and coming of age of a combined pool of techniques, to make inroads into law enforecement applications (Mena, 2003). *Data mining* has emerged indeed as a major area of research in computing, aiming at finding patterns and connections in huge databases[2] (e.g., Adriaans & Zantinge, 1996). This it does by massively resorting not only to standard *database technology*, but also to *statistical modelling*, and to several branches of *artificial intelligence*, mainly *pattern-matching* and *machine-learning*.

Types of data mining include, for example (Stranieri & Zeleznikow, 2005b):

• *Predictive data mining*: its aim is to learn from sample data in order to make a prediction. Techniques include: *neural networks, rule induction, linear, multiple regression.* See Table 6.1.1.1.
• *Segmentation*: its aim is to automatically group data into groups/clusters; to discover meaningful groups in sample data. Techniques include: *k-means clustering, self-organising maps.* See Table 6.2.1.2.

Table 6.2.1.1 An example of predictive data mining (by kind permission of Stranieri & Zeleznikow, 2005b)

Marriage	Length	Children	Percentage assets to wife
1	30 years	4	50%
2	20 years	2	20%
3	5 years	2	10%
4	10 years	1	70%
5	2 years	0	90

clustered together. If there are fewer than 35 offenders the SOM algorithm could place descriptions of the same offender across a number of cells", while typically some cells remain empty (Adderley & Musgrove, 2003b, pp. 30–31). A police sergeant received the table, and analysed individual cases, i.e., individual clusters, having been "given the brief to decide if there was sufficient evidence in the witness statements and for those crimes that had been solved to say whether there was a possible link between some of the crimes in each cluster" (ibid., p. 31).

[2] "Law-enforcement agencies across the US compile crime statistics using well-established standards such as the FBI's Uniform Crime Reporting System and its successor, the National Incident-Based Reporting System (www.fbi.gov/hq/cjisd/ucr.htm), as well as other criteria defined by jurisdictional needs and requirements" (Chen et al., 2004).

Table 6.2.1.2 An example of segmentation (by kind permission of Stranieri & Zeleznikow, 2005b)	Marriage	Length	Children	Percentage assets to wife
	1	30 years	4	50%
	2	20 years	2	70%
	3	5 years	2	10%
	4	3 years	1	70%
	5	2 years	0	90%

Table 6.2.1.3 An example of summarisation (by kind permission of Stranieri & Zeleznikow, 2005b): if length=30 Percent=50% (66%)	Marriage	Length	Children	Percentage assets to wife
	1	30 years	4	50%
	2	30 years	2	50%
	3	30 years	2	10%
	4	3 years	1	70%
	5	2 years	0	90%

- *Summarisation*: its aim is to automatically present data in a way that makes interpretation easier; that is to say, the aim is to help the user visualise patterns or find associations within the sample data. Techniques include: *associations, visualisation*. See Table 6.2.1.3.
- *Time series*, for forecasting;
- *Text mining.*

Within the scholarly discipline of AI & Law, data mining has not necessarily been applied to matters relating to legal evidence. One comes across such applications that are far away from the concerns of crime detection, or police intelligence or investigation. Take *knowledge discovery from databases* (*KDD*). An especially notable case of the application of *knowledge discovery from legal databases* (a subject covered by Stranieri & Zeleznikow, 2005a) is the prediction of judicial decisions in Australian family law, in order to assist couples that intend to divorce with negotiation and settling. This is a project developed by Andrew Stranieri and John Zeleznikow. This itemisation is reproduced by kind permission from Stranieri and Zeleznikow (2005a):

Field: Family Law in Australia
Task: Predict by percentage the split of assets
      a judge awards husband and wife
Mining technique: Neural network
Data selection: approximately 1000 unreported cases
Data pre-processing: some contradictions removed
Data transformation: restructuring using argument tree
Data mining: 20 neural networks
Evaluation: Resampling with each neural network,
      Prediction of unseen cases.

Another application of knowledge discovery to law, reported about in a brief paper by Pedro Feu Rosa (2000) and surveyed in Stranieri and Zeleznikow (2005a, pp. 12, 228), a Supreme Court Judge in Brazil initiated a program for the resolution of traffic accident disputes. It is called *Judges on Wheels*, which "involves the transportation of a judge, police officer, insurance assessor, mechanical and support staff to the scene of minor motor vehicle accidents. The team collects evidence, the mechanic assess the damage, and the judge makes a decision and drafts a judgement with the help of a program called the 'Electronic Judge' before leaving the scene of the accident. The 'Electronic Judge' software uses a KDD approach that involves data mining tools called neural networks" (Stranieri & Zeleznikow, 2005a, p. 12). Stranieri and Zeleznikow (2005a) itemised this as follows:

Field: Traffic accidents in Brasil
Authors: Feu de Rosa
Task: Predictive. Predict %outcome of traffic case. Used to help ensure
        consistency amongst Judges who spend more time on the road
Mining technique: Neural network
Data selection: initially synthetic commonplace cases, later actual cases
Data pre-processing: little detail
Data transformation: little detail
Data mining: 1 neural network
Evaluation: little detail

The application of *data mining* to police or Internal Revenue Service investigations has received an excellent treatment in depth in a book by Jesús Mena (2003), *Investigative Data Mining for Security and Criminal Detection*. In 2010, another book of his was forthcoming: *Behavioral Forensics: How to Conduct Machine Learning Investigations*. In the present Chapter 6, we clearly do not make an attempt to compete with those books. (The present chapter is likely to provide readers with motivation to read them, too.) We try here to integrate the subject of investigative data mining into the full picture that emerges from the book you are reading now.

Huge amounts of data, some of it potentially amenable to yield information relevant to crime investigation, pose a challenge that can be met by combining several categories of techniques[3] from computer science:

- *Link analysis* is an interactive technique, visualising graphically networks of entities and events. This may make it easier to grasp networks of irregular transactions, or of suspected offenders. See Sections 6.1.2 and 6.2, and Chapter 7 below. For example, in the United States, several government agencies use NETMAP[4]:

---

[3] Also including, e.g., *association rules*, for which see fn 36 in Chapter 3.

[4] NETMAP is a tool of ALTA Analytics (http://www.altaanalytics.com/). It can query databases by using the SQL query language. "The main shapes of NETMAP link charts are those of a wagonweel

"Financial crime analysts and investigators use tools like NETMAP to begin to define parts of financial transactions as they relate to individuals, organizations, and locations, including dates, amounts, institutions, sources, and ID-numbers", considering that "[j]ust in a day more than $1 trillion is wired through New York City alone" (Mena, 2003, p. 84).

- *Database* technology (e.g., for example, techniques handling *relational databases*), for organising the data of individual databases, and to carry out and basic kinds of retrieval (which are themselves embedded in sophisticated techniques from, e.g., *machine learning*: see below).
- *Data preparation* (manually) for the various data mining techniques; but also whatever computing technology offers for *data integration* and, if the data are multimedial, *data fusion* methods, so that benefits can be derived from combining different sources of information that moreover may be of different kinds.
- *Data warehousing*, i.e., conflating various sources of information (transactional, demographics) so that a cohesive view emerges of individuals (e.g., customers) of interest to the user. See Section 6.1.7.1 below.
- *Text mining*, a kind of data mining that incorporates *free-text information retrieval* and *natural-language processing* techniques, so that a mass of textual documents – notwithstanding its mainly being unstructured text[5] – can be probed into, looking for significant information: "Unlike traditional data mining, which deals with databases that follow a rigid structure of tables containing records representing specific instances of entities based on relationships between values set in columns,[6] text mining deals with unstructured data" (Mena, 2003, p. 8).[7] In the 2000s, data mining techniques were used, e.g., on the Enron database of emails, and this is an example of the need to handle data in the form of free text. Srihari (2009) discussed text mining for counterterrorism.

---

format, with color conveying very important factors", but is "also supports some additional layouts, including circular, column, row, row/column, bullseye, and Cartesian charts" (Mena, 2003, p. 101).

[5] Even though free-text may be inside a document that is itself divided into chapters and sections, and is therefore structured in that particular sense, such a body of text is nevertheless "unstructured" for the purposes of the search at hand. Structures has to emerge from the analysis.

[6] Values set in columns is what you get in a database relation, the columns corresponding to the attributes which are each a header of a column. It is by contract to tabular database, that we can speak of free-text databases.

[7] Mena discusses NASA's *Perilog* text mining tool that analysed thousands of free-form narrative reports on aviation accidents (Mena, 2003, pp. 128–130), and MITRE's *TopCat* text mining tool that goes through a collection of documents, identifies different topics, and displays the key players for each topic (ibid., pp. 130–132). *TopCat* can also be used with a *summarisation filter.* Automated summarisation is an active area of research: Mani (2001) is a book on the subject; Nissan (2003h) is a long review of that book, and we adapted it into a section below.

- *Pattern-recognition* techniques,[8] variously applied, and oftentimes resorting to *neural networks* or then to *genetic algorithms* (*evolutionary computing*).[9]
- *Statistical modelling* (modelling analyses include, especially, *linear regression*),[10] and *statistical prediction techniques.*
- *Neural networks* (see Section 6.1.13 below) are a popular kind of representation[11] for tasks involving *classification, prediction,* or *profiling,* and all three categories of application are quite important for investigative data mining; one advantage of neural networks for prediction over statistical methods such as regression, is that neural networks can manage with a relatively small training sample[12]; "this makes them ideal in criminal detection situations because, for example, only a tiny percentage of most transactions are fraudulent" (Mena, 2003, p. 9). According to the kind of neural networks adopted, we may have *supervised learning* or *unsupervised learning.* Supervised learning is (Callan, 1999, p. 225)[13]:

> A type of learning that can be applied when it is known to which class a training instance belongs. With supervised learning we know what the network should produce as output

---

[8] *Pattern recognition* is "The creation of categories from input data using implicit or explicit data relationships. Similarities among some data exemplars are contrasted with dissimilarities across the data ensemble, and the concept of data class emerges. Due to the imprecise nature of the process, it is no surprise that statistics has played a major role in the basic principles of pattern recognition" (Principe, Euliano, & Lefebvre, 2000, p. 643).

[9] *Genetic algorithms* (the subject of Section 6.1.16.1 in this book) are "Global search procedures, proposed by John Holland, that search the performance surface [as optimisation techniques are conceptualised as search in a multidimensional surface indeed], concentrating on the areas that provide better solutions. They use 'generations' of search points computed from the previous search points using the operators of crossover and mutation (hence the name)" (Principe et al., 2000, p. 642).

[10] *Linear regression* is the process of fitting a cloud of samples by a linear model. The *fitting* is done by minimising the sum of the square of the deviations.

[11] There exists many kinds of neural networks. For example, Principe et al. (2000) is a good textbook that comes along with a compact disk of computer simulations.

[12] Of course, neural networks are now part of the standard curriculum of computer science. But Mena explains nicely how the basic properties of neural networks are useful for investigative data mining: "A key concept about working with neural networks is that they [unless they are self-organising maps] must be trained, just as a child or a pet must, because this type of software is really about remembering observations. If provided an adequate sample of fraud or other criminal observations, it will eventually be able to spot new instances or situations of similar crimes. Training involves exposing a set of examples of the transaction patterns to a nneural-network algorithms; often thousands of sessions are recycled until the neural network learns the pattern. As a neural network is trained, it gradually becomes skilled at recognizing the patterns criminal behavior and features of offenders; this is actually done through an adjustment of mathematical formulas that are continuously changing, gradually converging into a formula of weights that can be used to detect new criminal behavior or other criminals" (Mena, 2003, p. 10). This kind of neural networks can be used for clustering individuals with similar profiles, and as mena points out, neural networks were used (recognising kerosene) in arson investigations in California, and more in general "to detect and match the chromatographic signature of chemical components" (ibid.).

[13] Apart from Callan (1999), other textbooks specifically devoted to *artificial neural networks* include, e.g., Zurada (1992).

for each training instance. If the network does not produce the correct output then the learning algorithm uses this information to adjust the network (usually by adapting the weights).

- *Unsupervised learning*,[14] which can be done by resorting to various techniques, one of which is *in self-organising maps*[15]: these are a kind of neural networks that do not require training at all; they are useful for detecting clusters in a mass of data.[16] In investigative data mining, *unsupervised learning* techniques have been

---

[14] See Section 6.1.13.14 below. Unsupervised learning in neural networks is the subject of a paper collection edited by Geoffrey Hinton and Terrence Sejnowski (1999). Duda, Hart, and Stork (2001b) provide a discussion of unsupervised learning and clustering. A nice concise formulation is found in the Wikipedia entry (http://en.wikipedia.org/wiki/Unsupervised_learning):

In machine learning, unsupervised learning refers to the problem of trying to find hidden structure in unlabeled data. Since the examples given to the learner are unlabeled, there is no error or reward signal to evaluate a potential solution. This distinguishes unsupervised learning from supervised learning and reinforcement learning.

Unsupervised learning is closely related to the problem of *density estimation* in statistics. However unsupervised learning also encompasses many other techniques that seek to summarize and explain key features of the data. Many methods employed in unsupervised learning are based on data mining methods used to preprocess data.

Approaches to unsupervised learning include:

- *clustering* (e.g., *k-means, mixture models, k-nearest neighbors, hierarchical clustering*),
- *blind signal separation* using *feature extraction* techniques for *dimensionality reduction* (e.g., *Principal component analysis, Independent component analysis, Non-negative matrix factorization, Singular value decomposition*).

Among neural network models, the *self-organizing map* (SOM) and *adaptive resonance theory* (ART) are commonly used unsupervised learning algorithms. The SOM is a topographic organization in which nearby locations in the map represent inputs with similar properties. The ART model allows the number of clusters to vary with problem size and lets the user control the degree of similarity between members of the same clusters by means of a user-defined constant called the vigilance parameter. ART networks are also used for many pattern recognition tasks, such as automatic target recognition and seismic signal processing.

---

[15] *Self-organising maps* were introduced by Kohonen (1990). Unlike most neural networks, Kohonen maps don't need supervised training. That is to say, they don't need to be taught what the correct output is. A tasks they are usually made to perform is *clustering* (by measuring distance), whereas other kinds of neural networks are rather suitable for *classification*. In applications to crime detection, neural networks with supervised training are "used when a sample of cases, profiles, or crimes is available for training a network to recognize the patterns of criminal behavior. For example, an auction site such as eBay.com could use this type of network to detect the probability of criminal activity because it probably has in its servers records of transactions where fraud was perpetrated" (Mena, 2003, p. 162). Solan, Horn, Ruppin, and Edelman (2005) described unsupervised learning of natural languages.

[16] Robert Callan pointed out (1999, p. 133): "The first decision to make when choosing a network model is the type of model, and this is dependent on whether or not the classification of training data is known. For example, training a system to recognize customers with poor credit rating is likely to involve supervised learning because a financial lender will have a record of whether a debt from a past customer has been paid. Sometimes there is no information as to the class into

used for clustering analysis,[17] such as in the U.S. CATCH project (Computer Aided Tracking and Characterization of Homicides), and Birmingham's West Midlands Police application to modelling the behaviour of sex offenders, or then, to burglaries by offenders who gain access to premises by deception.[18]

- *Classification trees.* "Classification and regression trees are machine-learning methods for constructing prediction models from data. The models are obtained by recursively partitioning the data space and fitting a simple prediction model within each partition. As a result, the partitioning can be represented graphically as a decision tree.[19] Classification trees are designed for dependent variables that take a finite number of unordered values, with prediction error measured in terms of misclassification cost. Regression trees are for dependent variables that take continuous or ordered discrete values, with prediction error typically measured by the squared difference between the observed and predicted values" (Loh, 2011, p. 14). Wei-Yin Loh's paper (2011) is an overview of the subject.[20]

---

which data fall, and sometimes the classification is fuzzy. For instance, it is often difficult to give precisely the state of health of a machine such as a helicopter. Currently much effort is being devoted to monitoring the health condition of helicopters. On-board sensors log information which is later downloaded to a database on the ground for analysis. Assuming that a helicopter operates most of its time in a good state of health, the downloaded information can be analysed to see if it varies significantly from previous flights. If there is something different in the data then it might be time to examine the aircraft more closely to see if a fault exists. Cluster analysis is often used in such situations. The Kohonen self-organizing feature map is an unsupervised neural network that has much in common with statistical clustering."

[17] Apart from traditional clustering techniques (see e.g. Kaufman & Rousseeuw, 2005), also consider approximate clustering, which is often appropriate for data mining, and includes *fuzzy clustering* (e.g., Joshi & Krishnapuram, 1998 for Web mining; and Feng & Chen, 2004 as used in image processing), and *rough clustering* (Lingras & Peters, 2011). These are respectively based on Lotfi Zadeh's *fuzzy set theory* (Zadeh, 1965) and Zdzislaw Pawlak's *rough set theory* (Pawlak, 1991). [Fuzzy approaches are the subject of Section 6.1.15 in thid book. Algorithms for rough set theory were presented by do Carmo Nicoletti and Quinteiro Uchôa (2001). Geng and Chan (2001) presented an algorithm for automatically generating a case base from a database by using similarity based rough approximation.] "Traditional clustering partitions a group of objects into a number of nonoverlapping sets based on a similarity measure. In real world, the boundaries of these sets or clusters may not be clearly defined. Some of the objects may be almost equidistant from the center of multiple clusters. Traditional set theory mandates that these objects be assigned to a single cluster. Rough set theory can be used to represent the overlapping clusters" (Lingras & Peters, 2011, p. 64). There also exists hybrid rough-fuzzy clustering (Maji & Pal, 2007; Mitra, Banka, & Pedrycz, 2006).

[18] The latter project has been described concisely in the very first note of Section 6.1.1 above, based on Adderley and Musgrove (2003a, 2003b).

[19] Lior Rokach and Oded Maimon's (2008) is the first book entirely dedicated to *decision trees* in *data mining.*

[20] *Tree-based methods* such as *decision trees* or *classification trees* are popular in machine learning. Cf. Kothari and Dong (2002), Chen, Wang, and Zhang (2011). "Almost all classification tree construction algorithms such as ID3 [(Quinlan, 1986)], C4.5 [(Quinlan, 1993)], and CART [(Breiman, Friedman, Olshen, & Stone, 1984)] employ a top-down heuristic search using recursive partitioning because the enumeration of all 2^n possible partitions is essentially intractable. Starting from a heterogeneous set (in terms of the variation in the class label or outcome variable)

- Other *machine-learning* techniques,[21] detecting patterns (segmenting and classifying the data according to a desired output), and yielding (for example) behavioural profiles of suspects.[22] Machine learning can be used "for extracting rules and decision trees from the data for predicting crimes and profiling

---

of training samples (root node), each feature (or predictor) is evaluated using a statistic to determine how well it classifies the training samples by itself. The best feature is selected to split the training samples to descendant nodes. The whole process is recursively repeated to split the descendant nodes until some prespecified stopping criteria are met. This search algorithm is greedy because it never backtracks to reconsider its previous choices. Usually, the tree-growing step is followed by a bottom-up pruning step, which removes unessential subree3 s to avoid overfitting. [. . .] The critical step in tree growing is to select the best feature to split a node." (Chen et al., 2011, pp. 55–56). Segal and Xiao remark (2011, p. 80): "Since the mid-1980s, tree-structured (or recursive partitioning) classification and regression methods have enjoyed widespread popularity. This followed the publication of the Classification and Regression Trees (*CART*) monograph [(Breiman et al., 1984)] that established a rigorous framework for such techniques, and convincingly illustrated one of their greatest virtues: interpretability. Tree-structured methods (TSM) produce interpretable prediction rules by subdividing data into subgroups that are homogenous with respect to both predictors and response. For continuous responses, as considered here, simple (terminal) subgroup summaries (typically means) serve as predictions. The interpretability of the attendant prediction rules derives from (1) the natural, recursive fashion by which predictors are employed in eliciting subgroups, (2) the accessibility of companion tree diagram schematics, and (3) the availability of predictor importance summaries. However, by the mid/late-1990s a serious deficiency of TSM was evident: modest predictive performance, especially in comparison with emerging, flexible competitors such as support vector machines (SVM) [on which, see in Sections 6.1.9.3, 6.2.1.3 and 8.7.3.1 in this book]. In a series of papers, Breiman developed a strategy for remedying this shortcoming: create an ensemble of trees, where each tree in the ensemble is grown in accordance with the realization of a random vector and obtain predictions by aggregating (voting) over the ensemble." In fact, Segal and Xiao's paper (2011) is about *multivariate random forests*. "Random forests seek to effect such correlation reduction [between the quantities being averaged] by a further injection of randomness. Instead of determining the optimal subdivision of a given subgroup of a (constituent) tree by evaluating all allowable partitions on all predictors, as is done with single-tree methods [as well as in a technique called] bagging [(Breiman, 1996)], a subset of the predictors drawn at random, is employed." (Segal & Xiao, 2011, p. 80).

Let us say something more about *bagging*. "Bagging is a method for improving the predictive power of classifier learning systems. It forms a set of classifiers that are combined by voting, by generating replicated bootstrap samples of the data. Bagging produces replicate training sets by sampling with replacement from the training instances. The multiple classifiers are then combined by voting to form a composite classifier. In bagging, each component classifier has the same vote" (Stranieri & Zeleznikow, 2005b). Cf. fn 31 below. Another method is *boosting*. By contrast to bagging (ibid.): "Boosting improves the predictive power of classifier learning systems by adjusting the weights of training instances. It manipulates the training data in order to generate different classifiers. Boosting uses all instances at each repetition, but maintains a weight for each instance in the training set that reflects its importance; adjusting the weights causes the learner to focus on different instances and so leads to different classifiers. The multiple classifiers are then combined by voting to form a composite classifier."

[21] For *machine learning*, see e.g. Mitchell (1997). It is significant that in the subtitle of their book *Data Mining*, Witten and Frank (2000) singled out machine learning: *Practical Machine Learning Tools and Techniques with Java Implementations.*

[22] Marketers value, and the public sometimes resents another application of data mining: *personalisation*, resulting in potential customers being targeted with personalised promotion (making the right offer at the right time), suiting the profile generated about them from data provided willingly or unwittingly.

perpetrators" (Mena, 2003, p. 220). With respect to ordinary computer programs, machine-learning algorithms offer the advantage of being able to improve their performance by acquiring experience at carrying out the task at hand, or to learn by being shown. Machine learning is most useful in order to automate a manual process, and in particular, this often is a process of searching. By questioning the data, machine-learning algorithms discover which attributes discriminate more, and are therefore more useful for classification. They are therefore useful for *segmenting a database*, by detecting key features or intervals. "Machine-learning software can segment a database into statistically significant clusters based on a desired output, such as the identifiable characteristics of suspected criminals or terrorists" (Mena, 2003, p. 11). An additional advantage of machine learning at detection, over the use of neural networks, is that whereas the latter's inner workings are hidden from the user (a black box), machine learning algorithms are more transparent: "they can generate graphical decision trees or IF/THEN rules, which an analyst can understand and use to gain important insight into the attributes of crimes and criminals" (ibid., p. 12). The branches of the decision tree each identify a cluster. Or then, the output may be IF/THEN rules, enabling (for example) an automated monitoring system to score individuals involved in transactions, and to issue (depending on the kind of circumstances) differently calibrated alerts.

- *Multiagent* technology[23] which enables to manage a society of autonomous *software agents*, themselves each comprising three basic abilities: communication skills, knowledge, and performing tasks. See Section 6.1.6 below.

Feature extraction is described nicely by Chaoji, Hoonlor, and Szymanski (2010):

> Within the data mining community, the term *feature extraction* is commonly used for techniques that identify features relevant to the application at hand. Within this context, the term feature has been loosely used for attributes of data that can range, for instance, from keywords for text documents to principle eigenvectors[24] for high dimensional genetic data. Feature extraction is broadly considered to be composed of two sub-tasks — *feature construction* and *feature selection* [(Guyon & Elisseeff, 2003)], each addressing one of the two main challenges of the problem. The first challenge results from the presence of a large amount of noise in the data which results in construction of ineffective features. The second challenge results from the large number of features usually generated. The features are ranked based on optimality criteria — such as information gain, kernel[25] and novelty detection — and only the top-ranked features are used to avoid the curse of dimensionality and enhance generalization capabilities [(Evangelista, Embrechts, & Szymanski, 2006)].

---

[23] A standard textbook is Wooldridge's (2002) *An Introduction to Multiagent Systems.*

[24] For *eigenvectors*, see in fn 26 below.

[25] S.v. *kernel methods*, Stranieri and Zeleznikow (2005a, Glossary) provide this definition (from the perspective of *machine learning*): "Kernel estimates smooth out the contribution of each observed data point over a local neighbourhood of the point. Nearest neighbour and locally weighted regression are approaches for approximating target functions. Learning involves storing the presented training data and when a new query instance is encountered, a set of similar related instances is retrieved from memory and used to classify the new query instance. The kernel function is the function of distance that is used to determine the weight of each training example.

The output of investigative data mining techniques may be obtained either on the initiative of the users, or then on the initiative of monitoring software, "data mining models which can issue alerts to security, law enforcement, and other regulatory personnel" (Mena, 2003, p. 8).

Mena's *Behavioral Forensics* has refined the conceptual classification and the terminology, by distinguishing (to say it with chapter headings in the table of contents) between "Extractive Forensics: Link Analysis and Text Mining", "Inductive Forensics: Clustering Incidents and Crimes", and "Deductive Forensics: Anticipating Attacks and Pre-Crime".[26]

Also *profiling* is deductive. This is *offender profiling*, also known as *criminal profiling*, or *psychological profiling*, or *criminal personality profiling*. It is based on past behaviours, and is carried out by criminal profilers in the employment of the police in order to identify suspects, as well as by forensic psychologists. Profiling, too, can usefully resort to pattern recognition techniques from data mining (Mena, 2003, p. 19). Profiling, however, must only be done downstream of the forensic analysis of all the available physical evidence. It is from the physical evidence that a criminal profiler can infer offender behaviour, victim characteristics (victimology), and crime-scene characteristics. It is quite important to profile the victims, too, not only the offenders. In his *Criminal Profiling: An Introduction to Behavioral Evidence Analysis*, Brent Turvey (1999) provided this definition: "A deductive criminal profile is a set of offender characteristics that are reasoned from the convergence of physical and behavioral-evidence patterns within a crime or a series of related crimes".

Apart from physical anthropology characteristics that the criminal profiler would try to guess out (age, body features, sometimes race), socio-cultural characteristics (marital status, occupation, living arrangements, communal or national background), props (vehicle driven), psychological traits (intelligence level, psychosexual maturity, motivating factors), personal past (arrest record), the profiler would also try to deduce provocation factors that may drive the suspect out, and which interrogation techniques are likely to work best with the suspect once apprehended. The profiler would also try to suggest appropriate interrogation techniques if the suspect is already in custody, or if the suspect was already identified and is about to be apprehended. Out of basic data features, several can be obtained with the help of demographic databases or demographic data providers. Mena (2003, pp. 20–22) identifies in such reliance on database what makes profiling a good application of data mining, and he further suggests that "the ideal profiling method is a hybrid of machine learning and human reasoning, domain experience, and expertise" (ibid., p. 21).

Whereas kernel methods define the degree of smoothing in terms of a kernel function and bandwidth, nearest neighbour methods let the data determine the bandwidth by defining it in terms of the number of nearest neighbours."

[26] Appendix A in Mena (2003, pp. 379–414) provides an amazing wealth of addresses on the Web, of interest to the subject of his book. That appendix is entitled "1,000 Online Sources for the Investigative Data Miner".

6.1.2 Social Networks, and Link Analysis

6.1.2.1 Social Networks and Their Visualisation

Social network analysis is a mathematical discipline applied to the social sciences, and it has its own forums, such as the journal *Social Networks*.[27] Social network analysis is the branch of sociology that deals with the quantitative evaluation of an individual's role in a group or community, by analysing the network of connections between that individual and others. The techniques of social network analysis are specifically designed to explore relational data (rather than attributive ones): the relational aspects of social structures. The discipline made its appearance in the mid-20th century, its mainstream being originally developed by sociometric analysts, by researchers from Harvard who modified some techniques of graph theory, and by anthropologists from Manchester who used these developments to investigate the structure of community relations.[28] Central concepts of social network analysis include: *centrality, density, components, cliques,* and *distances.* Sparrow (1991, pp. 264–265) listed and examined briefly six different notions of centrality[29] from the network analysis literature[30]:

---

[27] On *social network analysis* (*SNA*), see, e.g., Breiger's overview (2004), Linton Freeman's four-volume set (2007), Aggarwal (2011), Newman (2010), Scott (1991), Burt (1980), Newman (2003), Backstrom, Huttenlocher, Kleinberg, and Lan (2006), Kempe, Kleinberg, and Tardos (2003, 2005), and Lu, Korniss, and Szymanski (2009). Exploratory visualisation of social networks is the subject of, e.g., Brandes, Raab, and Wagner (2001), but within an application to decision-making research in a real-case study: they applied some SNA techniques for the study the patterns of decision making itself. They represented the process of decision making can be represented as the network of interactions between the actors involved in the process. This involved a mix of communication, policy network studies and status visualisation techniques. In their paper, Brandes et al. (2001) studied the privatisation, in East Germany, of the shipbuilding industry and of a major steel plant, EKO Stahl AG. Their aim was to find what kind of policy making structures evolved during the decision processes and how powerful are the actors' positions in these networks. Brandes et al. (2001) identified the actors who could make an impact on decisions on the privatisation in these cases, such as the European Commission, the federal ministries of finance and economics, parties within the state parliament, the board of directors and the supervisory board of the Treuhandanstalt, the local governments with enterprise sites, the metal workers' union, competitors in West Germany among others. Status visualisation was used in order to help to analyse the two types of ties which were identified as significant for policy making in these cases, namely "obligation of report" and "consideration of interest". I drew this example from a report by Popov (2003), from a project (*WaterTime*) in which I was involved myself (Nissan et al., 2004).

[28] For the history of the discipline, see e.g. Linton Freeman's (2004) *The Development of Social Network Analysis: A Study in the Sociology of Science.*

[29] Concerning *centrality,* also see, e.g., Pfeiffer and Neville (2011).

[30] For Sparrow's (1991) identification of which notions of centrality is applied in practice in link analysis diagrams used by crime analysis, see the text citing fn 210 towards the end of Section 6.2.5. Also see fn 61, towards the end of Section 6.1.2.3. On notions of centrality, cf. e.g. Freeman (2008).

1. *Degree*: the degree of a node in a social network is the number of other nodes to which it is directly linked, but if the graph is a directed network with arrows, then the degree is the number of paths coming from a node (rather than reaching the node).

2. *Betweenness*: "The 'betweenness' of a node is defined as the number of geodesics (shortest paths between two other nodes) which pass through it. It is a measure of how important any one node might be to effective communication within, or operation of, the network" (Sparrow, 1991, p. 264; cf. Freeman, 1979).

3. *Closeness*: "The concept of 'closeness' picks as central to a network the node which minimizes the maximum of the minimal path-lengths to other nodes in the network. That is, the central node becomes the node of minimum radius, where the radius of a node is defined as the longest of its shortest connecting paths to other nodes" (Sparrow, 1991, p. 264; cf. Freeman, 1979).

4. *Euclidean centrality after multidimensional scaling*: such centrality is apparent in two- or three-dimensional plots of the results of multidimensional scaling (cf. Kruskal & Wish, 1978).

5. *Point strength*: "A node's 'point strength's is defined as the increase in the number of maximal connected network subcomponents upon removal of that node. So it is a measure of how much network fragmentation would be caused by removal of that node" (Sparrow, 1991, pp. 264–265; Cf. Capobianco & Molluzzo, 1979/1980).

6. *Business*: the business of a node "is a measure of the local information content when the network is seen as a communication network" (Sparrow, 1991, p. 265).[31]

Sinai (2006) applied social network analysis to combating terrorism.[32] Schum (1987) discusses evidence and inference for the intelligence analyst. In criminal

---

[31] This notion of the business of a node in a network was defined by Stephenson and Zelen (1989). Sparrow explains (1991, p. 265): "To obtain some precise numerical scale upon which to measure 'business', one can imagine all nodes firing (transmitting) along each of their links once per unit time. Choose some retransmission ratio (between zero and one), whereby every received transmission is retransmitted one period later but with some loss of intensity, by each node. Keep the system firing repeatedly until the total information content of each node and each link reaches equilibrium. This will occur asymptotycally and monotonically both for directed and undirected networks. Then measure each node's total transmission intensity per unit time. The equilibrium transmission intensities represent useful relative, but not absolute, indicators of 'how busy' each node might be."

[32] It is interesting to note that social networks can be extracted that are not necessarily about real-life characters. Within computational linguistics, David Elson, Nicholas Dames, and Kathleen McKeown, all of them from Columbia University in New York, reported (Elson, Dames, & McKeown, 2010) about a project which resulted in a method for extracting social networks from literary fiction. Their application was to 19th-century British novels and serials. One of the novels is a story of murder in a rural setting, namely, the third edition of Thomas Hardy's *Tess of the d'Urbevilles* (1891). They also analysed the third edition of *Oliver Twist* by Charles Dickens (1837), which is of about a criminal gang; the first edition of Bram Stoker's *Dracula* (1897); and the first edition of Robert Stevenson's *The Strange Case of Dr. Jekyll and Mr. Hyde* (1987);

investigation, intelligence analysts oftentimes apply concepts from social networks, namely (Sparrow, 1991), criminal networks among individual suspects, gangs, bank accounts, and tools such as weapons and vehicles.

Sparrow (1991) discussed the application of social network analysis to criminal intelligence. In Sparrow's article, "Section 4 examines several network analytic concepts — for instance, centrality,[33] equivalence, strong and weak ties — and explores their application to law enforcement" (Sparrow, 1991, p. 253). Sparrow also remarked that as "criminal intelligence databases can be huge, with many thousands of nodes" (ibid., p. 261), this mandates the use of sparse matrix techniques in computation.[34] He also noted (ibid., p. 262) that because of the incompleteness of data on criminal networks, this requires the use of techniques for statistical inference from incomplete graphs (e.g., Frank, 1978; Friedkin, 1981). Criminal networks are

---

for all three novels, they categorised the setting as being urban. "We present a method to automatically construct a network based on dialogue interactions between characters in a novel. Our approach includes components for finding instances of quoted speech, attributing each quote to a character, and identifying when certain characters are in conversation. We then construct a network where characters are vertices and edges signify an amount of bilateral conversation between those characters, with edge weights corresponding to the frequency and length of their exchanges. In contrast to previous approaches to social network construction, ours relies on a novel combination of pattern-based detection, statistical methods, and adaptation of standard natural language tools for the literary genre. We carried out this work on a corpus of 60 nineteenth-century novels and serials, including 31 authors such as Dickens, Austen and Conan Doyle. In order to evaluate the literary claims in question, we compute various characteristics of the dialogue-based social network and stratify these results by categories such as the novel's setting. For example, the density of the network provides evidence about the cohesion of a large or small community, and cliques may indicate a social fragmentation. Our results surprisingly provide evidence that the majority of novels in this time period do not fit the suggestions provided by literary scholars, and we suggest an alternative explanation for our observations of differences across novels" (Elson et al., 2010, p. 138). In the visualisation produced by their software, those characters who loom large have their name enclosed in a large ellipse, whereas marginal characters appear in tiny ellipses. A shortcoming is that in order to read the name in the tiniest ellipse, I had to zoom to 800% in their paper's .pdf file in order to read the name 'Susan' in their figure 1, which shows the automatically extracted conversation network for Jane Austen's *Mansfield Park*.

[33] While discussing how crime analysts used to draw the social networks of organised crime, he mentioned that, among the other things, they were aiming at "representing 'centrality' within the organization by 'centrality' on the chart" (Sparrow, 1991, p. 256). Buth whereas he found this pictorially reasonable, he also pointed out: "But it employs a most unsophisticated concept of centrality, namely the selection of the point or points of 'maximum degree' (those with the most established connections). Moreover the context in which it is applied makes the use of maximum degree potentially misleading: the determination of centrality will depend upon *who you know most about*, rather than *who is central or pivotal in any structural sense*. The danger in this practice is that it may incline an agency to pay closest attention to those it already knows most about, individuals who may not in fact be the principal characters. The practice may therefore serve to perpetuate unfortunate and misleading biases in the initial intelligence collection" (ibid.).

[34] Writing around 1990, Sparrow pointed out: "Some network analysis algorithms do claim to be able to handle very sizeable networks. For example the NEGOPY program (Richards and Rice, 1981) claims to handle up to 30,000 links or so. But it contains an unfortunate reliance on a one-dimensional interim stage in the analysis of groups and cliques, which will inevitably render its results suspect when applied to networks of any complexity" (Sparrow, 1991, p. 262).

dynamic, not static. And their boundaries are fuzzy[35] (Sparrow, 1991, pp. 262–263), and "the fuzzy boundaries render precise global network measures (such as radius, diameter, even density) almost meaningless.[36] With the global measures go some, but not all, measures of centrality" (ibid., p. 263).

Brandes et al. (2001, section 1) remarked about the importance of *visualisation*, when researching social networks, since the early beginning of that discipline:

> From the very beginning, visualization has been an essential tool in the analysis of social networks. In his groundbreaking work, Moreno (1953)[37] relied extensively on graphical representations, and there is hardly any mentioning of alternatives to visual analysis of sociometric data. In fact, he attributes the breakthrough of the sociometric movement to a

---

[35] *Fuzzy* in the ordinary lay sense, not in the sense of fuzzy set theory. Fuzzy logic is the subject of Section 6.1.15 in this book.

[36] "Meaningless" as usually understood. Beside the points raised in the debate on probabilities in law, we may tentatively glean some insight from the following concept from discrete mathematics. Fred Roberts, a mathematician from Rutgers University who has specialised in applying discrete mathematics to social and biological systems, has defined *meanigless statements* as follows; I am quoting from a seminar abstract: "A statement involving scales of measurement is called *meaningless* if its truth or falsity can depend on the particular versions of scales that are used in the statement". He went on to "develop the mathematical foundations of a theory of measurement that will allow us to make the notion of meaningless statement precise", and to "give a variety of examples of meaningless statements. For example", he showed "that the conclusion that a given solution to a problem is optimal might be meaningless and in particular we will describe such results" from graph theory or operations research "for shortest path problems, for graph coloring problems arising from frequency assignments, and for scheduling problems". Roberts also considered "limitations (through functional equations) on the possible averaging functions which allow meaningful comparisons in different applications such as choosing new technologies, comparing the abilities of different groups of students, etc."

[37] Moreno's classic book *Who Shall Survive* was originally published in 1934 and later in 1953 and 1978. It is still considered a must for serious psychodrama students. This work was in the vanguard of sociology and social psychology as it developed prior to, during and following the Second World War. Jacob Levy Moreno (1889–1974) is considered to have been the father of psychodrama, sociometry, and group psychotherapy. René Marineau authored a biography of Moreno (Marineau, 1989). Moreno was born in Bucharest (the son of Moreno Nissim Levy, a merchant from Pleven, Bulgaria, where a plaque marks J. L. Moreno's ancestral home) and moved to Vienna as a child, where he became doctor of medicine. In his autobiography, Moreno claimed that while a medical student, in 1912, he told Sigmund Freud: "You meet people in the artificial setting of your office. I meet them on the street and in their homes, in their natural surroundings. You analyze their dreams. I give them the courage to dream again." He moved to the United States in 1925, and worked in New York, at Columbia University, and also at the New School of Social Research. "In 1932, Dr. Moreno first introduced group psychotherapy to the Americal Psychiatric Association. For the next 40 years he developed and introduced his Theory of Interpersonal Relations and tools for social sciences he called 'sociodrama', 'psychodrama', 'sociometry', and 'sociatry'. In his monograph entitled, 'The Future of Man's World', he describes how he developed these sciences to counteract 'the economic materialism of Marx, the psychological materialism of Freud, and the technological materialism' of our modern industrial age" (http://en.wikipedia.org/wiki/Jacob_L._Moreno). In the centennial year of Moreno's birth, 1989, the *Journal of Group Psychotherapy, Psychodrama & Sociometry* published its Vol. 42. Moreno's *Invitations to an Encounter*, of 1914, is considered to have been influential for Martin Buber's I-Thou philosophy. "Moreno is also widely credited as one of the founders of the discipline of social network analysis, the branch of sociology

showing of sociometric charts at the 1933 convention of the Medical Society of the State of New York (Moreno, 1953, p. xiii).

While early network analysis was largely based on plausible, yet informal, concepts and qualitative data exploration, a wealth of formal concepts has been subsequently developed to provide quantitative empirical evidence for substantive research questions. For a comprehensive overview of such methods see Wasserman and Faust (1994); Scott (2000). Sadly, visualization techniques have not kept up with this progress in measurement, leading to a divergence of analysis and graphical presentation that can be traced through the history of social network visualization (Klovdahl, 1981; Brandes, Kenis, Raab, Schneider, & Wagner [1999]; Freeman, 2000a).[38]

Brandes et al. (ibid.) advocated the visualisation not only of connections within a social network, but also of quantitative data:

While today visualizations are used to present network data, quantitative results of network analyses are still typically given in tabular form. However, aggregate indices in general are insufficient to fully appreciate and understand the structural information contained in network data. In network analysis, it is therefore desirable to integrate graphical presentation of the actual network and results from quantitative analyses.

Brandes et al. (ibid.) also made a remark about there only being a minority of social networks that can be mapped onto a geographical representation[39]

Many types of networks are traditionally visualized using point-and-line representations (Bertin, 1983). Since few networks have an underlying spatial layout, their elements need to be positioned in some other meaningful way. While the tedious work of manually positioning the elements is out of the question even for small to medium-size networks, the primary design principle implemented in currently available software for automatic layout is clarity. That is, the focus is on readability rather than visual communication of substantive content.

In addition to the inherent difficulty of laying out an abstract network in a readable way (see Di Battista et al., 1999; Kaufmann and Wagner, 2001 for overviews of algorithms for the visualization of networks in general), there is also the issue of confidence. Who is going to comfortably draw conclusions from complex aggregate data, if it is difficult to relate them to the original network data and if it is unclear how much the drawing of the network leads to wrong impressions and succeedingly to wrong interpretations?

At any rate, it does matter that there exist such situations that visualisation could exploit the spatial layout of the social network.

Brandes et al. (2001, section 2) also stated:

Commonly used network visualization tools such as Pajek (Batagelj and Mrvar, 1998), KrackPlot (Krackhardt et al., 1994), or MultiNet (Richards, 1999) are designed to produce general purpose visualizations focusing on the ease of perceiving connectedness

that deals with the quantitative evaluation of an individual's role in a group or community by analysis of the network of connections between them and others. His 1934 book *Who Shall Survive?* contains some of the earliest graphical depictions of social networks" (Wikipedia, ibid.).

[38] Freeman (2000a) was published in an e-journal. Cf. Freeman (2000b, 2005, 2009).

[39] Incidentally, Cornell University computer scientist Jon Kleinberg and his collaborators have published the paper 'Inferring Social Ties from Geographic Coincidences' (Crandall et al., 2010). Among the other things, Kleinberg has also published about *small-world* phenomena from an algorithmic perspective (Kleinberg, 2000a, 2000b, 2001, 2004, 2006).

information (i.e. the presence or absence of links between pairs of actors), or inherent symmetry. Node positions are typically determined using variants of the spring embedder (Eades, 1984), multidimensional scaling, or eigenvectors of network-related matrices such as the adjacency or Laplacian matrix. Pajek (Batagelj and Mrvar, 1998) provides the option to fix one or more dimensions of the layout space, e.g. by mapping one or more node indices to coordinates, but currently has no dedicated algorithm to produce readable visualizations given such constraints. Since the result of the status analysis cannot be taken into account with the common layout algorithms, status indices need to be represented by the size of nodes, by numerical labels, or separate from the drawing [see Fig. 6.1.2.1.1 and Table 6.1.2.1.1

Figure 6.1.2.1.1 shows the *Katz status index* for an example. (Among *centrality measures*, it is called *Katz centrality*.) Let us say something about it. It was introduced, in the journal *Psychometrika*, by the Detroit-born statistician Leo Katz (1914–1976), who originally applied it to a popularity context (Katz, 1953). To determine individual status, Katz considered how many people chose the most popular individual (which was current in indexes in use at the time of his research),

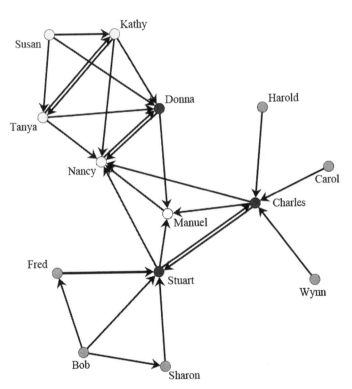

Fig. 6.1.2.1.1   A visualisation of an advice network (cf. Table 6.1.2.1.1), modified from figure 6 in Brandes et al. (2001),[40] where the nodes are coloured. It was obtained automatically. The type of the diagram is *stem-and-leaf.* The type of the network layout is *spring-embedder*

---

[40] The advice network in the figure is from an example made by David Krackhardt.

Table 6.1.2.1.1 Katz status index (based on figure 6 of Brandes et al., 2001)

1.00	Nancy	(Secretary)
0.66	Donna	(Supervisor)
0.57	Manuel	(Manager)
0.19	Stuart	(Supervisor)
0.17	Charles	(Supervisor)
0.08	Kathy	(Secretary)
	Tanya	(Secretary)
0.02	Fred	(Auditor)
	Sharon	(Auditor)
0.00	Bob	(Auditor)
	Carol	(Auditor)
	Harold	(Auditor)
	Wynn	(Auditor)
	Susan	(Secretary)

as well as (and this was novel) who is doing the choosing. Katz defined a matrix, **X**, whose column sums pertain to how many people choose the given individual. This is the *sociomatrix*, i.e., the *adjacency matrix* of the network under consideration. Katz noted that the elements of the powers of the sociomatrix, given by $\mathbf{X}^p$, provide the number of directed walks in the graph of length p from i to j. Katz (ibid., p. 40) noted that this equates to the indirect p-step choices (with $p > 1$) of a given individual by the group.[41] Katz assumed that longer walks inside a graph are less effective than shorter ones, and therefore he introduced an attenuation factor α, where $0 \leq \alpha \leq 1$. There is a criterion of choice of this attenuation factor.[42] His objective was to find the column sums of the matrix, as follows:

---

[41] To account for all possible walks, one raises the sociomatrix to the power of infinity.

[42] In the jargon of *matrix* operations, one can say that the value of the attenuation factor α has to be chosen such that it is smaller than the reciprocal of the absolute value of the largest *eigenvalue* of the adjacency matrix of the network under consideration. Let us explain *eigenvalue*. Consider a square matrix, i.e., an array with as many columns as its rows. A vector is a matrix with only one column, or only one row. The *eigenvectors* of a square matrix are those non-zero vectors that, after being multiplied by that square matrix, at most only have their *magnitude* (their numeric value, their length when drawn as an arrow) modified, but not their direction (when interpreting vectors in the sense of having a magnitude, a direction, and either sense). For each eigenvector, its *eigenvalue* is the factor (a *scalar*: just a number) by which the eigenvector changes when multiplied by the matrix. Let **X** be the square matrix. Then a non-zero vector **v** is an eigenvector of **X** if there is a scalar λ such that $\mathbf{X} \cdot \mathbf{v} = \lambda \cdot \mathbf{v}$ We say that the scalar λ is the eigenvalue of **Z** corresponding to **v**. If we draw the vector **v** in the plane of the perpendicular horizonatal axis and vertical axis (i.e., in Cartesian coordinates), we can see that matrix **X** acts by stretching the vector **v**, not changing its direction, so **v** is an eigenvector of **X**. The usual tabulation of a matrix or a vector is interpreted in n dimensions, instead of just two dimensions. A vector written as a column of n numerical values has to be imagined as drawn in a space of n dimensions, and a square matrix of n rows and n columns also has n dimensions. Here is an example from Wikipedia (http://en.wikipedia.org/wiki/Eigenvalues_and_eigenvectors). Let the matrix be called A and let it be as follows:

$$A = \begin{bmatrix} 2 & 1 \\ 1 & 2 \end{bmatrix}.$$

$$\mathbf{T} = \alpha\mathbf{C} + \alpha^2\mathbf{C}^2 + \alpha^3\mathbf{C}^3 + \cdots + \alpha^k\mathbf{C}^k + \cdots$$

In order to avoid the computation of matrix powers, Katz resorted to the *geometric series*, that is to say:

Then the vector $X = \begin{bmatrix} 3 \\ -3 \end{bmatrix}$ is an eigenvector with eigenvalue 1. Indeed,

$$Ax = \begin{bmatrix} 2 & 1 \\ 1 & 2 \end{bmatrix}\begin{bmatrix} 3 \\ -3 \end{bmatrix} = \begin{bmatrix} 2\cdot 3 + 1\cdot(-3) \\ 1\cdot 3 + 2\cdot(-3) \end{bmatrix} = \begin{bmatrix} 3 \\ -3 \end{bmatrix} = 1\cdot\begin{bmatrix} 3 \\ -3 \end{bmatrix}.$$

Now, consider that the adjacency matrix of a graph is a square matrix. The eigenvalue of a graph is the eigenvalue of its adjacency matrix. In fact, one also speaks of *eigenvalues of a matrix*. Let I be the $n \times n$ *identity matrix*, that is to say, a square matrix in which all values are zeroes, except a diagonal of ones. By det, one means the *determinant* of a matrix. The eigenvalues of the matrix A are the solutions λ of the equation $\det(A - \lambda\,I) = 0$ This equation is called the *characteristic equation* of A. Suppose that A is the following *diagonal matrix*:

$$A = \begin{bmatrix} a_{1,1} & 0 & \cdots & 0 \\ 0 & a_{2,2} & \cdots & 0 \\ \vdots & \vdots & \ddots & 0 \\ 0 & 0 & 0 & a_{n,n} \end{bmatrix},$$

then the characteristic equation reads

$$\det(A - \lambda I) = \det\begin{bmatrix} a_{1,1} & 0 & \cdots & 0 \\ 0 & a_{2,2} & \cdots & 0 \\ \vdots & \vdots & \ddots & 0 \\ 0 & 0 & 0 & a_{n,n} \end{bmatrix} - \lambda\begin{bmatrix} 1 & 0 & \cdots & 0 \\ 0 & 1 & \cdots & 0 \\ \vdots & \vdots & \ddots & 0 \\ 0 & 0 & 0 & 1 \end{bmatrix}$$

$$= \det\begin{bmatrix} a_{1,1} - \lambda & 0 & \cdots & 0 \\ 0 & a_{2,2} - \lambda & \cdots & 0 \\ \vdots & \vdots & \ddots & 0 \\ 0 & 0 & 0 & a_{n,n} - \lambda \end{bmatrix}$$

$$= (a_{1,1} - \lambda)(a_{2,2} - \lambda)\cdots(a_{n,n} - \lambda) = 0$$

The solutions to this equation are the eigenvalues $\lambda_i = a_{i,i}$ ($i = 1, \ldots, n$). The *determinant* det(**A**) or $|\mathbf{A}|$ of a square matrix **A** is a number encoding certain properties of the matrix. A matrix is invertible if and only if its determinant is nonzero. Its *absolute value* (i.e., regardless of sign) equals the area (in $\mathbf{R}^2$, that is to say, the space in two dimensions of all real numbers) or volume (in $\mathbf{R}^3$, that is to say, the space in three dimensions of all real numbers) "of the image of the unit square (or cube), while its sign corresponds to the orientation of the corresponding linear map: the determinant is positive if and only if the orientation is preserved. The determinant of 2-by-2 matrices is given by

$$\det\begin{pmatrix} a & b \\ c & d \end{pmatrix} = ad - bc.$$

When the determinant is equal to one, then the matrix represents an equi-areal mapping. The determinant of 3-by-3 matrices involves 6 terms (*rule of Sarrus*). The more lengthy *Leibniz formula* generalises these two formulae to all dimensions." This quotation concerning determinants is from http://en.wikipedia.org/wiki/Matrix_(mathematics)

$$\sum_{k=1}^{\infty} r^k = \frac{r}{1-r} , \quad r < 1$$

Katz substituted $r = \alpha C$ and from the previous two equations, he obtained

$$\mathbf{T} = (\mathbf{I} - \alpha \mathbf{C})^{-1} - \mathbf{I}$$

The conventional status index in use before the Katz status index divides the column sums by $(n-1)$, but Katz (1953, p. 42) divided the column sums of $\mathbf{T}$ by a value, m, reflecting the underlying technique adopted by Katz, and given by

$$m \cong (n-1)! \alpha^{(n-1)} e^{1/\alpha}$$

See the graph Fig. 6.1.2.1.2 and the corresponding choice matrix in Table 6.1.2.1.2. This was the example originally used by Katz (1953, p. 40). For the six actors A to F, one element corresponds to the original status vector

$$\mathbf{s} = [0.4\ 0.2\ 0.2\ 0.6\ 0.2\ 0.8].$$

Nodes F, D, and A (in descending order) are the actors with high in-degree. With regards to status, they dominate. By contrast, if we use Katz's measure of the status index, and we use as multiplier $\alpha = 0.5$, Katz's status vector is

$$\mathbf{s} = [0.47\ 0.04\ 0.04\ 0.41\ 0.22\ 0.45].$$

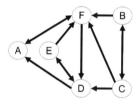

Fig. 6.1.2.1.2 The digraph (i.e., directed graph) associated with the Katz choice matrix of Table 6.1.2.1.2. From Katz (1953, p. 40)

Table 6.1.2.1.2 Katz choice matrix, from Katz (1953, p. 40)

$$\mathbf{C} = \begin{bmatrix} 0 & 0 & 0 & 0 & 0 & 1 \\ 0 & 0 & 1 & 0 & 0 & 1 \\ 0 & 1 & 0 & 1 & 0 & 1 \\ 1 & 0 & 0 & 0 & 1 & 0 \\ 0 & 0 & 0 & 1 & 0 & 1 \\ 1 & 0 & 0 & 1 & 0 & 0 \end{bmatrix}$$

Based on this status vector, actor A scores slightly higher than F, even though the in-degree of A is relatively low. Nevertheless, A dominates, because A was chosen by F and D, both of the actors with the highest in-degree.

A team in Seoul (Phuoc, Kim, Lee, & Kim, 2009), interested in a good ranking system for World Wide Web search engines, compared the Katz status index, an old model, to *PageRank*, which ranks webpages (Brin & Page, 1998; cf. Altman & Tenneholtz, 2005). PageRank was apparently names after one of its proponents, Larry Page. The patent was assigned to Stanford University. The algorithm is used by Google. Its mathematics is explained nicely on Wikipedia.[43] The theory behind PageRank is based on the assumption of a *damping factor*, and in this it resembles the Katz status index. In fact[44]:

> The PageRank theory holds that even an imaginary surfer who is randomly clicking on links will eventually stop clicking. The probability, at any step, that the person will continue is a damping factor d. Various studies have tested different damping factors, but it is generally assumed that the damping factor will be set around 0.85.
>
> The damping factor is subtracted from 1 (and in some variations of the algorithm, the result is divided by the number of documents (N) in the collection) and this term is then added to the product of the damping factor and the sum of the incoming PageRank scores.

The formula for the PageRank of node A while accounting for damping can be written as follows, based on the sum of the incoming PageRanks:

$$PR(A) = \frac{1-d}{N} + d \left(\frac{PR(B)}{L(B)} + \frac{PR(C)}{L(C)} + \frac{PR(D)}{L(D)} + \cdots \right).$$

$L(B)$ is the normalised number of outbound links of node B.

Brandes et al. (2001, section 2) went on to criticise their own figure 6, of which our Fig. 6.1.2.1.1 is a modification:

> Though the network diagram is very readable, it does not convey the interesting substantive information. Moreover, its design is inherently undirected (the picture would be the same even if some or all of the edge directions were reversed), and it is next to impossible to relate the status scores to the picture. Assume, for instance, we swap the status scores of Nancy and Manuel; the visualization would not provide any indication that something was wrong. This is in stark contrast to empirical evidence suggesting that network layout not only affects the ease of reading (Purchase et al., 1997), but has an influence on the understanding and interpretation of substantive content as well (McGrath et al., 1997). Consequently, Krackhardt (1996, p. 166) arranged the actors so that most nominations point in an upward direction, thus creating an informal advice hierarchy that yields an implicit notion of status [see Fig. 6.1.2.1.3].

---

[43] http://en.wikipedia.org/wiki/PageRank

[44] From Section "Damping Factor" in http://en.wikipedia.org/wiki/PageRank (accessed in May 2011).

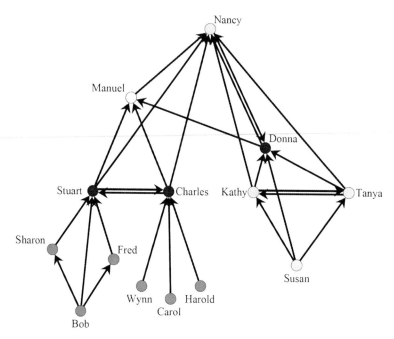

Fig. 6.1.2.1.3 A visualisation of an advice network (cf. Table 6.1.2.1.1 and Fig. 6.1.2.1.1), so arranged that most nominations are upward.[45] Modified from figure 7 in Brandes et al. (2001), itself an adaptation from Krackhardt (1996, p. 166). The arrangement is manual, as opposed to the automatically generated Fig. 6.1.2.1.1

6.1.2.2 Link Analysis

In Section 6.1.2.1, we considered *social network analysis*. Social network analysis has been applied, among the other things, to organised crime. United States Air Force's Major Jonathan T. Hamill has discussed (2006) a Ph.D. dissertation at the Air Force Institute of Technology in Ohio, *Analysis of Layered Social Networks*, in which section 2.3 (ibid., pp. 40–60) is "The Psychology of Terrorists", application to counterterrorism being the motivation for the project. Hamill's thesis is concerned with prevention of near-term terrorist attacks:

---

[45] "Though it works fine in this particular example, note that the above rule for vertical arrangement is error-prone in general, since the requirement of a maximum number of upward oriented connections may result in misleading visual explanations. A simple example of this kind is a network of actors whose connections form a directed cycle. Any one connection can be chosen as the single downward oriented one, but each choice results in a different vertical ordering of the actors" (Brandes et al., 2001). "Interpretation of relative status becomes unreliable, if not impossible, in visualizations based on a maximum number of upward pointing arcs, and only one notion of status is supported." (ibid.). Brandes et al. (2001) discussed shortcomings of various algorithmic solutions when organising a graph for visualisation, and proposed remedies for them.

To aid in this understanding, operations research,[46] sociological, and behavioral theory relevant to the study of social networks are applied, thereby providing theoretical foundations for new and useful methodologies to analyze non-cooperative organizations. Such organizations are defined as those trying to hide their structures or are unwilling to provide information regarding their operations; examples include criminal networks, secret societies, and, most importantly, clandestine terrorist organizations.

More generally, wherever individuals are organised, we can map their links by making their social network explicit, for example in order to better realise which advantage (i.e., which *social capital*) the individual derives from the network:

> In its simplest form, a social network is a map of specified ties, such as friendship, between the nodes being studied. The nodes to which an individual is thus connected are the *social contacts* of that individual. The network can also be used to measure *social capital* — the value that an individual gets from the social network. These concepts are often displayed in a social network diagram, where nodes are the points and ties are the lines.[47]

In the present Section 6.1.2.2, we consider *link analysis*, a technique which has become quite important for crime intelligence and crime investigation. Whereas link analysis is not to be confused with social network analysis (the two followed, in the respective research literature, different historical trajectories), they have come together: link analysis can benefit from social network analysis, borrowing from the latter, and applying, this or that formal device. Users watching on the screen the results returned by link analysis tools will see those results, not the mathematics of the underlying concepts from social network analysis, if these are borrowed indeed.

Link analysis is an interactive technique, visualising – in charts or maps or diagrams – networks of *entity-to-event* associations (e.g., tying a victim to a crime), as well as *entity-to-entity* (e.g., blood relative, or spouse, or place of birth, or owner of a firm), and *event-to-event* (e.g., tying emails to each other).[48] "Link analysis is the process of building up networks of interconnected objects or items over time and the use of special techniques and software tools for forming, examining, modifying, analyzing, searching, and displaying these patterns of behavior, especially for the investigative data miner" (Mena, 2003, p. 80).

Harper and Harris (1975) described, in the *Human Factors* journal, a link analysis technique, using graph and matrix representations. The early beginnings of the techniques were unrelated to the processing capabilities made available by information technology. Nor were such early applications of link analysis as reported, to crime investigations; rather, they were applications in the general discipline of *human factors* (Harper & Harris, 1975, p. 158):

---

[46] *Operations research* is the branch of mathematics concerned with techniques of optimisation. Also some methods from artificial intelligence are concerned with heuristic optimisation (*heuristic*, as what is found is not guaranteed to be the global optimum).

[47] Quoted from http://en.wikipedia.org/wiki/Social_network

[48] "Links, as well as nodes, may have attributes specific to the domain or relevant to the method of collection. For example, link attributes might indicate the certainty or strength of a realtionship, the dollar value of a transaction, or the probability of an infection" (Mena, 2003, p. 83).

Link analysis has proven to be a useful tool in human factors research and engineering. Probably the earliest formal application of the technique was by Gilbreth and Gilbreth (1917) who evolved a system for machine shop layout based upon distances traveled during assembly operations. Fitts, Jones, and Milton (1950) employed link analysis methods to study the eye movements of aircraft pilots during instrument landing approaches. Channell and Tolcott (1954) used the method to define and rank communication links in a Navy command and control system. Haygood, Teel, and Greening (1964) used a computer-based link analysis technique to resolve conflicts in equipment placement. Harris and Chaney (1969) employed link analysis as an aid to evaluate the design of complex electronic test equipment. Chapanis (1969), McCormick (1964), and Van Cott and Kinkade (1972) all describe the use of link analysis in their human factors reference books.

When used by law enforcement agencies, link analysis makes it easier for human users to grasp the social networks of suspected offenders.[49] "Link analysis is the first level by which networks of people, places, organizations, vehicles, bank accounts, telephone numbers, e-mail addresses, and other tangible entities can be discovered, linked, assembled, examined, detected, and analyzed" (Mena, 2003, p. 75).

Harper and Harris remarked (1975, pp. 158–159):

In applying link analysis to the organized crime problem, the focus is on determining the presence or absence of links among individuals. The data base usually consists of information in a variety of formats and types: investigation reports, arrest records, informant reports, surveillance reports, telephone toll-call records, financial statements, newspaper articles, and public records of many kinds. From the intelligence analyst's point of view, the strength of a link between two individuals is a matter of degree, depending upon the content and completeness of available information. At least three categories of links are needed in the application of link analysis to criminal intelligence: STRONG LINKS, WEAK LINKS, AND NO LINKS. An example of a strong link would be the link between a father and son observed frequently together. A weak link is considered as a relationship that is suspected but unconfirmed, or requires some inferential judgment. An example of a weak link would be a link established on the basis of frequent telephone calls made by an individual to a motel operated by a suspected crime figure.

By 2003, Mena was able to note: "Link analysis is already used to detect fraud by specialists in the insurance and telecom industries, as well as in the area of e-commerce" (Mena, 2003, p. 76). Some link analysis tools have "the capability of incorporating multimedia and some interactive *what-if* scenarios" (ibid.).[50]

---

[49] New ways of making or superposing diagrams, in the kid 19th century, were intended to help human experts in inferring connections: "Cholera was a forcing ground for new modes of data presentation, as in this chart correlating cholera and diarrhea deaths with meteorological variables. It was hoped that novel presentations may suggest inferences that would not have been apparent otherwise" (Hamlin, 2009, p. 157, caption of figure 9). There was no correlation, between the 1848 epidemic in England and weather conditions, and we can say that much at present even just looking at the superposed diagrams in that chart.

[50] Mena (2003) also notes difficulties: "Link analysis is a very labor-intensive method of data mining" (ibid., p. 85). "While these visual-link networks have proven useful to investigators, their manual construction has proven difficult when it involves hundred of thousands of transactions" (ibid., p. 76). "As with all data mining projects, extracting and preparing the data for analysis is commonly a major task. Transactional databases more often than not contain incomplete or inconsistent information, or multiple instances of the same entities because they are designed and

"Knowing and working at the right level of granularity is a very important part of preparing the data for link analysis" (ibid., p. 78). Link analysis is specialised per application. For example, *call detail records* (who is calling whom, and when) are analysed (this is called *dialed-digit analysis*) in order to fight wireless fraud, an application for which link analysis is also used in different manners (ibid., pp. 78–79). Another application is for counter-drug analysts (ibid., pp. 80–82). Mena noted (ibid., p. 5):

> Link-analysis technology has been used in the past to identify and track money-laundering transactions by the U.S. Department of the Treasury, Financial Crimes Enforcement Network (FinCEN). Link analysis often explores associations among large numbers of objects of different types. For example, an antiterrorist application might examine relationships among suspects, including their home addresses, hotels they stayed in, wire transfers they received and sent, truck or flight schools attended, and the telephone numbers that they called during a specified period. The ability of link analysis to represent relationships and associations among objects of different types has proven crucial in helping human investigators comprehend complex webs of evidence and draw conclusions that are not apparent from any single piece of information.

There is a problem of glut, when using link analysis as opposed to other methods of data mining: "Link analysis works best in situations where there is a limited number of observations, such as events (meetings) and entities (suspects). Its functionality begins to deteriorate once a large number of observations or transactions begins to populate a case file" (Mena, 2003, p. 86). This is because of the limited human ability to grasp what is being perceived, and link analysis, being a visualisation technique, is a help for perception, and less than helpful when it overloads it.

Link analysis is not suited for handling a mass of data based on aggregate statistical characteristics, something for which *neural networks* and *machine learning* are suited for instead. Besides, the latter two approaches construct predictive models: networks, for them, are a *model representation*, whereas for link analysis instead, networks are a *data representation* (ibid., p. 88).

It is possible however for a tool to combine link analysis with neural networks. The latter is resorted to, in order to detect trends hidden in data, by the *Trend Hunter* utility of the ATAC criminal analysis tool.[51] An advantage of ATAC is its wide interoperability. Mena (2003, section 3.11, pp. 88–104) enumerated and described various link analysis tools. Mena discussed at length and in detail instead the popular *Analyst's Notebook.*[52]

---

built for speed not analysis", but: "In order to map associations correctly it is necessary to first identify accurately the right individual in a database" (ibid., p. 77). *Consolidation* and *disambiguation* of transactions or individuals are necessary operations in data preparation for the purposes of link analysis (ibid., p. 78). We may add that worldwide, mistakes of identity have sometimes caused individuals to be denied credit, to be denied a job or even to lose their job (because of postings on the Web that the employer disliked), or to end up in prison – and this because of manual misidentification, apparently not involving link analysis.

[51] See http://www.bairsoftware.com/atac.htm The acronym ATAC is short for Automated Tactical Analysis of Crime.

[52] http://www.i2.co.uk/home.html The British firm, i2, had their software adopted by the FBI.

6.1.2.3 Link Analysis Tools for Criminal Investigation

A team at the University of Arizona in Tucson, whose members were Yang Xiang, Michael Chaub, Homa Atabakhsha, and Hsinchun Chen, described a project in the visualisation of criminal relationships (Xiang, Chau, Atabakhsh, & Chen, 2005). In their prototype system, called COPLINK Criminal Relationship Visualizer, they resorted to a hyperbolic tree view and a hierarchical list view. We are going to consider Coplink in some detail in Section 6.2.5. The visualisation tool from Xiang et al. (2005) is but an example from a class of tools. Xu and Chen (2004), also in Tucson, Arizona, proposed a technique for effective link analysis, resorting to "shortest-path algorithms,[53] priority-first-search (PFS)[54] and two-tree PFS, to identify the strongest association paths between entities in a criminal network" (ibid., p. 473). They remarked: "Efficiency of the two-tree PFS was better for a small, dense kidnapping network, and the PFS was better for the large, sparse narcotics network" (ibid.).

Mena (2003, section 3.11, pp. 88–104) described at some length such link analysis tools that are specifically tailored for assisting in criminal investigation. *Crime Workbench* is an intelligence management software product for criminal and fraud investigation;[55] there is a scaled down version, Crime Workbench Web, accessible from everywhere, and "amend at the intelligence analyst and law enforcement investigator on the move" (ibid., p. 100). *Daisy* is a link analysis too supporting a circular layout of nodes: these are connected by lines inside the circle, and are possibly surmounted by histograms outside the circle.[56] By contrast, the main layout of displays generated by NETMAP – a link analysis tool[57] used by several government agencies in the United States – are a wagonwheel format, while also supporting other layouts.

Mena noted that a unique feature of another tool, *Crime Link*,[58] "is its ability to generate a two-dimensional association matrix that basically shows *who knows*

---

[53] *Shortest-path algorithms* are a class within *graph search algorithms*. Shortest-path algorithms can identify the optimal paths between nodes in a graph, by examining link weights. Criminal networks in turn are represented as a graph.

[54] The priority-first-search algorithm "works by maintaining a shortest-path tree T rooted at a source node s. T contains nodes whose shortest distances from s are already known. Each node u in T has a parent, which is represented by p_u. A set of labels, d_u, is used to record the distances from the node u to s. Initially, T contains only s. At each step, we select from the candidate set Q a node with the minimum distance to s and add this node to T. Once T includes all nodes in the graph, the shortest paths from the source node s to all the other nodes have been found. PFS differs from the Dijkstra algorithm because it uses an efficient priority queue for the candidate set Q. With modifications, PFS can be used to compute the shortest paths from a single source node to a set of specified nodes in the graph." (Xu & Chen, 2004, p. 479).

[55] http://www.memex.com/cwbover.html

[56] Mena (2003, pp. 100–101). See http://www.daisy.co.uk/daisy.html

[57] http://www.altaanalytics/com/ MAPLING is discussed by Mena (2003) on pp. 101–102 and, as applied to money laundering investigations, on pp. 84–85.

[58] http://www.crimelink.com/

whom, who has done what, who has been where, etc." (ibid., p. 97). This is a triangular table, with one-line textual explanations (such as personal names, with their variants) shown perpendicularly to its diagonal, thus identifying the rows columns of the matrix. Those personal names are preceded by a bullet, if the row or column includes a bullet in at least one case. This enables to see who knows whom.

The *ORIONInvestigations* criminal data organiser can be integrated with the *ORIONLink* link analysis tool.[59] "A special feature of *ORIONLink* is its *what-if* mode, which allows objects and their connections to be hidden or restored on the fly, allowing for the viewing of their impact on the total organization, such as a terrorist cell or criminal gang" (Mena, 2003, p. 103).

Besides, Mena (ibid., p. 104) illustrates various possible applications (to money laundering investigations, to drug investigation, to insurance fraud investigations: there are further possibilities) of the *VisuaLink* link analysis software suite,[60] specifically devised for law enforcement users, and which comprises various data preparation components.

Harper and Harris (1975, p. 159) explained:

> The link analysis procedure centers round the production of an association matrix and a link diagram. The association matrix provides an array. of the relationships among any set of individuals; the notation in any cell of the matrix indicates the nature of the link — strong, weak, or none — between two individuals. The link diagram, the end product of the analysis, presents a graphic illustration of the relationships among the set of individuals. If some of the individuals are members of identifiable organizations, these organizations can also be incorporated into the diagram. The analysis is completed by [a] six-step approach.

The association matrix is triangular, and the same names identify the rows and the columns. The six steps were:

1. Assemble the available information;
2. Abstract information relevant to individual relationships and affiliations;
3. Prepare an association matrix,
4. Develop a preliminary link diagram;
5. Incorporate organizations in the diagram;
6. Refine the link diagram.

This was what Harper and Harris (1975) propose, and by the 2000s, software tools are also providing some more sophisticated functions. Nevertheless, basically computer tools for link analysis in criminal investigation are still organised according to that old template.

When they published their article, Walter Harper and Douglas Harris were affiliated with Anacapa Sciences, Inc., in Santa Barbara, California. Malcolm Sparrow remarked (1991, p. 254):

---

[59] http://www.oriosci.com/productinfo/Magic.html. These ORION tools are discussed in Mena (2003, pp. 102–103).

[60] http://www.visualanalytics.com/

Use of the Anacapa charting system, as developed by Anacapa Sciences Inc., Santa Barbara, California, is currently the predominant form of network analysis within law enforcement. It is used particularly frequently within major fraud investigations and by Organized Crime Squads, where understanding of large and sometimes sophisticated criminal enterprises is required.

Anacapa charts constitute a two-dimensional visual representation of link data (see Harper and Harris, 1975; Howlett, 1980; Klovdahl, 1981; Coady, 1985). They provide a method of making visual sense of a mass of data. They are also an extremely useful tool for communicating the results of analysis (and thus are used as briefing aids as well as aids for analysis). Anacapa charts generally depict individuals by small circles, and relationships by lines (solid or dotted according to whether the relationship is confirmed or unconfirmed). The charts may also show rectangles enclosing one or more individuals as a method of representing membership of corporations or institutions. They clearly show who is central, who is peripheral, and visually reveal chains of links connecting one individual to another. To a network analyst they look like typical network diagrams.[61]

Already in the mid-1980s, the FBI was working on the *Big Floyd* prototype (Bayse & Morris, 1987). Its application was to *template matching*, "a process which helps the analyst to determine whether or not a particular type of crime is likely to have been committed, or whether a particular pattern of criminal relationships is in existence" (Sparrow, 1991, pp. 258–259). Big Floyd used to perform (ibid., p. 259)

the regular functions of storage and retrieval of link data, encompassing links of many different specified types. It does an excellent job of facilitating the interaction between investigator and the visually displayed network, or selected subgraphs from it. It also has first class facilities to enable the investigator to re-order and interrogate the database.

Significantly "Big Floyd" also introduces a new dimension of analysis — namely the notion of template matching. Essentially, ingredients of a criminal network are superimposed on a model template for particular kinds of deduction (example "Smith is probably guilty of embezzlement"). The template is the encapsulation of an expert investigator's accumulated experience and knowledge about a particular type of offence. If the appropriate combination of linkages exist, the deduction is probably "true". The inferential system is used as a component of an Artificial Intelligence system for investigation of organized crime activities.

---

[61] We have seen in Section 6.1.2.1 that Sparrow (1991) listed six different concepts of network centrality, namely: *degree; betweenness; closeness; Euclidean centrality after multidimensional scaling; point strength*; and *business*. The boundaries of a criminal web are fuzzy, and Sparrow (1991) remarked: "The third and fourth (Closeness and Euclidean Centrality) become quite arbitrary if the network has arbitrary or fuzzy boundaries. But, in fact, Euclidean Centrality is probably closest to the reality of the Anacapa chart — where centrality on the chart equates with Euclidean centrality after a manual version of two-dimensional scaling — even though the practical determination of the starting (central) node was initially by its Degree" (ibid., p. 265). Moreover: "On balance it appears that the second, fifth and sixth notions of centrality (Betweenness, Point Strength, and Business) have greater relevance to the identification of network vulnerabilities than the others (Degree, Closeness, and Euclidean Centrality)" (ibid., p. 266).

6.1.2.4   Various Tools Applied to Criminal Intelligence

There exist a number of commercially available products for link analysis. Tools reported about in the research literature include the following. *Coplink* is a tool for criminal intelligence analysis which finds links in databases among such entities. Coplink performs data integration, pooling together the various information sources available (Hauck, Atabakhsh, Ongvasith, Gupta, & Chen, 2002; Chen, Zeng, Atabakhsh, Wyzga, & Schroeder, 2003; Chen et al., 2003; Xiang et al., 2005). Section 6.2.5 below is concerned with Coplink.

Drawing on experience gained with the Coplink project, Chen et al. (2004) presented a general framework for crime data mining. A project for FinCEN (Financial Crimes Enforcement Network) – the U.S. Treasury agency set up to detect money laundering – with the goal of developing a computer tool for identifying money laundering networks, by carrying out network link analysis, was reported about by Goldberg and Wong (1998). Links are created between records in databases of financial transactions, so that the networks can be detected of those individuals who made those transactions. Horn, Birdwell, and Leedy (1997) apply shortest-path algorithms to link individuals in the Link Discovery Tool. An overview was provided in a section in Zeleznikow, Oatley, and Leary (2005). Another paper on tools for crime detection from the same volume is by Atib and Zeleznikow (2005).

Leary (2004) presented FLINTS, short for Forensic Led Intelligence System. FLINTS, which was originally applied by the West Midlands Police with headquarters in Birmingham in England, is described in Chapter 7 in this book. FLINTS produces a graphical pattern of links, showing patterns of links between crimes and criminals. Data sources are both "hard" forensic data, such as DNA, fingerprints, and shoe-prints (the latter, a less weighty kind of evidence than the former two), and "soft" data, which are behavioural.

FLINTS III assists in identifying groups of offenders, by analysing offender networks, with the added feature of geographical profiling,[62] which enables police officers to locate crime hotspots. Comparative and seasonal analysis maps are produced. Leary, VanDenBerghe, and Zeleznikow (2003a, 2003b) described an application of the FLINTS model to financial fraud modelling. An example of a possible question to ask FLINTS is: "Show me the most prolific offender this year, and link the object to first level accomplices". An inference network helps with hypothesis generation concerning accomplices. Another system was tried by the Zurich police in Switzerland; it was developed by Olivier Ribaux.

6.1.2.5   Gianluigi Me's Investigation Strategy for Tackling Internet Child Pornography

Gianluigi Me, of the Third University of Rome, proposes an investigation strategy (Me, 2008) to tackle *internet child pornography*, "relying on the construction of a

---

[62] In applied psychology, there has been some criticism of false confidence in computerised geographical profiling methods. See Snook, Taylor, and Bennell (2005).

victim's picture database, based on straightforward considerations on the probability of finding a link between two different children. This link can represent the most important key to linking apparently different pedo-criminal phenomena for different pedophiles,[63] joining the same pedo-ring at the same level" (ibid., p. 423). "[E]ven if the number of [child pornography] victims is not known a priori" (ibid., p. 421), "we are looking for the probability of two pictures depicting the same child" (ibid.). Me remarked (ibid., p. 422):

> [T]he more you collect pictures with the identification data of the correspond[ing] criminal profile, the more probability you have of detecting the same child as a victim of two different criminals. This consideration creates a relationship link between two pedophiles, since the same child picture has been found in their virtual souvenir boxes: this reflects the affiliation to the same pedophile ring or the belonging to different rings where at least one person is in common.

The results of Me (2008) "can offer complementary benefit to the Situational Crime Prevention (SCP) approach to Internet CP [i.e., child pornography] and pedophilia, due to the increased risk to the pedophile when collecting the pictures and in order to improve the [law enforcement] capability to threaten the pedophiles. [...] SCP refers to a preventative approach that relies upon the reduction of the opportunities for crime, according to the emergent criminological theories focusing on the relationship between the offender and the actual environment where the crime takes place" (ibid., p. 419).

6.1.3 Assessing the Risk of Crimes

Part of the applications of investigative data mining are preventative, and go by the name *precrime data mining*. It is subserved by *behavioural profiling*, enabling the police to keep track of a social network of potential offenders, so that action would be taken before (further) crimes are committed.[64] In the words of Mena (2003, pp. 1–2):

> Investigative data mining is the visualization, organization, sorting, clustering, segmenting, and predicting of criminal behavior, using such data attributes as age, previous arrests, modus operandi, type of building, household income, time of day, geo code, countries visited, housing type, auto make, length of residency, type of license, utility usage, IP address, type of bank account, number of children, place of birth, average usage of ATM card, number of credit cards, etc.; the data points[65] can run into the hundreds. Precrime is the

---

[63] In Britain, the spelling *paedophile* is usual; the prefix *paedo-* stands for 'child', whereas the prefix *pedo-* properly stands for 'soil', as in *forensic pedology*, which is about the examination of soil traces in criminal investigation.

[64] Napier and Baker (2005; 3rd edn. 2009) provide an overview of criminal personality profiling.

[65] Of course, the multitude of attributes can be expected to be subdivided into clusters corresponding to entities or relations in some good database design. But it has been especially *relational database* technology that has enhanced the possibilities for analysis, unfettered by a predetermined notion of which kinds of transactions are envisaged.

interactive process of predicting criminal behavior by mining this vast array or data, using several AI technologies: [...]

Even before data mining came into the picture – with the objective of assessing risk, and an output consisting of predictive models or rules – security professionals did try to estimate the probability of crimes. The data resorted to were criminal statistics, as well as documentation over a given past period in the given area. For example, one would refer to the statistics of car thefts in a given fairly narrow area: a neighbourhood, or even just a building block.

Another category of precrime risk assessment is when it is necessary to profile an offender who may hit again, such as a serial killer. Serious crime analysts would try:

a *to prevent further crimes*: to identify cues that impinge upon the offender's future behaviour, apart from trying to identify the offender, and
b *to solve the crime*: to devise a good way to capture the offender while minimising the risk both to the public, and to law enforcement personnel.[66]

This is different from *crime analysis*, as being part of policing intended to prevent future crimes by studying the statistics of the historical data. It is not a given criminal episode that is to be solved, or a given offender who is to be captured, but the goal is instead to lower the risk of future crime, of given types and in a given geographical area.

6.1.4 Geographic Information Systems for Mapping Crimes

Geographical information systems have various purposes, as well as different presentations. Some are accessible the World Wide Web, and these called *Web-geographical information systems* (*Web-GISs*).[67] The design of such a tool "strongly requires methodological and operational tools for dealing with information distributed in multiple, autonomous and heterogeneous data sources, and a uniform data publishing methodology and policy over Internet Web sites" (De Antonellis, Pozzi, Schreiber, Tanca, & Tosi, 2005, p. 33).

We have already mentioned (in Section 6.1.2.2) that such a link analysis tool as Richard Leary's FLINTS (described in Chapter 7 below) enables, among the other things, geographic profiling, so that police officers can locate crime hotspots. *Geo-mapping tools* are sometimes used in order to look for potential associations

---

[66] In a police science journal, Badiru, Karasz, Karasz, and Holloway (1988) described the expert system AREST [sic]. Its application was to the profiling of suspects of armed robberies. In a technical report of the Canadian Police Research Centre, Valcour (1997) described InvestigAide B&E, an expert system whose purpose was to support the processing and investigation of breaking and entering cases, by assisting in gathering and recording case data, and providing such information as suspect characteristics.

[67] See, e.g., Zhong Ren and Ming Hsiang (2003), Worboys and Duckham (2004), Schreiber et al. (2003), De Antonellis et al. (2005), and Pühretmair and Wöβ (2001).

and trends in crime, but sometimes the purpose is different. Crime maps are also sometimes used by the police in their public relations – "Maps of crime are highly persuasive because people tend to instantly grasp graphs, believing what they can see" (Mena, 2003, p. 344) – even though, for sure, their use for investigators and for policy-makers is much more important.

For example, a local newspaper from South East London, the *News Shopper* (Bexley edition), on of 27 August 2008, published the following unsigned item on p. 4, under the headline "Online maps to show crime hot spots":

> Crime maps showing where and how often offences are committed could be seen on the internet from next month. The Met police is currently testing electronic crime mapping software and plans to launch the system in September, after a technical review. Interactive maps will sit alongside monthly crime statistics published on the Met's website. They will provide details on the number, rate and geographical location of crime types on a ward, borough and London-wide basis. According to the map, the crime rate in Bexley is below average for London, while in Bromley, Lewisham and Greenwich it is average.
>
> A test map can be viewed online at maps.met.police.uk By clicking on a borough, visitors can see figures for burglary, robbery and vehicle crime and figures from previous years. Crime maps have been used in the US — notably in Chicago, New York and Los Angeles — where police departments show incidents at a house-to-house level.

Then Jules Cooper in the *Bexley Times* on Thursday, 11 September 2008 announced on p. 7, under the headline "Net marks crime capital":

> A crime map of the capital has been launched on the internet by the Metropolitan Police Service. Burglaries, robberies and vehicle thefts are charted ward by ward on the map launched last Wednesday and each is graded by colour between high and low crime. The project is in its infancy and is expected to be expanded to show violent and sexual crimes, antisocial behaviour and the number of calls made to the police. By borough, Bromley, Bexley and Greenwich were all classed as having an 'average' rate of burglaries and robberies, whilst Westminster had the highest rate in London. No borough in London was classed as having 'low' crime. At the moment viewers can only view crime statistics of their sub-ward area of 633 houses, or of their borough. High crime sub-wards were shown to be clustered in Greenwich Peninsula and were also dotted around Woolwich, Thamesmead and Belvedere. However, areas of 'high' crime appear adjacent to 'lower than average' areas. [. . .]

As a matter of fact, crime maps at websites came to London several years after they did at major cities in the United States, where there also is a Web portal to the *geographic information systems* (*GIS*) of various police departments, at the website of CMRC: "In 1997 the National Institute of Justice established the Crime Mapping Research Center, whose goal is the promotion, researching, evaluation, development, and dissemination of GIS technology and the spatial analysis of crime" (Mena, 2003, pp. 344–345). Eventually, such maps were made accessible on the Internet, to anyone with a browser. Apart from urban crime maps, crime can also be mapped along roads (Kangas, Terrones, Keppel, & La Moria, 2003, p. 370, figure 12.10, and p. 372, figure 12.12).

The first AutoCarto conference was held in 1974 in Reston, Virginia: "this was the first in an important series of conferences that set the GIS research agenda"

(Longley, Goodchild, Maguire, & Rhind, 2001, p. 12, table 1.4).[68] The first issue of the *International Journal of Geographic Information* Science appeared in 1987. In 1988, TIGER (Topologically Integrated Geographic Encoding and Referencing) was announced and described by the U.S. Census Bureau, as being a follow-up from DIME (Dual Independent Map Encoding – Geographic Database Files), a data structure and street-address database for the 1970 census that they developed in 1967. "Low cost TIGER data stimulate[d] rapid growth in US business GIS" after 1988 (ibid., p. 13). The *MapQuest* commercial Internet mapping service was launched in 1996, "producing over 130 million maps in 1999" (ibid.). Let us say something about geographic information systems actually are. Longley et al. state (2001, pp. 11, 13):

> [...] GIS is a complex beast, with many distinct appearances. To some it is a way to automate the production of maps, while to others this application seems far too mundane compared with the complexities associated with solving geographic problems and support-ing spatial decisions, and with the power of a GIS as an engine for analyzing data and revealing new insights. Others see a GIS as a tool for maintaining complex inventories, one that adds geographic perspectives to existing information systems, and allows the geograph-ically distributed resources of a forestry or utility company to be tracked and managed. All of these perspectives are clearly too much for any one software package to handle, and GIS has grown from its initial commercial beginnings as a simple off-the-shelf package to a complex of software, hardware, people, institutions, networks, and activities that can be very confusing to the novice. A major software vendor as ESRI today sells many distinct products, designed to serve very different needs: a major GIS workhouse (ArcInfo), a sim-pler system designed for viewing, analyzing, and mapping data (ArcView), an engine for supporting GIS-oriented Web sites (ArcIMS), an information system with spatial extensions (ArcSDE) and several others.

"It is convenient to classify the main GIS software packages into six groups, based on their functionality and type: professional, desktop, hand-held, component, viewer, and Internet" (Longley et al., 2001, p. 171). For example, ESRI Press pub-lished *Serving Maps on the Internet* (Harder, 1998).[69] Table 1.3 on p. 10 in Longley et al. (2001) variously defines a GIS, according to the groups who find them useful: "a container of maps in digital form" (for the general public); "a computerized tool for solving geographic problems" (for decisions-makers, community groups, and planners); "a spatial decision support system" (for management scientists or oper-ations researchers); "a mechanized inventory of geographically distributed features and facilities" (for utility managers, transportation officials, or resource managers); "a tool for revealing what is otherwise invisible in geographic information" (for sci-entists or investigators); and "a tool for performing operations on geographic data that are too tedious or expensive or inaccurate if performed by hand" (for resource managers, planners, and cartographers).

---

[68] Foresman (1998) collects essays by the pioneers of geographic information systems about the history of the field.

[69] Also Plewe (1997) is concerned with geographic information systems accessible online on the Internet.

Crime maps are the subject of Mena's (2003) chapter 12, 'Mapping Crime: Clustering Case Work' (ibid., pp. 343–378). He begins by contrasting *top-down* vs. *bottom-up* approaches to crime mapping. When a human analyst explores (by using a computer tool) the features of crimes by different dimensions, this is a top-down approach. Mena correctly points out that this is a useful complement to the bottom-up approach to mapping crime, which is a machine-driven rather than human-driven analysis, and (by using data mining) clusters the data about crime automatically: "This type of map is driven by the criminal data itself and may lead to the discovery of new, previously unseen patterns and can provide very important insights that a human-driven analysis might miss" (ibid., p. 343). It must be said that sometimes maps may be deceptive: Monmonier's (1996) book is entitled *How to Lie with Maps*.

O'Looney's (2000) *Beyond Maps: GIS and Decision Making in Local Government* was concerned with GIS applications in local government, and a simplified classification from O'Looney appeared in Longley et al. (2001, table 2.1, pp. 34–35). There were three columns: "Inventory Applications (locating property information such as ownership and tax assessments by clicking on a map)", "Policy Analysis Applications (e.g. number of features per area, proximity to a feature or land use, correlation of demographic features with geological features)", and "Management/Policy-Making Applications (e.g. more efficient routing, modeling alternatives, forecasting future needs, work scheduling)". There was one row in the table for *law enforcement* indeed:

1. The cell of inventory applications to law enforcement stated: "Inventory of police stations, crimes, arrests, convicted perpetrators and victims; plotting police beats and patrol car routing; alarm and security system locations".
2. The cell of policy analysis applications to law enforcement stated: "Analysis of police visibility and presence; officers in relation to density of criminal activity; victim profiles in relation to residential populations; police experience and beat duties".
3. The cell management or policy-making applications to law enforcement stated: "Reallocation of police resources and facilities to areas where they are likely to be most efficient and effective[70]; creation of random routing maps to decrease predictability of police beats".

A distinction is to be made between visualisation on a geographical map of events that have actually occurred, and *geosimulation*. "Geosimulation (Benenson & Torrens, 2004) proposes the aggregation of Multi-Agent Systems (MAS) and Geographic Information Systems (GIS) for modeling and simulating urban phenomena" (Furtado & Vasconcelos, 2007, p. 57). Geosimulation "addresses an urban phenomena simulation model with a multi-agent approach to simulate discrete, dynamic, and event-oriented systems (Benenson & Torrens, 2004). In

---

[70] *Effectiveness* (less often, *efficacy*) denotes success at goal achievement. *Efficiency* denotes success at achieving goals while containing the expenditure of resources, including time.

Section 6.1.6.2, we are going to discuss the use of multiagent technology in the geosimulation of criminal dynamics in urban environments, for the purpose of training police officers.

It is important to realise that one can map crime visually, without actually displaying the data on a geographical map.[71] Kangas et al. (2003) is an article about CATCH (Computer Aided Tracking and Characterization of Homicides), a project of Battelle Memorial institute's Pacific Northwest Division in Richland, Washington state, and the Attorney General of Washington, Criminal Division. In CATCH, *Kohonen neural networks* (i.e., *self-organising maps*)[72] "learn to cluster similar cases from approximately 5,000 murders and 3,000 sexual assaults residing in the databases" (ibid., p. 365), using data from the HITS (Homicide Investigation Tracking System) database system, containing data about violent crimes primarily from the U.S. Pacific Northwest. CATCH itself, that comes in two versions – one for murders and one for sexual assaults – is a collection of tools that also include query tools and geographical maps. "The tools in CATCH are of two types. First, there are database mining tools to give the crime analyst a better understanding of the content of the database. Second, there are tools that let the analyst retrieve and

---

[71] Using data from Britain, Adderley and Musgrove (2003b) used self-organising maps (i.e., Kohonen neural networks) in order to model the behaviour of offenders who commit serious sexual assaults. Clustering resulted in the formation of profiles of offenders, some of which were then confirmed independently: some of them belonged to convicted offenders, whereas other profiles resulted in further investigation. It took Adderley and Musgrove ten weeks to achieve results that using conventional methods, would have taken 2 years (as was the case of an in-house study of the police). "When a specified offense occurs within the United Kingdom the force in which the offense occurred has the remit to forward full details to the NCF [i.e., the National Crime Faculty of the National Police Staff College at Bramshill, Hampshire] for subsequent entry into the Violent Crime Linkage Analysis System (ViCLASS) system" (*sic*, ibid., p. 350), "a relational database developed in 1991 by the Royal Canadian Mounted Police comprising 53 tables, not all of which are used in the United Kingdom" (ibid.).

Adderley and Musgrove (2003b) point out that sometimes the data are ambiguous; for example, in a particular gang rape, there was the initial intention to pick up a prostitute, sop the question as to whether she was specifically targeted is yes, in that she was a prostitute, but no, in that it need not have been specifically her (ibid., p. 353). After data preparation, model building followed. "A self-organizing map was selected because it has the ability to cluster similar records into the same cell, while producing a two-dimensional topological map showing the relationship of those records to near neighbors. This can be used to form larger clusters by merging neighboring cells" (ibid., p. 355). In this sense, a map is obtained, even though it does not look as a geographical map. For example, in their figure 12.4 on p. 356, they showed the clustering of 2,370 crimes on a 20×20 grid, and by adding straight lines manually, one can see three different areas, according to how the offender approached the victim: three manners "broadly categorized as cons, surprise, and blitz" (ibid., p. 356). As a particular case, clustering could also be on a geographical basis, but clearly Adderley and Musgrove (2003b) is about data visualisation, not about geographical crime mapping. Their article was published as part of Mena's (2003) chapter 12, "Mapping Crime", and the same is true of Kangas et al. (2003).

[72] *Self-organising maps* (*SOM*), or *Kohonen neural networks*, were invented by Teuvo Kohonen (1982). The nodes of the network (i.e., artificial neurons) learn to map points in an input space to coordinate in an output space (that is to say, from the set of the input nodes to the set of the output nodes). Lebbah, Bennani, and Rogovschi (2009) proposed an approach that considers the automated learning of self-organising maps as a mixture of Markov models.

compare specific crimes" (ibid., p. 367). In particular, it is possible to have a set of crimes to be placed on a geographical map as pins (e.g., along highways). "The user can select pins to view additional information about specific crimes" (ibid., p. 369). For example, two crimes were compared in a map (ibid., p. 372, figure 12.12), and this was done (ibid., p. 373):

> according to the sexual offender labels: Power Reassurance, Power Assertive, Anger Retaliatory, and Anger Excitation. The figure shows the individual weights assigned to each of the details and the four labels describing each of the two crimes. The details of the two crimes in the figure are sorted to bring the significant details to the top. The two crimes compared in the figure are both described to have "unusual ritual" and "blindfold" in common. These are two crime details that are relatively rare in the database and may suggest that the same offender committed these two crimes.

The weighting systems were developed by Robert Keppel, chief criminal investigator at the Attorney general in Washington. Keppel publishes both in specialist forensic forums (Keppel, 1995a; Keppel & Weis, 1997), and popular books about solving crimes and his experience at it (Keppel, 1995b, 1997).

6.1.5 Detection

6.1.5.1 General Considerations

Pro-active rather than passive crime detection (it is passive when denunciations are merely received) is adapted, of course, to the specific patterns that typify the different braches of criminal activity. Generally speaking, the gathering of intelligence is required, in order to enable effective policing, both in order to solve crimes, and in order to prevent them. This is distinct from crime investigation, and for intelligence analysis to be effective, it should not be made subservient to the contingencies of the investigation of this or that crime incident. See Section 4.5.1 below.

Ratcliffe (2005, p. 439, 2003) proposed a "3i Model" of the *intelligence-led policing* process. The three "I"s stand for "Interpret, Influence, Impact". The schema is redrawn here in Fig. 6.1.5.1.1.

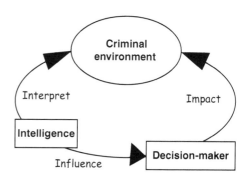

Fig. 6.1.5.1.1 Ratcliffe's 3i Model of the intelligence-led process

Mena (2003, chapter 9, "Criminal Patterns: Detection Techniques", pp. 275–299) begins by discussing the *modus operandi* (*MO*) of various kinds of crimes,[73] along with some known indicators of such crimes, and then turns to presenting a general methodology for detecting crimes by means of data mining. In practice, he customises for crime detection the CRISP-DM data mining model methodology (the Cross-Industry Standard Process–Data Mining), a standard that is widely adopted in industry. Mena tailors every phase of the process (understanding of the objectives, understanding of the data, data preparation, modelling, evaluation, and deployment) to crime detection in general, after having discussed in previous sections the specific problems and methods associated with particular categories of crime to be detected. The very possibility of suggesting a general methodology is a challenge, and trying to address this problem deserves appreciation. "There is no single template for detecting fraud, just as there is no one methodology for data mining" (ibid., p. 276). Moreover, not only old patterns, but also novel behaviour on the part of offenders is to be expected (ibid.):

> Criminal perpetrators, whether hackers or thieves, are creative and opportunistic individuals, and attempts to catch them cannot be based solely on how they have behaved in the past. An investigative data miner must look for old patterns, as well as new ones that may signal a new type or hack attack. For this reason, two typical analyses will be needed, one involving classification of known patterns and the other involving a clustering analysis in search of anomalies or outliers[74] in the data.

Moreover, *link analysis* is useful for the detection of offenders. Financial crimes is one area to which Mena devotes much attention. "The goal of data mining for a financial institution is the development of rules and models enabling it to reduce the number of fraudulent-transaction alerts to a volume that can be handled and investigated by, say, an audit group in a bank" (ibid., p. 276), with the proviso that one should expect offenders to take detection-avoidance action, based on what they expect the auditors' rules and procedures to be. Also "money launderers are

---

[73] Keppel (2005; 3rd edn. 2009) provides an overview of linking cases by modus operandi and signature of serial offenders.

[74] Rousseeuw and Hubert explain (2011, p.73) "In real data sets, it often happens that some observations are different from the majority. Such observations are called *outliers*. Outlying observations may be errors, or they could have been recorded under exceptional circumstances, or belong to another population. Consequently, they do not fit the model well. It is very important to be able to detect these outliers. In practice, one often tries to detect outliers using diagnostics starting from a classical fitting method. However, classical methods can be affected by outliers so strongly that the resulting fitted model does not allow to detect the deviating observations. This is called the *masking* effect. In addition, some good data points might even appear to be outliers, which is known as *swamping*. To avoid these effects, the goal of *robust statistics* is to find a fit that is close to the fit we would have found without the outliers. We can then identify the outliers by their large deviation from that robust fit." Rousseeuw and Hubert (2011) present an overview of robust statistical methods for detecting outliers, and of *outlier detection tools*. Cf. Su and Tsai (2011). The concept of *outlier* is familiar from *statistics*. Barnett and Lewis (1994) is a book on the subject. The definition given by Grubbs (1969) is: "An outlying observation, or outlier, is one that appears to deviate markedly from other members of the sample in which it occurs." Also see http://en.wikipedia.org/wiki/Outlier

believed to change their MOs frequently. If one method is discovered and used to arrest and convict a ring of criminals, activity will switch to alternative methods" (ibid., p. 280). "[M]oney launderers resemble individuals who engage in ordinary fraud: They are adaptive and devise complex strategies to avoid detection. They often assume their transactions are being monitored and design their schemes so that each transaction fits a profile of legitimate activity" (ibid.).[75]

Detection of crime perpetrated by using computers requires awareness of techniques for evading such detection. Strategies to evade computer forensic investigations are referred to by some authors (following Harris, 2006) as *anti-forensics*: the name *digital anti-forensics* has been given to strategies to evade computer forensic investigations, as well as ways to exploit critical failures in computer forensics software or in the reliability of computer security systems.

Whereas Mena (2003) insisted correctly that data mining for fraud detection should be combined with human expertise in order to make detection techniques flexible and evolving, arguably there are two classes of techniques that could be resorted to in addition, for the formalisation of the automated processing: one class is methods from artificial intelligence for handling *agents' beliefs*, including *nested beliefs* (i.e., beliefs that agents ascribe to each others), for which see Section 3.4 above. As to game theory, see Section 4.3.2.2 above.

It is crucial to understand that data mining identifying suspect cases in a data set can only be an *indicative* tool, not an *implicative* tool: data mining points out patterns or exceptions (*outliers*) to a pattern, and just because transactions or individuals are so identified is not evidence against suspect persons. Rather, investigation should follow, and validate a charge independently.

6.1.5.2 Complex Tools' Vulnerability to Manipulation by Perpetrators

Mena (2003) has an interesting treatment of methods for insurance fraud detection (ibid., sections 9.5. and 9.7), and these are summarised in a large table on pp. 286–287 in his book. In his section 9.6, Mena (2003) briefly discusses a case study, of death claims that did not add up. "A traditional auditing tool was first used as a

---

[75] Mena (2003, pp. 280–281) points out that the use of techniques derived from AI research, i.e., data mining, for the purpose of monitoring wire transfer traffic (so that suspicious transfers, typically related to money laundering, may be detected) was rejected by the 1995 OTA report – a report from September 1995, prepared by the Office of Technology Assessment (OTA) and commissioned by the Permanent Subcommittee on Investigations of the U.S. Senate committee on Governmental Affairs. "The OTA report rejected the use of data mining due in part to a lack of useful profiles, high cost, and privacy issues, but, most importantly, the major challenges in constructing an effective wire transfer analysis was related to the incomplete, spotty, and poor condition of the data, not the AI technologies. 'In several cases, technologies are available that would be appropriate for wire transfer analysis, but data and (government) expertise do not exist to make those technologies effective'" (Mena, 2003, p. 281). Mena claimed that however: "The post-9/11 environment is changing the priorities of years ago" (ibid.). The problem of the poor quality of the data, owing to ineffective standards, was being addressed by new legislation, with the data quality being improved enough for data mining being applied.

preprocessor to manipulate the files and sort the data", and so forth (ibid., p. 287). Then, a software product from WizSoft, WizRule, was used so that all the IF/THEN rules in the data set were searched and found. The level of unlikelihood of deviations was calculated, by that tool. Some cases that were pointed out by the tool were then investigated (ibid., p. 288).

In his section 9.5, 'Insurance Crimes', Mena (2003, pp. 281–286) considered in particular losses to Medicare in the United States, through improperly charged healthcare services.[76] Mena's discussion is rather detailed, and suited indeed for data mining, but in a sense, addresses a problem that in those particular forms,

---

[76] Consider moreover that a truthful claim may be sometimes ambiguously formulated. Partridge (1991) provides an example of a U.S. insurer misunderstanding a claim: Partridge's own son cut his knees (resulting in an injury that required several stitches), when on a trip to Gettysburg with the Boy Scouts. The father filled out an insurance form, and the insurer asked for confirmation because on the form, in the section where a short description of how the accident happened has to be supplied, the father had written: "Injury received while on the battlefield in Gettysburg, Pa." The insurer was puzzled because of the assumption that if you received an injury at a battlefield, then you were one of the combatants, and because no one still alive, let alone a minor, could have fought at the battle of Gettysburg (1–3 July 1863). This is a nice example of an ambiguous description which an artificial intelligence program with natural-language processing capabilities could be made to explain out: it is possible to receive an injury at a place where a battle had taken place in 1863, but if the person injured is a child around the year 1990, then presumably this wasn't during the famous battle. By itself, the claim may be quite truthful. Perhaps an employee at the insurer was taken aback, because of the expectation that some claims would be spurious, and perhaps this was a spurious claim making an outrageously false statement about the circumstances of the claimed injury, on the part of a claimant overconfident that anything goes.

Dan Sperber and Deirdre Wilson discussed the notion of *loose talk* (Sperber & Wilson, 1986), by means of an example they provide (Sperber & Wilson, 1990). "At a party in San Francisco, Marie meets Peter. He asks her where she lives, and she answers: 'I live in Paris'." Contrast this to a situation in which the location of the event when the occurance takes place is different: "Suppose Marie is asked where she lives, not at a party in San Francisco, but at an electoral meeting for a Paris local election". There is a difference, concerning the truth value of Marie's utterance, in terms of *relevance*. "It so happens that Marie lives in Issy-les-Moulineaux, a block away from the city limits of Paris. Her answer is literally false, but not blatantly so. If Peter presumed literalness, he will be misled". Yet, assumptions are warranted, that in terms of artificial intelligence could be represented in terms of a nesting of beliefs that agents ascribe to each other. It is not precise that Marie lives in Paris, in the sense that this is inside the city limits.

In his autobiography, politician David Ben Gurion (who was born in Russia in 1886, and in 1948 proclaimed the independence of the State of Israel) claimed that his father had been a lawyer. It has been pointed out that his father had never graduated from high school, and was living in a region where he could not earn a university degree (the son instead earned a law degree in Constantinople, and for that purpose learned Turkish). Rather, the father used to write letters in good Russian for those who could not write in that language (but perhaps could write in Yiddish instead), and carried out the functions of a notary, drew up contracts, and so forth. Did Ben-Gurion try to aggrandise his family background, by claiming that his father had been a lawyer? Perhaps taking such a view would be anachronistic. In the United States in the first half of the 19th century, and in rural parts of Russia until much later, the professional profile of an *ad hoc lawyer* was commonplace. Such a lawyer used to carry out some of the functions of a lawyer, such as drawing up contracts, or settling border disputes between farmers, but they hadn't a law degree. Claiming that an ad hoc lawyer was a lawyer is false, but historically it used to be a commonplace and non-malicious statement, other than in the big cities. But Ben-Gurion himself had earned a law degree at a university, so perhaps

is rather peculiar of the United States, where private providers of healthcare are sometimes conniving, but more generally grossly overcharge, for European sensibilities.

It must be said that the other side of the medal, with medical insurance world-wide, is that insurers are also known to behave unethically, and medical insurance expert witnesses tend to have a poorer reputation (including within the medical profession) than expert witnesses in most other domains. Sometimes quite justi-fied misgivings arise, that some such experts testify in a manner that suits the party that instructs them: either the insurer, or the patient.

Moreover, in the United Kingdom there is an ongoing trend, in that domain of expert testimonies, for the economically stronger party to require shortened pro-ceedings, such that their expert witnesses would not be cross-examined. Whereas the standard situation is that in general expert witnesses can be expected to be cross-examined ferociously, with the other party trying to shatter their credibility even when they are quite competent and irreproachable, it is unfortunately precisely in such categories of trials where expert testimony is (by public feeling) more suspi-cious, that the party instructing them, who may be an insurer, would try to insist that in order to contain expenses, the expert witness should not be required to appear in court. Private persons are likely to find this difficult to resist.

This arguably drastically reduces the public's confidence in the possibility of obtaining justice in cases of medical insurance claims disputed by the insurer. For sure, an expert who in order to suit the insurer instructing him or her claims, say, that the claimant would in all likelihood fully recover from an accident within six months, in theory could be exposed when after many years this prediction is proven wrong, especially when counterexpertise is in place (and was in place ab initio) to point out how the insurer's expert was methodologically at fault, or even could not have been in good faith. In practice however it is very difficult to expose an expert based on past cases, if the parties wronged alike, time after time, are private persons rather than corporations or institutions.

This kind of behaviour patterns makes Mena's (otherwise praiseworthy) recom-mendation problematic: "It is important that carriers have the intelligence to process claims with payment, recall them, cancel them, reduce them, or seek clarification from medical staff or patient" (ibid., p. 282). This would all be good and well if the insurer's pattern of behaviour is spotless. When it is not, this may be itself a pattern belonging to corporate culture. There is a risk that a data mining tool be presented as a magical black box, and ascribed probative weight that does not compete to it, either in order to discourage claimants, or even to mesmerise the court. Even worse, the tool itself may be manipulated fraudulently, by a corporate perpetrator confident enough that nobody would be both motivated enough and smart enough to detect the fraud. I am by no means claiming that such a situation is already in place anywhere, but I am presenting a worst-case scenario for when data mining will be widespread

---

his claiming what he did claim about his father, yet not pointing out that his father, though for practical purposes "a lawyer", had no degree, was not entirely innocent.

enough for rogues to emerge (like in other sectors)[77] who would sporadically bend technology (in this case, data mining) for their own unlawful purposes.

There already exist situations when fraud in simple software may be suspected: such as at a supermarket that, in contrast to its local competitors, quite often incurs small "errors", always to the detriment of customers as they pay (errors small enough for some clients to neglect to require that they would be made good, once they uncover the error), and there is the suspicion that this is not only because cashiers and other staff find themselves forced to conform to the corporate culture of their employer, but because digital equipment at the till was dishonestly manipulated centrally, away from the control of most staff.

Needless to say, digital manipulations of the latter kind, if they occur indeed at some supermarket's tills, affect algorithms and data much simpler than data mining technologies: for the very reason that these are often most effective when ensembles of models are combined,[78] and for the very reason that even the average information technologists may consider such systems daunting, let alone following how they run step by step,[79] data mining tools may be vulnerable to dishonest manipulation on the part of private corporate perpetrators. If such a scenario is ever to materialise,

---

[77] Mena (2003, p. 288) remarks that in telecommunications crime, outside criminals use either unwitting company personnel, or unscrupulous or venal employees to defraud the phone company.

[78] Less heterogeneous than *ensembles* of data mining models, in *committees* of artificial neural networks (ANNs) – also known as *committees of machines* – it is only neural networks that are combined. Different neural networks together vote on a given example. They are typically used as *classifiers*, i.e., machines that automatically divide input data into classes. *Committees* are "Ensembles of ANNs trained with the same data, often with different topologies, whose output is interpreted as a vote for the classification. Committees are appealing because they decrease the variance of the final decision, which is considered one of the most severe problems in semiparametric classifiers" (Principe et al., 2000, p. 640).

The usefulness of committees of neural networks consists of stabilising the results, by avoiding going astray after just a single neural network, as individual neural networks are subject to finding local minima during optimisation, thus missing resolutions that are globally better. It is as though on a surface with hills and valleys, if we are looking for a maximum, because of narrow vision we were to climb on a hill to the top, and not climb a mountain in another area. Even if the topology (architecture) of the neural network is the same, if we start with the same architecture and training but using different initial random weights, it is often the case that the behaviours of networks would be vastly different. Committees are a remedy to such variation.

Using committees of machines is similar to the method of *bagging* in machine learning. The difference is that in a committee of neural networks, one obtains the necessary variety of machines in the committee by training from different random starting weights. By contrast, in bagging the variety is obtained by training on different randomly selected subsets of the training data.

[79] In the final section in his book, a section entitled 'Alien Intelligence', Mena remarks about such software that evolves, breeds solutions, and learns on its own (2003, p. 376): "Sometime we can't follow its logic in detail, but we use these AI components because they are very accurate. This is what the renowned computer scientist and writer James Martin calls 'alien intelligence', which is a process executed on a computer that is so complex that a human can neither follow the logic step-by-step nor come to the same result by other means. We couldn't write a conventional program, for example, to spot fraud on millions of accounts in real time; we need neural networks to help us". The problem with neural networks is that they are notoriously opaque rather than transparent in how they run and reach results.

and if once it does, such an unfortunate development comes to be exposed, a major crisis in technology being trusted may ensue.

It is necessary to give this a thought already at present. A hint of how to address this could be that some mandatory procedures must apply, which themselves could not be tampered with. This kind of regulation is already in place at nuclear power plants, when validation software that carries out reactor core physics simulations must be run, after a design of how to reload fuel assemblies into the core has been produced.

At nuclear power plants, such mandatory procedures are motivated by a concern for safety. With corporate data mining, governmental regulation could enhance trust in proper use, discouraging the technology being misused fraudulently. For sure, data mining per se does not lend itself to criminal behaviour, but the risk is that because of the inner workings being beyond the understanding of non-IT or even some IT professionals, flawed or maliciously manipulated data mining tools would be misrepresented, in order to support unwarranted claims. The problem is only somewhat mitigated by the wide availability of commercial data mining kits, so that some similarity among tools is likely to occur, and this in turn enhances transparency up to a point.

6.1.6 Autonomous Agents

6.1.6.1 From Blackboard to Multiagent Systems

Multiagent systems constitute an independent topic at the intersection between distributed computing and artificial intelligence.[80] Multiagent technology[81] enables to manage a society of autonomous *software agents*, themselves each comprising three basic abilities:

- *communication skills* vis-à-vis other agents or human users;
- *knowledge*, either built-in (e.g., in a ruleset, or in a semantic network), or acquired by means of machine-learning techniques;
- *performing given tasks* (of which the ones relevant for investigative data mining are: information retrieval, filtering, monitoring, reporting),

and themselves each entrusted with tasks with may be specialising in sensing (and monitoring) vs. taking appropriate action,[82] or then in retrieval functions

---

[80] Textbooks on multiagent systems include Ferber (1999), Weiss (1999), Wooldridge (2002, 2nd edn.: 2009). Multiagent systems are sometimes combined with representations and techniques from, e.g. *logic* and *game theory* — this was shown in a book by Shoham and Leyton-Brown (2009) — or *algebra* (Amigoni & Continanza, 2012).

[81] See e.g. Wooldridge (2002); Wooldridge and Jennings (1995).

[82] A *security* application of this is the monitoring *digital signatures* provided by the use of swipe cards. If and when deviations from the norm are spotted, an alert is silently given, so that the card provider would monitor the card, just in case it was stolen.

(e.g., undertaking and carrying out given kinds of Web search), vs. in the analysis of what has been retrieved. Such software agents in turn may make use of other AI techniques, such as neural networks.[83] An example of *sensor agents* is such agents "that can read identity badges and detect the arrival and departure of users to a network, based on the observed user actions and the duration and frequency of use of certain applications or files" (Mena, 2003, p. 7). By contrast, *actor agents* may, e.g., create a profile, or "query a remote database to confirm access clearance" (ibid.).

An application of multiagent systems to crime investigation was reported about by Dijkstra, Bex, Prakken, and De Vey Mestdagh (2005).[84] It is about regulated information exchange during investigation between police forces. This is because (ibid., p. 133)

> in the European Union exchange of any personal data is regulated by privacy law and in the Netherlands exchange of crime investigation data between police departments is regulated by a special act. Typically, organisations must balance the goal to exchange as much information as possible with the obligation to stay within the law.

As they explained in the abstract:

> Interactions between police officers about information exchange are analysed as negotiation dialogues with embedded persuasion dialogues. An architecture is then proposed consisting of two agents, a requesting agent and a responding agent, and a communication language and protocol with which these agents can interact to promote optimal information exchange while respecting the law. Finally, dialogue policies are defined for the individual agents, specifying their behaviour within a negotiation. Essentially, when deciding to accept or reject an offer or to make a counteroffer, an agent first determines whether it is obligatory or permitted to perform the actions specified in the offer. If permitted but not obligatory, the agent next determines whether it is in his interest to accept the offer.

There is a multitude of applications of multiagent systems reported about in the scholarly literature. For example, Bivens, Gao, Hulber, and Szymanski (1999) reported about agent-based network monitoring. Szymanski and Chung (2001) reported about indexing the Web by means of agents, these being called *Web bots* (patterned after [*virtual*] *robot*). The latter application is an illustration of how multiagent technology can be combined with techniques from other domains, which in this particular case are information retrieval and text mining.

---

[83] In fact, the U.S. Treasury Department's Financial Crimes Enforcement Network (FinCEN), which tries to detect financial crimes, have a tool called FAIS (i.e., FinCEN Artificial Intelligence System), which "uses an agent to weed through this large data space" – namely, "all cash transactions involving dollar amounts of above $10,000", about ten million transactions a year – "and search for abnormalities and fraud through the use of neural network and link analysis" (Mena, 2003, p. 107).

[84] Dijkstra et al. (2005, p. 133) explained the context of their project "This research is part of an ongoing research project ANITA (Administrative Normative Information Transaction Agents), which aims at performing the fundamental research needed to develop a multi-agent system for regulated information exchange in the police intelligence domain [(De Vey Mestdagh, 2003)]."

A precursor of multiagent systems was what in AI from the 1980s was called the *blackboard* paradigm (it is still researched by some).[85] A problem is posted on the agenda inside the blackboard. Different knowledge sources (which now would be autonomous agents) check the blackboard, to see whether there is any (sub)problem the given knowledge source is competent for trying to solve. If a particular knowledge source is competent (which can be checked by means of that knowledge source's activation record, being a summary of what it is able to do), then that knowledge source tries its hand at it, and in the process may be faced with subproblems it cannot solve, so it posts such subproblems on the blackboard, for other knowledge sources to handle it if competent. See Figs. 6.1.6.1.1, 6.1.6.1.2, 6.1.6.1.3, 6.1.6.1.4, 6.1.6.1.5, 6.1.6.1.6, and 6.1.6.1.7. These are my own drawings, which convey notions drawn from Barbara Hayes-Roth's 1983 report on the blackboard architecture (Hayes-Roth, 1983; cf. 1985).

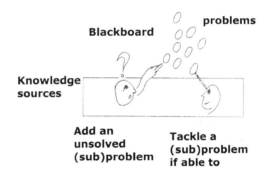

Fig. 6.1.6.1.1 Knowledge sources faced with (sub)problems in a blackboard architecture

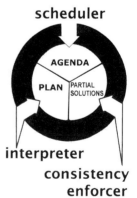

Fig. 6.1.6.1.2 An idealised schema of a blackboard (inside the circle) and of control components that access it (outside the circle)

---

[85] A blackboard-based approach has been reported in the late 2000s from the University of North Carolina at Charlotte (Liu, Yue, Wang, Raja, & Ribarsky, 2008; Yue, Raja, Liu, Wang, & Ribarsky, 2009; Yue, Raja, & Ribarsky, 2010).

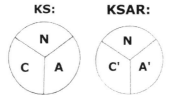

Fig. 6.1.6.1.3 Simplified schemata of (on the *left side*) a knowledge source (KS) in a blackboard architecture: N stands for the KS's name, C stands for the condition part of an *if-then* rule, and A stands for that rule's action part; and (on the *right side*) a knowledge source activation record (KSAR), which identifies a knowledge source. In the KSAR, too, N stands for the name of the KS (which is shared with the KSAR). C′ stands for the triggering condition of the KSAR, whereas A′ is the activity summary, i.e., a summary of proposed activities of the KS

Fig. 6.1.6.1.4 The control flow inside the blackboard architecture

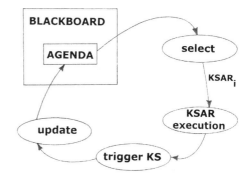

Fig. 6.1.6.1.5 The scheduler (inside the blackboard architecture) selects one of the pending actions from the agenda, where knowledge source activation records (KSARs) identify their respective knowledge sources (KSs). The scheduler identifies highest-performance tests. Once the scheduler has selected a given KSAR, the interpreter will execute the respective KS, of which a summary is provided in its KSAR

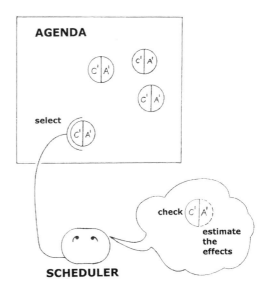

Fig. 6.1.6.1.6 Upon success
of the KS's condition's
validation, the interpreter
executes the action part of the
knowledge source, which in
turn modifies the blackboard

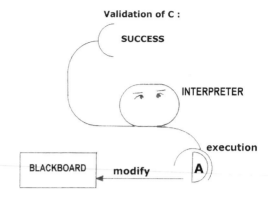

Fig. 6.1.6.1.7 To validate the
KS conditions, variables are
bound to values in the space
of partial solutions

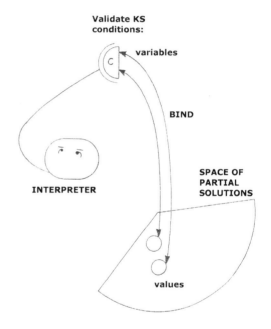

"The need for structured knowledge led to the earliest work that was recognizably multiagent systems: *blackboard systems*" (Wooldridge, 2002, p. 307).[86] "Blackboard systems were highly influential in the early days of

---

[86] The earliest implementation of blackboard systems was in the 1970s. An edited volume on the subject was published by Engelmore and Morgan (1988), and it quoted (ibid., p. 16; cf. Wooldridge 2002, p. 307) the blackboard metaphor as originally proposed by Newell (1962): "Metaphorically we can think of a set of workers, all looking at the same blackboard: each is able to read everything that is on it, and to judge when he has something worthwhile to add to it. This conception is [...] a set of demons, each independently looking at the total situation and shrieking in proportion to what they see fits their natures".

multiagent systems, but are no longer an area of major research activity" (Wooldridge, 2002, p. 308). Eventually, agents in multiagent systems took to communicate by *message passing*.

Blackboard systems have found application in legal computing: "GBB is an expert system shell based on the blackboard paradigm. It provides the blackboard database infrastructure, knowledge source languages and control components needed by a blackboard application. It is used in the construction of the CABARET legal knowledge based system" (Stranieri & Zeleznikow, 2005a, Glossary). Ashley's (1991) HYPO system (which modelled adversarial reasoning with legal precedents) was continued in the CABARET project (Rissland & Skalak, 1991), and the CATO project (Aleven & Ashley, 1997). Besides: "The PROLEXS project at the Computer/Law Institute, Vrije Universiteit, Amsterdam, Netherlands is concerned with the construction of legal expert shells to deal with vague concepts. Its current domain is Dutch landlord-tenant law. It uses several knowledge sources and the inference engines of the independent knowledge groups interact using a blackboard architecture" (Stranieri & Zeleznikow, 2005a, Glossary). PROLEXS is the subject of Walker, Oskamp, Schrickx, Opdorp, and van den Berg (1991) and of Oskamp, Walker, Schrickx, and van den Berg (1989).

Wooldridge (2002, p. 311) relates how the subcontracting[87] and negotiation metaphors emerged in multiagent systems research:

> In the late 1970s at Stanford University in California, a doctoral student called Reid Smith was completing his PhD on a system called the Contract Net, in which a number of agents ('problem solving nodes' in Smith's parlance) solved problems by delegating sub-problems to other agents (Smith, 1977, 1980a, b). As the name suggests, the key metaphor is that of sub-contracting in human organizations. The Contract Net remains to this day one of the most influential multiagent systems developed.[88] It introduced several key concepts into the multiagent systems literature, including the economics metaphor and the negotiation metaphor.

In fact, "the encounters that occur among computing elements in a multiagent system are *economic* encounters, in the sense that they are encounters between *self-interested* entities" (Wooldridge, 2002, p. 9). First of all, consider this general definition (Smith, 1980a, p. 1104):

> *Distributed problem solving* is the cooperative solution of problems by a decentralized and loosely coupled collection of knowledge-sources (*KS's*) (procedures, sets of production rules, etc.), located in a number of distinct processor nodes. The *KS's cooperate* in the sense that no one of them has sufficient information to solve the entire problem; mutual sharing of information is necessary to allow the group, as a whole, to produce an answer.

---

[87] See for example the treatment of the concept (from economics) of *incentive contracting* in an artificial intelligence framework, in a paper by Kraus (1996) that provides both a survey and a model.

[88] There are limitations, and proposed improvements. Fan, Huang, and Jin stated (2008, p. 603): "The CNP is a powerful coordination mechanism in multi-agent systems. However, the performance of the CNP degrades when the number of agents increases or the announcement is of high frequency. Hence, it has a problem of applicability to large-scale multi-agent systems. In order to overcome this problem, a personal assistant that may evaluate the other agents is proposed. It can avoid an announcement sent to redundant bidders, and only the best bidder sends the bid proposal."

By *decentralized* we mean that both control and data are logically and often geographically distributed; there is neither global control nor global data storage. *Loosely coupled* means that individual *KS's* spend most of their time in computation rather than communication.

In Reid Smith's contract net protocol (1980a), the basic messages are treated as follows. Let us start with task announcements (Smith, 1980a, p. 1106):

A node that generates a task normally initiates contract negotiation by advertising existence of that task to the other nodes with a **task announcement** message. It then acts as the manager of the task. A task announcement can be addressed to all nodes in the net (*general broadcast*), to a subset of nodes (*limited broadcast*), or to a single node (*point-to-point*). The latter two modes of addressing, which we call *focused ad-dressing*, reduce message processing overhead by allowing nonaddressed nodes to ignore task announcements after ex-amining only the **addressee** slot. The saving is small, but is useful because it allows a node's communication processor alone to decide whether the rest of the message should be ex-amined and further processed. It is also useful for reducing message traffic when the nodes of the problem solver are not interconnected with broadcast communication channels.

There are four main slots in a task announcement, in Smith's contract net proto-col: *eligibility specification, task abstraction, bid specification*, and *expiration time*. They are defined as follows (ibid.):

The **eligibility specification** is a list of criteria that a node must meet to be eligible to submit a bid. This slot reduces message traffic by pruning nodes whose bids would be clearly unacceptable. In a sense, it is an extension to the addressee slot. Focused addressing can be used to restrict the possible respondents only when the manager knows the *names* of appropriate nodes. The eligibility specification slot is used to further restrict the possible respondents when the manager is not certain of the names of appropriate nodes, but can write *a description* of such nodes.

The **task abstraction** is a brief description of the task to be executed. It enables a node to rank the task relative to other announced tasks. An abstraction is used rather than a complete description in order to reduce the length of the message.

The **bid specification** is a description of the expected form of a bid. It enables the manager to specify the kind of infor-mation that it considers important about a node that wants to execute the task. This provides a common basis for comparison of bids and enables a node to include in a bid only the information about its capabilities that is relevant to the task, rather than a complete description. This both simplifies the task of the manager in evaluating bids and further reduces message traffic.

The **expiration time** is a deadline for receiving bids. We assume global synchronization among the nodes. However, time is not critical in the negotiation process. For example, bids received after the expiration time of a task announcement are not catastrophic: at worst, they may result in a suboptimum selection of contractors.

Slot information is encoded in a high-level language understandable to all nodes, and called *common internode language*. It is supplemented with a programming language for transfer of procedures between nodes.

Another aspect of Smith's contract net protocol (CNET) is *task announcement processing* (Smith, 1980a, p. 1107):

In CNET, all tasks are typed. For each type of task, a node maintains a rank-ordered list of announcements that have been received and have not yet expired. Each node checks the eli-gibility specifications of all task announcements that it re-ceives. This involves ensuring that the conditions expressed in the specification are met by the node (e.g., MUST-HAVE

SENSOR). If it is eligible to bid on a task, then the node ranks that task relative to others under consideration.

Ranking a task announcement is, in general, a task-specific operation. Many of the operations involved in processing other messages are similarly task-specific. CNET defines a *task template* for each type of task. This template enables a user to specify the procedures required to process that type of task. In Appendix E we describe the roles of the required procedures, together with the default actions taken by CNET when the user chooses to omit a procedure.

Let us turn to *bidding*, in Smith's contract net protocol (ibid.):

announcement-ranking activity proceeds concurrently with task processing in a node until the task processor [...] completes processing of its current task and be-comes available for processing another task. At this point, the contract processor is enabled to submit bids on announced tasks. It checks its list of task announcements and selects a task on which to submit a bid. If there is only one type of task, the procedure is straightforward. If, on the other hand, there are a number of task types available, the node must select one of them. The current version of CNET selects the most recently received task (older tasks are more likely to have been already awarded).

An idle node can submit a bid on the most attractive task when either of the following events occur: 1) the node receives a new task announcement or 2) the expiration time is reached for any task announcement that the node has received. At each opportunity, the node makes a (task-specific) decision whether to submit a bid or wait for further task announcements. (In the *signal* task, a potential contractor waits for further an-nouncements in an attempt to find the closest manager.)

The template of a bid contains a *node abstraction slot.* That slot briefly describes which capacities the node has, that are relevant to the announced task. That same slot may also include a list of requirements: "Statements of this form are used by a bidder to indicate that it needs additional information if it is awarded the task." (ibid.).

Smith (1980a) also described how *bid processing* is done in his contract net protocol (ibid., p. 1107):

Contracts are queued locally by the manager that generated them until they can be awarded. The manager also maintains a rank-ordered list of bids that have been received for the task. When a bid is received, the manager ranks the bid relative to others under consideration. If, as a result, any of the bids are determined to be *satisfactory*, then the contract is awarded immediately to the associated bidder. (The definition of *satisfactory* is task-specific.) Otherwise, the manager waits for further bids.

Note that "a manager is not forced to always wait until the expiration time before awarding a contract" (Smith, ibid.). It may also be that at expiration time, the contract hasn't been awarded yet (Smith, 1980a, pp. 1107–1108):

If the expiration time is reached and the contract has not yet been awarded, several actions are possible. The appropriate action is task-specific, but the possibilities include: awarding the contract to the most acceptable bidder(s); transmitting another task announcement (if no bids have been received); or waiting for a time interval before transmitting another task announcement (if no acceptable bids have been received). This is in contrast to the traditional view of task allocation where the most appropriate node available at the time would be selected.

Successful bidders are informed that they are now con-tractors for a task through an **announced award** message. The **task specification** slot contains a specification of the data needed to begin execution of the task, together with any ad-ditional information requested by the bidder.

Once a contract is awarded, some data structures are used for communication between the contractor and the manager, and possibly also for communication with other nodes. In particular (Smith, 1980a, p. 1108):

> The *information message* is used for general communication between manager and contrac-tor during the processing of a contract. [...] The *report* is used by a contractor to inform the manager (and other report recipients, if any) that a task has been par-tially executed (an *interim report*) or completed (a *final report*). The *result description* slot contains the results of the execution. Final reports are the normal method of result communication. Interim reports, however, are useful when generator-style control is desired. A contractor can be set to work on a task and instructed to issue interim reports whenever the next result is ready. It then suspends the task until it is instructed by the manager to *continue* (with an information message) and produce another result.
>
> The manager can also terminate contracts with a *termination* message. The contractor receiving such a message terminates execution of the contract indicated in the message and all of its outstanding subcontracts.

Amigoni and Continanza (2012) address the problem of how to recruit agents to perform tasks:

> [W]e aim to contribute to the further methodological growth of multiagent systems by iden-tifying and formally studying a general problem that is related to the selection of agents to cope with given requests. More precisely, the problem we consider is to choose, or recruit, a subset of agents from a set of available agents, to satisfy a request. We call this problem the problem of recruitment of agents. The recruitment of agents is a general problem whose par-ticular instances pervade the whole field of multiagent systems: from the selection of agents, considered as primitive components, for forming a multiagent system (Weiss, 1999), to the assignment of goals (Durfee et al., 1987), to the allocation of tasks (Gerkey and Mataric, 2004), to the matchmaking between requested and available resources (Klusch and Sycara, 2001). The purpose of this paper, theoretical in its nature, is to introduce a novel formal approach to the problem of recruitment of agents. We characterize each agent by a set of functions it requires or it can perform. The request and the availability can be intended as two sets of agents. Broadly speaking, the problem of recruitment is thus to select a subset of the available agents in such a way the functions they can perform "cover" the functions of the requested agents. Some constraints can be imposed on the set of recruited agents, leading to the definition of different kinds of recruitment. We study the problem of recruit-ment of agents by adopting the algebraic formalism of lattices (Birkhoff, 1967; MacLane and Birkhoff, 1979). [...]

Amigoni and Continanza (2012) described five scenarios in which the problem of recruitment arises, either when multiagent systems are running, or even when they are being designed:

> In the field of multiagent systems, the problem of recruiting (selecting) the most suitable agents to satisfy a request arises in several situations. [...] The first scenario is related to the process of design and development of multiagent systems. Despite the lack of assessed methodologies for developing multiagent systems, it is widely recognized that agents have to be considered as reusable and composable items (Weiss, 1999). This idea pervaded the field since its early stages [...] One of the basic features that a methodology for developing multiagent systems is supposed to exhibit is the support to the reusability of agents as components. In this perspective, agents can be employed many times to compose different multiagent systems that address different applications. Several approaches

have been proposed for supporting the development of systems composed of reusable agents, ranging from agent platforms (Ricordel and Demazeau, 2000) to service-oriented approaches (Singh and Huhns, 2005). From the point of view of the designer of a multiagent system, it is important to have a way to determine which agents, among those available, are the most adequate for a given application. Hence, the problem is to select, to recruit, the available agents that are the most suitable to form the multiagent system. [...]

As to the scenarios when multiagent systems are running, they include, e.g., *goal assignment* (ibid.):

The second scenario is related to the well-studied problem of assigning goals in a multiagent system (Durfee et al., 1987). Generally speaking, the distribution of goals among the agents can be performed statically by the designer or dynamically during the activity of the system, according to some criteria. One of these criteria states that a goal must be assigned to the most suitable agent (see Weiss, 1999, Chapter 2). Such goal assignment problems are usually encountered in agent-based collaborative design systems (Parunak et al., 1997; Darr and Birmingham, 1996). The goal assignment problem can be considered as a recruitment problem in which the request is a set of "ideal" agents, each one exhibiting the abilities (i.e., functions or services) needed to reach a goal, whereas the availability is the set of "actual" agents (with their abilities) that are candidate to reach the goals.

Another scenario is with *subplan assignment* (ibid.):

The third scenario is related to the allocation of subplans to the agents (see Weiss, 1999, Chapter 3). This situation can be viewed as a special case of the previous one, in which the goal to be reached is to execute a subplan. The aim of the subplan allocation is to find an effective distribution of the subplans such that they are executed by the most adequate agents. [...]

Yet another scenario is with the *assignment of agents to tasks* (ibid.):

The fourth scenario generalizes the previous two and is related to the associations between agents and tasks to be performed. In this case, agents have some skills and some of these skills are required to perform tasks (see Weiss, 1999, Chapter 7). This problem is often encountered when the agents try to find collaboration partners (Gerkey & Mataric, 2004) and in role exchanging (Zhang & Hexmoor, 2002). More precisely, the problem involves a set of agents, a set of tasks to be fulfilled, and a utility function that measures the fitness of an agent for a task (which depends on the abilities of the agent and on the abilities need to perform the task). The objective is to find agents that can perform the tasks and that maximize (a function involving) utility. Once again, we can formulate this problem as an instance of the problem of recruitment by considering the request as a set of "ideal" agents that possess the abilities needed for executing the tasks and the availability as a set of "actual" agents that are present in the system.

And then there is the problem of *matchmaking* by means of *middle-agents* who moderate the requests (ibid.):

The last scenario is related to the problem of matchmaking, in which middle-agents connect service provider agents with requester agents in open environments (Klusch and Sycara, 2001; Pour Ebrahimi et al., 2004). This problem has found many solutions, including market-based approaches like contract net (Smith, 1980a) and fuzzy matching[89] (Ogston and Vassiliadis, 2002). Usually, these solutions associate a service provider to a requester, but do not fully address the case in which many service providers are needed to satisfy a request. Also matchmaking can be interpreted as a problem of recruitment by considering

---

[89] Fuzzy approaches are the subject of Section 6.1.15 in this book.

the request and the availability as sets of agents with the required and available services, respectively. [. . .]

In his discussion of agents in the context of investigative data mining, Mena (2003) is especially concerned with autonomous agent technology for intelligent retrieval from the Web or other sources (in a manner that conventional search engines cannot perform), based on different information types (e.g., documents in XML), to which they adapt their queries. Mena also discusses other applications of agents, e.g., as information-filtering agents (based on the security levels of users), and notification agents, giving special alerts to wireless devices. "When used in conjunction with other data mining technologies, [. . .] agents can assist investigators in accessing, organizing, and using current and relevant data for security deterrence, forensic analysis, and criminal detection" (Mena, 2003, p. 112). A case study in Mena's book is about a bio-surveillance agent for monitoring bio-terrorist attacks, and planned by DARPA[90] (ibid., section 4.10, pp. 117–120).

6.1.6.2　Multiagent Systems, Simulation and Geographic Space, in Tools for Training Police Officers

In Section 6.1.4, 'Geographic Information Systems for Mapping Crimes', we pointed out the distinction between visualisation on a geographical map of events that have actually occurred, and *geosimulation*. "Geosimulation (Benenson & Torrens, 2004) proposes the aggregation of Multi-Agent Systems (MAS) and Geographic Information Systems (GIS) for modeling and simulating urban phenomena" (Furtado & Vasconcelos, 2007, p. 57). Geosimulation "addresses an urban phenomena simulation model with a multi-agent approach to simulate discrete, dynamic, and event-oriented systems (Benenson & Torrens, 2004).

In geosimulated models, simulated urban phenomena are considered a result of the collective dynamic interaction among animate and inanimate entities that compose the environment. The Geographic Information System (GIS) is responsible for providing the 'data ware' in geosimulations" (ibid., p. 59). Gimblett (2002) is an edited volume about the integration of geographic information systems and agent-based modelling techniques for simulations, the applications being social or ecological.

Vasco Furtado and Eurico Vasconcelos (2007), of the University of Fortaleza in Brazil, have described the *ExpertCop* tutorial system, "a geosimulator of criminal dynamics in urban environments that aims to train police officers in the activity of preventive policing allocation" (ibid., p. 57). "In ExpertCop, the students (police officers) configure and allocate an available police force according to a selected geographic region, and then follow the simulation process" (ibid.).

The *Pedagogical Agent*, an intelligent automated tutor, helps the students to interpret the results, "by observing how crime behaves in the presence of the allocated preventive policing. The interaction between domain agents representing social

---

[90] DARPA is the United States' Defense Advanced Research Projects Agency.

entities such as criminals and police teams allocated by the students drives the simulation" (ibid.). The *Pedagogical Agent* "seeks to explain the model at the macro-level (global or emergent behavior) and micro-level (behavior of the agents individually)" (ibid.). "At the micro-level, the [Pedagogical A]gent uses the steps given in the decision-making process of each agent to explain individually each event that occurred in the simulation. At the macro-level, the [Pedagogical A]gent uses the data mining process to identify the system's patterns of behavior" (ibid., p. 78).

The architecture of *ExpertCop* comprises a user interface, a multiagent systems platform, a geographic information system, and a database. "The GIS is responsible for generating, manipulating and updating a map of the area on a small scale. The map contains geographical and statistical layers, representing the characteristics of the area such as streets, demographic density, traffic signs, slums, commercial areas, etc. The GIS agent makes it possible for the other system agents to interact with the map by creating patrol areas, identifying structures and distances, identifying the domain agent positions, plotting them and allowing them to move about the map" (ibid., p. 62).

"The criminals are the most important agents in the model" (ibid., p. 63), and "[t]heir internal architecture" consists of "three modules: perception, cognition and performance" (ibid.). "[S]pecific evaluation criteria are selected in the internal state, such as *risk, opportunity* and *reward*. [. . .] In the case of ExpertCop, only one type of evaluation is made, to commit a crime or not" (ibid., p. 64). "ExpertCop works only with robberies, thefts, and burglaries, which are types of crime influenced directly by preventive policing" (ibid.).

Risk is based on variables which include the type of crime (the risk level being "based on the type of punishment for the crime, on the level of experience and on the apparatus of the criminal" (ibid.)), the type of target –which "indicates the capacity of resistance against a crime" (ibid.), and that in *ExpertCop* is any of: "persons, vehicles, residences, gas stations, drugstores, lottery houses, banks and commercial establishments" (ibid., p. 66) – police presence, public illumination, and existence of escape routes (ibid.).

"*Benefit* is defined based on the type and amount of goods the target can offer" (ibid.). "*Personality* defines the criminal's 'courage' vis-à-vis the crime. When being created, a type of personality is randomly associated to the criminal (apprehensive, careful, fearless, and bold). A 'bold' criminal evaluates risk with fewer criteria, giving more weight to the benefit. But an 'apprehensive' criminal does the opposite, giving much more weight to risk" (ibid.).

Furtado and Vasconcelos further report (ibid.):

Another ongoing work aims at transforming ExpertCop into a decision-making support tool. In doing so, we are aware that the accuracy of the simulation model is essential. Therefore we have adopted a different approach for the crime simulation model. Instead of cognitive agents, criminals are reactive agents with behavior driven by real crime data and the statistical distribution of crime in urban areas. We model the criminal as distributed entities with the ability to demonstrate self-organization from their individual (local) activities as well as taking into consideration the influence of other criminals in the community where they live (Furtado et al., 2006). We are also designing an evolutionary approach that integrates with the simulation tool and is devised to assist police officers in the design of effective police patrol routes. Our approach is inspired by the increasing trend of hybridizing multi-agent systems with evolutionary algorithms. Our idea is to uncover strategies for police patrolling that cope with the dynamics of the crime represented by criminals that learn 'on the fly'. To uncover good police patrol routes in this context, we are integrating into the simulation model a genetic algorithm.[91] Preliminary experiences have shown that such an approach is very promising (Reis et al., 2006). Our long-term challenge is then to design and integrate educational strategies into a much more accurate crime simulation model.

CACTUS features another application of simulation to the training of police officers (Hartley & Varley, 2001). CACTUS is a multiagent simulation system. By using CACTUS, police officers are trained in managing public order events, and the tool is intended for helping them to develop strategic and contingency planning skills. There is simulation, and there is debriefing. The trainees use CACTUS collaboratively, as a team. A trainer acts as a facilitator, mediating among them, while they communicate among themselves the way they would doing in a real situation.

6.1.7 The Challenge of Handling a Disparate Mass of Data

6.1.7.1 Data Warehousing

Data warehousing is the "assembling a cohesive view of customers from multiple internal databases coupled with external demographic data sources", or also: "the practice of compiling transactional data with lifestyle demographics for constructing composites of customers and then decomposing them via segmentation reports and data mining techniques to extract profiles or 'views' or who they are and what they are" – a now standard notion from the computer science curriculum, but that here we have quoted as two definitions formulated by Mena (2003, pp. 4, 40), who noted that by the time he was writing, they had not yet been applied to criminal detection and security deterrence, and just yielded the potential of application to those areas.

Mena recommends (2003, p. 40) to test the data, using a subset of the entire data, and crucially, with a clear objective. With proper data mining, hidden patterns of behaviour of the persons involved will hopefully emerge. Some of the databases provide demographic data, or then credit data, but there also exist sources of criminal data, such as, in the United States, the National Law Enforcement Telecommunications System (NLETS), "a nationwide network that links all states and many federal agencies together for the exchange of criminal justice information" (Mena, 2003, p. 50), as well as the FBI's National Crime Information Center (NCIC). Other sources are DNA databases, and firearm databases. Yet another source is the log files generated by Web servers,[92] recording every transactions between the server and browsers. Moreover, servers write cookies to a browser's

---

[91] Genetic algorithms are the subject of Section 6.1.16.1 in this book.

[92] Tsai and Chan (2007) discussed the detection of cyber security threats in weblogs by using probabilistic models.

hard disk, so that the website can recognise returning visitors – something also enabled by another data set: Web bugs, i.e., invisible bits of code. These also alert if an email has been opened, or an embedded link was clicked on (Mena, 2003, pp. 57–59).

6.1.7.2 XML for Interoperability Between Data Sources

Typically, the databases you may find available, for them to be integrated into a *data warehouse* – this being (for our present concerns) in order to carry out investigative data mining – were devised for applications other than data mining. To provide interoperability among disparate systems, different kinds of data sets can be merged by using XML.[93] In particular, like for various other disciplines, XML standards have been developed for legal documents; this was done by non-profit organisations such as LegalXML.[94] Also see Leff (2001).

One resorts to XML syntax in order to mark up data, and the labels inserted come in pairs: it is like opening and closing a parenthesis. Such "parentheses" are typically nested inside each other. The nesting constitutes a hierarchy (a tree of attributes). The labels correspond to some semantics that we wish to convey to the computer about what these data are. Moreover, there are schemata that describe permissible structures of the nesting in the XML representation. This makes XML representations quite flexible.

In the 1980s, there was a school within database design research that advocated a kind of relational databases, such that the relations be not just flat tables, but would allow embedding. This was the *nested relations* school. In practice however, at the time that research community favoured shallow nesting, and developing the mathematics for handling this. By contrast, in XML and its parent-language, SGML, the depth of nesting is unlimited. SGML was originally devised for communicating structured documents.[95]

---

[93] The popularity of XML (Extensible Markup Language) stems from its role as a standard within Web technology (it was endorsed institutionally), and is reflected in a multitude of coding languages and applications making use of it, as well as in a literature comprising textbooks or reference books (Light, 1997; Holzner, 1998; Nakhimovsky & Myers, 2002), conference proceedings (Fuhr, 2006; Bressan, 2003; XML, 2002), and dissertations (Minh, 2007), as well as in reports in the information media.

[94] http://www.legalxml.org

[95] In the 1980s and later, this has also been the case of my own approach to nested relations: I advocated that the nesting should be deep and flexible, unlike in the mainstream of database design research into nested relations. This, along with the applicational thrust of what I had been developing, did not militate toward a favourable appreciation by the nested relations community of RAFFAELLO (my tool for retrieval from nested relations) and CuProS (Customization Production Systems) — itself, a ruleset- or formal grammar description of how the nesting of attributes is allowed to be within given types of nested relations). In retrospect, the applicational thrust of the RAFFAELLO project had been quite warranted: the quite similar concept of XML has at present a great appeal, for quite various applications, and the emergence of the World Wide Web has much favoured this.

Deep nested relations *could* be represented in some formal approaches from the 1980s and early 1990s, but it is the flexibility that eluded them. Nested relations emerged, in relational database

XML originated from the Standard Generalized Markup Language, SGML for short,[96] that was designed in the 1980s, and is defined in ISO Standard 8879. SGML enabled a formal definition of the component parts of a publishable data set, and when designed, it was primarily intended as a tool enabling publishable data (such as technical documentation) to be interchanged between, for example, authors or originators, and publishers. By the late 1980s, early digital media publishers had understood the versatility of SGML for dynamic information display. The main historical interest now of SGML is that it was simplified into XML, the Extensible Markup Language, that is at the foundation of the area of research known now as the *Semantic Web*: the use of a *semantic web* makes it possible for online textual (or multimedial) searches to find content based on meaning and context, as opposed to conventional search engines that only find documents containing specific user-defined words or phrases. Most of XML comes from SGML unchanged. Now XML is even appearing as a data type in some other languages.[97]

---

design research, out of the desire to generalise flat relations, so that hierarchically structured objects could be modelled directly. Paper collections appeared (Abiteboul, Fischer, & Schek, 1989; Özsoyoğlu, 1988). Normal forms were introduced for nested relations (Özsoyoğlu & Yuan, 1987), in the tradition of normal forms from relational databases.

Mark Levene introduced important variants of nested relations (Levene, 1992; Levene & Loizou, 1990). In particular, he combined the *universal relation model* – which allows the user to view the database as though it was just one flat relation, in the space of all attributes of the database: it was the subject of my early research (Nissan, 1982, 1983, 1987c) – with nested relations, into an approach called the *nested universal relation model* (Levene, 1992). Levene's model offered the following advantages: "Functional data dependencies and the classical notion of lossless decomposition are extended to nested relations and an extended chase procedure is defined to test the satisfaction of the data dependencies. The nested UR [i.e., universal relation] model is defined, and the classical UR model is shown to be a special case of the nested model.

This implies that an UR interface can be implemented by using the nested UR model, thus gaining the full advantages of nested relations over flat relations" (Levene, 1992, abstract). Levene's formalisation incorporated null values into the model. Also see Levene and Loizou (1993, 1994). Incidentally, apart from relational databases, Levene has also done (with Poulovassilis) some work on a nested-graph database model for representing and manipulating complex objects (Poulovassilis & Levene, 1994).

More recent work on nested relations includes Bertino, Catania, and Wong (1999) and Garani (2004, 2008). Georgia Garani (whose 2004 Ph.D. is from Mark Levene's department at Birkbeck College in London) distinguishes nested attributes as decomposable and non-decomposable (Garani, 2008). Overcoming a once popular maxim in nested relations research ("Unnesting and then nesting on the same attribute of a nested relation does not always yield the original relation"), Garani (2008) has proven that "for all nested relations, unnesting and then renesting on the same attribute yields the original relation subject only to the elimination of duplicate data".

[96] The literature about SGML includes Goldfarb (1990), Bryan (1997), Smith (1992), and Spivak (1996).

[97] SGML's and XML's idea of trees of data, that can be conceived of as embedded parentheses with an unlimited depth of nesting, described in a meta-schema, was also separately attained in the 1980 in the RAFFAELLO representation language, with its CuProS meta-representation language – on which, see now Nissan (2010c) and Nissan & El-Sana (2012). They were originally described in Nissan (1986, 1987a, 1988, 1999). The original application was to lexical databases (Nissan, 1988, 1999), catering and terminal food-processing (Nissan, 1987b), and law (Nissan, 1992) – the latter application being a combined representation of Italy's regional constitutions (*Statuti Regionali*).

There is one aspect of XML that was first formalised in XML (rather than SGML), but had been first successfully implemented in a number of projects, one of these being in lexicography: the software from the University of Waterloo, Canada, New Oxford English Dictionary Project. That aspect is the notion of *well-formedness*, as opposed to *validity*. Well-formedness enables parsing without a schema. By contrast, an XML document being valid means that it contains a reference to a schema (a Document Type Definition, or DTD), and abides by that schema. The schema itself is a grammar. There are various schema languages for XML. The oldest of these is DTD, that XML inherited from SGML. But XML DTDs are simpler than SGML DTDs.

It is typical for webpages to be coded in HTML: labels of HTML are interspersed within the textual content, and the identifiers of graphic material. HTML handles presentation, not content, which is what XML is supposed to do. If one was to search an HTML Web page for content, one could only look for the occurrences of given strings. This is because the only function of the syntax of HTML is to structure the presentation, regardless of the meaning of the content. In XML, instead, the syntax is meant to describe the semantics of the content, whereas a separate module, called a stylesheet, states how the syntactic units extracted from an XML document are to be displayed. It is not the case that the entire content of the stored data has to be displayed, only their layout will be different. In fact, it may be possible to only extract some of the information, as enclosed by given tags which constitute semantic attributes; it's the data retrieved in response to a query that will be displayed as instructed by the stylesheet, and the query itself is actually specified inside the stylesheet along with the specification of how to display the results.

Furthermore, as mentioned earlier, a separate module, called DTD (for Document Type Definition) will describe admissible structures of the semantic attributes with respect to each other, the way they can appear inside the XML document. That is to say, the DTD is the schema of a database, whose instances are the respective XML documents.

There are some minor problems with terminology, when dealing with both XML and databases, because the term 'attribute' and the term 'entity' are used differently in the XML literature and in the database literature. Here is a standard XML

As to the food processing project, this was a relatively minor project, punningly named FIDEL GASTRO (after *gastronomy*), and that I had my undergraduate students implement in 1987. It was considered valuable enough for a journal in hospitality management to publish a paper on this application to large kitchens. FIDEL GASTRO finds now a parallel in a function of the so-called Microsoft Home, introduced in 2004, and reportedly first inhabited by Bill Gates and his family. Even though the Microsoft Home uses radio-frequency identification tags for inventory tracking, the basic function is like that of my 1987 project. Barron (2004), describing the Microsoft Home, wrote: "The network knows, for example, what ingredients are available in the kitchen. If the makings for chocolate chip cookies are not at hand, it will suggest a recipe for oatmeal cookies, assuming these ingredients are on the shelf" – and this is precisely what FIDEL GASTRO was doing. Incidentally, bear in mind that catering is a subject complex enough to be taught at vocational schools, and that there exist textbooks, e.g. Kinton, Ceserani, and Foskett (1992).

definition for 'attribute': "A name-value pair, separated by an equals sign, included inside a tagged element that modifies certain features of the element. All attribute values, including things like size and width, are in fact text strings and not numbers. For XML, all values must be enclosed in quotation marks".

This is very much like some HTML declarations of tables, or of the inclusion of images, and the like. What is meant by 'attribute' in database terminology, is called an 'element' in the jargon of XML, and what in database terminology is "the value of the attribute", in XML is the content of the element. If a string, this is referred to as data of the PCDATA type. If, instead, something that is nested inside the current element, then this aggregate is made of sub-elements of that element.

Consider a database relation schema, whose attributes ("attributes" as meant in database terminology, that is, "elements" in XML) are:

FORENAMES
SURNAME
EMPLOYMENT
PLACE_OF_RESIDENCE
MARITAL_STATUS
DEPENDENTS
REFERENCES.

One straightforward way to represent in XML such a relation for the given individual, Donald Duck, would be to simply enclose the value of each relation attribute between two tags, <FORENAME> and </FORENAME>, and so forth:

```
<PERSON>
    <FORENAMES>      Donald        </FORENAMES>
    <SURNAME>        Duck           </SURNAME>
    <EMPLOYMENT>        unemployed     </EMPLOYMENT>
    <PLACE_OF_RESIDENCE> Duckburg </PLACE_OF_RESIDENCE>
    <PLACE_OF_BIRTH> Granny McDuck's Farm </PLACE_OF_BIRTH>
    <MARITAL_STATUS>    unmarried    </MARITAL_STATUS>
    <DEPENDENTS>      Hewey          </DEPENDENTS>
    <DEPENDENTS>      Louie          </DEPENDENTS>
    <DEPENDENTS>      Dewey          </DEPENDENTS>
    <REFERENCES>      Scrooge McDuck </REFERENCES>
    <REFERENCES>      Daisy Duck      </REFERENCES>
    <REFERENCES>      Mickey Mouse    </REFERENCES>
</PERSON>
```

Such a slavish rendering into XML of the database relation lifted from a relational database grossly underexploits the capabilities of XML. To start with, mainstream relational database technology stores the data in flat relations, that is, tables. In the 1980s and early 1990s, several database researchers tried to promote an alternative kind of relational databases, in which tables could be nested inside each other, or, to say it otherwise, attributes may be nested as being the value of another attribute. In artificial intelligence representations, too, frames usually are hierarchies of properties: the values are the terminal nodes in a tree with, say, three generations. Conceptually, such were some of the ideas that can be detected behind the rise of XML, as being a coding in which you can actually nest any levels of attributes inside each other. For example, the same XML file could store a much richer relation than the above, still for the individual whose name is Donald Duck:

```
<PERSON>
    <NAME>
      <FORENAME>  Donald  </FORENAME>
      <SURNAME>
          <CURRENT>  Duck   </CURRENT>
          <AS_RECORDED_AT_BIRTH>

                McDuck

  </AS_RECORDED_AT_BIRTH>
      </SURNAME>
    </NAME>
    <EMPLOYMENT_RECORD>
      <CURRENT_EMPLOYMENT>
        unemployed
      </CURRENT_EMPLOYMENT>
      <PREVIOUS_EMPLOYMENT>
          <CATEGORY>  sailor   </CATEGORY>
          <CATEGORY>  farm hand  </CATEGORY>
          <FROM>    1936     </FROM>
          <UNTIL>   1937     </UNTIL>
      </PREVIOUS_EMPLOYMENT>
      <PREVIOUS_EMPLOYMENT>
          <CATEGORY> factotum     </CATEGORY>
          <EMPLOYER> Scrooge McDuck </EMPLOYER>
          <WHEN>    often      </WHEN>
          <MODE> short-term informal contract </MODE>
      </PREVIOUS_EMPLOYMENT>
    </EMPLOYMENT_RECORD>
    <PLACE_OF_RESIDENCE>
        <TOWN>     Duckburg   </TOWN>
        <STATE>    California    </STATE>
    </PLACE_OF_RESIDENCE>
    <PLACE_OF_BIRTH>
        <PLACE> Granny McDuck's Farm  </PLACE>
        <COUNTY>    Duckburg    </COUNTY>
        <STATE>    California    </STATE>
    </PLACE_OF_BIRTH>
```

```
<MARITAL_STATUS> unmarried </MARITAL_STATUS>
<DEPENDENTS>
  <MINOR>
      <NEPHEW>    Hewey   </NEPHEW>
      <NEPHEW>    Louie   </NEPHEW>
      <NEPHEW>    Dewey   </NEPHEW>
  </MINOR>
  <SENIOR>
      <UNCLE>    Scrooge McDuck   </UNCLE>
  </SENIOR>
</DEPENDENTS>
<REFERENCES>    Daisy Duck    </REFERENCES>
<REFERENCES>    Mickey Mouse   </REFERENCES>
</PERSON>
```

The syntax of XML requires that the hierarchical structure have one and just one root, which here is PERSON. Let the XML code of the example given above be stored in a file called duck1.xml It will have to be preceded by two initial XML statements, respectively specifying under which version of XML and with which alphanumeric encoding that file has to be processed; and to which stylesheet type and given stylesheet file the given XML file should be linked:

```
<?xml version="1.0" encoding="UTF-8"?>
<?xml-stylesheet type="text/xsl" href="nicestyle3.xsl"?>
```

Now, let us define the DTD for the XML nested relation in which we stored information about Donald Duck. We want to state that:

- The root element is PERSON.
- The root element contains one NAME element.
- The root element contains zero or one elements of each of the following: EMPLOYMENT_RECORD, PLACE_OF_RESIDENCE, PLACE_OF_BIRTH (it may be absent for some reason), MARITAL_STATUS} (it also may be absent, for example if unknown, or not relevant, or even deliberately withheld), and MARITAL_STATUS may or may not include an element SPOUSE.
- The root element contains zero or more elements of each of the following: DEPENDENTS (not anybody has other people legally depending on him or her), REFERENCES.
- Each NAME element is expected to contain either one or more strings (the symbol standing for a string in a DTD is #PCDATA), or one or more FORENAME and one or more SURNAME, and moreover, these may contain just a value, or, then, zero or more CURRENT, PREVIOUS, and AS_RECORDED_AT_BIRTH. The symbol | stands for "or".
- Element EMPLOYMENT_RECORD may include one or more strings, or then, zero or more elements for CURRENT_EMPLOYMENT and for

PREVIOUS_EMPLOYMENT, and these possibly contain a further level of nest-ing, including zero or more CATEGORY elements and zero or one FROM, UNTIL, or WHEN elements.

- Elements PLACE_OF_RESIDENCE and PLACE_OF_BIRTH include some string, or zero or one PLACE, COUNTY, STATE}, and COUNTRY.
- DEPENDENTS may include some string, or zero or more of: MINOR, SENIOR.
- SPOUSE, REFERENCES, or elements inside MINOR or SENIOR may each include just a string, or a NAME element, or a LINK_TO_PERSON element.
- MINOR may include one or more of: CHILD, GRANDCHILD, NEPHEW, GREATNEPHEW, COUSIN.
- SENIOR may include zero or more of: PARENT, GRANDPARENT, UNCLE, GREATUNCLE, COUSIN (a child may be grown-up and thus no longer or minor age, yet be otherwise legally a minor).

The DTD is coded as follows.

```xml
<?xml version="1.0"?>
<!ELEMENT  PERSON  (NAME, EMPLOYMENT_RECORD+,
                    PLACE_OF_RESIDENCE+,
                    PLACE_OF_BIRTH+,
                    MARITAL_STATUS+,
                    DEPENDENTS*,
                    REFERENCES*)>
<!ELEMENT  NAME
            (#PCDATA+ | (FORENAME*, SURNAME*))>
<!ELEMENT  FORENAME
            (#PCDATA+ | (CURRENT*, PREVIOUS*,
                        AS_RECORDED_AT_BIRTH*))>
<!ELEMENT  SURNAME
            (#PCDATA+ | (CURRENT*,
                        PREVIOUS*,
                        AS_RECORDED_AT_BIRTH*))>
<!ELEMENT  CURRENT  (#PCDATA*)>
<!ELEMENT  PREVIOUS (#PCDATA*)>
<!ELEMENT  AS_RECORDED_AT_BIRTH  (#PCDATA*)>
<!ELEMENT  EMPLOYMENT_RECORD
            (#PCDATA+ | (CURRENT_EMPLOYMENT*,
                        PREVIOUS_EMPLOYMENT*))>
<!ELEMENT  CURRENT_EMPLOYMENT
        (#PCDATA+ | (CATEGORY*, FROM+, UNTIL+, WHEN+))>
<!ELEMENT  PREVIOUS_EMPLOYMENT
      (#PCDATA+ | (CATEGORY*, FROM+, UNTIL+, WHEN+))>
<!ELEMENT  PLACE_OF_RESIDENCE
```

```
                  (#PCDATA+ | (PLACE+, COUNTY+, STATE+, COUNTRY+))>
<!ELEMENT  PLACE_OF_BIRTH
                  (#PCDATA+ | (PLACE+, COUNTY+, STATE+, COUNTRY+))>
<!ELEMENT  MARITAL_STATUS (#PCDATA*, SPOUSE*)>
<!ELEMENT  DEPENDENTS (#PCDATA*, MINOR*, SENIOR*)>
<!ELEMENT  MINOR (#PCDATA*, CHILD*, GRANDCHILD*,
                            NEPHEW*, GREATNEPHEW*, COUSIN*)>
<!ELEMENT  SENIOR (#PCDATA*, PARENT*, GRANDPARENT*,
                            UNCLE*, GREATUNCLE*, COUSIN*)>
<!ELEMENT  SPOUSE   (#PCDATA*, NAME+, LINK_TO_PERSON)>
<!ELEMENT  LINK_TO_PERSON   (#PCDATA*)>
<!ELEMENT  CHILDN   (#PCDATA*, NAME+, LINK_TO_PERSON)>
<!ELEMENT  PARENT   (#PCDATA*, NAME+, LINK_TO_PERSON)>
<!ELEMENT  GRANDPARENT
                            (#PCDATA*, NAME+, LINK_TO_PERSON)>
<!ELEMENT  UNCLE (#PCDATA*, NAME+, LINK_TO_PERSON)>
<!ELEMENT  GREATUNCLE (#PCDATA*, NAME+, LINK_TO_PERSON)>
<!ELEMENT  NEPHEW   (#PCDATA*, NAME+, LINK_TO_PERSON)>
<!ELEMENT  GREATNEPHEW (#PCDATA*, NAME+, LINK_TO_PERSON)>
<!ELEMENT  COUSIN   (#PCDATA*, NAME+, LINK_TO_PERSON)>
<!ELEMENT  PLACE   (#PCDATA*)>
<!ELEMENT  COUNTY   (#PCDATA*)>
<!ELEMENT  STATE    (#PCDATA*)>
<!ELEMENT  COUNTRY  (#PCDATA*)>
<!ELEMENT  CATEGORY (#PCDATA*)>
<!ELEMENT  FROM     (#PCDATA*)>
<!ELEMENT  UNTIL    (#PCDATA*)>
<!ELEMENT  WHEN     (#PCDATA*)>
```

The meaning of the notation can be understood by comparing this code with the explanation with which it was foreworded. Ishikawa, Yokohama, Ohta, and Katayama (2005) discussed mining XML structures based on statistics. Lee and Hwang (2005) discussed a method for retrieving similar XML documents.

6.1.7.3 Ontologies

Structuring conceptual relations by using *ontology* languages (and XML can be adapted into such a task) is a development of what in AI from the 1970s and 1980s used to be *semantic networks*, i.e., networks drawn as graphs whose nodes are concepts, and whose arcs (edges) are labelled with relationships between those concepts. The application of *ontologies* has mushroomed, and at present there exists a body of research into *data mining with ontologies* (Nigro, González Císaro, & Xodo, 2008). Mena's (2003) *Investigative Data Mining for Security and*

Criminal Detection does not mention ontologies, but by the early 2010s the times are mature for considering ontologies as well, when devising applications for law enforcement.[98]

From the late 1960s to the 1980s, *semantic networks* have been a prominent kind of knowledge representation in artificial intelligence.[99] In 1975, Gary Hendrix introduced *partitioned semantic networks*, i.e., such semantic networks that apart from being drawn as graphs with nodes and labelled arcs, also allow arcs and nodes to be bundled together into spaces (drawn as rectangles), that are themselves joined by arcs (Hendrix, 1979).

Various kinds of semantic networks were developed during the 1970s and 1980s. During the 1990s and 2000s, semantic networks further spread, in practice becoming the conceptual centrepiece of *ontologies*. The two concepts are not identical, though, but the latter are rooted in the former. The stress in using ontologies is on uniform communication and shared understanding (Uschold & Grüninger, 2004). John Sowa was conspicuous in semantic or associative networks (Sowa, 1991, 1994, 2006), and he also turned to the discourse of ontologies, with its partly new terminology (Sowa, 1995). The term 'ontology' in computer science became popular in the 1990s, apparently following Gruber (1993, cf. 1995), but it was in use already in the 1980s within artificial intelligence. "A specification of a representational vocabulary for a shared domain of discourse — definitions of classes, relations, functions, and other objects — is called an ontology" (ibid., in the abstract).

The difference between semantic networks and ontologies as being a formalism for organising concepts is that the stress in ontologies is "shared understanding", for it to function as a unifying framework. Shared understanding is itself considered to be a requirement: for good communication; for identifying requirements for any system (e.g., software) to be developed so that it could be specified properly; and for interoperability, and possibly reuse and sharing, as well as so that formal representation would enable the automation of consistency checking, thus improving reliability.

We quote from Uschold and Grüninger (1996):

> '*Ontology*' is the term used to refer to the shared understanding of some domain of interest which may be used as a unifying framework to solve the above problems in the above-described manner. An ontology necessarily entails or embodies some sort of world view with respect to a given domain. The world view is often conceived as a set of concepts (e.g. entities, attributes, processes), their definitions and their inter-relationships; this is referred to as a *conceptualisation*. Such a conceptualisation may be implicit, e.g. existing only in someone's head, or embodied in a piece of software. [...] However, the more standard usage and that which we will adopt is that the ontology is an explicit account or representation of [some part of] a conceptualisation.

---

[98] Munn and Smith (2008) try to relate ontologies as being structured, automated representations developed within knowledge engineering (their examples are from medicine and biology), to *philosophical ontology*: in philosophy, ontology is the discipline concerned with how things in the world are divided into categories, and how these categories are related.

[99] Sowa (2006, 1991), Findler (1979), Lehmann (1992), Maida and Shapiro (1982), Woods (1975), Steyvers and Tenenbaum (2005).

What does an ontology look like? An [explicit] ontology may take a variety of forms, but necessarily it will include a vocabulary of terms and some specification of their meaning (i.e. definitions). The degree of formality by which a vocabulary is created and meaning is specified varies considerably. [...] A formal ontology is a formal description of objects, properties of objects, and relations among objects. This provides the language that will be used to express the definitions and constraints in the axioms. This language must provide the necessary terminology to restate the informal competency questions. If we are designing a new ontology, then for every informal competency question, there must be objects, attributes, or relations in the proposed ontology or proposed extension to an ontology, which are intuitively required to answer the question. [...]

Ontologies (Uschold & Grüninger, 1996, 2004) have become widespread, in applied computing, and there is much research ongoing within computer science.[100] There may be *domain ontologies*, that are specialised per specific domains, and *upper ontologies*, that are general common sense that applies across a wide range of domains. An important example of the latter is the CYC project (Lenat & Guha, 1990). One also speaks of *ontology engineering*, i.e., the set of techniques for building ontologies.[101] This is a subfield of knowledge engineering. Arrigoni Neri and Colombetti (2009) remarked:

An ontology designed to represent the knowledge about a specific domain is usually not directly suitable for esource [i.e., electronic source] metadata. In general, an ontology engineer designs the ontology as a collection of concepts, more or less organised in taxonomies. Then he uses language constructs to further constrain ontology interpretations and finally he fills its ontology with some relevant individuals. The result is that some domain terms are used as concepts, while others are used as individuals. The level of this division largely depends on designer preference and the specific goal the ontology is designed for.

There exist various special ontology languages (*OWL* is popular), and there are description logics for ontologies,[102] but one could also resort to general programming languages, such as *Prolog* or *Lisp*, in order to represent ontologies, or then one may store these in data structures, to be manipulated by languages such as *C++* or *Java*. For example, Astrova and Kalja (2008) reported about storing *OWL* ontologies in *SQL3* object-relational databases.[103]

An ontology (as meant in computer science) is a formal representation of a set of concepts and the relations among them, within a given domain (or in general common sense). Ontologies are important for the purpose of enabling knowledge sharing and reuse. Typically, an ontology includes individuals, classes of individuals (instances or objects), attributes of objects or classes, and relations. Relations are often drawn as arcs in a graph, whose nodes are individuals or classes. Moreover, there may also be *restrictions* (necessary conditions), and *if/then rules*, that augment

---

[100] E.g., see Staab and Studer (2009), Grüninger and Lee (2002), and Uschold (2005).

[101] E.g., see Gómez-Pérez, Fernández-López, and Corcho (2004), De Nicola, Missikoff, and Navigli (2009), Orgun and Meyer (2008), Gruber (1995), Lam (2007), and Toppano, Roberto, Giuffrida, and Buora (2008).

[102] Description logics for ontologies are the subject of Sattler (2003) and Baader et al. (2003).

[103] Conference series sometimes combine, in their scope, databases and ontologies (Catarci & Sycara, 2004; ODBASE, 2005).

the representation. There may be as well events, that change attributes or relations. And there may be axioms (but by these, when dealing with ontologies, one means not only a priori knowledge, but also the theory derived).

Just as methods from artificial intelligence have become mainstream and incorporated in some other areas of the practice of computing, the same has happened with ontologies. Traditionally and at present, too, ontologies are important in computational linguistics.[104] *WordNet* is a well-known monolingual English lexicon.[105] Another important area of application of ontologies is the Semantic Web.[106] There are applications of ontologies to information-providing dialogue-systems: in Sweden, Annika Flycht-Eriksson completed a doctoral dissertation (2004) on the design and use of ontologies in such systems.

Ontologies are also important for enterprise architectures, because of the need to communicate; e.g., they are a cost factor in enterprise integration (Goranson et al., 2002). Ontology-based integration of information is a main purpose of ontologies, and various approaches to doing this exist (e.g., Wache et al., 2001). Integrating disparate kinds of information can be quite difficult, all the more so if the data reside outside a single organisation. Access to remote data is essential for investigative data mining as desirable for law enforcement agencies. Large governmental agencies themselves have their own, different information systems. A "data-integration issue that may limit the type of information available for some investigative data mining projects" (Mena, 2003, p. 65) is the data residing in multiple, remote locations, "which may mean that these sources must be accessed via LANs, WANs, Intranet, dial-up, wireless, Internet, or proprietary closed, secured networks. This may mean that control and access is by a third party and the data is not in a centralized repository or data warehouse" (ibid.). But, we add, such disparateness is itself a possible area of application of ontologies.

---

[104] See Calzolari, Monachini, Quochi, Socia, and Toral (2010), Hirst (2004), Aussenac-Gilles and Sörgel (2005), and Poesio (2005). In a special sense, the motivation for developing ontologies in computer applications has an important precedent in the work of corporate terminologists (e.g., at Airbus), as opposed to state institutions that in some countries (e.g., France and Israel) approve terminology. Unlike at such state institutions, the knowhow of corporate terminologists comes close to concepts that are current in ontology development. In artificial intelligence, the emergence of ontologies was contextually different from the emergence of semantic networks, even though without a grasp of the latter, ontologies would not have emerged. Namely, the need for ontologies was felt when developing very large knowledge bases. But no matter how simple your artificial intelligence application, you are not unlikely to be using a semantic network, and actually *Prolog* students often learn that language by first programming some rudimentary semantic network. The work of terminologists proper has benefited from the burgeoning state of the art of ontologies as being an area of computer science.

[105] Concerning *WordNet*, see Fellbaum (1998), and see http://wordnet.princeton.edu/ Besides, Lenci et al. (2000) discussed SIMPLE, a framework for the development of multilingual lexicons.

[106] Berners-Lee, Hendler, and Lassila (2001) is a popularistic introduction to the Semantic Web. Also see Michael Uschold's (2003) "Where Are the Semantics in the Semantic Web?". Maedche and Staab (2001) reported about ontology learning from the Semantic Web. Fensel, van Harmelen, Horrocks, McGuinness, and Patel-Schneider (2001) discussed an ontology infrastructure for the Semantic Web. AAAI (2002) is a paper collection about ontologies and the Semantic Web.

Mena (2003, p. 65) also mentioned "the thorny issue of integrating multimedia formats, involving free-text data, as well as images, audio, e-mail, wireless data, and other binary objects". He remarked: "For counter-intelligence analyses, which need to deal with these types of information objects and formats, this is a very real data-integration and analysis issue", and ensuring a consistent framework "can be a real challenge when dealing with time-sensitive analyses and a need to implement solutions in real time" (ibid.).

Bear in mind however that even independently of explicit ontologies, but at any rate based on semantics and content, there exists a body of research into retrieval from video data; see, e.g., Shim and Shin's paper (2005) "Spatio-temporal modeling of moving objects for content- and semantic-based retrieval in video data". Within research on ontologies there is work concerned with multimedia. Ontologies have been developed for representing and annotating video-events (François, Nevatia, Hobbs, & Bolles, 2005).

Consider the graph in Fig. 6.1.7.3.1, being a detail from the screen (in Arrigoni Neri & Colombetti, 2009) of an ontology navigation based query. As can be seen, multimedial objects are described. Mario Arrigoni Neri of Nova Semantics has kindly supplied me with Fig. 6.1.7.3.2, showing in a clearer manner a subgraph of the one shown in the screenshot detail shown in Fig. 6.1.7.3.1. It is useful to realise that applications of ontologies to multimedia are extant: Kompatsiaris and Hobson (2008) published a paper collection on the theory and applications of semantic multimedia and ontologies. Song, Koo, Yoo, and Choi (2005) discussed an ontology for integrating multimedia databases. For sure, applications need not necessarily be what law enforcement agencies need. For example, there are applications to the cultural heritage: Vrochidis et al. (2008) reported about a hybrid ontology and visual-based retrieval model for cultural heritage multimedia collections. Image processing is one of the areas of application of ontologies: Anouncia and Saravanan (2007) discussed ontology-based process plan generation for image processing.[107]

---

[107] It is important to realise that any positive integer number of variables may be associated with individual pixels, and one may have *multivariate images*, requiring *multivariate image mining* (or *MVI mining*). Herold, Loyek, and Nattkemper (2011) provide an overview. They explain (ibid., p. 2): "Because of recent advances in sensor technology and a rapid increase in storage capacities, a growing number of intensity values can be recorded and associated with pixel coordinates using new imaging technologies. This growth in dimension can be observed in different scientific areas and this new category of images is referred to as multivariate images (MVIs). In these images, an almost arbitrary number of variables is associated with each pixel that represent, for instance, signal values at different time points or for different spectral bands or for different imaging parameters or modalities. Thus, these images can no longer be interpreted as gray value images or red, green, blue color images, and new information technologies are needed." Current applications are mainly to biomedical imaging. In particular, multivariate images result from different techniques, and include *multispectral images* in microscopy, *multifluorescence imaging* (or *multicolour imaging*: it "aims at precisely visualizing the location of molecules in a sample"), and *multimodal imaging*.

In *multispectral imaging*, a "biological sample is imaged for multiple wavelengths so that each signal, s_i ($i \in [1, n]$), represents the intensity of a pixel at a given wavelength λ_i. In general, a red, green, blue (RGB) image can be regarded as the most simple multispectral image stack with

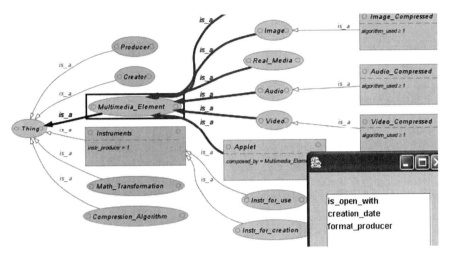

Fig. 6.1.7.3.1   A detail from a screen snapshot in Arrigoni Neri and Colombetti (2009)

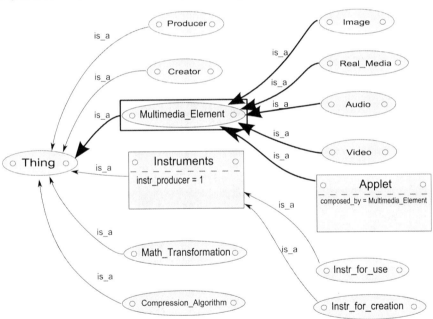

Fig. 6.1.7.3.2   A drawing kindly supplied by Mario Arrigoni Neri in September 2011

only three bands. Modern spectral imaging systems, however, allow to image signals over a wide wavelength range, with small increments" (ibid., p. 2).

Multifluorescence images result as "multiple molecules are selectively labeled by molecule-specific antibodies fused with a fluorophore and imaged by fluorescence microscopy. Each signal,

Importantly, ontologies have been developed within computing for law (see Section 6.1.7.4). For example, Lenzi, Biagioli, Cappelli, Sprugnoli, and Turchi (2009) reported about the LME project; their article is concerned with legislative metadata based on semantic formal models. Abrahams, Eyers, and Bacon (2009) discussed a structured storage of legal precedents using a minimal deontic ontology, for computer assisted legal document querying. A *crime emergency ontology event model* is the subject of Wang, Guo, Luo, Wang, and Xu (2005). Leary et al. (2003a, 2003b) discussed the goal of developing a *financial fraud ontology*. *Investigative data mining* also stands to benefit from ontologies, because data mining in combination with ontologies is a field entering maturity: all of the papers in a collection edited by Hector Oscar Nigro, Sandra González Císaro and Daniel Xodo (2008) are about data mining with ontologies. We have already mentioned that one of the applications of multiagent systems is for data mining. But ontologies can also subserve multiagent system technology: Hadzic and Chang (2008) discussed using *co-algebra* and *co-induction* to define ontology-based multiagent systems.

Ontologies have also been developed in such areas as software engineering, engineering,[108] electronic commerce (E-commerce),[109] biology and bioinformatics,[110]

---

s_i ($i \in [1, n]$) thus, reflects the intensity of a pixel for one molecule m_i. In recent years, the number of available specific antibodies has continuously been increasing, allowing to selectively label a large number of molecules. However, in most applications, only few molecules are labeled at once due to the spectral limitation of fluorescence microscopy" (ibid., pp. 2–3).

"Both multivariate imaging strategies mentioned so far can be summarized as intramodular imaging techniques, as the same imaging modality is used and changes in their parametrization, i.e., recorded wavelength or labeled molecule is applied to acquire the set of n different signals. However, MVI data can also be acquired by applying different imaging modalities" (ibid., p. 3). One speak then of *multimodal images*. "For example, bright field imaging can be combined with images obtained by dark field, phase contrast, and fluorescence imaging" (ibid.). Both in multi-modal imaging and in *intramodular imaging* (namely, multispectral imaging and multifluorescence imaging), "the acquired images hold the same resolution. This eases the process of image registration, i.e., spatially aligning all channels of the MVI to each other, which is the prerequisite for a meaningful MVI analysis" (ibid.). Moreover, "also modalities that acquire images of different spatial resolution can be combined such as optical microscopy and electron microscopy. Here, directly mapping the spatial location in different images is not possible, and sophisticated mapping techniques are required" (ibid.).

[108] Li, Yang, and Ramani (2009) described a methodology for engineering ontology acquisition and validation. Ciocoiu, Nau, and Grüninger (2001) were concerned with ontologies for integrating engineering applications. Grüninger and Delaval (2009) discussed a cutting process ontology for sheet metal parts. A paper by Paul van der Vet and Nicolaas Mars (1995) is a case study in ontologies for very large knowledge bases in materials science.

[109] Ding, Fensel, Klein, Omelayenko, and Schulten (2004) discussed the role of ontologies in E-commerce. A book by Gómez-Pérez et al. (2004) discussed applying ontologies to the areas of knowledge management, E-commerce, and the Semantic Web. Dieter Fensel published a book (2003) about ontologies for knowledge management and E-commerce.

[110] Calzolari et al. (2010) discussed an ontology for biology. Stevens, Wroe, Lord, and Goble (2004) were concerned with ontologies in bioinformatics.

biomedical informatics,[111] library science, document management systems,[112] and agriculture.[113] Even an attempt to developed a computational ontology of mind was reported.[114] Moreover, a Swiss prominent team in 3D computer graphics and virtual reality,[115] in Geneva and Lausanne, reported about an "ontology of virtual humans: incorporating semantics into human shapes".[116]

Mario Arrigoni Neri and Marco Colombetti, in a paper (2009) in e-learning – which among the other things, propose a graphical syntax for the well-known ontology language *OWL* – noted: "Learning objects paradigm is widely adopted in e-learning environments. Learning objects management can be improved using semantic technologies from ontology engineering and the semantic web", and: "Learning objects composition is one of the main challenges in e-learning management systems and can be improved exploiting ontological reasoning. The building of a course can be carried out in two phases, in the first one we compose concept

---

[111] Udo Hahn and Stefan Schulz (2004) discussed building a very large ontology from medical thesauri.

[112] Mitschick and Meissner (2008) are concerned with metadata generation and consolidation within an ontology-based document management system.

[113] The *International Journal of Metadata, Semantics and Ontologies* published a special issue entitled *Agricultural Metadata and Semantics* (Manouselis, Salokhe, & Johannes Keizer, 2009).

[114] By Ferrario and Oltramari (2004).

[115] See e.g. Magnenat Thalmann and Thalmann (1996, 2001, 2005). Cf. fn 291 below.

[116] Gutiérrez et al. (2005, 2007). Cf. Garcia-Rojas et al. (2008a, 2008b). "The context of this work is the search for realism and believability of Virtual Humans. Our contribution to achieve this goal is to enable Virtual Humans (VH) to react to spontaneous events in virtual environments (VE). In order to reflect the individuality of each VH, these reactions have to be expressive and unique. In this paper we present firstly a model of reaction based on personality traits. The model was defined using statistical analysis of real people reacting to unexpected events. We also consider that the emotional state is involved in the modulation of reactions, thus we integrate a model of emotion update. Secondly, we present a semantic-based methodology to compose reactive animation sequences using inverse kinematics (IK) and key frame (KF) interpolation animation techniques. Finally, we present an application that demonstrates how Virtual Humans can produce different movements as reaction to unexpected stimuli, depending on their personality traits and emotional state" (from the abstract of Garcia-Rojas et al., 2008b).

Whereas Garcia-Rojas et al. (2008b) were concerned with reactive behaviour, with expressive animation, and with semantics, Garcia-Rojas et al. (2008a) were rather concerned with inhabited virtual environments, with ontologies, with an authoring tool, and with visual programming. To say it with the abstract: "The creation of virtual reality applications and 3D environments is a complex task that requires good programming skills and expertise in computer graphics and many other disciplines. The complexity increases when we want to include complex entities such as virtual characters and animate them. In this paper we present a system that assists in the tasks of setting up a 3D scene and configuring several parameters affecting the behavior of virtual entities like objects and autonomous virtual humans. Our application is based on a visual programming paradigm, supported by a semantic representation, an ontology for virtual environments. The ontology allows us to store and organize the components of a 3D scene, together with the knowledge associated with them. It is also used to expose functionalities in the given 3D engine. Based on a formal representation of its components, the proposed architecture provides a scalable VR system. Using this system, non-experts can set up interactive scenarios with minimum effort; no programming skills or advanced knowledge is required."

level entities to obtain an outline of the course, then we fill such an outline with actual resources from the repository. Both phases can use ontology based models to capture specific domain knowledge" (ibid.).

Data organisation upstream of feeding them into a data mining tool (Pyle, 1999) can be facilitated by a special category of software: Mena (2003, section 2.16, pp. 68–72) reviewed several commercial software products specifically designed for data preparation. Arguably, it has meanwhile become realistic to also resort to ontologies. Mena (2003, section 2.17, pp. 72–74) argued for standardising crime reports. This may be quite difficult, because: "Police officers and investigators may use widely varying styles and formats in describing criminal scenes and modus operandi", and moreover, they may be spelling errors, as well as abbreviations (ibid., p. 72). Arguably, ontologies could do a lot to filter out such diversity, and extract a unified representation automatically or semi-automatically.[117]

---

[117] To give the flavour of what ontologies may look like, the following is excerpted from *TGMA: The mosquito anatomy morphology* (http://anobase.vectorbase.org/anatomy/mosquito_anatomy. obo), accessed in February 2009, and developed at IMBB in Greece for VectorBase (http://www. vectorbase.org is the homepage of the site where it is posted, with other such ontologies of ticks and malaria, at http://anobase.vectorbase.org/ontologies):

id: TGMA:0000051
name: postfrontal suture
def: "One of two sutures diverging from the coronal suture above the ocelli and separating the interocular space from the frons." [ISBN:0-937548-00-6]
comment: Fig 02,04,07,08 Abbr: pfs in ISBN:0-937548-00-6.
synonym: "frontal suture" RELATED [ISBN:0-937548-00-6]
is_a: TGMA:0001828 ! anatomical line
relationship: part_of TGMA:0000003 ! adult cranium

id: TGMA:0000052
name: postfrontal ridge
def: "The apodeme marked externally by the postfrontal suture." [ISBN:0-937548-00-6]
comment: Fig 05 Abbr: PR in ISBN:0-937548-00-6.
synonym: "frontal ridge" RELATED [ISBN:0-937548-00-6]
relationship: part_of TGMA:0000003 ! adult cranium

id: TGMA:0000053
name: adult postgena
def: "The lateral and ventral parts of the cranium behind the compound eye." [ISBN:0-937548-00-6]
comment: Fig 02,03,04,06 Abbr: PG in ISBN:0-937548-00-6.
synonym: "cheek" RELATED [ISBN:0-937548-00-6]
synonym: "gena" RELATED [ISBN:0-937548-00-6]
synonym: "gula" RELATED [ISBN:0-937548-00-6]
synonym: "gular region" RELATED [ISBN:0-937548-00-6]
synonym: "Kehle" RELATED [ISBN:0-937548-00-6]
synonym: "occiput" RELATED [ISBN:0-937548-00-6]
synonym: "temple" RELATED [ISBN:0-937548-00-6]
synonym: "tempus" RELATED [ISBN:0-937548-00-6]
is_a: TGMA:0001835 ! compound organ component
relationship: part_of TGMA:0000003 ! adult cranium

id: TGMA:0000054
name: postgenal seta

6.1.7.4 Legal Ontologies

Andrew Stranieri and John Zeleznikow

The present Section 6.1.7.4 is based on a section in Stranieri and Zeleznikow (2005a).[118] Whilst the World Wide Web is becoming a major source of information retrieval and a repository of legal knowledge, the uses of web mining to discover legal knowledge has been limited.[119] Zeleznikow (2002b) noted that currently, very few legal decision support systems are available on the World Wide Web. Much current research is focused upon using text mining for Homeland Security and Intelligence and Law Enforcement.

The Australasian Legal Information Institute (AustLII)[120] provides free Internet access to Australian legal materials. AustLII's broad public policy agenda is to improve access to justice through better access to information. To that end, AustLII has become one of the largest sources of legal materials on the net, with over 7 gigabytes of raw text materials and over 1.5 million searchable documents (by the early 2000s). It does not have any decision support systems on its Internet site.

The British and Irish Legal Information Institute (BAILII)[121] provides access to the most comprehensive set of British and Irish primary legal materials that are available for free and in one place on the Internet.

In Canada, the Canadian Legal Information Institute project (CANLII) aims at gathering legislative and judicial texts, as well as legal commentaries, from federal, provincial and territorial jurisdictions bin order to make primary sources of

---

def: "One of the setae occurring in a group on the postgena at the posteroventral area of the cranium." [ISBN:0-937548-00-6]
comment: Fig 02,04 Abbr: PgS in ISBN:0-937548-00-6.
synonym: "gular bristle" RELATED [ISBN:0-937548-00-6]
synonym: "gular chaeta" RELATED [ISBN:0-937548-00-6]
synonym: "postgenal hair" RELATED [ISBN:0-937548-00-6]
relationship: part_of TGMA:0000053 ! adult postgena

Another website worth visiting is http://www.ifomis.org/bfo/publications of Basic Formal Ontology (BFO).

[118] [A note by E. Nissan:] Valente (2005) has discussed types and roles of legal ontologies, and his paper followed in the same book an especially stimulating article on the use and reuse of legal ontologies by Breuker, Valente, and Winkels (2005). Also Gangemi, Sagri, and Tiscornia (2005), too, discussed legal ontologies. This was inside an edited volume that had *legal ontologies* in its subtitle. The volume editors were Benajmins, Casanovas, Breuker, and Gangemi (2005), and the papers in the volume were drawn from two meetings devoted to the Semantic Web and the legal domain: The International Workshop on Legal Ontologies and Web-Based Legal Information Management held in Edinburgh, Scotland, in June 2003 (John Zeleznikow had been directing a laboratory at the University of Edinburgh at the time), and the International Seminar on Law and the Semantic Web, held in Barcelona, Spain, in November 2003.

[119] *Web mining* was surveyed by Kosala and Blockeel (2000). Joshi and Krishnapuram (1998) discussed fuzzy clustering methods for web mining.

[120] www.austlii.edu.au

[121] www.bailii.org

Canadian law accessible on the Internet.[122] The large volume of legal information in electronic form creates a need for the creation and production of powerful
computational tools in order to extract relevant information in a condensed form.

The development of *legal ontologies* offers great opportunities for the development of legal decision support that draws on knowledge learnt using *knowledge
discovery from* databases (*KDD*) on the World Wide Web. As explained earliest
in this book, an ontology as an explicit conceptualization of a domain is defined
in Gruber (1995). Breuker, Elhag, Petkov, and Winkels (2002) claim that unlike
engineering, medicine or psychology, law is not ontologically founded. They claim
that law is concerned with constraining and controlling social activities using documented norms. They have developed a core upper level ontology LRI-core. This
ontology has over 200 concepts and has definitions for most of the anchors that
connect the major categories used in law: person, role, action, process, procedure,
time, space, document, information, intention, and so on. The main intended use is
supporting knowledge acquisition for legal domains, but a real test of its semantics
is whether it enables natural language understanding of common sense descriptions
of simple events, as in the description of events in a legal case documentation. This
is of the core principle of the Semantic Web initiative of WC3.

The development of legal ontologies has been examined by Bench-Capon and
Visser (1997). Ontologies have benefits for:

(a) knowledge sharing;
(b) verification of a knowledge base;
(c) knowledge acquisition; and
(d) knowledge reuse.

A formal legal ontology was built by Visser (1995) by developing a formal specification language that is tailored in the appropriate legal domain. He commenced
by using van Kralingen's theory of frame-based conceptual models of statute law
(van Kralingen, 1995). Visser uses the terms ontology and specification language
interchangeably. He claims an ontology must be:

(a) epistemologically adequate;
(b) operational;
(c) expressive;
(d) reusable; and
(e) extensible.

Visser chose to model the Dutch Unemployed Benefits Act of 1986. He created
a CommonKADS expertise model (Schreiber et al., 1999). Specifying domain
knowledge is performed by:

---

[122] http://www.canlii.org

(a) Determining the universe of discourse by carving up the knowledge into onto-logical primitives. A domain ontology is created with which the knowledge from the legal domain can be specified.
(b) The domain specification is created by specifying a set of domain models using the domain ontology.

A legal ontology based on a functional perspective of the legal system was developed by Valente (1995). He considered the legal system as an instrument to change or influence society in specific directions by reacting to social behaviour. The main functions can be decomposed into six primitive functions each of which corresponds to a category of primitive legal knowledge:

(a) Normative knowledge – which describes states of affairs that have a normative status (such as forbidden or obligatory);
(b) World knowledge – which describes the world that is being regulated, in terms that are used in the normative knowledge, and so can be considered as an interface between common-sense and normative knowledge;
(c) Responsibility knowledge – the knowledge which enables responsibility for the violation of norms to be ascribed to particular agents;
(d) Reactive knowledge – which describes the sanctions that can be taken against those who are responsible for the violation of norms;
(e) Meta-legal knowledge – which describes how to reason with other legal knowledge; and
(f) Creative knowledge – which states how items of legal knowledge are created and destroyed.

Valente's ontology, which he described as a Legal Information Server, allows for the storage of legal knowledge as both text and an executable analysis system interconnected through a common expression within the terms of the functional ontology. The key thrust of his conceptualisation is to act as a principle for organizing and relating knowledge, particularly with a view to conceptual retrieval.

Many organizations are now building legal ontologies to provide legal knowledge on the World Wide Web. The Dutch Tax and Customs Administration have developed the POWER (Program for an Ontology-based working environment for rules and regulations) research project (van Engers & Glasee, 2001). POWER develops a method and supporting tools for the whole chain of processes from legislation drafting to executing the law by government employees. The POWER program improves legislation quality by the use of formal methods and verification techniques.

CLIME, e-COURT and FFPOIROT are all legal ontology projects funded by the European Union. Because of the plethora of legal systems, there is a great need to develop legal ontologies that are applicable across the European Union.

In the CLIME project, a large-scale ontology was developed for the purpose of a web-based legal advice system MILE (Maratime Information and Legal Explanation). The system features both extended conceptual retrieval and normative assessment on international rules and regulations regarding ship classification

(Bureau Veritas) and maritime pollution (MARPOL). The user can formulate a case using a structured natural language interface. The interface uses only the terms available in the ontology, which ensures that the user formulates a query on a topic known to the system. The ontology also provides a means for adequate knowledge management of the rules and regulations.

The KDE (Knowledge worker Desktop Environment) project reused the CLIME ontology in a knowledge and workflow-management environment. In the KDE system, the CLIME ontology functioned as a domain ontology for the work of those associated with ship classification within the Bureau Veritas organization.

The CLIME knowledge base has two separate components:

(a) Domain – A domain ontology of the design, construction, maintenance, repair, operation and construction of ships. The domain ontology incorporates a small abstract top ontology, distinguishing things like artifacts, substances, agents and functions;
(b) Norms – A knowledge base of norms: mappings from rules in legal documents to deontic constraints that allow or disallow certain types of cases. These norms are often limited and incomplete interpretations of the norms expressed in the rules. The knowledge acquisition for the CLIME ontology can be split into two phases: (i) the conceptual retrieval phase in which the concepts and their relations are identified, created and defined, and (ii) the phase in which knowledge acquisition for normative assessment takes place.

The e-COURT project (Breuker, Valente, & Winkels, 2002) is a European project that aims at developing an integrated system for the acquisition of audio/video depositions within courtrooms, the archiving of legal documents, information retrieval and synchronized audio/video/text consultation. The focus of the project is to process, archive and retrieve legal documents of criminal courtroom sessions. In principle, these documents should be accessible via the World Wide Web. The system has the following major functions:

(a) Audio/Video/Text synchronization of data from court trials and hearings;
(b) Advanced Information Retrieval – multilingual, tolerant to vagueness. Statistical techniques are combined with ontology based indexing and search;
(c) Database management – multimedia documents support retrieval;
(d) Workflow management defines and manages rules for sharing relevant information and events among judicial actors; and
(e) Security management plays an important role to protect privacy information and to comply with national and international regulations about the interchange of criminal information.

The project is aimed at the semi-automated information management of documents produced during a criminal trial: in particular, the transcription of hearings. The structure of this type of document is determined by the debate/dialogue nature of the hearings, as well as by specific local court procedures. The developers identify and annotate content topics of a document. These annotations can vary from case descriptions in oral testimony to indictments in criminal law. Their first completed task was an ontology for Dutch criminal law, which served as a framework for ontologies on Italian and Polish criminal law.

FF-POIROT is a multi-million euro-dollar venture to develop European standards for the prevention, detection and successful investigation of financial fraud. The goal of the project is to build a detailed ontology of European Law, preventive practices and knowledge of the processes of financial fraud. The FF-POIROT project aims at compiling for several languages (Dutch, Italian, French and English) a computationally tractable and sharable knowledge repository (a formally described combination of concepts and their meaningful relationships) for the financial fraud domain. This knowledge source is being constructed in three ways:

(a) Having human experts analyze and model the domain(s), in particular identifying the most abstract notions;
(b) Using computers to automatically find relevant notions (the most specific ones) from existing documents and semi-structured corpora including the Internet (text mining);
(c) Having humans validate the automatically generated suggestions to combine/merge already existing similar knowledge sources (semi-automatically aligning).

The resulting environment is useful to at least three different and EU-relevant types of user communities:

(a) Investigative and monitoring bodies: benefit from the strongly enriched information retrieval made possible by linking e.g. internet or database search facilities to the FF-POIROT ontology in order to detect or investigate instances of attempted or actual financial fraud. Species of fraud (typologies) have been identified so that macro and micro-analysis can be undertaken, the results of which are then used as "templates of fraud". These templates can be stored, accessed and used to mine for new instances of fraud, conducted across linguistic and jurisdictional boundaries;
(b) Financial professionals: Accountants, auditors, banks, insurance agencies, government departments, regulators and financial experts will benefit from an "FF-POIROT-style" ontology using it as an authoritative concept base, extensively cross-linked (to other domains, systems and languages) and available for customised applications. Exploitation in this area could be as a high-tech service extending similar services and products (in particular with respect to accounting practices related to European VAT), currently already commercialised by at least two of FF-POIROT's users;
(c) Law enforcement: Police and other law enforcement agencies benefit by the availability of relevant parts of the FF-POIROT ontology – for example as an RDF-mapped Semantic Web resource, to support future police-oriented

query systems – in a non-technical user-friendly, attractive, and comprehensive manner. Additionally, sharing of information with investigative bodies and understanding of related documents will be substantially enhanced if such communication and documents are hyperlinked to a shared ontology. Optimising the investigation, discovery, prevention and reduction of complex frauds is being made routine and efficient.

The partners in the FF-POIROT projects include universities (in Belgium, Romania and the United Kingdom), software houses (in Belgium and Italy) and two industry partners, CONSOB and VAT Applications who wish to commercialize the consortium's results.

CONSOB is the public authority responsible for regulating the Italian securities market. It is the competent authority for ensuring: transparency and correct behaviour by securities market participants; disclosure of complete and accurate information to the investing public by listed companies; accuracy of the facts represented in the prospectuses related to offerings of transferable securities to the investing public; compliance with regulations by auditors entered in the Special Register. CONSOB conducts investigations with respect to potential infringements of insider dealing and market manipulation law. Within the FF-POIROT project, CONSOB is particularly interested in detecting and prosecuting companies that spread fraudulent information on the internet.

VAT Applications NV is a Belgian software company developing automated software to deal with issues surrounding Value Added Tax at a European level. It has packages for all countries and in eleven languages. The addition of ten new members to the European Union in 2004, has placed a further need for the development software packages to help compliance with VAT requirements across the European Union and the identification, prevention and reduction of fraud across jurisdictions.

The University of Edinburgh's Joseph Bell Centre for Forensic Statistics and Legal Reasoning has been performing the following tasks:

(a) Prepare for the construction and testing of the financial forensics repository using macro and micro analytical techniques;
(b) Gather information on how relevant authorities accumulate and analyse evidence of financial fraud, and analyse the tools auditors and accountants use to maintain up-to-date awareness of financial services regulations; and
(c) Collect requirements for the retained data, its validation and the applications needed to optimise the use of the information.

User requirements were collected by conducting structured interviews and using consortium expertise to accumulate necessary information for the construction and testing of a financial fraud ontology. Advice was obtained from end-users on how law enforcement agencies and investigative and regulatory bodies accumulate and analyse criminal evidence in domains of financial fraud, and analyse resources by which financial regulatory knowledge is available for auditing and accounting professionals.[123]

6.1.7.5 An Application of Ontologies to Eliminating Sensitive Information While Declassifying Documents: The Case of Accounts of Crime Investigation

Raskin, Atallah, Hempelmann, and Mohamed (2001) reported about the use of onotologies when manipulating documents being declassified, so that information that still must not be released be eliminated, and the wording reformulated so that it would not be included. Their project was intended to respond to a real need for handling masses of documents, because of a policy instituted in the mid-1995:

> Since Executive Order 12958, Classified National Security Information, signed by President Clinton on April 17, 1995, most U.S. Government agencies have faced a monumental problem of declassifying millions of pages of its documentation. Many agencies as well as other organizations and corporations are increasingly facing the need of downgrading or sanitizing information that they need or have to share with their various coalition partners, e.g., within the NATO alliance.

Raskin et al. (2001) listed different degrees of security requirements while declassifying documents. When the requirement is *weak declassification*, the problem is one of "dividing a set of documents into definitely open ones and others, with a reasonable degree of accuracy". When the requirement is *strong declassification*, the problem is one of "determining the status of each document as unclassified or classified without any margin of error". When the requirement is *downgrading/sanitizing*, the problem is more complex, as it involves "strong declassification coupled with a seamless modification of each classified document to an unclassified version". And finally, the most complex problem in this spectrum is when one has to carry out "*on-the-fly downgrading/sanitizing/surveillance*: filtering out electronic communication in real time." Some information is *top secret*, some other information is merely *secret*, and some other information is merely *confidential*.

> In partially automated textual declassification, there have been two primary approaches to the problem. The keyword-based approach is exemplified by the TapUltra-UltraStructure approach developed for the Department of Energy (see NRC, 1995; DPRC, 2000 in lieu of unavailable regular publications). The approach is based on an assumption that the classified element will appear as an anticipated word or string of words in the text. This assumption is not always correct, and the result is insufficient accuracy which is unlikely to be improvable in principle. The statistical tagging approach cleverly divides the entire corpus of documents into the training and testing subcorpora. Humans tag the training corpus in a variety of ways and divide it into classified and unclassified subsets. A sophisticated statistical procedure attempts then to relate certain tag clusters to the classified nature of a document and

---

[123] Leary et al. (2003a, 2003b) discussed the goal of developing a *financial fraud ontology*. Lenzi et al. (2009) reported about the LME project; their article is concerned with legislative metadata based on semantic formal models.

to tag the testing corpus automatically as well as to divide it into the classified and unclassified subsets. If this task is achieved with a high degree of accuracy, the approach succeeds (Hochberg, 1999, 2000).

"The existing approaches share an important principle: They do not try to follow the declassification rules for human workers because, of course, humans understand the rules and these approaches do not." By contrast, the *ontologic semantic* approach in Raskin et al. (2001) "both for text and for data, is based on the computer understanding of the information, which does make it possible to follow the prescribed declassification rules in every sensitive detail as well as to dynamically modify these rules."

> The ontological semantic approach (see Nirenburg and Raskin, 2004) uses three major static resources, the lexicon (see Nirenburg and Raskin, 1987, 1996; Viegas and Raskin, 1998), the ontology (see Mahesh, 1996), and the text-meaning representation (TMR) language (see Onyshkevych and Nirenburg, 1995). The lexicon contains words of a natural language, whose meanings are explained in terms of an ontological concept and/or its property. The ontology contains a tangled hierarchy of concepts, each containing a set of properties with filler specifications [...]. The TMR language composes the sentential meaning out of ontological concepts and their properties evoked by the words of the sentence with the help of a special formal syntax.

In the approach of Raskin et al. (2001), which was to only involve minimal analysis, the use of ontology is confined to crucial terms and concepts, with the "possible addition of a few domain-specific nodes and/or properties of nodes". The lexicon, too, is a resource only used for crucial terms, with the "possible but rare addition of a terminological lexical entry or sense". TMR was used primarily for crucial terms. Nevertheless, TMR, was to be ready for any paraphrase. The analyser was fully ready for any paraphrase. As to the text generator, it was to be used only for downgrading and surveillance.

Raskin et al. (2001) exemplified their method on several texts. A few of these were reports about criminal investigation. The text entitled "Dartmouth Murders" was " taken from the *Washington Post* archive section. It's about a murder that two teenagers committed at their school. They tried to escape after committing the crime, but they were caught." Raskin et al. (2001) assumed, for the sake of the example, that nothing is allowed to be mentioned that would help to identify the identity of the suspects, their age, or the nature of their crime. "For example, we have to delete the name 'Casey Purcell', simply because people knowing Purcell might know his friends and thus can figure out the identity of the suspects."

In another narrative text also downgraded in the exemplification of Raskin et al. (2001), also actually taken from the *Washington Post* archive, an employee in Massachusetts had shot dead seven colleagues in the offices of Edgewater, an Internet company. In order to hide the identity of the state inside the U.S. where the crime took place, the names of police officers and of people living there had to be suppressed. Their names were replaced with those persons' position. Moreover, in order to hide the identity of the company where the shooting took place, the name of the company and of the victims were suppressed, and the identity of the suspect had also to be suppressed, and so were even his imposing physical features. The word "e-business" was replaced with "this kind of business". Also the name of a neighbouring company was suppressed.

Raskin et al. (2001) mentioned unsolved problems, with literal as well as non-literal language. Concerning literal language, they stated:

> In sum, even with literal use of language, we have a number of yet unsolved issues:
> 1. Not everything can be deleted or replaced in a sentence, only elements clearly circum-scribed syntactically are interchangeable.
> 2. Information can lie at the "core" of a text, that is, the purpose of the text has been to relate that very information and elaborate on facets of it. This "central information" is obviously hard to obscure.
> 3. If too much information is deleted or replaced it becomes obvious that the text has been tampered with.
> 4. If the text is of any poetic or rhetoric nature, any change to the wording will affect it negatively. In view of the expected clients for this application this latter effect is hopefully of minor significance.

6.1.7.6 A Digression – *Maurice v. Judd* (New York, 1818): Is Whale Oil a Kind of Fish Oil? When the Jury Had to Decide About Ontology

In New York during the early Republic, there was a sea captain, whaleman, and whale oil man, named *Preserved Fish*. The family name *Fish* is unsurprising, for a New Englander from a fishing community; moreover, *fish* used to be a nickname for whalers. *Preserved* was his first name (by etymological motivation, it means the same as the Arabic first name *Maḥfuḍ*, which is also originally a passive participle). Preserved Fish was called as a witness for the defence, in a trial held in New York in 1818, *Maurice v. Judd*, the plaintiff being an inspector, James Maurice who insisted on also inspecting (for a fee) whale oil, whereas the law required that fish oil be inspected. The defendant was Samuel Judd, a wealthy oil merchant, who insisted that whale oil was not intended to be inspected, by current legislation.

A scientist – the distinguished New York physician-naturalist, Samuel Laptham Mitchill, with a record of service as a senator and state representative in Washington, and the one who had given the United States the name *Fredonia*, i.e., the land of the free – testified that the whale is not a fish.[124] Traders in marine oils claimed that when an order for fish oil is made, liver oil is supplied, not whale oil. Moreover, it was the quality of liver oil that was uneven, whereas the quality of whale oil was usually satisfactory.

Eventually, the jury found for the plaintiff, after the plaintiff's lawyer insisted that all those who claimed that a whale is not a fish, or that whale oil is not fish oil, were easterners, i.e., New Englanders, even though they may have been living in New York. There was antipathy between New Yorkers and New Englanders. The jury found for the plaintiff. This is the subject of a book by Burnett (2007).[125] Captain

---

[124] A book by Golan (2004) traces the history of *scientific expert testimony* in England and America.

[125] Another version of section 6.1.7.5 appears in a book review I wrote on Burnett (2007).

Fish was from New Bedford, in New England, and "had been for twenty years in New York" (ibid., p. 175). Burnett remarks (ibid., p. 164) that "the case of *Maurice vs. Judd* represented above all a showdown between two powerful groups of politically active and wealthy figures in the city of New York in the early nineteenth century: a clique of oil merchants and chandlers on the one hand, and a consortium of tanner-financiers on the other."

This court case is quite interesting in our own present context of discussing ontologies, because here we have an example of ontology being centrestage: in practice, this was what the jurors were asked to decide about. Moreover, as we are going to see, there are lots of nuances and distinctions; this should immunise readers against too simplistic a view of taxonomies, and therefore against inadequate, too rigid, ontologies insensitive to differences of usage.

Jurors were used to consider the whale as a kind of fish, and this was also what they gathered from the English translation of the Bible they were used to. (In the Hebrew original, the relevant lexicographical situation is quite complex, more than in translation, because translators already made classification choices.) Burnett points out (2007, pp. 8–9):

> *Maurice v. Judd* [...] presents a gloriously feisty public forum where competing parties deployed a wide range of skills, texts, and authorities in efforts to undermine (and sometimes to undergird) the edifice of contemporary taxonomy and classification. Nor are these different positions merely static: by following the citations marshaled by the diverse parties to the action I will show how knowledge of natural order and natural types "migrated" across different communities of expertise, and across geographical regions, thereby revealing how the "new philosophy" of the metropolitan (and largely French) classifying science made its way to American readers, and how such ambitious "systems" fared in confrontation with folk taxonomies, vernacular natural history, and biblical representations of creation. These trial transcripts thus dramatize just how unstable the science of natural order was in 1818, at least as viewed from lower Manhattan by readers who had access to a preponderance of the leading publications in Anglo-European natural history; indeed, it was by setting these texts against each other that opponents of the "new philosophy" could represent the science of classification as a house woefully divided, and by no means the architecture of the natural world. Having revealed the contingency of such "systems", the skeptics were positioned to defend the legitimacy of the taxonomic discriminations implicit in ordinary language and in social and political categories precipitated out of labor, law, and the market. The adversarial setting of the Mayor's Court dramatized these conflicts, and for historians of science and scholars of law generally interested in the relationship between legal systems and the production of knowledge, *Maurice v. Judd* is a mini-bonanza.

Traditionally in England, the whale was known as "royal fish": whales and sturgeons were so-called because they were the special possession of the throne since the 14th century (each beached whale had to go to the King), with the term "Fishes Royal" first appearing in a statute of 1325 (Burnett, 2007, p. 3). "We modern readers may need a reminder: in the late eighteenth and early nineteenth century the word 'fish' meant (as the 1817 Philadelphia edition of Samuel Johnson's *Dictionary of the English Language* stated clearly) 'an animal existing only in water'" (Burnett, 2007, p. 20). "And the author of the article in the *National Advocate* made the tacit taxonomy on which this taxonomy rested still more explicit: 'a whale *is* a fish, for the simple reason that it is not a beast or a bird'" (ibid., pp. 20–21).

The plaintiff's counsel invoked Scripture and the scriptural tradition, as well as ordinary language, as for example a peddler of "oysters, crabs, and clams" is called a "*fish*-monger" (Burnett, 2007, p. 21). "Moreover, by these lights, the whale was not just any fish. Rather, it was, as the Philadelphia *Lady's and Gentleman's Weekly Literary Museum and Musical Magazine* commented in its article on the trial, the very 'king of the scaly tribe', the *primogenitus* of the seas", as pointed out by Burnett (ibid., p. 21), who proceeds to show how this is supported by a "survey of juvenile literature and didactic volumes touching on natural history available in New York before 1819" (ibid., pp. 21–22). "Indeed, most Americans probably first encountered the whale in the context of nursery-rhyme natural theology: the ubiquitous *New England Primer* reserved the letter 'W' as an occasion to catechize Christian youths in the pervasive power of the Lord's calls, using a couplet that would have been quick to the tongue of every New Yorker in 1818, 'Whales in the sea / God's voice obey'" (ibid., pp. 22, 24). People were raised into a conception of ascribing beasts to the land, birds to the air, and fish to the water, and that the biggest fish of them all was not a fish was deeply against the grain.

During the last days of the year in 1818, the galleries of Mayor's Court were apparently quite crowded, and Burnett (ibid., p. 19) explains that it was so for the sheer fact that such a "paradox" could be debated:

> That same "paradox" guaranteed the coverage of the trial in a host of newspapers and periodicals in New York and beyond — eventually across much of the young Republic. The paradox in question was simply the proposition that a whale was *not* a fish. [. . .] Nor was this sense of surprise merely the theatrical special pleading of the plaintiff's counsel, [John Anthon,] who clearly had an interest in presenting his opponent's position as an egregious departure from habit, custom, and verity: published and unpublished responses to the trial support Anthon's assertion that the vast majority of Americans not only assumed that a whale was a fish, but were surprised to learn that the question could be debated.

"Anthon dismissed the notion of non-fish-whale oil as nothing more than a 'mere provincial usage' of New England, one that could be readily ignored" (Burnett, 2007, p. 175). New York's jurors were offered the rationale, as Burnett conveys the gist of it making it explicit, that a "secret confraternity had been giving silent shape to the case: these anomalous oath-takers, who had outrageously and vociferously vouched for mammalian cetes, were *not really New Yorkers*. They were, rather, 'easterners' — Boston men, long-boned New Englanders, [. . .]" (ibid., p. 174). "It was a subtle ploy, but an effective one, playing as it did on the Yankee–Knickerbocker rivalry that had stewed New York elites for a generation" (ibid., pp. 175–176). Judd's lawyers rose instantly to denounce to the jurors the use by the other party of "the contemptuous epithet of yankees" (ibid., p. 176).

When, in an earlier generation, Linnaeus had based his classification of plants on their reproductive organs, this was judged unseemly by some prudes. To New Yorkers, it seemed outlandish that in order to explain the difference between whales and fish, he would explain that fish ejaculate into the water, whereas whales have a huge male organ (even though, along with the distinction between cold and hot blood, and along with whales' lactation, this is quite an apt explanation, from the viewpoint of scientific zoology). As Burnett explains (2007, pp. 42–43):

These sallies at the categories of the naturalists [such as cetes having a horizontal tail, vs. the vertical tail of fish] left only delicate matters as the rationale for keeping whales out of the fish category: breasts and reproductive organs. When called to the stand, Dr. Mitchill would make much of these points, which were at the heart of the classification he had come to defend: male fish, he could show, had "no *penis intrans*" and, unlike the cetes, propagation among the cetes involved the casting of "the fecundating fluid" over ova deposited in a "nidus". These bedroom details, raised at the level of "philosophy", and set against the commonplace distinctions of the fish-market (and the sacred groupings of scripture), clearly struck many New Yorkers as grounds for a snicker: shortly after the trial, a satirical poem — there were to be a number of them — in the *Evening Post* invoked the city's preeminent naturalist with a sly dig at his prurient engagement with taxonomy, hailing him as

Mitchell, who sung the amours of fishes...

The two whalemen called as witnesses "disagreed emphatically on the question before the court" (Burnett, 2007, p. 95). Captain Preserved Fish took stand for the defendant, Samuel Judd. James Reeves testified for the plaintiff. Captain Fish, who "eventually became a director at the Bank of America" (ibid., fn 1), "hailed from New Bedford, the Massachusetts city that was in those very years displacing Nantucket as the gravitational center of the whaling industry in the United States" (ibid., p. 95). Like Mitchill, Fish insisted that whales were not fish because they breathed air. Reeves instead claimed he thought they might be able to breathe underwater (ibid., pp. 95, 97). During cross-examination, the plaintiff's lawyers eventually had Fish admit that a whale could breathe if its mouth was underwater but its nose above water, and Fish was dismissed.

Reeves, testifying for Maurice, "explained that it was the common habit of whalemen to call their quarry 'fish'" (ibid., p. 97). Once Reeves came under cross-examination, Judd's attorney asked him: if someone were to ask him for "fish oil", what would he give them? "Reeves had an easy answer: he would simply ask 'what kind of fish oil do you want?' since, from what he understood, the 'oil was named from the fish, as black fish, humpback, and whale oil'" (ibid., p. 98). Burnett (ibid., fn 8) points out "that the term 'whale' was itself ambiguous, and not uniformly used in the period to refer to all the large cetaceans". In particular, Burnett remarks, "Reeves here distinguishes between 'humpback' oil and 'whale' oil, despite the fact that the 50-foot humpback [. . .] certainly counts, by our lights, as a 'whale'" (ibid., fn 8). Again during his cross-examination, Reeves claimed: "I never heard any distinction between fish oil and whale oil, as talked of here to day, but always thought that fish oil included them all" (ibid., p. 98).

If Maurice's lawyers tried to awaken in the jurors their prejudices against New Englanders (ibid., pp. 174–176), Judd's lawyers appealed to their class sympathies, and "reminded jurors that in weighing the testimony from the practical whalemen, they would do well to recall that *Captain* (whale-not-a-fish) Fish had been 'master of a vessel in the trade', whereas *Mr.* (whale-a-fish-far-as-I-know) Reeves 'was but a common whaler who had made but three voyages' before the mast" (ibid., p. 177). The plaintiff's lawyers tried to get the judge to discount much of Fish's testimony because this former whaleman had become an oil merchant, and as such he had an interest in whale oil not having to be inspected (ibid., p. 145).

Significantly, obstacles were put in the way of testimony being heard about how lawmakers had intended the law to be understood (Burnett, 2007, p. 170):

> Responding to the exhortation to ascertain the intent of the legislators, Judd's lawyers went so far as to seek out and call as a witness the actual legislator who had chaired the committee responsible for the fish oil statute: Peter Sharpe, a city representative [the one of the city of New York] to Albany [. . .] but the court disallowed any part of Sharpe's testimony that purported to provide direct access to the assembly's will in passing the law, thereby hamstringing a potentially decisive defense witness. Sharpe was permitted, however, to dilate on what he "may happen to know as a member of the community".

Judd's lawyers referred again and again to legislative intent (ibid., p. 171). Among the other things, they noted "that if the law had really been meant to cover whale oils, then it was impossible to understand why no inspector had been assigned to Sag Harbor, the state's [i.e., New York state's] only great 'eastern' whaling depot", as indeed "the legislation called for the commissioning of three inspectors for the whole state, one for Albany, one for Troy, and one for 'the city of New-York, [sic] whose powers shall extend to, and include the village of Brooklyn'" (ibid., pp. 176–177). Burnett found (from advertisements from that period) that Sharpe sold at his shop in New York umbrella and parasol frames made of whalebone, so he "knew his whale products first hand!" (Burnett, 2007, p. 187, fn 65):

Lawmakers had been more receptive to the distinction between fish oil and whale oil, than the plaintiff, and eventually the jurors, were willing to concede. But the way the jurors found out was at odds with the conventions of the oil merchants (Burnett, 2007, p. 149):

> The assertion of Maurice and the plaintiff's-side witnesses — that "fish oil" was the general term and included all the oils of the sea creatures — thus did not conform, according to [Thomas] Hazard and his fellow merchants, to the usages of the market. Fish oil was fish oil. It was the oil derived from the livers of cod and other fish (hence the synonym "liver oil"), and if someone came into the shop and requested "fish oil", giving them whale oil, or porpoise oil, or elephant oil [obtained from sea elephants, i.e., elephant seals], or, of all things, *spermaceti oil* (generally double the price of good common whale oil, which traded at about the same price as standard grade liver oil) was unthinkable.
>
> Moreover, from the merchants' perspective, this was a distinction that had nothing to do with whether whales were fish. When queried on this matter, Hazard shrugged it off: he had been "lately told by a learned friend, that a whale was not a fish", but this was news to him, and he didn't really care, since it seemed to him that this had nothing to do with the law and its extortionate misapplication. On the subject of the cetacean's internal anatomy he had even less to offer: Did the whales too have a liver? He had no idea. He had never seen whale liver oil come to market, but that was all he could say. Similarly, the oil dealer John Russell, who had fifteen years in the trade, declared himself agnostic on the niceties of book taxonomy.

The purpose of the legislation had to do with the manufacturing process (ibid., p. 151):

> These manufacturing details were essential because they went to the heart of what was understood to be the purpose of the legislation at issue: to guard against adulterated and/or unacceptably impure "fish oil" coming to market. What was the "fish oil" that had long been the target of customer complaints? "Liver oil", according to the merchants, for the simple reason that it was by its nature a sloppy substance, of uneven quality, and thus very liable

to prompt dissatisfaction among purchasers. Such troubles, they asserted, were more or less unknown with expensive household illuminating oil like spermaceti, or the lubricant and lighting oils taken from porpoises and the ordinary whales. Generally tried out by fire in the process of their manufacture, these oils were comparatively uniform, consistently "dry" (without admixtures of water), and seldom occasioned any difficulty. With common "fish oil", the stuff oozed out of the livers of various groundfish, things were admittedly different. The products had different recent commercial histories as well [. . .]

Even the plaintiff, James Maurice the inspector, was apparently aware of this distinction. Burnett relates (ibid., p. 165):

With considerable sums of money on the line, much could hang on a stray word. Toward the end of the trial Judd's lawyers called James Maurice's former assistant, who gave testimony strongly suggesting that Maurice, the former oil man, had been obliged rapidly to shuffle his own nomenclature after taking up his new commission as the long arm of the fish oil law. Present while Maurice conducted one of his controversial early inspections on several barrels of whale oil, this witness testified that he had overheard someone ask Maurice casually whether he was inspecting "fish oil". To which the inspector, "answered no; but afterwards, looking up and correcting himself, said, yes."

Ultimate victory was Judd's, however, because the original statute was amended by the legislators in Albany, its language being revised. The bill, put forth by Sharpe, authorised the inspection of liver oil, and excepted sperm or whale oil from inspection (Burnett, 2007, p. 187). This was the initiative of Peter Sharpe, the state representative of the city of New York, who as a witness at the trial had "endeavored to inform the jury that the true intent of the legislature extended only to liver oil from bona fide fish" (ibid., p. 187). On appeal, the original verdict of the jury was upheld – the reasoning being that as the law was changed into excluding whale oil, this proved that it originally did include it – and Judd had to pay the fine and legal costs (ibid., p. 189). Judd was wealthy, and this was an acceptable price to pay for the new situation, which vindicated him and the other oil merchants and chandlers. Disgusted because of the restrictions imposed by the new legislation, Maurice turned in his commission as inspector, sold his real estate in the city of New York, and apparently moved out of town (ibid., p. 189).

6.1.7.7 Legal Modelling, and Financial Fraud Ontology Transnational Online Investment Fraud

Richard Leary, Wim Vandenberghe, and John Zeleznikow

The project described here was developed in the early 2000s while the present authors were affiliated with the Joseph Bell Centre for Forensic Statistics and Legal Reasoning of the University of Edinburgh. The project[126] combined legal ontology and financial fraud analysis, as well as knowledge analysis and user

---

[126] In 2003, it was the subject of two workshop presentations by the present three authors (Leary et al., 2003a, 2003b), and this section is based on one of these (Leary et al., 2003b). Moreover, there also have been other publications about the same subject, including a journal article with the same title as Leary et al. (2003b), but by John Kingston, Burkhard Schafer, and Wim

requirement analysis. The context was a European Commission funded project, FF POIROT (financial fraud prevention oriented information resources using ontology technology). Its partners included legal academics, computer science academics, linguists, software houses, and two user partners, CONSOB and VAT Applications (VAT@) who wished to commercialize the consortium's results.[127] It was named after follows in the detective star from fiction, Hercule Poirot, and it was its aim to provide *inter alia* law enforcement agencies with a novel approach to solve the financial fraud puzzle.

The task reported about, here, is the specification of the user requirements that define the functionality of the financial fraud ontology that had to be designed by the FF POIROT partners. The goal of the broader project was to build a detailed ontology of European Law, preventive practices and knowledge of the processes of financial fraud within the European Union. It aims at compiling for several languages (Dutch, Italian, French and English) a computationally tractable and sharable knowledge repository (a formally described combination of concepts and their meaningful relationships) for the financial fraud domain.

Financial fraud is growing faster than international trade. Frauds are *prima facie* more complex and involve larger sums than ever before. More than any other wrong-doing, fraud may involve both civil and criminal legal action. The focus of the FF POIROT project was quite deliberately on criminal fraud. Criminal fraud is clearly enough defined, requiring a deliberate misrepresentation or deception leading to some kind of improper pecuniary advantage. As financial fraud is a very broad field, we have to delineate it to very concrete subdomains that exist in the fraud area. Our initial focus is to examine cross-border Value Added Tax fraud within the EU and Investment fraud on the World Wide Web. This corresponds respectively to the domain expertise of VAT@ and CONSOB. The present Section 6.1.7.7 will only discuss investment fraud on the World Wide Web. The fraud may be committed or attempted in a number of ways.

In developing computer resources such as forensic ontologies, in particular as evidence support for transnational issues in Europe such as financial fraud, we need to be aware of the different legal systems in the European Union. Clearly such resources will also fulfil a strong documentary need for many *bona fide* orga-nizations that depend on meaningful insight in Europe's complex multi-national regulations. There is an urgent need to examine the various European legal systems when trying to build forensic ontologies in Europe. A major reason is that crimes are regularly being committed in transnational domains. This is certainly the case for the two subdomains of financial fraud under FF POIROT scrutiny. Forensic evi-dence, by definition, can be used in criminal or civil courts. However, in the FF POIROT project, we confine ourselves to an examination of ontologies for criminal

Vandenberghe (Kingston et al., 2004). Cf. Kingston et al. (2003), Kingston and Vandenberghe (2003), Vandenberghe, Schafer, and Kingston (2003).

[127] Commissione Nazionale per le Società e la Borsa (http://www.consob.it) and VATAT (http://www.vatat.com). They are respectively concerned with the share market, and with the Value Added Tax (VAT).

law. A major reason for taking this decision is the different burdens of proof in civil law when compared to criminal law.

One of the resources that were to be built was a partial ontology of financial fraud evidence. To illustrate the role and importance of an evidence ontology, consider that in the process of fact investigation many things are to be discovered including hypotheses (or possible conclusions), evidence, and arguments linking hypotheses and evidence. These arguments are generated in defence of the relevance and credibility of evidence and form the basis for subsequent assessments of the probative force of evidence. During fact investigation, of each episode of which is unique in law, we have hypotheses in search of evidence at the same time we have evidence in search of hypotheses. Also to be generated or discovered were arguments linking the evidence and hypotheses. FF POIROT did not cover these aspects of legal reasoning itself.

An important aspect of FF POIROT was the mining of (formal) ontology elements from unstructured or semi-unstructured re sources such as lexicons, text databases, XML documents, RDF schemes, law texts, and of course the Internet. This involves the processing of natural language, which however in the context of FF POIROT was be assumed to be an a priori limited to the above mentioned component domains. Language understanding is a process that traditionally is recognized to be the result of various kinds of knowledge: phonological, morphological, syntactic, semantic, pragmatic and world knowledge.

For the purposes of FF POIROT, it was possible to simplify the picture and to adopt a somewhat reduced view. Firstly, we can make abstract from the discourse level. Authors of legal documents or descriptive reports on forensic issues in general merely want to convey facts, and not to invoke emotions or to initiate actions by the reader. As such, we can limit our analysis to what in the speech-act literature is known as constative inscriptions, sentences uttered in a descriptive context, however without being too narrow as is the case in the traditional formal linguistic semantics scene where sentence-meaning is viewed as being exhausted by propositional content and is truth-conditionally explicable. Since multilingual resources were one of our main objectives, we could however hardly ignore morphology.

The involvement of this project with ontology technology had its roots in artificial intelligence on knowledge representation. Basic research had concentrated on formal aspects trying to determine the underlying fundamental notions of the way we view the world and its organization, to the point of involving and formalizing central ideas of philosophy. A notable practical effort is the attempted distributed development by the IEEE of a *Standard Upper Ontology* (*SUO*).[128] On the other hand, a lot of attention has been focused on the construction of ontologies from a software engineering perspective. Products of this research were the first partial methodologies for the specific development of ontologies such as METHONTOLOGY and techniques for semi-automatic ontology acquisition.

---

[128] http://suo.ieee.org

CYC and Ontolingua are best known, among the applied results achieved in the field. Ontolingua is based on *knowledge interchange format* (*KIF*) and considered an important and influential formalism with Lisp-like representation of ontologies, and was proposed as an ANSI standard and is also being used in the IEEE SUO effort cited above. We did not adopt this latter formalism in FF POIROT for its suspected lack of scalability to the size of the terminology databases and corpora we were expecting to mine, or the number of concepts we will need to align to in the project. Instead, we adopted a more "layered" approach for the FF POIROT ontology and its tool set inspired by the way "classical" large database systems are typically set up.

According to the well tried ontology base, we envisaged a set of "language independent" domain specific atomic facts, which we called *lexons*, and instances of their explicit interpretations. The latter in this way form a separate layer mediating between the ontology base and the application instances committing to the ontology. It is precisely this aforementioned separation in relational database systems that allows for the high efficiency and scalability of its management tools (DBMS), the sometimes huge size of the "models", and high volume transaction processing. Also, a number of well-known techniques from the database view and schema integration were to be evaluated and tested for alignment and merging of the different parts of the ontology. Since the ontology will be built up from components for the different subdomains (evidence, law and finance) the issue of scalability for ontology modeling were to be encountered in each of these three dimensions separately as well as across different domains when these subdomains are aligned and/or merged to create the financial forensics ontology.

Let us now turn to an abstract model of online investment fraud. In order to identify signals useful to the reduction of uncertainty associated with the presence of suspect solicitation agents on WWW, it is useful to be able to analyse the fraud in the form of an abstract model. This section will assess the potential of the fraud model and explain the methodology which supports the model. The objective of our legal model was that it should be helpful in the process of designing the financial fraud ontology.

In the tradition of Wigmore and Twining, the proposed method of knowledge modeling is by using inference networks of law. These are representations for complex probabilistic reasoning tasks often based on masses of evidence. This is highly useful as online investment fraud cases are notorious for huge data files to be investigated. The model is a directed acyclic graph; it is directed because it shows the direction of reasoning, or the direction of probabilistic influence among nodes on the network. It is acyclic because, following any reasoning path, you are never led back to where you started.

Further the model is an integrated logic based model. For the purposes of reasoning about evidence in fraud cases it seems to us there are three types of logic to take account of: logic of deduction, logic of induction; and logic of abduction. Depending upon the problem faced, any one or any combination of these forms of logic can be used. It is not a binary issue of logic or no logic.

It is essential that crime investigators work within a guiding frame so that certain items become evidence and certain other items can be discarded. The better they get at the art of solid reasoning, the more efficient they will be in solving their cases. Using logic to untangle complex scams and solve the complicated puzzles of crime means the difference between dead reckoning that can steer an investigator in the right direction and random guessing that can make things hopelessly confused.

The main idea of the model is that fraud cases can be broken down into three distinct layers of information. Firstly, a proposition (hypothesis) layer, secondly a law layer and thirdly the evidence layer. Any case will therefore have a layer of information about the hypothesis or case theory, for example, (X Defrauded Y), a layer of information about specific elements of law that need to be satisfied if a case of fraud is to be proven and, thirdly, there is an evidence layer comprising all the material facts and evidence that go to make up the facts of the case. The following is an abstract model of the different layers involved in constructing or assessing a legal case. Note that the chart provides the abstract model and the Key List describes the component parts of the model. See Fig. 6.1.7.7.1 and Table 6.1.7.7.1.

The abstract model is arrived at by asking a series of questions aimed at exposing the relationships between propositions of law and propositions of evidence. Although these questions appear in the form of a hierarchy above, when being used to discover the presence of a fraud within a tangible or intangible environment, they can be asked within any sequence including "top down" and "bottom up". Logic can therefore be both ex ante or ex post. In other words, we can move from facts to conclusions and from conclusions to facts. An investigation may be a waste of time and money, however valid its legal conclusion/hypothesis, if evidence is not gathered to support that conclusion.

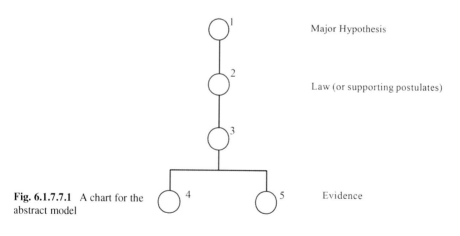

Fig. 6.1.7.7.1 A chart for the abstract model

Table 6.1.7.7.1 Key list

---

1. What is the ultimate intended aim (major hypothesis or proposition)
2. What is the substantive law that will be breached if the ultimate intended aim is reached
3. What are the acts or omissions that need to be undertaken (or not undertaken) if the ultimate intended aim is to be achieved?
4. What acts or omissions are generally seen if the ultimate intended aim is to be achieved?
5. What acts or omissions are generally not seen if the ultimate intended aim is to be achieved?

However, it should be borne in mind that in terms of completeness, no matter how thorough the query and search process is, there will always be unanswered questions and, no conclusion, no matter how well formulated, can ever account for all the facts we may potentially encounter. The evidence layer can become extremely complex for a number of reasons which will be explained henceforth.

We now turn to the *complexity of the evidence layer.* We articulate this in five points. Firstly, evidence or facts are always context specific. That is, the relevance of the evidence will be determined by the circumstances in which it is under consideration. Any item of evidence can be used for more than one purpose. It is not unusual for evidence to be used by different sides in a case for different purposes. A prosecutor may seek to use evidence of previous bad character to show that a suspect has a propensity for particular types of behaviour whereas the defence may seek to use the same evidence of previous bad character to demonstrate that the suspect has not offended for a considerable amount of time and is therefore reformed. In other circumstances, the defence may choose to use the same evidence to demonstrate that the suspect could not have fully participated in the crime because he was in prison during the preparatory stages of the offence.

Secondly, evidence never arrives in the hands of the user with its credentials made out. The relevance, credibility and weight of the evidence always has to be assessed and declared.

Thirdly, the user of evidence is always biased to some degree in the interpretation of evidence. Each user should be aware of their "standpoint" in using evidence and be prepared to declare it. Different persons have different standpoints each of which may result in a different interpretation of the evidence.

Fourthly, evidence is a word of association and therefore it can only be assessed by comparing, contrasting and juxtaposing it with other evidence and hypotheses. Hence, it is not possible to have a "single item of stand alone evidence." There is always other evidence.

Fifthly, all evidence can be broken down into smaller component parts. For example, an item of documentary evidence may be made up of paper, writing, ink, type face, a post mark, glue. The document may even have a fingerprint, a DNA stain or a discarded hair stuck to it. This atomistic view of evidence results in a situation where all evidence can be infinitely broken down into smaller and smaller parts which means that it can always be seen in the light of other evidence. This ancillary evidence about evidence can provide important insights into the relevance, credibility and weight of the evidence as a whole. A question for the user is always going to be "at what level of detail and at what level of granularity should the abstract model be considered to be complete?" This question is most important in fields such as criminal law. The reason is that it bears directly on the forensic standard "beyond a reasonable doubt". Regardless of how well a particular model appears to be formulated, there is always room for doubt. Facts are based on evidence and evidence always falls short of certainty.

Let us consider now *the role of evidence in argumentation.* Arguments are made up of *hypotheses*, sometimes called *propositions* or *case theories*, *chains* of directly relevant or indirectly relevant evidence and *generalizations*. Generalizations are generated by humans from perceived signals and stimulus in the environment. Generalizations may be presented by one person to another in circumstances where they become simply "accepted facts". These interactions take place between humans in the normal course of communication.

Others are formulated by direct perception of new signals by a single person. In reality, the process of reasoning from *evidence (signals)* to *hypothesis (case theory)* inevitably involves both. A useful way to think about generalizations is that they are clusters of signals assembled into forms that resemble an explanation or a story.

Because *generalizations* are constructed by the clustering of different forms of signals and stimulus from different sources of information, in the pursuit of different objectives and by different people, they exhibit highly subjective characteristics. This means that generalizations need to be managed with care. Understanding the fundamental steps in the construction of explanations and stories from mixtures of hypotheses, evidence and generalizations provides valuable insights into human decision-making. Furthermore, assessing the reliability of the grounds upon which an explanation is constructed provides a means to grade validity. Assessments about validity of explanations are inevitably uncertain and therefore can only be used as inferences towards to away from the hypothesis under consideration. That does not mean they are of limited use. If maximizing the frequency of desired outcomes as opposed to undesired outcomes is important, systematic methods have much to offer humans engaged in processes like investigation, decision making or the assessment of risk.

Generalizations are formulated by first and second hand exposure to information about events in the environment. We receive and process signals generated by these events and experiences and our sensory receptors process the signals into scenarios we can store and recover from memory. Views are generated about event types and often about causality. The purpose of this process in ways that can assist us in dealing with future. We formulate views of event are supported or negated by ancillary evidence. Evidence is therefore but one component used in the construction of legal arguments.

Inferences flow from items of evidence, generalizations and ancillary evidence towards or away from the hypothesis or proposition. Evidence therefore tends to support or tends to negate the hypothesis under consideration. Handling evidence in cases is therefore complex by virtue of the number of different ways the hypothesis, evidence, generalizations and ancillary evidence can be brought together.

In order to consider *the anatomy of the case as a whole*, we consider now a *case study*. Let us begin with *facts*. The following model was extracted from an actual case file of unauthorized online solicitation that occurred within the jurisdiction of the Italian financial market regulated by CONSOB.[129] The company Smallxchange, headquartered in the British Virgin Islands, aims to become an unofficial 24-h stock exchange on which any company in the world can be listed at no charge. In return the investors are asked to tender shares in exchange for a stake in the venture. The shares

---

[129] See CONSOB's weekly newsletter (October 2001).

would then be traded between partners in this unofficial stock exchange. Investors were solicited by a WWW Page advertising financial investment services (public offering of participation certificates).

In order to establish the efficacy of regulation of fraud on the Internet, it is necessary to consider whether CONSOB has appropriate jurisdiction.[130] CONSOB considered that its jurisdiction was asserted as Smallxchange targeted the national investment market of Italy. The soliciting agent was not licensed to trade as required under Directive 93/22/EEC (and its implementation in Italy: Legislative Decree 58) and false statements were made on the web page.

The illustration is an abstract model of the fraud. Note that the model is comprised of true claims (signals) as well as false claims. Refer to Fig. 6.1.7.7.2. Node 10 is a false statement aggravating the fact that the company, although properly constituted in law in UK, was not licensed to solicit investment services. This is a simple model but a more detailed model follows later. The chart in Fig. 6.1.7.7.2 depicts a simplified version of an investment scam online. In fact it could involve many more individuals, and so forth. There are three levels in the hierarchy. The top level, which only includes Node 1, corresponds to a *major hypothesis*. The middle level comprises a few nodes which correspond to *law* (or *supporting postulates*). The lowest level in the hierarchy, which comprises most nodes, corresponds to *evidence*. See a key list in Table 6.1.7.7.2. Next, refer to Fig. 6.1.7.7.3 and its respective

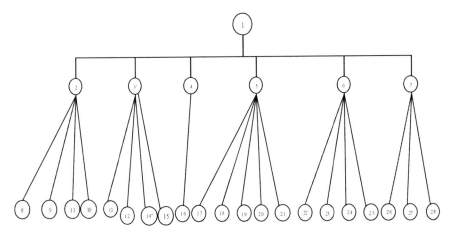

Fig. 6.1.7.7.2 A simplified version of an investment scam online: the low level of detail of the abstract model. The *numbers* refer to the number of a proposition on a key list of the evidence being charted. At the top level we find a major hypothesis, at the middle level, law (or supporting postulates), and at the lowest level, the evidence. See a key note in Table 6.1.7.7.2

---

[130] This must be considered separately from the regulator's ability to enforce its powers within such jurisdiction. For example, a securities regulator would first need to consider whether a security was being advertised or sold within its geographical jurisdiction and secondly, whether or not the person advertising the product was subject to their regulation.

Table 6.1.7.7.2 Key list

---

1. Smallxchange.Com Ltd is fraudulenty solicited investment services on the WWW
2. Targets the national market (i.e. the Italian public/investor market) (assertion of jurisdiction)
3. Smallxchange solicited securities services on WWW for investors
4. Requirement to inform Consob of its existence and to comply with minimal disclosure rules on technical details
5. Unauthorised sollicitation of investors (contra article 94 of Decree 58)
6. Unauthorised alternative trading system (contra article 102 of Decree 58)
7. Placing of unauthorised funds
8. An Italian ISP hosted the site
9. Most of the advertising was in Italian
10. Company is run by Italian executives
11. Possibility of paying in lira/euro
12. Non fulfilment
13. Web site lists shares for sale
14. Gianni Altieri was offered investment services by Smallxchange via email dated August 29, 2000.
15. http://www.smallXchange.com is a Web Site managed by Smallxchange Ltd.
16. http://www.smallXchange.com is hosted by Smallxchange Italia s.r.l.
17. Public offering of financial products
18. Shares of the companies listed on the stock exchange
19. Shares of the stock exchange in exchange for shares of the listed companies
20. Mutual fund shares
21'. Unauthorised public offering
22. Organization of a stock exchange
23. Quoted companies
24. Clearing house
25. Trading book
26. Placing of a fund
27. Asset management company
28. Fund name

---

key list in Table 6.1.7.7.3. Again, at the top level we find a major hypothesis, at the middle level, law, and at the lowest level, the evidence.

The abstract model lends itself to both macro and micro analysis. The model is a network of links and relationships between different items of evidence (signals). This allows finer analysis to be undertaken including the introduction of new signals. The analyzer of the case must however at some stage decide when to stop. The nature and characteristics of evidence signals means that the analyst could continue to analyze to ever smaller levels of detail.

The abstract model in Fig. 6.1.7.7.4 is a micro analysis of elements 7, 26, 27, 28, 36, 37 and 38 from the key list. Element 7 in the key list refers to a section of the law which demands that if the placing of unauthorized funds is to be proven, then an inducement to acquire securities must be shown to exist. Different sections of the abstract model can be broken down in this way to provide ever more detailed analysis.

An *evaluation of the abstract model* follows. The abstract model provides a number of benefits in the construction of fraud templates:

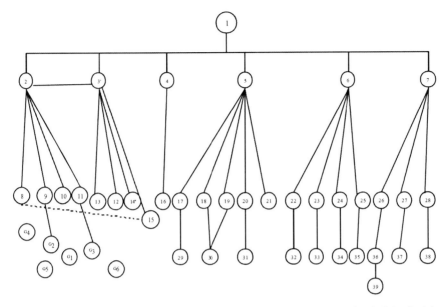

Fig. 6.1.7.7.3 A simplified version of an investment scam online: the higher level of detail of the abstract model. The *numbers* refer to the number of a proposition on a key list of the evidence being charted. G stands for *generalization*. At the top level we find a major hypothesis, at the middle level, law (or supporting postulates), and at the lowest level, the evidence. See a key note in Table 6.1.7.7.3

Table 6.1.7.7.3 Key list

1. Smallxchange.Com Ltd is fraudulenty solicited investment services on the WWW
2. Targets the national market (i.e. the Italian public/investor market) (assertion of jurisdiction)
3. Smallxchange solicited securities services on WWW for investors
4. Requirement to inform Consob of its existence and to comply with minimal disclosure rules on technical details
5. Unauthorised sollicitation of investors (contra article 94 of Decree 58)
6. Unauthorised alternative trading system (contra article 102 of Decree 58)
7. Placing of unauthorised funds
8. An Italian ISP hosted the site
9. Most of the advertising was in Italian
10. Company is run by Italian executives
11. Possibility of paying in lira/euro
12. Non fulfilement
13. Web site lists shares for sale
14. Gianni Alterie was offered investment services by Smallxchange via email dated August 29 2000.
15. http://www.smallXchange.com is a Web Site managed by Smallxchange Ltd.
16. http://www.smallXchange.com is hosted by Smallxchange Italia s.r.l.
17. Public offering of financial products
18. Shares of the companies listed on the stock exchange
19. Shares of the stock exchange in exchange for shares of the listed companies
20. Mutual fund shares
21'. Unauthorised public offering

Table 6.1.7.7.3 (continued)

22. Organization of a stock exchange
23. Quoted companies
24. Clearing house
25. Trading book
26. Placing of a fund
27. Asset management company
28. Fund name
29.–36. Etc.
37. Tricalpa Investment Inc.
38. Millenium Bug International
39. Etc
G_1 The presence of references to facts and circumstances concerning Italy in the site
G_2 The Employment of the Italian language
G_3 The indication of prices or amounts in Italian lire or Euro
G_4 The operations in Italy of intermediares through which it is possible to carry out or agree to the promotion or placement executed through the Internet
G_5 The spreading of information in Italy; it is included the execution of individualized or mass advertising or information campaigns in Italy, with the object similar to the site contents
G_6 The availability of the site through search motors specialized in Italy or Italian

- It uses rational principles for the combination of the key logical components in fraud: A proposition, the law, evidence and generalizations;
- It facilitates a method for combining key logic. Same "logic" in detection, prevention and prosecution;
- Provision of both holistic and atomistic (macro and micro) analysis of the key components in fraudulent activity. Consequently it facilitates to imagine all the sources of doubts that may lurk between the evidence;
- It ensures that the analysis of fraud cases is undertaken in a rational, repeatable way which can be conveyed to others for analysis and use (checking the coherence of your argument; convincing others of the relevance of an item of evidence);
- It provides the basic abstract model from which computational models can be constructed;
- It facilitates both "top down" and "bottom up" analysis of the key components in fraud.

We next concern ourselves with the *user requirements analysis*. What key features and requirements of the financial fraud ontology are important from the user's point of view? We set out a systematic requirements analysis by identifying and documenting the main needs of fraud investigators. We first consider the *method*, and *the breakdown of the users*.

Requirements gathering can be done using a number of different methods separately or in combination. We decided to organise the activities along three lines. First, we consulted the literature on financial fraud. To complement the literature review of the phenomenon of financial fraud to include the practice of fraud with VAT and fraud with securities, a number of structured interviews

Fig. 6.1.7.7.4 A micro
analysis of elements 7, 26,
27, 28, 36, 37 and 38 from the
key list

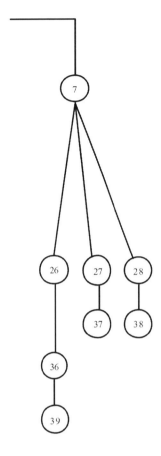

were conducted with representatives from several institutions in all three countries. Moreover, consortium expertise was used to accumulate necessary information for the construction and testing of a financial fraud ontology. Finally we had brainstorming sessions.

The ontology should at least be useful to three different and EU-relevant types of user communities:

- financial professionals: Accountants, auditors, banks, insurance agencies, government departments, regulators and financial experts
- Police and other law enforcement agencies
- Investigative and monitoring bodies

The emphasis is on defining what is required in terms of the information requirements rather than how the system should be physically implemented. Step one was to figure out what information would help investigators do their job better. Thus we start of with explaining the ontology functions. Then we will scrutinize the specific requirements for each fraud subdomain. Analogue with this is an analysis of the system attributes.

We start with *general strategic requirements*. The system has to be effective and efficient in deterring and preventing financial fraud. Central to achieving this is the identification of fraudulent activity from what is often a vast array of data. Eliminating legitimate activity from illegitimate activity is at the core of the problem, a fact that fraudsters know and use to hide illegal operations.

Illegitimate activity ranges from complex, organised and well thought through fraud to simple, disorganised and opportunist fraud. However, care needs to be taken not to assume that because a fraud is simple, disorganized and not particularly well planned that it will not have serious consequences. The www provides many examples of simple single frauds perpetrated for what may appear small financial gains. However, when these are added together, large amounts are often involved. This is used by fraudsters in both VAT fraud and Investment and Securities fraud. Single fraudulent transactions may involve small sums but when added together in the form of a "continuing fraudulent operation", massive sums of money can be involved and often over small timescales.

All fraud, complex or simple, involves at some stage of the process a breach of trust, confidence and fiduciary duty between a victim and a fraudster. Gaining and harnessing an understanding of this relationship and building it into the ontology, provides many opportunities for the identification of fraud. Refer to Table 6.1.7.7.4.

Let us consider, now, *temporal awareness of fraudulent actions*. Identifying different types of *Patterns* of fraudulent activity over time is a useful inquisitive technique for focusing the process of enquiry. A useful methodology is to develop a classification of events and activities that take place at different stages of fraud as the process unfolds. For example, events and activities that take place in before the fraud is committed (preparatory acts or omissions) events and activities that take place at the time the fraud is committed (*actus reus*) and finally, events and activities that take place after the commission of the fraud (consequential acts). See Fig. 6.1.7.7.5.

Table 6.1.7.7.4 Victims vs. fraudsters

Victim	Fraudster
Buyer	Seller
User	Supplier
Employee	Employer
Investor	Investment advisor
Principal	Agent
Beneficiary	Trustee
Manufacturer	Vendor
Stockholder	Executive
Customer	Broker

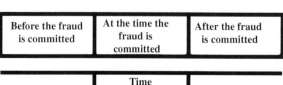

Fig. 6.1.7.7.5 Time in relation to fraudulent actions

A major task in fraud detection is constructing models of fraudulent behavior. This identifies key characteristics of fraud which can be used to prevent future frauds (online fraud detection) and for detection of past frauds (a posteriori fraud detection). It can also be used to identify ongoing fraud.

Fraud cases are notorious for their complexity. This complexity is usually caused by the complex nature and extent of the information involved. Said briefly, the law is often simple but the facts and evidence is often complex. Therefore, the ontology has to be able to manage and control the masses of data gathered during financial fraud investigations. This can aid the investigator to in focusing on relevant areas of law, the relevant facts in issue and the links and associations inherent in the evidence. Some associations between hypotheses, law and facts in a fraud model may be obvious, but others may be less so obvious. Simply modelling these relations is an important part of investigative methodology. Identifying what may be obvious and what may not be so obvious, lies at the heart of effective modelling and investigation. The way in which simply modelling and visualizing the relationships between the hypothesis under investigation, the law and the evidence, should not be under-estimated.

The following *top-level strategic requirements* were identified:

1. The user needs to be able to identify the species of fraud involved. This may be in terms of a legal definition but it will also be in terms of the methodology adopted to commit or even plan the fraud.
2. The user needs to be able to identify and express a hypothesis. The hypothesis will be in the form of some tentative explanation, a theory that requires explanation or some exposition. This exposition may or may not be able to account for the law and facts presented. In brief, the user must be able to identify associations between legal rules, facts and explanations gathered during investigations.
3. Pre-condition: to automate pattern searching to reveal previously unknown relationships.
4. The user must be able to streamline and standardize data capture, storage and analysis.
5. The user must be able to engage in the synthesis of probable and even possible models of fraud.
6. The user must have access to an information infrastructure for investigations
7. The user must be able to have access to information that is geographically specific.
8. The user must be able to have access temporal classifications and associations.
9. The system must provide clear audit trails.
10. The system must be sensitive to privacy and digital rights management.
11. The system has to work interoperable: the system has to take into account the different regulatory requirements, i.e. it has to work cross-jurisdictional; across the UK, Belgium and Italy. A system that will be deployed across multiple jurisdictions, faces the fact that no two law enforcement agencies store their incident data in exactly the same way. Thus it is important to have a data organization design that is flexible enough to be applied to any underlying data set.

12. A system should use standard and non-standard querying techniques so that it can be used to identify standard patterns of fraud and non-standard patterns of fraud.
13. The system has to incorporate knowledge from different domains.
14. The user has to be able to share information amongst regulators in the EU.
15. The system must be able to conduct querying on the basis of incomplete information.
16. The system needs to be able to be interoperable between agencies.
17. The system and users need to be able to use "Red Flags" and "Alerts" sensitive to fraud signals.
18. The system must be sensitive to both fuzzy and linear associations. Associations between facts and law are often fuzzy rather than linear.
19. The system has to look at multiple factors in a potential fraud case and select only those where it assumes a certain degree of likelihood of fraud for manual review.
20. The system has to include a kind of electronic case management system; to store and work on new cases. This includes a case chart; interests harmed; estimated losses; target; geography.
21. Investigators often need to be able to justify and document the manner in which they draw a conclusion. This is used in legal proceedings to justify subsequent actions. A search history should be designed to address this need.
22. The General User Interface (architecture) should be simple but adequate to achieve the requirements of the user.

The following points were taken into consideration:

- Confidentiality requirements;
- Privacy rights;
- Digital rights;
- Priority issues;
- Entities to be investigated;
- Periods to be covered in investigation;
- Authority to obtain information and access to premises and records;
- Identify key issues: consider: business activities; operating locations; trading record; management; audit reports; cash flow and financing;
- Decide on documentation to be seized: consider: evidential requirements;
- Range and location of documents to be seized;
- System scalability;
- Graphical User Interface (GUI) ergonomics.

Let us consider the user requirements for CONSOB type fraud. The main objective for CONSOB is a systematic and scalable "web crawler procedure". That is, closing the gap between inspection and enforcement in such a way that enables the user to detect more fraud with lower false positives. At the time we were developing the project CONSOB's procedure, which is fundamentally based on keyword-search, consisted of using different Internet search engines (such as Altavista, Googly, Yahoo, and so forth), as well as several meta-search engines. The search result is a list of web sites whose content is investigated by CONSOB's inspection officers in order to analyse and identify market abuse phenomena, abuse provisions of investment services and investment solicitation. The keywords are selected and combined to manually create complex queries on basis of the experience acquired during the ordinary supervision activity of the CONSOB's operative units. The use of the FF POIROT ontology in CONSOB's business case is related with the use of tools able to automate the query launching and to optimise the web information retrieval results. That is to say:

- Ability to examine possible fraudulent websites, and the links included on that website.
- The system has to be attached with several subject-specific thesauri, databases of term phrases with respect to the specific crime of fraudulent online investment solicitation.
- Finding suspected information on the World Wide Web: A web crawler (a proprietary search engine as opposed to general-purpose search engines) with a twofold search task: Which sites are selling securities AND which securities are being sold unlawful. Identification of traders in investment funds on the web. Identification of those traders who are not licensed. Proving that point above are engaged in trading in investment funds.
- A match program to compare the found pages with the search intention to filter out the irrelevant pages (lexicographically).
- Data manager; is responsible for the management of search results.
- A program to compare the search intention with web pages lexicographically to filter out irrelevant pages.
- Application of image processing technology in the search task.
- Facilities for organizing and managing search results should be provided.
- Semantic analysis of the selected pages shall be done to identify the pages containing crime information. First by a natural language processor and, then, by human experts.
- A central repository to store the relevant web sites after the semantic analysis. The system should keep a detailed history of the fraudulent website and changes to it to make the job easier for prosecutors (Collection of suspected information). A centralized database with a fraudster's name, method of operation, email address, URL, screen names, or other pertinent data would serve as a national repository for these crimes and criminals. As financial crimes conducted on the World Wide Web are particularly difficult to solve, but investigators linked through such a system could connect clues from various jurisdictions.
- If a page is verified as containing crime information, it will be processed automatically to abstract new concept terms that are to be added to the database for supporting further search.

The user requirements for combating VAT fraud were as follows. The main objective in fighting cross border VAT in the EU is to establish an effective system of mutual assistance and information exchange in order to ensure the proper functioning of the VAT system. A possible use case is an automatic and preferably a spontaneous exchange of information to help in the detection and prevention of fraud in intra-Community trade.

The system needs to enable two-way co-operation. This is in terms of maintaining and respecting legal authority of a European Union (EU) Member State but at the same time cooperating with other national authority's of other EU Member States. The Ontology would provide a solid base for the monitoring and enforcement of non-compliance of VAT laws. This should include:

- data integration within the same agency;
- data integration between different (national) agencies;
- data integration between two or more EU Member State agencies.

Fuzzy logic is central to the effective investigation and identification of tenuous and non-descript facts within a suspected or potential fraud. Distinguishing between probable, potential, accepted facts and frauds will enable and support better decision making and resource management.

The average life span of a VAT carousel fraud scheme is four months. After four months, the fraud organizer will make changes to the fraud scheme (adding companies, taking companies out, etc). Using fuzzy logic allows the system to adjust the profile dynamically as data are being analyzed. The output of the fuzzy logic system is twofold. First, a degree of likelihood of fraud is assessed by the fuzzy logic system. A second output variable gives an indication why a certain invoice claim was considered to be possibly fraudulent by the fuzzy logic system.

a. Active logic inference engine (VAT fraud à Customs & Excise have power of criminal investigation. While their counterpart in Belgium do not have this power. Only the police have the power to investigate in Belgium. You want to have the system to know this).
b. Contextual computing (building in the ability to learn from data should enable systems to apply individual context to decision making)
c. Recognise trends in VAT Fraud. Follow up developments in used techniques. Fraud control is played against opponents who think creatively, adapt continuously, and relish devising complex strategies. So a set of fraud controls that is perfectly satisfactory today may be of no use tomorrow, once the game has progressed a little. Maintaining effective fraud controls demands continuous assessment of emerging fraud trends and constant, rapid revision of trends.
d. The system has to be flexible: VAT fraudsters need only a few days or weeks at the most to change tactics once they find out a particular method is thwarted. For example, new buffer companies. Because fraud control is dynamic and continuously evolving, a static set of filters has only short-term value.
e. The investigator will analyse apparently random data such as invoices files to determine if some external agent (fraudster) is distorting the random nature of the data and leaving a noticeable pattern. Model has to make it feasible to distinct between simple irregularities and actual fraud.

f. System needs a typology of VAT fraud.

g. Multiple data sources (VIES, ICT listing, etc) are often used, each having different functions and user interfaces. This adds another dimension of difficulty for the end-user. One easy-to-use interface that integrates these different data sources is needed

h. The system has to recognise all national rules.

i. An ontology is needed to enable a correct and rapid analysis of the VAT regulations in different member states and to keep analytical activity up to date.

j. This cross linking to the various national statutes is highly relevant for VAT officers because VAT fraud often has a cross border element. It helps the VAT officer who does not understand the different languages concepts and their meaning.

k. Data mining: to identify deliberate falsification of data (invoices) held within external database sources (VIES, etc.).

l. Graphical/illustrative presentations of key issues assist users in understanding them. In the case of the UK, visualization will not only assist users. During a trial, the evidence of a fraud investigation is inevitably complex and mountainous. Presenting this information in court to a lay jury is frequently seen as one of the biggest hurdles in any case. Applying simple, clear graphics to illustrate complex commercial data or financial transactions can help a jury to understand highly intricate cases.

m. In fraud detection and investigation it is essential to develop a fraud risk profile in order to identify those areas that are vulnerable to fraud and to establish applicable and appropriate red flags.

n. Presenting the data in a way that it is easily understand by the judge, client, and so forth.

o. Running of multiple profiles. Indicators: rarely can fraudulent activity be detected through the use of a single profile. Similarly, the running of multiple profiles is normally time consuming and a drain on resources. For example, other profiles in VAT transactions may include post box service, and so on. As a result, the trend is increasingly towards fully automated systems that can repeatedly run all the know profiles.

p. Concerning VAT, a lot of the tasks are repetitive. For example, checks to ensure VAT numbers are valid. This should be automated so the investigator does not spend time running these tests.

A discussion of *meeting the requirements* follows. When the requirements are met the resulting environment will be useful to the above mentioned target audience in a way that:

1. Investigative and monitoring bodies will benefit from the strongly enriched information retrieval made possible by linking e.g. internet or database search facilities to the FF POIROT ontology in order to detect or investigate instances of attempted or actual financial fraud. Species of fraud (typologies) have been identified so that macro and micro analysis can be undertaken then used as "templates of fraud". These templates can be stored, accessed and used to mine for

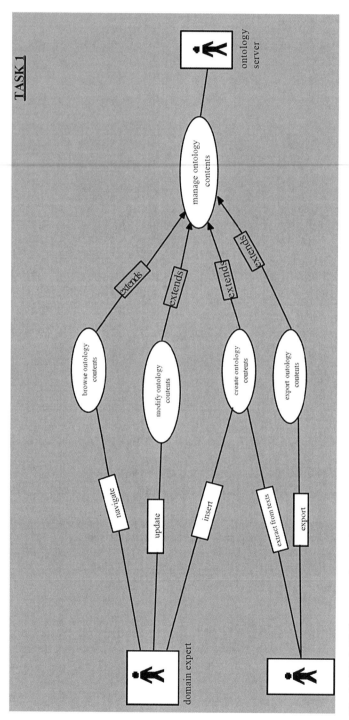

Fig. 6.1.7.7.6 UML use case diagram for Task 1

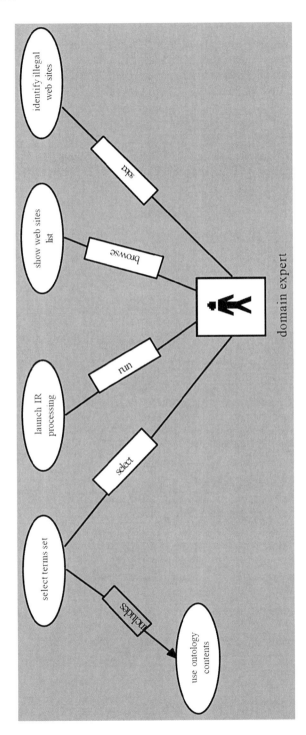

Fig. 6.1.7.7.7   UML use case diagram for Task 2

new frauds across linguistic and jurisdictional boundaries. In addition, they can use partial templates (bits of the model) to act as "attractors" or "magnets" which they can use to mine for data that might (when drawn together) amount to a fraud.

2. Financial professionals will benefit from an "FF POIROT style" ontology using it as an authoritative concept base, extensively cross-linked (to other domains, systems and languages) and available for customized applications. Exploitation in this area could be as a high-tech service extending similar services and products (viz. on European VAT in respect of accounting rules) currently already commercialized by at least two of FF POIROT's users.

3. Law enforcement: benefit by the availability of relevant parts of the FF POIROT

4. ontology; for example, as an RDF-mapped Semantic Web resource, to support *future*

5. *police-oriented query systems*, in a non-technical user-friendly, attractive, and comprehensive manner. Additionally, sharing of information with investigative bodies and understanding of related documents will be substantially enhanced if such communication and documents are hyperlinked to a shared ontology. Optimizing the investigation, discovery, prevention and reduction of complex frauds is being made routine and efficient.

Let us consider *use case decomposition*, for the CONSOB part of the project. The use case diagram in two parts, drawn in UML format,[131] shown in Figs. 6.1.7.7.6 and 6.1.7.7.7, represents the CONSOB showcase in terms of actors, use cases and interactions amongst them. Actors are users and external systems. In order to make these figures comprehensible, a short description of the scenario relevant to the use case identified is given hereafter.

This is mainly based on a document by Maria Vittoria Marabello of Knowledge Stones S.p.A., within the FF POIROT consortium. Task 1 consists of *accessing and editing the ontology contents*:

- *Manage the ontology contents*: This use case occurs each time the user wants to access and manage the contents of the domain specific ontology, extracted from texts by the *ontology extraction tool* (OET), integrated and made available by the project's ontology server.
- *Browse Ontology Contents*: This use case occurs when the user wants to navigate the ontology contents.
- *Create Ontology Contents*: This use case occurs when the user wants to update the ontology contents by manually creating new elements.
- *Modify Ontology Contents*: This use case occurs when the user wants to update the ontology contents by changing the available elements.
- *Export Ontology Contents*: This use case occurs when an upload of the domain specific ontology contents into the project's ontology server is required.

---

[131] UML is the Unified Modeling Language. This is a widespread language for such purposes.

Task 2 consists of *supporting the Web investigation*:

- *Select Terms Set*: This use case occurs each time the user wants to select a terms set to feed the information retrieval process, by means of which it is possible to identify financial frauds carried out through Web Sites.
- *Use Ontology Contents*: This use case occurs when the user wants to select a terms set to feed the information retrieval process. The terms set has to be part of the project's ontology validated contents.
- *Launch IR Processing*: This use case occurs whenever the user wants to start the IR process, in order to select a group of sites potentially carrying out a financial fraud.
- *Show Web Sites List*: This use case occurs each time the user wants to look at the list of sites produced by the IR process.
- *Identify Illegal Web Sites*: This use case occurs each time the user, by looking at the sites list produced by the information retrieval process, can carry out a Web Site inspection to identify the illegal services there proposed.

In the present Section 6.1.7.7, we have explained how we approached the tasks of setting the user requirements for a project envisaging the development of an ontology prototype concerning financial fraud. Whilst the initial prototype was to be designed to fulfil the requirements expressed here, it also had to be designed for flexibility, in order to allow easy modification and iterations based on use cases, user feedback and user-testing results. As this was an *initial* analysis of user requirements, there should always be scope for discussion on new necessities of the system.

6.1.8 Automatic Text (and Multimedia) Summarisation

6.1.8.1 An Overview

Automated summarisation may or may not be associated with *text mining*, but it is relevant for both investigative and judicial or juridic context.[132] Sometimes researchers who are engaged in the detection of crime, are also researching text mining or then the automated summarisation of large documents, which is the case of Christopher Yang, who has published about knowledge discovery and information visualisation for terrorist social networks (Yang, 2008), but has also published about the hierarchical summarisation of large documents (Yang & Wang, 2008).

Writing a summary is a cognitively demanding task for humans, who moreover can be expected to approach it in different ways, to varying degrees of satisfaction for their clients, who in turn apply criteria relevant for given purposes. All

---

[132] The present Section 6.1.8.1 on automated summarisation is an adaptation of Nissan (2003h).

the more so, good summarisation is an ambitious task for automated *NLP* (*natural-language processing*) systems. The sheer amount of information flowing in as online text makes the allocation of human time to process it prohibitive, in given contexts. Hence, the appeal of the prospect of having automated tools carrying out summarisation or, at the very least, the kind of sorting that goes under the name *story categorisation.*

For *news story categorisation systems,* already in the 1980s nice results could be shown, combining information retrieval and NLP: Hayes, Knecht, and Cellio (1988) reported about a tool that, while

> ["]not perform[ing] a complete semantic or syntactic analysis of the input stories" — a stream of news stories — was sophisticated enough to handle such lexicon that its super-ordinate semantic concepts would make for misleading predictions about the category in which the story belongs. "We were prepared for sports stories that looked like metals stories ("...*captured the gold medal at the summer Olympics*...") or like war/disorder stories ("...*the battle on center court at Wimbledon*..."). A more difficult challenge was posed by words and phrases that were good predictors of a particular topic but occurred randomly across all story types, sometimes with the same meaning, sometimes not. [...] Metaphorical language was also a problem — not use of fixed phrases (we had no trouble failing to assign the category **metals** to a story that contained the phrase *like a lead balloon*) — but rather creative metaphorical language. So, a story about a series of battles in the continuing disposable diaper war between Proctor and Gamble and its competitor was assigned to the disorders category.

Automatic summarisation is more demanding. In fact, it requires endowing the tool with enough understanding of the text, that another text be generated, conveying a sensibly identified gist of the input. When one has AI application in the legal or investigative domain in mind, it is a matter of course to point out that case summarisations are of paramount importance in the workings of the judiciary, both for a case at hand, and in the record of the past as subserving the construction of new cases that may obtain. Even more to the point, *text mining* for investigative purposes can greatly benefit from automatically generated summaries, which once they come to the attention of human analysts, would motivate them to read some given detected documents.

In the SALOMON project, Belgian criminal cases were summarised automatically and presented by a case profile. Case category, case structure and irrelevant text units are identified based on a knowledge base represented as a text grammar. Thematically important text units and key terms are selected by shallow techniques. These paragraphs are represented as weighted vectors and clustered. The system points the user effectively towards relevant texts. SOLOMON was described in Uyttendaele, Moens, and Dumortier (1998) and Moens, Uyttendaele, and Dumortier (1999). The next section, Section 6.1.8.2, is going to deal with projects specifically in text summarisation for law.

Inderjeet Mani (2001) provides a systematic introduction to automated summarisation techniques. Which strategies are applied by humans when confronted with the task of writing a summary is a subject discussed early on in the book, by way of its foundation: "the study of summarization by human abstractors provided a useful grounding for automatic summarization. It also became clear that in order to provide a constructive analysis of the field, covering a few critical issues in depth would be preferable to a broad compendium of the tremendous variety of work in summarization" (ibid., p. ix), so that as a survey Mani's book was not meant to be exhaustive.

As could be expected, Mani's own work in the field features prominently in the book, "because of the wealth of system detail I can tap for discussion of these basic issues" (ibid., p. ix). Particular approaches are illustrated in case studies, in view of adoption as a textbook (an aim subserved as well by the review sections placed at the end of chapters; they list and concisely define concepts by way of a recapitulation). The publisher's blurb notes that "the book also includes detailed assessments of evaluation methods and new topics such as multi-document and multimedia summarization", where "multimedia" concerns the input, the output, or both. In multi-document summarisation, "the summarizer identifies what's common across the documents, or different in a particular one" (ibid., p. 13).

In Mani (2001), chapter 1, "Preliminaries", introduces a variety of basic concepts, such as measures of semantic informativeness, or the relationships between indicative, informative, and evaluative or critical summaries. This distinction fits in the transformation stage, which in a general abstract architecture of a summariser, is intermediate between analysis (either generic or user-focused) and synthesis (of either fragments, or connected text).

Mani's chapter 2 is on human professional abstractors. There exists an ANSI standard of abstracting, for which Edward Cremmins was responsible. A book by Endres-Niggermeyer (1998) is a detailed empirical study of human abstractors. Chapter 2 of Mani's book describes, among the other things, how strategies of manual summarization make use of features, e.g. cue phrases (explicit statements of concern or conclusion in the input paper), and in-text summaries (which an author may introduce with "In summary". Location cues from the beginning or end of text units are considered "likely to carry theme-relevant information" (ibid., p. 32), and so is the title cue. Professional abstractors may as well revise author-supplied, computer-produced, or their own draft abstracts (ibid., p. 37). Mani's chapter 4 is on revision.

At the start of his chapter 3, "Extraction", Mani remarks: "For a computer program, extracts are obviously an easier target than abstracts, since the program does not have to create new text. Extraction is a relatively low-cost solution, compared to the additional knowledge resources required to construct sentential meanings or to generate text" (ibid., p. 45): analysis predominates, is shallow, "and rarely goes as deep as a sentiential semantics" (ibid., p. 45). Mani's chapter 5 shows that "extraction can fruitfully exploit a discourse-level analysis" (ibid., p. 45), "though the representation from the deeper analysis isn't present in the extracted result" (ibid., p. 45). Discourse-level analysis is necessary of abstraction, optional for extraction. "Since humans (professional abstractors are often given exemplars of abstracts as guides in training them [. . .], it makes sense to have machines do the same" (ibid., p. 45).

Unsurprisingly for a treatment of *discourse analysis*, an important part is played by *text cohesion* (Mani, ibid., chapter 5, section 2) and *text coherence* (ibid., section 3). It is a coherence relation of the *elaboration* kind that links "John can open Bill's safe" and "He knows the combination" As to cohesion: "The semantic relationships underlying cohesion are ubiquitous in text" (ibid., p. 93), and include "devices such as repetition, anaphora,[133] ellipsis, synonymy, etc." (ibid., p. 93). "Cohesive ties influence the comprehensibility and perhaps even the summarizability of texts" (ibid., p. 93). The discussion in "Cohesion graph topology" (this is the title of Mani's section 2.2) is based on Skorochod'ko's *Connectivity Criterion* ("The salience of a sentence is proportional to the number of sentences that are semantically related to it"), and *Indispensability Criterion*: "The salience of a sentence is proportional to the degree of change to the graph when the sentence is removed" (Mani, ibid., p. 95).

Text cohesion can be used for topic segmentation (Kozima's *Text Tiling* algorithm was devised for that), where: "A topic [...] could be thought of as a text segment that is about a single thing; this notion is somewhat different from the related notion of 'what the text is about'" (ibid., p. 102). *Lexical chains* are a related notion: "if we have one or more topical segments about a particular topic, a chain is a sequence of related words characterizing the topic" (ibid., p. 104). An algorithm for computing lexical chains was proposed by Barzilay and Elhadad (1999).

"An alternative approach to segmenting text into topical regions is to deal with relatively coarse-grained topics for discovering topical segments" (Mani, ibid., 105) – this is the beginning of Mani's section 2.3.3 – and statistical models have been used to that effect. Chapter 6 in Mani (2001), "Abstraction", discusses abstraction from templates (ibid., section 2), or by term rewriting (ibid., section 3), using event relations (ibid., section 4), using a concept hierarchy (ibid., section 5). This is followed by "Synthesis for Abstraction" (ibid., section 6), and this includes both extraction (ibid., section 6.3) and generation (ibid., section 6.4), which eventually results in surface realization (ibid., section 6.4.5). In his book, Mani noted (pp. 160–162):

> Recently, there has been a great deal of interest in statistical generation [...], to address the knowledge acquistion bottleneck in developing grammars of sufficient coverage for a particular application. Of particular interest here is the use of language modeling methods discussed in [Mani's own] Chapter 3 [i.e., 'Extraction']. Banko et al. (2000) use these methods to produce very short headline-summaries. Equation 6.6. describes the general form of their method — here H and D represent the bag of words in the headline and the document respectively. The equation reflects a mixture of several models using simple linear interpolation: it uses a linear combination of the conditional probability of a term occurring in a training headline given its occurrence in the corresponding document, the most likely ordering of terms in the document (i.e., using bigrams from a corpus rather than grammatical knowledge to influence word-ordering), and the length of the resulting summary.

---

[133] Resolving *anaphora* determines what determinative or possessive adjectives or pronouns (e.g. "this", "my", "yours"), or articles ("the"), or other indexicals (e.g., "yesterday"), refer to. Literally in Greek *anaphora* means "carrying back", and *anaphora* in the narrow sense means a reference backwards by a determinative, as opposed to *cataphora*, which refers forwards. In the usual, broader sense, *anaphora* encompasses both backward and foreword references.

The equation is as follows:

$$s^* = \arg\max(\; \alpha \sum_{i=1}^{n} \log(P(w_i \in H \mid w_i \in D)) \; +$$
$$\beta \sum_{i=2}^{n} \log(P(w_i \mid w_{i-1})) \; +$$
$$\gamma \log(P(len(H) = n)))$$

Experience of everyday life teaches us that when summarising anything, we must pay attention to critical information, and that there are different way for information to be conveyed to a fuller or lesser extent. The loss of information may be critical, for given purposes. There is an Arabic proverb that conveys the problematic nature of summaries; the chapter on Joseph in Egypt is the longest in the Koran, and the proverb sums it up: "A man lost his son, and found him". This is an accurate summary, and it is focal in view of expectations about what does matter for human emotions. But then consider this punning summary (which I am making up) of Joseph Conrad's novel *Lord Jim*: "Wishful sinking". The protagonist of that novel is a sailor who, believing the ship is about to sink, abandons it, and by so doing is dishonoured; he eventually recovers his honour because of the death he dies. It is only once you already know the plot, that you can appreciate the summary "Wishful sinking" (the belief that the ship was about to sink was not quite "wishful thinking", but being inaccurate, it comes close).

In Mani's chapter 7, "Multi-document summarization", among the other things we find: "The difference between informational equivalence and informational subsumption is really a matter of degree" (ibid., p. 175). Examples given in Mani (2001, chapter 7) are taken from Radev, Jing, and Budzikowska (2000). In particular (Mani, ibid., p. 175):

(7)   X was found guilty of the murder.

(8)   The court found X guilty of the murder of Y last August and sentenced him to life.

Mani remarked (ibid.):

Sentence (8) contains additional information, about the sentencer, the victim, the time of the sentencing, and the duration of the sentence. If the additional information is deemed important, (7) could be eliminated if substituted by (8). For example, "the court" may be viewed as less important, but if (8) had instead "the 5 white jurors" or "the tribunal", that may be deemed more important. [...] In this particular case, which is quite typical, the subsuming sentence (8) is longer. There can be cases where the subsuming sentence is of the same length, e.g., (9), or even shorter, e.g., (10). Since being sentenced implies being found guilty, (9) may be viewed as conveying all the information in (7), while also being of the same length.

(9)   Last August, X was sentenced to life for Y's murder.

(10)   X got life last August, for Y's murder.

Mani also remarked (ibid.): "Another criterion is *coverage*. A sentence in one article which subsumes multiple sentences in another article might be preferred to one which just subsumes a single sentence in the other article".

A case study, of biographical summarisation, appears in Mani's section 4 of chapter 7; in particular, section 4.4 (pp. 201–202) enumerates "the top-level components that can be involved in" a multi-document biographical summariser: (1) "a tokenizer for words and sentences, which outputs strings marked up with word and sentence boundaries"; (2) "a part-of-speech tagger, which outputs a part-of-speech for each word in a sentence"; (3) "a named-entity finder, which extends the word tokenization to include named entities along with within-document coreference relations among them"; (4) "a nominal tagger, which tags names like 'priest' as a person"; (5) "an anaphora resolver, which resolves pronouns like 'he', and definite NPs [i.e., noun phrases] like 'their leader'"; (6) "a cross-document coreference module, which decides whether two names (e.g., George Bush), each from a different document, describe the same entity or not"[134]; (7) "a syntactic analyzer,

---

[134] Let us develop here that example, which Inderjeet Mani proposed yet not develop himself in context. Disambiguating "George Bush" is usually between the father and the son, as both of them were presidents of the United States. Consider in addition that in the 1830s, in New York there was a professor of Hebrew by that name. For sure a newspaper or a news magazine you may have been browsing between 1980 and 2010 has not been referring to *that* George Bush. And of the two politicians, international news mentioning George Bush in the 1980s and early 1990s are likely to have been referring to the elder Bush, but in a Texan context the son, who was a governor, may have been referred to. Elsewhere, the text is likely to have pointed out that the son was meant, rather than the father: "Ann Richards [...] is running for reelection as Governor of Texas against George W. Bush, a Republican and the eldest son of the former President. [...] She derides him as 'all hat and no cattle'. [...] Her followers hand out bumper stickers saying: 'Don't elect the son-of-a-Bush'. They call him 'Shrub'", as reported by Ian Brodie in the London *Times* of 20 October 1994, p. 15, under the title "Lone Star governor struggles to uproot the Shrub".
Also in 1994, the 1830s George Bush was briefly discussed in a new scholary book from the United States (Ritterband & Wechsler, 1994). Columbia College (from the 1880s, Columbia University) suspended Hebrew instruction from 1799 "until 1830 when, perhaps responding to a movement to establish the rival University of the City of New York, it appointed the Rev. Samuel Turner, D.D. [...] to a professorship of Hebrew language and literature" (ibid., p. 12), but then the rival new university "soon appointed George Bush and Isaac Nordheimer to Hebrew and Arabic chairs, respectively. Nordheimer, one of America's first Jewish college professors, is oft noted for his Hebrew grammar. The work of Bush and Nordheimer allowed Turner to cease instruction at Columbia, though Nordheimer died within three years of his appointment" (ibid., p. 13). Endnote 54 on p. 243 explains: "The University of the City of New York apparently cornered the market on Hebrew instruction in New York. Turner wrote: 'When Nordheimer became known as a good Hebrew teacher, I felt it less incumbent on me to devote my time to this object. [*sic*] Since then I have never been required to give lessons in Hebrew, so that the professorship has become a sinecure' (quoted in Richard Gottheil, "Semitic Languages at Columbia", *Columbia University Bulletin* 19 [March, 1898], 94). Bush, not Nordheimer, taught Hebrew at the new institution." That much is related by Ritterband and Wechsler (1994) about that early George Bush.
In the *Catalogue of the Officers, Alumni, and Students of the University of the City of New York, 1839–40*, printed in New York by Hopkins and Jennings in 1840, and now accessible online (http://dspace.nitle.org/bitstream/handle/10090/1838/UnivofCityofNewYork1839_40_cat.PDF?sequence=1), one finds indeed: "GEORGE BUSH, Professor of Hebrew. ISAAC NORDHEIMER, P. D., Professor of the German Language and of Oriental Languages", listed among the (few) "Professors not of the Governing Faculty."

which provides syntactic analysis for a sentence or parts thereof"; (8) "a tagger for temporal expressions, which resolves dates and times like '3 pm on June 1st' and 'next Tuesday'"; (9) "an event-ordering component, which tags certain verbs with event indices along with a 'precedes' attributes [*sic*] indicating which event-indices succeed it temporally"; (10) "an appositive phrase extractor, which allows the identification of occupation and age descriptions associated with a person"; (11) "an event extractor, which finds events associated with a person"; (12) "an associated-people extractor, which computes a mutual information metric across named entities found in the collection to find people who are mentioned together significantly"; (13) "a biography aggregator, which merges biographical tuples [...]"; (14) "a text planner, which takes a table of descriptions of a person and decides what to say in each sentence" (Mani, 2001, p. 201); (15) "a realization component, which takes the input sentence representations and generates sentences" (ibid., p. 202).

Concerning what Mani calls "an associated-people extractor", I would like to refer to a related task, even though not in summarisation, that was described in by Marie-Daneille Demelas-Bohy and Monique Renaud (1995). Their paper was entitled "Instability, networks and political parties: a political history expert system prototype". It described computer-assisted attempts to ascribe party affiliation to the members of the 1880 National Convention of Bolivia; party affiliation was not stated in the parliamentary roll. Based on a few known affiliations of leading politicians, on the events stored in the database, on statements (if any record survives) by the individual members of parliament, on their known attitudes or relation toward other politicians, and so on, a computer program proposed individual party affiliations that in the main quite successfully match conclusions reached by the same authors qua historians without resorting to the computer. This amounts to a reconstruction of the Bolivian political class at the time. Mathematical research into social networks is relevant; refer to the *Social Networks* journal (1979–), and, e.g., to a book by Wasserman and Faust (1994).

Chapter 8 in Mani's book (2001) is entitled "Multimedia summarization", and shortly overviews the *summarization of dialog, of video, and of diagrams*. Section 3 (ibid.) is entitled "Summarization of video"; for example (ibid., p. 212):

> Current methods for processing broadcast news exploit information from the audio or closed-captioned text (silence, speaker changes, anchor-reporter handoffs, and content

---

Another Web search retrieved facsimile excerpts from a book being advertised, with the following, further information. Goldman clarifies the scholarly relation of Bush to Nordheimer (2004, pp. 163–164 in chapter 8): "Nordheimer died too young to realize his full scholarly potential — at the age of thirty-three he succumbed to the tuberculosis that had weakened him since his adolescence — his life and writings had considerable influence on the leading American Protestant Hebraists of the first half of the nineteenth century: Moses Stuart of Andover Theological Seminary, George Bush of New York University, and Edward Robinson of Union Theological Seminary."

This example of human-initiated search for information drives in the importance of incorporating some reasonably effective competence in natural-language analysis, not only in automatic summarization tools, but also in such text mining tools that demands on their output are not unambitious.

analysis), as well as video (anchor and logo detection, for example) to help determine what is salient. (The closed-captioned text is generated for the benefit of TV viewers who have hearing impairments.) The Broadcast News Navigator (BNN) system [(Merlino et al., 1997)] provides a tool for searching, browsing and summarizing TV news broadcasts from a variety of news sources (including some foreign language ones). In BNN, information extracted from the audio (silence, speaker changes), video (anchor and logo detection), and closed-captioning text (anchor-reporter handoffs) is used to segment the stream into news stories. BNN uses a number of mixed-media presentation strategies, combining key frames extracted automatically from the video with summaries of the accompanied closed-captioned text. These summaries contain a single sentence (extracted by weighting occurrences of proper name terms) along with key organizations, locations, and people involved. To minimize redundancy, clusters of related stories in the BNN stream or on the Internet are formed by means of cosine similarity vocabulary comparisons; only representative video segments from a cluster are shown.

Still in chapter 8 in Mani (2001), section 4 is "Summarization of diagrams", and section 5 is "Automatic multimedia briefing generation". Mani's chapter 9, "Evaluation", discusses intrinsic methods (quality and informativeness evaluations, e.g., of the fidelity to the source: in these, the system's performance is tested for its own sake), and extrinsic methods: "to determine the effect of summarization on some other task" (ibid., p. 241). Extrinsic methods include relevance assessment, reading comprehension, presentation strategies, and assessing the impact on end-users of a system mature enough to have any.

An early automatic summariser was DeJong's FRUMP (dealt with by Mani, 2001 on pp. 130–132), based on the representation of generalised event patterns by means of *scripts*, and coming from what used to be the Yale-based *conceptual-dependency* school of automated narrative understanding (for which, see Sections 5.2.8 and 5.2.9 above). FRUMP was originally described in DeJong (1979, 1982).[135]

---

[135] Another computer scientist with a record of early involvement in research into summarization tools is Udo Hahn, who is also prominent in research about *ontologies*. In his preface, Mani (2001) actually credits Hahn (ibid., p. x) as having jointly taught conference tutorials, on which the introduction of Mani's book is based. They co-authored Hahn and Mani (2000). When preparing the original draft of what is now the section you are reading, I chanced upon a copy of an old report by Hahn and Ulrich Reimer, 'Heuristic text parsing in TOPIC: Methodological issues in a knowledge-based text condensation system' (Bericht TOPIC–5/83, 2nd ed., Universität Konstanz), that was going to appear in the North-Holland *Proceedings of the 5th International Research Forum in Information Science*, Heidelberg, 1983. The task of TOPIC was described as being "the generation of condensates (abstracting)" (from German texts). "Parsing heuristics referring to cohesion and coherence of texts" were in the first place intended to generate indicative summaries. Mani's book (2001) discusses TOPIC on pp. 148–150: "The system applies shallow methods of parsing noun phrases in the text, relying on a lexicon which maps to a knowledge base of domain concepts. The system increases the activation weights of frames, slots, and slot values whenever they are referred to in the text. TOPIC counts how frequently references are made to a frame itself, to a slot of a frame, or to the slot value. Thus, *concept counting* is carried out, rather than counting words, word-stems or discourse referents [. . .]. For example, the salience of a slot is determined by the frequency of reference to that slot compared to the frequency of reference to all slots mentioned in the text. A frame is salient if the ratio of the number of its instances to the number of its active instances (an active frame is one which is referenced at least once in the text) is less than the number of its active instances. [. . .] These patterns of salience are applied to individual paragraphs, and

6.1.8.2 Text Summarisation Projects for Law

Andrew Stranieri and John Zeleznikow

Text summarisation[136] involves identifying, summarising and organising related text so that users can efficiently deal with information in large documents. Sparck Jones (1993) states that text summarisation consists of three steps:

- The text analysis step identifies the essential content of the source text resulting in a source text representation;
- In the transformation step the content of the source text is condensed either by selection or generalisation of what is important in the source. The selected and generalised information is captured in a summary representation; and
- The synthesis step involves drafting and generation of the summary text based upon the summary representation.

The SALOMON project represents seminal work in text summarisation for law, and is discussed next. The SALOMON project (Moens, 2000) automatically summarised Belgian criminal cases in order to improve access to the large number of existing and future court decisions. SALOMON extracts relevant text units from the case text to form a case summary. Such a case profile facilitated the rapid determination of the relevance of the case to be employed in text search. Techniques were developed for identifying and extracting relevant information from the cases.

A double methodology was used when developing SALOMON. First, the case category, the case structure and relevant text units were identified based on a knowledge base represented as a text grammar. Consequently, general data and legal foundations concerning the essence of the case were extracted. Secondly, SALOMON extracted informative text units of the alleged offences and of the opinion of the court based on shallow statistical techniques. The application of cluster algorithms based on the selection of representative objects has the potential for automatic theme recognition, text abstracting and text linking, even beyond the legal field.

A major part of the SALOMON research concerns automatic abstracting of text. Document abstracts generated automatically generally belong to two types (Sparck Jones, 1993). Firstly, the abstract is constructed for easy and fast determination

---

then topic descriptions are determined and aggregated over paragraphs, after which generalization operations are applied across the topic descriptions to create a hierarchical text graph. Using an interactive text graph navigation aid, a user is able to traverse the resulting text graph, varying the detail of the summaries [... O]ne can certainly ask how such a hypertext conceptual representation compares with a conventional text summary. [...] TOPIC could, in principle, certainly produce an extract summary, simply by weighting sentences based on the density of references to salient concepts".

[136] Section 6.1.8.2 is based on a section on text summarisation in Stranieri and Zeleznikow (2005a).

of relevance: it indicates whether the complete text version is of interest (indicative abstract). Secondly, the abstract is a document surrogate expressing the main contents of the document: its components may be used for text search and linking (informative abstract). In this way abstracting is related to indexing. A brief summary may serve as a complex structured index description.

The automatic generation of document abstracts has early been recognised as a potential area for automation (Luhn, 1958). At that time automatic text abstracting and indexing were strongly related. Attempts have been made to extract words, phrases, or sentences that reflect the content of the text. Index terms are weighted depending upon the occurrence in titles and headings (Salton, 1989) or upon occurrence frequencies in the text and/or text corpus (Salton & Buckley, 1988). Sentence scores are based on the number of significant and non significant words in it (Luhn, 1958), on location heuristics (Baxendale, 1958), or on the occurrence of positive or negative indicator phrases (Edmundson, 1969), or are computed as the sum of term weights after eliminating stop words (Earl, 1970). Sentences, the score of which surpasses a certain threshold value, are retained for summary purposes.

Moens, Uyttendaele, and Dumortier (1997) noted that until recently, automatic abstracting had been receiving little attention, apart from the application of artificial intelligence techniques in restricted text domains. With the current information overload, automation of text summarisation receives renewed interest. An example of the automatic generation of case summaries in the legal field and their use for information retrieval is FLEXICON (Fast Legal Expert Information CONsultant), reported about by Gelbart and Smith (1993). FLEXICON extracts relevant text units based on location heuristics, occurrence frequencies of index terms, and the use of indicator phrases.

Let us turn now to other applications of summarisation in law. Grover, Hachey, Hughson, and Korycinski (2003) report on a project, *Sum*, that applies automatic summarisation techniques to the legal domain. In their methodology, sentences from text are classified according to their rhetorical role in order that particular types of sentence can be extracted to form a summary. They describe some experiments with judgements of the House of Lords. They have performed automatic linguistic annotation of a small sample set and then hand-annotated the sentences in the set in order to explore the relationship between linguistic features and argumentative roles. They use state-of-the-art natural language processing techniques to perform the linguistic annotation using XML-based tools and a combination of rule-based and statistical methods. They focus on the predictive capacity of tense and aspect features for a classifier.

Farzindar and Lapalme (2004) describe a method for the summarization of legal documents helping a legal expert determine the key ideas of a judgment. Their approach is based on the exploration of the document's architecture and its thematic structures in order to build a table style summary for improving coherency and readability of the text. They present the components of a system, called *LetSum*, built with this approach, its implementation and some preliminary evaluation results. They were exploring methods for generating flexible summaries of legal documents, taking as their point of departure the approach to automatic summarisation of Teufel and Moens (2002). They were working with law reports for three main reasons:

i. The existence of manual summaries means that they have available to them evaluation material for the final summarization system;
ii. The existence of differing target audiences allows them to explore the issue of tailored summaries; and
iii. the texts have much in common with the academic papers that Teufel and Moens worked with, while remaining challengingly different in many respects.

The goals of Farzindar and Lapalme (2004) are similar to those of the SALOMON project (Moens et al., 1997), which also deals with summarisation of legal text. However, their choice of methodology is designed to test the portability of the Teufel and Moens approach to a new domain. Farzindar and Lapalme (2004) considered the processing of previous legal decisions and their summaries because a court order generally gives a solution to a legal problem between two or more parties. The decision also contains the reasons that justify the solution and constitute a law jurisprudence precedent from which it is possible to extract legal rules that can be applied to similar cases. To find a solution to a legal problem not directly indicated in the law, lawyers look for precedents of similar cases. For a single query in a database of law reports, one often receives hundreds of documents. Hence, legal professionals require summaries.

In Quebec, the French-speaking province of Canada, REJB (Répertoire électronique de jurisprudence du Barreau) and SOQUIJ (Société québecoise d'information juridique) are two organizations that provide manual summaries for legal resources, but these services very expensive. For example the price of only one summary with its full text, provided by SOQUIJ is \$C7.50. Some legal information systems have been developed by private companies such as QuickLaw in Canada and WESTLAW and LEXIS in the United States, however no existing system completely satisfies the specific requirements of this field.

One reason for the difficulty of this work is the complexity of the domain: specific vocabularies of the legal domain and legal interpretations of expressions produce many ambiguities. For legal judgments, Farzindar and Lapalme (2004) identify discursive structures for the different parts of the decision and assign some argumentative roles to them. The processing of a legal document requires detailed attention and it is not straight-forward to adapt the techniques developed for other types of document to the legal domain.

Their corpus contained 3500 judgments of the Federal Court of Canada.[137] They manually analysed 50 judgments in English and 15 judgments in French as well as their summaries written by professional legal abstractors. The average size of the documents that are input to their system are judgments between 500 and 4000 words long (2–8 pages), which form 80% of all 3500 judgments; 10% of the documents

---

[137] These are available in HTML at http://www.canlii.org/ca/cas/fct/

having less than 500 words (about one page) and so they do not require a summary. Only 10% of the decisions have more than 4000 words.

6.1.9 Text Mining

6.1.9.1 General Considerations

Information overload has motivated the emergence of both *data mining* and *text mining*. Pooled techniques for extracting fairly sophisticated kinds of information from large text corpora goes by the name *text mining*.[138] Solka remarked (2008, p. 94):

> Data mining on text has been designated at various times as statistical text processing, knowledge discovery in text, intelligent text analysis, or natural language processing, depending on the application and the methodology that is used [(Baeza-Yates & Ribeiro-Neto, 1999)]. Examples of text mining tasks include classifying documents into a set of specified topic areas (supervised learning), grouping documents such that each member of each group has similar meaning (clustering or unsupervised learning),[139] and finding documents that satisfy some search criteria (information retrieval).

The *text analytics* involved in text mining goes beyond conventional *information retrieval* from online text. Disciplinary areas involved include *information retrieval, computational linguistics (natural-language processing), knowledge management, data mining*, and in particular *machine learning*, as well as statistical methods. Besides, *link detection* is an approach to the analysis of text; it shares or makes use of various key elements of text mining. Moreover, the use of a *semantic web* enables text mining to find content based on meaning and context, as opposed to conventional search engines that only find documents containing specific user-defined words or phrases.

Typically, *statistical pattern learning* is resorted to, in order to discover patterns and items of interest.[140] The process of text mining typically involves inferring some structure, by a variety of means, such as parsing sentences and multi-sentence units by computational linguistic means. Data are modified, by both removal of some, and the insertion of some information (typically, tags which identify linguistic features), and inserted into a database. Once the data are thus structured, they are analysed, looking for patterns, or looking for items by learning patterns. Criteria or metrics of *relevance* and *interestingness* apply. Sometimes, tools are capable of analysing textual sources in multiple languages.

Tasks may include:

---

[138] Text mining is the subject of Berry's book (2003) and a survey by Solka (2008).

[139] See Section 6.1.13.14 below.

[140] *Statistical natural language processing* is the subject of Manning and Schutze (1999).

- *text categorisation*, i.e., determining what a given text is about (categorization can be made more efficient by resorting to concept mining: see below)[141];
- *text clustering*: clustering documents by topic (having converted text to quantitative data, one can use any of the clustering methods familiar to statisticians, or then use an encoding in graphs for the same purpose)[142];
- *concept mining (concept/entity extraction)*: identifying candidate word-senses inside text, resolving ambiguity by means of any out of a number of *disambiguation* techniques as known from computational linguistics, and then determining the concepts involved (using a thesaurus or an ontology), possibly using techniques based on *semantic similarity* between concepts;
- the generation of *ontologies* (one also talks about *granular taxonomies*);
- *automatic summarisation*;
- *entity relation modelling*: learning relations between named entities.

In order to carry out clustering, classification, and information retrieval on text, these being tasks involved in data mining, a notion of similarity between documents is needed. Solka pointed out (2008, p. 99):

> The most commonly used measure in text data mining and information retrieval is the cosine of the angle between vectors representing the documents [(Berry & Browne, 2005)]. Assume we have two document vectors $\vec{a}$ and $\vec{q}$, then the cosine of the angle between them, θ, is given by

$$cos(\theta) = \frac{\vec{a}^T \vec{q}}{||\vec{a}||_2 ||\vec{q}||_2},$$

> where $||\vec{a}||_2$ is the usual L_2 norm of vector $\vec{a}$. Note that larger values of this measure indicate documents are close together, and smaller values indicate the documents are further apart. We can easily apply this measure to the bigram proximity matrices by converting each matrix to a vector — for example by just piling each column on top of the other.

Nevertheless, a similarity measure may not be as convenient for use as a measure of distance. Solka continued (2008, p. 99):

---

[141] Sebastiani (2002) is a survey of machine learning in automated text categorisation. Cf., e.g., Esuli, Fagni, and Sebastiani (2008).

[142] Solka (2008) explained as follows the graph-based method (ibid., pp. 102–103): "One can cast the term-document matrix as a bipartite graph where the documents are on the left-hand-side of this graph, and the terms are on the right-hand-side. The graph is designated a bipartite graph because there are edges only between the documents and the terms. There are no edges between the documents or between the terms. Given this encoding one can view document clustering as a graph cut problem, where one attempts to divide a graph into two groups in such a way as to minimize the number of edges that pass between them. Approximate solutions to this problem can be obtained using a spectral decomposition of the graph Laplacian. A benefit of this approach is that it allows one to obtain a simultaneous clustering of terms and documents. This makes sense in that a clustering of terms would naturally induce a clustering of documents and a clustering of documents would induce a clustering of terms."

The cosine measure is a similarity measure rather than a distance. We are usually more comfortable working with distances, but we can easily convert similarities to distances. First, assume that we have organized our similarities into a positive-definite matrix C, where the ij-th element of this matrix indicates the similarity of the i-th and j-th documents. Then one way to convert this value to a Euclidean distance is to use the following formula [(Duda et al., 2001a)]:

$$d_{ij} = \sqrt{c_{ii} - 2c_{ij} + c_{jj}}.$$

Note that when two documents are the same $(c_{ii} = c_{jj})$ then the distance is zero.

An important book on text mining and link detection is Feldman and Sanger (2007), *The Text Mining Handbook: Advanced Approaches in Analyzing Unstructured Data.*[143] After introducing core text mining operations, and then text mining pre-processing techniques, the book proceeds with chapters on categorization, on clustering, on information extraction, on probabilistic models for information extraction, and on preprocessing applications using probabilistic and hybrid approaches. Next, a chapter about presentation-layer considerations for browsing and query refinement is followed with a chapter on visualization approaches. And finally, there are chapters on link analysis, and on text mining applications.

Some text mining tools are commercial, other tools are available on an open source basis, and still other tools are being used privately by institutions, corporations, or professionals from various categories. These include, e.g., academics, or then law enforcement or counterintelligence personnel.

Applications of text mining include:

- security (especially by monitoring textual data on the Internet);
- spam filters, which according to detected characteristics predict whether email messages are unwanted material, such as unsolicited advertisements;
- alert services, e.g. about scholarly literature (such as the biomedical literature, and social science);
- search and indexing;
- marketing;
- the media industry (through websites);
- obtaining feedback for movies distribution, by analysing the affectivity of words that appear in movie reviews, or in commercial product reviews (this is called *sentiment analysis*)[144];

---

[143] An older book on data mining is Han and Kamber (2001).

[144] The application to movie reviews was described by Pang et al. (2002), whereas Valitutti et al. (2005) were concerned with the development of affective lexical resources. Esxuli and Sebastiani (2010) reviewed *sentiment-quantification* methods (as opposed to *sentiment classification*) within *opinion mining*. Sentiment classification instead is the subject of Abbasi (2010). Also see, e.g., Argamon et al. (2009). Feldman, Fresko, Goldenberg, Netzer, and Ungar (2010) apply text mining to the analysis of product comparisons (concerning car models) on Web-supported product discussion boards:

- business intelligence solutions, using a news and company information content set;
- patent information (this is the case of the Thomson Data Analyzer);
- legal practice (as being an extension of information retrieval in the legal domain).

One of the application domains covered in Feldman and Sanger (2007) is counter-terrorism activities.[145] Another domain is business intelligence, and yet another one is genomics research. What makes text mining useful in a law enforcement or counter-intelligence context, is the possibility offered by text mining of building large dossiers of information about specific people and events. This greatly empowers intelligence analysts.

There are many text mining tools available. Mena (2003, section 5.8, pp. 141–157) surveyed several of them. For example, VisualText, a text mining toolkit from TextAI,[146] enables to develop custom-made text-analysers supporting various functions. "For those agencies or departments with an IT staff wishing to customize and build its own text analyzer, this kit is ideal" (Mena, ibid., p. 155). It supports both *shallow extraction* (the identification of names, locations, and dates in text), and *information extraction* of a more advanced king (extracting, correlating, and standardising content). Other supported functions include *indexing* of text (e.g., from the Internet), *filtering* (to determine whether a document is relevant), *categorisation* (what is the topic of documents?), *test grading* (for reading and matching prose), *summarisation* (to briefly describe contents), *automated coding* (e.g., for coding police reports), *natural-language querying* (so queries could be made in plain text), and *dissemination* (for routing documents to those persons who need them). Refer to the case studies in Sections 6.2.1 and 6.2.7.

There is increasing recognition that product reviews by consumers can provide important insight into how they view products, and that automated text analysis methods can be fruitfully used to extract such information [(Popescu & Etzioni, 2005; Dave, Lawrence, & Pennock, 2003)]. For example, the rapidly growing field of sentiment analysis looks to extract how authors feel about different products [(Kim & Hovy, 2006; Turney, 2002; Hu & Liu, 2004; Pang, Lee, & Vaithyanathan, 2002)]. Such work has tended to look at single products, in spite of the fact that many of the purchase decisions, and hence much of the marketing effort, is based on product comparisons. This paper describes a methodology for automatically analyzing products and comparisons between them. Given a (possibly ungrammatical) sentence such as "Sonata has soft ride similar to Camry and Accord" we automatically extract the products (Sonata, Camry and Accord) and what attributes they are compared on ("soft ride"). Our goal is to automatically determine which products are compared with each other, what attributes they are compared on, and which products are preferred on different attributes. We term this process "comparative sentiment analysis."

[145] Cf. Christopher C. Yang's (2008) 'Knowledge Discovery and Information Visualization for Terrorist Social Networks'.

[146] http://www.textanalysis.com

6.1.9.2 Examples of text Mining as Applied to Law

Andrew Stranieri and John Zeleznikow

This brief section is based on section 57 in chapter 10 of our book *Knowledge Discovery from Legal Databases* (Stranieri & Zeleznikow, 2005a). Text mining includes techniques for clustering documents, summarising and categorising documents and extracting information from text. A common application of text categorisation is the assignment of keyword lists to categorise cases. Typically legal publishers expend considerable resources to manually determine the most appropriate list of keywords for each published case. For example, judgments available online from WESTLAW the American legal publisher, are categorised manually into 40 high level categories such as bankruptcy.[147] Thompson (2001) described comparative trials with three different data mining techniques, one that applies clustering and two that involve classification by rule induction.

Other approaches that involve text mining involve sophisticated case matching techniques that are not simple examples of clustering or classification approaches because other processes are also involved. For example, Brüninghaus and Ashley (2003) sought to elicit case factors automatically from a summary of a case. The motivation for doing so was to enable the most time consuming phase of case based reasoning methods (Ashley, 1991), the elicitation of factors to be performed automatically. This involved sophisticated natural language parsing of sentences.

Yearwood (1997) reported a technique for the retrieval of similar cases. His work involves the automatic identification of which sections of refugee law judgments feature most prominently in the retrieval of cases that match a current one. This work was also successfully applied to more structured documents taken from hospital records (Yearwood & Wilkinson, 1997).

In the SALOMAN project (Moens et al., 1997; Moens, 2000) summary of a judgments was generated. This was done by combining text matching using information retrieval algorithms with expert knowledge about the structure of judgments. SPIRE, developed by Daniels and Rissland (1997) integrates a case based reasoner with information retrieval techniques to locate the passage within a document where a query concept is likely to be found.

Dozier, Jackson, Guo, Chaudhary, and Arumainayagam (2003) used text-mining techniques to create an on-line directory of expert witnesses from jury verdict and settlement documents. The supporting technologies that made the application possible included information extraction from text via regular expression parsing, record linkage through Bayesian based matching and automatic rule-based classification. Their research shows that text-mining techniques can be used to create useful special-purpose directories for individuals involved in legal proceedings.

---

[147] www.westlaw.com Accessed on 15 March 2004.

Common application areas of text mining include:

(a) *Homeland security and intelligence*:

  (i)   Analysis of terrorist networks.
  (ii) Rapid identification of critical information about such topics as weapons of mass destruction from very large collections of text documents and
  (iii) Surveillance of the Web, e-mails, or chat rooms.

(b) *Law enforcement* such as the structuring of narrative reports written by federal, state, and local law enforcement agents to aid the analytical process by identifying previously unnoticed trends, links, and patterns.

The Coplink project (Hauck et al., 2002), to which Section 6.2.5 in this book is devoted, does not use entity extraction techniques because they drew the data from a structured database system. Yet many police records systems contain large collections of unstructured text and structured case reports. These textual sources often contain volumes of information that are not captured in the structured fields. A research direction that was envisaged in that project is to develop textual mining approaches that support knowledge retrieval from such sources. The development of linguistic-analysis and textual-mining techniques for performing fine-grained content analysis could help to make intelligent use of large textual collections in police databases.

6.1.9.3 Support Vector Machines, and Their Use for Information Retrieval, Text Classification and Matching

Andrew Stranieri, John Zeleznikow, and Ephraim Nissan

This section is based on section 33 in chapter 6 and some other text in our book *Knowledge Discovery from Legal Databases* (Stranieri & Zeleznikow, 2005a). Support Vector Machines are learning machines that can perform binary classification (pattern recognition) and real valued function approximation (regression estimation) tasks. Support Vector Machines non-linearly map their n-dimensional input space into a high dimensional feature space. In this high dimensional feature space a linear classifier is constructed.[148]

As long as two classes are linearly separable, support vector machines determine the hyperplane in the n-dimensional feature space that maximises the margin between the examples of the classes. A new example is classified by computing to which side of the hyperplane the example belongs. The technique can be generalised to examples that are not linearly separable. Data is linearly separable if a straight line or plane can be drawn to separate examples into different types of outputs. Figure 6.1.9.3.1 illustrates the plot of points that represent X or Y. The shaded

---

[148] We are going to come back to support vector machines in Sections 6.2.1.3 and 8.7.3.1.

Fig. 6.1.9.3.1 Linear
separability of X or Y

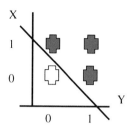

Fig. 6.1.9.3.2 Linear
nonseparability of X exor Y,
that is to say, of either X or Y

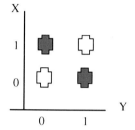

points represent the value 1 on (X OR Y). We see clearly that a straight line can be
drawn that separates those X and Y data points that have a value 1 on (X OR Y)
from those that have a value 0. In contrast, in Fig. 6.1.9.3.2 we see that a similar
straight line cannot be drawn: the *exclusive-Or function* (also called *exor*) is said to
be non-linearly separable.

Support Vector Machines are based on the structural risk minimisation principle
from computational learning theory (Vapnik, 1995). The idea of structural risk minimisation is to find a hypothesis **h** for which we can guarantee the lowest true error.
The true error of **h** is the probability that **h** will make an error on an unseen and
randomly selected test example. An upper bound can be used to connect the true
error of a hypothesis **h** with the error of **h** on the training set and the complexity
of **H**, the hypothesis space containing **h**. Support Vector Machines are a method for
creating functions from a set of labeled training data. The function can be a classification function if the output is binary or the function can be a general regression
function.

For classification, Support Vector Machines operate by finding a hypersurface
in the space of possible inputs. This hypersurface will attempt to split the positive
examples from the negative examples. The split will be chosen to have the largest
distance from the hypersurface to the nearest of the positive and negative examples.
Intuitively, this makes the classification correct for testing data that is near, but not
identical to the training data.

There are various ways to train Support Vector Machines. One particularly
simple and fast method is Sequential Minimal Optimisation. Sequential Minimal
Optimisation is a fast method to train Support Vector Machines. Training a Support

Vector Machine requires the solution of a very large quadratic programming optimisation problem. Sequential Minimal Optimisation breaks this large problem into a series of smallest possible problems. These small problems are solved analytically, which avoids using a time-consuming numerical optimisation.

Joachims (1998) states that support vector machines are based on the structural risk minimisation principle from computational learning theory (Vapnik, 1995)[149]. The idea of structural risk minimisation is to find a hypothesis **h** for which we can guarantee the lowest true error. The true error of **h** is the probability that **h** will make an error on an unseen and randomly selected test example. An upper bound can be used to connect the true error of a hypothesis **h** with the error of **h** on the training set and the complexity of **H**, the hypothesis space containing **h**. Support Vector Machines find the hypothesis **h** that approximately minimises this bound on the true error. The ability of Support Vector Machines to learn can be independent of the dimensionality of the feature space. Support Vector Machines measure the complexity of hypotheses based on the margin with which they separate the data, not the number of features. Thus generalisation can occur, in the presence of many features as long as the data is separable with a wide margin. We do this by using functions from the hypothesis space.

Joachims (1998) claimed that Support Vector Machines are excellent for classifying text because of their ability to deal with:

(a) High dimensional input space. When learning text classifiers, we have to deal with a very large number of features. Since Support Vector Machines use *overfitting* (which does not necessarily depend on the number of features), they have the potential to handle these large feature spaces.
(b) Few irrelevant features. One way to avoid high dimensional input spaces is to assume that most features are irrelevant. Feature selection tries to determine these irrelevant features. Text categorisation generally involves very few irrelevant features. Through a detailed example, Joachims (1998) showed that a classifier using only the worst features has a much better than random performance. Since it is unlikely that all the features are completely redundant, he conjectures that a good classifier should combine many features and that aggressive feature selection may result in a loss of information.
(c) Document vectors are sparse. For each document, the corresponding document vector contains only a few non-zero entries. Support Vector Machines are well suited for problems with dense concepts and sparse instances.
d) Most text categorisations are *linearly separable* and thus suitable for the use of Support Vector Machines.

Gonçalves and Quaresma (2003) have developed a methodology for the automatic *classification* of documents and applied it to a set of documents written in the

---

[149] Also see more recent publications by Thorsten Joachims of Cornell University, e.g. Joachims, Hofmann, Yue, and Yu (2009).

Portuguese language. Their methodology integrates support vector machines with natural language processing techniques, such as, lemmatization and part-of-speech tagging. They applied their research to a set of Portuguese juridical documents from the Attorney General's Office. This set is composed by 7089 documents and it is being manually classified by juridical experts into a set of concepts from a legal taxonomy. Their research only used part-of-speech information to eliminate words from the bag-of-words, but they reportedly intended to use syntactical and semantic information and to propose and evaluate specific kernels. They compared their Support Vector Method classification results with other machine learning algorithms, such as the C4.5 algorithm[150] and Naive Bayes, and also information retrieval measures, namely precision, recall, and f-measure. The obtained results showed to be, at least, equivalent with similar approaches and they proved to be adequate for the Portuguese language and for the legal domain.

Flexlaw, reported about by Smith et al. (1995), used a Vector Space Model for *matching*. It automatically constructed structured representations from text. Cases and other legal documents are represented by document profiles that preserve the meaning of legal text and contain all the information necessary and sufficient to match documents with a user's query.

In addition to improving legal text indexing and query formulation, the Flexlaw knowledge representation is a documentation tool that automatically generates case *headnotes* (which they call *flexnotes*). A *flexnote* consists of case header information, a classification of the subjects of law being used and a listing of these items. Gelbart and Smith (1993) contrasted Flexlaw with other information retrieval models:

(a) the Boolean model; and
(b) probabilistic models.

---

[150] The C4.5 algorithm (Quinlan, 1993) is an enhancement of ID3 that includes tools to (a) To deal with missing values on attributes and missing data, (b) for pruning decision trees, (c) dealing with continuous variables, (d) dealing with rule accuracy, (e) providing alternative measures for selecting attributes. The C5.0 algorithm is an enhancement of C4.5 that includes (a) *boosting* techniques (see below), (b) sophisticated ways to measure errors, (c) methods to facilitate scaling uyp an algorithm to perform on large datasets. The ID3 algorithm was developed by Quinlan (1986), and is a machine learning algorithm which induces a decision tree for classification problems. The tree is derived from examples in a training set. The ID3 algorithm uses an entropy-based measure known as *information gain*, as a heuristic for selecting the attribute that will best separate the samples into individual classes. The attribute becomes the 'test' or 'decision' attribute at the node. A handy presentation of decision tree techniques in data mining is provided by Rokach and Maimon (2008).

Boosting (Quinlan, 1996) improves the predictive power of classifier learning systems by adjusting the weights of training instances. It manipulates the training data in order to generate different classifiers. Boosting uses all instances at each repetition, but maintains a weight for each instance in the training set that reflects its importance; adjusting the weights causes the learner to focus on different instances and so leads to different classifiers. The multiple classifiers are then combined by voting to form a composite classifier. Boosting assigns different voting strengths to component classifiers on the basis of their accuracy.

They performed tests on 1,000 cases from British Columbia (Canada) dealing with economic loss. Their conclusions were:

(a) Flexlaw is superior to Boolean search in terms of the knowledge structuring, the user interface, the retrieval effectiveness and the ranking of relevant documents;
(b) Flexlaw, though based on the vector space model, is superior to the SMART implementation of the model in incorporating intelligent structuring of both documents and queries; and
(c) Flexlaw and the inference network model intelligently incorporate structure in the document and query representations offer elegant and easy-to-use interfaces, allow the incorporation of multiple information sources such as thesauri and produce a ranked list of relevant cases.

Support vector machines have also been used for *information retrieval*. Al-Kofahi, Tyrrell, Vachher, and Jackson (2001) view the task of retrieving similar cases as complex and must be achieved with the integration of more than one method. They used a large dataset of seven million cases and performed similarity matching by invoking a support vector machine trained with over 2000 cases. The support vector machine integrated similarity predictions based on a number of measures. Similarity based on title matching, calculated using optimisation theories from mathematical programming was one measure. Another measure estimated the probability that a example case in a Court A, would have a precedent in another court. The support vector machine was trained using a linear kernel and positive instances were weighted five times more strongly than negative cases. Results demonstrate that recall rates were comparable with those for humans and while precision was not quite at that level, it was sufficiently high to warrant the development.

Hu, Liao, and Vemuri (2003, p. 173, table V) drew a comparison between variants of support vector machines (SVMs). In a *standard SVM*, also called a *soft-margin SVM*, the *objective function* to be optimised is:

$$\Phi(\mathbf{w}) = \tfrac{1}{2}\mathbf{w}^T\mathbf{w} + C \sum_{i=1}^{\ell} \xi_i$$

(where $\mathbf{w}^T$ is the *transposed vector* of the *weights vector* $\mathbf{w}$), under these *constraints*:

$$y_i f(\mathbf{x}_i) \geq 1 - \xi_i$$

Let us digress in order to explain the concept of a *transposed vector*. A vector is usually written as a one-column array of values. It is a general case of a matrix. The *transpose* of an m-by-n matrix $\mathbf{A}$ is the n-by-m matrix $\mathbf{A}^T$ formed by turning rows into columns and vice versa. Therefore, the individual item found inside a matrix in the case in its jth row and ith column is the same as the element in the transposed matrix in its ith row and jth column:

$$\left(\mathbf{A}^T\right)_{i,j} = \mathbf{A}_{j,i}$$

For example:

$$\begin{bmatrix} 1 & 2 & 3 \\ 0 & -6 & 7 \end{bmatrix}^T = \begin{bmatrix} 1 & 0 \\ 2 & -6 \\ 3 & 7 \end{bmatrix}$$

In a *hard-margin SVM*, the objective function is:

$$\Phi(\mathbf{w}) = \tfrac{1}{2}\mathbf{w}^T\mathbf{w}$$

under these constraints:

$$y_i f(\mathbf{x}_i) \geq 1$$

When Vapnik first introduced the idea of a SVM (see e.g. in Vapnik, 1998), it was for the *separable* case (such that positive and negative samples can be separated by a unique optimal hyperplane with the largest margin), and it is this version, for the separable case, that is called a *hard-margin SVM*. By contrast, the generalised concept of a *soft-margin SVM* (or *standard SVM*) would also work for the *non-separable* case; it was introduced by Cortes and Vapnik (1995). This generalisation to the non-separable case was done by introducing some *training errors*, being *positive slack variables*:

$$\{\xi_i\} \quad i = 1, ..., \ell$$

The purpose of these is to find the best tradeoff between training error and margin. This is done by choosing an appropriate constant C associated with slack value. This endowed the soft-margin SVM with an error-tolerant property. The *slack term* in the objective function of the soft-margin SVM is the *sum of misclassification errors*:

$$\sum \xi_i$$

Its effect is that notwithstanding the good generalisation ability of the soft-margin SVM, a defect arises: "when trained with noisy data, the decision hyperplane might deviate from optimal position (without maximized separating margin)" (Hu et al., 2003, p. 173). "This leads to a complicated decision surface, which is known as the over-fitting problem" (ibid.). This motivated the introduction by Song, Hu, and Xie (2002) of a variant called robust SVM, originally applied to *bullet hole image classification*, something of interest to forensic science. The so-called *robust SVM* addressed the overfitting problem "by only minimizing the margin of the weight $\mathbf{w}$ instead of minimizing the margin and the sum of misclassification errors" (Hu et al., 2003, p. 173). In place of the soft-margin SVM's slack term

$$\{\xi_i\} \ i \ = \ 1, ..., \ell$$

in the robust SVM this other slack term was introduced:

$$\lambda D^2(\mathbf{x}_i, \mathbf{x}^*_{y_i})$$

λ is a non-negative pre-selected *regularisation parameter*. It measures the influence of averaged information, that is, distance to the class centre. As to

$$D^2(\mathbf{x}_i, \mathbf{x}^*_{y_i})$$

this is the normalised distance between data point $\mathbf{x}_i$ and the centre of the respective classes in the *feature space*. The centre of the respective classes is

$$(\mathbf{x}^*_{y_i}, \ y_i \ \in \ \{+1, -1\})$$

In the variant of SVM called *robust SVM* (this is the variant adopted by Hu et al., 2003), the objective function is the same as in a hard-margin SVM:

$$\Phi(\mathbf{w}) = \tfrac{1}{2}\mathbf{w}^T\mathbf{w}$$

but under these constraints:

$$y_i f(\mathbf{x}_i) \geq 1 - \lambda D^2(\mathbf{x}_i, \mathbf{x}^*_{y_i})$$

The motivation for introducing the robust SVM was a defect of the standard RSV (Hu et al., 2003, p. 173):

> The main idea of Support Vector Machines (SVMs) is to derive a hyperplane that maximizes the separating margin between two classes — the positive and the negative [...]. The promising property of SVM is that it is an approximate implementation of the Structure Risk Minimization principle based on statistical learning theory rather than the Empirical Risk Minimization method, in which the classification function is derived by minimizing the Mean Square Error over the training data set.
>
> One of the main assumptions of SVM is that all samples in the training set are independently and identically distributed (i.i.d.). However, in practice, the training data are often contaminated with noise. The noisy data makes the validity of this i.i.d. assumption questionable. The standard SVM training algorithm will make the decision surface deviate from the optimal position in the *feature space*. When mapped back to the *input space*, it results in a highly nonlinear decision boundary. Therefore the standard SVM is sensitive to noise, leading to poor generalization ability.

It is typical of *operations research* (i.e., the science of *optimisation*) that there the usual, *primal problems* (in *primal space*) have *dual problems* corresponding to them respectively. It is sometimes convenient to solve the *dual problem*, in *dual space*, instead of the primal problem. For the SVM variants, the dual problems are so-called *quadratic programming* (*QP*) optimisation problems. The dual space is the space of Lagrange multipliers α_i, (where $i = 1, \ldots, \ell$), whose values give the decision functions by computing the sign of

$$f(\mathbf{x}) = \sum_{\text{Support Vectors}} \alpha_i y_i K(\mathbf{x}_i, \mathbf{x}) + b$$

where b is the threshold value of the decision function (Hu et al., 2003, pp. 173–174). Hu et al. (2003, p. 174, table VI) gave the dual problems for support vector machines as follows. Let

$$\gamma_i = 1 - \lambda D^2(\mathbf{x}_i, \mathbf{x}^*_{y_i}))$$

Then in the dual problem for the soft-margin (i.e., standard) SVM, the objective function is:

$$W(\alpha) = \sum_{i=1}^{\ell} \alpha_i - \tfrac{1}{2} \sum_{i,j=1}^{\ell} \alpha_i \alpha_j y_i y_j k(\mathbf{x}_i, \mathbf{x}_j)$$

under these constraints:

$$\sum_{i=1}^{\ell} y_i \alpha_i = 0$$

$$0 \leq \alpha_i \leq C.$$

For the dual problem of the hard-margin SVM, the objective function is:

$$W(\alpha) = \sum_{i=1}^{\ell} \alpha_i - \tfrac{1}{2} \sum_{i,j=1}^{\ell} \alpha_i \alpha_j y_i y_j k(\mathbf{x}_i, \mathbf{x}_j)$$

under these constraints:

$$\sum_{i=1}^{\ell} y_i \alpha_i = 0$$

$$0 \leq \alpha_i.$$

For the dual problem of a robust SVM, the objective function is:

$$W(\alpha) = \sum_{i=1}^{\ell} \alpha_i \gamma_i - \tfrac{1}{2} \sum_{i,j=1}^{\ell} \alpha_i \alpha_j y_i y_j k(\mathbf{x}_i, \mathbf{x}_j)$$

under these constraints:

$$\sum_{i=1}^{\ell} y_i \alpha_i = 0$$

$$0 \le \alpha_i.$$

6.1.10 Stylometrics, Determining Authorship, Handwriting, and Questioned Documents Evidence

Various data mining techniques have been used in order to reduce very large feature sets down to optimal subsets (Liu & Motoda, 1998). For example, in *stylometric* analysis within text mining (e.g., in order to detect *sender deception* in email, when the actual sender disguises his or her identity), *writeprint characteristics* can be defined by a variety of features, which include *lexical features, syntactic features, structural features* (the latter relate to the overall structure of the author's writing), and *content-specific features.*

"If a researcher attempted to operationalize these categories of features by developing metrics to measure those features, the potential lists would be almost limitless. So, a first major step to comparing emails writeprints is developing a set of features that are discriminatory, measurable, and manageable." (Gray & Debreceny, 2006). "Adding more features to the analysis does not always improve discriminating power. de Vel, Anderson, Corney, & Mohay (2001) found that the performance of their analysis decreased when they increased the number of function words to 320 from 122." (ibid.).

"Li, Zheng, and Chen (2006) used the generic algorithm form of heuristic search to find the optimum subset of features. Starting with 270 features introduced in the prior paragraph, they found the optimum subset for identifying message authors includes 134 features. Their finding of 134 features is not universal; instead the results will vary depending on the textual materials being analyzed and the language used by the authors." (ibid.).

Sometimes what need be ascertained is the identity of a person, but – unlike eyewitness testimony, or fingerprints, or trying to match a description of a suspect to the police's database of mug shots (facial photographs) – it's the personal identity of an author or of the hand in which a document is written. Hypotheses of authorial identity concerning either a given text,[151] or a given physical copy of the

---

[151] There is a separate issue of how the authorial persona comes through, in a literary or other textual work, if it comes through at all. Consider for example Martial's *Liber spectaculorum* about the cruel arena game under the Flavian dynasty in Rome: both the Emperor's name, and the authorial persona are major absences from the *Liber Spectaculorum* (see Nissan, 2011d, section 2):

In Sec. 11 [of the general introduction to her book], Coleman [(2006)] addresses two features that set the *Liber spectaculorum* apart from the rest of Martial's oeuvre. Firstly, the 'I' composing the book is absent: "we constantly hear the author's voice, but his *persona* is entirely effaced" (lxxxii). The other term of the dual absence is that the epigrams were

text (a manuscript, or a typescript) may be made from the different perspectives of textual philologists, historians, and forensic expertise on forged documents, or on documents connected with perpetrators or victims. Forensic stylistics is one of the tools available for trying to satisfy that need. Literary studies, as well as history, are also interested in the problem of determining whether two different documents were authored by the same person.

The entry for "Questioned document examination" in Wikipedia[152] is useful, yet somewhat U.S.-centred. Section "Common tools of the trade" lists: excellent eyesight; handlens/loupe; stereomicroscope; and Video Spectral Comparator (VSC). The same entry states:

> The examination of handwriting to assess potential authorship proceeds from the *principle of identification* which can be expressed as: "Two writings are the product of one person if the similarities, when taken in combination, are sufficiently individual and there are no fundamental unexplainable differences."
> There are three stages in the process of examination. In brief, they are:
>
> 1. The questioned and the known items are analysed and broken down to directly perceptible characteristics.
> 2. The characteristics of the questioned item are then compared against the known standard.
> 3. Evaluation of the similarities and differences of the compared properties determines which ones are valuable for a conclusion. This depends on the uniqueness and frequency of occurrence in the items.

---

not received by a readership through the medium of a book (lxxxi): "Perhaps what caught [Titus'] approval was, instead, a *libellus* [i.e., booklet] that one day, together with similar *libelli* [booklets] celebrating spectacles under Domitian, would form the *liber* [i.e., book] from which our surviving collection was excerpted" (lxxxiv).

And as mentioned, there is the problem of identifying which Flavian emperor was the one relevant, among Vespasian's two sons and successors, namely, Titus and Domitian:

> In Sec. 6, Coleman tries to identify the emperor eulogised, but never identified in the epigrams: Titus? or Domitian? or both in turn? To Coleman, it "seems highly unlikely" that "a single emperor" was being honoured (lxxxiii). This "must remain a tantalizing puzzle" (lxiv). "[T]he atmosphere of immediacy in the second epigram is much better suited to Titus' inauguration [of the Flavian amphitheatre in Rome: the Coliseum] than to an event several years later, [...] and, given the parallels between the events of the *Liber spectaculorum* and the extant sources for Titus' inauguration, it seems perverse to postulate an entirely unattested ceremony under Domitian as the occasion celebrated in the book" (lix). Coleman dismisses another argument for ascription of the occasion to the reign of Domitian: "[T]he enmity towards Titus that is attributed to Domitian by hostile sources is a flimsy basis for supposing that he would object to the public circulation of a collection that celebrated spectacles associating both of them with" the Colosseum.

[152] http://en.wikipedia.org/wiki/Questioned_document_examination

ASTM Standard E2290-03 (Standard Guide for Examination of Handwriting) outlines the procedure followed by most reputable examiners.[153] Another method is provided online by the Forensic Expertise Profiling Laboratory (School of Human Biosciences, La Trobe University, Victoria, Australia). The method is divided into 11 modules which may be accessed via the FEPL website.[154]

Identifying an author, or, in particular, finding out whether ascribed authorship is correct, or whether two documents are by the same author[155] is an area of expertise which on occasion overlaps with forensic concerns. The detection of the forgery of manuscripts (fake letters and documents) is discussed by Rendell (1994). Sometimes, the longhand of the person who wrote is not available, because the text is typewritten (it is possible to trace a typescript to the individual typewriter), or then because it was written into a file and printed, or then because it already appeared in print before the introduction of information technology. Or, then, an ancient text may have been copied by hand by a chain of copyists. In that case, the determination

---

[153] From an American perspective, Michael Risinger – a legal scholar who tends to be critical of expert testimony in especially criminal (Risinger, 2007a) and occasionally civil cases – surveys court cases involving the reliability of handwriting identification expertise (Risinger– 2007b; cf. Risinger, Saks, Thompson, & Rosenthal, 2002). His paper (2007b, p. 477) "seeks to collect and separately describe and analyze every explicit decision by an American court on the reliability of handwriting identification expertise since the decision in *Daubert v. Merrell Dow Pharmaceuticals, Inc.*", i.e., 509 U.S. 579 (1993). "the cases listed here are by no means all of the cases since 1993 in whichhandwriting identification testimony by putative experts has been proffered or accepted" (Risinger, 2007b, p. 477). Risinger explained (ibid., pp. 478–479): "Most use of such expertise likely goes unremarked upon, or occurs in cases that never generate written opinions. In the vast majority of the reported cases involving such experts, the testimony is merely noted as part of a recitation of facts. These cases include substantial numbers of civil cases, often involving challenged signatures on wills or deeds, or insurance and other contract cases, but not uncommonly involving more complex issues. The volume should not be surprising. Estimates of the number of persons who offer such testimony in court, at least on occasion, ranges up to 5,000 or more, with some hundreds who do so regularly. The range of credentials and experience exhibited by these witnesses is also startling, and it is likely that most of the testimony that occurs in American courtrooms is by persons whose training and experience would be looked down upon by the accrediting body of the Osbornian establishment, the American Board of Forensic Document Examiners (ABFDE)."

Larry Miller (1984) expressed criticism of unintended bias on the part of forensic document examiners. He began his article by claiming (ibid., p. 407): "Questioned document examination, particularly handwriting/handprinting identification, lends itself readily to unintended bias on the part of the examiner. Questioned document examination is one of the few forensic science areas that depends primarily on a subjective analysis by the examiner. Most questioned document examiners atternpt to render analyses as poossible by using sophisticated measuring techniques. However, complete objectivity cannot be achieved because of (1) the situation in which the document examiner is summoned for analyses, and (2) the fact that most of the identification process involves a subjective opinion of the examiner." Larry Miller (1987) pointed out procedural bias in forensic science examinations of *human hair.* Again, this was because such evaluations are subjective.

[154] The FEPL website is at www.latrobe.edu.au/humanbio/forensic/method_online.htm

[155] See Joseph Rudman's overview (1997) of authorship attribution studies at the meet with humanities computing, and also see Hanlein (1998).

of authorship is based on stylometric features alone, along with whatever the text says which may clarify its origination.

Don Foster, whose academic affiliation is in literary studies, and who in his stylometric analyses uses his computer in order to search digital corpora, has shown in several case-studies between two covers of the same volume (Foster, 2001) how essentially the same approach was repeatedly applied by himself, when elucidating authorship in a literary studies context, and when assisting the police in tracking down, according to stylistic considerations, a perpetrator – the Unabomber – who left a copious textual trail.[156] The Unabomber, Ted (Theodore J.) Kaczynski, a former academic whose victims were scientists or engineers, was in other respects careful not to leave cues; for example, he used to sand batteries he was using in mail bombs, in order to remove labels. even kept shoes with smaller soles attached to the base in order to confuse investigators about his body size.

Don Foster helped the prosecution prove that the Umabomber's manifesto, "Industrial Society and Its Future", was written by Ted Kaczynski, a loner living in a cabin in the Montana Rockies. He used to identify his next few targets in works of biographical references, or in academic journals, he perused at university libraries. Ted Kaczynski was arrested in April 1996. In November 1996, the defence team invited Foster to join it. Foster inspected documents he was sent, and it appeared to him altogether likely that the defendant was the author of the manifesto, so he declined to assist (Foster, 2001, pp. 102–103). In March 1997, Foster was invited to join the prosecution team, and he examined reams of documents thoroughly. Even so, he was unaware at the time of Ted Kaczynski's 1979 "Autobiography" and of his journals, nor did he learn about books related to the Unabomber found inside Kaczynski's cabin (ibid., p. 104).

The defence team was assisted by other scholars. The most categorical and also the academically most prominent among these was University of California at Berkeley's linguist Robin Lakoff (she already was the author of six books, whereas Foster was at an earlier stage of his academic career).[157] Lakoff for example

---

[156] For a treatment of forensic stylistics in relation to authorship determination, also see McMenamin (1993), Aked (1994).

[157] Don Foster's stylometric analysis (see Foster, 2001, chapter 3) was important for identifying the Unabomber. The defence team attacked his five-page opinion (he had been instructed to keep it short) for giving no specific examples, and suggested that he hadn't read the documents at all. In the same sweep, the defence included a second declaration by Robin Lakoff, in which she admitted she had only read an affidavit, as well as just two of the two hundred documents on which Fitzgerald's analysis was based (Foster, 2001, p. 108).

Still, she claimed, her conclusions would not have been different. Understandably, Foster is bitter and sarcastic concerning this, in his book. Foster prepared a detailed opinion of fifty pages, that was not deemed necessary by the judge, who rejected the defence motion. There is a sense in which that decision of the court better established the credentials of stylometric analysis for judicial purposes, whereas Lakoff's own opinion was not so much a stylometric analysis, as an attack on the evidentiary merits of stylometric analysis.

Also the Ted Kaczynski's sister-in-law, Linda Patrik, a professor of philosophy, came to believe (during a stay of hers in Paris) she knew he was the Unabomber because of what he wrote and the way he wrote. Eventually Ted Kaczynski was quoted in the information press as blaming his brother David for being a Judas Iscariot.

dismissed, as evidence of common authorship, *double use of content-linked lexical choices* (Foster, 2001, pp. 104–105): double, because found in texts by the Unabomber and by the defendant. Foster points out in his book that *pace* Lakoff, it wasn't just that the topical word *electrodes* was hit upon. Rather, in a 1971 essay, Kaczynski fretted over the future prospect of *electrodes* being *inserted in the brain* in order to physically control emotions (Foster, 2001, p. 105). Foster remarked (ibid., p. 106):

> Discounting one by one the items of textual and linguistic evidence presented by Fitzgerald,[158] Professor Lakoff denied seeing the forest for the trees, dismissing each identified similarity as slight or circumstantial: Kaczynski and the Unabom [*sic*] subject, she concluded, wrote nothing that was not found in the ordinary language of law-abiding citizens. But Fitzgerald had made no claim for the uniqueness of any particular similarity between the T-docs and the U-docs.[159] It was the sheer magnitude and detail of the similarities between those documents that provided probable cause for a search of Kaczynski's Montana cabin.

Foster (2001, p. 106) easily rejects Lakoff's claim about discrepancies such as Kaczynski's having misspelled *chlorate* as "clorate" three times in a single document, whereas (Foster, ibid.):

> In his manifesto, the Unabomber twice spells *chlorate* correctly (FC[160] boasts of using "a *chlorate pipe bomb to blow* up Thomas Mosser" and "a *chlorate explosive ... to blow up* the genetic engineer Charles Epstein and the computer specialist David Gelernter").[161] The defence complained that this "important distinction between Ted's language ("clorate") and FC's ("chlorate") passed unnoticed by Fitzgerald. But Ted wrote "clorate" in 1970. By 1986, he had learned to spell *chloride* and *chlorine* (in his letters); one may guess that he also learned, by 1995, how to spell *chlorate*. And while Ted may have misspelled *chlorate* in 1970, he already recognized its potential usefulness. Like the Unabomber, Ted Kaczynski had a fantasy of making people "blow up", and with the same material: all three of those 1970 instances of "clorate" appear in an original short story of Ted called "How I Blew Up Harold Snilly",[162] submitted to *Harper's* for publication, and rejected.

---

[158] Supervisory Special Agent (SSA) James Fitzgerald of the FBI's National Center for the Analysis of Violent Crime.

[159] The T-docs are Ted Kaczynski's documents, whereas the U-docs are the Unabomber's documents.

[160] FC is how the Unabomber signed himself in his manifesto.

[161] Gelernter had developed the LINDA network software. He was critically wounded, as was Epstein, in June 1993 (cf. Foster, 2001, pp. 136–137). Gelernter was nearly blinded by the explosion. It was just after Gelernter went back to the U.S. after giving a seminar at the Department of Mathematics and Computer Science at Bar-Ilan University, in the Greater Tel-Aviv area. I was in the audience, at that talk of his. In an email circulated to the department's staff at Bar-Ilan, David Gelernter and his wife thanked us for our expression of solidarity, and suggested donations to the charity Esra.

[162] Here is an example of sheer coincidence: the name *Snilly* can be understood, in ancient Aramaic, to be a phrase of two words (*sni li*, a masculine singular passive participle followed by an inflected personal pronoun), meaning 'hateful to me'. This would be onomastically quite apt for a character being a person whom Ted Kaczynski's first-person narrator would want to blow up, and as the narrative was fiction, it is a name an author may aptly make up. But Kaczynski was utterly unlikely to know Aramaic, or that fine point from Aramaic.

Replace in all of the foregoing "hand" for "author" or "authorship", and then interest in a forensic context is at least as much obvious. The questions the expert is then asked to answer are like these ones: Was this signature forged? Is that text written by hand in a hand different than it is claimed to be? Blueschke and Lacis (1996) discussed an advanced technique for "the examination of the sequence of crossed lines, specifically, between ball point pen strokes (waterfast glycol and aqueous based inks) and faint typewritten impressions (produced by old, poor quality fabric ribbon)" (from the abstract); use was made of scanning electron microscopy (SEM) and photographic stereoscopic pairs. Huber and Headrick (1999) is a book on *handwriting identification.*

A relevant paper collection is Marinai and Fujisawa's (2008), *Machine Learning in Document Analysis and Recognition.* In the early 2000s, a team led by Sargur Srihari at the University of Buffalo[163] was developing a computer program with the task of determining the authorship of handwritten documents for forensic applications (Mena, 2003, pp. 363–364). "Providing a scientific basis for establishing the individuality of handwriting has become essential for admitting handwriting evidence in U.S. courts due to a number of recent rulings concerning expert testimony" (ibid., p. 363). Therefore, the automatic identification is useful, in that it can be explained based on measurable features. Cf. Zhang and Srihari (2004) and Ball, Kasiviswanathan, Srihari, and Narayanan (2010). Srihari and Leedham (2003) surveyed computer methods in forensic document examination. Srihari, Srinivasan, and Desai (2007) reported about questioned document examination using CEDAR-FOX, in the *Journal of Forensic Document Examination.*

Pu and Srihari (2010) reported about probabilistic measure for signature verification; cf. Srihari, Srinivasan, and Beal (2008) and Kalera, Srihari, and Xu (2004). Ball, Stittmeyer, and Srihari (2010) reported about an application to writer verification in historical documents. *Writer verification* is the task of determining whether two handwriting samples (a *known document* and a *questioned document*) were written by the same or by different writers. Ball and Srihari (2009) drew a comparison of statistical models for writer verification. They explained:

> We present a system for performing writer verification which captures the idea of writer uniqueness. Intuitively, the system works by pairwise comparing letters of the same class between the two documents and determining their similarity to one another (by computing a similarity distance). Two conditional probability estimates are then computed based on each distance — (i) the probability of the two characters being produced by a single writer (i.e., the distance being explained by normal variation) and (ii) the chance of characters being produced by two different writers. The *log-likelihood ratio* (LLR) is computed and is used to determine the strength of confidence for the opinion.
>
> A unique contribution of our method is our approach to generating the probability estimates. Our method captures the uniqueness of an individual writer by generating a probability distribution of distances between instances of character classes in the known

---

[163] http://www.cedar.buffalo.edu/index.html CEDAR is the Center of Excellence in Document Analysis and Recognition at the University of Buffalo. Publications are listed at, and sometimes can be downloaded from, http://www.cedar.buffalo.edu/papers/publications.html

document and the general population, as represented by a set of many samples. This intuitively captures how different a writer's sample is from the general population. While it might be desirable to generate this directly by determining the distribution of features on the writer's own samples, there will in practice often be few instances of character classes. By comparing with the general population, the uniqueness can be learned even when only a small set of characters is present.

Srihari, Ball, and Ramakrishnan (2009) reported about the identification of forgeries in handwritten petitions for ballot propositions. Srinivasan and Srihari (2009) discussed signature-based retrieval of scanned documents, and that article of theirs appeared in a paper collection about computer methods for counterterrorism. Manning and Srihari (2009) discussed computer-assisted handwriting analysis in combination with legal issues in U.S. courts. Srihari, Collins, Srihari, Srinivasan, and Shetty (2008) reported about the automatic scoring of short handwritten essays in reading comprehension tests. Srihari and Ball (2008) were concerned with writer verification of handwritten Arabic. Srihari, Ball, and Srinivasan (2008) reported about searching Arabic handwriting.

This kind of domain is known by the name *questioned documents evidence* (Levinson, 2000): there exist techniques for determining authenticity, age, ink and paper sources, equipment used, forgeries, alterations, and erasures, as well as, of course, handwriting identification.[164]

The Wikipedia entry for "Questioned document examination"[165] explains which kinds of documents are examined:

> Documents feature prominently in all manner of business and personal affairs. Almost any type of document may become disputed in an investigation or litigation. For example, a questioned document may be a sheet of paper bearing handwriting or mechanically-produced text such as a ransom note, a forged cheque or a business contract. Or it may be some material not normally thought of as a 'document'. Forensic document examiners define the word 'document' in a very broad sense as being any material bearing marks, signs or symbols intended to convey a message or meaning to someone. This encompasses traditional paper documents but also includes things like graffiti on a wall, stamp impressions on meat products, or covert markings hidden in a written letter, among other things. Some forensic document examiners limit their work to the examination and comparison of handwriting, but most of the forensic document examiners inspect the whole document.

Besides, consider *forensic linguistics. Forensic stylistics* is one facet of it. Bolelli (1993, p. 126) refers to the appointment of a linguist as an expert witness to advise the court whether a given word is an insult (in countries like Italy and the Netherlands, the court can appoint an expert witness above the parts, and such a role is called *amicus curiae* internationally, including in English-language treatments),

---

[164] Handwriting identification is the subject of Morris (2000).

[165] The literature on questioned documents includes Osborn (1929), Harrison (1958), Conway (1959), Hilton (1982), Huber and Headrick (1999), Ellen (2005), Morris (2000), Levinson (2001), Koppenhaver (2007), Köller, Nissen, Reiß, and Sadorf (2004) At www.bka.de/vorbeugung/pub/probabilistische_schlussfolgerungen_in_schriftgutachten.pdf German and English versions of Köller et al. (2004) can be downloaded.

but thus is just one out of an array of contexts in which the intervention of a *forensic linguist* may be relevant.

Levi (1994) discussed the role of the *linguist* as expert witness in North American courts. Forensic linguistics as a discipline[166] has a specialised forum, the Routledge journal *Forensic Linguistics*, first published in 1994. An aspect of forensic linguistics that has been researched is what is the effect of language sociolect (the language variety of this or that social class) and of language style, of powerful or powerless language, on impression formation in the courtroom, and on upon judgements of victims and villains.[167]

Later in this book, while shortly discussing disciplines of forensic science, we are going to consider *biometrics*, which strives to identify or authenticate personal identity as based on physical traits. Yet, even though this is relatively little known even among practitioners of biometrics itself, biometrics is also concerned with the identification of a person based on personal traits of verbal and nonverbal communication; it is a challenge to express the task algorithmically (Esposito, Bratanić, Keller, & Marinaro, 2007).

6.1.11 Classification, Clustering, Series Analysis, and Association in Knowledge Discovery from Legal Databases

Andrew Stranieri and John Zeleznikow

6.1.11.1 Classification

The aim of *classification* techniques is to group data into predefined categories. For example, data representing important case facts from many cases may be used to classify a new case into one of the pre-defined categories, pro-plaintiff or pro-defendant, which respectively comprise such cases that were decided for the plaintiff, and such cases that were decided for the defendant.

Techniques exist for the automatic discovery of knowledge in the form of rules that take the general form

IF   A and B and C
THEN D.

A number of researchers have applied *knowledge discovery from databases* (*KDD*) techniques to automatically extract IF-THEN rules from data in order to make a prediction. Wilkins and Pillaipakkamnatt (1997) examined large numbers of cases in order to estimate the number of days that are likely to elapse between the

---

[166] For forensic linguistics, see e.g. Coulthard (1992), Shuy (1993) – the latter, reviewed in Danet (1994) – O'Barr (1982), and Gibbons (1994).

[167] See Erickson, Lind, Johnson, and O'Barr (1978), Bradac, Hemphill, and Tardy, (1981), Gibbons, Busch, and Bradac (1991).

arrest of an offender and the final disposition of the case. The time to disposition depends on variables such as the charge, offender's age, and the county where the arrest was made. Values on more than 30 variables from over 700,000 records from 12 U.S. states were used. Rules were automatically extracted using the rule induction algorithm ID3. Although Wilkins and Pillaipakkamnatt (1997) themselves had hoped for rulesets that predicted the time to disposition more accurately than their results indicate, this study remains an impressive demonstration of the potential for KDD techniques to contribute to the delivery of legal services.

Vossos, Zeleznikow, & Hunter (1993) and Zeleznikow, Vossos, and Hunter (1994), in conjunction with a legal firm, developed the *Credit Act Advisory System, CAAS*. This is a rule based legal expert system that provides advice regarding the extent to which a credit transaction complies with the Credit Act 1984 (Vic), of Victoria in Australia. Although the majority of rules derive directly from the statute, some factors remain vaguely defined in the Act. For example, the factor "credit was for a business purpose" is not defined by the statute. In this instance, a rule induction algorithm was invoked to discover new rules from a database of facts from past cases that involved credit for a business purpose. A rule induction technique discovers rules from past cases where a judge had decided whether credit was extended for a business purpose. These rules help a user determine whether a new, current situation involves credit for a business purpose or not.

In Section 6.1.1 in this book, it was already mentioned that a brief paper by Pedro Feu Rosa (2000) – surveyed in Stranieri and Zeleznikow (2005a, pp. 12, 228: also the present section is based text in that same book) – was concerned with another application of knowledge discovery to law. Namely, a Supreme Court Judge in Brazil initiated a program for the resolution of traffic accident disputes. It is called *Judges on Wheels*. A judge, police officer, insurance assessor, mechanical and support staff are transported to the scene of minor motor vehicle accidents. The team collects evidence, the mechanic assess the damage, and the judge makes a decision and drafts a judgement with the help of a program called the *Electronic Judge* before leaving the scene of the accident. The *Electronic Judge* software uses a KDD approach that involves data mining by means of neural networks.

Neural networks tools learn patterns of decision making from judges in previous traffic accidents and suggest an outcome for the current accident that is consistent with previous ones. No rules are induced. Although, the judge is not obliged to follow the suggestion offered by the *Electronic Judge*, the software was being used by judges in 68% of traffic accidents in the state of Espirito Santo. The system plays an important role in enhancing the consistency of judicial decision-making.

Hobson and Slee (1994) studied a handful of cases from the U.K. Theft Act and used neural networks[168] to predict the outcome of theft cases. They used a series of leading cases in British theft law to train a network to predict a courtroom outcome. The results they obtained were less than impressive, which they attributed to flaws in the use of neural networks in legal reasoning. This criticism was unduly harsh.

---

[168] Cf. Hobson and Slee (1993), for the application of networks in the legal domain.

Neural networks have much to offer KDD. However, any application of KDD to data drawn from the legal domain must be carefully performed. Due attention is required, so that key assumptions made at each phase of the KDD process are clearly articulated and have some basis in jurisprudence. For example, the cases used in the Hobson and Slee study involved *leading cases*. We argue that leading cases are not well suited to a KDD exercise. See in Section 6.1.11.5 below.

Bench-Capon (1993b), drawing on hypothetical data from a social security domain, was guarded in his appraisal of the benefits of using neural networks to model reasoning in legal domains. Similar concerns regarding the use of neural networks in law have been advanced by Hunter (1994). However, as we shall demonstrate in subsequent chapters, the appropriate application of KDD involves steps that include data selection, data pre-processing, data transformation, data mining and evaluation. At each phase, assumptions that are consistent with jurisprudential theories must be made. If assumptions are clearly articulated and carefully drawn, neural networks, in addition to other KDD techniques can be adapted to provide accurate predictions.

Chen (2000a) described an automated detective that scans web pages for criminal activity. In that study, the data is text on a web page. Processes developed by Chen (2000a) seek to classify the page into one of two pre-defined categories, illegal or not illegal.

In the *Split Up* project (Stranieri, Zeleznikow, Gawler, & Lewis, 1999) – whose argument tree we considered in Section 6.11.6.1 in the present book – collected data from cases heard in the Family Court of Australia dealing with property distribution following divorce. The objective was to predict the percentage split of assets that a judge in the Family Court of Australia would be likely to award both parties of a failed marriage. Australian Family Law is generally regarded as highly discretionary. The statute presents a "shopping list" of factors to be taken into account in arriving at a property order. The relative importance of each factor remains unspecified and many crucial terms are not defined. The age, state of health and financial resources of the litigants are explicitly mentioned in the statute as relevant factors yet their relative weightings are unspecified. The Act clearly allows the decision-maker a great deal of discretion in interpreting and weighing factors.

The relative importance judges have placed on relevant factors in past cases can, to some extent be learnt with the use of KDD. This knowledge enables the user of Split Up to predict the outcomes of future cases. As we shall discuss throughout this work, important issues to be taken into account include which cases should be included in a KDD sample, how do we deal with cases in which a judge has perhaps erred, how do we evaluate the results of our systems, and how do we know which factors are important.

Oatley and Ewart (2003) described the OVER Project as a collaboration between West Midlands Police in England and the University of Sunderland that aimed to assist police with the high volume crime, burglary from dwelling houses. A software system they developed enables the trending of historical data, the testing of "short term" hunches, and the development of "medium" and "long term" strategies to burglary and crime reduction, based upon victim, offender, location and details of victimisations. The software utilises mapping and visualisation tools and is capable of a range of sophisticated predictions, tying together statistical techniques with theories from forensic psychology and criminology. The statistical methods employed (including multi-dimensional scaling, binary logistic regression) and data-mining technologies (including neural networks) are used to investigate the impact of the types of evidence available and to determine the causality in this domain. The final predictions on the likelihood of burglary are calculated by combining all of the varying sources of evidence into a Bayesian belief network. This network is embedded in the developed software system, which also performs data cleansing and data transformation for presentation to the developed algorithms.

Oatley, Ewart, and Zeleznikow (2006)[169] note that computer science technology that can support police activities is wide ranging, from the well known geographical information systems display ("pins in maps"), clustering and link analysis algorithms, to the more complex use of data mining technology for profiling single and series of crimes or offenders, and matching and predicting crimes. They present a discussion of data mining and decision support technologies for police, considering the range of computer science technologies that are available to assist police activities.

6.1.11.2 Clustering

The aim of *clustering* techniques is to group data into clusters of similar items. Whereas the aim of *classification* techniques is to group data into predefined categories, the aim of clustering techniques is to analyse the data in order to group the data into groups of similar data. For example, a clustering technique may group cases into six main clusters that an analyst would interpret in order to learn something about the cases.

In practice, legal data about persons, cases or situations is typically stored as text based documents rather than structured databases. Discovering knowledge by the automatic analysis of free text is a field of research that is evolving from information retrieval research and is often called text mining. Hearst (1999) proposes that text-mining involves discovering relationships between the contexts of multiple texts and linking this information together to create new information.

Many text-mining applications involve clustering. The application of a type of neural network known as *Self Organising Maps* (*SOM*) to group European Parliament cases into clusters has been described by Merkl and Schweighofer (1997), Schweighofer and Merkl (1999) and Merkl, Schweighofer, and Winiwarter (1999). Each cluster contains only cases that are similar according to the SOM. The SOM, used in this way have proven to accurately discover groupings for many thousands of cases.

In the SOM application Merkl et al. (1999) were interested in identifying clusters and the issue of selecting a cluster centre was not important. Pannu (1995) engaged

---

[169] Cf. Oatley, Zeleznikow, and Ewart (2004), Oatley and Ewart (2003).

in knowledge discovery by identifying the *centre point* in a cluster. This took the form of identifying a prototypical exemplar of pro-defendant and pro-plaintiff cases within a domain, i.e., such cases that were decided for the defendant or for the plaintiff. An exemplar pro-defendant case has features that are most like those cases in which the defendant won and most unlike the cases the defendant lost. This technique can be applied to assist a lawyer to structure an argument in a current case.

As Moens (2001) notes, a major group of techniques that involves *unsupervised learning* (a subject for which, see Section 6.1.14.14 below) is the clustering of objects that share common features. Cluster analysis is a multivariate statistical technique that automatically generates groups into data (Kaufmann & Rousseeuw, 2005, 1st edn. 1990). *Non-hierarchical clustering methods* partition a set of objects into clusters of similar objects. Hierarchical methods construct a tree-like hierarchy of objects with the root representing a cluster containing all the objects, the leaves representing the individual objects and the nodes containing the intermediate groupings. The technique of clustering supposes:

- An abstract representation of the object to be clustered, containing the features for the classification;
- A function that computes the relative importance (weight) of the features; and
- A function that computes a numerical similarity between the representations.

Clustering is employed to group terms that regularly co-occur in documents or to group documents if they discuss the same topic terms. A form of neural network, known as *self-organising maps* (*SOM*), have been successfully applied to text clustering. We discuss SOM in Section 6.1.14.15 below.

6.1.11.3 Series Analysis

The aim of *series analysis* is to discover *sequences within the data*. Sequences typically sought are *time series*. For example, past cases over a time period may be analysed in order to discover important changes in the way a core concept is interpreted by Courts. Very few studies have been performed that analyse sequences of data in law. However, the study by Rissland and Friedman (1995) provides a good indication of the potential utility in doing so. They collected data from U.S. bankruptcy cases over a ten-year period and asked whether knowledge discovery techniques could be applied to automatically discover significant shifts in judicial decision-making. Data represented variables known to be relevant for the concept of "good faith" in bankruptcy proceedings. Their aim was to discover a method for detecting a change in the way the concept of "good faith" was used by Courts. The onset of a leading decision was automatically detected from case data using a metric they devised.

6.1.11.4 Detecting Association Rules

The objective of *association* techniques is to discover ways in which data elements are associated with other data elements. For example, an association between the gender of litigants and the outcome of their cases may surprise analysts and stimulate hypotheses to explain the phenomenon. *Association rules* depict an association between specific variable values. For example, an association rule that claims that if gender is female, then case is won on 10% of cases highlights a link between two variables, gender and outcome. The link is not necessarily causal and may not even be interesting. Typically, the discovery of all possible association rules from data from many cases is computationally infeasible. However, an algorithm called *a priori* advanced by Agrawal, Imielinski, and Swami (1993) makes the automatic generation of rules tractable. Stranieri, Yearwood, and Meikl (2000) have illustrated that association rule generators can highlight interesting associations in a small dataset.

In an example of KDD in law that aims to analyse a legal domain rather than making specific predictions regarding judicial outcomes, Ivkovic, Yearwood, and Stranieri (2003) have generated association rules from over 300,000 records drawn from database of applicants for government funded legal aid in Australia. In that country, applicants for legal aid must not only pass an income and assets test but must also demonstrate that their case has some merit for success. Consequently considerable data is recorded about the applicant and the case.

The purpose of the association rules study performed by Ivkovic et al. (2003) was to determine whether this data mining technique could automatically analyse the data in order to identify hypotheses that would not otherwise have been considered. For example, as a result of this study, an association between the applicant's age and categories of legal aid applied requested was discovered. It can be summarised as follows: 89% of applicants between 18 and 21 applied for legal aid for criminal offences whereas 57% of applicants between 40 and 50 applied for aid for criminal offences. This result surprised experts in the field who did not expect young applicants to be so highly represented in criminal law matters. This result is not, of itself used to explain much, but is advanced to assist in the formulation of hypotheses to explain the associations observed.

The application of association rules is to suggest hypotheses from data, and such applications that are relevant to law are, for example:

- About population groups; for example, a hypothesis may be that most Western suburbs shoplifting is perpetrated by Northern suburb, young women.
- About case types; for example, a hypothesis may be that few family law cases where the husband has the children resulted in a 50:50 split.
- About Court practices or efficiencies; for example, a hypothesis may be that most cases that involved self-represented litigants who had professional jobs took longer to hear than those self-represented litigants without professional jobs.

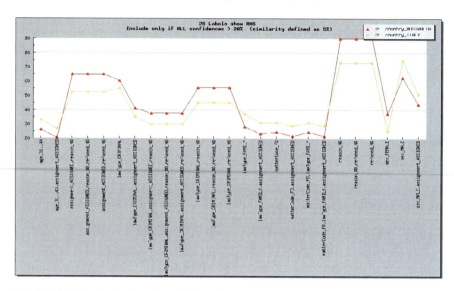

Fig. 6.1.11.4.1   Visualisation of association rules

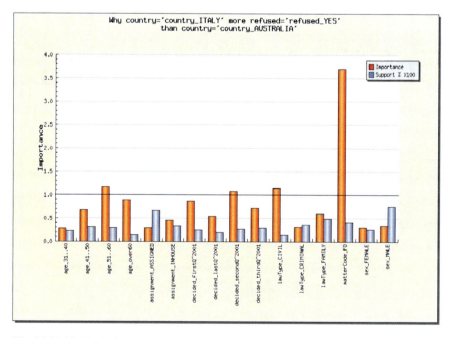

Fig. 6.1.11.4.2   Exploring hypotheses suggested by association rules

The four categories of KDD techniques – classification, clustering, series analysis and association detection – are useful categories in the practical process of applying KDD to data, because they help an analyst determine the desired outcome of a KDD exercise.

Figure 6.1.11.4.1 shows a example of visualisation of association rules. Figure 6.1.11.4.2 shows exploring hypotheses.

6.1.11.5 On Interestingness. Commonplace Cases, Rather Than Leading (Interesting, Landmark) Cases, Are Suitable in Training Sets for Legal Knowledge Discovery Algorithms

The vast majority of cases that come before a first instance decision maker in family law are never published, are never appealed, and establish no new principle or rule. They do not revolve around a new legal interpretation, nor do they involve circumstances that are legally interesting to experienced practitioners. They are commonplace cases.

Commonplace cases are suitable for the discovery of knowledge about how judges exercise discretion in family law, whereas landmark cases are not suitable. The distinction between commonplace and landmark cases is not one based on clear definitional categories since any case that is currently viewed as commonplace could conceivably be used in the future as a landmark case. For example, perhaps the most significant leading case in family law, Mallet vs Mallet[170] was not particularly extraordinary at the first instance court.

The trial judge in Mallet vs Mallet awarded 20% of the business assets from a long marriage to the wife after taking the contributions and needs of both parties into account. The Full Bench of the Family Court increased the wife's percentage split to 50% by making explicit the principle that equality should be the starting point. That Court commenced with 50% and deviated according to contributions and needs. Following this decision, the husband appealed to the High Court. The High Court overruled the Full Bench of the Family Court and reinstated the trial judge's decision. As indicated previously, this case became a landmark case in that it firmly endorsed unfettered trial Court discretion.

Although a case cannot be definitely categorised as either commonplace or landmark, the distinction between them is a useful one when applying selecting cases for inclusion in a KDD exercise. Most landmark cases are not suitable for the assembly of training sets for data mining, because these cases typically revolve around a definitional issue or they attempt to resolve a classification ambiguity so that a precedent for subsequent cases may be set.

Landmark cases heard by appeal courts typically establish a new rule or principle. In a domain where traditional *stare decisis*[171] is less influential than in

---

[170] (1984) 156 CLR 185

[171] *Stare decisis* is a fundamental principle in common law legal systems. The principle dictates that the reasoning, loosely, *ratio decidendi*, used in new cases must follow the reasoning used by

standard Common law domains, Appeal Courts can more readily be seen to establish broad principles or resolve classification ambiguities. For example, in the Full Court decision in the Marriage of Elias[172] a precedent was established that deemed entrepreneurial prowess as a form of contribution to a marriage. Debts have been admitted as negative contributions in *The Marriage of Anttman*.[173] Both these leading cases can be seen to refine the open textured concept of a contribution to a marriage.

The objective in applying machine learning in the discretionary domain of family law, which is what we did in the Split Up system, is to model the way, in which judges weight factors which are known to be relevant. A leading case may introduce a new factor that subsequent trial decisions must accommodate. Data about the factor could not have been recorded in cases prior to the landmark case. For example, prior to Elias, no trial judge would have mentioned a contribution in the form of entrepreneurial prowess, because that issue was not known to be relevant.

Hunter (1994) illustrated that most applications of neural networks as a data mining technique, to law, use landmark cases. For example, as mentioned earlier (in Section 6.1.11.1), Hobson and Slee (1994) used a series of leading cases in British theft law to train a network to predict a courtroom outcome. Results they obtained highlighted flaws in the use of neural networks in legal reasoning. However, we agree with Hunter in noting that their results are partly due to the use of landmark cases rather than commonplace cases.

A distinction between *commonplace* and *landmark decisions* can also be seen in the *ratio decidendi*, that is to say, the rationale of a decision. The ratio decidendi in reported and appellate Court decisions can be seen to have a different purpose from the ratio in commonplace cases. The purpose of the ratio of an appellate court judge is to convince subsequent trial judges to accept a change in the interpretation of legal principles or rules. This is so even if a case sets no dramatic precedent but reinforces existing, and commonly held principles. The purpose of the ratio in unreported cases is slightly different.

First instance decision makers aim to explain to litigants (and others) that the reasoning used was in accordance with the appropriate statutes and principles and that an appeal is not warranted. The ratio in unreported cases is thus more likely to reflect the reasoning actually used in assimilating all facts to determine a conclusion. The ratio in a reported case is more likely to revolve only around those facts that are contentious. The discussion centres on which of a number of possible interpretations of principles is most appropriate as a precedent for making future decisions.

---

decision-makers in courts at the same or higher level in the hierarchy. Stare decisis is unknown to civil law, where judgments rendered by judges only enjoy the *authority of reason. Traditional stare decisis* is when the same decision has to be taken as a higher court judging about the same facts. *Local stare decisis* is when the same decision has to be taken as the same court judging about the same facts. *Personal stare decisis* is when the same decision has to be taken as the same judge judging about the same facts.

[172] (1977) Fam LR, cited in [Ingleby, 1993].

[173] (1980) 6 Fam LR.

Commonplace cases are more appropriate than landmark cases, for inclusion in the training set of a data mining algorithm.[174] However, discerning a commonplace case from a landmark case is problematical given that a past commonplace case may become a future landmark case if it happens to be appealed or, perhaps even referred to, in an appealed decision. A concept of "interesting" (thus, of *interestingness*) is advanced in order to guide the discernment of a commonplace case from a land-mark case. If a case is not interesting, it is a commonplace case. For a first instance decision to be interesting it must:

(a) be appealed, or
(b) includes a new principle, rule or factor in its ratio decidendi, or
(c) exhibits an outcome vastly at odds with other similar cases.

It is not sufficient to admit only appealed cases to the category of interesting cases, because a litigant may choose to avoid an appeal for a variety of reasons. Thus, not all interesting cases are appealed.

The concept of *interestingness* of a case can be operationalised relatively easily by noting that senior judges of the Family Court make precisely this sort of judge-ment in deciding which cases are to be published by Court reporting services. These services do not publish the judgements of all cases, because the majority of cases are of little interest to readers. Thus, the more appropriate cases from which to extract data for inclusion in a training set are unreported cases. These cases are those in which a senior judge of the Family Court has ruled as uninteresting. These cases are not published, so it is difficult for a future practitioner to invoke one of these cases as backing for an argument.

Reported cases are of great importance for identifying relevant factors in the Split Up system. A reported case may set a precedent; invalidating a factor that had previously been considered relevant, or alternatively, it may introduce a new factor.

Accessing a random sample of cases is not straightforward and requires some assumptions. For example, the Family Court operates throughout Australia, yet it seems unreasonable to assume that decisions have no regional differences. A clas-sifier trained with data from one region may perform poorly when predicting a case from another region. Another assumption we make is that decisions made by appeal Courts are not necessarily representative of decisions made by first instance judges. We also make the assumption that decisions made more than 4 years ago are not necessarily representative of decisions made recently, or that are likely to be made in the near future. Data for the original Split Up project was gathered from unre-ported Family Court cases decided between 1992 and 1994 in the Melbourne region of Australia. Each of the cases examined was decided by one of eight different judges. Judgments from these eight judges were examined in preference to limiting ourselves to those from only one judge in order to encourage the network to mimic

---

[174] Such as neural networks or rule induction algorithms.

a composite of all judges and also because no one judge had decided a sufficient number of cases[175] during that period.

6.1.12 Inconsistent Data

Andrew Stranieri and John Zeleznikow

6.1.12.1 Reasons for Inconsistency

We discuss *data inconsistency*, based on our treatment of the subject in Stranieri and Zeleznikow (2005a). This is an important subject, for data mining. The viewpoint we are going to offer is that of knowledge *discovery from databases* (*KDD*) in law. Legal databases are likely indeed to contain records that reflect inconsistencies. A simple and hypothetical example illustrates this. Consider a task where the decision maker concludes outcome X whenever facts A, B and C are present. This may have occurred in many cases, so be captured many times in a legal database. However, if a new case decides Y from facts A, B and C, then this is at odds with the first pattern. The reasons for this can include:

(a) *Noise.* The data collection procedure was inaccurate.
(b) *Judicial error.* The decision maker may have erred.
(c) *Change.* Legislation, precedent cases (in common law countries) or judicial behaviour may have changed.

A concern with inconsistent data is important for the KDD process within law, because data-mining techniques might tend to learn incorrect or inappropriate patterns. For example, a data-mining technique will learn incorrect patterns if exposed to sufficiently many cases in which a judge had not followed personal or local stare decisis.[176] Similarly if elements of a case such as the length of the marriage are wrongly recorded in a database, the dataset is considered noisy. Furthermore, law is always in flux, so changes in legislation, precedents, judicial or community values will similarly impact on patterns learnt. In this Section 6.1.12, noise, error and change are discussed.

6.1.12.2 Noise and Outliers

Noise is typically assumed to consist of random discrepancies in data that are due to measurement anomalies and are not a feature of the distribution of data. For example, a faulty scanner may introduce noise into industrial data. Noise may explain outliers. Inconsistencies between the categorisation of values for the Split Up template, by the three raters in our Split Up project for assisting in negotiation in

---

[175] For both completeness and to train the neural network.

[176] See the definition of *stare decisis* in fn 106 above.

settling divorce cases[177] (Stranieri et al., 1999), introduce noise into the training sets. Eliot (1993) surveyed neural network research to point out that generalisation performance and training time degrade if the dataset contains noisy data. Liang and Moskowitz (1992) quantified the effect of noise on neural network performance and have introduced a method based on semi-markov models to detect noisy examples.

Data objects that are grossly different from or inconsistent with the remaining set of data are called *outliers*. Han and Kamber (2001) note that many data-mining algorithms attempt to minimise the influence of outliers or totally eliminate them. However, such action can lead to the loss of important hidden information – such as in the case of fraud detection, where outliers may indicate fraudulent activity.

The *outlier mining problem* can be viewed as two subproblems:

(a) define what data can be considered as inconsistent in a given data set; and
(b) find an efficient method to mine the outliers so defined.

The problem of defining outliers is nontrivial. If a *regression* model[178] is used for data modelling, than an analysis of the residuals can provide a good estimate for *extremeness*. The task is more difficult when finding outliers in *time-series data*, as they may be hidden in trend, seasonal or other cyclic changes. Data visualisation methods are weak in detecting outliers in data with many categorical attributes or in data of high dimensionality, since human eyes are good at visualising numeric data of only two to three dimensions.

Computer-based methods for outlier detection can be categorised into three approaches:

1. *Statistical-Based Outlier Detection*. This approach assumes a distribution or probability model for the given data set (*normal distribution*) and then identifies outliers with respect to the model using a discordancy test. Application of the test requires knowledge of the data set parameters (such as the assumed data distribution), knowledge of distribution parameters (such as the mean and variance) and the expected number of outliers. A statistical discordancy test examines two hypotheses: a working hypothesis and an alternative hypothesis. The hypothesis is retained if there is no statistically significant test supporting its rejection. A major drawback of the statistical approach is that most tests are for single

---

[177] Arno Lodder and john Zeleznikow provided an overview of computer-assisted dispute resolution (as being an alternative to litigation) in a book (Lodder & Zeleznikow, 2010). *Split Up* is the subject of section 5.4 in that book. The hybrid rule–neural approach of Split Up was described in Stranieri et al. (1999). Bellucci and Zeleznikow (2005) is concerned with the *Family Winner* decision-support system that supports mediators in family law.

[178] In *linear regression*, data is modelled using a straight line of the form

$$y = \alpha x + \beta$$

α and β are determined using the method of least squares. Polynomial regression models can be transformed to a linear regression model.

attributes, yet many data mining problems require finding outliers in multidi-mensional space. Moreover, the statistical approach requires knowledge about parameters of the data set, such as the data distribution. However, in many cases, the data distribution may not be known. Statistical methods do not guarantee that all outliers will be found for the cases where no specific test was developed, or the observed distribution cannot be adequately modelled with any standard dis-tribution. Wang and Gedeon (1995) described a statistical detection method and report improvements over other methods to detect and remove outliers. However, these methods are not trivial to implement and can be costly in terms of computer resources.

2. *Distance-Based Outlier Detection.* The notion of distance-based outliers was introduced to counter the main limitations imposed by statistical methods. Rather than relying on statistical tests, we can think of distance-based outliers as those objects who do not have "enough" neighbours, where neighbours are defined based on their distance from the given object. In comparison with statistical-based methods, distance-based outlier detection generalises the ideas behind discordancy testing for various standard distributions. Distance-based outlier detection avoids the excessive computation that can be associated with fitting the observed distribution into some standard distribution and in selecting discor-dancy tests. Several efficient algorithms for mining distance-based outliers have been developed:

   (i)   index-based algorithm;
   (ii) nested-loop algorithm; and
   (iii) cell-based algorithm.

3. *Deviation-Based Outlier Detection.* Deviation-based outlier detection does not use statistical tests or distance-based measures to identify exceptional objects. Instead, it identifies outliers by examining the main characteristics of objects in a group. Objects that deviate from this description are considered outliers.

In the next section we discuss judicial error as a source of contradictory data, particularly within a domain that affords a decision maker much discretion.

6.1.12.3 Judicial Error as a Source of Inconsistency

Judicial error is conceptualised differently by prevailing jurisprudential theories. Utilitarianism was first advanced by Jeremy Bentham.[179] Bentham argued that the purpose of a legal system is to advance the greatest degree of happiness to the great-est number of people. There is little place for natural law or natural rights in his legal philosophy. For utilitarians, an error in legal reasoning occurs if a judge determines

---

[179] Bentham (1748–1832) was a leading theorist in Anglo-American philosophy of law and one of the founders of *utilitarianism*. His most important theoretical work is the *Introduction to the Principles of Morals and Legislation* (1789), in which much of his moral theory – which he said reflected "the greatest happiness principle" – is described and developed.

an outcome which cannot, ultimately, contribute to the well being of the largest number of people.

According to perspectives advanced by Dworkin (1977, 1986), a judge errs, albeit in a minor way, by failing to discover the ideal way in which to apply precedents to a current fact situation. This view led to the concept of an ideal judge; a concept that was perhaps attacked most strongly by adherents to the critical legal studies movement.

For *legal positivists* such as Hart (1994), a judge may err by failing to discern a *core case* from a *penumbra case* or by failing to apply appropriate rules to resolve a current penumbra case. For German *conceptualists*, a judge errs by failing to reason deductively from facts to a conclusion.

The concept of judicial error that can be drawn from major theories of jurisprudence, pre-supposes a failure in adherence to the doctrine of stare decisis.[180] However, the type of stare decisis that most neatly fits into these theoretical perspectives advanced is what we define as traditional stare decisis.

The right of appeal in common law jurisdictions provides a safeguard against judicial error. However, the grounds for appeal against a first instance decision vary so markedly across jurisdictions that a general specification of erroneous decisions is very difficult. For instance, according to Dickey (1990), the acceptable grounds for appeal a first instance decision-maker in the Family Court of Australia include:

(a) a failure on the part of the trial judge to provide reasons for a judgement, or
(b) the use of an inappropriate principle in reaching a decision, or
(c) incorrect findings of fact or,
(d) the inappropriate weighting of factors.

The requirement to give reasons has been imposed on first instance judges by a number of High Court decisions. In these cases, traditional stare decisis was operative, in that the High Court was firm in laying down constraints to ensure trial judges included reasons for their decisions. Traditional stare decisis is also clear in the *Marriage of Gronow*[181] in establishing a right to appeal if the trial judge acted on a wrong principle or allowed irrelevant factors to influence her.

Another ground for appeal involves the inappropriate weighting of a relevant factor. We indicated above[182] that the High Court has been reluctant to fetter the discretion of trial judges by laying down guidelines to control the way in which factors are weighted. The fact that experienced practitioners can predict Family Court outcomes, demonstrates that personal stare decisis and local stare decisis apply in the Family Court of Australia.

This arises because of a desire on the part of first instance decision-makers to weight relevant factors in a manner that is consistent with the decisions of other

---

[180] See the definition of *stare decisis* in fn 106 above.

[181] (1979) 5 Fam LR 719.

[182] In the case Mallet vs Mallet (1984) 156 CLR 185.

judges. A hypothetical Family Court judge can be imagined as one who whenever she is presented with cases with identical facts, the judge would determine precisely the same percentage split of assets to both parties. That is, the exercise of discretion is perfectly consistent with other judges and, perfectly consistent with the same judge over time.

However, the ideal judge does not exist in the real world. Individual judges are not perfectly consistent with other judges, even on the same set of facts. An informal study with Family Court judges exposed to the same case facts, revealed substantial variance in percentage split outcomes. This concurs with experiences reported by family law practitioners. If it were possible to expose a large number of judges to the same set of facts, then we can imagine that a mean outcome would emerge and individual judgments would fall on both sides of the mean.

A conceptualisation of judicial error is important for the application of the knowledge discovery process to legal reasoning, because the goal of a machine learning system is to predict outcomes that judges will consider acceptable. The performance of such algorithms can be expected to degrade if exposed to large numbers of decisions in which a judge has actually erred.

If the entire set of cases used in a KDD exercise, contains a significant amount of errors, then data mining algorithms cannot be expected to accurately predict outcomes. But, how are we to determine whether an actual judicial outcome is an unacceptable exercise of discretion for the purposes of KDD? To what extent can two judges offer divergent decisions on cases with very similar findings of fact before one (or both) is considered to have erred? Furthermore, to which authority should we turn, to make this determination? We shall first discuss the issue of which authority is best placed to make a determination on acceptable bounds of discretion.

The most obvious authorities for the discernment of acceptable exercises of discretion from unacceptable exercises of discretion are appellate Courts. However, this authority is not totally suitable because decisions that fail local stare decisis may never be appealed for a variety of reasons including:

(a) An appeal to a higher court is expensive and the possible gain may not warrant the additional expense.
(b) Gender or other cultural factors may impact on the decision to appeal. For example, Alexander (1992) has illustrated that women tend to be more reluctant than men to continue conflict and are therefore more reluctant to pursue an appeal.

Furthermore, according to Kovacs (1992), a demonstration that a relevant factor was not given appropriate weight by a trial judge is extremely difficult to prove, because standards for the exercise of discretion in family law have not been laid down by the High Court. Experienced practitioners typically advise against an appeal unless a decision was patently unjust.

An appeal Court is not ideally situated to determine issues of local stare decisis,[183] because the main function of an appeal Court is to determine whether

---

[183] See the definition of *stare decisis* in fn 106 above.

a lower Court has appropriately applied legal rules and principles. The issue of determining local, or personal stare decisis is only indirectly addressed.

Schild (1998) explores these issues in depth when considering the field of the sentencing of Israeli criminals. To ensure more consistent sentencing decisions, he recommended the establishment of panels of experts specifically formed to provide feedback. This approach raises many issues that warrant discussion, but this is beyond our current scope.

The task at hand is pragmatic, in that we are concerned with the impact judicial error has on the knowledge discovery from database process. If some cases from which we collect data, fail to adhere to local (or personal) stare decisis, then datamining techniques cannot be expected to learn useful patterns.

Cases in the dataset that are inconsistent with other cases need to be identified and dealt with in the pre-processing phase. If the inconsistency is due to judicial error, then we are compelled to attempt to identify them and adopt a strategy such as modifying offending records, or removing or ignoring such records. If the inconsistency is due to a change in legislation or the emergence of a precedent case, then other mechanisms may need to be invoked.

Contradictory examples are, in general, examples that have different outcomes despite identical inputs. Contradictory cases are necessarily present in discretionary domains, because judges cannot be expected to weight factors in the same way on every case throughout their career. Nor can they be expected to be perfectly consistent with the weightings used by other judges.

6.1.12.4 Dealing with Contradictory Data: An Example from *Split Up*

There are a number of ways to deal with extreme contradictions. Most simply, the contradictions can be ignored. Wang and Gedeon (1995) note that a small proportion of contradictory examples will not dramatically effect the performance of a neural network. However, the performance of other data-mining techniques depends more heavily on the proportion of contradictory examples. The first step in dealing with contradictions, if they are not to be ignored, involves their detection. This is not trivial in a KDD exercise in law. The data in table illustrates sample contradictory data.

Marriage 1 and Marriage 2 in Table 6.1.12.4.1 have identical values on input attributes but differ dramatically on the value on the output attribute (percentage of assets awarded to the wife). A casual observer might conclude that these two records clearly contradict each other. However, Marriage 3 does not contradict Marriage 1 despite identical input values because the output percentage is 64 and not 65.

Consider transformation methods used in the Split Up project. A fundamental transformation performed on the values of variables is to map an ordinal value onto a binary string. That transformation assisted us in the deployment of neural networks for making predictions. Another benefit of the transformation adopted was that we could more easily develop a metric for determining the extent to which two examples are contradictory. We briefly describe the nature of variables and the transformation we performed in order to illustrate the metric.

Table 6.1.12.4.1 Sample contradictory data

Marriage number	Wife's age (years, months)	Wife's health	Age of eldest child	Suburb	Percentage of assets awarded to the wife
1	35,1	Good	4,1	Delacombe	65
2	35,1	Good	4,1	Delacombe	30
3	35,1	Good	4,1	Delacombe	64
4	35,5	Good	?	Delacombe	50
5	34,9	Good	4,2	Gold Point	40
6	34,9	Good	4,2	Sebas	40

An ordinal variable such as the contributions of the husband relative to the wife has five possible values, ["much more", "more", "same as", "less", "much less"]. This was mapped to a binary string 5 places long, where each character is either 1 or 0. The string [1,0,0,0,0] represents the value "much more" whereas the string, [0,0,1,0,0] represents between "the same as".

Two binary outcomes can be compared by noting the position of the set bit in each outcome. Thus, a binary outcome, [1 0 0 0 0], differs from [0 0 0 0 1] by four place units. The set bit in the second number is four places away from the set bit in the former outcome. We call this a four-place contradiction. The average number of examples across all 20 datasets in the Split Up study that had identical inputs and outputs that differed by three or more bit positions totalled 9.37% of the population. However, this ranged from 0% for one dataset to 29.4% for another.

Plausible explanations for the high proportions of contradictions in the financial resources dataset are illustrative of the kinds of issues that emerge when dealing with contradictory data:

(a) *Sampling error.* The sample drawn was not representative of the population of cases with respect to financial resources determination.

(b) *Local stare decisis.* Local stare decisis with respect to financial resources in the Melbourne registry is quite poor.

(c) *Incomplete knowledge.* Relevant factors that predict financial resources are missing. Salary, superannuation, business and resources from family or new partners may not be the only relevant items. Data collection occurred at the wrong level of granularity.

The most likely explanation for the quality of the datasets in the Split Up study is that of sampling error, because the sample size is so small it does not allow us to learn patterns. However, it is interesting to note that the factors considered relevant for determining financial resources are a matter of on-going controversy. One Family Court judge clearly indicated that resources a party receives from his or her family or new partners are irrelevant. However, domain experts are quite adamant that judges do indeed take this factor into account. One practitioner extols female clients to dress modestly for Court appearances in case judges take the view that the prospects for remarriage of a well-dressed divorcee are high and consequently the wife will have inflated financial resources prospects. This might lead to the judge concluding that a well groomed wife requires a lesser split of the common pool than a woman who is more modestly attired, because the judge believes the latter woman has greater future needs.

It is unwise to conclude that local stare decisis has failed merely because of the existence of contradictions. The number of contradictions reflects those examples with identical inputs and outputs that differed by more than 3 bit places. This is a rather crude measure of the level of contradictions. It may suffice for the data-mining purposes of identifying interesting patterns in datasets, but is not sufficient as the basis of sociological inferences.

A more sophisticated measure of contradictions would be to introduce a metric of input similarity. The criteria of 3 [or more bit] places may be too severe for some training sets and too relaxed for others. However, despite these considerations, it seems most plausible to assume that the anomaly noted in the financial resources network is due to sampling error.

6.1.12.5 Inconsistencies Due to New Legislation or Precedents

Broadly speaking, new legislation and new precedent cases impact on the way in which judges make decisions in the following ways:

(a) Making a factor relevant that was previously not mentioned in the decision-making context, or was previously considered irrelevant. So, for example, domestic violence in family law property proceedings was not a relevant consideration prior to Kennon v Kennon.[184]

(b) Making a factor that was once relevant, irrelevant. For example, the ethnic background of a child was once a factor in determining child welfare issues in Australia.[185] It often led to the forcible removal of many aboriginal children from their families. Ethnic background is now no longer considered relevant

(c) Changing the way an outcome is inferred without changing relevant factors. If a new factor is introduced as a relevant consideration by a statue or precedent, then cases prior to the precedent have no data collected about that factor and the way in which the factor impacts on the other factors may be so severe that it invalidates any previous knowledge gleaned from a KDD exercise. In this case, there is little alternative but to re-expose the data to the data-mining exercise. However, this course of action is problematic, because soon after the introduction of the new factor, there are very few cases decided where the factor plays a

---

[184] Kennon V. Kennon FLC 92-757 (1997).

[185] See for example, the Royal Commission into Aboriginal Deaths in Custody's *National Report*, vol. 1, p. 6 Accessible on at this website: http://www.austlii.edu.au/cgi-bin/disp.pl/au/journals/AILR/1997/disp269

prominent role. For example, even though domestic violence is clearly an issue in property proceedings since the case Kennon v Kennon, there have been such a small number of cases since that precedent that involve domestic violence, that the very little data exists.[186]

The constantly changing nature of law would seem, at first sight, to make KDD in law a fruitless process. However, this is not the case. The data transformation act, based on argumentation theories, and described in the next chapter, has the effect of decomposing a major problem into small units. Any change caused by the introduction of a relevant new factor, can be localised to one argument, without impacting on other arguments. It is however, the case that knowledge within the effected argument cannot be relied upon once a change occurs. However, we demonstrate in the next chapter that the impact of this change is not significant as long as argumentation is used to decompose the task into smaller units.

6.1.12.6 How to Deal with Inconsistent Data

Once detected, inconsistent data may be dealt with in one of three ways:

(a) All contradictory cases are removed from the dataset.
(b) No contradictory cases are removed from the dataset.
(c) Some contradictory cases are removed from the dataset, through the use of predefined criteria.

The strategy adopted in the Split Up project was to remove all contradictory cases from the dataset. Although this strategy is less than ideal, it avoids some of the drawbacks of other approaches.

Leaving contradictory examples in the dataset is not appropriate if the sample size is small. If sufficient data is collected, then we could have a greater confidence that the contradictions noted reflect the exercise of discretion in the population and are not anomalies due to the sample selected. For example, if the sample size is increased tenfold, then we would have considerably more confidence that the proportion of contradictions noted in the sample was the proportion that existed in the true population. This would mitigate toward leaving the contradictory cases in the dataset.

When presented with identical inputs, a neural network learns to produce an outcome that is between the contradictory outputs. Whilst this strategy is acceptable, it relies on the existence of substantially large datasets, which is often not feasible in law. The examples used in the Split Up system are by no means plentiful and sampling error cannot be ruled out. A concrete example may clarify this assertion.

---

[186] See for example the court case of Farmer and Bramley [2000] FamCA 1615 (13 December 2000). This reference is to a case in the Family Court of Australia.

The strategy of removing all contradictory examples is preferred to one in which we attempt to determine which of the contradictory cases are unacceptable exercises of discretion. Schild (1995) highlights the need for panels of experts and judges to regularly determine boundaries for acceptable exercises of discretion. Such a panel would have the authority to rule that one or more of the contradictory cases was unacceptable and thus mandate the removal of only those cases.

However, such panels do not exist in most fields of law. The authority to determine which of the contradictory outcomes are acceptable and which are unacceptable, does not reside with any one person or group. It should not be taken by data analysts engaged in the knowledge discovery process. If contradictory cases cannot remain in the dataset and unacceptable examples cannot be discerned from acceptable ones, then the relatively conservative strategy of removing all contradictory cases is the most appropriate one.In domains that are not appreciably less discretionary than Australian family law, it could be said that if two judges arrive at different conclusions after a finding of identical facts, then the judges are using different legal principles or standards. Simply removing contradictory cases from consideration when modelling a domain, runs the very serious risk that important rules, or principles that discern one case from another, are overlooked. However, as illustrated above, two judges in family law could conceivably agree on the facts of a case and also on the appropriate legal principles, yet still reach different conclusions. This is because the principal statute affords the first instance decision maker flexibility in the weighting and combining of factors.

Family law disputes are unusual in that any extreme exercise of discretion is equally undesirable if it favours the husband or the wife.[187] However, in other matters, an extreme exercise of discretion in favour of the plaintiff may be worse (or better) than one in favour of the defendant.

6.1.13 Rule Induction

Andrew Stranieri and John Zeleznikow

6.1.13.1 Preliminaries

An important data-mining algorithm we discuss in this section is *rule induction*. *Inductive reasoning* is the process of moving from specific cases to general rules. A rule induction system is given examples of a problem where the outcome is known. When it has been given several examples, the rule induction system can create rules that are true from the example cases. The rules can then be used to assess other cases where the outcome is not known. New knowledge can be inferred with rule induction. Once rules have been generated they can be reviewed and modified by

---

[187] In many legal domains, there is an onus on a specific party to prove its claims. For example, in criminal law, the prosecution must prove the defendant is guilty beyond reasonable doubt. In taxation law, the taxpayer must prove he met all the guidelines.

the domain expert, providing for more useful, comprehensive and accurate rules for the domain.

Data mining techniques derive from three different sources: artificial intelligence, inferential statistics and mathematical programming. Artificial intelligence research has contributed techniques such as neural networks, rule induction and association rules. Linear, logistic and multiple regression, in addition to algorithms such as K-means and K-medians have been developed by statisticians. Mathematical programming has contributed techniques such as the min-max method from optimisation theory.

The evaluation phase involves the evaluation and interpretation of knowledge discovered as a result of the data-mining phase. The evaluation of any legal system is fraught with theoretical and pragmatic obstacles. Assumptions regarding the nature of knowledge impact on how knowledge discovered using the process are evaluated.

6.1.13.2 Pattern Interestingness

As Han and Kamber (2001) state, a data mining system has the potential to generate thousands of patterns or rules. Not all of the patterns are useful or interesting. Hence we need to define what is an interesting pattern and how can we generate all the interesting patterns and only the interesting patterns.

A pattern is *interesting* if:

- the pattern is easily understood by humans;
- the pattern is valid (with some degree of certainty) on new or test data;
- the pattern is potentially useful;
- the pattern is novel.

A pattern is also interesting if it validates a hypothesis that the user wished to validate, or resemble a user's hunch. An interesting pattern represents knowledge.

Several objective measures of *pattern interestingness* exist, based on the structure of discovered patterns and of the statistics underlying them. The concepts of *support* and *confidence* are examples of objective measures of pattern interestingness. In general, each interestingness measure is associated with a threshold, which may be controlled by the user.

Although objective measures help identify interesting patterns, they are insufficient unless combined with subjective measures that reflect the needs and interests of a particular measure. Subjective interestingness measures are based on user beliefs in the data. These measures find patterns interesting if they are unexpected (contradicting a user's belief) or offer strategic information on which the user can act.

It is often unrealistic and inefficient for data mining systems to generate all of the possible patterns. Instead, user-provided constraints and interestingness measures should be used to focus the search. *Association rule mining* is an example where the use of constraints and interestingness measures can ensure the completeness of mining.

6.1.13.3 Features of, and Difficulties with, Rule Induction Systems

Rule induction algorithms discover rules that are intended to be applicable as generalisations from sample data. Although there are hundreds of *rule induction algorithms*, the one initially developed by Quinlan (1986), called ID3, involves the use of information theory and has been applied to many data-sets. At the basis of a rule induction system is an algorithm which is used to induce rules from a training set. Benefits of rule induction include:

(1) Rule induction has the ability to deduce new knowledge. A human may be able to list all the factors influencing a decision, but may not understand the impact of these factors;
(2) Once rules have been generated they can be reviewed and modified by the domain expert, providing for more useful, comprehensive and accurate rules for the domain.

There are, however, many difficulties in implementing rule induction systems:

(1) Some rule induction programs or training sets may generate rules that are difficult to understand;
(2) Rule induction programs do not select the attributes. Hence, if the domain expert

    a. chooses inappropriate attributes in the creation of the training set,
    b. there are inconsistent examples in the training set or,
    c. there are inadequate examples in the training set, then the rules induced are likely to be of little value;

(3) The method is only useful for rule-based, classification type problems;
(4) The number of attributes must be fairly small;
(5) The training set should not include cases that are exceptions to the underlying law. In law, this requirement may not be feasible;
(6) The training set must be sufficiently large to allow the rule induction system to make valid inferences;

We introduce some sample data in order to illustrate how ID3 works. Table 6.1.13.3.1 displays data related to the property division of six fictitious and overly simple marital splits from our *Split Up* software system for assisting in negotiations for settling a divorce (Zeleznikow & Hunter, 1994). The result attribute is for the percentage split of property obtained by the wife upon divorce.

A common technique for converting data into rules is to initially convert the training set into decision trees. Decision trees can then be converted into rules. A *decision tree* is an explicit representation of all scenarios that can result from a given decision. The root of the tree represents the initial situation, whilst each path from the root corresponds to one possible scenario. A more formal definition is that a decision tree is a problem representation in which:

Table 6.1.13.3.1 Data for property split in family law

Case	Is the property asset rich?	Any children?	Does the wife work?	Equal split
50	Yes	Yes	Yes	Yes
51	No	Yes	No	No
52	No	Yes	No	No
53	Yes	No	Yes	Yes
54	Yes	Yes	No	No
55	No	No	Yes	Yes
56	No	Yes	Yes	No

a. Each node is connected to a set of possible answers;
b. Each non-leaf node is connected to a test that splits its set of possible answers into subsets corresponding to different test results;
c. Each path carries a particular test result's subset to another node.

The exercise of manually extracting rules is difficult with three boolean variables but becomes quite impossible if there are many variables of various types. Furthermore, there is no way of knowing whether all rules have been extracted, or whether the set extracted is a good, or perhaps the best set that could have been extracted. The ID3 rule induction algorithm developed by Quinlan (1986) addresses these concerns by automatically inducing rules from large and complex data sets in a way that resorts to a theoretical construct to extract the best set of rules.

ID3 works by first building a decision tree from the data. Figure 6.1.13.3.1 illustrates a decision tree for the data in Table 6.1.13.3.1. The nodes of a decision tree are variables in the data set. For example, the top most or root node represents the feature *Children*. The arcs from each node are possible values of the variable the node represents. The leaves of the tree represent a distinct category or class of output variable, in this case *Equal split* to be classified.

The extraction of rules from a decision tree is trivial once a rule is generated from every path through the tree. For example, the rules that emerge from each path in Fig. 6.1.13.3.1 are:

- IF *Children* = *no* THEN *Equal split*
- IF *Children* = *yes* and *rich* = *no* THEN *no Equal split*
- If *Children* = *yes* and *rich* = *yes* and wife_works = no THEN *no Equal split*
- If *Children* = *yes* and *rich* = *yes* and wife_works = yes THEN *Equal split*

A number of different decision trees, and therefore, rules, can be derived from the same data set. Figure 6.1.13.3.2 illustrates a different decision tree from the same marital data in Table 6.1.13.3.1. This decision tree has wife works at the root of the tree. Rules derived are quite different from those in the decision tree of Fig. 6.1.13.3.1.

Fig. 6.1.13.3.1 Decision tree for marital data

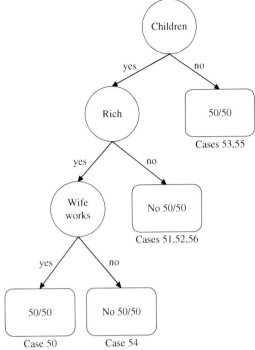

Fig. 6.1.13.3.2 Decision tree for marital data with wife works as root

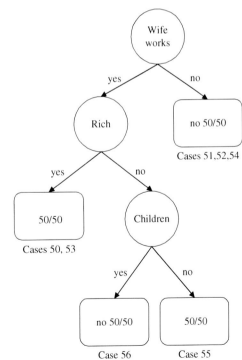

Fig. 6.1.13.3.3 Wife
working as root of the tree

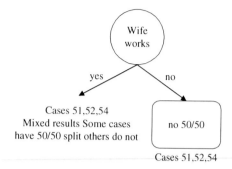

The ID3 algorithm builds a decision tree by following the same three steps:

1. Select an attribute as a node in the tree (often called selecting a feature to split on).
2. Split cases on that attribute's values.
3. Repeat 1 and 2 until leaves contain the same class.

Figure 6.1.13.3.3 illustrates the first stage of ID3 if the feature wife works is selected as the root of the tree. The cases on the no arc are all of the same class so the algorithm stops on that branch. The cases on the yes arc contain a mix of values for Equal split so the algorithm repeats using only those cases.

The key element of the ID3 algorithm is the use of *information theory* advanced by Shannon and Weaver (1949) for the selection of an attribute on which to split. ID3 also has an inductive bias favouring shorter decision trees. This follows the well known principle of *Occam's Razor*,[188] namely: *prefer the simplest hypothesis that fits the data.*

6.1.13.4 Examples of Rule Induction in Law

Vossos et al. (1993), in conjunction with a legal firm, developed the Credit Act Advisory System, CAAS. This is a rule based legal expert system that provides advice regarding the extent to which a credit transaction complies with the Credit Act 1984 (Vic). Although, the majority of rules derive directly from the statute, some factors remain vaguely defined in the Act. For example, the factor "credit was for a business purpose" is not defined by the statute.

IKBALS III (Zeleznikow et al., 1994) is an integrated rule-based/case-based reasoner that operates in the domain of Victorian (Australia) Credit Law. Whilst the deductive reasoner covers the total domain of Credit law, the analogical component is confined to advising as to whether a transaction is for a valid business purpose. In this instance, a rule induction algorithm based on ID3 is invoked to discover new rules from a database of facts from past cases that involved credit for a

---

[188] Developed by William of Occam circa 1320.

business purpose. A rule induction technique discovers rules from past cases where a judge had decided whether credit was extended for a business purpose. These rules help a user determine whether a new, current situation involves credit for a business purpose.

Large numbers of cases were examined by Wilkins and Pillaipakkamnatt (1997) in order to estimate the number of days that are likely to elapse between the arrest of an offender and the final disposition of the case. The time to disposition depends on variables such as the charge, the offender's age, and the county where the arrest was made. Values on more than 30 variables from over 700,000 records from 12 US states were used. Rules were automatically extracted using the ID3 rule induction algorithm. Although Wilkins and Pillaipakkamnatt (1997) themselves had hoped for rule sets that predicted the time to disposition more accurately than their results indicate, this study remains an impressive demonstration of the potential for KDD techniques to contribute to the effective delivery of legal services.

6.1.14   Using Neural Networks

Andrew Stranieri and John Zeleznikow

6.1.14.1   Historical Background

A *neural network* consists of many self-adjusting processing elements cooperating in a densely interconnected network. Each processing element generates a single output signal that is transmitted to the other processing elements. The output signal of a processing element depends on the inputs to the processing element: each input is gated by a weighting factor that determines the influence that the input will have on the output. The strength of the weighting factors is adjusted autonomously by the processing element as data is processed. Neural networks are particularly useful in law because they can deal with

(a) classification difficulties,
(b) vague terms,
(c) defeasible rules, and
(d) discretionary domains.

Whereas neural networks only became popular in computer science decades after traditional computing (*symbolic computing*) did, actually the history of neural networks can be traced back to the mid-century. In the present Section 6.1.13,[189] we are going to consider various kinds of neural networks, and to devote some attention to how they have been applied to law. Already before 1950, the enormous capacity for

---

[189] We are using some material especially from Stranieri and Zeleznikow (2005a).

humans to learn and adapt to new situations led a number of researchers to postulate that a machine, structured in a similar way to the brain, may also learn.

Neural networks resemble the brain in two respects:

1. Knowledge is acquired by the network through a learning process
2. Inter-neuron connection strengths known as weights are used to store the knowledge

Much of the impetus for neural networks came from a recognition that the human brain, structurally, is made of cells called neurons. Neurons are connected to other cells through fibres called axons. Neurons become activated electrically and transfer the electrical impulse down their axons to other neurons. The juncture between the axon and neuron is called a dendrite. The signal travelling along an axon is restricted to a greater or lesser degree by chemicals at the site of the dendrite. The rudimentary structure is illustrated in Fig. 6.1.14.1.1.

McCulloch and Pitts (1943) explored the idea that a machine, structured similarly to the brain, may also learn. They devised a cell that performed the function of a logical AND, and another that performed the function of logical OR. They suggested that higher level reasoning and learning could occur by the combined effect of numerous specialist AND or OR cells. Rosenblatt (1958) generalised the McCulloch and Pitts neural network. He developed a neural network called a *perceptron* that could learn a variety of functions including AND and OR. He did so by suggesting dynamic modification of the weights that represent the strength of interconnections amongst neurons.

Let us consider a perceptron network *topology*. There is a pattern of connections between neurons: 2 input nodes fully connected to 2 hidden nodes, fully connected to one output node. In neural networks, such nodes that are neither input nor output are called *hidden nodes*. There is an *activation function*, f, defined as follows (we give the numerical value by way of example):

If Activation ≥0.7 then Output = 1 else Output = 0

In Fig. 6.1.14.1.2, we see the input activation of the percetron, for given weights. The data of the output activation are shown in Table 6.1.14.1.1. This is how the neurons in the perceptron combine. Let us consider a different input; then in Fig. 6.1.14.1.3, we see the input activation of the percetron. The data of the output activation are shown in Table 6.1.14.1.2.

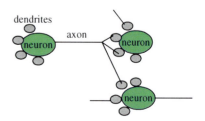

Fig. 6.1.14.1.1 Simple brain structure

Fig. 6.1.14.1.2 How neurons combine: input activation

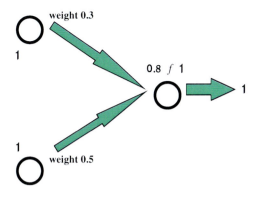

Table 6.1.14.1.1 The data of the output activation of the perceptron given the input of Fig. 6.1.14.1.2

Inputs		Outputs
1	1	1
1	0	0
0	1	0
0	0	0

Fig. 6.1.14.1.3 How neurons combine: input activation

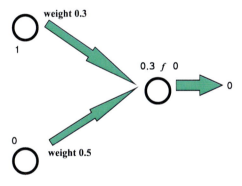

Table 6.1.14.1.2. The data of the output activation of the perceptron of Fig. 6.1.14.1.3

Inputs		Outputs
1	1	1
1	0	0
0	1	0
0	0	0

6.1.14.2 Feed Forward Networks

Neurons are grouped into layers or slabs (Zahedi, 1993). An input layer consists of neurons that receive input from the external environment whilst the output layer consists of neurons that communicate the output of the system to the user or the external environment. Designing the interactions among neurons is equivalent to programming a system to produce an input and produce the desired output. Designing a neural network consists of:

(a) Arranging neurons in various layers;
(b) Deciding the type of connections among neurons of different layers, as well as among the neurons within a layer;
(c) Deciding the way a neuron receives input and produces output;
(d) Determining the strength of connections within the network by allowing the network to learn the appropriate values of connection weights by using a training data set.

The neurons of one layer are always connected to the neurons of at least another layer. There are different types of layer-to-layer or inter-layer connections[190]:

 (i) *Fully connected* – each neuron on the first layer is connected to every neuron on the second layer;
(ii) *Partially connected* – a neuron on the first layer is connected to one or more neurons on the second layer;
(iii) *Feed forward* – the neurons on the first layer send their output to the neurons of the second layer, but they do not receive any input back from the neurons on the second layer;
(iv) *Bi-directional* – in addition to a set of connections going from neurons of the first layer to those on the second layer, there is another set of connections carrying the outputs of the neurons of the second layer into the neurons of the first layer;
(v) *Hierarchical* – the neurons of the lower layer communicate only with the neurons on the next level;
(vi) *Resonance* – in the resonance type of inter-layer connection, the two layers have bi-directional connection, with the added complexity that they continue sending messages across the connections a number of times until a certain condition is achieved.

Nodes in feed forward networks are organised in layers as depicted in Fig. 6.1.14.2.1. In a feedforward network, connections all lie in the same direction from the input layer to the output layer.

The first layer of nodes receives activation input into the network and is called the INPUT LAYER. The input nodes of feed forward networks become activated and forward their activation forwar to nodes in the next layer. Neurons in each layer feed activation forward to subsequent layers. In contrast, recurrent networks, to be discussed in the next section, pass their activation back to input and other nodes to form an internal feedback loop. Of the more than 200 different kinds of neural

---

[190] At http://en.wikipedia.org/wiki/Types_of_artificial_neural_networks many types of neural networks are briefly but usefully surveyed.

Fig. 6.1.14.2.1 Feed forward
neural network architecture
with four layers

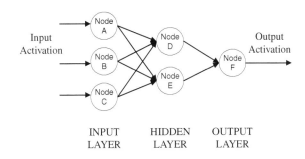

INPUT   HIDDEN   OUTPUT
LAYER   LAYER   LAYER

networks,[191] the feed forward networks are the most commonly used networks. The simplest feed forward network is called the *perceptron*.

Figure 6.1.14.2.2 illustrates a simple perceptron with three neurons. A perceptron has only two layers, an INPUT and an OUTPUT layer though any number of neurons may be defined in each of those two layers. When the two neurons on the left, A and B are activated, they pass their activation on to neuron C. The link between A and C and B and C is marked with a weight that acts to inhibit (or exalt) the signal. The activation coming into C is calculated by summing the inputs multiplied by the weight. For example, if we set the activation of nodes A and B to 1.0 then the activation reaching

$$C\ (1*0.8) + (1*\ 0.8) = 1.6\,\text{units},$$

where 0.8 is the weight between A and C and also between B and C. The activation leaving a node is not simply the activation entering the node. Rather, the raw input activation is passed through a function known as the activation function to determine the output. Rosenblatt (1958) advanced the following activation function:

if input is greater than a threshold
then the activation output is 1
else the activation output is 0.

Learning commences in a *perceptron* by setting weights to any random starting point. One by one, examples are presented to the network and a learning rule

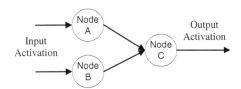

Fig. 6.1.14.2.2 Perceptron

---

[191] At http://en.wikipedia.org/wiki/Types_of_artificial_neural_networks a few of the many kinds of neural networks are surveyed.

determines whether the initial weights will produce the output required. If not, the learning rule modifies the weights. Training stops when a set of weights is found that produce the correct output for all inputs.

The *perceptron* learning rule is simple:

(a) If the output is correct then do not change any weight.
(b) If the output is too small then increase the active weight by a constant.
(c) If the output is too large then decrease the active weight by a constant.

Rosenblatt (1958) demonstrated that starting with any set of initial weights, the *perceptron* learning rule will incrementally modify weights until a set of weights that leads to the desired output is found. The constant, d, is called the learning rate and is generally set between 0 and 1. A large learning rate will modify weights each time by a large amount and lead to faster training. However, as we discuss below, this can also lead to sub-optimal training.

Let us consider the training of the *perceptron* initialised with weights as depicted in Fig. 6.1.14.2.2. The *perceptron* is required to learn from the data in Table 6.1.14.2.1, which contains the *training data*. The training itself is tabulated in Table 6.1.14.2.2.

The *perceptron* can be configured with any number of input and output nodes and the learning rule will still find a set of weights, if one exists, that maps the input into the outputs. A great deal of excitement surrounded the introduction of Rosenblatt's (1958) *perceptron* as a result of the breadth of applications imaginable. However, the excitement waned when Minsky and Papert (1969) illustrated how the *perceptron* fails to find a set of weights if the examples are non-linearly separable. This limits the application of *perceptrons* to little more than trivial problems.

Data is linearly separable if a straight line or plane can be drawn to separate examples into different types of outputs. Please refer again to the figures of Section 6.1.9.3 above, of which the first one illustrates the plot of points that represent X or Y. The shaded points represent the value 1 on (X OR Y). We see clearly that a straight line can be drawn that separates those X and Y data points that have a value 1 on (X OR Y) from those that have a value 0. In contrast, in the second figure of Section 6.1.9.3 we see that a similar straight line cannot be drawn. The exclusive-Or function is said to be non-linearly separable. Minsky and Papert (1969) demonstrated that the Perceptron cannot learn patterns that are non-linearly separable such as the exclusive-Or function.

Table 6.1.14.2.1 Training data for perceptron example

Example	A	B	C
1	1	1	1
2	1	0	0
3	0	1	0
4	0	0	0

Table 6.1.14.2.2 Perceptron training

Example	Input at A	Input at B	Weight A/C	Weight B/C	Raw input at C	Activation at C	Expect activation	Learning rule outcome
1	1	1	0.8	0.8	1.6	1	1	Correct. Leave weights unchanged
2	1	0	0.8	0.8	0.8	1	0	Output is too large so decrease the active weight
3	0	1	0.5	0.8	0.8	1	0	Output is too large so decrease the active weight
4	0	0	0.5	0.5	0.0	0	0	Correct output so leave weights unchanged
1	1	1	0.5	0.5	1.0	1	1	Correct output so leave weights unchanged
2	1	0	0.5	0.5	0.5	0	0	Correct output so leave weights unchanged
3	0	1	0.5	0.5	0.5	0	0	Correct output so leave weights unchanged
4	0	0	0.5	0.5	0.5	0	0	Correct output so leave weights unchanged

Rumelhart, Hinton, and Williams (1986a)[192] and Werbos (1974) demonstrated that non-linearly separable problems can be learnt by a neural network provided that there were at least three layers of neurons as depicted in Fig. 6.1.14.2.1. A network that has a hidden layer cannot be trained with the *perceptron* learning rule.

---

[192] Also see Rumelhart, Hinton, and Williams (1986b).

This is because the error of the nodes in the hidden (middle) layer cannot be known. The error on the output layer is known because the output desired is available in the data set and the network's output is known. However, the desired output on a hidden layer is unknown. Without knowing the error on hidden layers, the weights between input and hidden nodes cannot be adjusted.

6.1.14.3 Back Propagation of Errors

Rumelhart et al. (1986a) developed a new learning rule called the *Generalised Delta Learning Rule* or *back propagation of errors*. In this learning rule, the error on the hidden nodes, though not known, is estimated from the error at the output layer. The mathematics involved can be difficult but the intuition is straightforward. The error of hidden nodes is related to the error of nodes in the next layer. In fact, the error is a derivative of errors in the next layer. The hidden layer error is estimated as the derivative of the output layer error. Using the derivative of the output layer to estimate the hidden layer error turns out to work quite well.

The approach does however assume that the derivative can be calculated on all output values. In order to ensure this, Rumelhart et al. (1986a) applied an activation function that generated a continuous output. The most commonly used activation function is the *sigmoidal* or *S-curve function.*

Since its introduction, the multi-layer feedforward neural network trained with back propagation of errors has been applied in thousands of applications. Many neural network packages are available commercially and others are available as open source programs.[193]

6.1.14.4 Setting Up a Neural Network

Setting up a neural network involves determining a topology. A network topology is a specification of the number of neurons in the input layer, the output layer and in each of the hidden layers. Decisions regarding the number of nodes in the input and in the output layers depend on the way data is to be encoded for the network.

Data encoding refers to the format of data to be input to the neural network. For example, the percentage split argument in our Split Up system for automated assistance in settling divorces encodes:

- A percentage split outcome awarded to the husband, measured with 14 categories; [0–10%, 11–20%, 21–30%, 31–35%, 36–40%, 41–45%, 46–50%, 51–55%, 56–60%, 61–65%, 66–70%, 71–80%, 81–90%, 91–100%] as output.

---

[193] The Usenet news group comp.ai.neural-nets maintains a monthly posting of a Frequently Asked Question (FAQ) that lists packages available. Regardless of the package used, the use of a neural network involves two main steps; defining the network and training it with data. These steps are discussed in the next two sections.

- An input variable that represents the contributions the husband has made relative to the wife with values on a five point scale: [much more, more, same, less, much less].
- An input variable that represents the level of wealth of the marriage. This is also a five point scale: [very high, high, average, low, very little].
- An input variable that represents the future needs the husband has relative to the wife with values on a five point scale: [much more, more, same, less, much less].

Figure 6.1.14.4.1 illustrates the topology with 15 input nodes, 5 hidden nodes and 14 output nodes that implements the percentage split network in the Split Up study. Five of the input nodes encode values for the contribution variable. The next five encode the "needs" variable and the remaining five encode the "wealth" variable. A marriage where the judge considers the husband has contributed *much less* than the wife, has future needs *much more* than the wife and is of *average wealth* is encoded as [0,0,0,0,1,1,0,0,0,0,0,0,0,1,0]. This is quite a sparse encoding as the same values could be encoded in a far more compact way. For example, an encoding scheme illustrated in Table 3 could be used to encode the same case using only three input nodes as [–1,1,–0.5].

Table 6.1.14.4.1 shows a sample encoding in the Split Up system. More compact encoding schemes enable for the development of neural networks with fewer input nodes and connections to be designed. However, the compactness makes training more difficult.

Once the input and output encoding is determined, the next decision involves selecting the number of hidden layers and the number of nodes at each layer.

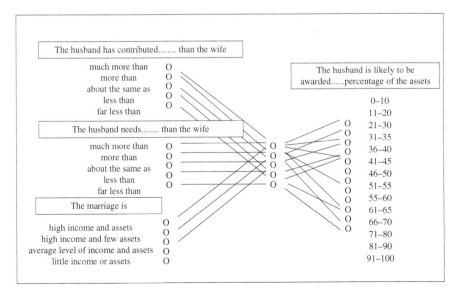

Fig. 6.1.14.4.1   Topology of percentage split network in Split Up

Table 6.1.14.4.1 Sample encoding in Split Up

Data value	Encoding
Much less	−1
Less	−0.5
Same	0
More	0.5
Much more	1
Very high income and assets	1
High income and assets	0.5
Average income and assets	0
Low income and assets	−0.5
Little income or assets	−1

Cybenko (1989) demonstrated that a single hidden layer is sufficient to approximate any (linear or non linear) continuous function. This means that any function between inputs and outputs can be approximated with a neural network that has only one hidden layer. This is not to say that the optimal number of hidden layers is one.

Haykin (1994) reviewed a body of research that has been devoted to the discernment of optimal network architectures. All of the approaches surveyed recognise a relationship between training set size and network size. However, a procedure that can be applied to determine the best topology for any data set has not been found. Lengers (1995) demonstrated a method based on trying many hundreds of different topologies using artificial intelligence search techniques.

Once a neural network topology is defined, training may commence. In the next section, processes are discussed to ensure training occurs effectively.

6.1.14.5 Training a Neural Network

Multi-layer feed-forward networks are commonly trained with the back-propagation of errors learning rule. Training involves exposing a network to a training set that is comprised of data examples, with known outputs. The learning rule adjusts the internal weights of a network in a direction that will minimise the errors made by the network on subsequent exposure to the examples. An *epoch* is completed when all training set examples are presented to the network. Typically, a network with many nodes and examples requires many hundreds, thousands or tens of thousands of epochs before the learning rule discovers a set of weights that will minimise the error made on classifying examples.

Training a neural network is as much art as science and requires the adjustment of many parameters during the training. A plot of the errors at each epoch is useful. This is depicted in Fig. 6.1.14.5.1. The error is often measured as the proportion of the training set examples that are incorrectly predicted by the network. For example, an error rate of 0.75 indicates that for 75% of examples in the training set, the output calculated by the neural network did not match the output that was observed in the training set. We see in Figure 6.1.14.5.1 that the error rate remained quite high for

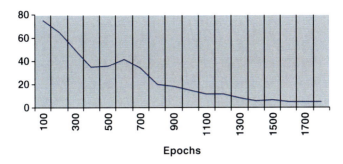

Fig. 6.1.14.5.1   Plot of error rate vs. epochs

the first 600 or so epochs. By epoch 1000 the rate was quite low. Furthermore, it did not alter terribly much between epoch 1300 and epoch 1700.

Training a neural network involves making decisions regarding the following parameters:

- Learning rate
- Momentum
- Bias term
- Stopping criteria

6.1.14.6 Learning Rate

The learning rate specifies the speed with which learning occurs. If this is too high, the weight matrix[194] may be caught in a local minima and never find the set of weights that corresponds to an optimal solution. Figure 6.1.14.6.1 depicts learning as the search for the set of weights that will realise the smallest error. The initial weights, typically selected at random, lead to large errors. As the learning rule adjusts the weights, the error of the network reduces, until no further reduction seems to occur during epoch after epoch. The weights at this point may be the best set that will be discovered; i.e. they represent global minima. However, this cannot be known with certainty because the weights may represent local minima. They do not change from epoch to epoch because any change leads to an error that is worse, so the learning rule re-adjusts the weights back to the local minima.

Many variants introduce additional parameters to tune. Others, such as *quickProp* Fahlman (1989) dynamically modify many of the parameters, including the learning rate.

---

[194] A *weight matrix* "is used to list the weight values (strengths) that exist in the network. The position of a weight within the matrix will define which units the weight connects. Sometimes, more than one weight matrix is used to describe the way in which the units are connected in a network. For example, if units are placed in layers then a single matrix might be used to describe the connections between two layers" (Callan, 1999, p. 226).

Fig. 6.1.14.6.1 Weight space
for error reduction

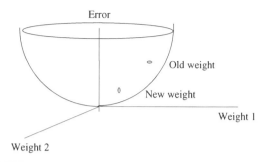

6.1.14.7 Momentum and Bias

There is no theoretical way of knowing whether the weights obtained are the best set possible or are an instance of weights stuck in local minima. The generalised delta rule includes a term known as the *momentum*, to add stability to a network and to guard against being caught in local minima. This term represents the extent to which weight values in previous epochs carry over into subsequent epochs. The user sets the momentum of the learning rule.

Momentum values are usually set between 0.3 and 1. A momentum term set too low will result in a network that may not be able to climb out of local minima regardless of the learning rate adjustments. In addition to momentum, terms known as *bias* represent constants that act as additional inputs to each node. The topology of the network, number of examples and the characteristics of the data all impact on these parameters.

A bias term is included in many implementations of neural networks and can be thought of as a fixed, constant input into each neuron. Bias terms are usually set between −1 and +1. Bias provides additional stability and restricts erratic learning behaviour. Modifying the bias term during training sometimes helps a network seemingly stuck at one error level to begin to make small gains on each epoch.

6.1.14.8 Training Stopping Criteria

Typically, training ceases when a fixed maximum number of epochs are reached or when the network performance has reached a threshold error level. A stopping criteria based on an error threshold is better than one based on number of epochs, but the error should be measured on examples not seen during training. The extent to which the trained network will generalise and perform correctly on cases not in the training set depends on the size and coverage of the training set, the architecture of the network and the complexity of the problem. Two extremes are to be avoided if adequate generalisation is to ensue: *undertraining* and *overtraining*.

Undertraining of a neural network occurs if the network is not exposed to enough examples. Learning is difficult in this situation simply because the training patterns available are not sufficiently representative of the true population of cases.

Another variation of the same extreme occurs if the network is not exposed to the training set for a sufficient number of epochs. The opposite extreme is known as *over-generalisation, overtraining* or *overfitting*. If a sufficiently large network has been exposed to an abundance of examples, far too many times, it can learn each input–output pair so well that it, in effect memorises those cases. The network classifies training set cases well but may not perform so well with cases not in the training set. The network is said to be *overtrained* or *overfitted*.[195]

The objective in training any neural network is to avoid either undertraining or overtraining. This can be achieved in various ways. In the Split Up project, this goal was achieved by pursuing the *cross-validation resampling method*.

However, perhaps the most important consideration in avoiding over-training or undertraining involves the discernment of a domain specific appropriate metric for measuring errors. A measure of classifier performance typically used in classifier training in non-legal domains is the number of examples correctly classified. As Weiss and Kulikowski (1992) point out, this measure of network performance may not be adequate for all domains. They suggest a metric that includes the costs of predicting a positive outcome when the actual outcome was negative (called *false positives*) and the risks associated with predicting a negative outcome when the actual outcome was positive (called *false negatives*).

For example, a network, trained to discern the presence or absence of a disease will ideally, err far more times on the side of predicting a disease when there is none present than it will err in missing a disease that is actually present. A False positive/False negative analysis of errors is not warranted in family law, because the direction of the error is not as critical as it is in medical diagnostic problems. A network that predicts the husband is to receive 60% of the property errs if the judge in the case actually awarded 55%. However, another network errs in a similar and in a no more or less damaging manner if it predicts the husband is to receive 50% of the assets. Thus, the direction of the error is not critical for our purposes.

The stopping criteria for neural networks that model legal domains are invariably subjective. It is unreasonable to expect perfect performance from neural networks in discretionary domains of law, because networks are trained on data from many judges, and thus cannot always exactly predict the outcome of any one judge on

---

[195] A nice exemplification of *overtraining* is found in the Wikipedia entry for "Artificial neural network" (http://en.wikipedia.org/wiki/Artificial_neural_network):

A common criticism of artificial neural networks, particularly in robotics, is that they require a large diversity of training for real-world operation. Dean Pomerleau, in his research presented in the paper "Knowledge-based Training of Artificial Neural Networks for Autonomous Robot Driving", uses a neural network to train a robotic vehicle to drive on multiple types of roads (single lane, multi-lane, dirt, etc.). A large amount of his research is devoted to (1) extrapolating multiple training scenarios from a single training experience, and (2) preserving past training diversity so that the system does not become overtrained (if, for example, it is presented with a series of right turns — it should not learn to always turn right). These issues are common in neural networks that must decide from amongst a wide variety of responses.

all cases. The measurement of the performance of a neural network, by counting the number of correctly classified examples, leads to a measure of network performance that may be too fine-grained for legal applications and thus increases the risk of over training. Given that a perfect performance is unlikely, other acceptable criteria must be adopted. There seems no theoretical basis to underpin such criteria, so acceptable criteria must be selected heuristically.

A good measure of a neural network's performance in a discretionary legal domain includes an indication of the magnitude of the error. An error of 5% either way when estimating a judge's decision about the percentage of marital assets to be awarded to the wife is, in our view, tolerable. On the other hand, a network which outputs a percentage split which deviates by 20% from that given by a judge, is assumed to have erred. Although the cut off point for declaring that an error has occurred is necessarily subjective it is important that a metric be discerned which can be applied consistently to all neural networks in the Split Up system.

The metric adopted in the Split Up study makes use of the following encoding scheme. Consider a network with five binary outputs. A network output of [1,0,0,0,0] for a particular example indicates that the first bit is set. If the actual output has the fifth bit set [0,0,0,0,1], we consider the network to have made an error of magnitude four. If the actual output sets two bits such as it would in [0,1,1,0,0] we take the average of the positions of the set bits. In this case we say the actual bit set is in position 2.5. If the expected output was [0,0,1,0,0] then the error is of magnitude 0.5 (i.e., in the range between 2.5 and 3). The use of an error heuristic based on the position of the set bit has advantages in that it is simple, easy to calculate and has a direct association with the interpretation placed on the bits. Encoding the five values "much more", "more", "about the same as", "less" and "much less" as bit string could be achieved with as few as three bits. However, a five bit number enables the position of the set bit to correspond directly with one of the values.

The error heuristic we use is central to the training of the neural networks used in the Split Up project. Training is halted in Split Up networks once the proportion of errors of magnitude three or more is observed to be 3% or less. An error of magnitude three represents a significant error for most neural networks. However, the cost of totally eliminating these errors is high, in that the additional training required increases the risk of overtraining.

A number of neural networks in legal domains have been trained successfully, although the use of neural networks in law is far from widespread. In the next section we review these attempts in order to argue that many neural networks have not been appropriately trained, and further inappropriate data has been used.

6.1.14.9 Application to Law of Neural Networks

Hunter (1994) notes that neural networks are essentially statistical. By this he means that associations between inferred outcomes and facts are represented as statistical associations captured as inter neuron weights. As such, connectionism derives support from the same jurisprudential theories as does any statistical method.

In the 1960s, Kort (1964) and Nagel (1964) both developed statistical methods for analysing cases. Their goal was to predict decisions. Both authors advanced methods for determining how the courts weighed individual facts to reach a decision. Kort's method was based on the solving of simultaneous equations in order to ascertain the weight of factors, while Nagel used discrimminant analysis. These authors validated their statistical approach by drawing on the jurisprudence of legal realists. As stated in chapter one, we claim that connectionism can be useful for resolving situations that involve open texture, yet their effectiveness depends on the type of open textured situation studied.

The classification of situations, characterised as open textured by Prakken (1993a), provides a useful framework for a survey of neural network approaches. We argue that neural networks are best applied to situations that involve the open texture inherent in judicial discretion though some inroads can also be made toward resolving classification difficulties. To recapitulate, Prakken (1993a) identifies situations characterised as open textured as those that involve classification ambiguities, defeasible rules or vague terms. We appended the situation characterised by judicial discretion to that list. In the following, we shall survey notable applications of neural networks to each of these open textured situations.

PROLEXS (Walker et al., 1991) operates in the domain of Dutch landlord-tenant law. It operates with four knowledge groups, each of which have their own knowledge representation language and dedicated inference engine:

- legislation: a rule-based system[196];
- legal knowledge;
- expert knowledge; and
- case law: using case-based retrieval.[197]

PROLEXS resorts to neural networks in case selection, case abstraction and credit assignment. The PROLEXS perceptron dealt with apartment suitability and had as its inputs the age of the tenant, the disability of the tenant, the quality of the apartment and the presence of an elevator. Various weights were assigned, and some learning was attempted. Rather than rely on manual specification of weights, the use of a perceptron allowed for automatic weight generation, avoiding the danger of manual specification of weights. The use of hidden layers in a neural network can improve the accuracy of the predictions generated by the network.

Borges, Borges, and Bourcier (2002) use neural networks to model the legal reasoning of judges at the Court of Appeal, Versailles, France. As does Hunter (1994),

---

[196] Historically within AI & Law, rule-based systems came under criticism because of too rigid interpretation of legislation, leaving no room for interpretation. Bench-Capon (1993a = 1994 [at a conference and a journal, both of them with Indira M. Carr as editor]) argued that rule-based representations of legal knowledge can nevertheless be acceptable, if the use made of the rules is sophisticated.

[197] For retrieving legal cases, see e.g. Zeng, Wang, Zeleznikow, and Kemp's (2005) "Knowledge Representation for the Intelligent Legal Case Retrieval".

they claim that one of the main obstacles to the use of neural networks in legal domains, is the inability of such networks to justify their decision making. They develop a multilevel perceptron justification algorithm. They claim that their models can be used for improving the self-justification process of a decision-maker and for predicting or suggesting new lines of reasoning based on implicit knowledge. Borges, Borges, and Bourcier (2002) use employment contracts cases. Borges et al. (2003) study the topography of a multilayer perceptron with backpropagation algorithm to improve connectionist classification.

Hobson and Slee (1994)[198] study a handful of cases from the U.K. theft act and also use neural networks to predict the outcome of theft cases. They used a series of leading cases in British theft law to train a network to predict a courtroom outcome. Results they obtained were less than impressive which they attributed to flaws in the use of neural networks in legal reasoning. This criticism was too harsh. Neural networks have much to offer knowledge discovery from databases (KDD). However, any application of KDD to data drawn from the legal domain must be carefully performed. Due attention is required so that key assumptions made at each phase of the KDD process are clearly articulated and have some basis in jurisprudence. For example, the cases used in the Hobson and Slee study involved leading cases. We believe that leading cases are not well suited to a KDD exercise involving neural networks.

6.1.14.10 Application to Classification

Bench-Capon (1993b) applied neural networks to a problem that involved open texture in the manifestation of classification difficulties. He identified six variables as inputs into a neural network that modeled the imaginary domain of social security entitlements in the United Kingdom. The output represented whether or not an applicant was entitled to social security benefits. The open texture in this domain manifested itself as difficulties inherent in classifying whether the applicant was entitled to social security benefits.

Presented with cases that were not used for training, the neural network was able to suggest an outcome that reflected the weightings of input variables in prior cases. However, limitations were apparent in that, in some cases the network was clearly in error. For example for every case in the training set that output a social security benefit, it had, as one of the inputs, the fact that the applicant was over a certain age. This was because the applicant's age was a limiting condition for the granting of a benefit. However, when dealing with some unseen cases, the neural network granted a benefit to some applicants under the limiting age.

A neural network cannot be guaranteed to perform correctly on cases that were not present in the training set. If trained appropriately, then we may estimate the proportion of all possible cases that will be classified correctly. However, we will not know with certainty which class of cases will be incorrectly classified. This

---

[198] We already referred to that study in Sections 6.1.11.1 and 6.1.11.5 above.

is not necessarily a condemnation of neural networks. The limiting condition in the Bench-Capon's study (1993b) is more aptly represented as a rule. Furthermore, the rule seems to be one, which is applied in an all or nothing, way: without any exceptions. In law, very few rules in operate in this way. The Bench-Capon study can thus be seen to apply neural networks to a classification task that is more obviously suited to a series of simple rules.

Warner (1994) does not explicitly claim that neural networks have the potential to resolve situations in law characterised by classification difficulties. Rather, he maintains that neural networks are appropriate to use in modelling law, because they exhibit the capacity to emulate the parallel reasoning process of a lawyer. He argues that legal problem solving behaviour is often described as a serial process that progresses in a step-by step fashion, from the initial problem description, to the goal of the reasoning. Yet, legal reasoning involves a parallel process of assimilating facts to reach partial solutions and assimilating partial solutions to reach a final solution. Warner's rationale for the use of neural networks in law is open to criticism, in that the distinction between problem solving performed in series and in parallel, is by no means clear. For instance, it is not clear why a parallel process should succeed in law where a serial process will fail. Furthermore, according to Hunter (1994), there is little support from jurisprudential theorists for the notion that legal reasoning is, in any sense, parallel.

Despite the shortcoming in the rationale that Warner (1994) uses to justify the use of neural networks, the actual task to which he applies neural network, is one that attempts to deal with classification difficulties in the domain of consideration in contract law. His network attempts to classify a case according to whether the contract involved a consideration. The uses of neural networks for modelling legal reasoning by Bench-Capon and Warner are similar, in that each of these authors applies neural networks to resolve classification difficulties; difficulties that contribute to a perception of law as open textured. The application of neural networks to legal reasoning by Philipps (1991) and by Thagard (1989) differ from these approaches, in that their studies can be seen to apply connectionism in an attempt to resolve defeasible rules.

6.1.14.11 Application to Rule Defeasibility

Philipps (1989) demonstrates how neural networks can assist in dealing with defeasible rules by examining a hypothetical example taken from Roman Law. The will of a hypothetical citizen whose wife was pregnant read:

> If a son is born to me let him be heir in respect of two thirds of my estate, let my wife be heir in respect of the remaining part; but if a daughter is born to me, let her be heir to the extent of a third; let my wife be heir to the remaining part.

This hypothetical will can be seen to involve two rules, one governing the distribution of the estate in the event of the birth of a daughter and the other governing the distribution of the estate in the event of the birth of a son. Rather than representing these rules as clauses in a logic program or rules in a rule based reasoner, Philipps trained a feed forward neural network with back-propagation of errors to deliver the correct output when exposed to scenarios that involved the birth of a boy and the birth of a girl, but not the birth of both. He then put forward a case that necessarily defeats these rules; one in which twins, a boy and a girl are born. In this case, the network that had not been exposed to this scenario during training, produced an outcome that indicated the mother receives two shares, the son receives three and the daughter receives four.

Philipps argues this outcome is reasonable, in that it represents an equilibrium based on past cases. However, Hunter (1994) points out that the notion of equilibrium with past cases is jurisprudentially flawed. There is no notion of moral correctness, nor any appeal to reason, that reflect higher principles. We agree with Hunter on this point, because we believe that, in this Roman Law example, reasoning is best modelled as deductions made from known legal rules. However, this is not the case in discretionary domains. Another instance of the application of connectionism for modelling defeasible rules in law can be seen in the work of Thagard (1989).

He proposed a theory of explanatory coherence that aims to model the way in which competing hypotheses are supported by available evidence. Some nodes in the network he developed represent propositions about each hypothesis. Other nodes represent available evidence. Links exist between evidential nodes and hypothesis nodes. Each has an associated weight that may be excitary or inhibitory. To determine which hypothesis has more support, the network is activated. Nodes feed activation (or inhibition) to other nodes which provide feedback to each other, until an equilibrium is reached. The network is then settled.

Thagard (1989) trialed his ECHO program (cf. Section 2.2.1 above in this book) on a murder case in which the competing hypotheses were X was innocent and X was guilty. Propositions associated with these hypothesis included C broke his hand punching X and C broke his hand falling on a rock. Thagard's propositions did not include rules from statutes or from legal principles, but could easily have been extended thus. Propositions that reflected statutes or principles would compete for activation with other propositions and those hypotheses that remained most active after the network settled, would be deemed to have, in Thagard's terms, more explanatory coherence.[199]

In this way, the Thagard approach can be interpreted as one which attempts to resolve those situations in law that are characterised as open textured, because of the presence of defeasible rules. The Thagard approach is certainly intuitively appealing, but requires much further research. Attempts by Thagard and Philipps to use neural networks to model reasoning with defeasible rules can be seen to be overly ambitious if we relate their attempts to the use of Toulmin argument structures (for which, see Sections 3.2 and 3.11 in this book).

Inputs and outputs of their neural networks correspond to datum and claim of the Toulmin Argument Structure. The force, rebuttal, warrant and backing cannot be represented using conventional connectionist systems. So, in the Roman law

---

[199] *Coherence in finite argument systems* is the subject of Dunne and Bench-Capon (2002).

example, commentators such as Hunter are unlikely to accept the neural network conclusion, because it cannot supply a warrant or supporting evidence. This does not point to a flaw with the use of connectionism in law, but, in our view only high-lights that the procedure used to infer a claim is only one component of the structure used to persuade a reader of the feasibility of the claim. This opacity of neural networks calls for an alternative provision of transparency for the advice given by a knowledge-based systems. This is why in our Split Up system, where calcula-tions are by means of neural networks, we have a separate automated generation of explanations for the output obtained by the neural networks.

6.1.14.12 Vagueness

Law is replete with terms that are vague.[200] A concept such as "within reasonable limits", specified in a statute, is labelled a vague term by Brkic (1985). What is "a reasonable period"? This is vague. The presence of vague terms was enough to entice Brkic (1985) to condemn the use of deduction to model legal reasoning. To our knowledge, connectionism has not been applied to tasks that involve vague terms.[201] Vague terms present difficulties, because there are a number of senses in which a term may be considered vague. A statutory concept such as "within reasonable limits" may signify that a decision-maker has recourse to an element of discretion in much the same way that a Family Court judge has some flexibility in distributing marital property. If all relevant principles, rules and factors were made clear to a decision maker who then had to weight the factors in order to determine whether a current case fell within reasonable limits, we would be inclined to regard the resolution of vague terms in much the same way as we see the allocation of discretion.

However, the above paragraph does not describe not all vague concepts appear-ing in statutes. A vague concept such as within reasonable limits, may be included in a statute, with no supplementary material that would assist a decision maker in defining the term. Legislative drafters often prefer this flexibility, so that Courts will lay down principles to guide future decision makers. A connectionist system can conceivably be developed that has, as inputs, the facts of a case and outputs one of a permitted number of uses of the vague concept. This use of connectionism is not dissimilar to the use of connectionism to resolve classification difficulties.

Transvaluationism is an account of *vagueness* proposed by philosopher Terry Horgan. Horgan states (2010, p. 67):

> The philosophical account of vagueness I call "transvaluationism" makes three fundamen-tal claims. First, vagueness is logically incoherent in a certain way: it essentially involves

---

[200] For example, see George Christie's (1964) "Vagueness and Legal Language". It is not merely the terms that are vague. Some concepts as well are confused and confusing, he argued concerning the concept "due process of law", in an article (Christie, 1984b) which aptly appeared in a book entitled *Les notions à contenu variable en droit*.

[201] It is not only terms that are vague. See Jonathan Yovel's discussion of vagueness in Section 4.6.2.2 above, in the context of his treatment of *relevance*.

mutually unsatisfiable requirements that govern vague language, vague thought-content, and putative vague objects and properties. Second, vagueness in language and thought (i.e., semantic vagueness) is a genuine phenomenon despite possessing this form of incoherence — and is viable, legitimate, and indeed indispensable. Third, vagueness as a feature of objects, properties, or relations (i.e., ontological vagueness) is impossible, because of the mutually unsatisfiable conditions that such putative items would have to meet.[202]

6.1.14.13 Application to Modelling Discretionary Legal Domains

The application of neural networks to the task of learning the way in which judges weight relevant factors in a *discretionary* domain[203] does not presume more from neural networks than they can deliver. As we have seen, the use of neural networks to resolve classification ambiguities or to mimic reasoning with defeasible rules makes questionable jurisprudential assumptions. We claim that neural networks can be appropriately applied to learn the way in which judges, have combined factors in past cases. To do this, we adopt a legal realist stance that variations displayed by individual judges on similar cases in a discretionary domain, are not the result of the application of different legal principles. However, a number of obstacles must be overcome if this paradigm is to be usefully applied. Hunter (1994) and Aikenhead (1996) identify prominent flaws in the way in which neural networks have been trained for use in past legal applications.

The concerns they raise focus on the explication deficiencies of neural networks, the assembly of appropriate data and methods used for the training of neural networks. We successively survey these concerns in order to describe the steps we have taken to ensure our neural networks are appropriately trained. The lack of explication facility inherent in the connectionist paradigm weighs heavily against their use in law. To overcome this problem we need to return to jurisprudence in order to discover how explanations fit into the scheme of legal reasoning.

The jurisprudence of the legal realism movement[204] is central to the application of the connectionist paradigm, in that this movement advocates a separation of

---

[202] More can be found s.v. "Transvaluationism" in the Glossary at the end of this book.

[203] *Discretionary*, as opposed to *mandatory*. In particular, as applied to judicial decision-making: what is up to the judge to decide, unfettered by mandatory rules, is discretionary. See Section 4.2.5. Meikle and Yearwood (2000) are concerned with the provision of support for the exercise of discretion, and how the need to avoid the risk of adversely affecting it when using a computer tool, inspired the structural design of EMBRACE, a decision support system for Australia's Refugee Review Tribunal. Leith (1998) has warned about the risks, with AI applications to law, that judicial discretion be restricted, if computer tools come to be involved in the judicial decision-making process.

[204] "Legal realists are jurisprudes for whom the reliance on rules is an anathema. They argue that judges make decisions for a range of reasons which cannot be articulated or at least are not apparent on the face of the judgement given" (Stranieri & Zeleznikow, 2005a, Glossary). See, e.g., Rumble (1965), in the history of ideas. Wilfrid Rumble began his paper by stating (ibid., p. 547, his brackets):

> Even now, the nature of American legal realism is the subject of widespread and often intense disagreement. Its significance has, to be sure, seldom been denied. Most jurists would agree with the evaluation of Mr. Justice Cardozo that "the most distinctive product of the last decade [the 1920's] in the field of jurisprudence is the rise of a group of scholars

the decision making process from the process of justifying that decision. Thus, reasoning to reach a conclusion and explaining that conclusion can be seen as two distinct processes. Drawing this distinction enables us to design a system that uses neural networks to infer conclusions and another system to explain the conclusions. A decision is made on the basis of facts inputted. We assume that rules and principles are not necessarily factors for arriving at a decision. However, rules, principles and the facts of a case, in addition to the decision itself, are necessary in order for a justification to be advanced.

Discretion, defined as the ability of individual judges to assign different relative weights to relevant factors is accommodated in the first phase, the reaching of a conclusion. The second phase, justification of the decision does not necessarily involve a reproduction of the reasoning steps nor does it necessarily require that all factors that were relevant, even if they are highly weighted, are reported as a justification of the decision.

A barrister who suspects that her client will condemn her performance, will be tempted to offer the client a conservative prediction. Yet, that factor cannot be included in an explanation without defeating the purpose. The justification phase necessarily requires a reference to rules or principles. Decisions explained without reference to established statutes or precedents are totally untenable in liberal democracies. Legal concepts are useful tools for justifying a decision and can be applied by an artificial reasoner to justify or explain any decision. A family law expert displays the same capacity. Given the same set of facts an expert is able to justify a property decision of 70% to the husband and yet, is also able to create a justification for an output of 50% to the husband for the same case.

6.1.14.14   Unsupervised Neural Networks

The neural networks we have previously discussed are *supervised neural networks.* This means that during training the network is presented with the example and the output is learnt for that example. For instance, during training of the Split Up percentage split network, input values for contributions, needs and wealth are presented to one network along with a percentage split of assets that the trial judge awarded in that case.

In supervised learning, the system developer tells the system what the correct is, and the system determines weights in such a way that once given the input it would produce the desired output. The system is repeatedly given facts about various cases, along with expected outputs. The system uses the learning method to adjust the weights in order to produce outputs similar to the expected results. The bulk of our discussion on neural networks for data-mining legal data sets involved a consideration of supervised neural networks.

---

styling themselves realists". Nonetheless, the contours of this "product" are still not universally agreed upon. Even the legal realists were baffled. The confession of one — "I do not know what it [legal realism] means" — has been echoed by others.

In *unsupervised learning* the neural network is not presented with inputs and outputs. Rather, the entire data set is presented to the network. The network is required to cluster examples into groups of similar examples. There are many types of unsupervised networks including Self-Organising Maps, Grossberg nets, In-star, out-star, Bi-directional Associational Maps and Hopfield networks (Hecht-Nielson, 1990). There is a variety of applications (either potential or actual) of unsupervised neural networks in data mining, including for the purposes of crime detection.Unsupervised neural networks known as *self-organising maps* or *Kohonen networks* have been applied in a text mining context by Merkl and Schweighofer (1997), Schweighofer and Merkl (1999) and Merkl et al. (1999). Self-organising maps will be discussed in the next section.

6.1.14.15 Text Clustering with Self-Organising Maps (Kohonen Neural Networks)

Kohonen (1982) first introduced *self-Organising maps* (*SOM*) or *Kohonen networks*. The basic SOM architecture consists of two layers of nodes as illustrated in Fig. 6.1.14.15.1. Each input is connected to every output node. A randomly assigned weight is associated with each connection. The inputs nodes represent feature values that distinguish one example from another.

The data miner sets the size of the SOM output grid. The SOM in Fig. 6.1.14.15.1 contains 25 nodes in a 5*5 configuration. There is no systematic way to determining the optimal size of an output grid. Trial runs with grids of varying sizes are generally performed until an appropriate configuration is adopted.

During training, feature vectors are presented to the SOM. Figure 6.1.14.15.2 illustrates the presentation of a first example that has values [5,5]. Those values represent activation that flows forward along each connection and are attenuated by the weight associated with each connection. The weights are initially set randomly. Each output node receives slightly different activation because the weights are initially different. One of the output nodes received the greatest activation and is called the *winner*. The weights between the input and the winner are increased so as to ensure the same node is the winner if the same input is presented again. Weights to nodes near the winner are also increased with the use of a *neighbourhood function* illustrated in Fig. 6.1.14.15.3. Figure 6.1.14.15.4 illustrates the presentation of the second example.

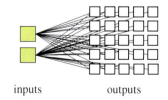

Fig. 6.1.14.15.1 Basic self organising map architecture

inputs   outputs

Fig. 6.1.14.15.2 Presentation
of an example to a SOM

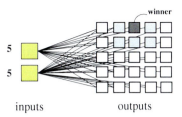

Fig. 6.1.14.15.3 Weights
strengthened after first
example

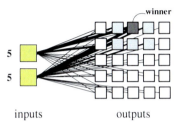

Fig. 6.1.14.15.4 Presentation
of second example

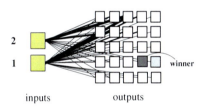

Fig. 6.1.14.15.5 Presentation
of a third example to SOM

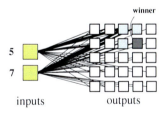

Figure 6.1.14.15.4 illustrates that a different node emerges upon presentation of quite different inputs. The weights between that winner and the inputs are strengthened. Figure 6.1.14.15.5 illustrates the presentation of an input that is more similar to the first instance than the second instance.

The winning node in Fig. 6.1.14.15.5 is closer to the winning node after presentation of the first example than the second example because the example [5,7] is more similar to [5,5] than it is to [2,1].

After repeated exposure to a sufficiently large number of cases, different areas on the output grid will reflect different clusters of examples. Manual examination is required in order to label regions on the grid to reflect the meaning of each cluster.

The distance between regions on the grid represents the similarity between clusters. For example, the top left region of the output grid in the study by Merkl and Schweighofer (1997) corresponded to cases that involved chemical weapons and was labelled "arms control". The bottom centre region was labelled "Human rights" and corresponded to documents on treaties and torture.

Merkl and Schweighofer (1997) applied a hierarchical variation to the standard SOM. Miikkulainen (1993) introduced a *hierarchical self organising map* where the output grid is used as an input grid to another SOM and that output is used as input to yet another SOM. This has benefits in that the higher-level grids represent more abstract clusters. More pragmatically, training time is substantially reduced. For example, the top level grid in the study by Merkl and Schweighofer (1997) discovered four key clusters in public international law: humanitarian law, human rights, environment law and other matters.

6.1.15 Using Fuzzy Logic

Andrew Stranieri and John Zeleznikow

Natural language has many terms that are used frequently but are not precisely defined. For example, the term "young man" is not precisely defined yet is useful in many contexts. Fuzzy logic models the way in which imprecise terms in rules can combine with other imprecise terms and imply conclusions which are also often not precisely defined. To appreciate fuzzy logic and its potential application in law, we must first understand its precursor, fuzzy set theory. Zadeh (1965)[205] introduced the idea of a fuzzy set as a more general form of classical sets. In classical set theory an element either is, or is not, a member of a set. The boundary that demarcates the set from other sets is crisp.

In fuzzy set theory, an element belongs to a set to a degree that ranges from 0, which is equivalent to not in the set, to 1, which means the element is clearly in the set. Values between 0 and 1 indicate varying degrees of membership. Table 6.1.15.1 illustrates elements that represent age in years of men. Alongside each element is a rating for the degree of membership of each element to the set "young man".

A person who is 15 years old is clearly a member of the young person set whereas the 25-year-old person is less clearly a member of the same set. Being 25 years old

Table 6.1.15.1 Degree of membership of "young person set"

Age in years	0	5	10	15	20	25	30	35	40	45	50	55	60
Degree of membership	1	1	1	1	0.9	0.7	0.6	0.4	0.3	0.2	0	0	0

---

[205] Also see, e.g., Yager and Zadeh (1994), Ross (1995).

would be very young for being a champion marathon runner, but quite old for being a champion swim sprinter.

We are not implying that there is uncertainty regarding the person's age. We may be quite certain the person is 25 yet express the view that the person is not unequivocally young.

Interpreting the degree of membership figure as an uncertainty about membership of the set is also misleading. We can be quite certain that a man aged 25 belongs to the set with a degree that can be quantified as 0.7.

Chen (2001) states that there are at least five important explanations on the role of fuzzy logic in data mining:

1. *Knowledge Granulation* – Fuzzy sets are conceptual extensions of set theory and are primarily geared towards various aspects of knowledge representation and predetermining most of the activities of data mining, especially knowledge granulation. Fuzzy sets are linguistic information granules capturing concepts with continuous boundaries. They are one of a number of contributing technologies towards data mining.
2. *Better Tolerance* – Fuzzy sets exploit uncertainty in an attempt to make system complexity manageable. Fuzzy logic can deal with incomplete, noisy and imprecise data and is helpful in developing better uncertain models of the data than is possible with traditional methods. Since fuzzy systems can tolerate uncertainty and utilise language-like vagueness to smooth data, they may offer robust, noise-tolerant models or predictions in situations where precise data is unavailable or too expensive.
3. *Data Classification* – Fuzzy logic works at a high level of abstraction and is thus useful for data mining systems performing classification (Han & Kamber, 2001).
4. *"Indirect" Contribution to Data Mining through its relationship with Artificial Neural Networks* – Fuzzy set theory by itself is neither a machine learning nor a data mining technique. However, fuzzy set theory does have a close relationship with the weights used in artificial neural networks.
5. *Increased chance of Knowledge Discovery Due to Vagueness* – Fuzzy set theory can be combined with other data mining and uncertain reasoning approaches. By allowing vagueness, the chance of uncovering hidden knowledge is enhanced.

As Phillips and Sartor (1999) note, a judge must decide on legally relevant situations, which can only be described in indeterminate terms. The decisions must be determinate and can often only be expressed as a numerical quantity. But what is indeterminancy? Indeterminancy is not uncertainty. To quote the Roman maxim — *Mater semper certa est, pater semper incertus* — one can never be certain that a man was the real father of a child, even if he was the mother's husband. But the concept of a father is certainly determinate. Phillips and Sartor (1999) argue that fuzzy logic is an ideal tool for modelling indeterminancy. Legrand (1999) has developed guidelines for the use of Fuzzy Logic to model legal reasoning.

Phillips (1993) has used fuzzy reasoning in modelling traffic accident law. Borgulya (1999) also uses fuzzy logic methods to model decisions made by judges regarding traffic accidents. He provides information for courts and lawyers about the seriousness of an actual case compared to previously tried cases. Xu, Kaoru, and Yoshino (1999) constructed a case-based reasoner to provide advice about contracts under the United Nations Convention on Contracts for the International Sale of Goods (CISG). Shapira (1999) investigates the attitude of Jewish law sources from the second to fifth centuries to the imprecision of measurement. He argues that the Talmudic sources were guided by primitive insights compatible with fuzzy logic presentation of the inevitable uncertainty involved in measurement.

6.1.16 *Using Genetic Algorithms in Data Mining*

Andrew Stranieri, John Zeleznikow, and Ephraim Nissan

6.1.16.1 Evolutionary Computing and Genetic Algorithms

Evolutionary computing refers to the task of a collection of algorithms based on the evolution of a population toward a solution of a certain problem. These algorithms can be used in applications requiring the optimisation of a certain multidimensional function. The population of possible solutions evolves from one generation to the next, ultimately arriving at a satisfactory solution to the problem.

The various algorithms differ in the way in which a new population is generated from the present one, and in how the members are represented within the algorithm. The two most significant evolutionary computing techniques are:

(1) *Genetic Algorithms* – Genetic algorithms are general-purpose search algorithms that use principles derived from genetics to solve problems. A population of evolving knowledge structures that evolve over time – through competition and controlled variation – is maintained. Each structure in the population represents a candidate solution to the concrete problem and has an associated fitness to determine which structures are used to form new ones in the competition. The new structures are created using genetic operators such as crossover and mutation. Genetic algorithms are very useful in search and optimisation problems, because of their ability to exploit the information accumulated about an initially unknown search space in order to bias subsequent searches into useful subspaces, namely their robustness.

(2) *Evolutionary Algorithms* – Evolutionary algorithms are computer-based problem solving systems that use computational models of evolutionary processes as key elements in their design and implementation. Examples include evolutionary programming, evolution strategies, classifier systems and genetic programming. Evolutionary algorithms share a common conceptual base of simulating the individual structures via processes of selection, mutation and reproduction.

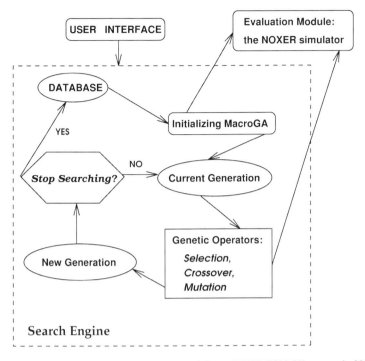

Fig. 6.1.16.1.1 The genetic algorithm in the control flow of FUELCON (Nissan et al., 2001)

For example, Fig. 6.1.16.1.1, which is from Nissan, Galperin, Soper, Knight, and Zhao (2001), shows the control flow of FUELCON, an expert system for designing how to refuel the core of a nuclear reactor. It is based on a genetic algorithm called *MacroGA*. Each individual solution is a configuration of fuel units (themselves assemblies of rods) in the grid which is the cross-section of the core of the reactor (in one-eighth symmetry). Solutions were evaluated by means of NOXER, a software tool in reactor physics. Figure 6.1.16.1.2, which is also from Nissan et al. (2001), shows how FUELCON's population of solutions (the "cloud" of solutions) eventually moves into a better region, and contains the optimal solution. The method was *macroevolution*, because the population of competitors is a population of clouds of solutions, thus a set of sets, a population of populations.

The following is quoted from Zhao, Knight, Nissan, Petridis, and Soper (1998), and explains the genetic algorithm in FUELCON (this was the doctoral project of Jun Zhao, supervised by Nissan and others):

In macroevolution, a number of species co-evolve. In the scheme of macroevolution we have adopted,

- A number of species are used, with no dominant species.
- Migration is controlled by a migration rate (or probability) determining when migration occurs, the number of migrants per migration (normally two), and a migration topology, such as the so-called ring or line topology.

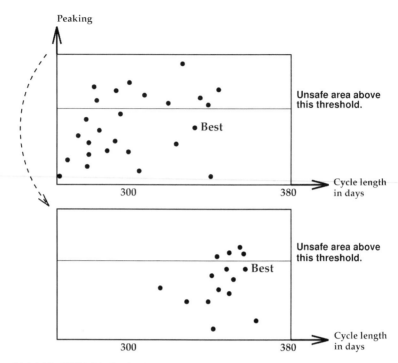

Fig. 6.1.16.1.2 FUELCON's cloud of solutions moves to a better region, and the optimal solution is found (Nissan et al., 2001). Each individual solution (which is a configuration of fuel in the core of the reactor) is shown as a *dot*

- Migrants are the best individuals in the source species, and they will compete with all the individuals within the destination species for survival; the same number of least fit individuals will then be removed.
- Each species has a different crossover and mutation rate, which are generated from a mutation rate range and a crossover rate range.
- The ranking selection method is applied to all species.
- It is only as a particular case, that all species may happen to use the same crossover and mutation operators.

More generally, such uniformity is not necessary (ibid.). The same paper also explained:

In the macro genetic algorithm, the first step is to initialize its parameters, and a set of species. At this stage, the probability of migration is set, each species is initialized in terms of selection operator, crossover operator, mutation operator, population size, and crossover and mutation rates. After initialization, all species evolve in parallel, and migrations take place at each generation. At each generation, the best individual is recorded and checked. If the current best individual is acceptable in terms of fitness, then a termination message, "Stop", is distributed to all species, and the macroevolution process comes to an end.

Here is an outline of how FUELCON works (ibid.):

1. Initialize the MacroGa with setup parameters, such as the number of species (sub-populations), the number of generations, population size for each species, etc.
2. Create the current generation, and evaluate the fitness for each individual in the population.
3. Apply the genetic operators to create a next generation.
4. Check whether an acceptable loading pattern has been found. If so, go to step 6.
5. Replace the current generation with the next generation, then save the search information (i.e., the best reload pattern), and go to step 3.
6. Save the final search results to the database, and stop.

The advantages of this macroevolution (in which we have a population of populations) were explained (ibid.) as stemming from:

(1) A set of weakly interacting species, allowing each species to concentrate on a separate area of the search space. The species can search their own regions aggressively (under high selection pressure) and hence quickly, without the risk of a premature loss of diversity.

(2) The use of different crossover and mutation rates in the various species, avoiding the problem of having to determine effective values for these parameters. The inclusion of rather high mutation rates in some of the species adds a strong hill-climbing element to the search, without generating a random one. Hill-climbing has been shown to be an effective ingredient in genetic algorithms; macro evolution allows its introduction in a natural way while gaining the advantage of point 1.

New parameters to be determined for effective performance appear however as the migration rate between species, and the number of individuals exchanged at each migration. Values for these parameters giving good performance were easy to determine however, confirming that macrogenetic algorithms are robust, requiring little parameter tuning for a new application.

The FUELCON project however involved no data mining. Cios, Pedrycz, and Swiniarski (1998) claimed that evolutionary computing is useful to data mining because it can be used to solve optimisation problems. The optimisation processes are based on a population of potential solutions rather than relying on a population of potential solutions rather than relying on a single search point being moved according to some gradient based or probabilistic search rules.

6.1.16.2 Genetic and Other Methods as Applied to Transforming Pre-processed Data Upstream of the Data Mining Phase

Data that has been selected and pre-processed may not necessarily be ready for exposure to a data-mining algorithm. Some transformation of the data may dramatically enhance the benefit of the subsequent data mining phase. Transformation can be performed in five ways:

(a) *Aggregation of data values.* This involves transforming values into categories or groups. Values on an age variable captured in years and months, for example, may be transformed into five pre-defined age groups. Aggregating values is also known as *binning* because it involves transforming values of a feature into a small number of categories.
(b) *Normalisation of data values.* A variable with large values measured, for instance in the thousands could dominate a variable with very small values measured in the thousandths in the data mining phase. Normalising involves transforming both sets of values so that they fall within the same range. Scaling values so that they fall within a specified range is particularly important if two or more features have vastly different ranges.
(c) *Feature reduction.* This involves the removal of features that are not relevant or make no sizeable contribution to the data mining exercise.
(d) *Example reduction.* Example reduction involves eliminating records from the data set. Data-sets in law are typically too small to contemplate example reduction.
(e) *Restructuring.* Restructuring involves decomposing the data-set into smaller parts for independent data mining exercises.

Restructuring a data set into smaller parts for independent mining exercises is particularly important for mining from data sets in law. This is due to the lack of availability of large data sets that reflect judicial reasoning. For example, 94 variables were identified by specialist family lawyers as relevant for determining property outcomes in Australian family law. A data mining exercise with so many variables requires data from many thousands of cases for meaningful results. However the mining exercise was decomposed into 35 independent, small and manageable data mining exercises. Most of these smaller exercises involved less than five variables, so that mining was possible, though not ideal, with data from around one hundred cases.

Feature reduction involves the removal of features that are irrelevant or will not contribute to the data mining exercise. Irrelevant features may clutter the data mining phase making the discovery of meaningful patterns difficult or at worst, impossible. There are three main ways that feature reduction is performed:

(a) *Expert heuristics.* Legal specialists well acquainted with the jurisdiction the data-set derives from often have a clear view of the extent to which a feature may be irrelevant and warrant removal. The articulation of a reason for each feature's relevance presents as a simple and effective, yet not foolproof mechanism for the identification of irrelevant features. In law, the relevance of a feature typically derives directly from a statute, precedent case, regulation or commonly accepted practice. However, this is not always the case. Most family law specialists claim the wife's hair color is irrelevant and should not play a role in mining aimed at predictive property split orders. In contrast, some specialists claim hair color is entirely relevant in property proceedings as judges may, correctly or not, regard that blond women have better prospects for re-marriage and therefore ought to be awarded fewer marital assets.

(b) *Statistical techniques.* Statistical techniques can be applied to the data-set to identify features that do not contribute to the prediction. *Principal components analysis (PCA)* is the technique most often used to determine such features. PCA involves the analysis of variance between features and the class variable in a prediction exercise. PCA requires specialist statistical software, since the calculations are cumbersome. PCA is applicable only to features that are numeric.[206]

(c) *Data mining.* The third approach used in feature reduction involves the application of a data mining technique in order to discover features that do not contribute to the mining. The *rule induction* algorithm is often applied in this way because features that are irrelevant do not appear in rules derived with this algorithm. Alternatively, *genetic algorithms* can be applied: see below.

Within category (c), we mention the application of genetic algorithms in a project related to our *Split Up* system for assisting in negotiations for marital splits. Skabar, Stranieri, and Zeleznikow (1997) applied the following method with excellent results. The search method they resorted to was *genetic algorithms.* These they used in order to look for the best subset of features of the Split Up data-set for neural network training. They found a subset of 17 features predicted percentage split in property proceedings as well as the original 94 featured data-set.

The use of expert heuristics is the best of the three approaches when using a data-set that derives from legal databases. The statistical and data-mining approach may yield counter-intuitive results that while correct, are not readily explained or accepted. For example, many of the features found to be unnecessary by Skabar (1997) in predicting percentage split outcomes such as the contributions made by the husband are central in statutes and common-sense reasoning in family law. Specialist lawyers, judges and other commentators explain virtually every judgement with reference to this feature. The fact that a data-mining method does not need this feature in order to make good predictions cannot be taken to mean that the feature is not taken seriously by judges in reaching decisions. It is more likely that this is an artefact that arises because the interdependence between this feature and other features results in accurate predictions when using a combination of other features.

---

[206] Suppose that we have N tuples from k-dimensional space to compress. Han and Kamber (2001) say PCA searches for c k-dimensional orthogonal vectors that can be best used to represent the data, where $c \leq k$. The original data is projected onto a much smaller space, resulting in data compression. PCA can be used as a form of dimensionality reduction. Unlike attribute subset selection, which reduces the attribute set size by retaining a subset of the initial set of attributes, PCA "combines" the essence of attributes by creating an alternative smaller set of variables. The initial data can then be projected onto this smaller set.

6.1.16.3 Nearest Neighbours Approaches and Their Integration with Genetic Algorithms

Below, we discuss evolutionary computing in order to illustrate an innovative use of genetic algorithms in law by Pannu (1995). However, before doing this we briefly overview the *k-nearest neighbour* algorithm that is required for an understanding of the approach which Pannu (1995) uses. According to Ripley (1996), the *k-nearest neighbour (k-NN)* algorithm is attributed to Fix and Hodges (1951). It is a relatively simple algorithm for classifying examples in a sample that uses two basic steps to classify each example:

1. Find the *k* nearest, most similar examples in the training set to the example to be classified
2. Assign the example the same classification as the majority of *k* nearest retrieved neighbours.

A trivial example involves classifying whether a young man is likely to be classified with an even split of marital property given the data in Table 6.1.16.3.1. Say the example to be classified is a young man represented as [1,0,1,0] and that k = 3. Assuming each feature is equally important, the three most similar examples are examples 1, 2 and 3. The majority of the k neighbours, (i.e examples 1 and 2) are classified. Even so the young man example will also be classified as receiving an even split.

Issues that need to be considered when using the k-NN algorithm include:

- *Choice of Similarity metric.* Typically a Euclidean distance metric is deployed such as

$$\Sigma \, (x_e - x_t)^2$$

where

$$x_e - x_t$$

is the difference between the example value and the a training set value for each feature. This can be modified by weighting each feature differently

Table 6.1.16.3.1 Sample data for k-th nearest neighbour example

Ex.	Age young	Age elderly	Sex male	Sex female	Split
1	1	0	1	0	Even
2	1	0	1	0	Even
3	0	1	1	0	Uneven
4	0	1	0	1	Uneven

$$\Sigma w(x_e - x_t^2)$$

This metric, which combines the difference between points linearly, is adopted.

- *Optimal choice of k.* The decision about the size of k must be made in advance. A large value of k introduces computational complexity, whereas a small value k is less accurate. Refinements of the algorithms involve dropping examples that are not needed to correctly classify the example.

Michie, Spiegelhalter, and Taylor (1994) illustrate that the k-NN compares favourably with respect to error rates in classification tasks against neural networks, Bayesian belief networks and linear or logistic regression. The k-NN approach is embedded in the genetic algorithm of Pannu (1995) discussed next.

Pannu (1995) applied genetic algorithms to discover a prototype, 'perfect' exemplar for cases with a specified outcome. Good exemplars for cases are useful because future cases can be mapped to exemplars with different outcomes to predict likely outcomes and to identify weaknesses in a case. Two elements are required in order to generate a good exemplar; a distance metric to measure the degree of similarity between one case and another, and a search procedure that can explore an very large number of possible exemplars to find the best one.

The approach Pannu (1995) used integrated k-th nearest neighbour distance metric with a genetic algorithm described by Kelly and Davis (1991). The distance metric computes a distance between two vectors. The distance algorithm was based on the k-th nearest neighbour algorithm.

For Pannu (1995), the vector elements were a 1 or a 0 and represented whether or not a factor was present in a case. A fitness function that sought to find a exemplar case did so by minimising the distance between itself and all other cases with the same outcome and by maximising the distance between itself and exemplars for cases that had different outcomes.

Evolutionary computing techniques have not been extensively applied in the legal domain though the work by Pannu (1995) indicates some possibilities. Quite recent data mining techniques broadly categorised as kernel machines are described in the next section, though these algorithms have not yet been applied to law.

6.2   Case Studies of Link Analysis and Data Mining

6.2.1   Digital Resources and Uncovering Perpetration: Email Mining, Computer Forensics, and Intrusion Detection

6.2.1.1   Email Mining

One form of *text mining* is *email mining*. In a section entitled "Email Text Mining", Gray and Debreceny (2006) remarked: "The text of the email is essentially unstructured. Minkov and Cohen (2006) notes that these characteristics of emails allow us to view a set of semistructured emails as a graph, with nodes representing

Fig. 6.2.1.1.1 A framework
for email data mining,
redrawn from Gray and
Debreceny (2006)

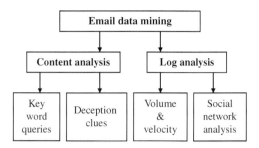

actors, temporality, subject matter and meetings. We can exploit these characteristics by employing a variety of techniques as illustrated in Figure [6.2.1.1.1]". Those techniques can be blended, and, e.g., one can analyse content (emails and their file attachments) while also analysing the log: for example, the social network of senders and recipients, possibly in relation to roles known from the structure of an organisation of which these are employees. "Within corporate email systems, it is relatively simple to match email recipients to corporate roles and responsibilities" (Gray & Debreceny, 2006).

From the *temporal mining of an email log*, volume and velocity are metrics that can be analysed. "Volume measures the number of emails a person sends and/or receives over a period of time. Velocity measures how quickly the volume changes. Gradual change would be low velocity and sudden jumps in volume would be high velocity" (Gray & Debreceny, 2006). This is potentially useful when trying to detect suspicious activities. "In terms of continuous monitoring of volume and velocity, the key issue is determining the optimum time intervals to sample the data" (ibid.). "Changes in velocity over time for no apparent reason may also indicate suspicious activities. The first task is to create a *baseline normal* profile and then changes in volume and velocity compared to the profile for no apparent reason may indicate suspicious activities" (ibid.).

Rolling histogram is a concept that has arisen in the literature concerning this. "Recognizing that the baseline profile can evolve over time, Stolfo, Creamer, and Hershkop (2006) use the term 'rolling histogram' to reflect the dynamic aspects of an employee's profile changing over time. The concept of the rolling histogram is like other moving averages where the profile is updated based on a moving window of a time interval (e.g., a twelve-week moving average)" (Gray & Debreceny, 2006). Stolfo et al. (2006) used software called Email Mining Toolkit (EMT). It is freely available.[207] It was developed at Columbia University, includes approximately 132,000 lines of Java code, and interfaces with relational databases.

Link and network monitoring is another kind of analysis of the log, in relation to the social network of the senders and the recipients within an organisation.[208] Gray and Debreceny (2006) remarked:

---

[207] http://www1.cs.columbia.edu/ids/emt/

[208] *Email surveillance* is the subject of, e.g., Browne and Berry (2005).

Once the networks and cliques are identified, continuous monitoring techniques could be used flag emails that fall outside the established patterns. For example, an email from a high-level executive to a warehouse worker, where no similar emails existed before, could be suspicious. Emails from employees to customer domains where the employee does not hold a position that normally communicates with customers would be suspicious. Unlike the monitoring of volume and velocity, link and network monitoring could be performed on a near real-time basis.

Another direction of research in *email mining* is *deception research*. Deception can be of the sender trying to deceive the addressee, of then of both of them in collusion trying to deceive their employer. Moreover, distinguish *sender deception* (lying about the sender's identity) from *content deception*.

6.2.1.2 The Enron Email Database as an Opportunity for Research

The Enron scandal spawned text mining research into the email database of Enron. In the words of Gray and Debreceny (2006):

A large corpus of emails from Enron was put into the public domain by the Federal Energy Regulatory Commission following its investigation of the corporation in relation to alleged manipulation of "electricity and natural gas markets in California and other Western states in 2000 and 2001." The original corpus contained 0.6m emails from 158 users (Klimt and Yang [2004a, 2004b]). These users included key participants in the events that brought down the corporation in 2001 [...] Elimination of [email] duplicates reduced the corpus to 0.2m messages; an average of 757 messages per user. They also worked to remove quotations of previous emails in subsequent emails in that thread. [...] The Enron email corpus has subsequently been transformed into a relational database format and published in MySQL format (Shetty and Adibi, 2004). [...] Exploring the emails may be undertaken by targeted analysis based upon known patterns, or by automated techniques. [...] Emails also provide a flavor of the relationship between the external auditors and Enron. A total of 466 emails in the corpus were sent from Enron email addresses to Andersen email addresses. A surprising proportion of these emails were comprised of jokes often in poor taste, event announcements and personal mail. There were 33 emails from Andersen email addresses to Enron email addresses. Again, many of these emails were related to matters other than the audit.

Research into the Enron email database has adopted various techniques, with different purposes. Gray and Debreceny (2006), whose viewpoint is that of auditors, mentioned that even such a rudimentary technique as looking for key words yielded results: "Emails could be searched for key words such as finder's fee, bribe, kickback, and similar words that could indicate questionable actions or overrides of controls. This would be cherry-picking the naive fraudsters. It is hard to believe that a fraudster would use such words in the company email, but they do as found by researchers who have explored the Enron email corpus" (ibid.). "Probably the most discussed continuous email monitoring is the *Carnivore* system developed by the FBI to scan emails in the United States. The CIA and NSA are assumed to have similar systems to monitor email traffic outside of the U.S. The difference being that the FBI needs a court order before it can monitor a specific person's email traffic in the U.S. By the way, companies do not need a court order to monitor employee emails." (ibid.).

One strand of research was intended to discover structures within the organisation. This is part of the discipline analysing social networks, in order to identify communities and model their evolution. The Enron email dataset was made available to the public,[209] and this has enabled research to flourish.[210] Gray and Debreceny (2006) pointed out:

> Research on automated understanding of the emails within the Enron corpus is still at a relatively early stage. A considerable amount of research has gone into understanding social network relationships within email data sets. Whilst this is an important first step in identifying key relationships that can be used for assurance purposes, social network analysis does not on its own allow identification of emails that may be critical to an assurance issue. As discussed above, there are also a variety of techniques to analyze the text within a corpus including natural language processing and machine learning. The next step is to match content analysis and social networks.

For those who "want to recognize a group of authors communicating in a specific role[211] within an Internet community, the challenge is recognize possibly different roles of an author within different communication communities. Moreover, each individual exchange in electronic communications is typically short, making the standard text mining approaches less efficient than in other applications" (Chaoji et al., 2010).[212] The textual corpus of Enron emails corpus is a suitable domain of application: "An example of such a problem is recognizing roles in a collection of emails from an organization in which middle level managers communicate both with superiors and subordinates. To validate our approach we use the Enron dataset which is such a collection" (Chaoji et al., 2010).

Wilson and Banzhaf (2009) applied a genetic algorithm to the discovery of social networks within the Enron email database. "Heer [jheer.org] has built a variety of tools that allow visual representations of several types of social networks including Friendster relationships (Vizter) and relationships expressed in Enron emails (Enronic). These tools are based on natural language processing techniques", and one of the tools, Enron Corpus Viewer, plots a graph being "a visual representation of the social networks embedded in the Enron corpus" (Gray & Debreceny, 2006).

Chapanond, Krishnamoorthy, and Yener (2005) developed such an analysis of the Enron email data. They constructed an email graph, and studies its properties by using *graph theoretical* and *spectral analysis* techniques. "The graph theoretical analysis includes the computation of several graph metrics such as degree distribution, average distance ratio, clustering coefficient and compactness over the email graph. The spectral analysis shows that the email adjacency matrix has a rank-2

---

[209] Enron Email Dataset, http://www-2.cs.cmu.edu/enron/ and later on at http://www.cs.cmu.edu/~enron/ (maintained by W. W. Cohen). Moreover, the following is also available: Enron Employee Status Record, at *http://isi.edu/~adibi/Enron/Enron Employee Status.xls*

[210] E.g., Klimt and Yang (2004a, 2004b). Keila and Skillicorn (2005), Diesner and Carley (2005), McCallum et al. (2005), and Priebe et al. (2005).

[211] Role identification in a corpus of emails is a special case of automated text categorization.

[212] Chaoji et al. (2008a, 2008b, 2010) and Goldberg et al. (2008) stem from the same team, led by Boleslaw K. Szymanski at the Rensselaer Polytechnic Institute, in Troy, New York state.

approximation. It is shown that preprocessing of data has significant impact on the results, thus a standard form is needed for establishing a benchmark data".

Goldberg et al. (2008) are concerned with "Social networks that arise spontaneously and evolve over time": "Their loose membership and dynamics make them difficult to observe and monitor". Goldberg et al. (2008) presented "a set of tools for discovery, analysis and monitoring evolution of hidden social groups on the internet and in cyberspace. Two complementary kinds of tools form a core of our approach. One [SIGHTS] is based on statistical analysis of communication network without considering communication content. The other [Recursive Data Mining] focuses on communication content and analyzes recursive patterns arising in it" (ibid.).

6.2.1.3 Discovering Social Coalitions with the SIGHTS Text Mining System

One of the tools presented by Goldberg et al. (2008) is SIGHTS (Statistical Identification of Groups Hidden in Time and Space). SIGHTS was "designed for the discovery, analysis, and knowledge visualization of social coalition in communication networks by analyzing communication patterns". The algorithms of SIGTHS "extract groups and track their evolution in Enron-email dataset and in Blog data. The goal of SIGHTS is to assist an analyst in identifying relevant information" (Goldberg et al., 2008).

SIGHTS has three main modules: Data Collection/Storage, Data Learning and Analysis, and Knowledge Extraction/Visualisation. The data sources are email data, or blogs, and it was envisaged to also include a link to chatrooms at a later stage. From the data sources, data are collected, and a semantic graph and metadata are stored in a database. "The Data Collection Modules operate on semantic graphs. The graphs are constructed by adding a node for each social network actor and a directed edge from sender's node to a recipient's node. The edges are marked with the time of the communication and, possibly, other labels. Some edge labels are only appropriate for specified types of graphs" (from section 2 of Goldberg et al., 2008).[213] Blog Collector is a module accessing blogs, one of the data sources.[214]

---

[213] "The user may have communication data existing in a variety of formats. SIGHTS handles the stand-alone input of a reasonable range of these formats in order to facilitate the introduction of new data into the program. Among these is a plain-text XML format which is well-documented. SIGHTS is also able to read from a database that is constructed according to specified guidelines. Blogs data is collected from LiveJournal.com blogs service provider. The semantic graph is constructed by creating a node for each blogger and the edge between any pair of bloggers who participated in the discussion in the comments of a post." (from section 2 of Goldberg et al., 2008).

[214] "Blogs collector monitors LiveJournal.com update feed and records the permanent address of the post. Two weeks after the date of the initial post, the blogs collector visits the page of the post and collects the thread of comments using the screen-scraping techniques. Blogs collector allows the establishment of 'interest filters' that can narrow the data collection to posts on a certain topic. Blogs collector provides the interface for the analyst to tag posts as interesting and not interesting that will create the training set for the interest learning program. This information is also stored in the database and is accessible to other modules of the application" (from section 2 of Goldberg et al., 2008).

The algorithm modules of SIGHTS interact with the database, retieving from it the semantic graph and metadata, and storing in it derived data. The algorithm modules include:

- Real Time Clustering,
- Leader Identification,
- Topic Identification,
- Cycle Group Analysis,
- Stream Group Analysis.

Interactive visualisation, through which users access the output of the algorithm, accounts for:

- Size vs Density plot,
- Graph of Clusters plot,
- Group Persistence view,
- Leaders and Group Evolution view,
- interactive Graph of Overlapping Clusters.

Goldberg et al. (2008, section 2) explained:

> Temporal group algorithms identify hidden groups in the stream of communications for the user specified time scales [(Baumes et al., 2006; Camptepe et al., 2005).] Noteworthy among them are the cycle model algorithms that identify all groups of users who persistently communicate over a time interval and the stream model algorithm that finds groups based on frequently communicating triples followed by merging correlated triples. Such groups usually communicate over multiple time intervals during the period of interest in a streaming fashion. Our algorithms also give the group structure hierarchy and can be modified to track evolution. An example of the evolution of a group found in the ENRON email data set is shown in

a figure comprising three graphs, which show the evolution of a part of the Enron organisational structure in the periods 2000–2002 (respectively, the graphs showed relations at Enron during September 2000–September 2001, March 2000–March 2001, and September 2001–September 2002). All three graphs represented frequent structures; and the nodes in the graph represent actors of the Enron community. Some of those nodes (*B, C, D, F*) were present in all three time-intervals.

In SIGHTS, there is an Opposition Identification Module. Its task is to identify "the positive and negative sentiments between pairs of bloggers based on the length and average size of the messages in the conversations that took place among them" (from section 2 of Goldberg et al., 2008). From LiveJournal.com, SIGHTS splits threads of comments into conversations between pairs of bloggers. "The module employs the Support Vector Machine classifier[215] that was trained using a data set that was manually created to determine the oppositions between bloggers using the

---

[215] Support vector machines are the subject of Section 6.1.9.3 in this book.

length of the conversation and the average length of the message in the conversation to determine whether bloggers opposed each other in a given conversation" (ibid.).

Bennett and Campbell (2000) provided a good introduction to *support vector machines* (*SVMs*). Ingo Steinwart and Andreas Christmann published a book (2008) on support vector machines. So did Campbell and Ying (2011), whose abstract states, among the other things:

> Support Vectors Machines have become a well established tool within machine learning. They work well in practice and have now been used across a wide range of applications from recognizing hand-written digits, to face identification, text categorisation, bioinformatics, and database marketing. In this book we give an introductory overview of this subject. We start with a simple Support Vector Machine for performing binary classification before considering multi-class classification and learning in the presence of noise.

An early definition of the concept was as follows: "The *support-vector network* is a new learning machine for two-group classification problems. The machine conceptually implements the following idea: input vectors are non-linearly mapped to a very high-dimension feature space. In this feature space a linear decision surface is constructed. Special properties of the decision surface ensures [*sic*] high generalization ability of the learning machine. [...] High generalization ability of support-vector networks utilizing polynomial input transformations is demonstrated" (Cortes & Vapnik, 1995, p. 173).

The Wikipedia entry[216] is usefully detailed. Here is its introduction:

> *Support vector machines (SVMs)* are a set of related supervised learning methods that analyze data and recognize patterns, used for classification and regression analysis. The original SVM algorithm was invented by Vladimir Vapnik and the current standard incarnation (soft margin) was proposed by Corinna Cortes and Vladimir Vapnik. The standard SVM takes a set of input data and predicts, for each given input, which of two possible classes the input is a member of, which makes the SVM a non-probabilistic binary linear classifier. Since an SVM is a classifier, then given a set of training examples, each marked as belonging to one of two categories, an SVM training algorithm builds a model that assigns new examples into one category or the other. Intuitively, an SVM model is a representation of the examples as points in space, mapped so that the examples of the separate categories are divided by a clear gap that is as wide as possible. New examples are then mapped into that same space and predicted to belong to a category based on which side of the gap they fall on.
>
> More formally, a support vector machine constructs a hyperplane or set of hyperplanes in a high or infinite dimensional space, which can be used for classification, regression, or other tasks. Intuitively, a good separation is achieved by the hyperplane that has the largest distance to the nearest training data points of any class (so-called functional margin), since in general the larger the margin the lower the generalization error of the classifier.
>
> Whereas the original problem may be stated in a finite dimensional space, it often happens that in that space the sets to be discriminated are not linearly separable. For this reason it was proposed that the original finite dimensional space be mapped into a much higher dimensional space, presumably making the separation easier in that space. SVM schemes use a mapping into a larger space so that cross products may be computed easily in terms of the variables in the original space, making the computational load reasonable. The cross products in the larger space are defined in terms of a kernel function $K(x,y)$ selected to suit the problem. The hyperplanes in the large space are defined as the set of points whose inner

---

[216] http://en.wikipedia.org/wiki/Support_vector_machine (accessed in April 2011).

product with a vector in that space is constant. The vectors defining the hyperplanes can be chosen to be linear combinations with parameters α_i of images of feature vectors that occur in the data base.

6.2.1.4 Recursive Data Mining

Recursive Data Mining, is "a text mining approach that discovers patterns at varying degrees of abstraction in a hierarchical fashion. The approach allows for certain degree of approximation in matching patterns, which is necessary to capture non-trivial features in realistic datasets. Due to its nature, we call this approach *Recursive Data Mining* (RDM)" (Chaoji et al., 2010). Goldberg et al. (2008) also described a complementary set of tools, using *Recursive Data Mining* (*RDM*). Those tools's task is "to identify frequent patterns in communication content such as email, blog or chat-room sessions". The approach of Goldberg et al. (2008) "enables discovery of patterns at varying degrees of abstraction, in a hierarchical fashion, and in language independent way". They "use RDM to distinguish among different roles played by communicators in social networks (e.g., distinguishing between leaders and members). Experiments on the Enron dataset, which categorize members into organizational roles demonstrate that use of the RDM dominant patterns improves role detection" (ibid., from the abstract). Szymanski and Zhang (2004) and Coull and Szymanski (2008) resorted to Recursive Data Mining for *masquerade detection* (within *intrusion detection* affecting computer resources)[217] and *author identification*. These are subjects investigated using various techniques by other authors (e.g., de Vel et al., 2001; Elsayed & Oard, 2006).

Goldberg et al. (2008) "used *Recursive Data Mining* (RDM) for distinguishing the roles of the communicators in a social group. In general, RDM discovers, in a recursive manner, statistically significant patterns in a stream of data. The key properties of the pattern discovery in RDM include: (i) no restriction of the size of gaps between patterns, (ii) recursive mining in which discovered patterns are replaced by the new token and the mining is repeated on the newly created string, (iii) tolerance to imperfect matching" (from section 1 of Goldberg et al., 2008).

In Recursive Data Mining, "In the first iteration, the algorithm captures statistically significant patterns from the initial sequences. The patterns obtained

---

[217] Greg Stocksdale of the National Security Agency Information Systems Security Organization defined *spoofing* as "Pretending to be someone else. The deliberate inducement of a user or a resource to take an incorrect action. Attempt to gain access to an AIS [i.e., Automated Information System] by pretending to be an authorized user. Impersonating, masquerading, and mimicking are forms of spoofing" (Mena, 2003, p. 429). More precisely, Stocksdale defined *mimicking* as "Synonymous with impersonation, masquerading, or spoofing" (in Mena, 2003, p. 424). Moreover, Stocksdale gloassary also includes an entry for *mockingbird*, defined as "A computer program or process that mimics the legitimate behavior of a normal system feature (or other apparently useful function) but performs malicious activities once invoked by the user" (ibid.). *Spoofing* instead of *masquerading* sometimes occurs indeed in the terminology of the research literature. For example, Gosh et al. (2005) discussed *InFilter*, a tool whose teask is "predictive ingress filtering" for the purpose of detecting *spoofed Internet Protocol* (*IP*) *traffic*.

are assigned new tokens. The initial sequences are re-written by collapsing each sequence pattern to its newly assigned token, while retaining the rest of the tokens. Next, the algorithm operates on the re-written sequences and continues to iterate through the pattern generation and sequence re-writing steps until either the sequences cannot be re-written further or a predefined number of iterations is reached." (Chaoji et al., 2010, section 4).

Goldberg et al. (2008, section 4) introduced the algorithm shown in Fig. 6.2.1.4.1, using not just one classifier for the entire process, but a different classifier for each level of RDM abstraction. "The process starts with a sliding window of predefined length passing over the input sequence one token at a time. At each stop, patterns with all possible combinations of tokens and gaps are recorded. When pass is completed, the recorded patterns are checked for frequency of their occurrence". In fact, not all patterns are of equal importance. "Some patterns could be either too specific to a certain text or insignificant because they contain very commonly occurring words. In either case, they are ineffective in classifying the mined text while adding to the computational cost of the algorithm. The 'usefulness' of a pattern is computed via a statistical significance test. A pattern is deemed significant if its frequency of occurrence (based on a unigram model) is larger than the expected number of occurrence in a random string. Patterns that are deemed insignificant are eliminated from further consideration." (ibid.).

"At each position in the sequence, the tokens in the significant patterns are matched against the tokens in the sequence" (ibid.). A *dominant pattern* at position j in the input sequence is that pattern whose matching score is the highest, starting at location j in the sequence. The matching score is calculated using this formula:

$$\text{score}\,(\mathcal{P}i, S_v j) = \begin{cases} 1 & \text{if } \mathcal{P}i = S_v j \\ \epsilon & \text{if } \mathcal{P}i = GAP, \epsilon < 1 \\ 0 & \mathcal{P}i \neq S_v j \end{cases}$$

Require: Set of sequences $\mathcal{S}$
Ensure: Sets of patterns (features) $\mathcal{L}$, one for each level
1: $\mathcal{L} = \{\}$
2: $i = 0$
3: $S = \mathcal{S}$ {Level-0}
4: **repeat**
5:   $\mathcal{P}_{ALL} = pattern\_generation(S)$
6:   $\mathcal{P}_{SIG} = sig\_patterns(S, \mathcal{P}_{ALL})$
7:   $\mathcal{D} = get\_domi\_patterns(S, \mathcal{P}_{SIG})$
8:   $\mathcal{L}_i = \mathcal{D}$
9:   i++
10:   $S = make\_next\_level(S, \mathcal{D})$ {Level-i}
11: **until** $\mathcal{M} == \emptyset \lor i == max\_level$
12: **return** $\mathcal{L}$

Fig. 6.2.1.4.1 Recursive Data Mining Algorithm 1 from Goldberg et al. (2008)

"$\mathcal{P}_i$ is the *i*th token of the pattern and *j* is an index over sequence *S*. ε is intended to capture the notion that a match with a gap is not as good as an exact match but much better than a mismatch." Goldberg et al. (2008) explain:

> During the second pass of the sequence at level *v*, the sequence for level *v*+1 is formed. The sequence corresponding to a dominant pattern is replaced by the new token for this dominant pattern. Unmatched tokens are copied from sequence S_v to the new sequence S_{v+1}.

"Like most supervised learning tools, RDM has two stages of processing — training and testing. The *training phase* starts with *pattern generation*, and follows by pattern selection through the *pattern significance assessment* step." (Chaoji et al., 2010, section 4). Goldberg et al. (2008, section 4) explain the training phase as follows:

> The training phase uses the dominant patterns generated at each level to construct an ensemble of classifiers, one for each level. The classifiers can be created from any machine learning method, such as Naïve Bayes or Support Vector Machine.[218] Given a set of input sequences, along with the class labels, dominant patterns are generated for each label starting at level 0 to level *max_level*. The union of all dominant patterns at a level *v* across all input sequences forms the set of feature for classifier at level *v*. For the ensemble of classifiers, the final posterior class probability is the weighted sum of the class probabilities of individual classifiers. Each classifier is assigned a weight that reflects the confidence of the classifier. The original input sequences are further split into a new training set and a tuning set. Each classifier in the ensemble trains its model based on the new training set. The confidence value of classifier at level *v*, *conf* (C_v), is defined as the relative accuracy on the tuning set. The testing phase follows the training phase in terms of the level by level operating strategy. [...]

Advantages of recursive data mining include there being no length restriction on the patterns formed: "This allows arbitrary size patterns to be discovered. Most of the other published techniques work on a fixed size window" (Chaoji et al., 2010, section 1); the ability of the method to also discover approximate, (i.e., similar) patterns; and that this method is *hierarchical*, the hierarchy resulting from the *recursive* processing: "This enables us to capture patterns at various levels of abstractions. Moreover, the hierarchical nature allows us to remove noisy symbols from the stream as we move from a lower level to a higher level in the hierarchy. This ultimately leads to discovery of *long range patterns* that are separated by long noisy intermediate segments." (ibid.).

In the Recursive Data Mining method, as explained in Chaoji et al. (2010), the total score for a pattern, starting at index *j* in *S*, is given by

$$\text{score}\,(\mathcal{P}, S_v[j]) = \sum_{i=1}^{|\mathcal{P}|} \text{score}(\mathcal{P}[i], S_v[j+i])$$

After the training phase, there is the testing phase. This is done level by level. Of the dominant patterns at level 0, the frequency is counted over the level 0 test sequence. This results in a vector of frequencies. It is the feature vector at level 0. Then the

---

[218] We have said something about support vector machines at the end of Section 6.1.2.3.

same is done at the next level. Let the level that has just been done be v. Then the next level sequence is generated, by applying the rewriting rules for dominant patterns. "This process continues till all levels of dominant patterns are exhausted. Each classifier in the ensemble classifies the test data and the final probability of class C given a sequence x is assigned based on the following weighing scheme

$$\mathbf{P}(C \mid x) = \sum_{i=1}^{\text{max\_levels}} \text{Conf}\,(C_i) \times \mathbf{P}_{C_i}(C \mid x)$$

where x is a test sequence and

$$\mathbf{P}_{C_i}(C \mid x)$$

is the posterior probability assigned by classifier C_i" (Goldberg et al., 2008, section 4).

6.2.1.5 The Disciplinary Context: A Brief Introduction to Computer Forensics

The foregoing in the present Section 6.2.1 is concerned with *email mining*, which is a technique within *text mining*, as well as within *computer forensics*. It is not necessarily the case that AI methods are used in the analysis of computer forensic evidence. The most obvious connection would be the discovery process and the data mining techniques used for example on the Enron database of emails indeed.

Dealing with *computer crime* requires expertise in computing, of course; e.g., in *computer security*. Nevertheless, when it comes to forensic investigation once a transgression was committed or is suspected, *computer forensics* (also known as *evidential computing*, or *forensic computing*) is not confined to computer crime alone. For example, evidence from a firm's computers may be seized so that forensic accountants examine the data.

Computer forensics[219] is the use of techniques that are specialised for the collection, identification, description, provision with security, retrieval, authentication, analysis, interpretation and explanation of digital information, when a case being investigated involves the use of computing or of a data carrier.[220] *Digital evidence*[221] is any digital information that could be used as evidence in a legal case. One also speaks of *digital crime*, and *digital forensics*.

---

[219] *Computer forensics* = French *investigation informatique*. Throughout this book, I haven't tried to provide equivalent terminology across languages, but let us exemplify here how terminology differs, in the case of French: unless you are told or were already aware, you could not just guess the French term correctly, based on the English term.

[220] *Data carrier* = French *support d'information*.

[221] *Digital evidence* = French *preuve numérique*.

We have already referred previously to digital forensics. This was when we discussed, in Section 4.3.4, the costs/benefits analysis of digital forensic investigations into digital crime.

The *hash value*[222] of some given digital information is generated by an algorithm applied to a file or to some logical or physical memory unit. The algorithm is such that it is impoosible to modify the digital information without the hash value also being modified. If the hash value was not modified, then it is assumed that the digital information was not modified. To be on the safe side, the hash value is calculated in two different manners, especially when it comes to hard disks.

Chain of evidence[223] in computer forensics is the recording of the stages of the inquiry (investigation), in order to guarantee that some given digital evidence is indisputably derived from some given digital information. The record describes how that digital information was preserved, gives its hash value, describes software and hardware used for preventing tampering (by rewriting), describes the operations carried out and the software employed, informs about incidents and especially about any modification of the digital information being analysed, lists the items of evidence collected, and provides the series numbers of the data carriers used for recording such evidence. For such a record to be a judicial document (which includes the inquiry documents of an examining magistrate), e.g., in France, it is necessary that the chain of evidence be requested by some judicial authoritiy, and that it be accompanied by a chain of custody.

The *chain of custody*[224] is a report or notes of the proceedings of the seizure or reception of some give digital information and of its support. It contains information about who had detained it previously (an owner, or user, or custodian), about the place and circumstances of this digital information being obtained, retrieved or transmitted, about the data carrier (including a physical description with a photograph, as well as the series number), and possibly a description consisting of metadata, the data structure, and the hash value. The chain of custody also specifies whether the data are accessible or otherwise, and whether there is a seal (with its identification). Also included are information about accompanying documents, the dates when the data carrier was opened and closed, mentions of any modification that has occurred (such as the suppression of a password), a description of how (if such is the case) the data carrier was returned (in terms of accessibility to data, to whether a label was applied, or to any seal). Also a photograph is included.

A *forensic copy*[225] is a whole copy, bit by bit, of digital information present on a data carrier, including blank spaces, precluded areas, and queues. The software used in order to obtain the forensic copy is specified. The forensic copy must have the some hash value as the original of which it is the copy; otherwise, the chain of evidence must specify the reasons for difformity.

---

[222] *Hash value* = French *empreinte numerique*, or *valeur de hachage*.

[223] *Chain of evidence* = French *rapport d'investigation*.

[224] *Chain of custody* = French *rapport de garde*.

[225] *Forensic copy* = French *copie-image*.

Forensic computing[226] is the subject of a book by Sammes and Jenkinson (2000) which deals with data security, but especially shows how information held in computer systems (that possibly was deliberately hidden, or then, subverted, for criminal purposes) can be recovered in such a way that its integrity cannot be challenged, legal issues associated with computer-generated evidence, and practices required to ensure its admissibility. A more recent book is Carrier's (2005) *File System Forensic Analysis.*[227] London-based Overill (2009) discussed the development of Master's modules in computer forensics and cybercrime for computer science forensic science students.[228]

A distinction has been made, in the literature, between *computer* and *digital forensics.* The name *digital anti-forensics* has been given at least as early as Shirani (2002) – and apparently made popular following an article by Harris (2006) of Purdue University[229] (cf. Rogers, 2005, also from Purdue) – to strategies to evade computer forensic investigations, as well as ways to exploit critical failures in computer forensics software or in the reliability of computer security systems. Harris wrote (2006, pp. S44–S45):

> Currently there is no unified definition for anti-forensics. This is not surprising however, since it is a relatively unexplored field. Several definitions are available and each has its own relative merits. Some of those definitions look only at specific segments of anti-forensics. Some have seen anti-forensics as simply breaking tools or avoiding detection (Foster and Liu, 2005) while others have only related anti-forensics to system intrusions (Shirani, 2002). [...]"Peron and Legary pinpoint anti-forensics as the attempt to "limit the identification, collection, collation and validation of electronic data" so that the crime investigation is hindered (Peron and Legary, 2005). This definition is not complete however, since it disregards the analysis of the evidence. Evidence analysis is essential to the forensic process; therefore, we must include it if we list each phase in our definition. Another definition by Grugq identifies antiforensics as "attempting to limit the quantity and quality of forensic evidence" (Grugq, 2005). This definition is useful as well, but it only considers the evidence and completely ignores the forensic process. If we combine Grugq's ideas with those of Peron and Legary, we can arrive at a concise yet precise definition of anti-forensics. In this paper, we will consider anti-forensics to *be any attempts to compromise the availability or usefulness of evidence to the forensics process.* Compromising evidence availability includes any attempts to prevent evidence from existing, hiding existing evidence or otherwise manipulating evidence to ensure that it is no longer within reach of the investigator. Usefulness maybe compromised by obliterating the evidence itself or by destroying its integrity.

---

[226] Kruse and Heiser (2002) is a book on computer forensics. As we couldn't delve, here, in computer forensics any further, we confined ourselves to just providing a few definitions, that were loosely adapted from Lerti (2006). Handling digital evidence in relation to computer crime is the topic of Casey (2000 [new edn., 2004], 2001) and Kanellis et al. (2006). McHugh (2001) provides a historical and methodological overview of intrusion detection in computer security.

[227] Cf. Carrier & Spafford's article (2004) "Event recostruction of digital crime scenes".

[228] Of course, the literature about *digital forensics* is vast. For example, Goel et al. (2005) discussed *Forensix*, a reconstruction system. Tang and Daniels (2005) discussed a framework for *distributed forensics.*

[229] I owe Dr. Jeimy Cano the information that the name *digital anti-forensics* has been in use (at least) since 2006, following an article at a conference by Harris (2006). Actually, the conference was at West Lafayette, Indiana, where Ryan Harris was based, pursuing a MS in information security from Purdue University.

Harris (2006, p. S45) enumerated four kinds of anti-forensic activities, namely, *evidence destruction, evidence source elimination, evidence hiding*, and *evidence counterfeiting*. Harris (ibid., table 1) classified common antiforensic methods as follows. *MACE alterations* involve destroying ("Erasing MACE information or overwriting with useless data"),[230] or counterfeting ("Overwriting with data which provides misleading information to investigators"). *Removing/wiping files* involves destroying ("Overwriting contents with useless data"), or hiding: "Deleting file (overwriting pointer to content)". *Data encapsulation* involves hiding: "Hiding by placing files inside other files". *Account hijacking* involves counterfeiting: "Evidence is created to make it appear as if another person did the 'bad act'". *Archive/image bombs* involve counterfeting: "Evidence is created to attempt to compromise the analysis of an image". In *disabling logs*, what is involved is source elimination: "Information about activities is never recorded".

While trying to suggest countermeasures, Harris recognised that the *human element* is likely to be the most difficult to handle. Harris (2006, p. S47, table 2) listed the following exploits of the various anti-forensic actions. For *MACE alteration*, the human element is: "Investigator may assume accuracy of dates and times". For *removing/wiping files*, the human elemewnt is: "Investigator may fail to examine deleted files". For *account hijacking*, the human element is: "Investigator may fail to consider whether the owner of the account was actually the person at the keyboard". Harris listed no human element for *archive/image bombs*. For *disabling logs*, he gave this human element: "Investigator may not notice mising log records".

In the next column in the table, Harris listed the forms that the *tool dependence element* takes in the various anti-forensic activities. For *MACE alteration*, the tool dependence element is: "Tools may not function with invalid or missing dates or times". For *removing/wiping files*, the tool dependence element is: "Methods of restoring deleted files are specific to the tool — so effectiveness may vary". For *account hijacking*, the tool dependence element is: "Tool may not be capable of extracting information that would aid investigator in determining who was in control of the account". For *archive/image bombs*, the tool dependence element is: "Improperly designed software may crash". For *disabling logs*, he gave this tool dependence element: "Software may not flag events that indicate logging was disabled".

In the third and last column in the table, Harris listed the forms that the *physical/logical limitations element* takes in the various anti-forensic activities. For *MACE alteration*, the element of physicial or logical limitations is: "Invalid dates and times make collating information from multiple evidentiary sources difficult or

---

[230] The New Technology File System (NTFS) is a file system developed and introduced by Microsoft in 1995 with Windows NT. As a replacement for the FAT file system, it quickly became the standard for Windows 2000, Windows XP and Windows Server 2003. NTFS keeps track of lots of *time stamps*. Each file has a time stamp for "Create", "Modify", "Access", and "Entry Modified". The latter refers to the time when the MFT entry itself was modified. These four values are commonly abbreviated as the *MACE values*. Other attributes in each NFT record may also contain timestamps that are of forensic value.

impossible". For *removing/wiping files*, the element of physical or logical limitations is: "Time required to restore wiped file contents may outweigh the evidentiary value of the data it contained". For *account hijacking*, the element of physical or logical limitations is: "Zombied computer accounts may produce so much indirection that it is almost impossible to actually find the origin of an attack. Lack of detailed information may keep investigator from determining actual account user". For *archive/image bombs*, the element of physical or logical limitations is: "Useful information might be located in the bomb itself, but outside the logical limitations of the investigator's system". For *disabling logs*, he gave this element of physical or logical limitations: "Missing data may be impossible to reconstruct".

Insecurity governance or *insecurity management* is a branch of information technology concerned with how to respond, on an organisational level, to threats to computer security. *Multimedia forensics* is specifically concerned with uncovering perpetrators of piracy targeting protected digital content or encrypted applications. Typically, perpetration consists of unauthorised music and movie copying, either for private use of for selling pirated copies, thus eating a big bite of the profit of the record industry and the movie studios. Chang-Tsun Li (of the University of Warwick, England), has published a book (Li, 2008) on state-of-the-art *pirate tracking software*. A particular technique, *traitor tracing*, can be applied to multimedia forensics, but the term has previously been used also in the literature about cryptography.

6.2.1.6 Digital Steganography

In Section 8.2.5, we are going to concern ourselves with *digital image forensics*, which consists of computational methods of detection of image tampering. It is worthwhile to also mention another discipline: *digital steganalysis* is a forensic activity within *digital steganography*, which itself also comprises the deeds of perpetrators, not only the attempts by investigators to uncover those deeds. "*Steganography* is the art and science of writing hidden messages in such a way that no one, apart from the sender and intended recipient, suspects the existence of the message".[231] *Steganography* also denotes a particular system of ascribing or claiming to decipher hidden messages.

The history of secret writings is the subject of Kahn (1967, 2nd edn., 1996). Steganographies were associated with mysticism and occult studies in the early modern period, and particularly, with claims in the writings of the German abbot

---

[231] http://en.wikipedia.org/wiki/Steganography "Generally, messages will appear to be something else: images, articles, shopping lists, or some other *covertext* and, classically, the hidden message may be in invisible ink between the visible lines of a private letter. The advantage of steganography, over cryptography alone, is that messages do not attract attention to themselves. Plainly visible encrypted messages — no matter how unbreakable — will arouse suspicion, and may in themselves be incriminating in countries where encryption is illegal. Therefore, whereas cryptography protects the contents of a message, steganography can be said to protect both messages and communicating parties." (ibid.).

Johannes Trithemius (1462–1516),[232] discussed by Noel Brann (1981, 1999, 2006), Arnold (1971, 2nd edn. in 1991), David Kahn (1967, 2nd edn. 1996), Umberto Eco (1995, in one of the sections of his chapter 6), and Walker (1958, pp. 86–90). Later early modern steganographers included Giovambattista della Porta (in his *De furtivis litterarum notis*, of 1563), Blaise de Vigenère (in his *Traité des chiffres*, of 1587), and Gustavus Selenus (in his *Cryptometrices et cryptographjiae libri IX*, of 1624).[233]

Regardless of that cultural context, generally speaking:

> Steganography has been used throughout history for secret communications. Criminals have always sought ways to conceal their activity in real, or physical space. The same is true in virtual, or cyber space. Digital steganography represents a particularly significant threat today because of the large number of digital steganography applications freely available on the Internet that can be used to hide any digital file inside of another digital file. Use of these applications, which are both easy to obtain and simple to use, allows criminals to conceal their activities in cyber space. In fact, the NIJ Guide for Electronic Crime Scene Investigation for First Responders[234] states that potential digital evidence in child abuse, child exploitation, and terrorism investigations includes information regarding steganography. Thus, steganography presents a significant challenge to those who investigate it because detecting hidden information and then extracting that information is very difficult and may be impossible in some cases.[235]

---

[232] "Until 1499 Trithemius' reputation rested primarily on his monastic, mystical and humanist writings. Then, in that year, his magical notoriety burst onto the historical stage like a lightning bolt, signaled by a 1499 letter to a Carmelite friend, Arnold Bostius (1445–1499), announcing the birth of the art of steganography, a form of cryptography ostensibly invoking angels for the conveyance of secret messages. Far from having himself invented the art therein described, Trithemius assured Bostius, he had been instructed in its principles through a divine revelation. Inasmuch as the intended recipient had deceased prior to the letter's arrival, the prior of his cloister gained access to its contents and, aghast at what he therein encountered, insti instigated the abbot's necromantic legend. If the unforeseen disclosure of the Bostius epistle can be said to have delivered the first serious blow to Trithemius's reputation, a second severe blow was inflicted in the following decade by the French scholar Carolus Bovillus (c. 1479–1553), who, following a 1503 Sponheim visit in which he was given access to the partially completed *Steganographia*, condemned its author in a widely circulated letter as a diabolically inspired sorcerer" (Brann, 2006, p. 1136).

[233] Of Trithemius' Latin treatise *Steganographia, hoc est, ars per occultam scripturam animi sui voluntatem absentibus aperiendi certa*, published in Frankfurt on the Main "ex officina typographica Matthiae Beckeri, sumptibus Joannis Berneri", in 1605, 1608, and 1621, there exists a partial English edition: *The Steganographia of Johannes Trithemius*, edited by Adam McLean, and translated by Fiona Tait, Christopher Upton and J. W. H. Walden. It was published in 1982 in Edinburgh, Scotland, in the Magnum Opus Hermetic Sourceworks.

[234] Generally speaking, concerning *first responding officers*, also called *first responders* (which strictly speaking is a broader category, as sometimes the earliest responders are members of the public), Miller (2003) writes: "The first responders at a crime scene are usually police officers, fire department personnel or emergency medical personnel. They are the only people who view the crime scene in its original condition. Their actions at the crime scene provide the basis for the successful or unsuccessful resolution of the investigation. They must perform their duties and remember that they begin the process that links victims to suspects to crime scenes and must never destroy the links" (ibid., p. 118).

[235] From http://www.sarc-wv.com/ This is the address of the site of the Steganography Analysis and Research Center within Backbone Security.

In fact:

> Steganography includes the concealment of information within computer files. In digital steganography, electronic communications may include steganographic coding inside of a transport layer, such as a document file, image file, program or protocol. Media files are ideal for steganographic transmission because of their large size. As a simple example, a sender might start with an innocuous image file and adjust the color of every 100th pixel to correspond to a letter in the alphabet, a change so subtle that someone not specifically looking for it is unlikely to notice it.[236]

Applications of digital steganography include the following[237]:

- Concealing messages within the lowest bits of noisy images or sound files.
- Concealing data within encrypted data or within random data. The data to be concealed is first encrypted before being used to overwrite part of a much larger block of encrypted data or a block of random data (an unbreakable cipher like the one-time pad generates ciphertexts that look perfectly random if you don't have the private key).
- Chaffing and winnowing.[238]

---

[236] http://en.wikipedia.org/wiki/Steganography

[237] From http://www.sarc-wv.com/ This is the address of the site of the Steganography Analysis and Research Center within Backbone Security.

[238] See http://en.wikipedia.org/wiki/Chaffing_and_winnowing "*Chaffing and winnowing* is a cryptographic technique to achieve confidentiality without using encryption when sending data over an insecure channel. The name is derived from agriculture: after grain has been harvested and threshed, it remains mixed together with inedible fibrous chaff. The chaff and grain are then separated by winnowing, and the chaff is discarded. The technique was conceived by Ron Rivest. Although it bears similarities to both traditional encryption and steganography, it cannot be classified under either category. This technique is remarkable compared to ordinary encryption methods because it allows the sender to deny responsibility for encrypting their message. When using chaffing and winnowing, the sender transmits the message unencrypted, in clear text. Although the sender and the receiver share a secret key, they use it only for authentication. However, a third party can make their communication confidential by simultaneously sending specially crafted messages through the same channel." An explanation of the workings (on which, variations exist) follows hereby (ibid.): "The sender (Alice) wants to send a message to the receiver (Bob). In the simplest setup, Alice enumerates the bits in her message and sends out each bit in a separate packet. Each packet contains the bit's serial number in the message, the bit itself (both unencrypted), and a message authentication code (MAC) whose secret key Alice shares with Bob. Charles, who transmits Alice's packets to Bob, interleaves the packets with corresponding bogus packets (called 'chaff') with corresponding serial numbers, the bits inverted, and a random number in place of the MAC. Charles does not need to know the key to do that. Bob uses the MAC to find the authentic messages and drops the 'chaff' messages. This process is called 'winnowing'. Eve, an eavesdropper located between Alice and Charles, can easily read Alice's message. But an eavesdropper between Charles and Bob would have to tell which packets are bogus and which are real (i.e., to *winnow*, or 'separate the wheat from the chaff'). That is infeasible if the MAC used is secure and Charles does not leak any information on packet authenticity (e.g., via timing). When an adversary requires Alice to disclose her secret key, she can defend with the argument that she used the key merely for authentication and did not intend to make the message confidential. If the adversary cannot force Alice to disclose an authentication key (which knowledge would enable the adversary to forge messages from Alice), then her messages will remain confidential. On the other hand, Charles does not even possess any secret keys that he could be ordered to disclose."

- Mimic functions convert one file to have the statistical profile of another. This can thwart statistical methods that help brute-force attacks identify the right solution in a ciphertext-only attack.
- Concealed messages in tampered executable files, exploiting redundancy in the i386 instruction set.
- Pictures embedded in video material (optionally played at slower or faster speed).
- Injecting imperceptible delays to packets sent over the network from the keyboard. Delays in keypresses in some applications (telnet or remote desktop software) can mean a delay in packets, and the delays in the packets can be used to encode data.
- Content-Aware Steganography hides information in the semantics a human user assigns to a datagram. These systems offer security against a non-human adversary/warden.
- Blog-Steganography. Messages are fractionalized and the (encrypted) pieces are added as comments of orphaned web-logs (or pin boards on social network platforms). In this case the selection of blogs is the symmetric key that sender and recipient are using; the carrier of the hidden message is the whole blogosphere.

Moreover, one also speaks of *network steganography* ("All information hiding techniques that may be used to exchange steganograms in telecommunication networks can be classified under the general term of network steganography"),[239] and of *printed steganography* (as the output of digital steganography may be in the form of printed documents): when using printed steganography, "A message, the *plaintext*, may be first encrypted by traditional means, producing a *ciphertext*. Then, an innocuous *covertext* is modified in some way so as to contain the ciphertext, resulting in the *stegotext*."[240]

> The ciphertext produced by most digital steganography methods, however, is not printable. Traditional digital methods rely on perturbing noise in the channel file to hide the message, as such, the channel file must be transmitted to the recipient with no additional noise from the transmission. Printing introduces much noise in the ciphertext, generally rendering the message unrecoverable. There are techniques that address this limitation, one notable example is ASCII Art Steganography.[241]

One sometimes talks about *fingerprints*, and a *fingerprint vault scheme*, in digital steganography: see Li, Niu, Wang, Jiao, and Sun (2005).

6.2.1.7 Digital Forensics and Bayesian Networks

Bayesian networks have been applied to the evaluation of evidence in digital forensic investigations (Kwan, Chow, Law, & Lai, 2008).[242] Moreover, Overill et al.

---

[239] http://en.wikipedia.org/wiki/Steganography "Contrary to the typical steganographic methods which utilize digital media (images, audio and video files) as a cover for hidden data, network steganography utilizes communication protocols' control elements and their basic intrinsic functionality. As a result, such methods are harder to detect and eliminate" (ibid.).

[240] http://en.wikipedia.org/wiki/Steganography

[241] http://en.wikipedia.org/wiki/Steganography

[242] Halliwell et al. (2003) built upon the application of Bayesian networks (BNs) to inferring the probability of defence and prosecution statements based on forensic evidence. Halliwell et al.

(2010b) have developed a *sensitivity analysis* for such an application. "A Bayesian network representing an actual prosecuted case of illegal file sharing over a peer-to-peer network has been subjected to a systematic and rigorous sensitivity analysis. Our results demonstrate that such networks are usefully insensitive both to the occurrence of missing evidential traces and to the choice of conditional evidential probabilities" (ibid., from the abstract). The study concerns a court case tried in Hong Kong, "involving the use of a BitTorrent (BT) peer-to-peer (P2P) network to act as the initial 'seeder' for illegally uploading a copyright protected audio-visual file for subsequent distribution was constructed and examined. In Hong Kong only the uploading of copyright protected material is prohibited whereas in the UK any activity infringing copyright is forbidden" (ibid., section 1). In order to carry out the sensitivity analysis, Overill et al. (2010b) proceeded as follows:

> We have systematically replaced the aggregated likelihoods from the original survey [(Kwan et al., 2008)] by the minimum and maximum values of the responses provided by the sample of 31 expert digital forensic investigators. We have removed 'outlier' values from this sample by discounting any single response lying at either extreme of the range. [...] In addition, we have simultaneously set all the likelihoods to their respective minimum and maximum values in turn.

It was claimed that the Bayesian network in the study for which the sensitivity analysis was carried out "is insensitive to the occurrence of missing evidence and also to the choice of evidential likelihoods to an unexpected degree." Overill, Silomon, and Chow (2010a) conceded than in extreme cases of missing evidential traces, much lower probabilities for the investigative hypothesis were found.

It must be said however that even with the sensitivity analysis, the Bayesio-skeptic general critique of Bayesian methods in a judicial contexts is not assuaged at all. The sensitivity analysis is to the satisfaction of statisticians, but this by itself does not prove that Bayesianism is safe for evaluating evidence in criminal cases, other than in the relatively harmless application to having the prosecutor assess whether to prosecute.

Potentially, and if taken per se, more interesting also for the Bayesian skeptics is another method from that same team, which tries to calculate *operational complexity* (Overill, Silomon, & Chow, 2010a). The very idea is tantalising, and a proper definition may satisfy perhaps also the Bayesian skeptics.

Nevertheless, the way Overill, Silomon, and Chow (2010a) defined and employed it, operational complexity is applied to the quantification of forensic evidential probabilities: "From the complexity of formation of a set of traces via a

---

(2003) noted: "This is an important development as it helps to quantify the meaning of forensic expert testimony during court proceedings, for example, that there is 'strong support' for the defence or prosecution position. Due to the lack of experimental data, inferred probabilities often rely on subjective probabilities provided by experts. Because these are based on informed guesses, it is very difficult to express them accurately with precise numbers. Yet, conventional BNs can only employ probabilities expressed as real numbers." (ibid., p. 42). This is oblivious to the critique of Bayesianism in law (see Sections 2.4 and 5.1 in this book). Halliwell et al. (2003) introduced an extension of probability theory, allowing to express *subjective probabilities* as *fuzzy* numbers.

specified route a measure of the probability of that route can be determined. By determining the complexities of alternative routes leading to the formation of the same set of traces, the odds indicating the relative plausibility of the alternative routes can be found" (ibid., from the abstract). Overill, Silomon, and Chow (2010a) exemplified this method of their by applying in the context of a digital forensic examination. The court case taken as a real case study is still the same that was tried in Hong Kong, about BitTorrent and the illegal upload of a copyright protected audio-visual file.

The *operational complexity model (OCM)* is described as follows:

The various *feasible routes* by which the recovered set of digital evidential traces could have been formed are first enumerated. For each feasible route k by which the set of digital evidential traces $\{E_i\}$ could have been formed the operational complexity of that route is given by:

$$C_k = KLM_k + CC_k$$

C_k is the operational complexity of each feasible route k. It is a measure which "comprises a cognitive complexity component specified by the GOMS-KLM model[243] [(Kieras, 2001)] and a suitably defined computational complexity (CC) [(Papadimitriou, 1994)] component." C_k is inversely related to p_k, i.e., its probability of occurrence:

The constant of proportionality is determined uniquely by the normalization condition on the sum of the probabilities over all feasible routes k:

$$p_k \propto C_k^{-1}$$

The constant of proportionality α reflects the units in which the complexity of each of the feasible routes k is measured, and is given by:

$$\sum p_k = 1$$

It should be noted here that while the OCM model makes use of a complexity metric it is not based on Shannon information theory [(Shannon & Weaver, 1949)], which would lead to an inverse exponential relation:

$$\alpha = \left(\sum C_k^{-1}\right)^{-1}$$

Let $\{E_i\}$ be a recovered set of digital evidential traces. Let H_k be the hypothesis that feasible route k was taken. Overill, Silomon, and Chow (2010a) combined their definitons as given above, with probabilistic calculations. The *posterior probability* of a feasible route k leading to the formation of $\{E_i\}$ is given by

---

[243] The GOMS (Goals, Operators, Methods, Selections) family of models of *cognitive complexity* includes the GOMS Keyboard-Level Model (KLM), developed by Kieras (2001), and which provides a tractable means of measuring human involvement in the operational process.

$$Pr(H_k|\{E_i\})$$

The *posterior odds* for two alternative routes k and k' leading to the formation of the same recovered set of digital evidential traces $\{Ei\}$ is then given by:

$$O(k:k') = Pr(H_k|\{E_i\}) / Pr(H_{k'}|\{E_i\})$$

Note that the odds are independent of the constant of proportionality since α appears linearly in both the numerator and the denominator.

In a digital forensics context, if H_k represents the prosecution's contention regarding the formation of $\{E_i\}$ and $H_{k'}$ is the defence's alternative contention, then the odds $O(k:k')$ provide a measure of the relative plausibility of the two competing hypotheses. More generally, if a total of n feasible routes are identified which are each capable of leading to the formation of the set of recovered traces, then the odds that feasible route k was taken are given by:

$$O(k) = Pr(H_k|\{E_i\}) / Pr(H_k^c|\{E_i\})$$

where H_k^c is the hypothesis that feasible route k was *not* taken, and involves summing the individual probabilities of the remaining $n-1$ feasible routes.

6.2.1.8 Intrusion Detection in Computer Resources A Glimpse of an Intruder's Modus Operandi

One of the areas of *computer forensics* is *intrusion detection.*[244] "An intrusion is when a hacker attempts top break into or misuse a computer system, Web site, or network. Yet another way to define an intrusion is any set of actions that attempt to compromise the integrity, confidentiality, or availability of a computer resource" (Mena, 2003, p. 301). "There are two types of potential intruders, the outside hacker and the inside one. Remarkably, FBI studies have revealed that 80% of intrusions and attacks come from within organizations" (Mena, 2003, p. 302). In the rest of Section 6.2.1, we are only going to discuss the subject selectively.

Mena (2003, section 10.2, pp. 302–309) provides an articulate, detailed description of the likely *modus operandi* of a hacker intent on intruding into a target system. See Fig. 6.2.1.8.1. Mena's description of the *intelligence* stage an intruder would carry out, enumerates such Web resources that the hacker may use in order to learn about the structure of a firm or organisation, and in order to detect possible openings for an intrusion. For example, security at the networks and webpages of the new acquisitions of a company are likely to lag behind the security at parent company. A distributed database, the *Domain Name Service* (*DNS*), mapping addresses and hostnames to each other, may be configured insecurely, and then an attacker may

---

[244] John McHugh (2001) provides a historical and methodological overview of intrusion detection in computer security.

Fig. 6.2.1.8.1 Stages in the *modus operandi* of an intentional system intrusion (based on text in Mena, 2003, pp. 302–303)

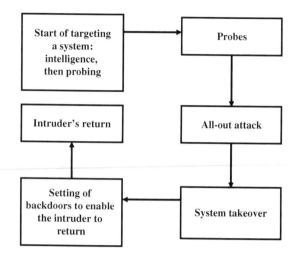

learn addresses, and then the map of the internal network of the firm or organisation that the attacker is targetting.

It is at the next stage, *scanning*, that the intruder may use automated discovery tools in order to carry out *ping sweeps* (sending *ping* requests, i.e., checks whether a system is alive, massively in parallel), and *port scans* (which may be done, e.g., by using a tool called *Nmap*, which determines which type of operating system a target computer is using).

At the next stage, *probing*, "an attacker will attempt to identify user accounts, network resopurces, users and groups, file-sharing lists, and applications" (Mena, 2003, p. 306). Mena explains which utilities an intruder may use for probing, on different operating systems. The next stage is attack, and Mena (ibid., p. 307) explains which utilities on different operating systems an intruder may use in order in order to eavesdrop for passwords, and would then break in.

At the next stage, the intruder would try to take *control* of the system. Mena (ibid., p. 307) explains which utilities an intruder would use in order to gain *administrator privileges*. And finally, the intruder would set *trapdoors*, "to secure privileged access, and enabling return", Mena explains (ibid., p. 308), proceeding to enumerate which tools a cybercriminal would be use at this last stage. For example, *netcat*, a tool for network debugging and exploration, "reads and writes data across network connections", is used "for planting remote-control, services", and "can create almost any kind of connection a perpetrator needs" (ibid.).[245]

---

[245] The research literature about *intrusion detection* is vast. See, e.g., e volume edited by Kreibich and Jahnke (2010).

6.2.1.9 A Classification of Intrusion Detection Systems

Intrusion detection systems (*IDS*) try to automatically detect break-ins, but also "a legitimate user misusing system resources" (Mena, 2003, p. 311). Coull, Branch, Szymanski, and Breimer pointed out (2003, p. 24):

> Standard security deployments such as firewalls, patched operating systems and pass-word protection are limited in their effectiveness because of the evolving sophistication of intrusion methods and their increasing ability to break through entry points of a guarded infrastructure [...]. An intrusion detection system (IDS) addresses the layer of security following the failure of the prior devices. This layer usually monitors any number of data sources (i.e., audit logs, keystrokes, network traffic) for signs of inappropriate or anomalous behavior. Since attacks occurring at this level are sophisticated enough to bypass entry point protection, advanced algorithms and frameworks for detection are required to prevent total subversion of critical resources. While no computer or network is entirely secure, intrusion detection is essential for any computer-based infrastructure, in which the value of its assets draws the attention of potential attackers.

Patterns of detection include *misuse intrusions*, vs. *anomaly intrusions*. (One also classifies the respective tasks into *penetration identification* vs. *anomaly detection*.) *Anomaly intrusions* can be detected based on a profile of the system being monitored. As an example,[246] consider Zhang, Zhu, Jeffay, Marron, and Smith (2008, p. 1):

> In the context of Internet traffic anomaly detection, we will show that some outliers in a time series can be difficult to detect at one scale while they are easy to find at another scale. In this paper, we develop an outlier detection method for a time series with long range dependence, and conclude that testing outliers at multiple time scales helps to reveal them. We present a multi-resolution anomaly detection (MRAD) procedure for detecting network anomalies.

As to *misuse intrusions*, being "well-defined attacks on known weak points of a system" (Mena, 2003, p. 309), they can be detected by data mining audit-trail information, using pattern matching (ibid.). Mena (2003, p. 311) suggests to use a hybrid program, combining both approaches, that "would always be monitoring the system for potential intrusions, but would be able to ignore spurious false alarms if they resulted from legitimate user actions" (ibid.). But false negatives, i.e., ignoring intrusive activities that are not anomalous, "is far more serious than the problem of false positives", i.e., false alarms (ibid., p. 310).[247] *Misuse detection schemes* look for attacks "in the form of a pattern or signature[248] so that even variations of

---

[246] Also see, e.g., Perdisci et al. (2009). They described the McPAD system.

[247] "It is not uncommon for the number of real attacks to be far below the false-alarm rate. Real attacks are often so far below the false-alarm rate that they are often missed and ignored" (http://en.wikipedia.org/wiki/Intrusion_detection_system).

[248] A *signature* is string of information that an intrusion detection sensor looks for in a packet sent through the network, and if the string matches the signature, then it is detected as an event in an intrusion detection context. Packets are small manageable pieces into which the data is broken up, so it could be sent through a network. A *signature-based intrusion-detection system* (*IDS*) "monitors packets in the Network and compares with preconfigured and predetermined attack patterns known as signatures. The issue is that there will be lag between the new threat discovered and Signature being applied in IDS for detecting the threat. During this lag time your IDS will

the same attack can be detected", but, "not unlike virus detection systems — they can detect many or all known attack patterns, but are of little use for as yet unknown attack methods" (ibid.). *Anomaly detection* tends to rely on techniques from artificial intelligence[249]:

> An *Anomaly-Based Intrusion Detection System* is a system for detecting computer intrusions and misuse by monitoring system activity and classifying it as either *normal* or *anomalous*. The classification is based on *heuristics* or rules, rather than patterns or *signatures*, and will detect any type of misuse that falls out of normal system operation. This is as opposed to signature based systems which can only detect attacks for which a signature has previously been created.
>
> In order to determine what is attack traffic, the system must be taught to recognize normal system activity. This can be accomplished in several ways, most often with *artificial intelligence* type techniques. Systems using *neural networks* have been used to great effect. Another method is to define what normal usage of the system comprises using a strict mathematical model, and flag any deviation from this as an attack. This is known as strict anomaly detection.
>
> Anomaly-based Intrusion Detection does have some short-comings, namely a high false positive rate and the ability to be fooled by a correctly delivered attack. Attempts have been made to address these issues through techniques used by PAYL and MCPAD.

Apart from *misuse IDSs*[250] and *anomaly IDSs*,[251] there also exist a different criterion of classification: *host-based IDS*,[252] also known as *event log viewer*, carrying out monitoring for suspicious activity by checking event logs from multiple

---

be unable to identify the threat" (http://en.wikipedia.org/wiki/Intrusion_detection_system). "Many attacks are geared for specific versions of software that are usually outdated. A constantly changing library of signatures is needed to mitigate threats. Outdated signature databases can leave the IDS vulnerable to new strategies" (ibid.).

[249] http://en.wikipedia.org/wiki/Anomaly-based_intrusion_detection_system

[250] *Misuse detection* is the subject of, e.g., Kinder et al. (2005) and Meier et al. (2005).

[251] *Anomaly detection* within intrusion detection is the subject of, e.g., Valeur et al. (2005); Latendresse (2005); Agbaria and Friedman (2005). The research literature about this subject is vast. Bear in mind however that *anomaly detection* is a broader subject, as the more general topic looms large in *data mining* research. "*Anomaly detection*, also referred to as *outlier detection*, refers to detecting patterns in a given data set that do not conform to an established normal behavior. The patterns thus detected are called anomalies and often translate to critical and actionable information in several application domains. Anomalies are also referred to as *outliers*, surprise, aberrant, deviation, peculiarity, etc. Three broad categories of anomaly detection techniques exist. Supervised anomaly detection techniques learn a classifier using labeled instances belonging to normal and anomaly class, and then assign a normal or anomalous label to a test instance. Semi-supervised anomaly detection techniques construct a model representing normal behavior from a given normal training data set, and then test the likelihood of a test instance to be generated by the learnt model. Unsupervised anomaly detection techniques detect anomalies in an unlabeled test data set under the assumption that majority of the instances in the data set are normal" (http://en.wikipedia.org/wiki/Anomaly_detection). As to computer security: "Anomaly detection for IDS is normally accomplished with thresholds and statistics, but can also be done with *soft computing* [i.e., neural, genetic, or fuzzy techniques], and inductive learning. Types of statistics proposed by 1999 included profiles of users, workstations, networks, remote hosts, groups of users, and programs based on frequencies, means, variances, covariances, and standard deviations" (ibid.). It was Dorothy Denning (1986) who introduced anomaly detection for intrusion detection systems.

[252] *Host-based intrusion detection* is the subject of, e.g., Dreger et al. (2005).

sources (Mena, 2003, p. 321). They operate in nearly real time, so "system faults are often detected quickly" (ibid.). "These host-based IDSs are ideal for detecting computer misuse from inside users or outsiders who have already infiltrated a network" (ibid.). Coull et al. explain (2003, p. 25):

> Traditionally, there have been two main classes of IDSs: hostbased and network-based systems. A host-based IDS monitors the detailed activity of a particular host. Depending on the specific IDS implementation, any number of data sources can be used to search for malicious activity. Solaris Basic Security Module (BSM) provides system call traces which are typically used as datasets for host-based IDSs [253]. For instance, when an analysis of the BSM data shows signs of an intrusion, the IDS alerts the system administrator of an attack. In other implementations, hostbased systems also use such identifying information as a user's keystrokes and command execution patterns.

By contrast, there exist *network-based IDSs*, and these monitor all network traffic. They monitor networks of computers as well as other devices, these being routers and gateways, that intruders tend to attack: "rather than using machine and process-oriented data, such as that from BSM, network-based IDSs primarily use data from network traffic in detecting intrusions." (Coull et al., 2003, p. 25). "A network-based IDSs view is restricted to what passes over a given line" (Mena, 2003, p. 321). In particular, *tcpdump* is a popular program for capturing network traffic. It can display or store every field belonging to a TCP packet.[254] Some IDSs are hybrids, that combine network-based and host-based intrusion-detection in the same package (Mena, 2003, p. 321).

Let us say something about the difference between intrusion detection systems (*IDS*) and *firewalls*. A firewall is a fence, without much discernment. A firewall is placed at the perimeter of a computer system.[255] An IDS can be placed outside the firewall, in order to gather information about an attack, as well as inside a firewall, in order to check information that goes out. A firewall, once it is turned on, shuts off all communication from outside (while not blocking outgoing connections from inside the system), and then turns back on some few well-chosen items. A firewall restricts access to designated points, but cannot detect whether by other criteria

---

[253] A document describing BSM is S.M. Inc.'s Sunshield *Basic Security Module Guide, Solaris*7 (Sun Part No. 8052635-10, October 1998).

[254] Available via anonymous FTP from ftp.ee.lbl.gov (by V. Jacobson, C. Leres, and S. McCanne, June 1989). ICP is the Transmission Control Protocol. The Internet is based (among the other things) on this protocol.

[255] A firewall is defined by Greg Stocksdale of the U.S. National Security Agency Information Systems security Organization as "A system or combination of systems that enforces a boundary between two or more networks. Gateway that limits access between networks in accordance with local security policy" (Mena, 2003, pp. 422–422). Stocksdale provided an example based on the UNIX operating systems: "The typical firewall is an inexpensive micro-based UNIX box kept clean of critical data, with many modems and public network ports on it, but just one carefully watched connection back to the rest of the cluster" (Mena 2003, p. 423). An *application level gateway* is defined by Stocksdale as "A firewall system in which service is provided by processes that maintain complete TCP [i.e., the Internet's Transmission Control Protocol] connection state and sequencing. Application level firewalls often re-address traffic so that outgoing traffic appears to have originated from the firewall, rather than the internal host" (Mena 2003, p. 419).

a communication from outside going through the designated points is legitimate. More generally, a firewall cannot by itself recognise attempts to break it. A fence around premises blocks intruders from walking it, but not from climbing on the fence, or digging under the fence. It is an IDS that has the task to recognise attacks. Moreover, a firewall is at the boundary, whereas an IDS may also recognise attacks inside the system.[256]

Malicious traffic analysis is necessary not only in traditional computer networks, but also in *wireless mobile ad hoc networks (MANET)*. These have a highly dynamic topology, without infrastructure. There may be *malicious intermediate nodes* in a MANET, and these constitute a threat both to security and to anonymity. Mizanur Rahman et al. (2008) proposed RINOMO, an anonymous on-demand routing protocol for MANETs. It is purported to be robust, and to both protect anonymity, and achieve security in MANETs. In order to obtain secure communication, legitimate nodes in the network need be authenticated.[257] Once they are authenticated, they

---

[256] "Though they both relate to network security, an intrusion detection system (IDS) differs from a firewall in that a firewall looks outwardly for intrusions in order to stop them from happening. Firewalls limit access between networks to prevent intrusion and do not signal an attack from inside the network. An IDS evaluates a suspected intrusion once it has taken place and signals an alarm. An IDS also watches for attacks that originate from within a system. This is traditionally achieved by examining network communications, identifying heuristics and patterns (often known as signatures) of common computer attacks, and taking action to alert operators. A system that terminates connections is called an *intrusion prevention system*, and is another form of an *application layer firewall*" (http://en.wikipedia.org/wiki/Intrusion_detection_system).

[257] Yu et al. (2008) discussed *biometric*-based user authentication in mobile ad hoc networks. "In high security MANETs, continuous authentication is desirable so that a system can be monitored for the duration of the session to reduce the vulnerability. Biometrics provides some possible solutions to the authentication problem in MANETs, since it has direct connection with user identity" (ibid., p. 5). They proposed to use not just one biometric technology, but *multimodal biometrics*, in order "to exploit the benefits of one biometric while mitigating the inaccuracies of another. We propose an optimal multimodal biometric-based continuous authentication scheme in MANETs" (ibid.).

"Biometrics, which refers to identifying an individual based on his or her physiological or behavioral characteristics, has the capability to reliably distinguish between an authorized person and an imposter. A biometric system can be operated in two modes: (1) verification mode and (2) identification mode (Jain et al., 2000). The former is called *person verification*, or *person authentication*. A biometric system operating in the verification mode either accepts or rejects a user's claimed identity, while a biometric system operating in the identification mode establishes the identity of the user without any claimed identity information" (Khuwaja, 2006, pp. 23–24). Jain et al. (1999) is a book on the subject. Bromby (2010) discussed how biometrics can aid certification of digital signatures. The most mature technique for person verification, or one of the most mature, is fingerprint-based identification. Other approaches are based on "face, hand geometry, iris, retina, signature, voice print, facial thermogram hand vein, gait, ear, odor, keystroke dynamics, etc." (Khuwaja, 2006, p. 24). For example, *iris recognition* is the subject of Li et al. (2002), Yunhong et al. (2003). *Retina recognition* is discussed by Yoichi Seto (2009).

Biometric fusion (or *information fusion in biometrics*: Ross & Jain, 2003) is "[t]he general method of improving performance via collection of multiple samples" (Rattani, Mehrotra, & Gupta, 2008, p. 485). *Multi-biometrics* is "[t]he ability to utilize multiple biometrics modalities (multimodal), instances within a modality (multi-instance), and/or algorithms (multi-algorithmic) prior to making a sepecific verification / identification or enrollment decision" (ibid.), where *enrollment* is "[t]he initial process of collecting biometric data from a user and then storing it in a template for later use" (ibid., p. 484).

can communicate by using *pseudo IDs*. The generation of pseudo IDs resorts to pairing-based cryptography. Mizanur Rahman et al. claimed (2009, p. 179):

> Nodes can generate their pseudo IDs independently and dynamically without consulting with system administrator. As a result, RINOMO reduces pseudo IDs maintenance costs. Only trust-worthy nodes are allowed to take part in routing to discover a route. To ensure trustiness each node has to make authentication to its neighbors through the designed anonymous authentication process. Thus, RINOMO safely communicates between nodes without disclosing node identities. It also provides different desirable anonymous properties such as identity privacy, location privacy, route anonymity, and robustness against several attacks.

6.2.1.10 Intrusion Detection by Means of Various Learning Techniques

Some IDSs resort to neural networks, for profiling (rather than for classification), whereas some other IDSs resort to machine learning algorithms (Mena, 2003, p. 322). Mena (ibid., section 10.7, pp. 313–318) presents a case study from the MITRE corporation, of the use of data mining for intrusion detection (their Data Mining in ID project). Data mining is called for, because of data overload. "Metalearning IDSs have been developed at Columbia University. Metalearning integrates a number of different classifiers. This type of IDS benefits from a multilayered approach in which machine learning and decision procedures detect intrusions locally" (Mena, ibid., p. 323).

Various approaches within machine learning have been applied to intrusion detection.[258] Zonghua Zhang and Hong Shen (2004) reported about the online training of *support vector machines*[259] for real-time intrusion detection. So did Kim and Park (2003). Hu et al. (2003) applied a variant, called *robust support vector machines*, to anomaly detection in computer security.[260] Another method in machine learning is *boosting*.[261] Webb (2000) introduced *multi-boosting*. The

---

[258] In Canada, the joint editor of the *Computational Intelligence* journal, Ali Ghorbani, and his collaborators (Ren, Stakhanova, & Ghorbani, 2010) have described an online *adaptive* approach to *alert correlation*. Bear in mind that apart from *machine learning* (which is part of *artificial intelligence*), there also exist adaptive control (which is part of *systems & control*, historically a different discipline within the mathematics of engineering, concerned with the modelling of *dynamic systems*).

[259] *Support vector machines* (*SVMs*) are the subject of Section 6.1.9.3 in this book.

[260] Hu et al. (2003) presented an application *robust support vector machines* (*RSVMs*), to anomaly detection over noisy data. They described as follows the advantage of RSVMs for the purposes of intrusion detection: "RSVMs effectively address the over-fitting problem introduced by the noise in the training data set. With RSVMs, the incorporation of an averaging technique in the standard support vector machines makes the decision surface smoother and controls the amount of regularization automatically [...]. Moreover, the number of support vectors of RSVMs is significantly less compared to those of standard SVMs. Therefore, RSVMs have a faster testing time" (ibid., p. 168). RSVMs were introduced by Song et al. (2002), who applied them to *bullet hole image classification*.

[261] "Boosting improves the predictive power of classifier learning systems by adjusting the weights of training instances. It manipulates the training data in order to generate different classifiers. Boosting uses all instances at each repetition, but maintains a weight for each instance in the

algorithm appeared ibid., in table 4 on p. 169. "MultiBoosting can be viewed as combining AdaBoost[262] with wagging.[263] It is able to harness both AdaBoost's high bias and variance reduction with wagging's superior variance reduction" (ibid., p. 159). Bie, Jin, Chen, Xu, and Huang (2007) applied that approach to intrusion detection:

> [T]raditional data mining based intrusion detection systems use single classifier in their detection engines. In this paper, we propose a meta learning based method for intrusion detection by MultiBoosting multi classifiers. MultiBoosting can form decision committees by combining AdaBoost with wagging. It is able to harness both AdaBoost's high bias and variance reduction with wagging's superior variance reduction.

Bie et al. explained (ibid., p. 811):

> MultiBoosting [(Webb, 2000)][264] can be considered as wagging (which is in turn a variant of bagging) committees formed by AdaBoost. A decision is made as to the size of sub-committees, and how many sub-committees should be formed for a single run. In the absence of an a-priori reason for selecting any specific values for those factors, MultiBoost takes a single committee size T and sets the number of subcommittees and the size of those sub-committees to square of T. Note that both these values must be whole numbers, it is necessary to round off the result. Deriving the values is achieved by setting a target final

---

training set that reflects its importance; adjusting the weights causes the learner to focus on different instances and so leads to different classifiers. The multiple classifiers are then combined by voting to form a composite classifier" (Stranieri & Zeleznikow, 2005b).

[262] "*AdaBoost*, short for Adaptive Boosting, is a machine learning algorithm, formulated by Yoav Freund and Robert Schapire [(1997)]. It is a meta-algorithm, and can be used in conjunction with many other learning algorithms to improve their performance. AdaBoost is adaptive in the sense that subsequent classifiers built are tweaked in favor of those instances misclassified by previous classifiers. AdaBoost is sensitive to noisy data and outliers. However in some problems it can be less susceptible to the overfitting problem than most learning algorithms. AdaBoost calls a weak classifier repeatedly in a series of rounds $t = 1, ...,T$ from a total T classifiers. For each call a distribution of weights D_t is updated that indicates the importance of examples in the data set for the classification. On each round, the weights of each incorrectly classified example are increased (or alternatively, the weights of each correctly classified example are decreased), so that the new classifier focuses more on those examples" (http://en.wikipedia.org/wiki/AdaBoost).

[263] *Wagging* is the subject of section 7.4.2.2. in Rokach and Maimon (2008). "Wagging is a variant of Bagging [Bauer and Kohavi (1999)] in which each classifier is trained on the entire training set, but each instance is stochastically assigned a weight" (ibid., Rokach & Maimon's brackets). Webb (2000, p. 161) explained *wagging*: "Wagging (Bauer & Kohavi, in press [1999]) is variant of bagging, that requires a base learning algorithm that can utilize training cases with differing weights. Rather than using random bootstrap samples to form the successive training sets, wagging assigns random weights to the cases in each training set. Bauer and Kohavi's (in press [1999]) original formulation of wagging used Gaussian noise to vary the instance weights. However, this can lead to some instance weights being reduced to zero, effectively removing them from the training set. Instead, following a suggestion from J. R. Quinlan (personal communication, May 1998) the new technique uses the continuous Poisson distribution to assign random instance weights. As the assignment of instance weights by bagging can be modeled by the discrete Poisson distribution, use of the continuous Poisson distribution can be viewed as assigning instance weights using an equivalent distribution to bagging, but over a continuous rather than discrete space."

[264] Contrast this to the theory of *multiclass boosting* of Indraneel Mukherjee and Robert Schapire (2011).

sub-committee member index, where each member of the final committee is given an index by starting from one. Due to too great or too low error, that allows the premature termination of boosting one sub-committee to lead to an increase in the size of the next sub-committee. An additional sub-committee is added with a target of completing the full complement of committee members if the last sub-committee is prematurely terminated. When this additional sub-committee also fails to reach this target, this process is repeated, adding further sub-committees until the target total committee size is achieved.

There exist applications of machine learning also to intrusion detection in *wireless sensor networks* (*WSNs*). Misra, Abraham, Obaidat, and Krishna (2009) described the LAID scheme. They applied *learning automata* for that purpose. The feedback is an *S*-shaped function: the feedback from the environment to the automaton is not crisp (completely favourable or completely unfavourable), but also any continuous value within those extremes.

6.2.1.11 Masquerading and Its Detection

Anomaly detection systems can detect previously unknown attacks, and therefore "anomaly-based systems are strongly applicable to masquerade detection" (Coull et al., 2003, p. 25). *Masquerading* is a security attack – one of the most damaging kinds of attacks indeed – "in which an intruder assumes the identity of a legitimate user. Many approaches based on Hidden Markov Models and various forms of Finite State Automata were proposed to solve this problem" (ibid., p. 24). Coull et al. explain (ibid.):

Masquerade attacks typically occur when an intruder obtains a legitimate user's password or when a user leaves their workstation unattended without any sort of locking mechanism in place. It is difficult to detect this type of security breach at its initiation because the attacker appears to be a normal user with valid authority and privileges. This difficulty underlines the importance of equipping computer systems with the ability to distinguish masquerading attacker actions from legitimate user activities.

The detection of a masquerader relies on a user signature, a sequence of commands collected from a legitimate user. This signature is compared to the current user's session. The underlying assumption is that the user signature captures detectable patterns in a user's sequence of commands. A sequence of commands produced by the legitimate user should match well with patterns in the user's signature, whereas a sequence of commands entered by a masquerader should match poorly with the user's signature. Designing algorithms to distinguish legitimate users and masqueraders based on user signatures has been extensively studied [(Maxion & Townsend, 2002; Schonlau et al., 2001)].

In particular (Coull et al., 2003, p. 25):

A seminal work by Schonlau et al. [(2001)] analyzes the performance of various masquerade detection methods. Results showed that the method yielding the lowest number of false alarms was *uniqueness*, which had a false positive rate of 1.4%. However, it had a false–negative rate of 60.0%. Another good performer was the *Bayes one-step Markov* with a false positive rate of 6.7% and a false negative rate of 30.7%. In another paper [(Maxion & Townsend, 2002)], Maxion and Townsend analyzed the sources of error made by the detection mechanisms covered by Schonlau et al. and proposed several improved methods, among which the *Naïve Bayes with updates* yielded excellent 1.3% of false positive rate with a respectable 38.5% of false negative rate.

Coull et al. (2003) – an article from Boleslaw Szymanski's team at Rensselaer Polytechnic Institute in Troy, NY – approaches masquerading detection by applying to that task "a new algorithm that uses pair-wise sequence alignment to characterize similarity between sequences of commands" (ibid., p. 24). "Sequence alignment has been extensively applied in the field of bioinformatics as a tool for comparing genetic material [(Gelfand, Mironov, & Pevzner, 1996; Goad & Kanehisa, 1982)]. Our algorithm, which is a unique variation of the classic Smith-Waterman algorithm [(Smith & Waterman, 1981)], uses a novel scoring scheme to construct a semi-global alignment. The algorithm produces an effective metric for distinguishing a legitimate user from a masquerader" (Coull et al., ibid.). "The novelty of our approach results from application of techniques used in bioinformatics for a pair-wise sequence alignment to compare the monitored session with the past user behavior. Our algorithm uses a semi-global alignment and a unique scoring system to measure similarity between a sequence of commands produced by a potential intruder and the user signature, which is a sequence of commands collected from a legitimate user." (ibid.). After testing, the team found that "that the described algorithm yields a promising combination of intrusion detection rate and false positive rate, when compared to the published intrusion detection algorithms" (ibid.).

Coull et al. (2003, p. 27) explained why they chose to depart from the Smith-Waterman algorithm:

> The problem with using a purely local alignment to characterize similarity between command sequences is that both a prefix and suffix can be ignored in both sequences. For intrusion detection, it is critical that we align the majority of the tested block of commands to the user's signature. If we were to allow a large prefix and large suffix of the tested block of commands to be ignored then the intrusion itself might be ignored.

Also using a purely global alignment algorithm would have been unsuitable (Coull et al., ibid.):

> The problem with using a purely global alignment is that there may be large portions of the signature that do not necessarily align with a segment of the user's commands. Thus, we want to design a scoring system that rewards the alignment of commands in the user segment but does not necessarily penalize the misalignment of large portions of the signature.

Let *UserSign* stand for the *signature sequence.* It represents the user's typical command behaviour. Let *IntrBlck* stand for the tested block, i.e., the block being tested for intrusion. This is the monitored command sequence, which may contain a possible subsequence of masquerader commands. "Since the *UserSig* is significantly longer than the *IntrBlck*, it is expected that most of the commands in the *UserSig* will not participate in the alignment" (Coull et al., 2003, p. 27). Coull et al. (ibid., p. 28, figure 4) modified the Smith-Waterman *local alignment alogirithm*, and proposed the following *semi-global alignment algorithm*:

```
Input: string UserSig of length m,
       string IntrBlck of length n
1. Initialize a matrix, D,
          of type integer
```

```
2.  for i=0 to m
3.  for j=0 to n
4.  if(j=0 or i=0)
5.  D[i][j]=0;
6.  else
7.  if(j=n or i=m)
8.  top=D[i][j-1];
9.  left=D[i-1][j];
10. else
11. top=D[i][j-1] - gUserSig;
12. left=D[i-1][j] - gIntrBlck;
13. if(top<0) top=D[i][j-1];
14. if(left<0) left=D[i-1][j];
15. diagonal=D[i-1][j-1] +
              matchScore(UserSigi-1,
                         IntrBlckj-1);
16. D[i][j]=maximum(top,left,diagonal);
17. return D[m][n];
```

Coull et al. (2003, p. 27) explained that in the beginning, this algorithm initialises a matrix of float. This matrix is used to store the score throughout the alignment process.

Each position (i, j) in the matrix corresponds to the optimal score of an alignment ending at *UserSig$_j$* and *IntrBlck$_j$*. This optimal score is computed by starting at the upper left corner of the matrix (i.e., at the point $(0,0)$) and then recursively making a step yielding the maximum from the three following options:

> Option 1 (diagonal step): The alignment score ending at position $(i-1,j-1)$ plus *matchScore*(UserSig$_i$,IntrBlck$_j$), which is a penalty or reward for aligning the UserSig's ith command with the IntrBlck's jth command.
> Option 2 (top-down step): The alignment score ending at position $(i, j-1)$ plus *gUserSig*, which is the penalty for introducing a gap into the UserSig, or
> Option 3 (left-right step): The optimal score ending at position $(i-1, j)$ plus *gIntrBlck*, which is the penalty for introducing a gap into the *IntrBlck*.

If Option 1 yields the largest value, then the optimal alignment matches *UserSig$_i$* with *IntrBlck$_j$*. If Option 2 or Option 3 yields the largest score, then the optimal alignment associates either *UserSig$_i$* or *IntrBlck$_j$* with a gap.

There are three essential parameters used in the scoring system. The *matchScore(UserSig$_i$,IntrBlck$_j$)* function returns a negative value if the two commands do not match well and a positive value if they do. The *gUserSig* and *gIntrBlck* are negative gap penalties associated with inserting gaps into the *UserSig* and *IntrBlck*, respectively.

This approach heavily penalises "any gaps that may be inserted into the user signature, as we do not want commands in the tested block to be aligned with gaps in the user's signature" (Coull et al., 2003, p. 29). Eventually, a paper by Coull and Szymanski (2008) in the journal *Computational Statistics and Data*

Analysis described further progress concerning sequence alignment for masquerade detection. Their method included the algorithm for alignment, enriched with "several scoring systems, methods for accommodating variations in user behavior, and heuristics for decreasing the computational requirements of the algorithm" (ibid., p. 4116). Another paper from Szymanski's team (Bivens, Palagiri, Smith, Szymanski, & Embrechts, 2002) applied *neural networks* to network-based intrusion detection. Another approach to intrusion detection was described by Branch, Bivens, Chan, Lee, and Szymanski (2002), from the same team: it resorted to *time dependent deterministic finite automata*.

6.2.1.12 Honeypots for Trapping Intruders

The goal of Honeynet Project[265] – reported about by Spitzner (2003a) – is trapping hackers, by providing them with so-called *honeypots*. Information on hackers is gathered "by deploying networks (called honeynets) around the world to be compromised" (ibid.). Honeynet is just one out of several projects resorting to networks of honeypots. The Honeynet Research Alliance coordinates honeynet research around the world. The seminal paper on honeypots was by Cheswick (1992),[266] of AT&T Bell Laboratories.[267] Cheswick's paper began as follows:

> On 7 January 1991 a cracker, believing he had discovered the famous sendmail DEBUG hole in our Internet gateway machine, attempted to obtain a copy of our password file. I sent him one. For several months we led this cracker on a merry chase in order to trace his location and learn his techniques. This paper is a chronicle of the cracker's "successes" and disappointments, the bait and traps used to lure and detect him, and the chroot [sic] "Jail" we built to watch his activities.

Basically, *honeypots* could be any out of various computer resources, such as a computer on a network, or a password file, or an entry in a database, or an Excel spreadsheet. Typically, research into honeypots has been concerned computers in a network which are used as an information system resource, the value of that resource lying in its unauthorised or illicit use. It is a computer unused by the legitimate users of the network: they don't know about it, so it is not involved in legitimate network traffic. The assumption is that any traffic it gets is malicious by definition, i.e., attacks. An attacker would think this is a normal computer. A log is maintained on a remote machine, of any interactions the honeypot gets. There are *low-interaction honeypots*, and *high-interaction honeypots*.[268]

---

[265] Papers about the project are posted at the website of the Honeynet Project, under the rubric "Know Your Enemy" Whitepapers (http://www.honeynet.org/papers/).

[266] Honeypots are the subject of, e.g., Provos and Holz (2007), Göbel et al. (2006), Spitzner, 2002, (2003b, 2004); Oudot (2003); Oudot and Holz (2004); Dulaunoy (2010); Crandall, Wu, and Chong (2005); Pouget and Holz (2005).

[267] By the late 2000s, Bill Cheswick was affiliated with the Department of Computer Science of Columbia University, in New York City.

[268] The presentation in the present Section 6.2.1.12 is partly based on a nicely organised slideshow by Claire O'Shea (2005), available on the Web.

Low-interaction honeypots are simple, low-cost, and low-risk (because an attacker never enters a real system). The information obtained by this kind of honeypots is limited however, there are new types of attacks such honeypots may miss, and moreover attackers may easily detect that this is a honeypot. In a low-interaction honeypot, what an attacker interacts with is a simulated computer, and one real machine may simulate various things, such as an entire network of *virtual honeypots*.

High-interaction honyepots are real systems running real services, and these serivces will be compromised. Interactions will be monitored and logged in detail, so detailed information would be obtained about what an attacker did. Moreover[269]:

Honeypots can be classified based on their deployment and based on their level of involvement. Based on the deployment, honeypots may be classified as

1. Production Honeypots
2. Research Honeypots[270]

What is used is the *fishbowl* analogy. In real life, a fish swims inside a fishbowl at home, and never gets out of a fishbowl, inside which it finds various props, such as rocks and plants. In a honeypot organised like a fishbowl, a framework has been set up, that provides data logging and also security for the host, because the attacker

---

[269] http://en.wikipedia.org/wiki/Honeypot_(computing) At that webpage, a few types of honeypots are briefly described. For example, some honeypots are specilised as *anti-spam tools*. Moreover: "An e-mail address that is not used for any other purpose than to receive spam can also be considered a spam honeypot. Compared with the term *spamtrap*, the term 'honeypot' might better be reserved for systems and techniques used to detect or counter attacks and probes. Spam arrives at its destination 'legitimately' — exactly as non-spam e-mail would arrive" (ibid.). The Honeypot Project, which is open-source, "uses honeypot pages installed on websites around the world. These honeypot pages hand out uniquely tagged spamtrap e-mail addresses. *E-mail address harvesting* and *spammers* can then be tracked as they gather and subsequently send to these spamtrap e-mail addresses" (ibid.). Moreover, there also exist *database honeypots*: "Databases often get attacked by intruders using *SQL Injection*. Because such activities are not recognized by basic firewalls, companies often use database firewalls. Some of the available SQL database firewalls provide/support honeypot architectures to let the intruder run against a trap database while the web application still runs as usual" (ibid.).

[270] "*Production honeypots* are easy to use, capture only limited information, and are used primarily by companies or corporations; Production honeypots are placed inside the production network with other production servers by an organization to improve their overall state of security. Normally, production honeypots are low-interaction honeypots, which are easier to deploy. They give less information about the attacks or attackers than research honeypots do. The purpose of a production honeypot is to help mitigate risk in an organization. The honeypot adds value to the security measures of an organization. *Research honeypots* are run by a volunteer, non-profit research organization or an educational institution to gather information about the motives and tactics of the *Blackhat* community [see http://en.wikipedia.org/wiki/Black_hat] targeting different networks. These honeypots do not add direct value to a specific organization. Instead they are used to research the threats organizations face, and to learn how to better protect against those threats. This information is then used to protect against those threats. Research honeypots are complex to deploy and maintain, capture extensive information, and are used primarily by research, military, or government organizations" (ibid.).

could not get out of the fishbowl into other parts of the host system. Appropriate *data control*, invisible to the attacker, should be in place to prevent harm done from inside the fishbowl to machines outside it. There is still a risk that such data control would not be successful, and that other machines in the host network would be at risk. This is a disadvantage. Inside the fishbowls, there are machines that we want the attacker to attack (setting this up effectively is difficult), so the attacker's interaction with them could be watched. This is done by *data capture*, also invisible to the attacker, and recording all of the attacker's activities while in the fishbowl. (Anything that implements data control and data capture is called a *honeynet*.) Such monitoring is time-intensive, which is a disadvantage, but a detailed profile of attack can be captured, and new types of attack can also be captured, and these are advantages. Another problem with honeypots, is that the attacker may use the honeypot for carrying out criminal activities, and the host would be blamed.

Usually, high-interaction honeypots are used for research purposes, and not for intrusion detection in operational systems, because setting up and maintaining high-interaction honeypots inside operational systems would be too expensive. Symantec's Decoy Server, as well as Honeynets, are examples of high-interaction honeypots. Most *honeypot research* is on the several ways to use a honeypot as part of a security system for the purposes of *intrusion detection and prevention*. Another use of honeypots is for *attack analysis*: by observing how attackers behave, hopefully better tools to guard against them could be developed.

Moreover, honeypots can be used as *decoys*. The host populates all unused addresses on one's network with honeypots, so the attacker would have to waste time to attack such honeypots. Automated ttacks by *malware* (malicious software, especially *worms*)[271] is slowed down by decoys. As to human attackers, they are both slowed down, and annoyed, and therefore hopefully discouraged.

Another use of honeypots is as *tarpits*, also intended to slow down an attacker. A tarpit allows an attacker to open a connection, but then reduced the window size to zero. The attacker cannot get any data through, and cannot close the connection, and this uses up resources on the attacker's system. For example, a tarpit may consist of an *open email relay*, that would entice spammers because they would expect to be able to send out spam through that anonymous mail relay. The tarpit however would respond very slowly, wasting the time of spammers. Moreover, such a honeypot may pretend it forwards the mail, but actually drop it, and human spammers would be duped into thinking they had been successful, whereas automated spammers would assume success and move on.

---

[271] A *worm* is defined by Greg Stocksdale of the U.S. National Security Agency Information Systems security Organization as an "Independent program that replicates from machine to machine across network connections often clogging networks and information systems as it spreadsds" (Mena, 2003, p. 430). In contrast, a virus is "a program that can infect other programs by modifying them to include a possibly evolved copy of itself" (Stocksdale, in Mena, ibid.).

A major use of honeypots is as *burglar alarms*, because once the honyepots are compromised, system administrators know that an attack is going on. There has been speculation with some evidence, that based on abnormal activity on the honeypots, attacks can be detected a few days in advance.

Yet another use of honeypots is as a so-called *honeycomb*, in *automatic signature generation*. It detects patterns, and created *intrusion detection signatures* faster than with *manual signature generation*. *Honeyd* is a low-interaction honeypots, and uses the honeycomb as a plug-in.[272] A single machine simulates the network stack of each machine in a group of virtual machines, and also simulates the physical network between them.

The Honeyd machine[273] has been used as a network decoy, for detecting worms, for capturing spam, and for providing a front end that selectively forwards packets[274] to high-interaction honeypots. What Honeyd tries to do, is to fool so-called *fingeprinting tools* (such as *Xprobe* and *Nmap*). What is meant by *fingerprinting* in intrusion detection, is testing a network behaviour.[275] Tools like Nmap generate a *fingerprint*, which looks like abstruse code, but typifies the behaviour of the network being tested.

---

[272] The concept of a *honeycomb* was introduced by Christian Kreibich and Jon Crowcroft (2004). Kreibich has also been working on *botnets* (Caballero, Poosankam, Kreibich, & Song, 2009). Juan, Kreibich, Lin, and Paxson (2008), whose team also included Kreibich, discussed a tool for offline and live testing of *evasion resilience* in network intrusion detection systems. Cf. Dreger, Kreibich, Paxson, and Sommer (2005), on *host-based intrusion detection*.

[273] Honeyd is available as an open source, at http://www.honeyd.org

[274] When data is sent through a network, the data is broken up in to small manageable pieces called *packets*.

[275] Moreover   (http://en.wikipedia.org/wiki/Application_protocol-based_intrusion_detection_ system): "An *application protocol-based intrusion detection system* (*APIDS*) is an *intrusion detection system* that focuses its monitoring and analysis on a specific application *protocol* or protocols in use by the computing system. [...] An APIDS will monitor the dynamic behavior and *state* of the protocol and will typically consist of a system or agent that would typically sit between a *process*, or group of *servers*, *monitoring* and analyzing the application protocol between two connected devices. A typical place for an APIDS would be between a *web server* and the *database management system*, monitoring the *SQL* protocol specific to the *middleware/business logic* as it interacts with the *database*." Monitoring dynamic behaviour on the part of an APIDS involves the following. "At a basic level an APIDS would look for, and enforce, the correct (legal) use of the protocol. However at a more advanced level the APIDS can learn, be taught or even reduce what is often an infinite protocol set, to an acceptable understanding of the *subset* of that application protocol that is used by the application being monitored/protected. Thus, an APIDS, correctly configured, will allow an application to be '*fingerprinted*', thus should that application be subverted or changed, so will the fingerprint change" (ibid.). In general, regardless of their being protocol-based or otherwise, there is a class of intrusion detection systems that are known as *middleware-level IDSs*. For example, Naess, Frincke, McKinnon, and Bakken (2005) discussed configurable middleware-level intrusion detection for embedded systems.

Honeypots and honeynets[276] can be used in combination with *automated monitoring tools*. These can look for suspicious activity and send out alerts. One such tool is *Swart*. It monitors log files for predefined patterns. It is at such tasks that *data mining* has a role to play. The honeypots gather data about network attacks, and any interaction with them is assumed to be an attack. It is in order to detect this or that attack, that *pattern matching* is resorted to. Still, the more sophisticated attacks are, the harder it is to catch them with honeypots. It has also been argued that making it possible to detect the presence of honeypots may prove to be a deterrent:

> Just as honeypots are weapons against spammers, honeypot detection systems are spammer-employed counter-weapons. As detection systems would likely use unique characteristics of specific honeypots to identify them, a great deal of honeypots in use makes the set of unique characteristics larger and more daunting to those seeking to detect and thereby identify them. This is an unusual circumstance in software: a situation in which *"versionitis"* (a large number of versions of the same software, all differing slightly from each other) can be beneficial. There's also an advantage in having some easy-to-detect honeypots deployed. Fred Cohen, the inventor of the *Deception Toolkit*, even argues that every system running his honeypot should have a deception port that adversaries can use to detect the honeypot. Cohen believes that this might deter adversaries.[277]

Some honeypot systems only target automated attacks by propagating malware, rather than attacks by human attackers. This is the case of the *Nepenthes* system.[278] Göbel, Hektor, and Holz (2006) discussed the collection of malware that spread automatically (such as network *worms* or *bots*) by using the Nepenthes low-interaction honeypot. The purpose is obtaining the malware itself, its binary code is downloaded and stored for further in-depth analysis. Nepenthes only simulates the vulnerable parts of a service, not the full service for an attacker to interact with. Human attackers would easily detect Nepenthes, whereas this tool is useful for interacting with propagating malware instead. The modules of Nepenthes include:

- *vulnerability modules* (which simulate the vulnerable parts of network services);
- *shellcode parsing modules* (these analyse the code received by a vulnerability module, which is in a low-level, machine-executable, assembly language, and extract information about the malware)[279];

---

[276] "Two or more honeypots on a network form a *honeynet*. Typically, a honeynet is used for monitoring a larger and/or more diverse network in which one honeypot may not be sufficient. Honeynets and honeypots are usually implemented as parts of larger *network intrusion detection systems*. A *honeyfarm* is a centralized collection of honeypots and analysis tools." Quoted from http://en.wikipedia.org/wiki/Honeypot_(computing)

[277] http://en.wikipedia.org/wiki/Honeypot_(computing) citing Fred Cohen's *Deception Toolkit* (in turn, accessed in 2006 at http://all.net/dtk/index.html).

[278] The source code of the nepenthes system is available from http://nepenthes.mwcollect.org

[279] "Shellcode parsing modules analyze the received payload and automatically extract relevant information about the exploitation attempt. Currently, only one shellcode parsing module is capable of analyzing all shellcodes received in the wild. The module works in the following way: First, it tries to decode the shellcode. Most shellcode is obfuscated with an XOR encoder. An XOR decoder is a common way to 'encrypt' the native shellcode in order to evade intrusion detection systems

- *fetch modules* (the information which is the output of the shellcode parsing modules is used by the fetch modules in order to download the malware from some remote location);
- *submission modules* (these handle the malware once it has been downloaded: they save its code to hard disk, or store it in a database, or send it to developers of antivirus software); and
- logging modules (information about the simulation is logged by these, so that patterns in the collected data could be detected and an overview provided).

There also is an *event-driven notification mechanism* in Nepenthes, so that the events triggered by each step of an attack be registered and reacted to.

> Traditional honeypots are servers (or devices that expose server services) that wait passively to be attacked. *Client Honeypots* are active security devices in search of malicious servers that attack clients. The client honeypot poses as a client and interacts with the server to examine whether an attack has occurred. Often the focus of client honeypots is on web browsers, but any client that interacts with servers can be part of a client honeypot (for example ftp, ssh, email, etc.).[280]

In particular, there again is the distinction between *high-interaction client honeypots* and *low-interaction client honeypots*, just as there is such a distinction concerning just traditional honeypots:

> High interaction client honeypots are fully functional systems comparable to real systems with real clients. As such, no functional limitations (besides the containment strategy) exist on high interaction client honeypots. Attacks on high interaction client honeypots are detected via inspection of the state of the system after a server has been interacted with. The detection of changes to the client honeypot may indicate the occurrence of an attack against that has exploited a vulnerability of the client. An example of such a change is the presence of a new or altered file.
>
> High interaction client honeypots are very effective at detecting unknown attacks on clients. However, the tradeoff for this accuracy is a performance hit from the amount of system state that has to be monitored to make an attack assessment. Also, this detection mechanism is prone to various forms of evasion by the exploit. For example, an attack could delay the exploit from immediately triggering (time bombs) or could trigger upon a particular set of conditions or actions (logic bombs). Since no immediate, detectable state change occurred, the client honeypot is likely to incorrectly classify the server as safe even though it did successfully perform its attack on the client. Finally, if the client honeypots are running in virtual machines, then an exploit may try to detect the presence of the virtual environment and cease from triggering or behave differently.[281]

---

and string-processing functions. After decoding the code itself according to the computed key, this module then extracts more information from the shellcode (e.g., credentials). If enough information can be reconstructed to download the malware from a remote location, this information is passed to the next type of module" (Göbel et al., 2006, p. 20).

[280] http://en.wikipedia.org/wiki/Client_honeypot

[281] Ibid. Several such systems are briefly described at that webpage. So are several *low-interaction client honeypots*. "Low interaction client honeypots differ from high interaction client honeypots in that they do not utilize an entire real system, but rather use lightweight or simulated clients to interact with the server. (in the browser world, they are similar to web crawlers). Responses from servers are examined directly to assess whether an attack has taken place. This could be done, for

6.2.2 The United States' Anti-Drug Network (ADNET)

Law enforcement agencies in the United States resort to ADNET (Anti-Drug Network), with data-mining assistance from the MITRE Corporation. This is briefly described by Mena (2003, section 7.5, pp. 210–212). The bodies that share data within ADNET include the U.S. Department of Defence, the U.S. Coast Guard, the Department of Justice, the Department of State, the Department of Treasury, the Federal Communications Commission, and the U.S. intelligence community.

A U.S. governmental source explains[282]:

> The ADNET program's mission is the implementation of information systems, technologies, and services at the secret and sensitive-but-unclassified level for Department of Defense, federal, state, local, and tribal law enforcement and partnering nations.
>
> ADNET supports the Deputy Assistant Secretary of Defense for counternarcotics and its mission of counter-narcoterrorism, including:
>
> - Statutory detection and monitoring
> - Demand reduction activities
> - Support to domestic and host nation law enforcement
> - Other missions that support the war on terrorism, readiness, national security, and security cooperation goals
> - ADNET provides application and customer enclave services to the counter-narcoterrorism communities of interest.

Another source, being a resource for the press, provides further detail:

> ADNET is a community of interest that provides command, control, communication, computer, and intelligence (C4I) capabilities to help the Department of Defense (DoD) and other federal, state, and local governments detect, monitor, and interdict activities related to narcotics trafficking and narco-terrorism (CNT). These efforts are directed by the Office of the Deputy Assistant Secretary of Defense for Counternarcotics and Global Threats.[283]

The same press resource from the U.S. government explains the capabilities and serivces of ADNET as follows:

> ADNET is the primary secure link among DoD, the Office of National Drug Control Policy, Federal Communications Commission, Homeland Security, National Guard (high intensity drug trafficking areas), intelligence community, Justice, and Treasury. Interagency groups leverage ADNET's secure and accredited operational infrastructures at the Secret and Sensitive But Unclassified (SBU) levels to complete CNT tactical and strategic missions. ADNET develops and operates critical information systems such as the Counterdrug Consolidated Database (CCDB), Webshare collaboration system, FORUM (request for

---

example, by examining the response for the presence of malicious strings. Low interaction client honeypots are easier to deploy and operate than high interaction client honeypots and also perform better. However, they are likely to have a lower detection rate since attacks have to be known to the client honeypot in order for it to detect them; new attacks are likely to go unnoticed. They also suffer from the problem of evasion by exploits, which may be exacerbated due to their simplicity, thus making it easier for an exploit to detect the presence of the client honeypot" (ibid.).

[282] See http://www.disa.mil/services/adnet.html

[283] See http://www.disa.mil/news/pressresources/factsheets/adnet.html

information), counter drug (CD) common operational picture (COP), and electronic mail to support these interagency groups.

These systems utilize ADNET's enterprise products and services which includes

- maintenance of six (6) separate architectures (development, test, user acceptance, continuity of operations (COOP), ADNET-Secret, and ADNET-SBU) for full life-cycle development;
- extensive security engineering to include design and implementation of security configurations and firewall and intrusion detection system monitoring and maintenance;
- certification and accreditation documentation to ensure compliance with DoD and customer policies for operating on Secret and SBU;
- full service network operations center and service desk to provide customer and technical support from the network to the customer's edge device;
- engineering and fielding of complete information systems to include telecommunications, hardware, software development, installation, security engineering, accreditation, training, network operations, and service desk.

ADNET manages a number of devices at customer locations consisting of workstations, routers, switches, firewalls, storage area networks, and servers in the Secret and Unclassified environments.

ADNET operates an unclassified information sharing portal technology system supporting the combatant commanders, federal, state, local, and foreign governments doing intelligence preparation of the battlefield, joint operations, operational evaluations, and interdiction. The El Paso Intelligence Center leverages the ADNET Unclassified portal to allow vetted users to access the National Seizure System.

Additionally, DoD's general counsel has authorized the ADNET program to host U.S. person data on their systems.

MITRE, Mena (2003) reported, was "working on a now-fielded prototype targeting system that analyzes passenger vehicle crossing data and develops data mining rules and tools that help operators perform real-time analysis to identify potential counternarcotics targets" (ibid., p. 211). In particular, MITRE was applying techniques from *machine learning.* "The objective is to provide end users with a system that will quickly indicate if an individual coming into the United States is worthy of further inspection" (ibid.). For an incoming car at the border, this is done via the licence plate. Based on this input, ADNET informs the customs system operator about the travel patterns of that car, and whether this trip is different – and suspicious (ibid., p. 210).

The following is quoted from MITRE (2001)[284]:

Anti Drug Network (ADNET): A middle-aged man in a light blue Mustang is on the way to enter the United States from Mexico through one of the numerous customs checkpoints along the southwest border. He is confident no one will suspect that he is transporting more than 10 pounds of heroin in secret compartments inside his vehicle; he has done it before and he plans to do it again and again.

---

[284] This text from MITRE (2001) was quoted by both Jesus Mena (2003), and Hakikur Rahman (2009, pp. 176–177).

But, a customs system operator at a site near El Paso, Texas, uses the Anti-Drug Network (ADNET) system to access data on the driver and his car via his license plate. It's just routine check and takes a few moments.

The agent quickly learns through a system that accesses a large data warehouse of information on crossings, seizures, and motor vehicles that the driver makes this trip on a regular basis, at a regular time, but this trip is different. She decides it is worth her time and trouble to continue the inspection. Ten minutes later, she finds more than a dozen small packages of white powder inside the vehicle. The drugs were seized and the driver was arrested.

Situations like this occur almost daily across the many ports of entry along the Mexican/U.S. border and other entry points into the United States. It may happen to many other countries and continents. Sophisticated data-sharing systems developed by the ADNET community (i.e., Department of Defense, U.S. Coast Guard, Department of Justice, Department of State, Department of Treasury, Federal Communications Commission, and the intelligence community) give U.S. drug and law enforcement officials a cache of information needed to track the flow of illegal narcotics and other dangerous substances into the country.

6.2.3 Investigating Internet Auction Fraud

6.2.3.1 What the Problem Is

Wikipedia has an informative entry for "Internet fraud",[285] with a usefully detailed classification.[286] Choo (2008) proposed a typology of organised crime groups on the Internet. Dawn Gregg and Judy Scott (2008) described a typology of complaints about eBay sellers: eBay is the world largest online auction website.[287] "In an *online*

---

[285] Fraud, regalrdless of the Internet, has been approached within AI & Law in respect of *ontologies*: Vandenberghe, Leary, and Zeleznikow (2003) discussed the goal of developing a *financial fraud ontology*.

[286] http://en.wikipedia.org/wiki/Internet_fraud

[287] http://www.ebay.com This is a generalised auction site, in the sense that customers are allowed to put up many different kinds of items for sale on the auction site. But in respect of the mode of bidding, eBay has a *forward auction* facility. What distinguishes an auction from other forms of selling is that the seller puts up the items for sale, without giving a fixed price. Moreover, an *auctioneer* manages the process. "There are several different types of auctions, the most common ones being an increasing bid auction (English auction), a decreasing bid auction (Dutch auction), and a price quantity pair auction. Auctions found their way onto the internet as early as 1995" (Chan et al., 2001b, p. 384). On the Internet, *increasing bid auctions* are known as *forward auctions*, whereas *decreasing bid auctions* are known as *reverse auctions*. In a forward auction, "the seller puts up an item for sale and specifies an acceptable minimu price or reserve price that he is willing to accept. The item is then posted on the auction site together with the minimum price and the bidding is kept open for a specified period. During this period, potential buyers bid for the item and the latest high bid is displayed (but not the identity of the bidder). When the specified period lapses, the highest bidder is required to purchase the item at the bid price. There are clearly defined rules for the auction site that the bidder and the seller of the item are required to adhere to" (ibid., pp. 384–385).

By contrast, at a reverse auction "the seller puts up an item for sale at a high price. The price of this item is progressively reduced until a potential buyer accepts the bid and the items are then deemed to have been sold to the buyer" (ibid., p. 385). "An example of a decresing bid auction

auction scheme, a fraudster starts an auction on a site such as eBay or TradeMe with very low prices and no reserve price, especially for typically high priced items like watches, computers, or high value collectibles. The fraudster accepts payment from the auction winner, but either never delivers the promised goods, or delivers an item that is less valuable than the one offered – for example, a counterfeit, refurbished, or used item."[288]

Gregg and Scott's (2008) categories include the sellers delivering goods not as requested by the buyer, or delivering goods of low quality, or goods without ancillary item or parts, or then goods being defective or damaged; moreover the goods supplied may be or black market items. In a so-called *accumulation* fraud, a seller builds up his or her reputation by making the initial investment of selling much low-value merchandise over a long period of time. Next, the seller presents an offer of expensive goods, but once buyers make their payment, they never get the expensive

---

site is Klik klok, which auctions gold and jewellery" (ibid., p. 386). The third kind of auction is a *price quantity pair auction*: it "has potential buyers making a bid for a certain quantity of an item at a certain price and sellers offering to sell a given quantity at a specified price. The buyer's bids are progressively increased and seller's 'asking' price progressively decresed until matching bids are obtained and the requisite quantity is then deemed to have been sold to the buyer at the right bid price" (ibid., p. 385). Sites like eBay are *C2C auction sites*, i.e., customer-to-customer sites, as opposed to *B2B auctions*, i.e., broker-to-broker auctions. One of the models of B2B auctions is "Use of a liquidation broker to sell excess items. In this case, the liquidation broker is essentially a third party auction site that does the auctioning for you" (ibid., p. 386). Otherwise, one may auction items at one's own website, or one may resort to "the auction facility on a virtual market site that one is a participant in to auction excess inventory" (ibid.). These, too, are B2B models, according to Chan et al. (2001b). As to C2C auction sites, they are any of three types: generalised auction sites (such as eBay), specialised auction sites, or *agent-based auction supporting sites*, i.e. "agent based services or search engines that will allow a buyer to specify an item, and the mobile agent or search engine would then visit relevant new sites returning information on where the item can be found. An example of this is www.usaweb.com" (ibid., p. 386).

[288] From section "Online auction and retail schemes" at http://en.wikipedia.org/wiki/Internet_fraud Online auction fraud is akin to online retail fraud. "*Online retail schemes* involve complete online stores that appear to be legitimate. As with the auction scheme, when a victim places an order through such a site, their funds are taken but no goods are sent, or inferior goods are sent. In some cases, the stores or auctioneers were once legitimate, but eventually stopped shipping goods after accepting customer payments. Sometimes fraudsters will use phishing techniques to hijack a legitimate member accounts on an online auction site — typically an account with a strongly positive online reputation — and use it to set up a phony online store. In this case, the fraudster collects the money, while ruining the reputation of the conned eBay member. When victims complain that they have not received their goods, the legitimate account holder receives the blame. A more subtle variation of online auction fraud occurs when a seller ships an item to an incorrect address that is within the buyer's ZIP code using the United States Postal Service's Delivery Confirmation service. This service does not require the recipient to sign for the package, but offers confirmation that the Postal Service delivered the package within the specified ZIP code. The item shipped is usually an empty envelope with no return address and no recipient name, just a street address different from that of the victim. The delivery of the envelope with the Delivery Confirmation barcode attached suffices for the Postal Service to record the delivery as confirmed. The fraudster can then claim the package has been delivered, and offer the Delivery Confirmation receipt as proof to support the claim." (ibid.).

goods they purchased. In his own discussion of frauds at eBay auctions, Wahab (2004) stated:

> With respect to forms of online auction fraud, there are several activities which constitute fraudulent behaviour including:
>
> *Non-delivery*: involves the seller placing an item up for bid when, in fact, there is either no item at all or the seller has no intention to sell. As a result, the item is never delivered to the buyer after he/she purchases the item.
>
> *Misrepresentation*: Occurs when the seller's purpose is to deceive the buyer as to the true value of an item by listing false information or using fake pictures of the item.
>
> *Non-payment*: Involves a buyer placing the highest bid and winning the auction, and as the merchandise is delivered no money is paid. The victim in this case is actually the seller.
>
> *Triangulation*: Involves three parties: the perpetrator, a consumer, and an online merchant. The perpetrator buys merchandise from an online merchant using stolen identities and credit card numbers. Then, the perpetrator sells the merchandise at online auction sites to unsuspecting buyers. Later, the police seize the stolen merchandise to keep for evidence, and the buyer and merchant end up the victims.
>
> *Fee stacking*: Involves adding hidden charges to the item after the auction is over to obtain more money. Instead of a flat rate for postage and handling, the seller adds separate charges for postage, handling, and shipping. As a result, the buyer has to pay more than anticipated.
>
> *Black-market goods*: These goods include copied software, music CD's, videos, etc. The goods are delivered without a box, warranty, or instructions. Auction sites such as eBay try to stamp out selling such items by prohibiting the selling of unauthorised copies of software, games, music, or video. Multiple violations of eBay's unauthorised copy policy could result in the suspension of your account.

Wahab (2004) also listed fraudulent kinds of bidding at online auctions:

> *Multiple bidding*: This occurs when a buyer places multiple bids (some high and some low) using different aliases. The multiple high bids cause the price to escalate, and scares off other potential buyers from bidding. Then, in the last few minutes of the auction the same buyer withdraws their high bids, only to purchase the item with their lowest bid. On eBay, it is not permitted to use secondary User IDs or other eBay members to artificially raise the level of bidding and/or price of an item. Equally, retracting bids is not allowed as a rule on eBay, as all bids are binding, except: sales of real estate or businesses, sales of items that are prohibited by law or by eBay's User Agreement, and other exceptional circumstances (typographical errors, significant change in the description of the item, inability to reach the seller, and unauthorised use of the buyers ID and password)
>
> *Shill bidding*: is the intentional sham bidding by the seller to drive up the price of his/her own item that is up for bid. This is accomplished by the sellers themselves and/or someone that is associated with the seller making bids to purposely drive up the price of the seller's item.
>
> *Shield bidding*: occurs when the buyer uses another email address or a friend (the shield) to drive up prices and discourage bids on an item she wants. At the last minute, the shield withdraws the high bid, allowing the buyer to win the item at a lower price. Most auction sites forbid retracting a bid once it's made, and on eBay shill and shield bidding is clearly prohibited.

Summing up the foregoing kinds of fraudulent behaviour, Wahab (2004) remarked: "Although one or more forms may be prevented under the auction site policies, the main concerns for online auction fraud lies in the non-delivery, delivery of defective goods or late delivery, failure to disclose all relevant information, and non-payment". Wahab (2004) listed the following factors in buyers' behaviour that make them vulnerable to fraud at online auctions:

(a) *Lack of knowledge*: where the buyer is not fully aware of the site policies or safe harbour principles. Many buyers act on the assumption that standard policies exist in all auction sites.

(b) *Payment Methods*: money orders or personal cheques were listed as methods of payment by 80% of the victims that reported Internet auction fraud. The National Consumers League found that most of the consumers who lost money in Internet auctions paid with a money order (48%), personal cheques (32%), or cashier's cheques (7%).

(c) *Negligence*: engaging in online auction activities has its stakes as well as its advantages. Thus, the lack of cautious conduct may very well result in becoming a victim of fraud. Buyers and sellers who do not act carefully by checking retail prices and information about each other, reading their feedback ratings, or using common sense in assessing the price of the item up for a bid, could become the perfect victims of fraud.

FADE (*Fraud and Abuse Detection Engine*) is a data mining system developed by the online auction site eBay in order to detect fraud perpetrator at its site (Mena, 2003, p. 254). Some unscrupulous sellers never supply the merchandise they sold, or then they misstate its features. Internet auction fraud has been ranked the highest amongst the reported fraud cases in electronic commerce (Ochaeta, 2008). Often fraudsters try to build up a reputation for themselves, by initially selling to or buying from traders with a good reputation, for a while, a lot of low priced or cheap products; or then they may sell to or buy from accomplices moderate value or expensive items. Morzy (2008) proposed algorithms for mining the reputation of participants of online auctions. Morzy identified further fraudulent practices, beside the ones described by Gregg and Scott (2008). Those practices considered by Morzy include *bid shilling*, that is to say, as seen earlier, the use of a false bidder identity to drive up the price of an item on behalf of the seller; and *bid shielding*: the perpetrators comprise a rolecalled the *shielder*, and a role of the one who is going to fraudulently win the auction. The shielder offers an artificially high bid for an item, so that other bidders be discouraged from competing for an item; then, at the last moment, the shielder withdraws the bid, and his or her accomplice, who is the second highest bidder, wins the auction. Chua and Wareham (2002, cf. 2004), concerned with self-regulation for online auctions, proposed a taxonomy, quoted by Kwan et al. (2010) and presented in two tables (Tables 6.2.3.1.1 and 6.2.3.1.2).

Kobayashi and Ito (2008) proposed a transactional relationship visualisation system in Internet auctions. Credit card phantom transactions in online auctions was discussed, from a fraud detection perspective, in Chae, Shim, Cho, and Lee (2007). Anonymacy and information asymmetry were identified by Sakurai and Yokoo (2003) and Chae et al. (2007) as being important factors in online auction fraud. A seller or a buyer might submit a false-name bid by pretending to be a potential buyer or seller, thus enabling the perpetrator to manipulate the supply-and-demand chain. Ku, Chen, and Chiu (2007a) proposed a data mining approach for internet auction fraud detection – "a simple method which is detected potential fraudster by social network analysis (SNA) and decision tree to provide a feasible mechanism of playing capable guardians in buyers' auction activities" – whereas Ku, Chen, Wu, and Chiu (2007b) were concerned with online gaming crime.

Table 6.2.3.1.1 Kinds of fraud perpetrated by sellers at online auctions

Seller as fraudster	
Bid shilling	Seller bids on own auctions to drive up the price
Misrepresentation	Seller intentionally misdescribes the item
Fee stacking	Seller adds hidden costs such as handling charges to the item after the auction ends
Failure to ship	Seller never sends the goods
Reproductions and counterfeits	Seller advertises counterfeit goods as the real thing
Triangulation fencing	Stolen goods are sold
Shell auction	Seller sets up an auction solely to obtain names and credit cards

Table 6.2.3.1.2 Kinds of fraud perpetrated by buyers at online auctions[289]

Buyer as fraudster	
Bid shielding	Two buyers collude on an auction. One bidder makes a low bid, while the second makes an inflated bid. Before the auction ends, the higher bidder withdraws
Failure to pay	Buyer never sends the money
Buy and switch	Buyer receives merchandise and refuses it. However, buyer switches original merchandise with inferior merchandise
Loss or damage claims	Buyer claims item was damaged and buyer disposed of it. Buyer wants money back

Jun Gu from the University of Edinburgh presented a case study of eBay, the online auction site (Gu, 2007), and included a table comparing eBay to Sotheby's, a traditional auction company. See Table 6.2.3.1.3. "The potential shopping risks for a consumer who purchases at Sotheby's and EBay could be inferred from [...] major differences as revealed in the [...] table" (Gu, 2007, p. 3).

Internet auction fraud is also a domain researched, e.g., by Kwan et al. (2010). That study, carried out by computer scientists at King's College London and the University of Hong Kong, is concerned with Internet auction fraud involving the

---

[289] Also consider *PayPal fraud* perpetrated by purchasers at eBay auctions. The following quotation is from section "PayPal fraud" at http://en.wikipedia.org/wiki/Internet_fraud "In a *collection in person PayPal scheme*, the scammer targets eBay auctions that allow the purchaser to personally collect the item from the seller, rather than having the item shipped, and where the seller accepts PayPal as a means of payment. The fraudster uses a fake address with a post office box when making their bids, as PayPal will allow such an unconfirmed address. Such transactions are not covered by PayPal's seller protection policy. The fraudster buys the item, pays for it via PayPal, and then collects the item from the victim. The fraudster then challenges the sale, claiming a refund from PayPal and stating that they did not receive the item. PayPal's policy is that it will reverse a purchase transaction unless the seller can provide a shipment tracking number as proof of delivery; PayPal will not accept video evidence, a signed document, or any form of proof other than a tracking number as valid proof of delivery. This form of fraud can be avoided by only accepting cash from buyers who wish to collect goods in person."

Table 6.2.3.1.3 Sotheby's vs. eBay (based on Gu, 2007)

	Sotheby's	eBay
Registration procedure for the buyer	Proof of identity (passport, driving license, etc.)	Providing a valid email address.
Registration procedure for the seller	1. Evaluating the item for a decision of acceptance. 2. Contracting with the seller if that item has been accepted.	1. Verifying the identity of Seller by phone or credit card. 2. Offering PayPal or a merchant account credit card as a payment method.
Liability distribution	The Sotheby's, the seller, and the buyer.	The seller and the buyer
Criteria for a decision of purchase	Descriptions and examinations of the specific item.	Descriptions only.

selling of faked goods in Hong Kong, and goods bearing false trade descriptions or forged trademarks.

Kwan et al. (2010) quoted from Ochaeta (2008) six steps in a safe Internet auction: (a) Initial buyers and sellers registration; (b) Setting up a particular auction event; (c) Scheduling and advertising; (d) Bidding (which handles the collection of bids from buyers); (e) Evaluation of bids and closing the auction; (f) Trade settlement. This last step involves payment, and the transfer of goods. At sites such as eBay, typically the seller is not the auctioneer, so the trade settlement step this final step involves the payment of fees to the auctioneer and other agents.

At the initial step, namely, the registration of the initial buyers and sellers, the authentication takes place of the trading parties. They exchange cryptography keys, and a profile is created for each trader. The profile states in which kinds of products the trader is interested, and possibly his or her authorized spending limits.

The second step, which is the setting up a particular auction event, consists of setting up of the protocol and rules of the auction. "Such rules include the descriptions of the items being sold or acquired, the type of auction being conducted (e.g. open cry, sealed bid, or Dutch), parameters negotiated (e.g. price, delivery dates, terms of payment), starting date and time of the auction, and the auction closing rules, etc." (Kwan et al., 2010).

At step (c), i.e., scheduling and advertising, typically involves items of the same category (such as art, or jewelry) being auctioned together on a regular schedule. This is done in order to draw the attention of potential buyers. "Popular auctions are sometimes mixed with less popular auctions. Items to be auctioned in upcoming auctions are also advertised. Potential buyers are notified of these upcoming events" (Kwan et al., 2010).

During the bidding step (i.e., step c), bids made by potential buyers are collected, the bid control rules of the auction are applied (involving minimum bid, bid increment, and deposits required with bids), and participants are notified when new higher bids are submitted. Next, step (d) consists of the evaluation of bids and the closing of the auction. Closing rules are implemented, and a notification is given to the winners and losers of the auction.

Whereas law enforcement agencies, the auction sites themselves, as well as newspaper articles advise users to be careful, to "be cautious at their end and perform background checks of sellers that they wish to transact with. Such suggestions however, require users to maintain constant vigilance and spend a considerable amount of time and effort in investigating potential dealers before carrying out a transaction" (Pandit, Chau, Wang, & Faloutsos, 2007, p. 202), this is not really helpful, and merely shifts the burden of responsibility to the users: "Such suggestions however, require users to maintain constant vigilance and spend a considerable amount of time and effort in investigating potential dealers before carrying out a transaction. To overcome this difficulty, self-organized vigilante organizations are formed, usually by auction fraud victims themselves, to expose fraudsters and report them to law enforcement agencies" (ibid.), but such grassroots efforts are not sufficient. Hence the usefulness of the advice a data mining tool, *NetProbe* (see in Sections 6.2.3.2 and 6.2.3.3), can give users by actually checking the stream of transactions of all users in order to identify likely fraudsters. "Specifically, NetProbe [. . .] is able to spot sellers that are prone to commit the 'non-delivery' type of fraud. idea is that such sellers usually have 'accomplices', that is, nodes with good reputation, who have never committed any fraud, but are willing to give good feedback scores to the fraudsters-to-be."[290]

There exist *reputation systems* (Resnick, Zeckhauser, Friedman, & Kuwabara, 2000; Resnick, Zeckhauser, Swanson, & Lockwood, 2003; Melnik & Alm, 2002), and these are used by the online auction sites. "But they are usually very simple and can be easily foiled" (Pandit et al., 2007, p. 202). Neverthelsss, reputation systems are applied extensively, and they do have an impact on patterns of behaviour: "In an overview, Resnick et al. [(2000)] summarized that modern reputation systems face many challenges which include the difficulty to elicit honest feedback and to show faithful representations of users' reputation. Despite their limitations, reputation systems have had a significant effect on how people buy and sell" (Pandit et al., 2007, p. 202). The following is quoted from a Wikipedia entry[291]:

A *reputation system* computes and publishes reputation scores for a set of objects (e.g. service providers, services, goods or entities) within a community or domain, based on a collection of opinions that other entities hold about the objects. The opinions are typically passed as ratings to a reputation center which uses a specific reputation algorithm to dynamically compute the reputation scores based on the received ratings.

Entities in a community use reputation scores for decision making, e.g. whether or not to buy a specific service or good. An object with a high reputation score will normally attract more business that an object with a low reputation score. It is therefore in the interest of objects to have a high reputation score.

Since the collective opinion in a community determines an object's reputation score, reputation systems represent a form of collaborative sanctioning and praising. A low score represents a collaborative sanctioning of an object that the community perceives as having

---

[290] From a project report by C. Faloutsos, at http://www.cs.cmu.edu/~christos

[291] http://en.wikipedia.org/wiki/Reputation_system

or providing low quality. Similarly, a high score represents a collaborative praising of an object that the community perceives as having or providing high quality. Reputation scores change dynamically as a function of incoming ratings. A high score can quickly be lost if rating entities start providing negative ratings. Similarly, it is possible for an object with a low score to recover and regain a high score.

Reputation systems are related to *recommender systems*[292] and *collaborative filtering*,[293] but with the difference that reputation systems produce scores based on explicit ratings from the community, whereas recommender systems use some external set of entities and events (such as the purchase of books, movies, or music) to generate marketing recommendations to users. The role of reputation systems is to facilitate trust (Resnick et al., 2000) (Jøsang, Ismail, & Boyd, 2007), and often functions by making the reputation more visible.

Reputation systems are often useful in large online communities in which users may frequently have the opportunity to interact with users with whom they have no prior experience or in communities where user generated content is posted like YouTube or Flickr. In such a situation, it is often helpful to base the decision whether or not to interact with that user on the prior experiences of other users.

Reputation systems may also be coupled with an incentive system to reward good behavior and punish bad behavior. For instance, users with high reputation may be granted special privileges, whereas users with low or unestablished reputation may have limited privileges.

Concerning types of reputation systems, the same entry explains concisely:

A simple reputation system, employed by eBay, is to record a rating (either positive, negative, or neutral) after each pair of users conducts a transaction. A user's reputation comprises the count of positive and negative transactions in that user's history.

More sophisticated algorithms scale an individual entity's contribution to other node's reputation by that entity's own reputation. PageRank is such a system, used for ranking web pages based on the link structure of the web. In PageRank, each web page's contribution to another page is proportional to its own pagerank, and inversely proportional to its number of outlinks.[294]

Reputation systems are also emerging which provide a unified, and in many cases objective, appraisal of the impact to reputation of a particular news item, story, blog or online posting. The systems also utilize complex algorithms to firstly capture the data in question but then rank and score the item as to whether it improves or degrades the reputation of the individual, company or brand in question.

6.2.3.2   Data Mining and Online Auction Fraud: Techniques in the Background of NetProbe

Jung, Han, and Suh (1999) applied case-based reasoning to the categorisation of the risk involved in electronic commerce transactions. A team from Carnegie Mellon

---

[292] See at http://en.wikipedia.org/wiki/Recommendation_system concerning *recommender systems*, also called *recommendation systems*. Cf. Leskovec, Singh, and Kleinberg (2006), "Patterns of Influence in a Recommendation Network".

[293] For *collaborative filtering*, see at http://en.wikipedia.org/wiki/Collaborative_filtering

[294] The algorithm of PageRank (Brin & Page, 1998) was already outlined, it was eventually realised, in the notion of Katz centrality in a social network (Katz, 1953). See Section 6.1.2.1 in this book. a team in Seoul (Phuoc et al., 2009), interested in a good ranking system for World Wide Web search engines, compared the Katz status index, an old model, to *PageRank*.

University – comprising Shashank Pandit, Duen Horng Chau, Samuel Wang, and Christos Faloutsos – described *NetProbe*, a fast and scalable data mining system which they designed and implemented, for fraud detection in online auction networks (Pandit et al., 2007).[295] Experiments with NetProbe as reported in Pandit et al. (2007) were conducted on a synthetic dataset of very large graphs with as many as 7,000 nodes and 30,000 edges. Experiments were also conducted on a real dataset crawled from the eBay online auction website. This real dataset was "with nearly 700,000 transactions between more than 66,000 users, where NetProbe was highly effective at unearthing hidden networks of fraudsters, within a realistic response time of about 6 minutes" (Pandit et al., 2007, p. 201). It is a recognised fact among scholars that the social networks, let alone the networks of transactions, of criminal organisations are dynamic. Pandit et al. (ibid.) came up with a solution: "For scenarios where the underlying data is dynamic in nature, we propose *Incremental NetProbe*, which is an approximate, but fast, variant of NetProbe. Our experiments prove that Incremental NetProbe executes nearly doubly fast as compared to NetProbe, while retaining over 99% of its accuracy".

Figure 6.2.3.2.1 shows an overview of the NetProbe system. NetProbe systematically analyses the transactions of users of online auction sites, and offers users the advantage that they can query the trustworthiness of any other user, and the query results are visually explained to the user through an interface. The general problem is that fraudsters build for themselves a reputation at the online auction site, by behaving correctly for a while. Once they hit, they are burnt out, but they can still trade through accomplices who still have a good reputation at the same auction site.

In NetProbe, users and transactions were modelled as a *Markov random field* (*MRF*) which is tuned for the detection of suspicious patterns generated by fraudsters. MRFs are suitable for such problem-solving about inference, that there is uncertainty in observed data.[296] A *Markov random field* (*MRF*) is a probabilistic

---

[295] A different team, Yungchang Ku, Yuchi Chen and Chaochang Chiu, also proposed a data mining approach for detecting potential fraudsters at online auction sites (Ku et al., 2007a). Their approach is based on social network analysis and on a decision tree. The intended users are prospective buyers.

[296] A now old book about Markov random fields is the one by Ross Kindermann and J. Laurie Snell (1980). MRFs have been discussed in the artificial intelligence literature about *belief propagation* (e.g., Yedidia, Freeman, & Weiss, 2003). Moreover, MRFs can be used for a wide variety of machine vision or image processing problems, e.g. Mitchell (2010), Li (2009), Jin, Fieguth, and Winger (2005, cf. 2006), Kato and Pong (2001), Feng and Chen (2004). Yuri Boykov, Olga Veksler and Ramin Zabih (1998) combined MRFs with *graph cuts*: they reduced stereo vision to a *multiway cut problem* on a certain graph. Boykov et al. (1998) "focus on MRFs with two-valued clique potentials, which form a generalized Potts model. We show that the maximum a posteriori estimate of such an MRF can be obtained by solving a multiway minimum cut problem on a graph. We develop efficient algorithms for computing good approximations to the minimum multiway, cut. The visual correspondence problem can be formulated as an MRF in our framework" (ibid., from the abstract). They also applied their "techniques to MRFs with linear clique potentials" (ibid.).

Also see Wu and Chung (2005a, 2005b): they "introduce[d] a novel energy minimization method, namely iterated cross entropy with partition strategy (ICEPS), into the Markov random field theory. The solver, which is based on the theory of cross entropy, is general and stochastic. Unlike some popular optimization methods such as belief propagation (BP) and graph cuts (GC),

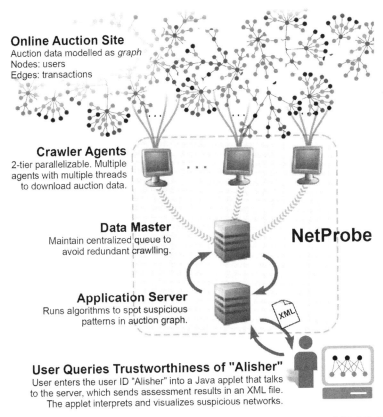

Online Auction Site
Auction data modelled as *graph*
Nodes: users
Edges: transactions

Crawler Agents
2-tier parallelizable. Multiple
agents with multiple threads
to download auction data.

Data Master
Maintain centralized queue to
avoid redundant crawlling.

NetProbe

Application Server
Runs algorithms to spot suspicious
patterns in auction graph.

XML

User Queries Trustworthiness of "Alisher"
User enters the user ID "Alisher" into a Java applet that talks
to the server, which sends assessment results in an XML file.
The applet interprets and visualizes suspicious networks.

Fig. 6.2.3.2.1 An overview of the NetProbe system. By kind permission of "Polo" Chau of Carnegie Mellon University, and by kind permission of the Secretariat of IW3C2 for the WWW conferences. From Pandit et al. (2007)

ICEPS makes no assumption on the form of objective functions and thus can be applied to any type of Markov random field (MRF) models. Furthermore, compared with deterministic MRF solvers, it achieves higher performance of finding lower energies because of its stochastic property. We speed up the original cross entropy algorithm by partitioning the MRF site set and assure the effectiveness by iterating the algorithm. In the experiments, we apply ICEPS to two MRF models for medical image segmentation and show the aforementioned advantages of ICEPS over other popular solvers [...]" (Wu & Chung, 2005a, from the abstract).

Hiroshi Ishikawa (2003) proposed a method to solve exactly a first order Markov random field optimization problem, more generally than available before. "The MRF shall have a prior term that is convex in terms of a linearly ordered label set. The method maps the problem into a minimum-cut problem for a directed graph, for which a globally optimal solution can be found in polynomial time. The convexity of the prior function in the energy is shown to be necessary and sufficient for the applicability of the method" (ibid., from the abstract).

Du, Li, Chen, Zhang, and Yao (2006) combined MRFs with the well-known *simulated annealing* optimisation technique (itself inspired by annealing in metallurgy, which involves heating and

model defined by local conditional probabilities. The concept is useful for devising contextual models with prior information: Markov random field theory is typically resorted to in order modeling context dependent entities (such as, in image processing within computer science, image pixels). Basically, an MRF is an undirected graph, that is to say, the edges between pairs of nodes are not arrows. Each node in a MRF can be in any of a finite number of states. The state of a node statistically depends upon each of its neighbours (i.e., those nodes to which the given node is connected by an edge), and upon no other node in the graph. A *propagation matrix*, symbolised as ψ, represents the dependency between a node and its neighbours in the given MRF. Each case $\psi(i, j)$ in the matrix has a value which is equal to the probability of a node i being in state j given that it has a neighbour in state i. If an assignment of states to the nodes in a MRF is given, then by using the propagation matrix it is possible to compute a likelihood of observing that assignment. The problem of inferring the maximum likelihood assignment of states to nodes, where the correct states for some of the nodes are possibly known before hand, is solved by those using MRFs by resorting to heuristic techniques,[297] and

---

controlled cooling) as well as with optimisation by means of a *genetic algorithm*, for the purposes of image segmentation. In annealing from metallurgy, the heat causes the atoms to become unstuck from their initial positions and wander randomly through states of higher energy. Their being cooled slowly gives them more chances of finding configurations with lower internal energy than the initial one. In simulated annealing, each step of the algorithm replaces the current solution by a nearby solution, chosen randomly with a probability that depends both on the difference between the corresponding function values and also on a global parameter called the *temperature*. The temperature is gradually decreased during the process. The dependency is such that the current solution changes almost randomly when the temperature is large, but increasingly *downhill* as the temperature goes to zero. Allowing *uphill* moves potentially saves the method from becoming stuck at *local optima*. (For convenience, this explanation is partly reworded from http://en.wikipedia.org/wiki/Simulated_annealing) *Uphill* and *downhill* belong to the standard terminology of *operations research* (i.e., *optimisation techniques*), as moving towards a minimum or a maximum is metaphorised as moving through rough terrain. The *Boltzmann machine* is a neural network that uses the idea of simulated annealing for updating the network's state (Ackley, Hinton, & Sejnowski, 1985).

[297] This is so because enumerating all states would be exponential in time, and because of the lack of any known theoretic method that would solve this problem for a general MRF. Wu & Chung explained (2005a, p. 230), concerning various methods (including *belief propagation*, or alternatively *simulated annealing*, or *iterated conditional modes*, or *graph cuts*, or *mean field approximation*, or *relaxation labelling*, or *graduated nonconvexity*), as well as their own application of *cross entropy*:

> One of the earliest efforts to optimize MRF objective functions was made by Kirkpatrick, Gellatt, and Vecchi [(1983)] who proposed the solver, simulated annealing (SA). SA can guarantee to converge to a global minimum as long as the temperature is decreasing slowly enough which makes SA too slow for practical use especially for clinical data. Another pioneering work was done by Besag [(Besag, 1986)], where the iterated conditional modes (ICM) was presented. This is a fast solver at the cost that it finds local optima in a neighborhood where only one site label is allowed to change. After those two methods, quite a few solvers were introduced [(Li, 2009, 3rd edn., this citation is to the previous edn. 2001)], such as mean field approximation (MFa), relaxation labeling (RL), graduated nonconvexity (GNC), etc. Recently two efficient and fairly accurate solvers, belief propagation (BP) [(Yedidia et al., 2003)] and graph cuts (GC) [(Boykov, Veksler, & Zabin, 2001)], were

an especially powerful heuristic method to do that is the *iterative message passing scheme* of the *belief propagation* algorithm.

In order to detect likely fraudsters, a *belief propagation* mechanism was resorted to in NetProbe, that algorithm being generally used in order to infer the maximum likelihood state probabilities of nodes in the MRF, given a propagation matrix and possibly a prior state assignment for some of the nodes. The standard notions about belief propagation are as follows:

- Let vectors be indicated in a bold font, as opposed to scalars. The kth element in a vector $\mathbf{v}$ is indicated as $\mathbf{v}(k)$.
- Let S be the set of possible states in which a node can be.
- Let $\mathbf{b}_n(\sigma)$ stand for the probability that node n is in state σ. That probability is called the *belief* that n is in state σ.
- Nodes pass *messages* to each other. Iterative message passing is how belief propagation works. "Let $\mathbf{m}_{ij}$ denote the message that node i passes to node j. $\mathbf{m}_{ij}$ represents i's opinion about the belief of j. At every iteration, each node i computes its belief based on messages received from its neighbors, and uses the propagation matrix to transform its belief into messages for its neighbors" (Pandit et al., 2007, p. 203). $\mathbf{m}_{ij}$ is a message vector. $\mathbf{m}_{ij}(\sigma)$ is the σth element of that vector.
- Let $N(i)$ be the set of nodes that are the neighbours of node i.
- Let k be a normalisation constant.

---

proposed. These two solvers are now often used for MRF models because they give good accuracy in an efficient way, which means they can find "global" optima within a rather large neighborhood while maintaining acceptable time complexity. [...] BP and GC are not applicable to all types of objective functions. They obtain their accuracy at the cost of function form restrictions. For example, standard BP is only proper for pairwise MRFs and generalized BP is either not for all functions [(Yedidia et al., 2003)]. So we cannot solve by BP such MRF models as FRAME [(Zhu, Wu, & Mumford, 1996, cf. 1998)] or multi-level logistic (MLL) with more than two sites in a clique [(Li, 2001)]. The same situation occurs for graph cuts because GC will work only when the energy function is regular [(Kolmogorov & Zabih, 2004)]. These may considerably limit the usage of the two popular solvers. In this paper, we proposed a new simple stochastic solver for MRF modeling, called cross entropy (CE). This idea is originated from the field of operations research to simulate rare events [(Rubinstein, 1997)]. This paper combines the idea of CE with MRF theory for the first time and applies the whole model to medical image segmentation. The CE solver is a general and stochastic optimization method that can be applied to any kind of MRF formulation. Unlike BP and GC, CE makes no assumption on the form of the objective function so it is able to solve more complicated MRF models. The efficient CE solver is completely insensitive to initialization and more importantly, as a stochastic method, CE tends to find more global optimum than deterministic solvers like BP.

Then this pair of value assignment formulae holds, in belief propagation:

$$\mathbf{m}_{ij}(\sigma) \;\;\leftarrow\;\; \sum_{\sigma'} \psi(\sigma',\sigma) \prod_{n \in N(i) \backslash j} \mathbf{m}_{ni}(\sigma')$$

$$\mathbf{b}_{i}(\sigma) \;\;\leftarrow\;\; k \prod_{j \in N(i)} \mathbf{m}_{ji}(\sigma)$$

The first formula states that the messages that node i passes to node j (that is to say, i's opinion about the belief of j in state σ) is assigned the value obtained by multiplying the sums of all the propagation matrix cells which are the likelihoods that a node is in state σ given that is has a neighbour in state σ', for the products (done for all such nodes n other than j that are i's neighbours) of node n's opinion about the belief of i in state σ'.

The second formula states that the belief of i in state σ (that is to say, the probability that node i is in state σ) is assigned as value a normalisation constant multiplied for the products of the messages that node j passes to node i (that is to say, j's opinion about the belief of i in state σ), for all such j that j is a neighbour of node i.

The standard algorithm is as follows: "Starting with a suitable prior on the beliefs of the nodes, belief propagation proceeds by iteratively passing messages between nodes based on previous beliefs, and updating beliefs based on the passed messages. The iteration is stopped when the beliefs converge (within some threshold), or a maximum limit for the number of iterations is exceeded" (Pandit et al., 2007, p. 203). "In case there is no prior knowledge available, each node is initialized to an unbiased state (i.e., it is equally likely to be in any of the possible states), and the initial messages are computed by multiplying the propagation matrix with these initial, unbiased beliefs" (ibid., fn 4).

Fraud detection as a domain of application of link analysis is related to two other application domains: *trust propagation*, and *authority propagation*. The latter's goal is to rank webpages by importance: a webpage is considered to be important, if webpages that are themselves considered important point to it. This kind of computation is carried out by *PageRank* (Brin & Page, 1998)[298] and by *HITS* (Kleinberg,

---

[298] Brin and Page were affiliated with Stanford University when they published that paper, in which they explained how Google crawls and indexes the Web. They explained: "Google is designed to crawl and index the Web efficiently and produce much more satisfying search results than existing systems. The prototype with a full text and hyperlink database of at least 24 million pages is available at http://google.stanford.edu/ To engineer a search engine is a challenging task. Search engines index tens to hundreds of millions of web pages involving a comparable number of distinct terms. They answer tens of millions of queries every day. Despite the importance of large-scale search engines on the web, very little academic research has been done on them. Furthermore, due to rapid advance in technology and web proliferation, creating a web search engine today is very different from three years ago. This paper provides an in-depth description of our large-scale web search engine — the first such detailed public description we know of to date. Apart from the problems of scaling traditional search techniques to data of this magnitude, there are new technical challenges involved with using the additional information present in hypertext to produce better search results" (from the abstract of Brin & Page, 1998).

1998).[299] By contrast, the goal of trust propagation is to distinguish good from bad websites, bad ones being those of scams (phishing), or ones with pornography. An example of a trust propagation system is *TrustRank* (Gyongyi, Molina, & Pedersen, 2004).[300] Pandit et al. (2007, p. 203) also stated affinity between their own project and that of Neville and Jensen (2003), Neville, Jensen, and Friedland (2003), and Neville et al. (2005), who respectively carried out automated classification of movies[301] and stock databases by aggregating features across

---

[299] In the conclusions section, Kleinberg (1998) stated, among the other things: "We began with the goal of discovering *authoritative pages*, but our approach in fact identifies a more complex pattern of social organization on the WWW [i.e., the World Wide Web], in which hub pages link densely to a set of thematically related authorities. This equilibrium between hubs and authorities is a phenomenon that recurs in the context of a wide variety of topics on the WWW. Measures of impact and influence in bibliometrics have typically lacked, and arguably not required, an analogous formulation of the role that hubs play; the www is very different from the scientific literature, and our framework seems appropriate as a model of the way in which authority is conferred in an environment such as the Web."

[300] Zoltan Gyongyi, Hector Garcia-Molina, and Jan Pedersen has published that article while at Stanford University. They explained: "Web spam pages use various techniques to achieve higher-than-deserved rankings in a search engine's results. While human experts can identify spam, it is too expensive to manually evaluate a large number of pages" (from the abstract of Gyongyi et al., 2004). As an alternative, the paper "propose[d] techniques to semi-automatically separate reputable, good pages from spam. We first select a small set of seed pages to be evaluated by an expert. Once we manually identify the reputable seed pages, we use the link structure of the web to discover other pages that are likely to be good. In this paper we discuss possible ways to implement the seed selection and the discovery of good pages" (ibid.). Experiments whose results were presented in the paper had been "run on the World Wide Web indexed by AltaVista and evaluate the performance of our techniques. Our results show that we can effectively filter out spam from a significant fraction of the web, based on a good seed set of less than 200 sites" (ibid.).

[301] Neville and Jensen (2003, p. 78): "In this paper, we introduce relational dependency networks (RDNs), an undirected graphical model for relational data. We show how RDNs can be learned and how RDNs and Gibbs sampling can be used for collective classification. Because they are undirected graphical models, RDNs can represent the cyclic dependencies required to express autocorrelation, and they can express a joint probability distribution, rather than only a single conditional distribution. In addition, they are relatively simple to learn and easy to understand. We show preliminary results indicating that collective inference with RDNs offers improved performance over non-collective inference that we term 'individual inference'. We also show that RDNs applied collectively can perform near the theoretical ceiling achieved if all labels of neighbors are known with perfect accuracy. These results are very promising, indicating the potential utility of additional exploration of collective inference with RDNs." In the example dataset from the movie domain, there are three types of objects: movies, studios, and actors (ibid., p. 83).

nodes in a graph.[302] Neville et al. (2005)[303] explained (ibid., from the abstract):

> We describe an application of relational knowledge discovery to a key regulatory mission of the National Association of Securities Dealers (NASD). NASD is the world's largest private-sector securities regulator,[304] with responsibility for preventing and discovering misconduct among securities brokers. Our goal was to help focus NASD's limited regulatory resources on the brokers who are most likely to engage in securities violations. Using statistical relational learning algorithms, we developed models that rank brokers with respect to the probability that they would commit a serious violation of securities regulations in the near future. Our models incorporate organizational relationships among brokers (e.g., past coworker), which domain experts consider important but have not been easily used before now.

---

[302] Besides, Pandit et al. (2007, p. 203) considered *graph mining* to be more remotely related to their own research on NetProbe. In particular, whereas NetProbe carries out systematic, large-scale checks on auction site user transactions, in graph mining either topologies are uncovered on the Web, or then fast algorithms are devised with the task of searching and mining for specific, or frequent graph patterns. Examples of such graph mining algorithms are embodied in tools such as *gSpan* (Yan & Han, 2002) for mining frequent subgraph patterns (cf. Yan, Zhu, Yu, & Jan, 2006) – a task which falls within *frequent pattern mining* (of which Han et al., 2007 is a survey) – and the *GraphMiner* system (Wang et al., 2005). Related algorithms were described in Pei, Jiang, and Zhang (2005), Yan, Zhou, and Han (2005), and Zeng, Wang, Zhou, and Karypis (2006). The latter proiposed a graph mining algorithm called *Cocain*.

Temporal data mining was surveyed by Laxman and Sastry (2006). Discovering frequent patterns in an *event sequence* fits in that area, whereas *episode mining* fits in both that area, and graph mining. "Discovering patterns in a sequence is an important aspect of data mining. One popular choice of such patterns are episodes, patterns in sequential data describing events that often occur in the vicinity of each other. Episodes also enforce in which order events are allowed to occur" (Tatti & Cule, 2010, from the abstract). "A pattern in a sequence is usually considered to be a set of events that reoccurs in the sequence within a window of a specified length. Gaps are allowed between the events and the order in which the events occur is often also considered important. Frequency, the number of sliding windows in which the episode occurs, is monotonically decreasing" (ibid., section 1). "The order restrictions of an episode are described by a directed acyclic graph (DAG): the set of events in a sequence covers the episode if and only if each event occurs only after all its parent events (with respect to the DAG) have occurred [...] Usually, only two extreme cases are considered. A parallel episode poses no restrictions on the order of events, and a window covers the episode if the events occur in the window, in any order. In such a case, the DAG associated with the episode contains no edges. The other extreme case is a serial episode. Such an episode requires that the events occur in one, and only one, specific order in the sequence. Clearly, serial episodes are more restrictive than parallel episodes. If a serial episode is frequent, then its parallel version is also frequent." (ibid.). Also see Tatti (2009), Zhou et al. (2010), Gwadera et al. (2005a, 2005b), Casas-Garriga (2003), and Mannila, Toivonen, and Verkamo (1997).

[303] Neville et al. (2005) was jointly authored by a computer scientists team from the University of Massachusetts at Amherst (Jennifer Neville, Özgür Şimşek, and David Jensen), and a team from NASD, the National Association of Securities Dealers (John Komoroske, Kelly Palmer, and Henry Goldberg). In 2011, Jennifer Neville was affiliated with Purdue University in West Lafayette, Indiana.

[304] NASD is in Washington, D.C. It was established in 1939. "NASD has a nationwide staff of more than 2,000, and its regulatory responsibility now includes 5,200 securities firms that operate more than 100,000 branch offices and employ 660,000 individual securities brokers" (Neville et al., 2005, section 2.1).

There may be an ethical and perhaps even legal problem with this, because a person may find him- or herself considered guilty by association. But what is being evaluated is not guilt, but reputation. Association with disreputable players tarnishes one's own reputation as well. NASD already had a database of brokers, called *CRD* (*Central Registration Depository*), in operation since 1981.[305]

Neville et al. (2005, p. 449) indicated the limitations of handcrafted rules in use at NASD before machine learning was applied:

> NASD currently identifies higher-risk brokers using a set of handcrafted rules. These rules are based on information intrinsic to the brokers such as the number and type of past violations. They do not exploit social, professional, and organizational relationships among brokers even though NASD experts believe this information is central to the task. Indeed, fraud and malfeasance are usually social phenomena, communicated and encouraged by the presence of other individuals who also wish to commit fraud [(Cortes et al., 2001)]. It is, however, difficult to accurately specify these patterns manually. As such, relational learning methods have the potential to improve current techniques.

Neville et al. (2005, p. 457) claimed that the findings of their own project supported the general beliefs at NASD, while reaching predictions differently:

> NASD staff began this project contending that information about the professional and organizational networks that connect brokers would provide useful information for determining their risk for serious violations of securities regulations. The results of this research have borne out those beliefs. Our relational models provide predictions that are competitive with, but significantly different from, the predictions provided by NASD's hand-tuned rules, which only examined brokers and their disclosures, ignoring additional relational information such as coworkers at present and past firms. These models show important potential for NASD's screening process. They identified higher-risk brokers not previously identified by the NASD rules, and thus provided additional targets for NASD examinations. Furthermore, being identified as higher-risk by both our models and the HRB model[306] model was found

---

[305] As stated by Neville et al. (2005, section 2.2): "CRD was established to aid in the licensing and registration of its broker-dealers and the brokers who work for them. CRD maintains information on all federally registered broker-dealers and brokers for the SEC [i.e., the U.S. Securities and Exchange Commission], NASD, the states, and other federally authorized private sector regulators, such as the New York Stock Exchange. Originally implemented in June 1981, CRD has grown to include data on approximately 3.4 million brokers, 360,000 branches, and 25,000 firms. For firms, CRD information includes data such as ownership and business locations. For individual brokers, CRD includes qualification and employment information. Information in CRD is self-reported by the registered firms and brokers, although incorrect or missing reports can trigger regulatory action by NASD."

[306] The HRB model is NASD's identification of *high-risk brokers* by handcrafted rules. Neville et al. explained (2005, section 3): "Currently, NASD generates a list of higher-risk brokers (HRB) using a set of handcrafted rules they have formed using their domain knowledge and experience. This approach has two weaknesses we aim to address. First, the handcrafted rules simply categorize the brokers as 'higher-risk' and 'lower-risk' rather than providing a risk-ordered ranking. A ranking would be more useful to examiners as it would allow them to focus their attention on brokers considered to have the highest risk. Second, NASD's handcrafted rules use only information intrinsic to the brokers. In other words, they do not utilize relational context information such as the conduct of past and current coworkers. NASD experts believe that organizational relationships can play an important role in predicting serious violations. For example, brokers that have had serious violations in the past may influence their coworkers to participate in future schemes. Furthermore,

to be more predictive of future problems than being identified by either model alone, thus permitting NASD to focus examinations on those most likely to have a serous violation in the near future. And finally, the probability estimates assigned to brokers by our models in general agreed with the subjective ratings of NASD examiners, thus the ranking provided by our models can be used to prioritize examiners' attention.[307]

We now go back to NetProbe. In NetProbe, the "key idea is to infer properties for a user based on properties of other related users. In particular, given a graph representing interactions between auction users, the likelihood of a user being a fraudster is inferred by looking at the behaviour of its immediate neighbors" (Pandit et al., 2007, p. 203). This is why trust propagation and authority propagation research are akin to the method of NetProbe. Some "non-trivial design and implementation decisions" were made by the Carnegie Mellon team "while developing NetProbe. In particular, we discuss the following contributions: (a) a parallelizable crawler that can efficiently crawl data from auction sites, (b) a centralized queuing mechanism that avoids redundant crawling, (c) fast, efficient data structures to speed up our fraud detection algorithm, and (d) a user interface that visually demonstrates the suspicious behavior of potential fraudsters to the end user" (Pandit et al., 2007, p. 202).

6.2.3.3 How NetProbe Works

In NetProbe, it was the transactions between users that were modelled as a graph, a *Markov random field* (*MRF*) indeed (we provided a definition for this in the previous subsection; see Section 6.2.3.2). Each node stands for a user. Each edge stands for one or more transactions between pairs of users. If there is an edge between two

---

some firms tend to be associated with continuous misconduct (i.e., they do not regulate their own employees and may even encourage violations). Lastly, higher-risk brokers sometimes move from one firm to another collectively, operating in clusters, which heightens the chance of regulatory problems. A model that is able to use relational context information has the potential to capture these types of behavior and provide more accurate predictions."

[307] Neville et al. (2005, p. 457) also indicated some limitations: "That said, the available data provide only relatively weak abilities to exploit the relational aspects of the domain. In CRD, individual brokers are directly related only through firms. Even branch relationships have to be inferred from address information, although this limitation will be obviated beginning this October [2005] when each broker will be systematically linked to a branch. More importantly, we do not know which individual brokers work together directly, nor what other social or organizational relationships they may share. To enhance their knowledge of potential links among individuals, NASD is investigating other recent technologies, most notably the NORA (Non-Obvious Relationship Awareness) system produced by Systems Research and Development, a Nevada-based company recently acquired by IBM. Such relationships could add substantially to the data analyzed in the work reported here, which could only use branch and firm relations present in CRD. The work reported here also exemplifies a framework that may be useful to projects that seek to develop screening tools to aid field examiners working in other domains such as health care, insurance, banking, and environmental health and safety. In such cases, development of a labeled training set may be impractical in the initial stages of a project. While the most accurate class labels would be the judgments of examiners, examiners' time is typically limited and organizations may be understandably skeptical about devoting large amount of examiners' time to labelling data sets."

nodes, this indicates that the two users for whom the two nodes stand, have trans-
acted at least once. Each node can be in one out of three states, namely, fraud,
accomplice, or honest, or then its state may be undetermined, in the sense that
NetProbe does not assign a state to that node. Pandit et al. (2007, p. 204) pointed
out the similarity to authority propagation as used in order to rank the importance
of webpages (see in the Section 6.2.3.2):

> As is the case with hyper-links on the Web (where PageRank [(Brin & Page, 1998)] posits
> that a hyper-link confers authority from the source page to the target page), an edge between
> two nodes in an auction network can be assigned a definite semantics, and can be used to
> propagate properties from one node to its neighbors. For instance, an edge can be inter-
> preted as an indication of similarity in behavior — honest users will interact more often with
> other honest users, while fraudsters will interact in small cliques of their own (to mutually
> boost their credibility). This semantics is very similar in spirit to that used by TrustRank
> [(Gyongyi et al., 2004)], a variant of PageRank used to combat Web spam. Under this
> semantics, honesty/fraudulence can be propagated across edges and consequently, fraud-
> sters can be detected by identifying relatively small and densely connected subgraphs (near
> cliques). However, our previous work [(Chau et al., 2006)] suggests that fraudsters do not
> form such cliques. [...] Instead, we uncovered a different *modus operandi* for fraudsters
> in auction networks, which leads to the formation of *near bipartite cores*.[308] Fraudsters
> create two types of identities and arbitrarily split them into two categories — *fraud* and
> *accomplice*. The fraud identities are the ones used eventually to carry out the actual fraud,
> while the accomplices exist only to help the fraudsters carry out their job by boosting their
> feedback rating. Accomplices themselves behave like perfectly legitimate users and interact
> with other honest users to achieve high feedback ratings. On the other hand, they also inter-
> act with the fraud identities to form near bipartite cores, which helps the fraud identities
> gain a high feedback rating. Once the fraud is carried out, the fraud identities get voided by
> the auction site, but the accomplice identities linger around and can be reused to facilitate
> the next fraud.

NetProbe uses the propagation matrix in order to detect *bipartite* cores in the graph.
In NetProbe, a particular propagation matrix was devised, so that the belief propagation mechanism would suite the behaviour of fraudsters and their accomplices.
The intuition (Pandit et al., 2007, pp. 204–205) was that a fraudster would avoid
linking to another fraudster. Rather, a fraudster would link heavily to accomplices.

---

[308] What is meant is that inside the graph which represents the online auction site, one expects to
find such subsets of the nodes (i.e., such subsets of the users), that the given subset is a *complete
bipartite graph*. That is to say, the given subset could be divided into two subsubsets, and each node
in either subsubset has edges linking it to all nodes in the other subsubset. If we replace "all" with
"one or more of the", then we would have a *bipartite graph* that is not a *complete bipartite graph*.
This is also a possibility that is relevant for detecting fraudsters and their accomplices at sites like
eBay. In the application at hand, which is to fraudsters at an online auction site, a fraudster is linked
to all of his or her accomplices, but two or more fraudsters may share accomplices. If a particular
fraudster is the only fraudster using his or her accomplices, that is to say, if the fraudster has
exclusive use of his or her accomplices, then one of the two subsubsets in the (complete) bipartite
core is a singleton set, i.e., such a set that it only contains one element. It may also be that if
the subsubset comprising the fraudsters comprises more than one fraudster, then the bipartite core
is *not* a complete bipartite graph, because it may be that one of the fraudsters in the fraudsters'
subsubset is only using some of the accomplices of another fraudster in that subsubset, and the
former fraudster may be using as well some accomplices that the latter fraudster is not using.

Table 6.2.3.3.1 NetProbe's propagation matrix

Neighbour state	Node state		
	Fraud	Accomplice	Honest
Fraud	ε	$1-2$	ε
Accomplice	0.5	2ε	$0.5-2\varepsilon$
Honest		$(1-\varepsilon)/2$	$(1-\varepsilon)/2$

An accomplice, instead, would link to both honest nodes, and fraudsters, but the accomplice has a higher affinity for fraudsters. As to honest nodes (i.e., innocent users), they link to honest nodes as well as to accomplices, because the honest user believes that the accomplice to be honest.

Pandit et al. (2007, p. 205) gave the table shown here as Table 6.2.3.3.1, and in particular, in their experiments they found it useful to set the value of ε to 0.05. Each case in the table denotes the probability that the given node is in the state identified by the column, given that this node itself has a neighbour in the state identified by the row.

In the running example shown in Figs. 6.2.3.3.1, 6.2.3.3.2, 6.2.3.3.3, 6.2.3.3.4, 6.2.3.3.5, and 6.2.3.3.6, the graph consists of users numbered from 0 to 14, and of these, nodes 7–14 are a bipartite core. All nodes are initially given the value "unbiased", in the sense that they are equally likely to be honest, or a fraudster, or

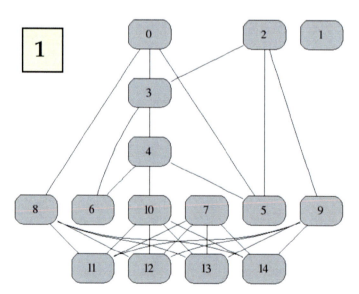

Fig. 6.2.3.3.1 Stage 1 in a sample execution of NetProbe. By kind permission of "Polo" Chau of Carnegie Mellon University, and by kind permission of the Secretariat of IW3C2 for the WWW conferences. Detail from a figure in Pandit et al. (2007). *Red triangles* represent fraudsters, *yellow diamonds* represent accomplices, *white ellipses* represent honest nodes, while *gray rounded rectangles* represent unbiased nodes

Fig. 6.2.3.3.2 Stage 2 in a sample execution of NetProbe. By kind permission of "Polo" Chau of Carnegie Mellon University, and by kind permission of the Secretariat of IW3C2 for the WWW conferences. Detail from a figure in Pandit et al. (2007)

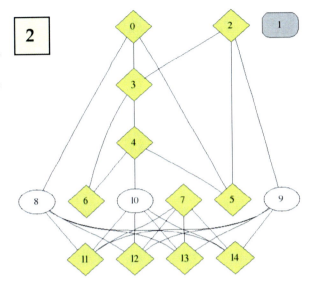

Fig. 6.2.3.3.3 Stage 3 in a sample execution of NetProbe. By kind permission of "Polo" Chau of Carnegie Mellon University, and by kind permission of the Secretariat of IW3C2 for the WWW conferences. Detail from a figure in Pandit et al. (2007)

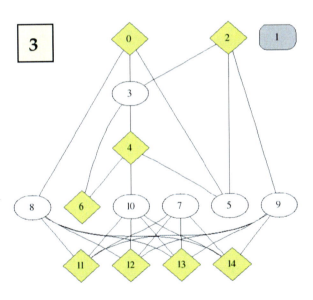

an accomplice. Pandit et al. (2007, p. 204, figure 2) resorted to the convention of depicting as red triangles the fraudsters, as yellow diamonds the accomplices, as white ellipses the honest nodes, and as gray rounded rectangles the unbiased nodes. By iteratively passing messages, the nodes affect each other's beliefs. Pandit et al. (2007, p. 205) explained:

Notice that the particular form of the propagation matrix we use assigns a higher chance of being an accomplice to every node in the graph at the end of the first iteration. These

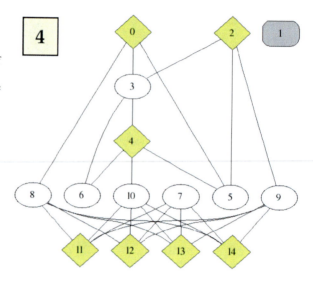

Fig. 6.2.3.3.4 Stage 4 in a sample execution of NetProbe. By kind permission of "Polo" Chau of Carnegie Mellon University, and by kind permission of the Secretariat of IW3C2 for the WWW conferences. Detail from a figure in Pandit et al. (2007)

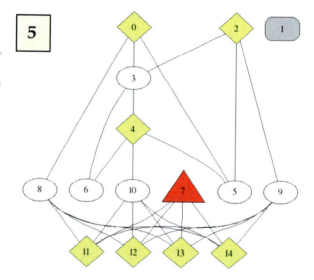

Fig. 6.2.3.3.5 Stage 5 in a sample execution of NetProbe. By kind permission of "Polo" Chau of Carnegie Mellon University, and by kind permission of the Secretariat of IW3C2 for the WWW conferences. Detail from a figure in Pandit et al. (2007)

accomplices then force their neighbors to be fraudsters or honest depending on the structure of the graph. In case of bipartite cores, one half of the core is pushed towards the fraud state, leading to a stable equilibrium. In the remaining graph, a more favorable equilibrium is achieved by labelling some of the nodes as honest. At the end of execution, the nodes in the bipartite core are neatly labeled as fraudsters and accomplices. The key idea is the manner in which accomplices force their partners to be fraudsters in bipartite cores, thus providing a good mechanism for their detection.

Goldberg et al. (2008), who were concerned with evolving social networks, remarked: "Their loose membership and dynamics make them difficult to observe

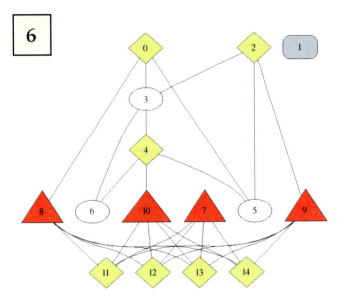

Fig. 6.2.3.3.6 Stage 6 in a sample execution of NetProbe. By kind permission of "Polo" Chau of Carnegie Mellon University, and by kind permission of the Secretariat of IW3C2 for the WWW conferences. Detail from a figure in Pandit et al. (2007)

and monitor". Sparrow (1991) among others recognised that criminal networks are dynamic, not static. All the more so, online auction sites burst with activity.[309] Pandit et al. (2007, p. 205) remark that in practice, given the very large size of the graph, it would be too strong a requirement if NetProbe had to propagate beliefs over the entire graph each and every time that a node (i.e., a user) or an edge (i.e., a transaction) is added to the network. In order for the users to get answers to their queries in real time when using NetProbe, the Carnegie Mellon team which developed NetProbe, also developed Incremental NetProbe, a version which allows approximation. This avoids wasteful recomputation from scratch of node beliefs. Incremental NetProbe incrementally[310] updates node beliefs as small changes occur in the graph. Figure 6.2.3.3.7 shows an example of Incremental NetProbe. The assumption, when using Incremental NetProbe, is that the addition of a new edge would only have a local effect. Incremental NetProbe works as follows (ibid.):

> Whenever a new edge gets added to the graph, the algorithm proceeds by performing a breadth-first search of the graph from one of the end points (call it *n*) of the new edge, up to a fixed number of hops *h*, so as to retrieve a small subgraph, which we refer to as the

---

[309] In fact, Prof. Christos Faloutsos (http://www.cs.cmu.edu/~christos), who supervised the development of NetProbe at Carnegie Mellon University, is also quite active in *graph mining*, and, in particular, in researching evolving graphs. See Section 6.2.4 below.

[310] In computer science, an *incremental* system is such that additions do not intrude into what was already there. This prevents having to do extensive changes to what one already had, once a new version is installed.

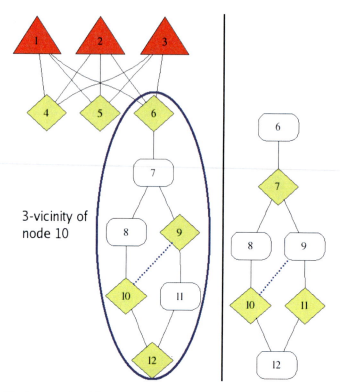

Fig. 6.2.3.3.7 An example of Incremental NetProbe. By kind permission of "Polo" Chau of Carnegie Mellon University, and by kind permission of the Secretariat of IW3C2 for the WWW conferences. From Pandit et al. (2007). *Red triangles* represent fraudsters, *yellow diamonds* represent accomplices, *white ellipses* represent honest nodes, while *gray rounded rectangles* represent unbiased nodes. An edge (shown as a *dotted blue line*) is added between nodes 9 and 10 of the graph on the left hand side. Normal propagation of beliefs in the 3-vicinity of node 10 (shown on the right hand side) leads to incorrect inference, and so nodes on the boundary of the 3-vicinity (i.e. node 6) should retain their beliefs

h-*vicinity* of *n*. It is assumed that only the beliefs of nodes within the *h*-vicinity are affected by addition of the new edge. Then, "normal" belief propagation is performed only over the *h*-vicinity, with one key difference. While passing messages between nodes, beliefs of the nodes on the boundary of the *h*-vicinity are kept fixed to their original values. This ensures that the belief propagation takes into account the *global* properties of the graph, in addition to the local properties of the *h*-vicinity.

6.2.3.4 A Non-Mining Model for Reasoning on the Evidence of Online Auction Fraud

At the end of Section 6.2.3.1, we mentioned a study about online auction fraud by Kwan et al. (2010). That study, carried out by computer scientists at King's College London an the University of Hong Kong, is concerned with Internet auction fraud involving the selling of faked goods in Hong Kong, and goods bearing false trade descriptions or forged trademarks. Let us elaborate about the original proposal in Kwan et al. (2010). Its approach is not from data mining. It is in probabilistic analysis, and strictly speaking, could be performed in theory on paper, maybe with a good calculator as help. We nevertheless dwell on this here, for the sake of representativeness, because it is often the case that AI systems for legal evidence include probabilistic analysis (notwithstanding the controversial status of Bayesianism for judicial purposes).

Kwan et al. (2010) proposed (basing themselves on several prosecuted cases) an investigation model for online auction fraud in selling of counterfeit goods using a Bayesian network approach. They made three ancillary hypotheses, substantiating the overall prosecution hypothesis that an online auction fraud crime has been committed. Namely, they hypothesised that perpetrators uploaded auction-related material, such as images or descriptions of the items. They hypothesised that manipulation (editing) of the corresponding auction item had taken place, such as adjusting the price. And they hypothesised that communication (e.g., by email or by instant messaging) had occurred between the seller and the buyer, concerning the auctioned fake item.

Those three sub-hypotheses are supported by 13 distinct evidential traces, again obtained from the responsible digital forensic examiners. Kwan et al. (2010) represented this in a Bayesian network model for the prosecution's main hypothesis and three ancillary hypotheses, with the related evidential traces; it is redrawn in Fig. 6.2.3.4.1. "This does not of itself substantiate the whole prosecution case. The auctioned item also has to be procured physically by the investigator and to be examined by the trademark owner in order to ascertain whether or not the item is counterfeit in nature" (ibid.).

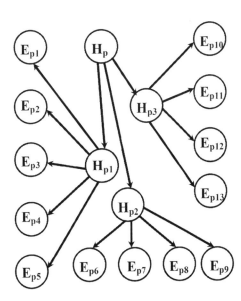

Fig. 6.2.3.4.1 A Bayesian network model, redrawn from Kwan et al. (2010), for prosecution hypotheses and evidential traces related to cases of online auction fraud

Note however that the approach in Kwan et al. (2010) is *not* from data mining. They intended it to be applied once suspects had already been identified, and were being prosecuted. In practice, they provided an interpretation of a typical case, being an abstraction of twenty cases that had actually been prosecuted in Hong Kong.

In Fig. 6.2.3.4.1, the prosecution hypotheses are as shown in Table 6.2.3.4.1. The evidential traces in Fig. 6.2.3.4.1 are as shown in Table 6.2.3.4.2.

Kwan et al. (2010) also developed a Bayesian network model for evaluating the relevance of the digital evidential trace, refreshenting the defence's scenarios; it is redrawn in Fig. 6.2.3.4.2.

In Fig. 6.2.3.4.2, the prosecution hypotheses are as shown in Table 6.2.3.4.3. The evidential traces in Fig. 6.2.3.4.2 are the same as in Fig. 6.2.3.4.2:

E_{d1} has the same definition as E_{p1},
E_{d2} has the same definition as E_{p2},
and so forth.

Table 6.2.3.4.1   The prosecution hypotheses in Fig. 6.2.3.4.1

H_p	The seized computer has been used as transaction tool for the fake item.
H_{p1}	Uploading of auction material related to the fake item has been performed.
H_{p2}	Manipulation of the corresponding auction item has been performed.
H_{p3}	Communication between the seller and the buyer on the fake auction item has occurred.

Table 6.2.3.4.2   The evidential traces in Fig. 6.2.3.4.1

E_{p1}	Material of the auctioned fake item (e.g., image file, text files, etc.) was found on the seized computer.
E_{p2}	Seller's account login record was retrieved from the auction site.
E_{p3}	Meta-data of a file found on the seized computer matched with that found on the auction site.
E_{p4}	IP address assigned to the seized computer matched with that which performed the data transfer.
E_{p5}	Internet history / cached contents for transferring the auctioned fake item material was found on the seized computer.
E_{p6}	Seller's account login record was retrieved from the auction site.
E_{p7}	IP address assigned to the seized computer matched with that logged into the auction site.
E_{p8}	Editing of an auction item has occurred (e.g., price adjustment) on the auction site.
E_{p9}	Enhanced material of an auction item (e.g., image file, text file, etc.) was found on the seized computer.
E_{p10}	Messages from auction site related to an auction item were found on the seized computer.
E_{p11}	Messages to/from the buyer related to an auction item were found on the seized computer.
E_{p12}	Address book containing covert investigator's email account was found on the seized computer.
E_{p13}	IP address assigned to the seized computer matched with that which performed the email communication.

Fig. 6.2.3.4.2 A Bayesian network model, redrawn from Kwan et al. (2010), for the defence's scenario, explaining out the same evidential traces which the prosecution interprets in terms of online auction fraud

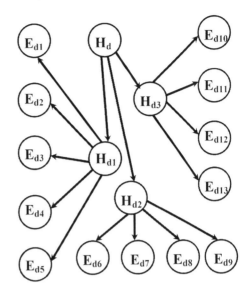

Table 6.2.3.4.3 The prosecution hypotheses are as shown in Table 6.2.3.4.3

H_d	The seized computer has been used as transaction tool for the fake item.
H_{d1}	Auction material related to the fake item was downloaded from the auction site.
H_{d2}	Manipulation of a non-fake item has taken place.
H_{d3}	Communication between the seller and the buyer on a non-fake auction item has occurred.

Kwan et al. (2010) – who did not acknowledge the misgivings that several important law scholars have concerning the application of Bayesianism to criminal cases – used a *likelihood rate* (*LR* for short), in the version devised by Evett (1993) in order to represent the situation where it is uncertain whether or not the evidence is a result of the suspect's activity:

$$LR = \frac{\Pr(E|H_p)}{\Pr(E|H_d)}$$

where E is the total digital evidence related to the crime. Kwan et al. (2010) claimed:

> In our simple Bayesian network models, the existence of each individual trace of digital evidence does not imply the existence of any other such traces. Since the evidential traces are mutually independent, their individual probabilities can be multiplied together to determine the probability of E given a root hypothesis. The prior probability values of the individual evidential traces for the online auction fraud models (both prosecution and defense) were obtained from a survey of the digital forensic examiners of the Hong Kong Customs & Excise Department, and are generally accepted values within this community of experts.

As calculated by Kwan et al. (2010), the LR of evidence for hypothesis H_{p1} against the evidence for hypothesis H_{d1} is:

$$\frac{\Pr(E|H_{p1})}{\Pr(E|H_{d1})} = \pi_{p1}/\pi_{d1} \quad \text{where}$$

$$\pi_{p1} = \Pr\left(E_{p1}|H_{p1}\right) \times \Pr\left(E_{p2}|H_{p1}\right) \times \Pr\left(E_{p3}|H_{p1}\right) \times$$

$$\times \Pr\left(E_{p4}|H_{p1}\right) \times \Pr\left(E_{p5}|H_{p1}\right)$$

$$\pi_{d1} = \Pr\left(E_{d1}|H_{d1}\right) \times \Pr\left(E_{d2}|H_{d1}\right) \times \Pr\left(E_{d3}|H_{d1}\right) \times$$

$$\times \Pr\left(E_{d4}|H_{d1}\right) \times \Pr\left(E_{d5}|H_{d1}\right)$$

which they calculated as:

$$\approx \frac{0.9 \times 0.75 \times 0.6 \times 0.75 \times 0.85}{0.9 \times 0.05 \times 0.6 \times 0.01 \times 0.01} \approx \frac{0.258}{0.0000027} \approx 95{,}600$$

Similarly, Kwan et al. (2010) calculated the LR values for H_{p2} against H_{d2} and H_{p3} against H_{d3}. It was especially for the prosecution's first sub-hypothesis that they found strong support. It cannot be however overemphasised that the concerns of scholars who are skeptic about Bayesianism in a judiciary context are important, and must be addressed. In Kwan et al. (2010) there is no mention of how controversial this topic is. There is one context however in which applying this kind of model would be unproblematic, and this is if the prosecution carries out such calculations when evaluating whether it has evidence strong enough for prosecuting. That is to say, this would just fit in a costs/benefits model.

6.2.4 Graph Mining for Malware Detection, Using Polonium

6.2.4.1 Preliminaries About Graph Mining

The leader of the team from Carnegie Mellon University that developed NetProbe, the tool for detecting fraudsters and their accomplices at online auction sites which we described in Sections 6.2.3.2 and 6.2.3.3 above, Prof. Christos Faloutsos,[311] is also quite active in *graph mining*. This is the area within data mining that is concerned with very large graphs.[312] Finding the mastermind of some activity within a graph is just one of the problems for which graph mining can be put to use. Another such use is modelling virus propagation, or how news propagates through blogs on the Web (this allows to understand the impact of blogs): the Blogosphere consists of blogs and posts (postings on a blog); there is a blog network, linking blogs, and (at a more detailed level) a post network, linking posts. Posts may be popular, but they tend to decay: post popularity drops off as days elapse since when the posting took place. Another task is finding patterns: rules, and outliers. Another problem is to understand how do real graphs look like, in social contexts involving very large

---

[311] See http://www.cs.cmu.edu/~christos

[312] See a long slide presentation, graphMining.ptt, at the same website.

graphs (such as the Internet map, or friendship networks, or protein interactions, of the food web in ecological systems, such as the smallmouth bass, which is a cannibalistic fish, along with leeches, phytoplankton, and zooplankton in Little Rock Lake).

A major side to Faloutsos' research on graph mining is the study of the temporal evolution of graphs. One application is tracking communities over time. In social network analysis, a static task is finding community structures. a dynamic task is monitoring community structure evolution, spotting abnormal individuals, or abnormal time-stamps. *Network forensics* is yet another application, the task being the identification of abnormal traffic pattern and finding out the cause.

One aspect of the temporal evolution of graphs is the study of *densification*, such as in affiliation networks (authors linked to their publications), or in patents being cited, or in physics papers citations. Another problem is, given a growing graph with such and such count of nodes, *generate* a realistic sequence of graphs that will obey all the static and dynamic patterns, such as power laws, or patterns about the diameter (a small diameter is a static pattern, whereas diameters shrinking or stabilising is a dynamic pattern). Faloutsos has been developing a generator in which such properties can be proven. For time evolving graphs, Faloutsos has applied tensors; these are multi-dimensional extensions of arrays, and there exist various decomposition methods for them, just as there exist decomposition methods for arrays.[313] Faloutsos and colleagues used tensor-based methods in order to spot patterns and anomalies on time evolving graphs, as well as for monitoring purposes, by application to streams.[314] *PeGaSus* is an open source Peta Graph Mining library, developed by Faloutsos and others, which performs typical graph mining tasks such as computing the diameter of the graph, computing the radius of each node, finding the connected components, and computing the importance score of nodes.

---

[313] In an overview of the application of tensor factorisations and decompositions in data mining, Morten Mørup explains (2011, p. 24): "Tensors, or multiway arrays, are generalizations of vectors (first-order tensors) and matrices (second-order tensors) to arrays of higher orders ($N > 2$). Hence, a third-order tensor is an array with elements $x_{i,j,k}$. Tensor decompositions are in frequent use today in a variety of fields ranging from psychology, chemometrics, signal processing, bioinformatics, neuroscience, web mining, and computer vision to mention but a few. Factorizing tensors have several advantages over two-way matrix factorization such as uniqueness of the optimal solution (without imposing constraints such as orthogonality and independence) and component identification even when only a relatively small fraction of all the data is observed (i.e., due to missing values). Furthermore, multiway decomposition techniques can explicitly take into account the multiway structure of the data that would otherwise be lost when analyzing the data by matrix factorization approaches by collapsing some of the modes. Tensor decompositions are in frequent use in psychometrics in order to address questions such as '*which group of subjects behave differently on which variables under which conditions?*'" Arguably, this may also be useful for data mining for investigative purposes or for criminal intelligence purposes.

[314] The projects of Faloutsos' team mentioned in Section 6.2.4.1 were described in See Tong, Faloutsos, and Jia-Yu Pan (2006); Tong and Faloutsos (2006); Leskovec, Kleinberg, and Faloutsos (2005); Leskovec, Chakrabarti, Kleinberg, and Faloutsos (2005); Leskovec and Faloutsos (2007); Sun, Tao, and Faloutsos (2006); Sun, Xie, Zhang, and Faloutsos, 2007).

6.2.4.2 The *Polonium* System

Esmaili, Safavi-Naini, Balachandran, and Pieprzyk (1996) applied case-based reasoning to the differentiation between hostile intrusions of computer systems and other anomalous transactions.[315] Duen Horng "Polo" Chau, of the Carnegie Mellon University team that developed NetProbe, also developed (in collaboration with Symantec, the world's leading security software provider) *Polonium*,[316] a tool for detecting malware.[317] A *malware instance* is defined as a program that has malicious intent. Computer viruses are just one kind of malware. Other kinds include worms, Trojan horses, rootkits, spyware, adware, and so forth.[318] Infected files are also considered malware. Chau, Nachenberg, Wilhelm, Wright, and Faloutsos (2010) claimed: "We evaluated it with the largest anonymized file submissions dataset ever published, which spans over *60 terabytes* of disk space",[319] with over 900 million files described in the raw data, from a total of 47,840,574 machines. Polonium resorts to graph mining. Like NetProbe, it also resorts to the belief propagation algorithm. "We adapted the algorithm for our problem. This adaptation was non-trivial, as various components used in the algorithm had to be fine tuned; more importantly, [. . .] modification to the algorithm was needed to induce iterative improvement in file classification." (Chau et al., 2010). A reputation-based approach was adopted. In a nutshell, "the key idea of the Polonium algorithm is that it infers a file's goodness by looking at its associated machines' reputations iteratively. It uses all files' current goodness to adjust the reputation of machines associated with those files; this adjusted machine reputation, in turn, is used for re-inferring the files' goodness." (ibid.).

The reputation-based approach adopted is a Symantec protection model that, for ever application that users may encounter computes a *reputation* score, and protects them from files whose score is poor. Various attributes contribute to reputation: whether an application comes from known publishers, whether it already has many users, and so forth. "Symantec has computed a reputation score for each machine based on a proprietary formula that takes into account multiple anonymous aspects of the machine's usage and behavior. The score is a value between 0 and 1" (Chau et al., 2010). Intuitions include: "Good files typically appear on many machines and bad files appear on few machines." (ibid.). Another intuition is what was called *homophilic machine–file relationships*: "We expect that good files are more likely to appear on machines with good reputation and bad files more likely to appear on

---

[315] Data mining has been applied to malware detection also by Muazzam Ahmed Siddiqui in his doctoral thesis discussed in Orlando, Florida (Siddiqui, 2008).

[316] The tool was probably named *Polonium* because of its association with the doctoral student "Polo" Chau, or at any rate the coincidence is apt, but the official explanation is that *Polonium* is an acronym for *Propagation Of Leverage Of Network Influence Unearths Malware*.

[317] See Chau et al. (2010), and an informal discussion in Chau (2011).

[318] At www.symantec.com/norton/security_response/malware.jsp Symantec provides definitions for kinds of malware.

[319] Emphasis in the original.

machines with low reputation. In other words, the machine-file relationships can be assumed to follow homophily." (ibid.).[320]

Computing *reputation* credibly was made possibly by the worldwide Norton Community Watch program, with millions of users contributing data anonymously. This is a huge file submissions dataset. The raw data undergo processing at Symantec, and then are fed into Polonium, which mines the data statistically, and machine learning is applied. "Each contributing machine is identified by an anonymized machine ID, and each file by a file ID which is generated based on a cryptographically-secure hashing function" (Chau et al., 2010). An undirected, unweighted bipartite graph of files and machines was generated "from the raw data, with almost 1 billion nodes and 37 billion edges (37,378,365,220). 48 million of the nodes are machine nodes, and 903 million are file nodes. An (undirected) edge connects a file to a machine that has the file. All edges are unweighted; at most one edge connects a file and a machine. The graph is stored on disk as a binary file using the *adjacency list* format" (ibid.); "we want to label a file node as good or bad, along with a measure of the confidence in that disposition" (ibid.).

Polonium computes the reputation for a given application, and is used in concert with other Symantec malware detection technologies. In the belief propagation algorithm as used in Polonium, belief corresponds to reputation. The Polonium team treated each file as a random variable X, whose value is

- either x_g (this being the "good" label)
- or x_b (this being the "bad" label).
- The probability $P(x_g)$ is the file goodness,
- whereas $P(x_b)$ is the file badness,

and the sum of the two probabilities is 1. Therefore, by knowing the value of one also knows the other. For each file i, the goal is to find the marginal probability

$$P\left(X_i = x_g\right),$$

that is the goodness of that file. Domain knowledge helps infer label assignments.

---

[320] Social influence is the subject of the papers in Forgas and Williams (2001). LaFond and Neville (2010) carried out *randomisation tests* for distinguishing *social influence* and *homophily effects*. A clear case where social influence is posited, is in the NASD beliefs that for determining the reputation of sock brokers, association with disreputable brokers is tarnishing, because one may be influenced into behaving irregularly like them (Neville et al., 2005). See fn 189 sqq. above. In artificial intelligence, Charlotte Gerritsen, Michel Klein and Tibor Bosse applied *agent-based simulation* to criminology: "A large group of offenders only shows criminal behaviour during adolescence. This kind of behaviour is largely influenced by the interaction with others, through social learning" (ibid., from the abstract). Their own study set to "to simulate social learning of adolescence-limited criminal behaviour, illustrated for a small school class. The model is designed in such a way that it can be compared with data resulting from a large scale empirical study" (ibid., from the abstract).

Terminology with the respective definitions include: *file ground truth* for "file label, good or bad, assigned by human security experts" (here, by file an executable file is meant); *known-good file* for "file with good ground truth"; *known-bad file* for "file with bad ground truth"; and *unknown file* for "file with unknown ground truth". "Symantec maintains a *ground truth database* that contains large number of *known-good* and *known-bad* files, some of which exist in our graph. We can leverage the labels of these files to infer those of the unknowns. The ground truth files influence their associated machines which indirectly transfer that influence to the unknown files" (Chau et al., 2010).

Moreover, the possibility of errors is recognised: in the case of Polonium, *True Positive (TP)* stands for "malware instance correctly identified as bad", as opposed to *False Positive (FP)* for "a good file incorrectly identified as bad". False positives are a price to pay that comes with some successful malware detection tools: Tesauro, Kephart, and Sorkin (1996), who applied neural networks, were able to detect "boot sector viruses" with over 90% true positive rate in identifying those viruses, but on the other hand this came at a 15–20% false positive rate. In Polonium, there is a tradeoff concerning false positives, that is expressed in how the belief propagation algorithm is made to stop.[321]

Virus signatures are virus profiles, or virus definitions. Malware detection comes in two major categories: *anomaly-based detection*, based on some presumed "normal" behaviour from which malware deviates; and *signature-based detection*, in which malware instances are detected because they fit some profiles (Idika & Mathur, 2007; Chau et al., 2010). It was Kephart and Arnold (1994) who first used data mining techniques to automatically extract virus signatures. Schultz, Eskin, Zadok, and Stolfo (2001) were among those who pioneered the application of machine learning algorithms (in their case, Naive Bayes and Multi-Naive Bayes) to classify malware.

In Naive Bayes, for a given sample we search for a class c_i that maximises the posterior probability

$$P\left(c_i \mid x;\ \theta'\right)$$

by applying Bayes rule. Then x can be classified by computing

$$c_l = \underset{c_i \in C}{\arg\max}\ \ P\left(c_i \mid \theta'\right) P\left(x \mid c_i; \theta'\right)$$

Concerning how belief propagation was applied in Polonium, Chau et al. (2010) explain:

> At a high level, the algorithm infers the label of a node from some prior knowledge about the node, and from the node's neighbors. This is done through iterative message passing between all pairs of nodes v_i and v_j. Let $m_{ij}(x_j)$ denote the message sent from i to j. Intuitively, this message represents i's opinion about j's likelihood of being in class x_j. The prior knowledge about a node i, or the prior probabilities of the node being in each possible class are expressed through the *node potential function* $\phi(x_i)$

---

[321] See an explanation in fn 207 below.

This prior probability is called a *prior*. Once the procedure execution is completed, the goodness of each file is determined: "This goodness is an estimated marginal probability, and is also called *belief*, or formally $b_i(x_i)$ ($\approx P(x_i)$), which we can threshold into one of the binary classes. For example, using a threshold of 0:5, if the file belief falls below 0:5, the file is considered bad" (ibid.). The messages are obtained as follows (ibid.):

> Each edge e_{ij} is associated with messages $m_{ij}(x_j)$ and $m_{ji}(x_i)$ for each possible class. Provided that all messages are passed in every iteration, the order of passing can be arbitrary. Each message vector m_{ij} is normalized over j (node j is the message's recipient), so that it sums to one. Normalization also prevents numerical underflow (or zeroing-out values). Each outgoing message from a node i to a neighbor j is generated based on the incoming messages from the node's other neighbors.

Let $N(i)$ be the set of nodes that are the neighbours of node i. Let k be a normalizing constant. Let the *edge potential* be notated as $\psi_{ij}(x_i, x_j)$; "intuitively, it is a function that transforms a node's incoming messages collected into the node's outgoing ones. Formally, $\psi_{ij}(x_i, x_j)$ equals the probability of a node i being in class x_i given that its neighbor j is in class x_j." (ibid.). The message-update equation is:

$$m_{ij}(x_j) \leftarrow \sum_{x_i \in X} \phi(x_i)\, \psi_{ij}(x_i, x_j) \prod_{k \in N(i) \backslash j} m_{ki}(x_i)$$

When the execution of the belief propagation algorithm ends,[322] the node beliefs are determined according to this formula:

$$b_i(x_i) = k\phi(x_i) \prod_{x_j \in N(i)} m_{ji}(x_i)$$

In Polonium, the intuition that good files are (slightly) more likely to appear on machines with good reputation and bad files (slightly) more likely to appear on machines with low reputation (that is to say, the *homophilic machine–file*

---

[322] "The algorithm stops when the beliefs converge (within some threshold. 10^{-5} is commonly used), or a maximum number of iterations has finished. Although convergence is not guaranteed theoretically for generally graphs, except for those that are trees, the algorithm often converges in practice, where convergence is quick and the beliefs are reasonably accurate." (Chau et al., 2010). In particular, in Polonium, there is a departure from how usually a belief propagation is made to terminate, and this involves how *true positive rates* (*TPR*) rather than *false positive rates* (*FPR*) are treated: "the Polonium algorithm's termination criterion is goal-oriented, meaning the algorithm stops when the TPR does not increase any more (at the preset 1% FPR). This is in contrast to Belief Propagation's convergence-oriented termination criterion. In our premise of detecting malware, the goal-oriented approach is more desirable, because our goal is to classify software into good or bad, at as high of a TPR as possible while maintaining low FPR — the convergence-oriented approach does not promise this; in fact, node beliefs can converge, but to undesirable values that incur poor classification accuracy. We note that in each iteration, we are trading FPR for TPR. That is, boosting TPR comes with a cost of slightly increasing FPR. When the FPR is higher than desirable, the algorithm stops" (ibid.).

Table 6.2.4.2.1 Edge potentials in polonium

$\psi_{ij}\left(x_i,\, x_j\right)$	x_i = good	x_i = bad
x_j = good	$0.5 + \varepsilon$	$0.5 - \varepsilon$
x_j = bad	$0.5 - \varepsilon$	$0.5 + \varepsilon$

relationships assumption) was converted into an edge potential defined according to Table 6.2.4.2.1, where the value of ε was set to 0.001.

Moreover, for machine nodes, the *node potential function* maps the reputation score computed by Symantec, into the machine's prior. That exponential mapping obeys the following formula (where k is a constant whose value is based on domain knowledge):

$$\text{machine\_prior} = e^{-k \times \text{reputation}}$$

This translates the intuition about what machine reputation contributes to the file reputation, into the machine prior. "Similarly, we use another *node potential function* to set the file prior by mapping the intuition that files that appear on many machines are typically good" (ibid.). This maps file prevalence into file prior. That is to say, the intuition about file goodness is translated into an unknown-file prior. And finally, the intuition about file ground truth is mapped into known-file prior: "For known-good files, we set their priors to 0.99. For known-bad, we use 0.01" (ibid.). "Note that no probability is ever 0, because it can 'zero-out' other values multiplied with them. A lower bound of 0.01 has been imposed on all probabilities. Upper bound is, therefore, 0.99, since probabilities of the two classes add up to 1" (ibid.).

When developing Polonium, the team modified the file-to-machine propagation between nodes of the graph: the edge potential based on the homophilic intuition is used in order "to propagate machine reputations to a file from its associated machines. Theoretically, we could also use the same edge potential function for propagating file reputation to machines. However, as we tried through numerous experiments — varying the ε parameter, or even 'breaking' the homophily assumption — we found that machines' intermediate beliefs were often forced to changed too significantly" (ibid.): what was happening, was that such change "led to an undesirable chain reaction that changes the file beliefs dramatically as well, when these machine beliefs were propagated back to the files. We hypothesized that this happens because for a machine's reputation (used in computing the machine node's prior) is a reliable indicator of machine's beliefs, while the reputations of the files that the machine is associated with are weaker indicators". Based on this hypothesis, the team found this solution: "instead of propagating file reputation directly to a machine", the had Polonium "pass it to the proprietary formula that Symantec uses to generate machine reputation, which re-compute a new reputation score for the machine". Experiments showed "that this modification leads to iterative improvement of file classification accuracy" (ibid.). Figure 6.2.4.2.1 shows an overview of the Polonium technology. Figure 6.2.4.2.2 shows the scalability of Polonium: the run time per iteration is linear to the number of edges.

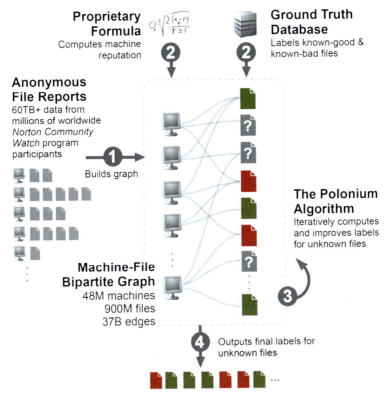

Fig. 6.2.4.2.1 An overview of the Polonium technology. By kind permission of "Polo" Chau from Carnegie Mellon University

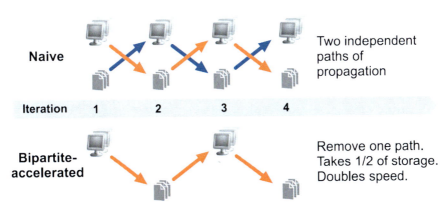

Fig. 6.2.4.2.2 The scalability of Polonium: the run time per iteration is linear to the number of edges. By kind permission of "Polo" Chau from Carnegie Mellon University

6.2.5 Link Analysis with Coplink

We have referred to the Coplink project in Section 6.1.2.4. *Coplink* is a tool for criminal intelligence analysis which finds links in databases among such entities. Coplink, developed by a team at the University of Arizona in collaboration with the Tucson police, performs data integration, pooling together the various information sources available (Hauck et al., 2002; Chen, Zheng, et al., 2003; Chen et al., 2003). It "evolved into a real-time system being used in everyday police work" (Hauck et al., 2002, p. 30). Drawing on experience gained with the Coplink project,[323] Chen et al. (2004) presented a general framework for crime data mining. Next, Xiang et al. (2005) described a prototype system called the COPLINK Criminal Relationship Visualizer.[324]

At the Tucson Police Department (TPD), records at the time consisted of about 1.5 million criminal case reports, containing details from criminal events spanning the period from 1986 to 1999 (Hauck et al., 2002, p. 31). Notwithstanding investigators being able, before Coplink became available, to access the Records management System (RMS) to tie together information, when it came to finding relationships inside the records they had to manually search the RMS data (ibid.).

In Coplink, a concept space is applied (ibid.):

> Coplink's underlying structure is the *concept space*, or automatic thesaurus, a statistics-based, algorithmic technique used to identify relationships between objects of interest. A concept space consists of a network of terms and weighted associations that assist in concept-based information retrieval within an underlying information space.
>
> In addition, co-occurrence analysis[325] uses similarity and clustering functions to weight relationships between all possible concept pairs. The resulting network-like concept space

---

[323] Coplink is accessible at http://ai.bpa.arizona.edu/coplink

[324] Also see Schroeder, Xu, Chen, and Chau (2007).

[325] Consider, within data mining, the task of *frequent pattern mining*, of which Han, Cheng, Xin, and Yan (2007) is a survey. They explained (ibid., p. 56): "Frequent patterns are itemsets, sub-sequences, or substructures that appear in a data set with frequency no less than a user-specified threshold. For example, a set of items, such as milk and bread, that appear frequently together in a transaction data set, is a *frequent itemset*. A subsequence, such as buying first a PC, then a digital camera, and then a memory card, if it occurs frequently in a shopping history database, is a *(frequent) sequential pattern*. A *substructure* can refer to different structural forms, such as subgraphs, subtrees, or sublattices, which may be combined with itemsets or subsequences. If a substructure occurs frequently in a graph database, it is called a *(frequent) structural pattern*. Finding frequent patterns plays an essential role in mining associations, correlations, and many other interesting relationships among data. Moreover, it helps in data indexing, classification, clustering, and other data mining tasks as well. Thus, frequent pattern mining has become an important data mining task and a focused theme in data mining research. Frequent pattern mining was first proposed by Agrawal et al. (1993) for market basket analysis in the form of association rule mining. It analyses customer buying habits by finding associations between the different items that customers place in their 'shopping baskets'. For instance, if customers are buying milk, how likely are they going to also buy cereal (and what kind of cereal) on the same trip to the supermarket? Such information can lead to increased sales by helping retailers do selective marketing and arrange their shelf space. Since the first proposal of this new data mining task and its associated efficient mining algorithms, there have been hundreds of follow-up research publications, on various kinds of extensions and

holds all possible associations between objects, which means that the system retains and ranks every existing link between every pair of concepts. Analysts frequently use this technique to develop domain-specific knowledge structures for digital-library applications.

In Coplink, detailed case reports serve as the underlying space, while concept derive from the meaningful terms that occur in each case. Concept space analysis easily identifies relevant terms and their degree of relationship to the seach term. The system output includes relevant terms ranked in the order of their degree of association, thereby distinguishing the most relevant terms from inconsequential terms. From a crime investigation standpoint, concept space anlysis can help investigators link known objects to other related objects that might contain useful information for further investigation — such as people and vehicles related to a given suspect.

Hauck et al. (2002, p. 31) listed three main steps involved in building a domain-specific concept space (CS). The first step consists of identifying document collections in the specific subject domain, and for the Tucson police, the collection was the case reports in the existing database. Each piece of information in the case reports database was categorised and stored in well-organised structures. At the second step, the terms were filtered and indexed (ibid., pp. 31–32):

A co-occurrence analysis captures the relationships among indexed terms. Developers then insert the resulting concept space into a database for easy manipulation with an appropriate algorithm. These last two steps were customized for the Coplink CS. After optimizing the code and tuning the database, building a Coplink CS takes approximately five hours, an acceptable period considering the TPD's requirements. [. . .] Term types in the CS concept space were divided into five main categories: Person, Organization, Location, Crime, and Vehicle. For the first four categories, only one piece of information such as a person's full name, street address, or crime type can function as a search term. For a vehicle, on the other hand, a single piece of information — such as color, make, or type — results in so many matches that using it as a search term would generate a flood of relevant terms. To avoid this problem, the Coplink CS combines two or more nonspecific vehicle terms into one composite term.

Hauck et al. (2002, p. 32) described how they applied co-occurrence analysis, by first identifying terms, and then computing the term frequency and document frequency for each term in a document, using a method proposed by Chen and Lynch (1992) for the automatic construction of networks of concepts characterising document databases.

The number of occurrences of term j in document i is the term frequency, tf_{ij} By contrast, the document frequency df_j is the number of socuments in a collection of N documents in which term j occurs. N is the total number of documents in a collection, whereas w_j is the weight of words in descriptor j. By d_{ij} one represents the combined weight of term j in document i. This is calculated as follows:

$$d_{ij} = tf_{ij} \cdot \log \left(N \cdot w_j / df_j \right)$$

applications, ranging from scalable data mining methodologies, to handling a wide diversity of data types, various extended mining tasks, and a variety of new applications."

Higher weights are assigned to such term types that are more descriptive and more important than others. Such higher weights are intended to ensure that relationships associated with these term types be always ranked reasonably. In particular, in the concept space of Coplink it was crime types that were assigned higher weights.

Term co-occurrence analysis was performed, according to Hauck et al. (2002, p. 32), based on the asymmetric cluster function, where W_{jk} are the similarity weights from term j to term k, whereas W_{kj} are the similarity weights from term k to term j, and where d_{ij} and d_{ik} are the combined weight of both descriptors j and k in document i:

$$W_{jk} = WeightingFactor(k) \cdot \left(\sum_{i=1}^{n} d_{ijk} \right) \bigg/ \left(\sum_{i=1}^{n} d_{ij} \right)$$

$$W_{kj} = WeightingFactor(j) \cdot \left(\sum_{i=1}^{n} d_{ikj} \right) \bigg/ \left(\sum_{i=1}^{n} d_{ik} \right)$$

Where *WeightingFactor* is used in order to penalise general terms, so that general terms be pushed down in the co-occurrence table, and is calculated according to the formulae:

$$WeightingFactor(k) = \log (N/df_k) / \log N$$

$$WeightingFactor(j) = \log (N/df_j) / \log N$$

The combined weights of descriptors were calculated according to the formulae:

$$d_{ijk} = tf_{ijk} \cdot \log (N \cdot w_j/df_{jk})$$

$$d_{ikj} = tf_{ijk} \cdot \log (N \cdot w_k/df_{jk})$$

"where tf_{ijk} represents the number of occurrences of both term j and term k in document i — we chose the smaller number of occurrences between the terms; df_{jk} represents the number of documents in a collection of N documents in which terms j and k occur together" (Hauck et al., 2002, p. 32).

Chen et al. (2004) described how three kinds of data mining are done in the Coplink project: *named-entity extraction*, *deceptive-identity detection*, and *criminal-network analysis*. Let us consider the first one first: "Our first data mining task involved extracting named entities from police narrative reports, which are difficult to analyze using automated techniques" (ibid., p. 53). The team deliberately chose challenging data: "We randomly selected 36 narcotics-related reports from the Phoenix Police Department that were relatively *noisy* — all were written in upper-case letters and contained many typos, spelling errors, and grammatical mistakes" (ibid.).

In order to carry out named-entity extraction, Hsinchun Chen's team used a modified version of the AI Entity Extractor system. In order to identify the names of persons, locations, and organisations in a document, that tool performs a three-step process. The first step consists of identifying noun phrases according to linguistic rules. At the second step, "the system calculates a set of feature scores for each phrase based on pattern matching and lexical lookup. Third, it uses a feed-forward/backpropagation neural network to predict the most likely entity type for each phrase" (ibid.).

The second data mining task for Coplink reported about in Chen et al. (2004) "involved automatically detecting deceptive criminal identities from the Tucson Police Department's database, which contains information such as name, gender, address, ID number, and physical description. Our detective consultant manually identified 120 deceptive criminal records involving 44 suspects from the database" (ibid.). In a case study, the team had developed a taxonomy for criminal identity deception. Based on that taxonomy, the team (ibid., pp. 53–54)

> selected name, birth date, address, and Social Security number to represent a criminal's identity and ignored other less reliable fields. Our method employed string comparators to compare values in the corresponding fields of each record pair. Comparators measure the similarity between two strings. We normalized the similarity values between 0 and 1, and calculated an overall similarity measure between two records as a Euclidean vector norm over the four chosen fields. A Euclidean vector norm is the square root of the sum of squared similarity measures and is also normalized between 0 and 1.
>
> We employed a holdout a holdout validation method using two-thirds of the data for training and the rest for testing. In the training stage, we tried threshold values ranging from 0.00 to 1.00 that differentiated between deceptive and non-deceptive records. We first determined the optimal threshold to be reached when the association decisions best matched our expert judgments, 0.48, then used this value to assess our algorithm's predicted association accuracy in the testing stage. [. . .] With this technique, law-enforcement officers can retrieve existing identity records relating to a suspect in their databases that traditional exact-match techniques often fail to locate.

As to the criminal-network analysis, Chen et al. (2004) used a concept-space approach of the kind described earlier in this section. With that technique, they extracted criminal relations from the incident summaries. The goal was to create a likely network of suspects. "Our data came from 272 Tucson Police Department incident summaries involving 164 crimes committed from 1985 through May 2002" (ibid., p. 54). In particular (ibid., pp. 54–55):

> Co-occurrence weight measured the relational strength between two criminals by computing how frequently they were identified in the same incident. We used hierachical clustering to partition the network between these subgroups. We also calculated centrality measures — degree, betweenness, and closeness[326] — to detect key members in each group, such as leaders and gatekeepers. [. . . D]ata mining uncovered 16 target gang members from the resulting network. In [a visualisation], the circles represent subgroups the system found, and they bear the labels of their leaders' names. A circle's size is proportional to the number of members in that subgroup. The thinckness of straight lines connecting circles indicates the strength of relationships between subgroups.
>
> We conducted a two-hour field study with three Tucson Police Department domain experts who evaluated the analysis's validity by comparing the results against their knowledge of gang organization. They confirmed that the system-found subgroups correctly

---

[326] For these concepts, see in Section 6.1.2.1 above; cf. in fn 14.

represented the real groups' organization. [...] Studying criminal networks requires additional data mining capabilities: entity extraction and co-occurrence analysis to identify criminal entities and associations, clustering and block modelling for discovering subgroups and interaction patterns, and visualization for presenting analysis results. One drawback of our current approach is that is generates mostly static networks. Given that criminal networks are dynamic, future research will focus on the evolution and precition of criminal networks.

The point that criminal networks are dynamic, and that techniques need be capable of dealing with that, was already made by Sparrow (1991). Efficient algorithms for searching graphs, and using Coplink's concept space, were discussed by Xu and Chen (2004), based in Tucson, Arizona, who used as a data set one year's worth of crime reports from the Phoenix Police Department. Their algorithms compute the shortest paths between two nodes in a graph, based on weighted links. They found that the efficiency of their algorithms differed, and whereas one algorithm was suitable for small and dense networks (such as kidnappers), another algorithm was efficient when the network is large and sparse, which is the case of narcotics networks.

At the University of Arizona in Tucson, Yang Xiang, Michael Chau, Homa Atabakhsha, and Hsinchun Chen described (Xiang et al., 2005) a project in the visualisation of criminal relationships: the Coplink Criminal Relationship Visualizer. They contrasted the use of two views, namely, a *hyperbolic tree* view, and a *hierarchical list* view. They explained (ibid., p. 76):

> The COPLINK Visualizer includes a hyperbolic tree view and a hierarchical list view implemented in Java. The hyperbolic tree was developed based on a freely available program written in Java (http://www.soi.city.ac.uk/~livantes/Research.html). Users can submit search terms to the system and the search terms have to be one of the five chosen entities, namely person, vehicle, organization, location, and incident/crime type.

They found the hyperbolic tree view to be more efficent for an "associate" task. Nevertheless, participants in the experiment generally found the hierarchical list view easier to use, apparently because they were more familiar with it. Opinions among the participants were divided as to which of the two views is more useful. The team proposed that both views are helpful, even though at some tasks the hyperbolic tree performs better. A hyperbolic tree view shows a hierarchy fanning out around the node which is the root of the tree. Viewers have the option to focus on one part of the tree, which is enlarged, whereas the rest of the tree is shown smaller and further away from the centre.

6.2.6 The EDS Project for the U.S. Federal Defense Financial Accounting Service

Mena (2003, section 7.7, pp. 213–219) describes a data mining project previously reported about in Vafaie, Abbott, Hutchins, and Matkovskly (2000), developed for the United States' Federal Defense Financial Accounting Service by prime contractor EDS Corporation and various subcontractors. An important aspect of that project was the application of machine learning techniques. The task was to develop a tool for detecting suspicious government financial transactions, because of the known occurrence of frauf in the vendor payment system. There was the problem of what to learn from, as the number of known cases from which to learn was not large, and moreover, data about these were incomplete. "Then, there is the problem that fraud is often hidden in large sets of legitimate translactions" (Mena, 2003, p. 213).

In establishing investigation goals, there was a concern with containing the costs. Whereas identifying suspicious payments was the primary goal, there was the constaint of maintaining a low false-alarm rate. "This cost concern is due to e limited number of examiners to investigate suspicious payments" (ibid.). Whereas the detection of suspicious financial transactions was the primary goal, other goals were also set, namely, that the data mining proicess to be developed could be generalised for use in other applications within the agency, and that knowledge transfer would be in place, so that the agency's existing staff could carry out the data mining process.

Having set the goals, the developers of the project took a step of knowledge discovery, i.e., they tried to understand the business methods involved, as well as the data, and the data were prepared. Initial exploratory analyses were performed, to enhance data preparation.

Next, the step was taken of assessing the modelling challenges (Mena, 2003, p. 214). Challenges included: "the data set is a very large payment database with incomplete information in the vendor payment data file" (ibid.); "payments are unlabeled and cannot be verified" (ibid.); and besides "there is a very small number of known fraud payments with instances of multiple payments from the same case" (ibid.). It was decided to use a cross-validation methodology, with several models (actually several modellers developed hundreds of models) using different data mining strategies. Then, a set of the best eleven models would be retained.

"The main strategy was to create multiple structured and random samples for training and testing of fraud detection models" (ibid.) Of the structured samples (called *splits*), eleven were for known fraud data. Each split had "taning, testing, and validation data subsets of 33 overlapping samples of fraud cases. In addition, 11 corresponding random splits were used with training, testing, and validation data subsets for non-fraud data of 33 non-overlapping sapmples of non-fraud" (Mena, 2003, p. 215). *Data balancing* required that the non-fraud set of samples be small enough, so that *false positives* be avoided (i.e., non-fraud transactions being taken to be fraud). "In addition to being split, the data was also rotated to ensure the validity of the models" (ibid.).

Classification algorithms generally differ, by their error rate, according to the data sets used, and how the data are structures has an impact on those error rates. In particular, in the project at hand, that much resulted from the step of evaluating the investigation algorithms. There was no clear winner, out of five algorithms (neural networks, logistic regression, linear vector, projection pursuit, and decision tree) on six datasets, because, for example, all five algorithms turned out to be first or second at least once, and of these, three algorithms were winners at least once, but four algorithms were worst at least once (ibid., pp. 215–216).

The next step was to select the investigation ensembles of models, because using just one model has shortcomings, depending on the non-exhaustive search by different algorithms for the best model, and because "iterative algorithms converge to local minima, such as neural networks" (ibid., p. 216). "Model ensembels make decisions by committee of algorithms" (ibid.).

Next, data were prepared for data mining: "some input and output data specifications are controlled via automated scripting" (ibid., p. 217). Next, the models were created and tested. The criteria for both their generation and their testing were multiple. The more fraud sensitive a model is, the better, but if the model is prone to false positives, this is a shortcoming. To make predictions more robust, the best models were combined.

The final step of the project as reported was to test the model on validation data. Which transactions were used for training, testing, and validation did much matter for the results obtained. But all in all, the ensemble tended to be a better classifier than any of its individual components (but not always) – it was found that "model ensembles mitigate risk compared to single-model solutions and that the ensemble, although not necessarily the best model, was always among the best, and rarely among the worst" (ibid., p. 219) – and "97% of known fraud cases were accurately detected in the validation data set sample" (ibid., p. 218). The models selected 1,217 suspicious transactions, so that the agency would carry out investigations to find out whether these were fraudulent payments.

6.2.7 Information Extraction Tools for Integration with a Link Analysis Tool, Developed in the Late 1990s by Sterling Software

Already by the late 1990s, text mining had results to show. During the 1990s, in the United States, several Message Understanding Conferences (MUC),[327] sponsored by DARPA,[328] were held. It built upon research in natural language automated understanding, an active and successful field in the 1970s and 1980s (See Section 5.2 above). The challenge was how to handle effectively masses of data. Traditionally, computer tools for understanding natural-language multi-sentence text had been successful, based on knowledge stored in long-term memory about narrow domains.

Douglas Lenat embarked upon the implementation of an enormous knowledge-base, CYC, of computational representations of items of common sense (Lenat & Guha, 1990), but that enterprise had its critics within the artificial intelligence scholarly community, at a time when the 1990s "AI Winter" was setting in, as leading AI scholars, and a multitude of teams worldwide, had become disenchanted with AI's near-term perspectives of taking on open-textured problems. Whereas the CYC

---

[327] By *messages*, what is intended is incoming documents whose text is *unformatted;* that is to say, they are *free-text*. The arrival of such textual records is referred to as *unformatted message traffick*.

[328] DARPA is the United States' Defense Advanced Research Projects Agency.

database is available online, had been historically important, and still has potential, arguable in practice the real breakthrough came with the proliferation of projects developing *ontologies*, for a multitude of application domains. One application is *financial fraud ontology* (Kingston, Schafer, & Vandenberghe, 2004). See Section 6.1.7.7 in this book.

Richard Lee of Sterling Software in McLean, Virginia, reported (Lee, 1998) about several tools for *information extraction* (*IE*) being developed by his firm. He claimed he had "demonstrated that the state of the art in Artificial Intelligence — specifically, Natural Language Understanding — is advanced enough that we can implement a practical Information Extraction tool which populates relational data bases with detailed information from free-text messages" (ibid., p. 67). Sterling Software's first system with an IE capability was the *Counter-Drug Intelligence System* (*CDIS*), "which was developed to support analysts tracking the entire spectrum of narcotics-related activities from crop cultivation and precursor chemical production to delivery of the drugs into the United States" (ibid., p. 66). At the core, there was a Sybase relational database. All the entity types involved were stored in that database, along with "a dozen narcotics-related event types" as well as "the full assortment of relations and roles" (ibid.). A second tool with an IE capability was specifically developed by Sterling Software for DARPA's MUC-6 (within the conference series mentioned earlier). "It extracted and templated information on Individuals, Organizations, Locations, Money, Dates, and Times, from Wall Street Journal articles" (ibid.). That tool was reported about in Lee (1995).

Sterling Software then developed a third tool with an IE capability, the *Migration Defense Intelligence Threat Data System* (*MDITDS*). At its core, there was a Memex database: "not, strictly speaking, a relational data base engine, but the design has separate tables for the primary entity types, a table for events, and the crucial Association table" (Lee, 1998, p. 66). MDITDS was to be combined with a link analysis tool, which was being developed by Orion Scientific (ibid.). A continuation tool was also been developed, around an Oracle relational database (ibid.), and with additional event types. A knowledge base was being developed for intelligence messages (ibid., p. 67).

Lee admitted (ibid., p. 66) that cross-sentence reasoning was still beyond the capability of his extraction tool: the tool had no problem, when handling a message about the arrival of an airplane carrying drugs, with realising that the drugs were seized, but the tool could not realise that the Movement event reported about was a transhipment involving both the aircraft and the drugs.

The handling of *coreference* (different instances within the text of referring to the same object or person) was to be improved (ibid., p. 67). "One limitation of the IE tool is that it makes no effort to decide whether an item it has found in a message is the 'same' as another item already in the data base; it errs on the side of assuming it is not" (ibid.). Nevertheless, Lee claimed that the generation of excess records could be handled once the IE tool was integrated with a link analysis tool: "It is up to the analyst to use various tools — including link analysis — to decide that the two records refer to the same item. This leads to a useful synergy between the two tools and the analyst" (ibid.).

Sterling Software was also developing the *Information Extraction Component* (*IEC*), with all the types of entities involved in the previous projects developed by the firm and mentioned here. In particular IEC, was endowed with "the various event types relevant to Counter-Terrorism analysts",[329] and it was to be delivered "with the knowledge bases needed for extracting from newswire articles" (ibid., p. 66).

All Sterling Software's tools with an IE capability except the project for MUC-6 were developed on contracts of the United States Department of Defense. All versions of Sterling Software's IE tool were reportedly developed using a natural-language processing tool, the *NLToolset*, produced by Lockheed-Martin (ibid., p. 67). Lee explained (ibid., p. 64):

> The IE operates by first looking for phrases containing all the references to the entities of interest, plus any date and time references. It then analyzes the phrases and clauses containing those references to find all the entity-to-entity associations (relations). It then analyzes the clauses for events of interest, assigning each entity reference, date and time in the clause to the appropriate role in the event. For each item found, it constructs a *frame* — a representationwhich categorizes each piece of pertinent information by putting it into the appropriate *slot*.

Once frames had been generated, to the extent that the extraction tool was able to identify coreference it merged those frames that refer to the same item. Next, those frames were converted into database records. "Typically, each frame is mapped to a single data base record, with each slot mapped to a data base field, but it is often more complicated" (ibid., p. 64).

Lee (1998, p. 65) provided an example whose input was this message:

> PILOT PABLO GARCIA, COLOMBIAN, PPT 2324224, ARRIVED AT MIAMI INTERNATIONAL AIRPORT ON 27 JUN 97. HE WAS ARRESTED BY U.S. CUSTOM AGENTS WHEN 300 KGS OF COCAINE WAS FOUND IN THE SPARE FUEL TANK OF HIS CESSNA FIREBAT.

---

[329] Lee (1998, p. 63) pointed out that event types had to be more specific per area of application, than the entities to be stored in the relational database. Entities of interest as listed, included: Individuals, Organisations (government, commercial, military, extralegal, and so forth), Places (of various grainsizes, ranging from street addresses to entire continents), Facilities (such as factories, airports, hotels, or warehouses), Documents (such as passports, driver's licenses, or bank book), Money, Vehicles (air, land, or sea), Drugs, and Weapons. By contrast (ibid.):

For Counter-Drug analysts, the events include:

- Processing, purchasing, transporting, etc of drugs
- Planning, meeting, or communicating about any of the above
- Arrest of traffickers or sezure of drugs, money, weapons, etc.

For Counter-Terrorism analysts, on the other hand, the events include:

- Killing, kidnapping, hostage-taking, etc of people
- Bombing, hijacking, etc of buildings and vehicles
- Buying, stealing, etc of weapons and money
- Training in weapons and tactics
- Arrest, conviction, punishment etc of terrorists

Lee claimed that "the frames would look something like this" (ibid.):

```
INDIVIDUAL:
      NAME: PABLO GARCIA
      OCCUPATION: PILOT
      CITIZENSHIP: COLOMBIA

DOCUMENT:
      TYPE: PASSPORT
      NUMBER: 2324224

PLACE:
      CITY: MIAMI
      COUNTRY: US

FACILITY:
      TYPE: AIRPORT
      NAME: MIAMI INTERNATIONAL AIRPORT

DATE:
      YEAR: 1997
      MONTH: 06
      DATE: 27

ORGANIZATION:
      NAME: CUSTOMS
      TYPE: LEA
      COUNTRY: US

DRUGS:
      TYPE: COCAINE
      QUANTITY: 300
      UNIT: KG

VEHICLE:
      TYPE: AIR
      MANUFACTURER: CESSNA
      MODELNAME: FIREBAT
      MODELNUMBER: XJ3

RELATION:
      TYPOE: HASDOC
      ENT1: <DOCUMENT>

RELATION:
      TYPE: LOCATED
      ENT1: <FACILITY>
      ENT2: <PLACE>
```

```
RELATION:
     TYPE: OWNS
     ENT1: <INDIVIDUAL>
     ENT2: <VEHICLE>

EVENT:
     TYPE: MOVEMENT
     AGENT: <INDIVIDUAL>
     DESTINATION: <PLACE>
     DESTFAC: <FACILITY>
     ENDDATE: <DATE>

EVENT:
     TYPE: ARREST
     ARRESTEE: <INDIVIDUAL>
     ARRESTER: <ORGANIZATION>
     PLACE: <PLACE>
     FACILITY: <FACILITY>
     BEGINDATE: <DATE>
     ENDDATE: <DATE>

EVENT:
     TYPE: SEIZURE
     SEIZEE: <DRUGS>
     SEIZER: <ORGANIZATION>
     PLACE: <PLACE>
     FACILITY: <FACILITY>
     BEGINDATE: <DATE>
     ENDDATE: <DATE>
```

This reflects an application of data structures (namely, frames with slots) which were already used in artificial intelligence in the 1970s and 1980s. What was not very developed as yet, was ontologies technology. Still, there is a continuity: we find in Lee's example both types (in event frames and relation frames), and instances of types (in the frames for individual, document, place, facility, date, organisation, drugs, and vehicle).

6.2.8 The Poznan Ontology Model for the Link Analysis of Fuel Fraud

A team at the Poznan University of Technology, in Poland, comprising Czeslaw Jędrzejek, Maciej Falkowski, and Maciej Smolenski, reported (Jedrzejek, Falkowski, & Smolenski, 2009) about an application of ontologies technology to link analysis for investigating scams involving chains of transactions made by a multitude of straw companies, and whose goal is fuel fraud.[330] In particular, what is involved is a kind of crime known as a fuel laundering scam. "This crime mechanism is to buy rebated oil (in Poland heating oil) from a licensed distributor and then mix it (i.e. add components) and sell to the retail market as duty paid diesel" (ibid., p. 83).

In order to avoid the considerably higher excise tax or duty on Diesel fuel, fraudsters process heating oil or agricultural oil by *fuel laundering* – i.e., by removing the dye identifying these, and adding components – into Diesel fuel that is suitable for engines. The lower-quality fuel thus obtained is then illicitly sold to drivers as Diesel fuel at a pump at gas stations. The cost of transforming the fuel is negligible, and as tax is avoided, the operators pocket the difference. This is a big sector on the black market, both in Poland and, e.g., in the United Kingdom.

The crime mechanism involves a flow of fuel, fuel components, and money, and this is masked by issuing fictitious invoices, either with or without payment. Whereas "the methods to hide the proceeds (i.e. executing the crime scheme) are very similar" (Jedrzejek et al., 2009, p. 81) – notwithstanding its also being true that "fraudsters may use many types of schemes, techniques and transactions to achieve their goals" so that "we need a conceptual model of fuel laundering crime of significant generality" (ibid.) – in the three major cases from Poland that the team studied "prosecutors had an enormous problem to uncover money flows from the source of money (profit centre) to sinks (where the money leaves companies and goes as cash to organizers of the scheme) and in retrospect, some of them did not even attempt to do this" (ibid.).

The purpose of the Poznan team's project was to develop adequate analytic tools to help with investigations and prosecutions. The tool developed is *FuelFlowVis*. The unwieldy difficulties with which the prosecutors were faced are explained in the paper: "This occurs because the use of traditional analysis tools (spreadsheets or non-semantic visualization tools) cannot provide information about chains of transactions — a separate binary relations' view does not give complete insight into the crime mechanism. The consequence of this fact is incomplete understanding of a crime mechanism" (ibid.).

The team was faced with the general problem of its being very difficult to model economic crime (cf. e.g. Chau, Schroeder, Xu, & Chen, 2007) for the purpose of developing a knowledge-based system. The team was also provides with an opportunity, as whereas data mining tools for investigating money laundering have become available, fuel laundering was still virgin territory for AI & Law as catering to the needs of national financial intelligence units.

The team mainly studied three large fuel laundering cases from the 2001–2003 period, that went to court in Poland in 2008. Data sources were incomplete, especially when it came to electronic data (these are often lost in the time lapsed since the crime being perpetrated, and the case going to court). Only for one of the three cases, a rather complete set of money transfers was available, along with the most

---

[330] Incidentally, e.g. Anne Alvesalo (2003) discusses the investigation of economic crime.

important invoice information. The lack of data for the other two cases — "we did not have the original wire transfer data; only the aggregated ones" (Jedrzejek et al., 2009, p. 81) — made it impossible to apply to them a particular data mining technique, namely: triggering rule-based red flags. Most defendants were changed with money laundering, or signing false documents, or fraudulently reclaiming VAT from the tax office, as well as with conspiracy, of tax evasion in the form of simple non-declaration of income, of false data in a tax statement, or of directing illegal activity performed by another person (ibid.).

The Poznan team developed a formal model of fuel laundering and money laundering, the model being based on a *minimal ontology* (coded in OWL). It is minimal, in the sense that the team deliberately only included there necessary concepts that follow in the logical order of uncovering facts about a crime (ibid., p. 82). That minimal ontology – which is itself structured as eight layers in fact-uncovering order (only five layers were shown in a table ibid.) — constitutes an application layer, which in turn is "embedded in an upper level ontology of criminal processes and investigation procedures" (ibid.).

Modules in the ontology include one (Person.owl) "describing persons as social entities and groups of persons" (ibid.); another module (Document.owl) "specifying legal meaning of documents and their content" (ibid.); a module LegalProvision.owl about legal acts and sanctions; the module intent.own about a person's intentions; the module Action.owl about activities; the module Object.owl describing goods, and in particular, fuels and the added components involved in fuel laundering; and moreover general concepts and relations were defined in the module MinimalModel.owl.

The taxonomy of concepts of the module Object.owl states that both DieselComponent and GasComponent are kinds of FuelComponent; that Diesel, Gas; and IllegalDiesel are kinds of Fuel; and that Fuel, FuelComponent, and HeatingOil are kinds of goods (ibid., p. 83).

The taxonomy of concepts of the module Person.owl states (ibid.):

- that MajorOwner, MinorOwner, and StrawOwner are kinds of Owner;
- that ManagementBoard is a kind of GroupOfPersonsCinnectedToCompany;
- that GroupOfPersonsCinnectedToCompany is a kind of GroupOfPersons;
- that GroupOfPersons, Fraudster, and PersonWhoFalsifiedDocument are a kind of PhysicialSubject;
- that IndirectManager is a kind of PersonNotConnectedToCompany;
- that Owner, DecisivePerson [sic], MiddleLevfelDecisivePerson, and OtherPersonRealatedToCompany are a kind of PersonConnectedToCompany;
- that Physical Subject, PersonConnectedToCompany, and PersonNotConnectedToCompany are a kind of Person;
- that HeadOfSingleUnit, HeadOfMultipleUnits, ChiefAdministrativePerson, ChiefAccountant, and DeputyHeadOfMultipleUnits are a kind of MiddleLevelDecisivePerson;

- thaty ChairmanOfTheBoard, MemberOfTheBoard, and DeputyPerson are a kind of DecisivePerson;
- and that Procurtent [sic] and OtherDeputy are a kind of DeputyPerson.

As can be seen, the concepts defined were such that were found to be useful on an ad hoc basis. For convenience in the exposition, Jedrzejek et al. (2009, p. 82) stated in *database relational notation* the most important concepts that at the time of their writing were functional in their FuelFlowVis tool.[331] This notation consists of the name of a relation, followed by a parenthesis containing a list of attributes. In turn, an attribute (such as Money-Transfer) may itself be a relation. That is to say, Jedrzejek et al. (ibid.) implicitly conceptualised their relational schema by allowing what in database research is known as *nested relations*[332]:

Flow (Money_Transfer,
      Invoice,
      Goods/Service)
Money_Transfer (From_Entity,
          To_Entity,
          Method_of_Transfer,
          Data,
          Value,
          Title-of-Transfer)
Method_of_Tranfer (Electronic_Transfer,
          Cash)
Fuel (Component_of_Gas,
      Gas,
      Component_of_Gas,
      Diesel)

Title_of_Transfer states what is the money transferred for, which is in order to obtain some given kind of goods in exchange. In link analysis as performed while investigating fuel laundering, that attribute is both important and problematic. "The crucial step is the unification of money transfer and invoice data, because perpetrators usually enter meaningless information in a 'title of payment field'" (ibid., p. 85).

The Poznan team's project resulted in a tool called *FuelFlowVis*. It is a "visual intelligent analytic tool" (ibid., p. 83). Its purpose is to support prosecutors in the management and building of evidence when handling a fuel laundering scam. "The tool serves to give an investigator an insight into size, timing and topology of transactions. This is controlled by various filters" (ibid., p. 84). Moreover, users are enabled to "inspect invoices or money transfers separately, or in a combined view,

---

[331] They actually store the data in a relational database, and queries are in SQL (ibid., p. 85).

[332] Concerning nested relations, see in fn 47 above, and in the text citing that footnote.

at various cales. Usually, one manipulates [the] left local panel and has a small size shaded overview in the right panel" one the screen, when in main application view (ibid.).

Link analysis is visualised in graphs, which are shown either in detail, or in a simplified view with just selected objects, or by showing aggregated relations (ibid.). In the link analysis diagrams, some graphs are *transfer diagrams*, and whereas the nodes represent persons, companies, or other entities, the connections between nodes are of the following types: fuel component invoices (shown in green), gas invoices (shown in blue), Diesel oil invoices (shown in red), or money transfers (shown in black).

Some other graphs are *roles of person's diagrams*, and the connections between nodes in these graphs are of the following types (ibid.): "Approve of electronic money transfer" (shown as a solid red line); "Cash transfer (Drawing cash on authorization or passing cash)" (shown as a dashed red line); "Real or informal ownership of a company (directing activities of a straw company owner)" (shown as a solid black line); "Informal management of a company" (shown as a dashed black line); and "Other activities" (shown as a blue line).

For a given node, *input neighbors* are such companies that transferred money or goods to the company represented by that given node, whereas by contrast *output neighbors* are such companies to which money or goods were transferred from the node considered (ibid., p. 85). The data mining capabilities of FuelFlowVis include also the search of paths, by means of a path algorithm (ibid.). The criminal organisation "consists of many straw companies, whose only rationale is to obscure patterns of transactions and move suspicion away of a mixing shop" (ibid., p. 86), where rebated fuel is fraudulently upgraded. In fact (ibid.):

> It has to be understood that although flow of money is real, operations are mostly fictitious — no change of material goods takes place. Similarly, for most operations, invoices were properly drawn pretending a legal operation, but actually the[y] were false. Phony companies have no real inbfrastructure, and most of the time invoices are produced by a scheme mastermind.

6.2.9 Fiscal Fraud Detection with the Pisa SNIPER Project

A team based in Pisa, Italy, and whose members are Stefano Basta, Fosca Giannotti, Giuseppe Manco, Dino Pedreschi and Laura Spisanti reported about the SNIPER project (Basta, Giannotti, Manco, Pedreschi, & Spisanti, 2009). SNIPER is an auditing methodology, applied to an area in fiscal fraud detection,[333] namely, the

---

[333] A comprehensive survey of research into the application of data mining to fraud detection was provided by Phua, Lee, Smith-Miles, and Gayler (2005). Cf. Kou, Lu, Sirwongwattana, and Huang (2004), Weatherford (2002).

detection of Value Added Tax (VAT) fraud. Such fraud can take various forms, such as underdeclaring sales, or overdeclaring purchases. Moreover, fraudulent claims are possible for credits and refunds, because "tax charged by a seller is available to the buyer as a credit against his liability on his own sales and, if in excess of the output tax due, refunded to him" (ibid., p. 27).

The team developing SNIPER aims at having a rule-based computer tool that by means of data mining, would "identify the taxpayers with the highest probability of being VAT defrauders, in order to support the activity of planning and performing effective fiscal audits" (ibid.). A major constraint is the limited auditing capability of the competent revenue agency: "In Italy for example, audits are performed on only 0.4% of the overall population of taxpayers who file a VAT refund request" (ibid.). The resulting *sample selection bias*, by which auditors focus on suspicious subjects, has the consequence that "the proportion of positive subjects (individuals who are actually defrauders in the training set is vast compared with that in the overall population" (ibid.). The same constraint on auditing capability also "poses severe constraints in the design of the scoring system" (ibid.), and "the scoring system should concentrate on a user-defined fixed number of individuals (representing the auditing capability of the agency), with high fraudulent likelihood and with a minimum false positive rate" (ibid.).

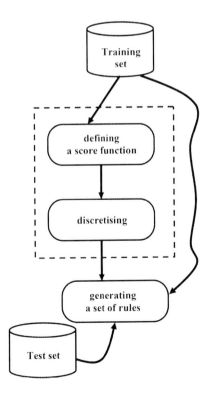

Fig. 6.2.9.1 The initial, preprocessing part of SNIPER's flowchart

The fraud detection scenario has several objective functions (i.e., criteria) to be optimised, "and a traditional classification system may fail in accomplishing such a multi-purpose task" (ibid.). These typical criteria were enumerated (ibid.):

- *Proficiency*: scoring and detection should not rely only on a binary decision boundary separating defrauders from non-defrauders. Rather, higher fraud amounts make defrauders more significant. For example, it is better to detect a defrauder whose fraud amounts to $1000 than one whose fraud amounts to $100.
- *Equity*: a weighting mechanism should highlight those cases where the fraud represents a significant proportion of the business volume. For example, an individual whose fraud amounts to $1000 and whose business volume is $100,000 is less interesting than an individual whose fraud amounts to $1000 but whose business volume is only $10,000.

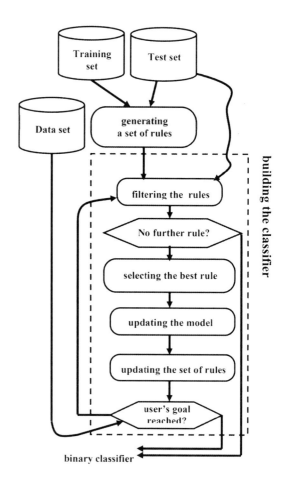

Fig. 6.2.9.2 The classifier-building part of SNIPER's flowchart

- *Efficiency*: since the focus is on refunds, scoring and detection should be sensitive to total/partial frauds. For example, a subject claiming a VAT refund equal to $2000 and entitled to $1800 is less significant than a different subject claiming $200 who is entitled to nothing.

Basta et al. (2009, p. 29) pointed out that

> In general, supervised techniques (using a training set of known fraudulent cases) based on hybrid or cost-sensitive classification suffer from low interpretability, which makes them inadequate for the problem at hand. In addition, the aforementioned problem of sample selection bias makes it difficult to devise a proper training set. Recently, semi-supervised and unsupervised methods have been proposed to partially overcome these drawbacks. Unfortunately, these techniques fail to provide interpretable explanations for the 'outlierness' of a fraudster.

Rather, the team opted for adopting a rule-based classification approach. This is because intelligible explanations made available to the auditors are more important than the scores themselves. By receiving explanations, auditors can get an idea of which behavioural mechanism behind the fraud to investigate. A drawback of rule-based classification techniques is that as, in the problem at hand, the underlying data distribution is such that occurrences of positive cases of fraud are rarely observed, the classifier would be poor at predicting accurately. In SNIPER, the approach is flexible, being "an ensemble method that combines the best of several rule-based baseline classification tools" (ibid.), each handling specific subproblems. The system should gradually learn a set of rules, and devise a scoring function. "Tuning the function allows different aspects of VAT fraud to be emphasized, from which baseline classification tools can then be trained in order to associate class labels to individuals according to their relevance to the aspect of interests" (ibid.). Bad rules, i.e., such rules that would degrade overall accuracy, are to be filtered out iteratively, until a final binary classifier is obtained, which advises whom to audit or not audit. Experiments were claimed to have shown SNIPER to be effective, outperforming traditional techniques (ibid.). In Figs. 6.2.9.1 and 6.2.9.2, I redrew the flowchart from Basta et al. (2009, p. 27, figure 1).

Chapter 7
FLINTS, a Tool for Police Investigation and Intelligence Analysis: A project by Richard Leary explained by its author

7.1 Introduction: Motivations and History of the Project

This chapter is the result of research conducted by myself into the benefits that can be gained by the application of a general theory and methodology for the process of obtaining, managing and using evidence in police investigation and intelligence analysis. Central to this thesis are methods and processes that help investigators and intelligence analysts to ask better questions. This introductory section presents a brief chronology of the development of those ideas and research. My standpoint was informed by having been a Detective Police Officer for a number of years in the United Kingdom.

My original ideas about improving police investigation and intelligence analysis came from ideas that involved the combination of different types of evidence. Furthermore, I had experimented with ideas about how we could improve police investigation and intelligence analysis by developing a better understanding about techniques for the reduction of "uncertainty" as presented in a paper at the First World Conference on Criminal Investigation and Evidence at the Hague in 1995. Uncertainty reduction (*entropy*) for me is at the heart of all good science and is the bedrock of rational systems of discovery. Something I remain convinced upon to this day.

In 1996, two additional papers were published in the Police Research Group's publication, *Focus*. The first was entitled *A Revolution in Criminal Investigation*, and concerned extending the application of forensic principles and genetic evidence within policing. The second was entitled *DNA: The Promise*; it challenged the traditional use of evidence, and proposed new ways for the systematic management and use of evidence in the investigation of multiple cases rather than solely of single cases. These three papers provided the ideas behind the systematic use of large collections of evidence, and helped I to formulate the original ideas underpinning a prototype system of software (called the "Forensic-Led Intelligence System", FLINTS) that became adopted by West Midlands Police. Prior to this, forensic evidence was almost exclusively used in the investigation of single, isolated events such as a burglary, a murder, or a rape, rather than in the routine investigation of linked series of crimes.

In 1996, I developed an interest in the methods of analysis and synthesis of evidence developed by John Henry Wigmore.[1] Although this approach was exclusively concerned with single, isolated cases, and was intended primarily for use by advocates preparing for court, it provided a foundational methodology for the charting of logical relations between evidence as an aid to developing powerful arguments. I also developed an interest in the science of complexity, which provided valuable ideas about how complex systems function and the way in which information in such systems behaves and can be used. That same year, I won the Forensic Science Society Scholarship and used that funding to continue this research into new ways of using and managing forensic evidence. Systemizing the combination of different evidence types and developing intelligence from forensic evidence were the focus of this work.

At this time, I was seeking to operationalise my research findings in the form of a system so as to accomplish two goals: to overcome five weaknesses identified in police investigation and practice, and to draw on the lessons learned from Wigmore, molecular biology, and complexity theory.

In 1998, I was appointed Scientific Officer to West Midlands Police and tasked to implement new methods of managing and using forensic evidence. In 1999, for the first time in the world, I and scientists from the Forensic Science service experimented with the use of highly sensitive technology for recovering DNA from surfaces that had merely been touched by humans. Although it was usual to recover DNA from visible samples, the experiment focused on material that was invisible to the human eye. The intelligence gained from this evidence was used to identify groups of criminals operating in networks. At this time, there was a national crime problem involving the defrauding of elderly citizens. Confidence tricksters were gaining access to the homes of elderly people on the pretext of being public officials, and using the opportunity to steal cheque books and other valuables. Using "supersensitive" recovery techniques, DNA was successfully recovered from door knockers, handles and other objects that had merely been touched by offenders. Applying new policy, procedures and techniques in accordance with the general theory and methodology described in this thesis, evidence was recovered that resulted in the detection of networks of criminals and crimes. This was later responsible for the prosecution of key people involved in organizing and committing these offences. The technique subsequently became a forensic service offered to investigators.

As a result of this work over a number of years I decided to implement some the main themes of the work into a software system. The resulting software was FLINTS. Mark Compton programmed the computer code under my guidance; I provided domain expertise that shaped how the programmer embodied the conceptual foundations behind my new approach to evidence management and implement it into the software.

---

[1] See Section 3.2 in this book.

In 1999, Nick Tofiluk, Chief Superintendent (later, Assistant Chief Constable) of the West Midlands Police, developed an interest in FLINTS and offered strategic assistance in overcoming organisational barriers to implementation of the system in the West Midlands Region. This resistance was an interesting reaction which I learnt greatly from. In essence, the resistance emanated from protectionist attitudes amongst some Detectives, Managers and the IT Department because adopting FLINTS meant (A) admitting that we could do things faster, cheaper and more effectively and (B) it involved the use of modern computing power and threatened job security. Whilst the former was true the latter was not. FLINTS merely ensured that humans could achieve more and be employed in the things they do best; reasoning, deciding, evaluating and decision making whilst the computer could access, count, sift, sort and process information at breath-taking speed. I and Nick agreed to work together and I was given great assistance in overcoming these organizational barriers. Responsibility for the development of the methodology and conceptual underpinnings continued to remain my own.

In 2002, I began work on a case study intended to develop a new approach to managing the problem of shifting contexts and standpoints in evidence management. In 2003, the first iteration of a new case study was programmed and used to simultaneously manage and analyse evidence in hundreds of cases of fraud. Lawyers involved in the original litigation had been unable to manage these cases without the application of the approach because the body of evidence was too vast for manual methods to succeed. Although the system, called MAVERICK, is outside the scope of this chapter, it uses a unique methodology to manage the way in which evidence is perceived and managed.

In 2004, using MAVERICK, I responded to requests in the provision of two important areas of assistance to law enforcement and financial organizations: First, I provided assistance in meeting the compliance obligations laid down by the Proceeds of Crime Act and Terrorism Act of 2000. This assistance was in terms of "disclosures" of material to the National Criminal Intelligence Service about suspected terrorist funding and financial crimes committed during organised crime involving fraud and deception. These disclosures were made on behalf of U.K. lawyers representing large corporate organisations who had been targeted with fraud. Second, I provided assistance in the management of a mixed mass of evidence concerning 2 million financial transactions suspected to contain material subject to the above legislation. My methodology and the MAVERICK software were used throughout.

7.2 Early Beginnings

The traditional approach to the management of evidence in policing has involved narrow conceptions of the way evidence is managed, analysed and used. My experience demonstrated that practitioners[2] adopted narrow views as well as uninspired

---

[2] This includes police officers, Crime Scene Investigators and lawyers.

approaches[3] towards the study and use of evidence as a science. This included the way that evidence should be collected and the many uses to which it could be put. A common experience was that whilst cases may appear to be overwhelming proven "on paper", by simply adopting another standpoint or considering an alternative explanation about some aspect of the case, an alternative view could be deemed not only plausible, but often persuasive. Often, this was the result of investigators treating and interpreting evidence only in the light of the hypothesis they were pursuing. Evidence is too often seen in light of the support it can give to a narrow or single hypothesis. Alternatives are not considered, or, if they are, they are dismissed too readily. Narrow or single hypotheses often appear in the form of a case theory. For example, the theory may propose that a particular act had been perpetrated by a particular individual, or that an event took place "in the following way", thereby favouring a particular explanation. This narrow view has implications not only for single cases, such as the investigation of historical events or crimes, but also for intelligence analysis and predictive enquiry. In terms of single cases, it creates barriers to the consideration of alternative explanations.

Evidence that may support an alternative theory may be ignored, resulting in the wrong conclusion being drawn. In terms of intelligence analysis, the narrow focus can prevent users of evidence from considering fruitful lines of enquiry that would potentially prevent a threat from becoming a reality. Simple explanations or those that appear obvious are considered at the expense of those more difficult to uncover. Collections of evidence often contain many layers of information in which indirect links and associations may not be immediately obvious. Accessing and testing these areas of our collections of evidence present many opportunities for the discovery of new knowledge.

This insight provided valuable lessons about the way evidence is sought, collected and used, and seemed crucial to developing a better approach. What seemed

---

[3] Following my appointment as a Detective in 1981 in the inner City of Birmingham, England, I found the lack of determination that some investigators adopted in the search for evidence in their investigations was surprising. In particular, the search for evidence in pursuit of one side of the story struck me. I cannot claim that this bias was borne of some high-grounded moral attitude, but rather, quite simply, of the futility of learning all sides of the story. It became apparent fairly early on that evidence is always available, in some form, somewhere, and it is only our determination and ingenuity in finding it that is in question. Furthermore, any collection of evidence eventually has to be tested by others. These may be Crown Lawyers, Defence Lawyers, a Jury or a Judge, and any suspect; therefore, I had a responsibility not only to satisfy my own view of the evidence, but also to demonstrate that I had tested arguments in favour of my hypothesis as well as those counter to it. This paid off many times, particularly in generating new sources of covert information from within the criminal fraternity. Balance and fairness demonstrates reliability, which was something that informants sought from an investigator when seeking to impart information, especially in cases involving violent or serious crime. Anticipating the opposing view, seeing evidence from different perspectives and demonstrating that evidence had been collected in support as well as negation of a hypothesis was crucial. Whilst it is never possible to overturn every possible stone, it *is* possible to demonstrate that one has overturned every *reasonable* stone, bearing in mind the available evidence and the issues under investigation.

to be missing was the development of a truly systematic forensic[4] attitude towards the management and use of evidence.

7.3 FLINTS 1

FLINTS is a modernised neo-Wigmorean approach to the management, analysis and use of evidence in pre-trial criminal fact investigations. It was designed on the basis of the methodology in this thesis to model the relationships between people, crime, locations, times and evidence in ways useful to analysts, investigators and policy makers. This kind of Wigmorean evidence modelling serves a number of purposes in the generation and discovery of knowledge. However, there are two principal purposes it is concerned with: first, the provision of understanding of the attributes of evidence we already possess about events that have already take place, and second, the provision of insights into evidence we do not yet possess, but need, and into events that may yet take place. At the end of this chapter, a case study in "linked burglary crime" is described, and the methodology and use of FLINTS are demonstrated.

Policing has suffered[5] from a lack of knowledge about the structural and intellectual questions surrounding the collection and use of evidence as a discipline and has therefore been unable to construct a conceptual framework and a set of operating principles that would allow police organisations to gain maximum knowledge from their collection of evidence.

The mechanisms I put forward in my doctoral dissertation to aid the modelling of relationships within networks of evidence are achieved by organising the systems and structures under which evidence is discovered, collected, considered and stored so that links and connections inherent in the evidence can be speedily established. This in turn aids the formation of new hypotheses and the elimination of old hypotheses. Questions can be asked of the system to draw on the complex combinations of evidence that already exist, but that are perhaps not readily known, as well as those combinations and connections not known to exist but that are strongly suspected to exist.

This demonstrates that although we may be in possession of information, we are often unaware of the evidence's existence, or, if we are aware of its existence, we are sometimes oblivious to its meaning and the links that exist within the information. The contribution that approaches like this can make to developing our understanding of the environment in which we operate is underestimated. What we "possess" and what we "know" are often very different. Establishing the difference between what

---

[4] To this end, *forensic* is meant to portray an interrogative, questioning approach. The *Shorter Oxford English Dictionary* defines the term as "pertaining to, connected with, or used in courts of law; suitable or analogous to pleadings in court, or a speech or written thesis maintaining one side or the other of a given question."

[5] I argued that much in chapter 1 of my doctoral dissertation.

we possess and what we know provides the ability to establish what we "do not possess" and "do not know". Optimising systems to undertake this function is crucial in getting the most benefit from the evidence collections we have. Applications for use of this approach are many.

Identifying links and connections between crimes and events that we know[6] have taken place and people that we believe are connected to these occurrences helps us to identify links and connections with other crimes, events and people that *may* be linked, but for which evidence is currently not available to justify, negate or sustain that belief.[7] Investigators can set out to establish whether sufficient evidence, even if not presently available, does exist in some form, somewhere, to justify or negate the hypothesis. This helps us to investigate crime not only on the basis of single events in time, but also on the basis of chains of events in time and space, and thus represents a whole new way of thinking about crime investigation and intelligence analysis. Let us imagine a series of ten crimes of burglary linked on the basis of DNA evidence.

Let us consider an example: a series of 10 crimes linked by a single DNA profile. Figure 7.3.1 illustrates that at each of the 10 crimes, DNA evidence in the form of a crime stain[8] was recovered. The hypothesis is formulated that these 10 events are linked because DNA recovered at each crime scene has produced the same genetic profile, namely that of suspect "A".

We can formulate a hypothesis that the donor of the DNA at each of the scenes of crime is the same person, even though we do not yet know their name.[9] In an effort

---

[6] Here, the term "know" does not mean a fact that has been established beyond challenge. It means instead "that which we are prepared to accept on the basis of reliable evidence currently in our possession".

[7] Challenge may come in the form of counter-arguments put forward by our adversaries or, just as importantly, counter-arguments we construct ourselves to test some argument that we are naturally persuaded by. The former is simple; adversaries or colleagues may favour another argument or explanation that they put to us in the form of a challenge, and we can deal with it on that basis. The latter is sometimes difficult because it involves constructing counter-assertions ourselves, often in the knowledge that we are already satisfied with the current explanation. The approach may go something like this: "Is this explanation or argument sustainable if new evidence were to be made available?" Alternatively, it may go like this: "Is my explanation or argument sustainable in the light of the following alternative hypothesis?" This thought process may involve considering a range of possible explanations or arguments ranging from that which is highly probable to that which is highly improbable. It may also involve considering that which is impossible. The reason for this is simple: that which is impossible on the basis of evidence currently available may become possible in the light of new evidence or some other explanation. The process may instead be as simple as viewing the evidence we currently have in a different light or from a different standpoint.

[8] *Crime stain* means DNA recovered in some form from a crime scene and that awaits matching against reference samples stored in a database. A match with one of these samples would enable the investigator or analyst to formulate a hypothesis that the individual may have had the "opportunity" to commit the crime. It does not necessarily mean that they *did* commit the crime.

[9] In addition to the problem of false positives and adventitious matches, investigators and analysts should also keep in mind that identical twins share the same DNA code. Identical twins (monozygotes) originate from a single embryonic cell and therefore share the same genomic DNA. Therefore, wherever monozygotic twins are suspected of involvement in a crime, both must be

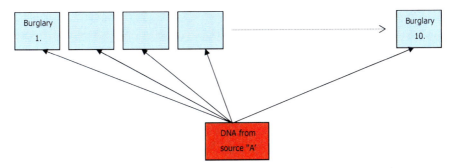

Fig. 7.3.1 A hypothetical series of 10 crimes linked by a single DNA profile

to identify the donor of the DNA, we might search for any matching DNA profiles from former suspects and convicted persons stored in the National DNA Database. However, it is possible that after the search, despite our establishing that the crimes appear to be linked, no profiles from suspects and convicted persons matched Profile A. We would then be left with the task of identifying the offender by other means.

7.4 Identifying "Unknown" Offenders

How can we set about identifying "unknown" offenders? We could sit around and hope that we "get lucky" or we could appeal for witnesses to the events in the hope that someone, somewhere, might have the evidence we need. One effective approach is to explore methods that reduce the level of uncertainty associated with the number of people in the database that could account for the DNA profile.[10]

We can create a "virtual offender" to account for the presence of DNA Profile A at the scene of each of the crimes and await other evidence that might indicate a legal identity. This can be done by systematically exploring the information we already possess to ascertain whether there are any indications anywhere in our systems as to the possible identity of the individual who possesses DNA Profile A. Not only might this produce a suggestion of their identity, it might also lead us to search for additional information in areas where we are likely to find useful indicators of the offender's true identity.

So far we have only considered DNA evidence recovered from each of the 10 crimes. There may be other evidence available that we have not considered. Fingerprints, footwear, tool marks, handwriting, hairs, fibres, witness evidence and

---

considered "suspects" and therefore both must be treated for the purposes of an investigation as requiring us to eliminate them from suspicion. The hypothesis that the virtual suspect or offender may be one of two identical twins must always be considered.

[10] The ideal position is to be able to eliminate all persons except one. Once we have reduced the uncertainty to a single individual, we can then use other evidential tests to challenge the reliability of the analysis and conclusion.

other clues may provide a suggestion about the likely identity of the suspect if we consider this evidence alongside the DNA.

Imagine that a fingerprint found at burglary 4 is identified as the index finger on the right hand of a known former burglar called Mr. George Smith. The question then arises: "Does George Smith have DNA profile A?" If he does, fingerprint evidence has suggested a method to establish the identity of the original donor of DNA profile A – possibly Mr. George Smith. If the answer affirms this, then Mr. George Smith may be asked to provide a DNA sample for comparison and, if matched to DNA recovered from one or more burglary scenes, asked to account for the presence of his DNA at each of the 10 scenes. Other evidence types can also be used in this way.

Many types of evidence can help us to identify people that we know exist in the population but for whom we have no means of distinguishing them as individuals. Used in combination, these sources of evidence present us with a range of possibilities to identify individuals uniquely. Some involve direct and some involve indirect chains of reasoning.

7.5 Systemising the Identification of Unknown Offenders

Policing and intelligence work has for too long approached the identification and elimination of suspects in a conceptually narrow way. The focus of attention has been on the use of names rather than a wider concept involving the use of *indicators of identity*.[11] Intelligence systems employed in law enforcement use names as the key identifier. The same is true of evidence systems used in fingerprint and other forensic databases.

The ability to systematically (and routinely) identify *persistent offenders* has great potential for decision-making and for optimising investigative effectiveness. Identifying those persons who commit most of the crimes in our systems offers greater returns on the investments we make in the deployment of staff and financial resources.

The use of a wide range of indicators of identity can be used rather than narrow, single indicators (typically only a name) to provide a more inquisitive methodology for identification. Rather than simply referring to offenders by either their name or as simply "unknown", they can be referred to as "virtual unknowns". They can be classified and catalogued in a database alongside indicators of the characteristics we do know. As the investigation of crime continues over time, we can explore different combinations and different inferential chains of links by using these indicators in combination to help us set about filling in the gaps in our knowledge. Researching

---

[11] This concentration on the use of a name as a means to identify people is surprising bearing in mind the large proportion of the population that share the same name. Some with the same name even share the same date of birth.

direct and indirect chains of links may eventually produce or suggest a possible indicator as a means of identification.

Let us consider this approach in detail. If we are satisfied from the available evidence that a crime has been committed, we can infer that someone who may (as yet) be unknown committed the crime. Unknown persons can be classified as "virtual suspects" simply by giving them a unique number to act as an identifier until their true identity is discovered. Once we have allocated a unique number to the "unknown", we can then think about them as a "virtual unknown" person. This provides us with a whole new way of thinking about the problem of identification. We can use a range of indicators about their characteristics, their identity or their personal circumstances to do so. Taken together, these indicators can provide the means to link different aspects of identity until one or more of those indicators provide a suggestion of a name.[12]

It is the ability to develop and navigate direct and indirect chains of inference between indicators that presents the opportunity to identity individuals. This is an example of a broader use of the concept of evidence and the wider uses to which it can be put to.

Table 7.5.1 is a *multidimensional identification index* designed to present a systematic approach to the use of a range of indicators to identify people.

Referring to Table 7.5.1, let us imagine that Event 2 was a burglary in which the offender shed hair. Subsequent DNA analysis of the hair produced a DNA profile. However, no reference sample of the offender existed in the National DNA Database, therefore the offender cannot be immediately identified by name. Genetic information gained from DNA profiling of the hair provided further information about the person's physical characteristics: their hair colour, eye colour, ethnic ancestry and height. These additional indicators are used to begin to fill gaps in the *virtual persons record* that may become useful to us.

The same DNA profile is found at Event 4, the theft of a motor vehicle. A witness to Event 4 states that the offender was seen to have a distinctive tattoo on his right forearm: an eagle and sword. He was aged between thirty and forty years, was a white European and had brown to red hair.

Because Event 4 revealed the same DNA profile as Event 2, we can begin to cross-reference specific details of *indicators* from Event 4 to Event 2.[13] The index demonstrates how we can use a method of cross-referencing evidence from one event to another so as to provide us with a system to navigate inferential links, gaining clues to the identification of individuals and even groups of individuals as we progress. In this example, it can be seen that the DNA recovered in Events 2 and

---

[12] A *virtual suspect or offender* is a person who is known to exist because evidence of their presence at a scene of crime has been discovered, but whose identity is yet to be established.

[13] For example, the original Indicators (DNA, tattoo, age and hair colour) that we discovered from Event 4 are marked with a red # sign. Because the same DNA profile was found at Events 2 and 4, we can infer that all details for Event 4 should also apply to Event 2. These inferred indicators are marked with a blue # sign.

Table 7.5.1 A multidimensional identification index

	Events, Crimes and People; 1-n				
Evidential indicators of identity	1	2	3	4	5
1. Sex					
2. Birth date or age		#		#	
3. Address zip code					
4. E-mail address, number					
5. Father's reference number					
6. Mother's reference number					
7. Male siblings					
8. Female siblings					
9. Height					
10. Eye colour					
11. Hair colour		#		#	
12. Ethnic origin		#		#	
13. Shoe size					
14. Biometric identifiers:					
(a) Eyes					
(b) Facial					
(c) Fingerprints (10)					
15. DNA profile		#		#	
16. Genetic characteristics:		#		#	
(a) Hair colour		#		#	
(b) Eye colour		#		#	
(c) Gender		#		#	
(d) Ethnic ancestry		#		#	
(e) Height		#		#	
17. Body marks; tattoos/scars		#		#	
18. Vehicle number					
19. Electoral roll number					
20. Nationality					
21. Passport number					
22. National Insurance Number					
23. Driving licence number					
24. Credit card number					
25. Taxation number					
26. Telephone number					
27. Cell phone number					
28. National Identification Number					
29. Associates with					
30. Employed by					
31. Educated at					
32. Related to					
33. Criminal convictions					
34. Occupation					
35. Name (legal/accepted)					

4 provided us with genetic information about the offender's physical characteristics and ancestral ethnicity, and these become a part of the index.

A search of the tattoo file in the multidimensional index reveals that two people are known to have a tattoo of this description: a male aged sixty-five years, of West Indian appearance and with a recorded name of Charles, and a thirty-two-year-old male of White European appearance called Finney. Neither had previously provided DNA profiles. The system could be automated to check for those persons within the population with indicators that match a tattoo as well as any other indicators available. This narrows down those in the system that could potentially match with the available information.

Computers can be used to manage and track the chains of connections produced by this kind of cross-referencing. Although the methodology is simple, the potential links involved soon become complex and require an efficient means of tracking and cross-referencing. This process helps us to eventually establish an identity using the conventional method of a legal name, ultimately reducing the uncertainty about the legal identity of the person of interest to us. Another useful attribute of this method is that the indicators of identity can be searched in predetermined ways involving one indicator or a combination of indicators to "cleave out" of the system configurations of information of interest to us. We may need to identify a white male, aged fifty to fifty-five years, with brown hair and blue eyes, and who drives a white BMW car. This may produce a range of potential suspects, some with known legal names and others still classified as "virtual unknowns". Again, the process of cross-referencing indicators, combining indicators and exploring inferential routes between records may produce an indicator of interest in determining a true identity.

Let us consider another aspect to this process. The evidence we have does not mean that the *virtual suspect or offender* was alone when the crimes were committed; they may have committed any one or any combination of these crimes with any number of other individuals. The index may provide evidence of links between individuals and hence their potential identity. Even the notion of virtual criminal networks can be used in this way. For example, we may have evidence in our system to suggest that a number of crimes have been committed, and by means of a range of indirectly linked indicators, a complex network of links between a group of people may be suggested. These groups can be used as sources of suggested names for elimination purposes. As with the fingerprint evidence at burglary 4 in Table 7.5.1, if we can establish an accomplice of our "virtual offender" acting in concert at (say) burglary 6, that evidence (whatever it may be)[14] may suggest a potential name for the donor of the DNA found at each of the 10 crimes.

---

[14] Evidence should always be subjected to questions about its reliability, relevance and probative force.

7.6 Link Detection

Modelling networks of offenders can assist in the identification of suspects and groups of suspects for crimes that may already have occurred and for crimes that are yet to occur if action is not taken. Let us consider how this can be done and how FLINTS can assist in this. Searching each of the 10 crimes for additional evidence types such as a fingerprint or tool mark or footwear impressions may give rise to suspicion about a group of suspects or even an additional single suspect who may also have been involved.

Figure 7.6.1 demonstrates how a multidimensional approach to evidence management and analysis can aid in the detection of links between series of crime evidence and people. The same approach can be used to detect links between groups of people, geographic locations and chronologies using different *mixtures* of evidence. Figure 7.6.1 is an illustration of a database of crimes that can be examined for linkages on the basis of different evidence types. Each square in the illustration represents one crime. Each blue square is a crime scene from which DNA of type A has been recovered. As already stated, these 10 crimes are potentially linked.

A useful question might concern which of the remaining crimes in the database are linked based on an analysis of a variety of evidence types and, importantly, which are linked on the basis of combined evidence types. If any other evidence type (for example, those listed in the illustration) can provide a suggestion of a linked suspect, then we can set out to implicate or eliminate that suspect based on the DNA evidence.

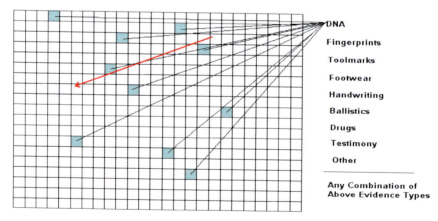

Fig. 7.6.1   A multidimensional approach to evidence management and analysis[15]

---

[15] A finger mark at linked crime 6 suggests the name "George Smith" as a suspect. Smith may possess DNA profile type A. If so, we can connect him with the series of 10 linked crimes. If he does not, one of his associates may. Other evidence types may indicate additional links between other crimes and Smith as well as other series of crimes and other suspects. Some of the new suspects may be connected to Smith as associates.

Inferential links may be discovered on the basis of high frequencies of offending in particular geographic areas or where a crime bears a particular *modus operandi*. These observations may reveal interesting patterns to consider as hypothetical links within the original linked series. This may reveal evidence that suggests suspects for consideration in the original series linked by means of DNA.[16] Using this idea, a search of the FLINTS system may reveal potential suspects on the basis of the frequency of crimes bearing striking similarities to the series of 10 that are believed to be linked.

Investigators and analysts can begin to discover and understand complex networks and connections between people, events, locations, times and evidence in ways not previously possible. FLINTS not only allows this to be done – it allows it to be done speedily, efficiently and with reliable and actionable results. In *Foucault's Pendulum*, Umberto Eco (1988, p. 225) describes an innate characteristic that exists in databases of information. This description by Eco could well have been a description of FLINTS:

> No piece of information is superior to any other. Power lies in having them all on file and then finding connections. There are always connections you have only to want to find them.

FLINTS is designed to act as an evidence integrator that brings together collections of evidence and arranges them in such a way that users can formulate questions. The principal objectives are to enable the marshalling of substance-blind sources of evidence that enable links between people, events, locations, times and evidence to be discovered by the process of analysis and questioning.

Figure 7.6.1 demonstrates the fundamental principle of integration, management and analysis of evidence around the key attractors of people, events, locations, times and evidence. If we begin from the left-hand side and work through the chart, we see that evidence is put into the system from various sources. These may be sources such as fingerprints and DNA, but in fact can be any class of information that we determine as reliable. *Accepted fact,* a concept well understood in law, has great potential in intelligence analysis. There are many facts about the way we live, work, behave and communicate that are generally available. These characteristics can be used as evidence in the form of *accepted fact* and treated in much the same way as DNA, fingerprints and other forensic evidence types.

Evidence of many kinds is integrated in the FLINTS database around the key attractors of people, events, locations, times and evidence so that links, associations and connectivity within the data can be detected. The system allows questions to be formulated in a structured way by investigators and analysts using a conventional computer that runs Microsoft Windows. Figure 7.6.2 is an illustration of the flow of evidence through FLINTS.

---

[16] One of those crimes may have been detected or there may be an item of evidence at any one of the crime scenes that may provide an insight into the identity of the "virtual suspect or offender".

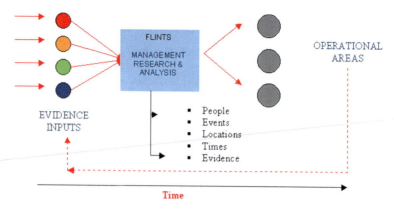

Fig. 7.6.2 The flow of evidence through FLINTS

7.7 The First Generation of FLINTS

The prototype FLINTS system began managing forensic evidence matches in the West Midlands Police department in April 1999 following a request from the force to use the system.[17] The system had been designed to demonstrate the benefits of its underlying concept[18] and used fingerprint and DNA evidence to do so. Evidence based on footwear, handwriting, tool marks and drugs were soon to follow. The system provided for the integration, management, analysis and performance measurement assessments as well as for the systematic allocation and management of enquiry work.[19] Protocols designed for key managers and key analytical tasks became part of the West Midlands Police strategic policy.

Forensic matches reported by departments for specific evidence types are input into FLINTS by means of a standard formula. For example, DNA matches reported by the National DNA Database, fingerprint matches reported by the West Midlands Fingerprint Bureau[20] and physical evidence matches such as footwear and tool marks reported by forensic laboratories are brought together in the FLINTS Bureau for entry into the underlying databases.

---

[17] This system was the prototype version of FLINTS.

[18] FLINTS was designed on the basis of *Intellogic* as an executable computer programme for use in forensic investigation. Other applications were not pursued as computer programmes at this stage.

[19] The enquiry work referred to is often called an *action package*. This package is a file of evidence produced by FLINTS that contains all the necessary evidence, photographs, plans and ancillary intelligence necessary to carry out an enquiry and usually leads to the arrest of a suspect. The suspect is normally the target in the action package.

[20] Fingerprint matches are input automatically, but their quality must be checked by the intelligence system's manager.

Strategic and analytical management tasks can be undertaken for a wide variety of purposes. Some of the tasks undertaken: maintaining a "tracking system" for the enquiry work allocated, assessing the performance of operational police areas by individual evidence types as well as by individual scene examiners, comparing evidence yields by operational areas and individuals, managing information about suspects identified, and comparing operational areas for trends.

7.8   Integration, Linking and Analysis Tools

From the initial implementation, it became apparent that FLINTS gives the user access to ranges and classifications of intelligence data about people, events, locations, times and evidence. The system enables the user to "visualise" the evidence in a number of ways that provides a range of perspectives on the data. Geographical visualisation, network visualisation and spreadsheets of varying kinds can be requested and presented in user-friendly ways. Wigmore recognised the power of visualising evidence for temporal analysis and the synthesis of arguments. FLINTS thus uses a Wigmorean approach in the development of scenarios of interest to the analyst and investigator.

Arthur Conan Doyle gave Sherlock Holmes a number of attributes important to his task that are rarely *all* seen at once in analysts and investigators in real life: keen curiosity, high native intelligence, a fertile imagination, powers of perception, a superb stock of knowledge and extreme ingenuity. In Arthur Conan Doyle's 1887 novel *A Study in Scarlet,* the first story to feature the character of Sherlock Holmes,[21] Holmes explains to Watson the difference between some of these attributes:

> I have already explained to you that what is out of the common is usually a guide rather than a hindrance. In solving a problem of this sort, the grand thing is to be able to reason backwards. That is a very useful accomplishment, and a very easy one, but people do not practice it much. In the every-day affairs of life it is more useful to reason forwards, and so the other becomes to be neglected. There are fifty who can reason synthetically for one who can reason analytically.

In *The Five Orange Pips*, Arthur Conan Doyle has Holmes explain to Dr. Watson the importance of understanding how chains of events can be studied and reasoned about. He says:

---

[21] "Although Conan Doyle wrote 56 short stories featuring Holmes, *A Study in Scarlet* is one of only four full-length novels in the original canon. The novel was followed by *The Sign of Four,* published in 1890. *A Study in Scarlet* was the first work of fiction to incorporate the magnifying glass as an investigative tool" (http://en.wikipedia.org/wiki/A_Study_in_Scarlet). The novel's quite negative portrayal of Mormons was heavily prejudiced and even libellous, as Conan Doyle allegedly eventually came to acknowledge (ibid.).

The ideal reasoner would, when he has once been shown a single fact in all its bearings, deduce from it not only all the chain of events which led up to it, but also all the results which would follow from it.

There are no formal rules in existence for *reasoning* and, if they did exist, they would represent a *logic of discovery.* Schum (1994, p. 479) believes that this illustrates what he calls *bottom up* and *top down* reasoning.[22] These are useful metaphors because they can aid investigators and analysts in understanding the frame of thinking in which they are operating.

FLINTS goes some of the way towards helping analysts and investigators develop their curiosity; because they are provided with high-quality data, and the system operates on the basis of questions, the user's imagination and perception of events, people, locations and times are important. This mass of knowledge and data is stocked, awaiting enquiry by users. Although FLINTS can never replace human powers of reasoning, it does provide a foundation and system from which users can access evidence, analyse it, synthesise questions and hypotheses, and visualise results in ways that are easily understood. In addition, the system then allows the results of those queries to be entered into the system as new inputs in the form of new questions in a circular and almost endless quest for new knowledge. The analyst and investigator can access substance-blind evidence about series of crimes, series and networks of active criminals, crime patterns, and areas where the frequency of crime is high. It can also identify travelling criminals. The system concentrates the mind of the user on using the weight of the evidence to link nodes rather than on the type of evidence involved.

Although by 2001 the Home Office was considering the potential of FLINTS and the approach underpinning the software to enhance the use and management of forensic evidence and intelligence nationally), a report from that year acknowledged that much more could be done to train users to get the best from the system.[23]

The FLINTS system has the potential to support substantial improvements in police efficiency and effectiveness in West Midlands. However, the force is far from using the system to its full capability. This includes the as yet untapped potential for FLINTS [to be used] as a senior strategic management information tool. West Midlands should therefore refine its

---

[22] Schum (1994) provides a diagram illustrating these processes. Their uses are in the generation and testing of hypotheses.

[23] FLINTS was adopted by the West Midlands Police, the Warwickshire Constabulary, the West Mercia Constabulary, the Staffordshire Police and the Hampshire Constabulary. The Tayside Police in Scotland and the Dorset Police are also considering adopting the system. The national body responsible for police technology – the Police Information Technology Organisation (PITO, a part of the Home Office) – are considering adopting the forensic module of FLINTS as a national system accessible to every police officer in England, Wales and Scotland. The system was recommended as a "best practice" by two of Her Majesty's Inspectors of Constabulary. The first, Keith Povey, afterward became Her Majesty's Chief Inspector of Constabulary; the second is Sir David Blakey. See also Management Summary, Home Office Policing and Reducing Crime Unit (2001) Evaluation of the Impact of the FLINTS Software System in West Midlands and Elsewhere (Home Office, United Kingdom).

FLINTS Project Plan so as to maximise its beneficial impact [...] This national potential includes the opportunity for forces to improve detection of crimes[24] committed by offenders across policing boundaries.[25]

7.9 Expanding FLINTS to Other Police Areas

In April 2001, following a recommendation from the Regional Forensic Science Group,[26] FLINTS began to manage forensic matches for West Mercia, Warwickshire and Staffordshire by means of a wide-area computer network linking the forces together. FLINTS gave the forces access to all West Midlands databases dealing with crime, incident handling[27] and custody data via FLINTS computer terminals of the type described towards the end of this chapter. In the future, it is predicted that each of these forces will also integrate all their current non-forensic databases of police information into FLINTS so as to realise the benefits that the West Midlands region is seeing. At present, the Midland Region communicates using high-bandwidth networking technology and shares all forensic intelligence data. It is the first Region to have adopted this approach. In Fig. 7.9.1, the current FLINTS communication channels are indicated by red lines; these represent the flow of data as in the original installation of FLINTS, at the West Midlands Police. However, note that these lines do not yet make for a complex system whereby each force can communicate with any other force or combination of forces as needs

---

[24] It should be noted that the reference is plural. This is an important feature of the rationale and design behind the FLINTS approach. FLINTS manages evidence and information about *volumes of crime* as well as single crimes. The traditional approach is based on managing evidence and information as single cases.

[25] There are 43 police forces in England and Wales. These are distributed and resourced on the basis of political boundaries, with separate Chief Officers and Police Authorities. Each force decides its own policy for crime investigation, detection and reduction as well as the structural arrangements for the delivery of the policing service to the community. There is a natural tendency to concentrate on crime committed within the force's boundaries, and crimes committed elsewhere attract less attention. This provides the strategic opportunity for criminals who are prepared to travel to commit crime with very little likelihood of being detected based on repetition of their offences. Criminals who reside in one police area and who travel to commit crime in other police areas are difficult to track and detect, and pose a serious threat to the community at large. Amongst other things, the National Criminal Intelligence Service (NCIS) was set up in 1996 to provide support to forces nationally in dealing with travelling criminals, yet no national system or ability to both monitor nominals (suspected persons), crimes they have links to, their associate networks and forensic evidence matches is capable of linking them with crimes and other persons. FLINTS could fill that gap.

[26] Forensic science and best practice is monitored jointly by a number of police and Forensic Science Service Regional User Boards. These operate across regional areas and serve a number of police forces. The Midland Region is served by boards for West Midlands, West Mercia, Staffordshire, and Warwickshire. It was chaired at the time by Mr. Peter Hampson, Chief constable of the West Mercia Police.

[27] The system is called *Command and Control Data*. This includes access to the emergency (999) system.

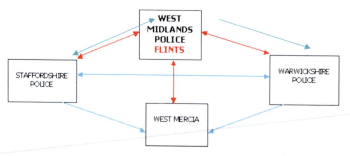

Fig. 7.9.1 Original (*red*) and envisaged (*blue*) communication channels

arise.[28] The next stage was to envisage an expanded capacity whereby each force would effectively input its data into one system, communicate in complex ways and make thorough use of feedback looping (the blue lines in Fig. 7.9.1).

In addition to these police services, a number of others expressed an interest in inputting their forensic match data into the system so that it can be shared in exchange for the improved analytical capability they would obtain.[29] This will enlarge the network and database, and will extend the system's analytical capability. The benefits of extending the system to other police forces will be the wide-scale integration of evidence managed in those force areas. As of April 2002, with the exception of the Midland Region and Hampshire, each evidence type was managed within isolated systems. The benefits of a substance-blind integration and treatment of evidence has yet to be realised in those areas. For example, police forces out-side the Midland Region cannot manage matches from their diverse evidence types within one system, they cannot access management information about matches with other evidence collections and they have yet to automate the preparation of Evidence and Intelligence "action packages". In short, Wigmorean approaches have yet to be adopted, but the tide is beginning to turn and FLINTS, with its ancestral foundations in Wigmorean analysis, is proving to be the catalyst for this change.

Access to accurate intelligence is central to being able to exercise good decision-making in policing. FLINTS provides this access through the integrated manage-ment of evidence as well as through a structured approach to the asking of questions of and about the evidence itself. Wigmore knew even in 1913, when he published his first edition of the *Principles of Judicial Proof* (Wigmore, 1913, 3rd edn. 1937) that

---

[28] Feedback loops involving an iterative process of hypothesis generation, testing and re-generation are limited. This type of process is important in the search for new knowledge in systems.

[29] Hampshire began using FLINTS in 2002, and as of April 2002, negotiations were underway to include Kent, Metropolitan Police, Tayside, South Wales, Dyfed Powys and Strathclyde. Two national Home Office projects, CRISP and VALLIANT, are studying the potential to link the databases of every police force. On 10 April 2002, the CRISP Project Team met with the West Midlands Police FLINTS Project Team, and subsequently reported that CRISP was considering using FLINTS as the central analytical tool for managing and interpreting the information.

the visualisation of evidence is crucial to gaining an understanding of the complex relationships and dependencies that exist in evidence. The ability to visualise links and networks is central to the ability to generate new knowledge about the evidence we possess and the hypotheses we are constructing by asking questions.

7.10   Volume Crimes and Volume Suspects: Not *Single* Events and *Single* Suspects

Police forces in the United Kingdom are based on geographical and political boundaries. Though there are benefits to the geographic organisation of the 43 police services in England and Wales, one drawback is the fragmentation of intelligence. Criminals can travel from one force area to another to commit crime, often frustrating intelligence strategies thereby. By identifying series of crimes linked on the basis of their rationale, the gathering and linking of provable evidence across wide geographical areas by means of intelligence networks enables the police service to operate in a target-rich environment and circumvent the problems brought on by geographical boundaries. Instead of second-guessing where crime is emerging, FLINTS can give up-to-date and reliable indications of areas where activity is likely to be most prolific and of those persons who are likely to be most active. FLINTS can also give its users specific as well as linked cases in which evidence exists to arrest offenders and often charge them with crimes. It can also be used to analyse, disrupt, fragment and control organised networks of criminals. FLINTS is proving to be a useful tool not only for crime detection in the Midlands but also nationally, serving as a targeting tool for the identification and disruption of criminal networks. Her Majesty's Inspector of Constabulary reported in 2000 that nationally:

> FLINTS has the capacity to link suspects with crimes that would not otherwise have been linked, for example, linking chequebook evidence from frauds with that from stolen vehicle crime [. . .] there is real potential for this system to be developed nationwide in the future. . . As FLINTS is developed it should be possible to utilise it to help identify series of offences which can then help to inform the tasking process. Potentially this database provides an exciting tool for crime investigation [. . .]

7.11   Performance Monitoring and System Identification

Identifying the outcomes of those processes by which evidence is managed and generated provides insights into new methods of generating and using evidence. As well as identifying outcomes of evidence generation processes such as fingerprint collection and DNA swabbing at scenes and classifying these outcomes by evidence type, FLINTS enables more complex configurations to be identified.

In 1999, as part of developing the treatment of evidence as a complex substance-blind commodity,[30] it became apparent that if DNA could be extracted from objects

---

30 The term *substance-blind evidence* is borrowed from Schum (1994).

merely touched by humans,[31] it could also be extracted from objects merely touched by persons committing crimes. This minute trace evidence had traditionally been thought to be beyond the ability of forensic science, but possible application areas now include crimes such as thefts of motor vehicles, deception, and fraud against elderly victims, in which offenders produce false identification papers and pose as government or public utility officials to gain access to the victim's home[32] to steal.

If DNA could be extracted from minute sources,[33] in this case faint and smudged fingerprints, it was proposed to the Forensic Science Service that in partnership with the West Midlands Police, an experiment should be run to recover minute traces by swabbing objects at crime scenes for DNA. These swabs would include DNA from objects merely touched by humans. For example, vehicle crimes would provide sources such as gear levers and steering wheels touched by the thieves. Thirty cases of burglary were targeted for the use of the Low Copy Number DNA technique and each involved elements of distraction tactics exercised against elderly victims.[34] National covert intelligence sources indicated[35] that a number of active individuals

---

[31] DNA profiling has developed rapidly in recent years to become more and more sensitive and discriminating. The Forensic Science Service (FSS) can now offer a specialist service that has major implications for police investigating not just the most serious current crimes, but also those that happened decades ago. DNA Low Copy Number (DNA LCN) is an extension of the routine FSS SGM Plus^{TM} profiling technique that enables scientists to produce DNA profiles from samples that contain very few cells, such as a single flake of dandruff or the residue left in a fingerprint. These profiles are fully compatible with those in the National DNA Database. DNA LCN profiles have been successfully generated from items such as discarded tools, matchsticks, nose and ear prints, weapon handles and ammunition casings in support of the FSS Major Crime Service. Given its high sensitivity, DNA LCN can be a particularly useful tool for investigating serious crimes when other profiling techniques have been exhausted or when options for forensic evidence appear to be limited. It can provide extremely valuable intelligence for Investigating Officers, but its context and interpretation need to be considered carefully. The relevance of a profile obtained through DNA LCN needs to be carefully considered, as it can offer valuable intelligence to police – but only within the framework of each individual case. DNA evidence, whether obtained through DNA LCN or another DNA SGN Plus^{TM} technique, is always corroborative and its significance will always depend on what else is known about the suspect.

[32] Elderly people are chosen as victims on the premise that they may experience difficulties in the recollection of identity. More disturbing is the premise that they will not be able to survive cross-examination. In one extreme case, a criminal admitted to me that elderly witnesses, especially the very elderly, may not survive long enough to give evidence in court.

[33] This method is known as *Low Copy Number DNA* because it recovers small traces and then amplifies the trace material into sufficiently large samples for profiling. Another term for the procedure is *supersensitive DNA*.

[34] A typical technique is to visit the victim with false identification and claim to be a member of one of the public utilities. Once inside the premises, the offender has expertise in locating the victim's cash savings. Many elderly victims do not use bank accounts. It is not unusual for several thousands of pounds to be stolen in cases of this sort. Many victims later die, but "proximity" in terms of causation of death is almost impossible to prove.

[35] Classified source.

were involved. As a result of using the Low Copy Number technique, DNA profiles were recovered from objects merely touched by the offenders that had committed the crimes. These were places such as door handles, door knockers, bells and so forth. As a result, 80% of the identified suspects were matched against DNA traces and later convicted and given prison sentences.[36]

7.12 Using FLINTS: A Tour of the System as the User Sees It

Here are three simple examples of the questions we might ask the system to deal with at the start of an exploration of the evidence. The precise nature of the question is a matter for the user to define, and will be determined by the type of problem and enquiry they face. This problem or enquiry might be very focussed and might search for particular items of information about specific people, events or locations. However, it might also be quite broad and search for strategic masses of data that could be used to formulate more focussed questions:

1. "Show me any links between suspect Mark Smith and any crimes."
2. "Show me robbery events over three months in Wolverhampton along with any links between those events and people."
3. "Show me a list of prolific offenders[37] and list them alphabetically."

The first two questions allow us to simply link people with crimes on the basis of evidence that we can prove to high standards of reliability, and the latter question enables the identification of those persons who repeatedly offend. Faced with answers to questions like these, we can set about deciding the most appropriate response to take in a rational and reliable way. The options may be to arrest the suspect, use covert surveillance, investigate the crimes or the people involved in detail, or engage in ampliative discovery by asking further questions to expand our field of knowledge around the people, events, locations, times and evidence itself. Let us look at the results of the questions we have posed above by accessing the FLINTS system. The illustrations below (Figs. 7.12.1 and 7.12.2) are taken from real questions asked of the database.

---

[36] The idea to use Low Copy Number DNA to find small traces of DNA left at scenes was raised at a meeting of Crime Scene Examiners in 1999 in the West Midlands Region. The hypothesis was that use could be made of the technique providing that a location could be identified where the offender was known to have touched some part of the scene. This would greatly assist the swabbing process and enhance the likelihood of recovery of trace material for DNA profiling. A national operation called "Operation Liberal" employs similar forensic techniques to target and identify burglary offenders where elderly victims are involved.

[37] That is, a list of people who have been linked by evidence to crimes on more than one occasion.

QUESTION 1

"Show me any links between suspect Mark Smith and any crimes."

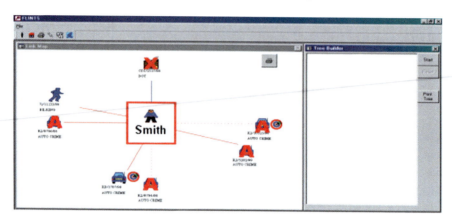

Fig. 7.12.1   An example of framing a question in FLINTS

QUESTION 2

"Show me all the robbery events in the last three months in Wolverhampton, along with any links between those events and people."

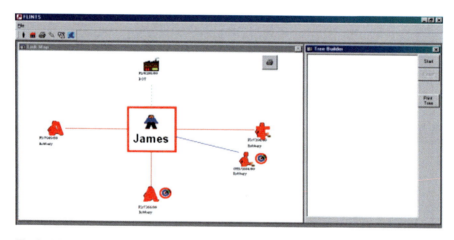

Fig. 7.12.2   A second example of framing a question in FLINTS

FLINTS has answered the question by presenting us with a modified Wigmorean chart illustrating the inferential dependencies by means of simple nodes and lines (arcs). We can see a node ("Smith") in the centre of the chart surrounded by seven other nodes around the outside of the chart that depict links to events (crimes) and other people (suspects). The arcs depict the inferential evidence – in this case, fingerprints and DNA. The dotted line depicts a partial fingerprint match.

Two charts result from this question. In the first (Fig. 7.12.2) we see that an individual called "James" has been selected by the database as the centre of an interesting network of four robbery offences and one burglary at a factory. Furthermore, one of the links is between the node for James, currently the centre of the network, and another individual node with a target sign adjacent to it. This indicates that there is a second network of links to be investigated in addition to those in the first chart. By asking the database for further information, we see in the second chart (Fig. 7.12.3) a set of links between the James node and another node bearing the name Massey. This tells us that James and Massey are implicated in yet another robbery.

The detection of volume offending is greater than expected. In another chart (Fig. 7.12.4), we can see that the node "Ford" has been identified by the system as a volume offender on the basis of forensic fingerprint evidence and DNA. He has been linked to twelve burglary offences at houses based on fingerprint evidence, to one offence of theft of a car based on fingerprint evidence, to three offences of burglary at houses based on DNA evidence, and to one offence of burglary at a dwelling house based on fingerprint and DNA evidence. If other evidence types such as footwear, tool marks, drugs, handwriting and so forth were added to the list, the volume and frequency might be even higher. Without FLINTS, it would not be possible to detect such complex linkages over time and geography by different evidence types.

The information contained in the charts presented thus far has been detailed at a micro level, with illustrations of links between certain sets of nodes. However, it is useful to be able to switch between a macro and micro view in the same way

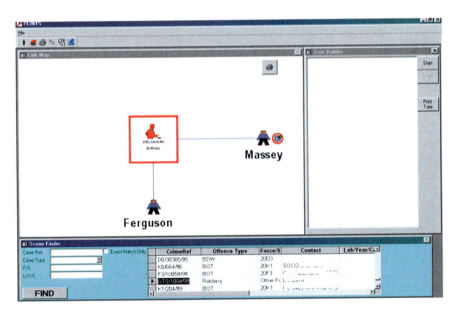

Fig. 7.12.3 Links being formed in FLINTS

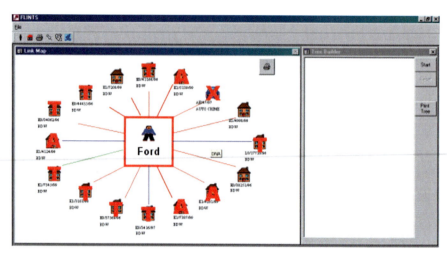

Fig. 7.12.4 The network of links around Ford

that we read a text – sometimes quickly, by scanning the text looking for key areas of interest, then slowly, reading the same text carefully, noting detailed meanings, relationships, connotations and implications. In the chart below (Fig. 7.12.5), we see a depiction of a "syllogistic tree" of *all* links in the database involving the node "Smith". This chart can help the analyst and investigator to understand networks of links that we should know already exist and networks of links that may exist but that have not yet been discovered. It can act as a prompt for asking further and better questions. For example, we can now ask ourselves a question such as:

> Faced with the following tree of links, and based on my knowledge of the prevalence and geography of crime elsewhere in the system [Fig. 7.12.6], what other links may exist between these nodes for which we do not yet have evidence?

Searching our database may begin with a simple question such as the one depicted for the node "Smith". The scenarios around Smith and other nodes of interest may begin to develop as we begin to ask further questions and receive answers to them that we can in turn use to formulate further questions. From this process, we begin to see emerging items and combinations of evidence.

The locations of events and crimes, as well as the locations that suspects and victims habitually go to or reside at (Fig. 7.12.6) should be regarded as prime material for intelligence generation. In this chart, the yellow dots refer to scenes of crimes and the red dot refers to the location or last known residence of the suspect for those crimes. Adding the dimensions of space and time to the range of tools provided by FLINTS has enabled analysts to examine crimes from the standpoint of the geographer. Clustering events by their locations begins to give us insights into the movements and activities of suspects and thus lets us synthesise potential as well as real links, raise propositions about events that suspects may have been involved in

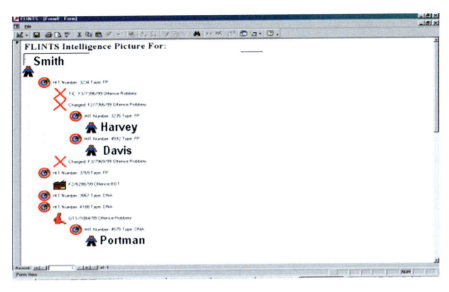

Fig. 7.12.5 Confirmed and rejected links in FLINTS

Fig. 7.12.6 A regional pattern of incidents and potential links

as well as events that are still emerging, look for crimes where there are elements of outstanding forensic evidence which we may use to either implicate or eliminate our sets of currently interesting suspects, and even identify vulnerable areas where victims are at greater risk. The chart containing the map (Fig. 7.12.6) illustrates these points.

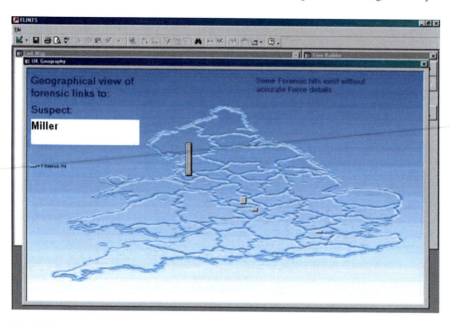

Fig. 7.12.7   A georeferenced view of forensic links to a suspect

In the illustrations in Figs. 7.12.6 and 7.12.7, and 7.12.8, we can see how we can adopt macro and micro views of geography to help us gain a better understanding of the characteristics and prevalence of the events and suspects we are currently interested in, or perhaps that we *should be* interested in given the emergence of new and interesting networks. Here, in our quest to gain insights into the activities of a node called "Miller", we learn that the suspect's links to crime span almost the length of the United Kingdom, notwithstanding the fact that his residence is in Liverpool. In this case, the events are burglary offences at factory premises from Liverpool in the northwest to the Midlands and on to London in the southeast. From this we may infer that the suspect has been using either the motorway network or the rail system to travel between events and crimes. Interestingly, one of the events in the series involves the theft of a car, so we may also infer that Miller has been stealing vehicles to undertake the journeys. Our next enquiry may be about vehicles stolen at or near the crimes in and around Liverpool, the Midlands and London.

One specific function the system undertakes is performance management by using various measures and indicators. In the following illustration (Fig. 7.12.8) we can see the way in which a variety of categories of data can be drawn together to allow managers to assess the relative performance of police departments. On the left-hand side can be seen a series of preformatted questions from "Unresolved

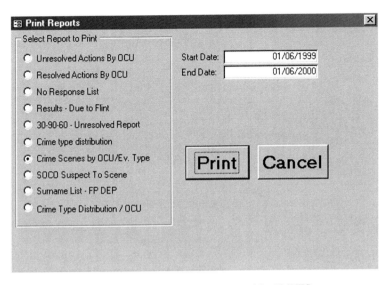

Fig. 7.12.8 Sample performance reports that can be generated by FLINTS

Actions by OCU"[38] to "Crime Type Distribution by OCU". The dates between the times of interest can be selected for the analysis and the resulting chart will reflect these dates.

The chart shown in Fig. 7.12.9 is the result of asking the system to measure and present the number of crime scenes, by operational area, in which matches[39] have been successfully achieved. Differences between areas can be evaluated, the way that scenes of crime examiners are used between different areas can be assessed, and the relative efficiency of staff in recovering evidence between different areas can also be assessed. If one area is achieving a high success rate, the others can examine the practices being adopted and try to emulate those achievements.

Other questions can be formulated to identify repeat offenders, and these questions can be used for strategic analysis and offender targeting. Offender targeting can be the concentration of both overt and covert means of monitoring the activities of key suspects within a population strongly suspected of involvement in series crime. One of the benefits of this function in FLINTS is the auditing and tracking capability that results from the analysis. This can help to justify decisions to third parties in later debates. In Table 7.12.1 we can see the answer to a question (where 'hits' means 'matches'):

Show me the evidential hits in FLINTS for 1.6.1999 for suspects with more than one hit.

---

[38] OCU is a police area called an *Operational Command Unit.*
[39] Police Forces use the term *hit* instead of *match.*

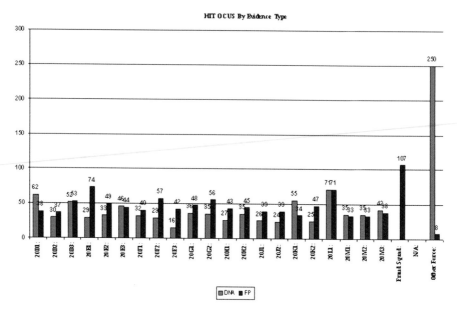

Fig. 7.12.9　A histogram of hit OCUs, by evidence type

Table 7.12.1　Answers to a question concerning evidential hits in FLINTS

Surname	Forename	Birth date	Crime	Crime no.	Evidence
Adams	Paul	12.3.77	Burglary	101010	DNA
Adams	Paul	12.3.77	Rape	1111010	DNA
Adams	Paul	12.3.77	Auto Theft	1011010	Fingerprint
Jones	David	17.11.52	Deception	11010001	Handwriting
Jones	David	17.11.52	Theft	1001111	Fingerprint
Jones	David	17.11.52	Theft	10010110	Tool mark
Jones	David	17.11.52	Theft	1001111	Footwear
Jones	David	17.11.52	Possess A	10010101	Drugs
Kelly	Bart	18.4.58	Burglary	11110001	DNA
Kelly	Bart	18.4.58	Burglary	11010001	Fingerprint
Kelly	Bart	18.4.58	Burglary	10110001	Footwear
Kelly	Bart	18.4.58	Burglary	11000001	DNA

In reality, the list in Table 7.12.1 would run to many pages. Lists can be prepared for different police areas and over different time spans, thereby giving different perspectives on the evidence. Note the squares filled in blue: for these squares, the crime reference numbers are the same, therefore Kelly and Jones may have committed this crime as accomplices. Fig. 7.12.10 illustrates how this correlation can be identified and brought to the attention of investigators.

In Table 7.12.2, we can see the result of asking the system to prepare a list of those scenes of crime that have been matched against suspects and list them by

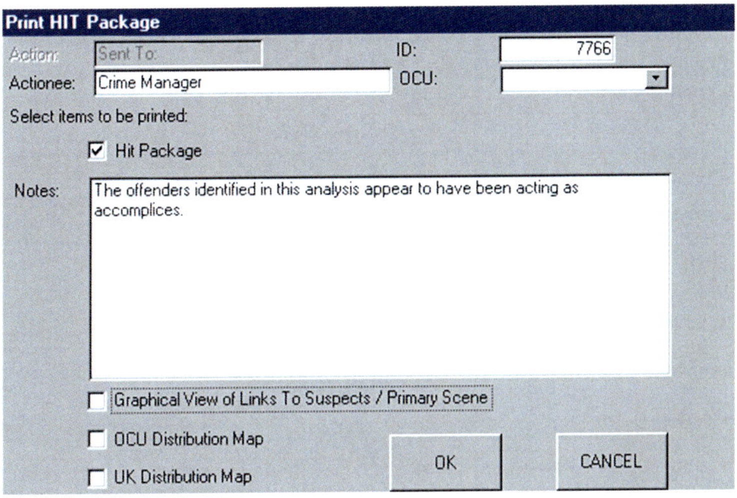

Fig. 7.12.10 A conclusion generated by FLINTS that calls a key finding (correlation) to the investigator's attention

operational area. In this case, we can see a list of persons identified as being suspects for single crimes as well series-linked crimes, along with the evidence type involved for the Sutton Coldfield area. The list has been abbreviated for illustration purposes.

Analysts, investigators and scene examiners can access their own reports as well as those of other areas to help formulate hypotheses about active offenders, crime types and the prevalence of particular suspects by area, crime type and density of offending.

The integrated approach to the management, analysis and synthesis of evidence now seen in the FLINTS system is enabling the police service to take a more sophisticated yet still pragmatic approach to the management and use of the evidence contained in police data systems. This approach permits analysts to solve problems that were known to exist yet that were too complex to tackle in the past.

A good example is the relationship between the incidence of crime and the illegal use of drugs, which has until now been *assumed rather than proven*. No reliable evidence has been produced to date to demonstrate this relationship, although intuitively many governments and police sources have claimed it to exist. Whilst there is evidence that many persons arriving in police custody are under the influence of drugs, the evidence to explain the networks of people and crimes involved has been too complex to even bring together let alone to analyse. FLINTS treats evidence and crimes in a substance-blind way. It is thus as applicable to the investigation of drug offences as it is to the investigation of burglary, rape, theft or homicide. Likewise, the evidence types it draws on are treated as "fuzzy" categories rather than "strictly deterministic" categories, and are equally applicable to DNA, fingerprints, footwear and a whole range of other forensic evidence types. Persuading the

Table 7.12.2 A listing of suspects with more than one hit

01/04/1999 to 19/04/1999
For Suspects with more than one hit

Surname	Fore Name(s)	DOB	Crime Number	Offence	Ev. Type
BOW	SHERMAN		G2/1151/99	BDW	DNA
BOW	SHERMAN		G1/13283/98	BDW	DNA
BRAD	ANTHONY		K1/1960/98	BOT	DNA
BRAD	ANTHONY		K1/4808/98	BOT	DNA
BRAD	ANTHONY		K1/1286/98	BOT	DNA
CARR	EDWARD		CH/874/98	Deception	FP
CARR	EDWARD		CH/1041/98	Deception	FP
ELM	JAMES		D2/7798/98	BDW	DNA
ELM	JAMES		D2/8499/98	BDW	DNA
FIN	MICHAEL		S1/9426/97	BOT	DNA
FIN	MICHAEL		S1/4283/97	BOT	DNA
FRA	DONALD		E3/5019/99	BOT	DNA
FRA	DONALD		F1/8926D/97	Criminal Damage	DNA
FRA	DONALD		F1/8926D/97	Criminal Damage	DNA
HAY	MARK		D3/375/99	Theft	FP
HAY	MARK		D0/19413/95	BDW	DNA

police service to treat evidence generically, in a substance-blind way, would pave the way to accessing a rich matrix of linked networks of people, events, times, locations and evidence.

A joint Government and Police Committee[40] chaired by a Minister asked early in 2001 that FLINTS be used to assist in identifying markets for the distribution of illegal drugs in the United Kingdom. Identifying those who travel across boundaries to commit a crime and who deal in drugs will aid the identification of travelling networks of criminals involved in drug trafficking or related offences. For example, at present there is no evidence available about those persons who engage in the illegal trafficking of drugs between the coastal towns of Sussex and the middle counties of England and Wales, yet there are data available that drug importation does take place

---

[40] The approach was made by Mr. Peter Hampson, QPM, Chief Constable, West Mercia Police, in February 2001.

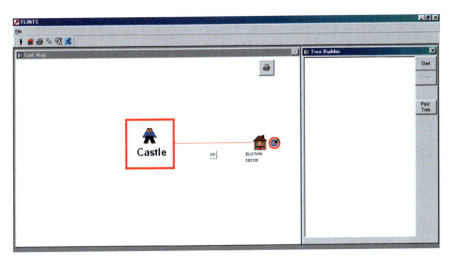

Fig. 7.12.11 Link between one suspect and evidence

on the southern coast and that the drugs arrive in the Midlands Region in smaller consignments. One way to tackle the problem of gaining a better understanding and real knowledge about this would be to apply the methods embodied in FLINTS.[41]

We can see how FLINTS, using a substance-blind approach to evidence, enables the system to be used for the analysis of drug networks. In this example (Fig. 7.12.11) we can see that the node "Castle" is linked to one offence of illegal possession of drugs on the basis of *fingerprint* evidence rather than a chemical drug analysis. Using fingerprint evidence in this way is an example of the substance-blind approach, and serves to illustrate how the use of one evidence type can inform the use of another. The fingerprint evidence involved came from the examination of paper wraps used to store the individual packs of drugs. The imaginative decision to use fingerprint analysis in this way was central to the ability to create a link to the networks.

However, we should also note from the chart that another network is operating behind the one visualised here. It is depicted by the "target" appearing against the crime node on the right of the screen. The system is telling us to look further because there are additional interesting links. In Fig. 7.12.12, the result of asking the system to present us with those additional links is illustrated. What we then see is that the node "Castle" is also linked to a node called "Kosko" and another node called "Castle". This latter node is in fact a brother of the first Castle. Probably the most interesting aspect of this analysis is not that we have fingerprint evidence presenting us with a scenario linking three formerly unknown associates but rather proving that none of the people involved in the network reside in the West Midlands Police area, where the drugs offence was committed.

---

[41] A substantial data set was being compiled to enter into FLINTS to establish the extent and weight of illegal drugs that reach markets and the magnitude of their people networks. A presentation of the findings to the Government was planned for Autumn 2001.

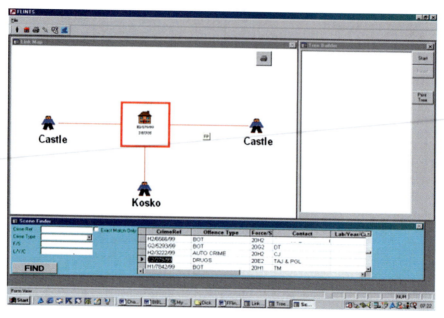

Fig. 7.12.12   Additional links suggested by FLINTS

An overview of the links between these nodes quickly demonstrates the extent of the network based solely on fingerprint evidence. Chemical analysis of the drug may reveal evidence of its source and original consignment. The use of evidence about telephone traffic among Castle, Kosko and Castle may reveal evidence of linked communications before, during and immediately after the events involving the handling of illegal drugs.

Figure 7.12.13 demonstrates how complex links between different people and different crimes can be identified using different but integrated evidence types and by using FLINTS in this way. These links would take very long periods of time to identify using conventional investigations. In this illustration, Williams has been linked to two offences of burglary at factory premises, three burglary crimes at domestic dwellings, one robbery and one theft of a car. It can also be seen that Kennedy and Tennison have been linked to the node marked with a large "X". This is, in fact, the same crime as the node marked with a "Y". This visual approach is thus a method to indicate quickly that Williams, Kennedy and Tennison may have committed at least one crime together whilst Williams has been implicated in another six crimes. The hypothesis suggests to the analyst that all three may have been operating together. Further links can then be explored by pressing the target icons depicted next to certain nodes. These indicate further lines of immediate enquiry available to the analyst. In this way, FLINTS allows the user to "surf" the connections and links inherent in the evidence. Figure 7.12.14 shows the police intelligence picture generated by FLINTS.

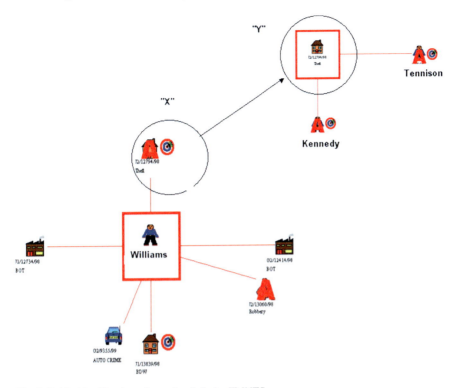

Fig. 7.12.13 Identification of complex links by FLINTS

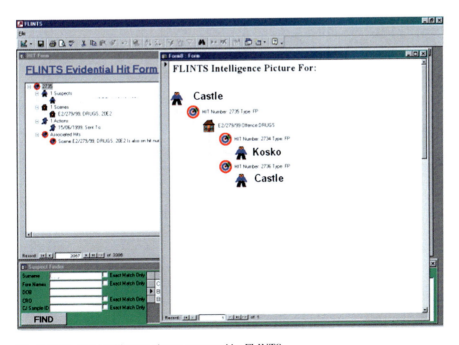

Fig. 7.12.14 The intelligence picture generated by FLINTS

7.13 The Intellectual Foundations of FLINTS

Large corporate bodies such as police forces have become far better at generating, transmitting, storing, and retrieving information than they have at making use of it to expose useful configurations and scenarios that can withstand repeated challenges and tests about the data's credibility and legality. Storing masses of data is *in itself* an unproductive pursuit because this does not automatically translate into masses of knowledge. Strategies and tools are needed to help the investigator and analyst make use of the evidence known to exist in order to discover evidence that may exist but that has not yet been discovered. One useful tool that will be described in detail later in this chapter is the ability to formulate useful questions. Good questions aid in the discovery of interesting configurations of evidence and chains of inferential reasoning from which useful conclusions can be drawn. Another useful tool that I will deal with later in this chapter is the formulation of stories to act as a mechanism for providing a structure in which configurations of evidence can be presented in a useful way. No matter how far-ranging and how thorough our search for evidence is, there will always be gaps and there will always be a degree of doubt. That doubt may be small and unpersuasive, but it will always be there to some degree.

In addition, strategies and tools are needed to aid us in the identification of known or suspected gaps in our knowledge as well as areas of weakness in our chains of reasoning. Circumstances often exist in which it is useful to be able to corroborate or negate an inference that we have drawn or are preparing to draw based upon evidence we currently possess. In this regard, we may see the following simple chains of reasoning (Figs. 7.13.1 and 7.13.2) depicted with black nodes and arcs that need to be tested by the search for evidence that will either corroborate or negate the node or arc. Corroborative evidence is depicted by red nodes and arcs, an approach borrowed from Schum (1994).

A number of the problems that policing faces in terms of the analysis and synthesis of evidence involve the manner in which evidence is managed and organised. Twining, Anderson and Schum are committed to the view that how well an organisation manages its existing thoughts and evidence will ultimately influence how well the organisation is placed to generate or discover new thoughts and new

Fig. 7.13.1 Simple chain of evidence generated by FLINTS

Fig. 7.13.2 Corroborated
chain of evidence generated
by FLINTS

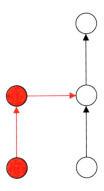

evidence that will prove useful to the problems they face. The strategies an organisation adopts in evidence management play a key role in its ability to discover new
evidence, new scenarios and new explanations. In addition, drawing defensible conclusions from databases will depend upon the quality of the information, its inherent
credibility and the probative force it delivers. Dealing with evidence in systems for
multiple-case analysis, as depicted so far, is subject to the same tests as dealing with
evidence handled in single cases in a traditional way. Successful investigation and
discovery depends not only upon strategies and methods designed to marshal our
information in ways useful and meaningful to solving our problems (as stated here),
but also upon the ability of the user of the evidence to keep in mind and continually
test for the evidence's credibility, relevance and reliability. Inference chains are only
as strong as their weakest link.

FLINTS symbolises a novel approach for marshalling evidence in pre-trial criminal investigations. The opportunity to exploit complex relationships and networks
of links between people suspected of involvement in criminal activity allows the
investigator at a tactical level and the police manager at a strategic level to identify threats and marshal finite resources more effectively and in direct response to
identified problems. Identifying the problems we face is the first step in solving
them. The deployment of resources and time is evidence-led and directed to specific
needs. Events can be connected or associated by virtue of their characteristics and
typology, which allow investigators to link events into chronological series. This is
not simply a matter of macro-level linking of high volumes of events over extended
time periods – it also enables investigators to undertake the micro-level analysis of
single events in the search for evidence. An item of evidence in one case may fill a
gap or even a series of gaps or part of a chronology in another case.

7.14 What Is It About FLINTS That Makes It Different?

FLINTS uses a modified form of Wigmore's method for the analysis and synthesis
of evidence in pre-trial investigations. The aim of the FLINTS approach and software is to introduce and develop a systematic method for the management of facts

founded upon the rational traditions of Francis Bacon, John Locke, John Stuart Mill and Stanley Jevons.

A frequent observation by practitioners using FLINTS for the first time is that it makes great use of "hard" evidence as opposed to the traditional approach in intelligence work, which relies more on the use of "soft" evidence. Though this description is useful, it can be misleading and problematic. The FLINTS approach and software was designed to make a distinction between tangible evidence such as fingerprints, blood samples, DNA profiles, footprints, drugs, firearms, and so on, and testimonial evidence from human witnesses. Examples here would be witnesses observing events and intelligence reports from informant agents.

This distinction is an important feature of the FLINTS approach. It draws on the differences between the attributes of the credibility of tangible evidence that differ from the attributes of the credibility of testimonial evidence in a number of ways important to this thesis. In the case of tangible evidence, we can draw on its authenticity and chain of custody as well as on the accuracy and reliability of the collection and sensing devices we use. Examples here might be DNA swabbing kits, electronic sensors, cameras, electrostatic lifting devices and sound recordings. In addition, we have the competence of those persons who operate and interpret these devices to draw upon. For testimonial assertions, we have to keep in mind the difficulties that surround the veracity, objectivity and observational sensitivity of human sources of evidence. Although this distinction is important, it does not mean that one form of evidence is naturally superior to another.

In its present form, FLINTS overcomes many of the investigative difficulties associated with attempts to link together different criminal activities, different people and different sources of evidence. One way of describing the utility of FLINTS is to say that it provides an elegant means for forming audit trails of related criminal activities.

7.15 A Case Study in Linked Burglary

One cannot overstress the importance of developing the *capacity* to ask good questions and how this differs from a *protocol* for asking good questions. Checklists for questions in the form of a protocol provide a good method of checking that certain things have been done, but investigators and analysts cannot operate effectively without basic training in good thinking. Evidence arrives in our hands from diverse sources, in diverse conditions and with varying levels of reliability. A modernised neo-Wigmorean approach has been incorporated in the form of computer software called FLINTS. Now let us explore a real-world scenario and the investigation of a series of burglary crimes using the methodology and software developed in this thesis.

This example is a real case of burglary, but with some fictional and additional hypotheses and evidential scenarios used to illustrate the potential of the methodology and of the use of FLINTS. The burglary scene depicted in the photograph (Fig. 7.15.1) presents many opportunities to recover physical, forensic and trace

Burglary Scene & Escape Route.

Arrows indicate sources of contact trace material. It is the scene examiner's job to locate and recover these materials.

Fig. 7.15.1   Annotated photograph of a burglary scene

evidence. The scene examination reveals that the door is open, having previously been left locked and secured by the victim earlier that day. There is also clear physical evidence of damage on the inside of the door, where some kind of tool appears to have been used. The lock has been forced open, which would allow an intruder to exit the premises. This evidence raises a hypothesis that the door could have been used as a point of exit and is therefore an ideal location for seeking contact trace material, but the question arises early on as to where the alleged offender entered the premises.

This question is central to our ability to detect the crime, because when people enter and leave premises, especially by the use of force, they may leave contact trace material behind as a result of their physical contact and proximity with objects that make up the fabric of the building. Windows, doors, furniture and objects that the intruder has touched provide excellent opportunities to recover evidence. Opportunities are presented to target searches for contact trace material that could provide evidence of the identity of the intruder, the clothes they were wearing and the kind of contact they had with the premises.

In the real case (the subject of the photograph), a search of the premises and grounds was made and the lower ground-floor casement window in the foreground of the photograph was found open and damaged. This raised a hypothesis that entry was gained by means of the open casement window. The hypothesis was supported by evidence that the owner of the property had left the premises locked and secured when she left for work earlier that day. There was no damage to the window locks when she had left home earlier that day and her jewellery and cash was now missing from a bedroom. Damage had been caused to furniture inside and a message in lipstick had been left on the dresser mirror that read "It is not over yet – we'll be back." Footwear marks were apparent in the soil below the window. On the kitchen work surface near the window that was believed to be the point of entry, there was a small smudge of red fluid that appeared to be blood. The fluid was located on the glass close to the forced lock. Another red fluid that may be blood was apparent on the kitchen work surface. A red fibre was snagged on the window ledge alongside some scuff marks, and was thought by the Scene of Crime Examiner to have been made by gravel embedded in the sole of a shoe when the intruder(s) entered.

Initially, the geography and extent of the scene of crime were thought to be the boundary of the premises. However, there was circumstantial evidence that the intruder(s) must have left the garden area by some means. On the pathway in the garden, a metal pole was found that the victim said was foreign to the scene. A hypothesis was raised that this might have been delivered into the scene by the intruder(s) as a tool to assist their entry into the building; as a result, the pole was recovered for examination at a laboratory.

The intruder(s) were not within the boundary of the property at the time the search was undertaken, and the gate remained locked and secure. It was hypothesised that they left by climbing the fence. A damaged shrub pointed out by the victim revealed a damaged fence panel. Directly above the panel, a fibre was found snagged on the top of the fence, but this time it was blue in colour. This gave rise to a series of new hypotheses: were there one, two or more offenders? If a single offender, were they wearing a red and a blue garment? Where did they go after climbing the fence?

Our observations of the scene should not be restricted to the house and garden. We can infer from the evidence available that the intruders probably left by climbing the fence. The scene now needs to be extended to encompass further pathways outside the perimeter of the garden. A "scene" can incorporate any place, any person or any "thing" that has been party to the events *prior to, at the time of* and even *after* the event under investigation.[42] The combination of events and times serves a number of purposes. One of them is the construction of stories to help us glue together the events we know about in a meaningful way that helps us to explain the events we do not know about but need to understand. The construction of stories such as

---

[42] Wigmore (1913, p. 149) dealt with "time and place" as a means of proof. "Proximity, on the part of the accused, as thus presented for consideration, may be, in itself, of various degrees, from mere vicinity, up to actual juxtaposition or contact. It may also be of various kinds, such as proximity to the person of the deceased, or to the scene of the crime, or both; and it may exist at different stages; as before the commission of the crime, or afterwards, or both before and after. The strongest form in which this circumstance can be presented, and the one which requires the least reasoning to give it effect, is undoubtedly that of the juxtaposition of the persons of the accused and deceased, proved, by actual observation to have existed both immediately before and immediately after the crime is perpetrated. These show presence at the moment of actual perpetration, with the greatest effect possible, short of direct evidence."

Fig. 7.15.2 A chronological
sequence of events

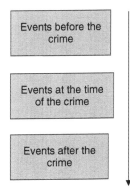

these helps us to search for evidence to either confirm or negate the evidence we
will produce to fill in our knowledge gaps. In addition to helping us tell stories and
discover new evidence, the stories provide an ideal form of classifying our search
for and interpretation of evidence. Figure 7.15.2 shows a Chronological sequence of
events.

A whole series of events can go into making up a "scene". People suspected
of involvement in the crime can and should be treated as potential crime scenes in
themselves, especially if they're a suspect or a victim, because they may have played
star roles as "actors" in the theatre of the crime. Victims in particular can provide
good evidence from their direct knowledge for two reasons: First, they have knowledge of events either before the crime was committed, at the time the crime was
committed, or some time after the crime was committed. Second, they often have
domain knowledge of the place, the time, the prevailing circumstances and even the
people who may have been involved and those who may not have been involved.
Victims often have a stock of ancillary knowledge useful to the provision of contextual evidence about the commission of the crime. Sometimes this knowledge will be
small, but often it will be more extensive than one might expect.

In the case we are investigating in the present example, the victim provided
important evidence about the condition of the premises before the crime was committed, and about how an intrusion and entry had changed the physical condition of
the building. She had also pointed out that the metal pole was foreign to the premises
and thought to have possibly been used as a tool to effect entry and discarded when
the intruders left. It is crucial that investigators and Scene of Crime Examiners fully
understand that the relevance, credibility and weight of any physical, forensic and
contact trace material will be directly conditioned by this type of evidence from a
victim or a witness. If a suspect is arrested as a result of fingerprints being identified
on the tool, that suspect might find it difficult to persuade us that the tool did not
belong to them but rather belonged to the owner of the premises or the victim.

It was decided that residents in houses opposite the "scene" may have witnessed
activity before, during or after the crime was committed. Perhaps they saw strangers
to the area loitering or climbing the fence, or heard the sounds of the window

and door being forced. We formed a hypothesis that the offender(s) had at some point climbed the fence, and that asking questions of residents near the scene could provide additional evidence. Who could have seen the offender(s) leaving or even entering the premises?

As a result of asking residents opposite the scene about the events of that day, we discovered an elderly lady who claimed to have seen two men climbing the fence and leaving the garden during the afternoon. She had been suspicious, so had watched them run, walk, then run again along the street towards a car parked nearby. One of them was carrying a black bag and she saw one of the men drop something. When he returned to pick it up, the other man forced him to carry on and leave the object. He threw it over the fence into the garden he had climbed out of, and that object appeared to be the pole found in the garden. The witness pointed out in the garden the direction in which the "pole" had been thrown and identified the metal tool in the garden on the pathway as being similar to the object she had seen thrown.

The object was recovered for forensic analysis, with emphasis placed on DNA and fingerprints in an attempt to identify the persons in possession of it earlier that day. Evidence was sought about the credibility of the witness. She said she had never experienced serious difficulties with her sight other than short-sightedness, but felt she could be sure of what she had seen. She did wear glasses for short-sightedness and had been wearing them at the time of the incident. The investigator might have chosen to question and confirm the credibility of the witness's evidence by asking her to repeat a car registration plate or some other unique object in the street under similar conditions to those under which the events were seen to unfold.

Control and elimination samples of DNA and of fingerprints were taken from the elderly witness and the victim to distinguish them from any foreign DNA and finger marks found on any of the exhibits recovered from the scene. During this exercise, the witness said that she had subsequently thought about the incident and now thought that she recognised the car the men had got into as one very similar to the car owned by the previous owner of the house. Also, one of the men appeared familiar in appearance, as if she had seen him before in the area. On being asked why she had not said so earlier, she replied that she had been concerned that she might have been wrong. This provides us with a good example of Schum's equivocation testimony.[43]

---

[43] Schum (1994, p. 107) provides a detailed methodology for assessing the relative strengths and weaknesses inherent in testimonial evidence provided by an eyewitness. The methodology serves to illustrate how important it is for investigators to bear in mind the attributes of evidence and the way in which reliability has to be *assessed* and not merely accepted. Schum's method is based on a non-statistical approach and involves asking a variety of questions about the behaviour of the witness relevant to assessing their credibility as well as other factors that might influence a person's credibility. Schum believes that most credibility-related questions fall into three main classifications or, as he calls them, "major attributes": veracity, objectivity and observational sensitivity. Let us assume that a witness "W" provides us with evidence that event "E" occurred. Let us further assume that the event did in fact take place and that "W" obtained evidence from his own senses causing "W" to *believe* that the event occurred – therefore, "W" *knows* that "E" occurred. We did not observe the event "E", so how are we to verify the account given by "W"? Because "W"

This gives rise to another hypothesis: that one of the offenders may have been the previous owner returning to the house to commit the crime. An enquiry with the victim reveals that she was involved in a dispute with the former owner about an outstanding sale of some of the contents that she had refused to pay for because they were substandard and faulty. She said that the dispute had become acrimonious, but did not believe that the former owner would burgle her home, even though she had been threatened on a previous occasion when she refused to withdraw her legal action. Instead, she had put this down to frustration about the legal action. However, as a precaution, she had reported it to her lawyer and he had written a letter to the former owner warning him about the consequences of any further actions involving threats and intimidation. This might provide important evidence about "motive".

Enquiries revealed that the former owner of the premises had a number of convictions for burglary of dwelling houses, two of which were offences similar in nature to the present crime – lower ground-floor windows had been forced open, escape was by means of a door to the rear, and there had been episodes of climbing on both occasions. He also had other convictions for violence and damage to property.

---

claims to have witnessed the event with his own senses, are we also to say we *know* that event "E" occurred? What we have really discovered is that "W" *claims to know* that event "E" occurred, not that event "E" actually did occur. In considering the testimony of "W" we are faced with a chain of inferences about what "W" believes, what "W" sensed and whether event "E" did occur. Schum demonstrates the decomposition of evidence when he tells us that we can also consider our own credibility in receiving the evidence from "W" because we are not passive in the receipt of evidence. If we question our own credibility, all we can really say is that we believe witness "W" told us that event "E" occurred. Let us examine this in detail to see what he means. In a diagram, one can see that "W" believes that "E" occurred based on the evidence of his senses, and this is depicted in the form of a chain of inferences. Each node in the chain indicates a point of uncertainty about what "W" tells us. If we include an assessment of our own ability to receive and convey the evidence of "W", then the inferential chain becomes much longer. Not only must we consider veracity, objectivity and observational sensitivity in respect of witness "W", we must also consider our own major attributes in the receipt and management of that evidence. This becomes increasingly important when dealing with evidence from questionable sources or when there are competing accounts of events from witnesses. Take, for example, intelligence sources where information is offered in return for favour or reward. The recruitment of intelligence sources from the criminal fraternity or from foreign countries for the receipt of intelligence should not be based simply on the ability of the source to provide information. A well-placed source in a criminal network of offenders or a foreign diplomat working as a defence attaché in a host country may well be in a position to provide timely, high-quality information. However, they may also be in a position to provide false or misleading information to undermine operations they have been recruited to oppose. Take, for example, a drug dealer providing the police with information. Though he may indeed have valuable information, he may also have a motive for "informing" on competing drug dealers who pose a threat to his own trade in illegal drugs. He may also provide the information to arrest many smaller drug dealers as a means of providing himself with a more open and exploitable market. In intelligence scenarios, a foreign source may provide valuable information about international negotiations concerning a new military capability. However, what is really being practised is a deception designed to distract attention away from new technology being developed in another area and that is of greater importance to that power. Schum (1994, p. 115) also provides a schematic diagram for depicting his classification of recurrent forms of evidence. He provides fifteen classifications.

The items of physical, forensic and contact trace material recovered included photographs of the suspected point of entry (the lower ground-floor window), the work surfaces in the kitchen (with suspected blood stains present), the footwear scuff mark to the window sill, damage inside the premises and the writing on the dresser mirror, the damage to the door suspected to be the point of exit, the garden area (including the metal pole on the pathway) and the fence suspected to have been climbed as an escape route. A photograph was also taken of the place at which the elderly witness said she saw the people climbing out of the garden. This provided evidence that she could indeed have seen what she claimed to have seen. Other items recovered included the suspected blood stains, the debris from the scuff marks, the metal tool, the fibre snagged on the window and the fibre snagged on top of the fence. A single footmark was found in the soil outside the casement window, and this was identified by the victim as a foreign mark. It was photographed and cast to reveal the size and weight of the shoe that created it to serve as evidence for comparison with any shoes later recovered from suspects. All the victim's shoes were examined for the presence of similar patterns to those in the flower bed in an attempt to eliminate extraneous evidence and reduce the potential number of sources of the mark.

Control samples were taken from all surfaces from which items had been recovered. For example, a control sample of soil from near the footmark, a sample of debris from the path, a control sample swab from the kitchen surface and glass (where the suspected blood was recovered) and a sample of wood from the window and fence for comparison with any clothing taken from suspects.

7.16 Forensic Decision-Making

The objective of the investigation was to discover the identity of the person(s) who committed the crime as well as the identity of the people seen climbing out of the garden. This was done to try to reduce the suspect population to as small a number as possible. From the available items of evidence the following hypotheses were constructed:

1. The premises had been entered by force, possibly via the casement window and by use of the metal tool recovered on the garden path.
2. One or both of the intruders had cut themselves in forcing the casement window, had bled onto the work surface inside the premises, and had scuffed the window sill with a shoe and grit from outside.
3. The premises had been searched and the mirror had been written on by the intruders with a message bearing relevance to an ongoing dispute.
4. The intruders had left by the open but now damaged door and climbed the fence to escape.
5. One of the intruders had thrown the metal tool away; it landed in the garden on the path.

Of prime interest was the identity of the former owner of the premises and whether he had both a motive[44] and the opportunity to commit the crime. In addition, it was important to determine whether there was any physical, forensic or contact trace material available to connect him to the enquiry or eliminate him. He was identified by the victim and her lawyer, and from this information his convictions were found, including the fact that he was already registered in the National DNA Database following a conviction three years previously for violence. This meant that simply submitting the suspected blood from the scene to the National DNA Database for profiling and comparison would provide valuable evidence about whether he had had an opportunity to commit the crime. Also, the elimination sample of the victim, who lived alone, would also have to be submitted to ensure that the suspected blood did not originate from her, however unlikely that might seem. Also of concern was the fact that a false positive might result in linking the former owner of the premises to the crime solely because he had lived there previously.

The DNA profiling process is very sensitive, and it could potentially pick up old genetic material from when the suspect was resident there. In an attempt to clear up this point, the victim reported that she had cleaned the surfaces almost daily with a surface cleaner and that the previous owner had not been present for eighteen months.

Whilst DNA profiling was being undertaken, including a comparison of the scene stains and the control samples from the witness and victim, enquiries were conducted into the background of the former owner of the burgled premises. Intelligence was received and later confirmed that at the time when the crime had been committed, the previous owner of the premises had been in police custody and then remanded to prison to await trial for a theft that was not connected with the burglary. This effectively provided an alibi for him and challenged the basis of the enquiry. There was no reason to question the honesty and credibility of the victim and the elderly witness, so the police were left with the task of identifying (from the population) who else might have committed the crime.

It was decided not to interview the former owner in prison on the following grounds. A hypothesis was considered that although he could not have committed the crime personally, he might know who had and might have been involved as a conspirator in arranging the crime. If questioned, then, he might forewarn the intruders so they could dispose of valuable forensic and trace evidence. No evidence was available to indicate who might have committed the crime, but blood recovered from the scene might link to someone already in the DNA database.

Five days after the submission of the suspected blood to the National DNA Database, the initial results were received by the police. The suspected blood from the kitchen work surface was confirmed to be blood, and wholly different from the victim's and witness's control samples, but it did not match with any person in the

---

[44] Evidence of *motive* is distinctly different from evidence of *opportunity*. One may have a motive to commit a crime, but that does not mean that the opportunity will present itself. Detectives sometimes mistake the two because motive and opportunity may on occasions converge, providing some additional probative force.

Database, including the former owner of the premises (the prime suspect). However, the FLINTS Co-Coordinator contacted the officer and informed him that one of the blood stains, although not matched to any person in the National DNA Database, did match with seven other DNA samples submitted from seven other crimes of burglary in the last two years as well as with samples from an offence of car crime.

Whilst no person had been matched, FLINTS now gave grounds for believing that the offender was a serial burglar responsible not only for this crime but for seven others. The problem now was to identify the offender. The National DNA Database was contacted and asked to confirm the gender[45] of the donor of the scene's blood samples and whether the two stains emanated from different donors. The Database confirmed that the donors were both male and were different people.

FLINTS was consulted in an effort to assist in identifying potential suspects for the series of nine crimes (eight burglary crimes and a car crime). In the mind of the investigator, the previous owner still had reason to be involved in the main burglary, so it was decided to begin the enquiry by identifying his network of associates. The investigator asked the system to follow five lines of enquiry and constructed the following questions:

1. Show me the links between the former suspect and any other known criminals in the system: what is the extent of his criminal network and who is in it?
2. Show me the geography of the nine crimes: where were they committed?
3. Show me a time line of the crimes: what is their chronology?
4. Show me all the burglary crimes committed in the area of the main crime: is any physical, forensic and contact trace evidence available in any of them?
5. Show me the current keeper of the car formerly owned by the former suspect: who has it now?
6. Show me the most prolific offender for burglary [in cases bearing the following features] in the area of. . . and over the time period of. . .

The answers to the questions provided the investigator with new evidence and emergent lines of enquiry. In answer to Question 1, it was revealed that the former suspect had a primary network of ten links to other criminals, all of whom he had been arrested with on previous occasions. In answer to Question 2, FLINTS told the investigator that the nine crimes fell within a radius of a spate of burglary crimes extending to 35 offences, all of which bore distinctive signatures in terms of the *modus operandi*. The answer to Question 3 was that all 35 offences had a regular pattern in that each was committed between 3.15 and 5 pm on a Tuesday or Thursday afternoon. The answer to Question 4 was that eleven of the crimes had various items of outstanding physical, forensic and trace evidence that could be submitted for

---

[45] The presence of X and Y chromosomes reveals that the genomic material comes from a man; the absence of a Y chromosome reveals that the donor was a woman. DNA markers used for criminal investigation routinely test for sex, but in my experience this eliminative test is not widely used despite its enormous value. For example, if a DNA profile is gained from material left at the scene of the crime, the gender test eliminates 50% of the suspect population from suspicion.

analysis and comparison with reference databases of people. Blood and finger marks were also available.

The answer to Question 5 gave the hoped-for breakthrough: the car was now registered to one of the associates in the primary network of the former suspect. He had incurred a Fixed Penalty Ticket for a parking violation on the day the main crime had been committed, and only three streets away near a shopping precinct. The payment of the Fixed Penalty Ticket had been made in the name of the current keeper of the car and via a bank account in the shopping precinct three streets away from the scene of the burglary. His DNA profile was not present in the National DNA Database. Two days before the burglary crime being investigated, he had visited the former suspect in prison.

Tangible grounds now existed to formulate a hypothesis that the current keeper of the car had committed the crime. This conclusion was reached on the basis of his former convictions for burglary in houses, his presence in the vicinity at the time the crime had been committed, the fact that he was the keeper of the vehicle seen by the witness in the same street the crime had been committed, and that he had no legitimate reasons for being inside the premises. The vehicle was now parked regularly outside his home address and used by him in the area. The decision was made to arrest the suspect (the current keeper of the car) in an attempt to recover evidence that would either eliminate or incriminate him. On arrest, his wardrobe was searched and a pair of blue denim trousers was found. These were bloodstained (Fig. 7.16.1); moreover, he had a cut to his right hand, and a red jumper was found along with a pair of shoes similar in pattern to that in the foot mark found in the soil outside the window.

At interview, he denied being involved in any burglary crimes at any time other than those of the crimes for which he had been convicted. He agreed to supply a DNA sample in the form of a mouth swab to eliminate him from the enquiry. The

Fig. 7.16.1 Bloodstained denim trousers. Are these consistent with having bled after climbing through a casement window?

DNA process would take five days, so it was important whilst he was in custody to use other evidence available to either eliminate him or implicate him.

The blue denim jeans were sent to the laboratory, and under microscopic analysis the fibres appeared similar to the fibre recovered from the fence, but because denim is a common fabric in clothing, a definitive conclusion of identity would be unlikely. The red fibre also resembled that recovered from the scene, but was a rare fibre and thus more discriminating than the denim. However, one pair of shoes was examined by a forensic scientist and compared with the shoe mark recovered from the soil bed (Fig. 7.16.2). The scientist reported that it was very similar (a close match), that there appeared to be blood on the shoes and that there were traces of debris in the sole. The scientist made a detailed examination and produced a statement identifying points of similarity in the pattern and distinguishing damaged sections that she said made the shoes unique.

Figure 7.16.2 shows footwear mark in blood, suitable for DNA swabbing and profiling. This may reveal the identity of a victim or the attacker who bled during the crime. The question arises whether the shoe was placed into the blood already present or blood was delivered to the floor from traces already on the shoe. Figure 7.16.3 shows the footwear used as evidence.

Those same damage marks on the sole were present in the soil cast taken at the scene. The suspect was later charged with the burglary on the basis of his presence in the area at the time the crime was committed as well as the fact that his shoes matched the foot mark outside the casement window at the point of entry.

Fig. 7.16.2 Footwear mark in blood suitable for DNA swabbing and profiling

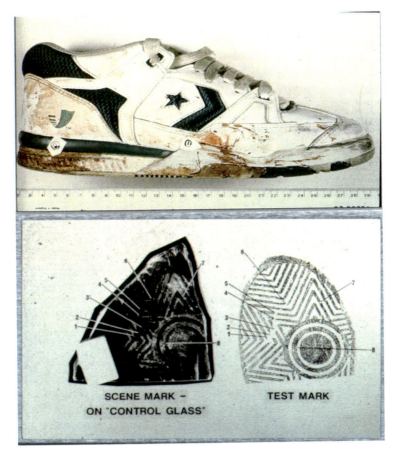

Fig. 7.16.3 Footwear used as evidence

He continued to deny involvement, although he admitted that he had knowledge of the dispute between his associate (as former owner of the property) and the victim. Faced with this evidence, he still declined to state who he had been with the day the crime had been committed and had no alibi evidence to offer.

His car was examined by a Scene of Crime Examiner, who revealed a number of finger marks in the front passenger area. These were sent for fingerprint examination with a suggestion that they be searched against the marks of the ten associates identified by FLINTS. One set of marks was identified as those of a third male. These in turn matched some outstanding finger marks at one of the linked burglary crimes. The third man was also arrested, and admitted his involvement in the original crime, saying that he had been recruited to settle a dispute between the former owner and the current owner of the premises.

Five days later, the National DNA Database reported that the DNA taken from the first man arrested and in custody matched that in all nine linked burglary crimes, including (based on the blood found on the kitchen work surface) the main crime and an additional theft of a motor vehicle. Furthermore, FLINTS now reported an additional link by means of fingerprint and handwriting evidence to a deception practised in a department store, where a cheque from a stolen book of 25 cheques had been used and presented fraudulently. The cheque book had been stolen during a car theft. The damage to the door in the main crime that was believed to have been the point of exit matched the edge of the metal pipe recovered from the garden path (Fig. 7.16.4).

The chart shown in Fig. 7.16.5 illustrates the crimes linked by forensic evidence to the suspect. The burglary and theft of the motor vehicle are linked by DNA evidence and the deception is linked by handwriting and fingerprint evidence. This chart demonstrates the links to those crimes that were the subject of a forensic link as well as links to an additional 35 potential offences of burglary that may have been linked to the suspect, depending upon the available evidence. Each of these crimes may have outstanding forensic material available for comparison with reference evidence against the main suspect as well as his associates. These could be

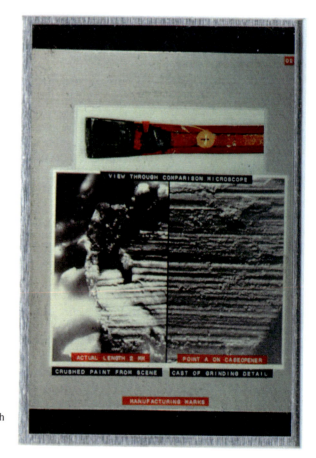

Fig. 7.16.4 Tool mark from the point of entry at the burglary scene. Microscopic comparison used to compare the tool mark in the paint with the tool recovered from the garden at the scene

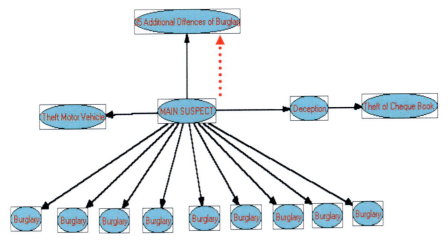

Fig. 7.16.5 Chart of links for the linked crimes and offender. This graph shows the topology of what can be interpreted as a Bayesian belief network

DNA, fingerprints, footwear, tool marks, firearms, handwriting, drugs, or, indeed, any forensic or physical contact trace material.

Analysis of the damage to the casement window and the door used to escape the premises revealed that the damage matched with the tip of the metal tool recovered from the path. A similar length of pipe was found in the boot of the car belonging to the suspect, and a comparison of the cut end sections of the two pieces revealed that they had once been a single pipe.

7.17 Second-Generation FLINTS

The discussion so far has centred on the conceptual ideas underpinning FLINTS and the prototype version built to prove those concepts in practice. The remainder of the chapter will be devoted to developments since testing of the prototype and a description of the newer version, now called FLINTS 2.

FLINTS 2 utilised the conceptual foundations of FLINTS 1, namely the systematic integration, analysis and use of information to inform the investigation and intelligence process. FLINTS 2 is an enhanced version of FLINTS 1 that allows access to information from a wider range of sources and allows this information to be manipulated in different ways. For example, new data sources include tables of information about arrested persons, about persons stopped and searched, and about vehicles. The new version also allows access to Command and Control[46] logs, and

---

[46] The Command and Control System is simply the computer that manages information about incidents and crimes reported to or attended by police. It contains details of each incident and the officers attending, as well as brief report details and times.

this enables information about incidents and crimes to be directly viewed and read on the screen.

FLINTS 2 was also built to incorporate advanced mapping software so that geographical analysis could be undertaken at a more atomistic level. Geographical analysis provides useful insights into the way in which information about events, people and time can be marshalled.

Two specific features of FLINTS 1 were enhanced because they have great potential for the future. The first, a "prolific (volume) offender search", offers the ability to analyse the activity of persistent offenders. The second, a crime "hot spot search", allows us to monitor the frequency with which crime occurs in different geographic areas. These functions allow the investigator or analyst to generate hypotheses about who in the known criminal population may be offending repeatedly and about the locations where crime seems to happen most. By combining these functions, the investigator or analyst can contemplate both detection and prevention strategies. Interventions can then be targeted more acutely and the results measured over time.

Two new search and analysis functions were added. The first allows a search to be made for addresses of interest, and the second allows searches to be conducted for vehicle license numbers and partial numbers. These searches can be used to answer obvious questions about people, addresses and vehicles, but they can also be used to answer less-obvious questions. For example, if we want to know the name of a man but all we have is a partial registration number of what is believed to be his brother's car, we can set about identifying the car, then the owner, then the owner's family members. We could use the address search to provide lines of enquiry to establish which family members live where and whether any of those addresses are of interest to us. Using these search functions together or in chains of questions, we are able to navigate around the data warehouse in search of information to substantiate or negate hypotheses or to open up and test new hypotheses. It is the interplay of good questions and thoughtful analysis that allows the system to be used to best effect.

Figure 7.17.1 is an illustration of the main functions of FLINTS 2. The key list in Table 7.17.1 identifies the functions which in Fig. 7.17.1 correspond to numbers. Another new feature is the ability to use electronic mail (e-mail) to communicate intelligence findings to other personnel. Actioning forensic matches between people and crimes can be done instantaneously, thereby informing staff of a developing hot spot or the identify of a prolific offender in real time. Just as importantly, the results of this communication can be received in real time.

FLINTS 2 is a "tailor made" system designed to support the West Midlands Police in undertaking their investigations and intelligence work. It is built on the

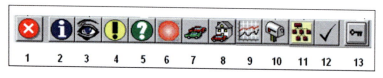

Fig. 7.17.1 The main functions offered by the FLINTS 2 toolbar

Table 7.17.1 Key list for Fig. 7.17.1

1 = Exit system.
2 = Management information.
3 = View graphical links.
4 = Prolific offender search.
5 = Names search.
6 = Hot spot search.
7 = Vehicle search.
8 = Address search.
9 = View management information.
10 = Mail system.
11 = View history.
12 = Enter hit results.
13 = Setup options.

same conceptual foundations as FLINTS 1, but uses wider sources of information. Links between people, crimes, locations and times are primarily based on forensic evidence, but incorporated into FLINTS 2 is the ability to use "accepted fact". Here, the term "accepted fact" refers to information that is collected in the course of routine work and that would not normally be challenged. For example, the following are examples of accepted facts: that Frederick James owns a Ford Fiesta with license number X123 GHF, and that Hugh Flannery was arrested with Frederick Prosser on 15 November 1999. Another accepted fact might be the details about a "stop and search" conducted by a police officer under the Police and Criminal Evidence Act. The fact that these events happened at a particular place, at a particular time, and involved particular people is not normally challenged. These sorts of facts therefore provide important links in chains of reasoning and seemed ideal for inclusion in the system. Introducing the term "accepted fact", which has been borrowed from the terminology of law, into intelligence work is an important step forward for law enforcement. It allows us to explain to intelligence personnel that the collection, analysis and use of everyday information can be extremely effective if the information is systemised and managed carefully; this is especially true where there is a mixed mass of information. However, the terminology also allows us to but remind personnel that information of any kind is always subject to tests of credibility, relevancy and probative force.

7.18 Access to the System: Searching or Surfing?

The traditional approach taken by intelligence organisations in Europe and North America has been based on a policy of a "need to know". This means that only those persons who "need to know" are allowed access to intelligence information. This has been an openly accepted policy, but one might ask "how do you know if you need to know before you have access to the information?" Evidence is only as good as the uses found for it, so giving wider and more open information access to staff offers a greater potential for the evidence contained in a database to be put to good use. That is, staff accessing the system will potentially discover new scenarios and combinations of evidence that in turn can be fed back into the system as new inputs. Wide-ranging and open access offers high-quality feedback benefits, but has to be balanced against the risks of misuse.

FLINTS may thus create a measure of tension because the very opportunity and ability to access the complexity inherent in combinations of evidence will nearly always justify the user in claiming that they have a "need to know". The nature of the policy currently operating in the West Midlands Region is currently classified as "sensitive", so it is not possible to publish it in this thesis. However, what can be said is that success was gained by applying for a policy of very wide-ranging access for users in order to ensure sufficient access to the complexity of linkages in the system. FLINTS now presents so many opportunities for linking that it is feasible to literally "surf" the system to discover links between crimes and suspects based on evidence that can be immediately acted upon. This is compatible with what Peirce ([1901] 1955, pp. 150–155) termed *abductive reasoning* and equates to acting on the basis of hypotheses that are mere hunches or insights, then recognising evidential opportunities presented as tests of their justification. The ability to formulate and ask questions speedily, then bring together the answers equally speedily while bearing in mind both what we have learnt and what we may want to learn if the opportunity presents itself is an example of Peirce's reasoning. The process is similar to the asking of questions followed by seeking evidence to either refute or confirm the hypothesis embedded in the questions.

Sir Edward Crew, the Chief Constable of the West Midlands region, commented about FLINTS that "the system is beginning to produce so many cases that a whole-sale re-evaluation needs to be taken about deployment of staff across the West Midlands. In some areas so many evidence leads and cases are being produced that there are insufficient staff in current structures to manage the arrests."[47]

Inappropriate access could present opportunities for corrupt practices and illegitimate use of the evidence. This problem has to be balanced against the need for wide-ranging and (as far as possible) open access to the system by investigators and analysts. The philosophy of this thesis and the design of the access system is therefore intended to support broad access but with security levels and passwords incorporated to prevent misuse.

Access to the FLINTS system cannot be gained until the user completes a log-in procedure, as shown in Fig. 7.18.1. Having negotiated the log-in procedure, users enter the system and gain access by negotiating a unique (individualised) password screen (Fig. 7.18.2). Passwords can be changed at regular intervals by the user or by system administrators to protect against security breaches. All changes are logged and tracked by means of audit trails. The toolbar at the top left corner of Fig. 7.18.2 is used to navigate through the system and to select the relevant options.

---

[47] Sir Edward Crew, addressing a meeting of the Jill Dando Institute of Crime Science and the West Midlands senior management team.

Fig. 7.18.1 Logging into the FLINTS system

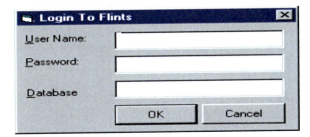

Fig. 7.18.2 The Toolbar in FLINTS 2

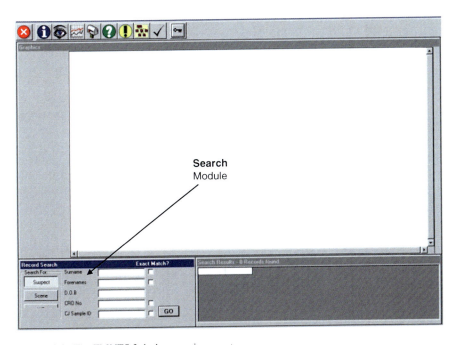

Fig. 7.18.3 The FLINTS 2 desktop environment

Once the user has negotiated the password and security system, they see the basic operating desktop (Fig. 7.18.3). This desktop gives the user the tools to undertake searches, analyse results and navigate the system.

7.19 Asking Questions About People and Suspects

Figure 7.19.1 illustrates the results of entering a suspect's name (here, "Tyler") into the system. Tyler may be of interest as part of an enquiry or in response to a request for intelligence information as part of someone else's enquiry.

In terms of suspects, any single field or combination of fields can be used to construct a search. Searches can be made by reference to surname, forenames, date of birth, criminal record number and DNA sample reference number. Names or identifying features (in any of the fields) can be selected and analysed further as the user's interest is raised.

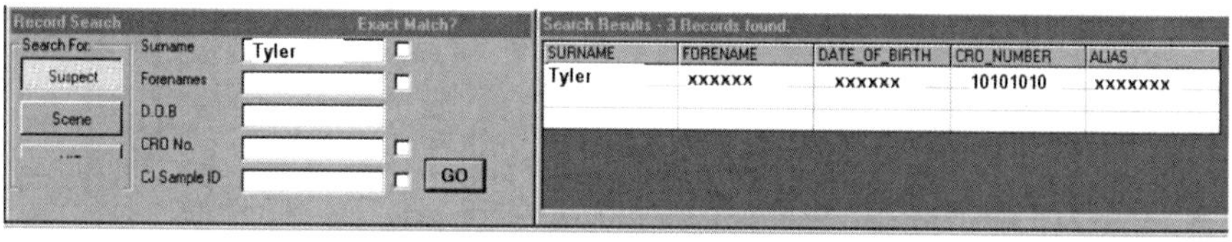

Fig. 7.19.1   The results of searching on a suspect name

7.20 Asking Questions About Crimes and Events

Crime types are coded into the system for ease of retrieval. Figure 7.20.1 illustrates the result of a search for *burglary dwelling crimes.* (These are coded as crime type BDW.) Once found, crimes on the list can be selected, viewed, cross-referenced and searched again to provide more details about each crime as progress is made. This search could result from trying to locate a crime of particular interest based on its *modus operandi* or other discriminating features.

Searches can also be done by geographic police area, such as a town, village, city or the whole of a police area. Geographic criteria entered into a search can change

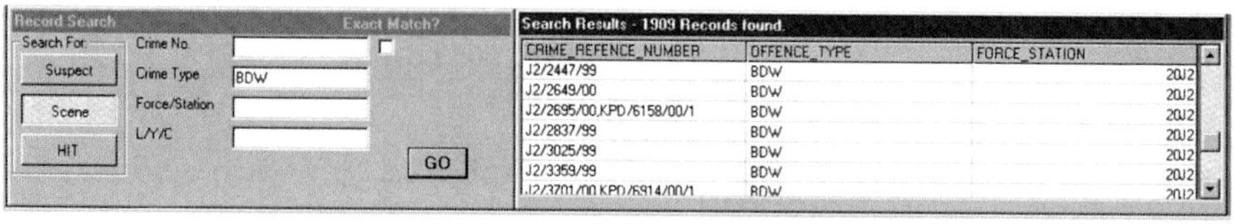

Fig. 7.20.1   The results for searching by code (here, for Burglary Dwelling Crimes)

Record Search | Exact Match? | Search Results - 238 Records found.

CRIME_REFENCE_NUMBER	OFFENCE_TYPE	FORCE_STATION	
AJ/989/98	DRUGS		20L2
CH/991/98	DECEPTION		20L2
F/121/96	BOT		20L2
F/79/96	BOT		20L2
J/104/96F	ROBBERY		20L2
J/173/98	CRIMINAL DAMAGE		20L2
JD/10442/96	ROW		20L2

Search For — Crime No. | Suspect | Crime Type | Scene | Force/Station 20L2 | HIT | L/Y/C | GO

Fig. 7.20.2 The results of searching based on a police area

the results enormously. Figure 7.20.2 illustrates a search of a police area called 20L2.[48] Again, crimes can be selected and analysed further as the user's interest is raised.

In terms of crimes, any single field or combination of fields can be used to construct a search. Searches can be made by reference to crime reference numbers, crime types, geographic locations and even laboratory references for forensic samples.

7.21 Displaying Modified Wigmorean Charts: Graphical Results in FLINTS

One of the most powerful intellectual tools that FLINTS 1 possessed was the ability to visually display links within the evidence stored in the system. This feature has been retained and enhanced in FLINTS 2. Having obtained a list of search results, the user can select the required entry, and the links within the evidence in the system will be illustrated. Figure 7.21.1 demonstrates this feature.

Prior to FLINTS, the task of bringing together the evidence to construct such a chart would have been very time-consuming. It would involve accessing many systems, as well as the arduous task of drawing a chart encompassing all the nodes and all the arcs. Apart from being time-consuming, the many actions required of the user to obtain the information and then construct the chart would involve the risk of error. The automated system in FLINTS 1 and 2 speeds this process up and reduces the risk of error. In addition, the process can be repeated time and time again as new and interesting scenarios or links are discovered. This means that immense amounts of information can be marshalled and tested in different ways as the process of discovery unfolds. Users can combine different strategies and different functions[49] to analyse, synthesise and hypothesise about relationships, links and networks of people and crimes of interest to the investigator's particular tasks. This process is unique to FLINTS 1 and 2.

Figure 7.21.1 provides an example of a search of the system and a graphical display of the result. Let us imagine that we have decided that a suspect called "Tyler" is of interest to us. In the top portion of the chart, we can see links between Tyler

---

[48] This area is a suburb of the West Midlands.

[49] Here, *function* simply means *questions*.

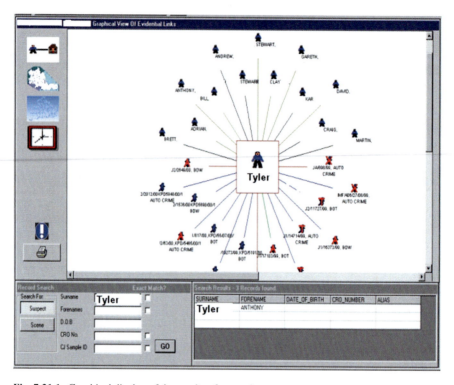

Fig. 7.21.1 Graphical display of the results of a search

and his former associates. These are people he has previously been arrested with or prosecuted with as a co-accused person. In the lower portion of the screen, we can see links to crimes based on inferences from forensic evidence. These present us with hypotheses about opportunity and will need to be tested alongside additional evidence. The different coloured lines refer to different evidence types or links.

I would like to stress my claim that the ability to manage, juxtapose and ask questions of evidence in a variety of ways provides valuable insights into interesting scenarios and possibilities. In Fig. 7.21.1, each forensic link is colour-coded and can be identified by placing the cursor on top of a line linking two objects or nodes together. Further information about each crime scene or person may be obtained by placing the cursor on top of the relevant icon. Additional information will appear that can then be presented in another graphical view.

On the left side of Fig. 7.21.1, the user can make use of a series of functions on a toolbar. This has been designed to display the evidence in a number of ways and to reveal interesting combinations of the evidence. Figure 7.21.2 is an expanded illustration of the toolbar itself. A key list is provided in Table 7.21.1.

The presence of evidence is not always the same as evidence of the validity of the inference one can draw from it. Checking evidence for authenticity is as important in FLINTS as it is in the management of evidence in single cases. Figure 7.21.3 is

Fig. 7.21.2 Enlarged view of
the results toolbar of
FLINTS 2

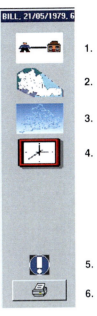

Table 7.21.1 A key list for
Fig. 7.36

1. Graphical chart function – people and events.
2. Graphical chart function – geography of crime.
3. National geography chart.
4. Temporal analysis of events.
5. Warning system
6. Print the graphic

Fig. 7.21.3 A sample
warning to confirm the
validity of links

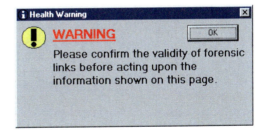

an illustration of the warning system that instructs the user to check the validity of the evidence before acting upon it.

This approach helps to eliminate errors in recording and in evidence interpretation, as well as false positives. Imagine the presence of a DNA match demonstrated visually to an investigator on a chart. Before the investigator decides to take action, they are prompted to check on the validity of the match by checking secondary

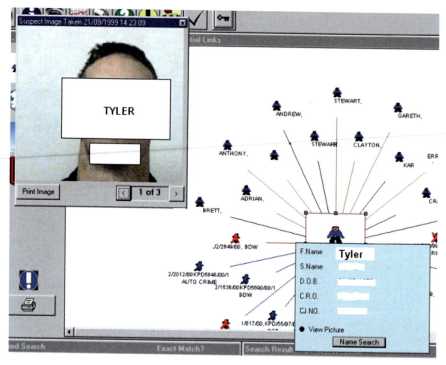

Fig. 7.21.4 FLINTS provides immediate access to photographs of suspects in its database

systems such as the National DNA Database or the Custody Records System in an attempt to uncover corroborative evidence.

As in Fig. 7.21.4, any available photographs of a suspect who appears in the chart can be viewed instantaneously. If there are a number of photographs available, they can be viewed chronologically. This has many uses, but one important one is the identification of unknown suspects.

7.22 Geographical Analysis

Figure 7.22.1 provides an enlarged view of the toolbar icons in Fig. 7.21.2, plus explanations of the features. Figure 7.22.2 provides an example of the map that can be generated by clicking the second map icon in Fig. 7.22.1.

Figure 7.22.2 is a map of the West Midlands Region and surrounding county police forces of Staffordshire, West Mercia and Warwickshire. Crimes committed by a network of linked offenders are plotted on the map to give an impression of the distribution of the crimes. This display can give analysts insights into the places where suspects and their associates habitually offend, and compare these locations with each person's place of residence. This chart could then be compared with and indeed overlaid by another chart dealing with undetected crimes. There may be some

(1) This icon can be selected to view a network of suspects geographically. In addition, links between suspects and crimes across England and Wales can be identified. The links are then presented in the graphics screen.

(2) This icon can be selected to view the West Midlands Region and surrounding areas.

(3) This icon can be selected to view the graphics screen.

Fig. 7.22.1 Icons for geographic analysis. (1) Icon for selecting geographic overview. (2) Icon for selecting a subset Area. (3) Icon for displaying the results for a selected view

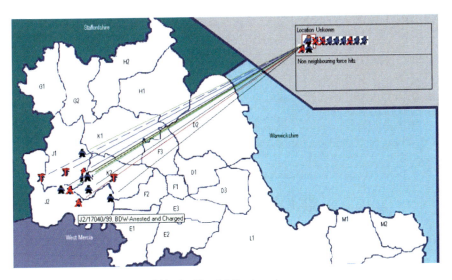

Fig. 7.22.2 Map of locations within the West Midlands region

correlation between those crimes known to have been committed by the identified network of persons and those crimes as yet undetected.

Figure 7.22.3 illustrates crimes that have been recorded across two police areas. This map display presents an opportunity to identify travelling criminals. Cylinders of various heights are used to give an impression of the number of crimes in each area. In this illustration, we have a hypothesis that a known offender, identified by means of DNA evidence, has been linked by forensic evidence to one crime in the West Midlands Region and another crime on the southern coast of England. Without FLINTS technology, these links could not be speedily identified during routine analytical work.

It illustrates crimes that have been recorded across two police areas.

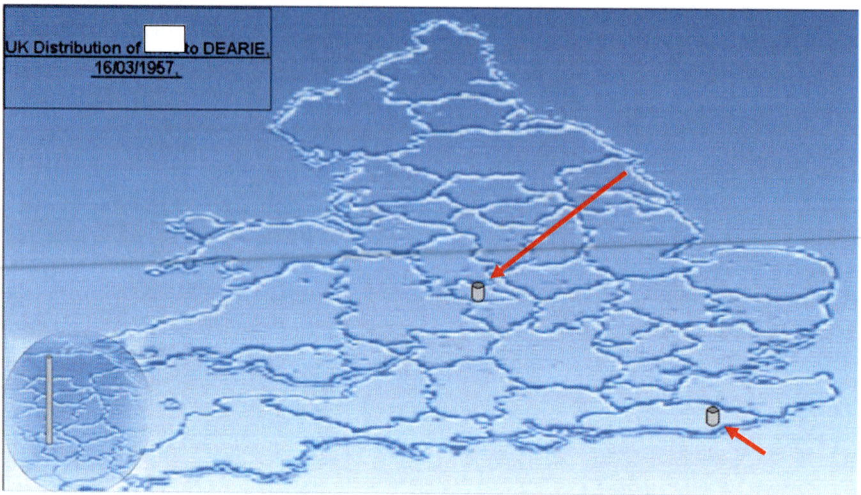

UK Distribution of _____ to DEARIE.
16/03/1957.

Fig. 7.22.3 Map of the West Midlands region and of crimes within the region

7.23 Temporal Analysis

FLINTS results can also be subjected to temporal analysis using the toolbar icon in Fig. 7.23.1.

The use of temporal analysis in intelligence work can provide useful evidence to infer "opportunity" and assess how groups of crimes may be connected with each other. This assists in the provision of hypotheses and ranges of questions that can be explored elsewhere in the system.

Linking these types of hypotheses with those connected with "virtual offenders and suspects" provides additional insights into the identification of those in the population who ought to be considered as more likely offenders and those who perhaps should not be so considered. Reducing the certainty attached to some suspects in

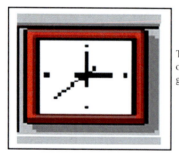

This icon can be selected to display a chronology of events, which can then be presented on the graphics screen.

Fig. 7.23.1 Icon used to select a chronological display

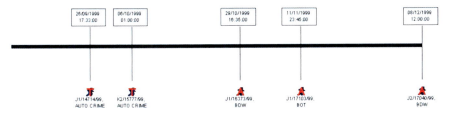

Fig. 7.23.2 Example of a typical chronology of crime for a suspect

the database is a useful method of indicating those who should be considered for further inductive eliminative exercises.

Figure 7.23.2 illustrates a chronology of crime for the suspect Tyler identified earlier in this chapter.

7.24 Prolific (Volume) Offenders Search

The prolific offender search function (Fig. 7.24.1) allows the user to ask the system questions designed to elicit information about persons who repeatedly commit crimes – that is, persons identified by evidence as doing so. The police, acting under Home Office instructions, classify these as "detections" and refer to them in a number of ways. Figure 7.24.2 illustrates the various ways in which these classifications are listed. These ways are called *disposal types*.

Prolific offenders can be identified by crime type, geography, and disposal type, as well as by reference to time. The results of searching under these criteria can be presented graphically in the form of a chart. This view has many uses in the construction and testing of hypotheses about crime and offenders.

Fig. 7.24.1 Searching for prolific (volume) offenders

Fig. 7.24.2 Disposal Types Used by FLINTS

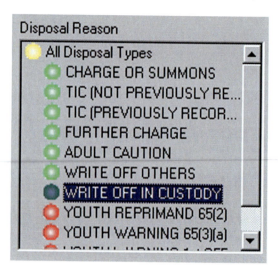

7.25 Using Geography to Identify Prolific Offenders

In the West Midlands Region, operational areas are known as Operational Command Units (OCUs). These OCUs are listed in groups or clusters called Divisions, and coded from A to M. Any one or a number of these areas can be selected to provide the basis for a geographic query. Figure 7.25.1 illustrates this.

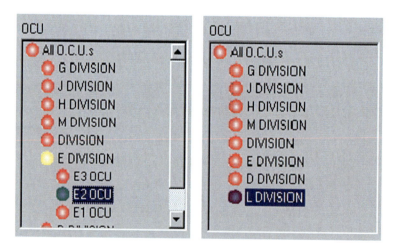

Fig. 7.25.1 List of available Operational Command Units (OCUs)

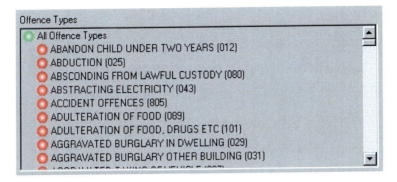

Fig. 7.25.2 List of available offence types

In addition, a single description or group of descriptions of crime can be selected to provide the offence type, as shown in Fig. 7.25.2.

For example, looking at Figs. 7.25.1 and 7.25.2 shows that we can select the E Division, the E2 OCU, and burglary crime during the last ninety days, by reference to where the crime was committed. This query (Fig. 7.25.3) would give us information about burglary crimes committed in E Division's E2 OCU during the last ninety days and let us view the information graphically. We could also select any one of the crimes to view the original report on screen directly to access additional information.

Figure 7.25.3 demonstrates the way in which the user is presented with a textual version of the question. This approach reminds the analyst at regular intervals about the question they are asking.

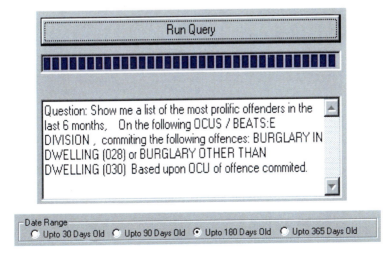

Fig. 7.25.3 The query definition dialog box

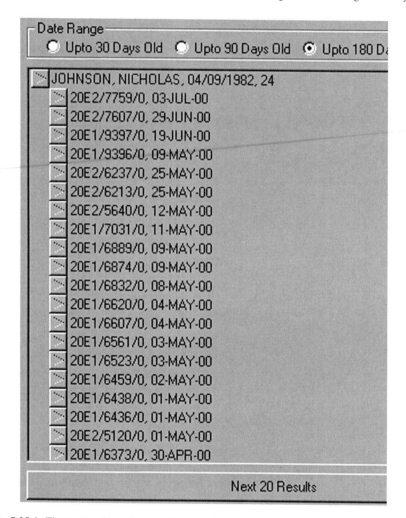

Fig. 7.25.4   The results of specifying a date range in a query

Figure 7.25.4 shows the results of a search. This screen allows the user to select items of interest from the results of the search for further searching or viewing in the graphical viewer.

Figure 7.25.5 is an example of the type of report that can be accessed using FLINTS 2 technology. The first illustration is a report concerning a crime included in the Crimes System and the second is a report concerning a Command and Control entry.

Fig. 7.25.5 The results of a query

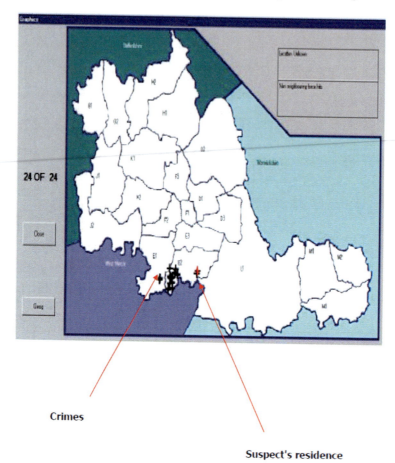

Crimes

Suspect's residence

Fig. 7.25.6   Graphical depiction (map)

A map can be presented to display the relationships between crimes committed
and events (indicated by black crosses) and the offender's address (indicated as a
red cross). See Fig. 7.25.6 for an example.

By integrating searches between functions, detailed information about individuals and crimes can be accessed speedily. This feature can again include photographic
details, as shown in Fig. 7.25.7.

All the links to this individual can displayed using the graphical viewer along
with information on their geography, chronology and associates.

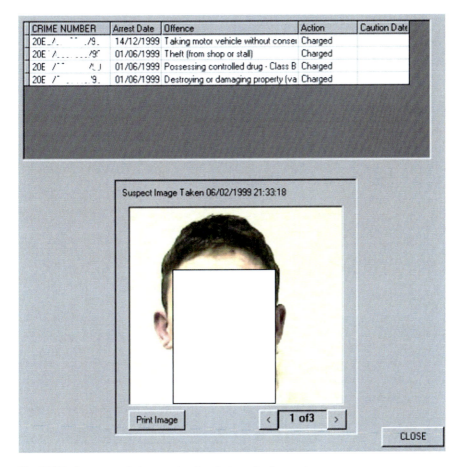

CRIME NUMBER	Arrest Date	Offence	Action	Caution Date
20E_/. ˙˙ ./9.	14/12/1999	Taking motor vehicle without conser	Charged	
20E ˙/. . . . . . ./9˙	01/06/1999	Theft (from shop or stall)	Charged	
20E /˙˙ /. J	01/06/1999	Possessing controlled drug - Class B	Charged	
20E /˙ . . . .'9.	01/06/1999	Destroying or damaging property (va	Charged	

Suspect Image Taken 06/02/1999 21:33:18

Print Image   < | 1 of3 | >

CLOSE

Fig. 7.25.7 Summary of crime results plus photograph of suspect

7.26 Hot Spot Searches

As illustrated in Fig. 7.26.1, the hot spot search function allows users to identify geographic areas where the frequency of crime is high. This can be done by reference to times, locations, and crime types, and can be compared with address details for prolific offenders. This provides a powerful analytical tool for strategic analysis of crime frequencies as well as a briefing tool for patrolling officers and investigators.

Figure 7.26.2 illustrates an example of using the hot spot feature to search for incidents rather than crimes. The address, the day, the date, the time, the reference number of the incident, the type of incident and any notes made by the reporting office can be accessed remotely by the analyst.

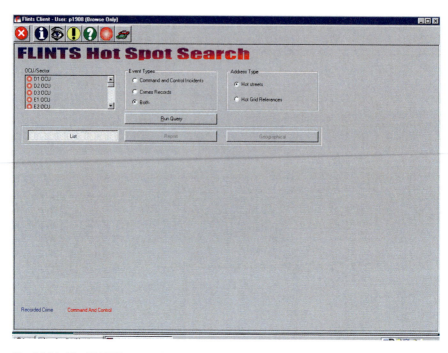

Fig. 7.26.1 The FLINTS search function for identifying hot spots

Fig. 7.26.2 Results of a hot spot search based on incidents rather than crimes

7.27 Vehicle Searching

FLINTS also offers a powerful tool for searching for vehicles (Fig. 7.27.1). The tool offers a range of options (Fig. 7.27.2). The results of vehicle searches appear in the form of lists from which the analyst can select those vehicles that appear to be of interest (Fig. 7.27.3).

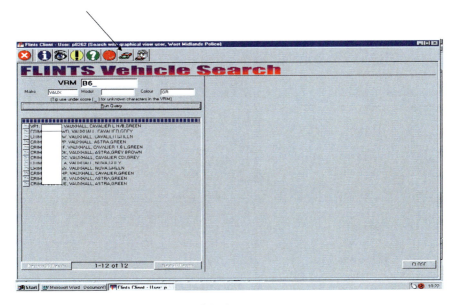

Fig. 7.27.1   The FLINTS vehicle search dialog box

Searches can be conducted on the basis of partial information, such as partial vehicle numbers, makes, models and colours.

Fig. 7.27.2   Options available in the FLINTS vehicle search

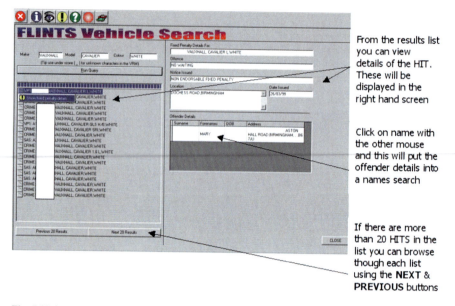

From the results list you can view details of the HIT. These will be displayed in the right hand screen

Click on name with the other mouse and this will put the offender details into a names search

If there are more than 20 HITS in the list you can browse though each list using the **NEXT** & **PREVIOUS** buttons

Fig. 7.27.3   The results of a vehicle search

7.28 Analytical Audit Trails

Using FLINTS 1 and 2 can involve navigating many inferential links between people, crimes, events, places and times. For example, a user may begin by searching for a suspect for a series of crimes but soon find themselves navigating links that change their priorities or produce unexpected opportunities to discover new issues of interest. The speed with which the system searches, retrieves information and then presents graphical charts can result in users "losing their way". Users can navigate so many links and find so many opportunities within charts that it can be difficult to know where the evidence trail started and how they arrived at a particular conclusion.

An audit trail has been built into the system to help users manage this potential confusion. This function can be activated by the user and will record as well as present audit trails. Figure 7.28.1 is an illustration of a *simple* audit trail. Audit trails can become long lists of links, depending on the analysis.

The function serves two purposes: First, it helps the analyst to maintain a log of analytical activity that allows the user to "backtrack" through the analysis. The analysis can also be repeated by following the audit trail if the occasion arises. Second, the function can help others to check how a particular conclusion was arrived at. For ease of interpretation, the example presented here is a simple one – but is nonetheless a real audit trail from FLINTS. In Fig. 7.28.2 we can see an example of a complex network of links between 37 suspects. The suspect at the

Fig. 7.28.1 The hierarchy of
links in a network of
associates

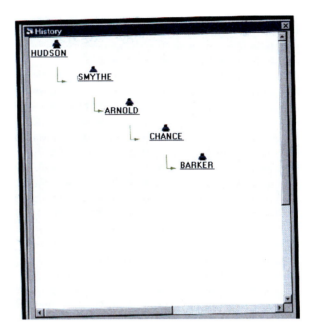

centre of the chart is called "Barker". The chart represents a series of links beginning with Hudson, then Smythe, Arnold, Chance and finally Barker. The original
search began with Hudson, but by navigating only three more steps the analysis
ended with an extensive network of linked criminals and crimes.

A valid question at this point might be: "What benefit has been gained by this
approach?" The answer is that at each level of search, a different chart was viewed
(similar to the one in Fig. 7.28.2). This approach can give many different perspectives and insights into many networks involving suspects, crimes, locations and
chronologies. Each of the five suspects from Hudson to Barker was viewed as a separate step in an analytical chain of reasoning. Each suspect, from Hudson through
to Barker, became a central node at each stage in the process. That is, they became
a central focus of the analysis, and all links known to exist between crimes and
suspects were displayed in a chart.

Those charts also appear similar to the one illustrated in Fig. 7.28.2. At each
stage, therefore, the analyst can decide where the analysis will journey next, and by
which route. Different routes will provide different results and different links. Many
unknown features and characteristics of networks between suspects and crimes
could be discovered in this manner.

Another answer to the question would be that Fig. 7.28.2 has four links between
suspects and burglary crimes (indicated by arrows). The suspects linked to these
crimes have been linked by means of forensic evidence and are thus liable to be
arrested on suspicion of committing those crimes. The hypothesis is that they had
the "opportunity" to commit those crimes. However, there are indirect links between

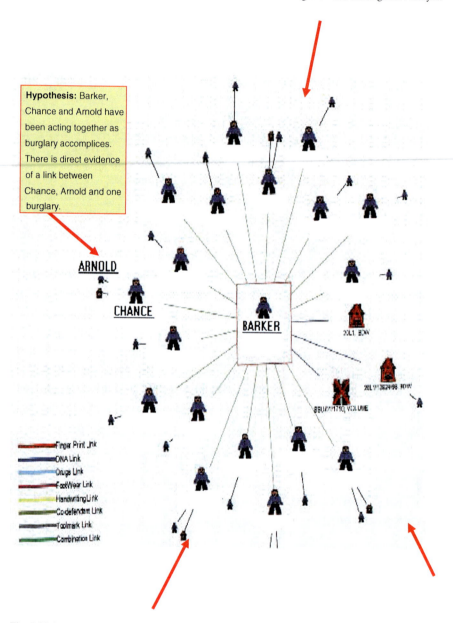

Fig. 7.28.2 List of links and hypothesis summary

other suspects and these crimes that may indicate different hypotheses. We could, for example, draw inferences about which suspects might be acting together in crime and which are not. These hypotheses can then be tested by performing other analytical work. This is an example of the way in which the system acts as a generator and tester of hypotheses. Some may be substantiated and some may not, but the important thing is the ability to ask the question. In this example (Fig. 7.28.2), we could formulate a hypothesis that Barker, Chance and Arnold have been acting together as burglars. There is direct evidence of a link between Chance and Arnold and one burglary. Other hypotheses of equal validity could also be formulated, but from even this brief analysis, Barker has already become a suspect of great interest to us.

There are seven links to crimes of burglary in this chart, of which three are linked directly to Barker and four are linked indirectly via another suspect. The chart presents many hypotheses for testing the possible involvement of Barker and others in crime as well as many opportunities for intelligence generation. Recording the way in which the chart was navigated might prove important to those we seek to persuade subsequently of the validity of our logic.

The potential to develop evidence marshalling can be appreciated if Fig. 7.28.2 is considered in the light of potential developments. In FLINTS 1 it was already possible to have a snapshot of all the links in FLINTS 1 at a given point in time using a set of predetermined *attractors*. For example, it was already possible to ask FLINTS 1 a complex question using several objects as attractors in a truncated chain.

The ability to navigate very complex layers of information and follow direct and indirect links like these using the powerful visualisation techniques demonstrated by FLINTS 1 and 2 provides great potential for the development of future systems.

Chapter 8
The Forensic Disciplines: Some Areas of Actual or Potential Application

8.1 Crime Scenario Modelling: The Dead Bodies Project, and a Scenario Space Generated Using an ATMS

8.1.1 Generating Crime Scenarios Automatically

Jamieson (2004) discussed the methodology of *crime scene investigation* (*CSI*), involving human scenarios.[1] Ross Gardner and Tom Bevel's (2009) *Practical Crime Scene Analysis and Reconstruction* addresses[2] every aspect of the analysis and reconstruction of the events surrounding a crime, and comprises an introduction and history of *crime scene analysis*, followed by theoretical and practical considerations, and then *event analysis*, this being a practical methodology for *crime scene reconstruction* (*CSR*). Event analysis in the form introduced and presented by Gardner and Bevel uses specially designed worksheets that cover internal, external, and terminal ballistics as they apply to understanding trajectories. Next, significant investigative questions of CSR are discussed in Gardner and Bevel (2009), before turning to *crime scene protocols* and their effect on reconstruction. This is followed by a chapter on *bloodstain pattern analysis*,[3] and then by a chapter by Matthew Noedel about shooting scene processing and reconstruction, a chapter by Scott Wagner on *forensic pathology* about *dead bodies*, in relation to CSR, and finally by chapters by Gardner and Bevel about writing crime scene reconstruction reports, about arguments and ethics, and about developing and using demonstrative exhibits in support of the crime scene analysis. The latter is about crime scene analysts testifying in court cases.

---

[1] Concerning fact investigation in general, see Binder and Bergman's book (1984), as well as, e.g., Zander (1979). In a British context, Cook and Tattersall (2008) is a pocket-sized handbook about the processes and actions involved in the role of Senior Investigating Officer. The issues covered comprise, among the other things, crime scene examination and investigative strategies.

[2] In the shorter compass of a book chapter, crime scene investigation is the subject of an introductory article by Marilyn Miller (2003, 3rd edn. 2009).

[3] For which, Section 8.8 below; it is also the subject of a book by those same authors (Bevel & Gardner, 2008, 3rd edn.).

E. Nissan, *Computer Applications for Handling Legal Evidence, Police Investigation and Case Argumentation*, Law, Governance and Technology Series 5, DOI 10.1007/978-90-481-8990-8_8, © Springer Science+Business Media Dordrecht 2012

Studies of crime scene investigation conducted in a cognitivist vein include Schraagen and Leijenhorst (2001) and Ormerod, Barrett, and Taylor, (2008). In an article entitled "Distributed Cognition at the Crime Scene", Chris Baber (2010) from the University of Birmingham discussed in the journal *AI & Society* a conceptualisation of *crime scene examination*, in terms of *distributed cognition*.[4] "In this paper, Distribution is defined by the number of agents involved in the criminal justice process, and in terms of the relationship between a Crime Scene Examiner and the environment being searched" (ibid., from the abstract). Baber's approach combines cognition and ergonomics. Baber pointed out (2010, p. 423):

> Crime Scene Examination presents an interesting and challenging domain in which to consider the notion of Distributed Cognition for the simple reason that it is not always apparent where the act of 'cognition' is situated. The ultimate aim of the criminal justice process, of course, is to acquire evidence which can be combined with information from other sources in order to produce a case that can be tried in Court. Contrary to its representation in popular fiction, the examination of a crime scene is unlikely to yield evidence that immediately links a suspect to a crime. Rather, the collection of evidence is part of a complex web of investigation that involves many individuals, each considering different forms of information in different ways.

Baber situates the role of *crime scene* examiner (*CSE*) within the criminal justice process (ibid.):

> The CSE is part of a much larger investigative system, each member of which has their own skills and roles (Smith et al., 2008). In a sense, Crime Scene Investigation involves sets of ad-hoc teams pursuing independent goals with quite limited overlap (Smith et al., 2008). Thus, there is typically a demarcation between roles. Having said this, the nature of this demarcation has been subject to significant shifting over the years, with the ongoing digitisation of Crime Scene Examination leading to further changes. For example, there used to be a specific role of Crime Scene Photographer whose function was to capture and process images of the crime scene (either prior to evidence recovery or at stages during the recovery process, depending on the nature of the crime). However, with the growing use of digital cameras by CSEs, this role has (in some Police Forces) changed. This has the interesting implication that the function of a photograph taken by the Crime Scene Photographer was to capture the scene as clearly as possible in order to aid discussion of the scene in Court (or during subsequent investigation), but the function of a photograph taken by the CSE could be to illustrate the evidence recovery process; [. . .]

---

[4] For this concept, see Dror and Hamard (2009). Baber remarks (2010, p. 424): "While I suggest that Crime Scene Examination necessarily involves several agents performing cognitive activity, this is not to argue that this results in an 'extended mind' across these agents; as Dror and Hamard (2009) point out, to argue for an extended mind is analogous to arguing for extended migraine – just because an event occurs in one brain does not inevitably mean that other brains will share this event. Dror and Hamard's (2009) argument is that one should not separate cognitive states from mental states. This criticism raises a core problem for the notion of 'Distributed Cognition', because it implies that cognition cannot be 'distributed' across agents because one cannot share mental states. A primary assumption of 'Distributed Cognition' is that it is not 'cognition' which is distributed so much as objects-in-the-world, which plays a role in supporting, structuring and aiding the activities of cognition."

Baber explains (2010, p. 426):

> What is happening in Crime Scene Examination is the mediation of cognition through the collection, manipulation and dissemination of a variety of artifacts; each artifact is interpreted in particular ways by the agents who come into contact with it. My argument will be that, for the various agents involved in this evidence chain, each artifact can 'afford' a particular set of responses, that is, the artifacts are resources for action, and the actions will be recognised by different agents according to their training and experience. I am using the notion of 'afford' in the sense introduced by Gibson (1977, 1979), as a form of perception–action coupling in which the physical appearance of an object in the world supports particular physical responses (e.g., a pebble 'affords' grasping in the hand).

Once recovered, evidence is shared (Baber, 2010, p. 429):

> The preceding discussion implies that the search of a scene is guided by experience, expectation and the ability to recognise items of evidential value. In this respect, the notion of Distributed Cognition can be interpreted in terms of the use of objects in the world as resources-for-action. The Crime Scene Examiner recognises objects as resources-for-action which may well differ from untrained observers. For example, while the untrained observer might assume that a pane of glass in a window could yield fingermarks, they might be less inclined to immediately assume that it could also yield footwear marks, and still less inclined to recognise its potential for yielding DNA (the latter two could arise from someone climbing in through the window, or from pressing their forehead against the window to see if anyone is at home).
>
> So far, this description looks very much like a process that involves the mental states of an individual; the CSE interprets the scene, recognising objects as resources-for-action, and then recovers the evidence. However, what makes the Crime Scene Examination process different from a Sherlock Holmes story is that the CSE submits the evidence for interpretation by other people. Indeed, it is unlikely for the CSE's notes and reports from the scene to include any deduction. Rather the report will be as descriptive as possible.[5] This representation, of the scene and its evidence, is passed along the recovery train. So we have a set of processes that could ostensibly represent the stimulus (or input) to a cognitive processing system. This processing is (formally) undertaken by people other than the CSE.

Prakken et al. (2003) discussed appropriate argument structures for reasoning about evidence in relation to hypothesising crime scenarios. It was a paper on using argumentation schemes for reasoning on legal evidence, mainly by way of an exploration of applying *Araucaria*, the argument visualisation system from the University of Dundee in Scotland,[6] to an analysis in the style of Wigmore Charts. Case-based

---

[5] Baber (2010, p. 430) concedes that there may be problems with striving to be objective by only providing descriptions, in that some useful information may be missed: "One could make a strong argument that this lack of information helps an analysis to be as objective as possible, by focussing only on the item at hand (and avoiding the potential for bias that Dror et al. (2005) demonstrated). On the other hand, it might be useful to have some knowledge of the item in situ, so as to decide how best to conduct analysis. If the Forensic Scientist had recovered the item herself then such information would be recalled by her, but when it is delivered in a batch of bags then such information is not obviously available. As an example of why this could be problematic, consider a finger-mark left on a window. This mark might not be detailed enough to form a print, but could indicate whether the window has been forced up or whether someone climbed down the window, knowing the orientation of the mark on the window can help decide how best to analyse it, but this might not have been provided in the evidence log."

[6] Araucaria is available for free at http://www.computing.dundce.ac.uk/staff/creed/araucaria

reasoning was applied by Toland and Rees (2005) to the task of recalling similar instances of volume crime, when confronted with a crime being investigated: the task was the identification of crimes with similar *modus operandi*, and the reasoning involved potential repeat offenders. Ribaux and Margot (1999) applied case-based reasoning to the categorisation of cases of burglary, with the retrieval of cases with similar profiles. The work reported about in Oatley et al. (2004) is concerned with assisting the police in detecting the perpetrators of burglary from homes, which is a high-volume crime with low detection rates; that project made use of a variety of data mining techniques, including: classification and association rules,[7] neural network clustering, survival analysis and Bayesian belief nets, case-based reasoning, as well as ontologies and logic programming.

A team that was initially led in Edinburgh by John Zeleznikow, in the early 2000s, worked on projects whose aim was to produce software tools assisting in the assessment of evidence in given limited, specialist domains. Jeroen Keppens and Burkhard Schafer were members of that team. Eventually, as various persons moved around to other affiliations, sequel projects emerged at different locations. The present section is concerned with one of those lines of research.

Keppens and Zeleznikow (2002, 2003) and Keppens and Schafer (2003a, 2003b, 2004) have reported about a project whose application is in post-mortem inquests, with the goal of determining whether death occurred through natural causes, homicide or suicide. In their Dead Bodies Project,[8] a so-called "truth maintenance system", or ATMS (a well-known AI approach to consistency)[9] is resorted to, in order to maintain a space of "possible worlds" which correspond to hypothetical scenarios. The architecture is shown in Fig. 8.1.1.1.

The project resorts to neither conventional expert systems, nor case-based reasoning. Any case is potentially unique. Crime investigation is very difficult to proceduralise. The design solution adopted for this project was to develop a model-based reasoning system, i.e., such a system that given a problem instance, a model of the problem is constructed, and a problem-independent technique is applied. In the same project, dynamic preference orderings are assigned to uncertain events. Default orderings may be overruled by inferred orderings.

An article by Keppens and Schafer (2005) "characterises an important class of scenarios, containing 'alternative suspects' or 'hidden objects', which cannot be

---

[7] A definition of *association rules* as a form of data mining is found in fn. 36 in Chapter 3.

[8] Ronald Wright (2005, 2nd edn.; 2009, 3rd death) provides an overview of the *investigation of traumatic deaths*.

[9] In Section 2.1.2 above (see in particular some historical information in fn. 1 in Chapter 1) we have already come across the approach known in artificial intelligence as *Assumption-based Truth Maintenance System* (*ATMS*). An ATMS is a mechanism that enables a problem solver to make inferences under different hypothetical conditions, by maintaining the assumptions on which each piece of information and each inference depends (de Kleer, 1986, 1988). The goal of computation with an ATMS is to find minimal sets of premises sufficient for the support of each node. One has to find all minimally inconsistent subsets (NOGOODSs), and to find all maximally consistent subsets (GOODSs).

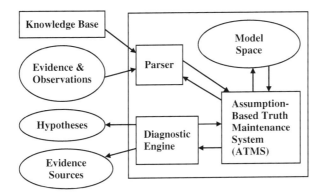

Fig. 8.1.1.1   The early architecture of the Dead Bodies Project of Keppens and Zeleznikow (2002, 2003)

synthesised robustly using conventional abductive inference mechanisms. The work is then extended further by proposing a novel inference mechanism that enables the generation of such scenarios."

Keppens and Schafer (2006) reported about a more advanced state of the same project applying artificial intelligence to crime scenario modelling. The prototype of a decision-support system was presented, for crime scenario construction. It is component events, rather than entire scenarios, that are stored. (By *scenario*, a description of a combination of events and situations is meant.) The component events are composed into useful scenarios by an algorithm. The input is a description of the available evidence. A network of plausible scenarios is then generated. Those scenarios in turn can be analysed, with the goal of devising effective evidence collection strategies. The algorithm was allegedly highly adaptable to unanticipated cases, by allowing a major crime being investigated to be matched by component events in several different ways. One advantage hoped for was the avoidance of such pitfalls of human reasoning as *premature case theories*, or rather *premature convergence*, such that police investigators tend to focus on the more likely suspects they had identified early on.[10]

---

[10] Keppens and Schafer (2006, section 2.1), citing McConville, Saunders, and Leng (1991) and Greer (1994). Once investigators think they already have the culprits, they tend to apply *confirmationism*, also known as *cognitive dissonance*, by which they privilege such information that confirm their preconceptions, and tend to disregard contrary evidence. "While the police service might pay lip service to a falsificationist model of rationality ('asking witnesses to come forward to eliminate them from the inquiry') existing reward structures make it difficult to implement this in practice. Our proposed system accounts for this by combining a 'backchaining' abductivist model of reasoning with a 'forward chaining' model that is based on the idea of indirect proof, sidestepping the issue of falsification and induction in a universe with only finitely many alternatives" (Keppens & Schafer, 2006, section 2.2). *Forward chaining* and its opposite, *backchaining*, are standard concepts from rule-based knowledge-based systems in artificial intelligence.

Therefore, that project belongs to a category of software tools known as *compositional modellers*, and introduced by Falkenhainer and Forbus (1991) in their paper 'Compositional modeling: finding the right model for the job'. Compositional modelling was also discussed by Keppens and Shen (2001). In compositional modellers, small, generic and reusable rules called *model fragments* capture a domain's first principles. These are "fundamental theories describing the behaviours and mechanisms that occur in the domain of interest [. . .]. The compositional modelling paradigm is adapted to the crime investigation domain by employing causal rules describing how combinations of assumed states and events lead to new states and events in plausible crime scenarios" (Keppens & Schafer, 2006).

Another category in which the system described by Keppens and Schafer (2006) is *abductive diagnosers*. In abductive diagnosis (Console & Torasso, 1991), what the conditions are of a physical system under investigation are determined by comparing observations as predicted by models, to such observations that are extracted from the real world. The generation of models, in an abductive diagnoser, is done by resorting to a knowledge base of *first principles* about the given domain. First principles are general rules, independent from the decision procedure, and in this they differ from the *heuristic rules* (i.e., *rules of thumb*) found in rule-based expert systems. In the project of Keppens and Schafer (2006),

> the first principles are expressed by means of causal rules describing how some states and events are triggered by other known or assumed states and events. The possible causes of a given set of available evidence are inferred by means of an abductive inference procedure. These causes form the hypothetical scenarios describing plausible crimes. Potential additional evidence that may confirm or contradict these scenarios is then deduced using the same causal rules. This abductive, first-principles based approach recognises that while the individual scenarios encountered in a major crime investigation may be virtually unique and vary widely, the underlying domain knowledge on evidence and the types of events that create it are not. It also encourages a principled hypothetico-deductive investigative methodology because it hypotheses all (known) possible causes of the available evidence, composes these causes into plausible scenarios and deduces additional evidence from the plausible scenario. This promotes consideration of many scenarios, instead of individual ones, in deciding on future investigative actions. Finally, the approach also allows making expert domain knowledge available to less experienced investigators.

The architecture of the decision-support system described by Keppens and Schafer (2006) is shown in Fig. 8.1.1.2. An *assumption-based truth maintenance system* (*ATMS*) is the central inference mechanism in this architecture. A *scenario space* is maintained by means of the ATMS. "All" possible scenarios that explain the available evidence are stored in the scenario space. The scenarios are represented as logic predicates; these predicates denote events and states, or causal relations between events and states. Causal relations between assumptions, states, and events are represented as *scenario fragments*, each of these being a tuple comprising a set of variables, a set of relations called *preconditions*, a set of relations called *postconditions*, and a set of relations called *assumptions*. There also is a representation of inconsistencies, e.g., "a person can not kill himself both with such an intention (i.e. in a suicide) and without this intention (i.e. in an accidental self-killing)"

Fig. 8.1.1.2 The architecture of the decision-support system described by Keppens and Schafer (2006), redrawn and rearranged from their figure 2. Data structures are shown in this figure as rectangles, whereas ellipses correspond to the inference mechanism

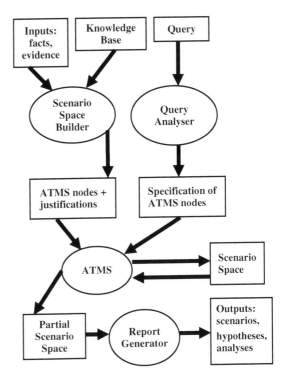

(Keppens & Schafer, 2006, section 4.4). The knowledge base comprises property definitions, a set of scenario fragments, and a set of inconsistencies. "*Property definitions* describe which types of predicate correspond to a symptom, fact, hypothesis or investigative action" (ibid., section 4.5). An example of scenario fragment is this one (Keppens & Schafer, 2006, section 4.3):

> if a person P suffers from ailment or injury C, C is the cause of death of P, and there is a medical examiner E, and assuming that E determines the cause of death of P and makes the correct diagnosis, then there will be a piece of evidence in the form of a cause of death report indicating that according to E, the cause of death of P is C.

Keppens and Schafer explained (2006, section 3.2):

> Once constructed, the scenario space is analysed through a series of *queries*. Queries are questions about the scenario space. Their answers are computed by extracting relevant parts from the scenario space and reported back in an understandable format. To interface between the human and scenario space, a *query analyser* translates standard types of user queries into a specification of ATMS nodes of interest, and a *report generator* provides the means to represent a partial scenario space back to the user.

What the scenario space is made to initially contain, is based on the initial set of given *facts* and *evidence*, and is constructed by means of a *knowledge base*.

For example, these five pieces of evidence appear in an example from Keppens and Schafer (2006): n_1: "A hanging corpse of a person identified as johndoe has been found"; n_{11}: "A report by a psychologist identified as frasier (n_{15}) stating that johndoe may have been suicidal prior to his death"; n_{14}: "The observation of suicide trial marks on the body of johndoe"; n_{16}: "The body of johndoe exhibits signs of petechiae" (i.e., small red to purple spots on the eyes or skin, caused by either disease or asphyxiation); n_{20}: "A report by a medical examiner identified as quincy (n_7) stating that the cause of death of johndoe was asphyxiation".

One possible scenario based on this evidence is suicide by hanging. For example, "The hanging corpse (n_1) and the summed cause of death (n_{20}) are the consequents of johndoe's hanging (n_5), which he was unable (unwilling) to end (n_4). The petechiae is caused by asphyxiation (n_{15}) resulting from the hanging. johndoe's suicide by hanging requires that johndoe is suicidal (n_7) and the last two pieces of evidence are a consequence of his suicidal state" (Keppens & Schafer, 2006, section 4.1).

Each scenario was represented as a *causal hypergraph*. A hypergraph is a generalisation of a graph, such that an edge may appear not just between two nodes, but between a set of nodes including two or more nodes. But scenarios were represented as directed acyclic hypergraph, whose nodes are events or states, whereas the edges are directed hyperarcs, each one from a set of at least one event or state, towards one and only one event or state. The scenario of suicide by hanging was shown in Keppens and Schafer (2006, figure 3), but we find it more convenient to translate here that hypergraph into a ruleset and a list of propositions. The ruleset is shown here in Table 8.1.1.1 (where $\wedge$ stands for *and*); each rule corresponds to one of the hyperarcs of the causal hypergraph of the scenario of suicide by hanging. The correspondence between node identifiers and particular propositions is listed in Table 8.1.1.2. In Table 8.1.1.1, each row stands for a directed hyperarc of the causal hypergraph, and here in the order we chose to reflect the arrangement in Keppens and Schafer's (2006) original diagram of their figure 3, from top to bottom. The meaning of the nodes is defined in Table 8.1.1.2.

Keppens and Schafer (2006, section 4.2) classify information by distinguishing *facts* ("pieces of inexplicable, certain information") from *evidence* ("information that is certain and explicable"), by distinguishing three kinds of "uncertain and

Table 8.1.1.1 The hyperarcs of the scenario of suicide by hanging (from figure 3 in Keppens & Schafer, 2006)

n_1	$\leftarrow$	$n_4 \wedge n_5$
n_{16}	$\leftarrow$	n_{15}
n_{20}	$\leftarrow$	$n_{15} \wedge n_{17} \wedge n_3 \wedge n_{18} \wedge n_{19}$
n_{15}	$\leftarrow$	n_5
n_{17}	$\leftarrow$	$n_4 \wedge n_5$
n_4	$\leftarrow$	n_6
n_5	$\leftarrow$	n_6
n_{21}	$\leftarrow$	n_6
n_{15}	$\leftarrow$	$n_2 \wedge n_{10} \wedge n_9 \wedge n_7$
n_6	$\leftarrow$	$n_7 \wedge n_8$
n_{14}	$\leftarrow$	$n_7 \wedge n_3 \wedge n_{13} \wedge n_{12}$

Table 8.1.1.2 Which event or state the nodes stand for

n_1:	observe(hanging-dead-body(johndoe))
n_2:	psychologist(frasier)
n_3:	medical-examiner(quincy)
n_4:	impossible(end(hanging(johndoe)))
n_5:	hanging(johndoe)
n_6:	suicide(johndoe, hanging)
n_7:	suicidal(johndoe)
n_8:	suicide-action(hanging, johndoe)
n_9:	psychological-examination(frasier, state-of-mind(johndoe))
n_{10}:	correct-diagnosis(frasier, state-of-mind(johndoe))
n_{11}:	psychological-evaluation(frasier, state-of-mind(johndoe), suicidal)
n_{12}:	medical-examination(quincy, body(johndoe))
n_{13}:	correct-diagnosis(quincy, body(johndoe))
n_{14}:	medical-report(quincy, body(johndoe), suicide-trial-marks)
n_{15}:	suffers(johndoe, asphyxiation)
n_{16}:	observe(eyes(johndoe), petechiae)
n_{17}:	cause-of-death(johndoe, asphyxiation)
n_{18}:	correct-diagnosis(quincy, cause-of-death(johndoe))
n_{19}:	medical-examination(quincy, cause-of-death(johndoe))
n_{20}:	medical-report(quincy, cause-of-death(johndoe), asphyxiation)
n_{21}:	suicidal-death(johndoe)

explicable" information (*uncertain states*,[11] *uncertain events*,[12] and *hypotheses*[13]), and by distinguishing three types of *assumptions*, i.e., of "uncertain and inexplicable information":

- *Default assumptions* describe information that is normally presumed to be true. In theory, the number of plausible scenarios that explain a set of available evidence is virtually infinite, but many of these scenarios are based on very unlikely presumptions. Default assumptions aid in the differentiation between such scenarios by expressing the most likely features of events and states in a scenario. A typical example of a default assumption is the presumption that a doctor's diagnosis of the cause of death of person is correct (e.g. n_{18}).
- *Conjectures* are the unknown causes of certain feasible scenarios (e.g. n_7). Unlike default assumptions, conjectures are not employed to differentiate between the relative likelihood of scenarios.
- Uncommitted *investigative actions*, i.e. possible but not yet performed activities aimed at collecting additional evidence, are also treated as assumptions. At any given stage in the investigation, it is *uncertain* which of the remaining uncommitted investigative actions will be performed. The reasoning required to perform such an action involves looking at its consequences instead of its causes, and therefore they are *not* (causally) *explicable*. As such, investigative actions assume a similar role as default assumptions and conjectures: i.e. they are employed to speculate about the plausible (observable) consequences of a hypothetical scenario.

---

[11] An example of *uncertain state* is node n_4, "johndoe was unable to end his hanging".

[12] An example of *uncertain event* is node n_{15}, "johndoe asphyxiated".

[13] An example of *hypothesis* is node n_{21}, "johndoe's death was suicidal".

8.1.2 The Structure of ATMS Inference in the Scenario Space Builder

The scenario-space builder instantiates scenario fragments as well as inconsistencies, into an ATMS. In the *initialisation phase*, an ATMS is generated that contains one node per piece of available evidence. Next, a *backward chaining phase* is executed. All plausible *causes* of the available evidence are added to the ATMS. A process is repeated, until exhausting all possible unifications[14] of individual consequents of a scenario fragment with a node already in the ATMS. That process does the following for each possible unification: it instantiates the antecedents and assumptions of that scenario fragment; the process adds a node to the ATMS for antecedent instance that does not already have a node; it adds an assumption node to the ATMS for each assumption instance that does not already have a node; and the process adds to the ATMS a *justification* (i.e. a rule like the rows in Table 8.1.1.1, but also added nodes such as assumption nodes can be included) "from the nodes corresponding to the antecedent and the assumption nodes corresponding to the assumptions, to the node corresponding to the consequent" (Keppens & Shafer, 2006, section 5.2.1).

Once the backward chaining phase is exhausted because action as described was taken for each possible unifications, execution enters the *forward chaining phase*.

---

[14] Take for example the syllogism "All men are mortal, and Socrates is a man; therefore Socrates is mortal". In predicate calculus, the three expressions

$$\forall X(man(X) \Rightarrow mortal\,(X)).$$
$$man(socrates).$$
$$man(socrates) \Rightarrow mortal(socrates).$$

respectively stand for "All men are mortal", "Socrates is a man", and "Socrates is a man, therefore Socrates is mortal". *Unification* is an algorithm that an automated problem solver can use in order to determine that socrates may be substituted for X. For it to apply inference rules, "an inference system must be able to determine when two expressions are the same or *match*. In propositional calculus, this is trivial: two expressions match if an only if they are syntactically identical. In predicate calculus, the process of matching two sentences is complicated by the existence of variables in the expressions. Universal instantiation allows universally quantified variables [that is: for all X] to be replaced by terms from the domain. This requires a decision process for determining the variable substitutions under which two or more expressions can be made identical (usually for the purpose of applying inference rules). Unification is an algorithm for determining the substitutions needed to make two predicate calculus expressions match" (Luger & Stubblefield, 1998, section 2.3.2., p. 68). "Generally, a problem-solving process will require multiple inferences and, consequently, multiple successive unifications. Logic problem solvers must maintain consistency of variable substitutions. It is important that any unifying substitution be made consistently across all occurrences of the variable in both expressions being matched" (ibid., p. 69). "Once a variable has been bound, future unifications and inferences must take the value of this binding into account. If a variable is bound to a constant, that variable may not be given a new binding in a future unification. If a variable X_1 is substituted for another variable X_2 and at a later time X_1 is replaced with a constant, then X_2 must also reflect this binding" (ibid.). Unification substitutions are combined and returned thanks to the composition of unification substitutions.

What this phase does, is adding to the ATMS all possible *consequences* of the plausible scenarios. Whereas the *backward chaining* phase repeated its process until exhausting all possible unifications of individual *consequents* of a scenario fragment with a node already in the ATMS, by contrast the *forward chaining* phase carries out the following process for each possible unification of the set of *antecedents* of a scenario fragment with a set of nodes already in the ATMS. That process instantiates the assumptions and consequents of that scenario fragment; the process adds an assumption node to the ATMS for each assumption instance that does not already have a node; the process adds to the ATMS a node for each consequent instance that does not already have a node; and the process adds to the ATMS a justification for each consequent instance, "from the nodes corresponding to the antecedent and the assumption nodes corresponding to the assumptions, to the node corresponding to the consequent instance"(Keppens & Shafer, 2006, section 5.2.1).[15]

The forward chaining process is repeated until exhausting all unifications of scenario fragment antecedents with sets of nodes in the ATMS. And finally, the *consistency phase* is carried out: "inconsistent combination of states and events are denoted as nogoods. This involves instantiating the inconsistencies from the knowledge base based on information in the ATMS and marking them as justifications for the nogood node." (ibid.). In the terminology of ATMS, a *nogood* is such a justification that has lead to an inconsistency, that is to say, from its node there is an arc $\rightarrow \perp$ and this implies that one of the propositions conjoined by *and* in the nogood must be false. With an ATMS, one has to find all minimally inconsistent subsets (NOGOODSs), and to find all maximally consistent subsets (GOODSs).

Keppens and Schafer (2004, section 3) pointed out similarities between what the ATMS does in their Dead Bodies project, and what a defence solicitor would do:

> In developing alternative scenarios consistent with the evidence, the ATMS performs some of the scrutiny a good defence solicitor would subject the prosecution case to. A defence solicitor has broadly speaking two strategies available to him. First, he can question the factual correctness or the legal admissibility of evidence presented by the prosecution. Second, he can accept the evidence at face value and argue that alternative explanations for their presence are possible that do not incriminate his client. We are concerned here primarily with this second strategy. However, it is here that we encounter a certain ambiguity, an ambiguity explicitly recognised by the Scots law of evidence. The defence has in fact again two strategies available to it. The first can be dubbed the "Perry Mason Stratagem". Like the fictitious advocate, the defence can pursue its own investigation and "point to the real culprit". In Scots law, this is known as the special defence of incrimination [Field & Raitt, 1996], recently used (unsuccessfully) in the Lockerbie trial

for an atrocity ascribed to an act of terror: an PanAm passenger aircraft exploded while flying over Scotland in 1988 because of a bomb on board.

---

[15] In the section 5.2.2 in their article, Keppens and Shafer (2006) supplied the formal algorithm for generating the scenario space.

This strategy has a number of psychological and legal advantages. The same reason that makes it the solution of choice for crime writers also works well with juries: no loose ends are left and the crime is avenged. Procedurally, it allows the defence to submit also other pieces of evidence. This corresponds to the "forward chaining" aspect of our ATMS: The party named by the defence will have interacted causally with the crime scene. This will have created evidence which can strengthen the defence case. This allows introduction of additional "suspect specific" evidence (such as alibi) evidence about other people, which otherwise might be ruled out as irrelevant. The defence of course need not prove the guilt of the other party; it only needs to establish it as a plausible alternative. [. . .]

8.1.3 An Extension with Bayesian Networks, Entropy, and Returned Evidence Collection Strategies

Keppens, Shen, and Lee (2005a) described an extension of the scenario space gener-ation, resorting to Bayesian modelling: "this paper shows a compositional modelling approach to synthesise and efficiently store a space of plausible scenarios within a Bayesian Network (BN) [. . .]. Furthermore, it presents an application of the maxi-mum entropy reduction technique to determine which investigative actions are most likely to reduce doubt" (ibid., section 1). In this extension of the work already described earlier in the present Section 8.1, scenario fragments also incorporate a set of probability distributions, one for each combination of the antecedent and assumption variables.

Thus, the following scenario states that if a victim V has petechiae on his eyes and the investigators examine V's eyes, then evidence of petechiae is discovered with a certain probability:

```
if {petechiae(eyes(V))}
assuming {examination(eyes(V))}
then {evidence(petechiae(V))}
distribution evidence(petechiae(V)) {
true, true -> true:0.99, false:0.01}
```

Keppens et al. (2005a, section 2.1) explained that, by adopting the nota-tion shown in Table 8.1.3.1, the general representation for a scenario fragment, incorporating probability distributions, is as follows:

Table 8.1.3.1 A notation for the predicates and values involved

$\{p_1, \ldots, p_k\}$	the set of antecedent predicates
$\{p_1, \ldots, p_m\}$	the set of assumption predicates
p_n	the consequent predicate
v_i	any of the values that variable p_i can take
q_j	a real value in the range $[0,1]$

```
if {p₁,...,pₖ}
assuming {pₗ,...,pₘ}
then {pₙ}
distribution pₙ {

        ⋮

    v₁,...,vₖ,vₗ,...,vₘ->vₙ₁ : q₁,...,vₙⱼₙ : qⱼₙ

        ⋮              }
```

By contrast, the general representation of an inconsistency is as a special kind of scenario fragment, as follows:

```
if {p₁,...,pₖ}
then {nogood}
distribution nogood {
    v₁,...,vₖ->⊤ : 1,...,⊥ : 0}
```

where $\top$ stands for the value *true*, and the reversed $\top$ stands for the value *false*. Moreover, in the knowledge base there also are prior distributions for assumed states and events. In order to enable the compositional modelling of Bayesian networks, presumptions concerning the scenario fragments include the presumption that the causal hypergraph is acyclic ("There are no cycles in the knowledge base": Bayesian networks are inherently acyclic), and the presumption that "*Any two probability distributions taken from two scenario fragments involving the same consequent variable are independent*. Intuitively, this assumption indicates that the outcome of an influence implied by one scenario fragment is not affected by that of another" (ibid.).

Entropy was adopted as a measurement of doubt, this being a concept from information theory. It is also adopted in machine learning (Mitchell, 1997) and in model-based diagnosis (Hamscher, Console, & de Kleer, 1992). Keppens et al. (2005a, section 3.2) explained that the entropy over an exhaustive set of mutually exclusive hypotheses

$$H = \{h_1,...,h_m\}$$

is given by:

$$\epsilon(H) = -\sum_{h \in H} P(h) \log P(h)$$

By resorting to conventional techniques from Bayesian networks, it is possible to compute the values $P(h)$. As in crime investigation, additional information is generated through evidence collection, Keppens et al. (ibid.) proposed that given e set of pieces of evidence

$$E = \{e_1 : v_1, \ldots, e_n : v_n\},$$

"the entropy metric of interest for the purpose of generating evidence collection strategies is the entropy over a set of hypotheses H", as per the formula:

$$\epsilon(H \mid E) = - \sum_{h \in H} P(h \mid E) \log P(h \mid E)$$

Conventional Bayesian network techniques allows computing the conditional probability values $P(h \mid E)$. Keppens et al. (ibid.) also proposed that selecting investigative

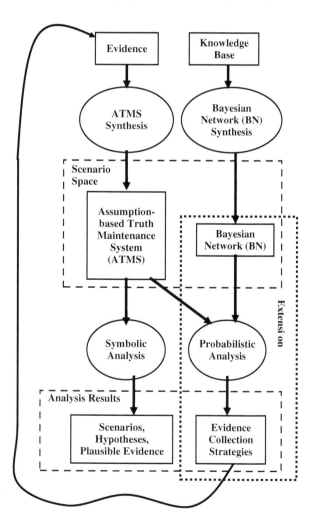

Fig. 8.1.3.1 The extended architecture, redrawn from Keppens et al. (2005b, section 3, figure 2): Bayesian networks appear in the knowledge representation, and evidence collection strategies appear in the output

actions from a given set A according to the following criterion is a useful evidence collection strategy:

$$\min_{a \in A} E(\epsilon(H \mid E), a)$$

They discussed minimal entropy-based evidence (EPE) collection in their section 3.3. They conceded however (Keppens et al., 2005a, in their section 3.4) that whereas that "technique guarantees to return an effective investigative action, it does not ensure globally optimal evidence collection". They proposed a remedy, in order to reduce the "likelihood of obtaining poor quality locally optimal evidence collection strategies". This is done by only "considering the EPEs after performing a sequence of actions", although this incurs computation overheads. They then proposed a simplified equation for that remedy. Next, they turned to discussing how to allow multiple evidence sets, or multiple hypothesis sets instead of just one.

In Fig. 8.1.3.1, we redraw from Keppens, Shen, and Schafer (2005b, section 3, figure 2) the architecture of their system, as extended with Bayesian networks in the knowledge representation, and with evidence collection strategies in the output.

8.1.4 Further Research

Jeroen Keppens

As argued by Schum (1994), a key aspect of evidential reasoning concerns the development of hypotheses. Indeed, as demonstrated by Aitken and Taroni (2004), probabilistic approaches to evidential reasoning tend to favour the statistics paradigm of hypothesis testing. This idea is not only useful when assessing evidence in court, it has been embraced by a part of the forensic science community, such as Cook, Evett, Jackson, Jones, and Lambert (1998), as a means to assess the probative force of evidence during the investigation of a (alleged) crime. But while hypotheses are readily available for testing once a case reaches court, the formulation of hypotheses during the investigative stage is not straightforward.

As argued by Keppens and Zeleznikow (2003), this requires what Peirce (1903) termed abduction or abductive reasoning. Keppens and Schafer (2006) have developed an abductive reasoning approach to produce the hypotheses required for evidential reasoning during a crime investigation. Being a knowledge based approach, it employs a knowledge base and a corresponding inference mechanism. The knowledge base consists primarily of generalised and reusable fragments of plausible scenario, such as one predicting the medical symptoms generated by a blow to the head and another indicating those resulting hitting one's head against the ground in a fall. Generally speaking, these scenario fragments express cause-effect relationships. The inference mechanism instantiates these scenario fragments to specific circumstances and combines them to compose plausible scenarios, which can then be analysed further.

The overall approach is inspired by earlier work on compositional modelling by Keppens and Shen (2004), an family of methods designed to generate formal models of real-world or hypothetical scenarios. Compositional modelling works on the idea that while the specific combination of circumstances contained within an individual scenario are relatively rare, and therefore difficult to generalise, the constituent elements appear rather more frequently. For example, while the circumstances of the murder of one of the victims of the serial killer Dr Harold Shipman might be relatively rare, the component elements such as injection with an overdose of diamorphine and the resulting evidence reoccur more frequently. Therefore, the use of compositional modelling helps to tackle, to some extent, significant knowledge acquisition problem involved with a system of this kind.

More recent developments in this strand of research have sought to further address the knowledge acquisition bottleneck and to allow more useful modes of inquire with the resulting scenario models. One extension concerns the modelling problem that arises when there are an unknown number of plausible instantiations. For example, an unknown number of unknown persons can be involved in a plausible crime scenario, such as the person a fingerprint belongs, the person who has been seen fleeing the scene of the alleged crime and the suspicious person observed in CCTV footage near the scene prior to the alleged crime. During the investigation it is not known whether this concerns three distinct individuals, two individuals (with two pieces of evidence referring to the same person) or just a single individual (to whom all evidence relates). Keppens and Shafer (2004, 2005) have proposed a *peg-unification* technique that involves representing all unknown instantiations as so-called pegs and employs an algorithm to explore all possible assumptions of equivalences between pegs simultaneously.[16]

---

[16] *Peg unification* is useful for *coreference resolution*. Keppens and Schafer explained (2003b, section 4):

> The task of identifying different references to the same entity is known as *coreference resolution* in computational linguistics. In the analysis of a discourse, it is important that references to the same entity are correctly associated with one another because each of the expressions that contains one of these references may add some information about the entity in question. For example, in the sentence "Every farmer who owns *a donkey*, beats *it*." "a donkey" and "it" refer to the same entity. The first half of the sentence conveys that the entities of interest are all donkeys owned by farmers. The second half of the sentence communicates that the entities of interest are beaten. Thus, the sentence as a whole imparts the knowledge that all donkeys owned by farmers are beaten.
>
> A wide range of techniques has been devised to perform coreference resolution tasks, such as the one illustrated in the example. The vast majority of these techniques specialise in examining texts for discourse analysis or information extraction. An important property of the existing approaches is that they tend to consider only a single possible solution at any one time, while the present problem domain requires a method that can represent and reason with multiple possible worlds simultaneously.

As to *pegs* (Keppens & Schafer, 2003b, section 4.1):

> The objective of this work is to identify possible references to the same unknown or partially specified entities in the scenario space. In order to correctly distinguish such entities, the notion of *pegs* is adopted from the literature on coreference resolution [(Karttunen,

Another extension of the work has augmented the original purely symbolic representation of scenarios with probabilities. More specifically, Keppens, Shen, and Price (2010) have devised a method to compose conventional conditional probability distributions from partial specifications thereof and incorporated the partial ones into the scenario fragments. This allows the original abductive reasoning approach

---

1976; Landman, 1986)]. Pegs refer to a specific entity whose exact identity remains unknown (or partially specified). In this paper, each peg is identified by an expression of the form _n, where n is a non-negative natural number. At the start of the scenario space generation algorithm $n = 0$, and n is incremented by 1 after each generation of a new peg. As such, each new peg is identified uniquely.

New pegs may be introduced into the scenario space during the instantiation of causal rules of the form if $\{A_n\}$ assuming $\{A_s\}$ then $\{c\}$, where An is a set of antecedent predicates, A_s is a set of assumption predicates and c is a consequent predicate. Whenever a rule, whose antecedent or assumption sentence contain variables that do not occur in the consequent sentence, is applied during the inverse modus ponens phase of the scenario space generation algorithm (i.e. step 2), then those variables are instantiated by pegs. Consider, for instance, applying inverse modus ponens on rule

> if $\{scene(S)\}$ assuming $\{person(P), took(P, G)\}$
> then $\{\neg evidence(recover(G, S))\}$

given the piece of evidence: ¬evidence(recover(handgun, home(victim)))}. The required substitution $\{G/handgun, S/home(victim)\}$ does not provide an instance for P. Here, P refers to an unknown entity and it is therefore substituted by a peg, say, _0. Therefore, the assumptions person(_0) and took(_0, handgun) are added to the scenario space. Similarly, pegs may also be introduced during the modus ponens phase of the scenario generation algorithm (i.e. step 3). In this case pegs are introduced when a rule whose consequent predicates contain variables that do not occur in the antecedent or assumption sentences, is applied.

Keppens and Schafer (2003b, section 4.2) explained *peg unification* as follows:

Because a peg refers to an unknown entity, it can be treated as a constant that uniquely identifies that entity, or it can be unified with a ground term, including another peg or terms containing other pegs. In the latter case, the unification is possible if it is hypothesised that the entity represented by the peg and the entity represented by the term unified to the peg are the same one. This hypothesis must therefore be made explicit by means of an assumption whenever an inference is made that depends on the unification of a peg and a ground term. In the remainder of this paper, such assumptions are referred to as *peg unification assumptions*.

In this paper, each peg unification assumption takes the form bind(_n, t), where _nψ is a peg and t is a ground term (which may include a peg). A peg unification assumption bind(_n, ψt) is added to the scenario space for each pair of predicates that can be matched using a substitution that contains a mapping of the form _n/t.

The binding relation implied by these assumptions is transitive. Therefore, peg unification can not only be assumed, but also be entailed by other peg unification assumptions. This knowledge is represented explicitly in the scenario space: for each pair of peg unification assumptions

$$bind(\_i, t_1(\ldots, \_j, \ldots)) \quad \text{and} \quad bind(\_j, t_2(\ldots, \_k, \ldots)),$$

the following new justification is added to the emerging scenario space:

$$bind(\_i, t1(\ldots, \_j, \ldots)) \wedge bind(\_j, t2(\ldots, \_k, \ldots))$$
$$\rightarrow bind(\_i, t_1(\ldots, t_2(\ldots, \_k, \ldots), \ldots))$$

to be used to produce Bayesian networks describing sets of plausible scenarios. Such a Bayesian network can, in turn, be employed to assess the usefulness of investigative actions based on the informativeness of the evidence they might produce. This extension also enables the knowledge engineer to express his/her lack of certainty regarding cause-effect relationships expressed by the scenario fragments.

However, the integration of probabilities with the approach potentially introduces a further knowledge acquisition challenge: the elicitation of suitable probabilities. Keppens (2007, 2009) has sought address this concern by employing qualitative and semi-quantitative abstractions of conditional probability tables. Fu, Boongoen, and Shen (2010) have independently developed another approach based on a similar idea, exploiting fuzzy sets[17] as a means of qualitative abstraction instead.

8.2 Processing Human Faces: A Panoply of Contexts

8.2.1 Computer Tools for Face Processing: Preliminary Considerations

Mike Redmayne of the London School of Economics in London, writing (Redmayne, 2002) in *The Modern Law Review*, describes a problematic case of face recognition on the part of a forensic expert: "Stephen Hookway was convicted of the robbery of a bank in Salford." (Salford is in the Greater Manchester area.) The following is quoted from Redmayne (ibid., pp. 23–24):

> The only evidence against him was the testimony of a "facial mapping" expert. The expert carried out a detailed examination of photographs of Hookway, and compared them to photographs of the robbery. He found a number of similarities between them. His findings were, he said, "very powerful support for the assertion that the offender was the appellant". He could not, however, say for sure that Hookway was the robber. "He conceded that, if a trawl were made through Manchester, it may be possible to find one or two people of similar appearance". The Court of Appeal acknowledged that, in the absence of a database, "it is impossible to know how many others may look the same as a particular accused". As in *Smith* [a case in which recognition depended on DNA evidence], relatives complicated the case: the defendant's brother was produced in court, at which the expert admitted that "he could not exclude the possibility that there was somebody else who closely resembled the

---

Scenario space generation first *unifies* the relevant sentences (i.e. the consequent of the causal rule during inverse modus ponens, the antecedents of the causal rule during modus ponens, or the inconsistent sentences of the constraint) with nodes in the emerging scenario space, and return the substitution σ required to achieve the unification. Next, scenario space generation *records* each binding that unifies a peg with a term in the scenario space and a newly created set A_p. Then, the process *instantiates* the remaining sentences (i.e. the antecedents and assumptions during inverse modus ponens or the assumptions and consequent during modus ponens) by applying the substitution σ and the process adds those that do not already exist in the scenario space as new nodes. And finally, scenario space generation *generates* a justification if applying a causal rule, or a nogood if applying a constraint.

[17] Fuzzy approaches are the subject of Section 6.1.15 in this book.

defendant". A similar point about the parity of evidence against Hookway and his brother can be made. Despite all this, the Court of Appeal refused to quash the conviction.

Victor S. Johnston and Craig Caldwell, of the Department of Psychology of New Mexico State University, Las Cruces, pointed out (Johnston & Caldwell, 1997):

> Humans are experts in facial recognition. They can recognize and discriminate between a very large number of faces seen over a lifetime, often following a single short exposure.[18] In contrast, humans have poor recall ability; they may not be able to recall the features of a close associate, or even a family member, in sufficient detail to construct a facial composite (Ellis, Davies, and Shepherd, 1986; Goldstein and Chance, 1981; Rakover and Cahlon, 1989). As a consequence, current facial composite procedures, which depend heavily on recall rather than recognition, may not be using the best approach for generating an accurate composite of a target face.

"Face processing touches upon a variety of contexts, and is investigated in different disciplines (Young & Ellis, 1989). Rakover and Cahlon (2001) is on face recognition in cognition and computation, and, while offering an overview of theories and models, it proceeds to present an original approach (the Schema Theory and the Catch Model) with criminological applications. It proposes a cognitive law of Face Recognition by Similarity (FRBS). Davies, Ellis, and Shepherd (1981), *Perceiving and Remembering Faces*, introduces issues in face recognition and its associated mental processes. Raymond Bruyer's edited volume (1986) provided an overview of the neuropsychology of face perception.

A forensic context is only one of the many facets of face recognition. The neuropsychology of face perception and face recognition is treated in Ellis et al. (1986). To psychologists, face recognition is a major challenge for human cognition. Apart from varying facial expressions, let alone disguises, even the views of a face when a head is rotated by different angles do not lend themselves to straightforward recognition on the part of humans exposed to such sights from real life, or by watching a video clip, or at a glance from photographs shot on the fly.

To human cognition, the challenge of recognising a given person in a photograph is not the same as recognising the face of a person who is standing in front of the cognitive agent. Face processing belongs in cognitive science as well as, in a different perspective, in computer science. Techniques from automated image recognition are involved in automated recognition or identity validation systems for security or other identification purposes (Nissan, 2003b, pp. 360–361).

8.2.2 Face Recognition Tools for Identification

8.2.2.1 Facial Recognition Classification, from a Database of Mug Shots

Face recognition is a major area within image processing, in computer science. To say it with Mena (2003, p. 167):

---

[18] There are studies in the psychology of eyewitness testimony that researched the effects of exposure duration on eyewitness accuracy and confidence (e.g., Memon, Hope, & Bull, 2003).

Facial recognition software works by measuring a face according to its peaks and valleys – such as the tip of the nose, the depth of the eye sockets – which are known as *nodal points*. A human face has 80 nodal points; however, facial recognition software may require only 14 to 22 to make a match, concentrating on the inner region of the face, which runs from temple to temple and just over the lip, called the "golden triangle". This is the most stable area because if an individual grows a beard, puts on glasses, gains weight or ages, this region tenjds not to be affected. The relative positions of these points are converted into a long string of numbers, known as a face print.

Databases of photographic images of suspects or convicted perpetrators are available to the police. Such photographs are usually *mug shots:* the face of the person is shown frontally. Suppose the police have a facial photograph of a suspect they are searching for. They want to identify that suspect, among the individuals whose mug shots are in the database.

For such a task of classification, the facial recognition tool of Attrasoft is useful (Mena, 2003, section 6.7, pp. 165–167). The firm, Attrasoft,[19] applies neural networks to tasks in facial recognition and, more generally, image processing. "Its facial recognition product is highly accurate, versatile, and capable of searching millions of images, easily handling over a terabyte of data" (ibid., p. 196).

The technique resorts to neural networks with supervised learning (i.e., the network is trained to recognised a predefined correct output). The tool is first *trained* to recognise the face of the suspect whose photograph is the input. This step is carried out by unsing the ImageFinder interface. The window of ImageFinder shows the Image, a toolbar (whose keys include: Train, Search, Classify, Batch, Example, Biometrics, and help), and an array of keys for various functions (for image processing, or for training or retraining, or for saving, sorting, classifying, undoing, and so forth).

In an example given by Mena (ibid., section 6.7), the given photograph is matched to a photograph of (apparently) the same man, smiling and wearing a hat. It also retrieved a photograph of the same man with a beard. What the user did, was to click on the *Train* button and wait a little bit until the message "Training End!" appears. Mena explains (ibid., p. 166):

> The user can modify the setting parameters, like blurring, sensitivity, external weight cut, image type, segment size, etc. Once training is complete, the system can be directed to go out and look for images that match the training sample, with the output having an integer, representing a similarity value. The higher the score between the training image(s) and the retrieved images, the better the match.

Another kind of situation is when the person is physically present, and a decision needs to be taken as to whether to let that individual in. In the United States, facial recognition systems are used by casinos, but it is potentially valuable for other kinds of situations when prescreening is necessary or advisable.

Similarity search for images can be specialised for human faces, which is the case of face recognition software. Bear in mind however that there is thriving research

---

[19] http://attrasoft.com

into general image similarity search. For example (*ERCIM News*, October 2010, p. 11), Andrea Esuli from ISTI-CNR in Pisa has been researching

> highly efficient similarity search, for which he has developed a novel algorithms based on prefix-permutation indexing. [. . . He] has turned this algorithm into a working search engine for images (http://mipai.esuli.it) that currently allows image similarity search on CoPhIR, the largest image dataset availbale for research purposes. Esuli's algorithm allows similarity searches to be conducted on CoPhIR in sub-second response times, a feat currently neither attained nor approached by competing systems.

In fact, MiPai is based on the PP-Index data structure for approximated similarity search (Esuli, 2009a, 2009b, 2010; Bolettieri et al., 2009). In the demo provided at Esuli's website, one can perform similarity search on the about 106 million images currently available in the CoPhIR collection.[20] Esuli explains[21]:

> The similarity measure used in this demo is based on a linear combination of the five MPEG-7 visual descriptors provided by the CoPhIR collection. The resulting concept of similarity is rather general, which is in line with the generalized nature of the images in the collection.
>
> This means that this may be considered a "general purpose" search system, where one may retrieve images globally similar to the one given as the query, for many aspects: color palette, distribution of colors in the image, presence of similar edges or textures.
>
> This does not means that this is an "all purpose" search system, i.e. you can't change the general similarity criterium with a more specific/specialized one. For example, you can't find shots of your cat climbing a wall given a shot of him sleeping on the sofa. You'll likely find shots of cats/dogs/teddy bears similar to your cat placed on a sofa similar to your sofa.

Efficiency comes at a cost, and a trade-off is made with accuracy[22]:

> One thing to be noted is that MiPai is an approximated method, thus the efficiency is paid with accuracy, i.e., the 100 selected images may not identify the exact (with respect to the MPEG–7 similarity measures) 100 most similar images. The MiPai algorithm offers multiple possibilities, both at index and search time, to trade efficiency for accuracy of results.

8.2.2.2 Reconstructing a Face from Verbal Descriptions: Mug Shots, vs. Sketches and Composites

Let us consider to faces in forensics in particular. Facial portraits, or *mugs*, may just be a photograph (a *mug* shot) of a suspect or convict; otherwise, if the portrait was made based on the verbal description of a victim or eyewitness, it used to be drawn by a sketch artist manually (such a portrait is sometimes called an *Identi-kit*). See Laughery and Fowler (1980) on the sketch artist and Identi-kit procedures for recalling faces, in a psychological perspective. An early example of a sketch produced manually in order to identify a perpetrator is from the Renaissance: a man and his child (who was to become a famous painter) were robbed, and on reaching

---

[20] http://cophir.isti.cnr.it/

[21] http://mipai.esuli.it

[22] http://mipai.esuli.it

the town of Bologna, the boy skilfully drew a sketch, based on which the authorities promptly identified the robbers.

An alternative to the sketch of a sketch artist is a *composite*, by which initially a photographic *photofit* was intended. The term *photofit* is still in use in the U.S., whereas in the U.K. the more general term *composite* is preferred. Research was conducted on the photofit method during the 1970s (Penry, 1974; Ellis, Shepherd, & Davies, 1975; Davies, Ellis, & Shepherd, 1978). Its shortcoming is that a face is composed of different photographic segments, for the eyes and for the mouth, and the separation lines are visible and interfere with recognisability. See Wogalter and Marwitz (1991), on the construction of face composites.

Photofit evidence is not without problems. It is "a method to obtain details of the appearance of a suspect, which when first introduced was expected to be more useful than it has proved" (Osborne, 1997, p. 308). "It was widely assumed that such photofit pictures were merely for incidental use in establishing a suspect that could then be put on an identification parade. A very strange result however occurred in the [English] case of *R* v *Cook* [1987] QB 417" (ibid.), and Osborne describes it as follows:

> In *Cook* the accused was convicted on the basis of a photofit prepared by the victim. After the photofit had been prepared the police arrested the suspect and put him in an identification parade. The victim identified him. In the course of the trial the photofit was put in evidence, the judge ruled it admissible as 'part of the circumstances of the identification'. This was upheld on appeal. It was considered that neither the hearsay rule [for excluding evidence] nor the rule against admission of a previous consistent statement applied to this situation because in preparing the photofit the officer was merely doing what a camera would have done. This result has been much criticised and it is suggested that it is wrong. A photofit is nothing like a camera because there is the interposition of human intelligence. It is suggested that a photofit is hearsay, just as a verbal description of the accused would have been and should have been ruled inadmissible. The decision however, has been upheld in another case, *R* v *Constantinou* (1989) 91 Cr App R 74, on somewhat similar facts.

In France, face composites (in French: *portrait robot*) were developed by a police chief in Lyons during the 1950s, and only consisted of three sliding parts (*bandes coulissantes*), respectively for the hair and forefront, the eyes and eyebrows, and the mouth and chin. A sketch artist used to complete the composites with scars or moles. Eventually the police in Paris adopted the American *identity kit*. From 1993, the French police resorts to computerised face composites, which in French are called *portrait robot informatisé* (Tribondeau, accessed 2006, s.v. *portrait robot*).

Internationally, there exist various computerised systems, including E-FIT, PROfit (CD-FIT), and Mac-A-Mug Pro.[23] These old computerised systems appear to be less satisfactory than the manual method, with faces drawn by a sketch artist. Apparently E-FIT is good at recognising the faces of famous persons, whereas PROfit is good for recognising faces of persons with low distinctiveness. In the CRIME-VUs project (see below), an attempt has been made to improve on those

---

[23] The E-FIT website is interesting; Amina Memon recommends it in her course handouts: http://www.visionmetric.com/index.php?option=com_content&task=view&id=17&Itemid=25

older systems. Bear in mind that composites are an *indicative tool* rather than an *implicative tool* (DNA evidence is an implicative tool, instead); nevertheless, composites are used in courtroom situations as evidence, even though it is not a weighty one.[24]

Johnston and Caldwell claimed (1997):

One of the most widely used systems for generating composite faces was developed by Penry (1974), in Britain, between 1968 and 1974. Termed "Photofit", this technique uses over 600 interchangeable photographs, picturing five basic features: forehead and hair, eyes and eyebrows, mouth and lips, nose, and chin and cheeks. With additional accessories, such as beards and eyeglasses, combinations can produce approximately fifteen billion different faces. Alternatives to Photofit include the Multiple Image-Maker and Identification Compositor (MIMIC), which uses film strip projections, Identikit, which uses plastic overlays of drawn features, and several computerized versions of the Photofit process, such as Mac-A-Mug Pro and Compusketch. Using Compusketch, a trained operator with no artistic ability can assemble a composite in less than an hour. Because of such advantages, computer aided sketching is becoming the method of choice for law enforcement agencies.

Nevertheless, there is a shortcoming (Johnston & Caldwell, 1997):

Systems such as Photofit and Compusketch depend on the ability of a witness to accurately recall the features of a suspect and to be aware of which features and feature positions of the generated composite require modification. Such systems may actually inhibit identification by forcing a witness to employ a specific cognitive strategy; namely, the recall of isolated features. Davies and Christie (1982) have shown that this single feature approach is a serious source of distortion, and Baddeley [(1979)] has concluded that any exclusively feature-based approach is misconceived.

Frowd et al. (2010a) explain:

Face recognition essentially emerges from the parallel processing of individual facial features and their spatial relations on the face (see Bruce & Young, 1986, for a review). In contrast, face production is traditionally based more on the recall of information: the description and selection of individual features. While we are excellent at recognising a familiar face, and quite good at recognising an unfamiliar one, we are generally poor at describing individual features and selecting facial parts (for arecent review, see Frowd, Bruce, & Hancock, [2008]).

---

[24] Frowd et al. (2005) presented what they referred to as being a forensically valid comparison of facial composite systems. Brace [sic], Pike, Kemp, Tyrner, and Bennet (2006) discussed whether the presentation of multiple facial composites improves suspect identification. Bruce [sic], Hancock, Newman, and Rarity (2002) had claimed that combining face composites yields improvements in face likeness. McQuiston-Surret, Topp, and Malpass (2006) discussed the use of facila composite systems in the United States. Frowd, McQuiston-Surret, Anandaciva, Ireland, and Hancock (2007) provided an evaluations of some systems for making facial composites, from the United States. Frowd, McQuiston-Surret, et al. (2007) tried to apply caricature in the attempt to improve the recognition of facial composites. Hasel and Wells (2006) claimed that applying morphing to facial composites helps with identifications, but Wells and Charman (2005) had claimed that building composites can harm lineup identification performance.

8.2.2.3 *FacePrints* for Generating Facial Composites

Caldwell and Johnston (1991) describe how a tool, *FacePrints*, based on an interactive genetic algorithm (GA) has been useful in assisting a witness to build a facial composite of a criminal suspect. That genetic algorithm[25] "can rapidly search a 'face-space' containing over 34 billion possible facial composites" (ibid., p. 416). An important feature of *FacePrints* is that it "relies on recognition rather than recall" (Johnston & Caldwell, 1997). *FacePrints* "begins by generating a set of thirty random binary number strings (genotypes) and developing these into composite faces (phenotypes)" (ibid.), where the binary string expresses a sequential set of coordinates in six position axes, corresponding to the shape and position of facial features. The witness views, one at a time, the thirty composites of the "first generation" of the algorithm, "and rates each face on a ten point scale according to its resemblance to the culprit" (ibid.); "the witness may not be aware of why any perceived resemblance exists" (ibid.). Then "the genotype of the fittest face and a second genotype, chosen in proportion to fitness from the remaining twenty-nine faces, are paired for breeding" (ibid.). In personal communication with the present author (13 December 1996), Victor S. Johnston remarked about the advantages of his approach: "The advantages of the GA are: 1. based on recognition rather than recall, 2. no interview required that could bias witness, 3. no exposure to mug shots. It is difficult to see how any bias could be introduced into a procedure that is driven only by the witness' recognition ability".[26]

8.2.2.4 The CRIME-VUs and EvoFIT Projects

Innovative tools for suspect recognition from facial composites include EvoFit (Frowd, Hancock, & Carson, 2004, 2010a)[27] and EFIT-V (Gibson, Solomon, Maylin, & Clark, 2009). In the United States, the leading tool is FACES. In South Africa, the ID software was developed (Tredoux, Nunez, Oxtoby, & Prag, 2006). "The basic operation of these 'recognition-based' systems is similar. They present users with a range of complete faces to select. The selected faces are then 'bred' together, to combine characteristics, and produce more faces for selection. When repeated a few times, the systems converge on a specific identity and a composite is 'evolved' using a procedure that is fairly easy to do: the selection of complete faces" (Frowd et al., 2010a). But (ibid.):

> One problem with the evolutionary systems is the complexity of the search space. They contain a set of face models, each capable of generating plausible but different looking faces. The models, which are described in detail in Frowd et al. (2004), capture two aspects of

---

[25] Genetic algorithms are the subject of Section 6.1.16.1 in this book.

[26] For the application of genetic algorithms to evolving facial images, also see Hancock (2000), Hancock and Frowd (2001).

[27] The EvoFIT website is at http://www.evofit.co.uk/ Charlie Frowd's website is at this other address: http://www.uclan.ac.uk/psychology/research/people/Frowd.html

human faces: *shape* information, the outline of features and head shape, and pixel intensity or *texture*, the greyscale colouring of the individual features and overall skin tone. The number of faces that can be generated from these models is huge, as is the search space. The goal then is to converge on an appropriate region of space before a user is fatigued by being presented with too many faces.

At the Face Perception Group (Faces Lab) at the Department of Psychology of the University of Stirling, in Scotland, the combination of facial composites, as well as sketches, and the effects of morphing between facial composites of the same depicted person, are studied in relation to effectiveness for recognition, in the framework of the CRIME-VUs project (Combined Recall Images from Multiple Experts and Viewpoints). The project, which was a predecessor of the EvoFIT project and produced an early version of the tool EvoFIT, had the aim of "examin[ining] the effectiveness of developing methods to construct and view composite images in 3D, and explor[ing] whether combining judgements from different witnesses could result in better composites" (Bruce & Hancock, 2002).

In CRIME-VUs, multiple techniques were resorted to, in forensically friendly format, and combining information from witnesses in different ways. One image processing technique used is morphing, for blending images into each other or to various degrees. Apparently the morph (of four composites) performs better than the best (and the worst) composite.

Hancock, Bruce, and Burton (1998) compared computer systems for face recognition with human perceptions of faces. Different image formats are compared, as to their impact on human and automatic face recognition, in Burton, Miller, Bruce, Hancock, and Henderson (2001). Bruce et al. (1999) were concerned with recognising persons from images captured on video. Importantly, in face recognition by humans, the recognition of unfamiliar faces (Hancock, Bruce, & Burton, 2000) is distinct from familiar face recognition (Burton, Bruce, & Hancock, 1999).

At the University of Central Lancashire (in Preston, northwest England) and the University of Stirling (in Scotland), Charlie Frowd and collaborators (Vicki Bruce, Peter Hancock, and Leslie Bowie, and others) has developed a novel "facial composite system", called *EvoFIT.* "Face construction by selecting individual facial features rarely produces recognisable images", whereas EvoFIT works by the repeated selection and breeding of complete faces" (Frowd et al., 2010a). EvoFIT is based on a holistic face coding scheme and an evolutionary interface[28]:

> Using this system, witness choose from a selection of faces that bear a resemblance to an assailant (a composite is 'evolved' over time by breading together the selected faces). In recent experiments, EvoFIT has outperformed other current composite systems (in the most recent realistic study, EvoFIT reached a level of naming roughly twice that of another UK composite system [...]). [...] EvoFIT has also been used in a criminal investigation, Operation Mallard (Northants). [...] (note that this system has the additional advantage that a verbal description is NOT required).

---

[28] The quotation is from http://www.psychology.stir.ac.uk/staff/cfrowd/index.php ABM is the industrial partner for EvoFIT; they also produce PRO-fit, one of the two facial composite systems used in the UK (the other one is E-FIT).

EvoFIT is now available for police and research use. It also has a construction 'wizard', rather like a wizard use to install software on a computer, and allows a composite to be constructed by a novice user. Please see www.evofit.co.uk

When a witness (or in general, a user) has to use EvoFIT, EvoFIT "presents users with screens of 18 such faces. Users select from screens of face shape, facial textures and then combinations thereof before the selected faces are bred together using a Genetic Algorithm,[29] to produce more faces for selection. This process is normally repeated twice more to allow a composite to be 'evolved'" (Frowd et al., 2010a).

Concerning a field trial of EvoFIT in 2007 with the Lancashire constabulary, developers claim[30]:

Given that it is not essential for a witness or victim to describe a face in detail to use EvoFIT, which was a limitation with previous composite systems, the number of potential crimes that can benefit from this technology is very large. To date, about 20 police personnel have been trained, and there has been great success in a range of crimes in Lancashire from theft to burglary to indecent assault [. . .]. Lancashire police are delighted with the effectiveness of the system. They are also using the new caricature animation format to present their EvoFITs of wanted persons to the public, a procedure that has been shown to substantially improve recognition rates.

Frowd et al. (2010a) "explored two techniques. The first blurred the external parts of the face, to help users focus on the important central facial region. The second, manipulated an evolved face using psychologically-useful 'holistic' scales: age, masculinity, honesty, etc. [. . .] Performance was best using both techniques". Frowd et al. (2010a) shows that the latest techniques, *external feature blurring* and *holistic tools*, enable a composite to be created from a two day-old memory of a face with fairly-good correct naming rates, 25%. This is compared to 5% from a traditional feature system under the same conditions. Charlie Frowd kindly provided for publication in this book, in August 2010, a screenshot of the first generation of faces from which the genetic algorithm of EvoFIT starts, as well as a screenshot showing the blur. Refer to Figs. 8.2.2.4.1 and 8.2.2.4.2.

Also, by the summer of 2010, Frowd's team had just finished developing a new interview for EvoFIT. It is called the *Holistic-CI*, and promotes an even better quality composite – a correct naming rate of 40%, which is clearly quite remarkable. The experiment for this is described in Frowd et al. (2010b). Frowd et al. (2010b) explain:

Facial composites are normally recovered from a witness's memory after a cognitive interview (CI). Here, we investigated the effect of different types of interview on composites produced from a newer evolving system, EvoFIT, which is based on the selection and breeding from arrays of complete faces. The holistic-cognitive interview (H-CI) promoted better likenesses and much more identifiable images than composites produced after the CI. Composites from both the hair-recall interview (HairI) and the holistic interview (HI) were identified similarly, and worse than composites from the CI.

---

[29] Genetic algorithms are the subject of Section 6.1.16.1 in this book.

[30] At http://www.evofit.co.uk/ (accessed in 2010).

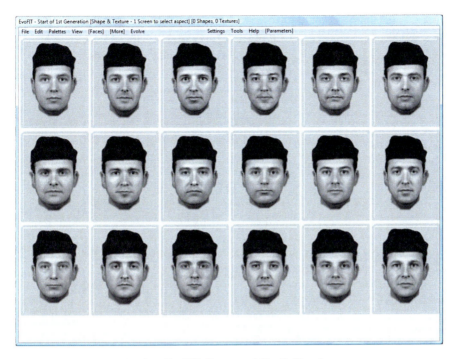

Fig. 8.2.2.4.1 A screenshot from EvoFIT. Courtesy of Charlie Frowd

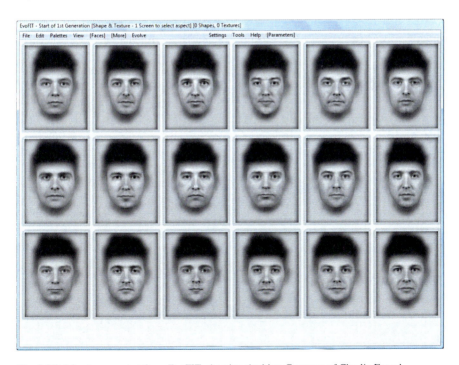

Fig. 8.2.2.4.2 A screenshot from EvoFIT, showing the blur. Courtesy of Charlie Frowd

Frowd explained (pers. comm., 19 August 2010) the relation between the CRIME-VUs and EvoFIT projects: "The CRIME-VUs project developed EvoFIT to a level where people could name the images at about 12% under the long delay. This gave us the evidence to take to the EPSRC government funding body to develop the blurring and the holistic tools, to essentially make it work as well as it does today".

8.2.3 Age-Progression Software and Post-Surgery Face Recognition

There is a different kind of application of computer graphics for face processing, that is in use in various contexts as explained below. It is *age-progression software*. Based on a facial image, this kind of software predicts how the particular person would age, or would have aged, for some parameter of assumed wear. To the police, age-progression software is potentially useful for the purposes of getting a better idea of how a given person would look, when trying to locate missing persons.

Aprilage Development Inc.[31] in Toronto produces the APRIL Age Progression Software is the only statistically based age progression software. This software generates a stream of aged images of faces from a standard digital photograph. The wrinkling/aging algorithms are based upon two sources: (a) published data regarding facial changes associated with aging; (b) research of several thousand people of all ages, ethnicities and lifestyle habits, even though the widening of the range of racial backgrounds was gradual, by segmenting additional populations: Version 2.4 (released in 2007) also included South Asian facial aging, and a Hispanic/Latino component was scheduled to be released soon afterwards. That same version also includes a 3D Component, which allows the user to work with an image of a face in various positions, in three dimensions. Version 2.4 reportedly enabled more flexibility with starting age: that version can age a child as young as 6, or an adult as old as seventy-two years of age. The same version also included a new flipbook feature, intended to improve the workflow for repetitive tasks.

Moreover, adjustment of the output images is possible, in order to take into account whether a person will age as a smoker versus a non-smoker (Smoking Simulation Software), if he or she adds excessive weight or experiences a high degree of unprotected sun exposure. APRIL ages an individual's face from adolescent to adulthood both as a non-smoker and as a pack-a-day consumer. It graphically predicts the premature wrinkling and unhealthy skin tone caused by cigarettes. The APRIL software was originally developed for use in science exhibits at Science Museums. Another context of use is as a health education tool, warning against smoking, obesity, and sun exposure (the latter possibly resulting in skin cancer: the

---

[31] http://www.aprilage.com "Founded in 1998, Aprilage Development Inc. has developed APRIL® Age Progression Software in association with the Ontario Science Centre and with the support of the National Research Council of Canada. The software is used in more than a dozen countries for health and science education, entertainment and product marketing."

software graphically predicts the premature wrinkling in the face by the effects of UV exposure). And indeed, the Roswell Park Cancer Institute in Buffalo, NY, was instrumental in helping develop the first version of APRIL.

Additional applications were envisaged, to assist in finding lost and missing children, and to help to identify criminals. In fact, APRIL can be used to help predict what an individual would look like after many years. For example, the tool could show how a pre-teen child who went missing may look as a teenager. APRIL was reportedly being used alongside a facial recognition software, for such applications to law enforcement and security. An application in a medical setting is that the software can be used in hospitals or in doctors' offices to illustrate how aging affects various medical, cosmetic, or surgical procedures. Reportedly, the tool was also being used at academic courses in gerontology.

Figures 8.2.3.1, 8.2.3.2, 8.2.3.3 and 8.2.3.4 were kindly supplied by Deirdre Hogan, Director of Sales at Aprilage, with permission to reproduce them here. These are pairs of images, the one on the left side in each pair being the photograph of a child or young adult, and the one on the right side in the same pair being a prediction of how that same individual would look as an adult or in old age. Respectively,

1. Figure 8.2.3.1 is file "gray_hair_example_Aprilage.jpg" from Aprilage, and shows normal aging of a white male young adult, the image on the right side showing him with grey hair, at age 72. The grey hair was obtained by applying the grey hair function.
2. Figure 8.2.3.2 is Aprilage's file "smoker-1-hi-res 45.JPG" and shows a girl, and how she would look aged 45, by assuming she smokes. The smoking factor was applied.

Fig. 8.2.3.1 Normal aging of a white male young adult (*left*), to age 72 (*right*). The grey hair was obtained by applying the grey hair function. Compliments of Aprilage Progression software (www. aprilage.com/www.age-me.com)

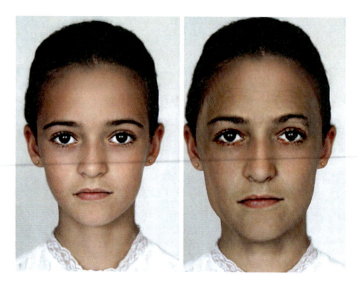

Fig. 8.2.3.2 A girl (*left*), and how she would look aged 45, by assuming she smokes. The smoking factor was applied. Compliments of Aprilage Progression software (www.aprilage.com/www.age-me.com)

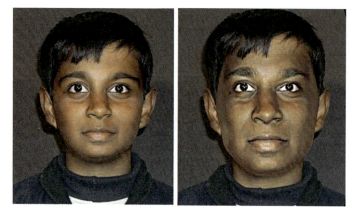

Fig. 8.2.3.3 A boy (*left*) of South Asian background, with a projection reflecting normal aging of the same person (*right*), the way he would look aged 60. The image of this person as an old man did not have the grey hair function applied. Compliments of Aprilage Progression software (www. aprilage.com/www.age-me.com)

3. Figure 8.2.3.3 is Aprilage's file "male SA org 2.5_3.jpg" and shows a boy of South Asian background, with a projection reflecting normal aging of the same person, the way he would look aged 60. The image of this person as an old man did not have the grey hair function applied.
4. Figure 8.2.3.4 is Aprilage's file "male Lat org 2.5._2.jpg" and shows a young male of Latino background, and how he would look with normal aging at age 70. The image as an old man did not have the grey hair function applied.

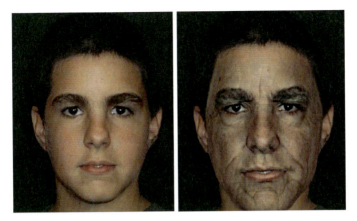

Fig. 8.2.3.4 A young male (*left*), and how he would look with normal aging at age 70 (*right*). The image as an old man did not have the grey hair function applied. Compliments of Aprilage Progression software (www.aprilage.com/www.age-me.com)

8.2.4 Facial Expression Recognition

Lisetti and Schiano (2000) reported about an automated facial expression recognizer they were developing. Moreover, they

> present some of the relevant findings on facial expressions from cognitive science and psychology that can be understood by and be useful to researchers in Human-Computer Interaction and Artificial Intelligence. We then give an overview of HCI applications involving automated facial expression recognition, we survey some of the latest progresses in this area reached by various approaches in computer vision (ibid., from the abstract).

They went on to "propose an architecture for a multimodal intelligent interface capable of recognizing and adapting to computer users' affective states" (ibid.). Their article is part of a multidisciplinary special issue of *Pragmatics & Cognition* on facial information processing in human cognition (Dror & Stevenage, 2000); see there, e.g., Anna Wierzbicka's (2000) "The semantics of human facial expressions".

8.2.5 Digital Image Forensics

Digital image forensics consists of computational methods of detection of image tampering. Such tampering is also done by computer (*digital forgeries*). Images typically portray people, and tools from image forensics work on models in three dimensions of the bodies that appear in the picture. Distinguish between computer models of the reasoning of and about deception, and computer techniques intended to enable the detection of forgeries, within forensic science. This is the case of a technique that maps inconsistencies in lighting in doctored, composite photographs, by associating a sphere with its own index of lighting with different regions of the photograph (Johnson & Farid, 2007a).[32]

The need for such technology was made acute by the spread and level of sophistication of digital imaging technology that can be used for manipulating digital images, including the production of photo hoaxes[33] or maliciously doctored photographs. Johnson & Farid remarked (2007a, p. 250):

> The field of digital forensics has emerged over the past few years to combat this growing problem. Several techniques have been developed to detect various forms of digital tampering. Statistical techniques have been developed for detecting cloning [(Fridrich et al., 2003; Popescu & Farid, 2004)]; splicing [(Ng & Chang, 2004)]; re-sampling artifacts [(Popescu & Farid, 2005a; Avcıbaş et al., 2004)]; color filter array aberration [(Popescu & Farid, 2005a)]; and disturbances of a camera's sensor noise pattern [(Lukáš et al., 2006)]. Optical techniques have been developed to detect chromatic aberrations [(Johnson & Farid, 2006a)], and geometric techniques for rectifying perspectively distorted planar surfaces [(Johnson & Farid, 2006b)]. More recently two related approaches have been developed for detecting inconsistencies in lighting [(Johnson & Farid, 2005, 2007b)]. Building specifically on this work, and more broadly on all of these forensic tools, we describe a new lighting-based digital forensic technique.

Johnson's dissertation (2007, p. 54) explains:

> Lighting environments can be captured by a variety of methods, such as photographing a mirror sphere [(Debevec, 1998)], or through panoramic photography techniques. These methods produce high dynamic range images, known as light probe images, that represent the lighting environment function $L(V)$. The spherical harmonic coefficients are computed by integrating the lighting environment function $L(V)$ against the corresponding spherical harmonic basis function [(Ramamoorthi & Hanrahan, 2001)]:

$$ l_{n,m} = \int_{\Omega} L(\vec{V}) Y_{n,m}(\vec{V}) \, d\Omega $$

---

[32] A popularistic introduction to this branch of image processing was provided by Hany Farid (2008), whereas Popescu and Farid (2005b) is a technical journal article, and Micah Kimo Johnson's dissertation (2007) is available online. Farid's team is at Dartmouth College.

[33] Johnson and Farid (2007a, figure 1) gave a poignant example, by showing a fake cover of a celebrity magazine. The original *Star* magazine cover showed actress Katie Holmes on the right side, with her left hand on the left shoulder of actor Tom Cruise. The cover headline claimed: "TOM & KATIE Are They Faking It?". The fake cover, instead, showed the paper's first author, Kimo Johnson, in place of Tom Cruise, and the pre-headline read "KIMO & KATIE". One could tell it was fake, however, because there was a shadow on the right side of Kimo's face, whereas there was mcuh light in the environment (as could be seen from Holmes' own face, and also from Cruise's face in the original). In Johnson (2007, p. 26), figure 3.1 shows a "photograph of the *American Idol* host and judges" which "is a digital composite of multiple photographs. The inconsistencies in the shape and location of the specular highlight on the eyes suggest that these people were originally photographed under different lighting conditions." Enlarged details show the eyes of the various persons in that photograph.

Johnson's dissertation (2007, pp. 54–55) shows several light probe images,[34] each on a sphere, and captured at places like inside Grace Cathedral in San Francisco, Galileo's Tomb and the Uffizi Gallery in Florence, and so forth. From each such light probe image, lighting environment coefficients were computed. Next, these lighting environment coefficients were each used to render a Lambertian sphere, characterising the respective lighting environment. Being *Lambertian* means that is reflects light isotropically (ibid., p. 7).[35] Johnson (ibid., p. 47, figure 4.4) showed how lighting environments could be rendered on spheres, by displaying the first three orders of spherical harmonics as functions on the sphere: from top to bottom, that figure showed the order zero spherical harmonic, $Y_{0,0}(\cdot)$; the three order one spherical harmonics, $Y_{1,m}(\cdot)$; and the five order two spherical harmonics, $Y_{2,m}(\cdot)$. "Irradiance describes the total amount of light reaching a point on a surface. For a Lambertian surface, the reflected light, or radiosity, is proportional to the irradiance by a reflectance term ρ. In addition, Lambertian surfaces emit light uniformly in all directions, so the amount of light received by a viewer (i.e., camera) is independent of the view direction. A camera maps its received light to intensity through a camera response function" (ibid., p. 48). Moreover, "the change in the intensity profile due to an increased exposure time t_2 can be modeled by a linear change to the profile of exposure time t_1" (ibid., p. 49). The relationship between image irradiance and intensity is expressed by a formula that can itself be rewritten in terms of spherical harmonics. Lighting environments can be estimated (ibid., section 4.1.3) and compared (ibid., section 4.1.4).

By introducing results, Johnson explained (2007, p. 54, section 4.2):

> We tested our technique for estimating lighting environment coefficients on synthetically generated images and real images of natural lighting environments. The synthetic images were rendered using the pbrt environment [(Pharr & Humphreys, 2004)] with data from a gallery of light probe images maintained by Paul Debevec [(1998)]. The natural images were obtained in two different ways. For the first set, we photographed a known target in a variety of lighting conditions. For the second set, we downloaded twenty images from Flickr, a popular image sharing website [[36]]. Results from four visually plausible forgeries are also presented. For all images, the lighting environment coefficients were estimated from the green channel of the image. Although all three color channels could be analyzed, we find that this is often unnecessary since the estimation is invariant to both multiplicative and additive terms.

---

[34] Light probe images by Paul Debevec, available at http://www.debevec.org/Probes.

[35] "The standard approaches for estimating light direction begin by making some simplifying assumptions about the surface of interest: (1) it is Lambertian (i.e., it reflects light isotropically); (2) it has a constant reflectance value; (3) it is illuminated by a point light source infinitely far away; and (4) the angle between the surface normal and the light direction is in the range $0°$–$90°$" (Johnson, 2007, p. 7).

[36] Flickr home page, at http://www.flickr.com.

In the discussion section in Johnson and Farid (2007a, section IV),[37] they pointed out the following, which is relevant to doctored images that show side by side persons who were originally not photographed together:

> When creating a composite of two of more people, it is often difficult to exactly match the lighting, even if the lighting seems perceptually consistent. The reason for this is that complex lighting environments (multiple light sources, diffuse lighting, directional lighting) give rise to complex and subtle lighting gradients and shading effects in the image. Under certain simplifying assumptions (distant light sources and diffuse surfaces), arbitrary lighting environments can be modeled with a 9-dimensional model. The model approximates the lighting with a linear combination of spherical harmonics. We have shown how to apporximate a simplified 5-dimensional version of this model from a single image, and how to stabilize the model estimation in the presence of noise. Inconsistencies in the lighting model across an image are then used as evidence of tampering.
>
> We showed the efficacy of this approach on a broad range of simulated images, photographic images, and visually plausible forgeries. In each case, the model parameters can be well approximated, from which differences in lighting can typically be detected. There are, however, instances when different lighting environments give rise to similar model coefficient – in these cases the lighting differences are indistinguishable.

In conclusion: "While any forensic tool is vulnerable to counter-measures, the precise matching of lighting in an image can be difficult, although certainly not impossible" (ibid.). The analysis of three forgeries (ibid., figure 12) associate differnetly shaded spheres characterising different lighting environments to different elements in the composite. For example, in one doctored photograph, ducks standing on the ground were added very close to players at a match. The shading effect on the spheres associated with two of the ducks are identical, but different from the shading effect on the spheres associated with two of the players. In another photograph, three men are standing side by side. The first one to the left is a football coach wearing sunglasses, a red shirt and white trousers. The other two men are soldiers holding rifles and wearing camouflage. The two spheres associated with the two soldiers have an identical shading effect, but the latter is different from that of the sphere associated with the football coach. Another photograph (ibid., figure 12) "is a forgery where the head of rapper Snoop Dogg has been placed on the body of an orchestra conductor" (with crossed arms, besuited, and with a white papillon; but the skin of a hand is that of a black person, like the face). Spheres rendered from the estimated lighting coefficients are associated with the head and the trunk, and the shading effect on the two spheres is different.

8.2.6 Facial Reconstruction from Skeletal Remains

Forensic *facial reconstruction* is the reproduction of an individual human's face from skeletal remains. To say it with Aulsebrook, Iscan, Slabbert, and Becker (1995): "Forensic facial reconstruction is the reproduction of the lost or unknown

---

[37] Understandably, Johnson and Farid's article (2007a) shares very much with the doctoral dissertation (Johnson, 2007).

facial features of an individual, for the purposes of recognition and identification. It is generally accepted that facial reconstruction can be divided into four categories: (1) replacing and repositioning damaged or distorted soft tissues onto a skull; (2) the use of photographic transparencies and drawings in an identikit-type system; (3) the technique of graphic, photographic or video superimposition; (4) plastic or three-dimensional reconstruction of a face over a skull, using modelling display".

Whereas Aulsebrook et al. (1995) is a review of "work done on both superimposition and plastic reconstruction", nevertheless "the authors believe that only the latter category can correctly be termed facial reconstruction". Computer-graphic techniques fit in categories (2), (3), and (4).

Caroline Wilkinson (2004) presents the Manchester method of forensic facial reconstruction. She also discusses how to reconstruct the faces of children. Her book collates all published facial tissue data, and describes tissue variations with reference to age, sex, stature and ethnic origin, for use by practitioners. Wilkinson also evaluates the accuracy of current methods.

There are factors which militate in favour of one candidate reconstruction rather than another one. In one case from England, in which a man's body was found at a stage of decomposition in which it looked like a lump of fat, two facial reconstructions were developed, one with a European likeness, and the other one with a Near Eastern likeness, whose appropriateness was suggested by the fact that on the teeth of the skull there were traces of *kat*, a recreational drug in common use in Yemen (and by some in Saudi Arabia). Eventually it was discovered that the man was a Yemeni-born grandfather who had been murdered by his own son.

In another case, a large set had been developed of possible face reconstructions for the body of a young woman, and when she was eventually identified, and it was possible to verify the accuracy of the reconstructions from photographs, it turned out that none of those reconstructions looked anywhere close to how she actually looked like when alive.

Not always facial reconstruction is for forensic purposes. A professor in Sheffield who reconstructed the face of ancient Egypt's Queen Nefertiti, related, at a workshop in Edinburgh in the summer of 2004, how after a television broadcast on that project of his, a lady phoned to inform him that he got it wrong. He conceded to her that there may be errors, but then she claimed: "**I** am Nefertiti". She promised she would send him evidence in support. John Prag and Richard Neave (1997) are concerned with reconstructing the facial appearance of ancient people; one of these is the famous King Midas, and another one is Philip II, the powerful father of Alexander the Great. The portrait of Philip II from coins provided cues for reconstruction. Another category also treated in the same book is ancient human remains retrieved from bogs. Prag and Neave's book caters to a broad audience, yet includes moderately technical detail. An early example is a sculpture of the head of Tamerlane (see Fig. 8.2.6.1): a "[p]ortrait head of Timur [was] made by the Soviet scholar M. M. Gerasimov. This sculpture is very accurate as it is based upon the skull found in Timur's grave. By closely studying such skulls and then working out the exact position of muscles, eyes, skin, hair and so on, Gerasimov pioneered the

Fig. 8.2.6.1 The portrait
head of Timur (i.e.,
Tamerlane), as reconstructed
by Mikhail Gerasimov

reconstruction of the portrait heads of long dead people" (Nicolle, 1990, p. 144, in a caption to a photograph).

Archaeologist and anthropologist Mikhail Mikhaylovich Gerasimov (1907–1970) "developed the first technique of forensic sculpture based on findings of anthropology, archaeology, paleontology, and forensic science. He studied the skulls and meticulously reconstructed the faces of more than 200 people, including Yaroslav the Wise, Ivan the Terrible, Friedrich Schiller and, most famously, Tamerlane" ([Gerasimov] 2007). Gerasimov's early work, from 1927 on, was on skulls of prehistoric or exotic humans. "It took a decade of studies and experiments to come close to individual portrait resolution quality of historical persons", yet "his first public work of this type is dated 1930", this being the "face of Maria Dostoyevskaya, mother of Fyodor Dostoyevsky" (ibid.). He worked on the skulls of Yaroslav the Wise in 1938, and of Tamerlane in 1941. "In 1953 the Soviet Ministry of culture decided to open the tomb of Ivan the Terrible and Gerasimov reconstructed his face" (ibid.). See Eve Conant's article (2003), and Mikhail Gerasimov's own *The Face Finder* (Gerasimov, 1971), originally of 1968. The earliest version of his memoirs appeared in Russian in 1949.

Facial reconstruction, as mainly developed for forensic purposes, when applied in an archaeological context has enabled even glaring departure with respect to ancient portraits (conditioned by cultural conventions) to be ascertained. Olga Wojtas (1996) reported that "[f]orensic techniques used by the police to establish the identity of unknown bodies have revealed what sixteenth-century Scottish humanist, classicist, historian and poet George Buchanan looked like. [...] Most of the portraits of the time pay tribute to his brain power by depicting a man with an enormous forehead, a literal "highbrow". But Buchanan's skull [...] is relatively small, with an average-sized forehead". Anatomist Matthew Kaufman "decided to find out whether any of the portraits were accurate", and then, having had the face reconstructed from a plaster cast, "was staggered" as "it turned out to be almost identical to a portrait of Buchanan now hanging in the Royal Society in London" and which, significantly, "avoids the convention of linking exceptional intellect to a large forehead". The newspaper report concludes with the interviewee remarking that head size as an indicator of intellect is a widespread belief. Nevertheless, a distinction is to be made between beliefs and pictorial or other culture-bound representational conventions.

It must be noted that whereas, when discussing forensic archaeology, we mentioned that there is a perception that this discipline is ahead in the application of scientific techniques to forensics for some applications, this is not the case of face reconstruction. An expert in forensic face reconstruction was skeptical, during her lecture at a workwhop in Edinburgh, of forensic archaeology precisely inasmuch face reconstruction is involved. In fact, in forensic face reconstruction, once human remains are identified and photographs of the dead person are obtained, it happens sometimes that face reconstructions that had been developed are found to be wide of the mark, and in some real case it can be seen that alternative reconstructions that had been proposed, could be seen to be quite different even before the identification was made. (It basically depends on the methods, and on assumptions.)

By contrast, no such validation is possible, when the face of a person from antiquity is reconstructed. In turn, this is different from peat bodies, which may be well conserved even after a millennium, and what one sees is a blackened face that is not a reconstruction; such is the case of the body of a garrotted man who was found in Denmark. His face, short facial hair, and hat are well preserved, but the mangling of his neck is an effect of his execution, before his body was thrown into the bog.

8.2.7   Considerations about Socio-Cultural Factors in Portraiture That Have Been Analysed with Episodic Formulae

In Section 5.3, we have been concerned with the representation of narratives by means of *episodic formulae*. One of the models that adopt that approach it TIMUR

(Nissan, 2008b). In Section 5.3.1, among the other things I explained that the analysis in TIMUR is of

> a perhaps apocryphal anecdote about the emperor Tamerlane. He invited three painters in turn, and commissioned from each, his own portrait. The first painter painted the king as a very handsome man, and Tamerlane had him beheaded, to punish him for his excessive flattery. The second painter represented the king realistically, if one means by that: warts and all. Tamerlane had him beheaded, as he found it intolerably offensive to see himself represented with hideous features. The third painter portrayed the king in the act of shooting an arrow, and did so "realistically", yet without revealing the physical defects, because the posture was such that these would not be apparent. How did the third painter portrait Tamerlane? In fact, in order to shoot the arrow from his bow, Tamerlane was kneeling down, so one would not notice that one leg was shorter. To aim, Tamerlane shut an eye, so one could not tell out the squint which affected his eyes (because you need to see both of them open, to tell out). This way, the life of the third painter was saved.

I also pointed out that this story of Tamerlane and the three painters involves fairly complex epistemic structures of belief and intentionality, and these are involved in the characters' reasoning about the human body of one of them, and about the depiction of that body in a portrait (i.e., in a given kind of representation). There are factors involving *ontologies:* Tamerlane shares with the three painters their all's being instances of kind 'human being', but, Tamerlane doesn't possess the specific skills associated with kind 'painter'. At any rate, he contracts out to painters the task of painting his portrait. The painters are utterly at his mercy, because his authority is absolute. Tamerlane, being an instance of kind 'absolute ruler', of which there only is (at most) one in a given polity, possesses a very high degree of authority on all other agents within the polity, and they in turn not only do not possess authority on him (except his doctor, if he considers him authoritative and follows his advice), but also hardly can resist his orders. Therefore, it is extremely dangerous for them to provoke his susceptibility, which is both affected by emotion, and is rational at the same time. He does not need to be concerned about the same in the reverse relation (unless he does so to so many and to such a degree, that the polity would rebel as well as his own otherwise obedient army).

Now refer to Fig. 8.2.7.1. This is figure 4 from Nissan (2008b, p. 574). The diagram shows an agent's mind, action, and structure, in relation to norms and to the potrait which in turn represents one of the agents, namely, Tamerlane. In section 3.6 of Nissan (2008b), 'Intentions and Effects of Portraying the Ruler' (ibid., pp. 546–555), I discussed eight examples from different cultures and historical periods, of cultural factors and effects associated with the portrait of a person in power. In section 3.15 in Nissan (2008b), 'Tamerlane Reading the Mind of Painter1' (ibid., pp. 564–565), episodic formulae express how Tamerlane may have reasoned about the first painter's own reasoning when choosing to paint him in the manner he did. The value of this kind of analysis is that is provides a formal means for representing reasoning about an individual's portrait, and also the fact that there is a difference between a portrait and an image unaffected by cultural factors. Even a photograph, for example a mug shot, carries an important luggage of cultural traditional conventions.

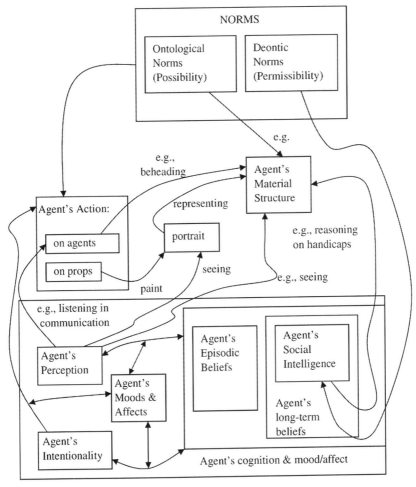

Fig. 8.2.7.1   An agent's mind, action, and structure, in relation to norms and to the portrait which in turn represents one of the agents. This is relevant for making sense of the story of Tamerlane and the three painters who, in turn, endanger themselves by painting his portrait

8.3 The Burgeoning Forensic Disciplines of Expert Opinion

8.3.1 General Considerations, and Some of the Specialties

Franke and Srihari (2008) provided an overview of *computational forensics*, at the very beginning of the proceedings of an international workshop about that domain. By *computational forensics*, what is meant is computer techniques for any discipline within forensic science.[38] Concerning the booming of forensic specialties, Hans Nijboer remarked[39] (2000, p. 3):

> [W]e can observe the fast development of forensic techniques and forensic specialties in the broader sense. Between archaeology or accountancy in its forensic form and the forensic zoology we indeed see over [one] hundred different forensic disciplines, of which some are well-established (like forensic psychiatry) and some have just started in developing 'objective' standards (shoe-print comparison)

– a development among whose critics he is.

> It has become clear that DNA based techniques are in fact not perfect but they are not too weak. But at the same time it was discovered that many techniques and methods lack a sound basis in a broader scientific sense. Very often objective standards and information about the validity and reliability of specific forensic techniques are simply unknown (ibid., p. 7).

Student enrolment is affected by the blooming of the forensic sciences.[40] An exception to the generally declining enrolment in chemistry at U.K. university departments, is the number of students who want to study forensic chemistry. In the present Section 8.3, we are going to raise some points concerning an array of forensic disciplines, combining forensic science, engineering-related issues, and forensic psychology. In the remaining sections of this chapter, we are going to deal with sample areas, each in turn. These areas in which computing or electronics, or sometimes more specifically knowledge-based systems of pattern-matching software, have actually been applied. Or then, they are areas in which there may be some potential for application.

Reliance on expert testimony may be problematic,[41] from the viewpoint of legal evidence theory, in that (in an Anglo-American perspective) there is a risk of tacitly

---

[38] *Computational forensics* is about what computing can do for forensic science. It should not be mistaken for *computer forensics* (itself part of *digital forensics*), i.e., the forensic discipline concerned with illegal actions involving a computer. In a sense, we find here a distinction similar to the one between *computational science* – i.e., *scientific computing:* what computing can do for science – and *computer science*, the science of computing.

[39] Nijboer's (2000) was an overview of current issues in legal evidence. In the tenth anniversary issue of the e-journal *International Commentary on Evidence*, published at Berkeley in California, Nijboer (2008) provided comparative comments on current issues in evidence and procedure from a Continental perspective, as have emerged during the 2000s. He "discusses three dimensions of generality in evidence and procedure: (1) generality of fundamental issues in evidence and fact-finding and insights about them across national borders, (2) generality of issues of criminal evidence across various relevant disciplines (and professions), and (3) generality with respect to specific issues of criminal evidence and its principles and rules addressing the various probanda of specific crimes (murder, theft, rape, arson, negligence causing a serious traffic accident, et cetera)." Nijboer (2008) made frequent references to case law of the European Court of Human Rights (ECHR).

[40] Brenner (2000) is a glossary of forensic science. James and Nordby (2003, 3rd edn. 2009) is an edited volume with overview chapters on various forensic disciplines. In that volume, Zeno Geradts (2005, 2nd edn.; 2009, 3rd edn.) provides an overview of the *use of computers in forensic science*.

[41] There is a literature about expert evidence. For example, Carol Jones (1994) is concerned with expert evidence in Britain.

shifting paradigm from fact-finding by courts because the court has freely formed an opinion (*free proof*), to some form of binding reliance on expert testimony. In itself, reliance on expert witnesses may be problematic, perhaps because they may be misunderstood, but also because, in all frankness, trained judges tend to have a better reputation that both lawyers (whose reviled variant is the "shyster"), and expert witnesses (whose reviled variant is reputed to be the "hired gun", or to no lesser degree the more benign, if unfortunately rather benighted, astrologer-type; at any rate, lawyers during cross-examination typically try to discredit the expert witness of the other side).

If the perspective we are to adopt is historical, it will be important to point out that *free proof* (that has its detractors, among legal theorists in Anglo-American jurisdictions) was an achievement, especially as meant, or in the form it took, in Continental Europe. It replaced the so-called *legal proof* (in Latin *probatio legalis*, in French *preuve legale*, in German *gesezliche Beweistheorie*), and emancipated the judicial evaluation of the evidence from the older law of proof. This also involved the demise of torture as means for obtaining evidence; torture was deemed necessary for obtaining proof as necessary, in turn, to secure conviction, according to the system of legal proof, as opposed to the system of free proof that replaced it. In Continental Europe, free proof replaced rules of *quantum and weight;* these did not use to be part of the English and American judiciary systems.

Another kind of problem is that some important areas of expert testimony, such as forensic psychology or psychiatry, are treated variably, according to the country in which the court is, apart from the diffidence that lawyers are claimed to have of psychologists (see, e.g., Nissan, 2001f). Whatever negative may happen without expert testimony? In a section entitled "Evidence sans Expert", barrister and consultant psychiatrist Mahendra (2007, p. 1490), writing in England, commented on a recent court case:

> That expert evidence plays a crucial role in modern litigation is well accepted. It is required by a court which acknowledges its lack of expertise on the relevant issues on which it requires the assistance of experts. But this does not mean that evidence which would normally be within the province of the expert is not present in the course of a trial even while no expert is present. This evidence may influence the judge and, where present, a jury.
>
> One such area concerns mental disorder which, being commonly found, may then play some part in these deliberations and, yet, may not be subject to expert opinion in these circumstances. As lay individuals are known to hold all manner of views, not all reliable or valid, on psychiatric matters there may be scope for misunderstanding and even injustice. The issue came up in *R v Osbourne* [2007] EWCA Crim 481, [2007] All ER (D) 206 (Mar).

Forensic psychology[42] is not necessarily about the state of mind of a perpetrator, or of a victim. It has important things to say about the reliability of identification from memory. Uncertainty about an identity turns out in a broad array of forms, when

---

[42] See for example a volume, *Forensic Psychology*, edited by Joanna Adler (2010, 2nd edn. [originally of 2004]). In that book, section 1, entitled 'Forensic Psychology in Context', comprises chapter 1, 'Forensic psychology: concepts, debates and practice', by Joanna R. Adler; and chapter 2, 'Public perceptions of crime and punishment', by Jane Wood and G. Tendayi Viki.

it comes to legal matters. Oftentimes, it is about personal identity: the identity of a human individual, possibly a culprit (not just in real life, but in whodunit fiction as well) or one otherwise liable, or, then, a victim. Identification is oftentimes required of witnesses.

The literature on the assessment of witness reliability is very extensive; writing about eyewitness identification would be a book in its own right.[43] In her 2008 course handouts in *Psychology, Law and Eyewitness Testimony* at her website at the University of Aberdeen in Scotland, psychologist Amina Memon has provided useful entry points into the scholarly literature: "Gary Wells (USA) has an excellent website containing numerous articles on eyewitness memory"[44]; "Maryanne Garry (New Zealand) provides access to all her publications on false memories".[45] "Loftus also provides access to her articles on misinformation and false memory as well as some good links".[46] "Paul Ekman makes his papers on deception available on his website".[47] "Gary Well's website [has] lots of good links"[48]; and so forth. Other

---

Section 2, 'Investigation and Prosecution', comprises chapter 3, 'USA and UK responses to miscarriages of justice', by Tom Williamson; chapter 4, 'The interpretation and utilisation of offender profiles: a critical review of 'traditional' approaches to profiling', by Laurence Alison and Emma Barrett. Section 3, 'Testimony and Evidence', comprises chapter 5, 'Eliciting evidence from eyewitnesses in court', by Mark R. Kebbell and Elizabeth L. Gilchrist; and chapter 6, 'The ageing eyewitness', by Amina Memon, Fiona Gabbert and Lorraine Hope. Section 4, 'Correlates of Criminality – sensations and substances', comprises chapter 7, 'The status of sensational interests as indicators of possible risk', by Vincent Egan; chapter 8, 'Drug use and criminal behaviour: indirect, direct or causal relationship?', by Ian P. Albery, Tim McSweeney and Mike Hough; and chapter 9, 'Drug arrest referral schemes and forensic perspectives on the treatment of addiction', by Andrew Guppy, Paul Johnson and Mark Wallace-Bell. Section 5, 'Persistent Offending', comprises chapter 10, 'Life-course persistent offending', by Alex R. Piquero and Terrie E. Moffitt; and chapter 11, 'Stalking, Lorraine Sheridan and Graham Davies'. Section 6, 'Intervention and Prevention', comprises chapter 12, 'Domestic violence: current issues in definitions and interventions with perpetrators in the UK', by Elizabeth L. Gilchrist and Mark Kebbell, chapter 13, 'Effective programmes to prevent delinquency', by Brandon C. Welsh and David P. Farrington; and chapter 14, 'Parenting projects, justice and welfare', by Anthony H. Goodman and Joanna R. Adler. Section 7, 'Punishment and Corrections', comprises chapter 15, 'Women in prison', by Nancy Loucks; and chapter 16, 'Applied psychological services in prisons and probation', by Graham Towl.

[43] For a treatment of the psychology of person identification, see Clifford and Bull (1978). In Bull and Carson (1995), the chapter 'Assessing the Accuracy of Eye-witness Identifications' (Cutler & Penrod, 1995) has long been a useful entry point to the subject. Eyewitness psychology (e.g., Loftus, 1974 sqq, Ross et al., 1994) is but one area of forensic psychology. The *American Journal of Forensic Psychology* was established in the early 1980s; the British *Journal of Forensic Psychiatry & Psychology*, at the end of that same decade.

[44] http://www.psychology.iastate.edu/faculty/gwells/homepage.htm (cf fn. 19in Chapter 4).

[45] http://www.vuw.ac.nz/psyc/staff/maryanne-garry/index.aspx

[46] http://www.seweb.uci.edu/faculty/loftus/

[47] http://www.paulekman.com/downloadablearticles.html

[48] http://www.psychology.iastate.edu/~glwells/

than concerning witnesses, forensic psychology may, e.g., concern the custody of children of divorced parents.[49] And then there is forensic psychiatry.[50]

Cutler and Penrod (1995) are concerned with eyewitness identification of criminals in the United States, and Ross, Read, and Toglia (1994) are likewise concerned with criminal investigations with adult witnesses. In Bull and Carson (1995), Daniel Yarmey's chapter (Yarmey 1995) 'Earwitness and evidence obtained by other senses' is also about the identification of a person, such as a perpetrator. Hammersley and Read (1993), which appeared in a volume on the identification of suspects and its psychology, deals with voice identification by humans and computers.[51]

Henry Lee's Crime Scene Handbook (Lee, Palmbach, & Miller, 2001) is devoted to how to conduct an investigation,[52] starting by protecting and managing a crime scene; the *Handbook* includes a chapter, "Logic Trees", that could justifiably be of interest to such computer scientists who are interested in formalising general reasoning for the purposes of assisting crime analysis. One of the case studies in that volume is on shooting scene reconstructions. For a treatment of science in the criminal investigations, see, e.g., Kaye (1995) and Saferstein (1995); the latter considers forensic ballistics,[53] chemistry, and medicine. Cook et al. (1998)

---

[49] For a U.S. perspective, see Ackerman (1995).

[50] See, e.g., Lonsdorf (1995), Belfrage (1995), Chiswick and Cope (1995), Faulk (1994), Lloyd (1995), Gunn and Taylor (1993). Eigen (1995) considers forensic psychiatry in the context of British history.

[51] Also see Hollien (1990), about voice in forensic contexts.

[52] Kaye's (1995) *Science and the Detective: Selected Reading in Forensic Science* is a useful introduction. Lane, Tingey, and Tingey (1993) is a specialised encyclopaedia, but in a rather popularistic perspective. As to the *Encyclopedia of Forensic Sciences* (Siegel, Knupfer, & Saukko, 2000), its 1440 pages contain more than 200 articles.

[53] Concerning forensic ballistics, http://en.wikipedia.org/wiki/Ballistics states the following: "In the field of forensic science, forensic ballistics is the science of analyzing firearm usage in crimes. It involves analysis of bullets and bullet impacts to determine the type. Rifling, which first made an appearance in the fifteenth century, is the process of making grooves in gun barrels that imparts a spin to the projectile for increased accuracy and range. Bullets fired from rifled weapons acquire a distinct signature of grooves, scratches, and indentations which are somewhat unique to the weapon used. The first firearms evidence identification can be traced back to England in 1835 when the unique markings on a bullet taken from a victim were matched with a bullet mold belonging to the suspect. When confronted with the damning evidence, the suspect confessed to the crime. The first court case involving firearms evidence took place in 1902 when a specific gun was proven to be the murder weapon. The expert in the case, Oliver Wendell Holmes, had read about firearm identification, and had a gunsmith test-fire the alleged murder weapon into a wad of cotton wool. A magnifying glass was used to match the bullet from the victim with the test bullet. Calvin Goddard, physician and ex-army officer, acquired data from all known gun manufacturers in order to develop a comprehensive database. With his partner, Charles Waite, he catalogued the results of test-firings from every type of handgun made by 12 manufacturers. Waite also invented the comparison microscope. With this instrument, two bullets could be laid adjacent to one another for comparative examination. In 1925 Goddard wrote an article for the Army Ordnance titled 'Forensic Ballistics' in which he described the use of the comparison microscope regarding firearms investigations. He is generally credited with the conception of the term 'forensic ballistics', though he later admitted

and Jamieson (2004) are important articles, proposing rational approaches to crime scene investigation. Dixon (1999) discusses police investigative procedures.

In situations which involve forensic scientists, sometimes human remains[54] are only an incomplete skeleton. Consider the problem of determining whether the person was a man or a woman. "The estimation of sex from skeletal remains is often difficult because of the great overlap of the ranges of the measurements between both sexes in general", in the words of Riepert, Drechsler, Schild, Nafe, and Mattern (1996, p. 140), a study whose "data from a large sample [being radiographs of the ankle] provide an objective basis for sex identification. The single measurement of the calcaneus length allows an estimation of sex with nearly 80% accuracy" (ibid.).

Sometimes, it is the identity of an object or other asset that is of interest; this, in turn, is amenable to the detection of the values of some attributes of the object, such as the owner, or geographic origin. To clarify the difference between (i) personal identification, (ii) the identification of attributes of a human individual other than one's unique identity as partly captured by one's full name, and (iii) the identification of attributes of an object other than ownership, consider such differences within the scope of the practice of one of the forensic disciplines: forensic entomology.[55]

Identifying a corpse is an example of (i), whereas identifying its whereabouts at death or shortly afterwards is an example of (ii). The latter is exemplified in the following quoted passage (Turner, 1987, p. 134), which, next, also illustrates (iii), concerning the geographic area of origin of a consignment of marijuana:

> Human corpses, whether they have been produced naturally or as the result of foul play, are processed by [...] insect decomposers in the same way as any other piece of carrion. Forensic entomology is concerned with interpreting the insect evidence. This involves providing information about the time of death, and possibly changes in the location of the body based on a study of the insects present in the corpse when it is found. A good illustration of this is provided by a Russian case history (Arutyunov, 1963, in Keh, 1984). Living fly larvae found on a partially skeletonized body in a seawater tank were identified as species that are intolerant of salt-water. It was therefore deduced that the body had been dumped in the tank only a short time before it was discovered. The age of the larvae suggested death occurred about 2 weeks prior to the finding of the corpse. These observations were confirmed by the murderer's confession. The victim had been shot 2 weeks previously and then the body had been moved by car and put into the tank the day before it was discovered.
>
> A detailed knowledge of insects, their habits, life histories and delectations have also been useful in solving less macabre forensic problems. In an interesting and well-publicized recent case [(Joyce, 1984)] the New Zealand police intercepted a large consignment of marijuana. When the usual chemical analyses failed to identify the source of the marijuana the consignment was examined for insects. The bodies of sixty insects were recovered and

---

it to be an inadequate name for the science. In 1929 the St. Valentine's Day Massacre led to the opening of the first independent scientific crime detection laboratory in the United States."

[54] Boddington, Garland, and Janaway (1987) and Cox and Mays (2000) are at the interface with forensic osteology within forensic pathology. In Krogman and İşcan (1986), the topic is the human skeleton in forensic medicine.

[55] Forensic entomology is the subject of Catts and Goff (1992), Catts and Haskell (1990), Keh (1984), Stærkeby (2002). An overview of forensic entomology is provided by Gail Anderson (2005, 2nd edn.; 2009, 3rd edn.).

from these entomologists were able to precisely pinpoint the origins of the marijuana to a region 200 km SW of Bangkok, near a stream or lake where fig trees and termites are found. As in the previous case the detailed entomological evidence was of paramount importance in convicting the suspects.

As seen, one of the areas of application of forensic entomology is in the service of *post mortem* analysis. Also related to the latter (within forensic pathology) – though not necessarily so, as there are other applications as well in criminal investigation – are techniques from the forensic analysis of soils and geological evidence: Junger (1996) set "to determine the discriminative qualities of the various procedures to discern at what point soils become indistinguishable from one another" (from the abstract).

> One hundred samples were collected from three different sites; a beach, an island isolated by a river, and a bus parking lot. The samples were analysed using color determination, particle size distribution analysis and mineralogical profiles of the twenty-five most common soil minerals. Of the three hundred samples examined, over one-half could be discriminated by color alone, the remainder needing only particle size distributions analysis for differentiation, negating the need for lengthy mineralogical examinations (ibid.).

Moreover – cost being a factor in decision-making about how to analyse the evidence – these tests required only "very inexpensive equipment", and the calculations were not demanding in terms of either training or cost (ibid.). Cole and Ackland (1994) provide case studies in homicide investigation, in respect of forensic pathology, and in a British context.

In general on legal medicine, see, e.g., Schneider, Nagano, and Geserick (1994). Legal medicine's aims (not confined to perpetrator identification) include, e.g., problems hospitals are faced with, in care for the critically ill newborn. Clements (1994) is on forensic obstetrics, in respect of safety and liability for malpractice in British law. Clark and Crawford (1994) is on the history of legal medicine and of medical jurisprudence. Sometimes, veterinary surgeons act as witnesses (BVA, 1979).

And then, there is (human) forensic odontology, or forensic dentistry (Bowers, 2002; Glass, 2005, 3rd edn. 2009). Whereas the dentist who used to have a person in care may help in identification by means of stored X-ray items, there is, as well, a different kind of application: "Bite marks left on human tissue and bitten material have become an important aspect of scientific evidence used for the conviction or acquittal of a suspect", to say it with the abstract of Nambiar, Bridges, and Brown (1995), where use of a computer program for shape analysis is described.

Forensic chemistry and toxicology,[56] while sometimes resorted to in relation to forensic medicine, have a wider range of applications. In general, note that particular classes of techniques find disparate applications in the forensic sciences. Bob Ardrey (1994) is concerned with mass spectrometry, for such purposes. Or, then, consider chromatographic analysis; Ian Tebbett (1992) is concerned with gas chromatography in forensic science.

---

[56] See Molina's (2009) *Handbook of Forensic Toxicology for Medical Examiners;* as well as, e.g., Pardue (1994), Cone and Deyl (1992).

Ukpabi and Peltron (1995) provide a review of the use of the scanning electron microscope is made in order to identify the cause of fibre damage, for application within "forensic textiles" (*sic*) as being an area of textile studies.[57] Trace evidence analysis is discussed in Deedrick (2001) concerning fabric processing, and in Ballou (2001) on fibre from wigs. Biermann and Grieve (1996) reported about a database of mail order garments and its statistical evaluation, for the forensic purpose of estimating the frequency of fibre types found in clothing. But see in Section 8.3.2.

8.3.2 Statistics Comes into the Picture

At the end of Section 8.3.1, we mentioned textile fibre types and their frequency as found in clothing. Allen and Pardo (2007a, pp. 116–119) offered a critique, in terms of the *reference-class problem* (see Section 2.4 above) of how probability theory was applied to juridical proof concerning carpet fibres in Finkelstein and Levin (2003). The problem, Allen and Pardo claim (2007a, pp. 117–118),

> arises from an ambiguity in the sentence, "Based on manufacturing records, an expert testifies the frequency of such fibers in carpets is less than 1 in 500." What does this mean? Whose records? Which records? Does the statistic refer to those who make a particular kind of carpet, or all U.S. manufacturers, or all manufacturers in the world? Or all carpets ever made in the history of the world to date? And once we know the class to which it applies, why is this the appropriate class in which to place Jones [a suspect, a neighbour of where a crime was perpetrated] and his carpet sample [i.e., carpet fibres taken from Jones's house, and matching an unusual carpet fibre found at the scene]? Is the fiber more or less prevalent in his part of the world, country, state, region, age group, gender, profession, socioeconomic class, and so on? Each of the different classes suggested by these questions would reveal different probabilities and likelihood ratios, but the evidence under consideration has not changed. Indeed, the evidence would likely have widely varying likelihood ratios. The probative value of the evidence cannot be simply the ratio derived from any arbitrarily chosen reference class. [...] A second problem with their conclusions concerns how the fiber evidence connects with other evidence.

In fact, had there been the case that there is (ibid., p. 119)

> conclusive evidence that the crime scene fiber had been planted after the fact to frame Jones would reduce the value of the fiber evidence to zero. Even if we have no evidence about this possibility, how do we know that it was brought from the suspect's home? Even if it was, how do we know that it was from carpeting in his home rather than, say, from having been picked up on the shoes of the actual perpetrator when he was at a party at the home of the person wrongly accused of the crime? These possibilities further show the disjunct between the value of evidence, on one hand, and the likelihood ratio calculated on the basis of a specified reference class, on the other. [... T]here may be no data for other plausible reference classes, which means that the mathematics can be done only by picking these or some variant. [...] Using the data one has does not kake the proffered analysis correct or true in some sense; instead, it is reminiscent of relying on the lamppost more for support than illumination.

---

[57] Those authors themselves were affiliated with the Department of Clothing and Textiles, at the Faculty of Human Ecology of the University of Manitoba in Winnipeg, Canada.

Statistics turns up in a multitude of contexts from forensic science. Actually, application in legal contexts dates back from the early modern period.[58] "Legal applications of probabilistic and statistical reasoning have a long history, having exercised such pioneers as Nicolas Bernoulli, Condorcet, Laplace, Poisson and Cournot (Zabell, 1988). After a period of neglect interest has resurfaced in recent years, and the topic has given rise to many challenging problems" (Mortera & Dawid, 2006).

> Many pioneers of probability and statistics, including the Bernoullis, Condorcet, Laplace, Poisson and Cournot, were motivated by problems of quantification and combination of legal evidence and judgement. But the trail they blazed became disused and overgrown as statisticians lost interest in such questions while legal evidence scholars confined themselves to issues of admissibility, precedent and other such formal rules, paying remarkably little attention to problems of interpretation. Very occasionally some aspect of statistical evidence or argument would break surface – significant legal cases include the 1865 Howland will case and the 1894 Dreyfus case – but it was not until the 1968 Californian case of People v. Collins, in which the prosecution presented a fallacious statistical argument in an attempt to magnify the impact of eye-witness identification evidence, that the issues became subject to serious discussion and argument. This stimulated what became known in the academic legal community as "the new evidence scholarship" [. . .] The probabilities debate remained academic until 1985 when, with the advent of DNA profiling and its numerical "random match probabilities", presentation of, and argument about, statistical evidence of various kinds started to become much more common in the courts (Dawid, 2004b).

Dawid and Mortera (1994) suggest a reason for the delay in the actual emergence of statistics in court: "The infamous trial *People v. Collins* (1975) was one of the first cases where statistical analysis of evidence was made. Unfortunately the analysis was so poor that it set back the introduction of statistical evidence in court for many years" (ibid., p. 2).[59]

A critic of Bayesianism in judiciary contexts, Ron Allen remarked about probability levels (Allen, 2008a, p. 320):

> The equally obvious probabilistic interpretation to give to these numbers is that they are relative frequencies, as propensity and classical accounts are plainly inapposite. That raises an immediate difficulty because virtually never is the data presented at trial in relative frequency formats, and even when it is (DNA evidence, good statistical evidence of disparate treatment), it must be combined with evidence that is not ("The defendant raped me", "I was treated in a way that people with different skin color were not").

Allen (2008a, pp. 320–321) proceeded to claim:

> The solution to this probelm appears equally obvious: subjective Bayesianism. One can translate impressions about evidence into subjective beliefs and then compute posterior probabilities in the light of new evidence. This not only maintains consistency among belief states, but has the added advantage of seeming to approximate what trials seem to be about, which is updating beliefs in the light of new evidence. Yet another advantage of

---

[58] See on this Nissan (2001b), reviewing Rosoni (1995).

[59] In the context of forensic science, see the book on Bayesian networks by Taroni et al. (2006), Aitken (1995), Aitken and Taroni (2004), Robertson and Vignaux (1995). An introduction to statistics for forensic scientists was authored by David Lucy (2005).

this approach is that it provides an answer to other important questions such as the meaning of relevance, prejudice, and probative value. "Relevance" means a likelihood ratio of anything other than 1:1; "prejudice" means that the evidence is likely to affect the rationality of appraising the likelihood ratio, and "probative value" means how far from a 1:1 ration the likelihood ratio is.

And yet: "I believe it is wrong allo the way down, from the most general questions of the basic structure of proof at trial to the most detailed question of the probative value of discrete pieces of evidence" (ibid., p. 321). In the rest of that paper, and in much of his published *oeuvre*, Allen shows why. His arguments are cogent, and cannot be safely ignored. We have given more space to them in other places throughout this book. At any rate, there is a raging controversy between those endorsing probabilisitc accounts of judicial proof, and those opposing that kind of approach. Computing scientists turning to modelling legal evidence can only ignore the controversy at their risk and peril.

Gastwirth and Miao (2009), concerned with race discrimination in employment practices, provided a statistical analysis of the data in disparate impact cases from the United States. They took issue with the specific rationale behind a court ruling, petitioners' brief, and respondent's brief. The petitioners were claiming reverse discrimination at a Fire Department after an examination was cancelled. Baldus and Cole (1980) is a book on statistical proof of discrimination.

David Kaye (1982) was concerned with statistical evidence of unlawful discrimination of various kinds: discrimination in *ad hoc* decision making, discrimination in the application of a rule, discrimination in the formulation of a rule, and discrimination in the operation of a rule. Michael Finkelstein (1980) discussed the judicial reception of multiple regression studies in race and sex discrimination cases. Kaye (1982, pp. 775–776) was especially concerned with

how statistical proof fits into discrimination litigation in two areas in which such evidence commonly is employed. The courts have relied heavily on statistical evidence in cases in which a criminal defendant alleges that he was indicted by an unconstitutionally selected grand jury or an unconstitutionally empanelled petit jury (Finkelstein, 1978, pp. 18–58). In essence, a claim of disparate treatment is presented, and statistical analysis of the pattern of selection is therefore appropriate. There is no constitutionally per-missible basis for systematically excluding, say, members of defendant's race from the population of citizens who are eligible for jury duty. Where direct evidence of dis-crimination is unavailable, statistical methods have been pressed into service.

Writing in 1980, Kaye concluded that, among the other things (1982, p. 782–783):

The courts tend to adopt a fairly realistic attitude to-ward such matters as defining the relevant population, and recent opinions reveal increasing awareness of classical hypothesis testing in evaluating measured differences. However, the process of drawing a conclusion for legal purposes entails an integration of statistical and non-quantitative information, making classical hypothesis testing inapposite to factfinding in litigation. A full-fledged Bayesian analysis of the probability of discrimination is theoretically more satisfying but is too controversial and, in a sense, too powerful to have much chance of becoming judicially accepted and of contributing to accurate decision making by judges or juries. Presenta-tion of the likelihood function avoids the objections to Bayesian inference, but a more mundane calculation of the probability that an observed difference would arise in the absence of dis-crimination might be more easily comprehended by a court. Such a calculation should be the starting point for any formal analysis, and consideration should be given to supplementing this calculation with fuller presentations, such as displays of prediction intervals and likelihood functions.

Houck (1999) discussed statistics in relation to trace evidence. "The inability to place a specific probability estimate on chance association has led to a widespread view that trace evidence is much weaker than DNA evidence, a problem which has been referred to as "the tyranny of numbers" [(Houck, 1999)].

However, as noted by Houck (1999, p. 3), "the tyranny of numbers is a consequence of an over-reliance on deduction and mathematics, and these ultimately limit a discipline by requiring it to fit in a preordained model. [. . .]" Bayesian statistical approaches have become popular in many branches of forensic science in recent years" (Pye, 2006, pp. 24–25). Pye further remarks (ibid., p. 25):

> Quantitative methods, including formal hypothesis testing, clearly have an important role to play in the assessment of all forms of trace evidence, but they can rarely provide a complete answer. Issues of "uniqueness", "rarity", "randomness" and "representativeness" in relation to trace evidence are usually difficult to quantify in an exact mathematical or meaningful statistical way. Statistical estimates of frequency of occurrence are usually context-dependent, based on the extent and timing of any sampling carried out, and on the methods used for sample collection and data analysis.
>
> As pointed out by Houck (1999), "context, is in fact, the crucial component to a proper grasp of the significance of trace evidence. Without context, we are communicating mere facts with no foundation of meaning, much in the way Poincar[é]'s pile of stones is not a house". The existence of a suitable context for the evaluation of the significance of trace evidence depends partly on the experience/knowledge of the trace evidence examiner, the availability of database information relating to the materials under examination, and the willingness of those instructing the forensic examiner to provide relevant information relating to the circumstances of the case. The examiner is not always provided with information which may have an important bearing on the assessment of the *evidential value* of the scientific findings. Partly for this reason, the examiner should, normally restrict his/her assessment to the likely *scientific significance* of any apparent similarity. The wider issue of evidential significance is more properly a matter for the court. Over the past fifteen years there have been great improvements.

Richard Overill and Jantje Silomon devoted a paper (2010) to what they term *digital metaforensics*, i.e., "quantifying the investigation" into digital crime cases (cf. Section 4.3.4 above). Their article, in line with those authors' record of research, resorts to statistics, and concerns (ibid., from the abstract):

> two related areas of digital forensics. The first involves quantifying the extent to which the recovered digital evidential traces support the prosecution's contention that a particular digital crime has been committed. The second addresses the issue of quantifying the cost-effectiveness of the digital forensic investigative process, in order to optimise the deployment of valuable and scarce resources for maximum efficacy.

Their thrust is to provide metrics that would appear to be more precise than such qualitative statements as "very likely".

> Not surprisingly, defence lawyers assigned to digital crime cases have become aware of this discrepancy and have attempted to exploit it to persuade the court that the prosecution does not possess evidence of sufficient probative value. However, the development of potentially

suitable methodologies and techniques for the quantitative interpretation of digital forensic
investigations is underway [. . .] and offers the prospect of bringing a degree of numerical
certitude to the recovered evidence in such cases.

It remains to be seen whether this is not merely an illusion. The skeptics concerning
Bayesianism in a judicial context may point out that merely quantifying does not
ensure that the quantification, apart from sounding grand, is also credible for good
reason.

8.3.3 Some More Forensic Disciplines

Apart from subserving legal medicine, forensic toxicology is also involved in environmental poisoning (Sigmund, 1995). Other forensic disciplines are concerned
with the environment; such is the case of forensic engineering for environmental
cases (Shuirman & Slosson, 1992), or, then, of forensic economics as applied to the
liability for environmental damages, caused by hazardous substances pollution.[60]
When it comes to engineering, there are fields of application (other than assessment
of environmental damage) which correspond to subareas of expertise within forensic
engineering. Forensic engineering may be in the realm of civil engineering (in cases
of structure collapse), or, for example, automotive engineering.[61] There is a role,
in court, for computer-aided accident reconstruction (Bohan, 1991). Johnson (1985)
was concerned with the (mis)interpretation of the causes of motorcycles collision
vis-à-vis driver behaviour.[62] A car crash involves impact. Another kind of impact is
involved in forensic ballistics.[63]

William Bodziak published (2000) the book *Footwear Impression Evidence*. He
also provided an overview of forensic footwear evidence in the form of a book chapter (2005b), preceded by a chapter (Bodziak, 2005a) concerning vehicles, namely,
about forensic tire impression and tire track evidence. Let us consider the Wikipedia
entry[64] for "Forensic footwear evidence". The incentive to resort to such expertise is

---

[60] Ward and Duffield (1992) is in a U.S. perspective.

[61] Within automotive engineering, Peters and Peters (1994) is relevant for U.S. law.

[62] Also see José Almirall's paper (2001), "Manslaughter Caused by a Hit-and-Run: Glass as
Evidence of Association".

[63] Sellier and Kneubuehl (1994) is in forensic ballistics, in a medical context.

[64] It is remarkable that there are concise, yet valuable introductions to various forensic science
disciplines, posted as entries on Wikipedia. These include a general entry "Forensic science"; various entries from the physiological sciences ("Forensic pathology", "Forensic dentistry", "Forensic
anthropology", "Forensic entomology"); entries with affinity to the social sciences ("Forensic
psychology", "Forensic psychiatry"); entries in other specdialisations ("Fingerprint analysis",
"Forensic accounting", "Ballistics", "Bloodstain pattern analysis", "DNA analysis", "Forensic
toxicology", "Forensic footwear evidence", "Questioned document examination", "Explosion
analysis"); entries on cybertechnology in forensics ("Information forensics", "Computer forensics"); entries related to engineering ("Forensic engineering", "Fire investigation", "Vehicular
accident reconstruction"); entries on people in forensics ("Edmond Locard", "Bill Bass");
and related articles ("Crime scene", "CSI effect", "Trace evidence"). For all of these, see

because of the availability of footprints. The problem is that how strong the evidence is is questionable. The same entry admits: "The Unabomber, Theodore Kaczynski, was known to keep shoes with smaller soles attached to the base in order to confuse investigators about the size of the suspects."[65] The introduction to a Wikipedia entry for "Forensic footwear evidence"[66] reads as follows:

> *Forensic footwear examination* is the study of footwear impressions evidence created. Such evidence is used in legal proceedings to determine the identities of persons at the crime scene. Footwear evidence is often the most abundant form of evidence at a crime scene and in some cases can prove to be as specific as a fingerprint. Initially investigators will look to identify the make and model of the shoe or trainer which made an impression. This can be done visually or by comparison with evidence in a database both methods focus heavily on pattern recognition and brand or logo marks. Information about the owner of any footwear can be gained from the analysis of wear patterns which are dependant on angle of footfall and weight distribution. Detailed examination of footwear impressions can help to link a specific piece of footwear to a footwear imprint as each shoe will have unique wear charateristics.

Perhaps the value of such evidence is especially for excluding suspects. Many people can be expected to wear shoes of the same model and size. Nevertheless, the shoe itself may be available, and more solid evidence can be obtained from it, for identifying the person who was wearing it: *"Footwear insole imprints* are imprints left in the inside of footwear caused by contact from the person's foot. Analysis of the insole imprints can be used to link a person(s) to a piece of footwear." Moreover:

> *Footwear trace evidence* is trace evidence that is recovered from footwear. Types of trace evidence that could be recovered include skin, glass fragments, body hair, fibres from clothing or carpets, soil particles, dust and bodily fluids. The study of this trace evidence could be used to link a piece of footwear to a location or owner.

For our present purposes, it is interesting that information technology is helpful in the form of *footwear databases:*

> Forensic investigators can use computerized footwear databases to quickly compare the class characteristics between footwear impression and outsole profile of footwear outsoles stored in the database. This greatly reduced the time required to match shoeprint to. Examples include the Footwear Intelligence Technology (FIT) launched by the Forensic Science Service (FSS) in February 2007. Such systems contains information on thousands of footwear patterns with daily updates from both manufacturers and police forces.

A team at the University of Buffalo led by Sargur Srihari reported (Ramakrishnan, Malgireddy, & Srihari, 2008; Ramakrishnan & Srihari, 2008) about shoe-print extraction from latent images, by resorting to *conditional random fields.*

---

http://en.wikipedia.org/wiki/ followed with the name of the entries, with each blank space replaced with an underscore.

[65] Don Foster's stylometric analysis (see Foster, 2001, chapter 3) was important for identifying the Unabomber. Also the latter's sister-in-law, a professor of philosophy came to believe she knew he was the Unabomber because of what he wrote and the way he wrote. See in Section 6.1.10, and in fn. 94 in Chapter 6 in particular.

[66] http://en.wikipedia.org/wiki/Forensic_footwear_evidence.

Let us turn to a few other specialties. If real estate is involved in a case, this may concern situations where a structure did or may collapse, or where there was a fire and structural engineering and fire simulation experts need investigate (either concerning negligence, or arson).[67] Their models in fire simulation within a building are in *computational fluid dynamics.* In less dramatic circumstances involving real estate, surveyors may testify as expert witnesses in court (Clarke, 1985; Watson, 1975).

Forensic accounting (e.g., for *fraud investigation*) is specialised per countries: see Lemar and Chilvers (1995) for Britain; Frank, Wagner, and Weil (1994) and Bologna and Lindquist (1995) for the U.S.A.; and Zier (1993) for Canada. The Wikipedia entry[68] remarks in the introduction:

> *Forensic Accounting* is the specialty practice area of accounting that describes engagements that result from actual or anticipated disputes or litigation. "Forensic" means "suitable for use in a court of law", and it is to that standard and potential outcome that Forensic Accountants generally have to work. *Forensic Accountants*, also referred to as *Forensic Auditors* or *Investigative Auditors*, often have to give expert evidence at the eventual trial. All of the larger accounting firms, as well as many medium-sized and boutique firms, have specialist Forensic Accounting departments. Within these groups, there may be further sub-specializations: some Forensic Accountants may, for example, just specialize in insurance claims, personal injury claims, fraud, construction, or royalty audits.

We have already seen how link analysis and data mining have been put to good use in order to uncover frauds: by mining email databases in the Enron case

---

[67] As http://en.wikipedia.org/wiki/Fire_investigation points out: "Fire investigation is one of the most difficult of the forensic sciences to practice. In most forensic disciplines, even the basic question of whether a crime has been committed is normally obvious. During a fire investigation, an entire process must be undertaken just to determine if the case involves arson or not. The difficulty of determining whether an arson fire has occurred or not arises because fires destroy evidence. A fire investigator looks at what is left behind after a fire and obtains information to piece together the events that occurred in the moments leading up to the fire. One of the challenging aspects of fire investigation is the multi-disciplinary base of the investigator's job. Fires can be caused by or involve most things people see or use. For this reason, fire investigators need to know not only basic science of fire behavior, but knowledge of many different areas of study (including construction, electricity, human behaviour, vehicles etc.) is helpful. If the fire origin has, for example, a gas appliance, an investigator should know enough about appliances to either include or exclude it as a possible cause of the fire. Fire investigators must also know their own limitations and call upon experts to assist when needed. Accordingly, fire investigators sometimes work with forensic electrical engineers (when examining electrical appliances, household wiring, etc.) or others skilled in forensic engineering (gas-powered appliances, air handling equipment, gas delivery systems, etc.)." Concerning certification of the experts, the same entry explains: "In the USA, some states require that fire investigators obtain certification as a Certified Fire Investigator (CFI). The International Association of Arson Investigators, a professional group of fire investigators, grants CFI certification. The National Association of Fire Investigators (NAFI), a professional association of fire and explosion investigators, offer several National Board Certified fire investigation certifications, including Certified Fire and Explosion Investigatior (CFEI), Certified Vehicle Fire Investigator (CVFI), and Certified Fire Investigation Instructor (CFII). For more information, please visit their website at http://www.nafi.org."

[68] http://en.wikipedia.org/wiki/Forensic_Accounting.

(Section 6.2.1), by trying to identify fraudsters and accomplices at online auction sites (Section 6.2.3), the U.S. Federal Defense Financial Accounting Service's EDS project (Section 6.2.6), and the tool for detecting fuel frauds developed in Poland (Section 6.2.8). The latter project is a case in point for how conventional forensic accounting is in practice powerless when faced with very complex flows of transactions, unless use is made of link analysis or data mining technology.

8.4 The Contribution to Forensic Science of Anthropology and Archaeology

8.4.1 Forensic Archaeology and Anthropology

Some interdisciplinary interfacing of forensics sometimes occurs with kinds of reconstruction other than forensic; for example, forensic archaeology applies techniques from archaeology to criminal investigation.[69] Forensic archaeology applies techniques from archaeology to criminal investigation: see Hunter et al. (1997). The following is quoted from a call for participation in a workshop on Archaeology and Forensic Science, held at the British Academy in London on 27 February 2007, in concomitance with the Council for British Archaeology's 2007 Winter General Meeting.

> Forensic archaeology is a relatively new concept in Britain and these presentations explore how archaeology in its many facets has developed from its traditional roots into the arena of criminal investigation. As these talks show, this is mostly, but not exclusively, concerned with searching for and excavating clandestine graves, including mass graves. Search involves systematic sequencing of various techniques including the use of aerial imaging, geophysical survey, as well as cadaver dogs but, unlike more traditional archaeology, is affected by the decay dynamic of buried human remains. Recovering modern buried human remains also poses problems in that the type of evidence needed can be very different from the evidence archaeologists and anthropologists normally identify. It also needs to be obtained within the constraints of a novel legal framework and presented in court. These issues are pursued and, using case studies, a number of different scenarios are outlined which detail the different methodologies used in excavation and the different types of evidence – archaeological, anthropological and environmental – that could be used to obtain a successful conviction.

The titles of the talks are indicative of how disciplines meet within forensic archaeology: "Archaeology and the crime scene", "Physical anthropology: forensic identification, trauma and case studies", "Geophysics: divergence, human decay dynamics and case studies", "Applications of ecology, botany, and palynology to criminal investigation". *Palynology* (see Section 8.5.5 below) is the study of pollen, in respect of morphology, biochemistry, and biogeography. The public consisted of archaeologists: active, retired, or students.

---

[69] See Hunter et al. (1997).

Even though the quotation given earlier states that forensic archaeology is rather new in Britain, it must be said that whereas in the United States, forensic science is strong in physical anthropology, apparently Britain is ahead in other disciplines for forensic identification (including of human remains), that are grounded in forensic archaeology. Various scientific disciplines contribute techniques to archaeology, and experts conversants with both archaeology and forensics find more rigour within the former disciplinary tradition, which has much to contribute to forensics.

In the rest of this chapter, as well as in Sections 8.4.2, 8.5.2, and 8.5.5, I am going to provide information from notes I took at the 2007 London workshop referred to. John Hunter of the University of Birmingham is an archaeologist who moved into forensic archaeology, and (like the other speakers from the workshop) assists the police and appears in court as an expert witness. He started his talk by dispelling the misconception that forensic archaeology (i.e., archaeology used in forensic environments) is forensic science used in archaeology.

Around a serious crime event, the incident is attended to by an array of professionals: the scene of crime officer, the senior investigating officer, the coroner, the Home Office pathologist, the Forensic Science Service, the scientific support manager, the Crown Prosecution Service, and others.

A common ground fo archaeology and forensic science is the search and recovery of human remains, skeletal analysis, and analytical science. Key divergences include: the timeframe of operation (archaeologists choose when going out, whereas a police investigation cannot be deferred, e.g., because of bad weather), hierarchies (Hunter referred to himself as being quite powerful within his archaeological team, whereas when he is called to assist the police, or is called to testify in court, the mutual positioning is different), a two-way knowledge base (which is not the case of archaeological practice), legal constraints (on disclosure), the role of the expert witness (as opposed to an archaeologist addressing scholars), and "publication" to a jury (as opposed to a peer-reviewed journal).

Concerning appearing in court as an expert witness, Hunter (like another speaker on the same day) pointed out that whereas one usually thinks about trials in terms of justice being done, actually trials are games, and the barrister who has been most persuasive, wins. It is the task of the barrister of the other side to try to ruin your professional reputation as an expert witness.

Moreover, unlike archaeology, forensic archaeology deals with the recent dead and the living. When dealing with graves, in archaeology it is necessary to distinguish between context and non-context. In contrast, in forensic archaeology is is necessary to distinguish between context and contamination. Preserving the integrity of the grave can facilitate finding out about identity, cause and manner of death, and the interval since death. Have the remains *been* buried (by somebody), or have they *become* buried? A buried body may cause different types of vegetation change: the vegetation is different from the surroundings, for example, either higher, or lower. It is lower on the grave than surrounding vegetation, is the grave was originally covered with stones. Apart from the vegetation change, there also is a topographic change. There can be expected to be a disturbance caused by body remains. There may be linkage between sites. The cues on (or in) the terrain may be artefactual, ecological, or ecofactual (e.g., intrusive vegetation).

There is a window of opportunity that should not be lost, when the police is looking for a body after a death presumed to be recent. After three weeks from death, the body is decaying, and this continues for other three weeks, during which the body is emitting temperature. Thermal imaging in order to find out a burial, when there has been a crime, needs to exploit that window of opportunity. Non-invasive imaging techniques are available, and recommended. The more invasive a forensic technique, the greater the risk of losing forensic evidence, because of various reasons. A non-invasive imaging technique can reconstruct the volume and shape (inside the ground) of a mass grave: how deep it is, how long, and so forth. This can be visualised by computer in three dimensions, as a volumetric model, and animated (by having the system of reference with the three axes rotate). The same example was made during the same workshop by Cheetam, in a talk about the forensic and archaeological application of survey methods from geophysics; the given volumetric model was developed by applying a technique that measures earth resistivity (see in Section 8.5.2 below).

Hunter pointed out that the search for a grave may have a positive outcome, i.e., recovery, or a negative outcome, i.e., elimination. It may be a search concerning a recent incident, with a named victim, with a suspect being identified, and with an unknown disposal site, yet with the body remains being recovered. Or then it may be an old incident, with no name to the victim, with no suspect, but with a specific location. An example of the latter kind of situation is the case of a witness who reports seeing (or that a relative had seen), thirty years before, a child being buried at a specific location. This is a more usual kind of intelligence.

When searching for a grave, there are distinctions to be made concerning spatial scope. It may be a search in the backgarden of a given urban house, using imaging techniques from geophysics. Or then, the scope may be broader, and aerophotography may be resorted to. It is only if and once the remains *are* found, that one can look into the matter and say whether there was a murder or not. Questions proper to ask include: How was the grave dug? Was it dug in a hurry, or carefully prepared? Is there foreign material in the grave? Did the perpetrator leave any traces in or around the grave? The grave is a very rich source of material. There is a pattern to how people tend to dispose of bodies. They tend to dispose of bodies in places they know. The expert in court only gives information. It is the barrister's task to interpret. For example, the expert may say whether the material taken out of the grave was taken off site, or whether the material found in the grave was put there from on-site or off-site.

Taphonomics studies decay. Analysis in taphonomics interacts with other disciplines. The expert is likely to ask the entomologist, the climatologist, and so forth. One of the examples illustrated by Hunter was a mass grave excavation, showing depositional events and taphonomic variables. One may find commingled, saponified remains. An important notion is joints: fifteen main points on the body. As mentioned earlier, a computer-generated section of the mass grave can be visualised in three dimensions and rotated (actually, such imaging matters because it delimits the outer contour of the mass grave).

8.4.2 Factors Involved in Forensic Anthropology

8.4.2.1 Preliminaries

The second lecture at the workshop on Archaeology and Forensic Science, held at the British Academy in London on 27 February 2007, was given by forensic archaeologist and anthropologist Corinne Duhig, affiliated with Anglia Ruskin University and with Wolfson College of the University of Cambridge, and a consultant for "Gone to Earth", a small firm (with three consultants in all, operating individually in the whole of Britain). The logo of "Gone to Earth is the profile of a fox excavating a bone. Actually, scavengers such as foxes (and crows) disturb burials and sometimes cause remains to be uncovered. It must be said that in Britain there is a policy different from policies from the Continent concerning foxes: as there is no rabies in the country, foxes are not systematically culled. Foxes are frequent in urban backgardens. (What they do to your garden may prompt unprinted expletives.)

By the late 2000s, body remains (even ancient) are more likely to be reported in the United Kingdom that it used to be a few decades ago. The forensic anthropologist's[70] (and apparently Duhig's own) breakdown of casework by type is: ca. 75% non-forensic (non human, or archaeological), the rest being forensic (homicide, suicide, misadventure, or open), or "other". Physical anthropology as applied to forensic identification, trauma and case studies, is different from physical anthropology as done in mainstream archaeology. The role of the forensic anthropologist is search and excavation, assistance to the Home Office Pathologist (who by the late 2000s has been more receptive to the anthropologists than, say, twenty years earlier), defleshing and reconstruction (a body still with soft tissue is reduced by the anthropologist to a skeleton, and then rebuilding is carried out; in archaeology, too, there is cleaning and rebuilding, but of course there is no recent soft tissue).

Then the anthropologist develops an anthropological profile for identification. A lot of it is exclusion; for example, the pathologist is notified by the anthropologist that the body does not match the profile. Other tasks of the anthropologist include skeletal trauma mapping, sequencing and interpretation, and taphonomic interpretation.[71] The remains may be fresh, or decomposing, or fully skeletonised, or burnt, or cremated (usually perpetrators don't know how to cremate well), or disrupted (e.g., because of a road accident, or an airplane crash), of dismembered (which was deliberately done by a perpetrator), or processed (by a perpetrator, to make the remains less identifiable).

---

[70] Marcella Sorg (2005; 3rd edn. 2009) provides an overview of *forensic anthropology*.

[71] William Haglund (2005; 3rd edn. 2009) provides an overview of *forensic taphonomy*, which is about burial.

The Big Four of identification are: ethnology, sex, age, and stature. Ethnology for the forensic anthropologist at present in the United Kingdom involves a greater range than archaeologically (as, e.g., now there are people from South Asia, the Far East, and sub-Saharan Africa in the country, and that wasn't the case in antiquity or the early Middle Ages). It is concerning the identification of sex and age, that anthropologists are most useful to the police. Homicide demographics involve mainly young adult males. This is very different from archaeological remains. As to stature, one ought to bear in mind two things:

(a) informant error, as people quite frequently overestimate the height of others, and moreover (especially males) their own stature;
(b) size for postulated activity, e.g., a required limb length to do something: the forensic anthropologist has to work out from length and angulation of limbs, whether it is possible for the given person to have done a given activity, e.g., movement. Could that child have extended an arm and picked up that given thing?

8.4.2.2 Ante-mortem Skeletal Pathology, and Para-, Peri-, and Post-mortem Traumas

As explained by Corinne Duhig in the same lecture, the identification of a person from body remains involves various factors. It depends on reliable record or recollection of informants, as well as preservation in remains. For *ante-mortem skeletal pathology*, the range of values includes: life-history trauma (battery, torture); evidential trauma; and non-trauma. Identification as based on preservation in remains also depends on epigenetic/non-metric traits (e.g., dental variables can be extremely variable); on body build (degree of muscularity: it depends on how much tissue you have, in the available remains); on handedness (was that person left-handed?); and on shoe size (the latter is something that is not asked in archaeology).

Let us turn to *"para-mortem" trauma*. This is a term invented by Duhig herself. Identifying para-mortem trauma properly has important implications at a criminal trial. Violence may have been directed at a person alive or perceived to be alive, or, in contrast, at or close to the time of death. Violence may have been for the purpose of homicide or suicide, or of causing pain, or of mutilation. Injuries may have been produced by blunt weapons, or by sharp weapons, or by projectiles. The latter, in turn, may include, e.g., bomb fragments. Moreover, para-mortem trauma may have resulted from accidental injury and death (e.g., in an air crash). Forensic anthropologists do not have the responsibility for determining the type of death.

Types of para-mortem trauma include: blunt trauma, sharp-weapon trauma, and projectile wounds. In particular, blunt trauma (which is involved, e.g., in crimes of passion) may be: simple depressed fracture of skull; various crushed features of skull; or fracture of the post-cranial skeleton (i.e., of the skeleton other than the skull). Kinds of post-cranial fracture importantly include defence injury to a forearm (as a person under physical attack usually rises the forearms to protect him- or herself).

Sharp-weapon trauma consists of incisions. These may be stab wounds (which tend to be on the edge of ribs), or cut/slash wounds. The latter often are superficial; they are common in accidents. As to projectile wounds, they may be entry wounds (more regular; if in the skull); or exit wounds (less regular, larger; if in the skull). Small calibre projectiles often stay in, and have no exit, so there would be an entry wound, but no corresponding exit wound. Holes in the skull, which in a forensic context are identified as projectile wounds, if found in archaeological remains instead, at first sight may be believed to be due to the skull being damaged because of defective preservation. For the forensic anthropologist analysing para-mortem trauma, it is important to determine *wound sequencing*, i.e., the direction and sequencing of wounds. May I add that this is interesting in view of *models of time* from artificial intelligence or, more broadly speaking, from computer science (see Section 8.4.2.3). Constraints preclude some candidate sequencing. This could be a promising direction for computer application to forensic anthropology.

Having dealt, with *para-mortem trauma*, let us turn to *peri-mortem trauma*. This concerns early decomposition stages. It also concerns violence directed at a body: dismemberment, defleshing, and so forth, as having been carried out by a perpetrator. It is also of interest to determine for which purpose, such violence directed at a dead body was carried out. And finally, there is *post-mortem trauma*. It concerns later decomposition stages. Post-mortem trauma may be due to human activity (accidental disturbance, or second burial), or to animal activity (damage, scattering), and so forth. Peri-mortem and post-mortem processing wounds include, e.g., cutting by blades or by saws, for the purpose of dismemberment.

8.4.2.3 A Digression on Formal Models of Time

An important class of temporal representations from artificial intelligence is such methods that are based on variants of *temporal logic.* We are not referring to formal representations of tense in natural language. Temporal logics are independent of natural language, and therefore are not directly concerned with tense. Temporal logics as used in artificial intelligence[72] were introduced by Allen (1983b, 1984, 1991),[73] and originally were only concerned with intervals (by means of an *interval calculus*, rather than with time points. Temporal logics have been used, for example,

---

[72] Within artificial intelligence, see e.g. Shoham and McDermott (1988) about temporal reasoning.

[73] A useful online survey of temporal logic is Galton (2008). van Benthem (1995) is more detailed and more technical; whereas van Benthem (1983, 2nd edn. 1991) is a book on temporal logic. Fisher, Gabbay, and Vila (2005) is a handbook. Cf. Antony Galton's book (1987) and critique (1990) of James Allen's *theory of action and time.* Also consider Alur, Henzinger, Kupferman (2002) *alternating-time temporal logic*, which eventually gave rise to Wooldridge and van der Hoek's (2005) *Action-based Alternating Transition Systems* (*AATS*), used by Bex et al. (2009) in order to represent reasoning about the narrative of an alleged crime (see Section 3.4.4.4 in this book).

Surveying the broader context of kinds of temporal representations, Fabio Alberto Schreiber explains (1994, section 3): "In the logicians' community there is a strong debate on the need of creating a non standard *Temporal Logic.* Scholars having mathematical and physical background and interests claim that times can be designated by terms in a first order theory, which is more

for tasks in engineering (e.g., Knight, Ma, & Nissan, 1999). In James Allen's interval calculus, there is a composition table of basic interval-to-interval relations, e.g., if they contain each other, or partly overlap. That approach to qualitative reasoning about time inspired Tony Cohn's approach to qualitative reasoning about space. It is based on Clarke's *calculus of individuals* and uses a set of eight basic relations on spatial regions, i.e., how one region connects to another. Cohn, Gooday, and Bennett (1995) compare structures in spatial and temporal logics. Cui, Cohn, and Randell (1992) show how space and time are both taken care of in their formalism. Cohn et al. (1994) show how temporal continuity is exploited in their qualitative spatial calculi. The papers Nissan (2001g, 1997b) are about formalisms of space, more broadly meant.

In Section 5.3.3.2 we considered *time granularity*, different *grainsizes* being, for example, a year or a day. Bettini et al. (2000), a book on time granularities and how they are processed in representations from computer science, in particular from the viewpoints of database design, of constraint reasoning, and of automated knowledge discovery. Also see Bettini, Wang, and Jajodia (2002); cf. Schreiber (1991, 1994).

By contrast to temporal logics, different kinds of representation were developed for linguistics by semanticists, in order to represent the semantics of *tense*, as intended by linguists: Alice ter Meulen's book (1995) was reviewed by Nissan (1998b), a review reworked into appendix B of Nissan (2011a). In her book, "temporal reasoning is considered a form of logical reasoning, in which quantificational force, binding, and context change are core concepts" (ter Meulen, 1995, p. 3). Her structured semantic objects are *Dynamic Aspect Trees* (*DATs*).

Computer science also has temporal representations for concurrency. One which is considerably complex, and is used to modelling concurrent computation, is is Tony Hoare's notation (and respective theoretical framework) known as *Communicating Sequential Processes (CSP)*, which he published in a book by the same title (Hoare, 1985). It is a powerful technique, and requires a good understanding of the theory behind it. A current textbook on the subject is Roscoe's *The Theory and Practice of Concurrency* (Roscoe, 1998). The latter book is about the untimed version of CSP, with modelling without measuring the passage of time. By contrast, for modelling also such measurements (in either real numbers, or as discrete time points), there exists a version of Hoare's approach that has been named *Times CSP*:

---

than adequate for time modeling. Besides [Bertrand] Russel and [Willard] Quine, these authors – referred often to as *detensers* – comprise [James] Allen, [Drew] McDermott, [Robert] Kowalski and others. People interested in linguistic aspect of logic, on the other hand, feel that time is tightly woven into languages, under the form of different tenses of the verb, and they relate modal to temporal notions [. . .] [Arthur] Prior and [Georg Hendrik] Von Wright belong to this *tensers* school. Just to show how things become complicate, we only mention that, in his theory of tense, [Hans] Reichenbach defines three different times for each tense: an *utterance* time, at which the sentence is expressed, a *reference* time, which we refer to in the sentence, and an *event* time, which is the object of the sentence".

it reinterprets CSP over time, records the exact time at which each event occurs, it associates with events non-negative real numbers.[74]

A simpler representation for concurrent processes and temporal constraints is *Petri nets*. Think of such a variant of a flipper game, that little balls (we are going to call them *tokens*) are scuttling along routes between obstacles, that can be figured out as being small doors, or closed valves (these we call *transitions*). There are one or more such conduits that each reaches such a valve (i.e., incoming arcs upstream of the transition), and one or more conduits that proceed forth from it (outgoing arcs downstream of the transition). In each conduit, there will be at most one ball at a time. One or more balls will stop at the transition, and this valve will not open, unless from each and every incoming arc, a ball has arrived. If all such balls are there, then the valve would open (i.e., the transition *fires*), and the balls would move further. There is a major departure with respect to the real physical world. In the latter, you would expect that if you had, say, three marbles right before the valve, and the valve opens, then beyond that valve those marbles will still be three balls. Not so with the kind of directed graphs that are known as *Petri nets*. If beyond the valve there only is one outgoing arc, then those three marbles would turn into just one marble, whereas if two arcs leave the open valve, then those three balls will become two: one for each outgoing arc. Petri nets are such directed graphs, that along every route (itself made up of arcs), there is an alternation of *places* (drawn as hollow circles), and *transitions* (drawn as a barrage: a short line drawn across). Moreover, *tokens* move through the graph according to rule we have described. See Fig. 8.4.2.3.1.

As I wrote in Nissan (2011a, appendix A):

Petri nets have proved to be a major paradigm for other computer application domains, e.g., for scheduling in manufacturing, or for logic validation when modelling digital systems. This has not been the case in legal computing. Petri nets were applied to legal systems

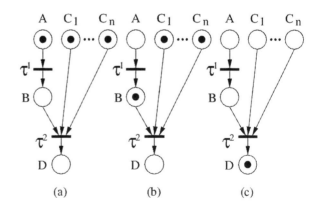

Fig. 8.4.2.3.1 Three successive states in the execution of a sample Petri net

(a)   (b)   (c)

---

[74] It is covered in a textbook by Steve Schneider (1999). Also see Schneider (2001). He has also co-authored a book on security protocols (Ryan, Schneider, Goldsmith, Lowe, & Roscoe, 2000).

in Holt and Meldman (1971).[75] In the literature of the discipline of artificial intelligence and law, a few papers are concerned with temporal structure (Bauer-Bernet, 1986; Poulin et al., 1992; Vila and Yoshino, 1995, 1998;[76] Knight, Ma, and Nissan, 1998), and Petri nets have been applied quite sporadically, less frequently than temporal logic, the latter being an approach in artificial intelligence which was introduced by Allen ([1983a, 1983b], 1984). Farook and Nissan (1998) have applied Petri nets to the representation of mutual wills. Valette and Pradin-Chézalviel (1998), in the same journal special issue as the former, applied time Petri nets to the modelling of civil litigation. Rossiter et al. (1993) described an application of Petri nets (within a formal model for quality assurance) to legal documentation organized as hypertext. Raskin et al. (1996) modelled by means of Petri nets, *deontic* states, i.e., states of obligation or permissibility.

For most purposes, the representation of *asynchronous, concurrent processes* is best suited by Petri nets indeed. The representation of concurrency among processes is not well suited by *finite state automata*, because for a large number of tasks, the number of states becomes unwieldy. Petri nets were originally defined by Petri in 1962 (Petri, 1966), and then refined and named after him by Holt (e.g., Holt, 1971; cf. Miller, 1973). Research into this paradigm developed during the 1970s and boomed in the 1980s. The literature is vast, with a choice of general works and a variety of proceedings. Among the books, see, e.g., Proth and Xie (1996), Peterson (1981), David and Alla (1992), Reutenauer (1990), Fernandez and Best (1988). Over the years, several different classes of Petri net formalisms were introduced, but we confined ourselves, in this article, to a simple application of the standard kind. As to fancy kinds of Petri nets, it may be that some amongst the present readership may find it useful to find about *predicate/transition nets* and then apply it in their own research (Genrich & Lautenbach, 1979). Reutenauer (1990) was concerned with the mathematics of Petri nets. Brown (1989a, 1989b) provides a treatment of Petri nets in terms of formal logic. In algebraic logic, the *box calculus* is a causal algebra with multilabel communication, within the Petri nets paradigm (Best & Hall, 1992; Esparza & Bruns, 1994). Olderog (1991) draws a comparison of three formalisms for representing concurrent processes; these include Petri nets.

8.4.2.4 Software Tools for Human Anatomy

There exists software for anatomy. For example, a workshop on the Mathematical Foundations of Computational Anatomy (MFCA'06) was held in September 2006

---

[75] Also by Anatol Holt, cf. Holt (1971, 1988). In Holt (1988), *diplans* were introduced, for the purposes of studying coordination in the workplace and of automation. "Diplans are the expressions of a new graphical language used to describe plans of operation in human organizations. With diplans, systems of constraint, which may or may not take the form of procedure definitions, can be specified. Among the special strengths of diplans is their ability to render explicit the interactive aspects of complex work distributed over many people and places – in other words, coordination. Diplans are central to coordination technology, a new approach to developing support for cooperative work on heterogeneous computer networks." (ibid., from the abstract).

[76] Cf. Vila and Yoshino (2005), and cf. Fisher et al. (2005) on temporal logics in AI.

in conjunction with the MICCAI'06 conference. Works in computational anatomy are also presented, for example, at the Annual International Conferences of the IEEE Engineering in Medicine and Biology Society (EMBS), and at the Annual Meetings of the International Society for Computer Assisted Orthopaedic Surgery (CAOS).

Arbabi, Boulic, and Thalmann (2007a, 2007b) described a fast method for finding the range of motion in the human joints, and in the hip joint in particular. The context is the diagnosis of hip disease: "Finding the range of motion for the human joints is a popular method for diagnosing", and the claim was made that it is both more trustworthy "and easier to find the range of motion by employing computer based models of the human tissues. In this paper we propose a novel method for finding range of motion for human joints without using any collision detection algorithm. This method is based on mesh classifying in a cylindrically segmented space" (Arbabi et al., 2007b, from the abstract). The method illustration was the determination of the range of motion in the human hip joint, but actually the method could be applied more generally to the joints in the human body.

From that same Swiss team in Lausanne, also see Abaci et al. (2007a), on object manipulation and grasping "in an object manipulation context. Our proposal is a novel method that combines a tubular feature classification algorithm, a hand grasp posture generation algorithm and an animation framework for human-object interactions. This method works on objects with tubular or elongated parts, and accepts a number of parameter inputs to control the grasp posture" (ibid., from the abstract).

Being able to model grasping by computer, as well as being able to determine by computer the range of motion in the human joints (even though this is for the purposes of diagnosis in vivo), is arguably relevant for questions akin to the one asked at the end of Section 8.4.2.1 above: "Could that child have extended an arm and picked up that given thing?".

The history of the project of modelling hip joints is related in the following, which is quoted from Magnenat-Thalmann and Gilles (2007, p. 25)[77]:

> Since 2002, Prof. Nadia Magnenat-Thalmann of the Swiss National Center of Competence in Research Co-Me has been leading a project on interactive clinical visualization for hip joint examination. The goals of this research are to build a 3D patient-specific functional model of the hip joint, of the hip joint, and to develop interactive tools allowing clinicians to examine hip behaviour. Such tools will be invaluable aids in diagnosis and treatment planning, particularly for osteoarthritis and impingement syndrome pathologies.

Also consider, e.g., *MuscleBuilder*, a computer-graphic modelling tool for human anatomy (Aubel & Thalmann, 2007; cf. 2000, 2001, and Gutiérrez et al., 2005, 2007). In cultural terms, this is an extension of the genre of anatomy handbooks, which itself is grounded in the history of the ideas, as well as of the arts. Jonathan Sawday's (1996) is a book in cultural history, concerned with the dissection of the human body in the culture of the English Renaissance, in relation to conceptualisations of the body in several domains, including the arts.

---

[77] Nadia Magnenat-Thalmann leads a team in Geneva, whereas Daniel Thalmann leads a team in Lausanne. Cf. in Section 5.2.15 above.

Take illustrations in anatomy handbooks, through history, as made by illustrators by observing dissected bodies. Bernez (1994) discussed the aesthetics of seventeenth-century Dutch painter Gérard de Lairesse's illustrations for Bidloo's *Anatomia Humani Corporis*. Bernez shows how anatomic drawings within the history of art actually reflected moralising intents, about life and death, on the part of the artists, and, paradoxically, aesthetic ideal as well. Bernez shows that de Lairesse's anatomic drawings are somehow amenable to a seventeenth-century Dutch genre he practised, the *Vanitas:* "Anatomy as Vanitas: the allegorical representations of life's brevity [. . .]" (ibid., p. 213). "The Vanitas was a genre of still-life painting in which certain objects representing the fruitfulness of nature or the value of human activities were contrasted with elements which evoked the triumph of death" (ibid.).

EnVision (2002) relates about a project led by Michael I. Miller, director of the Center for Imaging Science at Johns Hopkins University, concerning the application to neuroscience of computational anatomy:

> "Computational anatomy could be described as a digital textbook of anatomy, with all its variability in healthy humans, adjusted for things like gender, age, and ethnicity, and also in pathological situations that affect anatomy", said Grenander. "The main difficulty is that anatomical substructures form highly complex systems, with variation being the rule", Miller said. As he said in an interview published earlier this year [(Taubes, 2002)], "If machines can compute structures that are equivalent to the structures we see in the world, then we can begin to understand them. In computational anatomy, we now have equations that describe how tissues can grow and bend and morph and change. These equations seem to generate very realistic structures".

Miller's application is to the brain, a soft tissue, "to learn how tissues grow, assume new shapes, and 'morph' into mature structures" (ibid.). Miller is quoted as saying: "Our mathematical formulation deforms structures in a coordinate space, and thus the original structures are entirely recoverable computationally. That is the difference between morphing and morphometrics" (ibid.). In morphing, just a photometric transformation is carried out, without any coordinate system allowing recovery of the previous shape. "For the past decade, Miller's group has been developing computational methods to analyse gross anatomical structures in the human brain, with the objective of creating tools to help neuroscientists and diagnosticians learn from changes in brain substructures. The underlying mathematics are supplied by metric pattern theory, a formalism developed by Ulf Grenander in the Division of Applied Mathematics at Brown University" (ibid.).

Several of the short papers in the special issue on "The Digital Patient" of *ERCIM News* (April 2007) describe such projects that revolve around computational models of human anatomy, and being carried out in various European countries. For example, Xavier Pennec (2007) introduces a project applied to the brain (one of Pennec's partners in France is also a partner of Miller).[78]

---

[78] At http://www-sop.inria.fr/asclepios/projects/ARCBrainVar/ a description is found of Pennec's project.

Among the applications, two that are generally relevant for our present concerns include "the spatial normalization of subjects in neuroscience (ie mapping all the anatomies into a common reference system) and atlas-to-patient registration in order to map generic knowledge to patient-specific data" (Pennec, 2007). Arguably, atlas-to-patient mapping is relevant for computational anatomy to be of any use to forensic anthropology.

González Ballester, Büchler, and Reimers (2007) "are constructing advanced statistical digital models of bone shape and biomechanical properties. These models will lead to the design of a new breed of orthopacdic implants that will guarantee an optimal fit for the whole range of patients" (ibid., p. 27). "During this project, we have extended our ability to analyse the surface shape of anatomies to also include internal structures and bone density information. This results in a compact statistical description of the variability in bone shape and density, and the correlation between them" (ibid.). This suggests, I would say, that conceivably, some similar model could be of use to forensic anthropology and perhaps to forensic ballistics, in order to simulate what may have brought about the conditions observed in a dead human body in a forensic setting.

Computational models of human anatomy find expression also other than through the 3D visualisation of the anatomy. The simulation of pain in robotics has been reported about. Reportedly in the late 2000s, the University of Gifu was expecting to make use of a patient-robot for medical training, in particular in the palpation of patients, before having the trainees exercise in palpation directly on humans. The patient-robot was developed by Yuzo Takahashi. The robot has 24 internal sensors, and if touched in a body part (corresponding to a human body part), it speaks up and conveys the physical distress being simulated. Eight kinds of symptomatologyare recognised in the prototype, and the inclusion of more is envisaged. Its skin produces the sensation, when touched, of human skin.

Victor Ng-Thow-Hing is active both in robotics (e.g. Hauser & Ng-Thow-Hing, 2010), and in biomechanical anatomical models of human and animal bodies, a field in which he was supervised by Eugene Fiume in Toronto (Ng-Thow-Hing, 1994, 2001; Agur, Ng-Thow-Hing, Ball, Fiume, & McKee, 2003; Teran et al., 2005; Wu, Ng-Thow-Hing, Singh, Agur, & McKee, 2007). Musculotendon units were built by sketching interactively profile curves directly onto the bones; the curves can be subsequently adjusted to interactively edit the shape of the resulting muscle. As an alternative for producing an initial shape of the muscle, it is also possible to load into the system pre-built muscles from an anatomical library. The muscle models generated were used as *force actuators*, in a robotic simulation sense. The simulation framework allows muscles to be visualised, and the simulation combines the muscles with articulated skeletons. These are made up of rigid bones and of joints; there are various joint constraints.

Hutchinson, Ng-Thow-Hing, and Anderson (2007) applied an anatomical model to reconstruct the turning and running performance of the dinosaur *Tyrannosaurus rex*. This is an example of *computational palaeontology*. That model combined *mass models* as those used by Ng-Thow-Hing in *digital human modelling* at Honda, the *B-spline model* he was using for muscle, and generated a versatile shape primitive for estimating mass properties of body tissue. Just as he could do that for extant animal species or for humans, he was able to do that for the fossil species, and the model was validated with an ostrich carcass.

8.5 Aspects of the Contribution to Forensic Science of Geology, Geophysics, and Botany

8.5.1 Forensic Geology

Forensic geology (also called *geoforensics*, or *forensic geoscience*) is an important discipline, for criminal investigation as well as for the purposes of litigation, e.g. concerning environmental damages.[79] Laurance Donnelly (2003, p. 8) pointed out: "Over the past one hundred years or so, several crimes have been solved due to the expertise provided by geologists. However, due to the sensitive and confidential nature of police investigations, only occasionally are these reported in the scientific literature". In a 1893 German-language handbook for examining magistrates, "Hans Gross, a criminal investigator and professor of criminology [...] was one of the first to advocate the use of microscopes in mineralogical studies analysing 'dust' and 'dirt' on shoes and 'spots' on cloth" (Donnelly, 2003, pp. 8–9). This approach was "subsequently used by George Popp in 1904, during a murder investigation (the Eva Disch case), in Frankfurt, Germany" (ibid., p. 9). In France, Edmond Locard (1877–1966), a star of criminalistics who used inventively a variety of techniques (see Section 8.7.1 below), concerned himself with the analysis of dust traces, too, and described them at length (Locard, 1930). "The Federal Bureau of Investigation (FBI) have been using forensic geology since 1935, initially to help solve the Matson kidnapping case" (Donnelly, 2003, p. 9).

Turning to the 2000s, Bergslien et al. (2006) have been trying to apply field portable X-ray fluorescence (FPXRF) spectrometry to both forensic and environmental geology. "There are many environmental applications that may also intersect the forensic arena, such as tracking pollutants in the environment to their source" (ibid., p. 19). A forensic application they reported about "involves analysis of mineral and rock deposits on automobile tires, shoes, carpets etc. and direct comparison with materials found at the crime scene. Knowledge of compositional changes in geological formations may aid in tracing movements of a crime suspect or victim" (ibid.).

At the inaugural meeting of the Forensic geoscience Group of the Geological Society of London, on 20 December 2006 (Ruffell, 2006), Donnelly pointed out (Donnelly, 2006, pp. 3–4):

---

[79] Books on forensic geology, or geoforensics, as it is also called, include Pye and Croft (2004), Pye (2007), and Murray and Tedrow (1975).

There are a number of geologists in the UK, and internationally, who currently work with, or have recently worked with the police, other law-enforcers, environmental agencies and humanitarian organisations to help bring some types of crimes to successful conclusions. Some geoscientists have also been involved in forensic investigations in the mining, engineering, minerals and water sectors of industry, or during the investigations of geohazards (also known as natural disasters). The common ground for all these sub-disciplines is that geoscience practice and results may end up as part of a public, international or legal enquiry by government or in courts of law.

Forensic Geoscientists may be broadly divided into two principal fields, depending on their skills, expertise and capabilities. Firstly, there are the laboratory-based geologists who may include for example; geochemists, mineralogists, petrologists, micro-palaeontologists and isotope specialists. These may be involved with forensic investigations to; provide physical evidence for use in court, assist in an investigation, provide intelligence or identify the location of a crime scene. In short, geoscientists may link an offender (or object) to the scene or link the victim to an offender. Secondly, there are field-based geologists, who use their skills in exploration (including for example: geophysics, geochemistry, geomorphology, hydrogeology, environmental geology, remote sensing and geotechnics) to search the ground (to locate murder victim's graves, weapons and other objects).

As opposed to "[t]raditional police methods of finding graves [which] often involve large-scale 'finger-tip searches' and 'trial-and-error' excavations", which apart from inefficiency, "may even destroy evidence and ignore subtle ground disturbances", geologists "are trained to 'read the ground'" (Donnelly, 2003, p. 9).

Donnelly proceeds to enumerate the main geologists' techniques for crime scene investigations: the *mineralogical, petrological*, and *geochemical analysis* of rock and soil, or even *fossils* (resorting to palaeontology), for evidence in both criminal and civil cases.

Another method is the use of *geological maps* (and conceivably, *geographical information systems* produced by information technology, indeed a category within *geoinformatics* or *geomatics*, could be somewhat customised to reflect, e.g., ease to excavate).

In the UK, maps published by the British Geological Survey (BGS) have been used in police investigations to identify potential burial sites and topographic features mentioned in witness or suspect statements. Since search investigations were usually undertaken under a limited budget, geological maps can be used to eliminate areas of ground which are less likely to conceal buried objects [... E.g., in Kent, w]here the cretaceous bedrock was exposed, the use of a spade was considered unlikely. (Donnelly, ibid.).

McCann, Culshaw, and Fenning (1997) proposed that (in the words of Fenning & Donnelly, 2004, p. 11) "an initial desk or background study of the survey area" – as distinct from a visit to the site "in order to obtain what can only described a 'feel' of the site (i.e. putting the desk study into context)" – should collect all available relevant information about the site, including, among the other things, "Present and historical topographical maps, usually from the Ordnance Survey", "Geomorphological research studies and reports", "Present and historical geological survey maps and associated descriptive memoirs from the British Geological Survey", "Aerial and satellite photography, both current and historical", "Present and historical soil survey maps with surface vegetation detail", "Web search of the English Heritage database of geophysical survey results related to archaeological investigations (Linford, 2002)", "Library/web search for relevant scientific and press publications and photographs, including university research papers", "Information on the nature and physical properties of the survey target (e.g. buried metallic weapon, victim's discarded clothing, or buried human remains)" – in the words of Fenning and Donnelly (2004, ibid.), where the method of McCann et al. (1997) is adapted to forensic investigations.

Geomorphological observations enable to interpret "subtle natural ground distur-bances arising from the particular crime. These might include vegetation changes, undulations, spring lines, breaks in slope, convex and concave slopes, disturbed ground, periglacial deposits, the occurrence of loose soil, drag marks, and the com-paction of ground" (Donnelly, ibid.). The interpetation needs to discern whether these exhibit the effects of natural physical processes, or result from human activ-ity, "for example mining subsidence, waste disposal, tipping and digging" (ibid.). Besides, *remote sensing* is another category of forensic techniques from geology.

Several other techniques of forensic geology belong in *geophysics*, and are treated in Section 8.5.2 below; as we are going to see, geophysical techniques for forensic investigations involve information technology, and there appears to be an important potential for more applications of computing. Donnelly (2003) explains the basics of geophysics in a forensic context as follows: "Geophysical surveys pro-vide an alternative, more cost-effective method for locating disturbed ground and buried objects. Geophysical surveys measure the vertical and lateral variation of physical properties of the ground. These include electrical conductivity, magnetic, electromagnetic and gravity, etc. If a buried object provides a property contrast this can be used to detect its presence" (ibid., p. 9).

It is to be remembered that specialists from different disciplines are involved in the forensic science side of criminal investigations, whether on the crime scene, or afterwards (or before the scene of the crime is identified). "Search teams are inter-disciplinary and involve the integration of specialists such as ground search personnel, dog handlers, helicopter pilots, forensic scientists, pathologists, mountain rescue, photographers, divers, forensic anthropologists, forensic archaeologists and scene of crime examiners" (Donnelly, 2003, p. 11).

Donnelly (2003, pp. 10–11) provides a case study: the Moor Murders from the 1960s. Several young children were abducted and murdered, and the perpetrators buried them in unmarked graves on Saddleworth Moor, a remote region in the Pennines, Northern England, on the Lancashire and West Yorkshire border. In the mid 1980s the case was reopened, as not all children had been found. During the 1990s, Donnelly himself had been involved in the search for the last remaining body (Donnelly, 2002b, 2004). In personal communication (26 June 2007, reproduced by kind permission) he explained the background and latest developments:

I have been working with the Police for 13 years now. Originally, most of my work was undertaken covertly and without the knowledge of others outside the police. However, since my 2002 presentation at Westminster Palace (see *Geoscientist* [Donnelly] 2002[c]), on forensic geology, there has been a steady increase in UK geologists' involvement in forensic geology, including both research and case work. There are now several universi-ties, research organisations and consultancies. This is of course, fantastic news. Before this event there were a few geologists in the UK working with the Police, mainly involved with the identification of rock and soil for helping to solve some crimes.

My primary objective has, and continues to be, to find the grave of a young boy, I believe to be buried in a remote location in part of northern England. In December 2006 I set up the Geological Society of London Forensic Geoscience Group. The first inaugural meeting was held in London, in December 2006 (see attached). Working with the police has presented unique opportunities and enabled me to explain the skills, capabilities, expertise and role of geologists, in police and forensic investigations. As a result, there is now little doubt in the police the valuable role geology may bring to help solve/investigate a crime, but only if geologists' are incorporated properly, with both the police understanding the role of the geologists, and the geologists understanding the role of other investigators (and also his/her limit of expertise).

The setting up of the FGG, in the Geological Society of London [. . .] is aimed at advance the study and understanding of forensic geology. Our inaugural meeting, held at Burlington House in December 2006, was successful [. . .]. In October 2007, FGG are supporting the 'Soil Forensic Conference' in Edinburgh [. . .]. This event will give UK geologists the opportunity to discuss and debate the role of geologists with the police and to identify the ways forward for our profession.

In geology, there exist *soil fingerprinting techniques*, and these can be used for forensic applications. Consider the *SoilFit* project: "The UK SoilFit project (http://www.macaulay.ac.uk/soilfit/) [. . .] aims to integrate data from state-of-the-art soil fingerprinting methods with data currently held in spatially referenced soils databases. This approach could potentially improve both matching of evidential soil samples and prediction of probable geographical origin" (Dawson et al., 2006).

A decision support tool is being developed to assist the forensic scientist in selecting the most appropriate analytical strategy depending on sample size, type and condition. A software prototype has been written to process the data and identify, with probabilities, the soil type. This information is then fed into a prototype rulesbased GIS model to identify areas with appropriate soils, which can be narrowed down by layering intelligence of other spatial data (e.g. distance from roads, broad vegetation types). These prototypes have been built to demonstrate and evaluate the approach for crime investigation. (ibid.)

8.5.2 Techniques from Geophysics in Forensic Archaeology vs. in Archaeology

One branch of forensic geology is forensic geophysics. Geophysical survey consists of surveying the subsurface of the earth by the measurement of its physical properties. "An individual survey may take hours, days or months to complete. Geophysical surveys provide an alternative, more cost-effective method for locating disturbed ground and buried objects, but the choice of instrument, methodology and interpretation need to take several inter-related factors into account.

These include the physical properties of the target (human remains, buried ransom money, jewellery, weapons), the geological profile, depth of burial, topography, ground conditions, age of the burial and the experience and – of course – skills of the operators" (Donnelly, 2002a). Fenning and Donnelly (2004) remarked: "[I]n the last twenty years, the application of geophysical methods in archaeological surveying, plus advances in geophysical instrumentation and computing technology, has allowed geophysicists to conduct high-resolution surveys of the top 1–2 m below ground surface" (ibid., p. 11).[80]

The third lecture at the workshop on Archaeology and Forensic Science, held at the British Academy in London on 27 February 2007, was given by Paul Cheetham, on "Geophysics: Application to Forensic Science". Cheetham's affiliation is with the School of Conservation Science at Bournemouth University. His early formation was in statistics and computing, before he turned to geophysics. He is the foremost authority, in Britain, on geophysics application to forensic science. He started his lecture by pointing out that forensic science being fashionable sometimes causes journalists to describe as "forensic" excavations, such excavations which have nothing forensic about them and are archaeological (or possibly carried out for historical purposes, e.g., excavating remains of Napoleonic troops for the purposes of studying their body parasites). Nevertheless, he stressed, oftentimes archaeologists employ better techniques than forensic science.[81] He stated that he sometimes gasps at articles published in forensic science journals, because of how they lag behind things well established from scientific methods as applied to archaeology.

Moreover, in pursuing some directions of research, one may notice discontinuity in the forensic literature, e.g., three isolated papers (whose respective authors did not continue in the given direction) may not cite each other, and no referee apparently pointed that out, and moreover that technique is considerably more advanced as used in archaeology. Such a picture with sporadic papers in forensic science about techniques from geophysics that don't even cite each other, and of research projects being discontinued, was contrasted to the situation in archaeological science, that has a tradition of steady work building upon previous work, when it comes to applying techniques from geophysics.

What are the chances, for a given technique, to be applied again and again in crime scene investigation (or, for that matter, while assisting the scientific police)? "If you do it quicker and cheaper, the police will call you back". During his talk, Cheetam also specifically considered different techniques from geophysics, and the likely reasons why their ranking according to prominence for forensic science vs. archaeology is different.

The big growth area in geophysics has been in smaller scale higher-resolution near-surface survey in what is loosely termed applied engineering, environmental geophysics, or industrial geophysics. This rise has run coincident with a decline in mineral prospection. In a sense, this was an incentive for geophysics to change the direction of its main thrust for application.

Types of geophysics required for forensic science include: near-surface survey; delineation of discrete small features of the terrain (this requires good lateral resolution); and part of the recovery process. It is archaeological geophysics, which is leading. Forensic geophysics may learn from it. When surveying the subsurface of

---

[80] Also Bevan (1991) is concerned with the search for graves resorting to geophysics. By contrast, the approach to the detection of clandestine graves in Davenport et al. (1992) is multidisciplinary.

[81] See Gaffney and Gater (2003), Mellett (1996).

the earth by geophysical techniques, normally measurements are taken above the surface, and are non-intrusive. When the application is forensic, one looks for specific kinds of evidence (e.g., graves), not for anything (just defined by scale) as in archaeological geophysics. When what has to be found is bodies and neonates, such bodies are too small for most techniques from geophysics.

Methods from geophysics that are frequently used in archaeology include: magnetometry; earth resistivity; topsoil magnetic susceptibility; ground penetrating radar (not as good as the previous methods); and electomagnetics. The latter technique for archaeology was developed by the French; according to Cheetham, it is the Cinderella among those techniques. In contrast, forensically, the ranking of the techniques is different. Ground penetrating radar is a good technique, Cheetham stated, for forensic purposes. (Fenning and Donnelly (2004) describe it as enjoying popularity and acclaim in the forensic domain: see below).

Cheetham went on, remarking that earth resistivity can be used for looking for graves or for metal, but is not often used in forensic contexts (see below). Electromagnetics is often recommended, but is almost not used. Magnetometry is applies in metal detectors. Topsoil magnetic susceptibility is only employed for specific uses, within a forensic context, and ranks lower with respect to its rank among techniques for archaeology. We are going to be more precise further down in this chapter, thanks to an invaluable survey by Fenning and Donnelly (2004).

Forensic graves are very different from archaeological graves, in respect of the effectiveness of detecting graves and cremations with the most frequently used geophysical survey techniques. Ground penetrating radar works especially well in sand, rather than in other kinds of terrain. (Cheetham brought as an example a commercial ad for the technique, with a picture showing a demonstration on the sand in front of the Sphinx in Egypt. He pointed out that for an advert, it made sense, because this technique works very well in sand.) Ground penetrating radar is not good for finding small objects.[82] In archaeometry, ground penetrating radar is put to good use for intensively recording an area, slicing the data into images, possibly animating the images by *time-slice* (e.g., to show ancient cultivations or archaeological features). Our Section 8.5.3 is devoted to the concept of *time slicing*. Time-slicing from geophysics is applied, then, to archaeometry, using computational methods.

Earth resistivity, Cheetham claimed during his lecture, is the Cinderella of forensic techniques from geophysics. Nevertheless, Cheetham pointed out, it is a superbly reliable technique in archaeology, with variants: resistivity electrode arrays are applied to archaeology, even though they are cumbersome. Earth resistivity is good for finding graves. Nevertheless, it is almost never used in forensics, because it is regarded as a low technique by geologists: two hours were reported, for surveying a 7×6 m area. But in archaeology, better is done. Apparently there is no good reason for not applying the method in forensics: it is a matter of lack of investment.

---

[82] Also Fenning and Donnelly (2004) point out that, e.g., coins could be located at depths up to 0.5 m using a sophisticated instrument, but only larger objectsd would be detected if buried deeper (ibid., p. 15).

Reluctance to employ this method for forensic purposes has been its perceived slowness; nevertheless, in applications in archaeology this problem has been overcome. An important application of earth resistivity is in volumetric models, rotated by computer animation, of graves or mass grave. Cheetham brought as an example of application to mass graves the same computer graphic model we had already mentioned by reporting about Hunter's talk (see at the end of Section 8.4.1).

Table 1 in Fenning and Donnelly (2004, p. 12)[83] summarises features of various geophysical survey methods.

- The *seismic* method's measured parameter is the travel times of reflected/refracted seismic waves, and the 'operative' physical parameters are the density and elastic moduli that determine the propagation velocity of seismic waves. The seismic method "is either applied to layered geological structures or used to determine depth of bedrock beneath superficial deposits. As such, it is rarely applied in forensic geophysics where a distinct target, such as a buried human body, is the survey objective" (Fenning & Donnelly, ibid., p. 13).

- In the *gravity method*, the measured parameter is the spatial variations in the strength of the gravitational field of the Earth, whereas the operative physical parameter is "the density difference between local rocks and an air-filled cavity" (ibid.), and in fact it is "usually employed to detect subsurface cavities, such as caves, graves and disused mine shafts" (ibid.). Fenning & Donnelly (ibid.) describe the gravity method as costly, time-consuming, and rarely applied in forensic geophysics.

- In the *magnetic* method, the measured parameter is spatial variations in the strength of geomagnetic field, whereas the operative physical parameter is magnetic susceptibility and remanence. This method would not be forensically useful if a corpse was buried naked. "The naked human body has virtually no associated magnetic anomaly and, when buried, is very unlikely to be detected by a magnetic survey. However, a fully clothed body is a different matter. Clothing may include metal buttons, zip-fasteners, shoe eyelets and belt buckles, while pockets may contain spectacles, keys, pens and other ferrous metallic objects" (Fenning & Donnelly, ibid.).

- The [*electrical*] *resistivity* method comes in a range of techniques, which "[a]ll involve inserting four steel electrodes into the ground and measuring vertical and horizontal variation in resistivity" (ibid.). Or, then, a *multi-electrode* array is sometimes used. In the resistivity method, the operative physical parameter is electrical conductivity, whereas the measured parameters are earth resistance, polarisation voltages or frequency-dependent ground resistance.

- The *induced polarisation* method has the same measured parameters as the resistivity method, but the operative physical parameter is electrical capacitance in

---

[83] It is based on Kearey and Brooks (1984). Incidentally, a current edition of that book is Kearey, Brooks, and Hill (2002).

stead of conductivity. Reportedly, it is less effective and slower a method than resistivity surveys (ibid., p. 14).

- In the *self-potential* method, which is reportedly inexpensive (ibid.), the measured parameter is "naturally occurring ground [electrical] potential due to electrochemical reactions between different rock and groundwater levels and flow" (ibid.), and the operative physical parameter is electrical conductivity. Fenning & Donnelly (ibid.) suggest that, notwithstanding the lack of publications about using this method for forensic purposes of discovering dead bodies, the self-potential method has potential (our pun intended) in that domain.

- In the *electromagnetic* methods, the measured parameter is the response to electromagnetic radiation, whereas the operative physical parameters are electrical conductivity and inductance. "An effective and rapid surveying alternative to resistivity profiling is the electromagnetic inductive conductivity (IC) profiling method, which allows continuous recording of the subsurface conductivity at a walking pace. Electrical conductivity is the reciprocal of electrical resistivity" (ibid.). "No case histories relating to direct detection of buried human remains are known", but in the literature applications of the method were described, "in defining archaeological features such as graves and tombs" (ibid.).

- In the *ground-penetrating radar (GPR)* method (e.g., Hammon, McMechan, & Zeng, 2000; Mellett, 1996), the measured parameter is the response to high-frequency electromagnetic radiation, and the operative physical parameters are electrical conductivity and the dielectric constant. Whereas in the electromagnetic inductive conductivity method, "instruments are one-man, portable and operat[ing] in the frequency range of 10–15 kHz", "[t]he much higher frequency range of 25 MHz to 2 GHz is the realm of GPR which has received substantial publicity for its ability to produce high-resolution cross-sections of the surface" (Fenning & Donnelly, 2004, p. 14). Reportedly, Hildebrand, Wiggins, Henkart, and Conyers (2002), who "compared seismic reflection and GPR imaging over a dead pig buried in a wooden coffin at a test site in Illinois" (Fenning & Donnelly, 2004, p. 13), found that "the GPR survey was many times faster than the seismic reflection survey" (ibid.).

- Moreover, *metal detector* methods involve a "one-man, portable hand-held scanning devic[e] with an audible signal or meter output" (Fenning & Donnelly, 2004, pp. 14–15). The smaller the metal object, the shallower the underground range of the instruments. A large object would be detected even if buried somewhat deeper (ibid.).

- And finally, "[t]he advantages of using mobile multi-sensor systems in forensic studies are clearly apparent where there are large tracts of survey and copious detailed data points are required" (ibid.); such mutisensor systems consist of arrays of sensors "which can be man-carried or vehicle-mounted and walked/towed across site" (ibid.), sometimes making use of *differential global-positioning systems (DGPS)*.

The general rule for all those methods is that "[t]he physical property contrast between a target and the surrounding host material of soil and rocks is essential if geophysical methods are to be effective" (Fenning & Donnelly, 2004, p. 12). "In addition to an understanding of the capabilities of geophysical methods, it is essential that the limitations of these methods be clearly understood.

MacDougall et al. (2002) point out various limitations which can make areas unattractive for geophysical surveys" (Fenning & Donnelly, ibid.). For example, "gates, buildings, fences, overhead power cables, parked or moving vehicles and machinery", being "man-made metallic features at ground surface", are detrimental for a survey to be conducted, and so it the "[p]resence of man-made metallic and non-metallic features below ground surface e.g. cables, pipes, sewers, reinforced concrete" (ibid.). This is also the case of "[e]lectrical interference e.g. mobile phones, electrical machinery, power cables", of "[c]urrent construction or farming activities", of "[s]evere ground topography", of access problems such as bushes and vegetation, of the "[p]resence of farm animals", and of "[s]easonal factors e.g. tourists, weather" (ibid.).

Fenning and Donnelly's article (2004) has been invaluable for writing part of this section. That article also analyses three case histories. The interested reader is urged to refer to that paper. Whatever we have quoted from it here, can only be an appetiser, not the main course.

8.5.3 A Clarification About Time Slicing

Time-slicing (mentioned in the Section 8.5.2, with data from ground-penetrating radar) is a concept that occurs in a number of different disciplines. Time-slicing can be found in computer operating system design; in cinematography; in synchrotron radiation from physics; in power engineering; and so forth. In a computer's operating system which, on a serial machine, has to simulate the parallel execution of a large number of programs, this is achieved by means of time slicing: at each time slice, a small number of instructions are executed for each program, one at a time. If the strategy is that a fixed number of instructions is to be executed for each program at each time slice, longer programs will take more time slices. Other strategies are possible.

In contrast, in telecommunications, time slices (i.e., burst, or time slots when the data are transmitted) enable a reduction in power consumption, e.g., of mobile receivers, because when the relevant data are not available, the front end (i.e., the receiver) is switched off, and later on it is informed when to wake up, when the next burst (intended for it) is expected.

As to special effects in cinematography and computer animation, the Wikipedia entry for "Bullet time"[84] remarks that "Technical and historical variations of this effect have been referred to as time slicing, view morphing, flo mo, mort temps and virtual cinematography":

---

[84] http://en.wikipedia.org/wiki/Bullet_time (accessed in March 2007).

a computer-enhanced variation of slow-motion special effects used in some recent films and computer games. It is characterized both by its extreme permutation of time (slow enough to show normally imperceptible and un-filmable events, such as flying bullets) and by the ability of the camera angle – the audience's point-of-view – to move around the scene at a normal speed while events are slowed. This is almost impossible with conventional slow-motion, as the physical camera would have to move impossibly fast; the concept implies that only a 'virtual camera', often illustrated within the confines of a computer-generated environment such as a game or virtual reality, would be capable of 'filming' bullet-time types of moments.

In beam physics, a report in the *Advanced Light Source (ALS) News* (ALS News, 2000) stated that

[i]n early 1996, Alexander Zholents and Max Zolotorev of Berkeley Lab's Center for Beam Physics proposed the laser time-slicing technique as a way to achieve effective bunch lengths in the femtosecond range. At the heart of the proposal was the use of a high-power, femtosecond laser synchronized with the electron bunches so that a pulse of laser light passed collinearly with an electron bunch through an undulator or wiggler. The high electric field of the shorter laser pulse modulated a portion of the longer electron bunch, with some electrons gaining energy and some losing energy. Subsequently, when the energy-modulated electron bunch reached a bend magnet (or other section of the storage ring with a nonzero dispersion), a transverse separation occurred. A collimator or aperture selected the synchrotron radiation from the displaced bunch slices.

Later on, according to the results of Schoenlein et al. (2000), a Berkeley team – in the words of ALS News (2000) –

generated 300-femtosecond pulses of bend-magnet synchrotron radiation at the Advanced Light Source (ALS) with the aid of a laser 'time-slicing' technique. Their proof-of-principle experiment demonstrates that this technique is a viable one for producing ultrashort pulses of x rays. An ALS bend-magnet beamline will soon be commissioned that will be dedicated to time-resolved x-ray diffraction, EXAFS, and other techniques capable of probing the long-range and local structure of matter on a femtosecond time scale.

Readers conversant with artificial intelligence are likely to know about *slice* from the terminology of *naive physics:* that notion of *slice* was introduced in Patrick Hayes' (1985) so-called *ontology for liquids*, a naive physics model that can handle phenomena in fluid dynamics, and involves spatio-temporal histories of objects. On p. 90, Hayes wrote the following concerning the difference between the formal concepts of *history* and *situation*:

A history differs from a situation in being restricted spatially and extended temporally: it is a connected piece of space-time in which 'something happens', more or less separate from other such pieces. Histories, unlike situations, have a *shape*: much of [Hayes' treatment is] devoted to ways of describing their shape.

Examples of histories include the inside of a room during the afternoon, a horserace and the pouring of water from one cup into another. The idea is that a history shall contain an event, isolating it temporally and spatially from other events. We include the special case in which nothing happens at all. A *state* [...] is an instantaneous 'slice' of a history at a certain time-instant. [...] If h is a history and t a time-instant (we assume a global timescale od some sort with an inequality defined on it), the $h@t$ (read h at t) is the 'slice' of h at t. This is a state, that is, a spatial entity at a particular time.

8.5.4 From Soil to Scent: Between Current Practice and Imagining the Digital Potential

8.5.4.1 Scent-Detection, Odorology, Cadaver Dogs, and Gas Soil Surveying: The Detection of the Scent of an Individual, vs. the Detection of a Kind (Graves)

Tribondeau (accessed 2006) credits a country in Eastern Europe with the origination of a particular technique for identification, *odorology* (s.v. *odorologie*, quoted here in my own translation):

> Developed since recently by the French police, this practice, which appeared about thirty years ago in Hungary (where it enables solving over 4000 cases per year), enables the identification of perpetrators through their olfactive print (*empreinte olfactive*). Concretely, investigators places cotton ribbons on the scene of the crime; then these conserved inside hermetically closed phials. It just takes, for especially trained dogs, to sniff a piece of cloth imbued with the scent of a suspect who eventually turns up, and subsequently the various phials who are opened in front of these dogs. Like with explosives and narcotics, the dog will stop in front of the phial with the same scent as the suspect. In Hugary, over 18,000 olfactive prints are collected every year. A phial may last during at least ten years.

This is a further development of the widespread employment of dogs for *scent-detection*. The latter method is "Relatively nondestructive. Proven effective even 170 years after burial. Effective over water" (Davenport et al., 1992). These are advantages, whereas disadvantages are as follows: "Most effective when air, ground moist. Dog may be trained for other uses and not properly trained for this type of work; handler may overstate qualifications" (ibid.). Davenport et al. (1992) were concerned with the detection of clandestine graves, and the dogs used were *cadaver dogs*. Using dogs or pigs is also widespread for finding truffles underground, or the method is also in use for detecting landmines, typically for the purpose of demining an area. Davenport et al. (ibid.) had carried out experiments with the detection of pig carcasses, and adopted a multidisciplinary approach to their detection:

> Excessive heat causes some discomfort to the dog and this may affect the dog's ability to locate a scent. When the temperature is extremely high the dog will still locate the scent; however in most cases, it will need to be within approximately a meter of the source. Even if the temperature is high, the results will improve if the ground is moist. Extremely low temperatures also limit the dog's ability to detect the scent from a distance, especially if the source is buried. If the source is buried in snow with temperatures allowing only minimal melting, the dog must be directly over the source to locate it. If the temperature is warm enough to allow for significant melting the dog can locate the source from a greater distance.

Apart from scent-detection by cadaver dogs, also *soil gas* surveying was carried out (ibid.):

> The soil gas surveying performed at the research site holds promise of providing a useful, albeit labor intensive, technique to locate graves. Organic gases were detected within three meters of two of the grave sites; however, the investigators had the privilege of knowing in advance the locations of these sites. Soil gas surveying is best in soils with a low clay content (so as not to clog the probes) and over unfrozen ground.

What can possibly be the use of computing for the techniques mentioned in this chapter? Arguably, even unsophisticated computing methods can be used for the purposes of organisation and classification, e.g., of the dogs and their records. In odorology, such relatively unsophisticated methods from information technology may be nevertheless useful. On the other hand, it may be that chemical sensors as in *electronic noses* are not sophisticated enough; they would only pick up the sort of scent components they were devised to detect. Dogs are much more sensitive. Nevertheless, pattern matching methods, and perhaps data mining methods, from computing could perhaps complement the use of dogs. At any rate:

Despite the importance of the olfactory sense to mankind, the sense of smell in man is often considered the least refined of the human senses, far less sensitive than that of other animals. For example, the human nose possesses only about one million aroma receptors that work in tandem to process olfactory stimuli whereas dogs have about 100 million receptors that distinguish scents at least 100 times more effectively than the average human [(Ouellette, 1999)]. Furthermore, the ability to detect chemicals in the environment is critical to the survival of most prokaryotic and eukaryotic organisms. A clear indication of the importance of olfactory systems in higher eukaryotes is the significant proportion (up to 4%) of the genome that is devoted to encoding products used in building olfactory sensory tissues [(Firestein, 2001)]. The relatively low sensitivity and discrimination capabilities of the human nose, coupled with the common occurrence of olfactory fatigue, has led to the need for electronic instruments with sensors capable of performing repeated discriminations with high precision to eliminate human fatigue.[85]

There are smells that humans could not identify accurately, and electronic noses can, either more accurately or more safely. Electronic noses may not be as good as dog noses (but some are claimed to be as good instead, as we are going to see), but when the task is to smell such substances that would be dangerous even to such police dogs that regularly detect narcotics, electroni noses may be the solution. We devote the next section to electronic noses indeed.

8.5.4.2 Electronic Noses

Odour assessment in industry resorts to any of the following:

- human sensory analysis,
- chemosensors, or
- gas chromatography.

With *gas chromatography*, information is obtained about volatile organic compounds, "but the correlation between analytical results and actual odor perception is not direct due to potential interactions between several odorous components".[86] Moreover, the police resorts to police dogs; individuals searching for truffles resorts

---

[85] Wilson and Baietto (2009, p. 5101).

[86] http://en.wikipedia.org/wiki/Electronic_nose (when accessed in April 2011, it had been last modified in March of the same year).

to truffle dogs or pigs; and personnel searching for landmines may resort, among the other things, to dogs or even pigs, but in that case this is not only because the olfaction of such animals is superior to human olfaction, but also because casualties among such animals in case landmines detonate are more acceptable than human casualties. There also is a technique that resorts to wasps: "In the Wasp Hound odor-detector, the mechanical element is a video camera and the biological element is five parasitic wasps who have been conditioned to swarm in response to the presence of a specific chemical".[87]

Electronic sensing (or *e-sensing*) technologies aim at endowing devices with the capability of reproducing human senses using *sensor arrays* and *pattern recognition* systems. In e-sensing, an *electronic nose* is such a device that is intended to detect odours or flavours. One also speaks of *machine olfaction* in order to denote the automated simulation of the sense of smell. Electronic-nose technology[88] is the subject of a fifty-page survey by Alphus Wilson and Manuela Baietto (2009).

> Since 1982, research has been conducted to develop technologies, commonly referred to as electronic noses, that could detect and recognize odors and flavors. The stages of the recognition process are similar to human olfaction and are performed for identification, comparison, quantification and other applications. However, hedonic evaluation is a specificity of the human nose given that it is related to subjective opinions. These devices have undergone much development and are now used to fulfill industrial needs.[89]

Wilson and Baietto explain (2009, p. 5100):

> The sensor technology of artificial olfaction had its beginnings with the invention of the first gas multisensor array in 1982 [(Persaud & Dodd, 1982)]. Advances in aroma-sensor technology, electronics, biochemistry and artificial intelligence made it possible to develop devices capable of measuring and characterizing volatile aromas released from a multitude of sources for numerous applications. These devices, known as electronic noses, were engineered to mimic the mammalian olfactory system within an instrument designed to obtain repeatable measurements, allowing identifications and classifications of aroma mixtures while eliminating operator fatigue [[90]]. Unlike other analytical instruments, these devices allow the identification of mixtures of organic samples as a whole (identifiable to a source that released the mixture) without having to identify individual chemical species within the sample mixture [[91]]. Hundreds of different prototypes of artificial-nose devices have been developed to discriminate complex vapor mixtures containing many different types of volatile organic compounds (VOCs) [[92]]. These prototypes collectively represent various

---

[87] http://en.wikipedia.org/wiki/Electronic_nose   Also   see   http://en.wikipedia.org/wiki/Wasp_Hound

[88] Also see Pearce, Schiffman, Nagle, Nagle, & Gardner's (2002) *Handbook of Machine Olfaction: Electronic Nose Technology.*

[89] http://en.wikipedia.org/wiki/Electronic_nose.

[90] Davide, Di Natale, and D'Amico (1995); Pelosi and Persaud (1988); Persaud (1992); Persaud, Bartlett, and Pelosi (1993), Shirley and Persaud (1990); Shurmer (1990).

[91] Davide et al. (1995); Gardner (1991); Lonergan et al. (1996).

[92] Ouellette (1999); Yea, Konishi, Osaki, and Sugahara (1994).

electronic aroma detection (EAD) technologies that utilize different sensor types including metal-oxide [93], semiconductive polymers [94], conductive electroactive polymers [95], optical [96], surface acoustic wave [97] and electrochemical gas sensors [98].

These electronic noses are typically used for recognition, rather than quantification[99]:

---

[93] Egashira and Shimizu (1993); Nanto, Sokooshi, and Kawai (1993); Shurmer et al. (1989).

[94] Yim et al. (1993); Pisanelli, Qutob, Travers, Szyszko, and Persaud (1994).

[95] Lonergan et al. (1996); Freund and Lewis (1995); Hatfield, Neaves, Hicks, Persaud, and Tavers (1994); Persaud, Qutob, Travers, Pisanelli, and Szyszko (1994).

[96] Staples (1999).

[97] Again in Staples (1999).

[98] On pp. 221–245 in Gardner and Bartlett's (1999) *Electronic Noses: Principles and Applications*.

[99] But nevertheless, *olfactometers* (when used in one of the senses of that terms) are used to both qualify and quantify. The following is quoted from http://en.wikipedia.org/wiki/Olfactometer

> An *olfactometer* is an instrument typically used to detect and measure ambient odor dilution. Olfactometers are utilized in conjunction with human subjects in laboratory settings, most often in market research, to quantify and qualify human olfaction. Olfactometers are used to gauge the odor detection threshold of substances. To measure intensity, olfactometers introduce an odorous gas as a baseline against which other odors are compared. Many scientists use the term "olfactometer" to refer to a device used to study insect behavior in presence of an olfactory stimulus. It consists of a tube with a bifurcation (with "T" or "Y" shape) where an insect walks and decides between to choices, usually clean air versus air carrying an odor. This is why this device is also called dual choice olfactomenter. Alternatively, an *olfactometer* is a device used for producing aromas in a precise and controlled manner.

> The following sense (as defined ibid.) is unrelated to electronic noses: "A flow-olfactometer is a complex instrument for creation of well defined, reproducible smell or pain stimuli in the nose without tactile or thermal stimulation. Stimulus rise time is fast enough to allow for recording of Olfactory Evoked Potentials (OEPs)." This device "produces a constant heated and humidified flow of pure air. This air flow runs continuously to the subjects nose. For the length of the stimulus pulse the continuous air flow is replaced by a bloc of odorized air" (ibid.). Contrast this to *dynamic dilution olfactometers* (ibid.):

> > The new generations of dynamic dilution olfactometers quantify odors using a panel and can allow different complementary techniques:

> > - odor concentration and odor threshold determination
> > - odor suprathreshold determination with comparison to a reference gas
> > - hedonic scale assessment to determine the degree of appreciation
> > - evaluation of the relative intensity of odors
> > - allow training and automatic evaluation of expert panels

> > These analyses are often used in site diagnostics (multiple odor sources) performed with the goal of establishing odor management plans.

> A concept related to the latter is *electrogustometry*, i.e., the measurement of *taste threshold*, i.e., the minimum amount of electrical current required to excite the sensation of taste. When using an *electrogustometer*, current is made to pass through the tongue, and a metallic taste is perceived.

Conventional electronic noses are not analytical instruments in the classical sense and very few claim to be able to quantify an odour. These instruments are first 'trained' with the target odour and then used to 'recognise' smells so that future samples can be identified as 'good' or 'bad' smells. Electronic noses have been demonstrated to discriminate between odours and volatiles from a wide range of sources.[100]

Electronic noses have a range of applications including *at-line quality control*,[101] various tasks in research and development (R&D),[102] and in process and production departments.[103] A possible application is to olfactive nuisance monitoring, but typical applications have been in the food & beverage sector (e.g., in order to detect spoiled produce), or to flavour & fragrance, or to cosmetics & perfume, as well as to packaging, and in the pharmaceutical and chemical industries.

The working principle of an electronic nose is that is should mimic human (or at any rate, natural) olfaction (it is said sometimes: "the mammalian sense of smell"), and that is should do so as a *non-separative mechanism*. That is to say, an odour (if this is what the device is intended to detect) or a flavour (if this is the device's target instead) should be perceived as a *global fingerprint*. An electronic nose is an instruments that consists of the following:

- head space sampling,
- sensor array,
- pattern recognition modules.

The latter generate signal patterns which in turn are used for characterising odours. "As a first step, an electronic nose need to be trained with qualified samples so as to build a database of reference. Then the instrument can recognize new samples by comparing volatile compounds fingerprint to those contained in its database. Thus they can perform qualitative or quantitative analysis".[104] The architecture of the system is as follows[105]: "Electronic Noses include three major parts: a sample delivery

---

"Electrogustometric taste threshold depends on the duration of current pulse and area of contact of electrode and tongue" (http://en.wikipedia.org/wiki/Electrogustometry).

[100] http://en.wikipedia.org/wiki/Machine_olfaction (when accessed in April 2011, it had been last modified in February of the same year).

[101] As listed at http://en.wikipedia.org/wiki/Electronic_nose tasks of electronic noses within quality control include: conformity of raw materials, as well as of intermediate and final products; batch to batch consistency; detection of contamination, spoilage, or adulteration; origin or vendor selection; and monitoring of storage conditions.

[102] Tasks of electronic noses at R&D laboratories include: formulation or reformulation of products; benchmarking with competitive products; shelf life and stability studies; selection of raw materials; packaging interaction effects; simplification of consumer preference test (ibid).

[103] Tasks of electronic noses in process and production departments include: managing raw material variability; comparison with a reference product; measurement and comparison of the effects of manufacturing process on products; following-up cleaning in place process efficiency; scale-up monitoring; and the monitoring of cleaning in place (ibid.).

[104] http://en.wikipedia.org/wiki/Electronic_nose

[105] Ibid.

system, a detection system, a computing system". Electronic noses "generally comprise: an array of sensors of some type; the electronics to interrogate those sensors and produce the digital signals, and finally; the data processing and user interface software".[106] In particular[107]:

> The **sample delivery system** enables the generation of the headspace (volatile compounds) of a sample, which is the fraction analyzed. The system then injects this headspace into the detection system of the electronic nose. The sample delivery system is essential to guarantee constant operating conditions.

Let us turn to detection[108]:

> The **detection system**, which consists of a sensor set, is the "reactive" part of the instrument. When in contact with volatile compounds, the sensors react, which means they experience a change of electrical properties. Each sensor is sensitive to all volatile molecules but each in their specific way. Most electronic noses use sensor arrays that react to volatile compounds on contact: the adsorption of volatile compounds on the sensor surface causes a physical change of the sensor. A specific response is recorded by the electronic interface transforming the signal into a digital value. Recorded data are then computed based on statistical models.
>
> The more commonly used sensors include metal oxide semiconductors (MOS), conducting polymers (CP), quartz crystal microbalance, surface acoustic wave (SAW), and Metal Oxide Semiconductors- Field Effect Transistors (MOSFET), Based on Ion Mobility Spectrometry (IMS), Based on Optical Florescence.
>
> In recent years, other types of electronic noses have been developed that utilize mass spectrometry or ultra fast gas chromatography as a detection system.

The one remaining component of the architecture is the computing system:

> The **computing system** works to combine the responses of all of the sensors, which represents the input for the data treatment. This part of the instrument performs global fingerprint analysis and provides results and representations that can be easily interpreted. Moreover, the electronic nose results can be correlated to those obtained from other techniques (sensory panel, GC, GC/MS). Many of the data interpretation systems are used for the analysis of results. These include artificial neural network (ANN),[109] Fuzzy logic,[110] pattern recognition modules, etc.[111]
>
> The entire system being a means of converting complex sensor responses into an output that is a qualitative profile of the odour, volatile or complex mixture of chemical volatiles that make up a smell.[112]

---

[106] http://en.wikipedia.org/wiki/Machine_olfaction

[107] http://en.wikipedia.org/wiki/Electronic_nose

[108] Ibid.

[109] Neural networks are the subject of Section 6.1.14 in this book.

[110] Fuzzy logic is the subject of Section 6.1.15 in this book.

[111] http://en.wikipedia.org/wiki/Electronic_nose

[112] http://en.wikipedia.org/wiki/Machine_olfaction

A particular application of machine olfaction is to the discovery of explosives.[113] This is the case of the *Fido Explosives Detector.*[114] This is a tool of ICx Technologies, Inc.,[115] and is based on a proprietary technology invented in 2007 by Timothy Swager of the Massachusetts Institute of Technology. Fido detects trace levels of explosive materials. The name *Fido* reflects the claim that the device's performance at detecting explosives is comparable to that of highly trained explosives detection dogs. There are several configurations of the device: handheld, desktop, or robot-mounted. It has been integrated into both *Packbot* (of the firm iRobot) and *Talon* (of Foster-Miller), and put to use by the U.S. Army in both Iraq and Afghanistan.

The vapour pressure of the chemicals in explosives is low, and this makes the task of discovering explosives by means of an electronic nose more difficult (Jha & Yadava, 2010, p. 364):

> An electronic nose consists of chemical sensor array with pattern recognition system to detect and identify vapour prints of target chemical compounds in gaseous phase. Its applications range from monitoring of hazardous chemicals in the environment, detection of disease through body odour or breathe, smell sensing and monitoring of food degradation through bacterial metabolites emission, to detection of explosives and narcotics through sniffing of the suspects. The detection of trace vapours emanating from hidden explosives is of paramount importance to homeland security and forensics. The security applications include sniffing hidden bombs, landmines, and suspected baggages or persons. The forensic uses involve early identification of devices and contraband activities for prevention of difficult countermeasures later. However, developing a portable electronic nose technology for these purposes is a difficult task due to extremely low vapour pressure of most of the chemical compounds comprising modern explosives.

Moreover, there are environmental differences which complicate the challenge (ibid.):

---

[113] Electronic noses for the detection of explosives are the subject of Pamula (2003); Yinon (2003); Gardner and Yinon (2004); Jha and Yadava (2010). Of course, there are venues of research into the detection of explosives, other than resorting to electronic noses. For example, David Moore (2007) provided a survey of advances in trace explosives detection instrumentation. In particular, section 4.2 in Morre (2007) is concerned with *vapour concentration methods*, and also section 5 is on *trace vapour detection*. Wang (2004) discussed microchip devices for detecting terrorist weapons. Brenda Klock's project plan (2001) concerns aviation in the United States: her plan outlined "the field evaluation for threat detection in X-ray images of bags containing explosives at full and sub-certification weights" (ibid., from the abstract). "X-ray systems in airports are designed to display images of baggage and its contents, including guns, knives, other weapons, and explosives. X-ray systems include a function designed to maintain on-the-job vigilance. Threat Image Projection (TIP) was developed to increase the proficiency of the primary skills required of a screener to interdict threats at the checkpoint. TIP exposes screeners to images of threats (e.g., weapons or explosives) by randomly projecting these threat images onto passenger bags as the bags move through the X-ray system. Alternately, TIP can also project the image of an entire bag containing a threat when there is a suitable gap between passenger bags" (ibid., p. iv).

[114] http://en.wikipedia.org/wiki/Fido_Explosives_Detector   Also   see: http://www.icxt.com/products/detection/explosive/fido/

[115] http://www.icxt.com/

The reliable detection of explosives vapour signature or vapour prints at such low concentrations is a challenging task even for some most advanced detection techniques today. The difficulty is further compounded as the trace explosive vapours are usually camouflaged in complex background of several interfering volatile organic compounds. The compositions of latter vary wildly over various kinds of sites of interest. For example, ambient air over landmines will be drastically different from that near the body of a person boarding an aircraft hiding a bomb or a busy market place threatened with a hidden bomb.

It is far from being the case that only one class of methodologies is employed in electronic noses for detecting explosives. Jha and Yadava (2010) resort to a surface acoustic wave (SAW) platform (ibid., pp. 364–365):

> The reliable detection of explosives vapour signature or vapour prints at such low concentrations is a challenging task even for some most advanced detection techniques today. The difficulty is further compounded as the trace explosive vapours are usually camouflaged in complex background of several interfering volatile organic compounds. The compositions of latter vary wildly over various kinds of sites of interest. For example, ambient air over landmines will be drastically different from that near the body of a person boarding an aircraft hiding a bomb or a busy market place threatened with a hidden bomb. them all. Most interesting aspects of SAW sensors are their continuous upgradability in performance through increase in operation frequency, modification in device design, improvement in polymer interface18, and planar technology.

In the model reported about by Jha and Yadava (2010), pattern recognition is performed by means of a neural network[116] with error backpropagation. Actually their article "proposes simulated SAW sensor array model as a validation tool for pattern recognition algorithms" (ibid., p. 369). Data preparation was by dividing the output of each sensor by the respective vapour concentrations and frequency shifts due to polymer coatings. Let

$$\Delta f_{ij} \qquad C^i \qquad \Delta f_p^j$$

respectively stand for the output of each sensor, the respective vapour concentrations, and frequency shifts. Their logarithms are taken to define a new matrix as

$$\Delta f_{ij} \leftarrow \log(\Delta f_{ij} / C^i \Delta f_p^j)$$

This is followed by the step of this data matrix being mean-centred and variance-normalised with respect to the vapour samples for each sensor in the array. This is called *dimensional autoscaling* (Osuna & Nagle, 1999). It is implemented as

$$\Delta f_{ij} \leftarrow (\Delta f_{ij} - \overline{\Delta f_j}) / \sigma_j$$

---

[116] Neural networks are the subject of Section 6.1.14 in this book.

where

$$\overline{\Delta f}_{ij} = (1 / N) \sum_{i=1}^{N} \Delta f_{ij}$$

and

$$\sigma_j = \sqrt{(1 / N) \sum_{i=1}^{N} (\Delta f_{ij} - \overline{\Delta f}_j)^2}$$

"represents the column mean and standard deviation, respectively. Then, the denoising was done by truncating the full rank SVD [i.e., singular value decomposition] expansion of the redefined data matrix by a matrix of lower rank. The procedure implicitly assumes that the rank of the data matrix is lower than the number of sensors in the array. The details of SVD denoising are presented. The data matrix regenerated on the basis of truncated SVD approximates the original data with reduced noise. The preprocessed data matrix as explained above is then PCA [i.e., principal component analysis] processed, and the first few principal components are taken to define the set of features to represent vapour identities. The classification is done by artificial neural network based on the training by error backpropagation algorithm" (Jha & Yadava, 2010, p. 369).

There even exist an application of electronic noses to medical pathology. Dogs can smell some human diseases: "The connection between differences in the aroma of diseased vs. healthy human tissues and diagnostic detection of human pathogenesis is supported by studies using the extraordinarily keen olfactory abilities of well trained dogs whose sense of smell is one million times greater than human's in the ability to detect melanoma tissues [(Pickel, Manucy, Walker, Hall, & Walker, 2004)], bladder cancer [(Willis et al., 2004)], as well as lung and breast cancers [(McCulloch et al., 2006)]."(Wilson & Baietto, 2009, p. 5125). But electronic noses can also be used for the purposes of detecting diseases: "Many medical researchers have published experimental data in the last ten years to demonstrate the feasibility of using the electronic nose to diagnose human diseases and to identify many different pathogenic microorganisms through the detection of the VOCs [i.e. volatile organic compounds] they emit both in vitro and in vivo [(Casalinuovo, Di Pierro, Coletta, & Di Francesco, 2006)]" (Wilson & Baietto, 2009, p. 5125).[117]

One also talks about electronic tongues (Wilson & Baietto, 2009, p. 5134):

New emerging technologies are continually providing means of improving e-noses and EAD capabilities through interfaces and combinations with classical analytical systems for rapid discrimination of individual chemical species within aroma mixtures. E-nose instruments are being developed that combine EAD sensors in tandem with analytical detectors such as with fast gas chromatography (FGC) [118]. More complicated technologies such as

---

[117] Also see Persaud's (2005) 'Medical applications of odor-sensing devices'.

[118] Staples (2000).

optical gas sensor systems also may improve on traditional e-nose sensor arrays by providing analytical data of mixture constituents [119]. These technologies will have the capability of producing recognizable high resolution visual images of specific vapor mixtures containing many different chemical species, but also quantifying concentrations and identifying all compounds present in the gas mixture. Similar capabilities for identifying components of solid and liquid mixtures may be possible with devices called electronic tongues [120]. Several recent reviews provide summaries of electronic tongue technologies and discuss potential applications for food analyses [121].

Whereas Wilson and Baietto (2009) did not mention forensic science specifically, it stands to reason that electronic noses and electronic tongues could find there application as well.

8.5.5 Forensic Palynology

Patricia E. J. Wiltshire gave the fourth and last lecture, at the workshop on Archaeology and Forensic Science, held at the British Academy in London on 27 February 2007. The talk had the title "From Archaeology to CSI" (i.e., crime scene investigation), but the analysis of pollen or other plant remains (a field in which Europe is ahead of the United States, in forensic contexts) played an important part in it. The speaker (who was also introduced to the audience by a nickname, "Pollen Pat", by which colleague in the Forensic Science Service sometimes refer to her), is affiliated with the Forensic Science Service as well as with the University of Aberdeen. She has worked on about 200 crime cases, and often appears in court as an expert witness. Originally she was an environmentalist. From palynology (i.e., the analysis of pollen), she spread into all of forensic science, and in fact, that was the talk in which more, and the most shocking, photographs of decaying human bodies were shown. Nevertheless, it was a lucid, well-argued talk extolling the role of palynology in solving forensic cases.

As exemplified during the talk, these typically were cases of of murder. For example, a girl of 15 had been beaten to death. Her boyfriend was suspected, but he denied the charge, and denied he had been in a schoolyard where the girl was believed to have been beaten by a gang of youngsters. Nevertheless, Wiltshire found the pollen of a tree from his garden all over the body of the girl, as well as on the knees of the young man's trousers. He eventually got a life sentence, and his mother was convicted for covering up for him.

In some other cases brought as examples, no murder was involved; e.g., the speaker had advised the police whether some marks visible on a package had been

---

[119] White, Kauer, Dickinson, and Walt (1996).

[120] Winquist, Holmin, Krantz-Rülcker, Wide, and Lundström (2000); Söderström, Borén, Winquist, and Krantz-Rülcker (2003).

[121] Gutés, Céspedes, and del Valle (2007); Winquist (2008); Scampicchio, Ballabio, Arecchi, Cosio, and Mannino (2008).

made in Europe or in Mombasa, Kenya. In another case, she belied a rape accusation: a girl claimed she had been pushed on a garden wall, but none of the pollen from the wall appeared on her garments. In the case that concluded the talk, namely, the case of a man wounded in the bottom, the speaker enabled the police to recategorise what at first the police had been believed to be a vicious sex crime, with the criminal still at large. She advised them to wait, before taking that direction of inquiry. Pollen analysis enabled her to reconstruct how the critically wounded man, with two very long stabs entering his body from his anus, got those wounds. Apparently he had been drunk, and tried to climb on a wall at a park, but in so doing, he had impaled himself.

Wiltshire began her talk by pointing out that where microorganisms are inhibited, plant remains (seeds, leaves, stems, pollen, spores) can be preserved for thousands of years. In such cases, the taxonomical identification of the plant to which the well-preserved pollen belongs can be straightforward. Analysis of assemblages of these plant remains has allowed the reconstruction (or at least this is what some think) of ecological environments. Such ideal preservation does not obtain, in most cases, for pollen from archaeological or even recent, forensic contexts. Poor preservation makes it difficult to determine the taxonomical identification of pollen remains.

Botany has been used extensively in archaeology over the last thirty years, through macrofossil analysis and palynology. It can be applied to analysing the function of artefacts (food or medicine remains), or the function of features: retting (soaking), water and food storage, textiles. To be precise, palynology is the study of palynomorphs, i.e., any microscopic objects from the reproduction of plants, such as pollen grains, plant spores, fungal or fossil spores, and so forth. (Actually, palynology studies morphological, biochemical, and biogeographical aspects of these.) When palynology is forensic, it is interfaced to other forensic disciplines, some of them also from ecology, e.g., pedology, i.e., soil analysis. Clearly pedology is important for forensic purposes (e.g., for analysing soil in or around graves, or as traces found on shoes).

Palaeoecological pollen (e.g., as found in blank peat) is easy to identify, whereas, as mentioned, archaeological or forensic pollen is not, as it is in phases of decomposition. This is a problem, for the forensic application of palynology, because what is "forensic" must be defensible in court, and an expert witness is under attack by the barrister of the other side (whereas ethically, the duties of the prosecution expert witness are to the court, rather than to the police). Wiltshire mentioned an authority who once said that palynology is rubbish, because it cannot be proven. Forensic analysis has shown that palynology is very crude (whether paelaeoecological, or forensic). Still, the discipline is not alone in that situation. Take medicine. Ecology is not an absolute science; it is like medicine, in that you cannot test hypotheses. What you do have, is symptoms. The discipline not being exact hasn't prevented Wiltshire from working on about 200 crime cases. Some of her work is clandestine, and involves dressing up, e.g., as a shop assistant.

A forensic expert has to recognise anomalies, and one must know what *is* right, to know what is *not* right. An ecosystem can be recognised by proxy indicators of the place: wood, leaves, seeds, pollens, spores, diatoms, and so forth. Like in medicine, these are symptoms. From the state of the flora on which a human body fell, it was understood it (a dead girl) was dumped in early August.

Any proxy indicator picked up by an offender might be traced back to the source: this is *Locard's Principle*.[122] Petrol cans, because of static electricity, have palyno-logical indicators stick to them. Parasitic worm eggs of such worms that parasitise frogs are yet another proxy indicator, and they indicate that there must be a stream or pond. The worm eggs are secondary proxy indicators of frogs, and frogs are secondary proxy indicators of a stream or pond. Worm eggs do not belong in paly-nology, but by their very nature, they are relevant to the work of a forensic expert who is a palynologist. Palynology can be useful at all stages of decomposition of a corpse. Nevertheless, it is important to avoid contamination of the evidence while dissecting (like the crime scene or the perpetrator of a crime, also staff handling the evidence could leave traces, and it is paramount to be able to tell which is what.)

Let us broaden the discourse about palynology, before turning to software for that discipline. *Palynology* is the study of palynomorphs, both living and fossil. The term was introduced by Hyde and Williams (1944). *Actuopalynology* (as opposed to *palaeopalynology*) is "the study of palynomorphs which are either living, still retain their cell contents, or whose cell contents have been removed by maceration"; one of its branches is *forensic palynology* (used to "to determine the past location of items or persons based on the pollen and spores on or in them"). Note that whereas the antonym of *palaeopalynology* is *actuopalynology*, the antonym of *palaeontology* is *neontology* (i.e., the study of still extant or recent animal or vegetal taxa).

As to applications of *archaeological palynology* ("the analysis of pollen, spores, and other palynomorphs from archaeological sites"), they "include the reconstruc-tion of prehistoric diet, funary practices, artifact function and source, archaeological feature use, cultivation and domestication of plants, and human impact on vegeta-tion", according to definitions at a webpage by Owen Davis (1999). Archaeological palynology and quaternary palynology are part of *environmental palynology*, i.e., "The use of palynomorphs, their identification, distribution, and abundance to deter-mine past changes in the biota, climate, or surficial geology of an area" (ibid.). A distinct area is *stratigraphic palynology*, i.e., "The use of palynomorphs, their iden-tification, distribution, and abundance to correlate among sedimentary sequences of any age, or to provide chronological control for these sedimentary sequences" (ibid.); "the study of sedimentary sequences often includes both stratigraphic and environmental palynology" (ibid.). One of the areas of palynology is *mellisopaly-nology*, i.e., the study of pollen in honey or other bee products. Another area is *aeropalynology*. Another subdiscipline is *pollen analysis*.

According to a somewhat circular definition provided by Peter Hoen (1999), *palynomorph* are "A general term for all entities found in palynological prepara-tions"; with the useful addition that: "In addition to pollen grains and spores, the

---

[122] On Edmond Locard, a star in the history of French and world criminalistics, see in Section 8.7.1 below.

term encompasses acritarchs, dinoflagellates and scolecodonts, but not other micro-fossils, such as diatoms, that are dissolved by hydrofluoric acid". Therefore, the delimitation is according to a technique of analysis. According to a broad defini-tion, provided by Owen Davis (1999), *palynomorphs* "include pollen, embryophyte spores, algae, fungal spores, dinoflagellates [which are unicellular aquatic organ-isms], microforaminifera, chitinozoans [marine fossils, shaped like flasks, occurring individually or in chains, usually assumed to be animal remains], acritarchs [con-sisting of a central cavity enclosed by a wall of single or multiple layers and a chiefly organic composition], and amoebas. Thus, they "include both plant and ani-mal structures that are microscopic in size (from about 5 μm to about 500 μm), and are composed of compounds that are highly resistant to most forms of decay other than oxidation, being composed of sporopollenin, chitin, or related com-pounds. In the strict sense, palynomorphs are recognized as microscopic structures that are abundant in most sediments and sedimentary rocks, and are resistant to the routine pollen-extraction procedures including strong acids, bases, acetolysis, and density separation. In a broader sense, other microfossils sometimes are given 'courtesy appointments' as 'palynomorphs' even they do not survive routine pollen-extraction procedures" (Davis, 1999). The term *palynomorph* was introduced in Tschudy (1961).

References in forensic palynology include Bryant and Mildenhall (1996), Bryant, Jones, and Mildenhall (1996), and Faegri and Iversen (1989, p. 174 ff). Also refer to the webpage on forensic palynology of the California Criminalistic Institute,[123] to Terry Hutter's forensic palynology website,[124] to the website of Dallas Mildenhall's Foresic Services in New Zealand,[125] and to a website of Lynne Milne,[126] at the University of Western Australia.

There exist software resources for palynology. For example, the European Pollen Database (EPD) can be queries through its website.[127] It also publishes a newsletter. "The EPD is a relational database handled by Borland's (now Corel) PARADOX software. It contains raw data of pollen counts, C14 dates, geographical location and description of sites, lithological description of the records, chronologies, and bibliographic references. [. . .] The EPD tables can be downloaded and read directly either by PARADOX or by other software such as Microsoft Access. Single files are available in other formats (ASCII and Tilia)" (from the EPD main page), Tilia being "a free software program written by Eric Grimm", and on which, information is provided at the Tilia website.[128]

The EPD website refers to "Web tools provided by the World Data Center for Paleoclimatology [and used in order] to retrieve basic information about a site, as

---

[123] http://www.ns.net/cci/Reference/Pollen/pollen.htm

[124] http://www.geoscience.net/Forensic_Palynology.html

[125] http://www.gns.cri.nz/help/laboratory/foren.html

[126] http://science.uniserve.edu.au/faces/milne/milne.html

[127] http://www.ncdc.noaa.gov/paleo/epd/epd_main.html

[128] http://www.ncdc.noaa.gov/paleo/tilia.html

well as summary pollen diagrams: the Pollen Data Search Engine allows you search by P.I., place, or time; Webmapper is a visual map tool for locating data". The Pollen Data Search Engine is accessible online,[129] whereas at another address one can access Webmapper.[130] The EPD e-list is hosted at the University of Colorado.

Pierre A. Zippi's PAZ Software[131] develops Mac-supported (but allegedly cross-platform) specialty scientific software solutions, applications having been developed for geological, biostratigraphic and earth science. Biostratigraphic services, such as data analysis, paleo data digitisation, and charting, are available[132]; whereas Paleontology sample preparation services are available at another website of the same firm.[133] One of the products of PAZ software is Palynodata Table Maker 1.0, which (as advertised) "Converts unwieldy Palynodata references and taxa list to tab-delimited ASCII text files. The resulting tab-delimited text files may be imported into spreadsheets, databases or mail merge applications. Greatly increases the usefulness of this large stratigraphic database". TILIA.12 To Spread (for MacOS) is used to "convert older Tilia 1.12 ASCII data files to tab-delimited spreadsheet files. NAPDToSpread will convert Tilia 2.0 files to spreadsheets. Free with WellPlot"; and so forth. Stephen Juggins' webpage[134] provides information on more software for palynology.

8.5.6 Computing in Environmental Forensics

There exist applications of computing to environmental law (McBurney & Parsons, 2001; de Vey Mestdagh, 1999), and there exist computer tools for environmental forensics. The latter field is the subject of Murphy and Morrison (2002), which I reviewed (Nissan, 2003g). Practitioners of environmental forensics are concerned with chemistry, materials science, fluid dynamics, statistics, possibly biology, and they are required to know what the law is, how it works, and how they can construct and present their case effectively, which is typically but not exclusively when they are heard during litigation as expert witnesses. "Environmental forensic investigations frequently deal with the release of contaminants" (ibid., p. xiii). Site history (Bookspan, Gravel, & Corley, 2002, i.e., chapter 2 in Murphy & Morrison, 2002), e.g., at a landfill, requires acquiring documents, from archives or verbal depositions. I see a potential for dedicated software tools for assisting in this: not so much for retrieval (the paper trail is, after all, on paper, and archive material may well date back from before the computer era), as for organizing the development of the investigation report (Nissan, 2003g, p. 572).

---

[129] At http://www.ncdc.noaa.gov/paleo/ftp-pollen.html

[130] http://www.ncdc.noaa.gov/paleo/pollen.html

[131] In Garland, Texas. See the website http://www.pazsoftware.com/

[132] At the website http://www.biostratigraphy.com

[133] At the website http://www.paleolab.com

[134] Accessible at http://www.staff.ncl.ac.uk/stephen.juggins/int_nn.htm

Computing is explicitly covered in the next chapter in Murphy and Morrison (2002), as the need for aerial photos (current or historical) of a site lends the subject to that book's chapter 3 (i.e., Ebert, 2002),[135] on photogrammetry, photointerpretation, and digital imaging and mapping. Electronics is on occasion linked to chemical spillages: a case study (section 3.5.2 in that same book) involves circuit board fabrication plants.

Chapter 5 in Murphy and Morrison's book, namely, Philp (2002), is on isotope measurements. "Bulk isotopic values have been readily available for many years but one of the most significant analytical advances in geochemistry in the past few years has undoubtedly been the development of combined gas chromatography – isotope ratio mass spectrometry (GCIRMS)" (ibid., p. 111). Computing and plotters are conspicuous in such analyses.

When it comes to environmental forensics rather than just environmental science, there is a factor that need be considered, considering computer-assisted modelling as pertaining to various areas of environmental science. "There are currently in excess of 400 groundwater flow (advective) and contaminant transport models" (ibid., p. 338, which is in chapter 8: Morrison, 2002). "In the United States, it is estimated that computer-based predictions of contaminant transport influence legal and policy decisions involving the allocation of at least 1 billion dollars each year" (ibid., p. 339). Several sources of uncertainty affect models.

The calculation-intensive subsurface models (Morrison, 2002) include, e.g., vapour, liquid, colloidal, or cosolvent transport through pavement or soil. "Preferential flows" of infiltrating liquid exploit preferential pathways, either artificial (dry wells, cisterns, utility line backfill, etc.), or natural: "worm channels, decayed root channels [. . .], soil fractures, slickenslides, swelling and shrinking clays, highly permeable soil layers, and insect burrows" (ibid., p. 335). This is fertile ground for computational science ($\neq$ computer science).

"The origin of inverse modeling for contaminant transport in groundwater is predated by research in the heat transfer literature" (ibid., p. 339). Inverse (or reverse) models are also called "backward extrapolation models", "hindcasting" 125 (patterned after "forecasting"), and "backward random walk" (339). "In its simplest application, inverse modeling relies upon measured properties or contaminant concentrations to extrapolate to some point in the past, the age and the location of a contaminant release, most frequently by using geostatistical and optimization approaches" (ibid., p. 339). "In cases where light non-aqueous phase liquids (LNAPLs) are of interest, numerical models are available to predict LNAPL plume migration over time [. . .] and to age date the release using a direct estimate and nonlinear parameter estimation approach" (ibid., p. 342).

Potential sources of uncertainty affecting inverse models include: "The reasonableness of the sected porosity and hydraulic conductivity value(s)" (ibid., p. 343),

---

[135] James I. Ebert is an envirnmental and forensic scientist who is also a certified photogrammetrist, and a trained archaeologist and anthropologist who has taken part in a project in palaeoanthropology and environmental research at Olduvai Gorge in Tanzania.

"The consistency of the groundwater flow direction and velocity over time", "The validity of the selected hydraulic gradient(s) values over time and distance from the release", "The number of data points and time interval during which the data were collected", "The nature of the release (steady versus non-steady", "The loading rate" (possibly based on production records), "The value(s) selected for aquifer(s) thickness (model specific)", "The horizontal and transverse dispersivity values" (ibid., p. 343), "Contaminant retardation and/or degradation rates" (ibid., p. 344), "Identification of the leading edge of the contaminant plume (model specific)", "The effect of recharge/discharge rates (if applicable) of water into the system and its impact on plume geometry and contaminant velocity" (ibid., p. 344). Bear in mind that a court may have to decide on whether some aspect of the model was reasonable, e.g., rejecting the defendant's model. Robert D. Morrison, the author of Ch. 8 in the same book, actually provides legal illustrations for a few of the items listed above. This way, for the "effect of recharge/discharge rates", he states (ibid., p. 344):

> In the *Velsicol* case, for example, the court wrote, 'the district court rejected the defendant's water model as inaccurately under representing the extent of chemical contamination in the groundwater supply. In refuting the defendant's model, the court reasoned that Velsicol had failed to factor in the massive dumping of liquid waste, the ponding of water in the trenches, and the draw down on the aquifer caused by new homes.'

Chapter 9 in Murphy and Morrison (2002), "Forensic Air Dispersion Modeling and Analysis", features techniques such as the Gaussian plume model analysis. A "case study is a toxic tort in which the plaintiffs claimed dioxin and furan exposure" (ibid., p. 385). "Chapters 10 through 12 [in Murphy & Morrison (2002)] introduce statistical aspects associated with an environmental forensic investigation. Chapter 10 summarizes statistical tests for comparing data sets and evaluating temporal or spatial relationships. Chapters 11 and 12 present advanced pattern recognition techniques, of increasing utility within today's greater computing power. Chapter 11 discusses particulate pattern recognition techniques used for source identification" (ibid., p. xiv).

Thomas D. Gauthier's "Statistical Methods" (chapter 10 in Murphy & Morrison, 2002) points out that of the "variety of statistical analysis techniques[, m]ost examples in the literature involve rather sophisticated applications including principal components analysis and chemical mass balance receptor modeling (discussed elsewhere in [Murphy & Morrison, 2002]). These techniques are powerful analytical tools and provide useful insights for data interpretation but the results can be difficult to explain to a judge or jury" (ibid., pp. 391–392). "Relatively simple statistical analysis techniques can be used in environmental forensic investigations to compare data sets, characterize associations between variables, evaluate trends, and make predictions. Moreover, it is often possible to assign a degree of confidence to the results. This advantage is particularly useful in litigation scenarios where experts are often asked to assign a probability to the correctness of their opinion" (ibid., p. 425).

For the identification of air pollution sources, dispersion or receptor modeling (Watson & Chow, 2002, i.e., chapter 11 in Murphy & Morrison, 2002) is a relevant tool. Modeling small particles suspended in the air goes by the name "particulate pattern recognition". "Receptor models use the variability of chemical composition, particle size, and concentration in space and time to identify source types and to quantify source contributions that affect particle mass concentrations, light extinction, or deposition" (ibid., p. 430). Such models include, e.g., *multiple linear regression on chemical markers* (ibid., p. 432), *temporal and spatial correlation eigenvectors* (ibid., p. 433),[136] and (which is of particular interest in our present book) *neural networks* (ibid., section 11.2.6, pp. 433–434): "Training sets that have known source–receptor relationships are used to establish the linkages in the neural net that are then used to estimate source contributions for data sets with unknown relationships. The network assigns weights to the inputs that reproduce the outputs. Neural networks can provide functional relationships that are solutions to the MLR and CMB equations" (ibid., p. 433), i.e., respectively, to the multiple linear regression and to the chemical mass balance equations. Moreover (ibid., p. 434):

> Spectral analysis [...], intervention analysis [...], lagged regression analysis [...], and trend analysis [...] models separate temporal patterns for a single variable and establish temporal relationships between different variables. These models have been used to identify sources, to forecast future pollutant concentrations, and to infer relationships between causes and effects. It is especially important to include meteorological indicators in time series models [...] and to use data sets with comparable measurement methods and sampling frequencies.

Glenn Johnson, Robert Ehrlich, and William Full (2002, i.e., chapter 12 in Murphy & Morrison, 2002) provide an in-depth tutorial into the use of principal components analysis and receptor models in environmental forensics. Such numerical methods are used in order to determine the three parameters enumerated at the end of the following quotation (ibid., p. 462):

> The identification of chemical contaminant sources is a common problem in environmental forensic investigations. Successful inference of sources depends on sampling plan design, sample collection procedures, chemical analysis methods, and knowledge of historical industrial processes in the study area. However, in compex situations where multiple sources contribute similar types of contaminants, even careful project training and design may not be enough. If sources cannot be linked to a unique chemical species (i.e., a tracer chemical), then mapping the distributions of individual contaminant concentrations is insufficient to infer source. If, however, a source exhibits a characteristic 'chemical fingerprint' defined by diagnostic proportions of a large number of analytes, source inference may be accomplished through analysis of multiple variables; that is, through use of multivariate statistical methods. The objective of a multivariate approach to chemical fingerprinting is to determine (1) the number of fingerprints present in the system, (2) the multivariate chemical composition of each fingerprint, and (3) the relative contribution of each fingerprint in each collected sample.

Out of the spectrum of numerical methods from the past twenty years, more recently developed "procedures are designed to solve more general problems, which take

---

[136] For *eigenvectors*, see in fn. 24 in Chapter 6.

into account complications such as bad data, commingled plumes (i.e., mixing of source fingerprints), and the presence of sources not assumed or anticipated at the start of an investigation" (ibid., p. 462). "In terms of experimental design, the source apportionment problem in environmental forensic investigations falls between two extremes.

At one extreme, all potential sources are known in terms of their chemical composition, location, history, and duration of activity. At the other extreme, none of these are known with certainty. Chemicals at the receptor (e.g., estuary sediments, groundwater at a supply well) may be the result of activities long absent from the vicinity of the site" (ibid., p. 462). Morever (ibid., p. 463):

> In the first case (a priori knowledge of all sources) the problem is a relatively simple one. Appropriate sampling locations can be determined using a conventional experimental design, which is part of conventional experimental statistics. Determination of contribution of each source can be extracted using a variety of linear methods, such as chemical mass balance receptor models (see chapter 11 of [Murphy & Morrison, 2002]). However, even when the contributing sources are known, environmental forensic investigations often proven to be more complex than initially anticipated. Chemicals in the environment may not retain their original composition. [...] The result of degradation will be resolution of one or more fingerprints, not originally anticipated.

When knowledge is uncertain, or unavailable, *exploratory data analysis* is to be used. indeed (ibid., p. 463):

> At the other extreme, where nothing is known with certainty, potential sources may be suspected, but samples of the sources (i.e., fingerprint reference standards) may not have been collected, and may not exist in the literature. The industrial history of a region may be imperfectly known. Often, a small, low profile operation may be a major but completely overlooked source of contamination. For cases towards this end of the spectrum, we must take leave of the elegance of conventional experimental statistics, and move into the realm of exploratory data analysis (EDA). The fundamental difference between these two approaches (experimental statistics and EDA) is the former is associated with creation of explicit hypotheses, and evaluation of data in terms of well-defined tests and strong probabilistic arguments. In contrast, the objective of EDA is to find patterns, correlations and relationships in the data itself, with few assumptions or hypotheses [...]. If the fruits of an EDA result in a map where the concentrations of a multivariate fingerprint increase monotonically towards an effluent pipe, and the fingerprint composition is consistent with the process associated with that source, the obvious inference is that the potential source is the actual source. We recognize that we are not working in the realm of classical statistics or formal hypothesis testing, and that EDA is based on less rigorous probabilistic statement. However, such an approach should not be construed as 'second best'. In environmental forensic, an EDA approach may be the only valid option.

Besides, it is important to consider that there may be bad or questionable data: "Unfortunately such errors rarely manifest themselves as random noise. More often, they contribute strong systematic variability. If unrecognized, the result may be derivation of 'fingerprints' which have little to do with the true sources. Therefore, a necessary adjunct to any data analysis in environmental forensics is identification of outliers" (ibid., p. 464). Nevertheless, even "inclusion of vigilant outlier identification and data cleaning procedures" may "resul[t] in deletion or modification of data", and then "the data must be clearly identified, and justification for the action must be provided in the narrative that accompanies the analyses" (ibid.).

To infer the sources of contaminants and their contribution, receptor modeling as described in chapter 12 ofd Murphy and Morrison (2002) is used. The *receptor modeling problem* is formally introduced in section 12.1.2 (ibid., p. 464):

> The objectives are to determine (1) the number of chemical fingerprints in the system; (2) the chemical composition of each fingerprints; and (3) the contribution of each fingerprints in each sample. The starting point is a data-table of chemical measurements in samples collected from the receptor (e.g., estuarine sediments, ambient air in a residential area). These data are usually provided in spreadsheet form where rows represent samples and columns represent chemical analytes. To the multivariate data analyst this table is a matrix. We will refer to the original data table as the m row by n column matrix $\mathbf{X}$, where m is the number of samples and n is the number of analytes. We wish to know the number of fingerprints present (k) and chemical composition of each (objectives 1 and 2 above). This can be expressed as a matrix $\mathbf{F}$, which has k rows and n columns. We also wish to know a third matrix $\mathbf{A}$, which has m rows and k columns, and represents the contribution of each fingerprint in each sample (objective 3 above). Thus the following linear algebraic equation formally expresses the receptor modeling problem.

$$\underset{(m \times n)}{\mathrm{X}} = \underset{(m \times k)}{\mathrm{A}} \quad \underset{(k \times n)}{\mathrm{F}}$$
Matrix dimensions

Subsequent sections in chapter 12 are devoted to methodological categories and are themselves further subdivided rather densely. They include "Principal Components Analysis" (section 12.2) – the acronym is PCA – as applied to environmental chemometrics, and "Self-Training Receptor Modeling Methods" (section 12.3), which in turn includes

- polytopic vector analysis (PVA): this is an algorithm that evolved over forty years, and whose roots are "in principal components analysis, pattern recognition, linear algebra, and mathematical geology" (ibid., p. 498),
- the unique vector rotation method, and
- the so-called SAFER method (the acronym stands for Source Appointment by Factors with Explicit Restrictions), which "is used in extended self-modeling curve resolution" (ibid., p. 508).

"These three [of section 12.3 in Murphy & Morrison (2002)] are analogous in that (1) they do not require a training data set; (2) they are PCA based methods; (3) they involve solution of quantitative source appointment equations by development of oblique solutions in PCA space; and (4) each involves the use of non-negative constraints" (ibid., p. 498). In fact, this is a particular class of algorithms, in Johnson et al. (2002), that deserves special attention in the book your are reading now, which is specifically concerned with the uses of artificial intelligence for legal evidence. Machine learning, as well as self-training algorithms (such as in artificial neural networks) are well-known to artificial intelligence practitioners. But self-training methods are also known from multivariate statistical analysis. Section

12.3 in Johnson et al. (2002), "Self-training receptor modeling methods", is about "models designed to resolve three parameters of concern in a multivariate, mixed chemical system: (1) the number of components in the mixture, (2) the identity (i.e., chemical composition or fingerprints) of each component, and (3) the relative proportions of each component in each sample" (ibid., p. 497). Before Johnson et al. (2002), the full polytopic vector analysis (PVA) algorithm had not been set in any single paper (ibid., p. 498).

"PVA was developed for analysis of mixtures in the geological sciences, but it has evolved over a period of forty years, with different aspects of the algorithm presented in a series of publications, by a number of different authors" (ibid.). The originator was a palaeontologist, John Imbrie (1963), and this initially resulted in a series of Fortran programs. This eventually became CABFAC (*C*algary *a*nd *B*rown *FAC*tor Analysis), which "quickly became the most commonly used multivariate analysis algorithm in the geosciences" (ibid., p. 499). Later on, "William Full, as a PhD candidate at the University of South Carolina in the early 1980s, developed the DENEG algorithm, which allows end-members (sources) to be resolved without a priori knowledge of their composition, and without use of a training data set (Full et al., 1981, 1982)" (Johnson et al., 2002, p. 499). PVA involves resolution of oblique vectors as source compositions. This vector analysis is polytopic, because "PVA involves resolution of a $k - 1$ dimensional solid, a "simplex" or "polytope", within k dimensional principal component space" (ibid.). So if $k = 4$, the polytope is a tetrahedron. The algorithms at the core of PVA are implemented under default options in the commercial versions of the SAWVECA software of Residuum Energy, Inc., Dickinson, Texas. Johnson et al. explained (2002, pp. 506–507):

PVA is one 'self-training' method that allows source profiles to be derived in absence of *a priori* knowledge of their chemical composition, but other such methods have seen considerable application in environmental chemical data. One of these is target transformation factor analysis (TTFA), which developed within analytical chemistry/chemometrics rather than mathematical geology/geochemistry (Roscoe and Hopke, 1981; Gemperline, 1984; Hopke, 1989; Malinowski, 1991).

In TTFA, the subroutine that allows estimates of source composition in the absence of known sources is the unique vector rotation method [...]. This method begins by establishing a $n \times n$ matrix where each row vector is 100% of a single analyte (i.e. 'unique vectors'). In turn, each of these vectors is iteratively rotated within principal component space.

Moreover (Johnson et al., 2002, pp. 508–509):

Another receptor modeling method, SAFER (Source Apportionment by Factors with Explicit Restrictions) is used in extended self-modeling curve resolution (ESMCR: Henry and Kim, 1990; Kim and Henry, 1999). Unlike PVA and TTFA, ESMCR does not typically involve transformation to unit length. [...] The SAFER method begins by defining the 'feasible region' where the simplex vertices and edges may reside. The inner boundary of the feasible region is defined by the convex hull of the data cloud [...]. The non-negativity constraints on the analytes define the outer boundary of the 'feasible region'. [...] For a three-component sistem [...], a feasible mixing model may be defined by direct inspection of the data plotted in the principal component space, and manually located within the feasible region (this method is termed SAFER3D). A method of resolving higher dimensional mixing models has recently been described (Kim and Henry, 1999). That method calls on the use of additional explicit physical constraints. Examples of additonal constraints may include (1) total mass of samples, (2) *a priori* knowledge of a subset of contributing sources, (3) upper and lower limits on ranges or ratios of analyte compositions, or (4) constraints based on laws of chemistry (Kim and Henry, 1999). As was the case for the unique vector iteration method, SADER has been applied primarily in source apportionment studies in air (Henry et al., 1997).

8.6 Forensic Engineering

Forensic engineering is a discipline[137] practised by such engineers who appear in court as expert witnesses, or at any rate are involved in dispute resolution and have to develop hypotheses and argue for them in a legal setting, including in front of arbitration panels, or in mediation and conciliation; for the difference between trial, arbitration, and mediation, see Hohns (1987), from the perspective of the forensic engineer in construction related disputes. Specter (1987) provides the following definition: "Forensic engineering may be generalized as the art and science of practitioners who are qualified to serve as engineering experts in matters before courts of law and in arbitration proceedings" (ibid., p. 61). The definition on Wikipedia[138] is as follows:

> Forensic engineering is the investigation of materials, products, structures or components that fail or do not operate/function as intended, causing personal injury for example. The consequences of failure are dealt by the law of product liability. The subject is applied most commonly in civil law cases, although may be of use in criminal law cases. Generally the purpose of a forensic engineering investigation is to locate cause or causes of failure with a view to improve performance or life of a component, or to assist a court in determining the facts of an accident. It can also involve investigation of intellectual property claims, especially patents.

Forensic engineering typically concerns failure: the failure of structures, foundations, materials, or machinery, or of construction as a process. See, e.g., Lewis and Hainsworth (2006). The journal in the field is *Engineering Failure Analysis*. Construction related disputes are just one of the areas within forensic engineering, and involve civil engineers. A special area is automotive engineering, for investigating car crashes. "Forensic engineering involves more than engineers. We have on our roster chemists, architects, contract administrators, fire cause investigators, and experts in packaging, radiology and computer technology" (Garrett, 1987, p. 17).

---

[137] In James and Nordby (2005, 2nd edn.; 2009, 3rd edn.), a volume on forensic science, the chapters about forensic engineering comprise one about structural failures, by Randall Noon (2005a; 2009a, 3rd edn.), then a chapter about basic fire and explosion investigation, by David Redsicker (2005, 2009, 3rd edn.), and a chapter on vehicular accident reconstruction, by Randall Noon (2005b; 2009b, 3rd edn.).

[138] http://en.wikipedia.org/wiki/Forensic_engineering.

Typically, scholarship in the field concerns failure theories, hypothesis testing, and failure investigations. It also concerns legal problems, practices, and policy connected with the testimony of forensic engineers. Not only engineers, but also trial lawyers and insurance adjusters are involved. In 1987, Pergamon Press (now Elsevier) started to publish a journal in the domain, entitled *Forensic Engineering*. In the United States, there is the *Journal of the National Academy of Forensic Engineers*. *Expert* (1985) is a guide for forensic engineers, published by the Association of Soil and Foundation Engineers. Supranant (1988) is a textbook. Other books in forensic engineering include Noon (1992, 2000), and Lewis, Gagg, and Reynolds (2004). The latter was authored at the Open University in Britain, and it is interesting to see how the website of that institution promotes both its forensic service to external clients, and its curriculum in forensic engineering;[139] as can be seen, the academic disciplinary compartment is Materials Engineering, home the focus there is on product failure, and individual researchers are specialised in a rather narrow category of materials:

> Product failure has been studied in the Materials Engineering Department since its inception, and forms the basis of several courses presented by the department (T839 Forensic Engineering). The loose grouping of individuals study a very wide range of cases, from metal fatigue of crankshafts ([...]), stress corrosion or ozone cracking of fuel lines ([...]), breakage of glass bottle causing personal injury ([...]), failure of power hand tools ([...]) to infringement actions in medical devices and garden products ([...]). Cases are studied within a framework set by litigation, enquires by insurers, or companies and institutions. Work has also been funded by the Consumer Research Laboratories in order to improve the design of handpumps and rising mains for use in developing countries. Independent research by the group has revealed new and unsuspected failure modes in both traditional and entirely new materials. All members have had recent experience of court procedure and giving expert advice before tribunals. This group has links with the *Fracture and Fatigue* and *Residual Stress* groups in the department. [...]

"[T]he insurance industry and the legal profession [are] the primary users of forensic engineering services" (Garrett, 1987, p. 17). Clients typically require "quality technical people to help them solve the puzzle of 'What happened?'" (ibid., p. 17). "[Y]ou are hired by an insurance company, a lawyer, a builder, a manufacturer, or an irate or injured citizen" (Knott, 1987, p. 11). "We ask clients to refrain from deciding in advance what kind of an expert they need. They may ask for a metallurgist when what they really need is a traffic engineer. And they may need several experts, not just one" (Garrett, 1987, p. 18). "If your client is an insurance company, it is usually interested in proof that it should or should not pay a claim" (Knott, 1987, p. 11) "The work is done to determine the probable cause of a failure or an accident. The lawyer will have to prove the case in court, and a proof in law is not the same as a proof in engineering" (ibid.). There are different categories of what is to be proven, in such cases in which a forensic engineer may be called to testify. "The law has evolved into distinct arenas. For example, strict liability, negligence,

---

[139] http://materials.open.ac.uk/research/res_forensic.htm.

and warranty. You may be able to show that the manufacturer had a first-rate quality control program. This is an excellent defense in negligence but has absolutely no application in strict liability" (ibid.).

Software for engineering, especially simulations for *failure analysis*, or then software for *structural risk evaluation*, or software modelling the plasticity and fracture of solid materials, will be of use to the forensic engineer in some categories of cases. Importantly, the entry for "Forensic engineering" in Wikipedia makes a distinction between forensic science and forensic engineering:

> There is some common ground between forensic science and forensic engineering, such as scene of crime and scene of accident analysis, integrity of the evidence and court appearances. Both disciplines make extensive use of optical and scanning electron microscopes, for example. They also share common use of spectroscopy (infra-red, ultra-violet and nuclear magnetic resonance) to examine critical evidence. Radiography using X-rays or neutrons is also very useful in examining thick products for their internal defects before destructive examination is attempted. Often, however, a simple hand lens suffices to reveal the cause of a particular problem. Trace evidence is often an important factor in reconstructing the sequence of events in an accident. For example, tyre burn marks on a road surface can enable vehicle speeds to be estimated, when the brakes were applied and so on. Ladder feet often leave a trace of movement of the ladder during a slipaway, and may show how the accident occurred.

Section "methods" (ibid.) remarks:

> Methods used in forensic investigations include reverse engineering, inspection of witness statements, a working knowledge of current standards, as well as examination of the failed component itself. The fracture surface of a failed product can reveal much information on how the item failed and the loading pattern prior to failure. The study of fracture surfaces is known as fractography. Fatigue often produces a characteristic fracture surface for example, enabling diagnosis to be made of the cause of the failure. The key task in many such investigations is to identify the failure mechanism by examining the failed part using physical and chemical techniques. This activity is sometimes called root cause analysis. Corrosion is another common failure mode needing careful analysis to determine the active agents. Accidents caused by fire are especially challenging owing to the frequent loss of critical evidence, although when halted early enough can usually lead to the cause. Fire investigation is a specialist skill where arson is suspected, but is also important in vehicular accident reconstruction where faulty fuel lines, for example, may be the cause of an accident.

8.7 Individual Identification

8.7.1 The Cultural Context: The History of Identification Methods

It is important to understand the history of the use of fingerprints for identification purposes, in order to realise how the mutual expectations of law enforcers and of perpetrators have evolved. This in turn is potentially useful for the purposes of future AI tools that would reason about the evidence. Understanding the dynamics of how both law enforcers and perpetrators had to become more and more clever, makes one realise that one cannot come up as well with the ultimate technique of detection.

Hardware and software you may produce may prove useful for a while, or even for a long time, but requirements will change, and older techniques will either have to change, or have to be supplemented with something else. Within AI, the area concerned with how to reason with an agent's beliefs about the beliefs of another agent is known as *agents' beliefs* (e.g., Ballim, By, Wilks, & Liske, 2001; Barnden, 2001).

The following example shows how a course of action taken by perpetrators with the intention of suppressing the evidence, actually backfired. During the Troubles in Northern Ireland in the 1970s and 1980s, bombs prepared by terrorists sometimes contained the gloves they had been using. Their assumptions was that the blast would destroy the gloves, but it was not so. Law enforcers hoped to find, inside the remains of such gloves, the fingerprints of perpetrators – that is to say, evidence that the terrorists had placed inside the bombs by believing that by so doing, they would destroy the evidence.

Those fingerprints were detected, because of their coating of lipids (traces of the fat on the skin of fingertips). Radioactivity was used, in order to make that coating of lipids (fat from the fingertips) apparent, using a photographic technique or based on luminescence, and the former appeared to be better than the latter.[140] Let us recapitulate, with more technical details:

- The people making bombs would wear gloves.
- When they finished they would place the gloves with the device.
- The fingerprints (contrary to what the bombers had assumed) could then be recovered from the inside of the gloves.
- The radioactive SO2 (sulfur dioxide) absorbed could then be detected[141] by luminescence or by photographic techniques (using silver halides).[142] The graphite

---

[140] Around 1980s, such circumstances were still secret, but by 2010, when I was informed verbally, they were in the public domain.

[141] E.g., in Goode, Morris, and Wells (1979), a team from the Atomic Weapons Research Establishment of the British Ministry of Defence, based at Aldermaston, Berkshire, described the application of radioactive bromine isotopes for the visualisation of latent fingerprints. A vapour phase bromination procedure was investigated for reaction with unsaturated lipids present in a fingerprint deposit.

[142] The light-sensitive chemicals used in photographic film and paper are silver halides. A *silver halide* is one of the compounds formed between silver and one of the halogens, namely: silver bromide (AgBr), silver chloride (AgCl), silver iodide (AgI), and three forms of silver fluorides. As a group, they are often given the pseudo-chemical notation AgX. Silver halides, except for silver fluoride, are extremely insoluble in water.

"Silver halides are used in photographic film and photographic paper, as well as graphic art film and paper, where silver halide crystals in gelatin are coated on to a film base, glass or paper substrate. The gelatin is a vital part of the emulsion as the protective colloid of appropriate physical and chemical properties. Gelatin may also contain trace elements (such as sulfur) which increase the light sensitivity of the emulsion, although modern practice uses gelatin without such components. When absorbed by an AgX crystal, photons cause electrons to be promoted to a conduction band (de-localized electron orbital with higher energy than a valence band) which can be attracted by a sensitivity speck, which is a shallow electron trap, which may be a crystalline defect or a cluster of

fine powder for conventional fingerprint recording could not be used. The photographic techniques proved to be the most efficient.

A medal dated 1969, designed by Jiri Harcuba, was struck in Czechoslovakia, in bronze, silver, and for the first time, with a golden proof, for the centenary of the death of Jan Evangelista Purkyně, a physician considered the discoverer and founder of *dactyloscopy*, i.e., the identification of persons based on their fingerprints. (Defying the Soviet invasion, the Czech mint also struck Harcuba's medal, also dated 1969, commemorating Jan Palach, the student who set himself ablaze in protest.) Purkyně (1787–1869) is actually much better known as the father of histology: the middle cortex of the cerebellum were named *Purkinje cells*, after him. Outside the Czech Rebublic or Slovakia, his family name is usually spelled *Purkinje*.

No mention of Purkyně is made in the entry for "dactyloscopie" in Nathanaël Tribondeau's glossary of criminalistics (Tribondeau, accessed 2006). About the origination of the technique, it just states: "Utilisée pour la première fois en 1880 par l'Anglais William J. Herschel" ("Used for the first time by an Englishman, William J. Herschel"). He got an entry in his name: "Born in 1738 and deceased in 1922, he is the inventor, along with Francis Galton [Darwin's cousin], of dactyloscopy (the collection and analysis of fingerprints). It was looking for some surer means than just a signature, for the authentication of commercial documents, that this English official seconded to Bengal conceived of the idea, from 1880, of having his suppliers mark contracts with their fingerprints, to avoid future disputes. It was only later on, that this procedure was used by the scientific police, with the success we all know about" (my translation).

What Tribondeau does not say about the adoption by fingerprints in France, is related in an article by Jean-Marc Berlière (2005) about the Scheffer Affair, about the first conviction of a suspect, in France, revolving around on identification by fingerprints. Berlière explains that with the emergence, in the positivist era, of the realisation, turned into an obsession in France, that recidivists are responsible for most crimes (this actually came along with now discredited theory of Cesare Lombroso about the born criminal), perpetrators smarted up to the challenge, and

---

silver sulfide, gold, other trace elements (dopant), or combination thereof, and then combined with an interstitial silver ion to form silver metal speck" (http://en.wikipedia.org/wiki/Silver_halide).

Apart from applications to photography, experiments have been conducted for medical purposes: silver halide optical fibres for transmitting mid-infrared light from carbon dioxide lasers, allow laser welding of human tissue, as an alternative to traditional sutures. Another use is in the making of lenses, exploiting photochromism: Silver halides are also used to make corrective lenses darken when exposed to ultraviolet light. "When a silver halide crystal is exposed to light, a sensitivity speck on the surface of the crystal is turned into a small speck of metallic silver (these comprise the invisible or latent image). If the speck of silver contains approximately four or more atoms, it is rendered developable – meaning that it can undergo development which turns the entire crystal into metallic silver. Areas of the emulsion receiving larger amounts of light (reflected from a subject being photographed, for example) undergo the greatest development and therefore results in the highest optical density" (ibid.).

law enforcement was faced with the problem of how to identify a person who has been using several false names.

Alphonse Bertillon proposed for identification to consider the *identité anthropométrique*, based on measurements of the bones of adults. The French police adopted this technique in 1883. There is a sense in which it was of little help, as perpetrators were unlikely to leave their bones around, yet it was rather useful for identifying recidivists who were using a false name, provided they had been *bertillonnés*, i.e., had their anthropometric measurements taken before. On 16 February 1883, a recidivist was recognised for the first time, based on anthropometric measurements.

By the end of 1883, 49 ex-cons had been identified that way; 241 during the next year (ibid., p. 350, fn. 3). The technique featured, arousing much interest, at the international exposition of Paris of 1889. "Its zenith was when, in the spring of 1892, it enabled Bertillon to identify 'Ravachol', who at the time was terrifying Paris, with a Koenigstein who had been *bertillonné* at Saint-Étienne prison two years earlier" (ibid., p. 350, my translation). The technique could tell apart two dissimilar persons, but similar anthropometric data could not be ascribed with certainty to the similar person. This was a major flaw.

Fingerprints were to prove a better technique. Fingerprints were observed by Italian anatomist Marcello Malpighi (1628–1694). That Purkyně described fingerprints in 1823 is mentioned by Berlière (who wrongly Hispanicises his first name as *Juan*). So is empirical use in British-ruled India, as well as the role of the physician Henry Faulds, or the classifications developed by Francis Galton, Edward Henry, and Juan Vucetich during the 1890s.

Berlière relates the role which Bertillon had, in the first conviction in France based on fingerprints.[143] On 16 October 1902, the body of a male servant was discovered inside the Parisian apartment of a dentist. The motive appeared to be theft. On a broken glasscase, many fingerprints were found. On one side of the glass, there was the print of a thumb, the prints of three other fingers being on the other side: these were the fingerprints of a person who has held the glass after it was broken.

One difficulty was that the fingerprints were overlapping, because of the transparency of the glass. An advantage for Bertillon was that he got the fingerprints of four adjacent fingers of the right hand, i.e., the only hand for which fingerprints had been stored. Bertillon searched the archives, card by card, without classification criteria to guide the search, and identified Henri-Léon Scheffer, born in 1876, who had been arrested and had had his fingerprints taken on 9 March 1902.

Bertillon's report to the examining magistrate, stating this identification, is dated 24 October 1902. Berlière points out (p. 351, fn. 7) that this case is usually misrepresented as though it was the first time that a perpetrator was identified based only

---

[143] The historical origins of identification by fingerprints have been discussed, e.g., by Simon Cole (1999), a criminologist who is prominent among those who question the accuracy, sufficiency, and individuality of fingerprint identification.

on fingerprints. That was not the case, as an intimate relation had been discovered between the victim and Scheffer, and the latter had been among the suspects.

For Berlière, Bertillon's role in identification by fingerprints becoming an established technique is paradoxical, as Bertillon was aware of publications about fingerprints from other countries, yet had been quite reluctant to adopt this method, mainly because of the difficulty to classify fingerprints, but also because he considered them not to be distinctive enough (a laughable claim, vis-à-vis the weakness of his own anthropometric method). Locard was sarcastic about Bertillon in that respect. Edmond Locard (1877–1966) was a younger star of French criminalistics, who established France's first scientific police laboratory (*Laboratoire de Police scientifique*) in Lyons in January 1910, and published during the 1930s a *Traité de criminalistique* in seven volumes of lasting value to forensic laboratories worldwide. Locard's thesis on legal medicine is dated 1902.

Berlière remarks that stubbornness was a trait of Bertillon's personality, and that this played a role in his determined attitude against Dreyfus, when, an expert witness in court, he insisted on interpreting the graphological evidence unreasonably. Berlière points out that this was one reason Locard disliked Bertillon quite intensely. Berlière mentions a major error made by Locard himself: in 1945, a woman was sentenced to forced labour for life, having been identified by him as the anonymous Nazi collaborator who had denounced a partisan in the French Resistance; she was only freed after the error was recognised as such in 1956.

Locard himself developed (among the other things) *graphometrics*, and solved some cases based on graphological evidence; e.g., he solved a case in which a husband guided the hand of his dying wife in writing a will in his favour (in 1923, Locard published a paper about 'L'Écriture à la main guidée' in the *Revue de droit pénal et de criminologie et Archives internationales de médecine légale* in Bruxelles). Vols. 5 and 6 of Locard's *Traité de criminalistique* were published in 1935, and in fact they are entitled *L'Expertise des documents écrits*, being devoted to the analysis of written documents. Vol. 1 appeared in 1931, and was devoted to fingerprints and to other traces (*Les Empreintes et les traces dans l'enquête criminelle*). Vols. 3 and 4 appeared in 1932, and were about identification evidence (*Les Preuves de l'identité*).

Apparently Bertillon's endorsement of fingerprints came after the physician Lacassagne (one of the founders of criminalistics) and Galton had extolled to him the method. He remained reluctant to see his own method, based on anthropometric measurement, made obsolete by fingerprint identification. His successor who took over from him at the police, quoted by Berlière (p. 358), testified that in February 1914, upon Bertillon's death, out of the 1,200,000 cards held by the scientific police, only 60,000 had been classified based on the fingerprints. France adopted classification based on fingerprints considerably later than Argentina, the United Kingdom, and other countries (ibid.). Argentina was pioneering in criminalistics, and there actually is an anecdote (it was even related in the *Reader's Digest*) about Locard, in his student days, becoming enthralled with the discipline one day, when he was accompanying his medicine professor, the famous Lacassaigne. They had to wait because of the rain, and Lacassaigne gave him an Argentinean journal, asking Locard to translate an article for him on the spot. What Locard read on that occasion determined his professional future. Alexandre Lacassagne (1843–1924) became "Professeur de Médecine Légale" in 1880, and established research in the domain in Lyons, where it was carried further by Étienne Martin, Pierre Mazel, Jacques Bourret, as well as by his most famous continuator, Edmond Locard.[144]

In his memoirs of the First World War, 'Aziz Bek, Head of Intelligence of the Fourth Ottoman Army, described an episode, which started when a spy stole documents (being unable to photograph or copy them on the spot) and then returned them. The commander of the 43th Division in Syria had noticed the disappearance of the defence plans, and on their reappearance he would not touch them. He had a laboratory detect fingerprints, then discreetly obtained the fingerprints of all officers, soldiers and clerks at the division headquarters. A circular was distributed, that had to be signed and returned. This way, a signature would identify the fingerprints unwittingly left on the paper. This led to the identification of an officer and of a soldier, and further investigation uncovered their links to a spy ring ('Aziz Bek [1933–1937] 1991, pp. 116–117).

Twenty years earlier, a course of action such as this one hadn't been taken, in France, with the *bordereau* ascribed to Alfred Dreyfus, but then such forensic "expertise" that had been sought at the time, had the goal of confirming his alleged guilt, rather than discovering the actual identity of the spy. "Evidence" had included supposed similarities in the handwriting, as well as the fact that when Dreyfus was ordered to write down under dictation a text identical with that of the dossier, he was visibly shaking (who wouldn't, in his shoes?).

The example of the forensic "expertise" seeking to confirm that Dreyfus had written the given document, illustrates the pitfalls of *confirmationism* (tests seeking to confirm rather than disprove a hypothesis),[145] and more broadly, of tunnel thinking. The forensic experts were so committed to the claim that the suspect was guilty, that it was almost a foregone conclusion that they would find what they were looking for. This suggests that cognitive science and artificial intelligence research producing computational simulations of tunnel thinking could provide some clarification

---

[144] Berthold Laufer, who was the United States leading Sinologist during the first three decades of the twentieth century, also authored a report on the history of fingerprinting (Laufer, 1913, 1917). Berthold Laufer was born in Cologne, Germany, in 1874. After earning his doctorate at the University of Leipzig in 1874, Berthold Laufer moved on the following year to the United States. He had obtained an invitation to the American Museum of Natural History in New York City, thanks to the famous anthropologist Franz Boas (1858–1942). Laufer eventually became curator of Asiatic Ethnology and Anthropology at the Field Museum of Natural History, Chicago, where he had moved in 1907, leaving a lectureship in Anthropology and East-Asiatic Languages at Columbia University. He died in 1934, upon leaping from the roof of the hotel in which he lived in Chicago, but the mode of his demise goes unmentioned in Latourette's (1936) biographical memoir of Berthold Laufer for the U.S. National Academy of Sciences.

[145] *Confirmation bias* as occurring in the police interrogation rooms, see e.g. Kassin, Goldstein, and Savitsky (2003), Meissner and Kassin (2002), and Hill, Memon, and McGeorge (2008). Confirmationism is sometimes referred to as *cognitive dissonance*. This name for the concept was spread by a book by Leon Festinger (1919–1989), *A Theory of Cognitive Dissonance* (Festinger, 1957).

at the theoretical level, which would eventually be put to use in the design of tools for assisting with reasoning about the evidence. It would be blue sky research eventually finding (hopefully) practical application in a better design of tools. One possibility would be to develop an AI tool that would test protocols or possibly other software, trying to ensure that they are not marred by pitfalls of the kind mentioned earlier. In a sense, such pitfalls have already been sometimes argued to affect widespread techniques. The adoption of the Dempster-Shafer statistical technique is rather widespread in AI tools, but a major problem stemming from the adoption of Dempster-Shafer is that it is apparently tilted towards *confirmationism* instead of *falsificationism*.

8.7.2 DNA and Fingerprints

8.7.2.1 DNA Evidence: A Brief Introduction

Computational methods for determining individuality (Srihari & Su, 2008) encompass several domains in forensic science, from fingerprint analysis to handwriting recognition. In the 1990s and 2000s, DNA has become the evidence per excellence for personal identification. DNA evidence is usually considered to be hard evidence about a person's identity.[146] Nevertheless, DNA fingerprinting is not uncontroversial.[147] Concerning DNA evidence, consider the application to paternity claims.[148]

---

[146] An overview of techniques of DNA analysis is provided by Duncan, Tacey, and Stauffer (2005, 2nd edn.; 2009, 3rd edn.), whereas in the same volume, Susan Herrero (2005, 2nd edn.; 2009, 3rd edn.) provides an overview of legal issues in forensic DNA. DNA fingerprinting is treated, e.g., in Baldin (2005), Inman and Rudin (2002), National Research Council (1996), Stockmarr (1999), Lauritzen and Mortera (2002), Meester and Sjerps (2004), Easteal, McLeod, and Reed (1991), Krawczak and Schmidtke (1994), and Butler (2001). See a brief, yet important debate (Krane et al., 2008), with useful bibliographies by the various commentators, about *sequential unmasking* in DNA identification. It was republished in www.bioforensics.com under the rubric *forensic bioinformatics*.

[147] Roberts (1991) is about the controversy about DNA fingerprinting. Nielsen and Nespor (1993) is on human rights in relation to genetic data and screening, in various contexts.

[148] Of course, historically there was interest in ascertaining paternity even before medical knowledge and technology would enable such checks credibly. For example, discussing early modern English midwifery books, Mary Fissell remarks (2003, p. 65): "Midwifery books of the 1670s and 1680s were obsessed by the issues of fatherhood. How could you know the father of a child? In certain circumstances, such as illegitimate births, knowing the father had long been important. These texts devoted much more attention to resemblance between parents and their children than did previous midwifery texts. This crisis in paternity had multiple roots. There was no sudden increase in illegitimate births that might have prompted such an interest. Some of the crisis may be due to longer-term intellectual changes that gradually made similitude a happenstance rather than an indicator of profound connection. No longer did resemblance mean something important about relatedness." Fissell further explains (ibid., pp. 65–66): "The crisis can also be understood in political terms. In [the] 1670s and 1680s, the question of monarchical succession – the transmission from one generation to another – became ever more pressing. Charles II did not have any legitimate sons, and his brother James's Catholicism made him a highly problematic successor. The

An article by an Oslo-based team, Egeland, Mostad, and Olaisen (1997), describes PATER, a software system for probabilistic computations for paternity and identification cases, in cases where DNA profiles of some people are known, but their family relationship is in doubt. PATER is claimed to be able to handle complex cases where potential mutations are accounted for.

Another project resulted in, e.g., Dawid, van Boxel, Mortera, and Pascali (1999), Dawid, Mortera, and Pascali (2001), and Dawid, Mortera, and Vicard (2010), Vicard, Dawid, Mortera, and d Lauritzen (2008), and Vicard and Dawid (2006), specifically about the statistics of disputed paternity. A prominent statistician, Philip Dawid, now at the University of Cambridge, at the time when he was affiliated with University College, London was remarking as follows at his research interests webpage[149]:

I have been interested in the application of Probability and Statistics to a variety of subject areas, in particular to Medicine (especially medical diagnosis and decision-making), Crystallography, Reliability (especially Software Reliability) and, most recently, *Legal Reasoning*. I have acted as expert advisor or witness in a number of legal cases involving DNA profiling. This has led me to a thorough theoretical examination of the use of Probability and Statistics for *Forensic Identification*. I head an international research team focusing on the analysis of complex forensic DNA identification cases using Probabilistic Expert Systems. These legally inspired investigations have also highlighted the many logical subtleties and pitfalls that beset evidential reasoning more generally. To address these I have established a multidisciplinary research programme on *Evidence, Inference and Enquiry* [[150]] at University College London. This is bringing together researchers from a wide diversity of disciplinary backgrounds to seek out common ground, to advance understandings, and to improve the handling of evidence.

---

duke of Monmouth's rebellion (the duke being the king's illegitimate son), the Rye House Plot, the Popish Plot [i.e., a libel against Catholics leading to executions] – all kept political instability at the forefront of popular awareness. The high politics of legitimate succession moved right into the birthing room in the Warming Pan Baby scandal, which erupted when James II's wife, Mary of Modena, gave birth a male heir – or did she? She had had eight previous pregnancies, all stillbirths or very short-lived infants. This baby was full-term and healthy, and some observers claimed it was a fraud. They suggested that a healthy baby had been smuggled into the birthing room, concealed in a warming pan, and substituted for Mary's sickly or stillborn babe."

From antiquity to the mid eighteenth century, the *theory of maternal imagination* had currency. It claimed that white parents could have a black child (or vice versa) if the mother, at the time of conception, saw or imagined a man with the other skin colour. A pregnant woman seeing an image of St. John the Baptist wearing hairy skins (or himself hairy) was believed to have given birth to a hairy daughter, who was depicted on the frontispiece of several 17th and early eighteenth century midwifery books. Fissell discussed such imagery. And books sometimes even suggested, Fissell points out, that a woman could deceive her husband by imagining her husband while having intercourse with her lover, so her illegitimate child would resemble her husband rather than her lover.

[149] It can be accessed at http://www.ucl.ac.uk/~ucak06d/research.html Philip Dawid's work on identification evidence, disputed paternity, and in forensic statistics includes Dawid (1994, 1998, 2001a, 2001b, 2002, 2004a, 2005a, 2005b, 2008), Dawid and Mortera (1996, 1998), Dawid and Evett (1997, 1998), Dawid and Pueschel (1999), Dawid et al. (1999, 2001), Dawid, Mortera, Pascali, and van Boxel (2002), Dawid, Mortera, Dobosz, and Pascali (2003), Dawid, Mortera and Vicard (2006), Mortera, Dawid, and Lauritzen (2003), Vicard and Dawid (2004, 2006).

[150] www.evidencescience.org

The Wikipedia entry for "Genetic fingerprinting" contains much detail.[151] Its introduction states:

> Genetic fingerprinting, DNA testing, DNA typing, and DNA profiling are techniques used to distinguish between individuals of the same species using only samples of their DNA. Its invention by Dr. Alec Jeffreys at the University of Leicester was announced in 1985. Two humans will have the vast majority of their DNA sequence in common. Genetic finger-printing exploits highly variable repeating sequences called minisatellites. Two unrelated humans will be unlikely to have the same numbers of minisatellites at a given locus. In STR profiling, which is distinct from DNA fingerprinting, PCR is used to obtain enough DNA to then detect the number of repeats at several loci. It is possible to establish a match that is extremely unlikely to have arisen by coincidence, except in the case of identical twins, who will have identical genetic profiles.Genetic fingerprinting is used in forensic sci-ence, to match suspects to samples of blood, hair, saliva or semen. It has also led to several exonerations of formerly convicted suspects. It is also used in such applications as iden-tifying human remains, paternity testing, matching organ donors, studying populations of wild animals, and establishing the province or composition of foods. It has also been used to generate hypotheses on the pattern of the human diaspora in prehistoric times.

Genetic testing is subjected to regulations (ibid.):

> Testing is subject to the legal code of the jurisdiction in which it is performed. Usually the testing is voluntary, but it can be made compulsory by such instruments as a search warrant or court order. Several jurisdictions have also begun to assemble databases containing DNA information of convicts. The United States maintains the largest DNA database in the world: The Combined DNA Index System, with over 4.5 million records as of 2007. The United Kingdom, maintains the National DNA Database (NDNAD), which is of similar size. The size of this database, and its rate of growth, is giving concern to civil liberties groups in the UK, where police have wide-ranging powers to take samples and retain them even in the event of acquittal.

There exist computer tools for carrying out statistical analysis concerning DNA evi-dence. "[U]sing object-oriented Bayesian networks we have constructed a flexible computational toolkit, and used it to analyse complex cases of DNA profile evi-dence, accounting appropriately for such features as missing individuals, mutation, silent alleles and mixed DNA traces" (Mortera & Dawid, 2006, section 8, p. 26).[152] Aitken, Taroni, and Garbolino (2003) described their own graphical model for the analysis of possible cross-transfer of DNA material, affecting DNA profiles intended for use as evidence. They resorted to Bayesian networks.

---

[151] http://en.wikipedia.org/wiki/Genetic_fingerprinting

[152] The kind of situations across which one may come is illustrated, e.g., by *DNA mixtures:* "A *mixed DNA profile* is typically obtained from an unidentified biological stain or other trace thought to be associated with a crime. This commonly happens in rape cases, in robberies where an object might have been handled by more than one individual, and also in a scuffle of brawl. For a mixed DNA trace there is no constraint on the number of distinct alleles observed for each marker, since the trace might have been formed as a mixture of biological material from more than one person" (Mortera & Dawid, 2006, section 6.3, p. 16).

8.7.2.2 Statisticians' Disagreements About How to Evaluate DNA Samples

Whereas suspect recognition based on facial composites (let alone on an artist's sketch) is an *indicative tool*, DNA evidence and fingerprint evidence are *implicative tools*. Even though one would have thought that DNA evidence is one area in which the use of statistics faces less challenges than other uses of Bayesianism in law, actually statisticians' disagreements about how to evaluate DNA samples shows that here, too, there are severe problems.[153] Even though controversies about DNA evidence only very rarely reach the public, they received a popular treatment in two issues of Britain's *New Scientist* magazine in August 2010. The second report was introduced as follows (Geddes, 2010, p. 8):

> Last week, a *New Scientist* investigation showed how different forensic analysts can reach very different conclusions about whether or not someone's DNA matches a profile from a crime scene. This week we show how, even when analysts agree that someone could be a match for a piece of DNA evidence, the statistical weight assigned to that match can vary enormously.

In an inset, 'When lawyers question DNA' (on p. 9 in Geddes, 2010) in the special report on DNA evidence in the second issue, Scottish forensic scientist Alan Jamieson, who at scholars' conferences is often a wise and sobering voice about expert testimony, pointed out that defence lawyers can obtain the prosecution's statistical data concerning DNA samples, provided they are only permitted to use them in order to dispute them in the case at hand, and not for the purposes of other investigations and trials; and that moreover, if the case does not reach court, the refutations put forth by the defence would never reach to public domain.

The *New Scientist* report by Geddes (2010), 'What are the chances?', was subheadlined: "In the second part of our investigation, Linda Geddes shows that *the odds attached to a piece of DNA evidence can vary enormously*" (added emphasis). The article began with a case of conviction then still being appealed in California: "Charles Richard Smith has learned the hard way that you can prove almost anything with statistics. In 2009 a disputed statistic provided by a DNA analyst landed him with a twenty-five-year jail sentence". This was for sexual assault at a parking lot in Sacramento, CA, in January 2006, when a woman was forced into oral sex with the perpetrator. A swab of cells from Smith's penis showed his own DNA and that of another person, and indicated that he had been sexually intimate with an unknown person. The DNA analyst as "Smith's trial said the chances of the DNA coming from someone other than [the victim] were 1 in 15,000. But both the prosecution and the analyst's supervisor said the odds were more like 1 in 47", and a later review reduced this to 1 in 13, "while a different statistical method said the chance

---

[153] Criticism also comes from critics of the application of probability theory to juridical proof in general, such as Ron Allen: even though one would have thought that DNA evidence would be a "safer" domain for statisticians, it is not quite so. Allen and Pardo (2007a) offered a critique, in terms of the *reference-class problem* (see Section 2.4 above) of how probability theory was applied to juridical proof concerning DNA random-match evidence in Nance and Morris (2002, 2005).

of seeing this evidence if the DNA came from [the victim] is only twice that of the chance of seeing it come from someone else." Geddes (2010, p. 8) further remarked:

"Usually DNA evidence is pretty strong", says David Balding, a statistical geneticist at University College London, whose calculation puts the lowest probability on the link between Smith and [the victim]. "My point is that the number juries are provided with often overstates the evidence. It should be a smaller number".

On 15 May 1997, Odd O. Aalen from Norway posted a question, in an e-list about statistics in legal evidence[154]: "Does anybody on this list know about criminal court cases where purely statistical evidence has been the sole or major evidence, and where the defendant has been convicted on this basis? I am thinking here of purely numerical evidence as opposed to substantive proof and statistical calculations related to this". On that very day, a reply came from Robert Lempert, a well-known scholar from the University of Michigan: "There have by now been a couple of DNA cases like this". Arguably, this shows how important the debate on statistics is.

Another posting on the same day provided more detail. It was by Bernard Robertson, editor of *The New Zealand Law Journal*, and definitely a "Bayesian enthusiast" in the controversy about Bayesianism in law. He stated: "The case of Adams provides an interesting example as the only prosecution evidence was DNA while the defence produced some more conventional evidence which tended to point the other way and also produced Professor Donelly to explain how to use Bayes Theorem to reduce the posterior odds below 'beyond reasonable doubt'." Robertson pointed out that this generated publications in the legal literature in England.

In an article by mathematicians from Queen Mary and Westfield College, London – Balding and Donnelly (1995) – a contribution was made to clarify the role of the modes of statistical inference, in the controversy over the interpretation of DNA profile evidence in forensic identification. They claimed that this controversy can be attributed in part to confusion over which such mode of inference is appropriate. They also remark that whereas some questions in the debate were ill-posed or inappropriate, some issues were neglected, which can have important consequences. They propose their own framework for assessing DNA evidence,

in which, for example, the roles both of the population genetics issues and of the non-scientific evidence in a case are incorporated. Our analysis highlights several widely held misconceptions in the DNA profiling debate. For example, the profile frequency is not directly relevant to forensic inference. Further, very small match probabilities may in some settings be consistent with acquittal.

Besides, there is also another kind of risk with DNA evidence. "Even in DNA cases, there is always the possibility of lab error or planted evidence" (Allen, 2008a, p. 328, note 1). The presence of DNA or of fingerprints from a given person at the scene of a crime does not necessarily mean that the person they identify was involved at the crime. In England in 2011, a retired teacher was arrested, demonised by the media,

---

[154] bayesian-evidence@vuw.ac.nz

and then released in connection with the kidnapping murder of a young woman architect, as there was evidence indicating his presence where she lived, but he was the landowner. He may have had other opportunities of losing hair or leaving fingerprints at the place. Besides, DNA evidence may be mislabelled inside a laboratory. Or then, perpetrators may leave on purpose DNA evidence, perhaps hair, but even blood from a person they want to implicate.

There is even the risk of fake DNA. based on a paper by an Israeli team of scientists led by Dan Frumkin that had appeared in the journal *Forensic Science International: Genetics*, an unsigned item the British periodical *Criminal Law & Justice Weely*, Vol. 173, No. 34 (August 22, 2009) reported on p. 531, under the headline 'Fake DNA', that Frumkin's team had taken DNA from human hair was taken and multiplied many times, and that an enhanced sample of that DNA "was then inserted into blood cells that had been purged of their previous DNA. Dr Frumkin suggested that, in theory, criminals could use the technique to plant samples of blood or saliva at crime scenes to cover their tracks and implicate another party." One would not expect to find a sample of saliva at a crime scene other than by the victim or the perpetrator if they were alone and in some isolated place, but if DNA from hair could be planted inside saliva, then the very expectations about how saliva could occur at a crime scene means that perpetrators could frame somebody. "The researchers said that the use of DNA is often the key to proving the guilt or innocence of suspects and that by using the technique they had developed, genetic profiles could easily be synthesized" (ibid.), even though this is currently beyond the ability of your usual perpetrator.

8.7.2.3 Human Fingerprints

Let us turn to *human fingerprints*,[155] which as usually found in investigative contexts are of the hand palm, and in particular, of the tips of the fingers.[156] Steps involving identification by fingerprints are as follows:

- A particular person (suspect X) handles an object (an exhibit).
- That exhibit is exposed to the environment.
- The exhibit is eventually recovered and treated, revealing fingerprints.

---

[155] See, e.g., Jain and Maltoni (2003) and Champod, Lennard, Margot, and Stilovic (2004). Also see the discussion in, e.g., Stoney (1997), Cole (2001, 2004, 2005, 2006a, 2006b), Cole et al. (2008), Balding (2005), Saks and Koehler (2008).

[156] Sometimes, the terms *fingerprint* and *fingerprinting* are used metaphorically. We have already come across *soil fingerprinting techniques* in a project in forensic geology that resorts to a decision support system, at the end of Section 8.5.1. In Section 8.5.6, we considered *chemical fingerprints*, identifying an individual component in a mixture (taken to be a multivariate, mixed chemical system). Another metaphorical use of the term *fingerprint* is found in *digital steganography*, a discipline we dealt with in Section 6.2.1.5 (which itself spans more, thematically). One sometimes talks about fingerprints, and a fingerprint vault scheme, in *digital steganography*: see

- The developed fingerprints are imaged.[157]
- The images of the fingerprints are transferred to a database.
- The images of fingerprints are compared, and if this is done automatically, then a pattern matching algorithm is used.
- Suspect X is identified.

The introduction to the Wikipedia entry for "Fingerprint" states[158]:

> A *fingerprint* is an impression of the friction ridges of all or any part of the finger. A friction ridge is a raised portion of the epidermis [skin] on the palmar (palm and fingers) or plantar (sole and toes) skin, consisting of one or more connected ridge units of friction ridge skin. These ridges are sometimes known as "dermal ridges" or "dermal papillae".
>
> Fingerprints may be deposited in natural secretions from the eccrine glands present in friction ridge skin (secretions consisting primarily of water) or they may be made by ink or other contaminants transferred from the peaks of friction skin ridges to a relatively smooth surface such as a fingerprint card. The term fingerprint normally refers to impressions transferred from the pad on the last joint of fingers and thumbs, though fingerprint cards also typically record portions of lower joint areas of the fingers (which are also used to make identifications).

Fingerprint identification, based on traces left by the skin of some persons' finger tips, is much debated in the literature, and until the end of the twentieth century its accuracy was hardly questioned, once it had come to be accepted by the beginning of that century. As we are going to see, the probative value of fingerprint evidence is no longer as secure as it used to be, and we are going to come back to that. Itiel Dror and colleagues' paper "When emotions get the better of us: The effect of contextual top-down processing on matching fingerprints" (Dror, Péron, Hind, &

Li et al. (2005). In *forensic ballistics*, one speaks of *ballistic fingeprinting*. Also in intrusion detection within computer security, metaphorically one speaks of *fingerprints* and *fingeprinting* (Section 6.2.1.12), in relation to attempts to identify an intruder.

One sometimes speaks of fingerprinting for the identification of an individual rhinoceros. Amin, Bramer, and Emslie (2003) described experiments with "rhino horn fingerprint identification", i.e., "the identification of the species and origin of illegally traded or confiscated African rhino horn", using techniques of intelligent data analysis. Rhino horns are akin to compacted hair and fingernails, and their chemical composition refelcts what the animal has been eating throughout its life. In turn, the chemistry of the food is affected by climate and geology. The so-called *fingerprint* of a rhino horn is a combination of variable values. In the project reported about by Amin et al. (ibid.), *Discriminant Function Analysis* was the principal technique of data analysis used, the prediction of the category in which a given case belongs is obtained by deriving mathematical functions that provide the greatest possible discrimination among categories. The same paper discussed a further stage, at which it was intended to use artificial neural nets for classification, or the automatic induction of classification trees (for the latter, cf. Quinlan, 1986; Kothari & Dong, 2002; Siroky, 2009; Chen et al., 2011). Contrast the task in the rhino project, to the task of identifying an individual, which is the case of techniques for the recognition of cattle based on characteristics of the animal's back skin that are akin to fingerprints.

[157] A discussion of fingerprint development and imaging, with the chemistry involved in the development explained in clear detail, can be found in an excellent PowerPoint presentation posted online, and authored by Steve Bleay of Britain's Home Office Scientific Development Branch (Bleay, 2009).

[158] http://en.wikipedia.org/wiki/Fingerprint.

Charlton, 2005) is a paper in cognitive psychology, applied to how experts perform at matching fingerprints. Dror and Charlton (2006) and Dror et al. (2006) tried to identify the causes of why experts make identification errors. Dror and Rosenthal (2008) tried to meta-analytically quantify the *reliability* and *biasability* of forensic experts.

"On the palmar surface of the hands and feet are raised surfaces called friction ridges. The scientific basis behind friction ridge analysis is the fact that friction ridges are persistent and unique" (from the Wikipedia entry for 'Fingerprint'). The Wikipedia entry, which as accessed in late 2007, was detailed and engaging (our present readers are encouraged to access it), states:

> Fingerprint identification (sometimes referred to as *dactyloscopy)* or palmprint identification is the process of comparing questioned and known friction skin ridge impressions (see *Minutiae)*[159] from fingers or palms to determine if the impressions are from the same finger or palm. The flexibility of friction ridge skin means that no two finger or palm prints are ever exactly alike (never identical in every detail), even two impressions recorded immediately after each other. Fingerprint identification (also referred to as individualization) occurs when an expert (or an *expert computer system* operating under *threshold scoring* rules) determines that two friction ridge impressions originated from the same finger or palm (or toe, sole) to the exclusion of all others.
>
> A *known print* is the intentional recording of the friction ridges, usually with black printer's ink rolled across a contrasting white background, typically a white card. Friction ridges can also be recorded digitally using a technique called *Live-Scan*. A *latent print* is the chance reproduction of the friction ridges deposited on the surface of an item. Latent prints are often fragmentary and may require chemical methods, powder, or alternative light sources in order to be visualized.

Computerisation brought about major changes in the *modus operandi* of fingerprint identification. The following is quoted from the Wikipedia entry[160]:

> Before computerization replaced manual filing systems in large fingerprint operations, manual fingerprint classification systems were used to categorize fingerprints based on general ridge formations (such as the presence or absence of circular patterns in various fingers), thus permitting filing and retrieval of paper records in large collections based on friction ridge patterns independent of name, birth date and other biographic data that persons may misrepresent. The most popular ten print classification systems include the Roscher system, the Vucetich system, and the *Henry Classification System* [...]
>
> In the Henry system of classification,[161] there are three basic fingerprint patterns: Arch, Loop and Whorl. There are also more complex classification systems that further break down patterns to plain arches or tented arches. [...]

An explanation of fingerprint appearance is provided by Bistarelli, Santini, and Vaccarelli (2006, pp. 360–361, section 2.1):

> The most evident structural characteristic of a fingerprint is the pattern of interleaved ridges and valleys that often run in parallel. Ridges vary in width from 100 to 300 lm and the period of a ridge/valley cycle is typically about 500 lm. If analyzed at global level, almost

---

[159] http://en.wikipedia.org/wiki/Minutiae.

[160] http://en.wikipedia.org/wiki/Fingerprint.

[161] On which, see http://en.wikipedia.org/wiki/Henry_Classification_System.

all of the patterns exhibit one or more regions characterized by a distinctive shape and called *singular regions*. These regions can be classified into three typologies according to their shape: loop, delta, and whorl are characterized respectively by a ⌒, Δ, and *O* shape. A particular presence of these singular regions defines the whole fingerprint class: the five classes in Henry's scheme [(Jain & Maltoni, 2003)] are *arch, tented arch, right loop, left loop, and whorl*.

At local level, other important features called minutiae refer to ridge discontinuities. Minutiae ar sometimes called "Galton details",[162] in honor of the first person who categorized them and observed that they remain unchanged over the individual's entire life [(Lee & Gaensslen, 1991, 2nd edn. 2001)].[163] Most frequently, the minutiae types can be identified by terminations, where a ridge line ends, and bifurcations, where a ridge bifurcates forming a "Y" [...], even if several types have been observed, described by their shape (dot, island, hook, lake, ridge crossing and multiple bifurcations).

Another important point in the image, which can be used also to align the fingerprint images, is the "core point", corresponding to the center of the north most loop type singular region. In fingers without loop or whorl regions, the core is associated with the point of maximum ridge line curvature. The most important minutiae characteristics are the location coordinates inside the image, their form type (e.g. termination, bifurcation, island, etc.) and the orientation of the ridge (in degree) on which the minutia is found.

Advances in research make it possible to avoid having to develop the prints first, in order to examine fingerprints[164]:

> Within the Materials Research Centre, University of Swansea, UK, University of Swansea, UK, Professor Neil McMurray and Dr Geraint Williams have developed a technique that enables fingerprints to be visualised on metallic and electrically conductive surfaces without the need to develop the prints first. The technique involves the use of an instrument called a scanning Kelvin probe (SKP), which measures the voltage, or electrical potential, at preset intervals over the surface of an object on which a fingerprint may have been deposited. These measurements can then be mapped to produce an image of the fingerprint. [...]
>
> Currently, in crime scene investigations, a decision has to be made at an early stage whether to attempt to retrieve fingerprints through the use of developers or whether to swab surfaces in an attempt to salvage material for DNA fingerprinting. The two processes are mutually incompatible, as fingerprint developers destroy material that could potentially be used for DNA analysis, and swabbing is likely to make fingerprint identification impossible.
>
> The application of the new SKP fingerprinting technique, which is non-contact and does not require the use of developers, has the potential to allow fingerprints to be retrieved while still leaving intact any material that could subsequently be subjected to DNA analysis. [...]

In the United States (ibid.):

> The FBI manages a fingerprint identification system and database called IAFIS, which currently holds the fingerprints and criminal records of over fifty-one million criminal record subjects, and over 1.5 million civil (non-criminal) fingerprint records. U.S. Visit currently holds a repository of over 50 million persons, primarily in the form of two-finger records (by 2008, U.S. Visit is transforming to a system recording FBI-standard tenprint records).

---

[162] Psychologist and anthropologist Francis Galton (1821–1911), Charles Darwin's cousin.

[163] Allegedly, the first edition was a bestseller of Lee and Gaensslen's (1991) *Handbook of Fingerprint Recognition*. The second edition, of 2001, is a major revision. A more recent handbook is *Handbook of Fingerprint Recognition* by Davide Maltoni, Dario Maio, Anil K. Jain, and Salil Prabhakar (2003, 2nd edn. 2009).

[164] http://en.wikipedia.org/wiki/Fingerprint.

Most American law enforcement agencies use Wavelet Scalar Quantization (WSQ), a wavelet-based system[165] for efficient storage of compressed fingerprint images at 500 pixels per inch (ppi). [. . .] For fingerprints recorded at 1000 ppi spatial resolution. law enforcement (including the FBI) uses JPEG 2000 instead of WSQ. [. . .]

8.7.2.4 Fingerprints from Dead Bodies

Sometimes forensic fingerprinting specialists are faced not with the task of pinpointing a live suspect criminal from the fingerprints he or she left, but rather with trying to achieve identification for a dead body, based on the skin of the finger tips. Take the case of mummified bodies. "The identification of mummified bodies places high demands on the skills of a forensic fingerprinting specialist. From a variety of methods, he must be able to choose the most appropriate one to reproduce the skin ridges from fingers, which are often shrunk and deformed", as stated in the English abstract of a paper by Ineichen and Neukom (1995), of the Zurich cantonal police: their "article introduces and discusses a method for indirect fingerprinting. In this method, a negative cast of the mummified fingertip is first produced with a silicon mass. This 3-dimensional negative is then filled with several layers of a white glue/talc mixture, until a skin-thick positive is attained. Using this artificial skin it is possible to reproduce, in a relatively short time, a fingerprint which is free of disturbing skin wrinkles and deformities" (ibid.).

The problem with using fingerprints from dead bodies is that deformation can be expected to be much worse that the elastic deformation that normally affects fingerprints from living persons. Bear in mind that fingers are in three dimensions, whereas fingerprints appear on a surface. Computer methods for fingerprint matching (the fingerprints having been left by persons while alive) have to cope with the problem of elastic deformation. In dead bodies, the deformation caused by decay is plastic, not just elastic. That is to say, the shape that the fingertip has taken will not revert to the previous shape the way that the finger tip of a living person, when pressed against a surface, is going to go back to its previous shape when not pressed.

8.7.2.5 The Problem of Assessing Fingerprint Sufficient Similarity

Are fingerprints really reliable? The courts in the United States and elsewhere have usually been rather unresponsive to challenges to identification accuracy. But there is another problem with the use of *latent prints*, i.e., of such fingerprints that were found at a crime scene (Cole, Welling, Dioso-Villa, & Carpenter, 2008, p. 167):

[A]side from being unresponsive to the question of accuracy, the individuality issue is problematic in its own right (Saks & Koehler, 2008). It is commonly said that the 'individuality' or 'uniqueness' of friction ridge skin is one of the 'fundamental premises' of latent print individualization (Moenssens, 1999).[166] Such discussions generally treat this premise as

---

[165] See http://en.wikipedia.org/wiki/Wavelet_Scalar_Quantization
[166] Cf. Moenssens (2003).

one that has been satisfied – i.e. the 'individuality' of friction ridge skin is 'known' or 'proven'. By this, it would appear that fingerprint proponents mean that the exact duplication of any area of friction ridge skin is extremely unlikely. But such an assertion has little meaning without knowing the conditions under which extreme similarity would be considered 'duplication', what scale of area of friction ridge skin is being discussed and at what level of resolution friction ridge skin is observed. Assertions of 'uniqueness' or 'individuality' could, for all we know, mean nothing more than that, when analysed at the level of molecules, no two areas of friction ridge skin will duplicate exactly. Such a statement is undoubtedly true not only of friction ridge skin, as well as many other objects in the world, but also of little value in measuring how accurately source attributions can be made from those objects by human experts using visual analysis.

For practical legal purposes, mere non-duplication is not what really matters. Rather (ibid.):

> Obviously, what is wanted is not the mere assertion of non-duplication, but, rather, measurements of the variability of different areas of friction ridge skin and, crucially, multiple images derived from the same areas of friction ridge skin. In short, the issue is not so much the individuality of an area of friction ridge skin itself, but rather the range of variability of legible impressions that can be produced by a given area of friction ridge skin relative to the range of impressions that could be produced by analogous areas of friction ridge skin from different individuals.
>
> Perhaps most importantly, it makes little sense to discuss the 'individuality', or even the 'variability', of 'fingerprints' as if it were a quality that inhered in friction ridge skin. These qualities can only exist in conjunction with some sort of perceptual system, whether human or mechanical.

Let us consider the common task of identifying suspect perpetrators, based on prints left by their fingers, in the British context. In the words of a scholar based in London, Mike Redmayne (2002, p. 25):

> Fingerprint experts have no statistics on which to base their conclusions. There is a large degree of consensus that individual fingerprints are unique, and that a certain number of similarities between two prints proves identity beyond almost any doubt. But there are no figures on which to base these judgments: no way of quantifying the cut-off point at which sufficient similarity proves identity. David Stoney has written perceptively about the process of fingerprint identification. He suggests that, on perceiving enough points of identity, the expert makes a 'leap of faith' and becomes 'subjectively certain' of identity. In many countries there is a convention that a particular number of points is required before a match is announced. In England and Wales, the magic number was long sixteen. Latterly, few people saw much logic in the 'sixteen points' rule, and it was abandoned in 2001. But the convention helps to explain why, when the expert in *Charles* went to court on just twelve points, his evidence was vulnerable to a *Doheny*-style challenge.

The *Doheny* case is one in which identification revolved on the DNA evidence. Also from England and Wales, it was judged in 1997 by the Court of Appeal, "which after agonising over" the risks of misconceptions on the part of jurors of what DNA evidence stands for (Redmayne, 2002, p. 20),

> hit upon an ingenious solution. Rather than explaining the subtle but important distinction between the probability of guilt given the DNA evidence and the probability of the DNA evidence given guilt in semantic terms, it would provide a simple illustration to convey the key issues [...]. Its sample jury instructions for DNA cases proceeds as follows:

> Members of the jury, if you accept the scientific evidence called by the Crown, this indicates that there are probably only four or five white males in the United Kingdom from whom that semen could have come. The defendant is one of them. If that is the position, the decision you have to reach, on all the evidence, is whether you are sure that is was the defendant who left that stain or whether it is possible that it was one of the other small number of men who share the same DNA characteristics.

The quotation, previously given, about fingerprints, as taken from Redmayne (2002, p. 25), is about the case of Neil Charles, convicted of robbery and false imprisonment, and the principal evidence about whom was a fingerprint; moreover, "[t]here was circumstantial evidence to link him to the crime scene – he had been seen acting suspiciously nearby earlier in the day, and [closed-circuit TV] cameras caught him in the area later on" (p. 25). "The defence strategy was simple: to get the expert think of his testimony in *Doheny* terms, so as to draw out an admission that Charles was just one of *n* men who might have left the print" (p. 25). "But the Court of Appeal would not allow two experts to explore these issues further because they had not been called at trial. In any case, it did not think the *Doheny* analogy apt because 'the Crown's case did not rest on any random occurrence ratio [sc. match probability]'." (ibid., p. 25, Redmayne's brackets).

Redmayne remarks that fingerprint identification is such powerful evidence that perhaps "really there is no room for a *Doheny* argument. The expert makes the leap of faith, leaving no quantifiable gap over which the jury must jump [. . .]. But as the match threshold moves down from 16 points, there is less room for complacency" (ibid., p. 26). There has been contention about the admissibility of fingerprint evidence. Yvette Tinsley, from the Victoria University of Wellington, New Zealand, discussed a possible reform of identification procedures (Tinsley, 2001).

Scotland's Fingerprint Inquiry[167] is likely to have repercussions also outside Scotland, in the long term. The Inquiry Report was expected in 2011. Oral hearings took place in the summer and autumn of 2009. On 14 March 2008, Scotland's Cabinet Secretary for Justice, Kenny MacAskill, announced a public judicial inquiry (set up by Scottish ministers under the Inquiries Act 2005). Its remit has been to investigate the steps taken to verify the fingerprints associated with the case of *H.M. Advocate* v. *McKie* in 1999, and related matters.

The background is as follows. Charged for the murder of Marion Ross, David Asbury was convicted in May 1997, and the prosecution case against him included fingerprint evidence. During the investigation into the murder, a fingerprint was found on the doorframe of the bathroom in Marion Ross's home. That fingerprint (which became known as "Y7"), was identified as belonging to Shirley McKie, a serving police officer involved in the murder investigation. During Asbury's trial, McKie denied that the fingerprint was hers. After the murder trial, she was prosecuted for perjury: the charge was that she had lied while giving evidence on oath, because of what she had said in her evidence at David Asbury's trial. The evidence before the jury at McKie's trial

---

[167] http://www.thefingerprintinquiryscotland.org.uk

included evidence from defence fingerprint experts that Y7 was not her fingerprint. The jury, unanimously, found Shirley McKie not guilty of perjury. The identification of Y7 was made, originally, by officers of the Scottish Criminal Record Office. Various fingerprint experts have expressed differing views as to whether Y7 is the fingerprint of Shirley McKie. In August 2000 David Asbury was granted interim liberation pending an appeal against his conviction for murder. His conviction was quashed in August 2002. The Crown did not oppose his appeal. Shirley McKie raised an action for damages arising from the identification of Y7 as her fingerprint. It was settled out of court by the Scottish Ministers, without admission of liability, in February 2006.[168]

The Scottish government set up the Fingerprint Inquiry to fulfil its commitment to hold an independent, public, judicial inquiry into the circumstances surrounding the Shirley McKie case. The Fingerprint Inquiry's[169] terms of reference, as agreed by the Scottish Ministers, are as follows:

- To inquire into the steps that were taken to identify and verify the fingerprints associated with, and leading up to, the case of HM Advocate v. McKie in 1999
- to determine, in relation to the fingerprint designated Y7, the consequences of the steps taken, or not taken, and
- to report findings of fact and make recommendations as to what measures might now be introduced, beyond those that have already been introduced since 1999, to ensure that any shortcomings are avoided in the future.

An editorial (Koehler, 2008) in a special issue of the journal *Law, Probability and Risk*, by Jonathan Koehler from Arizona State University in Tempe, began by noting:

Ten years ago, the notion that a top academic journal should publish an exchange on the scientific validation of fingerprint evidence would have been a non-starter. Until then, all but a few self-interested defendants and defence attorneys believed that when a fingerprint examiner matched a crime scene print (a latent print) to a suspect's reference print, the evidence was absolute and irrefutable. A fingerprint match proved identity if not guilt. Today, however, scientists, attorneys and others are taking a hard look at the forensic sciences in general and fingerprint evidence in particular. The oft-repeated claims that fingerprints are unique and that the source of fingerprint fragments can be identified with certainty have received special attention.[170]

---

[168] The quotation is from the webpage "About the Inquiry: Background" at the site of the inquiry itself, at http://www.thefingerprintinquiryscotland.org.uk/inquiry/23.html

[169] Set up under the Inquiries Act 2005, it is one of the first inquiries under that Act to use the Inquiries (Scotland) Rules 2007.

[170] The uniqueness claim was rejected by Balding (2005), Cole (2004) and Saks and Koehler (2008). Koehler noted (2008, p. 85): "Kaye (2003) points out the serious flaws in a study that some rely on as proof of fingerprint uniqueness. As for the certainty of fingerprint identifications, the data (not surprisingly) show that fingerprint examiners are fallible. Many commit false-positive and false-negative errors in proficiency tests and in casework (Cole, 2005, 2006a, 2006b). Indeed, some critics argue that there is no scientific reason to believe that fingerprint examiners can make reliable identifications at all (Epstein, 2002)." A bibliography of legal scholarship rejecting the validity of fingerprint identification can be found in the long very last footnote of Cole (2009), and it should be looked up there.

In an article from the United States cautious about the reliability of fingerprint evidence, Cole et al. (2008) began by pointing out: "Efforts to harness computer fingerprint databases to perform studies relevant to fingerprint identification have tended to focus on 10-print, rather than latent print, identification or on the inherent individuality of fingerprint images." (ibid., p. 165). That is to say (ibid., p. 166):

> Latent print individualization is a forensic technique that endeavours to attribute a 'mark' (a crime scene or 'latent' print) to the 'friction ridge skin' (the corrugated skin that covers human fingers, palms and soles) of an individual. Such attributions are currently achieved through a visual comparison of the mark with an exemplar 'print' whose origin is known. These attributions are made by human latent print examiners (LPEs). Computer algorithms (Automated Fingerprint Identification Systems or AFIS) are often used to search large databases for 'candidate' prints to present to the examiner, but there is neither an agency or a jurisdiction that currently allows a computer system to make *latent* print attributions nor an algorithm that claims an ability to make such attributions. This is not the case for 10-print attributions, in which the source of a set of 10 'inked', or intentionally recorded, prints is attributed. Such attributions are sometimes made by computer algorithms (Cherry & Imwinkelried, 2006).
>
> Professional LPEs are restricted to three conclusions: individualization, inconclusive and exclusion (Scientific Working Group on Friction Ridge Analysis Study and Technology, 2003).[171] Thus, the only 'inclusionary' conclusion – i.e. the only conclusion that implicates a suspect – is the conclusion of 'individualization'. 'Individualization', in turn, is defined as the claim that a particular area of friction ridge skin is the only possible source of a particular mark (Scientific Working Group on Friction Ridge Analysis Study and Technology, 2003). In other words, all other possible sources have been eliminated as possible sources of the mark.

Cole et al. (2008) questioned *accuracy*, i.e., how often it is that individualisations based on latent prints are correct: "Does the accuracy vary predictably in response to particular variables, such as, say, the amount of information contained in the mark or the skill level of the examiner?" (ibid., p. 166). They also questioned *sufficiency:* "How much consistent friction ridge detail is it necessary to find, in order to support a conclusion of individualization?" (ibid.). Their third question concerned *individuality:* "How rare are the various friction ridge features used in latent print analysis within various populations? How rare are various combinations of friction ridge features? How similar are the most similar areas of friction ridge skin, of some specified size?" (ibid.). Cole et al. (2008, pp. 166–167):

> There have been essentially no empirical studies addressing the accuracy questions (Haber & Haber, 2003, 2008), although some preliminary studies are now beginning to be undertaken (Wertheim et al., 2006; Langenburg, 2004; Haber & Haber, 2006). Purported answers to the sufficiency question are known to have been legislated rather than derived from empirical data (Champod, 1995; Evett & Williams, 1996; Cole, 1999). Current professional guidelines developed in the United States mandate an essentially circular definition of 'sufficiency': 'Sufficiency is the examiner's determination that adequate unique details of the friction skin source area are revealed in the impression' (Scientific Working Group

---

[171] Tthe Scientific Working Group on Friction Ridge Analysis, Study and Technology (SWGFAST) was established in 1995, and its mission is to establish consensus guidelines and standards for the forensic examination of friction ridges. See http://www.swgfast.org/ Several resports are posted at that site.

on Friction Ridge Analysis Study and Technology, 2002, section 1.5). The most sustained scholarly attention has been devoted to individuality, but much of it has focused on demonstrating or asserting the mere fact of the absolute non-duplication of complete fingertip-sized areas of friction ridge skin, rather than on measuring the degree of variability. This is true of both of the two major strands of fingerprint research. Statistical research focused on estimating the probability that exact duplicate areas of friction ridge skin (usually complete fingertips) exist (Pankanti et al., 2002; Stoney, 2001). Anatomical research focused on detailing the formation of friction ridge skin, while occasionally commenting that this process was sufficiently complex to support an assumption of non-duplication as a 'working principle' (Cummins & Midlo, 1943; Wilder & Wentworth, 1918; Wertheim & Maceo, 2002).

Nonetheless, defenders of latent print individualization have tended to seek to shift the debate to individuality when pressed concerning accuracy, a tendency that one of us has elsewhere called 'the fingerprint examiner's fallacy', the argument that the accuracy of a source attribution technique may be inferred from the uniqueness or variability of the target object (Cole, 2004, 2006b). [...]

What Cole et al. (2008) themselves did, was to carry out experiments measuring how accurate an automated fingerprint matching system was at identifying the source of *simulated latent* print (i.e., fingerprints taken, as though, from a crime scene, while actually having been obtained for the purposes of the experiment). The computer system carried out the task of a human latent print examiner fairly weel, except in that it (like presumably the human expert) tended to produce false positives (ibid., p. 165): "there are non-mate images that scored very highly on the AFIS's[172] similarity measure. These images would be susceptible to erroneous conclusions that would be given with a very high degree of confidence. Not surprisingly, the same was also true of the simulated latents which contained less information." They claimed that this is useful for assessing human experts, too: "We suggest that measuring the accuracy and potential for erroneous conclusions for AFISs might provide a basis for comparison between human examiners and automated systems at performing various identification tasks" (ibid.).[173]

8.7.3 Computational Techniques for Fingerprint Recognition

8.7.3.1 General Considerations

Research in *biometrics* within computer science has found various applications,[174] and in particular, identification by means of fingerprints is no longer confined to use by the police. In the words of Bistarelli et al. (2006, pp. 359–360):

---

[172] *AFIS* stands for "automated fingerpint identification system".

[173] Incidentally, note that Srihari, Srinivasan, and Beal (2008) discussed the discriminability of the fingerprints of twins. Sargur Srihari's team at the University of Buffalo is active in both computer-assisted handwriting recognition, and computer-assisted fingerprint recognition.

[174] For example, see fn. 177 in Chapter 6.

The term "biometrics" is commonly used today to refer to the authentication of a person by analyzing his/her physical characteristics (like fingerprints) or behavioral characteristics (like voice or gait). Since these characteristics are unique to an individual, their measurement provides a more reliable system of authentication than ID cards, keys, passwords, or other traditional systems while accessing restricted areas in office buildings and factories, or controlling the security of computer networks, electronic commerce, and banking transactions. The reason is that all these secret keys can be easily stolen or cloned to steal the personal identity, or they can also be forgotten by the owner preventing the whole identification process. Biometric characteristics are, instead, generally more difficult to duplicate and they naturally always "follow" the owner. Moreover, an advantage of biometrics is that they cannot be lent (like a physical key), and thus, they [guarantee the owner's] on-site presence.

   The most common biometric techniques are signature verification, retinal analysis, facial analysis, fingerprint verification, hand geometry, and voice verification. These technologies are comparable by the aid of several indicators, such as permanence (measurement should be invariant with time), uniqueness (different values for different persons), universality (everyone should have this trait), acceptability (if people are willing to accept this technology), performance (the recognition accuracy and system requirements) and circumvention (how [easy it is] to fool the system). Fingerprint matching is one of the most diffused biometric techniques used in automatic personal identification, because of its strong reliability and its low implementation cost; moreover, it is also the most mature and explored technology of all [biometric techniques].

Computational fingerprint recognition techniques – examining the pattern of ridges and furrows in fingerprints, and their *minutiae points*, that is to say, *ridge ending* and *ridge bifurcation* – are an active area within image processing. Na, Yoon, Kim, and Hwang (2005) discussed the shortcoming of such techniques. Brislawn, Bradley, Onyshczak, & Hopper (1996) described the FBI compression standard for digitised fingerprint images. Criminal investigation is just one of the area in which fingerprints are used for identification. "The fingerprint sensors are becoming smaller and cheaper, and automatic identification based on fingerprints is becoming an attractive alternative/complement to the traditional methods of identification" (Khuwaja, 2006, p. 25), not only in criminal investigation, but, along with other so-called *biometric* methods employed in *personal authentication systems*, and based on an individual person's body or sometimes behavioural features, also in e-banking, e-commerce, smart cards, and access to sensitive databases, and sometimes for access into premises with security requirements. The procedure is not without problems. Khuwaja remarks (ibid., pp. 24–25):

The quality of the finger image is the most significant factor in a reliable process (Emiroglu and Akhan, 1997; Jiang et al., 2001). One aspect of fingerprint identification systems, which largely has been overlooked, is the need for a determination on a pixel-by-pixel basis of the reliability of the information. In an image, one region might be highly reliable, while another is not. Sets of information must be extracted from an image by the system, a process known as encoding. This process is made difficult by the fact that different prints of the same finger may be substantially different due to effects such as (a) pressure; increased pressure leads to ridge joining and decreased pressure leads to ridge breaking. (b) dirt and moisture; this can cause phantom joints; (c) elasticity of the skin; the whole image can become sheared and distorted; (d) background; the latent may be taken from a complex background, both in relif and pattern; (e) inking; the amount of ink used to take finger impressions significantly affects the images; and (f) smudging; often regions of the print image are smudged.

Moreover, when fingerprints are scanned, there may be imperfections in the images (ibid., p. 25). Such imperfect images "require some preprocessing before the features on them can be extracted. The imperfections in the images manifest themselves in the form of noncontinuous regions and noncontinuous ridges (Costello, Gunawardena, & Nadiadi, 1994). These areas need either to be enhanced or ignored for valid recognition of the fingerprint" (Khuwaja, ibid.)

Automatic fingerprint identification systems are widely used, and there exist several pattern matching techniques applied to matching fingerprints, but the matching is time-consuming. There exists a series of Fingerprint Verification Competitions (FVC), in which the systems entered by competitors are tested on databases, and the performance is in terms of authentication reliability and speed.

Apart from the time it takes to match fingerprints, another problem is deformation. Hao, Tan, and Wang (2002, section 1) explain this as follows:

> In most [automatic fingerprint identification systems], the representation of fingerprints is based on minutiae such as ridge ending and ridge bifurcation, with each minutia being characterized by its locations and orientation. With this representation, the matching problem is reduced to a point pattern matching problem. In the ideal case described by Jain et al. (1997), the matching can be accomplished by simply counting the number of spatially overlapping minutiae. But in practice, the sensing system maps the three-dimensional finger on to two-dimensional images. Once the location, pressure and direction of impression change, the mapping will change accordingly, which inevitably leads to nonlinear deformation of fingerprint images. Two fingerprint images may have translation, rotation or even nonlinear deformation between them. If the time span between two impressions is long, the images may also change due to cuts on finger or skin disease.
>
> In most systems, fingerprint is represented with a set of minutiae which is called template. The representation itself may be noisy due to presence of spurious minutiae and absence of genuine minutiae. Also, the properties of minutiae such as the location and orientation may be inaccurately estimated due to image degradation and imperfect preprocessing.
>
> Considering all these situations, a good fingerprint matching algorithm should meet the following two criteria:

- Be robust to all kinds of possible deformation which are commonly observed in fingerprints and are hard to model.
- Be robust to small perturbation on minutiae and minutiae properties.

Terje Kristensen (2010) reported about a computer application to fingerprint identification, intended to reduce the matching time. To carry out classification a Support Vector Machine (SVM) algorithm[175] was resorted to. "The given fingerprint database is decomposed into four different subclasses and a SVM algorithm is used to train the system to do correct classification. The classification rate has been estimated to about 87.0% of unseen fingerprints. The average matching time is decreased with a factor of about 3.5 compared to brute force search applied" (ibid.).

---

[175] Support vector machines or vector support machines are the subject of Section 6.1.9.3. Moreover, we have said something about support vector machines at the end of Section 6.1.2.3.

A variety of approaches is encountered in the scholarly literature of automated fingerprint matching. For example, Chen and Kuo (1991) applied *tree matching*. Isenor and Zaky (1986) resorted to *graph matching* in order to solve the problem of *elastic deformation*. The matching is based on *euclidean distance* in Jain, Prabhakar, Hong, and Pankanti (2000) as well as Lee and Wang (1999), who represented the fingerprint with texture information extracted by *Gabor filters*.

In image processing, a *Gabor filter*, named after Dennis Gabor, is a linear filter used for edge detection. Frequency and orientation representations of Gabor filters are similar to those of the human visual system, and they have been found to be particularly appropriate for texture representation and discrimination. In the spatial domain, a 2D Gabor filter is a Gaussian kernel function modulated by a sinusoidal plane wave. The Gabor filters are self-similar: all filters can be generated from one mother wavelet by dilation and rotation.[176]

---

[176] From Wikipedia (http://en.wikipedia.org/wiki/Gabor_filter). The impulse response of a Gabor filter "is defined by a harmonic function multiplied by a Gaussian function. Because of the multiplication-convolution property (Convolution theorem), the Fourier transform of a Gabor filter's impulse response is the convolution of the Fourier transform of the harmonic function and the Fourier transform of the Gaussian function. The filter has a real and an imaginary component representing orthogonal directions. The two components may be formed into a complex number or used individually" (ibid.). With the convention that "λ represents the wavelength of the sinusoidal factor, θ represents the orientation of the normal to the parallel stripes of a Gabor function, ψ is the phase offset, σ is the sigma of the Gaussian envelope and γ is the spatial aspect ratio, and specifies the ellipticity of the support of the Gabor function" (ibid.), the Gabor filter is given by the following formulae. As a complex number:

$$g(x, y; \lambda, \theta, \psi, \sigma, \gamma) = \exp\left(-\frac{x'^2 + \gamma^2 y'^2}{2\sigma^2}\right) \exp\left(i\left(2\pi\frac{x'}{\lambda} + \psi\right)\right)$$

The real component is:

$$g(x, y; \lambda, \theta, \psi, \sigma, \gamma) = \exp\left(-\frac{x'^2 + \gamma^2 y'^2}{2\sigma^2}\right) \cos\left(2\pi\frac{x'}{\lambda} + \psi\right)$$

The imaginary component is:

$$g(x, y; \lambda, \theta, \psi, \sigma, \gamma) = \exp\left(-\frac{x'^2 + \gamma^2 y'^2}{2\sigma^2}\right) \sin\left(2\pi\frac{x'}{\lambda} + \psi\right)$$

where

$$x' = x\cos\theta + y\sin\theta$$

and

$$y' = -x\sin\theta + y\cos\theta$$

Fasel, Bartlett, and Movellan (2002) compared Gabor filter methods for another problem in pattern-matching that is relevant for biometrics, namely, the *automatic detection of facial landmarks.*[177]

Jain, Ross, and Prabhakar (2001) combined texture features and minutiae features, while being specifically interested in solid-state fingerprint sensors: in fact, these only provide a small contact area "for the fingertip, and, therefore, sense only a limited portion of the fingerprint. Thus multiple impressions of the same fingerprint may have only a small region of overlap. Minutiae-based matching algorithms, which consider ridge activity only in the vicinity of minutiae points, are not likely to perform well on these images due to the insufficient number of corresponding points in the input and template images. We present a hybrid matching algorithm that uses both minutiae (point) information and texture (region) information for matching the fingerprints" (ibid., from the abstract).

Kovács-Vajna (2000) combined triangular matching and dynamic time warping to tolerate nonlinear deformation of fingerprints.[178] Tan and Bhanu (2006) applied genetic algorithms[179] to fingerprint matching. The genetic algorithm "tries to find the optimal transformation between two different fingerprints. In order to deal with low-quality fingerprint images, which introduce significant occlusion and clutter of minutiae features, we design a fitness function based on the local properties of each triplet of minutiae" (ibid., from the abstract). They found that their approach compares favourably with an approach based on mean-squared error estimation.

Ito, Nakajima, Kobayashi, Aoki, and Higuchi (2004) proposed an algorithm for fingerprint matching, which resorts to the *Phase-Only Correlation* function. It uses phase spectra of fingerprint images, and we are going to devote to it a special subsection (see Section 8.7.3.3). Kong, Zhang, and Kamel (2006) were concerned with *palmprint identification*, and for that purpose, they resorted to *feature-level fusion;* as they explained in the abstract:

> Multiple elliptical Gabor filters with different orientations are employed to extract the phase information on a palmprint image, which is then merged according to a fusion rule to produce a single feature called the Fusion Code. The similarity of two Fusion Codes is measured by their normalized hamming distance. A dynamic threshold is used for the final decisions. A database containing 9599 palmprint images from 488 different palms is used to validate the performance of the proposed method.

---

[177] The article by Fasel et al. (2002) "presents a systematic analysis of Gabor filter banks for detection of facial landmarks (pupils and philtrum). Sensitivity is assessed using [...] a non-parametric estimate of sensitivity independent of bias commonly used in the psychophysical literature. We find that current Gabor filter bank systems are overly complex. Performance can be greatly improved by reducing the number of frequency and orientation components in these systems. With a single frequency band, we obtained performances significantly better than those achievable with current systems that use multiple frequency bands. [...]" (ibid., from the abstract).

[178] Cf. Kovács-Vajna, Rovatti, and Frazzoni (2000); Farina, Kovács-Vajna, and Leone (1999); and cf. Zs. Kovács-Vajna, "Method and Device for Identifying Fingerprints", U.S.A. Patent No. US6,236,741, filing date: 19.02.1997, issued: 22.05.2001; Zs. Kovács-Vajna, "Method and Device for Identifying Fingerprints Using an Analog Flash Memory", U.S.A. Patent No. US6,330,347, filing date: 28.07.1998, issued: 11.12.2001.

[179] Genetic algorithms are the subject of Section 6.1.16.1 in this book.

Ying Hao, Tieniu Tan, and Yunhong Wang, from the National Lab of Pattern Recognition at the Institute of Automation of the Chinese Academy of Sciences in Beijing, proposed an algorithm for fingerprint matching that is based on error propagation (Hao et al., 2002). They remarked that traditional methods treat fingerprint matching "as point pattern matching, which is essentially an intractable problem due to the various nonlinear deformations commonly observed in fingerprint images" (ibid., from the abstract). According to their own method (ibid.):

> Firstly, ridge information and Hough transformation are adopted to find several pairs of matching minutiae, the initial correspondences, which are used to estimate the common region of two fingerprints and the alignment parameters. Then a MatchedSet which includes the correspondence and its surrounding matched minutiae pairs is established. The subsequent matching process is guided by the concept of error propagation: the matching errors of each unmatched minutiae are estimated according to those of its most relevant neighbor minutiae. In order to prevent the process from being misguided by mismatched minutiae pairs, we adopt a flexible propagation scheme.

The matching algorithm they proposed comprises three steps (ibid., section 2). In the first step, each and every minutia "in the reference template is matched with each minutiae in the input template and all resulting potential correspondences are used to find several most reliable one, the initial correspondences, using Hough transformation" (ibid.). In the second step, "all minutiae surrounding the correspondence are matched and those minutiae pairs whose matching error are less than certain thresholds are added to the MatchedSet" (ibid.). In the third step, the algorithm adjusts "the matching error of each unmatched minutia according to the information provided by the MatchedSet recursively until the number of elements in MatchedSet stops increasing. A conformation process which checks the consistency of the matching errors of elements in the MatchedSet is made to label and remove the mismatched minutiae after each iteration" (ibid.). The MatchedSet is initialised after the two templates have been aligned and the common region estimated. Error threshold are chosen with care, so that only reliable pairs are added to the initial MatchedSet (ibid., section 2.3).

Arun Abraham Ross (2003) developed, under Anil Jain's supervision, a "hybrid fingerprint system that utilizes both minutiae points and ridge feature maps to represent and match fingerprint images" (from the abstract of the thesis). For image filtering, Ross used Gabor filters (Ross, 2003, section 2.3). Filtered images were underwent *tessellation* (i.e., mosaicking), for ridge feature mapping (ibid., section 2.4 and chapter 3). A deformable model was resrted to, in order to account for the elasticity of fingertips. Ross explained (ibid., in the abstract of the thesis):

> The hybrid matcher is shown to perform significantly better than a traditional minutiae-based matcher. The ridge feature maps extracted by this technique have also been used to align and register fingerprint image pairs via a correlation process, thereby obviating the need to rely on minutiae points for image registration. To address the problem of partial prints obtained from small-sized sensors, a fingerprint mosaicking scheme has been developed. The proposed technique constructs a composite fingerprint template from two partial fingerprint impressions by using the iterative control point (ICP) algorithm that determines the transformation parameters relating the two impressions. To mitigate the e_ect of nonlinear distortions in fingerprint images on the matching process, an average deformation

model has been proposed. The model is developed by comparing a fingerprint impression with several other impressions of the same finger and observing the common ridge points that occur in them. An index of deformation has been suggested in this context to aid in the selection of an 'optimal' fingerprint impression from a set of impressions. Finally, techniques to combine fingerprint information with the other biometric traits of a subject (viz., face and hand geometry) are presented.

The mosaicking is because of the following problem (Ross, 2003, pp. 55–56):

> [T]he average number of minutiae points extracted from a Digital Biometrics optical sensor (500 × 500 image at 500 dpi) is 45 compared to 25 minutiae obtained from a Veridicom sensor image (300 × 300 image at 500 dpi). This loss of information affects the matching performance of the veriffcation system – the relatively small overlap between the template and query impressions results in fewer corresponding points and therefore, results in higher false rejects and/or higher false accepts.

The remedy is as follows (Ross, 2003, pp. 56–57):

> To deal with this problem, we have developed a fingerprint mosaicking scheme that constructs a composite fingerprint template using evidence accumulated from multiple impressions. A composite template reduces storage, decreases matching time and alleviates the quandary of selecting the "optimal" fingerprint template from a given set of impressions. In the proposed algorithm, two impressions (templates) of a finger are initially aligned using the corresponding minutiae points. This alignment is used by a modified version of the well-known iterative closest point algorithm (ICP) to compute a transformation matrix that defines the spatial relationship between the two impressions. The resulting transformation matrix is used in two ways: (a) the two template images are stitched together to generate a composite image. Minutiae points are then detected in this composite image; (b) the minutia sets obtained from each of the individual impressions are integrated to create a composite minutia set.

8.7.3.2   Bistarelli, Santini, and Vaccarelli's Algorithm, Suiting the Hardware Constraints of a Smartcard Architecture

A team from Pisa and Pescara, Italy, comprising Stefano Bistarelli et al., proposed (2006) what they called "a light-weight fingerprint matching algorithm that can be executed inside the devices with a limited computational power" (ibid., p. 359). Their implementation is on a smartcard, and is support by the Java Card[TM] platform.[180] In devising their algorithm, they based in on "on the minutiae local structures (the "neighborhoods"), that are invariant with respect to global transformations like translation and rotation" (ibid.). Such local structure information

---

[180] On which, see http://www.javacardforum.org/ See Chen (2000b) about the architecture of Java Card. "Performing a biometric verification inside a smartcard is notoriously difficult, since the processing capabilities of standard smartcard processors are limited for such a complex task. With *Match-on-Card* (MoC) technology, the fingerprint template is stored inside the card, unavailable to the external applications and the outside world. In addition, the matching decision is securely authenticated by the smartcard itself, in this way, the card has only to trust in itself for eventually unblocking stored sensitive information, such as digital certificates or private keys for digital signature. Our verification MoC algorithm was developed to work in this very strictly bounded environment" (Bistarelli et al., 2006, p. 359).

about the minutiae characteristics, i.e., ridge pattern micro-characteristics, spares the system the need to pre-align the processing fingerprint templates, "which would be a difficult task to implement inside a smartcard" (ibid., p. 360). The CPU (i.e., the central processing unit) of a smartcard pose limitations: "matching on smartcard environment is bounded by the hardware simplicity (CPU limitations first of all), and thus waiting for a complete minutiae match could lead to a waiting time which is too long for the user. In our algorithm we solve this problem by stopping the computation as soon as it is possible to assert, with satisfactory confidence, that the considered templates belong to the same fingerprint" (ibid., p. 367).

"The main characteristic of the algorithm is to have an asymmetric behavior, in respect to the execution time, between correct positive and negative matches" (ibid., p. 359). Correct positive martches are when the same fingerprint is recognised. Correct negative matches are when two different fingers left the prints. The asymmetric execution time "is because the match procedure stops immediately when few minutiae pairs result in a positive match. If this check does not succeed, for example if the two fingers are different, or if the two acquisitions of the same finger are very disturbed, the procedure is fully executed (lasting longer) and the match decision is taken only at its end" (ibid., p. 360). Bistarelli et al. explained (2006, p. 367):

> Our proposed matching algorithm computes how much the neighborhood of a minutia in the candidate template is similar to the neighborhood of each minutia in the reference template. At the end of this scan step, the two most similar minutiae (those whose "similarity value" is the lowest) are matched and then discarded from subsequent scan phases concerning other different minutiae of the candidate template. All these similarity measures are summed together during the process and, at the end, the algorithm can decide if the two templates match by applying a threshold on this global score.

The problem with smartcard hardware limitations is solved "by stopping the computation as soon as it is possible to assert, with satisfactory confidence, that the considered templates belong to the same fingerprint" (ibid.). In fact, the "algorithm stops as soon as it finds some minutiae pairs (i.e. a number between 2 and 5) matching with a very good average similarity value, or even immediately when only the last examined minutiae pair has a matching value lower than a very rigourous threshold. Otherwise, if these two conditions are not true, the algorithm explores all the minutiae pairings space" (ibid.).

We translate into text the flowchart in Bistarelli et al. (2006, p. 367, figure 6). The input of the algorithm is the candidate minutia C from a candidate template. C is taken to be matched. The reference template is also taken as input, and each of its minutiae is called R (where "the minutia information exactly corresponds to its neighborhood features: the terms 'minutia' and 'neighborhood' can be used as synonyms, since to match a minutia we need to match its neighborhood", ibid.).[181]

---

[181] "The algorithm scans sequentially the minutiae of the reference template until a good match for the input minutia is found. Both candidate and reference minutiae lists are stored according to the increasing minutia reliability value: in this way we try to stop the procedure more quickly by scanning a reduced portion of the template minutiae lists. In fact, a minutia with a high reliability in a given template, when not cut away by partial overlapping, will probably have a high reliability

Step 1. Initially, minutia R in the reference template is taken, and *MinutiaDissimilarity* is initialised to zero.

Step 2. Take neighbour I or R.

Step 3. Take neighbour J of C.

Step 4. Is J matched? If yes, increment J by one and go to Step 3. If no, go to **Step 5**.

Step 5. Find *NeighDissimilarity* between I and J. This corresponds to these four substeps (Bistrarelli et al., 2006, p. 368), where (ibid., p. 366) *Ed* stands for "euclidean distance" (between the central minutia and its neighbour), *Dra* stands for "distance relative angle" (this is the angle between a segment which joins two minutiae points,[182] and the central minutia ridge direction), *Oda* stands for "orientation difference angle" (this is the difference angle between the central minutia orientation angle and the neighbour ridge orientation angle),[183] and *Rc* stands for "ridge count" between the central minutia and its neighbour (See Fig. 8.7.3.2.1):

1. To find the difference in absolute value between corresponding features:

$$EdDiff = |Ed_1 - Ed_2|,$$
$$rcDiff = |Rc_1 - Rc_2|,$$
$$draDiff = |Dra_1 - Dra_2|$$

and

$$odDiff = |Oda_1 - Oda_2|.$$

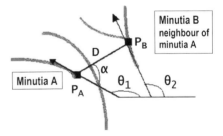

Fig. 8.7.3.2.1 Features of the minutiae. Redrawn from figure 5 of (Bistarelli et al., 2006)

also in other templates obtained from the same finger. Thus, the stopping conditions can be met earlier than in a casual disposition of the minutiae in the list. Moreover, it is obviously better to prematurely stop the procedure with few but 'good' minutiae than with low quality ones. The minutia of the reference template matched in this way, is then marked as 'already matched' and is not considered in the successive iterations." (Bistarelli et al., 2006, p. 368).

[182] Such as the ending of one ridge, and a bifurcation point of two other ridges close by.

[183] The orientation difference angle is the difference between two angles, which are each an angle between a horizontal straight line, and the straight line that is tangent to the respective ridge (thus being the central minutia ridge direction) at the given minutia point (such as the ending of the ridge, or a bifurcation point). It is the minutia point being one of the two ends of the segment we mentioned concerning the distance relative angle.

2. To check that every feature difference value is below the corresponding acceptance threshold; if only one difference value exceeds the relative threshold, the two neighbors cannot correspond in the two respective neighborhoods (*edDiff* must not be greater than the limit set by *edDiffThr, rcDiff* than *rcThr, edDiff* than *draThr* and *odDiff* than *odThr*). The set of the four feature difference thresholds can be globally defined as the features *bounding box*, which makes the algorithm tolerant to small non-linear distortions.

3. To multiply each feature difference for the corresponding eight value: thus,

$$edWghtDiff = edDiff \times edWght,$$

$$rcWghDiff = rcDiff \times rcWght,$$

$$odWghtDiff = odDiff \times odWght$$

and

$$draWghtDiff = draDiff \times draWght.$$

The different weight alues are necessary to attribute more importance to the features that match better such as, in our test experience, the euclidean distance. Before multiplying for the weight value, we have normalized the feature differences with respect to the bounding box thresholds (to have homogenous values).

4. To sum together all the four weighted differences to represent the global dissimilarity between the two neighbors:

$$NeightDissimilarity = edWghtDiff$$

$$+rcWghtDiff$$

$$+draWghtDiff$$

$$+odWghtDiff.$$

Step 6.   Is BBox, i.e. the bounding box, OK? If yes, go to **Step 7.** If no, discard *NeighDissimilarity*, then increment *J* by one and go to **Step 3.**

Step 7.   Is *J=LastNeigh* verified? If yes, go to Step 8. If no, increment *J* by one and go to **Step 3.**

Step 8.   Match *I* and *J* with best *NeighDissimilarity:*

the algorithm finds for the first neighbor of the reference minutia, the most similar neighbor in the input minutia among those satisfying the bounding box checks; the most similar is the one for which the algorithm finds the lowest *NeighDissimilarity* value" (ibid., p. 368). "The chosen most similar neighbor in the reference minutia is then marked and not considered while matching other neighbors" (ibid.).

"The obtained *NeighDissimilarity* value is then added to the global similarity
score between the minutiae, *MinDissimilarity*" (ibid., p. 368)

$$MinutiaeDiss+ = NeighDissimilarity$$

Moreover:

Increment by one the value of *NM*, that is the number of neighbours
matched.

Step 9.   Is the *NM=N* verified? That is to say: has the required minimum number
N of neighbours been matched?

Step 10.   Match *R* and *C*. (*MatchCost* is a temporary average.)

$$MatchCost = MinutiaeDiss/NM$$
$$MinutiaeMatched + +$$

That is to say:

"if the neighborhoods of the two *R* and *C* minutiae have been matched
[...], the *MinDissimilarity* score between *M* and *N* is finally divided by the
number of matched neighbor pairs and then added to the global dissimilarity value between the candidate and reference templates: the *MatchCost*.
The number of matched minutiae *MinutiaeMatched* is then incremented"
(ibid., p. 368).

Step 11.   Are stop conditions verified? If yes, return a successful match. If no,
repeat this procedure with the next candidate minutia *C*.

Step 12.   Is *I=LastNeigh* verified? That is to say:

"at the end of the two neighborhoods scanning and if the procedure has found
less than *N* matching neighbor pairs between the two minutiae ("Yes" case [to
the test *I=LastNeigh*]), these two minutiae can not be considered as matching
because their neighborhoods agree on too few points of evidence to be a reliable pair, even if their *MinDissimilarity* value is very low. Thus, the following
minutia *R* in reference template has to be checked ("No" case in [the test of
Step 13]), but if there are no more minutiae *R* to be examined, the entire procedure [...] is repeated for the next minutia *C* in the decreasing reliability order
of the candidate template." (ibid., p. 368).

If yes, go to **Step 13.** If no, increment *J* by one and go to **Step 3.** That is
to say: if no, the procedure is repeated for all the other neighbours in the
minutia of the reference template, excluding the ones already marked.

Step 13.   Is *R=LastMin* verified? If yes, repeat this procedure with the next
candidate minutia C. If no, increment R by one and go to **Step 1.**

8.7.3.3 The Tohoku Algorithm for Fingerprint Matching Based
on Band-Limited Phase-Only Correlation

Tatsuo Higuchi's team at Tohoku University and Tohoku Institute of Technology
published (Ito et al., 2004) an algorithm for fingerprint matching, which resorts

to the *phase-only correlation* (*POC*) function.[184] It uses phase spectra of fingerprint images. The algorithm was claimed to be "highly robust against fingerprint
image degradation due to inadequate fingertip conditions" (ibid., p. 682). It was also
claimed that it "exhibits efficient identification performance even for difficult fingerprint images that could not be identified by the conventional matching algorithms"
(ibid.). They experimented with the technique they developed, and carried out comparisons to other techniques, by using a prototype (from Yamatake Corporation)
of a fingerprint verification system with a pressure-sensitive sensor; the fingerprint
database was with fingerprints from employees of the 700-strong staff of Yamatake
Corporation.

Given two $N_1 \times N_2$ images (such as two fingerprints to be compared), $f(n_1, n_2)$
and $g(n_1, n_2)$, let their index ranges be:

$$n_1 = -M_1 \ldots M_1 \qquad (\text{where } M_1 > 0)$$

$$n_2 = -M_2 \ldots M_2 \qquad (\text{where } M_2 > 0)$$

Let us consider those two functions' respective two-dimensional *discrete Fourier
transforms*, $F(k_1, k_2)$ and $G(k_1, k_2)$:

$$F(k_1, k_2) = \sum_{n_1, n_2} f(n_1, n_2) W_{N_1}^{k_1 n_1} W_{N_2}^{k_2 n_2}$$

$$= A_F(k_1, k_2) e^{j\theta_F(k_1, k_2)},$$

and

$$G(k_1, k_2) = \sum_{n_1, n_2} g(n_1, n_2) W_{N_1}^{k_1 n_1} W_{N_2}^{k_2 n_2}$$

$$= A_G(k_1, k_2) e^{j\theta_G(k_1, k_2)},$$

where the ranks of k_1 and k_2 are defined as:

$$k_1 = -M_1 \ldots M_1 \qquad (\text{where } M_1 > 0)$$

$$k_2 = -M_2 \ldots M_2 \qquad (\text{where } M_2 > 0)$$

and where

$$W_{N_1} = e^{-j\frac{2\pi}{N_1}}$$

$$W_{N_2} = e^{-j\frac{2\pi}{N_2}}$$

---

[184] The concept was used earlier by e.g. Kuglin and Hines (1975), and Kenji, Aoki, Sasaki,
Higuchi, and Kobayashi (2003).

Moreover, the operator

$$\sum\nolimits_{n_1,n_2}$$

stands for

$$\sum\nolimits_{n_1=-M_1}^{M_1} \sum\nolimits_{n_2=-M_2}^{M_2}.$$

$A_F(k_1,k_2)$ and $A_G(k_1,k_2)$ are *amplitude components*. By contrast,

$$e^{j\theta_F(k_1,k_2)}$$

and

$$e^{j\theta_G(k_1,k_2)}$$

are *phase components*. The following formula gives the *cross spectrum*, $RFG(k_1,k_2)$, of the two two-dimensional discrete Fourier transforms, $F(k_1,k_2)$ and $G(k_1,k_2)$:

$$R_{FG}(k_1,k_2) = F(k_1,k_2)\overline{G(k_1,k_2)}$$
$$= A_F(k_1,k_2)A_G(k_1,k_2)e^{j\theta(k_1,k_2)}$$

In the latter formula, $\overline{G(k_1,k_2)}$ stands for the complex conjugate of $G(k_1,k_2)$. By definition, we denoted in that same formula the phase difference as follows:

$$\theta(k_1,k_2) = \theta_F(k_1,k_2) - \theta_G(k_1,k_2)$$

Moreover, the operator

$$\sum\nolimits_{k_1 k_2}$$

stand for

$$\sum\nolimits_{k_1=-M_1}^{M_1} \sum\nolimits_{k_2=-M_2}^{M_2}.$$

The ordinary $r_{fg}(n_1,n_2)$ is the correlation function

$$r_{fg}(n_1,n_2) = \frac{1}{N_1 N_2} \sum_{k_1,k_2} R_{FG}(n_1,n_2) W_{N_1}^{-k_1 n_1} W_{N_2}^{-k_2 n_2}$$

and is the two-dimensional *inverse discrete Fourier transform*. The *normalised cross-phase spectrum*, also called the *normalised cross-spectrum*, is given by definition by the following formula:

$$\hat{R}_{FG}(k_1,k_2) = \frac{F(k_1,k_2)\overline{G(k_1,k_2)}}{|F(k_1,k_2)\overline{G(k_1,k_2)}|}$$
$$= e^{j\theta(k_1,k_2)}.$$

The phase-only correlation function is given by the formula:

$$\hat{r}_{ff}(n_1, n_2) = \frac{1}{N_1 N_2} \sum_{k_1, k_2} W_{N_1}^{-k_1 n_1} W_{N_2}^{-k_2 n_2}$$

$$= \delta(n_1, n_2)$$

$$= \begin{cases} 1 & \text{if } n_1 = n_2 = 0 \\ 0 & \text{otherwise.} \end{cases}$$

As a particular case, if the two images are identical, if follows from the latter formula that their phase-only correlation function is the *Kronecker delta function*, $\delta(n_1, n_2)$. In the application at hand, it is two fingerprints that are compared. Ito et al. (2004) found it advantageous to resort for that purpose to the phase-only correlation function, as opposed to the ordinary correlation function, because of how accurate the phase-only correlation function is in image matching: it exhibits a much higher discrimination capability. In fact, when it is plotted as a surface in three dimension, the phase-only correlation function gives a distinct sharp peak when the two images being compared are similar to each other, whereas the peak drops significantly if the two images are not similar. Also with ordinary correlation, there is a peak if the two images are similar or identical, and the peak is not there is the two images are not similar, but with the phase-only correlation the difference is much sharper. "Other important properties of the POC function used for fingerpint matching is that it is not influenced by image shift and brightness change, and it is highly robust against noise" (Ito et al., 2004, p. 683).

In section 3 of Ito et al. (2004), the definition of phase-only correlation function was modified into a *band-limited POC function*, one that is dedicated to fingerprint matching tasks. Meaningless high-frequency components in the calculation of the cross-phase spectrum were eliminated from the new definition. Depending on the fingerprint image, if the ranges of the *inherent frequency band* are given by

$$k_1 = -K_1 \ldots K_1 \qquad (\text{where } 0 \leq K_1 \leq M_1)$$

$$k_2 = -K_2 \ldots K_2 \qquad (\text{where } 0 \leq K_2 \leq M_2)$$

– where the parameters K_1 and K_2 can be automatically detected by image processing – the effective size of the *frequency spectrum* is given by the formulae

$$L_1 = 2K_1 + 1$$

$$L_2 = 2K_2 + 1.$$

The *band-limited phase-only correlation function* was defined as follows:

$$\hat{r}_{fg}^{K_1 K_2}(n_1, n_2) = \frac{1}{L_1 L_2} \sum_{k_1 = -K_1}^{K_1} \sum_{k_2 = -K_2}^{K_2} \hat{R}_{FG}(k_1, k_2)$$

$$\times W_{L_1}^{-k_1 n_1} W_{L_2}^{-k_2 n_2},$$

where

$$n_1 = -K_1 \ldots K_1$$

$$n_2 = -K_2 \ldots K_2.$$

Ito et al. remarked (2004, p. 684):

> Note that the maximum value of the correlation peak of the band-limited POC function is always normalized to 1 and is not depending on the frequency band size L_1 and L_2. The shape of the band-limited POC function for the two identical images is always the Kronecker's delta function $\delta(n_1, n_2)$. Also, note that the original POC function can be represented as

$$\hat{r}_{fg}(n_1, n_2) = \hat{r}_{fg}^{M_1 M_2}(n_1, n_2).$$

As an alternative method for defining a frequency-selective POC function, had the Tohoku team adopted instead some adequate *low-pass filter* to the cross-phase spectrum, this would have resulted in the shape and height of the correlation peak depending on the type of the low-pass filter (Ito et al., 2004, pp. 684–685, citing Kenji et al., 2003), and what is more, this would have required fitting a model peak function to the correlation array, in order to evaluate the similarity between images, whereas with the band-limited POC function this is not required (Ito et al., 2004, p. 685).

Ito et al. (2004, p. 685, figure 5) give an example in which the original POC function would give a false negative, that is to say, when a registered fingerprint was matched to an impostor's fingerprint, the original POC limited gave a peak. By contrast, the band-limited POC function, for the same input pair of fingerprint, gave no peak. Therefore, the band-limited POC function is more reliable – it discriminates much better – than the original POC function, for the purposes of fingerprint matching.

The algorithm for fingerprint matching using the band-limited POC function takes an input $f(n_1, n_2)$, i.e. the registered fingerprint image, and $g(n_1, n_2)$, i.e. the fingerprint image to be verified. The output is a matching score between $f(n_1, n_2)$ and $g(n_1, n_2)$. The steps of the algorithm are as follows (Ito et al., 2004, p. 686):

Step 1. Store in advance a set of rotated images $f_\theta(n_1, n_2)$ of $f(n_1, n_2)$ over the angular range

$$-\theta_{max} \leq \theta \leq \theta_{max}.$$

with an angle spacing 1°.
Step 2. Calculate the POC function

$$\hat{r}_{f_\theta g}^{M_1 M_2}(n_1, n_2)$$

between $f_\theta(n_1, n_2)$ and $g(n_1, n_2)$.

Step 3. Calculate the rotation angle

$$\Theta = \arg\max_{\theta}\{S_1^{M_1 M_2}[f_\theta, g]\}$$

by evaluating the similarity between $f_\theta(n_1, n_2)$ and $g(n_1, n_2)$, in order to select the rotation-normalised image $f_\Theta(n_1, n_2)$.

Step 4. Estimate image displacements (τ_1, τ_2) between $f_\Theta(n_1, n_2)$ and $g(n_1, n_2)$ from the peak location of

$$\hat{r}_{f_\Theta g}^{M_1 M_2}(n_1, n_2)$$

Step 5. Extend the size of $f_\Theta(n_1, n_2)$ and $g(n_1, n_2)$ by τ_1 and τ_2 pixels for n_1 and n_2 directions, to obtain $f'(n_1, n_2)$ and $g'(n_1, n_2)$.

Step 6. Extract the effective fingerprint regions $f''(n_1, n_2)$ and $g''(n_1, n_2)$ from $f'(n_1, n_2)$ and $g'(n_1, n_2)$.

Step 7. Detect the inherent frequency band (K_1, K_2) from the two-dimensional discrete Fourier transforms of $f''(n_1, n_2)$.

Step 8. Calculate the band-limited POC function

$$\hat{r}_{f''g''}^{K_1 K_2}(n_1, n_2)$$

Step 9. Compute the *matching score*

$$S_P^{K_1 K_2}[f'', g'']$$

(by summing the highest peaks of the band-limited POC function: there may be several peaks, because elastic deformation causes them to be produced: see below), and then give the matching score as output, and terminate the execution of the algorithm.

In their experiments, Ito et al. explain (2004, p. 686), they used $\theta_{max} = 20°$. They also explained (ibid.):

In many cases, the band-limited POC function has multiple peaks, which is caused by elastic fingerprint deformation. The fingerprint image can expand or contract when a fingertip contacts with the sensor surface. Each portion of the fingerprint image will be shifted independently, which means several sub-domains in the image are moving individually. In this case, the POC function produces several peaks corresponding to the multiple translated sub-domains. The height of every correlation peak reflects the matched area of each sub-domain. Hence, we decide to employ the sum of these peaks as an evaluation criterion in order to make the proposed matching algorithm robust against elastic deformation.

8.8 Bloodstain Pattern Analysis, and the Use of Software for Determining the Angle of Impact of Blood Drops

8.8.1 The Basics

Do not confuse *DNA profiling* and *bloodstain pattern analysis* (*BPA*).[185] In order to carry out the latter (which some prefer to call *blood spatter analysis*), the analyst (or examiner) has to consider, for each blood pattern, factors including the number of blood patterns in the environment (e.g., on the floor and the walls inside a room), dispersion, shape, size, volume, orientation, and location. What is reconstructed (if reconstruction is successful, but not always this is feasible) is the events that occurred during the criminal incident. The analyst has to classify the bloodstain pattern, and then to associate that pattern back to a source event, that is conjectured to have unfolded at the crime scene. Concerning BPA, the Wikipedia entry[186] provides this usefully concise information:

> Bloodstain pattern analysis (BPA) is one of several specialties in the field of forensic science. The use of bloodstains as evidence is not new, however the application of modern science has brought it to a higher level. New technologies, especially advances in DNA analysis, are available for detectives and criminologists to use in solving crimes and apprehending offenders. The science of bloodstain pattern analysis applies scientific knowledge from other fields to solve practical problems. Bloodstain pattern analysis draws on biology, chemistry, maths, and physics among scientific disciplines. As long as an analyst follows a scientific process, this applied science can produce strong, solid evidence, making it an effective tool for investigators.

---

[185] Bloodstain pattern analysis is the subject of a valuable short introduction by Louis Akin (2005), of books by Tom Bevel and Ross Gardner (2008), and by Stuart James and William Eckert (1999), whereas the book by James et al. (2005a) is more recent (whereas their James et al., 2005b is an overview article about the recognition of bloodstain patterns). MacDonell (1993) is still cited sometimes, in the 2000s, in such studies that also cite more recent literature. Cf. MacDonell and Bialousz (1979). Stuart James also edited a paper collection on the subject (James, 1999). With respect to the second edition of 2002, the third edition of Bevel and Gardner's book (2008) includes new chapters that "detail a true taxonomic classification system, with a supporting decision map to aid analysts in the field; a specific methodology based on scientific method; conducting experiments in support of bloodstain pattern analysis; anatomical issues associated to bloodstain pattern analysis; issues surrounding the examination of clothing in bloodstain pattern analysis; as well as a chapter detailing the various presumptive testing and enhancement techniques for bloodstains" (ibid., from the summary). The contents of the third edition include: Bloodstain pattern analysis: its function and a historical perspective – Bloodstain pattern terminology – Bloodstain classification – A methodology for bloodstain pattern analysis – The medium of blood – Anatomical considerations in bloodstain pattern analysis – Determining motion and directionality – Determining the point of convergence and the area of origin – Evaluating impact spatter bloodstains – Understanding and applying characteristic patterns of blood – Bloodstained clothing issues – Presumptive testing and enhancement of blood – Documenting bloodstains – An introduction to crime scene reconstruction and analysis [this is also the subject of a book by those same authors: Gardner and Bevel (2009)] – Presenting evidence – Experimentation in bloodstain pattern analysis – Dealing with the risk of bloodborne pathogens – Appendix A weight/measurement conversion table – Appendix B: Trigonometric functions and their application in bloodstain pattern analysis.

[186] http://en.wikipedia.org/wiki/Bloodstain_pattern_analysis.

Bloodstain pattern categories include: *passive bloodstains, projected bloodstains,* and *transfer/contact bloodstains.* The same Wikipedia entry explains: "The definitions used below are from the suggested IABPA terminology list". In particular: "Passive bloodstains are those stains created by the force of gravity". *Passive drops* are "Bloodstain drop(s) created or formed by the force of gravity acting alone". *Drip pattern* denotes "A bloodstain pattern which results from blood dripping into blood". *Flow pattern* is "A change in the shape and direction of a bloodstain due to the influence of gravity or movement of the object". *Pool pattern* is "A bloodstain pattern formed when a source of blood is stationary for a period of time".

"A projected stain occurs when some form of energy has been transferred to a blood source". The respective terminology includes:

> *Low Velocity Impact Spatter (LVIS)* – A bloodstain pattern that is caused by a low velocity impact/force to a blood source.
> *Medium Velocity Impact* Spatter *(MVIS)* – A bloodstain pattern caused by a medium velocity impact/force to a blood source. A beating typically causes this type of spatter.
> *High Velocity Impact Spatter (HVIS)* – A bloodstain pattern caused by a high velocity impact/force to a blood source such as that produced by gunshot or high-speed machinery.
> *Cast-Off Pattern* – A bloodstain pattern created when blood is released or thrown from a blood-bearing object in motion.
> *Arterial Spurting* (or *Gushing*) *Pattern* – Bloodstain pattern(s) resulting from blood exiting the body under pressure from a breached artery.
> *Back Spatter* – Blood directed back towards the source of energy or force that caused the spatter.
> *Expiratory Blood* – Blood that is blown out of the nose, mouth, or a wound as a result of air pressure and/or air flow which is the propelling force.

"A transfer or contact stain is produced when an object with blood comes in contact with an object or surface that does not have blood. It may be possible to discern the object that left the blood impression." The respective terminology includes: *wipe pattern*, this being "A bloodstain pattern created when an object moves through an existing stain, removing and/or altering its appearance"; and *swipe pattern*, this being "The transfer of blood from a moving source onto an unstained surface. Direction of travel may be determined by the feathered edge."

> As indicated above, there are other terms currently used in BPA and different ways of classifying bloodstain patterns. For example there is a debate over the misnomer of the LVIS, MVIS, and HVIS as it relates to the physical term 'velocity'. A sub-committee of the SWGSTAIN [i.e., the Scientific Working Group on Bloodstain Pattern Analysis] has been tasked with addressing the terminology issues and develop a taxonomy for bloodstain patterns.

When it comes to *velocity impact stains*, the same entry explains:

> Contrary to what the name states, the terms low-, medium-, and high-velocity impact spatter do not describe the velocity of the blood droplets as they fly through the air. The variation in the 'velocity' is meant to describe the amount of energy transferred to a blood source in order to create the stains. Velocity is a speed (m/s) with a direction. Often the terms force and energy are quoted in conjunction with the unit ft/s or m/s which is an incorrect. Force is related to velocity and mass (N or 1 kg $\cdot$m$\cdot$s-2). Energy (work) is related to the force exerted on an object (J or N$\cdot$m or kg$\cdot$m2$\cdot$s-2).

Physical considerations apply: "Once blood has left the body it behaves as a fluid and all physical laws apply". In particular, *gravity* "is acting on blood (without the body's influence) as soon as it exits the body. Given the right circumstances blood can act according to ballistic theory." *Viscosity* "is the amount of internal friction in the fluid. It describes the resistance of a liquid to flow". *Surface tension* "is the force that gives the ability to blood to maintain its shape".

Blood spatter flight characteristics do matter: "Experiments with blood have shown that a drop of blood tends to form into a sphere in flight rather than the artistic teardrop shape. This is what one would expect of a fluid in freefall. The formation of the sphere is a result of surface tension that binds the molecules together. This spherical shape of blood in flight is important for the calculation of the angle of impact (incidence) of blood spatter when it hits a surface. That angle will be used to determine the point from which the blood originated which is called the Point of Origin or more appropriately the Area of Origin.[187] A single spatter of blood is not enough to determine the Area of Origin at a crime scene. The determination of the angles of impact and placement of the Area of Origin should be based on the consideration of a number of stains and preferably stains from opposite sides of the pattern to create the means to triangulate."

It is important to determine *angles of impact*.

As mentioned earlier a blood droplet in freefall has the shape of a sphere. Should the droplet strike a surface and a well-formed stain is produced, an analyst can determine the angle at which this droplet struck the surface. This is based on the relationship between the length of the major axis, minor axis, and the angle of impact. A well-formed stain is in the shape of an ellipse [See Fig. 8.8.1.1]. Dr. Victor Balthazard, and later Dr. Herbert Leon MacDonell,[188] realized the relationship of the length-width ratio of the ellipse was the function of the sine of the impact angle. Accurately measuring the stain will easily result in the calculation the impact angle. [. . .] Because of the three-dimensional aspect of trajectories there are three angles of impact, α, β, and γ. The easiest angle to calculate is *gamma* (γ). Gamma is simply the angle of the bloodstain path measured from the true vertical (plumb)[189] of the surface [. . .] The next angle that can be quite easily calculated is *alpha* (α). Alpha is the impact angle of the bloodstain path moving out from the surface (see [Fig. 8.8.1.2] with alpha at the top by the stain). The third angle to be calculated is *beta* (β). Beta is the angle of the bloodstain path pivoting about the vertical (z) axis [. . .] All three angles are related through the equation quoted below.

Let L be the length of the ellipse, that is to say, its major axis. Let W be the width of the ellipse, that is its minor axis. Let α be the angle of impact. Those variable are related by the equation

$$\sin \alpha = W/L$$

---

[187] The *point of origin* is also called the *point of hemorrhage*. Louis Akin "prefers to use the term *point of hemorrhage* to distinguish the area from which the blood was disgorged from other *points of origin*, the latter phrase being a widely used term in blood spatter, ballistics, crime, and accident scene investigation and reconstruction. Although most experts use the word *point*, the word *area* is a more conservative one to use" (Akin, 2005, p. 7).

[188] The author of MacDonell (1993).

[189] The plumb line is parallel to the z axis, in a Euclidean space in three dimensions.

Fig. 8.8.1.1 Upward moving
bloodstain showing proper
ellipse placement[190]

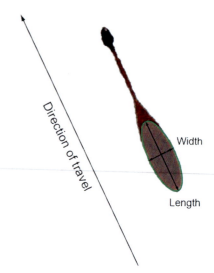

Fig. 8.8.1.2 Angles of
impact[191]

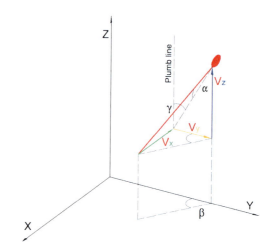

Therefore,

$$\alpha = \arcsin\,(W/L)$$

The three angles α, β, and γ are related by this equation:

$$\tan\beta = (\tan\alpha)\,/\,(\tan\gamma)$$

---

[190] In the public domain; http://en.wikipedia.org/wiki/File:BPA_ellipse_example.png Image made by Kevin Maloney.

[191] In the public domain; http://en.wikipedia.org/wiki/File:BPA_AOI.png Image made by Kevin Maloney.http://upload.wikimedia.org/wikipedia/en/9/91/BPA_AOI.png is the full resolution version.

Measurements need be carried out with diligence and accuracy by the bloostain pattern examiner (analyst). "In the past analysts have used a variety of instruments. Methods currently used include:

- Viewing loop with an embedded scale in 0.2 mm increments or better that is placed over the stain. The analyst then uses a scientific calculator or spreadsheet to complete the angle calculations.
- Bloodstain Pattern Analysis (BPA) software that superimposes an ellipse over a scaled close-up image of an individual bloodstain. The programs then automatically calculates the angles of impact" (from the Wikipedia entry).

8.8.2 Software

There exists *bloodstain analysis software* for calculating the angles of impact, in bloodstain pattern analysis:

> Accurately measuring the stain and calculating the angle of impact requires due diligence of the analyst. In the past analysts have used a variety of instruments. Methods currently used include:
>
> > Viewing loop with an embedded scale in 0.2 mm increments or better that is placed over the stain. The analyst then uses a scientific calculator or spreadsheet to complete the angle calculations.
> >
> > Bloodstain Pattern Analysis (BPA) software that superimposes an ellipse over a scaled close-up image of an individual bloodstain. The programs then automatically calculates the angles of impact.

Using software produces a very accurate result that is measurable and reproducible. One software product for bloodstain pattern analysis is the *Crime Scene Command* program,[192] produced by On Scene Forensics in Austin, Texas, and which is claimed to be easy to use. The originator of Crime Scene Command is Louis L. Akin. There is an *On Scene Blood Spatter Calculator*, for use on homicide scenes. A testimonial by a forensic instructor, Thomas Hanratty, from Milwaukee, Wisconsin, found at the producer's website, for *Crime Scene Command*, claims: "An officer, either a first responder[193] or a detective, merely plugs in a few measurements and the dreaded math calculations are performed for him/her. Best of all, a record is generated of a

---

[192] See http://www.onsceneforensics.com/Crime_Scene_Command.htm

[193] Concerning *first responding officers*, also called *first responders* (which strictly speaking is a broader category, as sometimes the earliest responders are members of the public), Miller (2003) writes: "The first responders at a crime scene are usually police officers, fire department personnel or emergency medical personnel. They are the only people who view the crime scene in its original condition. Their actions at the crime scene provide the basis for the successful or unsuccessful resolution of the investigation. They must perform their duties and remember that they begin the process that links victims to suspects to crime scenes and must never destroy the links" (ibid., p. 118).

wealth of materials, if the entire program is used; including witnesses, suspects, an evidence log, photo log and bloodstains. And it's all in one complete report."

The key benefits claimed by On Scene Forensics for *Crime Scene Command* are as follows.[194] The software

- Makes a record of the case information as a number one report.
- Serves as a scene personnel log showing the name, agency, badge number, time in and out, of each person who enters the scene.
- Makes a detailed record of the circumstances surrounding the death of the victim:
  - Weather conditions
  - Environmental conditions
  - Position of victim
- Performs all bloodstain computations instantly including:
  - Angle of impact in degrees
  - Point of origin
  - Transfer stain description and location
- Performs all bullet trajectory computations from a bullet hole in a solid surface including:
  - Gives caliber of bullet
  - Angles of impact in degrees
  - Trajectory path
- Suspect page records all information on the suspect.
- Records evidence found at the scene in a printable log.
- Records photographs taken at the scene in a printable log.
- Records witness statements, res gestae statements, and officers' notes on scene.
- Easy to read permanent record can be stored as a word document on hard drive or disk, and printed, faxed, or emailed.
- Can be used as notes when testifying.

8.8.3 Point or Area of Origin

The description at the end of the previous subsection refers, among the other things, to to *point-of-origin calculations*. Apart from the angles of impact, another thing that needs to be calculated is the *area of origin* indeed. The IABPA definition is: "Point (Area) of Origin – The common point (area) in three-dimensional space to which the trajectories of several blood drops can be retraced." The *area of origin* is shown in Fig. 8.8.3.1. "The area of origin can give a general location [(Bevel & Gardner, 2008, p. 195)] or relative posture [(James et al., 2005a, p. 219)] of a bleeding victim

---

[194] Also see Sections 8.8.4 and 8.8.5.

who has received a blow. In the literature, there are several limits used for area-of-origin calculations. These include a tennis ball, a grapefruit, a soccer ball, and a basketball" (Maloney, Killeen, & Maloney, 2009, p. 518).

The Wikipedia entry for "Bloodstain Pattern Analysis" explains:

> The *area of origin* is the area in three-dimensional space where the blood source was located at the time of the bloodletting incident. The area of origin includes the area of convergence with a third dimension in the z direction. Since the z-axis is perpendicular to the floor, the area of origin has three dimensions and is a volume.
>
> The term *point of origin* has also been accepted to mean the same thing. However it has been argued, there are problems associated to this term. First, a blood source is not a point source. To produce a point source the mechanism would have to be fixed in three-dimensional space and have an aperture where only a single blood droplet is released at a time, with enough energy to create a pattern. This does not seem likely. Second, bodies are dynamic. Aside from the victim physically moving, skin is elastic and bones break.

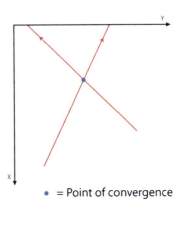

Fig. 8.8.3.1 Area of origin.[195] The *blue area* represents a volume in three-dimensional space. The area of origin is the area in that space to which the trajectories of several blood drops can be traced

● = Point of convergence

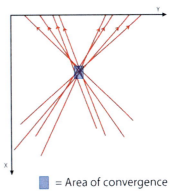

Fig. 8.8.3.2 Point of convergence[196]

■ = Area of convergence

---

[195] In the public domain; http://en.wikipedia.org/wiki/File:BPA_Origin.gif (animation). Image made by Kevin Maloney in 2005.

[196] In the public domain; http://en.wikipedia.org/wiki/File:BPA_POC.png Image made by Kevin Maloney.

Fig. 8.8.3.3 Area of
convergence[197]

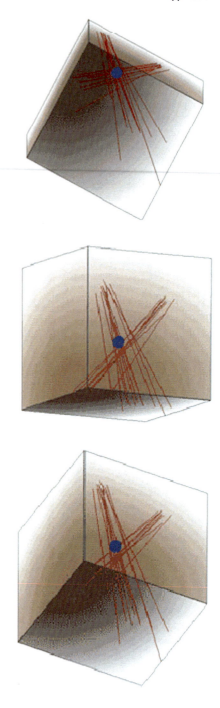

[197] In the public domain; http://en.wikipedia.org/wiki/File:BPA_AOC.png Image made by Kevin
Maloney.

Once a force is applied to the body there will be an equal and opposite reaction to the force applied by the aggressor (Newton's third law of motion). Part of the force will move the blood source, even a millimetre, and change the origin while it is still producing blood. So the source becomes contained in a three-dimensional volume, or region. As with the area of convergence, the area of origin is easily calculated by using BPA software. There are other longer, mathematical methods of determining the area or origin, one of which is the tangential method.

Other important concepts are the *point of convergence* and the *area of conve1rgence.* "The point of convergence is the intersection of two bloodstain paths, where the stains come from opposite sides of the impact pattern" (from the Wikipedia entry). See Fig. 8.8.3.2. "The area of convergence is the box formed by the intersection of several stains from opposite sides of the impact pattern" (ibid.). See Fig. 8.8.3.3. "To determine the point/area of convergence an analyst has to determine the path the blood droplets travelled. The tangential flight path of individual droplets can be determined by using the angle of impact and the offset angle of the resulting bloodstain. 'Stringing' stains is a method of visualising this. For the purpose of the point of convergence, only the top view of the flight paths is required. Note that this is a two-dimensional (2D) and not a three-dimensional (3D) intersection" (ibid.). "In the past, some analysts have drawn lines along the major axes of the stains and brought them to an area of convergence on the wall. Instead of using a top-down view, they used a front view. This provides a false point/area of convergence" (ibid.).

8.8.4 More Concerning Software

On Scene Forensics provides for *Crime Scene Command*[198] this description of the program at a glance:

This user friendly program installs in seconds and is easy to use without having to attend special classes. The program does all the trigonometric calculations necessary to determine the angle of impact and point of origin for blood spatter, the angle of impact and trajectory for bullet holes, and to estimate the time of death at a homicide scene. There is a crime scene log to enter the name, identification, agency, and purpose for everyone who enters the crime scene. There are separate pages for witnesses, victims, the scene environment, as well as death information for the pathologist. The program will estimate the time of death within four hours for the 18 hours after death.

Photographs of the crime scene, the individual bloodstains, and bullet holes, and items of evidence can be stored with each stain or pattern. The entire program and all the reports it generates can be printed with a single click of a mouse.

The software makes a permanent record of the crime scene that can be stored to hard drive printed as a Word document, faxed, or emailed. The printed reports can be used as bench notes and used on the stand to refresh memory and they satisfy the requirement for a scientific record of crime scene reconstruction.

---

[198] See Sections 8.8.2 and 8.8.5.

The Crime Scene Command program also includes screens for recording witness statements and making notes at the scene.

Crime Scene Command is meant to be used at the crime scene and is best installed on a laptop computer so that it can be taken to the scene. It is designed to be user friendly to patrol officers and not just to specially trained technicians. The program can be used at any crime scene, not only homicide scenes.

We have referred (in Section 8.8.2) to software products of On Scene Forensics. Another software product for bloodstain pattern analysis is *HemoSpat*, from a Canadian firm, FORident Software Inc.[199] Its owener and lead developer is Andy Maloney. He developed the software, whereas his brother Kevin Maloney is the firm's expert in bloodstain pattern analysis (but neither a co-owner, nor an employee; he is affiliated with the Forensic Identification Section of the Ottawa Police Service). At its website for *HemoSpat*, the firm claims that it is more efficient than the competing *BackTrack* software, because the latter "forces the analyst to follow specific steps which kaes it difficult and time consuming to correct mistakes or allow others to review your work. BackTrack does not allow you to use angled surfaces and has problems with current digital image sizes". By contrast, "*HemoSpat* maintans the analytical data from each project making peer review and verification possible." Like *Crime Scene Command*, that tool, too, is claimed to be easy to use. Version 1.3 of *HemoSpat* was released in September 2009, and version 1.4.1. was released in January 2011. The firm's website also states: "The March/April 2011 issue of the *Journal of Forensic Identification* contains an article titled 'One-Sided Impact Spatter and Area-of-Origin Calculations'. This is the result of a combined effort of FORident Software, L'Institut de Recherche Criminelle de la Gendarmerie Nationale in Paris, France, and the Forensic Identification Section of the Ottawa Police Service in Ottawa, Canada." To say it with the abstract of Maloney, Nicloux, Maloney, and Heron (2011):

It is common practice when calculating area of origin from impact spatter to use stains from both "sides" of the pattern – stains to the left and to the right of the blood source. Impact spatter at crime scenes, however, often provides the analyst with bloodstain patterns that are not as pristine as those created in a controlled environment. One situation that may arise is impact spatter consisting of stains from only one side of the pattern because of the removal of an object after the impact, such as a door or a person, or because the stains from one side are not on a planar surface. This study looks at a method of calculating the area of origin using stains from only one side of the pattern and shows that these partial patterns may still provide usable calculations to determine the area of origin.

Maloney et al. (2011, p. 132) explain how the practical need arises:

Bloodstain analysts must work with the data they are presented with at the crime scene, regardless of quantity or quality. Sometimes this means eliminating partial impact patterns because too few stains may be found for a regular analysis. This study demonstrates that at least some incomplete impact patterns – "one-sided" patterns – need not be eliminated from the analysis of the scene because they can still provide an acceptable calculation of the area of origin.

---

[199] See http://hemospat.com/index.php FORident Software Canada, Inc., 132-207 Bank St., Ottawa, Ontario, Canada K2P 2N2. Their email address is inf@hemospat.com

Some articles published by the Maloney brothers in the *Journal of Forensic Identification* can be downloaded from Andy Maloney firm's website. Maloney et al. (2011) is one of these. Another paper is 'The Use of Hemospat to Include Bloodstains Located on Nonorthogonal Surfaces in Area-of-Origin Calculations' (Maloney et al., 2009), abstracted as follows:

> Determining the origin of impact patterns at crime scenes can be a challenge when there is limited or less-than-ideal information. This is made even more difficult if the analyst cannot incorporate data from nonorthogonal and orthogonal surfaces in the same analysis. Using HemoSpat software for impact pattern analysis allows analysts to remove several limitations, maximize the use of this information, and produce precise and reliable results.

By contrast (Maloney et al., 2009, p. 514):

> Historically, bloodstain pattern analysts using forensic software for area-of-origin calculations had to exclude nonorthogonal (angled) surfaces from their calculations. Analysts could not incorporate orthogonal and nonorthogonal surfaces at the same time in their analyses [(Eckert & James, 1993, pp. 152–154; Carter, 2001b)].

Maloney et al. pointed out (2009, p. 523):

> The task of analyzing bloodstains on nonorthogonal surfaces is made easier by using the HemoSpat software. This allows the analyst to remove objects from the scene, analyse them in a controlled and safe environment, and incorporate the data in an area-of-origin calculation.

From the same website, one can also download a white paper (FORident Software, 2009) about the validation of HemoSpat. The goal was "to validate the accuracy of the HemoSpat bloodstain analysis software against an accepted standard and to examine the reproducibility of the results." This was done in collaboration with the Royal Canadian Mounted Police (RCMP). A comparison was made with the *BackTrack* computer program for bloodstain pattern analysis. Kevin Maloney had earlier participated in the validation of BackTrack (Carter et al., 2005). Maloney, Carter, Jory, and Yamashita (2005) is concerned with the representation in three dimensions of bloodstain pattern analysis. Both BackTrack and HemoSpat use the *tangent method* outlined by Carter (2001a). Carter (2001b) is an electronic book on the computer-assisted directional analysis of bloodstain patterns, and is provided with the BackTrack Suite. "The users have more direct control over the ellipse in HemoSpat using the mouse, whereas BackTrack requires the user to enter numbers to adjust the ellipse" (FORident Software, 2009, p. 3).

8.8.5 Effects of Velocity on Blood Drops and Blood Spatter

Louis L. Akin

8.8.5.1 Introduction

The software Crime Scene Command (CSC)[200] by On Scene Forensics was created in response to complaints by law enforcement officials that blood pattern software

---

[200] See Sections 8.8.2, 8.8.4, and 8.8.5.

programs were difficult to learn and required classroom instruction. CSC is intended to be user friendly enough for a person with only a basic knowledge of blood patterns to use. It automatically calculates the angle of impact and area of origin and averages the area of origin for several impact stains. The program has additional features such as a scene personnel log, evidence collection log, and separate tabs for information on victims, suspects and witnesses including statements. It also calculates bullet trajectories. Its only drawback is that it does not produce a 3-dimensional diagram like the others do, but that complexity is what requires classroom instruction or a nerd to operate the programs and was left out to produce a fast, reliable, easy to learn and user friendly program.

Through a variety of schools, classes, and seminars, homicide detectives and crime scene technicians or criminalists are garnering a level of expertise that has not previously existed in law enforcement. New technologies, sciences, and applied sciences are available for detectives and criminalists to use in solving crimes and apprehending offenders. Blood pattern analysis may require special schooling and expertise. However, blood pattern evidence collection is an example of an applied science that a homicide detective or first responding police officer can learn to use at a scene without having to become an expert in the field.

Blood spatter interpretation or analysis itself may be compared to tracking. It may take considerable training to reach the level of a tracker who can say that a footprint was made two days before by a pigeon-towed 180 male who has bunions. It does not require that level of training or expertise to be able to look at a footprint and determine which way the person was going. Just pick out the heel and toe.

Likewise, although an expert may be able to see things in the blood pattern that the first responding officer at a crime scene doesn't, a responder can preserve the evidence and take the measurements of the stains in a pattern just as he does at an accident scene. He or she could even learn to determine generally where a victim was positioned by looking at the blood spatter the same way he could tell which way a footprint is going.

A basic understanding of blood spatter analysis will also allow the first responding officer to assist in correctly collecting and preserving blood stain data at the scene. Fortunately, the principles and procedures to learn are not complicated, and while it is easier to use software to make the calculations, the basic principles can be learned from a source as brief as this article and applied by using a hand held calculator. Some critical determinations, such as establishing the point of convergence that shows where the victim was standing can be done without use of a calculator at all.

This basic understanding is important, because the interpretation of blood spatter patterns and other evidence at crime scenes may reveal critically important information such as:

- The positions of the victim, assailant, and objects at the scene during the attack.
- The type of weapon that was used to cause the spatter.
- The number of blows, shots, stabs, etc. that occurred.

- The movement and direction of victim and assailant, after bloodshed began.
- It may support or contradict statements given by witnesses (James & Eckert, 1999, pp. 10–11).

The investigator may use blood spatter interpretation to determine:

- What events occurred.
- When and in what sequence they occurred.
- Who was, or was not, there.
- What did *not* occur.

The lists of precisely what information can be learned by the interpretation of blood stain patterns are similar for Bevel and Gardner (2002), James and Eckert (1999), Hueske (1999), Akin (2004), and Sutton (1998).

8.8.5.2 Photography, and Traditional Determination of Velocities of Blood Spatter

Without a doubt, the most important thing to at a crime scene in regard to blood spatter analysis is to photograph the scene and the blood spatter. The photographs should all be made at a 90 degree angle from the surface on which the blood stains are found and a scale should always be in the photograph so the viewer can tell the size of the drops in the pictures.

The velocity of the blood spatter when it strikes a surface is a reasonably reliable indicator of the speed of the force that set the blood in motion in the first place. The velocity is that of the force causing the blood to move rather than of the speed of the blood itself and it is measured in feet per second (fps); high velocity blood, for instance, *may* be caused by a bullet moving at 900 fps, medium velocity blood spatter may be caused by a spurting artery or by a blunt instrument striking the already bloody head or limb of a victim.

Low velocity stains are produced by normal gravity and the stains are generally 3 mm or larger. It is usually the result of blood dripping from a person who is still, walking, or running, or from a bloody weapon. Dripping blood falls at a 90° angle and forms a 360° circumference stain when it hits a flat surface, depending, of course, on the texture of the surface. See Fig. 8.8.5.2.1 for an example of low velocity spatter.

Medium blood spatter is produced by an external force of greater than 5 fps and less than 25 fps. The stains generally measure 1–3 mm in size. Blood stains this size are often caused by blunt or sharp force trauma, that is, knives, hatchets, clubs, fists, and arterial spurts. They might also result from blood being cast off a weapon or other bloody object.

Most medium velocity blood found at crime scenes will be created by blood flying from a body as a result of blunt or sharp force or the body colliding with blunt or sharp surfaces. It may be the result of a punch, a stab, or a series of blows. A void space may be created by anything that blocks the blood from falling on the

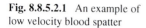

Fig. 8.8.5.2.1 An example of
low velocity blood spatter

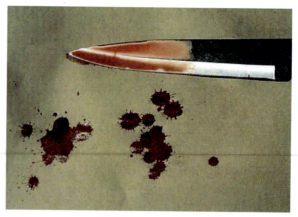

surface where it would have normally landed. The object creating the void may be either the victim or the attacker's body or a piece of furniture that was moved. See Fig. 8.8.5.2.2 for an example of medium velocity spatter.

High velocity blood spatter is produced by an external force greater than 100 fps and the stains tend to be less than 1 mm. The pattern is sometimes referred to as a mist. High velocity patterns are usually created by gunshots or explosives, but may also be caused by industrial machinery or even expired air, coughing, or sneezing. In any case, the spatter tends to be tiny drops propelled into the air by an explosive force. High velocity droplets travel the least far because of the resistance of the air against their small mass. See Fig. 8.8.5.2.3 as an example of high velocity spatter.

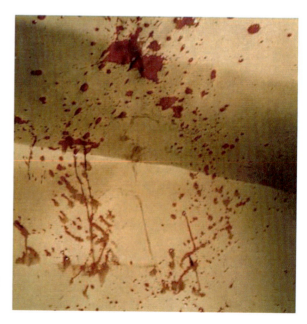

Fig. 8.8.5.2.2 An example of
medium velocity blood
spatter

Fig. 8.8.5.2.3 An example of
high velocity blood spatter

8.8.5.3 Blood Spatter Flight Characteristics

Experiments with blood have shown that a drop of blood tends to form into a sphere
rather than a teardrop shape when in flight. The formation of the sphere is a result
of surface tension that binds the molecules together.

Fresh blood is slightly more viscous than water, and like water it tends to hold
the spherical shape in flight rather than a tear drop shape as seen in cartoons.

This spherical shape of a liquid in flight is important for the calculation of the
angle of impact (incidence) of blood spatter when it hits a surface. That angle will

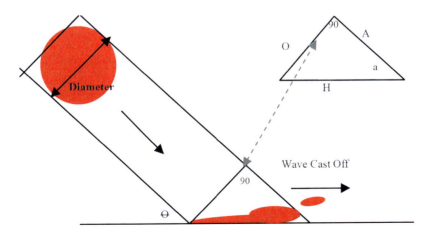

Fig. 8.8.5.3.1 Side view of blood drop in air, and then striking a flat surface

be used to determine the point from which the blood originated which is called the Point of Origin or as this author prefers, the Point of Origin (PO).

Generally, a single spatter of blood is not enough to determine the Point of Origin at a crime scene. The determination of the Angle of Impact and placement of the PO should be based on the consideration of a number of spatters and preferably spatters that will provide an arc of reference points in order to create a triangulation effect.

The process for determining the Angle of Impact is not complicated. When a drop of blood strikes a flat surface the diameter of the drop in flight will be equivalent to the width of the spatter on the surface as seen in Fig. 8.8.5.3.1. The length of the spatter will be longer, depending on the angle at which the drop hit. The following diagram will help the reader to understand this concept.

8.8.5.4 Point of Convergence (POC)

For purposes of instruction, we will consider a case in which a fan shape blood pattern is found on a floor as the result of a gun shot wound to the head. When blood disperses in various directions from a wound the blood drops will tend to fan out. As the drops strike the floor, they will elongate into oval shapes. An imaginary line drawn through the middle of the oval shape lengthwise will run back to the area where the blood came from.

If lines are drawn through several of the blood spatters as in Fig. 8.8.5.4.1 the lines will cross at the point where the person was standing. That point is called the Point of Convergence and will be flat on the floor (if that is where the spatter is located). Somewhere above that point is where the blood originated. If the victim was shot in the head, it may be 4–6 feet (roughly the height of an average person) above that point. Where the blood left the person's body is called the Point of Origin

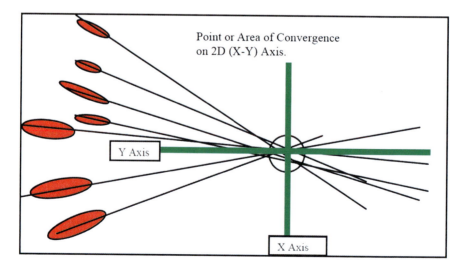

Fig. 8.8.5.4.1 Lines through the central axes of the spatter cross at the Point of Convergence

as previously mentioned. To find the Point of Origin (PO), first determine the two-dimensional Point of Convergence (POC) on the floor as seen in Fig. 8.8.5.4.1.

8.8.5.5 Determining the Angle of Impact (AOI), and the Point of Origin

The next step in the process is to determine the Angle of Impact (AOI) for representative bloodstains. Specialized blood spatter calculator software that performs all the calculations automatically is available from online vendors, but for those who do not mind doing the trigonometry all the calculations can be done on an ordinary hand held scientific calculator or even by the use of printed copies of arc sine tables.

The Angle of Impact is the angle at which the blood drop hit the floor. It can be determined by taking the inverse arc sin of the width divided by the length ratio of an individual blood spatter.

If using software just enter the width and length into the table on the screen and the calculation will be done automatically. If using a hand held calculator, divide the length of the drop into its width, then take the arc sinee which is the second function on a hand held calculator (or just look on a trigonometric functions table) to get the degrees of the AOI.

For example, if a drop measures 0.5 mm wide and 1.0 mm long, dividing 1.0 into 0.5 would give a ratio of 0.5. The arc sin of 0.5 is 30 degrees. Find that by using the cosecant function on the calculator, or by looking at an arc sinee table. This calculation determines that the blood drop hit the ground at 30 degrees and it is already known that it came from the Point of Convergence.

Measure the distance from the individual drop to the Point of Convergence and multiply that number by the *tangent* (TAN) of the Angle of Impact. This calculation (by the Theorem of Pythagoras) will tell how high up the spatter originated from. The following paragraph explains this more thoroughly.

The *Point of Origin* (PO) is located above the Point of Convergence (POC) on the perpendicular axis. In this case that would be 90 degrees perpendicular to the floor. It is the point from where the blood was disgorged from the body. To determine where that point is located first measure the distance from each blood stain along its central axis to the POC. Then take the TAN of the degrees AOI. Third, multiply the TAN of the AOI by the distance. Measure that distance from the floor up the perpendicular axis and you will arrive at the Point of Origin.

In conclusion, *blood pattern analysis experts* can develop vast amounts of information from the patterns of blood at a crime scene. First responding officers and homicide detectives will be more aware of the value of blood spatter evidence if they understand the fundamentals of pattern analysis. Additionally, *first responding officers* and *detectives* can glean a great deal of information themselves at the scene without becoming experts and they can assist the experts later with the data that they gathered at the scene. If the blood spatter evidence is properly photographed and if accurate measurements are taken of the length and width of the individual spatters and the distance from each spatter to the Point of Convergence, the analyst can later make the necessary calculations based on that data and draw conclusions from them. If the measurements and photographs are not taken, critical information may be lost forever.

Chapter 9
Virtopsy: The Virtual Autopsy*

9.1 Introduction

9.1.1 Preliminary Considerations

In forensic medicine, autopsy remains the gold standard for determining the cause and manner of death. An autopsy consists of two parts. First, an external examination is performed, in which all external findings are documented with photographs and in a written report. Second, the body is opened for the internal examination. All organs are removed, inspected, measured, and sampled for histology, in order to identify pathologies that lie within the organs. All internal findings are added to the written report.

This approach has some disadvantages. Due to its invasiveness, important evidence can be destroyed. In cases of advanced decomposition, liquefied organs lose their structural integrity if their surrounding body cavity is opened. Additionally, some cultural and religious belief systems prohibit the autopsy procedure.

The quality of the final report highly depends on the skills of the investigator to find and appropriately describe the findings. Findings that are overlooked, or conclusions that are poorly formulated, translate into a loss of evidence, that cannot be corrected once the body is buried.

The Virtopsy project began in 2000, at the Institute of Forensic Medicine of the University of Bern, in Switzerland. Its aim is to apply high tech methods from the fields of measurement engineering, automation and medical imaging to create a complete, minimally invasive, reproducible and objective forensic assessment method. The data generated can be digitally stored or quickly sent to experts without a loss of quality. If new questions arise, the data can be revised even decades after the incident.

In the rest of this chapter, the techniques used in the Virtopsy procedure are described, including: post-mortem computed tomography (PMCT) and post-mortem computed tomography angiography (PMCTA), post-mortem magnetic

---

*This chapter is contributed by Lars C. Ebert, Thomas Ruder, David Zimmermann, Stefan Zuber, Ursula Buck, Antoine Roggo, Michael Thali, and Gary Hatch.

resonance imaging (PMMR) and minimally invasive tissue and liquid sampling as means for documenting internal findings. These results can be combined with and surface scanning and photogrammetry which document the external findings. Following the introduction of the techniques, we explain the different ways of presenting the data, depending on the audience. Finally, the impact and acceptance of Virtopsy within the Swiss justice system is discussed.

9.1.2 Indications for Virtopsy

The Virtopsy approach is applied to a majority of the cases that undergo forensic evaluation at our institute. The additional information acquired through postmortem imaging prior to autopsy is often used to plan the autopsy, confirm autopsy findings and allow for a second-look if further questions arise in during the forensic investigation.

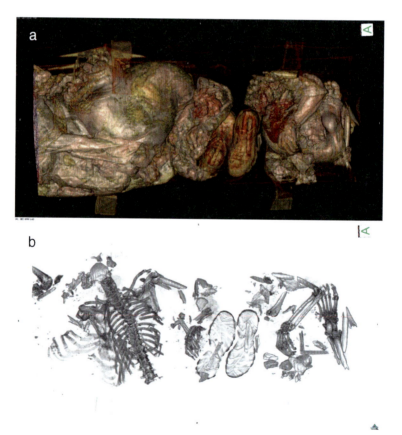

Fig. 9.1.2.1 Volume reconstructions of a CT scan of a train suicide victim (Osirix, Osirix foundation, Switzerland). (**a**) Surface reconstruction. (**b**) Bone reconstruction for quick assessment of the completeness of the body

Fig. 9.1.2.2 Volume rendering of a gunshot victim (Leonardo, Siemens, Germany). Highly x-ray dense materials such as the shotgun pellets and artificial hip joint are automatically color coded to aid with better perception

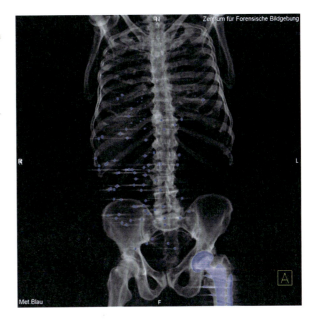

In all cases of uncertain or unknown identity, the whole corpse of the decedent is scanned for radiologic identification through comparison of ante-mortem data with post-mortem CT. In the case of train-pedestrian incidents, CT data is useful to identify missing organs or skeletal parts (Fig. 9.1.2.1). Additionally, CT is able to detect and, depending on the density of the object, identify foreign bodies such as medical implants (useful for identification) or projectiles and bullet fragments (relevant to the forensic investigation) (Fig. 9.1.2.2) . All homicides, deaths under the age of 18 years of age, and complicated cases are also evaluated with the Virtopsy method.

9.2 Technical Aspects of Virtopsy: Imaging Modalities and Techniques

9.2.1 The Virtobot System

Some tasks in forensic imaging are either repetitive or require a high accuracy. Automation could help to increase the quality of examinations and reduce costs. At the Institute of Forensic Medicine in Bern, we developed a robotic system to satisfy these needs. The so-called *Virtobot* (Ebert et al., 2010) is a 6-axes industrial robot, that is mounted onto an external axis along with the computed tomography couch (CT couch), so it can access the entire scannable volume (Fig. 9.2.1.1). It has a changeable end-effector and can therefore mount different tools. We incorporated a surgical navigation system to allow for a closed loop robot control. Currently modules for automated surface scanning and minimally invasive biopsy exist.

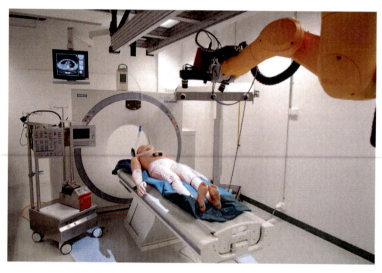

Fig. 9.2.1.1 *Right to left*: The Virtobot system with mounted surface scanner, optical tracking system for biopsy, CT scanner and heart-lung machine for post-mortem CT angiography

9.2.2 Photogrammetry and Surface Scanning

The exact three-dimensional recording of the body surface with all injuries as well as the documentation of suspected injurious objects (Thali, Braun, & Dirnhofer, 2003) – including for example vehicles – is carried out with the GOM TRITOP/ATOS III System (Gesellschaft für Optische Messtechnik mbH, Germany). This system delivers a high resolution, three-dimensional scan of the object. It can be employed for true-color 3D digitizing of smallest injuries as well as larger objects such as cars or trucks.

GOM TRITOP is an industrial optical measuring system, based on the principle of digital image-photogrammetry (Luhmann, Robson, Kyle, & Harley, 2006).[1] It is used for full-automatic, highly accurate measurements of 3D coordinates of discrete object points.

The flexible GOM ATOS III optical measuring machine is based on the triangulation principle. Two cameras observe striped patterns projected onto the object.

---

[1] Luhmann et al. (2006) is a standard reference on close range photogrammetry, "which uses accurate imaging techniques to analyse the three-dimensional shape of a wide range of manufactured and natural objects. Close range photogrammetry, for the most part entirely digital, has become an accepted, powerful and readily available technique for engineers and scientists who wish to utilise images to make accurate 3-D measurements of complex objects" (ibid., from the blurb). The mathematics of close range photogrammetry handles orientation, digital image processing, and the reconstruction of a model in three dimensions. Imaging technology includes both hardware and software. Important topics include targeting and illumination.

Up to four million highly precise 3D coordinates are then calculated from each single measurement. The measurements from different views are transformed into one coordinate system using reference targets to capture the whole objects surface. Next, a high resolution polygon mesh of the object surfaces is generated.

In forensic applications the color information of the measured object is very important for further analyses. The corresponding color value from the photogrammetric recordings is assigned in the TRITOP software to each point of the 3D surface model created in ATOS, resulting in a colored 3D model of the object.

For optimizing work flow, the surface scanner can be mounted to the Virtobot system and from there, it digitalizes the body surfaces of the deceased automatically. This system significantly decreases scanning times and only one operator is required. By using automation, a constant quality of the scans can be maintained, since the process is operator independent. A module for automated photogrammetry is currently in development.

9.2.3 Post-mortem Computer Tomography (PMCT)

9.2.3.1 CT Scanners

A CT scanner makes measurements of the x-ray attenuation through a predefined plane of a cross section of the body. The resulting dataset is a 3D volume consisting of volume pixels (voxels). In helical CT imaging, an x-ray tube rotates around the body, while the body is continuously moved through the gantry (Kalender, Seissler Klotz, & Vock, 1990). Since the resulting data are a set of 2D projections, the x-ray density of each voxel is then calculated by using filtered backprojection. The resulting voxels contain the information about the attenuation of x-ray that is displayed as density, measured in Hounsfield units (HU). 0 HU have been defined to be equivalent to the density of water, −1000 HU (i.e., one thousand below zero) to the density of air. The density of all other organic and inorganic materials vary individually and are used to distinguish between different tissues. On regular CT scanners HU range from −1000 to +3070, but the upper limit may be extended to be +30710 HU. Multislice scanners have a row of several detectors to decrease scanning times and therefore motion artifacts. Dual Source CTs make use of two perpendicular x-ray sources with different energy levels and allow for better differentiation of dense materials.

Typical resolution achieved with standard CT scanners is about 0.5–1.5 line pairs/mm. This means that objects of about 0.5 mm can be discerned. Standard post-mortem full body CT scans with a slice thickness of 1.25 mm and an increment of 0.7 mm consist of around 1500 single images (512*512 pixel in plane resolution).

The fact that CT imaging is based on x-ray attenuation allows for excellent assessment of osseous lesions such as fractures, collections of gas such as vascular gas embolism or detection of foreign bodies. The comparison of individual HU values of different foreign bodies may assist to identify if a given foreign body is metallic or non-metallic. Three dimensional image reconstruction software applications such as multi planar reformation (MPR) can display gunshot wound trajectories. The assessment of organ injuries with CT falls short of the sensitivity and specifity of MR imaging or autopsy, however, large organ lacerations can be detected. The volume of a fluid or gas collection can be measured (Jackowski et al., 2004) and the weight of organs can be estimated (Jackowski et al., 2006) based on voxel size.

9.2.3.2 Identification by Means of CT Scanning

CT scanning is a common examination performed in clinical radiology, which provides an ample pool of ante-mortem studies for use in cases of unknown identification. With the increased use of medical imaging techniques in clinical medicine, an increasing number of ante-mortem datasets is available. Prominent landmarks in these scans, such as the paranasal sinuses, but also medical implants such as dental implants, bone screws and plates, pacemakers and others can be used for comparison with post-mortem CT datasets for identification. By using maximum intensity projections, post-mortem CT datasets can be compared to ante-mortem 2D x-ray projections, or ante-mortem CT datasets. These techniques are reliable, even if the body has damages due to trauma or putrefaction. The advantages of these techniques are their quickness, reliability and low costs compared to other means of identification such as DNA analysis.

9.2.4 Magnetic Resonance Imaging (MRI)

Magnetic resonance imaging (MRI) is a medical imaging technique. In contrast to CT, MRI is not based on x-rays but uses a strong magnetic field. The strength of the magnetic field is measured in Tesla [T], and current MR units work with 1.5 T or 3 T magnets, creating a magnetic field that is roughly 50,000–100,000 times more powerful than the magnetic field of the earth.

In medical imaging MRI is based on the magnetization of hydrogen atoms in the body. Hydrogen atoms consist of a single proton and a single electron. When placed in a strong magnetic field, the protons of the hydrogen atom align themselves, similar to compass needles, along the axis of the magnetic field (B_0). In order to create an MR image, a short radio frequency (RF) pulse is emitted, altering the alignment of the protons by flipping the axis of the protons out of the magnetic field (B_0).

The time a given proton needs to realign along the axis of the magnetic field after the emission of a RF pulse is called spin-lattice relaxation time (T1). The RF pulse not only flips all protons out of the axis of the magnetic field, is also synchronizes the phase of each individual proton spin. The desynchronization of the spins after the emission of the RF pulse is called spin-spin relaxation time (T2). Tissue differentiation on MR images is based on the individual relaxation times T1 and T2 of different tissues.

MRI provides greater contrast for soft tissues than CT and is therefore useful for neurological, cardiovascular, and musculoskeletal imaging. In the post-mortem setting, MRI is a powerful adjunct to CT, its ability to visualize soft tissue organs complements the ability of CT to visualize osseous lesions.

However, there are a few important differences between ante-mortem and post-mortem MRI. The absence of motion artifacts in the post-mortem setting allows for better depiction of anatomical details. The assessment of the cardiovascular system in living patients, involves not only the morphology but also the function of the heart – an aspect that obviously cannot be evaluated in post-mortem MRI. After the cessation of cardiac motion, gravity causes fluids to pool in the dependent parts of the body and the corpuscular elements of fluids, such as blood cells will sediment within the vascular bed. The relaxation times T1 and T2 are both temperature dependent and image contrast may change with decreasing body temperature of a decedent (Fig. 9.2.4.1).

Also note the following shortcomings or limitation:

- With respect to CT, MRI is more time consuming and the time needed for post-mortem MRI may vary significantly, ranging from less than 1 h for focused regional imaging to several hours for whole body MRI.
- MRI scanning is limited to cases that do not involve metallic fragments or MRI incompatible implants. A prior CT scan can help to search for these types of foreign bodies.

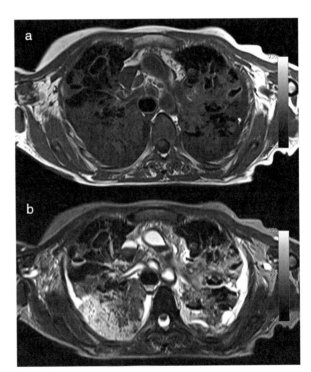

Fig. 9.2.4.1 Two different MRI scans showing a case of tuberculosis. (**a**) T1 weighted scan with bright fat and dark water content. (**b**) T2 weighted image with bright water content

9.2.5 Post-mortem CT Angiography

The assessment of the vascular bed and lesions of the vascular bed in non-contrast CT studies is very limited. In living patients the visualization of the vessels is achieved by intravascular injection of a contrast medium. The blood circulation distributes the contrast medium to the peripheral vessels and the internal organs, before it is excreted through the kidneys.

For the post-mortem setting, a non-dynamic CT angiography has been developed using the roller pump of a modified heart-lung machine to distribute the contrast medium in the vascular system. Vascular access is gained through a cut-down at the level of the femoral vessels.

- For visualization of the arterial system, a tube is inserted into the femoral artery and contrast medium is injected at a constant pressure. A second tube is inserted in the femoral vein, to drain and collect the overflowing blood from the venous system. Imaging is performed immediately after the instillation of the contrast medium.
- For visualization of the venous system, the injection and drainage tube are simply switched and the procedure and imaging are repeated.

Fig. 9.2.5.1 Volume reconstruction of a CT angiography (Osirix). The surrounding tissue has been virtually removed to expose the arterial system. This image shows a case of aortic dissection

In contrast to ante-mortem angiography, an important portion of the fluid components of blood have leaked out of the vessels and sedimented into the dependent portions of the body. This fluid has to be replaced for the post-mortem angiography and the contrast medium is therefore diluted with a high molecular hydrophilic or lipophilic solution:

- polyethylene glycol (PEG), discussed by Ross et al. (2008),
- or diesel oil, discussed by Grabherr et al. (2006).

Using a high molecular solution rather than a small molecular solution as a volume expander for the contrast medium, prevents leakage out of the vessel wall and subsequent edema.

Post-mortem CT angiography allows for excellent visualization of the entire vascular system of a decedent (Fig. 9.2.5.1). Vascular injuries and extravasation of contrast medium can thereby be diagnosed based solely on imaging. Intraabdominal or thoracic hemorrhages can be traced back to the lacerated vessel/s. Small vascular lesions that can be difficult to visualize during autopsy, may be identified after CT-angiography.

9.2.6 Tissue/Liquid Sampling

In order to define pathologies on a cellular level, a histological examination on tissue samples can be performed. For this technique, the tissue sample is sliced, stained and evaluated under a microscope. During autopsy, a tissue sample is retrieved by cutting a piece from each organ. Apart from the invasiveness of this approach, the quality of the samples is relatively poor, since it can be contaminated with other tissues or body fluids. Several techniques for minimally invasive tissue and liquid sampling have been developed or adapted from clinical medicine by the Virtopsy group.

The standard procedure for minimally invasive sampling involves placing an *introducer needle* to the exact location the tissue sample should retrieved from. A biopsy gun retrieves the tissue sample though the introducer needle. Three methods to place the introducer needle have been used at our institution: CT guided, navigated, and robotic needle placement.[2]

- In CT guided needle placement, the needle is placed by a radiologist under real-time fluouroscopic guidance inside the x-ray beam. Since CT only displays one slice of the body, accurate needle placement is limited by the possible gantry

---

[2] CT guided need placement is discussed in Aghayev et al. (2007). Navigated needle placement is discussed in Aghayev et al. (2008). Robotic needle placement is discussed in and Ebert et al. (2010).

tilt. Additionally, it comes with radiation exposure for the radiologist. These problems lead to the implementation of a technique based on surgical navigation.

- In surgical navigation, arrays of infrared markers are attached to every tool and anatomic structure that should be navigated. A tracking system then accurately determines the three-dimensional position of each marker. Based on this information and a CT dataset, a computer system tells the user where the needle is in 3D space, relative to a defined target, and guides the user to the target. This method works without radiation exposure to the radiologist, but requires training and skill on the part of the operator.
- In order to completely eliminate the human factor, a biopsy module was developed for the Virtobot system. It can automatically and precisely place introducer needles based on trajectories planned with CT data.

9.2.7 Virtopsy Workflow

The workflow of a Virtopsy is case specific. Depending on the individual case history, the Virtopsy team decides what image modalities are required to answer the forensic questions concerning the cause of death (Fig. 9.2.7.1). In forensic cases where the body displays patterned injuries or if reconstructive questions are opened, a colored 3D documentation of the body surface is recorded.

Using the Virtobot system, the entire body is documented with photogrammetry and surface scanning. Two scalebars and An array of optical and radiopaque markers are applied to the body. For the following photogrammetry, a series of photographs are taken from different positions. The TRITOP software automatically processes the photos and calculated the exact 3D coordinates of the uncoded reference markers as well as the camera positions. This data is exported to the surface scanners ATOS software to subsequently perform the surface scan of the object. Furthermore, the photographs are used for texturing of the surface model. If the Virtobot is used for scanning, the robotic system approaches different predefined positions in space and the attached surface scanner measures the topology automatically. In order to get a complete scan of the body, it has to be turned from supine to prone.

After external documentation, a CT scan is performed. Since the radiopaque markers are visible in the surface scan as well as the CT scan, data from both modalities can be merged into one set of data. In case of suspected vascular injuries or internal hemorrhage, a CT angiography is performed after accessing the femoral arteries and connecting the heart lung machine.

If the body has shown to be free of ferromagnetic foreign bodies such as metal fragments in the CT scans, it is moved to the adjacent MRI suite for an MRI scan. Depending on the suspected pathology, the proper sequences are selected. After finishing the imaging procedures, the body is ready for the standard legal examination. Based on the data gathered during medical imaging, the autopsy approach can be planned.

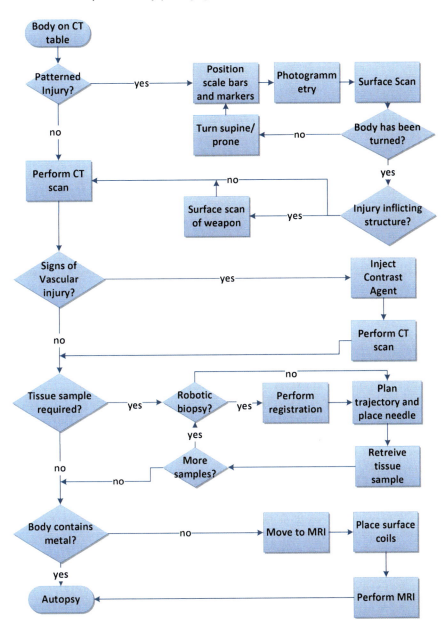

Fig. 9.2.7.1   Workflow of a standard Virtopsy

9.3 Visualisation: The Main Concepts for Storage, Processing and Visualization of Medical Image Data

9.3.1 Data Storage

Modern radiological scanners generate vast amounts of data. To ensure intra-operability between different manufacturers, the DICOM[3] (Digital Imaging and Communication in Medicine) standard was introduced in the early 1990s. The standard not only defines how data is stored, but also the necessary communication protocols. CT and MRI datasets consist of a three-dimensional array of volume pixels (voxels). In CT imaging, each voxel has a size and a Hounsfield value, e.g. an x-ray density. In MRI imaging, the value of a voxel is unitless but otherwise stored in the same format. Surface scanning usually generates three-dimensional polygon meshes. Different standard formats exist for storing polygon meshed, the one most commonly used especially in conjunction with rapid prototyping techniques is STL.

Medical imaging data is stored and analyzed by radiologists using a *Picture Archiving and Communication System* (*PACS*). PACSs communicate with medical imaging hardware using the DICOM standard and provide backup services for data integrity. Additionally, dedicated workstations offer different tools for visualization. The configuration as well as the available functions depend on how it is being used and how it can optimally be integrated into the workflow of an institute.

9.3.2 Imaging in Two Dimensions (2D Imaging)

Standard means of looking at medical imaging volume datasets are transversal, cross-sectional cuts. Since current computer screens only can display up to 256 shades of gray, only a selected segment of the 3070 values of the standard Hounsfield scale can be displayed at a time. This is achieved by applying a technique called *windowing*. In windowing, a range of Hounsfield values is defined and transformed to grayscale values. Higher values are depicted as white, lower values as black. By using different windows, different tissues or pathologies can be visualized. They are named to by the tissue that is seen best, i.e. soft tissue, lung, and bone window (Fig. 9.3.2.1).

Modern workstations allow the user to change the plane of the image (the angle of the cutting plane through the volume of data) in realtime. This allows for views that follow local anatomies rather than transversal cuts. If necessary, curved cuts are possible to follow the course of vessels or generate panoramic dental views, so-called *orthopantomograms* (Fig. 9.3.2.2). For diagnostic purposes, PACSs allow the user to measure distances and surface areas on reconstructed planes.

---

[3] http://medical.nema.org/

Fig. 9.3.2.1 The same axial cut in a CT dataset with different window levels, giving information about different tissues. (**a**) Soft tissue window. (**b**) Lung window. (**c**) Bone window

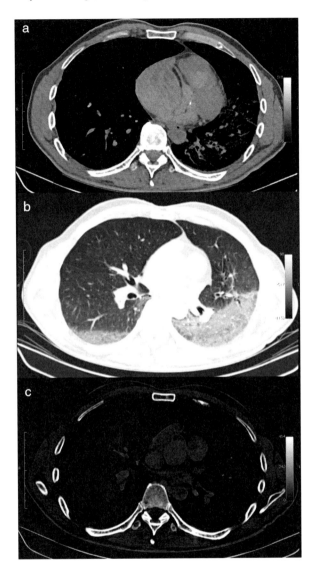

9.3.3 Imaging in Three Dimensions (3D Imaging)

Cross sectional imaging is only able to provide two-dimensional views of data that is actually three-dimensional. All PACSs feature a multi planar reformation (MPR) tool, that allows the user to reformat images in the axial, coronal and sagittal image plane. MPR permits localization in three simultaneous planes as well as the exact adjustment of CT exams, for instance to match follow-up exams with a previous study or for the assessment of complex findings (Fig. 9.3.3.1).

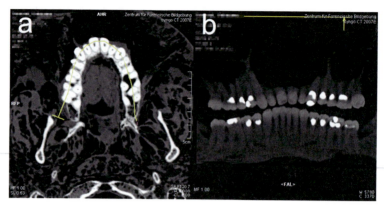

Fig. 9.3.2.2 Dental reconstruction for comparison with ante-mortem images (Leonardo). (**a**) Curve along which the orthopantomogram is calculated. (**b**) MIP orthopantomogram along the path in a

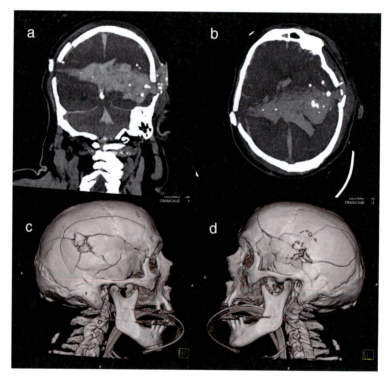

Fig. 9.3.3.1 Gunshot to the head. (**a**) Coronal image (MPR) along the bullet trajectory displaying entry wound (*left*) and exit wound (*right*). (**b**) Axial view of the bullet trajectory. (**c**) Volume reconstruction of the entry wound displaying the bone damage (Leonardo). (**d**) Volume reconstruction of the exit wound (Leonardo)

An other technique to display a dataset as a whole is the so-called volume rendering. Similar to windowing, a transparency and a color is assigned to each voxel, based on its Hounsfield value. The function defining this mapping is called transfer function. Since the x-ray densities of different tissues are known, predefined transfer functions allow the depiction of bone, soft tissue and skin in colour.

Different shaders allow for a better three-dimensional perception of the generated images. Some special shaders are used for specific task. While standard volume rendering techniques take all transpacencies and colors of voxels along a ray into account, Maximum Intensity Projection (MIP) only uses the highest value. This allows for excellent skeletal, angiographic, and metallic detail. A Minimum Intensity Projection on the other hand only uses the lowest Hounsfield value, which best displays gas collections inside the body.

9.3.4 Animation

Unlike medical imaging data, surface scanning produces textured 3D polygon meshes. Since polygon models are easier to manipulate than volume datasets, it allows repositioning of the models and the reconstruction of a sequence of events based on injury patterns and other facts.

For this task, dedicated animation software such as 3D studio MAX (from Autodesk, USA) is used. The polygon models (bones, surface etc.) can be imported directly. A virtual bone system for animation (biped) can be created and adapted to the properties of the polygon model that is to be animated. The biped consists of a set of joints that are linked to each other and have the same range of motion as the corresponding real joint. Bipeds are relatively easy to animate compared to polygon models with thousands or even millions of polygons. The polygon model is now linked to the *biped* (*rigging*) and every motion on the biped is copied to the polygon model (Fig. 9.3.4.1).

For animation, the biped can be put into different postures at different point in times, the animation is then calculated by interpolating between these postures. This technique is called *keyframing*. It is important to note that animation should be used carefully and should only show motions or positions that are based on facts.

There is in the scholarly literature some discussion of how jurors (in jurisdictions with a jury) may be affected by viewing computer animations: this may be facilitating, but unless special care is taken, there is some risk of prejudicial effects (Kassin & Dunn, 1997).[4]

---

[4] Schafer and Keppens (2007), who were discussing computer animation in the context of computer-assisted teaching in evidence courses, have remarked: "In this animation, two competing theories that both claim to account for the evidence are modelled side by side. According to the prosecution, the evidence found was produced by a cold-blooded killing, according to the defence, it was caused by events more consistent with the assumption of self defence. As we can see from the models, only the defence hypothesis produces the type of evidence that was found, in particular it accounts for the bullet trajectory found in the victim. The user can directly change the

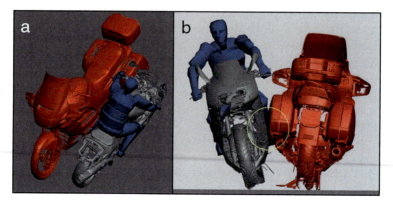

Fig. 9.3.4.1 Biped reconstruction of a traffic accident based on surface scans of the motorcycles. The positions during impact have been reconstructed by combining damages on the vehicle with injury patterns documented by photogrammetry, surface scanning and CT

9.3.5 *Segmentation*

Volume estimations in medical image datasets are possible with a technique called segmentation. In segmentation, each voxel in a dataset is assigned to a material. This way, each organ, pathology, gas collection, fluid collection or tissue can be assigned to a material. Since the volume of a single voxel is known, the volume of all voxels belonging to a material can be calculated. By combining this information with a known density of the tissue, even the weight of organs can be estimated.

Depending on the modality and the pathology or tissue to segment, automatic, semi-automatic and manual techniques exist. In manual segmentation all voxels of a specific material have to be selected by hand. Semi-automatic methods such as region growing and line wire algorithms assist the user to quickly select similar

---

position of the people involved, the computer calculates how this would have affected the evidence that was created. The scientific knowledge that underlies these models is complex. To calculate the relevant trajectories requires knowledge of geometry and kinetics, to reason about the ability of the accused to shoot from a specific position requires biological, biomechanical and medical knowledge. How much can a hand holding a heavy gun rotate? What would the recoil do to the ligaments? Moreover, it is not contested knowledge, and hence of little interest to the lawyer pleading the case. Nonetheless, the manipulation of the relevant parametric and geometric equations is taken care of by the computer. The user only needs to manipulate the physical objects (victim, gun, accused) to test different theories and explanations. To hide expert knowledge in this way does create problems if these models are used as evidence, in particular if they are used in an adversarial, partisan context. There is also the danger that computing constraints add facts that are either not established, or not established in legally permissible ways (Selbak, 1994; Kassin & Dunn, 1997; Menard, 1993). In our example for instance, the jury may be subconsciously swayed by the facial expressions of the animates, even though they have not been introduced through a witness into the court proceedings. These problems in using computer models in courts are however an advantage when using them for teaching. Without the need for time consuming mathematical preparation, students can be directly exposed to critical scientific thinking and substantive forensic subjects."

structures. Fully automatic methods are usually organ specific, sensitive to artifacts and contrast changes inside the dataset and fail to deliver data in decomposed bodies or in cases with significant pathologies or extensive damages.

Some software packages such as animation software require polygon meshes and cannot be use with on volume datasets directly. For visualization involving animation, the selected materials can be converted into a 3D polygon mesh by using the marching cubes algorithm. A combination of volume and polygon based rendering can then be used to demonstrate the relevant pathologies.

9.3.6 Image Fusion

Different modalities are used in Virtopsy. Each modality has a specific field of application with respect to different pathologies. In order to get a complete picture and correlate injuries visible in different modalities, it may be necessary to fuse different datasets and combine their information (Thali, Braun, Wirth, Vock, & Dirnhofer, 2003).

Since all datasets have their own independent local coordinate system, a co-registration has to be performed. The standard means of registration is a paired-point registration, where a set of markers is visible in both modalities. The markers are selected in both modalities and the transformation is calculated by minimizing the distance error between the paired point. If the surfaces are similar enough, surface matching can be performed instead.

9.3.7 Rapid Prototyping

Another application of segmentation is rapid prototyping. *Rapid prototyping* is actually a broader concept from *software engineering* – and it is often adopted while developing in a principled manner software systems in general – but in the present context it refers to a group of techniques that quickly generate physical models based on *Computer Aided Design* (*CAD*) data in small quantities.

State of the art methods for rapid prototyping are *stereolithography* and *3D printing*. Both techniques build up the physical model layer by layer. While stereolithography uses a liquid resin, which is selectively hardened by ultraviolet (UV) light, 3D printing spreads layers of powder onto a table and selectively binds them with colored glue. Unlike milling techniques, these techniques allow for the creation of occluded structures (internal cavities). 3D printing additionally delivers fully colored models.

Rapid prototyping cannot work with volume datasets, requiring polygon meshes and therefore will only work in conjunction with data that is prepared using segmentation techniques. Rapid prototyping techniques can be used for educational purposes or to present medical findings in a way, that is easily understood by medical laypersons, which is a common scenario in forensic investigations (Dolz, Cina, & Smith, 2000).

9.3.8 Post-mortem vs. Ante-mortem Imaging

Even though medical imaging techniques used in Virtopsy are the same as methods used in clinical medicine, interpretation of post-mortem image data sets has some differences. Changes common in deceased individuals can be mistaken for pathologies. This includes, but is not limited to: collections of gas due to decomposition, clotted blood and internal lividity. MRI scans change their appearance, if the body temperature is too low. Therefore it is advisable that post-mortem studies be evaluated by radiologists who are experienced in post-mortem imaging.

9.3.9 Medical Image Data for Radiologists and Pathologists

Traditionally, radiologists look at volume datasets using transverse cuts either through the body, or through single organs. The possibility to measure distances and surfaces is of additional diagnostic value. The slice stack is browsed through several times with different window levels, in order to view each tissue with the most appropriate contrast.

If necessary, for instance in cases of train suicides, a volume rendering can help to quickly perform an inventory of all body parts. For special purposes such as dental identification, methods such as MIP or VRT are used. Since the use of post-mortem CT angiography alters the liquid levels in vessels, volume measurements performed during autopsy are not reliable after such an intervention. In those cases, segmentation techniques are used instead.

MIP stands for *Maximum Intensity Projection*, whereas *VRT* stands for *Volume Rendering Techniques*. An explanation for both follows.

- *Volume rendering* displays the dataset as a whole, thereby providing a better perception of the three-dimensional structure of a CT dataset. So-called transfer functions are applied to the Hounsfield values[5] to derive voxel properties,

---

[5] Hounsfield units are a measure of density. For example Aamodt et al. stated (1999, p. 143): "Our aim was to assess in Hounsfield units (HU) the CT density of the inner cortical surface of the proximal femur after this bone had been removed. One HU is defined as a number on a density scale in which the X-ray absorption of water has been assigned the value of zero and the air the value of −1000."

http://en.wikipedia.org/wiki/Hounsfield_scale provides this definition: "The *Hounsfield scale*, named after Sir Godfrey Newbold Hounsfield, is a quantitative scale for describing radiodensity. [...] The Hounsfield unit (HU) scale is a linear transformation of the original linear attenuation coefficient measurement into one in which the radiodensity of distilled water at standard pressure and temperature (STP) is defined as zero Hounsfield units (HU), while the radiodensity of air at STP is defined as −1000 HU. For a material X with linear attenuation coefficient μ_X, the corresponding HU value is therefore given by

$$HU = \frac{\mu_X - \mu_{\text{water}}}{\mu_{\text{water}} - \mu_{\text{air}}} \times 1000$$

such as color and transparency. (A *voxel* is the volume unit, just as a *pixel* is a unit in the plane, in two-dimensional images.)

- *Maximum intensity projection* (*MIP*) is a way of presenting CT datasets by only displaying the voxel with the highest value along a projection ray. Information about the three-dimensional structure is lost, but it allows comparing CT datasets to orthopantomograms for dental identification.

Orthopantomograms, also called *orthopantograms*, *OPG*, or *panorex*, are not known to the non-specialist by that name, but the thing they name is familiar to dentists' patients, as they are a panoramic scanning *dental X-ray* of the upper and lower jaws, showing in two dimensions a half-circle from ear to ear. One advantage of such *panoramic* images is their coverage is broad, capturing both facial bones and the teeth, and another advantage is that also patients find the image is easy to understand. Such images can even be made in patients who cannot open their mouth, as the image is shot by introducing in the mouth a flat plastic spatula: dentists ask patients to bite on it, and the process takes about one minute. It is not only on living individuals that such dental X-rays can be taken, and they are useful indeed for identifying bodies. *Dental radiology* uses either *film technology* (which requires a chemical development process, and with the film on either a flat cassette, or a rotating cylinder), or *digital technology*. The first dental panoramic digital systems were designed in 1985–1991. In 1995, Signet, a French firm, introduced DXIS, the first dental digital panoramic X-rays system available on the market. In 1997, Siemens followed, with SIDEXIS. Since then, many manufacturers have been offering their own panoramic digital systems for dental X-rays.[6]

---

where μ_{water} and μ_{air} are the linear attenuation coefficients of water and air, respectively. Thus, a change of one Hounsfield unit (HU) represents a change of 0.1% of the attenuation coefficient of water since the attenuation coefficient of air is nearly zero. It is the definition for CT scanners that are calibrated with reference to water. *Rationale*[:] The above standards were chosen as they are universally available references and suited to the key application for which computed axial tomography was developed: imaging the internal anatomy of living creatures based on organized water structures and mostly living in air, *e.g.* humans. [. . .] The Hounsfield scale applies to medical grade CT scans but not to cone beam computed tomography (CBCT) scans."

The HU of air is –1000; the HU of fat is –120; the HU of water is 0; the HU of blood is +30 to +45; the HU of muscle is +40; the HU for contrast is +130; the Hu of bone is +400 or more (ibid.). "A practical application of this is in evaluation of tumors, where, for example, an adrenal tumor with a radiodensity of less than 10 HU is rather fatty in composition and almost certainly a benign adrenal adenoma" (ibid.). Something about the history of the technology: "CT machines were the first imaging devices for detailed visualization of the internal three-dimensional anatomy of living creatures, initially only as tomographic reconstructions of slice views or sections. Since the early 1990s, with advances in computer technology and scanners using spiral CT technology, internal three-dimensional anatomy is viewable by three-dimensional software reconstructions, from multiple perspectives, on computer monitors. By comparison, conventional X-ray images are two-dimensional projections of the true three-dimensional anatomy, i.e. radiodensity shadows. It was established by Sir Godfrey Newbold Hounsfield, one of the principal engineers and developers of computed axial tomography (CAT, or CT scans)." (ibid.).

[6] http://en.wikipedia.org/wiki/Orthopantomogram states the following concerning the equipment: "Dental panoramic radiography equipment consists of a horizontal rotating arm which holds an

9.3.10 Medical Image Data for Medical Laypersons

If radiological data has to be presented to non-medical professionals, grayscale transverse cuts as used by radiologists are insufficient, since interpretation of these data requires experience and training. This is especially important in forensics, since

---

X-ray source and a moving film mechanism (carrying a film) arranged at opposed extremities. The patient's skull sits between the X-ray generator and the film. The X-ray source is collimated toward the film, to give a beam shaped as a vertical blade having a width of 4–7 mm when arriving on the film, after crossing the patient's skull. Also the height of that beam covers the mandibles and the maxilla regions. The arm moves and its movement may be described as a rotation around an instant center which shifts on a dedicated trajectory. The manufacturers propose different solutions for moving the arm, trying to maintain constant distance between the teeth to the film and generator. Also those moving solutions try to project the teeth arch as orthogonally as possible. It is impossible to select an ideal movement as the anatomy varies very much from person to person. Finally a compromise is selected by each manufacturer and results in magnification factors which vary strongly along the film (15–30%). The patient positioning is very critical in regard to both sharpness and distortions."

The image is formed as follows (ibid.): "Normally, the person bites on a plastic spatula so that all the teeth, especially the crowns, can be viewed individually. The whole orthopantomogram process takes about one minute. The patient's actual radiation exposure time varies between 8 and 22 seconds for the machine's excursion around the skull. The collimation of the machine means that, while rotating, the X-rays project only a limited portion of the anatomy onto the film at any given instant but, as the rotation progresses around the skull, a composite picture of the maxillo-facial block is created. While the arm rotates, the film moves in a such way that the projected partial skull image (limited by the beam section) scrolls over it and exposes it entirely. Not all of the overlapping individual images projected on the film have the same magnification because the beam is divergent and the images have differing focus points. Also not all the element images move with the same velocity on the target film as some of them are more distant from and others closer to the instant rotation center. The velocity of the film is controlled in such fashion to fit exactly the velocity of projection of the anatomical elements of the dental arch side which is closest to the film. Therefore they are recorded sharply while the elements in different places are recorded blurred as they scroll at different velocity."

There is image distortion (ibid.): "The dental panoramic image suffers from important distortions because a vertical zoom and a horizontal zoom both vary differently along the image. The vertical and horizontal zooms are determined by the relative position of the recorded element versus film and generator. Features closer to the generator receive more vertical zoom. The horizontal zoom is also dependent on the relative position of the element to the focal path. Features inside the focal path arch receive more horizontal zoom and are blurred; features outside receive less horizontal zoom and are blurred. The result is an image showing sharply the section along the mandible arch, and blurred elsewhere. For example, the more radio-opaque anatomical region, the cervical vertebrae (neck), shows as a wide and blurred vertical pillar overlapping the front teeth. The path where the anatomical elements are recorded sharply is called 'focal path'."

Digital dental radiology, using electronic sensors and computers, offers advantages (ibid.): "One of the principal advantages compared to film based systems is the much greater exposure latitude. This means many fewer repeated scans, which reduces costs and also reduces patient exposure to radiation. Lost X-rays can also be reprinted if the digital file is saved. Other significant advantages include instantly viewable images, the ability to enhance images, the ability to email images to practitioners and clients (without needing to digitize them first), easy and reliable document handling, reduced X-ray exposure, that no darkroom is required, and that no chemicals are used."

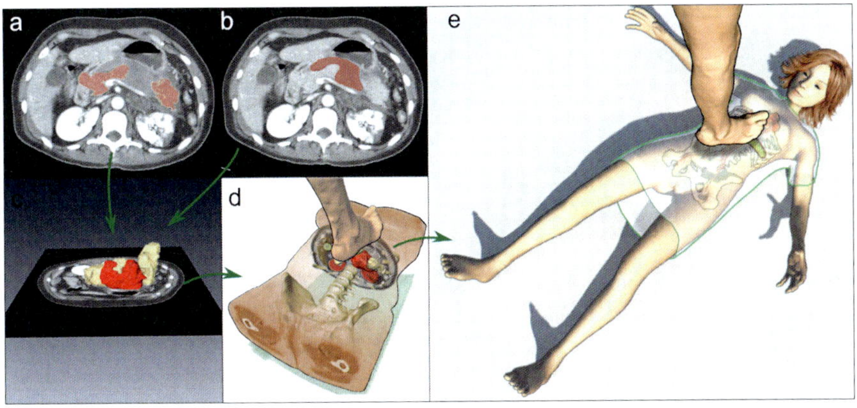

Fig. 9.3.10.1 Visualizing a pancreatic rupture after kick to the chest. (**a**) Segmented pancreas. (**b**) Segmented extravasated blood. (**c**) Polygon model of the segmented pancreas and blood. (**d**) Combination of volume rendering and polygon models. Transparent soft tissue is displayed by volume rendering. Bone, pancreas and blood are displayed as polygon models. (**e**) Final result of the reconstruction that can be put into a virtual crime scene, based on the physical evidence found

lawyers, judges and the jury are not accustomed to this kind of data. A rather simple way of depicting axial cuts is by coloring and labeling different organs. Additionally, a volume rendering showing the plane can help with better orientation.

3D imaging is especially useful for presenting information to an audience of medical laypersons, since it is self-explanatory in most cases. While bone fractures can be displayed directly using volume rendering techniques, some injuries require a combination of segmentation, polygon rendering and volume rendering. Additionally, 3D images can be combined with additional information such as force vectors, position of weapons or attackers during attack, if this is supported by evidence (Fig. 9.3.10.1).

9.4 Virtopsy and the Swiss Justice System

9.4.1 Advantages of Virtopsy in Court

Court members are normally laypersons with respect to forensic medical issues. For them, pictures of conventional autopsy can be distasteful and difficult to interpret. A real autopsy is, honestly, a rather grim process. On the other hand, Virtopsy pictures allow for a more or less abstract look at the inside of a human being. Therefore, Virtopsy pictures are routinely less distasteful and/or disturbing for court members. These types of pictures are more easily understandable, are normally less error prone (e.g. left side / right side confusion), enable three-dimensional color coded reconstructions and provide excellent visualization of given anatomy.

Furthermore, three-dimensional images can easily be shown in court rooms and interactively discussed with court members and other relatives of the deceased. Since Virtopsy data can be stored, with no loss of quality, they can be reused years after they have been made in case additional questions arise, possibly averting the need for exhumation. Virtopsy methods in general are non-destructive, which obviates the possibility of destroying evidence during the procedure.

9.4.2 Virtopsy in the Current Legal System and Practice of Switzerland

Notwithstanding the foregoing, and in particular, notwithstanding these advantages in dealing with criminal cases, Virtopsy is not yet anchored within the present Swiss legal system, meaning the Virtopsy technique is actually not specifically mentioned, in either acts of law or decrees. Moreover, prevailing case law and legal doctrine theory has yet to deal with this forward looking approach in forensic investigation.

The Virtopsy technique is based on research, ongoing for nearly a decade; however it is not yet part of the standard operating procedures of the Swiss Academy of Legal Medicine, which develops the guidelines that define due diligence in the field. On the other hand, the technique is part of the training program for future forensic pathologists at several Swiss universities. These seemingly disparate facts indicate that Virtopsy is not yet an element of what would be considered best practice in Switzerland.

However, the technology is used within certain areas of Switzerland, where the technique is implemented and well established (i.e., the Institute of Forensic Medicine at the University of Bern and its catchment area: the cantons of Bern, Aargau and Solothurn, and in the Canton Wallis, the district Oberwallis). Members of the legal practice in Bern, and in more and more in other cantons such as Lausanne and Zurich, take advantage of the new technique and apply it in conjunction with expert testimony as well evidence that helps to establish the burden of proof in criminal cases.

9.4.3 Criminal Procedure in Switzerland: The Legal Basis for Virtopsy Imaging Methods?

9.4.3.1 Background

Since January 1, 2011 a new, national Swiss Code of Criminal Procedure (SCCP) has been in effect. In Switzerland, the penal authorities include the following: in criminal prosecution the police, the office of the District Attorney, misdemeanor penal authorities, as well as several Courts such as trial court, the appeal board and appeal court at the cantonal level, and the Federal Supreme Court of Switzerland at the national level. Article 14 of the SCCP allows each canton to organize its own trial courts (such as circuit court, district court, and county court, etc.).

Article 328 of the SCCP,[7] which deals with procedure at the lowest court level, contains no specific regulation regarding the conduct of jury trails, which are therefore not yet instituted in Switzerland. Hence, professional judges preside over the courtroom in Switzerland.

9.4.3.2   Legal Basis for Virtopsy in Switzerland

Virtopsy is primarily used for identification of the deceased and for post-mortem investigations of extraordinary deaths (which include offenses, suicides, accidents and unclear deaths). The main Article in SCCP is Article 253, section 3 of which prescribes: "Otherwise, if there is a suspicion of criminal activity, or the identification of a body is in question, the district attorney may take possession of the body and direct further investigations, at times including an autopsy".[8] At this point an interpretation of the law is indispensable, according to the relevant rules of interpretation (grammatical, historical, systematical and teleological interpretation element). Under these rules further investigations cover also medical imaging method like a CT or MRI and other Virtopsy methods. This is the legal basis for the application of Virtopsy tools in criminal prosecution in cases of death.

On the other hand, imaging methods can also be used to investigate injuries of living persons (victims of crime or defendants), identification or cases of drug smuggling.. Articles 249 to 252 of the SCCP regulate the search and examination of living people. Articles 249, 250 concern the examination of the surface and therefore includes the use 3D surface scanning. Articles 251, 252 concern examination of the inside of the body, and are therefore relevant to CT and MRI examinations.[9]

These Articles of the SCCP constitute the basis to perform examinations with Virtopsy and imaging methods in Switzerland. We should add that Article 197 Section 1, subparagraph c of the SCCP implies that a compulsory examination like those named for cases of either (extraordinary) death or of living people (victims of a crime or defendants), have to be the "mildest method" possible. The non- or minimally-invasive methods of Virtopsy better satisfy this regulation when compared to full-invasive autopsy.

9.4.3.3   Evidence Law in Switzerland

In general, the key article of law relevant to Virtopsy in Swiss Evidence Law is Article 139 of the SCCP. All means of evidence that science and experience have shown to be valid for discovering the truth are to be utilized in an investigation. Virtopsy and its imaging methods are such means of evidence; especially because of the fact that imaging methods are non- or minimally-invasive and hence better

---

[7] See Niklaus Schmid's (2009) *Handbuch des Schweizerischen Strafprozessrechts*, N 380.

[8] Article 253 Section 3 Swiss Code of Criminal Procedure (SCCP).

[9] Articles 249–252 Swiss Code of Criminal Procedure (SCCP).

preserve body integrity and human dignity than the classical examinations such as invasive autopsy.

Imaging methods such as CT, MRI or surface scanning are scientifically accepted, in both medicine and surveying. It is the choice of the expert to decide which methods or examinations are necessary to provide an expert opinion.[10] In our opinion, the forensic expert opinion of the 21st century should include all reasonable and available means of evaluation, including medical imaging methods. However, Virtopsy methods do not meet the criteria for exclusion of evidence under Article 140 SCCP.[11]

According to Article 76 Section 4 SCCP the statements of experts can be recorded using technical aids such as images. Hence the use of images is explicitly approved by legislation for use court.[12]

In Switzerland the prosecuting authorities bear the burden of proof. The party of the proceedings, hence the prosecuting attorney as well as the defense can file requests to present evidence. The defending attorney is only bound to the interests of his client. He has the same rights as the defendant himself. The defense can collect its own evidence. Therefore it would be possible for the defending attorney to ask for expert testimony, which might Virtopsy methods.

Additionally, hospital CT and MRI can be used for forensic purposes. There is no ranking of evidence, but a so-called free consideration of evidence by the judge. All means of evidence are basically considered equal, although some evidence seems to be especially trustworthy like evidence produced by electronic equipment. The conviction of the judge is not based on the external but interior authority of a mean of evidence. Free consideration of evidence by the judge is limited, however and may be dependant on expert testimony.

Experts assist the penal authority by imparting their specialist knowledge, as relevant to the case at hand. Experts must deliver results and opinions based on a contentious and state of the art application of the scientific method.[13] The expert is the assistant of the penal authority (prosecuting attorney and court) in his field of expertise, rather like *amicus curiae* in Common law Countries. She or he does not make legal judgements or comments about the evidence. The experts have to possess special knowledge and skills in their respective field of expertise.

A legal inspection (a.k.a the external examination) of the body and the autopsy are performed by forensic experts or by an institute of forensic medicine.[14] During a Virtopsy a radiology expert does a reading of the CT or MRI images and surveying engineers perform surface scans. It is possible therefore for several experts to be employed in the same trial.

---

[10] Schmid Niklaus, N 944 f.

[11] Article 140 Swiss Code of Criminal Procedure.

[12] Article 76 Section 4 Swiss Code of Criminal Procedure (SCCP).

[13] Schmid Niklaus, N 929 f.

[14] Article 253 Section 3 Swiss Code of Criminal Procedure (SCCP).

In Switzerland there is no standing directory of court experts. However according to Article 183 Section 2 SCCP, the Swiss Federation or the cantons can employ permanent or official experts for some special fields, (e.g. the forensic, radiology, and engineering experts of the Institute of Forensic Medicine of the University of Bern). Furthermore, it is mandatory that experts are completely independent and impartial.[15] Both prosecuting authorities and defendants have the opportunity to comment on the qualifications of the expert and the content of the expert report in advance.[16] Hence, there is the possibility of an objection for both sides according to Article 393 SCCP.[17]

The impartial and independent, professional judge has to follow the rule of consideration of evidence and may not give more weight to the visually impressive, intuitive and exact nature of 3D-pictures of the Virtopsy. But in other countries, particularly where juries are involved, the impressive 3D renderings may have considerable sway.

According to Article 189 SCCP[18] if an expert opinion is unconvincing, imprecise, contrary to accepted expectations, or incomplete – in short, if there is any doubt regarding the correctness of the expert opinion – the judge can order a second opinion or an clarification from the first expert opinion. In such cases, Virtopsy has the advantage of the digital nature of the data, which allows for submission anywhere in the world to obtain second expert opinions.

To summarize, the Virtopsy and its imaging methods can be principally used as evidence by either the prosecution or the defense. The professional judge can also request viewing. The images must be annotated by expert commentary by an expert and must be included in the report in an "image folder". The image folder augments classical examination methods such as autopsy in court.

---

[15] Schmid Niklaus, N 936.

[16] Schmid Niklaus, N 937 f.

[17] Schmid Niklaus, N 940 f.

[18] SCHMID, N 951 f.

Chapter 10
Concluding Remarks

In this book, an attempt has been made to capture an array of subjects which all deserve attention, when techniques from computing are applied to the modelling of legal evidence, or then of argumentation, or of both. One chapter covers the treatment of tools for representing and processing narratives as known from natural-language processing. It has become a bulky book, and it originally started as an overlong paper. Looking back on the evolution of what has come to be this book, I doubt I would have had ab initio the courage to undertake such a comprehensive exposition. I owe much to the referees, who encouraged me to abound with the presentation of techniques, as opposed to a more superficial overview. For the very reason that this book tries to cover so much, we had to deal with tools or with discussing problems that have contingently or more fundamentally arisen within different jurisdictions.

This long trip took us from some general and historical considerations (Chapter 1) to an early encounter with models of forming an opinion (Chapter 2), and more specifically with modelling adjudicators' shifts of opinion (belief revision). We then turned (Section 2.2) to models of reasoning about a charge and about a given explanation (in ECHO), or of generating an explanation as exonerating as possible (in ALIBI). In the rest of Chapter 2 we could not avoid the crux of much mathematical and computational modelling of reasoning about legal evidence, namely, we had to come to terms with there being a fierce and well-argued controversy about Bayesianism concerning juridical proof.

We devoted Chapter 3 to the modelling of argumentation. We also discussed there agents' beliefs. Next, in Chapter 4 we discussed various aspects of computer assistance for organisational aspects. We began Chapter 4 with procedural-support systems for organising the evidence, and then proceeded to some criminal justice information systems, next to a discussion of the evaluation of costs and benefits while preparing a case (but also costs and benefits of argumentation itself). In Section 4.4, we discussed factors affecting the suitability or the reliability of eyewitnesses, and in particular we considered a computer tool, ADVOKATE. In Section 4.5, we considered various matters concerning policing. We considered

E. Nissan, *Computer Applications for Handling Legal Evidence, Police Investigation and Case Argumentation*, Law, Governance and Technology Series 5, DOI 10.1007/978-90-481-8990-8_10, © Springer Science+Business Media Dordrecht 2012

organisational problems of police intelligence systems. Then we discussed the handling of the suspects. We discussed polygraph tests (a deeply controversial tool). We also discussed lineups, and computerised versions of identity parades. We concluded Chapter 4 with a discussion of relevance. We then devoted Chapter 5 to the formal or computational modelling of narratives, whereas Chapters 6 and 7 are about link analysis and data mining techniques.

A panoply of forensic disciplines and their respective tools are the subject of Chapter 8, starting with crime scenario modelling, then continuing with computer processing of human faces, which occurs in various contexts, such as the generation of facial composites. We then discussed various forensic disciplines: forensic anthropology and forensic archaeology, forensic geology, physics, and botany, and then environmental forensics and, more briefly, forensic engineering. We then turned to individual identification by DNA and fingerprint evidence. We discussed problems affecting such evidence. We also presented two different computational models for fingerprint-matching. The Virtopsy team in Bern contributed Chapter 9, about how to conduct a virtual autopsy by means of computer imaging, before carrying out an invasive physical autopsy: planning the latter by means of the virtual autopsy is useful in order to make it less invasive. Also the presentation of evidence in court is facilitated by means of the VIRTOPSY technique.

Let us take an overarching view of the broad set of domains we have been considering. Introducing our present work, relations among disciplinary areas were outlined. It is befitting at this stage to consider again, in increasing degrees of detail, the relations of containment among different disciplinary areas, and how they contribute to each other. Therefore, please refer to Figs. 10.1, 10.2, and 10.3.

It has been a long journey, throughout this bulky book. The sheer scope of the enterprise makes it very difficult for the end result to always prove satisfactory, and this is why two chapters were entrusted to specialists of a specific domain, and the other chapters, too, are interleaved, here and there, with outer contributions. It is my hope that readers will agree that it has been a worthwhile journey, and that it opened new views, whether the reader is a specialist or a new learner.

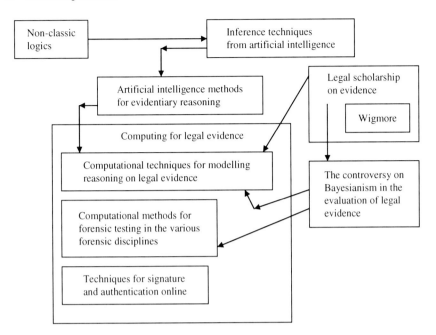

Fig. 10.1 Contributing or containment relations among disciplinary areas

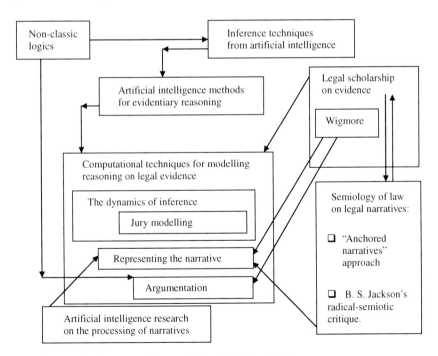

Fig. 10.2 Contributing or containment relations in further detail

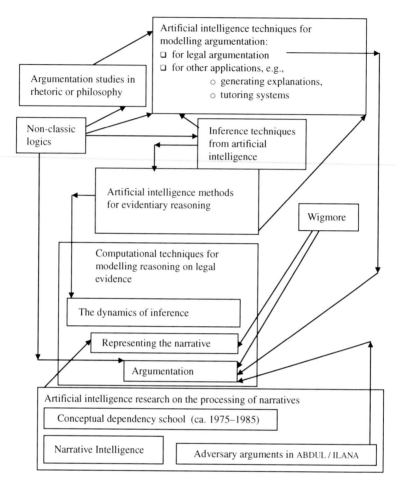

Fig. 10.3 Contributing or containment relations with a focus on computational models of argumentation and their application to law

Appendix: Glossary

This glossary defines such relevant concepts that are drawn from law (whether or not they were treated in the chapters of this book), or from computing (especially artificial intelligence), or argumentation, provided that they were mentioned in some relevant chapter. Tools are defined, if they had been mentioned or discussed in the book. So are abstract concepts, but not names of persons.

Importantly, with a few exceptions (in biometrics and concerning facial composites), this glossary does not cover forensic science or engineering, or forensic psychology or medicine. Much nomenclature had been introduced in the chapters about data mining or the forensic disciplines. Here and there, some passage in the glossary has appeared in sections in Nissan (2008a). This is the case of entries concerning: character evidence, logic and law, the doctrine of chances, *mens rea*, and hearsay.

There was little point to try and replicate, here, definitions for concepts from forensic science that can be found in Brenner's *Forensic Science Glossary* (2000). Even in such areas that were covered, there is no claim of completeness in this glossary. Sometimes a concept was developed more, simply because the present author was so inclined. It is hoped at any rate that this glossary will prove helpful, supplementing or presenting in a different manner such material that was expounded in the chapters of this book. There being a detailed Subject Index is intended to much facilitate access.

Abductive inference A mode of inference, theorised by Charles Peirce. It departs from deductive inference. See Section 2.2.1.6 above. "*Abduction*, or *inference to the best explanation*, is a form of inference that goes from data describing something to a hypothesis that best explains or accounts for the data. Thus abduction is a kind of theory-forming or interpretive inference" (Josephson & Josephson, 1994, p. 5).

ABDUL/ILANA A tool developed by computational linguists. It was an AI program that used to simulate the generation of adversary arguments on an international conflict (Flowers et al., 1982).

Actus reus The actual performance of a forbidden action, or that action itself, as opposed to the intention (*mens rea*).

Ad hominem argument Such an argument that attacks the person who is claiming the truth of a proposition, in order to attack that proposition. Ad hominem arguments are the subject of Walton (1998b).

Adjudicative fact-finding Judicial decision-making (returning a verdict, as distinct from the later stage, of sentencing). Sometimes different kinds of courts can be alternative venues for adjudication for the same case, apart from the option of turning to arbitration rather than a court of justice. Moreover, sometimes alternative venues are known to have a tendency to adjudicate differently. A U.S. taxpayer disagreeing with the Inland Revenue Service (IRS) has four venues of appeal. Two of these require that before turning to them, the taxpayer pay up front what the IRS demands, whereas the other two venues can be approached without paying in advance the disputed tax bill, but these other venues are known to be more biased against the taxpayer. Without paying in advance, a taxpayer can request a conference with an IRS appeals officer, but such officers are Treasury employees, and clearly favour the IRS. Also without paying in advance, a taxpayer can appeal to the U.S. Tax Court, but in 1989 it issued split decisions 55% of the time (i.e., the finding was a compromise), and that kind of court only decided 4% of cases in favour of taxpayers. But if taxpayers pay up front what the IRS requests and then sue in order to recover, then two venues are open: the U.S. Claims Court (which in 1989 favoured taxpayers in 8% of cases), and the U.S. District Court: in 1989 it found for the taxpayers in 18% of cases, and so appears to be the venue least unfavourable to taxpayers (Topolnicki & MacDonald, 1991, p. 84). In a different domain, contracts are sometimes drawn by specifying which geographic jurisdiction is to adjudicate in case of litigation, and not infrequently (especially when the parties are from different countries), the parties expect that adjudication at one's own place may prove to be more favourable. Thus, sometimes the parties reason as though as the ideal of perfect objectivity of adjudicators was an ideal at variance with actual practice.

Admissionary rules Typically in the U.S. law of evidence: rules about which kinds of evidence can be admitted and heard in court. As opposed to *exclusionary rules*.

ADR See **alternative dispute resolution**.

Adversarial A type of criminal procedure, which is typical of Anglo-American jurisdictions. As opposed to the *inquisitorial* system. During the 1990s, some countries on the European Continent with an inquisitorial system have to some degree shifted towards an adversarial system. In Britain, public inquiries are in theory inquisitorial, rather than adversarial. See **inquisitorial**.

Adversary argument One of two classes of arguments (the other class being *persuasion* arguments), "depending on the goals and expectations of the participants. [...] In [...] *adversary* arguments, neither participant expects to persuade or be persuaded: The participants intend to remain adversaries, and present their arguments for the judgment of an audience (which may or may not actually be present). In these arguments, an arguer's aim is to make his side look good while making the opponent's look bad" (Flowers et al., 1982, p. 275). The ABDUL/ILANA program models such arguers (ibid.).

ADVOKATE A computer system for the evaluation of the credibility of eyewitness evidence (Bromby & Hall, 2002). It is described in Section 4.4 in this book.

Age-progression software A kind of computer graphic software, useful to the police for the purposes of locating missing people, in that it predicts how a given person (based on an old photograph) would have aged meanwhile. See Section 8.2.3.

Agent beliefs Models from AI for treating them were applied to modelling the reasoning about legal evidence, in Ballim et al. (2001) and Barnden (2001). This area is called *attribution* in psychology. See Section 3.4

AI See **Artificial intelligence**.

AI & Law Artificial intelligence as applied to law, this being an established discipline both within legal computing and within artificial intelligence.

ALIAS A particular multi-agent architecture, with abductive logic-based agents. It was applied to the modelling of reasoning on the evidence in a criminal case, in Ciampolini and Torroni (2004), using LAILA, a language for abductive logic agents. See Section 2.2.1.5.

Alibi In the proper, legal sense of the term, an alibi states an alternative location. Loosely speaking, one sometimes uses the term more generally, to refer to an alternative, exonerating account provided by a criminal suspect, or by a defendant being tried. It disconfirms a claim which is essential for the accusers for them to prove the charge. "The defence of alibi presupposes that the accused was somewhare else when the offence happened. If he does not remember where he was, then he can give no particulars. If he was alone at the time, he must still give such particulars as he can of where he was and when" (Osborne, 1997, p. 135). See Section 2.2.2.8.

ALIBI A computer system developed by Nissan and his students in various prototypes as early as Kuflik et al. (1989). In an AI perspective, it is a planner which produces alternative explanations, and with respect to an input accusation, it seeks exoneration or a lesser liability. See Section 2.2.2.

Alternative dispute resolution (ADR) In civil cases, *case disposition* (q.v.) includes, among the other options: the court finding for one of the parties, or settlement out of court, or *alternative dispute resolution.* The latter may be either *arbitration*, or *binding* or *nonbinding mediation.*

Ambiguity aversion "Ambiguity aversion is a person's rational attitude towards probability's indeterminacy. When a person is averse towards such ambiguities, he increases the probability of the unfavorable outcome to reflect that fear. This observation is particularly true about a criminal defendant who faces a jury trial" (from an extended abstract of Segal & Stein, 2006). "Because most defendants are ambiguity-averse, while the prosecution is not, the criminal process systematically involves and is thoroughly affected by *asymmetric ambiguity-aversion*" (ibid.). Indeed: "The prosecution, as a repeat player, is predominantly interested in the conviction rate that it achieves over a long series of cases. It therefore can depend on [...] general probability as an adequate predictor of this rather. The defendant only cares about his individual case and cannot depend on this general probability". Because of the ambiguity, from the defendant's perspective, of his individual probability of conviction, "[t]he defendant consequently increases this probability to reflect his fear of that ambiguity" (ibid.). "Asymmetric ambiguity-aversion foils criminal justice. The prosecution can exploit it by forcing defendants into plea bargains that are both inefficient and unfair. Because plea bargain is a predominant method of case-disposition across the United States, this exploitation opportunity is particularly pernicious" (ibid.).

Amicus curiae In some countries, an expert witness above the parts, appointed by the court.

Anchored narratives (or **AN** for short) The *theory of anchored narratives* was proposed by Wagenaar et al. (1993). The central idea of this approach is that juridical proof is organized around plausible narratives where "plausibility" is determined by the relationship between the story offered at trial and the background knowledge/common sense of the decision maker. A shortcoming of the theory of anchored narratives is that has no operationalization of "not guilty".

In the theory of anchored narratives, narrative (e.g., the prosecution's claim that John murdered his wife) is related to evidence (e.g., John's fingerprints on the murder weapon) by a connection that must be satisfactory for the narrative to hold once the evidence is accepted: "[...] triers of fact [i.e., judges or, in some countries, the jury] reach their decisions on the basis of two judgments; first an assessment is made of the plausibility of the prosecution's account of what happened and why, and next it is considered whether this narrative account can be anchored by way of evidence to common-sense beliefs which are generally accepted as true most of the time" (Jackson, 1996, p. 10). For the story to be comprehensively anchored, each individual piece of evidence need be not merely plausible, but safely assumed to be certain, based on common-sense rules which are probably true (see **generalisations**). Critics point out that this begs the question: generalizations only hold with some degree of probability, if this can be pinpointed. Moreover, Ron Allen pointed out that in the theory of anchored narratives, there is no operationalization of "not guilty" or "not liable". His own related, but earlier work is free from that fault. See Section 5.1.2.

Anti-forensics Strategies to evade computer forensic investigations, in: *digital anti-forensics* (q.v.). See Section 6.2.1.5.

Appeal The right to appeal against a judgment is an ancient Roman principle. It was renewed during the Middle Ages. For example, in Montpellier, a town (now in southwestern France) which obtained privileges of autonomy from the Crown of Aragon, "appeal procedure was used from 1204 [and the town] enacted in 1212 a statute fixing a time limit for first and second appeals exclusively to their [local authorities]. But the kings in France, the counts in Provence swiftly monopolised the competency concerning "final appeals"; and by the end of the XIIIth century, it became impossible for the towns to keep such powers" (Gouron, 1992, pp. 34–35). The reverse of the medal, if the right of some judiciary authorities not to have their judgment appealed against: historically in the United States, one of various meanings that *freedom of proof* – "a slippery term" (Twining, 1997, p. 462) – used to have (unlike the current sense: see **free proof**) was this one: "freedom from hierarchical controls over fact-finding: for example freedom of triers of fact from appeal or review by a superior authority" (ibid., p. 448). Countries have a hierarchy of courts, and appeal is to a higher court.

Appeal to expert opinion See *Expert opinion, Appeal to.*

Applicant In some kinds of trial, this is the plaintiff; then the name for the defendant is *respondent.* The term *applicant* is used in the procedure of employment tribunals in England and Wales. In the *Civil Procedure Rules 1993*, in England and Wales, the term *plaintiff* was replaced with *claimant* (thought to be a more transparent, and more widely understood term: the same reform excised other traditional terms as well).

Araucaria A relatively widespread tool for visualising arguments (Reed & Rowe, 2001, 2004). It was developed at thew University of Dundee, in Scotland. The software is freely available. It was also discussed in chapters 11 and 12 in Walton, Reed, and Macagno (2008). See Section 3.7.

Arbitration In civil cases, a form of *case disposition* (q.v.). Like *mediation*, arbitration is a form of *alternative dispute resolution* (that is, alternative to the courts).

AREST A particular expert system, described by Badiru et al. (1988), and whose application was the profiling of suspects of armed robbery. See in the notes of Section 6.1.3.

Argumentation How to put forth propositions in support or against something. An established field in rhetorics, within AI & Law it became a major field during the 1990.

ArguMed Verheij (1999, 2003) described the *ArguMed* computer tool for visualising arguments. It was described by Verheij (1999, 2003). One of its peculiarities is the concept of *entanglement* (q.v.). See Section 3.7.

Argumentation layers Prakken and Sartor (2002) usefully "propose that models of legal argument can be described in terms of four layers. The first, *logical* layer defines what arguments are, i.e., how pieces of information can be combined to provide basic support for a claim. The second, *dialectical* layer focuses on conflicting arguments: it introduces such notions as "counterargument", "attack", "rebuttal" and "defeat", and it defines, given a set of arguments and evaluation criteria, which arguments prevail. The third, *procedural* layer regulates how an actual dispute can be conducted, i.e., how parties can introduce or challenge new information and state new arguments. In other words, this level defines the possible speech acts, and the discourse rules governing them. Thus the procedural layer differs from the first two in one crucial respect. While those layers assume a fixed set of premises, at the procedural layer the set of premises is constructed dynamically, during a debate. This also holds for the final layer, the *strategic* or *heuristic* one, which provides rational ways of conducting a dispute within the procedural bounds of the third layer" (Prakken & Sartor, ibid., section 1.2). See Section 3.8.

Arraignment In criminal cases: "All trials on indictment begin with the 'arraignment' which consists of formally putting the counts in the indictment to the accused and inviting him to plead [i.e., to plead guilty or not guilty] to each.

The jury are not empanelled at this stage and in most [English] courts the procedure is that matters are 'listed to plead' where nothing else is dealt with but the taking of the plea" (Osborne, 1997, p. 138), Exceptionally (in England) if solicitors write to the Crown Prosecution Service and to the court "that there is categorically to be a not guilty plea, the matter may be listed for trial without this preliminary stage" (ibid.).

Artificial intelligence (AI) Chapter 1 in Patrick Winston's (1984) popular textbook explained (ibid., pp. 1–2):

> There are many ways to define the field of Artificial Intelligence. Here is one:
>
> - Artificial Intelligence is the study of ideas that enable computers to be intelligent.
>
> But what is intelligence? Is it the ability to reason? Is it the ability to acquire and apply knowledge? Is it the ability to perceive and manipulate things in the physical world? Surely all of these abilities are part of what intelligence is, but they are not the whole of what can be said. A definition in the usual sense seems impossible because intelligence appears to be an amalgam of so many information-representation and information-processing talents.
>
> Nevertheless, the goals of Artificial Intelligence can be defined as follows:
>
> - One central goal of Artificial Intelligence is to make computers more useful.
> - Another central goal is to understand the principles that make intelligence possible.

Nissan (1991, section 1) introduced the bipolarity of goals of artificial intelligence as follows, in a rather florid style catering to a broad audience:

> In the framework of a discussion about the epistemology of computing, Bernard Stiegler (1986) employs a metaphor based on the myth of *Epimetheus and Prometheus.* According to that myth, Epimetheus endowed animals with various qualities, but forgot man. Unfledged and defenceless, to survive, man had to be endowed with reason by Prometheus, who sacrificed himself in the process. Here, this metaphor is going to be transposed onto the following idea, different from Stiegler's: the AIer [i.e., the practitioner or scholar of artificial intelligence] is an Epimetheus who yearns for becoming Prometheus for the machine. Because of the very nature of the different interests catered to by the two terms in the binomial *science* and *technology*, the technologist relishes his or her Epimethean role. Rational, industrial criteria justify this, and are justified themselves by the social-cultural pattern that produced, e.g., Edison (and for which, see, e.g., Jenkins, 1987, section II). So far, computer technology has endowed the machine with new attributes, just as the myth has Epimetheus endowing the spectrum of animal species with various combinations and dosage of faculties, that – albeit non-ratiocinative – are suitable for orienting them in the natural environment. No *actual* system – scientific prototypes, or industrial applications that computing has produced, escapes Epimetheus' limits. Not only [that]: nowadays, we [are] witness[ing] a trend in computing that aims at the *mainstreamization*, in computing practice, of AI methods, that are adapted by making them more similar to traditional algorithmic programming. The idea is, that you can describe objects in cohesive clusters, or adopt the AI technique of defining and searching a constraint space of possibilities, with just practical aims, with no cognitive preoccupations (or with just ergonomically [i.e., labour-facilitating] motivated cognitive preoccupations). Aristocrats of AI science may turn up their nose at such down-to-earth interests, when wearing the gown of [fundamental] research, but actually that possible attitude does not exclude taking interest, as a side occupation, in applied projects,

hopefully rentable. Scientific and technological interests each have a specific dignity: admitting the criteria of practice is *not* degradation, it is not tantamount to the guilt of Peer Gynt, who in Ibsen's drama [of 1867] wears a tail to gain [acceptance into] the Trolls' country.

[Whatever] the computer system – implemented or extrapolated as feasible – we were to consider, we are condemned to spot there, at most, Epimetheus' gift – a task-dependent suitability – while being reluctant to consider the system as being *already* intelligent, with no double quotes. This does not necessarily imply a mind/mechanism or soul/matter dualism, even though it may culturally motivate some dependency or counter-dependency (the latter claiming, *because* this runs against dualism, that intelligence *can* be achieved, with a certain technical paradigm, or more in general).

Dissatisfaction with given AI artifacts matches the criteria of Promethean eschatology, practically impossible to please on the ground of all cognitive desiderata. Realistically, such criteria have to be drastically simplified to be coped with step by step, and then they have to be gradually redefined more tightly, while we progress on the alternative trestles of widening the *technical can-do space* and of gaining more *scientific insight*. The\c arbitrariness of technical representation shapes, and provisionally delimits, scientific conception, but the latter, in turn, provides feedback for technological development. Awareness that scientific conceptions are a product of *social constructivism*, not just an *objective* product of either occasional serendipity or methodic [perspiration], is helpful to protect the scientist from overly enthusiasm. However, new adepts not always appreciate that, which can explain why in certain domains (e.g., linguistics), AI often becomes an *obtrusive* tool, or even a new theory on its own, instead of being recognized as being a versatile, non-partisan testbed where *representation* subserves *theory*, does not *replace* it.

Different research taxonomies of AI are surveyed by Hall and Kibler (1985); cf. Ringle (1979, 1983). Anyway, AI is most often conceived as fitting in a spectrum between the two ends: simulation of cognition as being the main concern, and the working, but cognitively indifferent tool. The contrast between science and technology – as we witness it in AI, notwithstanding the headway made by the tandem since the Seventies eternalizes distance to be covered; this is easily admitted, once we draw a comparison with the history of science and technology during the positivism era, when distances were thought to be smaller than they later proved to be (and when the [20th] century was figured out by extrapolating into "triumph" current "militant" conceptions of the [19th] century). Nowadays, there is the factor of *impatience*, as Latour (1986) has pointed out: "used to precede, engineers find it uneasy to follow [folk expectations], instead of just stupefy".

What is most specific in the contrast, inside AI, between technological opulence and scientific eschatology, is tightly bound to a terminological choice, that took sides with only one element of the binomial: by naming the discipline *artificial intelligence* (or, less explicitly and more modestly, *AI*), the distance left to be covered has been seized by the wrong end. A practical, concrete, down-to-earth choice (the nearest end), could have been: defining a *cumulative, open-ended* meter, *callidiority* (from Latin *callidior*, i.e. "smarter [than]").

This meter has both the merit and the fault of sparing technology the lashing of cognitive science ambitions, as the callidiority meter measures only past steps, not relativeness with respect to an Omega Point. Yet, such meter could cost ungluing the binomial. For technology, it may mean sinking into marshes – [in] the eyes of AI *scientists* – similar to those that, for up-to-date programmers [since the 1980s], COBOL [programming-language] administrative data processing has become. Production-system based commercial products would be repeated *ad nauseam*, acritically, as a this-worldly relish of a mortal fallen angel, nearly deaf to the *Memento mori* admonition of newly underfunded basic research. Several AIers fear such an *AI Winter*, that could stem out of premature industrial disillusion, after too feverish a fashion. [And indeed, it took place during the 1990s, with blue-sky research on open-ended problems no longer being funded the way it used to be during the 1980s. The very term *expert system* went out of favour, then being replaced with *intelligent system*.] On the other hand, ungluing the binomial is a scenery that by now cognitive scientists, AI researchers, and the scientific culture of AI cannot afford to accept. Indeed – and this is the fundamental importance of AI – AI as implemented or to be implemented is, nowadays, the testbed that makes theories materialize. Intellect hopes in the advantages of matter. Once we have started considering it feasible to bring the Heavenly Jerusalem down to the Earthly one, not to loose hold has become a cultural imperative.

Association rules "Association rules represent relationships between items in very large databases" (Chan et al., 2001b). Association rules are discovered by means of *data mining* (for which, see Chapter 6).

> An example would be "given a marker database, it was found that 80% of customers who bought the book 'XML for beginners' and 'internet programming' also bought a book on 'Java programming'." If X and Y are two sets of disjoint terms, then an association rule can be expressed as conditional implication $X \Rightarrow Y$ i.e. the occurrence of the set of items X in the market basket implies that the set of items Y will occur in this market basket. Two important aspects of an association rule are confidence and support [...]. The confidence of an association rule r: $X \Rightarrow Y$ is the conditional probability that a transaction contains Y given that it contains X, i.e. confidence $(X \Rightarrow Y) = P(X,Y)/P(X)$. The support of an association rule is the percentage of transactions in the database that contains both X and Y, i.e., Support $(X \Rightarrow Y) = P(X,Y)$. The problem of mining association rules can be stated simply as follows: Given predefined values for minimum support and minimum confidence, find all association rules which hold with more than minimum support and minimum confidence." (Chan et al., 2001b, p. 278, citing Agrawal & Srikant, 1994 for the definition of confidence and support).

ATT-Meta A system for agents' simulative reasoning by agents on each other, which deals with agents' beliefs in respect of a formal approach to uncertain reasoning about them. Barnden (2001) applies it to reasoning about legal evidence.

Attribution In psychology: how people (and computational cognitive models) reason about their own beliefs and the ones they ascribe to others. In AI, this area is called *agents' beliefs*. See Section 3.4.

Auxiliary probative policy (rules of) A category of rules excluding or restricting the use of admitted evidence. As opposed to *rules of extrinsic policy*. In interpretations of the American law of evidence, according to Wigmore's terminology, *rules of auxiliary probative policy* are such exclusionary rules that are intended to promote rectitude of decision, avoiding unreliability or alleged prejudicial effect.

AVBPA *Audio and Video-Based Biometric Person Authentication*: an acronym for the name of a series of conferences in biometrics.

AVERs The visualisation component of the architecture of a sense-making software tool for crime investigation, as envisaged by Bex et al. (2007). AVERs was "implemented as a web front-end to an SQL database. A case can be represented visually through multiple views; in this paper we will focus on the two graphical views, that is, the evidence view and the story view" (section 6 ibid.). Ideally, they wanted to design a more sophisticated tool than such *investigative analysis software*. Their approach to the story of the prosecution and the defence is qualitative, and does not resort to probabilistic quantification. It fits within logical and computer science research into argumentation, but this is combined with reasoning about stories and evidence. See Section 5.4.

Background generalisations See *generalisations*.

Backup evidence question In argumentation studies, Walton's (1997) *Appeal to Expert Opinion* offered (ibid., pp. 211–225) an argumentation scheme for "Argument for Expert Opinion", then reproduced in Walton et al. (2008, pp. 381–382). See s.v. *Expert opinion, Appeal to* above. The expert source is E; the subject domain is S; and A is a proposition about which E claims to be true (or false). The backup evidence question is: "Is E's assertion based on evidence?". It is articulated in three detailed subquestions: "What is the internal evidence the expert herself used to arrive at this opinion as her conclusion?"; "If there is external evidence – for example, physical evidence reported independently of the expert – can the expert deal with this adequately?"; "Can it be shown that the opinion given is not one that is scientifically unverifiable?".

Bail "Bail is the release of a person subject to a duty to surrender to custody in the future" (Osborne, 1997, p. 95). In English law, the Bail Act 1976 provides that "a defendant who fails without reasonable cause to surrender to custody is guilty of the offence of absconding", and it lies on the defendant to prove reasonable cause (e.g., sudden serious illness, or an accident on the way to court, for which evidence must be given). The Bail Act 1976 abolished the "common practice to grant an accused bail 'on his own recognisance'. This was a fixed sum of money which the accused did not have to provide at the time of granting bail but which, should he fail subsequently to surrender to custody would be forfeited" (Osborne, ibid.).

Bayes, naïve For a given sample we search for a class c_i that maximises the posterior probability

$$P(c_i \mid x \,;\, \theta')$$

by applying Bayes rule. Then x can be classified by computing

$$c_l = \underset{c_i \in C}{\arg\max} \; P(c_i|\theta')P(x|c_i;\theta')$$

Also see **naïve Bayesian classifiers**.

Bayes' theorem When dealing with a hypothesis H, and some evidence E, Bayes' theorem states:

$$P(H|E) = P(E|H)P(H)/P(E)$$

this can be read as follows: the *posterior probability* $P(H|E)$, i.e., the probability that H is true given E, is equal to the product of the *likelihood* $P(E|H)$, i.e., the probability that E given the truth of H, and the *prior probability* $P(H)$ of H, divided by the *prior probability* $P(E)$ of E.

Bayesian debate A controversy among legal scholars, concerning legal evidence and the use of statistics, and in particular of Bayes' theorem. See Sections 2.3 and 5.1. On statistics in DNA evidence, see Section 8.7.2.2.

Bayesian enthusiasts Such legal scholars of evidence or forensic statisticians who strongly support the use of Bayes' theorem as a foundation for statistical analysis as applied to legal evidence. Opposed by the Bayesio-skeptics. Note that whereas some in both camps accept these labels, there also are objections, and *Bayesians* vs. *skeptics* are more acceptable labels.

Bayesian networks A Bayesian network is a directed acyclic graph (i.e., a graph without loops, and with nodes and arrows rather than direction-less edges), such that the nodes represent propositions or variables, the arcs represent the existence of direct causal influences between the linked propositions, and the strengths of these influences are quantified by conditional probabilities. Whereas in an *inference network* the arrow is from a node standing for evidence to a node standing for a hypothesis, in a Bayesian network instead the arrow is from the hypothesis to the evidence. In an inference network, an arrow represents a relation of support. In a Bayesian network, an arrow represents a causal influence, and the arrow is from a cause to its effect.

Judea "Pearl has always argued for a subjective degree of belief interpretation of the probabilities in Bayesian networks" (ibid.), these being a formalism he introduced and developed in a series of papers in the 1980s, leading to a book (Pearl, 1988). Judea Pearl's "departure from standard Bayesianism arises because he thinks that prior probability distributions are inadequate to express background knowledge, and that also needs to use causal judgments which cannot be expressed in probabilistic terms" (Gillies, 2004, p. 284).[1]

Bayesian reasoning or Bayesian updating or Bayesian conditionalisation The use of the formula of Bayes' theorem in order to go from the *prior probability* $P(H)$ of a hypothesis H, to the *posterior probability* $P(H|E)$ of H, i.e., the probability that the hypothesis H is true, given the evidence E.

Bayesianism "*Bayesianism* is, roughly speaking, the view that relating hypotheses to evidence can be solved by bayesian reasoning" (Gillies, 2004, p. 287).

Bayesianism (Imperialistic) A charge made, by supporters of alternative systems of probability, or then by those suspicious of probabilities altogether, not only in a legal scholarship context: Imperialistic Bayesianism consists of the attitude of the Bayesian who dismisses (too quickly, the charge claims) any approach to uncertainty that is not based on Bayes' Theorem.

---

[1] Dechter, Geffner, and Halpern (2010) is a jubilee volume honouring Judea Pearl.

Bayesio-skeptics Such legal scholars of evidence who have misgivings about the validity or desirability of Bayes' theorem, or even of other probabilistic or statistical formalisms, in the analysis of the evidence of given criminal cases (while not necessarily opposed to such use in civil cases). The term *skeptics* is more widely acceptable, being less charged, albeit less specific.

Bench trial A trial in which the verdict is given by some (trained, professional) judge or judges, instead of by a jury (i.e., popular judges). In some countries there are no jury trials. In countries with jury trials, there are as well bench trials, which apply in different categories of cases.

Beyond a reasonable doubt. The standard for deciding to convict, in a criminal case. The corresponding Latin formula is: *in dubio pro reo* ("If in doubt, find for the defendant"). In contrast, in a civil case the standard for the verdict is less demanding: *more likely than not.* See **utility**. "Proof beyond a reasonable doubt is such proof as precludes every reasonable hypothesis except that which it tends to support and which is wholly consistent with the defendant's guilt and inconsistent with any other rational conclusion" (Stranieri & Zeeleznikow, 2005a, Glossary, s.v. *Proof beyond reasonable doubt*). In contrast, "Proof by a fair preponderance of the evidence is the standard of proof required in civil cases; a decision is made according to that evidence which as a whole is more credible and convincing to the mind and which best accords with reason and probability" (ibid., s.v. *Proof by a fair preponderance of the evidence*).

In the *Carneades* argumentation tool (Gordon & Walton, 2006; Gordon et al., 2007), without sticking to the legal sense of the phrase, the strongest *standard of proof* for an argument was defined to be BRD (*beyond reasonable doubt*): "A statement meets this standard iff it is supported by at least one defensible pro argument, all of its pro arguments are defensible and none of its con arguments are defensible". Cf. **Scintilla of evidence**, and **Preponderance of the evidence**.

A curious effect of the different standards for criminal and civil cases can be seen in the 1995 case of celebrity sportsman O. J. Simpson, that at a criminal trial, a jury on 4 October 1995 found not guilty of the murder of his ex-wife and her friend (a June day in 1994, Nicole Brown Simpson and Ron Goldman had been stabbed to death outside her Brentwood home in California), yet later on, in 1997, was considered "responsible" for their deaths by a civil court that ordered him to pay compensation (not paid because of bankruptcy). This is further complicated by the rule against *double jeopardy*: a defendant in the United States cannot be tried all over again. In late November 2006, Simpson's book entitled *IF I did it, Here's How it Happened* was announced amid an outcry. Publication was decided upon on 1 July 2007, but the family of the male victim acquired the rights to the revenue (e.g., Hunt, 2007). Nevertheless, basically it is quite correct that the justice system cannot afford other than a very demanding standard of proof at criminal trials.[2]

---

[2] In early October 2008, thirteen years to the day after his acquittal from the charge of murder, the former football star was convicted of armed robbery, in the context of an event that he claimed was

Another example is that of actor Robert Blake, who in 2002 was arrested for the murder of his wife Bonnie Lee Bakley, one year after her murder. Retired stuntman Ronald "Duffy" Hambleton testified against Blake, claiming that he had tried to hire him to kill his wife. Blake was acquitted of murder in 2005, but her family filed a civil suit and Blake was found to be liable for her murder. In an appeal, the prosecution suggested that detectives failed to investigate whether associates of Christian Brando (who the woman had been claiming, in a letter to him, had fathered her baby) may have murdered Bakley. Hambleton was one of Brando's associates, and a witness claimed that Brando (who had an alibi) haid said "Somebody should put a bullet in that bitch's head". This makes it all the more interesting, that Blake was found liable by a civil court, after being acquitted by a criminal court.

This other example is from the U.K., and concerns the Omagh bombing,[3] in Northern Ireland (i.e., Ulster). It killed 29 people in 1998. The police failed to secure a criminal conviction. Only one man, Sean Hoey, faced criminal charges over the Omagh killings, and he was acquitted in December 2007. Another man, Colm Murphy, was found guilty in Dublin's Special Criminal Court of conspiring to cause the Omagh bombing, but his conviction was later quashed. On 8 June 2009, four men were found to be responsible for the terrorist attack, and the Real IRA was found liable, in a landmark civil case brought by relatives of the victims at Belfast High Court. They had sued five men (one of them was cleared), as well as the Real IRA as an organisation, for up to £14 million.

The case opened in April 2008. Evidence for the case was heard (until March 2009) in both Belfast and Dublin, thus making legal history. It took Mr Justice Morgan three months to sift through the evidence. Those sued were Michael McKevin (the leader of the Real IRA), Liam Campbell, Colm Murphy, and Seamus Daly (these four were found responsible), as well as a man who was cleared, Seamus McKenna (the evidence against him came from his estranged wife, who was eventually considered an unreliable witness).

The judge awarded more than £1.6 million in damages to 12 named relatives who took the action. Much of the evidence was obtained by an undercover FBI agent, David Rupert, who infiltrated the Real IRA. Records and traces on two phones used by the bombers on the day of the attack were important evidence, and the judge deemed it proved that Campbell and Daly were in possession of the phones before and after the attack. Quite importantly, the burden of proof was as required in a civil case, and it is in this context that one has to understand the judge's statement that he considered the case against Campbell overwhelming.

Big Floyd A ink analysis tool of the FBI (Bayse & Morris, 1987), with inferential capabilities, and applying the notion of template matching for detecting the likelihood that particular types of crimes were committed. See Section 6.1.2.3.

---

an attempt to recover his own property. One wonders whether the jury could have been insensitive to the highly publicised previous case. See *Trial by the media.*

[3] *Omagh* is pronounced *Oma.* The town of Omagh is in County Tyrone.

Biometrics "Biometrics, which refers to identifying an individual based on his or her physiological or behavioral characteristics, has the capability to reliably distinguish between an authorized person and an imposter. A biometric system can be operated in two modes: (1) verification mode and (2) identification mode (Jain et al., 2000). The former is called *person verification*, or *person authentication*. A biometric system operating in the verification mode either accepts or rejects a user's claimed identity, while a biometric system operating in the identification mode establishes the identity of the user without any claimed identity information" (Khuwaja, 2006, pp. 23–24). Jain, Bolleand, and Pankanti (1999) and Li and Jain (2009) are books on the subject. Bromby (2010) discussed how biometrics can aid certification of digital signatures.

The most mature technique for person verification, or one of the most mature, is fingerprint-based identification (Isobe, Seto, & Kataoka, 2001; Seto, 2002). Other approaches are based on "face, hand geometry, iris, retina, signature, voice print, facial thermogram, hand vein, gait, ear, odor, keystroke dynamics, etc." (Khuwaja, 2006, p. 24). For example, *iris recognition* is the subject of Li, Yunhong, and Tan (2002), Yunhong, Tan, and Jain (2003). *Retina recognition* is discussed by Yoichi Seto (2009).

Biometric fusion (or *information fusion in biometrics*: Ross & Jain, 2003) is "[t]he general method of improving performance via collection of multiple samples" (Rattani et al., 2008, p. 485). *Multi-biometrics* is "[t]he ability to utilize multiple biometrics modalities (multimodal), instances within a modality (multi-instance), and/or algorithms (multi-algorithmic) prior to making a specific verification/identification or enrollment decision" (ibid.), where *enrollment* is "[t]he initial process of collecting biometric data from a user and then storing it in a template for later use" (ibid., p. 484). See Section 8.7 on *individual identification*.[4]

Blackboard systems "A blackboard system is a group of knowledge modules collaborating with each other by way of a shared database (blackboard), in order to reach a solution to a problem. Its basic components are: the blackboard, knowledge sources (independent modules that collectively contain the knowledge required to solve the problem) and a control mechanism (or scheduler) which directs the problem-solving process by deciding which knowledge source is most appropriately used at each step in the solution process. The knowledge sources have a condition part and an action part. The condition component specifies the situations under which a particular knowledge source could contribute to an activity. The scheduler controls the progress toward a solution in blackboard systems, by determining which knowledge sources to schedule next, or which problem sub domain to focus on" (Stranieri & Zeleznikow, 2005a, Glossary) See Section 6.1.6.1 in this book. Blackboard systems have found application in legal computing: "GBB is an expert system shell based on the blackboard paradigm. It provides the blackboard database infrastructure, knowledge source

---

[4] In particular, see Section 8.7.3.1. Also see in the last footnote of Section 6.2.1.9.

languages and control components needed by a blackboard application. It is used in the construction of the CABARET legal knowledge based system" (Stranieri & Zeleznikow, 2005a, Glossary). Ashley's (1991) HYPO system (which modelled adversarial reasoning with legal precedents) was continued in the CABARET project (Rissland & Skalak, 1991), and the CATO project (Aleven & Ashley, 1997). Besides: "The PROLEXS project at the Computer/Law Institute, Vrije Universiteit, Amsterdam, Netherlands is concerned with the construction of legal expert shells to deal with vague concepts. Its current domain is Dutch landlord-tenant law. It uses several knowledge sources and the inference engines of the independent knowledge groups interact using a blackboard architecture" (Stranieri & Zeleznikow, 2005a, Glossary). Blackboard systems are the subject of Hayes-Roth (1985) and of Engelmore and Morgan (1988).

Blue ribbon jury Specially qualified jury, instead of a jury whose members are ordinary members of the public. This is one of several possible remedies to *trial complexity* (Hewer & Penrod, 1995, p. 533).

Bolding-Ekelöf degrees of evidential strength Introduced in Bolding (1960), Ekelöf (1964). Åqvist (1992) proposed a logical theory of legal evidence, based on the Bolding-Ekelöf degrees. Shimony and Nissan (2001) restated Åqvist's approach in terms of the probabilistic version of Spohn's (1988) *kappa calculus* as developed in AI research. (The *kappa value* of a *possible world* is the *degree of surprise* in encountering that possible world, a degree measured in non-negative integer numbers.)

Burden of proof (or **persuasion burden**). Which party in a trial should prove or disprove a given claim. "There is a distinction between the evidential and legal burden of proof" (Jefferson, 1992, p. 19). In criminal cases, the defendant's "burden is called the evidential burden or onus of proof. The prosecution's burden is the legal one" (ibid.). See **Evidential burden** (as well as **onus of proof**) and **Legal burden**. The burdens of proof are also important in scientific inquiry; Scientific uncertainty and burdens of proofs in, respectively, scientific practice and environmental law are discussed – from the vantage point of the philosophy of science – in Lemons et al. (1997). Allen and Pardo assert (2007a, p. 108, fn 1), concerning formalisation, that

> there are attempts to defend an expected-utility approach to burdens of persuasion with an argument that is valid if, but only if, burdens of persuasion apply to cases as a whole (the defendant is liable or not, guilty or not), but this is false; they apply to individual elements (Allen, 2000).

Burden, evidential One of the two kinds of **burden of proof**, as opposed to **legal burden**. In criminal law in England, "[i]n most offences the Crown does not need to negative [sic] any defence the accused might have. It has to show the actus reus and mens rea, if any. If the defendant wishes to rely on a defence, he must raise it and show evidence in support, as Lord Diplock said with regard to mistake in *Sweet v Parsley* [1970] AC 132. The same can be said about self-defence, provocation, automatism and duress" (Jefferson, 1992, p. 19).

There is a distinction between the evidential and legal burden of proof. The difference may be illustrated by reference to automatism [...]. Before the accused can rely on this defence, he must put forward some evidence that he was acting automatically when he, say, hit his lover over the head with a heavy ashtray. The evidence might consist of a witness's saying that he saw what happened or a psychiatrist's drafting a report. In legal terms he has to adduce or lead evidence. If he does not adduce such evidence, his plea will fail at that stage and the prosecution does not have to lead evidence that his plea should not succeed. If he does, the prosecution has to disprove that he was acting automatically. His burden is called the evidential burden or onus of proof. The prosecution's burden is the legal one. (ibid.).

Burden, legal One of the two kinds of *burden of proof*, as opposed to *evidential burden*. In criminal law in England, "before the accused can rely on [a given] defence, he must put forward some evidence [to that effect]. If he does not adduce such evidence, his plea will fail at that stage and the prosecution does not have to lead evidence that his plea should not succeed. If he does, the prosecution has to disprove [what he claimed in his defence]. His burden is called the evidential burden or onus of proof. The prosecution's burden is the legal one" (Jefferson, 1992, p. 19).

In most area of the criminal law the prosecution must prove both the *actus reus* and the *mens rea* "beyond reasonable doubt". [...] The same principle applies to most defences. The prosecution has, for example, to disprove duress and self-defence. Older cases to the contrary are no longer authoritative. To this principle there are three exceptions.

Insanity For the accused to have this defence he must show that he was insane at the time of the offence. The standard of proof is on the "balance of probabilities". That phrase means in effect that if it is more likely than not that the accused was insane, he has the defence. [...] The legal reason assigned for this exception is that every person is presumed to be sane; [...]. The effect is that if the jurors are not certain either way, the accused does not have this defence.

Parliament expressly placing the burden on the accused [...] Parliament can alter the burden by statute and has done so on several occasions [for given kinds of offence and defendant's defence]. [...] Where Parliament places the burden of proof on the accused, the standard of proof is on the balance of probabilities, unless Parliament states otherwise.

"*Exception, exemption, proviso, excuse or qualification*" in a statutory offence [... In a case for the possession of morphine,] Lord Ackner held that Parliament could place the burden of proof on the accused either expressly or "by necessary implication". When deciding whether the burden was by implication on the accused, the court had to look not just for the language of the enactment but also at its substance and effect. The practical consequences could also be investigated. [...] On the facts the prosecution had merely to obtain an analyst's report [which is not a burdensome task for the prosecution]. Therefore, the burden remained on the Crown. [...] Where Parliament places the burden of proof on the accused, he bears the legal burden and not just the evidential one. [...] The types of argument utilised in *Hunt* will be used in later cases to decide whether an exception in a statute places the burden of proof on the accused. Doing so has to be justified and could not be justified simply on the basis of the grammar of the section containing the offence. In deciding whether Parliament intended to place the burden on the accused one should look at the practicalities. If one side would have serious difficulties in proving something, there was an inference that that party did not bear the burden. It was also a factor whether the crime was serious or not. If it was serious, it was more likely than not that the prosecution bore the onus. The burden was not likely to be placed on the accused, for it ought not easily to be held that Parliament did not intend to protect the innocent. (Jefferson, ibid., pp. 19–22).

CABARET A computer system for argumentation from AI & Law (Rissland & Skalak, 1991). See Section 3.9.1. **Blackboard systems** (q.v.) have found application in legal computing: "GBB is an expert system shell based on the blackboard paradigm. It provides the blackboard database infrastructure, knowledge source languages and control components needed by a blackboard application. It is used in the construction of the CABARET legal knowledge based system" (Stranieri & Zeleznikow, 2005a, Glossary). Ashley's (1991) HYPO system (which modelled adversarial reasoning with legal precedents) was continued in the CABARET project (Rissland & Skalak, 1991), and the CATO project (Aleven & Ashley, 1997).

CACTUS A piece of software (a simulation system based on a multi-agent architecture) for training police officers in managing public order events, while communicating as they would in a real situation (Hartley & Varley, 2001). See at the end of Section 6.1.6.2.

Carneades A computer tool, implemented using a functional programming language and Semantic Web technology, based on a particular formal model of argumentation (Gordon & Walton, 2006). See Section 3.7.

Case-based learning Learning from case studies, in an educational setting (Williams, 1992). It has provided inspiration for *case-based reasoning* in artificial intelligence. Leake (1996) remarked (citing Williams, 1992): "Although case studies already play a useful role in legal and medical education, students using them generally do not confront the complexity of real episodes and do not have the opportunity to act to execute, evaluate, and revise their solutions".

Case-based reasoning (CBR) A methodology in artificial intelligence, that instead of matching rules from a ruleset to a situation at hand, tries to match it to some entry from a pool of past cases, by calculating how close they are according to various features (e.g., Leake, 1996; Veloso & Aamodt, 1995). This is similar to, and at least in part overlapping with, *analogical reasoning* (Veloso, 1994). Stranieri and Zeleznikow (2005a) provide this definition:

> Case based reasoning is the process of using previous experience to analyse or solve a new problem, explain why previous experiences are or are not similar to the present problem and adapting past solutions to meet the requirements of the present problem.

The contrast between *rule-based* and *case-based* intelligent systems from artificial intelligence should not be mistaken for the contrast between such legal jurisdictions that mainly judge based on precedent (which is the case of Anglo-Saxon countries), and such jurisdictions (such as France) where adjudication is mainly based on rules as stated in law as made by legislators.

Moreover, the two opposite pairs do not overlap even when either rule-based or case-based reasoning is adopted in intelligent software systems applied to the legal domain. Bain's JUDGE system (Bain, 1986, 1989a, 1989b) is, among the other things, a tool whose AI mechanism is case-based reasoning. It adopts a hybrid approach involving both rule based and case based systems. JUDGE is a cognitive model of judges' decision-making when sentencing (and indeed it was based on interviews with judges).

Also see **model-based case-based reasoning paradigm**.

CaseMap A commercial software tool for organizing the evidence. It is produced by CaseSoft, an American firm (www.casesoft.com) See *procedural-support systems*, and Section 4.1.1.

Case disposition The manner a case is concluded, i.e., in criminal cases, by conviction, by acquittal, or by plea bargain (a predominant mode in the United States), or by the prosecution's decision not to prosecute, or by the alleged victim withdrawing the charges, or by the defendant dying or becoming incapacitated during the trial. In civil cases, case disposition includes: by the court finding for one of the parties, or by settlement out of court, or by *alternative dispute resolution* (either *arbitration*, or *binding* or *nonbinding mediation*), or by withdrawal of one of the parties (i.e., an employee who cannot afford to pay legal expenses so s/he could have his or her day in court at an employment tribunal), or by forgival and reconciliation.

CATO A computer system for argumentation from AI & Law (Aleven & Ashley, 1997). See Section 3.9.1.

Chances, doctrine of See **doctrine of chances**.

Character In reference to *evidence of disposition and character*: "The word 'disposition' is used to denote a tendency to act think or feel in a particular way. The word 'character' may include disposition, or sometimes mean 'general reputation' or merely the question of whether or not the accused has a criminal record" (Osborne, 1997, p. 313). See **character evidence**, and see **evidence of disposition**.

Character vs. action In argumentation: Walton et al. (2008, p. 330) describe argumentation schemes relating an agent's character to an agent's actions. In particular, §31.3, "Abductive Scheme for Argument from Action to Character", is as follows:

> *Premise*: Agent *a* did something that can be classified as fitting a particular character quality.
> *Conclusion*: Therefore, *a* has this character quality.
> Critical Questions
> CQ1: What is the character quality in question?
> CQ2: How is the character quality defined?
> CQ3: Does the description of the action in question actually fit the definition of the quality?

By contrast, §31.4, "Scheme for Argument from Character to Action (Predictive)" is as follows:

> *Premise*: Agent *a* has a character quality of a kind that has been defined.
> *Conclusion*: Therefore, if *a* carries out some action in the future, this action is likely to be classifiable as fitting under that character quality.

Critical Questions
CQ1: What is the character quality in question?
CQ2: How is the character quality defined?
CQ3: Does the description of the action in question actually fit the definition of the quality?

Thus, in both cases the critical questions are the same. Walton et al. (2008, pp. 330–331) added this comment:

> *Comment*: Even though the critical questions are the same for both, the predictive scheme for argument from character to action needs to be distinguished from the retro-ductive scheme that reasons from character to a particular action, and these two schemes need to be distinguished from the argument from a past action to an agent's character.

Their §31.5, 'Retroductive Scheme for Identifying an Agent from a Past Action' (ibid., p. 331) is as follows:

> *Factual Premise*: An observed event appears to have been brought about by some agent *a*.
> *Character Premise*: The bringing about of this event fits a certain character quality Q.
> *Agent Trait Premise*: *a* has Q.
> *Conclusion*: *a* brought about the event in question.

Cf. in Walton's *Legal Argumentation and Evidence* (2002, p. 44). Douglas Walton devoted a book to character evidence (Walton, 2006b).

Character evidence Arguments in favour or against a party in a trial, based on flattering or unflattering biographical data. According to the jurisdiction, use of such evidence is not always permitted. *Evidence of prior convictions* is a form of *evidence of disposition and character.* Another form is *uncharged conduct*, by which *uncharged misconduct* is intended: such past misconduct for which no charges were brought. There is much debate about the question of whether evidence of prior convictions has sufficient probative value to be heard by the trier of fact (a jury or a trained judge). At least in some cases (typically, against suspect child-molesters), it may be helpful to point toward what may have been the factual proof, to let it be known that the defendant had already been convicted of the same kind of offence. Nevertheless, in the law of evidence in some countries, exclusionary rules about which evidence can be used apply: *rules of extrinsic policy* give priority to other values (such as the protection of personal rights) over rectitude of decision. It is important to bear in mind that *legal truth* and *factual truth* are not identical. Yet, even withholding from a jury the information that the defendant had prior convictions, such a policy does not extend to a claim that police officers and law enforcement personnel should forego the use of prior convictions, while carrying out criminal investigations. Such a claim has been made, and goes by the name of *jury observation fallacy.*

Osborne (1997, p. 319) remarks about English law: "The general rule was that the character of any party in a civil case, or any witness in any case, is open to attack. The purpose of such attack is of course to show that the party or witness should not be believed". Yet "the fundamental rule [. . .] is that the prosecution may not for the purpose of proving an accused's guilt adduce evidence

of the character of the defendant whether of previous behaviour, previous convictions, or general reputation. The reason is obviously the extreme prejudice
to the accused in the eyes of the jury. The main exception to this is the use of
the 'similar fact' principle" (ibid.). See **similar fact evidence**. Osborne remarks
(ibid.):

> It has been recognised from the 18th century that an accused could call witnesses to
> speak to his good character, or cross-examine prosecution witnesses in order to get
> them to do so. This was exceptional and was intended as an additional protection for an
> accused, who could not testify before 1898. The important point to note however is that
> *character is indivisible*. One cannot assert a good character for one type of behaviour
> without the prosecution having the right to cross-examine or call evidence about other
> aspects of one's character. [...] It [is] not open to an accused to put only half of his
> character in issue.

The defendant loses his shield (his protection from bad character evidence) if
he makes *imputations* on the character of the prosecutor or of prosecution witnesses, but determining what is an imputation is not easy. See **shield**, and see
imputation.

"There were numerous cases in the period 1990–1993 which left unclear what
direction the judge [to the jury] the judge should give in respect of a defendant
with good character who chooses not to testify" (ibid., p. 320). Should good
character only, or primarily instead, affect credibility? If it only affects credibility, then as the defendant didn't testify, good character evidence is of no use. It
is useful, instead, if it is admitted by the court that good character is capable of
being relevant to innocence.

Allen and Pardo (2007a) offered a critique, in terms of the *reference-class
problem* (q.v.) of how probability theory was applied to juridical proof concerning character impeachment evidence in Friedman (1991).

Within research into argumentation, see Douglas Walton's (2007) *Character
Evidence: An Abductive Theory.*

Claimant In civil cases in England and Wales, the party that turns to the courts for
adjudication against another party. In the *Civil Procedure Rules 1993*, the term
plaintiff was replaced with *claimant* (thought to be a more transparent, and more
widely understood term: the same reform excised other traditional terms as well).

Common law In countries like Britain there are both *statutory law*, i.e., laws passed
by parliament, and *common law*, i.e., the body of sentences passed by judges,
and that serve as precedent. On the European Continent, what really matters is
statutory law, and the courts must abide by it when adjudicating.

Complexity (of a trial), or complex litigation Such features that may push a
case beyond a jury's ability, because a difficult challenge is posed to reasoned
decision-making. Tidmarsh (1992) and Hewer and Penrod (1995, p. 531) discuss *substantive definitions* of trial complexity, i.e., based on the substance of
a case (e.g., antitrust, securities and takeover litigation, or commercial disputes,
and products liability torts, or sometimes breach of contract cases); *procedural definitions* of trial complexity (e.g., complexity during the pre-trial phase,
complexity during the trial, complexity in the implementation or administration
of remedies following the verdict, and complexity arising from the number of

parties); and *"laundry list" definitions* (based on the number of parties, the number of witnesses, the presence of a class action, the existence of a product liability claim, the presence of related cases involving multiple or complex factual or legal issues, the extent of discovery).

Hewer and Penrod (1995, p. 533) recommend the following actions in order to alleviate problems arising from trial complexity according to three dimensions, namely, *complex evidence, complex law*, and *voluminous evidence* (for short henceforth: E, L, V): Better organisation of voluminous evidence (E, V); Explain complex legal issues more clearly (L); Limit the volume of evidence (E, V); Limit the time for presentation of evidence (E, V); Stipulate to facts before the trial (E, V); Allow fewer trial interruptions (V); Provide jury with notebooks including pictures and information about witnesses and exhibits (E, V); Allow juror note-taking (E, L, V); Allow jurors to question witnesses (E); Instruct the jurors prior to the evidence (E, L); Provide jurors with written copy of the judge's instructions (L); More thorough responses to juror questions during deliberations (E, L, V); Specially qualified (blue ribbon) juries (E, L, V); Special masters, i.e., neutral experts to assist jury (E, L, V); Special verdict forms with detailed questions for the jury to answer (L); Judge commenting or summarising of evidence (E, V); Greater reliance on summary judgement (E, L, V); Bifurcation of issues (E, V); Bifurcation of parties (V).

We have dealt with complexity in another sense in Section 6.2.1.7: the *GOMS* (*Goals, Operators, Methods, Selections*) family of models of *cognitive complexity* includes the *GOMS Keyboard-Level Model* (*KLM*), developed by Kieras (2001), and which provides a tractable means of measuring human involvement in an operational process.

Composites Composite images of human faces, used for suspect identification. Facial portraits, or *mugs*, typically are not composites, but rather a photograph (*mugshots*), or then portraits of suspects are, drawn by a sketch artist manually, based on a verbal description of a victim or eyewitness (*Identi-kit* procedures). An alternative to mugs and to artist's sketches is a *composite*, by which initially a photographic *photofit* was intended. The term *photofit* is still in use in the U.S., whereas in the U.K. the more general term *composite* is preferred. Old computerized systems for composites include E-FIT, PROfit (CD-FIT), and Mac-A-Mug Pro. An advanced tool is CRIME-VUs. See Section 8.2.2.

In non technical language, especially in the media, the differences between the various kinds of pictorial or photographic support for suspect identification tend to be blurred, and also the status of the person sought is imprecise. For example, in Italian the media would refer to *fotografie di pregiudicati*, e.g., literally, "photographs of ex-cons", whereas in Israeli Hebrew mug shots are often referred to informally as *foto-rétsakh*, i.e., literally, "photo-murder".[5] Such descriptors are grossly imprecise. (The Hebrew for "composite" is *klasterón*.)

---

[5] I received the following (impressionistic) explanation for how the term *foto-rétsakh* came into being – denoting not only mugshots, but also such passport-sized photographs that are perceived to resemble the police's mugshots. In the 1940s and 1950s, one method of shooting facial photographs

Such images are sometimes made public, not only in order to track down a person wanted on suspicion of a crime, or some youngster or old and forgetful person who has disappeared. Police may release an artist's impression of the face of a dead person they want to identify. That is to say, they already have him or her, but are unaware of that person's identity. The same may apply to a sufferer of amnesia.

Compusketch A system for assisting a witness in approximating his or her description of the facial features of a criminal suspect. It is a computerised version of the Photofit process. See Section 8.2.2.

Computational forensics Computer techniques subserving any discipline within forensic science. See Frank and Srihari (2008). *Computational forensics* should not be mistaken for **computer forensics** (q.v.).

Computer crime Crime that exploits the vulnerability of computer systems, and takes place through breaches of *computer security*. See Section 6.2.1.5.

Computer forensics Another name for *forensic computing*. Also see **digital forensics**. See Section 6.2.1.5. This is quite different from what is meant by **computational forensics** (q.v.).

Computer investigation Actions undertaken, either by the police or by an organisation that experienced computer crime, in order to identify suspect perpetrators as well as in order to find out they managed to evade computer security measures.

Computer security A discipline that provides a preventative response to *computer crime*.

Confabulation A defect of testimony: the witness is also inferring, not merely reporting. *Confabulation* in depositions may occur because witnesses discussed their recollections, and this had an effect on what they later think they remember. In particular, if it was two eyewitnesses who saw the same event and then discussed it, this may influence what they later claim to remember; this is sometimes referred to as *memory conformity*.

Confirmationism An approach to questioning witnesses, which seeks to confirm a given account. It is a flawed approach, and Voltaire lampooned it. *Confirmation bias* as occurring in the police interrogation rooms, see e.g. Kassin et al. (2003), Meissner and Kassin (2002), and Hill et al. (2008).

Confrontation right The right of a defendant to confront his accusers in court.

Consistency question In argumentation studies, Walton's (1997) *Appeal to Expert Opinion* offered (ibid., pp. 211–225) an argumentation scheme for "Argument for Expert Opinion", then reproduced in Walton et al. (2008, pp. 381–382). See s.v. Expert opinion, *Appeal to* above. The expert source is E; the subject domain is S;

---

was to have a man who had to be photographed introduce his head into a hole in a black curtain. The resulting photograph supposedly appeared to portray a murderer. But perhaps this explanation I was given in 2010 is a rationalisation *ex post facto*, which makes it appear as though it was a passport-sized photograph that was initially called *foto-rétsakh*. More plausibly, the term denoted mugshots ab initio, and it was only by metaphorical interpretation of the thing denoted (i.e., the *signified*, as opposed to the *signifier*, which is the word itself), that the term was also applied by some to passport-sized photographs with a dark backdrop (especially of an old kind), if that.

and *A* is a proposition about which *E* claims to be true (or false). The consistency question is: "Is *A* consistent with what other experts assert?". It is articulated in two subquestions: "Does *A* have general acceptance in *S*?"; "If not, can *E* explain why not, and give reasons why there is good evidence for *A*?".

Contrary-to-duty obligations A norm is violated, yet there are norms about how to deal with such a situation of violation. S.v. **time** in this Glossary, we consider some procedural constraints on temporal sequence at a trial, and how they can be allowed sometimes to be violated. Wishing to model this in terms of AI techniques, it makes sense to resort to techniques concerning contrary-to-duty obligations. Contrary-to-duty obligations are sometimes called *reparational obligations*, when the concept is concerned (as it often has been in the scholarly work of logicists within research into deontic logic) as *remedial obligation* for a state of affairs contravening a previous obligation; see, e.g., Parent (2003).

A related example is that known by philosophers as the one of the *gentle murderer*: one shall not murder, but if he does, let him do it gently; "gentle murder" is also called the *Forrester paradox* (Forrester, 1984). Research on contrary-to-duty obligations is related to *conditional obligations*; on the latter, see Chellas (1974), and on the relation between the two classes of obligations, see Tomberlin (1981). Horty (1993) deals with both classes in terms of nonmonotonic deontic logic.

For a discussion of contrary-to-duty obligations (or *contrary-to-duty imperatives*), see e.g. Carmo and Jones (2002), which is an encyclopedic entry, as well as Chisholm (1963), Åqvist (1967), Hage (2001), Carmo and Jones (1996), Prakken and Sergot (1996, 1997), and Governatori and Rotolo (2002). An approach that resorts to *Petri nets* (a graph representation expressing constraints on temporal precedence) for the representation of deontic states (i.e., states of obligation), including contrary-to-duty obligations, has been proposed in Raskin et al. (1996). By the same team, the paper by van der Torre and Tan (1999) is on contrary-to-duty reasoning. Ursu and Zimmer (2002) are concerned with the representation of duty and contrary-to-duty statements, in computer-aided design tools of the class of critiquing intelligent design assistants. Examples given by Ursu and Zimmer in section 4, of a *secondary* (contrary-to-duty) obligation that comes into effect when the *primary obligation* is violated, include: "Preferred design: uniform wall thickness should be used", yet: "When unavoidable" – i.e., when walls must have a different thickness – "transition from one wall thickness to another should always be as smooth as possible". Or then this other example: "There must be an alternative escape route from all parts of the building. However, in the following situations a single route is acceptable".

Convince Me A computer tool for supporting argumentation (Schank & Ranney, 1995). It is one of the tools reviewed in van den Braak et al. (2006) It is based on Thagard's Theory of Explanatory Coherence (e.g., Thagard, 2000a). The arguments consist of causal networks of nodes (which can display either evidence or hypotheses), and the conclusion which users draw from them. *Convince Me* predicts the user's evaluations of the hypotheses based on the arguments produced, and gives a feedback about the plausibility of the inferences which the users draw.

Coplink A tool for criminal intelligence analysis, developed for the Tucson police at the University of Arizona, and performing *network link analysis*. See Section 6.2.5.

Corpus (plural: **corpora**) A collection of documents. For example, corpora are what *information retrieval* tools and *text mining* search automatically. See Section 6.1.9.

Corroborative evidence "Corroborative evidence is that which independently tends to support or confirm other evidence" (Osborne, 1997, p. 303). "The general rule [in England] has always been that evidence does not require corroboration and that the court may act on the uncorroborated evidence of one witness alone, however serious the charge" (ibid.). Still in English law:

> Until 1995, however, there were individual classes of cases where the type of evidence, or the type of witness, were deemed inherently "suspect" in some way so as to require extra caution from a court before it considered its verdict. The law on corroboration evolved in a haphazard and piecemeal way and was burdened with difficult technicalities. Classically, three kinds of witness were thought to be sufficiently suspect to require corroboration of their evidence before there could be a conviction, namely children, accomplices, and victims of a sexual offence. There were, in addition, rules which indicated that corroboration should generally be looked for in any case where a witness might have some personal motive for wishing to secure the conviction of the accused, for example someone who had a grudge against the accused, or who might himself have fallen under suspicion of the crime in question. In these cases, a judge would have to remind the jury, in very technical terms, of the risk of convicting on the evidence of the "suspect" witness and then go on to describe what items of evidence could have the technical quality of corroboration on the particular facts of the case. Judges were notoriously prone to get aspects of corroboration wrong, either by directing the jury with insufficient force about the risks of acting without corroboration, or by misidentifying items of evidence in the case which they might say were technically capable of amounting to corroboration but which in fact lacked the necessary quality (ibid.).

Reform abolished the requirement for corroboration of evidence from given categories of witnesses, and also the requirement for the judge to give a warning to the jury ceased to be mandatory and became discretionary (ibid., pp. 304–305).

Criminal trial (as opposed to *civil trial*). In Anglo-American jurisdictions, the sequence is as follows. Initially, there is the *indictment*. Then, the accused is asked to plea *guilty* or *not guilty*. If the defendant pleas guilty (which typically is because of a *plea bargain*), the court hears the facts from the prosecution (with no need to present evidence), then the defence may intervene, and finally the sentence is given. If the defendant pleas not guilty, the case will have to be prosecuted. There is an adjournment to an agreed date. Then the adjourned hearing takes place, following *adversarial* lines (as typical of the *common law* system of Anglo-American jurisdictions). There is the prosecution's opening speech. Then the prosecution calls witnesses. For each prosecution witness, there is an *examination in chief* of the witness on the part of the prosecution, followed by *cross-examination* of the witness by the defence, and sometimes there is *re-examination* on the part of the prosecution. Then there is the close of the prosecution case. (Now the defence may submit that there is no call to answer. If the court accepts this, then the defendant is discharged. Otherwise:) Defence calls witnesses. For each one of the defence witnesses, there is an *examination in chief* of the witness by the defence, then *cross-examination* on the art of the prosecution, and sometimes *re-examination* by the defence. Then there is the defence's closing speech to the bench. Now the prosecution may have one more speech, but if this is the case, then the defence must have the last word. Now the factfinders (either lay magistrates, i.e., jurors, or one or more stipendiary magistrates, e.g., trained, professional judges) retire to consider their decision. (if there is a jury, the jury receives instructions from the judges before it retires.) Then the magistrates return and give the verdict (and state no reason). If the verdict is *not guilty*, then the defendant is discharged. If the verdict is *guilty*, then the court hears the facts from the prosecution (with no need to present evidence), and next the defence may intervene. Finally, the sentence is given. See *utility*, and *beyond a reasonable doubt.*

CRIME-VUs A project which produced EvoFIT (under the lead of Charlie Frowd), a computer graphic tool for suspect identification, and validated it with techniques from experimental psychology. The project was conducted at the University of Central Lancashire in Preston, and the Faces Lab of the University of Stirling, Scotland. The approach combines facial composites, sketches, and morphing between facial composites. See Section 8.2.2.4.

Cross-examination Questioning of one of the parties, or of a witness called by one of the parties at a trial, by the other party's lawyer. See **examination**. During cross-examination, not always questions are direct. Implication and innuendo are often effective. By accumulating details, it is in their *final statement to the court* (also called *final argument*, or more often *closing arguments*) that lawyers propose an account that puts facts in relation to each other, make characterisations, and draw conclusions.

CSI Crime scene investigation.

Daedalus A tool for supporting the activities of the *sostituti procuratori* (examining magistrates and then prosecutors) in the Italian judiciary. Developed by Carmelo Àsaro. A related tool is *Itaca.* See *procedural-support systems*, and Section 4.1.3.

DART A tool for supporting argumentation (Freeman & Farley, 1996), which was applied to legal situations also by Gulotta and Zappalà (2001). See Section 3.7.

Dead Bodies Project A project (Zeleznikow & Keppens, 2002, 2003; Keppens & Schafer, 2003a, 2004, cf. 2005, 2006) intended to help at *inquests* aiming at ascertain the causes of death, when *prima facie* a crime cannot be ruled out. See Section 8.1.

Decision tree A conditional structure of flow control. Decision trees (as well as IF/THEN rules) are automatically extracted from databases by *machine-learning* tools. Several machine-learning commercial products that primarily produce decision trees were described by Mena (2003, section 7.9, pp. 221–229):

- AC (http://www.alice-soft.com)
- Attar XperRule (http://www.attar.com/)
- Business Miner (http://www.businessobjects.com)

- C5.0 (http://www.rulequest.com/), also a rule-extractor; for expecially large databases (its algorithm is also used in SPSS's Clementine)
- CART (http://www.salford-systems.com), also a rule-extractor; very powerful and accurate, but relatively slow, and for numeric data only
- Cognos Scenario[6]
- Neurosciences aXi Decision Tree[7]
- SPSS Answer Trees[8]
- as well as several free decision tree software tools.[9]

Deafeasibility Carbogim et al. (2000) presented a comprehensive survey of defeasible argumentation. In this book, we have dealt with *defeasibility* in Sections 3.3 and 3.9.1. "Nonmonotonic reasoning [q.v.], because conclusions must sometimes be reconsidered, is called *defeasible*; that is, new information may sometimes invalidate previous results. Representation and search procedures that keep track of the reasoning steps of a logic system are called *truth maintenance systems* or TMS. In defeasible reasoning, the TMS preserves the consistency of the knowledge base, keeping track of conclusions that might later need to be questioned" (Luger & Stubblefield, 1998, p. 270).

Defence In court, and previously during the preparations for the trial, the formal standing (and actions taken in that role) of the accused (the defendant) and of his lawyers on his behalf (but he may be representing himself, without resorting to a lawyer).

Defendant The party against whom the *plaintiff* (who in particular may be the *prosecution*) turns to the courts for adjudication. In some kinds of trial, the names are *applicant* for the plaintiff, and *respondent* for the defendant.

Dempster-Shafer theory In statistics and in artificial intelligence: "Dempster-Shafer theory [Shafer, 1976] has been developed to handle partially specified domains. It distinguishes between uncertainty and ignorance by creating belief functions. Belief functions allow the user to bound the assignment of probabilities to certain events, rather than give events specific probabilities. Belief functions satisfy axioms that are weaker than those for probability theory. When the probabilistic values of the beliefs that a certain event occurred are exact, then the belief value is exactly the probability that the event occurred. In this case, Dempster-Shafer theory and probability theory provide the same conclusions" (Stranieri & Zeleznikow, 2005a).

Deontic, deontology Pertaining to duty and permissibility. Deontic logic has operators for duty. Deontological arguments appeal to principles of right or wrong, ultimate (rather than *teleological*) principles about what must, or ought or must not or ought not to be or be done.

---

[6] http://www.cognos.com/products/scenario/index.html

[7] http://www.neurosciences.com

[8] http://www.spss.com/spssbi/answertree/

[9] Such free software tools are linked to from the data mining portal www.kdnuggets.com

Deontic logic A modal logic of obligation and permission. Established in the 1940s. It was especially prominent in AI & Law research from the 1970s. See, e.g., Nissan (2008a), Åqvist (1984, 1986), Jones and Sergot (1992). Also see **contrary-to-duty obligations**.

Digital anti-forensics Strategies to evade computer forensic investigations, as well as ways to exploit critical failures in computer forensics software or in the reliability of computer security systems. Section 6.2.1.5.

Digital forensics A discipline that provides techniques and strategies for tackling crime involving digital media.

Digital forgeries Forged items involving digital media, such as images. They are to be detected by *digital forensics*, or in particular *digital image forensics*. See Section 8.2.5.

Digital image forensics See *image forensics*.

Discretion The faculty of making a choice, rather than being compulsively directed. In the legal context, there is e.g., **prosecutorial discretion** (q.v.). But there also is *judicial discretion*. Duke University's George Christie began 'An Essay on Discretion' (Christie, 1986) by stating (ibid., p. 747):

> Few terms have as important a place in legal discourse as "discretion". Despite the importance of the term, however, those who use it do not agree on its meaning. It is universally accepted that discretion has something to do with choice; beyond this, the consensus breaks down.
>
> If there is little agreement about the meaning of discretion, there is even less agreement about its desirability. Indeed, participants in the judicial process and observers of that process take a schizophrenic view of discretion. Sometimes they praise it and sometimes they execrate it.

In particular, there is a distinction between *primary discretion* and *secondary discretion* (ibid., pp. 747–748):

> In the judicial context, [Maurice] Rosenberg distinguishes between primary discretion and secondary discretion. Primary discretion arises when a decision-maker has "a wide range of choice as to what he decides, free from the constraints which characteristically attach whenever legal rules enter the decision process." Used in this sense, discretion can mean simply that a person has the authority to decide. Courts, judges, and legal scholars often use the term *discretion* in this sense, referring simply to authority to decide, or unconstrained choice.

That is Rosenberg's *primary discretion*. Moreover (Christie, ibid., pp. 748–749; the brackets are Christie's):

> Rosenberg contrasts the primary form of discretion with "the secondary form, [which] has to do with hierarchical relations among judges."
>
> The secondary form of discretion enters the picture when the system tries to prescribe the degree of finality and authority a lower court's decision enjoys in the higher courts. Specifically, it comes into full play when the rules of review accord the lower court's decision an unusual amount of insulation from appellate revision. In this sense, discretion is a review-restraining concept. It gives the trial judge a right to be wrong without incurring reversal.

> In the limiting case, the choice made by a person exercising primary discretion is by
> definition the correct choice. The correctness of the choice cannot be attacked because
> there are no external criteria on which to base such an attack. When secondary discretion
> is involved, one can attack the correctness of the choice, although the authority of the
> person to make that choice cannot be attacked. Thus secondary discretion involves the
> authority to make the wrong decision.

Christie mentions two examples Rosenberg gave, from college football, and notes: "In both cases, everyone agreed that the officials were clearly wrong; but, in both instances, no redress for those errors was possible" (ibid., p. 749). Rosenberg however was "concerned with the effect of secondary discretion on appellate courts' treatment of certain contested rulings of trial courts, particularly procedural rulings such as denials of motions for new trials" (Christie, ibid.). However, as "in any hierarchically organized bureaucracy, there are limits to the amount of perverseness that superiors are prepared to tolerate in their subordinates" (ibid.), practically "Rosenberg's secondary discretion – the authority to make wrong decisions – usually boils down to the authority to make decisions to which reviewing authorities will accord a presumption of correctness." (ibid.) Nevertheless: "The reviewing authority will intervene only if the initial decisionmaker *abused* his discretion" (ibid.). Christie conceded (ibid., fn 12):

> Behind this linguistic formula, of course, lie the difficult questions: How perverse must
> the initial decision be before it will be said to be an abuse of discretion? And are there
> any objective criteria for deciding degrees of abuse?

Christie then proceeded to remark about when the two kinds of discretion merge, and what the difference is (ibid., 749–750):

> A cynic might contend, however, that Rosenberg's notion of secondary discretion
> merges with what he calls primary discretion when an inferior is given the authority to
> make wrong choices that cannot be overturned. There is no practical difference between
> the authority to make whatever decision one chooses and the authority to make decisions
> that will be enforced even if they are felt to be wrong. Indeed, primary and secondary
> discretion do sometimes seem to merge at the edges, but one clear distinction exists –
> different types of criticism can be leveled at decisions made under different types of
> discretion.

Also consider *strong discretion*: "According to Dworkin, strong discretion characterises those decisions where the decision-maker is not bound by any standards and is required to create his or her own standards" (Stranieri & Zeleznikow, 2005a, Glossary). Stranieri and Zeleznikow (2005a) also explained:

> [Dworkin 1977] presents a systematic account of discretion by proposing two basic
> types of discretion, that he called strong discretion and weak discretion. Weak discretion
> describes situations where a decision-maker must interpret standards in her own way,
> whereas strong discretion characterises those decisions where the decision-maker is not
> bound by any standards and is required to create his or her own standards. [MacCormick,
> 1981] does not dispute this conceptualisation but contends that Dworkin's distinction
> between typologies is one of degree and not of type.

Discretionary As opposed to *mandatory*. In particular, as applied to judicial decision-making: what is up to the judge to decide, unfettered by mandatory rules. See Section 4.2.5. However, see the entry for **discretion** above. Kannai, Schild, and Zeleznikow (2007) offer an artificial intelligence perspective on legal discretion. Meikle and Yearwood (2000) are concerned with the provision of support for the exercise of discretion, and how the need to avoid the risk of adversely affecting it when using a computer tool, inspired the structural design of EMBRACE, a decision support system for Australia's Refugee Review Tribunal. Leith (1998) has warned about the risks, with AI applications to law, that judicial discretion be restricted, if computer tools come to be involved in the judicial decision-making process.

Meikle and Yearwood (2000) classify legal decision-making in four quadrants, according to two operational dimensions: "One dimension is the extent to which a system should either be an "outcome predictor" (a highly convergent aim) or should give access to diverse resources about the issues of interest (a highly divergent aim). This is the *predictive–descriptive* dimension. The other is the extent to which a system either needs to support discretion (by permitting complete autonomy, perhaps because the domain has no constraints) or needs to support weak discretion (by permitting only that allowable within prescribed constraints). This is the *strong–weak discretion* dimension" (Meikle & Yearwood, 2000, p. 101).

It was proposed that EMBRACE, as well as Bench-Capon's PLAID (Bench-Capon & Staniford, 1995), may be placed in the quadrant characterised by strong discretion and descriptiveness (instead of predicted outcome, which when there is strong discretion lets the user override the prediction either partly or altogether). We argue that the evolution of *Daedalus* is from weak to strong discretion (provided that validation steps are safeguarded), and that the approach is descriptive, whereas predictiveness is avoided out of a concern to ensure fairness to the suspects.

Also see Lara-Rosano and del Socorro Téllez-Silva's article (2003) on fuzzy[10] support systems for discretionary judicial decision making.

Disposition "The word 'disposition' is used to denote a tendency to act think or feel in a particular way. The word 'character' may include disposition, or sometimes mean 'general reputation' or merely the question of whether or not the accused has a criminal record" (Osborne, 1997, p. 313). See **evidence of disposition**.

DNA evidence An important use (yet not the only use) of such evidence is for the purposes of identifying perpetrators. See Section 8.7.2.

Dock identification "An old practice, now disapproved [in England], is the so-called 'dock identification' [. . .] where a witness is asked if the man seen at the scene of the crime is present in court. There will clearly be a tendency to look at the man in the dock and pick him just because he is there in that position" (Osborne, 1997, p. 305). "Obviously there is no theoretical objection to a witness testifying that the accused is the man he saw commit the crime. This is direct evidence by a first-hand observer. [Yet], where this happens (i.e. where the witness sees the accused at the trial for the first time after the offence) it is known as a 'dock

---

[10] Fuzzy logic is the subject of Section 6.1.15 in this book.

identification' and is frowned on except in exceptional circumstances" (ibid.). A remedy is *identification parades*, for which, see Section 4.5.2.3.

Doctrine of chances The odds that a new event is just a coincidence, in view of similar past events. In legal scholarship, it is discussed along with **uncharged conduct** as being a kind of **character evidence**, and in particular with the somewhat different concept of **similar fact evidence** (see s.vv.). Sometimes an expert witness would err clamorously with the statistics: "Forensics and expert witness investigations currently have a high profile in the media, principally in the field related to medical practitioners. The discrediting of evidence provided in the notorious Sally Clark case by Professor Sir Roy Meadows, has made many 'experts', not only medical, but also those operating in different professions, stop and take stock of how we undertake expert witness work, be it within the realm of Civil or Criminal Law" (Smith, 2006). In Britain, Sally Clark, a lawyer by profession, lost her apparently healthy firstborn son, aged $2\frac{1}{2}$ months, to sudden death in December 1996, and then, in January 1998, also her second baby, aged two months, in similar circumstances. She was convicted in November 1999 (by a 10–2 majority) of smothering her two babies; she was sentenced to prison for life, and spent years in prison after her second baby died, in circumstances similar to the death of her firstborn son. Meadows had claimed that there was only one chance in 73 million for this to be a coincidence (no witness qualified in statistics was in court); in so claiming, the Leeds professor was shockingly inaccurate, as the death of siblings is not necessarily statistically independent. Eventually, the mother was released and the expert witness disgraced. After a while, he was reintegrated in the medical profession, and shortly afterwards Mrs. Clark died in her early forties. (In another British case, a young woman was able to refute a similar charge, by bringing evidence that her maternal lineage, traced back to India, had a story of infant death.) A prominent forensic statistician, Philip Dawid, has discussed the Sally Clark case ([2003] EWCA Crim 1020) in Dawid (2004b), which is highly readable even for ones with little mathematical background. A more technical paper is Dawid (2001b). Also see Dawid (2005b, Sec. 4.3 and in particular, Sec. 4.3.1). Already in January 2000, Stephen Watkins' editorial, 'Conviction by Mathematical Error?', was published in the *British Medical Journal.* Dawid finds that both Meadows' and Watkins' calculations were flawed. He was an expert witness in statistics for the defence at the appeal hearing.

Arguably the expert witness's testimony against Sally Clark had been influenced by a case in the United States, in which several babies of the same mother had been believed to have died of cot death, yet she was eventually convicted of having killed them herself.

The following quotations are quoted from Nissan (2001c, section 3: 'The Doctrine of Chances & Uncharged Conduct'); at the time, I was kindly referred to these by Peter Tillers (p.c., 9 Feb. 2000). In the *New York Times*, George Judson (1995) reported from Owego, N.Y., that a defendant, who was a "48-year-old woman accused of smothering her five infant children a quarter of a century ago, was convicted of their deaths today in Tioga County Court. In 1972, a leading medical journal cited the deaths of two infants from rural New York, 'MH' and

'NH', as compelling evidence that Sudden Infant Death Syndrome ran in families. Today, a jury found that the babies [...] were murdered by their mother, as were two brothers and a sister before them". The defendant "had confessed to state troopers last year that she had smothered her babies", "a chilling and detailed confession", yet according to her she "had testified that she made the confession only to end hours of questioning by state troopers, saying that her children had simply stopped breathing, sometimes even as she fed them" (ibid.). According to the confession, the babies crying spells were the trigger; in contrast, she "suggested in her confession", the boy she and her husband adopted afterwards is alive as "unlike the five others, he had survived his crying spells because his father was out of work and at home during his infancy, and she had not been left to cope with the child alone". The five murder verdicts are of murder by depraved indifference (i.e., without the conscious intention to kill). The Hoyt case from upstate New York "was striking [...] also for the family's place at the center of research" which at the time was prominent in promoting a medical theory on cot deaths (ibid.). "But to a forensic pathologist in Dallas, [...] the death of five children in one family from SIDS was statistically impossible, and she believed that [the aforementioned] research was leading pediatricians to disregard danger signs within some families" (ibid.). Benderly (1997) approaches the effect of the Hoyt diagnosis of old and recent multiple murder verdicts from the viewpoint of scientific error and its effects on subsequent research. Williams (1996), referring to the Hoyt case, pointed out: "Criminal defense lawyers know how difficult it is to overcome a confession in a criminal trial, for juries find it hard to fathom why anyone would falsely implicate oneself". "Confessions are usually used as ground truth but are not 100 per cent reliable" (Vrij, 1998a, p. 89); even "people considered as guilty by virtue of a confession may actually be innocent, as some innocent people do confess" (ibid.).

Prof. Tillers also kindly referred me (p.c., 9 Feb. 2000) to the "famous case 'Brides in the Bath'": "Rex v. Smith, 11 Cr. App. R. 229, 84 L.J.K.B.[11] 2153 (1915) (husband perhaps drowned a number of wives to recover insurance proceeds; at first sight the drownings were accidental but...)". Prof. Tillers also referred me to the news from the *New York Times* of Sunday, March 19, 1995; in the words of the report – from Hot Sulphur Springs, Colorado – "A woman whose 11 marriages earned her the nickname the Black Widow was convicted on Friday of torturing and killing her ninth husband" (NYT, 1995). This particular husband had "hired a private investigator when he began to suspect that she was lying about how many times she had been married", and had intended to sue her for fraud and emotional distress. She was divorced from all previous husbands, except the eighth (her marriage to the ninth was annulled for that very reason), and "except for an elderly man who died of natural causes", and this includes her having divorced (twice) from "the lawyer who helped her avoid questioning in the 1972 shooting death of her third husband". In closing arguments, defense

---

[11] *L.J.K.B.* stands for *Law Journal Reports, Kings Bench.*

lawyers denied there was any physical evidence to dismiss the alibi of the two defendants (the woman and her boyfriend, also convicted, had claimed they had been away, camping). As to the admissibility of character evidence, it is remarkable that the two defendants were convicted even though "[t]estimony about her previous marriages was not allowed during her trial" (ibid.).

Moreover, Prof. Peter Tillers kindly sent me an article by a professor of Law from the University of California at Davis, Edward Imwinkelried (1990), a paper which "has an extensive discussion of the American view of the 'doctrine of chances'". Imwinkelried's paper, "The use of evidence of an accused's uncharged misconduct to prove *mens rea*: the doctrines that threaten to engulf the character evidence prohibition", states: "The admissibility of uncharged misconduct evidence is the single most important issue in contemporary criminal evidence law. The issue has figured importantly in several of the most celebrated criminal trials of our time". The introduction starts by describing a hypothetical case in which: "The accused is charged with homicide. The indictment alleges that the accused committed the murder in early 1990. During the government's case-in-chief at trial, the prosecutor calls a witness. The witness begins describing a killing that the accused supposedly committed in 1989. The defense strenuously objects that the witness's testimony is 'nothing more than blatantly inadmissible evidence of the accused's general bad character'. However, at sidebar the prosecutor makes an offer of proof that the 1989 killing was perpetrated with 'exactly the same modus operandi as the 1990 murder'. Given this state of the record, how should the trial judge rule on the defense objection?" (Imwinkelried, ibid.).

Federal Rule of Evidence 404(b), "which is virtually identical to Military Rule 404(b)" (the paper was published in the American *Military Law Review*), "forbids the judge from admitting the evidence as circumstantial proof of the accused's conduct on the alleged occasion in 1990. [...] Thus, the prosecutor cannot offer the witness's testimony about the 1989 incident to prove the accused's disposition toward murder and, in turn, use the accused's antisocial disposition as evidence that the accused committed the alleged 1990 murder". Yet, the judge is permitted "to admit the evidence when it is relevant on a noncharacter theory", as "uncharged misconduct evidence 'may, however, be admissible for other purposes, such as proof of motive, opportunity, intent, preparation, plan, knowledge, identity, or absence of mistake or accident'. In our hypothetical case, the trial judge could allow the prosecutor to introduce the 1989 incident to establish the accused's identity as the perpetrator of the 1990 killing. If the two killings were committed with the identical, unique modus operandi, the uncharged incident is logically relevant to prove the accused's identity as the perpetrator of the charged crime without relying on a forbidden character inference. Hence, the judge could properly admit the testimony with a limiting instruction identifying the permissible and impermissible uses of the evidence" (Imwinkelried, ibid.).

"Unless the judge clearly explains the law governing stipulations, a juror might suspect that any accused who knew enough about the crime to stipulate to the *mens rea* must have been involved personally in the crime. [...] When the question is the existence of the *mens rea*, the prosecutor ordinarily has a much more compelling need to resort to probative uncharged misconduct evidence. [...] The character evidence prohibition is violated when we permit a prosecutor to rely on the theory depicted in [Imwinkelried's] Figure 2 to justify the admissibility for uncharged misconduct evidence. [...] The courts should admit uncharged misconduct evidence under the doctrine to prove *mens rea* only when the prosecutor can make persuasive showings that each uncharged incident is similar to the charged offense and that the accused has been involved in such incidents more frequently than the typical person. [...]" (Imwinkelried, ibid., quoted the way it is excerpted in the the summary).

Imwinkelried's (1990) stated purpose in his paper "is to describe and critique [...] two lines of authority. The first section of the article discusses one line, namely, the case law advancing the proposition that the first sentence in Rule 404(b) [namely: 'Evidence of other crimes, wrongs, or acts is not admissible to prove the character of a person in order to show action in conformity therewith'] is automatically inapplicable whenever the prosecutor offers uncharged misconduct to support an ultimate inference of mental intent rather than physical conduct. The next section of the article analyses the second line of authority. That line includes the decisions urging that under the doctrine of objective chances, the prosecutor routinely can offer uncharged misconduct on a non-character theory to prove intent. Both lines of authority are spurious, and both represent grave threats to the continued viability of the character evidence prohibition".

Double-counting the evidence If the same item of evidence is then used again to make the evidence weightier, this is an example fo double-counting (Robertson & Vignaux, 1995, section 6.2, p. 95):

> Each piece of evidence must be considered only once in relation to each issue, otherwise its effect is unjustifiably doubled. However, this does not mean that once an intem of evidence has been used by one decision-maker for one purpose it cannot be used by another decision-maker for another purpose. Thus, the fact that the police have used an item of evidence to identify a suspect does not mean that the court cannot use it to determine guilt.

If a defendant is treated as though his or her guilt were likelier, for the very fact that this suspect is being tried, this is an example of the evidence being double-counted (ibid.):

> Of course, the court must not use the fact that the accused is in the dock as evidence of guilt and then also consider the evidence produced, since to do so would be to double-count the evidence which led to the arrest and which is also used in court. Wigmore cautioned jurors "to put away from their minds all the suspicion that arises from the arrest. the indictment and the arraignment".

This does not mean that the evidence on which the arrest was made, or on which this suspect was identified and retained in the first place, should be given a lesser weight, in order to compensate (ibid.):

> Fear of double-counting evidence has misled some about the weight of the evidence which caused the suspect to come under suspicion. A man might be stopped in the street because he is wearing a bloodstained shirt and we are now considering the value of the evidence of the shirt. It has been suggested that because this was the reason

for selecting this particular suspect we should change the way the evidence should be thought about, that it is less useful than if the suspect was arrested on the basis of other evidence.

This is not correct. The power of the evidence is still determined by the ratio of the two probabilities of the accused having a bloodstained shirt if guilty and if not guilty. It is just that there happens to be less evidence in one case than the other. When the suspect is stopped because of a bloodstained shirt there may be no other evidence. When the suspect is arrested on the basis of other evidence and then found to have a bloodstained shirt, the likelihood ratio for the bloodstained shirt is to be combined with a prior which has already been raised by the other evidence. Once again the power of an item of evidence is being confused with the strength of the evidence as a whole.

Doxastic Of or pertaining to belief.

Doxastic attitude An attitude of holding some belief.

Doxastic logic A modal logic of belief. In doxastic logic (or *logic of belief*), belief is treated as a modal operator. A doxastic logic uses Bx to mean "It is believed that x is the case." Raymond Smullyan (1986) defined several types of reasoners.[12] An *accurate reasoner* never believes any false proposition (modal axiom **T**). An *inaccurate reasoner* believes at least one false proposition. A *conceited reasoner* believes his or her beliefs are never inaccurate. A conceited reasoner will necessarily lapse into an inaccuracy. A *consistent reasoner* never simultaneously believes a proposition and its negation (modal axiom **D**). A *normal reasoner* is one who, while believing p, also *believes* he or she believes p (modal axiom **4**). A *peculiar reasoner* believes proposition p while also believing he or she does not believe p. A peculiar reasoner is necessarily inaccurate but not necessarily inconsistent. It can be shown that a conceited reasoner is peculiar. The converse of a normal reasoner is a *stable reasoner.* If a stable reasoner ever believes that that he or she believes p, then he or she really believes p. A *modest reasoner* never believes B$p{\to}p$ (that is, that believing p entails that p is true), unless he or she believes p. A *timid reasoner* does not believe p (being afraid, as though, to believe p) if he or she believes that believing p entails believing something false. A *queer reasoner* is of type G and believes he or she is inconsistent, but is wrong in this belief. A *type G reasoner* is a reasoner of type 4 (see below) who believes he or she is modest.

According to Löb's Theorem, any reflexive reasoner of type 4 is modest. If a consistent reflexive reasoner of type 4 believes that he or she is stable, then he or she will become unstable: she will become inconsistent. A reasoner is of type 4 if he or she is of type 3 and also believes he or she is normal. A reasoner is of type 3 if he or she is a normal reasoner of type 2. A reasoner is of type 2 if he or she is of type 1, and if for every p and q he or she (correctly) believes: "If I should ever believe both p and $p{\to}q$ (p implies q), then I will believe q." A type 1 reasoner has a complete knowledge of propositional logic: he or she sooner or later believes every tautology, i.e., any proposition provable by truth

---

[12] This was summarised in http://en.wikipedia.org/wiki/Doxastic_logic (to which we are indebted for the concepts in this entry).

tables (modal axiom **N**). If a type 1 reasoner ever believes p and believes $p \rightarrow q$ (p implies q) then he or she will eventually believe q (modal axiom **K**).

A *type 1* reasoner* is somewhat more self-aware that a type 1 reasoner. In fact, a type 1* reasoner believes all tautologies; his or her set of beliefs (past, present and future) is logically closed under *modus ponens*,[13] and for any propositions p and q, if he or she believes $p \rightarrow q$, then he or she will believe that if he or she believes p then he or she will believe q.

Dynamic uncertain inference Snow and Belis (2002) analysed "a celebrated French murder investigation" (p. 397), namely, the case of which Omar Raddad was convicted in Nice, in 1994, and then pardoned, the conviction being very controversial (the victim's body was found with, near it, a sentence accusing Raddad written on the floor, scrawled in the victim's blood). Snow and Belis (2002) "apply ideas about credibility judgments structured by graphs to the problem of dynamic uncertain inference. By *dynamic*, we mean that assessments of credibility change over time without foreknowledge as to the types of evidence that might be seen or the arguments that the [crime] analyst might entertain over time" (ibid., p. 397), in contrast with such "kind of belief change that occurs" when the possible outcomes of experiments "are typically known before one learns the actual outcomes" (ibid., pp. 397–398).

ECHO A computer tool, based on artificial neural networks, for abductive reasoning, developed by Paul Thagard and first applied to the modelling of reasoning on the evidence in a criminal case in Thagard (1989). See Section 2.2.1.

EMBRACE A decision support system for Australia's Refugee Review Tribunal.

Entanglement A concept expressing an undercutting move in argumentation, in Verheij's (1999, 2003) *ArguMed* computer tool for visualising arguments (see Section 3.7). It was described by Verheij (1999, 2003). In the words of Walton et al. (2008, p. 398):

> In ArguMed, undercutting moves, like asking a critical question, are modelled by a concept called entanglement. The question, or other rebuttal, attacks the inferential link between the premises and conclusion of the original argument, and thereby requires the retraction of the original conclusion. On a diagram, entanglement is representated as a line that meets another line at a junction marked by an X.

Entrapment Such circumstances of obtainment of evidence that the perpetrator was deceived, by being allowed or even enabled or incited to commit an offence, with law enforcement personnel present or even participating.[14] Osborne (1997, p. 298) remarked that in England, some cases

> clearly established that, even when policemen acting in plain clothes and participating in a crime go too far and incite criminals to commit offences which would otherwise not have been committed, the law of evidence will not be used to discipline the police.

---

[13] In logic, modus ponens states that from p being true and $p \rightarrow q$, we can deduce that q is true. As to $p \rightarrow q$, this is a *rule* (also called *clause*) such that "If p is true, then q is true"; q is a *logical consequence* of p.

[14] See in the notes of Section 4.5.2.1 in this book.

> There is no defence of "entrapment" known to English law and the law of evidence could not be used to create such a defence by the device of excluding otherwise admissible evidence. Where police had gone too far, the question of their misconduct will be dealt with in police disciplinary proceedings; but insofar the accused was concerned, entrapment would only be relevant to mitigate the sentence imposed, not to the question of admissibility.

Epistemic paternalism According to philosopher of knowledge Alvin Goldman (1991), the attitude by which the rules of evidence prescribe that the jurors will not be provided with some of the evidence. See Section 4.3.2.2.

Evidence-based crime prevention Crime prevention policy and practice as ideally being based on scientific evidence from criminology within the social sciences, rather than the crime policy agenda being driven by political ideology and anecdotal evidence (Farrington, Mackenzie, Sherman, & Welsh, 2006). *Evidence* in the phrase under consideration is not to be understood as *legal evidence.*[15]

Evidence discourse Presenting or discussing the evidence, and in particular legal evidence, especially from the viewpoint of discourse analysis. Other disciplinary viewpoints are possible. In an article in a law journal, a scholar from the University of Bristol, Donald Nicolson (1994), discussed epistemology and politics in mainstream evidence discourse, from the viewpoint of critical legal theory, "in relation to three core concepts: truth, reason and justice" (ibid., p. 726). "The main contention of this article is that, given both its intellectual ancestry and political function, mainstream discourse of evidence can best be understood as a form of positivism. This 'fact positivism' is to the study and practice of fact-finding what legal positivism is to the study and practice of law. Both encourage the view that the task of lawyers and adjudicators is neutral and value-free. Both focus attention on logic, whether of rules or of proof, and away from the inherently political and partial nature of law and facts" (ibid.).

Evidence, theory of juridical Conventional, vs. the one advocated by Allen (1994), whose "theory of juridical evidence is designed to replace the conventional theory – that the necessary and sufficient conditions of evidence are provided by the rules of evidence – with the thesis that evidence is the result of the interaction of the intelligence and knowledge of the fact finder with the sum of the observations generated during trial. If the conventional theory is true, the rules of evidence should provide a complex and relatively thorough statement of the grounds for the admission of evidence. They do not", as "The general rules of relevancy provide virtually no comprehensible criteria for admission and exclusion", whereas Allen's own theory of juridical evidence provides a set of necessary and sufficient conditions for admissibility (Allen, 1994, p. 630).

Evidence, law of The set of rules that regulate which evidence should be admissible in court. The following is quoted from my own discussion (Nissan, 2001c) of Twining (1997):

---

[15] Of course, evidence matters for various disciplines. For example, in the paper collection *Evidence*, edited by Bell, Swenson-Wright, and Tybjerg (2008), there are chapters on evidence in law, history, or science.

William L. Twining's 'Freedom of proof and the reform of criminal evidence', relevant for common law, is quite valuable because of the depth vision afforded by the author's charting recent and broader trends of legal theory in Anglophone countries. To Twining, the critics of the common law of evidence, recommending simplification and reduction in scope of its rule, "have won the argument, albeit in a slow and piecemeal fashion. One result is, as I have argued elsewhere, that the common law of evidence is much narrower in scope and of much less practical importance than the discourse of commentators, educators and practitioners has typically suggested" (441). A second trend, "which has proceeded much further in England" than in the U.S. (442), "has been the disaggregation of 'The Law of Evidence' into several bodies of law: Criminal Evidence, Civil Evidence and, increasingly, rules of evidence in tribunals, arbitration and other fora are treated as distinct" (442). "A further result of this trend has been a growing recognition that problems of proof, information handling, and 'evidence' arise at all stages of legal processes" (443). [...] In *Preliminary Treatise of Evidence at Common Law* (1898), "a Harvard scholar, James Bradley Thayer, advanced an interpretation of the law of evidence which has been accepted by most commentators as the classic statement of the modern common law" (Twining: 450), and based on two principles (ibid., from Thayer: 530): "That nothing is to be received which is not logically probative of some matter requiring to be proved" (the exclusionary principle), and: "That everything which is thus probative should come in, unless a clear ground of policy or law excludes it" (the inclusionary principle). In Wigmore's and others' reception, rules excluding or restricting the use of admitted evidence are either intended to promote rectitude of decision (avoiding unreliability or alleged prejudicial effect), these being Wigmore's "rules of auxiliary probative policy"; or, instead – these being exclusionary "rules of extrinsic policy" – they "give priority to other values over rectitude of decision" (Twining: 450). As per Twining's "interpretation, the Thayerite view is that the common law of evidence is a disparate series of exceptions to a principle of free proof" (Twining: 453), it being "broadly true that surviving English law of evidence conforms to the Thayerite model" (463).

Evidence of character See **character evidence**.

Evidence of disposition A category of evidence that fits into the broader category of *evidence of disposition and character*, and consists of evidence that a particular person has a tendency to act, think, or fell in a particular way. "Evidence of disposition is in general inadmissible for the prosecution both because it is not necessarily logically relevant to the issue of the accused's guilt of the offence with which he is now charged and also because it is clearly highly prejudicial to the accused for the jury to be told of his previous disposition. The risk is that the average jury will lose sight of everything else in the case apart from the striking revelation of the accused's bad character" (Osborne, 1997, p. 313), and if the defendant has convictions for "crimes in the past that are notoriously impopular with the public", there may "be a tendency in laypersons to wish to punish the accused again for his former crimes whatever his guilt of the present offence" (ibid.). Moreover, "drinking and quarrelling are not per se crimes" (ibid.), yet they are disposition, and using such traits of the accused in court is not admissible: in England, "evidence of the misconduct of the accused on another occasion *may not be given if its only relevance* is to show a general disposition towards wrongdoing or even a general disposition to commit the type of crime of which he is now accused" (ibid.). "The exception to the general rule is the case of so-called 'similar fact' evidence" (ibid.). See **similar fact evidence**. Moreover, an exception to the inadmissibility of evidence of bad character or disposition of the accused in a criminal case, is that the prosecution has the right to cross-examine in order to obtain such evidence, and the right to adduce such evidence, if the defendant has claimed good character. The prosecution has the right of rebuttal.

Evidence of opinion The kind of evidence provided by an *expert witness*, whereas in contrast: "The general rule is that a witness may only testify as to matters *actually observed* by him and he may not give his *opinion* on those matters. The drawing of inference from observed facts is the whole function of the trier of fact, i.e., in a criminal case the jury" (Osborne, 1997, p. 333) in countries where criminal cases are adjudicated at *jury trials* rather than by trained judges at *bench trials*.

Evidence, requirement of total A principle in the philosophy of science. See Section 4.3.2.2. There exist a weak and a strong version:

> (W-RTE) A cognitive agent X should always fix his beliefs or subjective probabilities in accordance with the total evidence in his possession at the time.

> (S-RTE) A cognitive agent X should collect and use all available evidence that can be collected and used (at negligible cost).

There also is a "control" version, formulated but rejected by Alvin Goldman (1991):

> (C-RTE) If agent X is going to make a doxastic decision concerning question Q, and agent Y has control over the evidence that is provided to X, then, from a purely epistemic point of view, Y should make available to X all of the evidence relevant to Q which is (at negligible cost) within Y's control.

In a social or legal context, the latter principle is improper, because harmful experimentation on human, as well as invasion of privacy, are objectionable. *Exclusionary rules of evidence* are another such example that the *requirement of total evidence* does not apply. Goldman calls such aspects of the philosophical discussion knowledge *social epistemics*. See Section 4.3.2.2.

Evidence, theory of "The distinction between the structure of proof and a theory of evidence is simple. The structure of proof determines what must be proven. In the conventional [probabilistic] theory [which Ron Allen attacks] this is elements to a predetermined probability, and in the relative plausibility theory [which Ron Allen approves of] that one story or set of stories is more plausible than its competitors (and in criminal cases that there is no plausible competitor). A theory of evidence indicates how this is done, what counts as evidence and perhaps how it is processed" (Allen, 1994, p. 606).

Evidential burden See **Burden, evidential**.

Evidential computing Another name for *forensic computing*.

Evidential damage doctrine A doctrine advocated by Ariel Porat and Alex Stein's *Tort Liability Under Uncertainty* (2001). It proposes to shift the *persuasion burden* (i.e., the *burden of proof*) to the defendant, in such cases that a tort plaintiff cannot adequately prove his or her case (and would currently lose the case) because the defendant's wrongful actions impair the plaintiff's ability to prove the facts underlying the plaintiff's lawsuit for damage (any damage actionable in torts). Such situations that would fall under the evidential damage doctrine, include any action in which the defendant's negligence is established, but causation is indeterminate. For example, toxic exposure, or environmental torts, or such medical malpractice cases in which the doctor was negligent but the patient had a preexisting condition.

Evidentialism In epistemology (the philosophy of knowledge), "a thesis about epistemic justification, it is a thesis about what it takes for one to believe justifiably, or reasonably, in the sense thought to be necessary for knowledge" (Mittag, 2004). Evidentialism is defined by this thesis about *epistemic justification*:

> (EVI) Person *S* is justified in believing proposition *p* at time *t* if and only if *S*'s evidence for *p* at *t* supports believing *p*.

Mittag points out (ibid.): "Particular versions of evidentialism can diverge in virtue of their providing different claims about what sorts of things count as evidence, what it is for one to have evidence, and what it is for one's evidence to support believing a proposition". What is evidence, for evidentialism? Mittag explains:

> Evidence for or against *p* is, roughly, any information relevant to the truth or falsity of *p*. This is why we think that fingerprints and DNA left at the scene of the crime, eye-witness testimony, and someone's whereabouts at the time the crime was committed all count as evidence for or against the hypothesis that the suspect committed the crime. The sort of evidence that interests the evidentialist, however, is not just anything whatsoever that is relevant to the truth of the proposition in question. The evidentialist denies that such facts about mind-independent reality are evidence in the sense relevant to determining justification. According to (EVI) only facts that one *has* are relevant to determining what one is justified in believing, and in order for one to *have* something in the relevant sense, one has to be aware of, to know about, or to, in some sense, "mentally possess" it. The sort of evidence the evidentialist is interested in, therefore, is restricted to mental entities (or, roughly, to mental "information"). In addition, it is only *one's own* mental information that is relevant to determining whether one is justified in believing that *p*. For example, *my* belief that Jones was in Buffalo at the time the crime was committed is not relevant to determining whether *you* are justified in believing that Jones committed the crime.

There exist objections to evidentialism. For example: even "though one once had good evidence for believing, one has since forgotten it. Nevertheless, one may continue to believe justifiably, even without coming to possess any additional evidence. Evidentialism appears unable to account for this" (Mittag, 2004). Of course, "I forgot what the evidence is" would not make a good impression in a courtroom, but *justifying belief* in the philosophy of knowledge does not necessarily has the same standards of evidence one would expect in civil or criminal courts.

Another objection, which is relevant also for the theory of evidence in law, refuses to identify *probability* with *justification* of belief in a given proposition. One's evidence *supporting* a proposition may be modelled by means of some theory of probability, but this is contentious. Mittag explains (ibid.):

A body of evidence, *e*, supports believing some proposition *p* only if *e* makes *p* probable. If we suppose for simplicity that all of the beliefs that constitute *e* are themselves justified, we can say that *e* supports believing *p* if and only if *e* makes *p* probable. However, one might argue that, even with this assumption, one's evidence *e* can make *p* probable without one being justified in believing that *p*. If this is so, the resulting evidentialist thesis is false.

Alvin Goldman, for example, has argued that the possession of reasons that make *p* probable, all things considered, is not sufficient for *p* to be justified (*Epistemology and Cognition*, 89–93). The crux of the case he considers is as follows. Suppose that while investigating a crime a detective has come to know a set of facts. These facts do establish that it is overwhelmingly likely that Jones has committed the crime, but it is only an extremely complex statistical argument that shows this. Perhaps the detective is utterly unable to understand how the evidence he has gathered supports this proposition. In such a case, it seems wrong to say that the detective is justified in believing the proposition, since he does not even have available to him a way of reasoning from the evidence to the conclusion that Jones did it. He has no idea *how* the evidence makes the proposition that Jones did it likely. Thus, the evidentialist thesis, so understood, is false.

The appeal to probability and statistics here is not essential to this sort of objection, so it would be a mistake to focus solely on this feature of the case in attempting to respond. [. . .]

Evidential reasoning A major area within artificial intelligence since the 1970s, as well as a prominent area within legal scholarship, in contrast within AI & Law it only emerged as a conspicuous area since around 2000.

Evidential strength There are quantitative approaches for modelling evidential strength. See **Bolding-Ekelöf degrees of evidential strength**.

EvoFIT A tool for suspect identification, resorting to a genetic algorithm[16] refining a population of facial composites. EvoFIT was developed within the CRIME-VUs project. The team working on EvoFIT is led by Charlie Frowd of the University of Central Lancashire. See Section 8.2.2.4.

Examination or examination in chief Questioning of a witness called by one of the parties at a trial, by the lawyer of the same party. It is followed by cross-examination by the lawyer of the other party, and then possibly by re-examination by the lawyer of the party that called the given witness. Moreover, also a judge can ask questions. More in general, *examination* (as opposed to *examination in chief*) refers to the questioning in court, at any stage, of the parties to a trial, or of their witnesses, by any qualified questioner (a lawyer of the some party or of the other party, or a judge, or the other party if he represents himself without a lawyer).

It is important not to confuse examination in court, with questioning by the police during investigation. Legal proceedings only start once the investigation stage ends: once a suspect is charged, the police can no longer question him or her. *Post-charge questioning* (on the part of police investigators) of terrorism suspects, possibly extended to other categories of criminals, was considered by the British government in November 2007, drawing criticism from civil liberties groups.

---

[16] Genetic algorithms are the subject of Section 6.1.16.1 in this book.

During investigation, questioning seeks to uncover information. This is not the case in court. Both when a party is examined in court by his own lawyer, and when the other party is cross-examined, in practice the purpose of the questioning is *not* to discover new information (which lawyers dread in court, as it is a risk), but rather to cause the examinee to reply in such a manner that would diminish the prospects of the success of the party against whom the questioning lawyer is pitted. Only when it is a judge who is asking questions, the questioning is genuine, i.e., seeking information not previously known to the questioner. Hickey (1993) discussed presupposition under cross-examination.

The following anecdote was related by American legal scholar Roger Park during a talk he gave in Amsterdam in December 1999. During the 19th century, a lawyer at a trial hoped to expose the bad character of the man he was questioning (see **character evidence**.). He asked him whether he had ever been in prison. The man replied that he had. Then the lawyer asked him about the circumstances of this happening. The man explained that he had been made a prisoner by the Indians (Native Americans). The effect was opposite to that intended by the lawyer: given the worldview of both lay and trained judges in the United States in the 19th century, the implication was that the examinee was of good character, a hero. This illustrates the dangers, for a lawyer and the party he or she represents, if the questions are such that information not previously known to the lawyer emerges. Importantly, persons being questioned in court must stick to giving answers without digressing. This is a major constraint, and therefore the lawyer examining the party he represents or that party's witnesses, has the duty to skilfully ask such questions that would enable all those important facts to emerge that would enable the lawyer to construct an effective argumentation. Jackson (1994, p. 70) pointed out:

> Consider, for a moment, the very basic process of courtroom examination. Legal theory tells us that the barrister is not giving evidence; he or she is merely asking questions. The evidence is given entirely by the witness. But both linguistic analysis and the philosophy of language (specifically, the theory of speech acts) show that this is an unrealistic account. Grammatically, no doubt, the barristers are asking questions, not making statements. But a question, from the viewpoint of speech act analysis, is an act requesting new information. It is commonly (though not universally) so used at the investigation stage. But the elicitation of new (to him/her) information is precisely what the barrister is *not* seeking to do. It is a commonplace in the training of barristers that they should never ask a question to which they do not already know the answer – more accurately, to which they do not think they know what the witness's answer will be. So questioning by the barrister has a quite different function, the function of presenting an argument, engaging in a battle, sometimes even making claims of fact.

Jackson then discusses "each of these three functions" (ibid.). Take asserting facts: "A barrister who made straightforward factual claims, in the grammatical form of assertions, would readily be pulled up short" [by the judge] (ibid., p. 71). Therefore, assertions are made "[a]ssuredly not up front", but "e.g. through the presuppositions of questions". "Of course, the barrister is not on the stand, giving evidence on oath. But it is precisely because his factual statements have *not* thereby been problematised that they become, when uttered, all the

more persuasive" (ibid.). "Not one of these techniques I have briefly described –
Socratic questioning (constructing a narrative argument); engagement in battle
(destroying the witness rather than the story); stating facts (by presupposition) –
is regarded as unprofessional": quite on the contrary. "[C]riminal investigators
should not be inhibited from what they see as the legal constraints on what can
be said in court from pursuing a full narrative or holistic account", as that is what
it takes to persuade the court, and that without incurring in "the shyster lawyer
syndrome" by which an unscrupulous lawyer is preferable to a respectable one
(ibid., p. 71). Characterizations are involved, e.g. as hostile examinations by a
barrister "seek to evoke stereotypes of respondents, not simply responses" (ibid.,
p. 70). It is still Jackson who states (ibid., pp. 70–71):

> I wish here to make a distinction between cross-examination which is designed to
> destroy the story, and cross-examination which is designed to destroy the witness. It
> is the latter with which I am concerned. It may be illustrated through the "Don't know"
> pattern. The barrister may ask the witness a series of questions, to which s/he antici-
> pates that the witness does not know the answer. These questions may relate to matters
> of quite marginal relevance. But the repetition of "Don't know" by the witness in respect
> of even marginal matters will create, and is designed to create, in the minds of the jury
> an image of a "Don't know" witness. It is an example of a simple rhetorical technique,
> *pars pro toto* – which evokes one of the basic narrative assumptions of everyday life: we
> do not rely upon what is said by people who appear not to know what they are talking
> about. Trite, maybe. Illogical, certainly. But immensely powerful.

Here is an example of *pars pro toto* negatively affecting a person's perceived
credibility, in the television appearance of that person as being a guest, or "victim" (as guests at broadcasts are called in the slang of the trade). "Believing
himself off screen, the victim keeps his head still, but surreptitiously swivels his
eyes – perhaps for a glimpse of the audience, or the clock, or for a peep at the
monitor. Immediately, by chance or by malicious design, the camera switches
to him and he looks shifty, cunning and wicked" (Janner, 1984, p. 147). This is
because of a stereotype about swivelling eyes. Viewers are made to see the "victim" swivelling his eyes, that precise moment being highlighted, yet in the stream
of events this may have been innocent and unimportant, rather than evidence
about his truthfulness when making a specific statement, or about his character
in general.

Exchange principle (Locard's) Anyone or anything entering a crime scene takes
something of the scene with them, and leaves something of themselves behind
when they depart.

Exclusionary principle In the American law of evidence, according to a formulation originally proposed by James Bradley Thayer, the principle "That nothing
is to be received which is not logically probative of some matter requiring to be
proved". See also **inclusionary principle**.

Exclusionary rules Typically in the U.S. law of evidence: rules about which kinds
of evidence must be excluded and not heard in court. As opposed to *admissionary
rules*. See **(rules of) extrinsic policy** and **(rules of) auxiliary probative policy**,
i.e., kinds of exclusionary rules.

Some kinds of evidence are excluded as a matter of policy. Sometimes, for reasons of policy, the law of some given jurisdiction may choose to disregard evidence that by common sense would prove adultery. By the law of England and Wales, until Parliament reformed family law in 1949, this was the case of evidence that could prove adultery because of lack of access of the husband, if a child was nevertheless born. Prior to 1949, such evidence was not admissible.

Sir Douglas Hogg, in his role as barrister in *Russell v. Russell* in 1924 (he had ceased to be Attorney-general earlier that year), had already tried to obtain admissibility for such evidence. "The question for the House of Lords was whether evidence of non-access might be given in divorce proceedings by one spouse with the result of bastardizing a child of the marriage. The answer was of great importance, not only to the parties to the suit, the sole evidence of the wife's adultery being the testimony of the husband that he did not have access to his wife at any time when the child could have been conceived, but also to all those who were interested in the proceedings in the Divorce Court, either as possible parties or as practitioners" (Heuston, 1964, p. 458).

The House of Lords decided the case ruled such evidence inadmissible: it "held that on grounds of decency and public policy the law prohibited the introduction of such evidence." (ibid.). Hogg had admitted that the evidence would be inadmissible in a legitimacy case, but "Hogg's argument was that the rule prohibiting the introduction of such evidence had never been applied to a case in which the object of the suit was to dissolve the bond of marriage on the ground of adultery, it only applied where there was a marriage in existence and the legitimacy of a child born in wedlock was in question" (ibid.). Hogg argued that "Where the issue is adultery the birth of a child is mere accident" (quoted ibid.). "This ingenious argument was rejected by the majority of the House, Lord Finlay saying: 'To what an extraordinary state would the admission of this evidence in the present case reduce the law of England! The infant may be illegitimate for the purpose of proving adultery; but legitimate for the purpose of succeeding to property or a title!'" (ibid.). Writing in an American journal on legal evidence, Hans Nijboer (2008) provided comparative comments on current issues in evidence and procedure from a Continental perspective, as have emerged during the 2000s. He

> finds that while legal scholars are increasingly communicating with legal scholars in other countries and scientists from other fields, there is a simultaneous counter-tendency toward adoption of crime-specific rules of substantive law and evidentiary measures for specific kinds of crime (such as protection of witnesses in rape cases, where the protection complicates the fact-findings process). He concludes from this that there is a tension between greater generality in regard to the first two dimensions and increasing specificity in regard to the third.

Expert evidence Evidence as supplied by an expert witness. The expert's *expert opinion* is part of the evidence in a case.

Expert opinion, Appeal to In argumentation studies, Walton's (1997) *Appeal to Expert Opinion* offered (ibid., pp. 211–225) an argumentation scheme for "Argument for Expert Opinion", then reproduced in Walton et al. (2008, pp. 381–382). Its major premise is: "Source E is an expert in subject domain S containing proposition A." The minor premise is: "E asserts that proposition A is true (false)." The conclusion is: "A is true (false)." Walton accompanied this with critical questions to be asked, and these come in different categories: **expertise question, field questions, opinion questions, trustworthiness questions, consistency questions**, and **backup evidence questions** (q.v.).

Expert witness A witness called to give testimony in court not because of having been involved in the facts of the case being tried, but because of his or her professional expertise in one of the forensic sciences, bearing on the evaluation of specific elements. Cf. s.v. *Witness vs. expert testimonies*. An expert witness is called to provide *evidence of opinion*.

"[T]he seminal 1993 United States Supreme Court decision *Daubert v. Merrell Dow Pharms.*[17] [is] now widely described as the most important expert evidence decision ever written by the Supreme Court" (Cole 2009, p. 111). "Broadly speaking, *Daubert* [...] might be said to concern 'the problem of expertise'" (*ibid.*, p. 112) namely (*ibid.*):

> Given that courts have long allowed expert witnesses to testify—and given the increasing use of such experts—how are courts to evaluate the testimony of proffered "experts"? Ought anyone who claims the mantle of expertise be permitted to testify in that guise? Or, should courts police claims to the title of "expert" by permitting only those experts deemed legitimate to testify? American courts have long tended toward the latter view; *Daubert* made this commitment (in the federal courts and in the many jurisdictions that subsequently adopted *Daubert* or *Daubert*-like rules) explicit. But, this preference only generates another philosophical dilemma: how are courts supposed to adjudicate claims to expertise when many, if not all, of those claims by their very nature are so technical that legally-trained judges cannot reasonably be expected to be competent to sit in judgment upon them? In other words, the law faces a specific instance of the question asked by the philosophical field known as "epistemology": how does one certify knowledge as legitimate?

In Britain, not always an expert witness has to appear in court in person, and sometimes it is enough for the expert to provide a report. Nevertheless, typically an expert witness must be ready to be cross-examined and to defend the credibility of his or her opinion on the matter at hand, and his or her professional credibility. An evidently biased expert witness would impress the court unfavourably. Like lawyers, expert witnesses, too, sometimes have a poor image: the lawyer being perceived to be a "shyster", and the expert witness – a "hired gun".

A philosopher, Ghita Holmström-Hintikka (2001), applied to legal investigation, and in particular to *expert witnesses* giving testimony and being interrogated in court, the Interrogative Model for Truth-seeking that had been developed by Jaakko Hintikka for use in the philosophy of science. A previous paper of hers (Holmström-Hintikka, 1995), about expert witnesses, appeared in the journal *Argumentation*.

---

[17] *Daubert v. Merrell Dow Pharms., Inc.*, 509 U.S. 579 (1993).

Bond, Solon, and Harper (1999) is a practical guide for expert witnesses. Carol Jones (1994) is concerned with expert evidence in Britain. Chris Pamplin, the editor of the *UK Register of Expert Witnesses* (http://www.jspubs.com), "analyse[d] the results of a major survey of the expert witness marketplace" and among the other things, remarked (Pamplin, 2007a, pp. 1480–1481):

> Another change over the years that many experts will find more welcome is the reduction in the number of cases for which they are required to give their evidence in court. It is now altogether exceptional for experts to have to appear in court in "fast-track" cases, and it is becoming less and less likely in those on the "multi-track". In 1997 we recorded that the average frequency of court appearances was five times a year; some four years later this had dropped to 3.8; it now stands at 3.1.

If this is convenient for the expert witnesses (their worst-case scenario is being cross-examined in court and leaving the court with their reputation in shatters), it must be said that justice may be the loser, in the interest of efficiency, if expert witnesses are not challenged in court every time that they deserve to. The "oracular" expert witness ought to be a nightmare for justice. Yet, case management requires that there will be a limit on how much evidence is to be obtained. In Pamplin's words (2007b, p. 1488):

> Limiting the amount and scope of expert evidence has long been one of the functions of the case management procedures of the civil courts. The time and expense involved in the provision of expert evidence means that the courts must have regard to the proportionality of any request. Indeed, the court should refuse permission where reasons for the request are viewed as frivolous.
>
> However, given that the need for additional evidence is sometimes critical to the court's ability to make an informed decision, and that the expert evidence itself is often of a highly technical nature, two questions arise:
>
> * How should the courts deal with such requests?
> * How much influence should the experts or the parties have upon the court's decision?
>
> If an expert feels that there is insufficient evidence before the court to prove or disprove a case, does the expert have discretion to request that further tests be carried out? If so, what is the expert's role in that evidence-gathering process? These were questions considered recently by the Family Court. [In *Re M (a child)* [2007] EWCA Civ 589, [2007] All ER (D) 257 (May), a case that contrasts with *Re W (a child) (non-accidental injury: expert evidence)* [2007] EWHC 136 (Fam), [2007] All ER (D) 159 (Apr). And also at an employment tribunal: *Howard v Hospital of St Mary of Furness* [2007] All ER (D) 305 (May).]

Expert witnesses do not only intervene in courts. Once instructed by a client, they (e.g., forensic engineers advising about product liability) may advise the client about the strength of their case. The client may renounce litigation, or give in to the plaintiff by settling out of court.

"Selecting the right expert may be crucial in court" (Holland, 2007)."An expert who can guarantee availability during the trial, and who can respond to any additional requests promptly will stand out from the other candidates" (ibid.,

p. 1486). "Ideally solicitors would like the expert to be recommended by a colleague, a barrister or client, as this is the best evidence that the expert is up to the job. Many [London] City firms also have internal databases of experts" (ibid.).

> With a little application, there is much a prospective expert candidate can do to satisfy these criteria. However, the expert should always bear in mind that the expert's role is to provide impartial assistance to the court or tribunal. In addition to the criteria above, another paramount factor is the independence of the expert from the appointing party. If the expert is not perceived to be independent, the judge will not give credit to his evidence and opinions and this could be damaging to the client's case. (ibid., p. 1487).

Moreover, expert testimony may be involved in *alternative dispute resolution*, this being either *arbitration*, or *binding* or *non-binding mediation*. (see **case disposition**.) Baria Ahmed (2007) points out:

> A potential expert in alternative dispute resolution (ADR) may adopt a range of roles: an expert consultant may form part of the advocacy team; a party retained expert may provide an opinion on the instructing party's position; the parties may instruct a neutral expert, appointed through an independent body such as the Royal Institute of British Architects, chosen by the parties jointly or appointed by the mediator or arbitrator; finally, the appointed mediator or arbitrator may themselves be an independent expert in light of their experience in the subject matter of the dispute. In the case of Early Neutral Evaluations and Expert Determinations, the neutral expert is tasked with providing either an "opinion" on the applicable law or a "decision" on the facts. [...] ADR processes, however, permit a non-traditional use of experts. The mediator, for example, may request that the expert makes a presentation of their views with all other participants present, or bring the parties' retained experts together without their respective clients to review findings, or choose to test their opinions in open/closed meetings.

An American legal scholar, Erica Beecher-Monas (2008), argued that during the 2000s, "courts throughout the common law system have taken an increasingly antithetical approach to expert testimony." She contrasted civil cases and criminal cases. In the former, but also

> in criminal DNA identification cases, courts appear to be actively engaged in scrutinizing the scientific testimony that comes before them. Defense attorneys appear to have little difficulty in challenging questionable scientific testimony. Research scientists are brought into the discourse as experts for the parties or the court. Courts are articulating the bases for their admissibility decisions, and these decisions are being reviewed on appeal.

She pointed out that the situation was different in criminal cases other than involving DNA: "In the criminal cases, however, where criminal identification procedures other than DNA are concerned, each of the participants in the legal process has failed." She found that prosecutors were not particular about how credible their expert witnesses were:

> Prosecutors repeatedly present experts whose testimony they have reason to know is (at best) dubious. Defense attorneys fail to bring challenges to the scientific validity of even patently flawed expert testimony. Courts, when challenges do arise, fail to engage in serious gatekeeping. And reviewing courts refuse to find shoddy gatekeeping to be an abuse of discretion. The consequence of this antithetical approach to admissibility, is

that the rational search for truth, in which the adversary system is supposedly engaged, is taken seriously only in civil cases.

So the problem was not only with the prosecutors. She conceded that "the civil courts are busy minutely scrutinising scientific studies proffered as the basis for expert testimony" but in criminal cases other than DNA, in stark contrast, "the criminal courts are admitting into evidence testimony (again, with the exception of DNA) for which those studies have never been done." The critique expressed by Beecher-Monas (2008) is not isolated. The American legal scholar Michael Risinger[18] (2007a) sarcastically gave his paper,[19] concerning the courts admitting expert testimony of dubious value,[20] a title reminding of the atom bomb's fictional enthusiast Dr. Strangelove: D. Michael Risinger, 'Goodbye to All That, Or a Fool's Errand, By One of the Fools: How I Stopped Worrying About Court Responses to Handwriting Identification (And 'Forensic Science' in General) and Learned to Love Misinterpretations of *Kumho Tire v. Carmichael*'.[21] Itiel

---

[18] From the Seton Hall University School of Law, in Newark, New Jersey.

[19] It is followed by an Appendix which is an article in its own right (Risinger, 2007b). Cf., e.g., Risinger et al. (2002). Both of these are concerned with expert testimony in handwriting identification.

[20] Risinger's paper (2007a) is described in its abstract as (among the other things) "a picaresque romp through the author's career, much of which has been spent coming to grips with the realities of forensic science, and the courts' abdication of their role as gatekeepers in judging the reliability of prosecution-proffered expertise." Moreover, "the article illustrates how the lower federal courts have managed to ignore or misinterpret *Kumho Tire v. Carmichael* in such a way as to create a jurisprudence of expertise wholly at odds with the clear mandate of the Supreme Court, often by converting decisions with no precedential status into precedents of breathtaking breadth." Michael Risinger has criticised dubious forensic expertise (especially in handwriting identification) in his articles as early as the 1980s.

[21] Cole (2009), responding to Risinger (2007a), remarked in a footnote: "On a completely irrelevant note: the first part of Professor Risinger's title refers to Robert Graves's memoir *Goodbye to All That*, whose discussion of the experience of being gassed in the First World War indirectly inspired my undergraduate thesis on German preparations for chemical warfare between the two world wars." Let me add that the intertextual reference in the second part title of Risinger's article is to the title of a black comedy film from 1964, on the nuclear scare, in which Peter Sellers played three major roles. It is the film *Dr. Strangelove or: How I Learned to Stop Worrying and Love the Bomb*, commonly known as *Dr. Strangelove*, directed, produced by Stanley Kubrick; the screenplay was jointly written by him with Peter George and Terry Southern. It was based on *Red Alert* by Peter George. Eventually in the plot, on board of an airplane with a damaged radio (so it cannot be recalled), "Aircraft commander Major T. J. 'King' Kong (Slim Pickens) goes to the bomb bay to open the damaged doors manually, straddling a nuclear bomb as he repairs arcing wires overhead. When he effects his electrical patches, the bomb bay doors suddenly open, the bomb releases and Kong rides it to detonation like a rodeo cowboy, whooping and waving his cowboy hat. The H-bomb explodes and [in automated retaliation, the Soviet Union's] Doomsday Device's detonation is inevitable" (quoted from http://en.wikipedia.org/wiki/Dr._Strangelove Also see http://www.filmsite.org/drst.html about the same film). The motif of the man riding a shot bomb like a cowboy apparently was after a real-life episode. The protagonist was Harry DeWolf, a future vice admiral and Chief of Staff of the Royal Canadian Navy. After retiring, he published a memoir under the title 'My Ride on a Torpedo' (DeWolf 1966), which he began by mentioning that when he retired, "a newspaperman commenting on my service career wrote that I had once ridden a torpedo

Dror and colleagues' paper "When emotions get the better of us: The effect of contextual top-down processing on matching fingerprints" (Dror et al., 2005) is a paper in cognitive psychology, applied to how experts perform at matching fingerprints. Dror and Charlton (2006) and Dror, Charlton, and Péron (2006) tried to identify the causes of why experts make identification errors. Dror and Rosenthal (2008) tried to meta-analytically quantify the *reliability* and *biasability* of forensic experts.

Some jurisdictions encourage conferences of experts sitting side by side and giving testimony together: this is the case of Australia's Federal Court (see **hot-tubbing**) sometimes at a **public inquiry** (q.v.) in Britain, which are inquisitorial (see **inquisitorial**, towards the end of that entry).

ExpertCop A piece of software (a geosimulator, combining simulation and a geographic information system) for training police officers in allocating police presence in given urban environments, for the purpose of preventing crime (Furtado & Vasconcelos, 2007). See Section 6.1.6.2.

Expertise question In argumentation studies, Walton's (1997) *Appeal to Expert Opinion* offered (ibid., pp. 211–225) an argumentation scheme for "Argument for Expert Opinion", then reproduced in Walton et al. (2008, pp. 381–382). See s.v. **Expert opinion, Appeal to** above. The expert source is E; the subject domain is S; and A is a proposition about which E claims to be true (or false). The expertise question is: "How credible is E as an expert source?". It is articulated in five detailed subquestions: "What is E's name, job or official capacity, location and employer?"; "What degrees, professional qualifications, or certification by licensing agencies does E hold?"; "Can testimony of peer experts in the same field be given to support E's competence?"; "What is E's record of experience, or other indications of practiced skill in S?"; "What is E's record of peer-reviewed publications or contributions to knowledge in S?".

Extrinsic policy (rules of) A category of rules excluding or restricting the use of admitted evidence. As opposed to *rules of auxiliary probative policy*. In interpretations of the American law of evidence, according to Wigmore's terminology,

---

like a cowboy around the deck of a destroyer" (*ibid.*, p. 167). This was on 2 July 1940, aboard the Canadian destroyer *St. Laurent*. DeWolf was skipper, with the rank of lieutenant commander. A young torpedoman who was painting a torpedo lifted the safety catch and pulled back the firing lever. The torpedo leaped free toward the stern, and in frenzy butted causing damage, and at any moment its safety device could be unwound to arm the dormant warhead, which would then explode on contact. The torpedo "would lurch forward with each motion of the ship. It would lurch forward with each motion of the deck; then, as the deck became level, the torpedo would stop, like a bull in the ring, undecided in which direction to make its next charge" (*ibid.*, p. 170). The torpedo rolled against the guardrails, and DeWolf and another officer tried to hold it there, and his colleague "ran to get a key to turn off the compressed air that was driving the propellers", but the ship rolled, the torpedo rolled away, and DeWolf "straddled it, and grabbed hold of the guardrail" (*ibid.*). "As the torpedo advanced, I resisted as much as I could, while going forward hand over hand along the guardrail with my legs locked on the maverick" (*ibid.*, pp. 170, 172). "These antics, no doubt, led to the story of 'riding the torpedo'" (*ibid.*, p. 172). Two colleagues arrived at the scene, wrestled the torpedo steady, and the air was turned off (*ibid.*).

rules of extrinsic policy are such exclusionary rules that give priority to other values over rectitude of decision. These are rules which are not so much directed at ascertaining the truth, but rather which serve the protection of personal rights and secrets.

Eyewitness testimony Historically, the preferred kind of evidence (e.g., by biblical law it is the only admissible kind of testimony). Othello states this request to Iago: "Give me the ocular proof" (*Othello*, III.iii.365). James Ogden (1992) remarks that this request was echoed (comically, for that matter) in late seventeenth-century plays. Ogden states: "*Othello* was one of the most popular plays after the Restoration; some twenty revivals are recorded. Thomas Rymer [(1692)] noted that 'from all the Tragedies acted on our English Stage, *Othello* is said to bear the Bell away'. To Rymer himself it was 'a Bloody Farce' which 'may be a lesson to Husbands, that before their Jealousie be Tragical, the proofs may be Mathematical'".

One of the major areas in eyewitness testimony is *identification evidence.* Psychological research has shown that eyewitness testimony is fraught with problems, and that it is precisely the most confident witnesses that may be prone to errors.

FacePrints A project and tool of Johnston & Caldwell at New Mexico State University, for assisting a witness to build a facial composite of a criminal suspect. See Section 8.2.2.

Facial reconstruction The forensic reproduction of an individual human's face from skeletal remains. Computer-graphic tools exist which support this task. See Section 8.2.6.

Facticity Law's commitment to relate as validly as possible to occurrences and events outside itself (and which took place in the past), normally requiring various mechanisms of representation based on some sort of truth by correspondence.

Fact positivism As defined by Donald Nicolson (1994), it "is to the study and practice of fact-finding what legal positivism is to the study and practice of law. Both encourage the view that the task of lawyers and adjudicators is neutral and value-free. Both focus attention on logic, whether of rules or of proof, and away from the inherently political and partial nature of law and facts" (ibid., p. 726).

Factfinders Also called *triers of fact.* In a judicial context: the judicial decision-makers who are empowered to give the verdict; i.e., the *jury* (jurors are also called *lay triers of fact*, or *lay factifinders*, or *lay magistrates*, or then *popular judges*, the latter, e.g., at the Assizes in Italy) in a *jury trial*, or the professional judge or judges (also called a *stipendiary magistrate*), in a *bench trial* (a trial with no jury). In a jury trial, before the juror retire to consider their decision, the judge instructs the jury about how to go about the decision-making process. In the United States, instructions to the jury tend to be a standard formula, whereas in England, judges tend to produce an elaborate speech to the jury, highly customized for the case at hand. Also see **Jury**.

Factual truth The past cannot be reproduced or relived. It can only be reconstructed. Moreover, there are factors – such as *rules of extrinsic policy* to exclude use of some kinds of evidence, such rules being intended to privilege some values (e.g., the protection of personal rights) over the *rectitude of decision* as aiming at the factual truth, or even considerations in terms of cost/benefits – that militate for there consciously there being an increased likelihood of a gap between the factual truth, and the *legal truth* that will result from the verdict.

Factum probandum (plural: *facta probanda*) That which is to be demonstrated by means of the *factum probans* (or of several *facta probantes*).

Factum probans (plural: *facta probantes*) Evidence in support of a *factum probandum.*

FADE (Fraud and Abuse Detection Engine) A data mining system developed by the online auction site eBay in order to detect fraud perpetrator at its site (Mena, 2003, p. 254).

False positive At a criminal trial, a false positive is a wrong conviction,[22] whereas a *false negative* is a wrong acquittal. In data mining software tools for the detection of suspicious transactions, a false positive is a false alarm, whereas

---

[22] Already Borchard's book (1932) was concerned with wrongful convictions; it is significant that is was published by Yale University Press. Cf. Leo (2005). http://www.innocenceproject.org/ is a website that documents real life cases of miscarriages of justice. Clive Walker and Keir Starmer's edited book (1999) *Miscarriage of Justice: A Review of Justice in Error* examines the various steps within the criminal justice system which have resulted in the conviction of the innocent, and suggests remedies to avoid such situations in the future. The perspective is especially that of England and Wales. There are two initial chapters in Part I, "The nature of miscarriages of justice", and these are chapter 1, "The Agenda of Miscarriages of Justice", and chapter 2, "Miscarriages of Justice in Principle and Practice", both of them by Clive Walker. Part II, "The Criminal Justice Process in England and Wales and Miscarriages of Justice", comprises chapter 3, "Police Investigative Procedures", by David Dixon; chapter 4, "The Right to Legal Advice", by Andrew Sanders and Lee Bridges; chapter 5, "The Right to Silence", by Keir Starmer and Mitchell Woolf; chapter 6, "Forensic Evidence", by Clive Walker and Russell Stockdale; chapter 7, "Disclosure: Principles, Processes and Politics", by Ben Fitzpatrick; chapter 8, "Public Interest Immunity and Criminal Justice", by Clive Walker with Geoffrey Robertson; chapter 9, "Trial Procedures" by John Jackson; chapter 10, "The Judiciary", by Clive Walker with James Wood; chapter 11, "Post-conviction Procedures", by Nicholas Taylor with Michael Mansfield; chapter 12, "Victims of Miscarriages of Justice", by Nicholas Taylor with James Wood; and chapter 13, "The Role and Impact of Journalism", by Mark Stephens and Peter Hill. This is followed by Part III, "Miscarriages of Justice in Other Jurisdictions", which comprises chapter 14, "Miscarriages of Justice in Northern Ireland", by Brice Dickson; chapter 15, "Miscarriages of Justice in the Republic of Ireland", by Dermot Walsh; chapter 16, "Miscarriages of Justice in Scotland", by Clive Walker; and chapter 17, "The French Pre-trial System" by John Bell. Part IV, "Miscarriages of Justice in Summary", comprises chapter 18, "An Overview", by Helena Kennedy and Keir Starmer. An earlier edition, entitled *Justice in Error*, appeared in 1993. Between the two editions, there had been intervening reforms in England and Wales. The 1999 book, *Miscarriages of Justice*, considers these reforms, and considers whether the concerns expressed earlier have been adequately addressed. The chapters in the 1993 version were: "The criminal justice process in England and Wales and miscarriages of justice", which comprises chapters 3 to 13: "Police Investigative Procedures: Researching the Impact of PACE" by Clive Coleman, David Dixon, and Keith Bottomley; "The Right to Legal Advice" by Andrew Sanders and Lee Bridges; "The Right to Silence" by Fiona McElree and Keir Starmer; "Forensic Evidence" by Russell Stockdale and Clive Walker; "Prosecution Disclosure – Principle, Practice and Justice" by Patrick O'Connor; "Trial Procedures" by John Jackson; "Post-conviction Procedures" by Michael Mansfield and Nicholas Taylor; "The Prevention of Terrorism Acts" by Brice Dickson. Next, Part III, "Miscarriages of Justice in Other Jurisdictions", comprises chapters 14 to 17: "Miscarriages of Justice in the Republic of Ireland" by Dermot Walsh; and "The French Pre-trial System" by John Bell.

a false negative is an undiscovered case. With data mining, Mena remarks (2003, p. 221):

> Often an alert of a suspected crime needs verification by human personnel and may require special processing, such as putting a transaction in a special queue or status. A false positive needs special attention and time, while a false negative may cause further losses. In other words, the costs of both are different. However, in both instances, consideration must be given that doing nothing is the worst possible action and option facing a business, government agency, or law enforcement unit. The cost of doing nothing may, in time, be the most expensive option of all, especially in situations involving the destruction of trust, data, systems, property, and human life.

Field question In argumentation studies, Walton's (1997) *Appeal to Expert Opinion* offered (ibid., pp. 211–225) an argumentation scheme for "Argument for Expert Opinion", then reproduced in Walton et al. (2008, pp. 381–382). See s.v. *Expert opinion, Appeal to* above. The field source is *E*; the subject domain is *S*; and *A* is a proposition about which *E* claims to be true (or false). The expertise question is: "Is *E* an expert in the field that *A* is in?". It is articulated in four detailed subquestions: "Is the field of expertise cited in the appeal [to expert opinion] a genuine area of knowledge, or an area of technical skill that supports a claim to knowledge?"; "If *E* is an expert in a field closely related to the field cited in the appeal, how close is the relationship between the expertise in the two fields?"; "is the issue one where expert knowledge in *any* field is directly relevant to deciding the issue?"; "Is the field of expertise cited an area in which there are changes in techniques or rapid developments in new knowledge, and, if so, is the expert up to date in these developments?".

Final submissions The final speeches to the bench of the lawyers for both parties, before the court decides about the case.

FinCEN (Financial Crimes Enforcement Network) The U.S. Treasury agency set up to detect money laundering. A project for FinCEN, whose goal is to identify money laundering networks, by carrying out network link analysis, was reported about by Goldberg and Wong (1998). Links are created in databases of financial transactions.[23]

Fingerprints The fingerprints of human hands are, relatively to other *biometric* features, more reliable characteristics of an individual person, "because of their immutability and individuality [. . .]. Immutability refers to the permanent and unchanging character of the pattern on each finger from before birth until decomposition after death. Individuality refers to the uniqueness of ridge details across individuals; even our two hands are never quite alike. Fingerprint techniques have the benefit of being a passive, nonintrusive identification system and have the additional advantage to use low-cost standard capturing devices (Espinosa-Duró, 2002)" (Khuwaja, 2006, p. 25). In biometrics, also *palmprints* are used, of the entire palm of a hand (Kumar, Wong, Shen, & Jain, 2003). In the 2000s, a trend

---

[23] See Section 6.1.2.2 and fn. 36 in Chapter 6.

became felt, in scholarship, to question the reliability of fingerprint evidence. See Sections 8.7.2 and 8.7.3.

Fingerprint identification The identification, by specialized forensic experts (*fingerprint experts*), or the identity of an individual whose fingerprints are available. There is a debate as to how many similarities between two prints proves identity beyond almost any doubt. See Sections 8.7.2 and 8.7.3. *Fingerprint identification* is not the same as *fingerprint verification*. Both kinds require *fingerprint recognition*. By analogy with fingerprints of a person's hand being unique identifiers, DNA identification techniques have been called *DNA fingerprinting*. Also in intrusion detection within computer security, metaphorically one speaks of *fingerprints* and *fingeprinting* (Section 6.2.1.12), in relation to attempts to identify an intruder.

Fingerprint compression Digitised fingerprint cards are held, e.g., by the FBI, in massive quantities, so when digitized, image compression is required. Compression, however, should not be such that features necessary for matching would be lost. "Because fingerprint ridges are not necessarily continuous across the impression due to minutiae, ridges endings, or bifurcations, the information needed to determine that one fingerprint matches another resides in the fine details of the minutiae and their relationships. Consequently, these details have to be retained for matching algorithms" (Khuwaja, 2006, p. 25). Compression techniques use, e.g., wavelet packets (Khuwaja, 2004).

Fingerprint matching algorithms Computational algorithms from image processing, that match a given input fingerprints card against either a single stored fingerprints card (in *fingerprint verification*), or a fingerprints database (in *fingerprint identification*). Some fingerprint matching algorithms use neural networks (e.g., Leung, Leung, Lau, & Luk, 1991; Khuwaja, 2006). "One advantage of any neural network, which performs a fingerprint recognition task, is that it will learn its own coarse-grained features; thus, precise locations do not form any part of an input set (Hughes & Green, 1991)" (Khuwaja, 2006, p. 26). See Section 8.7.3.

Fingerprint recognition Such image processing, possibly computational, that fingerprints are analysed, and matched against a pool of fingerprint cards.If the process is computational on digitised images, fingerprint matching algorithms are applied. The purpose may be either *fingerprint identification*, or just *fingerprint verification*. The finer level is *minutiae detection*, as opposed to coarse-grained features such as ridges in a fingerprint image.

Fingerpring scanning An input technique for digitized fingerprint databases, that transforms extant *fingerprint cards* (as used in manual processing and recognition) into digitized images.

Fingerprint sensors Equipment for an input technique for taking a person's fingerprints, by obtaining a digitized fingerprint image directly from that person. Igaki, Eguchi, and Shinzaki (1990) described a *holographic fingerprint sensor.*

Fingerprint verification A person who claims a given identity has his or her fingerprints checked. The outcome is binary: either acceptance, or rejection. This is less processing-intensive than the *fingerprint identification* of suspects, and is more typical of situations when security measures are taken, in order to prevent undue access, i.e., in *fingerprinting for security*, an application for which a *personal authentication system* is used.

FLINTS A software tool for criminal intelligence analysis. It performs *network link analysis*, and developed by Richard Leary, who originally applied it in the West Midlands Police. See Chapter 7.

Foil At an *identity parade* (i.e., a *lineup*), or then in a *photoarray*, any out of several look-alikes, known to be innocent, and who appear alongside the suspect. The eyewitness is made to identify the suspect, but without a bias (such as suggesting that the perpetrator is actually one of those persons). Wells (1993) suggested criteria for minimising *foil bias*. See Section 4.5.2.3.

Forensic computing A discipline that provides techniques and strategies for *computer investigations*, in response to *computer crime*. Also known as *evidential computing*, or *computer forensics*. The latter is distinguished from *digital forensics*. See Section 6.2.1.5.

Forensic sciences Various scientific specialties (such as chemistry, areas within medicine, psychology, handwriting analysis, fingerprint analysis, and so forth) when applied for the purposes of crime analysis and fact investigation, or for evaluations for the use of the court. There is a multitude of such specialties, with an increasing role in court. Sometimes globally referred to as in the singular: *forensic science*.

Forensic test A test applying any of the forensic sciences.

Free proof Historically in Continental Europe (in the Romanist tradition), *free proof* – in German *frie Beweiswurdigung*, in French *l'intime conviction* – pertains to the evaluation of the evidence, according to a system which replaced the so-called *legal proof* (in Latin *probatio legalis*, in French *preuve legale*, in German *gesezliche Beweistheorie*), and emancipated the judicial evaluation of the evidence from the older law of proof (this also involved the demise of torture as means for obtaining evidence). In Continental Europe, free proof replaced rules of *quantum and weight*; these did not use to be part of the English and American judiciary systems.

In the United States, in the context of Common Law systems from Anglo-Saxon countries), *free proof* or *freedom of proof* (not a term of art in England) historically lent itself to several different usages, but in current discussions in legal scholarship in the U.S.: freedom of triers of facts (i.e., factfinders, judicial decision-makers) from *exclusionary rules* affecting the evidence. See Twining (1997), Stein (1996).

Generalisations Or *background generalisations*, or *background knowledge*, or *empirical generalisations*: common sense heuristic rules, which apply to a given instance a belief held concerning a pattern, and are resorted to when interpreting the evidence and reconstructing a legal narrative for argumentation in court.

Geoinformatics or geomatics The science and technology of gathering, analysing, interpreting, distributing and using geographic information. It encompasses surveying and mapping, remote sensing, geographic information systems (GIS), and the Global Positioning Systems (GPS).

Guilty plea Typically, in criminal procedure in Anglo-American jurisdictions, the option a defendant is offered, to admit guilt on the part of the defendant at the beginning of a trial, and this typically in connection with a *plea bargain* being offered, with an explicit grant of sentencing concessions (a lighter sentence) for such a plea. In countries in Continental Europe, typically there was no possibility of a guilty pleas, prosecution was obligatory instead of discretionary, and plea bargaining was not envisaged, and was frowned upon.

Handwriting identification A discipline (Morris, 2000) which in the context of the forensic sciences, is part of the domain of *questioned documents evidence* (Levinson, 2000). See Section 6.1.10.

Hearsay Stated imprecisely: verbal statements attributed to others, or rumours. It is not admitted as evidence in court, if the person to whom the statement is ascribed could be called as a witness[24] (See Sections 4.6.1 and 2.5.1). More precisely, the *hearsay rule* (in English and American law) "requires a court to exclude any written or oral statement not made in the course of the proceedings which is offered *as evidence of the correctness of the matter asserted*. A statement which is relevant independently of the real intention of the speaker or the truth of what is stated is not adduced for a testimonial purpose and is therefore outside the scope of the rule" (Pattenden, 1993, p. 138). In fn. 2 ibid., Rosemary Pattenden clarifies "independently of the real of the speaker": "For example, in a contract case a person is contractually bound if he makes an oral statement which a reasonable man would regard as an acceptance of a proffered offer, even though he did not intend by his words to accept the offer". In fn. 3, she explains "or the truth of what is stated": "For example, a statement offered to prove that the declarant could speak or a statement which it is alleged is libellous. The distinction between 'original' and 'testimonial' use of an out-of-court statement is not, however, absolute. The statement 'I am alive' asserts and demonstrates the same thing".

As to the rationale behind the hearsay rule (which she challenges), Pattenden states:

> The basis of the hearsay rule is supposedly the dangers which attach to the use of statements not made by witnesses within the confines of the courtroom where the declarant can be subjected to immediate cross-examination. However, when the question of admitting an out-of-court assertion arises in a criminal trial, no attempt is ever made to measure the real danger which the statement presents to the fact-finding process. Instead the court concentrates on conceptual issues – is the statement being used testimonially? If the answer is yes, does it fall within one of the narrow and inflexible common law

---

[24] Also consider that a broader category is *out-of-court witness statements* (Heaton-Armstrong et al., 2006), which also include statements made to the police by a witness or defendant who also has to give testimony in court.

exceptions to the rule (all of which were created before the end of the nineteenth century) or one of the more recent, but equally limited, statutory exceptions to the rule. If the answer to the second question is no, the evidence is automatically rejected. There is never any question of weighing the probative value of the evidence against the risk of unreliability (Pattenden, ibid., p. 138).

Craig Osborne (1997) remarked: "It is apparent when reading reports of decided cases that courts not always appreciate the existence of a hearsay problem", as "there are also instances of the very existence of any problem at all being overlooked" (ibid., p. 254). "It is by no means the case that words said outside court and repeated in it will amount to hearsay. What matters is whether the statement from the speaker outside court is *tendered to prove the truth of its contents*" (ibid., p. 255). *Express assertions* are excluded by the hearsay rule (ibid.):

> With express assertions there must be an intention to communicate, thus non-verbal behaviour such as nods, gestures, pointing or signs may well amount to an express asssertion when what the person making the sign did is recounted to the court by another witness. As there must however, be some intention to communicate nobody has ever suggested that, say, a footprint, or yawning is subject to the hearsay rule.

Implied assertions are problematic. "This is where the maker of the statement did not intend to assert any particular fact" (ibid., p. 256). "The reason why it has often been suggested that these kind [sic] of statements ought to be admissible as exceptions to the hearsay rule is that there is a smaller risk of untruthfulness with implied assertions. [. . .] The authorities in England are not entirely conclusive" (ibid.).

For the United States, Ron Allen has claimed (2008a, p. 326):

1. The rules of evidence favour admissibility even in the face of legitimate claims of irrelevancy. The standard bearer here is of course the Supreme Court's decision in *Old Chief v. U.S.* [519 U.S. 171 (1997)], but that simply acknowledged the obvious truth of the narrative structure of proof at trial.
2. This narrative structure is enhanced by liberal admission of evidence, and even the rule once claimed as the embodiment of the exclusionary practices of Anglo-American law – the hearsay rule – has morphed into a rule of admission (Allen, 1992). All statements by parties are admissible, for example, no matter when or under what conditions made, as are all present sense impressions and statements of states of mind or physical conditions. Business records and government reports all come in readily, along with 35 or so other categories of admission. If none of the formal exceptions work, the courts may make up ad hoc exceptions to facilitate admission (Federal Rule of Evidence 807). Although there are some technical exclusionary rules, in reality, like hearsay, they often make promises that they do not keep. Another wide ranging example is the character evidence rules which promise exclusion but permit generous admissibility due to provisions such as FRE 404(b).

An expert system dealing with the hearsay rule is the *Hearsay Rule Advisor* (*HRA*). It was developed as an LL.M. project by Susan Blackman (1988), under the supervision of Marilyn MacCrimmon (1989). That expert system "provides advice on whether a statement comes within the definition of hearsay and if so, whether the statement comes within an exception to the general rule excluding hearsay statements" (MacCrimmon, ibid., p. 468). The initial questions the user is asked by this expert system – MacCrimmon explains (ibid., pp. 467–468) –

> classify exceptions based on the context of the trial (whether the declarant is available to testify and the type of trial, civil or criminal). This part of the program eliminates some exceptions as more facts become known. At this time the exceptions included in the program are: dying declarations, declarations against interest, declarations in the course of duty, and business documents (British Columbia only). Hearsay exceptions in the HRA are classified on the basis of four dimensions: EVENT, PERCEIVE, BELIEVE [and] INTEND. First the system searches for an approximate match between the user's facts and the events in the system. Once a match is found, the user is asked questions designed to assess whether the three dimensions of PERCEIVE, BELIEVE and INTEND for a particular exception are satisfied by the user's facts. These questions are tailored to fit the EVENT identified so that the system does not waste time with irrelevant or inapplicable questions. These dimensions fit the story model of Pennington and Hastie with the proviso that I assume that belief states are encompassed by the definition of psychological states as is implicit in [their examples]. Legal liability often turns on whether a person knows, thinks, believes certain things and not simply on whether they are in a particular emotional state.
>
> We begin with the declarant as the principal actor. The action is the making of the statement. The EVENT is defined as the events which initiate the required belief states which initiate the goal of telling the truth. Thus for dying declaration the initiating events are the declarant is wounded, and the declarant is dying. It is assumed that these events initiate the belief that the declarant is saying that initiates the goal of telling the truth. For the exception, declarations in the course of duty, the initiating events are the declarant is performing a duty and others are relying on his or her actions which initiate the belief state that the declarant expects to be discovered if he or she makes an error which in turn initiates the goal of avoiding censure by his or her employer.
>
> The dimensions of PERCEIVE [and] BELIEVE may be related to states of the world which enable the declarant to make a true statement. Circumstances which facilitate accurate perceptions are often required. [. . .] INTEND focuses on the facts of the specific case being considered in order to establish the requisite belief state. [. . .]

It is quite important to understand that different jurisdictions can be expected, generally speaking, to treat hearsay, too, differently. Take the Italian context (Ferrua, 2010, section 19):

> Suppose P gave witness in court concerning what (being crucial for convicting defendant Q) he was told by N, and that the latter, called as witness, is taking advantage of the right to avoid this being a next of kin, or at any rate, that N refuses to reply or does not appear at the hearing, and therefore deliberately avoids being cross-examined. There is no doubt that the guilt of the defendant cannot be proven based on statements that N may have made during the inquiry. But what are we to say concerning what N related to P, who provided indirect testimony?
>
> True, P is not avoiding being cross-examined, but should we allow conviction based on P's testimony, which reproduces verbatim what N's related, arguably amounts to admit it based on N's statements, who always deliberately avoided being cross-examined. The only conceivable way to deny this would be to claim that the "statements" referred to by the criterion of evaluation[25] are only the ones made during the trial, by

---

[25] This is merely a criterion of evaluation ("criterio di valutazione"), not an exclusionary rule ("regola di esclusione probatoria").

strict analogy with what is in force concerning the cross-examination rule [under the Italian jurisdiction].[26]

At any rate, the Court of Cassation in Italy ruled on 4 October 2004 that indirect testimony is only inadmissible ("l'inutilizzabilità della testimonianza indiretta"),[27] as per "articolo 195 commi 3 e 7 c.p.p.", if the primary source is not indicated, or if it was requested by one of the parties that primary source be called as witness, and it was not (except because of death, infirmity, or because the person cannot be found). In particular, the Court of Cassation ruled that indirect testimony is admissible, and has to be considered, in such a case that the primary source resorted to the right not to reply, while being a defendant tried for a related crime.[28]

Hot-tubbing A particular approach to expert witnesses, known by that name especially with reference to a practive at Australia's Federal Court, but also known (although not by that name) from public inquiries in Britain (see s.v. *Inquisitorial*, towards the end of that entry). In a comparative review, Erica Beecher-Monas (2008) explained:

> In Australia, [...], the Federal Court has encouraged (through its court rules) both "hot-tubbing" and joint conferences of experts. In the joint conference court rules, judges attempt to control expert witness partisanship by directing expert witnesses to confer, or to produce a document identifying the matters on which the experts agree and those on which they disagree. Under the "hot-tubbing" rules, experts testify together in court, responding to questions from attorneys and each other, as well as the judge. Judges may also appoint their own witnesses, although they rarely do so in criminal trials.

There is a difference between hot-tubbing and joint conferences of experts, in respect of lawyers' interventions (ibid.):

> "Hot-tubbing" is also known as taking concurrent evidence. In this procedure, the experts for both sides simultaneously take the stand in court and question each other about their opinions on the record. They are also subject to questioning by the court

---

[26] The original text from Ferrua (2010) is concerned with the second part of "art. 111 comma 4 Cost.", and it is as follows: "Supponiamo che *P* abbia testimoniato in giudizio su quanto, decisivo per la colpevolezza dell'imputato *Q*, gli ha confidato *N* e che quest'ultimo, chiamato a deporre, si avvalga della facoltà di astensione come prossimo congiunto o, comunque, rifiuti di rispondere o diserti il dibattimento, sottraendosi così per libera scelta al contraddittorio. Nessun dubbio che la colpevolezza dell'imputato non possa essere provata in base alle dichiarazioni eventualmente rilasciate da *N* nell'indagine preliminare. Ma che dire per quanto raccontato a *P*, che ha deposto come teste indiretto? È vero che *P* non si sottrae al controesame, ma consentire la condanna sulla base della sua testimonianza, dove è testualmente riprodotto il racconto di *N*, non equivale forse a consentirla sulla base delle dichiarazioni di *N* che si è sempre sottratto per libera scelta al contraddittorio? La sola via per rispondere negativamente sarebbe, per l'appunto, di sostenere che le 'dichiarazioni' a cui si richiama il criterio di valutazione siano solo quelle costituite nel processo, in stretta analogia con quanto vale per la regola del contraddittorio."

[27] The notion of *inutilizzabilità*, i.e., *inadmissibility* of criminal evidence, was discussed in an Italian context in Gambini (1997) and in Grifantini (1993, 1999).

[28] An attempt at formalisation of the reasoning about hearsay was made by Tillers & Schum in "Hearsay Logic" (1992).

and the lawyers. Hot-tubbing, in contrast to joint conferences of experts, permits the participation of legal counsel in exchanges among the experts.

Moreover, with *hot-tubbing* the parties have a say concerning procedure (ibid.):

In joint conferences, experts are supposed to work together (with only the experts present) to prepare a document probing areas of agreement and disagreement, to be submitted to the court. In its pristine form, a joint conference will exclude lawyers. In practice, however, there appears to be some flexibility – and the parties may have some ability to modify the joint conference procedure. For example, in one antitrust case, the parties refused to participate in a "hot tub" procedure and agreed to a joint conference only if they could treat the joint conference as mere negotiations, so that any communication or joint report could only be admissible with consent of the parties. If the parties can play such a significant role, it is questionable how far a joint conference can go toward solving the problem of partisan experts.

HUGIN A piece of Belief Net software, using which Neil and Fenton (2000) carried out calculations in order to present probabilistic legal arguments, concerning the **Jury Observation Fallacy** (q.v.).

HYPO A computer system for argumentation, fairly well-known in the discipline of AI & Law (Ashley, 1991). See Section 3.9.1. HYPO "is a case based reasoner developed by Ashley and Rissland at University of Massachusetts at Amherst. It analyses problem situations dealing with trade secrets disputes, retrieves relevant legal cases from its database, and fashions them into reasonable legal arguments. It has turned out to be the benchmark on which other legal case based reasoners have been constructed" (Stranieri & Zeleznikow, 2005a, Glossary).

IBIS An Issue-Based Information System that supports decomposing problems into issues. *QuestMap* (Carr, 2003) is a computer tool for supporting argumentation. It is based on IBIS, mediates discussions, supports collaborative argumentation, and creates information maps, in the context of legal education.

Identikit A system for generating composite faces, for the purposes of assisting a witness to describe the features of a criminal suspect. *Identikit* uses plastic overlays of drawn features. See Section 8.2.2.

Identity parade Also called *line-up*, or *identification parade*. A suspect stands in a line alongside *foils*, i.e., persons known to be innocent and who look alike, and the victim or witness has to identify the suspect. A computerised version is *ID parade discs*, on which video clips from a database appear, along with a video clip showing the suspect. See Section 4.5.2.8. In contrast, it is usually undesirable to have a *dock identification*, when the witness sees at the trial the accused for the first time after the offence. Even for such a case in which there was a parade, being an "identification procedure between crime and trial at which the witness has picked out the accused to assist the police", Osborne (1997, p. 305) raises a problem with *hearsay* (evidence admissibility rules include exclusionary rules which incloude the hearsay rule, as well as the rule against admission of a previous consistent statement):

If the witness confirms at the trial that he has previously picked out the accused, is he not, in effect, testifying as to a prior consistent statement? Moreover the hearsay implications are compounded if some other person is called to confirm that the witness picked out the accused at the identification parade. The point is inadequately analysed and it is far from clear as to whether the courts have acknowledged the hearsay problem at all. See, e.g., *R* v *Osbourne and Virtue* [1973] 1 QB 678 where the witnesses in court could not remember whom they had picked out at an identification parade. A police inspector who had been present was allowed to testify about what had happened at the parade without the court acknowledging the hearsay point (Osborne, ibid.).

It may be that computer tools for use at identity parades may incorporate some function for recording the outcome with a given witness in such a way that would be useful in court, but it may depend on the jurisdiction (e.g., it would be in agreement with the "philosophy" of validating steps in Asaro's *Daedalus* in Italy, as opposed to Anglo-American procedural law). It would be interesting to see whether how the software caters to validation may in turn result in something objectionable. Thereofore, it would be useful to have a legal professional involved in discussions, during the software requirement analysis and design phase.

IFS (Internet Fraud Screen) A data mining tool giving credit-card fraud alerts, developed by CyberSource for Visa U.S.A. for matching fraud transactions. IFS "uses a combination of rule-based modeling and neural-network modeling techniques" (Mena, 2003, p. 271). IFS's "profile scores look at more than a dozen different information items, including the customer's local time and the risk associated with the customer's e-mail host. CyberSource also provides e-retailers with an IFS report that includes risk profile codes, address verification systems (AVS) codes, and other relevant information to help e-merchants calibrate their risk thresholds and score settings. This helps the e-business subscribers to control the level of risk they want to operate under" (ibid.).

Image forensics A branch of forensic science whose goal is the detection of *image tampering*. The tampering is typically done by computer (*digital forgeries*), and the computational methods for detection (*digital image forensics*) belong to image processing within signal processing. See Farid (2008), Popescu and Farid (2007), Johnson (2007). We have discussed such techniques in Section 8.2.5.

Imputation A charge, including a charge possibly implied by a defendant while attacking the credibility of others, and affecting their *character*. (See **character evidence**.). In a section entitled "Imputations on the character of the prosecutor or his witnesses or on the deceased victim of the alleged crime", Osborne (1997, p. 323) explains that before *Selvey* v *DPP* [1970] AC 304, in English law "there was a problem as to whether the accused lost his shield [i.e., its being inadmissible for the prosecution to adduce bad character evidence about him, or to ask such questions during cross-examination that would aim at proving his bad character] by making imputations on prosecution witnesses which were necessary to *develop his defence*, or whether he only lost it if the imputations were *merely to attack* their credibility". For example, it may be that a defendant would need to claim that it actually was "a prosecution witness who actually committed the offence" (ibid.). In *Selvey* v *DPP*, the House of Lords held that prosecution is allowed to cross-examine "the accused as to character where he casts imputations on prosecution witnesses either in order to show their unreliability or where he does so in order to establish his defence" (Osborne, ibid., p. 324), yet with exceptions: "In a rape case the accused can allege consent without losing his shield", "If what is said amounts in reality to no more than a denial of the charge then an accused does not lose his shield", and "There is an unfettered judicial discretion to exclude cross-examination as to character even if strictly permissible but there is no general rule that this discretion should be exercised in favour of the accused even where the nature of his defence necessarily involves his attacking prosecution witnesses" (ibid.). "The difficult question which is for the judge to decide is: 'What is an imputation?' The courts have tried, not always with great success, to draw a distinction between what is merely a *denial* of the charge by the accused in forceful language and what amounts to an imputation" (ibid.). For example, if a defendant claiming that a witness is "a liar", should this be merely treated as a denial of the charge, or is it to be treated as an imputation, because "this may in effect be an allegation of perjury"? (ibid.).

Inclusionary principle In the American law of evidence, according to a formulation originally proposed by James Bradley Thayer, the principle "That everything which is thus probative should come in, unless a clear ground of policy or law excludes it". See also **exclusionary principle**.

Independent Choice Logic (ICL) Poole (2002) applied this formalism to legal argumentation about evidence. The formalism can be viewed as a "first-grade representation of Bayesian belief networks with conditional probability tables represented as first-order rules, or as a [sic] abductive/argument-based logic with probabilities over assumables" (p. 385).

Inductive reasoning "Inductive reasoning is the process of moving from specific cases to general rules. A rule induction system is given examples of a problem where the outcome is known. When it has been given several examples, the rule induction system can create rules that are true from the example cases. The rules can then be used to assess other cases where the outcome is not known" (Stranieri & Zeleznikow, 2005a, Glossary).

Inference The process of deriving conclusions from premises.

Inference engine "An inference engine is that part of an expert or knowledge based system that contains the general (as opposed to specific) problem solving knowledge. The inference engine contains an interpreter that decides how to apply the rules to infer new knowledge and a scheduler that decides the order in which the rules should be applied" (Stranieri & Zeleznikow, 2005a, Glossary).

Inference network "The inference net model is a probabilistic retrieval model; since it uses a probability ranking principle. It computes Pr(I|document), which is the probability that a user's information need is satisfied given a particular document" (Stranieri & Zeleznikow, 2005a, Glossary).

Inquest In Britain: a judicial or official inquiry, usually before a jury, typically in order to identify the causes of a death, in case this is not certified by a physician, or where the possibility of a crime cannot be ruled out a priori. The *Dead Bodies Project* (developed by Jeroen Keppens and others during the 2000s) has been described in Section 8.1.

Inquiry See **investigation**.

Inquisitorial A type of criminal procedure, which is typical of many European countries on the Continent. As opposed to the *adversarial* system, typical of Anglo-American jurisdictions. The adversarial system features a symmetry between the parties, whereas in the inquisitorial system the court is rather structurally aligned with the prosecution *vis-à-vis* the defendant, yet the court is to be convinced and adjudicates. It is of interest to consider how professionals used to the adversarial system perform, when they have to abide by the inquisitorial system. In England and Wales, as well as in Scotland, whereas the adversarial system characterises court proceedings, *public inquiries* are in theory inquisitorial (see **public inquiry**). This is also the case of the *Coroner's court.* Professor Sir Ian Kennedy, who chaired the public inquiry (which lasted two years and nine months, from 1998 until 2001) into the conduct of children's heart surgery at the Bristol Royal Infirmary between 1984 and 1995, and he described in a paper (Kennedy, 2007) his experience in that capacity. In 2005, Parliament passed the Inquiries Act, but the paper is general enough to retain interest even under the new regime of public inquiries (ibid., p. 15). In the interest of openness, information technology (IT) was resorted to (ibid., p. 14):

> The Inquiry needed to be completely open so that everyone could see and hear the same evidence. This was achieved by the use of IT with scanning of all the documents: this came to over 900,000 pages. A "Core Bundle" of relevant documents was prepared as a CD available to all legal representatives.[29] The daily proceedings could be seen at three separate locations as well as Bristol. It was also vital to create a website (this received over 1 million hits during the Inquiry and won a prestigious NHS[30] prize).

The approach was inquisitorial, and therefore (ibid., p. 38):

> In keeping with its inquisitorial approach, the Inquiry made it clear that there were no "parties", no "sides", to advance their particular view of events. Witnesses were called by the Inquiry and were the Inquiry's witnesses. They were there to assist the Inquiry. They were not there to score points in their own favour or against others. Legal representatives initially found these challenging propositions. They were used to taking sides on behalf of a client. But, gradually, they understood.

---

[29] In a section about the use of information technology, Kennedy explained (2007, pp. 41–44): "By scanning all relevant documents into the Inquiry's data-base, it was possible to ensure that the Inquiry, and particularly its legal team, could have access to all the relevant evidence collected at the earliest possible stage, and in a manageable form on computers. The creation of a CD containing the 'Core Bundle' achieved the same effect for both the Panel and the legal representatives of all those involved in the Inquiry. Witnesses' statements, and comments on them, were equally added to the database and were thus accessible to those involved. Once they began, the hearings were effectively 'paper free'. Counsel to the Inquiry, and other legal representatives on the occasions on which they addressed the Inquiry, were simply able to identify the unique code given to each document for it to be transmitted onto the computer screens of the panel, other lawyers and onto the screens available to the public. It was estimated that, by not having to search through shelves of box files to find the relevant document and the[n] pass it around to all, the Inquiry was able to accomplish anything from a quarter to a third more work on an everage day of hearings."

[30] National Health Service.

Its being inquisitorial in a country used to the adversarial system, it is challenging for those conducting the inquiry, as well as to the lawyers (ibid., pp. 37–38):

> It is often said that Public Inquiries are inquisitorial by nature. But the reality often is otherwise. One explanation is that those chairing Inquiries are usually unfamiliar with how to translate the idea into practice. Moreover, since they are very commonly judges, their first instinct is to revert to what is familiar and convert the Inquiry's proceedings into a courtroom. And courtrooms, in England, are not characterized by an inquisitorial approach (with the exception of the Coroner's court). Rather they are characterized by what can be described, perhaps a little provocatively, as a gladiatorial approach. The gladiators are the lawyers, usually counsel. The judge watches and gives the thumbs up, or down, at the end. Lawyers provide a further explanation to why the proceedings, though theoretically inquisitorial, soon take on an inquisitorial quality. This is because lawyers also are familiar with courts and the procedure of courts. It comes as no surprise that they will seek to treat the Inquiry as if it were just another court.

This has also to do with how the process of arriving at the legal truth is conceived of (ibid., p. 38), as the lawyers' attitude during the Inquiry

> also rests on a fundamental premise, particularly of counsel, that there only is one way to discover the truth and that it is through the cut and thrust of examination and cross-examination. Leave aside the fact that we have already seen that the concept of a single "truth" may be self-delusionary, the approach misses the point of what the Inquiry is seeking to do. It is not seeking to paint a picture just in black and white; that something happened and something else did not, that someone did wrong. It does not occupy a binary world of right and wrong, good and bad. What it is trying to do is understand, and understanding rarely comes in black and white. Furthermore, whatever else may emerge from gladiatorial contest, understanding rarely does.

Some lawyers are counsel to the inquiry, whereas some other persons are the legal representatives of groups and organisations involved in the inquiry (ibid., p. 39). The most prominent duty of counsel to the inquiry is "to take witnesses appearing before the Inquiry through their evidence", ensuring that "the Inquiry heard both the witness' account, any challenges to it and their responses to these challenges" (ibid.). Counsel to the Inquiry also organise the material collected by the inquiry. As to legal representatives, what they do during the hearings of an inquiry different from what they would be doing in court. This is because the procedure of the inquiry as defined by Kennedy for the Bristol Public Inquiry does not envisage that it would be the legal representatives who would examine and cross-examine the witnesses: it was up to the counsel to the inquiry to do so (ibid., pp. 39–40). In fact, "there is no *right*, as such, to cross-examination of witness (usually by lawyers) at a Public Inquiry. The Inquiry must, of course, behave fairly at all times" (ibid., p. 40). "The position of the Inquiry was simple. It wanted to hear witnesses telling their stories, rather than have the story filtered through the interventions of their legal representatives, who might seek to gloss over this, or over-emphasise that, out of their perception of what it was good for the Inquiry to hear" (ibid., p. 41).

Also the status of expert witnesses was that of an amicus curiae, called to assist the Inquiry (at a bench trial, especially under the inquisitorial system, it would be to assist the court): "Just like other witnesses, experts also were the

Inquiry's experts. They gave evidence to assist the Inquiry in its task", rather than representing one of the two sides in the adversarial system (ibid., p. 38). "They were advised as to the assistance that the Inquiry needed and gave their evidence accordingly, whether in the hearings, or in the conduct of several analytical studies carried out by the Inquiry" (ibid.). Nevertheless, this being Britain (ibid., pp. 38–39):

> Again, this was unfamiliar territory to legal representatives. They were used to experts appearing for one "side" or another. They urged that the expert should brief them and then they would question a particular witness, or advise the Inquiry, in the light of what they gleaned from the expert's briefing. I indicated that the Inquiry wished to hear from the experts and did not wish to hear their views "second hand", through counsel. I went further, and said that the Inquiry would benefit from experts taking part in the hearings at the same time as other witnesses, so that the Inquiry could test arguments as they were put, and witnesses could refer to experts as peers, sitting alongside them, in discussing areas of technical expertise.

(This is like **hot-tubbing**, q.v., at Australian courts.) Bear in mind that the public inquiry was about a hospital, and whereas some physicians were regular witnesses or were being investigated, some other physicians were called as expert witnesses. Therefore (ibid., p. 39):

> This they did, and the Inquiry would sometimes listen spellbound as expert and witness discussed matters of significant complexity, whether it was the correct response to a particular anatomical anomaly in the heart, or why paediatric intensive care was different from the care of adults, or how a particular statistical conclusion could be arrived at. [...] They made it plain that honest professionals could legitimately differ. [...]

Insecurity governance or insecurity management A branch of information technology concerned with how to respond, on an organisational level, to threats to *computer security.*

Instructing party The client of either a lawyer or an expert consultant (an expert witness). The lawyer or the consultant is *instructed* by the client.

Interesting case In law: "For a first instance decision to be interesting it must: 1) be appealed, or 2) includes a new principle, rule or factor in its ratio decidendi, or 3) exhibits an outcome vastly at odds with other similar cases" (Stranieri & Zeleznikow, 2005a, Glossary). Not the same as **landmark case** (q.v.).

Interesting pattern In knowledge discovery from databases (KDD) and in data mining: "A pattern is interesting if it is a) easily understood by humans, b) valid (with some degree of certainty) on new or test data, c) potentially useful and d) novel. A pattern is also interesting if it validates a hypothesis that the user sought to confirm" (Stranieri & Zeleznikow, 2005a, Glossary).

InvestigAide B&E An expert system (Valcour, 1997) for the Canadian Police, whose purpose was to support the processing and investigation of breaking and entering cases, by assisting in gathering and recording case data, and providing such information as suspect characteristics.

Investigation Actions undertaken, typically by the police, in order to identify criminal suspects, or the extent of criminal activities. In the Unites States, the term *investigation* is used. In Britain, it is *inquiry.*

Itaca A tool, modelled after **Daedalus** (q.v.), for the Court of Cassation in Rome, under contract to Siemens, as per the design of Mr. Justice Carmelo Àsaro (who when a prosecutor in Lucca, developed *Daedalus* single-handedly). See **procedural-support systems**, and Section 4.1.3.

Jury or lay factfinders In some countries, a group of citizens, not trained judges, who adjudicate trials of some categories of crime. In Anglo-Saxon countries, the judge can instruct the jury, but does not participate in the determination of the verdict. In Italy, some cases are heard by a mixed court (first introduced in colonial Libya), of trained judges and jurors, and after the verdict is given, the justification of the verdict must also be given: it is written by a trained judge, who – if outvoted by the jurors – may write a so-called *sentenza suicida*, i.e., a deliberately flawed justification in order to bring about an appeal. In Anglo-Saxon jurisdictions, a *retrial* may be ordered if some stringent conditions are met. Also see **factfinders**.

Jury observation fallacy A claim, so named, against the use of knowledge of prior convictions of a criminal suspect. See **character evidence**. Fenton and Neil (2000) tried to support this claim by making use of Bayesian networks to present probabilistic legal arguments. Adrian Bowyer summarised this stance in a letter published in the latest issue of June 2001 of the *London Review of Books* (*LRB*), a letter immediately signalled in an e-list posting by Mike Redmayne:

> Writing about Labour's proposal in its Criminal Justice White Paper that defendants' past convictions should be revealed to juries, John Upton (LRB, 21 June) fails to mention the Jury Observation Fallacy. According to this, if a jury finds someone not guilty on the evidence presented in court – in other words, without taking previous convictions into account – the fact that this defendant has previous convictions for similar crimes usually makes it more, not less, probable that he or she is indeed innocent of this particular crime. This is because, when a crime is committed, the police quite reasonably go out and feel the collars of those with previous convictions for similar crimes. They therefore tend to fish in a highly non-representative pool, rather than picking suspects from the general population. This tips the probabilities in the defendant's favour to an extent that is not outweighed by the likelihood of a certain fraction of past offenders becoming recidivists. If the defendant is considered innocent on the facts of the case, then his past convictions should be seen as evidence not so much of guilt as of the failures of police procedure.

Mike Redmayne (a legal scholar of the London School of Economics, quite at home with probabilistic modelling) was unconvinced by some of the assumptions made. In a posting discussing Fenton and Neil (2000) at an e-list,[31] he claimed:

> Your conclusion is sensitive to the probability that a defendant will be charged given a previous conviction and no hard evidence. If the probability is less than 1 in 200, the fallacy disappears. One point about this is that there are further screening stages between charge and trial, and even between trial and acquittal (the judge can be asked to certify that there is "a case to answer"). It would be very difficult for a case to get to the jury when (more or less) the only evidence against a defendant is that he has previous convictions for crimes similar to the one with which he's now charged. If there is other

---

[31] bayesian-evidence@vuw.ac.nz

evidence against the defendant, surely that affects your conclusion, because it increases the probability of guilt?

There is also likely to be evidence against a defendant other than a previous conviction because most suspects come to police attention independently of their having previous convictions. They may have been caught in the act, or, very often, reported by a member of the public – e.g. the victim.

A few cases will get to court when there is very little evidence other than the defendant's similar previous convictions. At this point, I wasn't sure quite what you meant by "similar" in your model. Similarity can include more than a crime being of the same legal category. It can include similarities in modus operandi, geographical proximity, and so forth. It is where previous convictions have this sort of similarity (sometimes called "striking similarity") that a case may get to the jury on previous convictions alone. (I also suspect that the police rely on such similarities when deciding which suspects to arrest.) If "similar previous conviction" is expanded in this manner, mightn't previous convictions have more probative value than you allow? These are obviously points about the operational reality of the criminal justice system, and you can't be blamed for not mentioning them. [...]

Jury research Thriving among psychologists in North America. It has produced various models of jurors' decision-making, as well as empirical results. See Section 2.1.7.

Kappa calculus In AI: a formalism introduced by Spohn (1988). The *kappa value* of a *possible world* is the *degree of surprise* in encountering that possible world, a degree measured in non-negative integer numbers. The probabilistic version of the kappa calculus was applied in Shimony and Nissan (2001) in order to restate Åqvist's (1992) logical theory of legal evidence, which Åqvist based on the *Bolding-Ekelöf degrees of evidential strength* (Bolding, 1960; Ekelöf, 1964). See Section 2.6.

Knowledge acquisition "Knowledge acquisition is the transfer and transformation of potential problem-solving expertise from some knowledge source to a program" (Stranieri & Zeleznikow, 2005a, Glossary).

Knowledge based system "A knowledge based system is a computer program in which domain knowledge is explicit and contained separately from the system's other knowledge" (Stranieri & Zeleznikow, 2005a, Glossary).

Knowledge discovery "Knowledge discovery is the non trivial extraction of implicit, previously unknown and potentially useful information from data" (Stranieri & Zeleznikow, 2005a, Glossary).

Knowledge engineering "Knowledge engineering involves the cooperation of domain experts who work with the knowledge engineer to codify and make explicit the rules or other reasoning processes that a human expert uses to solve real world problems" (Stranieri & Zeleznikow, 2005a, Glossary).

Knowledge engineering paradox "The knowledge engineering paradox is that the more competent domain experts become, the less able they are to describe the knowledge they use to solve problems" (Stranieri & Zeleznikow, 2005a, Glossary).

Knowledge engineering process "The knowledge engineering process is the process of transferring knowledge from the domain experts to the computer system.

It includes the following phases: knowledge representation, knowledge acquisition, inference, explanation and justification" (Stranieri & Zeleznikow, 2005a, Glossary).

Knowledge representation "Knowledge representation involves structuring and encoding the knowledge in the knowledge base, so that inferences can be made by the system from the stored knowledge" (Stranieri & Zeleznikow, 2005a, Glossary).

Legal burden See **Burden, legal**.

LAILA A language for abductive logic agents, used in ALIAS, a multi-agent architecture. It was applied to the modelling of reasoning on the evidence in a criminal case, in Ciampolini and Torroni (2004). See Section 2.2.1.5.

Landmark case In law (and by extension, in case-based reasoning within artificial intelligence): "A landmark case is one which alters our perception about knowledge in the domain – landmark cases are comparable to rules. Landmark cases are the basis of analogical reasoning" (Stranieri & Zeleznikow, 2005a, Glossary). Not the same as **interesting case** (q.v.).

Learning "Learning is any change in a system that allows it to perform better the second time on repetition of the same task drawn from the same population" (Stranieri & Zeleznikow, 2005a, Glossary).

Legal positivism "Legal positivists believe that a legal system is a *closed logical system* in which correct decisions may be deduced from predetermined rules by logical means alone" (Stranieri & Zeleznikow, 2005a, Glossary).

Legal realism "Legal realists are jurisprudes for whom the reliance on rules is an anathema. They argue that judges make decisions for a range of reasons which cannot be articulated or at least are not apparent on the face of the judgement given" (Stranieri & Zeleznikow, 2005a, Glossary). See, e.g., Rumble (1965).[32]

---

[32] Wilfrid Rumble began the first footnote in his paper by pointing out: "There is no infallible method to determine who is a legal realist. The most authoritative list is probably that compiled by Karl Llewellyn in 1931, with the assistance of Jerome Frank and Felix S. Cohen. See Llewellyn, *Jurisprudence: Realism in Theory and Practice* (Chicago, 1962), 74–76" (Rumble, 1965, p. 547, fn. 1). Karl N[ickerson] Llewellyn (1893–1962) was professor at the University of Chicago Law School. His work focused mostly on the topic of legal realism. Llewellyn (1962, repr. 2008) is a compilation of his writings from the 1930s through the 1950s. "Oliver Wendell Holmes, Jr., book, *The Common Law*, is regarded as the founder of legal realism. Holmes stated that in order to truly understand the workings of law, one must go beyond technical (or logical) elements entailing rules and procedures. The life of the law is not only that which is embodied in statutes and court decisions guided by procedural law. Law is just as much about experience: about flesh-and-blood human beings doings things together and making decisions. Llewellyn's version of legal realism was heavily influenced by [Roscoe] Pound and [Oliver Wendell] Holmes [Jr.]. The distinction between 'law in books' and 'law in action' is an acknowledgement of the gap that exists between law as embodied in criminal, civil, and administrative code books, and law. A fully formed legal realism insists on studying the behavior of legal practitioners, including their practices, habits, and techniques of action as well as decision-making about others. This classic study is a foremost historical work on legal theory, and is essential for understanding the roots of this influential perspective" (Llewellyn, ibid., from the 2008 publisher's blurb).

Lex posterior "Lex posterior is the legal principle that states the later rule has precedence over the earlier rule" (Stranieri & Zeleznikow, 2005a, Glossary).

Lex specialis "Lex specialis is the legal principle that states the priority is given to the argument that uses the most specific information" (Stranieri & Zeleznikow, 2005a, Glossary).

Lex superior "Lex superior is the legal principle that states that a ruling of a higher court takes precedence over one made by a lower court" (Stranieri & Zeleznikow, 2005a, Glossary).

Liability Being legally bound or responsible. One category of liability is a defendant's criminal liability. Another category is tort liability, which, e.gt., includes products liability torts and claims. Liability issues arising from the use of expert systems in the field of law were discussed by Karin Alheit (1989), as a particular case of liability in relation to the use of expert systems, for which, see Zeide and Liebowitz (1987). Alheit pointed out, in general concerning knowledge-processing software, that "[t]here exists a tremendous litig[ation] potential over their use, misuse, and even non-use" (Alheit, ibid., p. 43, referring to Zeide and Liebowitz 1987).

Linear regression "In linear regression, data is modelled using a straight line of the form $y = \alpha x + \beta$. α and β are determined using the method of least squares. Polynomial regression models can be transformed to a linear regression model" (Stranieri & Zeleznikow, 2005a, Glossary).

Lineup Also called *identity parade*. A suspect stands in a line alongside *foils*, i.e., persons who look alike, and the victim or witness has to identify the suspect. A computerised version is *ID parade discs*, on which video clips from a database appear, along with a video clip showing the suspect. See Section 4.5.2.3.

Lineup instructions Instructions given to eyewitness before an identification lineup. It is essential that such instructions must not be suggestive. For example, witnesses must not be given the impression that the perpetrator is believed to be one of the persons lines up; in fact, it may be that all of them are innocent. See Section 4.5.2.3.

Link Analysis Network link analysis arose in human factors research, originally in order to determine the layout of machine shops in American industry during the First World War (Gilbreth & Gilbreth, 1917). Link analysis is currently supported by computer tools. One of its applications is to crime investigation, and it is conducted by intelligence analysts. Its aim is to discover crime networks, to identify the associates of a suspect, to track financial transactions (possibly by data mining), to detect geographical patterns (possibly by kind of crime), and so forth. In Coady's words (1985),

> Link Analysis is the graphic portrayal of investigative data, done in a manner to facilitate the understanding of large amounts of data, and particularly to allow investigators to develop possible relationships between individuals that otherwise would be hidden by the mass of data obtained.

See Chapters 6 and 7.

Litigation Risk Analysis A proprietary method of Marc B. Victor, for quantifying legal and factual uncertainties by assuming probabilities, for constructing a decision tree, and for using it in order to evaluate the risks of litigation. See Section 4.3.2.3.

Local stare decisis "Local stare decisis is the tendency of judges to be consistent with the decisions of other members of their own region (or registry)" (Stranieri & Zeelznikow, 2005a, Glossary).

Logic In *How to Do Things with Rules*, William Twining and David Miers (1976, pp. 140–142) made the following remarks about the relation between logic and law; these remarks are of lasting value:

> The place of formal logic in legal reasoning is one of the most problematic topics in Jurisprudence. [...] First, it is important to realize that the term "logic" is used, even by philosophers, in a number of different senses. [...] Secondly, even where "logic" is confined to reasoning leading to necessary conclusions, very general questions of the kind "what is the role of logic in legal reasoning?" are ambiguous and misleadingly simple. For example, this question has been variously intepreted to mean: "To what extent do judges and advocates *explicitly* resort to deduction in justifying their decisions?"; "To what extent can judgments and other examples of argument towards conclusions of law be *reconstructed* in terms of formal logic?"; "To what extent is it feasible to resort to deductive-type arguments in legal reasoning?"; or "To what extent is it *desirable* to do so?", or even: "What illumination can be gained by applying the techniques of formal logic to examples of legal reasoning?" All these questions are different, although they are related to each other. They are complex questions; beware of glib answers to them.
>
> Thirdly, there is an unfortunate tendency in juristic controversy to present answers to some of these questions as disagreements between extremists. For instance, it is not uncommon to contrast a view that a legal system is a closed and complete system of rules from which all conclusions on points of law in particular cases can be deduced as a matter of logical necessity (sometimes referred to as "the slot-machine model") with the dictum of Mr Justice Holmes [(Holmes, 1881, p. 1)] that "(t)he life of the law has not been logic, it has been experience", which can be interpreted to mean that deductive logic plays no role at all in legal reasoning. Stated in this extreme form, both views are patently absurd. It is encouraging to find that few jurists who have been accused of adopting the slot-machine model have been guilty of any such crudity and that even a cursory reading of Holmes reveals that he was concerned to show that logic is only one of a number of factors in "determining the rules by which men should be governed" rather than to deny that it had, or should have, any influence in this respect.

The reference to Holmes is to Oliver Wendell Holmes, the Younger (1841–1935), who was a progressive judge in the U.S. Supreme Court. Twining & Miers go on to quote from an essay by Anthony Gordon Guest [(1961, pp. 195–196)]: "arguments need not be cast in a strictly syllogistic form, provided that they exhibit a logical structure. In the dialectic of the law, logic has an important part to play at a stage when a suggested rule has to be tested in order to discover whether or not its adoption will involve the contradiction of already established legal principles. [...]". Then, Twining & Miers (ibid., p. 142) offer a caveat concerning *arguments about inconsistency*: "Such arguments need to be treated with caution for a number of reasons: First, it is quite common for some kind of rules to 'hunt in pairs'. [...] Secondly, arguments about 'inconsistency' and 'contradiction' may often be more appropriately expressed as arguments about what constitutes an appropriate level of generality for a rule or a concept in a particular context". Maxims that point in contradictory directions exist in the common law; they 'hunt in pairs' indeed, and the phenomenon is termed *normative ambiguity* (ibid., p. 210). Twining & Miers illustrate this phenomenon with pairs of proverbs (e.g., "Too many cooks spoil the broth", but "Many hands make light work": ibid.). They go on to list legal examples (ibid., pp. 210–211), then they remark (ibid., p. 212):

> First, one must be wary of exaggerating the extent and the importance of normative ambiguity. Often the canons of interpretation may give clear and explicit guidance in a given case, especially where several canons cumulatively support the same conclusion. The difficulties tend to arise where several factors have to be weighes against each other as they favour different results. Secondly, it is important to distinguish between rule-statements which are logical contradictories and those which merely have different tendencies. [...] Moreover there are typically no rules dictating which of two canons is to prevail in such situations. Thus, just as they have carefully avoided laying down strict rules for determining the *ratio decidendi* of a case, so the common law judges have left themselves a fairly wide leeway of discretion in legislative interpretation. The canons indicate factors to be taken into account in deciding a particular case, but do not indicate precisely what weight should be given to such factors.

Loose talk An important concept for the evaluation of the truthfulness of a proposition. Cf. philosopher Terry Horgan account of vagueness he called **transvaluationism** (q.v.) Whereas in court, it is recognised that sometimes people speak other than literally, or with various degrees of precision, and yet are not lying, arguably also advanced natural-language processing capabilities, with which some legal software may be eventually endowed, ought to recognise that much.

Let us consider Dan Sperber and Deirdre Wilson's notion of *loose talk* (Sperber & Wilson, 1986), by means of an example they provide (Sperber & Wilson, 1990). "At a party in San Francisco, Marie meets Peter. He asks her where she lives, and she answers: 'I live in Paris'." Contrast this to a situation in which the location of the event when the occurance takes place is different: "Suppose Marie is asked where she lives, not at a party in San Francisco, but at an electoral meeting for a Paris local election". There is a difference, concerning the truth value of Marie's utterance, in terms of *relevance* (relevance for discourse, not the relevance of evidence). "It so happens that Marie lives in Issy-les-Moulineaux, a block away from the city limits of Paris. Her answer is literally false, but not blatantly so. If Peter presumed literalness, he will be misled". Yet, assumptions are warranted, that in terms of artificial intelligence could be represented in terms of a nesting of beliefs that agents ascribe to each other. It is not precise that Marie lives in Paris, in the sense that this is inside the city limits.

> In ordinary circumstances, however, Mary's answer is quite appropriate, and not misleading. How come? This is easily explained in terms of relevance theory. A speaker wants, by means of her utterance, to make her hearer see as true or probable a certain set of propositions. Suppose these propositions are all quite easily derivable as implications of a proposition Q. Q however has also other implications whose truth the speaker does not believe and does not want to guarantee. Nevertheless, the best way of achieving her

aim may be for her to express the single proposition Q, as long as the hearer has some way of selecting those of its logical and contextual implications that the speaker intends to convey and of ignoring the others.

This example, Sperber and Wilson claim, reflects quite a general phenomenon:

> Our claim is that such a selection process is *always* at work, is part, that is, of the understanding of *every* utterance. Whenever a proposition is expressed, the hearer takes for granted that some subset of its implications are also implications of the thought being communicated, and aims at identifying this subset. He assumes (or at least assumes that the speaker assumed) that this subset determines sufficient cognitive effects to make the utterance worth his attention. He assumes further (or at least assumes that the speaker assumed) that there was no obvious way in which achieving these effects might have required less effort. He aims at an interpretation consistent with these assumptions, i.e. consistent with the principle of relevance. When this criterion determines a single interpretation (or closely similar interpretations with no important differences between them) communication succeeds.

For Peter to interpret the answer Marie gave him while in San Francisco, various things are relevant, and the city limits of Paris are not among them. Marie can predict how Peter will understand her answer.

> In our example, Peter will be able to infer from Mary's answer quite an amount of true or plausible information: that Marie spends most of her time in the Paris area, that Paris is familiar to her, that she lives an urban life, that he might try to meet her on his next trip to Paris, and so on. It it such cognitive effects which make Marie's utterance sufficiently relevant to be worth his processing effort, in a way Marie manifestly may have anticipated. So, Peter is entitled to assume that Mary intended him to interpret her utterance in this way. Peter would be mislead by Marie's answer only if he were to conclude from it that she lives within the city limits of Paris. However it is clear that Marie had no reason to assume that Peter would have to derive such a conclusion in order to establish the relevance of her utterance. Therefore her utterance does not warrant it.

Marie's answer can be expected to be loosely understood. "This loose understanding does not follow from a strictly literal interpretation having been first considered and then discarded in favor of looseness [...]. In fact, at no point is literalness presumed". When does it become relevant to understand literally? Suppose that it was in Paris, and for the purposes of a Paris local election, that Marie had stated that she lives in Paris. "If she answers that she lives in Paris, the proposition expressed will itself be crucially relevant, hence the utterance will be understood literally, and Marie will have lied". In fact: "An utterance may be literally understood, but only at the end rather than at the beginning of the comprehension process, and only when relevance requires it". The procedure is actually the same: "The same procedure – derive enough cognitive effects to make up an interpretation consistent with the principle of relevance – yields in some cases a literal interpretation, in others a loose one. In other cases still, it yields a figurative interpretation".

Mac-a-Mug Pro A system for assisting a witness in approximating his or her description of the facial features of a criminal suspect. It is a computerized version of the Photofit process. See Section 8.2.2.

Machine learning A branch of artificial intelligence and of data mining. Basically, machine learning enables AI systems to improve their performance, by augmenting their knowledge. "Most machine-learning based software products are capable of generating decision trees or IF/THEN rules. Some are capable of producing both" (Mena, 2003, p. 221). Mena describes:

- Several products that primarily produce *decision trees* (ibid., section 7.9, pp. 221–229);
- Several *rule-extracting tools* (ibid., section 7.10, pp. 229–232);
- Several *machine-learning software suites* (Mena, 2003, section 7.11, pp. 233–248):

  - ANGOSS (http://www.angoss.com)
  - Megaputer (http://www.megaputer.com)
  - Prudsys (http://www.prudsys.de/discoverer)
  - Oracle data mining suite[33]
  - Quadstone (http://www.quadstone.com)
  - SAS (http://www.sas.com); cf. de Ville (2006).
  - SPSS (http://www.spss.com/spssbi/clementine)
  - Teradata Warehouse Miner (http://www.teradata.com)
  - thinkAnalytics (http://www.thinkanalytics.com)

MarshalPlan A computer tool prototype of David Schum and Peter Tillers, supporting the organization of the evidence, and combining Wigmore Charts, an algebraic approach, and hypertext. Entering its fully operational phase around 2005, yet the project started in the early 1990s. See **procedural-support systems**, and see Section 4.1.1.

Mechanical Jurisprudence An article by For Roscoe Pound[34] (1908) was entitled "Mechanical Jurisprudence". For the concept this title expresses, cf. Christie (1984a). Pound opposed the ossification of legal concepts into self-evident truths. By *mechanical jurisprudence*, which he called that way and he condemned, Pound referred the the wooden application of previous precedents to the facts of cases without regard to the consequences. For Pound, the logic of previous precedents alone would not solve jurisprudential problems. In opposition to mechanical jurisprudence, Pound offered his theory of *sociological jurisprudence*. Pound (1908) declared:

> Herein is the task of the sociological jurist. Professor Small defines the sociological movement as "a frank endeavor to secure for the human factor in experience the central place which belongs to it in our whole scheme of thought and action." The sociological movement in jurisprudence is a movement for pragmatism as a philosophy of law; for

---

[33] http://www.oracle.com/ip/analyze/warehouse/datamining

[34] The much cited American legal scholar Nathan Roscoe Pound (1870–1964) was Dean of Harvard Law School from 1916 to 1936. He also was the first one to receive a Ph.D. in botany from the University of Nebraska, which was in in 1898.

the adjustment of principles and doctrines to the human conditions they are to govern rather than to assumed first principles; for putting the human factor in the central place and relegating logic to its true position as an instrument.

One sentence in Pound (1908) resonates with current endeavours to treat law by means of artificial intelligence:

Undoubtedly one cause of the tendency of scientific law to become mechanical is to be found in the average man's admiration for the ingenious in any direction, his love of technicality as a manifestation of cleverness, his feeling that law, as a developed institution, ought to have a certain ballast of mysterious technicality.

Note however that it is not the purpose of AI to change legal conceptions. It is AI that has to adapt itself, when applied to law, to what legal scholars advocate. Pound (1908) claimed: "Jurisprudence is last in the march of the sciences away from the method of deduction from predetermined conceptions."

Mediation In civil cases, a form of **case disposition** (q.v.). Like *arbitration*, mediation is a form of *alternative dispute resolution* (that is, alternative to the courts). Mediation can be either *binding* or *non-binding*.

Memory conformity If two eyewitnesses who saw the same event then discussed it, this may influence what they later claim to remember. More in general, one has *confabulation* (which is undesirable) when the witness is also inferring, not merely reporting. Concerning the latter, see, e.g., Memon and Wright (1999); Gabbert et al. (2003, 2004); Luus and Wells (1994); Meade and Roediger (2002); Meudell et al. (1995); Principe and Ceci (2002); Skagerberg (2007).

Mens rea The intention to transgress on the part of the defendant, and how specifically it is (if at all) intended to transgress. As opposed to *actus reus*, which is the performance of a forbidden action. Sometimes the intention does not match the action performed. A cardinal doctrine of English criminal law is expressed by the maxim: *Actus non facit reum nisi mens sit rea*, i.e., "An act does not itself constitute guilt unless the mind is guilty". "The maxim draws attention to the two essential elements of a crime" (Curzon, 1997, p. 21): "the physical element (the *actus reus*), i.e. the prohibited *conduct* [...] (the so-called 'condition of illegality')", and "the mental element (the *mens rea*), i.e. the *condition of mind* [...] (the so-called 'condition of culpable intentionality')" (ibid.). "Some writers suggest a third element – absence of a valid defence, i.e. a defence which might reduce or negate defendant's criminal liability" (ibid.).

Models of time as known from artificial intelligence are potentially relevant for modelling such situations, because of the requirement of a temporal coincidence of *actus reus* and *mens rea*, and this can hold over an interval; the following casenote is quoted from Curzon (ibid.):

In *Fagan* v. *MPC* (1969), X accidentally drove his car on to Y's foot; he then deliberately left it there for a few minutes. X was charged with assault [...] and claimed that there was no coincidence of act and intent. It was held that X's conduct in driving the car on to Y's foot and allowing it to remain there constituted a continuing act; the assault was committed when X decided to leave the car on Y's foot. James J[ustice] stated: "It is not necessary that *mens rea* should be present at the inception of the *actus reus*; it can be imposed on an existing act. On the other hand, the subsequent inception of *mens*

rea cannot convert an act which has been completed without *means rea* into an assault"
(Curzon, ibid.).

"Before 1935, [in English law] it was said that where the accused had caused the victim's death, he had to show that he did not have the *mens rea* for murder. This burden was placed on the prosecution in *Woolmington* v *DPP* [1935] AC 462" (Jefferson, 1992, p. 23). "Under the influence of *DPP* v *Smith* [1961] AC 290 (HL) it was thought that a person intended to do what the natural consequences of his behaviour were. In legal terms a man was presumed to intend the natural consequences of his behaviour. If this presumption was ever irrebutable, s. 8 of the Criminal Justice Act 1967 abolishes it" (ibid.).

Take involuntary manslaughter. "If death has occurred but the defendant did not possess an intent to kill or cause grievous bodily harm, then providing the action or omission was not totally accidental and therefore blameless, any ensuing prosecution will be for manslaughter" (Bloy, 1996, p. 159). The following categories are enumerated by Bloy (ibid.): *unlawful act manslaughter, reckless (subjective) manslaughter*, and *gross negligence.* For the former:

> The modern definition was expressed by the House of Lords in *Newbury and Jones* (1976). Lord Salmon said an accused was guilty of manslaughter if it was proved that he intentionally did an act which was unlawful and dangerous and that the act inadvertently caused death. In deciding whether or not the act was dangerous the test is would "all sober and reasonable people" recognise that it was dangerous, *not* whether the *accused* recognised it as such. (Bloy, ibid.).
>
> The test [for the dangerous character of the act] is clearly based upon an objective assessment of the circumstances. For example, what conclusions might a reasonable person be expected to reach about the impact of a burglary, late at night, where the occupant of the property is not far short of his 90th birthday? If it is to be reasonably expected that he has a weak heart, or [is] in poor health, then the act of burglary immediately becomes a dangerous act. If however, the reasonable person would not suspect that the victim might in some way be vulnerable to the type of enterprise which is undertaken then a manslaughter conviction is unlikely to be secured on the basis that the act is not a dangerous act. (Bloy, pp. 162–163).

For manslaughter as being the outcome of *gross negligence*, in English law: "The decision of the House of Lords in *Adomako* (1994) is of great significance in helping to clarify the ambit of gross negligence manslaughter and whether or not recklessness is a relevant concept within this species of manslaughter" (Bloy, ibid., p. 166). A patient undergoing surgery suffered a cardiac arrest and subsequently died, because the anaesthetist "failed to notice that an endotracheal tube had become disconnected from the ventilator supplying oxygen to the patient" (ibid., p. 167). "The time period between the disconnection occurring and the [anaesthetist] noticing that this was the cause of the problem was six minutes. [The anaesthetist] was charged with manslaughter and convicted It was not denied by the appellant that he had been negligent but it was his contention that his conduct was not criminal" (ibid.). Bloy (ibid.) explains the attitude of the Court of Appeal and then of the House of Lords, which both dismissed Adomako's appeal:

The Court of Appeal treated the issue as one of breach of duty and stated the ingredients of involuntary manslaughter by breach of duty to be:

- the existence of a duty;
- the breach of the duty causing death; and
- gross negligence on the part of the accused which the jury considered justified a criminal conviction;

In respect of the *mens rea* the Court of Appeal was of the opinion that proof of any of the following states of mind might convince a jury that a defendant had been grossly negligent:

- indifference to an obvious risk of injury to health;
- actual foresight of the risk coupled with the determination to run it;
- an appreciation of the risk coupled with an intention to avoid it but also coupled with such a high degree of negligence in the attempted avoidance as the jury considered justified the conviction; and
- inattention or failure to advert a serious risk which went beyond "mere inadvertence" in respect of an obvious and important matter which the defendant's duty demanded he should address.

Twining and Miers (1976), while discussing *normative ambiguity* (see our entry for **logic**) provide examples of pairs of maxims pointing in different directions. The following pair is about *mens rea* (ibid., p. 211): "All statutory criminal offences are presumed, irrespective of their wording to include a *mens rea* requirement" (*Sweet* v. *Parsley* [1970] A.C. 132), but: "The presumption that all statutory offences include a *mens rea* requirement may be rebutted by the seriousness of the conduct to be prohibited" (*R.* v. *St Margaret's Trust* [1958] 1 W.L.R.[35] 522). Also see Fitzgerald (1961) "Voluntary and involuntary acts", and Hart's (1961b) "Negligence, mens rea and criminal responsibility". Throughout the history of law, there has been variation in how intention has been treated *vis-à-vis* liability (e.g., Jackson, 1971). Jackson (2010) points out:

> Legal doctrine does not require proof that the *mens rea* "caused" the *actus reus*; what it requires (normally) is (merely) that the *mens rea* exists "contemporaneously" with the *actus reus* – in order that we may attribute to the latter the appropriate moral opprobrium, i.e. to show from the offender's intention the required immorality of his act.

Meter-models Quantitative models of the jurors' decision-making process. In such models, the verdict decision is based on the comparison of a meter reading of the final belief, to a threshold to convict. Different classes of such models include probabilistic models, algebraic models, stochastic models, and such modelling that is based on AI formalisms for belief revision. In the algebraic approach, belief updating is additive, whereas in probabilistic models is multiplicative. See Sections 2.1.1 and 2.1.6.

---

[35] *W.L.R.* stands for the *Washington Law Review.*

MIMIC Short for the name *Multiple Image-Maker and Identification Compositor.* A system for generating composite faces, for the purposes of assisting a witness to describe the features of a criminal suspect. MIMIC uses film strip projections. See Section 8.2.2.2.

Minutiae detection Part of *fingerprint recognition*, and a prerequistie for *fingerprint matching algorithms*. This is a finer level than coarse-grained features such as ridges in a fingerprint image. See, e.g., Jiang et al. (2001), Espinosa-Duró (2002). See Section 8.7.

Model-based case-based reasoning paradigm Within case-based reasoning, in artificial intelligence: "The model based approach assumes that there is a strong causal model of the domain task. It generally involves selecting among partially matched cases, in which symbolic reasoning is used to determine the difference between the given problem and the retrieved cases" (Stranieri & Zeleznikow, 2005a, Glossary).

Modus ponens In logic, a form of inference by which if P→Q holds and P holds, then Q holds.

Multi-agent system In artificial intelligence, an approach such that intelligent behaviour is coordinated among a number of separate intelligent agents, these being autonomous software modules (sometimes embodied in robots). They are called *autonomous agents*. A precursor was the *blackboard* paradigm (for which, see **blackboard systems**). See Section 6.1.6.

Multimedia forensics A branch of forensics concerned with uncovering perpetrators of piracy targeting protected digital content or encrypted applications. Typically, perpetration consists of unauthorised music and movie copying, either for private use of for selling pirated copies, thus eating a big bite of the profit of the record industry and the movie studios. Chang-Tsun Li (of the University of Warwick, England), has published a book (Li, 2008) on state-of-the-art *pirate tracking software*. A particular technique, *traitor tracing*, can be applied to multimedia forensics, but the term has previously been used also in the literature about cryptography. See Sections 8.2.5 and 6.1.2.5.

Naïve Bayesian classifiers "Naïve Bayesian classifiers assume the effect of an attribute value on a given class is independent of the other attributes. Studies comparing classification algorithms have found that the naïve Bayesian classifier to be comparable in performance with decision tree and neural network classifiers" (Stranieri & Zeleznikow, 2005a, Glossary). For a given sample we search for a class c_i that maximises the posterior probability

$$P(c_i \mid x \; ; \; \theta')$$

by applying Bayes rule. Then x can be classified by computing

$$c_l = \underset{c_i \in C}{\arg \max} \quad P(c_i|\theta')P(x|c_i;\theta')$$

Nearest neighbour algorithm "The nearest neighbour algorithm is used in information retrieval where data that is closest to the search is retrieved. To perform this search, we need a 'metric' (distance function) between the occurrence of each piece of data. The kth nearest neighbour algorithm classifies examples in a sample by using two basic steps to classify each example: (a) Find the k nearest, most similar examples in the training set to the example to be classified; (b) Assign the example the same classification as the majority of k nearest retrieved neighbours" (Stranieri & Zeleznikow, 2005a, Glossary).

Negotiation "Negotiation is the process by which two or more parties conduct communications or conferences with the view to resolving differences between two parties. This process might be formal or mandated as in legal and industrial disputes, semi-formal, as in international disputes or totally informal as in the case of two prospective partners negotiating as to how they will conduct their married life" (Stranieri & Zeleznikow, 2005a, Glossary).

Network representation schemes "A network representation scheme is a knowledge representation scheme using graphs, in which nodes represent objects or concepts in the problem domain and the arcs represent relations or associations between them. Semantic networks are an example of a network representation scheme" (Stranieri & Zeleznikow, 2005a, Glossary).

Neural networks "A neural network receives its name from the fact that it resembles a nervous system in the brain. It consists of many self-adjusting processing elements cooperating in a densely interconnected network. Each processing element generates a single output signal which is transmitted to the other processing elements. The output signal of a processing element depends on the inputs to the processing element: each input is gated by a weighting factor that determines the amount of influence that the input will have on the output. The strength of the weighting factors is adjusted autonomously by the processing element as data is processed" (Stranieri & Zeleznikow, 2005a, Glossary). "Neural networks are particularly useful in law because they can deal with a) classification difficulties, b) vague terms, c) defeasible rules and d) discretionary domains" (ibid.). See Section 6.1.14.

Network topology "A neural network topology is a specification of the number of neurons in the input layer, the output layer and in each of the hidden layers" (Stranieri & Zeleznikow, 2005a, Glossary).

Nonmonotonic reasoning Such reasoning that it is not true that adding new information would never make the set of true statements to decrease. This is a standard concept in artificial intelligence. As a textbook explains " (Luger & Stubblefield, 1998, p. 269):

> Traditional mathematical logic is *monotonic*: It begins with a set of axioms, assumed to be true, and infers their consequences. If we add new information to this system, it may cause the set of true statements to increase. Adding knowledge will never make the set of true statements decrease. This monotonic property leads to problems when we attempt to model reasoning based on beliefs and assumptions. In reasoning with uncertainty, humans draw conclusions based on their current set of beliefs and assumptions. In reasoning with uncertainty, humans draw conclusions based on their current set of beliefs;

however, unlike mathematical axioms, these beliefs, along with their consequences, may change as more information becomes available. *Nonmonotonic reasoning* addresses the problem of changing belief. A nonmonotonic reasoning system handles uncertainty by making the most reasonable assumptions in light of uncertain information. It then proceeds with its reasoning as if these assumptions were true. At a later time, a belief may change, necessitating a reexamination of any conclusions derived from that belief.

Obligation See **deontic logic**, and **contrary-to-duty obligations**.

Ontology "An ontology as an explicit conceptualisation of a domain" (Stranieri & Zeleznikow, 2005a, Glossary). See Sections 6.1.7.3 and 6.1.7.4. "Legal ontologies are generalised conceptual models of specific parts of the legal domain. They provide stable foundations for knowledge representation" (Mommers, 2003, p. 70). For example, Mommers (2003) presented an ontology "based on an analysis of the relation between the legal domain and knowledge about that domain. It is explained how knowledge in the legal domain can be analysed in terms of three dimensions (acquisition, object and justification), and how these dimensions can be employed in alternative designs for collaborative workspaces" (ibid.). Boer, van Engers, and Winkels (2003) discussed using ontologies in order to compare and harmonise legislation.[36]

Onus of proof The same as **evidential burden**. See **Burden, evidential**. "In any given scenario the onus of proof indicates the degree of certainty for a given outcome to occur. In a criminal case in Common Law countries such proof must be beyond reasonable doubt, whereas in most civil cases in such countries, the proof required is by a fair preponderance of the evidence (i.e. more than 50% likely to occur)" (Stranieri & Zeleznikow, 2005a, Glossary). Jefferson explains (1992, p. 19):

> There is a distinction between the evidential and legal burden of proof. The difference may be illustrated by reference to automatism [. . .]. Before the accused can rely on this defence, he must put forward some evidence that he was acting automatically when he, say, hit his lover over the head with a heavy ashtray. The evidence might consist of a witness's saying that he saw what happened or a psychiatrist's drafting a report. In legal terms he has to adduce or lead evidence. If he does not adduce such evidence, his plea will fail at that stage and the prosecution does not have to lead evidence that his plea should not succeed. If he does, the prosecution has to disprove that he was acting automatically. His burden is called the evidential burden or onus of proof. The prosecution's burden is the legal one.

---

[36] "In the E-POWER project relevant tax legislation and business processes are modeled in UML to improve the speed and efficiency with which the Dutch Tax and Customs Administration can implement decision support systems for internal use and for its clients. These conceptual models have also proven their usefulness for efficient and effective analysis of draft legislation. We are currently researching whether conceptual modeling can also be used to compare 'similar' legislation from different jurisdictions to improve the capacity of the Dutch Tax and Customs Administration to react to future consequences of increased movement of people, products, and money between EU member states and increased harmonization between tax authorities in Europe. In addition, addressing the problem of comparing models is also expected to improve our methodology for modeling legislation." (Boer et al. 2003, p. 60).

Open-textured legal predicate "Open textured legal predicates contain questions that cannot be structured in the form of production rules or logical propositions and which require some legal knowledge on the part of the user in order to answer" (Stranieri & Zeeleznikow, 2005a, Glossary).

Opinion question In argumentation studies, Walton's (1997) *Appeal to Expert Opinion* offered (ibid., pp. 211–225) an argumentation scheme for "Argument for Expert Opinion", then reproduced in Walton et al. (2008, pp. 381–382). See s.v. *Expert opinion, Appeal to* above. The expert source is E; the subject domain is S; and A is a proposition about which E claims to be true (or false). The opinion question is: "What did E assert that implies A?". It is articulated in four detailed subquestions: "Was E quoted as asserting A? Was a reference to the source of the quote given, and can it be verified that E actually said A?"; "If E did not say A exactly, then what did E assert, and how was A inferred?"; "If the inference to A was based on more than one premise, could one premise have come from E and the other from a different expert? If so, is there evidence of disagreement between what the two experts (separately) asserted?"; "Is what E asserted clear? If not, was the process of interpretation of what E said by the respondent who used E's opinion justified? Are other interpretations plausible? Could important qualifications have been left out?".

Outlier A major anomaly, a notable departure from a pattern. Outliers may be a useful indicator for the purposes of crime detection. See Chapter 6. "Data objects that are grossly different from or inconsistent with the remaining set of data are called outliers" (Stranieri & Zeleznikow, 2005a, Glossary).

Overfitting "Overfitting occurs when the data mining method performs very well with data it has been exposed to but performs poorly with other data" (Stranieri & Zeleznikow, 2005a, Glossary).

Overtraining of neural networks "A neural network over-trains if it has been exposed to an abundance of examples, far too many times. In this case it can learn each input-output pair so well that it, in effect, memorises those cases. The network classifies training set cases well, but may not perform so well with cases not in the training set" (Stranieri & Zeleznikow, 2005a, Glossary).

Palmprints In biometrics, the print of the entire palm of a hand (Kumar et al., 2003), instead of just *fingerprints*. This is used in personal authentication systems, but is not practical in criminal investigation, as it is only seldom that a suspect would leave an entire palmprint, rather than fingerprints. See Section 8.7.

PATER A software system for probabilistic computations for testing paternity claims (Egeland, Mostad, & Olaisen, 1997). See Section 8.7.2.1.

Pattern recognition "The creation of categories from input data using implicit or explicit data relationships. Similarities among some data exemplars are contrasted with dissimilarities across the data ensemble, and the concept of data class emerges. Due to the imprecise nature of the process, it is no surprise that statistics has played a major role in the basic principles of pattern recognition" (Principe et al., 2000, p. 643).

PEIRCE-IGTT A piece of software: an abductive inference engine from artificial intelligence, developed by a team led by John Josephson. One of its applications was to the modelling of reasoning on the evidence in a criminal case. See Section 2.2.1.5.

Pentitismo In the Italian criminal justice system, an arrangement on the part of the prosecution, by which some political terrorist or member of the Mafia who was himself highly liable, were permitted to turn into a **state witness** (q.v.) against other defendants. There is some similarity to the *supergrass* system of Britain.

In Italy, a somewhat equivalent system is the *pentitismo*: in the late 1970s, as well as during the 1980s and still during trials held during the 1990s, on occasion a "repentant" terrorist would act as state witness against one or more defendants. Such a witness used to be called a *pentito*, or a *superpentito*. Sometimes the deal drew strong criticism, and in all fairness, defeated justice, such as when the murderer of a journalist obtained, by turning state witness, his own liberty, as well as that of the woman who had been his girlfriend before they were separately arrested in different circumstances. Once released, he immediately proceeded to wed another woman. One photograph that was highly visible in the mass media showed him talking, and, inside the same frame, the grim face of the father of the journalist whose murder justice had renounced punishing. It has also happened that the sincerity of a *superpentito*, securing convictions, was quite dubious. This was the case of the state witness during the Sofri case (for the 1972 terrorism-related killing of a police inspector), as well as of a witness from the Mafia against former prime minister Andreotti, who was convicted for the violent death of a journalist. Also the testimony of a state witness who had raped and murdered in the Circeo case, securing the convictions of other far rightists for a bombing with massive casualties in Bologna (it took place on 2 August 1980), appears to be discredited.

Personal authentication systems Systems for verifying the personal identity of a person, using biometric characteristics; e.g. using fingerprints with *digital signature technologies* (Isobe et al., 2001; Seto 2002).

Personal stare decisis "Personal stare decisis is the tendency of judges to be consistent with themselves" (Stranieri & Zeleznikow, 2005a, Glossary).

Persuasion argument One of two classes of arguments (the other one being *adversary* arguments), "depending on the goals and expectations of the participants. [It] consists of arguments in which the participants are motivated to reach a common agreement, for example in order to solve some problem": "the participants are both willing to be persuaded as well as trying to persuade" (Flowers et al., 1982, p. 275). This is relevant for computer tools for supporting negotiation.

Persuasion burden See **burden of proof**.

Photoarray An alternative to a *lineup* at which a suspect and foils are physically present and standing alongside each other. In a photoarray, the eyewitness is made to see a set of photographs instead. Also called *photospread*. An alternative is such an identity parade that there is no physical presence, but the eyewitness is made to see video clips of the suspect and foils. See Section 4.5.2.3.

Photofit A system for assisting a witness in approximating his or her description of the facial features of a criminal suspect. See Section 8.2.2.

Pirate tracing software A kind of software subserving *Multimedia forensics*, for uncovering perpetrators of piracy targeting protected digital content or encrypted applications. See Sections 8.2.5 and 6.1.2.5.

Plaintiff The party that turns to the courts for adjudication against another party (the defendant). In some kinds of trial (at employment tribunals in England and Wales), the names are: *applicant* for the plaintiff; *respondent* for the defendant. In the *Civil Procedure Rules 1993*, in England and Wales, the term *plaintiff* was replaced with *claimant* (thought to be a more transparent, and more widely understood term: the same reform excised other traditional terms as well).

Plausibility, relative "The distinction between the structure of proof and a theory of evidence is simple. The structure of proof determines what must be proven. In the conventional [probabilistic] theory [which Allen attacks] this is elements to a predetermined probability, and in the relative plausibility theory [which Ron Allen approves of] that one story or set of stories is more plausible than its competitors (and in criminal cases that there is no plausible competitor). A theory of evidence indicates how this is done, what counts as evidence and perhaps how it is processed" (Allen, 1994, p. 606). See Allen (1991, 2008a, 2008b).

Plausible inference "Polya developed a formal characterisation of qualitative human reasoning as an alternative to probabilistic methods for performing commonsense reasoning. He identified four patterns of plausible inference: inductive patterns, successive verification of several consequences, verification of improbable consequences and inference from analogy" (Stranieri & Zeleznikow, 2005a, Glossary).

Plea A statement made in court by other party in argument of the case. In particular, in Anglo-American criminal procedure,[37] the answer given by the defendant at the start of the trial, after the indictment. The answer is either *guilty*, or *not guilty.*

Plea bargain In Anglo-American criminal procedure, and in countries influenced by that system: an offer which the prosecution has a discretion to make, so that in return for a *guilty plea* at the start of the trial (before evidence is submitted to the court), the defendant is offered sentencing concessions (a lighter sentence). Bargaining about the sentence also takes place if one of the defendants is offered the option to become a prosecution witness against other defendants. In countries on the European Continent, it used to be the case that there could be no plea bargaining. *Plea bargaining* applies in criminal cases, and should not be mistaken for a *settlement out of court*, stopping the proceedings in the trial of a civil case.

Police science A field encompassing all aspects of law enforcement, focusing on the factors that affect crime and the police response to crime (Greene, 2006). One aspect of this discipline is the generation or refinement of methods of investigation, enabled by technological advances.

---

[37] Kamisar, LaFave, Israel, and King (2003) covers criminal procedure in the United States of America.

Polygraph testing Testing by means of hardware equipment, recording levels of arousal while the person tested is being questioned. Various methods exist. Polygraph testing and polygraph evidence are admitted in some countries (such as the United States), while being frowned upon for good reason in some other countries (including the United Kingdom). See Section 4.5.2.1. In the U.S., the Polygraph Protection Act of 1888 banned most polygraph tests for personnel selection purposes; the police in the U.S. resorts to such tests extensively during investigation. In some other countries (e.g., in the U.K.), the police is not allowed to use polygraph tests.

Post-charge questioning Questioning of a suspect on the part of the police, after legal proceedings have started. This is not supposed to happen. Legal proceedings only start once the investigation stage ends: once a suspect is charged, the police can no longer question him or her. *Post-charge questioning* (on the part of police investigators) of terrorism suspects, possibly extended to other categories of criminals, was considered by the British government in November 2007, drawing criticism from civil liberties groups.

Preponderance of the evidence On balance, the evidence seems to favour adjudication one way rather than in the other. This standard of proof is weaker than *beyond reasonable doubt.* Without sticking to the legal sense of these phrases, in the *Carneades* argumentation tool (Gordon & Walton, 2006), a standard of evidence stronger than *scintilla of evidence* and weaker than *beyond reasonable doubt* is The second weakest is PE (preponderance of the evidence): "A statement meets this standard iff its strongest defensible pro argument outweighs its strongest defensible con argument". A stronger standard (yet weaker than BRD, *beyond reasonable* doubt) is DV, which is defined as follows: "A statement meets this standard iff it is supported by at least one defensible pro argument and none of its con arguments is defensible".

Principal component analysis In statistical data analysis: "Principal components analysis (PCA) is the technique most often used to identify features that do not contribute to the prediction from a data-set. PCA involves the analysis of variance between features and the class variable in a prediction exercise. PCA requires specialist statistical software, since the calculations are cumbersome. PCA is applicable only to features that are numeric" (Stranieri & Zeleznikow, 2005a, Glossary).

Principled negotiation "Principled negotiation promotes deciding issues on their merits rather than through a haggling process focussed on what each side says it will and will not do" (Stranieri & Zeleznikow, 2005a, Glossary).

Prior convictions (evidence of) See **character evidence** (of which this is a kind); **jury observation fallacy.**

Private privilege The rule by which some categories of witnesses cannot be compelled to disclose certain kinds of information or documents.This includes protection from *self-incrimination*, either for the accused – who under English law "may not be asked questions which tend to show that he may be guilty of any other offence than that with which he is presently charged" (Osborne, 1997,

p. 338) – and for other witness: "In a criminal case no witness can be compelled to answer any question which would, in the opinion of the judge, have a tendency to expose the witness to any criminal charge" (ibid.). Another kind of private privilege is *legal professional privilege*, by which lawyer–client communications, as well as communications with third parties for the purpose of actual or pending litigation, are protected from disclosure. Yet, the client may waive this privilege, and direct his or her lawyer accordingly. Moreover, communications to facilitate crime or fraud are not privileged.

Privilege A rule that protects some kinds of communication or material documents from disclosure at trial or during a police investigation. There is *private privilege*, and there is *public interest privilege.*

Probabilistic information retrieval models "Probabilistic information retrieval models are based on the probability ranking principle which ranks legal documents according to their probability of relevance to the query given every available source of information. The model estimates the probability of relevance of a text to the query, on the basis of the statistical distribution of terms in relevant and irrelevant text, given an uncertainty associated with the representation of both the source text and the information need, as well as the relevance relationship between them" (Stranieri & Zeleznikow, 2005a, Glossary).

Probability Donald Gillies (2004, p. 286) provides this usefully concise explanation:

> Probability theory originated from the study of games of chance, and these still afford a good illustration of some of the basic concepts of the theory. If we roll a fair dice, the probability of getting 5 is 1/6. This is written $P(5)=1/6$. A *conditional probability* is the probabilities of a result given that something else has happened. For example, the probability of 5 given that the result was odd, is no longer 1/6, but 1/3; while the probability of 5 given that the result was even, is no longer 1/6, but 0. A conditional probability is written $P(A|B)$. So we have $P(5|\text{odd})=1/3$, and $P(5|\text{even})=0$. A related concept is *independence*. Two events A and B are said to be *independent* if the conditional probability of A given B is the same as the probability of A, or, in symbols, if . Successive rolls of a die are normally assumed to be independent, that is to say, the probability of getting a 5 is always the same, namely 1/6, regardless of what results have appeared so far. An important concept for probability in AI is *conditional independence. A* and B are said to be *conditionally independent* given C, if $P(A|B\&C) = P(A|C)$.

Also see **Probability, prior and posterior**.

Probability, objective "An *objective probability* is one which is supposed to be a feature of the objective world, such as mass or electrical charge. A well-known objective interpretation of probability is the frequency interpretation. For example, to say that the probability of 5 is 1/6 on this interpretation is taken to mean that, in a long series of rolls of the die, the result 5 will appear with a frequency of approximately 1/6. Those who adopt this interpretation estimate their probabilities from frequency data" (Gillies, 2004, p. 287).

Probability, prior and posterior With reference to Bayes' theorem, which when dealing with a hypothesis H, and some evidence E, states:

$$P(H|E) = P(E|H)P(H)/P(E)$$

this can be read as follows: the *posterior probability* $P(H|E)$, i.e., the probability that H is true given E, is equal to the product of the *likelihood* $P(E|H)$, i.e., the probability that E given the truth of H, and the *prior probability* $P(H)$ of H, divided by the *prior probability* $P(E)$ of E. A synonym of *prior probability* is *a priori probability*. A synonym of *posterior probability* is *a posteriori probability*.

Probability, subjective It "is taken to be the measure of the degree of belief of a particular individual that some event will occur. For example, if I say that my subjective probability that it will rain in London tomorrow is 2/3, this means that I believe to degree 2/3 that it will rain in London tomorrow. A woman's degree of belief can be measured by the rate at which she is prepared to bet, or her betting quotient. It can be shown that, starting from this way of measuring belief, the standard axioms of probability can be derived. An application of the subjective theory of probability to Bayesianism produces what is known as *subjective Bayesianism*. Here $P(H)$ is taken to represent the prior degree of belief of Mr. R, say, that H is true, while $P(H|E)$ represents his posterior degree of belief in H after he has come to know evidence E. A rational man on this approach changes his degree of belief in the light of new evidence E from $P(H)$ to $P(H|E)$, where the value of $P(H|E)$ is calculated using Bayes Theorem" (Gillies, 2004, p. 287).

Probative value "Probative value is a relational concept that expresses the strength with which evidence supports an inference to a given conclusion. It is a crucial concept for determining admissibility (see Fed[eral] R[ules of] Evid[ence] 403, which instructs judges to exclude evidence when its probative value is substantially outweighed by its prejudicial, confusing, or duplicative effect) and for determining whether parties have satisfied their burdens of proof" (Allen & Pardo, 2007a, p. 108, fn. 2).

Procedural *Procedural*, as opposed to *substantive*, as opposed to *procedural*, pertains to how to administer the judiciary process. For example, the order in which the parties and their witnesses testify belongs in procedure.

Procedural representation scheme In artificial intelligence: "A procedural representation scheme is a knowledge representation scheme in which knowledge is represented as a set of instructions for solving a problem. Examples of procedural representation schemes include production rules", i.e., IF-THEN rules (Stranieri & Zeleznikow, 2005a, Glossary).

Procedural-support systems A category of computer tools for assisting humans in handling court cases. "Procedural-support systems are AI & Law programs that lack domain knowledge and thus cannot solve problems, but that instead help the participants in a dispute to structure their reasoning and discussion, thereby promoting orderly and effective disputes" (Prakken & Renooij, 2001). "When procedural-support systems are to be useful in practice, they should provide support for causal reasoning about evidence" (ibid.). Available operational tools include *CaseMap, MarshalPlan*, and (in Italy) *Daedalus*. See Section 4.1.

Production rule In artificial intelligence: a rule consisting of a *condition part* (or *left-hand part*) and an *action part* (or *right-hand part*). It is also called an *IF-THEN rule*.

Production rule system In artificial intelligence: "Production rule systems are expert systems which consist of a set of production rules, working memory and the recognise-act cycle (also known as the rule interpreter)" (Stranieri & Zeleznikow, 2005a, Glossary).

PROLEXS "The PROLEXS project at the Computer/Law Institute, Vrije Universiteit, Amsterdam, Netherlands is concerned with the construction of legal expert shells to deal with vague concepts. Its current domain is Dutch landlord-tenant law. It uses several knowledge sources and the inference engines of the independent knowledge groups interact using a blackboard architecture" (Stranieri & Zeleznikow, 2005a, Glossary). See Section 6.1.14.9 in this book, and s.v. **blackboard systems.** PROLEXS is the subject of Walker, Oskamp, Schrickx, Opdorp, and van den Berg (1991) and of Oskamp et al. (1989).

Prosecutorial discretion The choice being left to the prosecutor (in some jurisdictions, especially in the Anglo-American adversarial system), whether to prosecute or not, and if not, to propose a *plea bargain.* As opposed to *obligatory prosecution*, which until recently used to be common in Continental Europe. Prosecution, as being the decision to charge a suspect with a crime, is the subject, e.g., of books by Miller (1969) and by Jacoby, Mellon, Ratledge, and Turner (1982). Cf. Kingsnorth, MacIntosh, and Sutherland (2002).[38] **Discretion** (q.v.) is a broader concept.

Public inquiry As public inquiries in Britain are inquisitorial, as opposed to the adversarial system that characterises the courts, the impact of this contrast is explained at the entry for **inquisitorial.** As early as the Bristol Public Inquiry in the late 1990 (it was chaired by Sir Ian Kennedy: see **inquisitorial**), "the Inquiry established a process whereby the statements of witnesses who were not to be called were made available on the Inquiry's website, together with the comment, if any, of someone identified by the Inquiry's lawyers as having been the object of criticism in the statement" (Kennedy, 2007, p. 37). That was also the case of witnesses that were called to give oral evidence before the Inquiry, but then their statements with the comments were not posted at the website until the

---

[38] Flowe et al. (2010) pointed out: "Prosecutors have the discretion to determine whether a suspect will be charged and what charges the suspect should face (Bordenkircher v. Hayes, 1978). Prosecutors also have a legal and ethical obligation to protect felony suspects who are not just innocent-in-fact, but who are also innocent-in-law (California District Attorneys Association, 1996). Charges should not be filed even if the prosecutor has a personal belief in the suspect's guilt. Rather, issuing decisions should be guided by whether the evidence in the case is legally sufficient and admissible. Previous archival research has found that felony charges are more likely to be issued if there is physical evidence to support the allegations (Albonetti, 1987; Feeney, Dill, & Weir, 1983; Jacoby et al., 1982; Miller, 1969; Nagel, & Hagan, 1983) and if the crime is serious, such as when a victim has been injured (Kingsnorth et al., 2002). Factors that may lead prosecutors to not file charges include: A primary aggressor has not been identified (e.g., the California Primary Aggressor Law requires a primary aggressor be identified), the suspect is thought to be innocent, or there are 'interests of justice' concerns, such as the suspect will provide testimony in a more serious case (Silberman, 1978). Despite the fact that much research has been carried out examining the relationship between evidentiary factors and felony issuing decisions, little is known about the role that eyewitness identification evidence may play in prosecution."

witness had given oral evidence. That way, the contributions of the various witnesses were known in advance. This made it possible to schedule the witness' appearance accordingly. Resorting to a website did away with *Salmon letters* (ibid.):

> Not only was this [web-supported procedure] fair to all, but it allowed the Inquiry to take account of and explore differences of view when questioning witnesses. Moreover, it meant that the Inquiry could avoid a procedure known as the issuing of "Salmon letters", named after Lord Justice Salmon who chaired the Royal Commission on Tribunals in 1966. The purpose of "Salmon letters" was to put individuals on notice should they have been criticised in evidence. It was a procedural response to the evidence heard, designed to ensure fairness. I took the view that it reflected an approach which equated Public Inquiries with judicial proceedings. It was, therefore, inappropriate and, moreover, unnecessary. Fairness could be maintained in a far more coherent and sensible way. In effect, the "Salmon letters" procedure introduced an unnecessary formal step into the proceedings, which commonly provoked legal to-ing and fro-ing. By getting witnessed to reveal and confront their various accounts well in advance, everyone knew where they stood. There was no need to have resort to some additional, and time-consuming, and, frankly, out-dated procedural mechanism.

Public interest privilege Also called *public interest immunity*. A category of *privilege*, by which "evidence is excluded because of some public interest in withholding it which outweighs the usual public interest in open litigation" (Osborne, 1997, p. 340). A lesser legal concept than *privilege* is *confidentiality*, and it, too, is such that communications in professional–client relationships are sometimes protected (which is, instead, a right, and is considered *private privilege*, for the client of a lawyer). "[O]ne originally separate basis of public privilege which has merged somewhat into the mainstream is the rule that no question may be asked in proceedings which would tend to lead to the identification of any person who has given information leading to the institution of a prosecution" (ibid., p. 342).

Questioned documents evidence Evidence from forensic tests (Levinson, 2000), concerning the authenticity of documents or parts thereof, of their authorship ascription, of their date, or of the hand in which they are written. There exist techniques for determining authenticity, age, ink and paper sources, equipment used, forgeries, alterations, and erasures, as well as *handwriting identification*, the latter being the subject of Morris (2000). See Section 6.1.10. The following is quoted from the introduction to the useful entry for 'Questioned document examination' in Wikipedia[39]:

> **Questioned document examination** (QDE) is known by many names including *forensic document examination, document examination, diplomatics, handwriting examination*, and sometimes *handwriting analysis*, although the latter name is not often used as it may be confused with graphology. Likewise a forensic document examiner is not to be confused with a graphologist, and vice versa. The questioned document division of a crime lab is sometimes referred to as "QD" in popular media.
>
> The task of forensic document examination is to answer questions about a disputed document using a variety of scientific processes and methods. Many examinations involve a comparison of the questioned document, or components of the document, to a

---

[39] http://en.wikipedia.org/wiki/Questioned_document_examination

set of known standards. The most common type of examination involves handwriting wherein the examiner tries to address concerns about potential authorship.

One task of a forensic document examiner is to determine if a questioned item originated from the same source as the known item(s), then present their opinion in court as an expert witness. Other tasks include determining what has happened to a document, determining when a document was produced, or deciphering information on the document that has been obscured, obliterated or erased.

Professional organisations include the American Society of Questioned Document Examiners (ASQDE), the American Academy of Forensic Science (AAFS), the Southwestern Association of Forensic Document Examiners (SWAFDE), and the Southeastern Association of Forensic Document Examiners (SAFDE) in the U.S.A.; the Canadian Society of Forensic Science (CSFS); the Australasian Society of Forensic Document Examiners (ASFDE) in Australia and Asia; the Gesellschaft für Forensische Schriftungtersuchung (GFS) in Frankfurt (Germany); the Asociación Profesional de Peritos Calígrafos de Cataluña (in Spain); the National Association of Document Examiners (NADE); the Association of Forensic Document Examiners (AFDE); and so forth.

Questioning During police investigations, the process of asking suspects, or actual or potential witnesses, such questions that seek to uncover information. This is quite different from *examination* in court. It is important not to confuse examination in court, with questioning by the police during investigation. Legal proceedings only start once the investigation stage ends: once a suspect is charged, the police can no longer question him or her. *Post-charge questioning* (on the part of police investigators) of terrorism suspects, possibly extended to other categories of criminals, was considered by the British government in November 2007, drawing criticism from civil liberties groups.

Questmap A computer tool for supporting argumentation (Carr, 2003). *QuestMap* is based on IBIS, mediates discussions, supports collaborative argumentation, and creates information maps, in the context of legal education. Collaborative problem identification and solving is the purpose of IBIS, an Issue-Based Information System. Problems are decomposed into issues. See Section 3.7.

Ratio decidendi The rationale of a decision made by an adjudicator in a court case. The ground or reason for the decision. The point in a case that determines the judgement. "*Ratio decidendi* is Latin for the "reasons for decision", that is the legal reasons why the judge came to the conclusion that he or she did. It is the fundamental basis for the rule of law in common law systems. Stare decisis says that the ratio decidendi will apply to subsequent cases decided by courts lower in the hierarchy" (Stranieri & Zeleznikow, 2005a, Glossary).

Reason!Able A computer tool for supporting argumentation (van Gelder, 2002). Some tools envisage collaboration among users, yet *Reason!Able* only has one user per session. It guides the user step-by-step through the process of constructing an argument tree, containing claims, reasons, and objections, the latter two kinds being complex objects which can be unfolded to see the premises. See Section 3.7.

Rebutter A defendant's answer in matter of fact (about the accusation and the evidence) to a plaintiff's (or, in particular, prosecution's) *surrejoinder.* (See **replication**.)

Reference-class problem Allen and Pardo (2007a, p. 109) find that scholarship which applies probability theory to juridical proof

> suffers from a deep conceptual problem that makes ambiguous the lessons that can be drawn from it – the problem of reference classes. The impolications of this problem are considerable. To illustrate the problem, consider the famous blue bus hypothetical. Suppose a witness saw a bus strike a car but cannot recall the color of the bus; assume further that the Blue Company owns 75 percent of the buses in the town and the Red Company owns the remaining 25 percent. The most prevalent view in the legal literature of the probative value of the witness's report is that it would be determined by the ratio of the Blue Company buses to Red Company buses, whether this is thought of as or plays the role of a likelihood ratio or determines information gain (including an assessment of a prior probability) [. . .] But suppose the Red Company owns 75 percent (and Blue the other 25 percent) of the buses in the county. Now the ratio reverses. And it would do so again if Blue owned 75 percent in the state. Or in the opposite direction: it would reverse if Red owned 75 percent running in the street where the accident occurred (or on that side of the street) and so on. Or maybe the proper reference class has to do with safety standards and protocols for reporting accidents. Each of the reference classes leads to a different inference about which company is more likely liable, and nothing determines the correct class, save one: the very event under discussion, which has a likelihood of one and which we are trying to discover.

"The blue bus hypothetical [. . .] exemplifies the general implications of reference classes, and those implications would hold for practically any attempt to quantify a priori the prbative value of evidence" (ibid., p. 113).

Regression In statistics: "In linear regression, data is modelled using a straight line of the form $y = \alpha x + \beta$. α and β are determined using the method of least squares. Polynomial regression models can be transformed to a linear regression model." (Stranieri & Zeleznikow, 2005a, Glossary).

Rejoinder The defendant's answer to the plaintiff's *replication.* (See **replication**.)

Relevance Pertinence of a piece of evidence, for the purposes of proving that which is to be proven in court, as a criterion for such evidence to be heard or excluded instead. Yovel (2003) provided a mildly formalised treatment, with a notation in *MicroProlog* style, of what in legal scholarship about evidence is known as *relevance.* See Section 4.6 in this book. Here is a definition from a legal textbook on evidence: "The purpose of calling evidence in court is to try to prove certain facts to be true. Evidence which assists in this process is relevant and that which does not assist is irrelevant. It is the first rule of evidence, and one to which there are no exceptions, that irrelevant evidence is never admissible in court. This does not mean that relevant evidence is always allowed, because sometimes the court disallows it despite its relevance. The greater proportion of this book is about rules which limit the extent to which relevant evidence can be used" (Templeman & Reay, 1999, p. 1). Modern theories of relevance are the subject of Tillers (1983). Also see Richard Lempert's (1977) 'Modeling Relevance'.

There also exist other senses of *relevance*: in *sensitivity analysis* from statistics, including when it is applied to legal evidence, "An item of evidence is called 'relevant' to a hypothesis is observing the evidence changes the probability that the hypothesis is true" (Levitt & Laskey, 2002, p. 375). Moreover, for the *relevance of an utterance*, see in the entry for **loose talk** in this Glossary.

Teun van Dijk (1989) describes the concept of relevance as it applies to a class of modal logics broadly called "relevance logics" as a concept grounded firmly in the pragmatics, and not the semantics or syntax of language. Within a discursive community, the data items in a generic argument must be relevant to the claim to the satisfaction of members of the community. The purpose of van Dijk's article was stated as follows (ibid., p. 25):

> In this paper an attempt will be made to provide a general and informal discussion of "relevance" and related notions from this linguistic point of view. More particularly, it will be argued that the relevance requirement must be satisfied by any compound sentence, viz. by all connectives, and by any coherent discourse, i.e. not only deductive or argumentative, in natural language. Although such a claim might have feed-back in the philosophy of logic, we will be concerned with the applications of some recent ideas from relevance logics in the explicit characterization of these properties of natural language.

Reparational obligations See **contrary-to-duty obligations**.

Replication In American law: the plaintiff's (or the prosecution's) reply to the "defence", intended as the original statement of the defendant or his defence lawyer (or team of lawyers). The plaintiff's *replication* may prompt an answer in matters of fact, called the defendant's *rejoinder*, which may prompt the plaintiff's *surrejoinder*, which may prompt the defendant's *rebutter*, which may prompt that plaintiff's *surrebutter*.

Resolution "Resolution is a semi-decidable proof technique for first order predicate calculus, which given an unsatisfiable well formed formula, proves it to be unsatisfiable. If the well formed formula is not unsatisfiable, there is a possibility that the algorithm may not terminate" (Stranieri & Zeleznikow, 2005a, Glossary).

Respondent In some kinds of trial, the defendant; then the name for the plaintiff is *applicant*.

Rule base (or **ruleset**). "The rule base of a legal (or indeed any) rule based expert system is that part of the system in which the rules are stored. It is kept separate from the other part of the expert system, the inference engine" (Stranieri & Zeleznikow, 2005a, Glossary).

Rule-based expert system "A rule based expert system is a collection of rules of the form : IF condition(s) THEN action. Rule based systems include production rule systems, and some would argue, logic based systems as well" (Stranieri & Zeleznikow, 2005a, Glossary).

Rule-extracting tools A category of *machine learning* tools. Several commercial rule-extracting tools were described by Mena (2003, section 7.10, pp. 229–232):

- AIRA (http://www.godigital.com.br), and Excel add-on
- DataMite,[40] for relational databases
- SuperQuery (http://www.azmy.com)
- WizWhy (http://www.wizsoft.com)

---

[40] http://www.lpa.co.uk/ind_top.htm

Salmon letters See **public inquiry**.

Scheme *Argumentation schemes* are "predefined patterns of reasoning. A single scheme describes an inference, the necessary prerequisties for that inference, and possible critical questions that might undercut the inference" (van den Braak & Vreeswijk, 2006).

Scintilla of evidence A tenuously probative piece of evidence, enough to motivate probing further, searching for more evidence. Without sticking to this sense of the phrase, in the *Carneades* argumentation tool the weakest standard of evidence is SE (*scintilla of evidence*): "A statement meets this standard iff it is supported by at least one defensible pro argument".

Secondary obligation See **contrary-to-duty obligations**.

Sensitivity analysis An analysis of how given pieces of evidence being available, would affect the demonstrability of given claims. It can be used when evaluating litigation risk: see Section 4.3.1. It can be useful for a costs/benefits analysis of whether to obtain some piece of evidence: see Section 4.3.2. Levitt and Laskey (2002, Sections 1.4.4 and 1.5.4) discussed and exemplified such a sensitivity analysis, in the context of their analysis of the evidence in a murder case by means of Bayesian networks (BNs). Their example concerns the French case in which Omar Raddad was convicted in 1994 of murdering his employer, but then pardoned because of how controversial the case was. Levitt & Laskey (ibid., p. 375) wrote:

> The BN knowledge representation can capture useful quantitative behaviour regarding alternative explanations for the same items of evidence. For example, the relevance of items of evidence regarding Raddad depends on their relationship in the evidential argument implied by the BN, and [...] they can change as evidence accrues. In particular, the evidence of Raddad's location at the time of the murder is co-dependent with the evidence from the examiner's testimony about the time of death. The relevance of one depends dynamically on the other, and they co-vary as evidence is accrued to the global evidential argument about Raddad's guilt or innocence that is modelled by [a given] BN [...]. This introduction of the examiner's testimony [...] does not change the probability of Raddad's guilt. That is, the evidence is not relevant to Raddad's guilt given the evidence accrued up to that point. The examiner's report becomes relevant when we accrue the evidence that Raddad was with his relatives on Monday. In the presence of the examiner's report, the evidence provides an alibi and greatly reduces the probability of guilt. Subsequently, the evidence regarding a possible typographical error of the recording of the day of the death changes the relevance of Raddad's alibi for his whereabouts on Monday from very strongly relevant to very weakly relevant.
>
> The process of exploring complex models to identify subtleties such as this can be facilitated by computational tools, which are in turn enabled by the sophisticated representational and inferential capabilities of the modular BNFrag [i.e., Bayesian network fragments] architecture described in this Article. For example, sensitivity analysis can be used to examine the impact of changes in modeling assumptions of the strength of relevance of evidence to hypothesized conclusions. [...] The term sensitivity analysis has multiple, related, but different definitions in the literature on statistics and scientific experimentation. [... W]e illustrate the use of a particular sensitivity analysis, sometimes called an "importance measure," specifically to compute a measure of the weight or relevance of evidence items to a BN query. An item of evidence is called "relevant" to a hypothesis is observing the evidence changes the probability that the hypothesis is true. [...]

Sentenza suicida In Italy: a justification of a verdict written by a trained judge in a deliberately flawed manner, so that an appeal trial would necessarily take place, thus overturning a verdict given by jurors who outvoted that judge at a *mixed court* (nonexistent in Anglo-Saxon countries): see **jury**.

Settlement out of court In a civil case, an agreement among the parties not to continue in the case being litigated. It involves a compromise as to compensation. A settlement out of court should not be mistaken for *plea bargaining*, which applies in criminal cases.

Shield For a defendant in a criminal case: such protection that makes it inadmissible for prosecution to cross-examine in order to obtain bad character evidence, or to adduce such evidence. See **character evidence**, and see **imputation**. Situations in which the defendant loses his shield include such that come into being if he claims good character for himself, or bad character for prosecution witnesses (or for the prosecutor).

Shield bidding A form of malpractice related to *online auction fraud*. It is also known as *bid shielding*. It "occurs when the buyer uses another email address or a friend (the shield) to drive up prices and discourage bids on an item she wants. At the last minute, the shield withdraws the high bid, allowing the buyer to win the item at a lower price. Most auction sites forbid retracting a bid once it's made, and on eBay shill and shield bidding is clearly prohibited" (Wahab, 2004). See Section 6.2.3.

Shilling A form of malpractice related to *online auction fraud*. It is known as *bid shilling*, or *shill bidding*. "The ability to disguise identity, revoke bids, and maintain multiple on-line identities may facilitate undesirable practices like *shilling*. Shilling is where sellers arrange for false bids to be placed on the items they are selling. Sellers place the bid themselves by using multiple identities or by using confederates. The idea is to force up the cost of a winning bid and encourage interest in the auction" (Mena, 2003, p. 256). "*Shill bidding*: is the intentional sham bidding by the seller to drive up the price of his/her own item that is up for bid. This is accomplished by the sellers themselves and/or someone that is associated with the seller making bids to purposely drive up the price of the seller's item." (Wahab, 2004). Cf. **shield bidding.** See Section 6.2.3.

Similar fact evidence An exception to the rule which in criminal law prevents the disclosure of evidence of disposition and character (see **evidence of disposition**). In England, "the law will permit the prosecution to adduce evidence of previous misconduct where its nature, *modus operandi* or some other circumstance, shows an unmistakable similarity to the offence charged. This must be strong enough to go beyond any question of coincidence so as to lead the jury to conclude 'this is the work of the same man'" (Osborne, 1997, pp. 313–314). For a somewhat different concept, see **doctrine of chances**.

Situation theory A formal theory that considers actors within the situation in which they are.

> Situation Theory grew out of attempts by Jon Barwise in the late 1970s to provide a semantics for "naked-infinitive" perceptual reports such as "Claire saw Jon run". Barwise's intuition was that Claire didn't just see Jon, an individual, but Jon doing

something, a situation. Situations are individuals having properties and standing in relations. A theory of situations would allow us to study and compare various types of situations or situation-like entities, such as facts, events, and scenes. One of the central themes of situation theory of meaning and reference should be set within a general theory of information, one moreover that is rich enough to do justice to perception, communication, and thought. By now many people have contributed by the need to give a rigorous mathematical account of the principles of information that underwrite the theory.[41]

Slate A particular computer tool; it supports human users' reasoning by argumentation (Brigsjord, Shilliday, Taylor, Clark, & Khemlani, 2006).

Slot-machine model An extreme logicist view of a legal system. See **logic**.

Smurfing "the breaking up of large sums of money into smaller units, and subsequent passing of each segment through multiple accounts. Used by money launderers, the practice is designed to make the money trail extremely difficult to follow" (Sparrow, 1991, p. 252, fn. 1). See Chapter 6.

Social epistemics Social aspects of the philosophy of knowledge, according to Alvin Goldman (1987a, 1987b). Because of such social aspects, the *requirement of total evidence* is an invalid principle, and an example of contravening on it is *exclusionary laws of evidence* in court: jurors are not given all the evidence, and Goldman (1991), who approves of this, calls this *epistemic paternalism.*

SPLIT-UP "SPLIT-UP is a hybrid rule based/ neural network system developed at La Trobe University that uses textbooks, heuristics, expert advice and cases to model that part of the Family Law Act 1975 (Australia) which deals with property division. Explanation is provided through the use of Toulmin argument structures" (Stranieri & Zeleznikow, 2005a, Glossary. It was they who developed SPLIT-UP).

Stare decisis Stare decisis is a fundamental principle in common law legal systems. The principle dictates that the reasoning, loosely, *ratio decidendi,*[42] used in new cases must follow the reasoning used by decision-makers in courts at the same or higher level in the hierarchy. Stare decisis is unknown to civil law, where judgments rendered by judges only enjoy the *authority of reason.*

Traditional stare decisis is when the same decision has to be taken as a higher court judging about the same facts.

Local stare decisis is when the same decision has to be taken as the same court judging about the same facts.

---

[41] From the summary of Aczel, Israel, Katagiri, and Peters (1993). "Situation theory is the result of an interdisciplinary effort to create a full-fledged theory of information. Created by scholars and scientists from cognitive science, computer science and AI, linguistics, logic, philosophy, and mathematics, it aims to provide a common set of tools for the analysis of phenomena from all these fields. Unlike Shannon-Weaver type theories of information, which are purely quantitative theories, situation theory aims at providing tools for the analysis of the specific content of a situation (signal, message, data base, statement, or other information-carrying situation). The question addressed is not how much information is carried, but what information is carried" (from the publisher's blurb of Aczel et al. 1993).

[42] The ground or reason for the decision. The point in a case that determines the judgement.

Personal stare decisis is when the same decision has to be taken as the same judge judging about the same facts.

State witness One of the intended defendants in a criminal case, who having been offered a deal by the prosecution, turns into a witness, allied with the prosecution, against at least one defendant. This is not only the case of minor offenders. Sometimes offenders with a heavy liability are offered to become state witnesses, or at any rate to inform investigators in such a manner that would secure convictions. In Britain, a state witness is said to be giving *Queen's evidence.*

In Britain, a *supergrass* may be a very important informer, not necessarily a state witness. The supergrass system in Britain emerged in 1972, and in its heyday years it was used against armed robbers in London. It also was used to combat terrorism in Northern Ireland. The first police informer within the supergrass system was Bertie Smalls, who shopped hundreds of associates in 1976; the operation was masterminded by Scotland Yard detective Tony Lundy.

In Italy, a somewhat equivalent system is the *pentitismo*: in the late 1970s, as well as during the 1980s and still during trials held during the 1990s, on occasion a "repentant" terrorist would act as state witness against one or more defendants. Such a witness used to be called a *pentito*, or a *superpentito.* Sometimes the deal drew strong criticism, and in all fairness, defeated justice, such as when the murderer of the journalist Walter Tobagi obtained, by turning state witness, his own freedom, as well as that of the woman who had been his girlfriend before they were separately arrested in different circumstances. Once released, he immediately proceeded to wed another woman. One photograph that was highly visible in the mass media showed him talking, and, inside the same frame, the grim face of the father of the journalist whose murder justice had renounced punishing. It has also happened that the sincerity of a *superpentito*, securing convictions, was quite dubious. This was the case of the state witness during the Sofri case (for the 1972 terrorism-related killing of a police inspector), as well as of a witness from the Mafia against Italy's former prime minister Giulio Andreotti, who was convicted for the violent death of a journalist. Also the testimony of a state witness who had raped and murdered in the Circeo case, securing the convictions of other far rightists for a bombing with massive casualties in Bologna, appears to be discredited.

Statistically oriented case-based reasoning paradigms In artificial intelligence: "In statistically oriented case based reasoning paradigms, cases are used as data points for statistical generalisation. The case based reasoner computes conditional probabilities that a problem should be treated similarly to previously given cases" (Stranieri & Zeleznikow, 2005a, Glossary). See **case-based reasoning**.

Statistical reasoning "In contrast to symbolic reasoning, statistical reasoning derives its results by checking whether or not there is a statistical correlation between two events. Examples of statistical reasoning include neural networks and rule induction systems. Whilst rule based systems are considered to be examples of symbolic reasoning; the rules are often derived using statistical tests" (Stranieri & Zeleznikmow, 2005a, Glossary).

Statutory law In countries like Britain there are both *statutory law*, i.e., laws passed by Parliament, and *common law*, i.e., the body of sentences passed by judges, and that serve as precedent. "Statutory law is that body of law created by acts of the legislature – in contrast to constitutional law and law generated by decisions of courts and administrative bodies" (Stranieri & Zeleznimkow, 2005a, Glossary).

Stevie An argumentation-based computer tool intended for supporting criminal investigation. Stevie enables analysts to view evidence and inferences, The program is described as distilling out of that information coherent *stories* which are "hypothetical reconstructions of what might have happened", and which are defined as "a conflict-free and self-defending collection of claims" which moreover is temporally consistent (van den Braak & Vreeswijk, 2006). See Section 3.10.2.

Story A narrative: see Chapter 5. In *Stevie*, a *story* is "a conflict-free and self-defending collection of claims" which moreover is temporally consistent (van den Braak & Vreeswijk, 2006). See Section 3.10.2.

Story model Of Nancy Pennington and Reid Hastie (1986, 1988, 1992, 1993), for modelling jurors' decision making. It is based on the information processing paradigm from cognitive psychology.

Striking similarity A strong similarity between a crime to previous convictions of a criminal suspect or defendant, such that the crime under trial and the ones from previous convictions are in the same legal category, and shared similarities such as the *modus operandi*, geographic proximity, and so forth. It is where there is such "striking similarity", that a case may get to the jury on previous convictions alone. See *jury observation fallacy*.

Substantive *Substantive*, as opposed to *procedural*, pertains to the rules of right administered by a court, rather than to how to administer it.

Supergrass In Britain, an informer whose collaboration is extremely fruitful for police investigators. Such an informer may or not be a **state witness** (q.v.). The latter is always the case, instead, of Italy's **pentitismo** (q.v.). The supergrass system in Britain emerged in 1972, and in its heyday years it was used against armed robbers in London. It also was used to combat terrorism in Northern Ireland. The first police informer within the supergrass system was Bertie Smalls, who shopped hundreds of associates in 1976; the operation was masterminded by Scotland Yard detective Tony Lundy.

Surrebutter or surrebuttal A plaintiff reply to a defendant's *rebutter.* (See *replication.*)

Surrejoinder A plaintiff reply to a defendant's **rejoinder.** (See **replication**.)

Teleological Of an argument (as opposed to *deontological* reasoning): of a "[reason given for acting or not acting in a certain way may be on account of what so acting or not acting will bring about. [. . .] All teleological reasoning presupposes some evaluation" (MacCormick, 1995, p. 468).

Text mining "sometimes alternately referred to as *text data mining*, roughly equivalent to *text analytics*, refers to the process of deriving high-quality information from text. High-quality information is typically derived through the divining of patterns and trends through means such as statistical pattern learning. Text mining usually involves the process of structuring the input text (usually parsing, along with the addition of some derived linguistic features and the removal of others, and subsequent insertion into a database), deriving patterns within the structured data, and finally evaluation and interpretation of the output. 'High quality' in text mining usually refers to some combination of relevance, novelty, and interestingness. Typical text mining tasks include text categorisation, text clustering, concept/entity extraction, production of granular taxonomies, sentiment analysis, document summarisation, and entity/relation modelling (i.e., learning relations between named entities)".[43] See Chapter 6. Commercial tools include:

- AeroText – provides a suite of text mining applications for content analysis. Content used can be in multiple languages.
- Attensity – hosted, integrated and stand-alone text mining (analytics) software that uses natural language processing technology to address collective intelligence in social media and forums; the voice of the customer in surveys and emails; customer relationship management; e-services; research and e-discovery; risk and compliance; and intelligence analysis.
- Autonomy – suite of text mining, clustering and categorisation solutions for a variety of industries.
- Basis Technology – provides a suite of text analysis modules to identify language, enable search in more than 20 languages, extract entities, and efficiently search for and translate entities.
- Endeca Technologies – provides software to analyse and cluster unstructured text.
- Expert System S.p.A. – suite of semantic technologies and products for developers and knowledge managers.
- Fair Isaac – leading provider of decision management solutions powered by advanced analytics (includes text analytics).
- Inxight – provider of text analytics, search, and unstructured visualisation technologies. (Inxight was bought by Business Objects that was bought by SAP AG in 2008).
- LanguageWare – text analysis libraries and customisation tooling from IBM.
- LexisNexis – provider of business intelligence solutions based on an extensive news and company information content set. Through the recent acquisition of Datops LexisNexis is leveraging its search and retrieval expertise to become a player in the text and data mining field.
- Nstein Technologies – text mining solution that creates rich metadata to allow publishers to increase page views, increase site stickiness, optimise SEO, automate tagging, improve search experience, increase editorial productivity, decrease operational publishing costs, increase online revenues. In combination with search engines it is used to create semantic search applications.

---

[43] Based upon the Wikipedia entry http://en.wikipedia.org/wiki/Text_mining (the way it was in late July 2010).

- SAS – solutions including SAS Text Miner and Teragram – commercial text analytics, natural language processing, and taxonomy software leveraged for Information Management.
- Silobreaker – provides text analytics, clustering, search and visualisation technologies.
- SPSS – provider of SPSS Text Analysis for Surveys, Text Mining for Clementine, LexiQuest Mine and LexiQuest Categorize, commercial text analytics software that can be used in conjunction with SPSS Predictive Analytics Solutions.
- StatSoft – provides STATISTICA Text Miner as an optional extension to STATISTICA Data Miner, for Predictive Analytics Solutions.
- Thomson Data Analyzer – enables complex analysis on patent information, scientific publications and news.

Open source resources include[44]:

- GATE – natural language processing and language engineering tool.
- UIMA – UIMA (Unstructured Information Management Architecture) is a component framework for analysing unstructured content such as text, audio and video, originally developed by IBM.
- YALE/RapidMiner with its Word Vector Tool plug-in – data and text mining software.
- Carrot2 – text and search results clustering framework.

Time *Legal time* is a debated issue in legal theory (e.g., Jackson, 1998b), as well as in AI & Law.[45] For the latter, see a thematic journal issue (Martino & Nissan, 1998) devoted to temporal representation for legal applications. In our present context, it is worth mentioning especially the treatment of a crime narrative in section 5 (pp. 233–238) in Gian Piero Zarri's article (Zarri, 1998) in that journal issue. Zarri described and applied his NKRL system of representation of time, causality and intentionality. Poulin, Mackaay [sic], Bratley, and Frémont (1989) described a "time specialist" software – using "intervals as the basic temporal element" (ibid., p. 747) – as well as a language, EXPERT/T, based on a temporal logic for legal rules. Temporal logics are popular in AI (Fisher et al., 2005; Knight et al., 1999). Also see "Time in automated legal reasoning" by Vila and Yoshino (2005). For another formalism that is oriented, instead, to the semantic representation of verbal tense, Alice ter Meulen's trees for temporal representation, stemming from theoretical semantics, refer to a book review by Nissan

---

[44] http://en.wikipedia.org/wiki/Text_mining

[45] Moreover, the *recency effect* is debated in psychology, in relation to legal evidence (Furnam, 1986).

(1998b). One of the products of CaseSoft,[46] an American firm producing software for legal professionals, is the *TimeMap* chronology-graphing software.
Let us consider constraints on *temporal sequence* in a criminal trial in Anglo-American jurisdictions. The phases of such a trial are as follows:

Indictment;
The accused is asked to plea guilty or not guilty;

- If the defendant pleas guilty – plea-bargain:

    1. The court hears the facts from the prosecution (with no need to present evidence);
    2. Defence may intervene;
    3. Sentence.

- If the defendant pleas not guilty, the case will have to be prosecuted;

    1. Adjournment to an agreed date;
    2. Adjournment hearing (following adversarial lines);
    3. Prosecution opening speech;
    4. Prosecution calls witnesses;

        4.1. Examination in chief;
        4.2. Cross-examination;
        4.3. (sometimes) re-examination;

    5. Close of the prosecution case;
    6. (The defence may submit that there is no case to answer. If the court accepts this, the defendant is discharged. Otherwise:)
    7. Defence calls witnesses:

        7.1. Examination in chief;
        7.2. Cross-examination;
        7.3. (sometimes) re-examination;

    8. Defence's closing speech to the bench (= closing arguments = final submissions);
    9. (Prosecution may have one more speech, but then defence must have the last word.)
    10. The magistrates retire to consider their decision (the decision is taken either by a bench of lay magistrates, i.e., a jury, or a stipendiary magistrate, i.e., a trained judge);

        if the fact-finders are a jury, before they retire they are given final instructions by the judge;

    11. The magistrates return and give a verdict (and state no reason);

        11a. If the verdict is "not guilty", then the defendant is discharged;
        11b. If the verdict is "guilty", then:

            11b.1. The court hears the facts from the prosecution (with no need to present evidence);
            11b.2. Defence may intervene;
            11b.3. Sentence.

---

[46] http://www.casesoft.com

How is the delivery of the evidence affected, by the constraints on the temporal sequence of the phases of a trial? There are important implications for the possibility to introduce evidence. Consider for example employment tribunals in England and Wales (thus, we are not dealing now with criminal cases). The Applicant (i.e., the plaintiff) gives his statement, which is read aloud by himself, or silently by the Court. He is then examined by his barrister (he has one, unless he is representing himself), and then cross-examined by the Respondent's barrister. (If the Applicant is an employee, then the Respondent will typically be his employer.)

Some new evidence, not found in the written statement and in the bundle of documentary evidence, may emerge when the Applicant is asked questions as a witness. Cross-examination of the Applicant is followed sometimes by his being subjected to re-examination by his own side's barrister, and then (also optionally) the Court may ask him questions. Then, all witnesses for the Applicant undergo (each in turn) the same cycle of giving their respective statement, being examined, cross-examined, possibly re-examined, and asked questions by the Court. Next, the same happens for the Respondent.

A major problem for the Applicant arises, if witnesses for the defence present new evidence when examined and cross-examined, as the Applicant's barrister may be unaware on the spur of the moment of what to ask next to such an item of evidence emerging, whereas the (former) employee being the Applicant would be quite able, cognitively but not procedurally in the trial, to ask such questions that would expose untruthful evidence when it is submitted by the defence's witnesses when examined or cross-examined. Procedural constraints prevent the Applicant himself from intervening (unless he has no barrister and is representing himself, which in other respects would be a big disadvantage), let alone making a further statement giving evidence in response to the defence's witnesses. (This is not formally forbidden, but in practice this is strongly and tacitly discouraged, because of how complicate the trial would become.)

A further disadvantage for the Applicant is if after he and his witnesses have finished giving evidence, the barrister for the defence submits some further item of documentary evidence (this may be very important, and deliberately withheld for the purposes of an "ambush"): the Court may criticise such a move, yet accept that the new evidence be added to the bundle. The Applicant's barrister may protest, or refrain from doing so if he or she deems that protesting would be impolitic. Even when summing up in the end, the barrister for the Applicant will be unable to introduce new information as evidence, even though the Applicant may have such information that is relevant or even crucial.

It happens sometimes that by agreement between the parties, a witness for the Applicant will be able to give evidence after one or more witnesses of the Respondent, because the witness being late is cogently unable to come before (e.g., if he has to fly from abroad). Nevertheless, it is up to the parties and to the Court to agree about this. It may be of advantage to the Applicant, if the late witness for the Applicant will be asked questions (possibly, even by the Court) that would enable to assess some evidence that had previously been introduced by a witness for the Respondent. This way, such evidence may be refuted, that would not have been otherwise, because of procedural constraints.

The situation with a late witness for the Applicant is such that procedural constraints on the temporal sequence are overridden because of the agreement between the parties, which enables that witness give evidence after one or more of the witnesses for the Respondent. Out of courtesy, the Court may then instruct the defence that if the defence would like to call back its witnesses that had given evidence before, *after* the late witness of the Applicant, this request would be granted. The defence may then renounce this (perhaps in order not to be perceived as having been put at a disadvantage).

Another way for time constraints to be involved, is that the hearing at the tribunal is booked several months in advance, and one's barrister will have to be paid according to the expected length of the hearing. One tactic of the Respondent may be to cause their witnesses (including ones who do not really introduce important evidence) use more time than expected, so that a new additional hearing, months away, will have to be booked, at which some more witnesses of the Respondent will give evidence, then the Applicant's barrister will sum up, and the Respondent's barrister will sum up. At this additional hearing, the Applicant will have to be silent, not being able to introduce more evidence. Booking another hearing may be beyond what is affordable to the more impecunious party, which oftentimes is an employee of a big corporation. This may in practice compel the Applicant to accept a settlement.

Yet another problem is that sometimes employment tribunals (a president and two further members) are double-booked by the administration of the tribunals, and they themselves only learn about this early during the hearing. For the more impecunious party, this is a major burden, making it more likely that one more hearing will have to be booked. This, too, militates towards the more impecunious party being more likely to accept a settlement.

All of this is interesting both legally, and for AI modelling. The temporal sequence conditions how the evidence can be introduced, and whether evidence can be given in reply. Techniques from AI can represent this. Yet, AI practitioners need know about such procedural constraints. Importantly, there are less exclusionary rules on evidence at employment tribunals in England and Wales, than there are on criminal evidence.

In employment cases, a first deadline applies to the submission of which documentary evidence will go into the bundle. The solicitors of the two parties reach an agreement. Exceptionally (as seen earlier) some new document may be submitted during the hearing, subject to the discretion of the Court. Some time after the bundle of documentary evidence is finalised, the two parties exchange witness statements. This must be simultaneous, in order to avoid that a last-minute change is done in the statement that comes late, so that it would respond to some "surprise" in store in the statement of the other party that arrived early. Exceptionally, on the day after the exchange of statements it may happen that the solicitors for the defence claim to the solicitor of the Applicant that they forgot to email or to fax one of the witnesses statements. The Applicant may renounce to protest, considering that the Court may override the protest.

All of this is fertile ground for AI modelling. Temporal constraints are so important, at a hearing, that they may make or break a case.

We have explained such situations, that a constraint is not satisfied, but then a standard arrangement is adopted. This can be modelled in terms of **contrary-to-duty obligations** (q.v.).

Toulmin's model A widespread model of argument structure (Toulmin, 1958). It consists of the following parts: Data (the premises), Claim (the conclusion), Qualifier (the modality of how the argument holds), Warrant (support for the argument), Backing (support for the Warrant), and Rebuttal (an exception). See Section 3.2.

Traitor tracing A technique applied to *pirate tracking software*, within *multimedia forensics*. The term *traitor tracing* has previously been used also in the literature about cryptography. See Section 6.2.1.5.

Transvaluationism An account of *vagueness* proposed by philosopher Terry Horgan. Cf. **loose talk** (q.v.). Vagueness in statements given in court is usually recognised not to amount to untruthfulness. Horgan (2010, p. 67) states:

> The philosophical account of vagueness I call "transvaluationism" makes three fundamental claims. First, vagueness is logically incoherent in a certain way: it essentially involves mutually unsatisfiable requirements that govern vague language, vague thought-content, and putative vague objects and properties. Second, vagueness in language and thought (i.e., semantic vagueness) is a genuine phenomenon despite possessing this form of incoherence – and is viable, legitimate, and indeed indispensable. Third, vagueness as a feature of objects, properties, or relations (i.e., ontological vagueness) is impossible, because of the mutually unsatisfiable conditions that such putative items would have to meet.

An important concept in Horgan's treatment is that of sorites sequence, an example of which is "a sequence of men each of whom has a tiny bit more hair on his head than his predecessor" (when applying vagueness to the descriptor *bald*). Horgan explains (2010, pp. 70–71):

> A second essential feature of vagueness is what I call "boundarylessness" – a term I adopt from Sainsbury (1990). This feature, which obtains with respect to a sorites sequence, involves the simultaneous satisfaction by the sequence of the following two conditions:

> > *The Difference Condition*: Initially in the sorites sequence there are items with a specific status and every predecessor of an item with this status has the same status. Eventually in the sequence there are items with the polar-opposite status, and every successor of an item with this status has the same status. No item in the sequence has both the initial status and the polar-opposite status.
> > *The Transition Condition*: There is no determinate fact of the matter about status-transitions in the sorites sequence.

> Examples of polar-opposite statuses are baldness vs. nonbaldness, heaphood vs. nonheaphood, satisfying the predicate "is bald" vs. satisfying the expression "is not bald", truth vs. falsity.

The Transition Condition needs further conceptual unpacking. It involves, essentially, two conceptual aspects or dimensions, one individualistic and the other collectivistic.

The Individualistic Same-Status Principle (*ISS Principle*): Each item in the sorites sequence has the same status as its immediate neighbors.

The Collectivistic Status-Indeterminacy Principle (*CSI Principle*): There is no correct overall distribution of statuses to the items in the sequence.

The ISS Principle is so called because it involves items in the sequence considered individually – each considered in relation to its immediate neighbors. The CSS Principle is so called because it involves the items in the sequence considered collectively. Both principles are essentially involved in the idea of boundarylessness – the idea of an absence of sharp boundaries.

TreeAge Pro Decision tree software, for performing a Litigation Risk Analysis. See Section 4.3.1.

Trial by mathematics Originally, the title of Tribe (1971), about the Bayesian approach to modelling judicial decision-making in criminal cases. Nevertheless, the phrase is likelier to occur in polemical contexts.

Triangulation A form of *online auction fraud* (see Section 6.2.3). "Involves three parties: the perpetrator, a consumer, and an online merchant. The perpetrator buys merchandise from an online merchant using stolen identities and credit card numbers. Then, the perpetrator sells the merchandise at online auction sites to unsuspecting buyers. Later, the police seize the stolen merchandise to keep for evidence, and the buyer and merchant end up the victims" (Wahab, 2004).

Triers of fact See *factfinders*. Jurors are *lay triers of fact*.

Trustworthiness question In argumentation studies, Walton's (1997) *Appeal to Expert Opinion* offered (ibid., pp. 211–225) an argumentation scheme for "Argument for Expert Opinion", then reproduced in Walton et al. (2008, pp. 381–382). See s.v. *Expert opinion, Appeal to* above. The expert source is E; the subject domain is S; and A is a proposition about which E claims to be true (or false). The trustworthiness question is: "Is E personally reliable as a source?". It is articulated in three more detailed subquestions: "Is E biased?"; "Is E honest?"; "Is E conscientious?".

Truth maintenance system (*TMS* for short) Within artificial intelligence, such representation and search procedures that keep track of the reasoning steps of a logic system. "Nonmonotonic reasoning [q.v.], because conclusions must sometimes be reconsidered, is called *defeasible*; that is, new information may sometimes invalidate previous results. [...] In defeasible reasoning, the TMS preserves the consistency of the knowledge base, keeping track of conclusions that might later need be questioned" (Luger & Stubblefield, 1998, p. 270).

Uncharged conduct or uncharged misconduct A kind of bad character evidence: such past behaviour for which no charges were brought. See **character evidence**.

Utility One theoretical approach to adjudication is in terms of utility: see Friedman (1997, pp. 277–278); Lempert (1977, pp. 1021, 1032–1041). Let there be two options: plaintiff (**p**) wins, i.e., the court finding for the plaintiff, or defendant (**d**) wins, i.e., the finding is for **d**.

It would seem wisest to select the option with the greater expected utility. The formulae are:

$$EU(p) = P(\Pi) \times U(p,\Pi) + P(\Delta) \times U(p,\Delta)$$

and

$$EU(d) = P(\Pi) \times U(d,\Pi) + P(\Delta) \times U(d,\Delta),$$

"where $EU(p)$ and $EU(d)$ represent the expected utilities of judgments for the plaintiff and the defendant, respectively; $P(\Pi)$ represents the probability that the facts are such that the plaintiff is entitled to judgment, and $P(\Delta)$ represents the comparable probability with respect to the defendant" (Friedman, p. 277). Of the two arguments of the (social) utility function U, the first one represents the winner ("the party who receives the judgment"), and the second one stands for the party that in truth deserves to win ("the party who is in fact entitled to judgment"). "Thus, for example, $U(p,\Delta)$ equals the social utility of a judgment for the plaintiff when the truth, if it were known, is such that the defendant should receive judgment. $U(p,\Pi)$ and $U(d,\Delta)$ must each have greater utility than $U(p,\Delta)$ and $U(d,\Pi)$; it is helpful to assume that the first pair has positive utility and the second pair has negative utility" (ibid., pp. 277–278). The *standard of persuasion* $O(\Pi)$ is the degree of confidence when $EU(p) = EU(d)$. The *plaintiff wins* is optimal "only if the fact-finder's degree of confidence in the plaintiff's case is at least as great as this level" (ibid., p. 278), if it is a civil case.

$$O(\Pi) = P(\Pi)/(1 - P(\Pi)) =$$
$$(U(d,\Delta) - U(p, \Delta)/(U(p, \Pi)) - U(d,\Pi))$$

In contrast, in a criminal case the standard is *beyond a reasonable doubt*. The negative utility of wrongly convicting an innocent, $U(p,\Delta)$, "far exceeds any of the other utilities in magnitude" (ibid., p. 278). In civil cases, the usual conception is that $U(p,\Pi) = U(d,\Delta)$ and that $U(p,\Delta) = U(d,\Pi)$. "This means that the standard of persuasion, expressed in odds, equals 1, or 0.5 expressed as a probability. This, of course, is the familiar 'more likely than not', or 'balance of probabilities', standard" (ibid., p. 278).

Virtopsy A computational technique developed by a team in Bern, Switzerland, for carrying out "a virtual autopsy": information acquired through post mortem imaging prior to autopsy is often used to plan the autopsy, confirm autopsy findings and allow for a second look if further questions arise in during the forensic investigation. See Chapter 9.

Voir dire The jury selection process, with safeguards: the parties can have prospective jurors rejected, as a safeguard intended to weed out such jurors that are perceived to be prone to be biased. "Courts in the USA permit attorneys much more latitude in jury selection (voir dire) than do criminal court procedures world-wide" (Cutler & Penron, p. 208). Nevertheless, "US federal courts and many state courts (e.g. Massachusetts, California) perform the most perfunctory voir dire and do not permit attorneys to ask questions about jurors' attitudes. Indeed, judges in these courts are not obligated to permit attorneys to ask any questions during voir dire" (ibid.). This is a severe limitation on voir dire as a safeguard, and attorneys are in a sense forced to rely on stereotypes about categories of prospective jurors, rather than on informed evaluations. Moreover, *voir dire* also applies to the acceptance of an *expert witness* being opposed by the opposing attorney. In the words of Knott (1987, p. 14):

> The opposing attorney will ask questions that will show that you have limited expertise in the specific field at hand, and therefore your testimony should be limited or disallowed. The attorney is really trying to prevent certain opinions from being introduced and is doing it on the grounds that your expertise does not extend into that area. He or she will ask you questions and, on the basis of your answers, will move to reject you as an expert.
>
> Note: You will not be allowed to say anything more in your defense. The judge will assume the answers you gave during voir dire were complete. Your attorney may ask you additional questions to clear up the confusion, but don't count on it. Note that if the opposing attorney is successful, he or she may have destroyed you and your client's case.

Weight (evidential) The probative value of the evidence.

Wigmore Charts A graphic method of structuring legal arguments, currently conspicuous in some more formal approached within legal evidence scholarship; first introduced by American jurist John Henry Wigmore in the *Illinois Law Review*, 8 (1913), 77. See Section 3.2.

Witness: two-witness rule Mandated by Biblical law for capital cases: two eyewitnesses are necessary, and circumstantial evidence or other evidence is not valid. This rule has been influential. Bernard Jackson, who discussed the matter at length in Jackson (1977), explains (Jackson, 1990, p. 18):

> [T]he two-witness rule of the Bible has been widely adopted in countries influenced by Canon law, as indeed have some of the necessary means of avoiding its rigours. When the medieval Canon lawyers sought to construct an institution of corroboration by similar fact evidence (*testes singulares*), they justified their argument by analysis of the facts of the story of Susannah, found in the Apocrypha to the Hebrew Bible. True enough, they said, Susannah could not be rightly convicted when one elder said that she committed adultery under an oak while the other said it was under a holm tree. But that was only because the two elders had claimed to have observed the event *together*. Had they not made this claim, their evidence would not have been regarded as logically contradictory: for though adultery may not be committed simultaneously under two different trees, it may be so committed successively. Moreover, we all know (so the Canon law doctors argued) that adultery with the some lover is an act which is prone to be repeated – *factum iterabile* – unlike some other crimes against Canon law, such as the murder of a Bishop (especially the same Bishop). I have traced the use of this argument for corroboration by similar fact evidence from a Canonist *Summa* of the mid-12th century, written in Bologna, to English treason trials of the 17th century, and a famous divorce case of the same period, which then became one of the principal foundations for the so-called *Moorov* doctrine which Lord Hailsham so fully read into his speech in the House of Lords in the modern leading case of *Kilbourne*.

In Jewish law, this argument would not have been valid for conviction in a criminal case, and two eyewitnesses would have still been necessary, who witnessed the same event and reported about it with no contradiction.

Witness vs. expert testimonies Evidence as given by individuals who have knowledge of specific details in a legal narrative at hand, as opposed to evidence given by professionals (expert witnesses) based on their professional expertise.

References

AAAI. (2002). *Ontologies and the semantic web: Papers from the AAAI workshop, Edmonton, AB, Canada, July 2002*. American Association for Artificial Intelligence. Edmonton, AB: AAAI Press.

Aamodt, A., Kvistad, K. A., Andersen, E., Lund-Larsen, J., Eine, J., Benum, P., et al. (1999). Determination of the Hounsfield value for CT based design of custom femoral stems. *The Journal of Bone & Joint Surgery*,[47] *81-B*(1), 143–147. http://web.jbjs.org.uk/cgi/reprint/81-B/1/143.pdf

Aarne, A., & Thompson, S. (1928). *The types of the folktale: A classification and bibliography* (A. Aarne, Trans. and S. Thompson, Enlarge) (FF Communications, Vol. 74.) Helsinki: Suomalainen Tiedeakatemia = Academia Scientiarum Fennica, 1928. 2nd revision: (FF Communications, Vol. 75, No. 184), 1961. Reprints: 1973, 1964, 1981. Another reprint: B. Franklin, New York, 1971. Aarne's German original was *Verzeichnis der Märchentypen*.

Abaci, T., Mortara, M., Patane, G., Spagnuolo, M., Vexo, F., & Thalmann, D. (2005). Bridging geometry and semantics for object manipulation and grasping. In *Proceedings of workshop towards Semantic Virtual Environments (SVE 2005)*. Also, Report VRLAB CONF 2005 021. Lausanne: Virtual Reality Lab at the Swiss Federal Institute of Technology. http://infoscience.epfl.ch/getfile.py?recid=99017&mode=best

Abbasi, A. (2010, July/August). Intelligent feature selection for sentiment classification. In H. Chen (Ed.), *AI and opinion mining, part 2*, under the rubric Trends & Controversies. *IEEE Intelligent Systems, 25*(4), 75–79.

Abelson, R. P. (1979). Differences between belief and knowledge systems. *Cognitive Science, 3*, 355–366.

Abelson, R. P. (1995). *Statistics as a principled argument*. Hillsdale, NJ: Lawrence Erlbaum Associates.

Abiteboul, S., Fischer, P. C., & Schek, H.-J. (Eds.). (1989). *Nested relations and complex objects in databases*. Lecture Notes in Computer Science, Vol. 361. Berlin: Springer.

Abrahams, A. S., Eyers, D. M., & Bacon, J. M. (2009). Structured storage of legal precedents using a minimal deontic ontology, for computer assisted legal document querying. *International Journal of Metadata, Semantics and Ontologies, 4*(3), 196–211.

Ackerman, M. J. (1995). *Clinician's guide to child custody evaluations*. New York: Wiley.

Ackermann, W. (1956). Begründung einer strengen Implikation. *Journal of Symbolic Logic, 21*(2), 113–128. http://www.jstor.org/stable/2268750

Ackley, D. H., Hinton, G. E., & Sejnowski, T. J. (1985). A learning algorithm for Boltzmann machines. *Cognitive Science, 9*, 147–169.

---

[47] This is the journal of the British Editorial Society of Bone and Joint Surgery.

Aczel, P., Israel, D., Katagiri, Y., & Peters, S. (Eds.). (1993). *Situation theory and its applications*, (Vol. 3). CSLI Lecture Notes, Vol. 37. Stanford, CA: Center for the Study of Language and Information (CSLI).[48]

Adderley, R., & Musgrove, P. (2003a). Modus operandi modeling of group offending: A case study. Section 6.12 In J. Mena (Ed.), *Investigative data mining for security and criminal detection* (pp. 179–195). Amsterdam & Boston: Butterworth-Heinemann (of Elsevier).

Adderley, R., & Musgrove, P. (2003b). Modeling the behavior of offenders who commit serious sexual assaults: A case study. Sec. 12.4 In J. Mena (Ed.), *Investigative data mining for security and criminal detection* (348–362). Amsterdam & Boston: Butterworth-Heinemann (of Elsevier).

Adderley, R., & Musgrove, P. B. (2003c). Clustering burglars: A case study. Section 1.15 In J. Mena (Ed.), *Investigative data mining for security and criminal detection* (pp. 24–37). Amsterdam & Boston: Butterworth-Heinemann (of Elsevier).

Adler, J. R. (Ed.). (2004). *Forensic psychology: Concepts, debates and practice*. Cullompton: Willan Publishing (distrib. Routledge). 2nd edition: 2010.

Adriaans, P., & Zantinge, D. (1996). *Data mining*. Reading, MA: Addison Wesley.

Agharia, A., & Friedman, R. (2005). A replication- and checkpoint-based approach for anomaly-based intrusion detection and recovery. At the second international workshop on Security in Distributed Computing Systems (SDCS). In *Proceedings of the 25th International Conference on Distributed Computing Systems Workshops (ICDCS 2005 Workshops)*, 6–10 June 2005, Columbus, OH. IEEE Computer Society 2005, pp. 137–143.

Aggarwal, C. C. (2011). *Social network data analysis*. Berlin: Springer.

Aghayev, E., Ebert, L. C., Christe, A., Jackowski, C., Rudolph, T., Koval, J., et al. (2008). CT based navigation for post-mortem biopsy: A feasibility study. *Journal of Forensic Legal Medicine, 15*(6), 382–387.

Aghayev, E., Thali, M. J., Sonnenschein, M., Jackowski, C., Dirnhofer, R., & Vock, P. (2007). Post-mortem tissue sampling using computed tomography guidance. *Forensic Science International, 166*(2/3), 199–203.

Agrawal, R., Imielinski, T., & Swami, A. (1993). Mining association rules between sets of items in large databases. In *Proceedings of the 1993 ACM SIGMOD international conference on management of data (SIGMOD'93)*, Washington, DC, pp. 207–216.

Agrawal, R., & Srikant, R. (1994). Fast algorithms for mining association rules. In *Proceedings of the 20th international conference on Very Large Data Bases (VLDB'94)*, Santiago, Chile, pp. 487–499.

Agur, A., Ng-Thow-Hing, V., Ball, K., Fiume, E., & McKee, N. (2003). Documentation and three-dimensional modelling of human soleus muscle architecture. *Clinical Anatomy, 16*(4), 285–293.

Ahmed, B. (2007). Role players: Baria Ahmed looks at the many functions the expert may fulfil in ADR. In *Expert Witness Supplement* to *The New Law Journal, 157*(7294) (London, 26 October 2007), 1485.

Aikenhead, M. (1996). The uses and abuses of neural networks in law. *Santa Clara Computer and High Technology Law Journal, 12*(1), 31–70.

Aitken, C. (1995). *Statistics and the evaluation of evidence for forensic scientists*. Chichester: Wiley.

Aitken, C., & Taroni, F. (2004). *Statistics and the evaluation of evidence*. Chichester: Wiley.

Aitken, C., Taroni, F., & Garbolino, P. (2003). A graphical model for the evaluation of cross-transfer evidence in DNA profiles. *Theoretical Population Biology, 63*(3), 179–190.

Aked, J. P. (1994). *Individual constancies in written language expression*. Ph.D. Thesis, University of Glasgow.

---

[48] These are the *Proceedings of the Third International Conference on Situation Theory and Its Applications* Oiso, Japan, November 1991.

Akin, L. L. (2004). *Blood spatter interpretation at crime and accident scenes: A step by step guide for medicolegal investigators*. Austin, TX: On Scene Forensics.

Akin, L. L. (2005). Blood interpretation at crime scenes. *The Forensic Examiner*, Summer 2005, 6–10. http://www.onsceneforensics.com/PDFs%20Forms/ACFEI_BLOOD_SPATTER_AKIN. pdf

Albonetti, C. (1987). Prosecutorial discretion: The effects of uncertainty. *Law and Society Review, 21*, 291–313. doi://10.2307/3053523.

Alchourrón, C. E., Gärdenfors, P., & Makinson, D. (1985). On the logic of theory change: Partial meet contraction and revision functions. *The Journal of Symbolic Logic, 50*, 510–530.

Alcoff, L. M. (2010). Sotomayor's reasoning. *The Southern Journal of Philosophy, 48*(1), 122–138.

Aleven, V., & Ashley, K. D. (1997). Evaluating a learning environment for case-based argumentation skills. In *Proceedings of the sixth international conference on artificial intelligence and law*. New York: ACM Press, pp. 170–179.

Alexander, R. (1992). Mediation, violence and the family. *Alternative Law Journal, 17*(6), 276–299.

Alexander, R. (2000). *Reflections on gender in family law decision making in Australia*. Ph.D thesis, Faculty of Law, Monash University, Clayton, VIC.

Alexy, R. (1989). *A theory of legal argumentation*. Oxford: Clarendon Press.

Alheit, K. (1989). Expert systems in law: Issues of liability. In A. A. Martino (Ed.), *Pre-proceedings of the third international conference on "Logica, informatica, diritto: Legal expert systems"*, Florence, 1989 (2 vols. + Appendix) (Vol. 2, pp. 43–52). Florence: Istituto per la Documentazione Giuridica, Consiglio Nazionale delle Ricerche.

Alker, H.R., Jr. (1996). Toynbee's Jesus: Computational hermeneutics and the continuing presence of classical Mediterranean civilization. Chapter 3 In H. R. Alker Jr. (Ed.), *Rediscoveries and reformulations: Humanistic methodologies for international studies*. (Cambridge Studies in International Relations, Vol. 41, pp. 104–143) Cambridge: Cambridge University Press. Extracted and revised from Alker et al. (1985).

Alker, H. R., Jr., Lehnert, W. G., & Schneider, D. K. 1985. Two reinterpretations of Toynbee's Jesus: Explorations in computational hermeneutics. In G. Tonfoni (Ed.), *Artificial intelligence and text-understanding: Plot units and summarization procedures* (pp. 49–94). Quaderni di Ricerca Linguistica, Vol. 6. Parma, Italy: Edizioni Zara.

Al-Kofahi, K., Tyrrell, A., Vachher, A., & Jackson, P. (2001). A machine learning approach to prior case retrieval. In *Proceedings of the eighth International Conference on Artificial Intelligence and Law* (ICAIL'01), St. Louis, MO. New York: ACM Press, pp. 89–93.

Allen, J. F. (1983a). Recognizing intentions from natural language utterances. Chapter 2 In M. Bradie & R. C. Berwick (Eds.), *Computational models of discourse* (pp. 108–166). Cambridge, MA: MIT Press.

Allen, J. F. (1983b). Maintaining knowledge about temporal intervals. *Communications of the ACM, 26*, 832–843.

Allen, J. F. (1984). Towards a general theory of action and time. *Artificial Intelligence, 23*(2), 123–154.

Allen, J. F. (1991). Time and time again: The many ways to represent time. *International Journal of Intelligent Systems, 6*, 341–355.

Allen, M., Bench-Capon, T., & Staniford, G. (2000). A multi-agent legal argument generator. In *Proceedings of the eleventh international workshop on Database and Expert Systems Applications (DEXA 2000)*, September 2000, Greenwich, London. New York: IEEE Computer Society, pp. 1080–1084.

Allen, R., & Redmayne, M. (Eds.). (1997). *Bayesianism and Juridical Proof*, special issue, *The International Journal of Evidence and Proof, 1*, 253–360. (London: Blackstone)

Allen, R. J. (1986). A reconceptualization of civil trials. *Boston University Law Review, 66*, 401–437.

Allen, R. J. (1991). The nature of juridical proof. *Cardozo Law Review, 13*, 373–422.

Allen, R. J. (1992). The hearsay rule as a rule of admission. *Minnesota Law Review, 76*, 797–812.

Allen, R. J. (1994). Factual ambiguity and a theory of evidence. *Northwestern University Law Review, 88*, 604–640.

Allen, R. J. (1997). Rationality, algorithms and juridical proof: A preliminary inquiry. *International Journal of Evidence and Proof, 1*, 254–275.

Allen, R. J. (2000). Clarifying the burden of persuasion and Bayesian decision rules: A response to Professor Kaye. *International Journal of Evidence and Proof, 4*, 246–259.

Allen, R. J. (2001a). Artificial intelligence and the evidentiary process: The challenges of formalism and computation. *Artificial Intelligence and Law, 9*(2/3), 99–114.

Allen, R. J. (2001b). Clarifying the burden of persuasion and Bayesian decision rules: A response to Professor Kaye. *International Journal of Evidence and Proof, 4*, 246–259.

Allen, R. J. (2003). The error of expected loss minimization. *Law, Probability & Risk, 2*, 1–7.

Allen, R. J. (2008a). Explanationism all the way down. *Episteme, 3*(5), 320–328.

Allen, R. J. (2008b). Juridical proof and the best explanation. *Law & Philosophy, 27*, 223–268.

Allen, R. J., & Lively, S. (2003 [2004]). Burdens of persuasion in civil cases: Algorithms v. explanations. *MSU Law Review, 2003*, 893–944.

Allen, R. J., & Pardo, M. S. (2007a). The problematic value of mathematical models of evidence. *Journal of Legal Studies, 36*, 107–140.

Allen, R. J., & Pardo, M. S. (2007b). Probability, explanation and inference: A reply. *International Journal of Evidence and Proof, 11*, 307–317.

Allen, R. J., & Pardo, M. S. (2008). Juridical proof and the best explanation. *Law & Philosophy, 27*, 223–268.

Almirall, J. (2001). Manslaughter caused by a hit-and-run: Glass as evidence of association. Chapter 7 In: M. M. Houck (Ed.), *Mute witnesses: Trace evidence analysis*. London: Academic.

ALS News. (2000). Laser time slicing promises ultrafast time resolution. *ALS News*, 156 (July 12, 2000, last updated on September 30, 2002), report posted at *The Advanced Light Source* website at http://www.als.lbl.gov/als/science/sci_archive/femto2.html Retrieved in March 2007.

Alston, W. P. (1989). *Epistemic justification*. Ithaca, NY: Cornell University Press.

Alston, W. P. (2005). Perception and representation. *Philosophy and Phenomenological Research, 70*, 253–289.

Altman, A., & Tenneholtz, M. (2005). Ranking systems: The PageRank axioms. In *EC '05: Proceedings of the 6th ACM conference on Electronic Commerce (EC'05)*, Vancouver, Canada, 5–8 June 2005, pp. 1–8. http://stanford.edu/~epsalon/pagerank.pdf

Alur, R, Henzinger, T. A., & Kupferman, O. (2002). Alternating-time temporal logic. *Journal of the ACM, 49*(5), 672–713.

Alvarado, S. J. 1990. *Understanding editorial text: A computer model of argument comprehension*. Boston and Amsterdam: Kluwer. Cf. an earlier version at ftp://ftp.cs.ucla.edu/tech-report/198_-reports/890045.pdf

Alvesalo, A. (2003). Economic crime investigators at work. *Policing & Society, 13*(2), 115–138 (Taylor & Francis).

Amgoud, L., Caminada, M., Cayrol, C., Doutre, S., Lagasquie-Schiex, M.-C., Modgil, S., et al. (2004). Argument-based inference. In J. Fox (Ed.), *Theoretical Framework for argumentation* (pp. 3–46). ASPIC Consortium.

Amgoud, L., & Maudet, N. (2002). Strategical considerations for argumentative agents. In S. Benferhat & E. Giunchiglia (Eds.), *Proceedings of the 9th international workshop on Non-monotonic Reasoning (NMR)* (pp. 399–407). Toulouse, France: IRIT.

Amigoni, F., & Continanza, L. (2012, in press). A lattice-based approach to the problem of recruitment in multiagent systems. *Computational Intelligence*.

Amin, R., Bramer, M., & Emslie, R. (2003). Intelligent data analysis for conservation: Experiments with rhino horn fingerprint identification. *Knowledge Based Systems, 16*(5–6).

Amos, W. (1985). *The originals: Who's really who in fiction*. London: Cape.

Anderson, A. R. (1960). Completeness theorems for the system E of entailment and EQ of entailment with quantification. *Zeitschrift für mathematische Logik und Grundlagen der Mathematik, 6*, 201–216.

Anderson, A. R. (1967). Some nasty problems in the formal logic of ethics. *Nous, 1*, 354–360.

Anderson, A. R., & Belnap, N. D. (1975). *Entailment: The logic of relevance and necessity* (Vol. 1). Princeton, NJ: Princeton University Press.

Anderson, A. R., & Dunn, J. M. (1992). *Entailment: The logic of relevance and necessity* (Vol. 2). Princeton, NJ: Princeton University Press.

Anderson, G. S. (2005). Forensic entomology. In S. H. James & J. J. Nordby (Eds.), *Forensic science: An introduction to scientific and investigative techniques* (2nd ed.). Boca Raton, FL: CRC Press. Also in 3rd edition, 2009.

Anderson, M., & Perlis, D. (2005). Logic, self-awareness and self-improvement: The metacognitive loop and the problem of brittleness. *Journal of Logic and Computation, 15*(1), 21–40.

Anderson, T., Schum, D., & Twining, W. (2005). *Analysis of evidence: How to do things with facts. Based on Wigmore's science of judicial proof.* Cambridge, UK: Cambridge University Press.

Anderson, T., & Twining, W. (1991). *Analysis of evidence: How to do things with facts.* (With a teacher's manual.) London: Weidenfeld & Nicolson[49]; Boston: Little, Brown & Co., 1991; Evanston, IL: Northwestern University Press, 1998. [The 2nd edn. (extensively revised) is Anderson et al. (2005).]

Anderson, T. J. (1999a). The Netherlands criminal justice system: An audit model of decision-making. Chapter 4 In M. Malsch & J. F. Nijboer (Eds.), *Complex cases: Perspectives on the Netherlands criminal justice system* (pp. 47–67). (Series: Criminal Sciences). Amsterdam: THELA THESIS.

Anderson, T. J. (1999b). On generalizations: A preliminary exploration. *South Texas Law Review, 40*.

André, E., Rist, T., & Müller, J. (1998). Integrating reactive and scripted behaviors in a life-like presentation agent. In K. P. Sycara & M. Wooldridge (Eds.), *Proceedings of the second international conference on autonomous agents* (pp. 261–268). New York: ACM Press.

[Anon.] (2001). Rediscovery of long lost birds. (Rediscovery of rare birds makes us aware of the importance of micro-habitats for saving an endangered species.) *Deccan Herald* (Bangalore, India), Sunday, October 14, 2001. http://www.deccanherald.com/deccanherald/oct14/sh5.htm

Anouncia, S. M., & Saravanan, R. (2007). Ontology based process plan generation for image processing. *International Journal of Metadata, Semantics and Ontologies, 2*(3), 211–222.

Antoniou, G. (1997). *Nonmonotonic reasoning with incomplete and changing information.* Cambridge, MA: The MIT Press.

Antoniou, G., Billington, D., Governatori, G., Maher, M. J., & Rock, A. (2000). A flexible framework for defeasible logics. In *Proceedings of the 17th national conference on artificial intelligence and 12th conference on innovative applications of artificial intelligence*, Austin, TX. Cambridge, MA: MIT Press for the AAAI Press, pp. 405–411.

Antoniou, G., Billington, D., & Maher, M. J. (1999). The analysis of regulations using defeasible rules. In *Proceedings of the 32nd Hawaii international conference on systems science.* Maui, Hawaii, p. 225.

Appelbaum, P. S., & Kemp, K. N. (1982). The evolution of commitment law in the nineteenth century: A reinterpretation. *Law and Human Behavior, 6*(3/4), 343–354.

Appling, D. S., & Riedl, M. O. (2009). Representations for learning to summarise plots. In *Intelligent narrative technologies, II: Papers from the AAAI spring symposium*, 2009.

Åqvist, L. (1967). Good Samaritans, contrary-to-duty imperatives, and epistemic obligations. *Noûs, 1*, 361–379.

Åqvist, L. (1984). Deontic logic. In D. Gabbay & F. Guenthner (Eds.), *Handbook of philosphical logic*, vol. 2: *Extensions of classical logic* (pp. 605–714). Dordrecht: Reidel (Kluwer).

Åqvist, L. (1986). *Introduction to deontic logic and the theory of normative systems.* (Indices. Monographs in Philosophical Logic and Formal Linguistics, 4.) Naples, Italy: Bibliopolis.

---

[49] There was a preliminary circulation draft already in 1984.

Åqvist, L. (1992). Towards a logical theory of legal evidence: Semantic analysis of the Bolding-Ekelöf degrees of evidential strength. In A. A. Martino (Ed.), *Expert systems in law* (pp. 67–86). Amsterdam: North-Holland.

Arbabi, E., Boulic, R., & Thalmann, D. (2007a). A fast method for finding maximum range of motion in the hip joint. In *Computer assisted orthopaedic surgery: 7th annual meeting of CAOS, international proceedings* (pp. 497–500). [*CAOS'07*.] Germany: Pro BUSINESS, on behalf of the International Society for Computer Assisted Orthopaedic Surgery[50]. Also, Report VRLAB-CONF-2007-139. Lausanne: Virtual Reality Lab at the Swiss Federal Institute of Technology. http://infoscience.epfl.ch/getfile.py?recid=109304&mode=best

Arbabi, E., Boulic, R., & Thalmann, D. (2007b). A fast method for finding range of motion in the human joints. In *Proceedings of the 29th annual international conference of the IEEE Engineering in Medicine and Biology Society (EMBS'07)*,[51] Lyon, France, August 23–26, 2007. Also, Report VRLAB-CONF-2007-140. Lausanne: Virtual Reality Lab at the Swiss Federal Institute of Technology.

Ardrey, B. (1994). *Mass spectrometry in the forensic sciences.* (VG Monographs in Mass Spectrometry.) Manchester: Fisons Instruments.

Argamon, S., Bloom, K., Esuli, A., & Sebastiani, F. (2009). Automatically determining attitude type and force for sentiment analysis. In Z. Vetulani & H. Uszkoreit (Eds.), *Responding to information society challenges: New advances in human language technologies* (pp. 218–231). Lecture Notes in Artificial Intelligence, Vol. 5603. Berlin: Springer.

Arnold, K. (1971). *Johannes Trithemius (1462–1516).* Würzburg, West Germany: Kommissionsverlag Ferdinand Schoningh. 2nd edn. (1991).

Aron, J. (2012, January 14). Software could spot face-changing criminals. *New Scientist, 213*(2847), 18–19.

Arrigoni Neri, M., & Colombetti, M. (2009). Ontology-based learning objects search and courses generation. In E. Nissan, G. Gini, & M. Colombetti (Eds.), *Marco Somalvico memorial issue*, Special issue of *Applied Artificial Intelligence, 23*(3), 233–260.

Arthaber, A. (1929). *Dizionario comparato di proverbi e modi proverbiali in sette lingue: italiana, latina, francese, spagnola, tedesca, inglese, greca antica.* Milan: Hoepli (repr. 1972; curr. repr. 1991).

Artikis, A., Sergot, M., & Pitt, J. (2003). An executable specification of an argumentation protocol. In G. Sartor (Ed.), *Proceedings of the ninth International Conference on Artificial Intelligence and Law (ICAIL 2003)*, Edinburgh, Scotland, 24–28 June 2003 (pp. 1–11). New York: ACM Press.

Arutyunov. (1963). See citations inside Keh (1984).

Asaro, C., Nissan, E., & Martino, A. A. (2001). DAEDALUS: An integrated tool for the Italian examining magistrate and the prosecutor. A sample session: Investigating an extortion case. *Computing and Informatics, 20*(6), 515–554.

Asher, N., & Sablayrolles, P. (1995). A typology and discourse semantics for motion verbs and spatial PPs in French. *Journal of Semantics, 12*(2), 163–209.

Ashley, K. (1991). *Modeling legal argument: Reasoning with cases and hypotheticals.* Cambridge, MA: The MIT Press (Bradford Books).

Astrova, I., & Kalja, A. (2008). Storing OWL ontologies in SQL3 object-relational databases. In *Proceedings of the eighth conference on applied informatics and communications*, Rhodes, Greece, August 20–22, 2008, pp. 99–103.

Atib, H., & Zeleznikow, J. (2005). A methodology for constructing decision support systems for crime detection. In R. Khosla, R. J. Howlett, & L. C. Jain (Eds.), *Knowledge-based intelligent information and engineering systems: Ninth international conference, KES 2005, Melbourne,*

---

[50] http://www.caos-international.org/

[51] http://www.embc07.ulster.ac.uk/

Australia, September 14–16, 2005, Proceedings, Part IV (pp. 823–829). (Lecture Notes in Computer Science, Vol. 3684.) Berlin: Springer.

Atkinson, J. M, & Drew, P. (1979). *Order in court: The organization of verbal interaction in judicial settings*. Atlantic Highlands, NJ: Humanities Press.

Atkinson, K., Bench-Capon, T., & McBurney, P. (2005a). Generating intentions through argumentation. In F. Dignum, V. Dignum, S. Koenig, S. Kraus, & M. Wooldridge (Eds.), *Proceedings of the fourth international joint conference on Autonomous Agents and Multi-agent Systems (AAMAS 2005)*, Utrecht, The Netherlands (pp. 1261–1262). New York: ACM Press.

Atkinson, K., Bench-Capon, T., & McBurney, P. (2005b). A dialogue game protocol for multi-agent argument over proposals of action. In K. Sycara & M. Wooldridge (Eds.), *Argumentation in Multi-Agent Systems*, special issue of the *Journal of Autonomous Agents and Multi-Agent Systems, 11*(2), 153–171.

Atkinson, K., Bench-Capon, T., & McBurney, P. (2005c). Persuasive political argument. In F. Grasso, C. Reed, & R. Kibble (Eds.), *Proceedings of the fifth international workshop on Computational Models of Natural Argument (CMNA 2005)*, at *IJCAI 2005*, Edinburgh, Scotland.

Atkinson, K., & Bench-Capon, T. J. M. (2007a). Argumentation and standards of proof. In *Proceedings of the 11th International Conference on Artificial Intelligence and Law (ICAIL 2007)*, Stanford, CA, June 4–8, 2007. New York: ACM Press, pp. 107–116.

Atkinson, K., & Bench-Capon, T. J. M. (2007b). Practical reasoning as presumptive argumentation using action based alternating transition systems. *Artificial Intelligence, 171*(10–15), 855–874.

Aubel, A., & Thalmann, D. (2000). Realistic deformation of human body shapes. In *Proceedings of computer animation and simulation 2000*, Interlaken, Switzerland, 2000 (pp. 125–135). Posted at http://vrlab.epfl.ch/Publications of the Virtual Reality Lab at the Swiss Federal Institute of Technology in Lausanne.

Aubel, A., & Thalmann, D. (2001). Efficient muscle shape deformation. In N. Magnenat-Thalmann & D. Thalmann (Eds.), *Deformable avatars* (pp. 132–142). Dordrecht, The Netherlands: Kluwer.

Aubel, A., & Thalmann, D. (2005). MuscleBuilder: A modeling tool for human anatomy. *Journal of Computer Science and Technology*. Posted at http://vrlab.epfl.ch/Publications of the Virtual Reality Lab at the Swiss Federal Institute of Technology in Lausanne.

Audi, R. (1994). Dispositional beliefs and dispositions to believe. *Noûs, 28*(4), 419–434.

August, S. (1991). *ARIEL: An approach to understanding analogies in arguments*. Technical Report 910051, Computer Science Department. Los Angeles, CA: University of California, Los Angeles. ftp://ftp.cs.ucla.edu/tech-report/1991-reports/910051.pdf

Aulsebrook, W. A., Iscan, M. Y., Slabbert, J. H., & Becker, P. (1995). Superimposition and reconstruction in forensic facial identification: A survey. *Forensic Science International, 75*(2/3), 101–120.

Aumann, R. J. (1987). Correlated equilibrium as an expression of Bayesian rationality. *Econometrica, 55*, 1–19.

Aune, B. (1975). Vendler on knowledge and belief. In K. Gunderson (Ed.), *Language, mind, and knowledge* (pp. 391–399). (Minnesota Studies in the Philosophy of Science, 7). Minneapolis, MN: University of Minnesota Press.

Aussenac-Gilles, N., & Sörgel, D. (2005). Text analysis for ontology and terminology engineering. *Applied Ontology, 1*(1), Amsterdam: IOS Press, pp. 35–46.

Avcıbaş, İ., Bayram, S., Memon, N., Sankur, B., & Ramkumar, M. (2004). A classifier design for detecting image manipulations. In *2004 International Conference on Image Processing, ICIP '04* (Vol. 4, pp. 2645–2648).

Avery, J., Yearwood, J., & Stranieri, A. (2001). An argumentation based multi-agent system for eTourism dialogue. In A. Abraham & M. Köppen (Eds.), *Hybrid information systems: Proceedings of the first international workshop on Hybrid Intelligent Systems (HIS 2001)*, Adelaide, Australia, December 11–12, 2001 (pp. 497–512). Advances in Soft Computing series. Heidelberg, Germany: Physica-Verlag (of Springer-Verlag).

Aylett, R., Louchart, S., Tychsen, A., Hitchens, M., Figuereido, R., & Delgado Mata, C. (2008). Managing emergent character-based narrative. In *INTETAIN '08: Proceedings of the 2nd international conference on INtelligent TEchnologies for Interactive EnterTAINment*. Institute for Computer Sciences, Social-Informatics and Telecommunications Engineering (ICST), Brussels, Belgium. New York: ACM.

Aziz Bek. (1991 [1933–1937]). *Intelligence and Espionage in Lebanon, Syria and Palestine during the World War (1913–1918)*, Hebrew trans., ed. E. Tauber. ('Iyyunim ba-Machtarot u-va-Meri, vol. 7.) Ramat-Gan, Israel: Bar-Ilan University Press, and Tel-Aviv: [Originally, the MS (either originally in Turkish and translated, or ghost-written) was published in Arabic, ed. F. Midani, in the Beirut newspaper *Al Ḥarār* (1932), then in book form (1933); further memoirs appeared in the Beirut newspaper *Ṣawṭ Al Ḥarār* (1936), then in book form (1937). Stauber's annotated Hebrew translation includes an introduction.]

Azuelos-Atias, S. (2007). *A pragmatic analysis of legal proofs of criminal intent*. Amsterdam: Benjamins.

Baader, F., Calvanese, D., McGuinness, D. L., Nardi, D., & Patel-Schneider, P. F. (Eds.). (2003). *The description logic handbook: Theory, implementation, and applications*. Cambridge, England: Cambridge University Press.

Baber, C. (2010). Distributed cognition at the crime scene. *AI & Society, 25*, 423–432. doi://10.1007/s00146-010-0274-6

Backstrom, L., Huttenlocher, D., Kleinberg, J., & Lan, X. (2006). Group formation in large social networks: Membership, growth, and evolution. In *Proceedings of the 12th ACM SIG KDD international conference on knowledge discovery and data mining* (pp. 44–54).

Backway, H. (2007). Video replacing identity parades. *News Shopper*, Bexley edition (South East London), 28 February, p. 8.

Baddeley, A. D. (1979). Applied cognitive and cognitive applied psychology: The case of face recognition. In L. G. Nilsson (Ed.), *Perspectives on memory research*. Hillsdale, NJ: Lawrence Erlbaum Associates.

Badiru, A. B., Karasz, J. M., & Holloway, R. T. (1988). Arest: [sic] Armed robbery eidetic suspect typing expert system. *Journal of Police Science and Administration, 16*(3), 210–216.

Baeza-Yates, R., & Ribeiro-Neto, B. (1999). *Modern information retrieval*. Boston: Addison Wesley.

Bain, W. M. (1986). *Case-based reasoning: A computer model of subjective assessment*. Ph.D. thesis. New Haven, CT: Computer Science Department, Yale University.

Bain, W. M. (1989a). JUDGE. In C. K. Riesbeck & R. C. Schank (Eds.), *Inside case-based reasoning* (pp. 93–140). Hillsdale, NJ: Lawrence Erlbaum Associates.

Bain, W. M. (1989b). MICROJUDGE. In C. K. Riesbeck & R. C. Schank (Eds.), *Inside case-based reasoning* (pp. 141–163). Hillsdale, NJ: Lawrence Erlbaum Associates.

Bainbridge, D. (1991). *CASE: Computer assisted sentencing in magistrates' courts*. Paper presented at the *BILETA Conference 1991*.

Balding, D. J. (2005). *Weight-of-evidence for forensic DNA profiles*. Chichester: Wiley.

Balding, D. J., & Donnelly, P. (1995). Inferring identity from DNA profile evidence. *Proceedings of the National Academy of Sciences, USA, 92*(25), 11741–11745.

Baldus, D., & Cole, J. W. L. (1980). *Statistical proof of discrimination*. Colorado Springs, CO: Shepard's/McGraw-Hill.

Ball, E., Chadwick, D. W., & Basden, A. (2003). The implementation of a system for evaluating trust in a PKI environment. In O. Petrovic, M. Ksela, M. Fallebblock, & C. Kittl (Eds.), *Trust in the network economy* (pp. 263–279). Berlin: Springer.

Ball, G. R., Kasiviswanathan, H., Srihari, S. N., & Narayanan, A. (2010). Analysis of line structure in handwritten documents using the Hough transform. In *Proceedings of the SPIE 17th conference on document recognition and retrieval*, San José, CA, January 2010, pp. DRR 1–10.

Ball, G. R., & Srihari, S. N. (2009). Comparison of statistical models for writer verification. In *Proceedings of the SPIE 16th conference on document recognition and retrieval*, San José, CA, January 2009, pp. 7247OE 1–8.pdf.

Ball, G. R., Stittmeyer, R., & Srihari, S. N. (2010). Writer verification in historical documents. In *Proceedings of the SPIE 17th conference on document recognition and retrieval*, San José, CA, January 2010. Downloadable from http://www.cedar.buffalo.edu/papers/publications.html

Ball, W. J. (1994). Using Virgil to analyse public policy arguments: A system based on Toulmin's informal logic. *Social Science Computer Review, 12*(1), 26–37.

Ballim, A., & Wilks, Y. (1991). *Artificial believers: The ascription of belief.* Hillsdale, NJ: Erlbaum.

Ballim, A., By, T., Wilks, Y., & Liske, C. (2001). Modelling agent attitudes in legal reasoning. *Computing and Informatics, 20*(6), 581–624.

Ballim, A., Wilks, Y., & Barnden, J. (1990). Belief ascription, metaphor, and intensional identification. Chapter 4 In S. L. Tsohatzidis (Ed.), *Meanings and prototypes: Studies in linguistic categorization* (pp. 91–131). London: Routledge, with a consolidated bibliography on pp. 558–581.

Ballou, S. (2001). Wigs and the significance of one fiber. Chapter 2 In M. M. Houck (Ed.), *Mute witnesses: Trace evidence analysis*. London: Academic.

Balsamo A., & Lo Piparo A. (2004). *La prova 'per sentito dire'. La testimonianza indiretta tra teoria e prassi applicativa*. Milan: Giuffrè.

Banko, M., Mittal, V. O., & Witbrock, M. J. (2000). Headline generation based on statistical translation. In *Proceedings of the 38th meeting of the Association for Computational Linguistics (ACL'2000)*, pp. 318–325.

Barb, A. A. (1972). Cain's murder-weapon and Samson's jawbone of an ass. *Journal of the Warburg and Courtauld Institutes* (London), *35*, 386–389.

Barber, H., & Kudenko, D. (2008). Generation of dilemma-based interactive narratives with a changeable story goal. In *INTETAIN '08: Proceedings of the 2nd international conference on INtelligent TEchnologies for Interactive EnterTAINment*. Institute for Computer Sciences, Social-Informatics and Telecommunications Engineering (ICST), Brussels, Belgium. New York: ACM.

Bargis, M. (1994). *Le dichiarazioni di persone imputate in un procedimento connesso*. Milan: Giuffrè.

Barnden, J. A. (2001). Uncertain reasoning about agents' beliefs and reasoning. *Artificial Intelligence and Law, 9*(2/3), 115–152.

Barnett, V., & Lewis, T. (1994). *Outliers in statistical data* (3rd ed.). New York: Wiley.

Baron, J. (1994). Nonconsequentialist decisions. With open peer commentary and the author's response. *Behavioral and Brain Sciences, 17*(1), 1–42.

Barron, J. (2004). In a futuristic house, speak clearly and carry a manual. *Daily Telegraph*, London, 28 October 2004, on p. 7 in *The New York Times* selection supplement.

Barragán, J. (1989). Bargaining and uncertainty. In A. A. Martino (Ed.), *Pre-proceedings of the third international conference on "Logica, informatica, diritto: Legal expert systems"*, Florence, 1989 (2 vols. + Appendix) (Vol. 1, pp. 49–64). Florence: Istituto per la Documentazione Giuridica, Consiglio Nazionale delle Ricerche.

Barwise, J. (1993). Constraints, channels and the flow of information. In P. Aczel, D. Israel, Y. Katagiri, & S. Peters (Eds.), *Situation theory and its applications* (Vol. 3, pp. 3–27). (CSLI Lecture Notes, Vol. 37.) Stanford, CA: Center for the Study of Language and Information (CSLI)[52].

Barzilay, R., & Elhadad, M. (1999). Using lexical chains for text summarization. In I. Many & M. T. Maybury (Eds.), *Advances in automatic text summarization* (pp. 111–121). Cambridge, MA: The MIT Press.

Basden, A., Ball, E., & Chadwick, D. W. (2001). Knowledge issues raised in modelling trust in a public key infrastructure. *Expert Systems, 18*(5), 233–249.

---

[52] These are the *Proceedings of the Third International Conference on Situation Theory and Its Applications*, Oiso, Japan, November 1991. Cf. Aczel et al. (1993).

Basta, S., Giannotti, F., Manco, G., Pedreschi, D., & Spisanti, L. (2009). SNIPER: A data mining methodology for fiscal fraud detection. In *Mathematics for Finance and Economy*, special issue of *ERCIM News*, 78 (July), 27–28. Accessible at the webpage http://ercim-news.ercim.org/ of the European Research Consortium for Informatics and Mathematics.

Batagelj, V., & Mrvar, A. (1998). Pajek: Program for large network analysis. *Connections, 21*(2), 47–57.

Bates, J. (1992). Virtual reality, art, and entertainment. *Presence: The Journal of Teleoperators and Virtual Environments, 1*(1), 133–138.

Bates, J., Loyall, A. B., & Reilly, W. S. (1992). Integrating reactivity, goals, and emotion in a broad agent. In *Proceedings of the fourteenth annual conference of the cognitive science society.* http://www-2.cs.cmu.edu/afs/cs.cmu.edu/project/oz/web/papers/CMU-CS-92-142.ps

Bauer, E., & Kohavi, R. (1999). An empirical comparison of voting classification algorithms: Bagging, boosting, and variants. *Machine Learning, 35*, 1–38.

Bauer-Bernet, H. (1986). Temporal aspects of the formalization and computerization of law. In A. A. Martino & F. Socci Natali (Eds.), *Automated analysis of legal texts: Logic, informatics, law* (pp. 451–472). Amsterdam: North-Holland.

Baumes, J., Goldberg, M., Hayvanovych, M., Magdon-Ismail, M., & Wallace, W. A. (2006). Finding hidden groups in a stream of communications. In *Proceedings of the IEEE international conference on Intelligence and Security Informatics (ISI–2006)*, pp. 201–212.

Baxendale, P. B. (1958). Machine-made index for technical literature: An experiment. *IBM Journal of Research and Development, 2*(4), 354–361.

Bayles, M. D. (1990). *Procedural justice: Allocating to individuals.* Dordrecht, The Netherlands: Kluwer.

Bayse, W. A., & Morris, C. G. (1987). FBI automation strategy: Development of AI applications for national investigative programs. *Signal Magazine*, May.

Beatie, B. A. (1976). "Romances traditionales" and Spanish Traditional Ballads: Menéndez Pidal vs. Vladimir Propp. *Journal of the Folklore Institute, 13*(1), 37–55. (Indiana University).

Beecher-Monas, E. (2008). Paradoxical validity determinations: A decade of antithetical approaches to admissibility of expert evidence. *International Commentary on Evidence, 6*(2), Article 2. http://www.bepress.com/ice/vol6/iss2/art2

Behrman, B. W., & Davey, S. L. (2001). Eyewitness identification in actual criminal cases: An archival analysis. *Law and Human Behavior, 25*, 475–491.

Behrman, B. W., & Richards, R. E. (2005). Suspect/foil identification in actual crimes and in the laboratory: A reality monitoring analysis. *Law and Human Behavior, 29*, 279–301.

Bekerian, D. A. (1993). In search of the typical eye-witness. *American Psychologist, 48*, 574–576.

Belfrage, H. (1995). Variability in forensic psychiatric decisions: Evidence for a positive crime preventive effect with mentally disordered violent offenders? *Studies in Crime and Crime Prevention, 4*(1), 119–123.

Belis, M. (1973). On the causal structure of random processes. In R. J. Bogdan & I. Niiniluoto (Eds.), *Logic, language, and probability* (pp. 65–77). Dordrecht, The Netherlands: Reidel (now Spinger).

Belis, M. (1995). Causalité, propension, probabilité. *Intellectica*, 1995/2, 21, 199–231. http://www.intellectica.org/archives/n21/21_11_Belis.pdf

Belis, M., & Snow, P. (1998). An intuitive data structure for the representation and explanation of belief and evidentiary support. In *Proceedings of the seventh international conference on Information Processing and Management of Uncertainty in knowledge-based systems (IPMU 1998)*, Paris, 6–10 July 1998. Paris: EDK, pp. 64–71.

Bell, A., Swenson-Wright, J., & Tybjerg, K. (Eds.). (2008). *Evidence.* (Darwin College Lectures Series.) Cambridge: Cambridge University Press.

Bell, B. E., & Loftus, E. F. (1988). Degree of detail of eyewitness testimony and mock juror judgments. *Journal of Applied Social Psychology, 18*, 1171–1192.

Bell, B. E., & Loftus, E. F. (1989). Trivial persuasion in the courtroom: The power of (a few) minor details. *Journal of Personality and Social Psychology, 56*, 669–679.

Bellucci, E., & Zeleznikow, J. (2005). Developing negotiation decision support systems that support mediators: A case study of the Family_Winner system. *Artificial Intelligence and Law, 13*(2), 233–271.

Belnap, N., & Perloff, M. (1988). Seeing to it that: A canonical form for agentives. *Theoria, 54,* 175–199. Reprinted with corrections in Kyberg, H. E., Loui, R. P., & Carlson, G. N. (Eds.). (1990). *Knowledge representation and defeasible reasoning* (pp. 167–190). Dordrecht: Kluwer.

Bem, D. J. (1966). Inducing belief in false confessions. *Journal of Personality and Social Psychology, 3,* 707–710.

Ben-Amos, D. (1980) The concept of motif in folklore. In V. J. Newall (Ed.), *Folklore studies in the twentieth century: Proceedings of the centenary conference of the folklore society* (pp. 17–36). Royal Holloway College, 1978. Woodbridge, England: Brewer, Rowman and Littlefield.

Bench-Capon, T. J. M. (1993a). In defence of rule based representations for legal knowledge based systems. In I. M. Carr (Ed.), *Proceedings of the 4th national conference on law, computers and artificial intelligence*, Exeter, England, 21–22 April 1993. Cf. Bench-Capon (1994).

Bench-Capon, T. J. M. (1993b). Neural networks and open texture. In *Proceedings of the fourth International Conference on Artificial Intelligence and Law (ICAIL'93).* New York: ACM Press, pp. 292–297.

Bench-Capon, T. J. M. (1994). In defence of rule based representations for legal knowledge based systems. *Law, Computers and Artificial Intelligence, 3*(1), 15–28. Cf. Bench-Capon (1993a).

Bench-Capon, T. J. M. (1997). Argument in artificial intelligence and law. *Artificial Intelligence and Law, 5,* 249–261.

Bench-Capon, T. J. M. (1998). Specification and implementation of Toulmin dialogue game. In J. C. Hage, T. Bench-Capon, A. Koers, C. de Vey Mestdagh, & C. Grutters (Eds.), *Jurix 1998: Foundation for legal knowledge based systems* (pp. 5–20). Nijmegen, The Netherlands: Gerard Noodt Institut.

Bench-Capon, T. J. M. (2002). Agreeing to differ: Modelling persuasive dialogue between parties without a consensus about values. *Informal Logic, 22*(3), 231–245.

Bench-Capon, T. J. M. (2003a). Try to see it my way: Modelling persuasion in legal discourse. *Artificial Intelligence and Law, 11*(4), 271–287.

Bench-Capon, T. J. M. (2003b). Persuasion in practical argument using value based argumentation frameworks. *Journal of Logic and Computation, 13*(3), 429–448. http://www.csc.liv.ac.uk/~tbc/publications/jcl03.pdf

Bench-Capon, T. J. M., Coenen, F., & Leng, P. (2000). An experiment in discovering association rules in the legal domain. In *Proceedings of the eleventh international workshop on Database and Expert Systems Applications (DEXA 2000)*, Greenwich, London, September 2000. New York: IEEE Computer Society, 2000, pp. 1056–1060.

Bench-Capon, T. J. M., Doutre, S., & Dunne, P. E. (2007). Audiences in argumentation frameworks. *Artificial Intelligence, 171*(1), 42–71.

Bench-Capon, T. J. M., & Dunne, P. E. (2005). Argumentation in AI and law: Editors' introduction. (Special issue.) *Artificial Intelligence and Law, 13,* 1–8.

Bench-Capon, T. J. M., & Dunne, P. E. (2007). Argumentation in artificial intelligence. *Artificial Intelligence, 171,* 619–641.

Bench-Capon, T. J. M., Freeman, J. B., Hohmann, H., & Prakken, H. (2003). Computational models, argtumentation theories and legal practice. In C. Reed & T. J. Norman (Eds.), *Argumentation machines: New frontiers in argument and computation* (pp. 85–120). Dordrecht, The Netherlands: Kluwer.

Bench-Capon, T. J. M., Geldard, T., & Leng, P.H. (2000). A method for the computational modelling of dialectical argument with dialogue games. *Artificial Intelligence and Law, 8,* 233–254.

Bench-Capon, T. J. M., Lowes, D., & McEnery, A. M. (1991). Argument-based explanation of logic programs. *Knowledge Based Systems, 4*(3), 177–183.

Bench-Capon, T. J. M., & Staniford, G. (1995). PLAID: Proactive legal assistance. In *Proceedings of the fifth International Conference on Artificial Intelligence and Law (ICAIL'95)*, College Park, MD, May 1995, pp. 81–87.

Bench-Capon, T. J. M., & Visser P. R. S. (1997). Ontologies in legal information systems: The need for explicit specifications of domain conceptualizations. In *Proceedings of the sixth International Conference on Artificial Intelligence and Law (ICAIL'97)*, New York: ACM Press, pp. 132–141.

Benderly, B. L. (1997). Turning a blind eye to mad science. (Review of: R. Firstman & J. Talan, *The Death of Innocents*, Bantam.) *The Washington Post*, November 17, 1997, final edn., Section "Style", p. C08.

Benenson, I., & Torrens, P. M. (2004). Geosimulation: Object-based modeling of urban phenomena. *Computers, Environment and Urban Systems, 28*(1/2), 1–8.

Benferhat, S., Cayrol, C., Dubois, D., Lang, J., & Prade, H. (1993). Inconsistency management and prioritized syntax-based entailment. In *Proceedings of the 13th International Joint Conference on Artificial Intelligence (IJCAI'93)*, pp. 640–645.

Benferhat, S., Dubois, D., & Prade, H. (2001). A computational model for belief change. In M. A. Williams & H. Rott (Eds.), *Frontiers in belief revision* (pp. 109–134). (Applied Logic Series, 22). Dordrecht: Kluwer.

Benajmins, V. R., Casanovas, P., Breuker, J., & Gangemi, A. (Eds.). (2005). In *Proceedings of law and the semantic web [2005]: Legal ontologies, methodologies, legal information retrieval, and applications.* (Lecture Notes in Computer Science, Vol. 3369.) Berlin: Springer.

Ben-Menahem, Y. (1990). The Inference to the best explanation. *Erkenntnis, 33*(3), 319–344.

Bennett, B. (1994). Spatial reasoning with propositional logics. In J. Doyle, E. Sandewall, & P. Torasso (Eds.), *Principles of Knowledge Representation and reasoning: Proceedings of the fourth international conference (KR94)*. San Francisco: Morgan Kaufmann.

Bennett, K. P., & Campbell, C. (2000). Support vector machines: Hype or Hallelujah? *SIGKDD Explorations, 2*(2), 1–13. New York: ACM Press.

Bennett, W. L., & Feldman, M. S. (1981). *Reconstructing reality in the courtroom: Justice and judgement in American culture*. New Brunswick, NJ: Rutgers University Press; London: Tavistock.

Bennun, M. E. (1996). Computerizing criminal law: Problems of evidence, liability and *mens rea. Information & Communications Technology Law, 5*(1), 29–44.

Bergslien, E., Bush, P., & Bush, M. (2006). Application of field portable Xray fluorescence (FPXRF) spectrometry in forensic and environmental geology: Theory and examples (abstract). In A. Ruffell (Ed.), *Abstract book of geoscientists at crime scenes: First, inaugural meeting of the Geological Society of London*, 20 December 2006 (pp. 17–20). London: Forensic Geoscience Group. http://www.geolsoc.org.uk/pdfs/FGtalks&abs_pro.pdf.

Berlière, J.-M. (2005). L'Affaire Scheffer: une victoire de la science contre le crime? La première identification d'un assassin à l'aide de ses empreintes digitales (octobre 1902). *Les Cahiers de la sécurité, 56*(1), 349–360. Posted at http://www.inhes.interieur.gouv.fr/fichiers/CS56BerliereINHES2005.pdf by the Institut national des hautes études de sécurité (INHES), France.

Berners-Lee, T., Hendler, J., & Lassila, O. (2001). The semantic web. *Scientific American, 284*(5), 34–43.

Bernez, M. O. (1994). Anatomy and aesthetics: Gérard de Lairesse's illustrations for Bidloo's *Anatomia Humani Corporis*. In M. Baridon (Ed.), *Interfaces: Image, texte, langage*, 5 (pp. 207–229). Dijon, France: Université de Bourgogne.

Berry, M., & Browne, M. (2005). *Understanding search engines: Mathematical modeling and text retrieval (Software, Environments, Tools)*. Philadelphia, PA: SIAM.

Berry, M. W. (2003). *Survey of text mining: Clustering, classification, and retrieval*. Berlin: Springer.

Bertin, J. (1983). *Semiology of graphics: Diagrams, networks, maps*. Madison, WI: University of Wisconsin Press.

Bertino, E., Catania, B., & Wong, L. (1999). Finitely representable nested relations. *Information Processing Letters, 70*(4), 165–173.

Besag, J. (1986). On the statistical analysis of dirty pictures. *Journal of the Royal Statistical Society, Series B, 48*, 259–302.

Besnard, P., & Hunter, A. (2008). *Elements of argumentation.* Cambridge, MA: The MIT Press.

Best, E., & Hall, J. (1992). *The box calculus: A new causal algebra with multilabel communication.* (Technical Report Series, 373.) Newcastle upon Tyne, England: University of Newcastle upon Tyne, Computing Laboratory.

Bettini, C., Jajodia, S., & Wang, S. (2000). *Time granularities in databases, data mining, and temporal reasoning.* Berlin: Springer.

Bettini, C., Wang, X. S., & Jajodia, S. (2002). Solving multi-granularity temporal constraint networks. *Artificial Intelligence, 140*(1/2), 107–152.

Bevan, B. W. (1991). The search for graves. *Geophysics, 56,* 1310–1319.

Bevel, T., & Gardner, R. M. (2008). *Bloodstain pattern analysis, with an introduction to crime scene reconstruction* (3rd ed.). (CRC Series in Practical Aspects of Criminal and Forensic Investigations.) Boca Raton, FL: CRC Press (of Taylor & Francis). The 1st edn. was of 1997, and the 2nd edn. was of 2002.

Bex, F., Bench-Capon, T., & Atkinson, K. (2009). Did he jump or was he pushed? Abductive practical reasoning. *Artificial Intelligence and Law, 17*(2), 79–99. http://www.computing.dundee.ac.uk/staff/florisbex/Papers/AILaw09.pdf

Bex, F. J. (2011). *Arguments, stories and criminal evidence: A formal hybrid theory.* (Law and Philosophy Series, 92.) Dordrecht, The Netherlands: Springer.

Bex, F. J., & Bench-Capon, T. (2010). Persuasive stories for multi-agent argumentation. In *Proceedings of the 2010 AAAI fall symposium on computatonal narratives.* AAAI Technical Report FS-10-04. (AAAI Fall Symposium Series.) Menlo Park, CA: AAAI Press, Menlo Park, CA, pp. 4–5 (sic). http://www.aaai.org/ocs/index.php/FSS/FSS10/paper/view/2174/2840 http://www.computing.dundee.ac.uk/staff/florisbex/Papers/AAAI-TBC10.pdf

Bex, F. J., & Prakken, H. (2004). Reinterpreting arguments in dialogue: An application to evidential reasoning. In T. F. Gordon (Ed.), *Legal knowledge and information systems. JURIX 2004: The seventeenth annual conference* (pp. 119–129). Amsterdam: IOS Press.

Bex, F. J., Prakken, H., Reed, C., & Walton, D. N. (2003). Towards a formal account of reasoning about evidence: Argumentation schemes and generalisations. *Artificial Intelligence and Law, 12,* 125–165. http://www.computing.dundee.ac.uk/staff/florisbex/Papers/AILaw03.pdf

Bex, F. J., Prakken, H., & Verheij, B. (2006). Anchored narratives in reasoning about evidence. In T. M. van Engers (Ed.), *Legal knowledge and information systems. JURIX 2006: The nineteenth annual conference* (pp. 11–20). Amsterdam: IOS Press.

Bex, F. J., van den Braak, S. W., van Oostendorp, H., Prakken, H., Verheij, H. B., & Vreeswijk, G. A. W. (2007). Sense-making software for crime investigation: How to combine stories and arguments? *Law, Probability & Risk, 6,* 145–168. http://www.computing.dundee.ac.uk/staff/florisbex/Papers/LPR07.pdf The same article with diagrams in colour: http://www.cs.uu.nl/research/projects/evidence/publications/lpr07submitted.pdf

Bex, F. J., van Koppen, P. J., Prakken, H., & Verheij, B. (2010). A hybrid formal theory of arguments, stories and criminal evidence. *Artificial Intelligence and Law, 18*(2), 123–152. http://www.cs.uu.nl/groups/IS/archive/henry/Bexetal10.pdf http://www.computing.dundee.ac.uk/staff/florisbex/Papers/AILaw10.pdf

Bex, F. J., & Walton, D. (2010). Burdens and standards of proof for inference to the best explanation. In R. Winkels (Ed.), *Legal knowledge and information systems. JURIX 2010: The 23rd annual conference* (pp. 37–46). (Frontiers in Artificial Intelligence and Applications, 223.) Amsterdam: IOS Press.

Bie, R., Jin, X., Chen, C., Xu, C., & Huang, R. (2007). Meta learning intrusion detection in real time network. In *Proceedings of the 17th international conference on artificial neural networks,* Porto, Portugal. Berlin: Springer, pp. 809–816.

Biermann, T. W., & Grieve, M. C. (1996). A computerized data base of mail order garments: A contribution toward estimating the frequency of fibre types found in clothing. Part 1: The system and its operation. Part 2: The content of the data bank and its statistical evaluation. *Forensic Science International, 77*(1/2), 75–92. Amsterdam: Elsevier.

Binder, D. A., & Bergman, P. (1984). *Fact investigation: From hypothesis to proof* (American Casebook Series.). St Paul, MN: West Publ.

Binmore, K. (1985). *Modelling rational players, Part 1* (ICERD Discussion Paper). London: London School of Economics.

Binsted, K., Bergen, B., Coulson, S., Nijholt, A., Stock, O., Strapparava, C., et al. (2006). Computational humor. *IEEE Intelligent Systems, 21*(2), 59–69. http://doc.utwente.nl/66729/

Biondani, P. (2010, June 10). Giustizia Bocciata. (Subheadline: Prescrizione breve. Garanzie fasulle. Ricorsi infiniti. Formalismi. Condanne non eseguite. Un rapporto europeo indica i veri problemi dei nostri tribunali.) *L'espresso, 56*(23), 73–74.

Birkhoff, G. (1967). *Lattice theory* (3rd ed.) (Colloquium Publications, 25). Providence, RI: American Mathematical Society. Reprinted 1984.

Bistarelli, S., Santini, F., & Vaccarelli, A. (2006). An asymmetric fingerprint matching algorithms for Java Card™. *Pattern Analysis Applications, 9*, 359–376. doi://10.1007/s10044-006-0048-4

Bivens, A., Gao, L., Hulber, M. F., & Szymanski, B. (1999). Agent-based network monitoring. In *Proceedings of the autonomous agents99 conference, workshop 1, agent based high performance computing: Problem solving applications and practical deployment*, Seattle, WA, May 1999, pp. 41–53.

Bivens, A., Palagiri, C., Smith, R., Szymanski, B., & Embrechts, M. (2002). Network-based intrusion detection using neural networks. In *Proceedings of intelligent engineering systems through Artificial Neural Networks ANNIE-2002*, St. Louis, MO, Vol. 12. New York: ASME Press, 2002, pp. 579–584.

Black, H. C. (1990). *Black's law dictionary*. St. Paul, MN: West Publishing Company.

Black, J. B., & Wilensky, R. (1979). An evaluation of story grammars. *Cognitive Science, 3*, 213–229.

Blackman, S. J. (1988). *Expert systems in case-based law: The rule against hearsay*. LL.M. thesis, Faculty of Law, University of British Columbia, Vancouver, BC.

Blair, D., & Meyer, T. (1997). Tools for an interactive virtual cinema. In R. Trappl & P. Petta (Eds.), *Creating personalities for synthetic actors: Towards autonomous personality agents.* Heidelberg: Springer.

Blair, J. P. (2005). A test of the unusual false confession perspective using cases of proven false confessions. *Criminal Law Bulletin, 41*, 127–144.

Bleay, S. (2009). *Fingerprint development and imaging: Fundamental research to operational implementation*. PowerPoint presentation, 1 July 2009. Home Office Scientific Development Branch, Sandridge, England. Posted at the website of the Higher Education Academy, York Science Park, York, England. Retrieved in 2010 at http://www.heacademy.ac.uk/assets/ps/documents/FORREST/2009/presentations/k2_bleay.pdf

Block, A. (1994). *Space, time, and organised crime*. New Brunswick, NJ: Transaction.

Bloy, D. (1996). *Criminal law* (2nd ed.) (Lecture Notes Series). London: Cavendish.

Blueschke, A., & Lacis, A. (1996). Examination of line crossings by low KV scanning electron microscopy (SEM) using photographic stereoscopic pairs. *Journal of Forensic Science, 41*(1), 80–85.

Boba, R. (2003). *Problem analysis in policing*. Washington, DC: Police Foundation. http://www.policefoundation.org/pdf/problemanalysisinpolicing.pdf

Boba, R. (2005). *Crime analysis and crime mapping*. Thousand Oaks, CA & London: Sage.

Bobrow, D., & Winograd, T. (1977). An overview of KRL, a knowledge representation language. *Cognitive Science, 1*(1), 3–46.

Bodard, F., Hella, M., Poullet, Y., & Stenne, P. (1986). A prototype ADP system to assist judicial decision making. In A. A. Martino, F. Socci Natali, & S. Binazzi (Eds.), *Automated analysis of legal texts, logic, informatics, law* (pp. 187–210). Amsterdam: North-Holland.

Boddington, A., Garland, A. N., & Janaway, R. C. (Eds.). (1987). *Death, decay and reconstruction: Approaches to archaeology and forensic science*. Manchester: Manchester University Press.

Bodenhausen, G. V. (1988). Stereotypic biases in social decision making and memory: Testing process models of stereotype use. *Journal of Personality and Social Psychology, 55*, 726–737.

Bodziak, W. J. (2000). *Footwear impression evidence.* Boca Raton, FL: CRC Press.

Bodziak, W. J. (2005a). Forensic tire impression and tire track evidence. Chapter 18 In S. H. James & J. J. Nordby (Eds.), *Forensic science: An introduction to scientific and investigative techniques* (2nd ed.). Boca Raton, FL: CRC Press. Also in 3rd edition, 2009.

Bodziak, W. J. (2005b). Forensic footwear evidence. Chapter 19 In S. H. James & J. J. Nordby (Eds.), *Forensic science: An introduction to scientific and investigative techniques* (2nd ed.). Boca Raton, FL: CRC Press. Also in 3rd edition, 2009.

Boer, A., van Engers, T., & Winkels, R. (2003). Using ontologies for comparing and harmonizing legislation. In G. Sartor (Ed.), *Proceedings of the ninth International Conference on Artificial Intelligence and Law (ICAIL 2003)*, Edinburgh, Scotland, 24–28 June 2003 (pp. 60–69). New York: ACM Press.

Bohan, T. L. (1991). *Computer-aided accident reconstruction: Its role in court* (SAE Technical Paper Series (12 p.)). Warrendale, PA: Society of Automotive Engineers (SAE).

Bolding, P. O. (1960). Aspects of the burden of proof. *Scandinavian Studies in Law, 4,* 9–28.

Bolelli, T. (1993). Figlio mio figlio di cane. In his *L'italiano e gli italiani: Cento stravaganze linguistiche* (pp. 126–128). Vicenza, Italy: Neri Pozza Editore. (Originally, in *La Stampa* Turin, 11 January 1991)

Bolettieri, P., Esuli, A., Falchi, F., Lucchese, C., Perego, R., & Rabitti, F. (2009). Enabling content-based image retrieval in very large digital libraries. In *Proceedings of the second workshop on very large digital libraries*, 2 October 2009, Corfu, Greece. Pisa, Italy: DELOS, an Association for Digital Libraries, pp. 43–50.

Bologna, J., & Lindquist, R. J. (1995). *Fraud auditing and forensic accounting: New tools and techniques* (2nd ed.). New York: Wiley.

Bond, C., Solon, M., & Harper, P. (1999). *The expert witness in court: A practical guide.* Crayford, Kent: Shaw & Sons.

Bondarenko, A., Dung, P. M., Kowalski, R., & Toni, F. (1997). An abstract argumentation-theoretic approach to default reasoning. *Artificial Intelligence, 93*(1/2), 63–101.

BonJour, L. (1998). The elements of coherentism. In L. M. Alcoff (Ed.), *Epistemology: The big questions* (pp. 210–231). Oxford: Blackwell.(page numbers are referred to in the citation as in Alcoff.) (Originally, In: BonJour, L. (1985). *Structure of empirical knowledge* (pp. 87–110). Cambridge, MA: Harvard University Press)

Bookspan, S., Gravel, A. J., & Corley, J. (2002). Site history: The first tool of the environmental forensic team. Chapter 2 In B. L. Murphy & R. D. Morrison (Eds.), *Introduction to environmental forensics* (pp. 19–42). San Diego, CA & London: Academic.

Boone, K. B. (Ed.). (2007). *Assessment of feigned cognitive impairment: A neuropsychological perspective.* New York: Guilford Press.

Borchard, E. M. (1932). *Convicting the innocent: Errors of criminal justice.* Garden City, NY: Garden City Publishing Company, Inc.; New Haven, CT: Yale University Press.

Borges, F., Borges, R., & Bourcier, D. (2002). A connectionist model to justify the legal reasoning of the judge. In *Proceedings of fifteenth international conference on legal knowledge based system.* Amsterdam: IOS Publications, pp. 113–122.

Borges, F., Borges, R., & Bourcier, D. (2003). Artificial neural networks and legal categorization. In *Proceedings of sixteenth international conference on legal knowledge based system.* Amsterdam: IOS Publications, pp. 11–20.

Borgulya, I. (1999). Two examples of decision support in the law. *Artificial Intelligence and Law, 7*(2/3), 303–321.

Bourcier, D. (1995). Une approche sémantique de l'argumentation juridique. *Revue L'année sociologique.* Paris: PUF (June).

Bowers, M. C. (2002). *Forensic dentistry: A field investigator's handbook.* London: Academic.

Boykov, Y., Veksler, O., & Zabin, R. (1998). Markov random fields with efficient approximations. In *Proceedings of the IEEE conference on Computer Vision and Pattern Recognition (CVPR)*, Santa Barbara, CA, 23–25 June 1998. New York: IEEE Computer Society, pp. 648–655.

Boykov, Y., Veksler, O., & Zabin, R. (2001). Fast approximate energy minimization via graph cuts. *IEEE Transactions on Pattern Analysis and Machine Intelligence (IEEE PAMI), 23*, 1222–1239.

Brace, N., Pike, G., Kemp, R., Tyrner, J., & Bennet, P. (2006). Does the presentation of multiple facial composites improve suspect identification? *Applied Cognitive Psychology, 20*, 213–226.

Bradac, J. J., Hemphill, M. R., & Tardy, C. H. (1981). Language style on trial: Effects of 'powerful' and 'powerless' speech upon judgements of victims and villains. *Western Journal of Speech Communication, 45*, 327–341.

Bradfield, A. L., & Wells, G. L. (2000). The perceived validity of eyewitness identification testimony: A test of the five Biggers criteria. *Law and Human Behavior, 24*, 581–594.

Bradfield, A. L., Wells, G. L, & Olson, E. A. (2002). The damaging effect of confirming feedback on the relation between eyewitness certainty and identification accuracy. *Journal of Applied Psychology, 87*, 112–120.

Brady, R. (Ed.). (2003). *Relevant logics and their Rivals, II*. Aldershot: Ashgate. Vol. 1 is Routley et al. (1983).

Brainerd, C. J., & Reyna, V. F. (2004). Fuzzy-trace theory and memory development. *Developmental Review, 24*, 396–439

Branch, J., Bivens, A., Chan, C.-Y., Lee, T.-K., & Szymanski, B. (2002). Denial of service intrusion detection using time dependent deterministic finite automata. In *Proceedings of research conference*. Troy, NY, October 2002.

Brandenburger, A., & Dekel, E. (1987). Rationalizability and correlated equilibria. *Econometrica, 55*, 1391–1402.

Brandes, U., Kenis, P., Raab, J., Schneider, V., & Wagner, D. (1999). Explorations into the visualization of policy networks. *Journal of Theoretical Politics, 11*(1), 75–106.

Brandes, U., Raab, J., & Wagner, D. (2001). Exploratory network visualization: Simultaneous display of actor status and connections. *Journal of Social Structure, 2*(4). http://www.cmu.edu/joss/content/articles/volume2/BrandesRaabWagner.html

Brann, N. L. (1981). *The Abbot Trithemius (1462–1516): The renaissance of monastic humanism*. Leiden, The Netherlands: Brill.

Brann, N. L. (1999). *Trithemius and magical theology: A chapter in the controversy over occult studies in early modern Europe*. Albany, NY: SUNY Press.

Brann, N. L. (2006). Trithemius, Johannes. In W. J. Hanegraaff with A. Faivre, R. van den Broek, & J.-P. Brach (Eds.), *Dictionary of Gnosis and Western esotericism* (pp. 1135–1139). Leiden, The Netherlands: Brill.

Branting, K., Callaway, C., Mott, B., & Lester, J. (1999). Integrating discourse and domain knowledge for document drafting. In *Proceedings of seventh international conference on artificial intelligence and law*. New York: ACM Press, pp. 214–220.

Branting, K. L. (1994). A computational model of ratio decidendi. *Artificial Intelligence and Law, 2*, 1–31.

Bratman, M. (1987). *Intention, plans and practical reason*. Cambridge, MA: Harvard University Press.

Breeze, A. (1992). Cain's jawbone, Ireland, and the prose *Solomon and Saturn. Notes and Queries, 39*(4), 433–436. (*Notes and Queries* Vol. 237, new series, Oxford University Press.)

Breiger, R. L. (2004). The analysis of social networks. In M. Hardy & A. Bryman (Eds.), *Handbook of data analysis* (pp. 505–526). London: Sage.

Breiman, L. (1996). Bagging predictors. *Machine Learning, 24*, 123–140.

Breiman L., Friedman J. H., Olshen, R. A., & Stone, C. J. (1984). *Classification and regression trees*. Belmont, CA: Wadsworth; New York: Chapman and Hall; San Mateo, CA: Morgan Kaufmann.

Brenner, J. C. (2000). *Forensic science glossary*. Boca Raton, FL: CRC Press.

Bressan, S. (Ed.). (2003). *Efficiency and effectiveness of XML tools and techniques [EEXTT] and data integration over the web: Revised papers from the VLDB workshop, at the 28th very large data bases international conference*, Hong Kong, China, 2002. Berlin: Springer.

Breuker, J., Elhag, A., Petkov, E., & Winkels, R. (2002). Ontologies for legal information serving and knowledge management. In *Proceedings of Jurix 2002: 15th annual conference on legal knowledge and information systems*. Amsterdam, The Netherlands: IOS Press, pp. 73–82.

Breuker, J., Valente, A., & Winkels, R. (2005). Use and reuse of legal ontologies in knowledge engineering and information management. In V. R. Benajmins, P. Casanovas, J. Breuker, & A. Gangemi (Eds.), *Proceedings of law and the semantic web [2005]: Legal ontologies, methodologies, legal information retrieval, and applications* (pp. 36–64). (Lecture Notes in Computer Science, Vol. 3369.) Berlin: Springer.

Brewka, G., Prakken, H., & Vreeswijk, G. (2003). Special issue on computational dialectics: An Introduction. (Special issue.) *Journal of Logic and Computation, 13*, 317–318.

Brigham, J. C. (1981). The accuracy of eyewitness evidence: How do attorneys see it? *The Florida Bar Journal, November*, 714–721.

Brin, S., & Page, L. (1998). The anatomy of a large-scale hypertextual web search engine. In *WWW 1998: Proceedings of the seventh international conference on world wide web*, pp. 107–117.

Bringsjord, S., & Ferrucci, D. A. (2000). *Artificial intelligence and literary creativity*. Mahwah, NJ: Erlbaum. [On the BRUTUS project.]

Brigsjord, S., Shilliday, A., Taylor, J., Clark, M., & Khemlani, S. (2006). Slate: An argument-centered intelligent assistant to professional reasoners. At the *Sixth International Workshop on Computational Models of Natural Argument*, held with *ECAI'06* Riva del Garda, Italy, August 2006.

Brislawn, C. M., Bradley, J. N., Onyshczak, R. J., & Hopper, T. (1996). The FBI compression standard for digitized fingerprint images. In *Proceedings of the international society for optical engineering*, Denver, CO, pp. 344–355.

Brkic, J. (1985). *Legal reasoning: Semantic and logical analysis*. New York: Peter Lang.

Bromby, M. (2002). To be taken at face value? Computerised identification. *Information & Communication Technology Law Journal, 11*(1), 63–73.

Bromby, M. (2003, February 28). At face value? The use of facial mapping and CCTV image analysis for identification. *New Law Journal, 153*(7069), 302–304.

Bromby, M. (2010). Identification, trust and privacy: How biometrics can aid certification of digital signatures. *International Review of Law, Computers and Technology, 24*(1), 1–9.

Bromby, M. C., & Hall, M. J. J. (2002). The development and rapid evaluation of the knowledge model of ADVOKATE: An advisory system to assess the credibility of eyewitness testimony. In T. Bench-Capon, A. Daskalopulu, & R. Winkels (Eds.), *Legal knowledge and information systems, JURIX 2002: The fifteenth annual conference* (pp. 143–152). Amsterdam: IOS Publications.

Bromby, M., MacMillan, M., & McKellar, P. (2003). A common-KADS representation for a knowledge based system to evaluate eyewitness identification. *International Review of Law Computers and Technology, 17*(1), 99–108.

Bromby, M., MacMillan, M., & McKellar, P. (2007). An examination of criminal jury directions in relation to eyewitness identification in commonwealth jurisdictions. *Common Law World Review, 36*(4), 303–336.

Brooks, K. M. (1996). The theory and implementation of one model for computational narrative. In W. Hall & T. D. C. Little (Eds.), *ACM multimedia '96*, Boston, MA (pp. 317–328). New York: The Association of Computing Machinery.

Brooks, K. M. (1999). *Metalinear cinematic narrative: Theory, process, and tool*. PhD dissertation in Media, Arts and Sciences (advisor: G. Davenport). Cambridge, MA: Program in Media Arts and Sciences, School of Architecture and Planning, Massachusetts Institute of Technology. http://xenia.media.mit.edu/~brooks/dissertation.html

Brooks, K. M. (2002). Nonlinear narrative structures for interactive TV. In M. Damásio (Ed.), *Interactive television authoring and production 2002* (pp. 43–56). Lisbon, Portugal: Universidade Lusófona de Humanidades e Tecnologias.

Brown, C. T. (1989a, June). *Relating Petri nets to formulae of linear logic* (Internal report, CSR-304-89). Edinburgh, Scotland: Department of Computer Science, University of Edinburgh.

Brown, C. T. (1989b, November). *Petri nets as quantales*. Internal report, CSR-314-89. Edinburgh, Scotland: Department of Computer Science, University of Edinburgh.

Browne, M., & Berry, M. W. (2005). Email surveillance using nonnegative matrix factorization. In *Proceedings of the SIAM international conference on data mining, SIAM workshop on link analysis, counterterrorism and security*. Philadelphia, PA: SIAM.

Bruce, V., & Hancock, P. (2002). *CRIME-VUs: Combined recall images from multiple experts and viewpoints*. Scotland: Department of Psychology, University of Stirling. http://www.stir.ac.uk/Departments/HumanSciences/Psychology/crimevus/index.htm

Bruce, V., Henderson, Z., Greenwood, K., Hancock, P. J. B., Burton, A. M., & Miller, P. I. (1999). Verification of face identities from images captured on video. *Journal of Experimental Psychology: Applied, 5*(4), 339–360.

Bruce, V., Ness, H., Hancock, P. J. B., Newman, C., & Rarity, J. (2002). Four heads are better than one: Combining face composites yields improvements in face likeness. *Journal of Applied Psychology, 87*(5), 894–902.

Bruce, V., & Young, A. W. (1986). Understanding face recognition. *British Journal of Psychology, 77*, 305–327.

Brüninghaus, S., & Ashley, K. (2001). Improving the representation of legal case texts with information extraction methods. In *Proceedings of the 8th International Conference on Artificial Intelligence and Law (ICAIL'01)*, St. Louis, Missouri. New York: ACM Press, pp. 42–51.

Brüninghaus, S., & Ashley, K. (2003). Predicting outcomes of casebased legal arguments. In *Proceedings of the 9th International Conference on Artificial Intelligence and Law (ICAIL'03)*, Edinburgh, Scotland. New York: ACM Press, pp. 233–242.

Bruyer, R. (Ed.). (1986). *The neuropsychology of face perception and facial expression*. (Neuropsychology and Neurolinguistics Series.) Lillington, NC: Psychology Press.

Bryan, M. (1997). *SGML and HTML explained* (2nd ed.). Harlow, Essex: Addison Wesley Longman.

Bryant, V. M., Jr., Jones, J. G., & Mildenhall, D. C. (1996). Studies in forensic palynology. Chapter 23G In J. Jansonius, & D. C. McGregor (Eds.), *Palynology: Principles and applications* (pp. 957–959). American Association of Stratigraphic Palynologists Foundation Vol. 3.

Bryant, V. M., Jr., & Mildenhall, D. C. (1996). Forensic palynology in the United States of America. *Palynology, 14*, 193–208.

Bryson, J., & Thórisson, K. R. (2000). Dragons, bats and evil knights: A three-layer design approach to character based creative play. *Virtual Reality, 5*(2), 57–71.

Buber, M. (1947). *Tales of the Hasidim: The Early Masters* (Trans. by O. Marx from the German: *Die Erzahlungen der Chassidim*). London: Thames and Hudson, 2 vols., 1956–1961; New York: Schoken, 1947, 1961, 1975, 1991.

Budescu, D. V., & Wallsten, T. S. (1985). Consistency in interpretation of probabilistic phrases. *Organizational Behaviour and Human Decision Processes, 36*, 391–405.

Bugental, D. B., Shennum, W., Frank, M., & Ekman, P. (2000). "True lies": Children's abuse history and power attributions as influences on deception detection. In V. Manusov & J. H. Harvey (Eds.), *Attribution, communication behavior, and close relationships* (pp. 248–265). Cambridge: Cambridge University Press.

Bull, R. (1979). The influence of stereotypes on person identification. In D. P. Farrington, K. Hawkins, & S. M. Lloyd-Bostock (Eds.), *Psychology, law and legal processes* (pp. 184–194). London: Macmillan.

Bull, R., & Carson, D. (1995). *Handbook of psychology in legal contexts*. Chichester: Wiley.

Burgoon, J. K., & Buller, D. B. (1994). Interpersonal deception: IV. Effects of deceit on perceived communication and nonverbal behavior dynamics. *Journal of Nonverbal Behavior, 18*, 155–184.

Burnett, D. G. (2007). *Trying leviathan: The nineteenth-century New York court case that put the whale on trial and challenged the order of nature*. Princeton, NJ: Princeton University Press.

Burt, R. S. (1980). Models of social structure. *Annual Review of Sociology, 6*, 79–141.

Burton, A. M., Bruce, V., & Hancock, P. J. B. (1999). From pixels to people: A model of familiar face recognition. *Cognitive Science, 23*(1), 1–31.

Burton, A. M., Miller, P., Bruce, V., Hancock, P. J. B., & Henderson, Z. (2001). Human and automatic face recognition: A comparison across image formats. *Vision Research, 41*, 3185–3195.

Butler, J. M. (2001). *Forensic DNA typing: Biology and technology behind STR markers.* London: Academic.

BVA. (1979). *Veterinary surgeons acting as witnesses in RSPCA prosecutions.* London: BVA Publications (British Veterinary Association).

Byrne, M. D. (1995). The convergence of explanatory coherence and the story model: A case study in juror decision. In J. D. Moore & J. F. Lehman (Eds.), *Proceedings of the 17th annual conference of the cognitive science society* (pp. 539–543). Hillsdale, NJ: Lawrence Erlbaum.

Caballero, J., Poosankam, P., Kreibich, C., & Song, S. X. (2009). Dispatcher: Enabling active botnet infiltration using automatic protocol reverse-engineering. In E. Al-Shaer, S. Jha, & A. D. Keromytis (Eds.), *Proceedings of the 2009* [i.e., 16th] *ACM conference on Computer and Communications Security (CCS 2009)*, Chicago, IL, November 9–13, 2009 (pp. 621–634). New York: ACM Press.

Cabras, C. (1996). Un mostro di carta. In C. Cabras (Ed.), *Psicologia della prova* (pp. 233–258). Milan: Giuffrè.

Caldwell, C., & Johnston, V. S. (1991). Tracking a criminal suspect through 'face-space' with a genetic algorithm. In R. Belew & L. Booker (Eds.), *Proceedings of the fourth international conference on genetic algorithms* (pp. 416–421). San Mateo, CA: Morgan Kaufmann.

Callan, R. (1999). *The essence of neural networks.* Hemel Hempstead: Prentice Hall Europe.

Callaway, C. (2000). *Narrative prose generation.* Ph.D. thesis, North Carolina State University. http://tcc.itc.it/people/callaway/pubs.html

Callaway, C. B., & Lester, J. C. (2001). Narrative prose generation. In *Proceedings of the 17th International Joint Conference on Artificial Intelligence (IJCAI'2001)*, Seattle, WA, 2001, pp. 1241–1248.

Callaway, C. B., & Lester, J. C. (2002). Narrative prose generation. *Artificial Intelligence, 139*(2), 213–252.

Callen, C. R. (2002). Othello could not optimize: Economics, hearsay, and less adversary systems. In M. MacCrimmon & P. Tillers (Eds.), *The dynamics of judicial proof: Computation, logic, and common sense* (pp. 437–453). (Studies in Fuzziness and Soft Computing, Vol. 94). Heidelberg: Physica-Verlag.

Calzolari, N., Monachini, M., Quochi, V., Socia, C., & Toral, A. (2010). Lexicons, terminologies, ontologies: Reflections from experiences in resource construction. In N. Dershowitz & E. Nissan (Eds.), *Language, culture, computation: Essays in honour of Yaacov Choueka* Vol. 2: *Tools for text and language, and the cultural dimension* (in press). Berlin: Springer.

Caminada, M., Doutre, S., Modgil, S., Prakken, H., & Vreeswijk, G. A. W. (2004). Implementations of argument-based inference. In J. Fox (Ed.), *Review of argumentation technology: State of the art, technical and user requirements* (pp. 2–13). ASPIC Consortium.

Campbell, C., & Ying, Y. (2011). Learning with support vector machines. *Synthesis Lectures on Artificial Intelligence and Machine Learning, 5*(1), 1–95. Published online in .pdf in February 2011 by Morgan and Claypool in the United States.[53] doi://10.2200/S00324ED1V01Y201102AIM010

Camptepe, A., Goldberg, M., Magdon-Ismail, M., & Krishnamoorthy, M. (2005). Detecting conversing groups of chatters: A model, algorithms and tests. In *Proceedings of the IADIS international conference on applied computing 2005*, pp. 145–157.

---

[53] See http://www.morganclaypool.com/doi/abs/10.2200/S00324ED1V01Y201102AIM010 Until early 2011, there were five issues available, published between 2007 and February 2011.

Camurri, A., & Ferrentino, P. (1999). Interactive environments for music and multimedia. *Multimedia Systems, 7*(1), 32–47.

Canter, D. (2000). Offender profiling and criminal differentiation. *Legal and Criminological Psychology, 5*, 23–46.

Capobianco, M. F., & Molluzzo, J. C. (1979/80). The strength of a graph and its application to organizational structure. *Social Networks, 2*, 275–284.

Capstick, P. H. (1998). *Warrior*. New York: St. Martin's Press.

Caputo, D., & Dunning, D. (2006). Distinguishing accurate identifications from erroneous ones: Post dictive indicators of eyewitness accuracy. In R. C. L. Lindsay, D. F. Ross, J. D. Read, & M. P. Toglia (Eds.), *Handbook of eyewitness psychology: Memory for people* (pp. 427–451). Mahwah, NJ: Lawrence Erlbaum Associates.

Carbogim, D., Robertson, D., & Lee, J. (2000). Argument-based applications to knowledge engineering. *The Knowledge Engineering Review, 15*(2), 119–149.

Carbonell, J. (1979). *Subjective understanding: Computer models of belief systems*. Ph.D. thesis, Technical Report YALE/DCS/tr150. Computer Science Department, Yale University, New Haven, CT.

Carbonell, J. (1981). POLITICS; Micro POLITICS. Chapters 11 and 12. In R. G. Schank & C. K. Riesbeck (Eds.), *Inside computer understanding: Five programs plus miniatures* (pp. 259–307 and 308–317). Hillsdale, NJ: Erlbaum.

Carbonell, J. G., Jr. (1978). POLITICS: Automated ideological reasoning. *Cognitive Science, 2*(1), 27–51.

Carenini, G., Grasso, F., & Reed, C. (Eds.). (2002). *Proceedings of the ECAI-2002 workshop on computational models of natural argument*, at *ECAI 2002*, Lyon, France.

Carenini, G., & Moore, J. (1999). Tailoring evaluative arguments to user's preferences. In *Proceedings of the seventh international conference on User Modeling (UM-99)*, Banff, Canada.

Carenini, G., & Moore, J. (2001). An empirical study of the influence of user tailoring on evaluative argument effectiveness. In *Proceedings of the 17th International Joint Conference on Artificial Intelligence (IJCAI 2001)*, Seattle, WA.

Carmo, J., & Jones, A. (1996). A new approach to contrary-to-duty obligations. In D. Nute (Ed.), *Defeasible deontic logic* (pp. 317–344). (Synthese Library, 263.) Dordrecht: Kluwer.

Carmo, J., & Jones, A. (2002). Deontic logic and contrary-to-duties. In D. Gabbay & F. Guenthner (Eds.), *Handbook of philosophical logic* (Vol. 8, 2nd ed., pp. 265–343). Dordrecht, The Netherlands: Kluwer.

Carofiglio, V., & de Rosis, F. (2001a). Ascribing and weighting beliefs in deceptive information exchanges. In M. Bauer, P. J. Gmytrasiewicz, & J. Vassileva (Eds.), *User modeling 2001* (pp. 222–224). (Springer Lecture Notes in Artificial Intelligence, 2109). Berlin: Springer.

Carofiglio, V., & de Rosis, F. (2001b). Exploiting uncertainty and incomplete knowledge in deceptive argumentation. In *Computational science, ICCS 2001* (pp. 1019–1028). (Lecture Notes in Computer Science, 2073). Berlin: Springer.

Carofiglio, V., de Rosis, F., & Grassano, R. (2001). An interactive system for generating arguments in deceptive communication. In F. Esposito (Ed.), *Proceedings of AI*IA 2001: Advances in artificial intelligence* (pp. 255–266). (Springer Lecture Notes in Artificial Intelligence, 2175). Berlin: Springer.

Carr, C. S. (2003). Using computer supported argument visualization to teach legal argumentation. In P. A. Kirschner, S. J. Buckingham Shum, & C. S. Carr (Eds.), *Visualizing argumentation: Software tools for collaborative and educational sense-making* (pp. 75–96). London: Springer.

Carr, D. (2008). Narrative explanation and its malcontents. *History and Theory*,[54] *47*, 19–30.

---

[54] The journal *History and Theory* is published in Middletown, Connecticut by Wesleyan University, and is distributed in New York & Chichester, West Sussex, England, by John Wiley & Sons.

Carrier, B. (2005). *File system forensic analysis*. Upper Saddle River, NJ: Addison-Wesley Professional.

Carrier, B., & Spafford, E. (2004). Defining event reconstruction of digital crime scenes. *Journal of Forensic Sciences, 49*(6), 1291–1298.

Carroll, G., & Charniak, E. (1991). *A probabilistic analysis of marker-passing techniques for plan recognition*. Technical Report CS-91-44, Computer Science Department. Providence, RI: Brown University.

Carter, A. L. (2001a). The directional analysis of bloodstain patterns theory and experimental validation. *Canadian Society for Forensic Science Journal, 34*(4), 173–189.

Carter, A. L. (2001b). *Carter's compendium for bloodstain analysis with computers: Directional analysis of bloodstain patterns*. Ottawa, ON: Forensic Computing of Ottawa Inc. BackTrack Analysis page (electronic book provided with BackTrack Suite).

Carter, A. L., Illes, M., Maloney, K., Yamashita, A. B., Allen, B., Brown, B., et al. (2005). Further Validation of the backtrack^{TM} computer program for bloodstain pattern analysis: Precision and accuracy. *IABPA News,*[55] *21*(3), 15–22.

Carter, D. L. (2004). *Law enforcement intelligence: A guide for state, local, and tribal law enforcement agencies*. Washington, DC: Office of Community Oriented Policing Services, U.S. Department of Justice. http://www.cops.usdoj.gov/files/ric/Publications/leintelguide.pdf

Caruso, S. (2001). Una sorta di "confronto all'americana" ante litteram nel bìos di S. Elia Speleota da Reggio (BHG 581). In *Miscellanea di studi in memoria di Cataldo Roccaro*, special issue of *Pan: Studi del Dipartimento di Civiltà Euro-Mediterranee e di Studi Classici, Cristiani, Bizantini, Medievali, Umanistici*, 18/19. Palermo, Sicily: Università degli Studi di Palermo. Posted at the journal's website at: http://www.unipa.it/dicem/html/pubblicazioni/pan2001/pan10-2001.pdf

Casalinuovo, I. A., Di Pierro, D., Coletta, M., & Di Francesco, P. (2006). Application of electronic noses for disease diagnosis and food spoilage detection. *Sensors, 6*, 1428–1439.

Casas-Garriga, G. (2003). Discovering unbounded episodes in sequential data. In *Proceedings of the Seventh European Conference on Principles and Practice of Knowledge Discovery in Databases (PKDD 2003)*, pp. 83–94.

Casey, E. (2000). *Digital evidence and computer crime: Forensic science, computers, and the internet*. London: Academic. New edn., 2004.

Casey, E. (Ed.). (2001). *Handbook of computer crime investigation: Forensic tools and technology*. London: Academic.

Cassel, J., & Ryokai, K. (2001). Making space for voice: Technologies to support children's fantasy and storytelling. *Personal and Ubiquitous Computing, 5*, 169–190.

Cassell, J., Sullivan, J., Prevost, S., & Churchill, E. (Eds.). 2000. *Embodied conversational characters*. Cambridge, MA: MIT Press.

Cassinis, R., Morelli, L. M., & Nissan, E. (2007). Emulation of human feelings and behaviours in an animated artwork. *International Journal on Artificial Intelligence Tools, 16*(2), 291–375. Full-page contents of the article on p. 158.

Castelfranchi, C., & Falcone, R. (1998). Towards a theory of delegation for agent-based systems. *Robotics and Autonomous Systems, 24*, 141–157.

Castelfranchi, C., & Falcone, R. (2000). Trust and control: A dialectic link. *Applied Artificial Intelligence, 14*, 799–823.

Castelfranchi, C., & Falcone, R. (2010). *Trust theory: A socio-cognitive and computational approach*. Chichester: Wiley.

Castelfranchi, C., & Poggi, I. (1998). *Bugie, finzioni e sotterfugi*. Florence: Carocci.

Castelfranchi, C., & Tan, Y. (2002). *Trust and deception in virtual societies*. Dordrecht, The Netherlands: Kluwer.

---

[55] The journal is published by the International Association of Bloodstain Pattern Analysts (IABPA). See http://iabpa.org

Castelle, G., & Loftus, E. F. (2001). Misinformation and wrongful convictions. In: S. D. Westervelt & J. A. Humphrey (Eds.). *Wrongly convicted: perspectives on failed justice* (pp. 17–35). Newark, NJ: Rutgers University Press.

Catarci, T., & Sycara, K. (2004). *Ontologies, databases, and applications of semantics (ODBASE) 2004 international conference*. Berlin: Springer.

Catts, E. P., & Goff, M. L. (1992). Forensic entomology in criminal investigations. *Annual Review of Entomology, 37*, 253–272.

Catts, E. P., & Haskell, N. H. (1990). *Entomology & death: A procedural guide*. Clemson, SC: Joyce's Print Shop.

Cavazza, M., Charles, F., & Mead, S. J. (2001). Narrative representations and causality in character-based interactive storytelling. In *Proceedings of CAST01, living in mixed realities*, Bonn, Germany, September 2001, pp. 139–142.

Cavazza, M., Charles, F., & Mead, S. (2002a). Planning characters' behaviour in interactive storytelling. *Journal of Visualization and Computer Animation, 13*(2), 121–131.

Cavazza, M., Charles, F., & Mead, S. J. (2002b). Character-based interactive storytelling. *IEEE Intelligent Systems, 17*(4), 17–24.

Cavazza, M., & Donikian, S. (Eds.). (2007). *Proceedings of the fourth international conference on virtual storytelling: Using virtual reality technologies for storytelling (ICVS'07)*. New York: ACM.

Cayrol, C. & Lagasquie-Schiex, S. (2006). Coalitions of arguments in bipolar argumentation frameworks. At the *Seventh international workshop on computational models of natural argument*.

Chadwick, D. W., & Basden, A. (2001). Evaluating trust in a public key certification authority. *Computers and Security, 20*(7), 592–611.

Chadwick, D. W., Basden, A., Evans, J., & Young, A. J. (1998). Intelligent computation of trust. Short paper at the *TERENA Networking Conference '98 (TNC'98)*, Dresden, 5–8 October 1998. TERENA, the Trans-European Research and Education Networking Association.

Chae, M., Shim, S., Cho, H., & Lee, B. (2007). An empirical analysis of fraud detection in online auctions: Credit card phantom transactions. In *HICSS 2007: Proceedings of the 40th annual Hawaii international conference on system sciences*.

Chaib-Draa, B., & Dignum, F. (Eds.). (2002). Trends in agent communication language. Special issue of *Computational Intelligence, 18*, 89–101.

Chaiken, S. (1987). The heuristic model of persuasion. In M. P. Zanna, J. M. Olson, & C. P. Herman (Eds.), *Social influence: The Ontario symposium* (Vol. 5, pp. 3–39). Hillsdale, NJ: Erlbaum.

Chaiken, S., Liberman, A., & Eagly, A. H. (1989). Heuristic and systematic information processing within and beyond the persuasion context. In J. S. Uleman & J. A. Bargh (Eds.), *Unintended thought* (pp. 212–252). New York: Guilford Press.

Chaiken, S., Wood, W., & Eagly, A. H. (1996). Principles of persuasion. In E. T. Higgins & A. Kruglanski (Eds.), *Social psychology: Handbook of basic mechanisms and processes* (pp. 702–742). New York: Guilford Press.

Champod, C. (1995). Edmond Locard – Numerical standards and 'probable' identifications. *Journal of Forensic Identification, 45*, 136–163.

Champod, C., Lennard, C., Margot, P., & Stilovic, M. (2004). *Fingerprints and other ridge skin impressions*. Boca Raton, FL: CRC Press.

Chan, H., Lee, R., Dillon, T., & Chang, E. (2001). *E commerce: Fundamentals and applications*. Chichester: Wiley.

Chan, J. (1991). A computerised sentencing system for New South Wales courts. *Computer Law and Practice, 1991*, 137 ff.

Chan, J., Brereton, D., Legosz, M., & Doran, S. (2001). *E-policing: The impact of information technology on police practices*. Brisbane, QLD: Criminal Justice Commission.

Chance, J. E., & Goldstein, A. G. (1995). The other-race effect and eyewitness identification. In S. L. Sporer, R. S. Malpass, & G. Köhnken (Eds.), *Psychological issues in eyewitness identification* (pp. 153–176). Hillsdale, NJ: Lawrence Erlbaum Associates.

Channell, R. C., & Tolcott, M. A. (1954). Arrangement of equipment. In supplement to *Human Factors in Undersea Warfare*. Washington, DC: National Academy of Sciences, National Research Council.

Chaoji, V., Hoonlor, A., & Szymanski, B. K. (2008a). Recursive data mining for author and role identification. In *Proceedings of the third Annual Inormation Assuarance Workshop ASIA'08*, Albany, NY, June 4–5, 2008, pp. 53–62.

Chaoji, V., Hoonlor, A., & Szymanski, B. K. (2008b). Recursive data mining for role identification. In *Proceedings of the fifth international Conference on Soft Computing as Transdisciplinary Science and Technology CSTST'08*, Paris, France, October 27–31, 2008, pp. 218–225.

Chaoji, V., Hoonlor, A., & Szymanski, B. K. (2010). Recursive data mining for role identification in electronic communications. *International Journal of Hybrid Information Systems, 7*(3), 89–100. Also at: http://www.cs.rpi.edu/~szymansk/papers/ijhis.09.pdf

Chapanis, A. (1969). *Research techniques in human engineering*. Baltimore, MD: John Hopkins Press.

Chapanond, A., Krishnamoorthy, M. S., & Yener, B. (2005). Graph theoretic and spectral analysis of Enron email data. *Computational & Mathematical Organization Theory, 11*(3), 265–281.

Charles, J. (1998). AI and law enforcement. *IEEE Intelligent Systems, January–February*, 77–80.

Charniak, E. (1972). *Toward a model of children's story comprehension*. Technical Report AI TR 266. Cambridge, MA: Artificial Intelligence Laboratory, Massachusetts Institute of Technology. ftp://publications.ai.mit.edu/ai-publications/pdf/AITR-20266.pdf

Charniak, E. (1977a). Ms. Malaprop, a language comprehension program. In *Proceedings of the fifth international conference on artificial intelligence*.

Charniak, E. (1977b). A framed PAINTING: The representation of a common sense knowledge fragment. *Cognitive Science, 1*, 355–394.

Charniak, E. (1983). Passing markers: A theory of contextual influence in language comprehension. *Cognitive Science, 7*, 171–190.

Charniak, E. (1986). A neat theory of marker passing. In *Proceedings of the fifth national conference on artificial intelligence*. Menlo Park, CA: AAAI Press, pp. 584–588.

Charniak, E. (1991). A probabilistic analysis of marker-passing techniques for plan-recognition. In B. D'Ambrosio & P. Smets (Eds.), *UAI '91: Proceedings of the seventh annual conference on uncertainty in artificial intelligence*, July 13–15, 1991, University of California at Los Angeles, Los Angeles, CA (pp. 69–76). San Mateo, CA: Morgan Kaufmann.

Charniak, E., & Shimony, S. E. (1990). Probabilistic semantics for cost-based abduction. In *Proceedings of the 11th annual national conference on artificial intelligence (AAAI'90)*. Menlo Park, CA: AAAI Press, pp. 106–111.

Charniak, E., & Shimony, S. E. (1994). Cost-based abduction and MAP explanation. *Artificial Intelligence, 66*, 345–374.

Charniak, E., & Wilks, Y. (1976). *Computational semantics*. New York: North-Holland.

Chau, "P." [= D. H.] (2011). Catching bad guys with graph mining. In *The Fate of Money*. An issue of *Crossroads: The ACM Magazine for Students, 17*(3), 16–18.

Chau, D. H., Nachenberg, C., Wilhelm, J., Wright, A., & Faloutsos, C. (2010). Polonium: Tera-scale graph mining for malware detection. In *Proceedings of the second workshop on Large-scale Data Mining: Theory and Applications (LDMTA 2010)*, Washington, DC, 25 July 2010. http://www.ml.cmu.edu/current_students/DAP_chau.pdf

Chau, D. H., Pandit, S., & Faloutsos, C. (2006). Detecting fraudulent personalities in networks of online auctioneers. In *Proceedings of the European Conference on Machine Learning (ECM) and Principles and Practice of Knowledge Discovery in Databases (PKDD) 2006*, Berlin, 18–22 September 2006, pp. 103–114.

Chau, M., Schroeder, J., Xu, J., & Chen, H. (2007). Automated criminal link analysis based on domain knowledge. *Journal of the American Society for Information Science and Technology, 58*(6), 842–855.

Chellas, B. F. (1974). Conditional obligation. In S. Stenlund (Ed.), *Logical theory and semantic analysis* (pp. 23–33). Dordrecht: Reidel.

Chen, H., Chung, W., Xu, J. J., Wang, G., Qin, Y., & Chau, M. (2004). Crime data mining: A general framework and some examples. *IEEE Computer, 37*(4), 50–56.

Chen, H., & Lynch, K. J. (1992). Automatic construction of networks of concepts characterizing document databases. *IEEE Transactions on Systems,* Sept./Oct. 1992, 885–902.

Chen, H., Schroeder, J., Hauck, R., Ridgeway, L., Atabakhsh, H., Gupta, H., et al. (2003). COPLINK Connect: Information and knowledge management for law enforcement. In *Digital Government: Technologies and Practices,* special issue, *Decision Support Systems, 34*(3), 271–285.

Chen, H., Zeng, D., Atabakhsh, H., Wyzga, W., & Schroeder, J. (2003). COPLINK managing law enforcement data and knowledge. *Communications of the ACM, 46*(1), 28–34.

Chen, P. (2000a). An automatic system for collecting crime on the Internet. *The Journal of Information, Law and Technology (JILT), 3* (online). http://elj.warwick.ac.uk/jilt/00-3/chen.html

Chen, X., Wang, M., & Zhang, H. (2011). The use of classification trees for bioinformatics. *Wiley Interdisciplinary Reviews (WIREs): Data Mining and Knowledge Discovery, 1*(1), 55–63. doi://10.1002/widm.14

Chen, Z. (2000b). *Java card technology for smart cards: Architecture and programmer's guide.* Boston: Addison-Wesley.

Chen, Z. (2001). *Data mining and uncertain reasoning: An integrated approach.* New York: Wiley.

Chen, Z., & Kuo, C. H. (1991). Topology-based matching algorithm for fingerprint authentication. In *Proceedings of 25th annual IEEE international carnahan conference on security technology,* pp. 84–87.

Cherry, M., & Imwinkelried, E. J. (2006). A cautionary note about fingerprint analysis and reliance on digital technology. *Judicature, 89,* 334–338.

Cheswick, B. (1992). An evening with Berferd: In which a cracker is lured, endured, and studied. In *Proceedings of the Winter Usenix Conference,* San Francisco, 1992, pp. 163–174. Published again in several places elsewhere. Retrieved in May 2011 http://www.cheswick.com/ches/papers/berferd.pdf

Chisholm, R. M. (1963). Contrary-to-duty imperatives and deontic logic. *Analysis, 24,* 33–36.

Chisholm, R. M. (1965). The problem of empiricism. In R. J. Swartz (Ed.), *Perceiving, sensing, and knowing.* Berkeley, CA: University of California Press.

Chiswick, D., & Cope, R. (Eds.). (1995). *Seminars in practical forensic psychiatry.* (Royal College of Psychiatrists, College Seminars Series.) London: Gaskell.

Choo, R. K. K. (2008). Organised crime groups in cyberspace: A typology. *Trends in Organized Crime, 11,* 270–295.

Choudhary, A.N., Honbo, D., Kumar, P., Ozisikyilmaz, B., Misra, S., & Memik, G. (2011). Accelerating data mining workloads: Current approaches and future challenges in system architecture design. *Wiley Interdisciplinary Reviews (WIREs): Data Mining and Knowledge Discovery, 1*(1), 41–54. doi://10.1002/widm.9

Christie, G. C. (1964). Vagueness and legal language. *Minnesota Law Review, 48,* 885–911.

Christie, G. C. (1984a). Mechanical jurisprudence. In *The guide to American law: Everyone's legal encyclopedia* (Vol. 7, pp. 321–322). St. Paul, MN: West Publishing Company. 12 vols., 1983–1985.

Christie, G. C. (1984b). Due process of law: A confused and confusing notion. In C. Perelman & R. Vande Elst (Eds.), *Les notions à contenu variable en droit* (Travaux du Centre National Belge de Recherche de Logique.) (pp. 57–79). Brussels: E. Bruylant.

Christie, G. C. (1986). An essay on discretion. *Duke Law Journal, 1986*(5), 747–778. http://scholarship.law.duke.edu/cgi/viewcontent.cgi?article=1017&context= faculty_scholarship&sei-redir=1#search=""Duke+law+journal"+Christie+"an+essay+on+ discretion""

Christie, G. C. (2000). *The notion of an ideal audience in legal argument.* Dordrecht: Kluwer. Also in French, *L'Auditoire universel dans l'argumentation juridique* (G. Haarscher, Trans.). Belgium: E. Bruylant, 2005.

Christopher, S. (2004). A practitioner's perspective of UK strategic intelligence. In J. H. Ratcliffe (Ed.), *Strategic thinking in criminal intelligence* (1st ed.). Sydney, NSW: Federation Press.

Chua, C. H., & Wareham, J. (2002). Self-regulation for online auctions: An analysis. In *ICIS 2002: Proceedings of international conference on information systems*.

Chua, C. H., & Wareham, J. (2004). Fighting internet auction fraud: An assessment and proposal. *IEEE Computer, 37*(10), 31–37.

Church, A. (1951). The weak theory of implication. In A. Menne, A. Wilhelmy, & H. Angell (Eds.), *Kontroliertes Denken: Untersuchungen zum Logikkalkül und zur Logik der Einzelwissenschaften* (pp. 22–37). Munich: Kommissions-Verlag Karl Alber.

Cialdini, R. (1993). *Influence: Science and practice* (3rd ed.). New York: HarperCollins.

Ciampolini, A., & Torroni, P. (2004). Using abductive logic agents for modelling judicial evaluation of criminal evidence. *Applied Artificial Intelligence, 18*(3/4), 251–275.

Ciocoiu, M., Nau, D. S., & Grüninger, M. (2001). Ontologies for integrating engineering applications. *Journal of Computing and Information Science and Engineering, 1*(1), 12–22.

Cios, K. J., Pedrycz, W., & Swiniarski, R. (1998). *Data mining methods for knowledge discovery*. Boston: Kluwer.

Clark, M., & Crawford, C. (Eds.). (1994). *Legal medicine in history*. Cambridge History of Medicine. Cambridge: Cambridge University Press.

Clark, P. (1991). *A model of argumentation and its application in a cooperative expert system*. Ph.D. thesis, Department of Computer Science, Turing Institute, University of Strathclyde, Glasgow, Scotland.

Clark, R. A., & Delia, J. G. (1976). The development of functional persuasive skills in childhood and early adolescence. *Child Development, 47*, 1008–1014.

Clark, S. E., & Wells, G. L. (2007). On the diagnosticity of multiple-witness identifications. *Law and Human Behavior, 32*, 406–422. Published online on 18 December 2007. doi://10.1007/s10979-007-9115-7

Clarke, P. H. (1985). *The surveyor in court*. London: Estates Gazette.

Clarke, R. V., & Eck, J. (2005). *Crime analysis for problem solvers in 60 small steps*. Washington, DC: Office of Community Oriented Policing Services, U.S. Department of Justice. http://www.popcenter.org/Library/RecommendedReadings/60Steps.pdf

Clarke, R. V., & Felson, M. (1993). Introduction: Criminology, routine activity, and rational choice. In R. V. Clarke & M. Felson (Eds.), *Routine activity and rational choice*. (Advances in Criminological Theory, 5.) New Brunswick, NJ: Transaction Publishers.

Clay, M., & Lehrer, K. (Eds.). (1989). *Knowledge and skepticism*. Boulder, CO: Westerview Press.

Clements, R. V. (1994). *Safe practice in obstetrics and gynaecology: A medico-legal handbook*. Edinburgh: Churchill Livingstone.

Clifford, B., & Bull, R. (1978). *The psychology of person identification*. London: Routledge.

Coady, W. F. (1985). Automated link analysis: Artificial Intelligence-based tool for investigators. *Police Chief, 52*(9), 22–23.

Cocker, M. (1990). *Soldier, scientist and spy*. London: Secker & Warburg. London: Mandarin, 1990.

Cocker, M. (2000). *Soldier, scientist, spy . . . fraud*. (sound cassette, recorded from BBC Radio 4, 11.00–11.30am, 26 December 2000.) London: BBC.

Cohen, D. (2005). Arguments that backfire. In D. Hitchcock (Ed.), *The uses of argument* (pp. 58–65). Hamilton, ON: OSSA.

Cohen, F. (2009). Two models of digital forensic analysis. In *Proceedings of the fourth international IEEE workshop on Systematic Approaches to Digital Forensic Engineering (SADFE-2009)*, Oakland, CA, 21 May 2009, pp. 42–53.

Cohen, F. S. (1935). Transcendental nonsense and the functional approach. *Columbia Law Review, 35*(6), 809–849. http://www.jstor.org/stable/1116300

Cohen, L. E., & Felson, M. (1979). Social change and crime rate trends: A routine activity approach. *American Sociological Review, 44*, 588–608.

Cohen, L. J. (1977). *The probable and the provable*. Oxford: Oxford University Press.

Cohen, P. (1985). *Heuristic reasoning about uncertainty: An artificial intelligence approach*. London: Pitman.

Cohen, P. R., & Levesque, H. J. (1990). Intention is choice with commitment. *Artificial Intelligence, 42*(2/3), 213–261.

Cohn, A. G., Gooday, J. M., & Bennett, B. (1995). A comparison of structures in spatial and temporal logics. In R. Casati & G. White (Eds.), *Philosophy and the cognitive sciences* (pp. 409–422). Vienna: Holder-Pichler-Tempsky.

Cohn, A. G., Gotts, N. M., Cui, Z., Randell, D. A., Bennett, B., & Gooday, J. M. (1994). Exploiting temporal continuity in qualitative spatial calculi. In R. G. Golledge & M. J. Egenhofer (Eds.), *Spatial and temporal reasoning in geographical information systems*. Amsterdam: Elsevier.

Colby, K. M. (1975). *Artificial paranoia*. Oxford: Pergamon Press.

Colby, K. M. (1981). Modeling a paranoid mind. *The Behavioral and Brain Sciences, 4*(4), 515–560.

Colby, K. M. (1983). Limits on the scope of PARRY as a model of paranoia. [Response to Manschreck (1983).] *The Behavioral and Brain Sciences, 6*(2), 341–342.

Cole, D. J., & Ackland, P. R. (1994). *The detective and the doctor: A murder casebook*. London: Hale.

Cole, S. A. (1999). What counts for identity? The historical origins of the methodology of latent fingerprint identification. *Science in Context*,[56] *12*, 139–172.

Cole, S. A. (2001). *Suspect identities: A history of fingerprinting and criminal identification*. Cambridge, MA: Harvard University Press.

Cole, S. A. (2004). Grandfathering evidence: Fingerprint admissibility rulings from Jennings to Llera Plaza and back again. *American Criminal Law Review, 41*, 1189–1276.

Cole, S. A. (2005). More than zero: Accounting for error in latent print identification. *Journal of Criminal Law and Criminology, 95*, 985–1078.

Cole, S. A. (2006a). The prevalence and potential causes of wrongful conviction by fingerprint evidence. *Golden Gate University Law Review, 37*, 39–105.

Cole, S. A. (2006b). Is Fingerprint identification valid? Rhetorics of reliability in fingerprint proponents' discourse. *Law Policy, 28*, 109–135.

Cole, S. A. (2009). *Daubert* revisited. Don't shoot the messenger by one of the messengers: A response to Merlino et al. *Tulsa Law Review, 45*, 111–132. http://www.tulsalawreview.com/wp-content/uploads/2010/10/Cole.Final_.pdf

Cole, S. A., Welling, M., Dioso-Villa, R., & Carpenter, R. (2008). Beyond the individuality of fingerprints: A measure of simulated computer latent print source attribution accuracy. *Law, Probability and Risk, 7*, 165–189.

Coleman, K. M. (Ed.). (2006). Martial, *Liber spectaculorum* [so on the jacket, vs. frontispiece: *M. Valerii Martialis Liber spectaculorum*], edited with introduction, translation [from Latin into English] and commentary. Oxford: Oxford University Press.

Colombetti, M., Gini, G., & Nissan, E. (2007). Guest editorial: Marco Somalvico Memorial Issue. *International Journal on Artificial Intelligence Tools, 16*(2), 149–159.

Colombetti, M., Gini, G., & Nissan, E. (2008a). Guest editorial: Papers in sensing and in reasoning (Marco Somalvico Memorial Issue). *Cybernetics and Systems, 39*(4), 305–309.

Colombetti, M., Gini, G., & Nissan, E. (2008b). Guest editorial: Robotics, virtual reality, and agents and their body: A special issue in memory of Marco Somalvico. *Journal of Intelligent and Robotic Systems, 52*(3/4), 333–341.

Colwell, K., Hiscock-Anisman, C., Memon, A., Woods, D., & Yaeger, H. (2006). Strategies of impression management among deceivers and truth tellers: How liars attempt to convince. *American Journal of Forensic Psychology, 24*(2), 31–38.

Colwell, K., Hiscock-Anisman, C., Memon, A., Rachel, A., & Colwell, L. (2007). Vividness and spontaneity of statement detail characteristics as predictors of witness credibility. *American Journal of Forensic Psychology, 25*, 5–30.

Combrink-Kuiters, C. J. M., De Mulder, R. V., & van Noortwijk, C. (2000). Jurimetrical research on judicial decision-making: A review. At *Intelligent Decision Support for Legal Practice (IDS*

---

[56] *Science in Context* is a journal published by Cambridge University Press.

2000). In *Proceedings of the international ICSC congress "Intelligent Systems & Applications" (ISA 2000),* Wollongong, NSW, Australia, December 2000 (Vol. 1, pp. 109–117). Wetaskiwin, AB: ICSC Academic Press.

Conan Doyle, A. (1987). See Doyle (1887).[57]

Conant, E. (2003). Man of 1,000 faces: The forensic genius of Mikhail Gerasimov. *Archaeology, 56*(4). The Archaeological Institute of America, July/August 2003.

Cone, E. J., & Deyl, Z. (Eds.). (1992). *Toxicology and forensic applications.* Special issue, *Journal of Chromatography, B: Biomedical Applications, 580*(1/2). Amsterdam: Elsevier.

Conklin, J., & Begeman, M. L. (1988). gIBIS: A hypertext tool for exploratory policy discussion. *ACM Transactions on Office Information Systems, 4*(6), 303–331.

Conley, J. M., & O'Barr, W. M. (1998). *Just words: Law, language and power.* Chicago: University of Chicago Press.

Conley, J. M., & O'Barr, W. M. (1990). *Rules versus relationships: The ethnography of legal discourse.* Chicago: University of Chicago Press.

Console, L., & Torasso, P. (1991). A spectrum of logical definitions of model-based diagnosis. *Computational Intelligence, 7*(3), 133–141.

Conte, R., & Paolucci, M. (2002). *Reputation in artificial societies. Social beliefs for social order.* Dordrecht: Kluwer.

Conway, J. V. P. (1959). *Evidential documents.* Springfield, IL: Charles C. Thomas.

Cook, R., Evett, I., Jackson, G., Jones, P., & Lambert, J. (1998). A model for case assessment and interpretation. *Science and Justice, 38,* 151–156.

Cook, T., & Tattersall, A. (2008). *Blackstone's senior investigating officer's handbook.* Oxford: Oxford University Press.

Cooper, J. (2008). Net marks crime capital. *Bexley Times* (South East London, of the Kentish Times Group), 11 September, p. 7, col. 5.

Cope, N. (2003). Crime analysis: Principles and practice. In T. Newburn (Ed.), *Handbook of policing* (pp. 340–362). Cullompton: Willan Publishing.

Cope, N. (2004). Intelligence led policing or policing led intelligence? Integrating volume crime analysis into policing. *British Journal of Criminology, 44*(2), 188–203.

Correira, A. (1980). Computing story trees. *American Journal of Computational Linguistics, 6*(3/4), 135–149.

Cortes, C., Pregibon, D., & Volinsky, C. (2001). Communities of interest. In *Proceedings of the fourth international symposium of intelligent data analysis.*

Cortes, C., & Vapnik, V. (1995). Support-vector networks. *Machine Learning, 20,* 273–297.

Costa, M., Sousa, O., & Neves, J. (1999). Managing legal precedents with case retrieval nets. In H. J. van den Herik, M.-F. Moens, J. Bing, B. van Buggenhout, J. Zeleznikow, & C. Grütters (Eds.), *Legal knowledge based systems. JURIX 1999: The twelfth conference* (pp. 13–22). Nijmegen, The Netherlands, Gerard Noodt Instituut (GNI).

Costello, B. D., Gunawardena, C. A., & Nadiadi, Y. M. (1994). Automated coincident sequencing for fingerprint identification. In *Proceedings of the IEE colloquium on image processing for biometric measurement,* London, pp. 3.1–3.5.

Coull, S., Branch, J., Szymanski, B. K., & Breimer, E. (2003). Intrusion detection: A bioinformatics approach. In *Proceedings of the 19th annual computer security applications conference,* Las Vegas, NV, December 2003, pp. 24–33.

Coull, S., & Szymanski, B. K. (2008). Sequence alignment for masquerade detection. *Computational Statistics and Data Analysis, 52*(8), 4116–4131.

Coulthard, M. (1992). Forensic discourse analysis. In M. Coulthard (Ed.), *Advances in spoken discourse analysis* (pp. 242–258). London: Routledge.

---

[57] In fact, Sir Arthur Conan Doyle was the son of Charles Doyle, who illustrated the book when it first appeared in book form, in 1888.

Cox, M., & Mays, S. (Eds.). (2000). *Human osteology in archaeology and forensic science.* London: Greenwich Medical Media.

Cox, M. T. (1994). Machines that forget: Learning from retrieval failure of mis indexed explanations. In A. Ram & K. Eiselt (Eds.), *Proceedings of the sixteenth annual conference of the cognitive science society* (pp. 225–230). Hillsdale, NJ: LEA. http://mcox.org/Papers/mach-forget.ps.gz

Cox, M. T. (1996a). *Introspective multistrategy learning: Constructing a learning strategy under reasoning failure.* Doctoral dissertation. Technical Report GIT-CC-96-06. Atlanta, GA: College of Computing, Georgia Institute of Technology. http://hcs.bbn.com/personnel/Cox/thesis/

Cox, M. T. (1996b). An empirical study of computational introspection: Evaluating introspective multistrategy learning in the Meta-AQUA system. In R. S. Michalski & J. Wnek (Eds.), *Proceedings of the third international workshop on multistrategy learning* (pp. 135–146). Menlo Park, CA: AAAI Press. http://mcox.org/Ftp/eval-paper.ps.Z

Cox, M. T. (2005). Metacognition in computation: A selected research review. *Artificial Intelligence, 169*(2), 104–114.

Cox, M. T. (2007a). Perpetual self-aware cognitive agents. *AI Magazine, 28*(1), 32–45.

Cox, M. T. (2007b). Metareasoning, monitoring and self-explanation. In *Proceedings of the first international workshop on metareasoning in agent-based systems at AAMAS 2007.* Also: Technical report. Cambridge, MA: BBN Technologies, Intelligent Computing, pp. 46–60. http://mcox.org/Papers/self-explan7.pdf

Cox, M. T., & Raja, A. (2007). *Metareasoning: A manifesto.* Technical Report: BBN Technical Memo, BBN TM 2028. Cambridge, MA: BBN Technologies, Intelligent Computing.

Cox, M. T., & Ram, A. (1999). Introspective multistrategy learning: On the construction of learning strategies. *Artificial Intelligence, 112,* 1–55.

Cozman, F. J. (2001). *JavaBayes: Bayesian networks in Java.* http://www-2.cs.cmu.edu/~javabayes/

Crandall, D., Backstrom, L., Cosley, D., Suri, S., Huttenlocher, D., & Kleinberg, J. (2010, December 28). Inferring social ties from geographic coincidences. *Proceedings of the National Academy of Sciences, 107*(52), 22436–22441. http://www.pnas.org/content/early/2010/12/02/1006155107.full.pdf+html

Crandall, J. R., Wu, S. F., & Chong, F. T. (2005). Experiences using Minos as a tool for capturing and analyzing novel worms for unknown vulnerabilities. In K. Julisch & C. Krügel (Eds.), *Detection of Intrusions and Malware, and Vulnerability Assessment: Proceedings of the second international conference (DIMVA 2005),* Vienna, Austria, July 7–8, 2005 (pp. 32–50). (Lecture Notes in Computer Science, Vol. 3548.) Berlin: Springer.

Crittendon, C. (1991). *Unreality: The metaphysics of fictional objects.* Ithaca, NY: Cornell University Press.

Cross, R., & Tapper, C. (1985). *Cross on evidence* (6th ed.). London: Butterworth.

Crump, D. (1997). On the uses of irrelevant evidence. *Houston Law Review, 34,* 1–53.

Cui, Z., Cohn, A. G., & Randell, D. A. (1992). Qualitative simulation based on a logical formalism of space and time. In *Proceedings of AAAI-92.* Menlo Park, CA: AAAI Press, pp. 679–684.

Culhane, S. E., & Hosch, H. M. (2002). *An alibi witness's influence on jurors' verdicts.* University of Texas-El Paso.[58] [Cited before publication in a passage I quoted from Olson & Wells (2002).]

Culhane, S. E., & Hosch, H. M. (2004). An alibi witness's influence on juror's decision making. *Journal of Applied Social Psychology, 34,* 1604–1616.

Culhane, S. E., & Hosch, H. M. (2005). Law enforcement officers serving as jurors: Guilty because charged? *Psychology, Crime and Law, 11,* 305–313.

Culhane, S. E., Hosch, H. M., & Weaver, W. G. (2004). Crime victims serving as jurors: Is a bias present? *Law and Human Behavior, 28,* 649–659.

---

[58] At the time, Scott Culhane was pursuing there a doctoral degree in legal psychology.

Cullingford, R. E. (1978). *Script application: Computer understanding of newspaper stories.* Technical Report YALE/DCS/tr116. New Haven, CT: Computer Science Department, Yale University.

Cullingford, R. E. (1981). SAM (Ch. 5); Micro SAM (Ch. 6). In R. G. Schank & C. K. Riesbeck (Eds.), *Inside computer understanding: Five programs plus miniatures* (pp. 75–119 and 120–135). Hillsdale, NJ: Erlbaum.

Cummins, H., & Midlo, C. (1943). *Finger prints, palms and soles: An introduction to dermatoglyphics.* Philadelphia, PA: Blakiston.

Curzon, L. B. (1997). *Criminal law* (8th ed.). London: Pitman.

Cutler, B. L. (Ed.). (2009). *Expert testimony on the psychology of eyewitness identification* (American Psychology-Law Society Series.) New York: Oxford University Press.

Cutler, B. L., & Penrod, S. D. (1995). Assessing the accuracy of eye-witness identifications. Chapter 3.3 In R. Bull & D. Carson (Eds.), *Handbook of psychology in legal contexts* (pp. 193–213). Chichester: Wiley.

Cutler, B. L., Penrod, S. D., & Martens, T. K. (1987). The reliability of eye-witness identifications: The role of system and estimator variables. *Law and Human Behavior, 11*, 223–258.

Cybenko, G. (1989). Approximation by superpositions of a sigmoidal function. *Mathematics of Control, Signals and Systems, 2*, 303–314.

Dagan, H. (2007). The realist conception of law. *Toronto Law Journal, 57*(3), 607–660.

Dahlgren, K., McDowell, J., & Stabler, E. P., Jr. (1989). Knowledge representation for common-sense reasoning with text. *Computational Linguistics, 15*(3), 149–170. http://acl.ldc.upenn.edu/J/J89/J89-3002.pdf

Dalton, R. (2005). Ornithologists stunned by bird collector's deceit. *Nature, 437*, 302–303. http://www.nature.com/news/index.html

Danet, B. (1994). Review of R. W. Shuy, *Language crimes: The use and abuse of language evidence in the courtroom* (Oxford: Blackwell, 1993), in the *Journal of Language and Social Psychology, 13*(1), 73–78.

Daniels, J. J., & Rissland, E. L. (1997). Finding legally relevant passages in case opinions. In *Proceedings of the sixth international conference on artificial intelligence and law*, Melbourne, Australia. New York: ACM Press, pp. 39–46.

Darling, S., Valentine, T., & Memon, A. (2008). Selection of lineup foils in operational contexts. *Applied Cognitive Psychology, 22*, 159–169.

Darr, T., & Birmingham, W. (1996). An attribute-space representation and algorithm for concurrent engineering. *Artificial Intelligence for Engineering Design, Analysis and Manufacturing (AI EDAM), 10*(1), 21–35.

Dauer, F. W. (1995). The nature of fictional characters and the referential fallacy. *The Journal of Aesthetics and Art Criticism, 53*(1), 32–38.

Daugherty, W. E., & Janowitz, M. (1958). *A psychological warfare casebook.* Baltimore, MD: John Hopkins Press, for Operations Research Office, Johns Hopkins University. Now available from Ann Arbor, MI: University Microfilms International (UMI) books on demand.

Dauglas, M. (1993). Emotion and culture in theories of justice. *Economy and Society, 22*(4), 501–515.

Dave, K., Lawrence, S., & Pennock, D. M. (2003). Mining the peanut gallery: Opinion extraction and semantic classification of product reviews. In *WWW 2003: Proceedings of the 12th international conference on world wide web.*

Davenport, G., & Murtaugh, M. (1997). Automatic storyteller systems and the shifting sands of story. *IBM Systems Journal, 36*(3), 446–456.

Davenport, G., Bradley, B., Agamanolis, S., Barry, B., & Brooks, K. (2000). Synergistic storyscapes and constructionist cinematic sharing. *IBM Systems Journal, 39*(3/4), 456–469.

Davenport, G. C., France, D. L., Griffin, T. J., Swanburg, J. G., Lindemann, J. W., Tranunell, V., et al. (1992). A multidisciplinary approach to the detection of clandestine graves. *Journal of Forensic Science, 37*(6), 1445–1458. (Also, posted at http://www.terraplus.ca/case-histories/dave1.htm)

David, R., & Alla, H. (1992). *Petri nets and Grafcet: Tools for modelling discrete event systems.* New York: Prentice Hall. Translation of: *Du Grafcet aux reseaux de Petri.*

Davide, F. A. M., Di Natale, C., & D'Amico, A. (1995). Self-organizing sensory maps in odour classification mimicking. *Biosensors and Bioelectronics, 10,* 203–218.

Davies, G. M., & Christie, D. (1982). Face recall: An examination of some factors limiting composite production accuracy. *Journal of Applied Psychology, 67*(1), 103–109.

Davies, G. M., Ellis, H. D., & Shepherd, J. W. (1978). Face identification: The influence of delay upon accuracy of Photofit construction. *Journal of Police Science and Administration, 6*(1), 35–42.

Davies, G. M, Ellis, H. D., & Shepherd, J. W. (1981). *Perceiving and remembering faces.* New York: Academic.

Davis, D., & Follette, W. C. (2002). Rethinking the probative value of evidence: Base rates, intuitive profiling, and the "postdiction" of behavior. *Law and Human Behavior, 26,* 133–158.

Davis, D., & Follette, W. C. (2003). Toward an empirical approach to evidentiary ruling. *Law and Human Behavior, 27,* 661–684.

Davis, G., & Pei, J. (2003). Bayesian networks and traffic accident reconstruction. *Proceedings of the ninth international conference on artificial intelligence and law,* Edinburgh, Scotland (pp. 171–176). New York: ACM Press.

Davis, O. (1999). *Palynomorphs.* At the website whose address is Retrieved in March 2007 http://www.geo.arizona.edu/palynology/ppalydef.html

Dawid, A. P. (1994). The island problem: Coherent use of identification evidence. Chapter 11 In P. R. Freeman & A. F. M. Smith (Eds.), *Aspects of uncertainty: A tribute to D. V. Lindley* (pp. 159–170). Chichester: Wiley.

Dawid, A. P. (1998). Modelling issues in forensic inference. In *1997 ASA proceedings,* Section on Bayesian Statistics, pp. 182–186. Alexandria, VA: The American Statistical Association.

Dawid, A. P. (2001a). Comment on Stockmarr's 'Likelihood ratios for evaluating DNA evidence when the suspect is found through a database search' (with response by A. Stockmarr). *Biometrics, 57,* 976–980.

Dawid, A. P. (2001b). *Bayes's theorem and weighing evidence by juries.* Research Report 219, April. Department of Statistical Science, University College London.

Dawid, A. P. (2002). Bayes's theorem and weighing evidence by juries. In R. Swinburne (Ed.), *Bayes's theorem. Proceedings of the British Academy, 113,* 71–90.

Dawid, A. P. (2004a). Which likelihood ratio? (Comment on 'Why the effect of prior odds should accompany the likelihood ratio when reporting DNA evidence', by R. Meester & M. Sjerps). *Law, Probability and Risk, 3,* 65–71.

Dawid, A. P. (2004b). *Statistics on trial.* Research Report 250, December. London: Department of Statistical Science, University College London. Then published as: Statistics on trial. *Significance, 2*(2005), 6–8.

Dawid, A. P. (2005a). Probability and statistics in the law. In Z. Ghahramani & R.G. Cowell (Eds.) *Proceedings of the tenth international workshop on artificial intelligence and statistics,* January 6–8 2005, Barbados. (Online at http://tinyurl.com/br8fl).

Dawid, A. P. (2005b). Probability and proof. On-line Appendix to *Analysis of evidence* (2nd ed., pp. 119–148), by T. J. Anderson, D. A. Schum, & W. L. Twining. Cambridge: Cambridge University Press. Posted at http://tinyurl.com/7g3bd, 94 pp.

Dawid, A. P. (2008). Statistics and the law. In A. Bell, J. Swenson-Wright, & K. Tybjerg (Eds.), *Evidence.* Cambridge.: Cambridge University Press, pp. 119–148. Also: Research Report 244, May 2004, Department of Statistical Science, University College London, May 2004.

Dawid, A. P., & Evett, I. W. (1997). Using a graphical method to assist the evaluation of complicated patterns of evidence. *Journal of Forensic Science, 42,* 226–231.

Dawid, A. P., & Evett, I. W. (1998). Authors' response to 'Commentary on Dawid, A. P. and Evett, I. W. Using a graphical method to assist the evaluation of complicated patterns of evidence. *J. Forensic Sci.* (1997) Mar; 42(2): 226–231' by Ira J. Rimson. *Journal of Forensic Science, 43,* 251.

Dawid, A. P., Hepler, A. B., & Schum, D. A. (2011). Inference networks: Bayes and Wigmore. Chapter 5 In: A. P. Dawid, W. L. Twining, & D. Vasilaki (Eds.), *Evidence, inference and enquiry* (to appear). Oxford: Oxford University Press.

Dawid, A. P., & Mortera, J. (1994). *Elementary Watson!: Coherent analysis of forensic evidence.* Research Report 136, May. Department of Statistical Science, University College London.

Dawid, A. P., & Mortera, J. (1996). Coherent analysis of forensic identification evidence. *Journal of the Royal Statistics Society, B, 58*, 425–443.

Dawid, A. P., & Mortera, J. (1998). Forensic identification with imperfect evidence. *Biometrika, 85*, 835–849. Correction: *Biometrika*, 86 (1999), p. 974.

Dawid, A. P., Mortera, J., Dobosz, M., & Pascali, V. L. (2003). Mutations and the probabilistic approach to incompatible paternity tests. In B. Brinkmann & A. Carracedo (Eds.), *Progress in forensic genetics 9: Proceedings from the 19th congress of the international society for forensic haemogenetics* (pp. 637–638). (International Congress Series, Vol. 1239.) Amsterdam: Elsevier Science.

Dawid, A. P., Mortera, J., & Pascali, V. L. (2001). Non-fatherhood or mutation? A probabilistic approach to parental exclusion in paternity testing. *Forensic Science International, 124*, 55–61.

Dawid, A. P., Mortera, J., Pascali, V. L., & van Boxel, D. W. (2002). Probabilistic expert systems for forensic inference from genetic markers. *Scandinavian Journal of Statistics, 29*, 577–595.

Dawid, A. P., Mortera, J., & Vicard, P. (2006). Representing and solving complex DNA identification cases using Bayesian networks. In *Progress in forensic genetics 11 (Proceedings of the 21st international ISFG congress)*. International Congress Series, Vol. 1288. Amsterdam: Elsevier Science, pp. 484–91. doi:10.1016/j.ics.2005.09.115

Dawid, A. P., Mortera, J., & Vicard, P. (2010). Paternity testing allowing for uncertain mutation rates. In A. O'Hagan & M. West (Eds.), *The Oxford handbook of applied bayesian analysis* (pp. 188–215). Oxford: Oxford University Press.

Dawid, A. P., & Pueschel, J. (1999). Hierarchical models for DNA profiling using heterogeneous databases (with Discussion). In J. M. Bernardo, J. O. Berger, A. P. Dawid, & A. F. M. Smith (Eds.), *Bayesian statistics 6* (pp. 187–212). Oxford: Oxford University Press.

Dawid, A. P., van Boxel, D. W., Mortera, J., & Pascali, V. L. (1999). Inference about disputed paternity from an incomplete pedigree using a probabilistic expert system. *Bulletin of the International Statistics Institute, 58*, 241–242. Contributed Papers Book 1.

Dawson, L., Macdonald, L., Ball, J., & "other members of the SoilFit team". (2006). Integration of soil fingerprinting techniques for forensic application (abstract). In A. Ruffell (Ed.), *Abstract book of geoscientists at crime scenes: First, inaugural meeting of the Geological Society of London* 20 December 2006 (p. 23). London: Forensic Geoscience Group. http://www.geolsoc.org.uk/pdfs/FGtalks&abs_pro.pdf.

Daye, S. J. (1994). *Middle-class blacks in Britain*. Basingstoke: Macmillan.

De Antonellis, V., Pozzi, G., Schreiber, F. A., Tanca, L., & Tosi, L. (2005). A Web-geographical information system to support territorial data integration. In M. Khosrow-Pour (Ed.), *Encyclopedia of information science and technology* (4 Vols., pp. 33–37). Hershey, PA: Idea Group Publishing. http://home.dei.polimi.it/schreibe/papers/encyclopedia deafin.pdf (*sic*: /schreibe/ not /schreiber/)

Debevec, P. (1998). Rendering synthetic objects into real scenes: Bridging traditional and image-based graphics with global illumination and high dynamic range photography. In *SIGGRAPH '98: Proceedings of the 25th annual conference on computer graphics and interactive techniques*. New York: ACM Press, pp. 189–198.

de Cataldo Neuburger, L., & Gulotta, G. (1996). *Trattato della menzogna e dell'inganno*. Milan: Giuffrè.

Dechter, R., Geffner, H., & Halpern, J. Y. (Eds.). (2010). *Heuristics, probability and causality: A tribute to Judea Pearl*. London: College Publications.

Deedrick, D. W. (2001). Fabric processing and "nubs". Chapter 1 In M. M. Houck (Ed.), *Mute witnesses: Trace evidence analysis*. London: Academic.

Deffenbacher, K. A., & Loftus, E. F. (1982). Do jurors share a common understanding concerning eyewitness behaviour? *Law and Human Behavior, 6*, 15–29.

Dehn, N. (1981). Memory in story invention. In *Proceedings of the 3rd Annual Conference of the Cognitive Science Society*. Berkeley, CA: Cognitive Science Society, pp. 213–215.

Dehn, N. (1989). *Computer story-writing: The role of reconstructive and dynamic memory* (Technical Report YALE/DCS/tr712). New Haven, CT: Computer Science Department, Yale University.

DeJong, G. F. (1979). *Skimming stories in real time: An experiment in integrated understanding*. Ph.D. thesis, Technical Report YALE/DCS/tr158. Department of Computer Science, Yale University, New Haven, CT.

DeJong, G. F. (1982). An overview of the FRUMP system. In W. G. Lehnert & M. H. Ringle (Eds.), *Strategies for natural language processing* (pp. 149–176). Hillsdale, NJ: Erlbaum.

de Kleer, J. (1984). Choices without backtracking. In *Proceedings of the fourth national conference on artificial intelligence*, Austin, TX. Menlo Park, CA: AAAI Press, pp. 79–84.

de Kleer, J. (1986). An assumption-based TMS. *Artificial Intelligence, 28*, 127–162.

de Kleer, J. (1988). A general labeling algorithm for assumption-based truth maintenance. In *Proceedings of the 7th national conference on artificial intelligence*, pp. 188–192.

Delannoy, J. F. (1999). Argumentation mark-up: A proposal. In *Proceedings of the workshop: Towards standards and tools for discourse tagging*, Association for Computational Linguistics, pp. 18–25. Article W99-0303 in the online version of the proceedings, accessible in *ACL Anthology* (at http://acl.ldc.upenn.edu//W/W99/).

Del Boca, A. (1987). *Gli italiani in Africa orientale* (Vol. 4). Bari & Rome: Laterza. Repr. Milan: Mondadori, 1996, 2001. The series of 4 vols. was first published by Laterza (Vol. 1: 1976, Vol. 2: 1980, Vol. 3: 1986, Vol. 4: 1987). The current edition is Mondadori's (Vol. 1: 1999, Vol. 2: 2000, Vol. 3: 2000, Vol. 4: 2001).

Demelas-Bohy, M.-D., & Renaud, M. (1995). Instability, networks and political parties: A political history expert system prototype. In E. Nissan & K. M. Schmidt (Eds.), *From information to knowledge: Conceptual and content analysis by computer* (pp. 228–260). Oxford: Intellect Books.

De Nicola, A., Missikoff, M., & Navigli, R. (2009). A software engineering approach to ontology building. *Information Systems, 34*(2), 258–275.

Denney, R. L., & Sullivan, J. P. (Eds.). (2008). *Clinical neuropsychology in the criminal forensic setting*. New York: Guilford Press.

Denning, D. (1986). An intrusion detection model. In *Proceedings of the seventh IEEE symposium on security and privacy*, May 1986, pp. 119–131.

DePaulo, B. M., & Kashy, D. A. (1998). Everyday lies in close and casual relationships. *Journal of Personality and Social Psychology, 74*(1), 63–79.

DePaulo, B. M., Kirkendol, S. E., Tang, J., & O'Brien, T. P. (1988). The motivational impairment effect in the communication of deception: replications and extensions. *Journal of Nonverbal Behavior, 12*(3), 177–202.

DePaulo, B. M., Lanier, K., & Davis, T. (1983). Detecting the deceit of the motivated liar. *Journal of Personality and Social Psychology, 45*(5), 1096–1103.

DePaulo, B. M., LeMay, C. S., & Epstein, J. A. (1991). Effects of importance of success and expectations for success on effectiveness at deceiving. *Personality and Social Psychology Bulletin, 17*(1), 14–24.

DePaulo, B. M., Lindsay, J. L., Malone, B. E., Muhlenbruck, L., Charlton, K., & Cooper, H. (2003). Cues to deception. *Psychological Bulletin, 129*, 74–118.

DePaulo, B. M., & Pfeifer, R. L. (1986). On-the-job experience and skill at detecting deception. *Journal of Applied Social Psychology, 16*, 249–267.

DePaulo, B. M., Stone, J. I., & Lassiter, G. D. (1984). Deceiving and detecting deceit. In B. R. Schlenker (Ed.), *The self and social life* (pp. 323–370). New York: McGraw-Hill.

de Rosis, F., Castelfranchi, C., & Carofiglio, V. (2000). On various sources of uncertainty in modeling suspicion and how to treat them. In *Proceedings of the workshop on deception, fraud and trust in agent societies*, At the *Autonomous Agents 2000 Conference*, pp. 61–72.

Dershowitz, A. M. (1986). *Reversal of fortune: Inside the von Bülow case*. New York: Random House.

de Vel, O., Anderson, A., Corney, M., & Mohay, G. (2001). Mining E-mail content for author identification forensics. *SIGMOD Record, 30*(4), 55–64.

de Vey Mestdagh, K. (1999). Can computers administer the law? An expert system for environmental permit law. In *Proceedings of legal knowledge based systems: JURIX 1999*. Nijmegen, The Netherlands: Gerard Noodt Instituut, pp. 134–135.

De Vey Mestdagh, C. N. J. (2003). Administrative Normative Information Transaction Agents (ANITA): Legitimacy and information technology, the best of two worlds. In *Access to knowledge and its enhancements: Proceedings of the ToKeN2000 symposium*, Delft University of Technology, Delft, The Netherlands, 21 February 2003.

de Ville, B. (2006). *Decision trees for business intelligence and data mining: Using SAS enterprise miner*. Cary, NC: SAS Publishing.

Devlin, P. (1976). *Report to the secretary of state for the Home Department of the Departmental Committee on Evidence of identification in criminal cases*. London: HMSO.

Dewey, J. (1929). *Experience and nature* (2nd ed.). LaSalle, IL: Open Court.

DeWolf, H. (1966). My ride on a torpedo. *Reader's Digest, 89*(531), July, U.S. edition for American service personnel abroad, pp. 167–171.

Diaz, R. M. (1981). *Topics in the logic of relevance*. Munich: Philosophia Verlag.

Díaz-Agudo, B., & González-Calero, P. A. (2003). Knowledge intensive CBR through ontologies. *Expert Update, 6*(1), 44–54.

Díaz-Agudo, B., Gervás, P., & Peinado, F. (2004). A case based reasoning approach to story plot generation. In *Advances in case-based reasoning. Proceedings of the 7th european conference on case based reasoning*, Madrid, 30 August – 2 September 2004. (Lecture Notes in Artificial Intelligence, Vol. 3155.) Berlin: Springer, pp. 142–156.

Di Battista, G., Eades, P., Tamassia, R., & Tollis, I. G. (1999). *Graph drawing: Algorithms for the visualization of graphs*. Englewood Cliffs, NJ: Prentice-Hall.

Dick, J. P. (1987). Conceptual retrieval and case law. In *Proceedings of the first international conference on artificial intelligence and law*, Boston. New York: ACM Press, pp. 106–115.

Dick, J. P. (1991). *A conceptual, case-relation representation of text for intelligent retrieval*. Ph.D. thesis, University of Toronto, Toronto, ON.

Dickey, A. (1990). *Family law* (2nd ed.). Sydney: The Law Book Company Ltd.

Diesner, J., & Carley, K. (2005). Exploration of communication networks from the Enron email corpus. In *Proceedings of the SIAM international conference on data mining, SIAM workshop on link analysis, counterterrorism and security*. Philadelphia, PA: SIAM.

Dijkstra, P., Bex, F. J., Prakken, H., & De Vey Mestdagh, C. N. J. (2005). Towards a multi-agent system for regulated information exchange in crime investigations. *Artificial Intelligence and Law, 13*, 133–151. http://www.computing.dundee.ac.uk/staff/florisbex/Papers/AILaw05.pdf

Ding, Y., Fensel, D., Klein, M. C. A., Omelayenko, B., & Schulten, E. (2004). The role of ontologies in eCommerce. In S. Staab & R. Studer (Eds.), *Handbook on ontologies* (pp. 593–616). International Handbooks on Information Systems. Berlin: Springer.

Dintino, J. J., & Martens, F. T. (1983). *Police intelligence systems in crime control*. Springfield, IL: Charles C. Thomas.

Dix, J., Parsons, S., Prakken, H., & Simari, G. (2009). Research challenges for argumentation. *Computer Science: Research and Development, 23*(2009), 27–34.

Dixon, D. (1999). Police investigative procedures. In C. Walker & K. Starmer (Eds.), *Miscarriage of justice: A review of justice in error* (2nd ed.). London: Blackstone Press.

do Carmo Nicoletti, M., & Quinteiro Uchôa, J. (2001). A family of algorithms for implementing the main concepts of the rough set theory. In A. Abraham & M. Köppen (Eds.), *Hybrid information systems: Proceedings of the first international workshop on Hybrid Intelligent Systems (HIS 2001)*, Adelaide, Australia, December 11–12, 2001 (pp. 583–595). Advances in Soft Computing Series. Heidelberg: Physica-Verlag (of Springer-Verlag), 2002.

Dolan, C. (1989). *Tensor manipulation networks: Connectionist and symbolic approaches to comprehension, learning, and planning*. Technical Report 890030. Los Angeles, CA: Computer Science Department, University of California. ftp://ftp.cs.ucla.edu/tech-report/198_-reports/890030.pdf

Doležel, L. (1972). From motifeme to motifs. *Poetics, 4*, 55–90.

Dolnik, L., Case, T. I., & Williams, K. D. (2003). Stealing thunder as a courtroom tactic revisited: Processes and boundaries. *Law and Human Behavior, 27*(3), 267–287.

Dolz, M. S., Cina, S. J., & Smith, R. (2000). Stereolithography: A potential new tool in forensic medicine. *American Journal of Forensic Medicine and Pathology, 21*(2), 119–123.

Domike, S., Mateas, M., & Vanouse, P. (2003). The recombinant history apparatus presents terminal time. In M. Mateas & P. Sengers (Eds.), *Narrative intelligence* (pp. 155–173). Amsterdam: Benjamins.

Domshlak, C., & Shimony, S. E. (2003). Efficient probabilistic reasoning in Bayes nets with mutual exclusion and context specific independence. In *Special Issue on Uncertain Reasoning (Part 1)*, in the *International Journal of Intelligent Systems, 19*(8), 703–725.

Donnelly, L. J. (2002a, May). Finding the silent witness. *Geoscientist, 12*(5), 16–17. The Geological Society of London.

Donnelly, L. J. (2002b). Earthy clues. Geologists can help the police to solve serious crime. *The Times*, London, Monday 5th August 2002, p. 10, T2.

Donnelly, L. J. (2002c, May). Finding the silent witness: How forensic geology helps solve crimes. All-Party Parliamentary Group for Earth Science, Westminster Palace, Houses of Parliament. The Geological Society of London. *Geoscientist, 12*(5), 24.

Donnelly, L. J. (2003, December). The applications of forensic geology to help the police solve crimes. *European Geologist: Journal of the European Federation of Geologists, 16*, 8–12.

Donnelly, L. J. (2004, March–April). Forensic geology: The discovery of spades on Saddleworth Moor. *Geology Today, 20*(2), 42. Oxford: Blackwell.

Donnelly, L. J. (2006). Introduction & welcome. In A. Ruffell (Ed.), *Abstract book of geoscientists at crime scenes: First, inaugural meeting of the Geological Society of London*, 20 December 2006 (pp. 3–5). London: Forensic Geoscience Group. http://www.geolsoc.org.uk/pdfs/FGtalks&abs_pro.pdf

Doob, A. N. (1978). *Research Paper on the Canadian Juror's View of the Criminal Jury Trial*. Publication D-88 of the Law Reform Commission of Canada, Ottawa, ON, 1978. Also, microfiche, Buffalo, NY: Hein, 1984.

Doob, A., & Park, N. (1987–1988). Computerized sentencing information for judges: An aid to the sentencing process. *Criminal Law Quarterly, 30*, 54–72.

Doob, A. N. (1990). *Sentencing aids: Final report to the Donner Canadian foundation*. Toronto, ON: Centre of Criminology, University of Toronto.

Doob, A. N., Baranek, P. M., & Addario, S. M. (1991). *Understanding justices: A study of Canadian justices of the peace*. Research Report 25. Toronto, ON: Centre of Criminology, University of Toronto.

Dore, A., & Vellani, S. (1994). Materiali lateniani nelle collezioni del Museo Civico Archeologico di Bologna. *OCNUS: Quaderni della Scuola di Specializzazione in Archeologia, 2*, 43–51.

Doyle, A. C. (1887). *A study in scarlet*. In *Beeton's Christmans annual*. Ward, Lock (illustrated by D. H. Friston). Then in book form: Ward, Lock & Co., 1888 (illustrated by C. Doyle); 2nd edn., 1889 (illustrated by G. Hutchinson); 1st American edn., J. B. Lippincott & Co., 1890. Reprinted, e.g. London: Murray, 1967.

Doyle, J. (1979). A truth maintenance system. *Artificial Intelligence, 12*, 231–272.

Dozier, C., Jackson, P., Guo, X., Chaudhary, M., & Arumainayagam, Y. (2003). Creation of an expert witness database through text mining. In *Proceedings of the nineth international conference on artificial intelligence and law*, Edinburgh, Scotland. New York: ACM Press, pp. 177–184.

DPRC. (2000). Website of the Declassification Productivity Research Center, George Washington University, Washington, DC. http://dprc.seas.gwu.edu/dprc5/research_projects/dwpa_n.htm

Dragoni, A. F., & Animali, S. (2003). Maximal consistency, theory of evidence, and Bayesian conditioning in the investigative domain. *Cybernetics and Systems, 34*(6/7), 419–465.

Dragoni, A. F., Giorgini, P., & Nissan, E. (2001). Distributed belief revision as applied within a descriptive model of jury deliberations. In a special issue on "Artificial Intelligence and Law", *Information & Communications Technology Law, 10*(1), 53–65.

Dragoni, A. F., & Nissan, E. (2004). Salvaging the spirit of the meter-models tradition: A model of belief revision by way of an abstract idealization of response to incoming evidence delivery during the construction of proof in court. *Applied Artificial Intelligence, 18*(3/4), 277–303.

Dreger, H., Kreibich, C., Paxson, V., & Sommer, R. (2005). Enhancing the accuracy of network-based intrusion detection with host-based context. In K. Julisch & C. Krügel (Eds.), *Detection of intrusions and malware, and vulnerability assessment: Proceedings of the Second International Conference (DIMVA 2005)*, Vienna, Austria, July 7–8, 2005 (pp. 206–221). Lecture Notes in Computer Science, Vol. 3548. Berlin: Springer.

Dror, I., & Hamard, S. (2009). *Cognition distributed: How cognitive technology extends our minds.* Amsterdam: Benjamins.

Dror, I. E., & Charlton, D. (2006). Why experts make errors. *Journal of Forensic Identification, 56*, 600–616. http://www.bioforensics.com/sequential_unmasking/Dror_Errors_JFI.pdf

Dror, I. E., Charlton, D., & Péron, A. (2006). Contextual information renders experts vulnerable to making erroneous identifications. *Forensic Science International, 156*, 74–78. http://www.bioforensics.com/sequential_unmasking/Dror_Contextual_FSI_2006.pdf

Dror, I. E., Péron, A., Hind, S.-L., & Charlton, D. (2005). When emotions get the better of us: The effect of contextual top-down processing on matching fingerprints. *Applied Cognitive Psychology, 19*(6), 799–809. http://www.bioforensics.com/sequential_unmasking/Dror_emotions.pdf

Dror, I. E., & Rosenthal, R. (2008). Meta-analytically quantifying the reliability and biasability of forensic experts. *Journal of Forensic Sciences, 53*(4), 900–903. http://www.bioforensics.com/sequential_unmasking/dror_meta-analysis_JFS_2008.pdf

Dror, I. E., & Stevenage, S. V. (Eds.). (2000). *Facial information processing: A multidisciplinary perspective.* Special issue of *Pragmatics & Cognition, 8*(1). Amsterdam: Benjamins.

Du, X., Li, Y., Chen, W., Zhang, Y., & Yao, D. (2006). A Markov random field based hybrid algorithm with simulated annealing and genetic algorithm for image segmentation. In L. Jiao, L. Wang, X. Gao, J. Liu, & F. Wu (Eds.), *Advances in natural computation: Second international conference (ICNC 2006)*, Xi'an, China, September 24–28, 2006 (pp. 706–715). *Proceedings, Part I.* (Lecture Notes in Computer Science, Vol. 4221). Berlin: Springer.

Duda, R. O., Hart, P. E., & Stork, D. G. (2001a). *Pattern classification* (2nd ed.). New York: Wiley Interscience.

Duda, R. O., Hart, P. E., & Stork, D. G. (2001b). Unsupervised learning and clustering. Chapter 10 in their *Pattern classification* (2nd ed.). New York: Wiley Interscience.

Dulaunoy, A. (2010). *Honeynets: Introduction to Honeypot/Honeynet technologies and its historical perspective.* ASBL CSRRT-LU (Computer Security Research and Response Team, Luxembourg) http://www.csrrt.org/ January 15, 2010 http://www.foo.be/cours/dess-20092010/honeynet-intro.pdf (accessed in May 2011).

Duncan, G. T., Tacey, M. L., & Stauffer, E. (2005). Techniques of DNA analysis. In S. H. James & J. J. Nordby (Eds.), *Forensic science: An introduction to scientific and investigative techniques* (2nd ed.). Boca Raton, FL: CRC Press. Also in 3rd edition, 2009.

Dundes, A. (1975). From etic [sic] to emic units in the structural study of folklore. In A. Dundes (Ed.), *Analytic essays in folklore* (pp. 61–72). Studies in Folklore, 2. The Hague, The Netherlands: Mouton. (Originally: From etic to emic units in the structural study of folktales. *Journal of American Folklore*, 75 (1962), pp. 95–105)

Dung, P. M. (1995). On the acceptability of arguments and its fundamental role in non-monotonic reasoning, logic programming and n person games. *Artificial Intelligence, 77*(2), 321–357.

Dung, P. M., Thang, P. M., & Hung, N. D. (2010). Modular argumentation for modelling legal doctrines of performance relief. *Argument & Computation, 1*(1), 47–69.

Dunn, J. M. (1986). Relevance logic and entailment. In F. Guenthner & D. Gabbay (Eds.), *Handbook of philosophical logic* (Vol. 3, pp. 117–124). Dordrecht, The Netherlands: Reidel (now Springer). Rewritten as Dunn & Restall (2002).

Dunn, J. M., & Restall, G. (2002). Relevance logic and entailment. In F. Guenthner & D. Gabbay (Eds.), *Handbook of philosophical logic* (New Edition, Vol. 6, pp. 1–128). Dordrecht, The Netherlands: Kluwer (now Springer). A revised version of Dunn (1986).

Dunne, P. E. (2003). Prevarication in duspute protocols. In G. Sartor (Ed.), *Proceedings of the ninth International Conference on Artificial Intelligence and Law (ICAIL 2003)*, Edinburgh, Scotland, 24–28 June 2003 (pp. 12–21). New York: ACM Press.

Dunne, P. E., & Bench-Capon, T. J. M. (2002). Coherence in finite argument systems. *Artificial Intelligence, 141*(1/2), 187–203. http://www.csc.liv.ac.uk/~tbc/publications/ulcs-01-006.pdf

Dunne, P. E., & Bench-Capon, T. J. M. (Eds.). (2005). *Argumentation in AI and law*. (IAAIL Workshop Series, 2.) Nijmegen, The Netherlands: Wolff Publishers.

Dunne, P. E., Doutre, S., & Bench-Capon, T. J. M. (2005). Discovering inconsistency through examination dialogues. In *Proceedings of the 18th International Joint Conferences on Artificial Intelligence* (IJCAI'05), Edinburgh, pp. 1560–1561. http://ijcai.org/search.php

Durandin, G. (1972a). *Les fondements du mensonge*. Paris: Flammarion.

Durandin, G. (1972b). La publicité en tant qu'idéologie. In *Revue des travaux de l'Académie des Sciences Morales et Politiques*(2ème trimestre, pp. 101–124).

Durandin, G. (1977). *De la difficulté à mentir*. Paris: Publications de la Sorbonne, and Louvain, Belgium: Nauwelaerts.

Durandin, G. (1978). La manipulation de l'opinion. In *Revue des travaux de l'Académie des Sciences Morales et Politiques* (pp. 143–173).

Durandin, G. (1982). *Les mensonges en propagande et en publicité*. Paris: Presses Universitaires de France (PUF).

Durandin, G. (1993). *L'information, la désinformation et la réalité*. (Collection "Le psychologue".) Paris: Presses Universitaires de France (PUF).

Durfee, E., Lesser, V., & Corkill, D. (1987). Coherent cooperation among communicating problem solvers. *IEEE Transactions on Computers, 36*(11), 1275–1291.

Dworkin, R. (1977). *Taking rights seriously*. Cambridge, MA: Harvard University Press.

Dworkin, R. (1986). *Law's empire*. London: Duckworth.

Dyer, M. G. (1983a). *In-depth understanding: A computer model of integrated processing of narrative comprehension*. Cambridge, MA: The MIT Press.

Dyer, M. G. (1983b). The role of affect in narratives. *Cognitive Science, 7*, 211–242.

Dyer, M. G. (1987). Emotions and their computations: Three computer models. *Cognition and Emotion, 1*(3), 323–347.

Dyer, M. G. (1991a). Symbolic neuroengineering for natural language processing: A multi-level research approach. In J. Barnden & J. Pollack (Eds.), *High-level connectionist models* (pp. 32–86). Norwood, NJ: Ablex.

Dyer, M. G. (1991b). Goal/plan analysis of text with distributed representations. In *Proceedings of international workshop on fundamental research for the future generation of natural language processing*. ATR Interpreting Telephony Research Laboratories, Kyoto International Community House, Kyoto, Japan, July 23–24, pp. 33–48.

Dyer, M. G. (1995). Connectionist natural language processing: A status report. Chapter 12 In R. Sun & L. Bookman (Eds.), *Computational architectures integrating neural and symbolic processes* (pp. 389–429). Boston & Dordrecht, The Netherlands: Kluwer.

Dyer, M. G., Flowers, M., & Wang, Y. A. (1992). Distributed symbol discovery through symbol recirculation: Toward natural language processing in distributed connectionist networks. Chapter 2 In R. Reilly & N. Sharkey (Eds.), *Connectionist approaches to natural language understanding* (pp. 21–48). Hillsdale, NJ: Lawrence Erlbaum Associates.

Dysart, J. E., Lindsay, R. C. L., MacDonald, T. K., & Wicke, C. (2002). The intoxicated witness: Effects of alcohol on identification accuracy. *Journal of Applied Psychology, 87*, 170–175.

Eades, P. (1984). A heuristic for graph drawing. *Congressus Numerantium, 42*, 149–160.

Earl, L. L. (1970). Experiments in automatic extracting and indexing. *Information Storage and Retrieval, 6*, 313–334.

Easteal, S., McLeod, N., & Reed, K. (1991). *DNA profiling: Principles, pitfalls and potential.* Chur, Switzerland: Harwood.

Ebert, J. I. (2002). Photogrammetry, photointerpretation, and digital imaging and mapping in environmental forensics. Chapter 3 In B. L. Murphy & R. D. Morrison (Eds.), *Introduction to environmental forensics* (pp. 43–69). San Diego, CA & London, U.K.: Academic.

Ebert, L. C., Ptacek, W., Naether, S., Fürst, M., Ross, S., Buck, U., et al. (2010). Virtobot: A multi-functional robotic system for 3D surface scanning and automatic post mortem biopsy. *International Journal of Medical Robotics, 6*(1), 18–27.

Eck, J. E., & Spelman, W. (1987). *Problem solving: Problem-oriented policing in newport news.* Washington, DC: Police Executive Research Forum.

Eckert, W. G., & James, S. H. (1993). *Interpretation of bloodstain evidence at crime scenes.* Boca Raton, FL: CRC Press. [Later, Eckert & James (1999).]

Eco, U. (1989). *Foucault's Pendulum* (W. Weaver, Trans.). London: Secker & Warburg, 1989. (Italian original: *Il pendolo di Foucault*, Milan: Bompiani, 1988).

Eco, U. (1995). *The search for the perfect language* (in The Making of Europe series), Oxford: Blackwell; London: FontanaPress, 1997. English translation from *La ricerca della lingua perfetta nella cultura europea.* Rome: Laterza, 1993 (in the series Fare l'Europa), 1996 (Economica Laterza, 85). Other translations, Paris: du Seuil (French); Munich: Beck (German); Barcelona: Editorial Crítica (Spanish & Catalan).

Ecoff, N. L., Ekman, P., Mage, J. J., & Frank, M. G. (2000). Lie detection and language loss. *Nature, 405*, 139.

Edmundson, H. P. (1969). New methods in automatic extracting. *Journal of the Association for Computing Machinery, 16*(2), 264–285.

Edwards, D., & Potter, J. (1995). Attribution. Chapter 4 In R. Harré & P. Stearns (Eds.), *Discursive psychology in practice* (pp. 87–119). London and Thousand Oaks, CA: Sage.

Egashira, M., & Shimizu, Y. (1993). Odor sensing by semiconductor metal oxides. *Sensors & Actuators, 14*, 443–446.

Egeland, T., Mostad, P., & Olaisen, B. (1997). A computerised method for calculating the probability of pedigrees from genetic data. *Science & Justice, 37*(4), 269–274. http://www.nr.no/~mostad/pater

Egeth, H. E. (1993). What do we not know about eyewitness identification? *American Psychologist, 48*, 577–580.

Egger, S. A. (1990). *Serial murder: An elusive phenomenon.* New York: Praeger.

Eggert, K. (2002). Held up in due course: Codification and the victory of form over intent in negotiable instruments law. *Creighton Law Review, 35*, 363–431. http://papers.ssrn.com/sol3/papers.cfm?abstract_id=904656

Eigen, J. P. (1995). *Witnessing insanity: Madness and mad-doctors in the English court.* New Haven, CT: Yale University Press.

Einhorn, H. J., & Hogarth, R. M. (1985). Ambiguity and uncertainty in probabilistic inference. *Psychological Review, 92*, 433–461.

Ekelöf, P. O. (1964). Free evaluation of evidence. *Scandinavian Studies in Law* (Faculty of Law, Stockholm University), *8*, 45–66.

Ekman, P. (1981). Mistakes when deceiving. *Annals of the New York Academy of Sciences, 364*, 269–278.

Ekman, P. (1985). *Telling lies.* New York: Norton.

Ekman, P. (1988a). Lying and nonverbal behavior: Theoretical issues and new findings. *Journal of Nonverbal Behavior, 12*, 163–175.

Ekman, P. (1988b). Self deception and detection of misinformation. In J. S. Lockhard & D. L. Paulhus (Eds.), *Self-deception: An adaptive mechanism?* (pp. 229–257). Englewood Cliffs, NJ: Prentice-Hall.

Ekman, P. (1989). Why lies fail and what behaviors betray a lie. In J. C. Yuille (Ed.), *Credibility assessment* (pp. 71–81). Dordrecht, The Netherlands: Kluwer.

Ekman, P. (1996). Why don't we catch liars? *Social Research, 63*, 801–817.

Ekman, P. (1997a). Lying and deception. In N. L. Stein, P. A. Ornstein, B. Tversky, & C. Brainerd (Eds.), *Memory for everyday and emotional events* (pp. 333–347). Hillsdale, NJ: Lawrence Erlbaum Associates.

Ekman, P. (1997b). Deception, lying and demeanor. In D. F. Halpern & A. E.Voiskounsky (Eds.), *States of mind: American and post-soviet perspectives on contemporary issues in psychology* (pp. 93–105). New York: Oxford University Press.

Ekman, P., & Frank, M. G. (1993). Lies that fail. In M. Lewis & C. Saarni (Eds.), *Lying and deception in everyday life* (pp. 184–200). New York: Guilford Press.

Ekman, P., & Friesen, W. V. (1969). Nonverbal leakage and clues to deception. *Psychiatry, 32*, 88–105.

Ekman, P., & Friesen W. V. (1974). Detecting deception from body or face. *Journal of Personality and Social Psychology, 29*(3), 288–298.

Ekman, P., Friesen, W. V., & O'Sullivan, M. (1988). Smiles when lying. *Journal of Personality and Social Psychology, 54*, 414–420.

Ekman, P., & O'Sullivan, M. (1989). Hazards in detecting deceit. In D. Raskin (Ed.), *Psychological methods for investigation and evidence* (pp. 297–332). New York: Springer.

Ekman, P., & O'Sullivan, M. (1991a). Facial expression: Methods, means and moues [sic]. In R. S. Feldman & B. Rime (Eds.), *Fundamentals of nonverbal behavior* (pp. 163–199). Cambridge: Cambridge University Press.

Ekman, P., & O'Sullivan, M. (1991b). Who can catch a liar? *American Psychologist, 46*, 113–120.

Ekman, P., & O'Sullivan, M. (2006). From flawed self-assessment to blatant whoppers: The utility of voluntary and involuntary behavior in detecting deception. *Behavioral Sciences and the Law, 24*, 673–686.

Ekman, P., O'Sullivan, M., & Frank, M. (1999). A few can catch a liar. *Psychological Science, 10*, 263–266.

Ekman, P., O'Sullivan, M., Friesen, W. V., & Scherer, K. R. (1991). Face, voice and body in detecting deception. *Journal of Nonverbal Behavior, 15*, 125–135.

Eliot, L. B. (1993). Prefilter your neurons. *AI Expert, 8*(7), 9.

Ellen, D. (2005). *Scientific examination of documents: Methods and techniques* (3rd ed.). Boca Raton, FL: CRC Press.

Ellis, H. D., Davies, G. M., & Shepherd, J. W. (1986). Introduction: Processes underlying face recognition. In R. Bruyer (Ed.), *The neuropsychology of face perception and facial expression* (pp. 1–38). Hillsdale, NJ: Lawrence Erlbaum Associates.

Ellis, H. D., Shepherd, J. W., & Davies G. M. (1975). An investigation of the use of the Photofit technique for recalling faces. *British Journal of Psychology, 66*(1), 29–37.

Elsayed, T., & Oard, D. W. (2006). Modeling identity in archival collections of email: A preliminary study. At the *Third Conference on Email and Anti-Spam, CEAS 2006*, Mountain View, CA, July 27–28, 2006.

Elsner, M., Austerweil, J., & Charniak, E. (2007). A unified local and global model for discourse coherence. In C. L. Sidner, T. Schultz, M. Stone, & Ch. X. Zhai (Eds.), *Human Language Technology conference of the North American Chapter of the Association of Computational Linguistics, proceedings (HLT-NAACL 2007)*, Rochester, NY, April 22–27, 2007. The Association for Computational Linguistics, 2007, pp. 436–443.

Elsner, M., & Charniak, E. (2008). You talking to me? A corpus and algorithm for conversation disentanglement. In *ACL 2008, Proceedings of the 46th Annual Meeting of the Association for Computational Linguistics*, Columbus, Ohio, June 15–20, 2008. The Association for Computer Linguistics, 2008, pp. 834–842.

Elson, D. K., Dames, N., & McKeown, K. R. (2010). Extracting social networks from literary fiction. In *Proceedings of the 48th annual meeting of the association for computational linguistics*, Uppsala, Sweden, 11–16 July 2010, pp. 138–147.

Emiroglu, I., & Akhan, M. B. (1997). Preprocessing of fingerprint images. In *Proceedings of the IEE European conference on security and detection*, Hertfordshire, England, pp. 147–151.

Endres-Niggermeyer, B. (1998). *Summarizing information*. Berlin: Springer.

Engel, M. (1992). Is epistemic luck compatible with knowledge? *Southern Journal of Philosophy, 30*, 59–75.

Engelmore, R., & Morgan, T. (Eds.). (1988). *Blackboard systems*. Reading, MA: Addison-Wesley.

EnVision (2002). Computational anatomy: An emerging discipline. *EnVision, 18*(3). National Partnership for Advanced Computational Infrastructure. http://www.npaci.edu/enVision/v18.3/anatomy.html

Epstein, R. (2002). Fingerprints meet Daubert: The myth of fingerprint "science" is revealed. *Southern California Law Review, 75*, 605–657.

Eraly, A. (2004). *The Mughal Throne: The Saga of India's great emperors*. London: Weidenfeld & Nicolson, 2003; London: Phoenix (of Orion Books), 2004, pbk. = 2nd edn. of *Emperors of the Peacock Throne: The Saga of the Great Mughals*, Penguin Books India, 1997, 2000.

ERCIM News. (2007). *The digital patient*. Special issue, *ERCIM News*, 69 (April). The papers in this issue can be downloaded from the site http://www.ercim.org/publication/Ercim_News/ of the European Research Consortium for Informatics and Mathematics.

ERCIM News. (2010). Andrea Esuli winner of the 2010 ERCIM Cor Baayen Award. *ERCIM News*, 83 (October), 11.

Erickson, B., Lind, A. E., Johnson, B. C., & O'Barr, W. M. (1978). Speech style and impression formation in a court setting: The effects of 'powerful' and 'powerless' speech. *Journal of Experimental Social Psychology, 14*, 266–279.

Ericson, R. V. (1981). *Making crime: A study of detective work*. Toronto, ON: Butterworths.

Ernst, D. R. (1998). The critical tradition in the writings of American legal history. Y*ale Law Journal, 102*, 1019–1044.

Erwin, D. H., & Droser, M. L. (1993). Elvis taxa. *Palaios, 8*, 623–624.

Eshghi, K., & Kowalski, R. (1989). Abduction compared with negation by failure. In G. Levi & M. Martelli (Eds.), *Sixth international conference on logic programming* (pp. 234–254). Cambridge, MA: MIT Press.

Esmaili, M., Safavi-Naini, R., Balachandran, B., & Pieprzyk, J. (1996). Case-based reasoning for intrusion detection. At the *IEEE twelfth annual computer security applications conference*, pp. 214–223.

Espar, T., & Mora, E. (1992). L'Expertise linguistique dans le procès pénal: langage et identité du sujet. *International Journal for the Semiotics of Law, 5*(13), 17–37.

Esparza, J., & Bruns, G. (1994). *Trapping mutual exclusion in the box calculus*. (LFCS Report Series, ECS-LFCS-94-295.) Edinburgh, Scotland: LFCS, Department of Computer Science, University of Edinburgh.

Espinosa-Duró, V. (2002). Minutiae detection algorithm for fingerprint recognition. *IEEE AESS Systems Magazine, 2002*, 264–266. The Aerospace & Electronic Systems Society of the Institute of Electrical and Electronics Engineers.

Esposito, A., Bratanić, M., Keller, E., & Marinaro, M. (2007). *Fundamentals of verbal and nonverbal communication and the biometric issue*. (NATO Security Through Science Series: Human and Societal Dynamics, 18.) Amsterdam: IOS Press.

Esuli, A. (2009a). PP-Index: Using permutation prefixes for efficient and scalable approximate similarity search. In *Proceedings of the seventh workshop on Large-Scale Distributed Systems for information retrieval (LSDS-IR'09)*, Boston, MA, 2009, pp. 17–24. http://www.esuli.it/fp-content/attachs/publications/LSDS-IR09.pdf

Esuli, A. (2009b). MiPai: using the PP-Index to build an efficient and scalable similarity search system. In *Proceedings of the second International Workshop on Similarity Search and Applications (SISAP'09)*, Prague, 2009, pp. 146–148.

Esuli, A. (2010). PP-Index: Using permutation prefixes for efficient and scalable similarity search. In *Proceedings of the eighteenth Italian Symposium on Advanced Database Systems (SEBD 2010)*, Rimini, Italy, 2010, pp. 318–325.

Esuli, A., & Sebastiani, F. (2010). Sentiment quantification. In H. Chen (Ed.), *AI and opinion mining, part 2*, under the rubric Trends & Controversies. *IEEE Intelligent Systems, 25*(4), July/August 2010, 72–75.

Esuli, E., Fagni, T., & Sebastiani, F. (2008). Boosting multi-label hierarchical text categorization. *Information Retrieval, 11*(4), 287–313.

Evangelista, P. F., Embrechts, M. J., & Szymanski, B. K. (2006). Taming the curse of dimensionality in kernels and novelty detection. In A. Abraham, B. Baets, M. Koppen, & B. Nickolay (Eds.), *Applied soft computing technologies: The challenge of complexity*. Berlin: Springer.

Evett, I. W. (1993). Establishing the evidential value of a small quantity of material found at a crime scene. *Journal of the Forensic Science Society, 33*(2), 83–86.

Evett, I. W., & Williams, R. L. (1996). A review of the sixteen points fingerprint standard in England and Wales. *Journal of Forensic Identification, 46*, 49–73.

Expert. (1985). EXPERT: *A guide to forensic engineering and service as an expert witness* (47 pp). Silver Springs, MD: The Association of Soil and Foundation Engineers (47 pp.).

Faegri, K., & Iversen, J. (1989). *Textbook of pollen analysis*. Fourth Edition by K. Faegri, P. E. Kaland, & K. Krzywinski. New York: Wiley. First edition, Copenhagen: Munksgaars, 1950.

Fahlman, S. E. (1989). Faster-learning variations on back-propagation: An empirical study. In D. Touretzky, G. Hinton, & T. Sejnowski (Eds.), *Proceedings of the 1988 connectionist models summer school* (pp. 38–51). San Mateo, CA: Morgan Kaufmann.

Fakher-Eldeen, F., Kuflik, T., Nissan, E., Puni, G., Salfati, R., Shaul, Y., et al. (1993). Interpretation of imputed behaviour in ALIBI (1 to 3) and SKILL. *Informatica e Diritto* (Florence), Year 19, 2nd Series, *2*(1/2), 213–242.

Falkenhainer, B., & Forbus, K. (1991). Compositional modeling: finding the right model for the job. *Artificial Intelligence, 51*, 95–143.

Fan, G., Huang, H., & Jin, Sh. (2008). An extended contract net protocol based on the personal assistant. In *ISECS international colloquium on computing, communication, control, and management, 2008. CCCM '08*. Guangzhou, China, 3–4 August 2008. Los Alamitos, CA: IEEE, Vol. 2, pp. 603–607.

Farber, P. L. (1977). The development of taxidermy and the history of ornithology. *Isis, 68*, 550–566.

Farid, H. (2008, June). Digital image forensics. *Scientific American*, 42–47.

Farina, A., Kovács-Vajna, Z. M., & Leone, A. (1999). Fingerprint minutiae extraction from skeletonized binary images. *Pattern Recognition, 32*(5), 877–889.

Farley, A. M., & Freeman, K. (1995). Burden of proof in legal argumentation. In *Proceedings of the fifth international conference on artificial intelligence and law*. New York: ACM Press, pp. 156–164.

Farook, D. Y., & Nissan, E. (1998). Temporal structure and enablement representation for mutual wills: A Petri-net approach. In A. A. Martino & E. Nissan (Eds.), *Formal models of legal time*, special issue, *Information and Communications Technology Law, 7*(3), 243–267.

Farrington, D., Mackenzie, D. L., Sherman, L., & Welsh, B. C. (Eds.). (2006). *Evidence-based crime prevention*. London: Routledge.

Farzindar, A., & Lapalme, G. (2004). Legal texts summarization by exploration of the thematic structures and argumentative roles. In *Text summarization branches out conference held in conjunction with the association for computational linguistics 2004*, Barcelona, Spain, July 2004. http://www.iro.umontreal.ca/~farzinda/FarzindarAXL04/pdf

Fasel, I. R., Bartlett, M. S., & Movellan, J. R. (2002). A comparison of Gabor filter methods for automatic detection of facial landmarks. In *Proceedings of the fifth international conference on automatic face and gesture recognition*, Washington, DC, May 2002, pp. 242–246.

Faught, W. S. (1975). Affect as motivation for cognitive and conative processes. In *Proceedings of the fourth international joint conference on artificial intelligence*, Tbilisi, Georgia, USSR, pp. 893–899.

Faught, W. S. (1978). Conversational action patterns in dialogs. In D. A. Waterman & F. Hayes-Roth (Eds.), *Pattern-directed inference systems* (pp. 383–397). Orlando, FL: Academic.

Faulk, M. (1994). *Basic forensic psychiatry* (2nd ed.). Oxford: Blackwell Scientific.

Feeney, F., Dill, F., & Weir, A. (1983). *Arrests without conviction: How often they occur and why.* Washington, DC: Government Printing Office.

Feinbert, S., Blascovich, J. J., Cacioppo, J. T., Davidson, R. J., Ekman, P., et al. (2002, October). *The polygraph and lie detection.* National Research Council. Washington, DC: National Academy of Sciences.

Feldman, R., Fresko, M., Goldenberg, J., Netzer, O., & Ungar, L. (2010). Analyzing product comparisons on discussion boards. In N. Dershowitz & E. Nissan (Eds.), *Language, culture, computation: Essays in honour of Yaacov Choueka* (2 vols.), Vol. 1: *Theory, techniques, and applications to e-science, law, narratives, information retrieval, and the cultural heritage* (in press). Berlin: Springer.

Feldman, R., & Sanger, J. (2007). *The text mining handbook: Advanced approaches in analyzing unstructured data.* Cambridge: Cambridge University Press.

Fellbaum, C. (1998). *WordNet: An electronic lexical database (Language, Speech, and Communication).* Cambridge, MA: The MIT Press.

Felson, M. (1992). Routine activities and crime prevention: Armchair concepts and practical action. *Studies on Crime and Crime Prevention, 1,* 30–34.

Feng, Y., & Chen, W. (2004). Brain MR image segmentation using fuzzy clustering with spatial constraints based on Markov random field theory. In G.-Z. Yang & T. Jiang (Eds.), *Medical imaging and augmented reality: Proceedings of the second international workshop (MIAR 2004),* Beijing, China, August 19–20, 2004 (pp. 188–195). Lecture Notes in Computer Science 3150. Berlin: Springer.

Fenning, P. J., & Donnelly, L. J. (2004). *Geophysical techniques for forensic investigations* (pp. 11–20) (Geological Society of London Special Publication, 232).

Fensel, D. (2003). *Ontologies: A silver bullet for knowledge management and electronic commerce.* Seacaucus, NJ: Springer.

Fensel, D., van Harmelen, F., Horrocks, I., McGuinness, D. L., & Patel-Schneider, P. F. (2001). OIL: An ontology infrastructure for the Semantic Web. *IEEE Intelligent Systems, 16*(2), 38–45.

Fenton, N. E., & Neil, M. (2000). The jury observation fallacy and the use of Bayesian networks to present probabilistic legal arguments. *Mathematics Today: Bulletin of the Institute of Mathematics and its Application (IMA), 36*(6), 180–187. Paper posted on the Web at http://www.agena.co.uk/resources.html

Ferber, J. (1999). *Multiagent systems: An introduction to distributed artificial intelligence.* Reading, MA: Addison-Wesley.

Fernandez, C., & Best, E. (1988). *Nonsequential processes: A petri net view* (EATCS Monographs on Theoretical Computer Science, 13). Berlin: Springer.

Ferrario, R., & Oltramari, A. (2004). Towards a computational ontology of mind. In *Proceedings of the international conference on Formal Ontology in Information Systems (FOIS 2004),* November 2004. Amsterdam: IOS Press, pp. 287–297.

Ferrua, P. (2010). Il giudizio penale: fatto e valore giuridico. In P. Ferrua, F. Grifantini, G. Illuminati, & R. Orlandi (Eds.), *La prova nel dibattimento penale* (4th ed., in press), Turin, Italy: Giappichelli. The third edition appeared in 2007, 2007, p. 293 ff.

Festinger, L. (1957). *A theory of cognitive dissonance.* Evanston, IL: Row Peterson. Reissues of the same edition, Stanford, California: Stanford University Press, 1962, 1970; London: Tavistock Publications, 1962. Revised and enlarged German translation: *Theorie der kognitiven Dissonanz* (1978).

Feu Rosa, P. V. (2000). The Electronic Judge. In *Proceedings of the AISB'00 symposium on artificial intelligence & legal reasoning,* 17 April 2000 (at the *2000 Convention of the Society for the Study of Artificial Intelligence and the Simulation of Behaviour*), Birmingham, England, 17 April 2000, pp. 33–36.

Field, D., & Raitt, F. (1996). *Evidence.* Edinburgh, Scotland: W.Green.

Fikes, R. E., & Nilsson, N. J. (1971). STRIPS: A new approach to the application of theorem proving to problem solving. *Artificial Intelligence, 2*, 89–205, 189–208.

Fillmore, C. J. (1968). The case for case. In E. Bach & R. T. Harms (Eds.), *Universals in linguistic theory*. New York: Holt, Rinehart and Winston.

Findlay, M., & Duff, P. (Eds.). (1988). *The jury under attack*. London: Butterworths.

Findler, N. V. (Ed.). (1979). *Associative networks: Representation and use of knowledge by computers*. New York: Academic.

Finkelstein, M. (1978). *Quantitative methods in law*. New York: The Free Press.

Finkelstein, M. (1980). The judicial reception of multiple regression studies in race and sex discrimination cases. *Columbia Law Review, 80*, 737–754.

Finkelstein, M. O., & Levin, B. (2003). On the probative value of evidence from a screening search. *Jurimetrics Journal, 43*, 265–290.

Fiorelli, P. (1953–1954). *La tortura giudiziaria nel diritto comune* (2 vols) ("Ius nostrum": Studi e testi pubblicati dall'Istituto di Storia del diritto italiano dell'Università di Roma, 1 & 2.). Milan: Giuffrè.

Fiorenza, E. (1977). *Re Cecconi: La morte assurda*. ("Instant book" series.) Rome: Editore Centro dell'Umorismo Italia.

Firestein, S. (2001). How the olfactory system makes sense of scents. *Nature, 413*, 211–218.

Fischhoff, B., & Beyth, R. (1975). "I knew it would happen": Remembered probabilities of once-future things. *Organizational Behavior and Human Performance, 13*, 1–16.

Fisher, M., Gabbay, D., & Vila, L. (Eds.). (2005). *Handbook of temporal reasoning in artificial intelligence* (electronic resource; Foundations of Artificial Intelligence, 1). Amsterdam: Elsevier.

Fissell, M. E. (2003). Hairy women and naked truths: Gender and the politics of knowledge in *Aristotle's Masterpiece*. In *Sexuality in early America*, special issue of *The William and Mary Quarterly*, Third Series, *60*(1), 43–74. Published by the Omohundro Institute of Early American History and Culture. http://www.jstor.org/stable/3491495

Fitts, P. M., Jones, R. E., & Milton, J. L. (1950, February). Eye movements of aircraft pilots during instrument landing approaches. *Aeronautical Engineering Review, 9*.

Fitzgerald, P. J. (1961). Voluntary and involuntary acts. In A. G. Guest (Ed.), *Oxford essays in jurisprudence*. Oxford: Oxford University Press. Corrected edn., Oxford: Clarendon Press, 1968.

Fitzmaurice, C., & Pease, K. (1986). *The psychology of judicial sentencing*. Manchester: Manchester University Press.

Fix, E., & Hodges, J. L. (1951). *Discriminatory analysis, nonparametric discrimination consistency properties*. Technical Report 4. Randolph Field, TX: U.S. Air Force.

Flowe, H. D., Finklea, K. M., & Ebbesen, E. B. (2009a). Limitations of expert psychology testimony on eyewitness identification. In B. L. Cutler (Ed.), *Expert testimony on the psychology of eyewitness identification* (pp. 220–221). American Psychology-Law Society Series. New York: Oxford University Press. doi://10.1093/acprof:oso/9780195331974.003.003

Flowe, H. D., Mehta, A., & Ebbesen, E. B. (2009b). *The role of eyewitness identification evidence in felony case dispositions*. Leicester, England: School of Psychology, Forensic Section, University of Leicester. Draft of June 2010. http://www2.le.ac.uk/departments/psychology/ppl/hf49/FloweMehtaEbbesenDraftJune10.pdf

Flowers, M., McGuire, R., & Birnbaum, L. (1982). Adversary arguments and the logic of personal attacks. Chapter 10 In W. Lehnert & M. Ringle (Eds.), *Strategies for natural language processing* (pp. 275–294). Hillsdale, NJ: Lawrence Erlbaum Associates.

Flycht-Eriksson, A. (2004). *Design and Use of ontologies in information-providing dialogue systems*. Ph.D. Thesis. Linköping Studies in Science and Technology, Vol. 875. Dissertation, no. 874. Linköping, Sweden: Department of Computer and Information Science, University of Linköping.

Foresman, T. W. (Ed.). (1998). *The history of geographic information systems: Perspectives from the pioneers*. Upper Saddle River, NJ: Prentice Hall PTR.

Forgas, J. P., & Williams, K. D. (Eds.). (2001). *Social influence: Direct and indirect processes.* Lillington, NC: Psychology Press.

FORident Software. (2009). *HemoSpat validation.* [A white paper.] FORidenti Software Technical Paper. Ottawa, ON: FORident Software. 9 August 2009. http://hemospat.com/technical_papers/pdf/FORident%20Software%20Technical%20Paper%20-%20HemoSpat%20Validation.pdf

Forrester, J. W. (1984). Gentle murder, or the adverbial Samaritan. *Journal of Philosophy, 81,* 193–197.

Foster, D. (2001). *Author unknown: On the trail of anonymous.* London: Macmillan; with respect to New York: Holt, 2000, the U.K. edition is corrected, and includes as well the new Ch. 7, on current British journalism.

Foster, J. C., & Liu, V. (2005). *Catch me if you can.* In Blackhat briefings. http://www.blackhat.com/presentations/bh-usa-05/bh-us-05-foster-liu-update.pdf (The web link did no longer seem to work in the summer of 2011; contact Blackhat for a copy)

Fox, F. (1971, April). Quaker, Shaker, rabbi: Warder Cresson, the story of a Philadelphia mystic. *Pennsylvania Magazine of History and Biography,* 147–193.

Fox, J. (1986). Knowledge, decision making and uncertainty. Chapter 3 In W. A. Gale (Ed.), *Artificial intelligence and statistics* (pp. 57–76). Reading, MA: Addison-Wesley.

Fox, J., & Parsons, S. (1998). Arguing about beliefs and actions. In A. Hunter & S. Parsons (Eds.), *Applications of uncertainty formalisms* (pp. 266–302). Berlin: Springer.

Fox, R., & Josephson, J. R. (1994). Software: PEIRCE-IGTT. In J. R. Josephson & S. G. Josephson (Eds.), *Abductive inference: Computation, philosophy, technology* (pp. 215–223). Cambridge: Cambridge University Press.

Fox, S., & Leake, D. (2001). Introspective reasoning for index refinement in casebased reasoning. *Journal of Experimental and Theoretical Artificial Intelligence, 13*(1), 63–88.

François, A. R. J., Nevatia, R., Hobbs, J., & Bolles, R. C. (2005). VERL: An ontology framework for representing and annotating video events. *IEEE MultiMedia, 12*(4), 76–86.

Frank, O. (1978). Sampling and estimation in large social networks. *Social Network, 1,* 91–101.

Frank, M. G., & Ekman, P. (1997). The ability to detect deceit generalizes across different types of high-stake lies. *Journal of Personality and Social Psychology, 72,* 1429–1439.

Frank, M. G., & Ekman, P. (2003). *Nonverbal detection of deception in forensic contexts: Handbook of forensic psychology.* New York: Academic.

Frank, P. B., Wagner, M. J., & Weil, R. L. (1994). *Litigation services handbook: The role of the accountant as expert witness. 1994 cumulative supplement.* New York: Wiley.

Frank, S. L., Koppen, M., Noordman, L. G. M., & Vonk, W. 2003. Modeling knowledge-based inferences in story comprehension. *Cognitive Science, 27,* 875–910.

Franke, K., & Srihari, S. N. (2008). Computational forensics: An overview. In *Computational forensics: Proceedings of the international workshop,* Washington, DC (pp. 1–10). (Lecture Notes in Computer Science, 5158). Berlin: Springer.

Freeman, J. B. (1991). *Dialectics and the macrostructure of arguments.* Berlin: Floris Publications.

Freeman, K. (1994). *Toward formalizing dialectical argumentation.* Ph.D. thesis, Department of Computer Science and Information Science, University of Oregon.

Freeman, L. C. (1979). Centrality in social networks: Conceptual clarification. *Social Networks, 1,* 215–240.

Freeman, L. C. (2000a). Visualizing social networks. *Journal of Social Structure, 1*(1). This article is posted at Freeman's website at http://moreno.ss.uci.edu/79.pdf and also at the journal's website at http://www.cmu.edu/joss/content/articles/volume1/Freeman.html http://www.heinz.cmu.edu/project/INSNA/joss/vsn.html

Freeman, L. C. (2000b). Visualizing social groups. In *American Statistical Association 1999 Proceedings of the Section on Statistical Graphics,* 2000, pp. 47–54. http://moreno.ss.uci.edu/80.pdf

Freeman, L. C. (2004). *The development of social network analysis: A study in the sociology of science.* Vancouver, BC: Empirical Press. Translated into Japanese by R. Tsuji and published as 社会ネットワーク分析の発展. Tokyo: NTT Publishing Co., 2007. Translated into Italian by

R. Memoli and published as *Lo sviluppo dell'analisi delle reti sociali. Uno studio di sociologia della scienza*. Milano: Franco Angeli, 2007. Translated into Chinese by Wang Weidong and published as 社会网络分析发展史. Beijing: China Renmin University Press, 2008.

Freeman, L. C. (2005). Graphical techniques for exploring social network data. In P. J. Carrington, J. Scott, & S. Wasserman (Eds.), *Models and methods in social network analysis*. Cambridge: Cambridge University Press. http://moreno.ss.uci.edu/86.pdf

Freeman, L. C. (2007). *Social network analysis* (4 Vols.). London: Sage.

Freeman, L. C. (2008). Going the wrong way on a one-way street: Centrality in physics and biology. *Journal of Social Structure, 9*(2). This article is posted at Freeman's website at http://moreno.ss.uci.edu/joss.pdf and also at the journal's website at http://www.cmu.edu/joss/content/articles/volume9/Freeman.html

Freeman, L. C. (2009). Methods of social network visualization. In R. A. Meyers (Ed.), *Encyclopedia of complexity and systems science*. Berlin: Springer. http://moreno.ss.uci.edu/89.pdf

Freeman, K., & Farley, A. M. (1996). A model of argumentation and its application to legal reasoning. *Artificial Intelligence and Law, 4*(3/4), 157–161.

Freund, M. S., & Lewis, N. S. (1995). A chemically diverse conducting polymer-based electronic nose. *Proceedings of the National Academy of Sciences USA, 92*, 2652–2656.

Freund, Y., & Schapire, R. E. (1997). A decision-theoretic generalization of on-line learning and an application to boosting. *Journal of Computer and System Sciences, 55*(1), 119–139.

Fridrich, J.,[59] Soukal, D., & Lukáš, J. (2003). Detection of copy-move forgery in digital images. In *Proceedings of digital forensic research workshop*, August 2003.

Friedkin, N. (1981). The development of structure in random networks: An analysis of the effects of increasing network density on five measures of structure. *Social Networks, 3*, 41–52.

Friedman, R. D. (1991). Character impeachment evidence: Psycho-Bayesian analysis and proposed overhaul. *UCLA Law Review, 38*, 637–691.

Friedman, R. D. (1997). Answering the Bayesioskeptical challenge. In R. Allen & M. Redmayne (Eds.), *Bayesianism and juridical proof* (pp. 276–291). London: Blackstone (With a consolidated bibliography: pp. 354–360). Special issue, *The International Journal of Evidence and Proof, 1*, 253–360.

Friedman, R. D., & Park, R. C. (2003). Sometimes what everybody thinks they know is true. *Law and Human behavior, 27*, 629–644.

Frisch, A. M., & Perlis, D. (1981). A re-evaluation of story grammars. *Cognitive Science, 5*(1), 79–86.

Frowd, C. D., Bruce, V., & Hancock, P. J. B. (2008). Changing the face of criminal identification. *The Psychologist, 21*, 670–672.

Frowd, C. D., Bruce, V., Ross, D., McIntyre, A., & Hancock, P. J. B. (2007). An application of caricature: How to improve the recognition of facial composites. *Visual Cognition, 15*, 954–984.

Frowd, C. D., Carson, D., Ness, H., Richardson, Morrison, L., McLanaghan, S., et al. (2005). A forensically valid comparison of facial composite systems. *Psychology, Crime & Law, 11*, 33–52.

Frowd, C. D., Hancock, P. J. B., & Carson, D. (2004). EvoFIT: A holistic, evolutionary facial imaging technique for creating composites. *ACM Transactions on Applied Psychology (TAP), 1*, 1–21.

Frowd, C. D., McQuiston-Surret, D., Anandaciva, S., Ireland, C. G. & Hancock, P. J. B. (2007). An evaluation of US systems for facial composite production. *Ergonomics, 50*, 187–198.

Frowd, C. D., Pitchford, M., Bruce, V., Jackson, S., Hepton, G., Greenall, M., et al. (2010a). The psychology of face construction: Giving evolution a helping hand. *Applied Cognitive Psychology*. doi:10.1002/acp.1662.

---

[59] This is Jessica Fridrich. Also Juri Fridrich is at the Computer Science Department of Dartmouth College in Hanover, New Hampshire. They both work in the given domain of research.

Frowd, C., Nelson, L., Skelton, F., Noyce, R., Heard, P., Henry, J., et al. (2010b). Interviewing techniques for Darwinian facial composite systems. Submitted.

Fu, X., Boongoen, T., & Shen, Q. (2010). Evidence directed generation of plausible crime scenarios with identity resolution. *Applied Artificial Intelligence, 24*(4), 253–276.

Fuhr, N. (Ed.). (2006). *Advances in XML information retrieval and evaluation: 4th international workshop of the initiative for the evaluation of XML retrieval, INEX 2005*, Dagstuhl Castle, Germany, November 28–30, 2005. Revised and Selected Papers. (Lecture Notes in Computer Science, Vol. 3977.) Berlin: Springer.

Fulford, R. (2005). Utopian ends, murderous means. *The National Post*, Toronto, 8 January 2005. http://www.robertfulford.com/2005-01-08-pfaff.html

Full, W. E., Ehrlich, R., & Bezdek, J. C. (1982). Fuzzy QModel: A new approach for linear unmixing. *Journal of Mathematical Geology, 14*, 259–270.

Full, W. E., Ehrlich, R., & Klovan, J. E. (1981). Extended Qmodel [sic]: Objective definition of external end members in the analysis of mixtures. *Journal of Mathematical Geology, 13*, 331–344.

Fung, T. H., & Kowalski, R. (1997). The IFF proof procedure for abductive logic programming. *Journal of Logic Programming, 33*(2), 151–165.

Furnam, A. (1986). The robustness of the recency effect: Studies using legal evidence. *The Journal of General Psychology, 113*(4), 351–357.

Furtado, V., Melo, A., Menezes, R., & Belchior, M. (2006). Using self-organization in an egent framework to model criminal activity in reponse to police patrol routes. In G. Sutcliffe & R. Goebel (Eds.), *Proceedings of the 19th international florida artificial intelligence research society conference* (pp. 68–73). Menlo Park, CA: AAAI Press.

Furtado, V., & Vasconcelos, E. (2007). Geosimulation in education: A system for teaching police resource allocation. *International Journal of Artificial Intelligence in Education, 17*, 57–81.

Gabbay, D., & Woods, J. (2003). *Agenda relevance: A study in formal pragmatics*. Amsterdam: North-Holland.

Gabbert, F., Memon, A., & Allan, K. (2003). Memory conformity: Can eyewitnesses influence each other's memories for an event? *Applied Cognitive Psychology, 17*, 533–544.

Gabbert, F., Memon, A., Allan, K., & Wright, D. (2004). Say it to my face: Examining the effects of socially encountered misinformation. *Legal and Criminological Psychology, 9*, 215–227.

Gabbert, F., Memon, A., & Wright, D. B. (2006). Memory conformity: Disentangling the steps towards influence during a discussion. *Psychonomic Bulletin and Review, 13*, 480–485.

Gaffney, C., & Gater, J. (2003). *Revealing the buried past: Geophysics for archaeologists*. Gloucester: Tempus Publishing.

Gaines, D. M. (1994). *Juror simulation*. BSc Project Report, Computer Science Department, Worcester Polytechnic Institute.

Gaines, D. M., Brown, D. C., & Doyle, J. K. (1996). A computer simulation model of juror decision making. *Expert Systems With Applications, 11*(1), 13–28.

Galasinski, D. (1996). Pretending to cooperate: How speakers hide evasive actions. *Argumentation, 10*, 375–388.

Galindo, F. (1996). Sistemas de ayuda a la decisión jurídica. ¿Son posibles? *Actas (Volumen I), II Congreso Internacional de Informática y Derecho*, Mérida, Spain, April 1995 (Mérida: UNED, Centro Regional de Extremadura). Published as: *Informática y Derecho*, Vol. 9/10/11, Part 1, 1996, pp. 631–650.

Galitsky, B. (1998). *A formal scenario and metalanguage support means to reason about it*. Technical report 98-28. New Brunswick, NJ: DIMACS. ftp://dimacs.rutgers.edu/pub/dimacs/TechnicalReports/TechReports/1998/98-28.ps.gz

Galitsky, B. (1999). *Narrative generation for the control of buyer's impression*. Technical Report. Technical report 98-28. New Brunswick, NJ: DIMACS.

Gallagher, T. (1998). Lost and found. *Living Bird*, Spring 1998. http://www.birds.cornell.edu/Publications/livingbird/spring98/OwletSp98.htm

Galton, A. P. (1987). *Temporal logics and their applications*. London: Academic.

Galton, A. P. (1990). A critical examination of Allen's theory of action and time. *Artificial Intelligence, 42*, 159–188.

Galton, A. P. (2008). Temporal logic. *Stanford Encyclopedia of Philosophy* (entry revised from an original version of 1999). http://plato.stanford.edu/entries/logic-temporal/

Gambini, R. (1985). *Il plea bargaining tra 'common law' e 'civil law'*. Milan: Giuffrè.

Gambini, R. (1997). Inutilizzabilità (dir. proc. pen.). In *Enciclopedia del diritto, Aggiornamento* (Vol. 1). Milan: Giuffrè.

Gan, H. (1994). Understanding a story with causal relationships. In Z. W. Raś & M. Zemankova (Eds.), *Methodologies for intelligent systems: 8th international symposium, ISMIS'94*. Charlotte, North Carolina, October 16–19, 1994 (pp. 265–274). Lecture Notes in Artificial Intelligence, Vol. 869. Berlin: Springer.

Gangemi A., Sagri, M. T., & Tiscornia, D. (2005). A constructive framework for legal ontologies. In V. R. Benajmins, P. Casanovas, J. Breuker, & A. Gangemi (Eds.), *Proceedings of law and the semantic web [2005]: Legal ontologies, methodologies, legal information retrieval, and applications* (pp. 97–124). (Lecture Notes in Computer Science, Vol. 3369). Berlin: Springer.

Garani, G. (2004). *A temporal database model using nested relations*. Ph.D. Dissertation, Computer Science and Information Systems Engineering. London: Birkbeck College, University of London.

Garani, G. (2008). Nest and unnest operators in nested relations. *Data Science Journal, 7*, 57–64.

Garcia-Rojas, A., Gutiérrez, M., & Thalmann, D. (2008a, July). Visual creation of inhabited 3D environments: An ontology-based approach. *The Visual Computer, 24*(7–9), 719–726. Also, Report VRLAB-ARTICLE-2008-062. Lausanne: Virtual Reality Lab at the Swiss Federal Institute of Technology.

Garcia-Rojas, A., Gutiérrez, M., & Thalmann, D. (2008b). Simulation of individual spontaneous reactive behavior. In *Proceedings of the seventh international conference on Autonomous Agents and Multiagent Systems (AAMAS)*,[60] Estoril, Portugal, May 12–16, 2008, pp. 143–150. Also, Report VRLAB-CONF-2008-150. Lausanne: Virtual Reality Lab at the Swiss Federal Institute of Technology. http://infoscience.epfl.ch/getfile.py?recid=125120&mode=best

Gärdenfors, P. (1988). *Knowledge in flux: Modeling the dynamics of epistemic states*. Cambridge, MA: MIT Press.

Gärdenfors, P. (1992). Belief revision: An introduction. In P. Gärdenfors (Ed.), *Belief revision* (pp. 1–28). Cambridge Tracts in Theoretical Computer Science, Vol. 29. Cambridge, UK: Cambridge University Press.

Gardner, A. von der Lieth. (1987). *An artificial intelligence approach to legal reasoning*. Cambridge, MA: The MIT Press.

Gardner, J. W. (1991). Detection of vapours and odours from a multisensor array using pattern recognition: Principal component and cluster analysis. *Sensors & Actuators, 4*, 109–115.

Gardner, J. W., & Bartlett, P. N. (1999). *Electronic noses: Principles and applications*. Oxford: Oxford University Press.

Gardner, J. W., & Yinon, J. (Eds.). (2004). *Proceedings of the NATO advanced research workshop on electronic noses and sensors for the detection of explosives*. (NATO Science Series 2003, Vol. 159). Dordrecht: Kluwer.

Gardner, R. M., & Bevel, T. (2009). *Practical crime scene analysis and reconstruction*. With contributions by M. Noedel, S. A. Wagner, & I. Dalley. (CRC Series in Practical Aspects of Criminal and Forensic Investigations.) Boca Raton, FL: CRC Press.

Garfield, B. (2007). *The Meinertzhagen mystery: The life and legend of a colossal fraud*. Washington, DC: Potomac Books.

Garnham, A. (1983). What's wrong with story grammars? *Cognition, 15*, 145–154.

Garrett, R. E. (1987). The overlooked business aspects of forensic engineering. *Forensic Engineering, 1*(1), 17–19.

---

[60] http://www.ifaamas.org

Garrioch, L., & Brimacombe, E. (2001). Lineup administrators' expectations: Their impact on eyewitness confidence. *Law & Human Behavior, 25,* 299–315.

Garry, M., Manning, C., Loftus, E. F., & Sherman, S. J. (1996). Imagination inflation: Imagining a childhood event inflates confidence that it occurred. *Psychonomic Bulletin and Review, 3,* 208–214. Posted on the Web at: http://faculty.washington.edu/eloftus/Articles/Imagine.htm

Garven, S., Wood, J., Malpass, R., & Shaw, III, J. (1998). More than suggestion: The effect of interviewing techniques from the McMartin Preschool case. *Journal of Applied Psychology, 83,* 347–359.

Gastwirth, J. L., & Miao, W. (2009). Formal statistical analysis of the data in disparate impact cases provides sounder inferences than the U.S. government's 'four-fifths' rule: An examination of the statistical evidence in *Ricci v. DeStefano. Law, Probability and Risk, 8,* 171–191. doi:10.1093/lpr/mgp017

Gauthier, T. D. (2002). Statistical methods. Chapter 12 In B. L. Murphy & R. D. Morrison (Eds.), *Introduction to environmental forensics* (pp. 391–428). San Diego, CA & London: Academic.

Gearey, A. (2005). Law and narrative. In D. Herman, M. Jahn, & M.-L. Ryan (Eds.), *Routledge encyclopedia of narrative theory* (pp. 271–275). London: Routledge, 2005 (hbk), 2008 (pbk, avail. Sept. 2007).

Geddes, L. (2010, August 21). What are the chances? ([pre-headline:] Special report: DNA evidence; [subheadline:] In the second part of our investigation, Linda Geddes shows that the odds attached to a piece of DNA evidence can vary enormously). *New Scientist, 207*(2274), 8–10. With an inset: 'When lawyers question DNA', on p. 9.

Geiger, A., Nissan, E., & Stollman, A. (2001). The Jama legal narrative. Part I: The JAMA model and narrative interpretation patterns. *Information & Communications Technology Law, 10*(1), 21–37. [Part II is Nissan (2001c).]

Gelbart, D., & Smith, J. C. (1993). FLEXICON: An evaluation of a statistical model adapted to intelligent text management. In the *Proceedings of the fourth international Conference on Artificial Intelligence and Law (ICAIL'93),* Amsterdam. New York: ACM Press, pp. 142–151.

Gelfand, M., Mironov, A., & Pevzner, P. (1996). Gene recognition via splices sequence alignment. *Proceedings of the National Academy of Sciences USA, 93,* 9061–9066.

Gemmell, J., Lueder, & Bell, G. (2003). The MyLifeBits lifetime store. In *Proceedings of the 2003 ACM SIGMM workshop experiential telepresence (ETP).* New York: ACM Press, pp. 80–83.

Gemperline, P. J. (1984). A priori estimates of the elution [sic] profiles of pure components in overlapped liquid chromatography peaks using target transformation factor analysis. *Journal of Chemical Information and Computer Sciences, 24,* 206–212.

Geng, L., & Chan, C. W. (2001). An algorithm for automatic generation of a case base from a database using similarity-based rough approximation. In A. Abraham & M. Köppen (Eds.), *Hybrid information systems: Proceedings of the first international workshop on Hybrid Intelligent Systems (HIS 2001),* Adelaide, Australia, December 11–12, 2001 (pp. 571–582). Advances in Soft Computing Series. Heidelberg: Physica-Verlag (of Springer-Verlag), 2002.

Genrich, H., & Lautenbach, K. (1979). Predicate/transitions nets. In W. Brauer (Ed.), *Net theory and application* (Lecture Notes in Computer Science, 84). Berlin: Springer.

Geradts, Z. (2005). Use of computers in forensic science. Chapter 26 In S. H. James & J. J. Nordby (Eds.), *Forensic science: An introduction to scientific and investigative techniques* (2nd ed.). Boca Raton, FL: CRC Press. Also in 3rd edition, 2009.

Gerard, S., & Sansonnet, J.-P. (2000). A spatio-temporal model for the representation of situations described in narrative texts. In *Proceedings of NLP 2000,* pp. 176–184.

Gerasimov, M. (1971). *The face finder.* London: Hutchinson.

Gerasimov, M. M. (about) (2007). *Mikhail Gerasimov.* Biographical Wikipedia [English] http://en.wikipedia.org/wiki/Mikhail_Gerasimov. Last modified on 24 April 2007, when accessed in August 2007. A Russian entry (Михаи́л Миха́йлович Гера́симов) is also available under http://ru.wikipedia.org/wiki/

Gerkey, B., & Mataric, M. (2004). A formal analysis and taxonomy of task allocation in multi-robot systems. *International Journal of Robotics Research, 23*(9), 939–954.

Gerritsen, C., Klein, M. C. A., & Bosse, T. (2009). Agent-based simulation of social learning in criminology. In *Proceedings of the [First] International Conference on Agents and Artificial*

Intelligence, ICAART 2009, Porto, Portugal, 19–21 January 2009, area 1: Artificial intelligence, paper 8.

Gervás, P., Díaz-Agudo, B., Peinado, F., & Hervás, R. (2005). Story Plot Generation based on CBR. In the *AI-2004* special issue, *Knowledge-Based Systems*, 18(4/5), 2005: 235–242. Previously in the *Proceedings of the 24th Annual International Conference of the British Computer Society's Specialist Group on Artificial Intelligence (SGAI). Applications and Innovations in Intelligent Systems*, Cambridge, England, 13–15 December 2004, (WICS Series) Berlin: Springer, Vol. 12, pp. 36–46.

Gervás, P., Lönneker-Rodman, B., Meister, J. C., & Peinado, F. (2006). Narrative models: Narratology meets artificial intelligence. In R. Basili & A. Lenci (Eds.), *Proceedings of satellite workshop: Toward computational models of literary analysis*. At the *Fifth International Conference on Language Resources and Evaluation*, Genoa, Italy, 22 May 2006, pp. 44–51.

Ghosh, A., Wong, L., Di Crescenzo, G., & Talpade, R. (2005). InFilter: Predictive ingress filtering to detect spoofed IP traffic. At the *Second International Workshop on Security in Distributed Computing Systems (SDCS)*, in: *Proceediongs of the 25th International Conference on Distributed Computing Systems Workshops (ICDCS 2005 Workshops)*, 6–10 June 2005, Columbus, Ohio. IEEE Computer Society, pp. 99–106.

Gibbons, B., Busch J., & Bradac J. (1991). Powerful versus powerless language: Consequences for persuasion, impression formation, and cognitive response. *Journal of Language and Social Psychology, 10*(2), 115–133.

Gibbons, J. (1994). *Language and the law.* (Language in Social Life Series). London: Longman.

Gibson, J. J. (1977). The theory of affordances. In R. Shaw & J. Bransford (Eds.), *Perceiving, acting and knowing* (pp. 67–82). Hillsdale, NJ: Erlbaum.

Gibson, J. J. (1979). *The ecological approach to visual perception.* Hillsdale, NJ: Erlbaum.

Gibson, S. J., Solomon, C. J., Maylin, M. I. S., & Clark, C. (2009). New methodology in facial composite construction: From theory to practice. *International Journal of Electronic Security and Digital Forensics, 2,* 156–168.

Gigerenzer, G., & Selten, R. (Eds.). (2001). *Bounded rationality: The adaptive toolbox.* Cambridge, MA: The MIT Press.

Gilbert, D. T., & Malone, D. S. (1995). The correspondence bias. *Psychological Bulletin, 117,* 21–38.

Gilbert, M. (2002). Informal logic, argumentation theory & artificial intelligence: Introduction. (Special issue.) *Informal Logic, 22,* 191–194.

Gilbert, M., Grasso, F., Groarke, L., Gurr, C., & Gerlofs, J.-M. (2003). "The Persuasion Machine": Argumentation and computational linguistics. Chapter 5 In C. Reed & T. Norman (Eds.), *Argumentation machines: New frontiers in argument and computation* (pp. 121–174). Dordrecht: Kluwer.

Gilbreth, F. B., & Gilbreth, L. M. (1917). *Applied motion study.* New York: Sturgis and Walton.

Gillies, D. (2004). Probability in artificial intelligence. Chapter 21 In L. Floridi (Ed.), *The blackwell guide to the philosophy and computing and information* (pp. 276–288). (Blackwell Philosophy Guides, 14). Oxford & Malden, MA: Blackwell.

Gilman, S. L. (1975). "Das-ist-der-Teu-fel-si-cher-lich": The Image of the Black on the Viennese Stage from Schikaneder to Grillparzer. In *Festschrift for Heinz Politzer* (pp. 78–106). Tübingen, Germany: Nimemeyer. Reprinted in Gilman (1982a).

Gilman, S. L. (1982a). *On blackness without blacks: Essays on the image of the black in Germany.* (Yale Afro-American Studies). Boston: G. K. Hall.

Gilman, S. L. (1982b). *Seeing the insane: A cultural history of psychiatric illustration.* New York: Wiley Interscience. Republished as a Wiley Paperback, 1985.

Gilman, S. L. (1984). Jews and mental illness: Medical metaphors, anti-Semitism and the Jewish response. *Journal of the History of the Behavioral Sciences, 20,* 150–159. Reprinted in his *Disease and Representation: Images of Illness from Madness to AIDS.* Ithaca, NY: Cornell University Press. (Also in Italian, Bologna: Il Mulino, 1993.)

Gilman, S. L. (1985). *Difference and pathology: Stereotypes of sexuality, race, and madness.* Ithaca, NY: Cornell University Press.

Gilman, S. L. (1986a). *Jewish self-hatred: Anti-semitism and the hidden language of the jews.* Baltimore, MD: The Johns Hopkins University Press. Paperback edn., 1990.

Gilman, S. L. (1986b). Black sexuality and modern consciousness. In R. Grimm & J. Hermand (Eds.), *Blacks and German culture* (pp. 35–53). Madison, WI: University of Wisconsin Press. Reprinted in Gilman, S. L. (1988). *Disease and representation: Images of illness from madness to AIDS.* Ithaca, NY: Cornell University Press; Paperback edition, 1988; Second edition, 1991; Second paperback edition, 1991; Italian translation, Bologna: Il Mulino, 1993; Japanese translation, Tokyo: Arino Shobo, 1996.

Gilman, S. L. (1991). *The Jew's body.* New York: Routledge.

Gilman, S. L. (1993a). *The case of Sigmund Freud: Medicine and identity at the Fin de Siècle.* Baltimore, MD: The Johns Hopkins University Press. Paperback, 1994.

Gilman, S. L. (1993b). Mark Twain and the diseases of the Jews. *American Literature, 65,* 95–116. Also In B. Cheyette (Ed.), *Between "Race" and culture: Representations of the Jew in English and American literature.* Stanford, CA: Stanford University Press, 1996, pp. 27–43. Also in: M. Moon & C. N. Davidson (Eds.), *Subjects and Citizens: Nation, Race, and Gender from "Oroonoko" to Anita Hill.* Durham, NC: Duke University Press, pp. 271–292.

Gilman, S. L. (1994a). Psychoanalysis and anti-semitism: Tainted greatness in a professional context. In N. Harrowitz (Ed.), *Tainted greatness: Anti-semitism, prejudice, and cultural heroes* (pp. 93–108). Philadelphia, PA: Temple University Press.

Gilman, S. L. (1994b). The Jewish nose: Are Jews white? or the History of the nose job. In L. J. Silberstein & R. L. Cohn (Eds.), *The other in Jewish thought and history: Constructions of Jewish culture and identity* (pp. 364–401). New York: New York University Press.

Gilman, S. L. (1995). Otto Weininger and Sigmund Freud: Race and gender in the shaping of psychoanalysis. In N. Harrowitz & B. Hyams (Eds.), *Jews and gender: Responses to Otto Weininger* (pp. 103–121). Philadelphia, PA: Temple University Press.

Gilman, S. L. (1996a). *Smart Jews: The construction of the idea of Jewish superior intelligence at the other end of the bell curve.* Lincoln: The University of Nebraska Press. Paperback edn., 1997.

Gilman, S. L. (1996b). Smart Jews in fin-de-siècle Vienna: 'Hybrids' and the anxiety about Jewish superior intelligence – Hofmannsthal and Wittgenstein. *Modernism/Modernity, 3,* 45–58. Reprinted in: R. Block & P. Fenves (Eds.), *The spirit of Poesy: Essays on Jewish and German literature and thought in honor of Géza von Molnar.* Evanston, IL: Northwestern University Press, 2000, pp. 193–207.

Gilman, S. L. (1996c). *The Bell Curve,* intelligence, and the virtuous Jews. In J. L. Kincheloe, S. R. Steinberg, & A. D. Gresson III (Eds.), *Measured lies: The bell curve examined* (pp. 265–290). New York: St. Martin's Press. Reprinted in *Discourse,* 19(1), 58–80 (1996).

Gilman, S. L. (1999). By a nose: On the construction of 'foreign bodies'. *Social Epistemology, 13,* 49–58.

Gilman, S. L. (Ed.). (2006). *Race and contemporary medicine: Biological facts and fictions.* Special issue. *Patterns of Prejudice,* 40. Also published as a book, London: Routledge, 2007.

Gilmore, G. (1979). Formalism and the law of negotiable instruments. *Creighton Law Review, 13,* 441–461. Also, New Haven, CT: Yale Law School, Faculty Scholarship Series, Paper 2564. http://digitalcommons.law.yale.edu/fss_papers/2564 or: http://digitalcommons.law.yale.edu/cgi/viewcontent.cgi?article=3612&context=fss_papers&sei-redir=1#search="Gilmore+"Formalism+and+the+law+of+negotiable""

Gimblett, H. R. (2002). *Integrating geographic information systems and agent-based modelling techniques for simulating social and ecological processes.* Oxford: Oxford University Press.

Giovagnoli, A., & Pons, S. (Eds.). (2003). *L'Italia repubblicana nella crisi degli anni Settanta: Tra guerra fredda e distensione.* Soveria Mannelli (prov. Cosenza, in Calabria, Italy): Rubbettino.

Gladwell, M. (2005). *Blink: The power of thinking without thinking.* New York: Little, Brown and Company.

Glass, R. T. (2005). Forensic odontology. Chapter 6 In S. H. James & J. J. Nordby (Eds.), *Forensic science: An introduction to scientific and investigative techniques* (2nd ed.). Boca Raton, FL: CRC Press. Also in 3rd edition, 2009.

Goad, W., & Kanehisa, M. (1982). Pattern recognition in nucleic acid sequences: A general method for finding local homologies and symmetries. *Nucleic Acids Research, 10*, 247–263.

Göbel, J., Hektor, J., & Holz, T. (2006). Advanced honeypot-based intrusion detection. In *Login:* (sic), December 2006, pp. 17–25. http://www.usenix.org

Goble, L. (1999). Deontic logic with relevance. In P. McNamara & H. Prakken (Eds.), *Norms, logics and information systems* (pp. 331–346). Amsterdam: ISO Press.

Goel, A., Feng, W.-C., Maier, D., Feng, W.-C., & Walpole, J. (2005). Forensix: A Robust, high-performance reconstruction system. At the *Second International Workshop on Security in Distributed Computing Systems (SDCS)*, In: *Proceedings of the 25th International Conference on Distributed Computing Systems Workshops (ICDCS 2005 Workshops)*, 6–10 June 2005, Columbus, OH. IEEE Computer Society, pp. 155–162.

Golan, T. (2004). *Laws of men and laws of nature: The history of scientific expert testimony in England and America*. Cambridge, MA: Harvard University Press.

Goldberg, H. G., & Wong, R. W. H. (1998). Restructuring transactional data for link analysis in the FinCEN AI system. In D. Jensen & H. Goldberg (Eds.), *Artificial intelligence and link analysis. Papers from the AAAI Fall Symposium*, Orlando, FL.

Goldberg, M., Hayvanovych, M., Hoonlor, A., Kelley, S., Magdon-Ismail, M., Mertsalov, K., et al. (2008). Discovery, analysis and monitoring of hidden social networks and their evolution. At the *IEEE Homeland Security Technologies Conference*, Boston, MA, May 12–13, 2008, pp. 1–6.

Golden, R. M., & Rumelhart, D. E. (1993). A parallel distributed processing model of story comprehension and recall. *Discourse Processes, 16*, 203–237.

Goldfarb, C. F. (1990). *The SGML handbook*, edited and introduced by Y. Rubinsky. Oxford: Clarendon Press, 1990, repr. 2000.

Goldin, H. E. (1952). *Hebrew criminal law and procedure*. New York: Twayne.

Goldman, A. I. (1986). *Epistemology and cognition*. Cambridge, MA: Harvard University Press.

Goldman, A. I. (1987a). Foundations of social epistemics. *Synthese, 73*(1), 109–144.

Goldman, A. I. (1987b). The cognitive and social sides of epistemology. In A. Fine & P. Machamer (Eds.), *PSA 1986* (Vol. 2, pp. 295–311). East Lansing, MI: Philosophy of Science Association.

Goldman, A. I. (1991). Epistemic paternalism: Communication control in law and society. *The Journal of Philosophy, 88*(3), 113–131.

Goldman, A. I. (1992). *Liaisons: Philosophy meets the cognitive and social sciences*. Cambridge, MA: The MIT Press.

Goldman, R. P. (1990). *A probabilistic approach to language understanding*. Technical Report CS-90-34, Computer Science Department. Providence, RI: Brown University.

Goldman, S., Dyer, M. G., & Flowers, M. (1988). Representing contractual situations. In C. Walter (Ed.), *Computer power and legal language: The use of computational linguistics, artificial intelligence, and expert systems in law* (pp. 99–118). New York: Quorum Books.

Goldman, S. R., Dyer, M. G., & Flowers, M. (1985). Learning to understand contractual situations. In *Proceedings of the ninth International Joint Conference on Artificial Intelligence (IJCAI'85)*, Los Angeles, CA, 18–24 August 1985. San Mateo, CA: Morgan Kaufmann Publ. http://ijcai.org/search.php

Goldman, S. R., Dyer, M. G., & Flowers, M. (1987). Precedent-based legal reasoning and knowledge acquisition in contract law. In *Proceedings of the first International Conference on Artificial Intelligence and Law (ICAIL'87)*, Boston, MA, pp. 210–221.

Goldman, Sh. (2004). *God's sacred tongue: Hebrew & the American imagination*. Chapel Hill, NC: University of North Carolina Press.

Goldsmith, R. W. (1986). The applicability of an evidentiary value model to judicial and prosecutorial decision making. In A. A. Martino, F. Socci Natali, & S. Binazzi (Eds.), *Automated analysis of legal texts, logic, informatics, law* (pp. 229–245). Amsterdam: North-Holland.

Goldsmith, R. W. (1989). Potentialities for practical, instructional and scientific purposes of computer aids to evaluating judicial evidence in terms of an evidentiary value model. In A. A. Martino (Ed.), *Pre-proceedings of the third international conference on "Logica, Informatica, Diritto: Legal Expert Systems"*, Florence, 1989 (2 vols. + Appendix) (Vol. 1, pp. 317–329). Florence: Istituto per la Documentazione Giuridica, Consiglio Nazionale delle Ricerche.

Goldstein, A. G., & Chance, J. E. (1981). Laboratory studies of face recognition. In G. Davies, H. Ellis, & J. Shepherd (Eds.), *Perceiving and remembering faces* (pp. 81–104). New York: Academic.

Goldstein, H. (1990). *Problem-oriented policing*. New York: McGraw-Hill.

Gómez-Gauchía, H., & Peinado, F. (2006). Automatic customization of non-player characters using players temperament. In S. Göbel, R. Malkewitz, & I. Iurgel (Eds.), *Proceedings of the third international conference on Technologies for Interactive Digital Storytelling and Entertainment (TIDSE)*, Darmstadt, Germany, 4–6 December 2006 (pp. 241–252). (Lecture Notes in Computer Science, 4326). Berlin: Springer.

Gómez-Pérez, A., Fernández-López, M., & Corcho, O. (2004). *Ontological engineering: With examples from the areas of knowledge management, e-commerce and the semantic web*. Berlin: Springer.

Gonçalves, T., & Quaresma, P. (2003). A preliminary approach to the multilabel classification problem of Portuguese juridical documents. In *Proceedings of EPIA'03, the Eleventh Portugese Conference on Artificial Intelligence*, Beja, Portugal, 4–7 December 2003. (Lecture Notes in Computer Science.) Berlin: Springer, pp. 435–444.

González Ballester, M. A., Büchler, P., & Reimers, N. (2007). Combined statistical model of bone shape and biomechanical properties for evidence-based orthopaedic implant design. In *The Digital Patient*, special issue of *ERCIM News*, 69 (April), 27–28. Accessible at the webpage http://ercim-news.ercim.org/ of the European Research Consortium for Informatics and Mathematics.

Good, I. J. (1960). The paradox of confirmation. *The British Journal for the Philosophy of Science, 11*(42), 145–149.

Good, I. J. (1983). On the principle of total evidence. In his *Good thinking*. Minneapolis, MN: Minnesota University Press.

Goode, G. C., Morris, J. R., & Wells, J. M. (1979). The application of radioactive bromine isotopes for the visualisation of latent fingerprints. *Journal of Radioanalytical [and Nuclear] Chemistry, 48*(1/2), 17–28.

Goodrich, P. (1986). *Reading the law*. Oxford: Blackwell.

Goodrich, P. (2005). Narrative as argument. In D. Herman, M. Jahn, & M.-L. Ryan (Eds.), *Routledge encyclopedia of narrative theory* (pp. 348–349). London: Routledge, 2008 (pbk).

Goranson, H. T., Chu, B. T., Grüninger, M., Ivezic, N., Kulvatunyou, B., Labrou, Y., et al. (2002). Ontologies as a new cost factor in enterprise integration. In *Proceedings of ICEIMT 2002*, pp. 253–263.

Gordon, T. F. (1995). The Pleadings Game: An exercise in computational dialectics. *Artificial Intelligence and Law, 2*(4), 239–292.

Gordon, T. F., Prakken, H., & Walton, D. N. (2007). The Carneades model of argument and burden of proof. *Artificial Intelligence, 171*, 875–896.

Gordon, T. F., & Walton, D. (2006). The Carneades argumentation framework: Using presumptions and exceptions to model critical questions. At *The Sixth International Workshop on Computational Models of Natural Argument*, held together with *ECAI'06*, Riva del Garda, Italy, August 2006.

Gouron, A. (1992). Medieval courts and towns: Examples from Southern France. *Fundamina: A Journal of Legal History, 1*, 30–45.

Governatori, G., & Rotolo, A. (2002). A Gentzen system for reasoning with contrary-to-duty obligations: A preliminary study. In A. J. I. Jones & J. Horty (Eds.), *ΔEON'02: Sixth international workshop on deontic logic in computer science*, Imperial College, London, May 2002 (pp. 97–116).

Grabherr, S., Djonov, V., Friess, A., Thali, M. J., Ranner, G., Vock, P., et al. (2006). Postmortem angiography after vascular perfusion with diesel oil and a lipophilic contrast agent. *AJR: American Journal of Roentgenology, 187*(5), W515–523.

Grady, G., & Patil, R. S. (1987). An expert system for screening employee pension plans for the Internal Revenue Service. *Proceedings of the first international conference on artificial intelligence and law* (pp. 137–143). New York: ACM Press.

Granhag, P. A., & Strömwall, L. A. (2004). *Detection deception in forensic contexts.* Cambridge: Cambridge University Press.

Grant, J., Kraus, S., & Perlis, D. (2005). A logic-based model of intention formation and action for multi-agent subcontracting. *Artificial Intelligence, 163*(2), 163–201.

Grasso, F. (2002a). Would I lie to you? Fairness and deception in rhetorical dialogues. In R. Falcone & L. Korba (Eds.), *Working notes of the AAMAS 2002 workshop on "Deception, Fraud and Trust in Agent Societies"*, Bologna, Italy, 15 July 2002. The article can be downloaded from http://www.csc.liv.ac.uk/~floriana/pub.html

Grasso, F. (2002b). Towards computational rhetoric. *Informal Logic Journal, 22*(3), 225–259.

Grasso, F., Cawsey, A., & Jones, R. (2000). Dialectical argumentation to solve conflicts in advice giving: A case study in the promotion of healthy nutrition. *International Journal of Human-Computer Studies, 53*(6), 1077–1115.

Grasso, F., Rahwan, I., Reed, C., & Simari, G. R. (2010). Introducing *argument & computation. Argument & Computation, 1*(1), 1–5.

Grasso, F., Reed, C., & Carenini, G. (Eds.). (2004). *Proceedings of the fourth workshop on Computational Models of Natural Argument (CMNA IV)* at *ECAI 2004*, Valencia, Spain.

Gray, G. L., & Debreceny, R. (2006). Continuous assurance using text mining. At the *12th world continuous auditing & reporting symposium.* Posted at the Rutgers Accounting Web (raw.rutgers.edu): http://raw.rutgers.edu/docs/wcars/12wcars/Continuous_Assurance_Text_Mining.pdf

Greene, J. R. (2006). *The encyclopedia of police science* (3rd ed.). London: Routledge.

Greenwood [=Atkinson], K., Bench-Capon, T., & McBurney, P. (2003). Towards a computational theory of persuasion in law. In G. Sartor (Ed.), *Proceedings of the ninth International Conference on Artificial Intelligence and Law (ICAIL 2003)*, Edinburgh, Scotland, 24–28 June 2003 (pp. 22–31). New York: ACM Press.

Greer, S. (1994). Miscarriages of criminal justice reconsidered. *Modern Law Review, 58*, 71.

Gregg, D. G., & Scott, J. E. (2008). A typology of complaints about eBay sellers. *Communications of the ACM, 51*(4), 69–74.

Gregory, F. (1998). There is a global crime problem. *International Journal of Risk, Security and Crime Prevention, 3*, 133–137.

Grey, T. (1983). Langdell's orthodoxy. *University of Pittsburgh Law Review, 45*, 1–53.

Grey, T. C. (1999). *The new formalism.* Stanford Law School Public Law and Legal Theory Working Paper, No. 4 (SSRN 200732). Stanford, CA: University of Stanford.

Grice, H. P. (1975). Logic and conversation. In P. Cole & J. Morgan (Eds.), *Syntax and semantics*, Vol. 3: *Speech acts* (pp. 41–58). Orlando, FL: Academic.

Grice, H. P. (1981). Presupposition and conversational implicature. In: P. Cole (Ed.), *Radical pragmatics* (pp. 183–198). New York: Academic Press.

Grifantini, F. M. (1993). Inutilizzabilità. In *Digesto delle Discipline Penalistiche* (4th ed., Vol. 7). Turin, Italy: Utet.

Grifantini, F. M. (1999). Utilizzabilità in dibattimento degli atti provenienti dalle fasi anteriori. In AA.VV., *La prova nel dibattimento penale.* Turin: Giappichelli.

Griffiths, P. E. (2003). Emotions. Chapter 12 In S. P. Stich & T. A. Warfield (Eds.), *The Blackwell guide to philosophy of mind* (pp. 288–308). Oxford: Blackwell.

Grosz, B. (1977). *The representation and use of focus in dialogue understanding.* Technical Note No. 151. Menlo Park, CA: Stanford Research Institute.

Grosz, B., & Kraus, S. (1996). Collaborative plans for complex group action. *Artificial Intelligence, 86*(2), 269–357.

Grover, C., Hachey, B., Hughson, I., & Korycinski, C. (2003). Automatic summarisation of legal documents. In *Proceedings of the ninth International Conference on Artificial Intelligence and Law (ICAIL 2003)*, Edinburgh, Scotland. New York: ACM Press, pp. 243–251.

Grubbs, F. E. (1969). Procedures for detecting outlying observations in samples. *Technometrics, 11*, 1–21.

Gruber, T. R. (1993). A translation approach to portable ontology specifications. *Knowledge Acquisition, 5*(2), 199–220.

Gruber, T. R. (1995). Towards principles for the design of ontologies used for knowledge sharing. *International Journal of Human-Computer Studies, 43*(5–6), 907–928. (Originally in N. Guarino & R. Poli (Eds.). (1993). *International workshop on formal ontology*, Padova, Italy. Revised August 1993. Technical report KSL-93-04, Knowledge Systems Laboratory, Stanford University, Stanford, CA. Often cited, without page-numbers, as though it appeared in N. Guarino & R. Poli (Eds.), *Formal ontology in conceptual analysis and knowledge representation*. Dordrecht: Kluwer. Actually published in a special issue on Formal Ontology in Conceptual Analysis and Knowledge Representation (Ed. N. Guarino & R. Poli), *International Journal of Human-Computer Studies, 43*(5–6), 907–928).

Grugq. (2005). *The art of defiling: Defeating forensic analysis*. In Blackhat briefings. http://www. blackhat.com/presentations/bh-usa-05/bh-us-05-grugq.pdf (The web link did no longer seem to work in the summer of 2011; contact Blackhat for a copy).

Grüninger, G., & Delaval, A. (2009). A first-order cutting process ontology for sheet metal parts. In *Proceedings of FOMI 2009*, pp. 22–33.

Grüninger, M., & Lee, J. (2002). Ontology applications and design: Introduction. In a special issue of *Communications of the ACM, 45*(2), 39–41.

Gu, J. (2007). Consumer rights protection on the online auction website – Situations and solutions: A Case study of EBay. *BILETA 2007 Annual Conference*, University of Hertfordshire, 16–17 April 2007. British and Irish Law, Education and Technology Association (BILETA). 8 pages. http://www.bileta.ac.uk/Document%20Library/1/Consumer%20Rights%20Protection% 20on%20the%20Online%20Auction%20Website%20-Situations%20and%20Solutions% 20-%20A%20Case%20Study%20of%20EBay.pdf

Gudjonsson, G. H. (1992). *The psychology of interrogations, confessions and testimony*. New York: Wiley. New edition: 2003.

Gudjonsson, G. H. (2001). False confessions. *The Psychologist, 14*, 588–591.

Gudjonsson, G. H. (2006). Disputed confessions and miscarriages of justice in Britain: Expert psychological and psychiatric evidence in the Court of Appeal. *The Manitoba Law Journal, 31*, 489–521.

Gudjonsson, G. H. (2007). Investigative interviewing. In T. Newburn, T. Williamson, & A. Wright (Eds.), *Handbook of criminal investigation* (pp 466–492). Cullompton: Willan Publishing.

Gudjonsson, G. H., & MacKeith, J. A. C. (1982). False confessions: Psychological effects of interrogation. In A. Trankell (Ed.), *Reconstructing the past: The role of psychologists in criminal trials* (pp. 253–269). Deventer, The Netherlands: Kluwer.

Gudjonsson, G. H., & Clark, N. K. (1986). Suggestibility in police interrogation: A social Psychological Model. *Social Behavior, 1*, 83–104.

Gudjonsson, G. H., & Sigurdsson, J. F. (1994). How frequently do false confessions occur? An empirical study among prison inmates. *Psychology, Crime, and Law, 1*, 21–26.

Gudjonsson, G. H., Sigurdsson, J. F., Asgeirsdottir, B. B., & Sigfusdottir, I. D. (2006). Custodial interrogation, false confession, and individual differences: A national study among Icelandic youth. *Personality and Individuals Differences, 41*, 49–59.

Gudjonsson, G. H., Sigurdsson, J. F., Asgeirsdottir, B. B., & Sigfusdottir, I. D. (2007). Custodial Interrogation: What are the background factors associated with claimed false confessions? *The Journal of Forensic Psychiatry and Psychology, 18*, 266–275.

Gudjonsson, G. H., Sigurdsson, J. F., & Einarsson, E. (2004). The role of personality in relation to confessions and denials. *Psychology, Crime and Law, 10*, 125–135.

Guest, A. G. (1961). Logic in the law. In A. G. Guest (Ed.), *Oxford essays in jurisprudence* (pp. 176–197). Oxford: Oxford University Press; Corrected edn., Oxford: Clarendon Press, 1968(in 1961 edition).

Guidotti, P. (1994). Use of precedents based on reasoning by analogy in a deductive framework. In I. Carr & A. Narayanan (Eds.), *Proceedings of the fourth national conference on law, computers and artificial intelligence* (pp. 56–69). Exeter, England: Exeter University Centre for Legal Interdisciplinary Development (EUCLID).

Gulotta, G. (2004). Differenti tattiche persuasive. In G. Gulotta & L. Puddu (Eds.), *La persuasione forense: strategie e tattiche* (pp. 85–148). Milan: Giuffrè, with a consolidated bibliography on pp. 257–266.

Gulotta, G., & Zappalà, A. (2001). The conflict between prosecution and defense in a child sexual abuse case and in an attempted homicide case. In D. M. Peterson, J. A. Barnden, & E. Nissan (Eds.), *Artificial intelligence and law*, special issue, *Information and Communications Technology Law, 10*(1), 91–108.

Gunn, J., & Taylor, P. J. (1993). *Forensic psychiatry: Clinical, legal and ethical issues.* Oxford & Boston: Butterworth-Heinemann.

Gutebier, T., Schmidt, M. A., & Rogers, S. P. (1989). *An annotated bibliography on preparation, taxidermy, and collection management of vertebrates with emphasis on birds.* (Special publication of Carnegie Museum of Natural History, 15). Pittsburgh, PA: Carnegie Museum of Natural History.

Gutés, A., Céspedes, F., & del Valle, M. (2007). Electronic tongues in flow analysis. *Analytica Chimica Acta, 600*, 90–96.

Gutiérrez, M., García-Rojas, A., Thalmann, D., Vexo, F., Moccozet, L., Magnenat-Thalmann, N., et al. (2007). An ontology of virtual humans: Incorporating semantics into human shapes. *The Visual Computer, 23*(3), 207–218.

Gutiérrez, M., Thalmann, D., Vexo, F., Moccozet, L., Magnenat-Thalmann, N., Mortara, M., et al. (2005). An ontology of virtual humans: Incorporating semantics into human shapes. In *Proceedings of the workshop towards Semantic Virtual Environments (SVE05)*, Villars, Switzerland, March 2005, pp. 57–67. Posted at http://vrlab.epfl.ch/Publications of the Virtual Reality Lab at the Swiss Federal Institute of Technology in Lausanne.

Güven, S., Podlaseck, M., & Pingali, G. (2005). PICASSO: Pervasive information chronicling, access, search, and sharing for organizations. In *Proceedings of the IEEE 2005 Pervasive Computing conference (PerCom 2005)*. Los Alamitos, CA: IEEE Computer Society Press.

Guyon, I., & Elisseeff, A. (2003). An introduction to variable and feature selection. *Journal of Machine Learning Research, 3*, 1157–1182.

Gwadera, R., Atallah, M. J., & Szpankowski, W. (2005a). Reliable detection of episodes in event sequences. *Knowledge and Information Systems, 7*(4), 415–437.

Gwadera, R., Atallah, M. J., & Szpankowski, W. (2005b). Markov models for identification of significant episodes. In *Proceedings of the SIAM International Conference on Data Mining (SDM 2005)*, pp. 404–414.

Gyongyi, Z., Molina, H. G., & Pedersen, J. (2004). Combating web spam with TrustRank. In *Proceedings of the 30th Very Large Data Bases international conference (VLDB 2004)*, Toronto, Canada, August 29–September 3, 2004. An older version of that paper had appeared as a technical report of Stanford University.

Haber, L., & Haber, R. N. (2003). Error rates for human fingerprint examiners. In N. K. Ratha & R. Bolle (Eds.), *Automatic fingerprint recognition systems* (pp. 339–360). New York: Springer.

Haber, L., & Haber, R. N. (2006). Letter Re: A report of latent print examiner accuracy during comparison training exercises. *Journal of Forensic Identification, 56*, 493–499.

Haber, L., & Haber, R. N. (2008). Scientific validation of fingerprint evidence under daubert. *Law, Probability and Risk, 7*, 87–109.

Habermas, J. (1981). *The theory of communicative action.* London: Beacon Press.

HaCohen-Kerner, Y. (1997). *The judge's apprentice.* Ph.D. Thesis (in Hebrew, with an English abstract). Ramat-Gan, Israel: Department of Mathematics and Computer Science, Bar-Ilan University.

HaCohen-Kerner, Y., & Schild, U. J. (1999). The judge's apprentice. In B. Knight & E. Nissan (Eds.), *Forum on case-based reasoning*, thematic section in *The New Review of Applied Expert Systems, 5*, 191–202.

HaCohen-Kerner, Y., & Schild, U. J. (2000). Case-based sentencing using a tree of legal concepts. In *Time for AI and society: Proceedings of the AISB'00 symposium on artificial intelligence and legal reasoning*, 2000. The Society for the Study of Artificial Intelligence and the Simulation of Behavior, UK, pp. 9–16.

HaCohen-Kerner, Y., & Schild, U. J. (2001). Case-based sentencing using a tree of legal concepts. In D. M. Peterson, J. A. Barnden, & E. Nissan (Eds.), *Artificial intelligence and law*, special issue of *Information and Communications Technology Law*, 10(1), 125–135.

HaCohen-Kerner, Y., Schild, U. J., & Zeleznikow, J. (1999). Developing computational models of discretion to build legal knowledge based systems. In *Proceedings of the seventh international conference on artificial intelligence and law, ICAIL99*, Oslo, 1999. New York: ACM, 1999, pp. 206–213.

Hadzic, M., & Chang, E. (2008). Using coalgebra and coinduction to define ontology-based multi-agent systems. *International Journal of Metadata, Semantics and Ontologies*, 3(3), 197–209.

Hafstad, G., Memon, A., & Logie, R (2004). The effects of post-identification feedback on children's memory. *Applied Cognitive Psychology*, 18, 901–912.

Hage, J. (2001). Contrary to duty obligations: A study in legal ontology. Chapter 8 In B. Verheij, A. R. Lodder, R. P. Loui, & A. Muntjewerff (Eds.), *Legal knowledge and information systems. JURIX 2001: The fourteenth annual international conference*, University of Amsterdam, December 13–14, 2001. (Frontiers in Artificial Intelligence and Applications, 70). Tokyo: Ohmsha.

Haglund, W. D. (2005). Forensic taphonomy. Chapter 8 In S. H. James & J. J. Nordby (Eds.), *Forensic science: An introduction to scientific and investigative techniques* (2nd ed.). Boca Raton, FL: CRC Press. Also in 3rd edition, 2009.

Hahn, U., & Mani, I. (2000). The challenges of automatic summarization. *IEEE Computer*, 33(11), 29–36.

Hahn, U., & Schulz, S. (2004). Building a very large ontology from medical thesauri. In S. Staab & R. Studer (Eds.), *Handbook on ontologies* (pp. 133–150). (International Handbooks on Information Systems). Berlin: Springer.

Haïm, S. (1956). *Persian-English proverbs*. Tehran [sic]: B. & D. Beroukhim Booksellers.

Hall, R. P., & Kibler, D. F. (1985). Differing methodological perspectives in artificial intelligence research. *The AI Magazine*, 6(3), 166–178.

Halliwell, J., Keppens, J., & Shen, Q. (2003). Linguistic Bayesian Networks for reasoning with subjective probabilities in forensic statistics. In G. Sartor (Ed.), *Proceedings of the ninth International Conference on Artificial Intelligence and Law (ICAIL 2003)*, Edinburgh, Scotland, 24–28 June 2003 (pp. 42–50). New York: ACM Press.

Halpin, H., & Moore, J. D. (2010). Event extraction in a plot advice agent. In *ACL-44 Proceedings of the 21st International Conference on Computational Linguistics and 44th annual meeting of the Association for Computational Linguistics*. http://portal.acm.org/citation.cfm?doid=12201275.1220283

Halpin, H. R. (2003) *The plots of children and machines: The statistical and symbolic semantic analysis of narratives*. MSc. thesis. Edinburgh, Scotland: School of Informatics, University of Edinburgh. http://www.semanticstories.org/thesis/mscthesis.pdf

Hamblin, C. L. (1970). *Fallacies*. London: Methuen.

Hamblin, C. L. (1971). Mathematical models of dialogue. *Theoria*, 37, 130–155.

Hamill, J. T. (2006). *Analysis of layered social networks*. Ph.D. dissertation. Report AFIT/DS/ENS/06 03. Graduate School of Engineering and Management, Air Force Institute of Technology (Air University). Available online at both these addresses: http://www.afit.edu/en/docs/ENS/dissertations/Hamill.pdf http://www.au.af.mil/au/awc/awcgate/afit/hamill_layered_social_networks.pdf

Hamilton, D. L., & Rose, T. L. (1980). Illusory correlation and the maintenance of stereotypical beliefs. *Journal of Personality and Social Psychology*, 39, 832–845.

Hamkins, J. D., & Löwe, B. (2008). The modal logic of forcing. *Transactions of the American Mathematical Society*, 360, 1793–1817.

Hamlin, C. (2009). *Cholera: The biography*. (Biographies of Disease Series). Oxford: Oxford University Press.

Hammersley, R., & Read, J. D. (1993). Voice identification by humans and computers. In S. L. Sporer, R. S. Malpass, & G. Köhnken (Eds.), *Suspect identification: Psychological knowledge, problems and perspectives*. Hillsdale, NJ: Lawrence Erlbaum Associates.

Hammon, W. S., McMechan, G. A., & Zeng, X. (2000). Forensic GPR-finite-difference simulation of responses from buried remains. *Journal of Applied Geophysics, 45*, 171–186.

Hamscher, W., Console, L., & de Kleer, J. (Eds.). (1992). *Readings in model-based diagnosis*. San Mateo, CA: Morgan-Kaufmann.

Han, J., Cheng, H., Xin, D., & Yan, X. (2007). Frequent data mining: Current status and future directions. In *Data Mining and Knowledge Discovery, 10th Anniversary Issue*, of *Data Mining and Knowledge Discovery, 15*, 55–86. http://www.cs.ucsb.edu/~xyan/papers/dmkd07_frequentpattern.pdf

Han, J., & Kamber, M. (2001). *Data mining: Concepts and techniques*. San Francisco: Morgan Kaufmann.

Hanba, J. M., & Zaragoza, M. S. (2007). Interviewer feedback in repeated interviews involving forced confabulation. *Applied Cognitive Psychology, 21*(4), 433–455.

Hancock, P. J. B. (2000). Evolving faces from principal components. *Behaviour Research Methods, Instruments and Computers, 32*(2), 327–333.

Hancock, P. J. B., Bruce, V., & Burton, A. M. (1998). A comparison of two computer-based face recognition systems with human perceptions of faces. *Vision Research, 38*, 2277–2288.

Hancock P. J. B., Bruce, V., & Burton, A. M. (2000). Recognition of unfamiliar faces. *Trends in Cognitive Sciences, 4*(9), 330–337.

Hancock, P. J. B., & Frowd, C. D. (2001). Evolutionary generation of faces. In P. J. Bentley & D. W. Corne (Eds.), *Creative evolutionary systems*. London: Academic.

Hand, D. J., Mannila, H., & Smyth, P. (2001). *Principles of data mining (Adaptive computation and machine learning)*. Cambridge, MA: MIT Press.

Handler Miller, C. 2004. *Digital storytelling: A creator's guide to interactive entertainment*. Burlington, MA: Focal Press.

Hanlein, H. (1998). *Studies in authorship recognition: A corpus-based approach*. (European University Studies, Series 14: Anglo-Saxon Language and Literature, 352). Frankfurt/M: Peter Lang, 1999. (Originally: doctoral dissertation, Universität Augsburg, 1998.)

Hao, Y., Tan, T., & Wang, Y. (2002). An effective algorithm for fingerprint matching. In *TENCON '02. Proceedings. 2002 IEEE region 10 conference on computers, communications, control and power engineering*, 28–31 October 2002, Vol. 1, pp. 519–522. Also, technical report, National Laboratory of Pattern Recognition, Institute of Automation, Chinese Academy of Sciences, Beijing. http://nlpr-web.ia.ac.cn/english/irds/papers/haoying/tencon.pdf

Harder, C. (1998). *Serving maps on the internet*. Redland, CA: ESRI Press.

Harley, E. M., Carlsen, K. A., & Loftus, G. R. (2004). The "saw-it-all-along" effect: Demonstrations of visual hindsight bias. *Journal of Experimental Psychology: Learning, Memory, and Cognition, 30*, 960–968.

Harman, G. (1986). *Changes in view: Principles of reasoning*. Cambridge, MA: The MIT Press.

Harman, G. H. (1965). Inference to the best explanation. *Philosophical Review, 74*(1), 88–95.

Harman, G. H. (1968). Enumerative induction as inference to the best explanation. *Journal of Philosophy, 65*(18), 529–533.

Harper, W. R., & Harris, D. H. (1975). The application of link analysis to police intelligence. *Human Factors, 17*(2), 157–164.

Harris, M. D. (1985). *Introduction to natural language processing*. Reston, VA: Reston Publ. Co.

Harris, R. (2006). Arriving at an anti-forensics consensus: Examining how to define and control the anti-forensics problem. At the *Digital Forensic Research Workshop 2006: The 6th annual DFRWS 2006*, Lafayette, Indiana, 14–16 August 2006. Article published in *Digital Investigation*, 3S, pp. S44–S49 (Amsterdam: Elsever). http://www.dfrws.org/2006/proceedings/6-Harris.pdf

Harris, D. H., & Chaney, F. B. (1969). *Human factors in quality assurance.* New York: Wiley.

Harrison, J. M. (1964). *Bird taxidermy.* London: Percival Marshall & Co., 1964. With an addendum (by J. Harrison): Newton Abbot (U.K.) & North Pomfreth, Vermont: David & Charles, 1976.

Harrison, W. R. (1958). *Suspect documents: Their scientific examination.* New York: Praeger.

Hart, H. L. A. (1961a). *The concept of law.* Oxford: Clarendon Press.

Hart, H. L. A. (1961b). Negligence, mens rea and criminal responsibility. In A. G. Guest (Ed.), *Oxford essays in jurisprudence.* Oxford: Oxford University Press. Corrected edn., Oxford: Clarendon Press, 1968.

Hart, H. L. A. (1994). *The concept of law* (2nd ed.). Oxford: Clarendon Press.

Hartley, J. R. M., & Varley, G. (2001). The design and evaluation of simulations for the development of complex decision-making skills. In T. Okamoto, R. Hartley, Kinshuk & J. P. Klus (Eds.), *Proceedings of the IEEE international conference on advanced learning technology: Issues, achievements and challenge* (pp. 145–148). IEEE Computer Society.

Hartwig, M., Granhag, P. A., Strömwall, L. A., & Doering, N. (2010). Impression and information management: On the regulation of innocent and guilty suspects. *The Open Criminology Journal, 3,* 10–16.

Hartwig, M., Granhag, P. A., Strömwall, L. A., & Vrij, A. (2005). Detecting deception via strategic disclosure of evidence. *Law and Human Behavior, 29,* 469–484.

Hasan-Rokem, G. (1996). *The web of life: Folklore in rabbinic literature – The Palestinian aggadic midrash Eikha Rabba* (in Hebrew: *Riqmat-Ḥayyim*), Tel-Aviv: Am Oved. English translation (by B. Stein): Stanford, 2000.

Hasel, L. E., & Wells, G. L. (2006). Catching the bad guy: Morphing composite faces helps. *Law and human behavior, 31,* 193–207.

Hastie, R. (Ed.). (1993). *Inside the juror: The psychology of juror decision making.* (Cambridge Series on Judgment and Decision Making). Cambridge: Cambridge University Press, 1993 (hard cover), 1994 (paperback).

Hastie, R., Penrod, S. D., & Pennington, N. (1983). *Inside the jury.* Cambridge, MA: Harvard University Press.

Hatfield, J. V., Neaves, P., Hicks, P. J., Persaud, K. C., & Tavers, P. (1994). Toward an integrated electronic nose using conducting polymer sensors. *Sensors & Actuators, 18,* 221–228.

Hauck, R. V., Atabakhsh, H., Ongvasith, P., Gupta, H., & Chen, H. (2002). COPLINK concept space: An application for criminal intelligence analysis. In *Digital Government,* special issue of *IEEE Computer, 35*(3), 30–37.

Hauser, K., & Ng-Thow-Hing, V. (2010). Randomized multi-modal planning for precision pushing on a humanoid robot. Chapter 9 In K. Harada, E. Yoshida, & K. Yokoi (Eds.), *Motion planning for humanoid robots* (pp. 251–276). Berlin: Springer.

Hawkins, K. (1992). The use of legal discretion: Perspectives from law and social science. In K. Hawkins (Ed.), *The uses of discretion.* Oxford Socio-Legal Studies. Oxford: Clarendon Press.

Hayes, P. J. (1985). Naive physics I: Ontology for liquids. Chapter 3 In J. R. Hobbs & R. C. Moore (Eds.), *Formal theories of the commonsense world.* Norwood, NJ: Ablex.

Hayes, P. J., Knecht, L. E., & Cellio, M. J. (1988). A news story categorization system. In *Proceedings of the second ACL conf. on applied natural language processing,* 1988, pp. 9–17. Reprinted in K. Sparck Jones & P. Willett (Eds.). (1997). *Readings in information retrieval.* San Francisco: Morgan Kaufmann, pp. 518–526.

Hayes-Roth, B. (1983). *The blackboard architecture: A general framework for problem solving.* Report No. HPP-83-30, Stanford Heuristic Programming Project (which was to become the Knowledge Systems Laboratory, in Palo Alto), of Stanford, CA: Stanford University.

Hayes-Roth, B. (1985). A blackboard architecture for control. *Artificial Intelligence, 26,* 251–321.

Hayes-Roth, B., & van Gent, R. (1997). Story-making and improvisational puppets. In W. L. Johnson (Ed.), *Autonomous Agents '97.* (pp. 1–7)Marina del Rey, CA. New York: ACM Press.

Haygood, R. C., Teel, K. S., & Greening, C. P. (1964). Link analysis by computer. *Human Factors, 6,* 63–70.

Haykin, S. (1994). *Neural networks: A comprehensive foundation*. New York: Macmillan.

Hearst, M. (1999). Untangling text data mining. In *Proceedings of the 37th annual meeting for computational linguistics* (pp. 3–10). New York: ACM Press.

Heaton-Armstrong, A. Wolchover, D., & Maxwell-Scott A. (2006). Obtaining, recording, and admissibility of out-of-court witness statements. In A. Heaton-Armstrong, E. Shepherd, G. Gudjonsson & D. Wolchover (Eds.), *Witness testimony. Psychological, investigative and evidential perspectives* (pp. 171–209). Oxford: Oxford University Press.

Hecht-Nielson, R. (1990). *Neurocomputing*. Reading, MA: Addison-Wesley.

Heckerman, D. (1997). Bayesian networks for data mining. *Data Mining and Knowledge Discovery, 1*, 79–119.

Henrion, M., Provan, G., Del Favero, B., & Sanders, G. (1994). An experimental comparison of numerical and qualitative probabilistic reasoning. In R. Lopez de Mántaras & D. Poole (Eds.), *Uncertainty in artificial intelligence: Proceedings of the Tenth Conference*, July 1994. San Mateo, CA: Morgan Kaufmann pp. 319–326.

Hendrix, G. G. (1976). *Partitioned networks for modelling natural language semantics*. Dissertation. Austin, Texas: Department of Computer Sciences, The University of Texas.

Hendrix, G. G. (1979). Encoding knowledge in partitioned networks. In N. V. Findler (Ed.), *Associative networks: Representation and use of knowledge by computers* (pp. 51–92). New York: Academic.

Henry, R. C., & Kim, B. M. (1990). Extension of self-modeling curve resolution to mixtures of more than three components. Part 1: Finding the basic feasible region. *Chemometrics and intelligent Laboratory Systems, 8*, 205–216.

Henry, R. C., Lewis, C. W., & Collins, J. F. (1994). Vehicle related hydrocarbon source composition from ambient data: The GRACE/SAFER method. *Environmental Science and Technology, 28*, 823–832.

Henry, R. C., Spiegelman, C. H., Collins, J. F., & Park, J. F. [sic] (1997). Reported emissions of organic gases are not consistent with observations. *Proceedings of the National Academy of Sciences USA, 94*, 6596–6599.

Hepler, A. B., Dawid, A. P., & Leucari, V. (2007). Object-oriented graphical representations of complex patterns of evidence. *Law, Probability & Risk, 6*, 275–293. doi:10.1093/lpr/mgm005

Her Majesty's. . . (1998/99). Information technology. Chapter 5 *In*: Her Majesty's chief inspector of constabulary for scotland report for 1998/99. http://www.scotland.gov.uk/library2/doc05/cicr-11.htm

Herold, J., Loyek, C., & Nattkemper, T. W. (2011). Multivariate image mining. *Wiley Interdisciplinary Reviews (WIREs): Data Mining and Knowledge Discovery, 1*(1), 2–13. doi://10.1002/widm.4

Herrero, S. (2005). Legal issues in forensic DNA. In S. H. James & J. J. Nordby (Eds.), *Forensic science: An introduction to scientific and investigative techniques* (2nd ed.). Boca Raton, FL: CRC Press. Also in 3rd edition, 2009.

Heuston, R. F. V. (1964). *Lives of the lord chancellors, 1885–1940*. Oxford: Clarendon Press.

Hewer, L., & Penrod, S. D. (1995). Jury decision-making in complex trials. Chapter 6.3 In R. Bull & D. Carson (Ed.), *Handbook of psychology in legal contexts* (pp. 527–541). Chichester: Wiley.

Hewstone, M. (1989). *Causal attribution: From cognitive processes to cognitive beliefs*. Oxford: Blackwell.

Heylighen, F. (1999). Advantages and limitations of formal expression. *Foundations of Science, 4*(1), 25–56.

Hickey, L. (1993). Presupposition under cross-examination. *International Journal for the Semiotics of Law, 6*, 89–109.

Hildebrand, J. A., Wiggins, S. M., Henkart, P. C., & Conyers, L. B. (2002). Comparison of seismic reflection and ground penetrating radar imaging at the controlled archaeological test site, Champaign, Illinois. *Archaeological Prospection, 9*, 9–21.

Hill, C., Memon, A., & McGeorge, P. (2008). The role of confirmation bias in suspect interviews: A systematic evaluation. *Legal & Criminological Psychology, 13*, 357–371.

Hilton, J. L., & Fein, S. (1989). The role of diagnosticity in stereotype-based judgments. *Journal of Personality and Social Psychology, 57*, 201–211.

Hilton, O. (1982). *Scientific examination of questioned documents.* Amsterdam & New York: Elsevier Science Publishing Co.

Hinton, G., & Sejnowski, T. J. (Eds). (1999). *Unsupervised learning: Foundations of neural computation.* Cambridge, MA: MIT Press.

Hinz, T., & Pezdek, K. (2001). The effect of exposure to multiple lineups on face identification accuracy. *Law and Human Behavior, 25*, 185–198.

Hirschman, L., Light, M., Breck, E., & Burger, J. D. (1999). Deep read: A reading comprehension system. In *Proceedings of the 37th annual meeting of the association for computational linguistics.*

Hirst, G. (2004). Ontology and the lexicon. In S. Staab & R. Studer (Eds.), *Handbook on ontologies* (pp. 209–230). (International Handbooks on Information Systems). Berlin: Springer.

Hitchcock, D., & Verheij, B. (2005). The Toulmin model today: Introduction to the special issue on contemporary work using Stephen Edelston Toulmin's layout of arguments. *Argumentation, 19*, 255–258.

Ho, D. (1998). Indigenous psychologies: Asian perspectives. *Journal of Cross-Cultural Psychology, 29*(1), 88–103.

Ho, Sh.-Sh., & Talukder, A. (2009). Utilizing spatio-temporal text information for cyclone eye annotation in satellite data. *IJCAI Workshop on Cross-Media Information Mining, at the International Joint Conference on Artificial Intelligence (IJCAI'09)*, July 2009.

Hoare, C. A. R. (1985). *Communicating sequential processes.* (Prentice Hall Series in Computer Science). Hemel Hempstead, Hertfordshire, England: Prentice Hall.

Hobbs, D. (1998). There is not a global crime problem. *International Journal of Risk, Security and Crime Prevention, 3*, 139–146.

Hobbs, J. R., Stickel, M. E., Appelt, D. E., & Martin, P. (1993). Interpretation as abduction. In F. C. N. Pereira & B. J. Grosz (Eds.), *Natural language processing* (pp. 69–142). Cambridge, MA: MIT Press. Paper posted on the Web at http://www.ai.sri.com/~hobbs/interp-abduct-ai.ps

Hobbs, P. (2007). Judges' use of humor as a social corrective. *Journal of Pragmatics, 39*(1), 50–68.

Hobson, J. B., & Slee, D. (1993). Rules, cases and networks in a legal domain. *Law, Computers & Artificial Intelligence, 2*(2), 119–135.

Hobson, J. B., & Slee, D. (1994). Indexing the Theft Act 1968 for case based reasoning and artificial neural networks. In *Proceedings of the fourth national conference on law, computers and artificial intelligence*, Exeter, England, p. 96.

Hochberg, J. (1999). Statistical approaches to automatic identification of classified documents. Paper delivered at the CRL/NMSU *International Symposium on New Paradigms in Knowledge and Information Processing*, Las Cruces, NM, December 13. Cited in a quotation from Raskin et al. (2001).

Hochberg, J. (2000). *Automatic identification of classified documents.* Paper delivered at the CERIAS Security Seminar, Purdue University, West Lafayette, IN, February 25. Cited in a quotation from Raskin et al. (2001).

Hoen, P. (1999). *The glossary: Part 4 (P–R).* Laboratory of Palaeobotany and Palynology, University of Utrecht. Retrieved in March 2007 http://www.bio.uu.nl/~palaeo/glossary/glos-p4.htm. Part of his *Glossary of Pollen and Spore Terminology*, 2nd edn. (http://www.bio.uu.nl/~palaeo/glossary/glos-int.htm). First edition (LPP Contribution Series, No. 1, 1994) was by W. Punt, S. Blackmore, S. Nilsson, & A. Le Thomas [sic].

Hogarth, J. (1988). *Sentencing database system: User's guide.* Vancouver, BC: University of British Columbia.

Hohns, H. M. (1987). The place of forensics in engineering. *Forensic Engineering, 1*(1), 3–5.

Holland, B. (2007). Picking the firm favourite: Selecting the right expert can be crucial in court. In *Expert Witness Supplement* to *The New Law Journal*, 157(7294) (London, 26 October 2007), pp. 1486–1487.

Hollien, H. F. (1990). *The acoustics of crime: The new science of forensic phonetics.* New York: Plenum.

Holmes, O. W., Jr. (1881). *The Common Law*. London: Macmillan; Boston: Little, Brown, 1881 (now in .pdf on the Web, in the HeinOnline Legal Classics Library: www.heinonline.org). With a new introd. by T. Griffin, New Brunswick, N.J.: Transaction, 2005. Also, ed. M. D. Howe, Boston: Little, Brown, 1948, 1963, Cambridge, MA: Belknap Press of Harvard University Press, 1963, Oxford: Oxford University Press, 1963, & London: Macmillan, 1968. Also as part of O. W. Holmes, Jr., *The Common Law & Other Writings* (Collected Legal Papers), Birmingham, AL: Legal Classics Library, 1982.

Holmström-Hintikka, G. (1995). Expert witnesses in legal argumentation. *Argumentation, 9*(3), 489–502.

Holmström-Hintikka, G. (2001). Expert witnesses in the model of interrogation. In A. A. Martino & E. Nissan (Eds.), *Software, Formal models, and artificial intelligence for legal evidence*, special issue of *Computing and Informatics, 20*(6), 555–579.

Holstein, J. A. (1985). Jurors' interpretation and jury decision making. *Law and Human Behavior, 9*, 83–100.

Holt, A. W. (1971). Introduction to occurrence systems. In E. L. Jacks (Ed.), *Associative information techniques* (pp. 175–203). New York: American Elsevier.

Holt, A. W. (1988). Diplans: A new language for the study and implementation of coordination. *ACM Transactions on Information Systems (TOIS), 6*(2), 109–125.

Holt, A. W., & Meldman, J. A. (1971). Petri nets and legal systems. *Jurimetrics, 12*(2), 65–75.

Holzner, S. (1998). *XML complete*. New York: McGraw-Hill.

Home Office. (2003). *Police and Criminal Evidence Act 1984. Codes of Practice A–E Revised Edition*. Her Majesty Stationary Office (HMSO).

Hopke, P. K. (1989). Target transformation factor analysis. *Chemometrics and Intelligent Laboratory Systems, 6*, 7–19.

Horgan, T. (2010). Transvaluationism about vagueness: A progress report. *The Southern Journal of Philosophy, 48*(1), 67–94.

Horie, C. V., & Murphy, R. G. (1988). *Conservation of natural history specimens: Vertebrates. Proceedings of the short course at Manchester University*. Manchester, England: University of Manchester Department of Environmental Biology and the Manchester Museum.

Horn, R., Birdwell, J. D., & Leedy, L. W. (1997). Link discovery tool. In *Proceedings of the counterdrug technology assessment center's ONDCP/CTAC international symposium*, Chicago, IL, August 18–22.

Horry, R., & Wright, D. B. (2008). I know your face but not where I saw you: Context memory is impaired for other race faces. *Psychonomic Bulletin & Review, 15*, 610–614.

Horsenlenberg, R., Merckelbach, H., & Josephs, S. (2003). Individual differences and false confessions: A conceptual replication of Kassin and Kiechel (1996). *Psychology, Crime and Law, 9*, 1–18.

Horty, J. F. (1993). Deontic logic as founded on nonmonotonic logic. In J.-J. Meyer & R. Wieringa (Eds.), *Deontic logic in computer science*. Basel: Baltzer. = *Annals of Mathematics and Artificial Intelligence, 9*, 69–91.

Horty, J. F., & Belnap, N. (1995). The deliberative stit: A study of action, omission, ability and obligation. *The Journal of Philosophical Logic, 24*, 583–644.

Horwich, P. (1982). *Probability and evidence*. Cambridge, MA: MIT Press.

Houck, M. M. (1999). Statistics and trace evidence: The tyranny of numbers. *Forensic Science Communications, 1*(3), 1–8.

Hovy, E. (1987a). *Generating natural language under pragmatic constraints*. Ph.D. dissertation, Yale University technical report YALEU/CSD/RR#521.

Hovy, E. (1987b). Generating natural language under pragmatic constraints. *Journal of Pragmatics, 11*(6), 689–719.

Hovy, E. (1988a). *Generating natural language under pragmatic constraints*. Hillsdale, NJ: Erlbaum.

Hovy, E. (1988b). Pauline: An experiment in interpersonal, ideational, and textual language generation by computer. In *Proceedings of the 15th international systemics congress*, East Lansing, MI.

Hovy, E. (1988c). Two types of planning in language generation. In *Proceedings of the 26th annual meeting of the Association for Computational Linguistics (ACL'88)*, State University of New York, Buffalo, NY, 1988, pp. 179–186.

Hovy, E. (1988d). Planning coherent multisentential texts. In *Proceedings of the 26th annual meeting of the Association for Computational Linguistics (ACL'88)*, State University of New York, Buffalo, NY, pp. 163–169.

Hovy, E. (1991) Approaches to the planning of coherent text. In C. L. Paris, W. R. Swartout, & W. C. Mann (Eds.), *Natural language generation in artificial intelligence and computational linguistics* (pp. 83–102). Dordrecht, The Netherlands: Kluwer.

Hovy, E. (1993) Automated discourse generation using discourse structure relations. *Artificial Intelligence, 63*(1/2), 341–385.

Howe, C. J., Barbrook, A. C., Spencer, M., Robinson, P., Bordalejo, B., & Mooney, L. R. (2001). Manuscript evolution. *Endeavour, 25*(3), 121–126.

Howe, M., Candel, I., Otgaar, H., Malone, C., & Wimmer, M. C. (2010). Valence and the development of immediate and long-term false memory illusions. *Memory, 18*, 58–75. http://www.personeel.unimaas.nl/henry.otgaar/HoweOtgaar--%20MEMORY%202010.pdf

Howe, M. L. (2005). Children (but not adults) can inhibit false memories. *Psychological Science, 16*, 927–931.

Howlett, J. B. (1980). Analytical investigative techniques: Tools for complex criminal investigations. *Police Chief, 47*(12), 42–45.

Hu, M., & Liu, B. (2004). Mining and summarizing customer reviews. In *Proceedings of the 10th ACM SIG KDD international conference on knowledge discovery and data mining*, pp. 168–177.

Hu, W., Liao, Y., & Vemuri, V. R. (2003). Robust support vector machines for anomaly detection in computer security. In *Proceedings of the International Conference on Machine Learning and Application (ICMLA 2003)*, pp. 168–174. doi://10.1.1.87.4085

Huard, R .D., & Hayes-Roth, B. (1996). *Children's collaborative playcrafting*. Technical Report KSL-96-17. Stanford, CA: Stanford Knowledge System Laboratory.

Huber R. A., & Headrick A. M. (1999). *Handwriting identification: Facts and fundamentals*. Boca Raton, FL: CRC Press.

Hueske, E. E. (2002). *Shooting incident investigation/Reconstruction tranining manual*.

Hughes, P. A., & Green, A. D. P. (1991). The use of neural networks for fingerpring classification. In *Proceedings of the second IEEE international conference on neural networks*, University of Sussex, England, pp. 79–81.

Hulstijn, J., & Nijholt, A. (Eds.). (1996). *Automatic interpretation and generation of verbal humor: Proceedings of the 12th twente workshop on language technology*, Twente, 1996. Enschede, The Netherlands: University of Twente.

Hunt, L. (2007). Goldman gets the last word on OJ. In her column 'In the frame'. *The Daily Telegraph* (London), 5 July 2007, p. 25.

Hunter, D. (1994). Looking for law in all the wrong places: Legal theory and neural networks. In H. Prakken, A. J. Muntjewerff, A. Soeteman, & R. Winkels (Eds.), *Legal knowledge based systems: Foundations of legal knowledge systems (Jurix'94)* (pp. 55–64). Lelystad, The Netherlands: Koninklijke Vermende.

Hunter, D., Tyree, A., & Zeleznikow, J. (1993). There is less to this argument than meets the eye. *Journal of Law and Information Science, 4*(1), 46–64.

Hunter, J. R., Roberts, C., & Martin, A. (with Heron, C., Knupfer, G. and Pollard, M.). (1997). *Studies in crime: An introduction to forensic archaeology*. London: Batsford, 1995, 1996; London: Routledge, 1997.

Hutchinson, J. R., Ng-Thow-Hing, V., & Anderson, F. C. (2007). A 3D interactive method for estimating body segmental parameters in animals: Application to the turning and running performance of *Tyrannosaurus rex. Journal of Theoretical Biology, 246*(4), 660–680.

Hutton, N., Tata, C., & Wilson, J. N. (1994). Sentencing and information technology: Incidental reform? *International Journal of Law and Information Technology, 2*(3), 255–286.

Hyde, H. A., & Williams, D. W. (1944). The right word. *Pollen Analisis Circulars, 8*, 6.

Iacoviello, F. M. (1997). *La motivazione della sentenza penale e il suo controllo in cassazione.* Milan: Giuffrè.

Iacoviello, F. M. (2006). Regole più chiare sui vizi di motivazione. In *Il Sole 24 Ore, Guida al Diritto*, 10/2006, p. 96.

IACP. (2002). *Criminal intelligence sharing: A national plan for intelligence-led policing at the local, state, and federal levels.* Alexandria, VA: Office of Community Oriented Policing Services and the International Association of Chiefs of Police. Executive summary available to download from http://it.ojp.gov/documents/NCISP_executive_summary.pdf

Idika, N., & Mathur, A. P. (2007). a survey of malware detection techniques. Technical report, Department of Computer Science, West Lafayette, IN: Purdue University.

Igaki, S., Eguchi, S., & Shinzaki, T. (1990). Holographic fingerprint sensor. *Fujitsu Scientific Technical Journal, 25*, 287–296.

Ilan, T. (2005). Rachel, wife of rabbi Akiva. *Jewish Women: A Comprehensive Historical Encyclopedia.* At the *Jewish Women's Archive.* http://jwa.org/encyclopedia/article/rachel-wife-of-rabbi-akiva

Imbrie, J. (1963). *Factor and vector analysis programs for analyzing geologic data.* Tecnical Report no. 6. Office of Naval Research, U.S.A., 83 pp.

Imwinkelried, E. J. (1990). The use of evidence of an accused's uncharged misconduct to prove mens rea: the doctrines that threaten to engulf the character evidence prohibition. *Military Law Review* [Washington, D.C.: Headquarters, Dept. of the Army, Supt. of Docs.], *130*(Fall 1990), 41–76.

Inbau, F. E., Reid, J. E., Buckley, J. P., & Jayne, B. C. (2001). *Criminal interrogation and confessions* (4th ed.). Gaithersberg, MD: Aspen.

Ineichen, M., & Neukom, R. (1995). Daktyloskopieren von mummifizierten Leichen [in German; Dactyloscopy of mummified bodies; with German and English summaries]. *Archiv für Kriminologie, 196*(3/4), 87–92. Our quotation is from the English summary, as reproduced in *Forensic Science Abstracts*, Section 49, 22(2) (1996): p. 57, sec. 4, §395.

Ingleby, R. (1993). *Family law and society.* Sydney: Butterworths.

Inman, K., & Rudin, V. (2002). *An introduction to forensic DNA analysis.* Boca Raton, FL: CRC Press.

Isenor, D. K., & Zaky, S. G. (1986). Fingerprint identification using graph matching. *Pattern Recognition, 19*, 111–112.

Ishikawa, H. (2003). Exact optimization for markov random fields with convex priors. *IEEE Transactions on Pattern Analysis and Machine Intelligence (IEEE PAMI), 25*(10), 1333–1336. http://doi.ieeecomputersociety.org/10.1109/TPAMI.2003.1233908

Ishikawa, H., Yokohama, S., Ohta, M., & Katayama, K. (2005). On mining XML structures based on statistics. In R. Khosla, R. J. Howlett, & L. C. Jain (Eds.), *Knowledge-based intelligent information and engineering systems: 9th international conference, KES 2005*, Melbourne, Australia, September 14–16, 2005, *Proceedings, Part I* (pp. 379–390). (Lecture Notes in Computer Science, Vol. 3684). Berlin: Springer.

Isobe, Y., Seto, Y., & Kataoka, M. (2001). Development of personal authentication system using fingerprint with digital signature technologies. In *Proceedings of the 34th Hawaii International Conference on System Sciences (HICSS-34)*, Hawaii, Track 9. IEEE Computer Society, http://computer.org/proceedings/hicss/0981/volume%209/0981toc. htm; http://computer.org/proceedings/hicss/0981/volume%209/09819077abs.htm

Ito, K., Nakajima, H., Kobayashi, K., Aoki, T., & Higuchi, T. (2004). A fingerprint matching algorithm using phase-only correlation. *IEICE Transactions on Fundamentals, E87-A*(3), 682–691. (IEICE stands for 'The Institute of Electronics, Information and Communication Engineers').

Ivkovic, S., Yearwood, J., & Stranieri, A. (2003). Visualising association rules for feedback within the legal system. In *Proceedings of the ninth International Conference on Artificial Intelligence and Law (ICAIL 2003)*, Edinburgh, Scotland. New York: ACM Press, pp. 214–223.

Izard, C. E. (1971). *The face of emotion.* New York: Appleton-Century-Crofts.

Izard, C. E. (1977). *Human emotions.* ("Emotions, Personality, and Psychotherapy" Series). New York: Plenum.

Izard, C. E. (1982). Comments on emotion and cognition: Can there be a working relationship?. In M. S. Clark & S. T. Fiske (Eds.), *Affect and cognition*. Hillsdale, NJ: Lawrence Erlbaum.

Jackowski, C., Thali, M., Sonnenschein, M., Aghayev, E., Yen, K., Dirnhofer, R., et al. (2004). Visualization and quantification of air embolism structure by processing postmortem MSCT data. *Journal of Forensic Science, 49*(6), 1339–1342.

Jackowski, C., Thali, M. J., Buck, U., Aghayev, E., Sonnenschein, M., Yen, K., et al. (2006). Noninvasive estimation of organ weights by postmortem magnetic resonance imaging and multislice computed tomography. *Investigative Radiology, 41*(7), 572–578.

Jackson, B. S. (1971). Liability for mere intention in early Jewish law. *Hebrew Union College Annual, 42*, 197–225.

Jackson, B. S. (1977). Susanna and the singular history of singular witnesses. *Acta Juridica* (1977), 37–54 (*Essays in Honour of Ben Beinart*).

Jackson, B. S. (1988a). *Law, fact and narrative coherence*. Merseyside (Liverpool, England): Deborah Charles Publications.

Jackson, B. S. (1988b). Narrative models in legal proof. *International Journal for the Semiotics of Law, 1*(3), 225–246.

Jackson, B. S. (1990). *The teaching of Jewish Law in British Universities*. A lecture given at the Institute of Advanced Legal Studies on 26th June 1990. The Second Jewish Law Fellowship Lecture. Oxford: The Yarnton Trust, for the Oxford Centre for Postgraduate Hebrew Studies and the Institute of Advanced Legal Studies. Typeset at Merseyside (Liverpool, England): Deborah Charles Publications.

Jackson, B. S. (1994). Towards a semiotic model of professional practice, with some narrative reflections on the criminal process. *International Journal of the Legal Profession, 1*(1), 55–79. Abingdon, UK: Carfax (later part of Taylor & Francis).

Jackson, B. S. (1995). *Making sense in law*. Liverpool: Deborah Charles Publications.

Jackson, B. S. (1996). 'Anchored narratives' and the interface of law, psychology and semiotics. *Legal and Criminological Psychology, 1*, 17–45. The British Psychological Society.

Jackson, B. S. (1998a). Bentham, truth and the semiotics of law. In M. D. A. Freeman (Ed.), *Legal theory at the end of the millennium* (pp. 493–531). (Current Legal Problems 1998, Vol. 51). Oxford: Oxford University Press.

Jackson, B. S. (1998b). On the atemporality of legal time. In F. Ost & M. van Hoecke (Eds.), *Temps et Droit. Le droit a-t-il pour vocation de durer?* (pp. 225–246). Brussels: E. Bruylant.

Jackson, B. S. (1998c). Truth or proof?: The criminal verdict. *International Journal for the Semiotics of Law, 11*(3), 227–273.

Jackson, B. S. (2010). Review of: S. Azuelos-Atias, *A Pragmatic Analysis of Legal Proofs of Criminal Intent* (Amsterdam: Benjamins, 2007). *International Journal for the Semiotics of Law, 22*(3), 365–372.

Jacoby, J., Mellon, L., Ratledge, E., & Turner, S. (1982). *Prosecutorial decision making: A national study*. Washington, DC: Department of Justice, National Institute of Justice.

Jacovides, M. (2010a). Experiences as complex events. *The Southern Journal of Philosophy, 48*(2), 141–159.

Jacovides, M. (2010b). Do experiences represent? *Inquiry, 53*, 87–103.

Jain, A. K., Bolleand, R., & Pankanti, S. (1999). *Biometrics: Personal identification in networked society*. Norwell, MA & Dordrecht, Netherlands: Kluwer.

Jain, A. K., Hong, L., Pankanti, S., & Bolle, R. (1997). An identity-authentication system using fingerprint. *Proceedings of the IEEE, 85*(9), 1365–1388.

Jain, A. K., & Maltoni, D. (2003). *Handbook of fingerprint recognition*. Berlin: Springer.

Jain, A. K., Prabhakar, S., Hong, L., & Pankanti, S. (2000). Filterbank-based fingerprint matching. *IEEE Transactions on Image Processing, 9*(5), 846–859.

Jain, A. K., Ross, A., & Prabhakar, S. (2001). Fingerprint matching using minutiae and texture features. In *Proceedings of Image Processing International Conference (ICIP)*, Thessaloniki, Greece, 7–10 October 2001, Vol. 3, pp. 282–285.

Jain, R. (2003). Multimedia electronic chronicles. "Media Vision" column in *IEEE Multimedia*, July 2003, pp. 111–112.

Jain, R. (2008). EventWeb: Events and experiences in human centered computing. *IEEE Computer*, February 2008, pp. 42–50.

Jain, R., Kim, P., & Li, Z. (2003). Experiential meeting system. In *Proceedings of the 2003 ACM SIGMM workshop experiential telepresence* (ETP). New York: ACM, pp. 1–12.

James, S. H. (Ed.). (1999). *Scientific and legal applications of bloodstain pattern interpretation.* Boca Raton, FL: CRC Press.

James, S. H., & Eckert, W. G. (1999). *Interpretation of bloodstain evidence at crime scenes* (2nd ed.). Boca Raton, FL: CRC Press.

James, S. H., & Nordby, J. J. (Eds.). (2003). *Forensic science: An introduction to scientific and investigative techniques* (1st ed.). Boca Raton, FL: CRC Press. 2nd edition, 2005. Also published in the 3rd edition, 2009.

James, S. H., Kish, P. E., & Sutton, T. P. (2005a). *Principles of bloodstain pattern analysis* (3rd ed.). Boca Raton, FL: CRC Press.

James, S. H., Kish, P. E., & Sutton, T. P. (2005b). Recognition of bloodstain patterns. In S. H. James & J. J. Nordby (Eds.), *Forensic science: An introduction to scientific and investigative techniques* (1st ed.) [with that title of the book]. Boca Raton, FL: CRC Press. Also in 3rd edition, 2009.

Jameson, A. (1983). Impression monitoring in evaluation-oriented dialog: The role of the listener's assumed expectations and values in the generation of informative statements. In *Proceedings of the eighth International Joint Conference on Artificial Intelligence (IJCAI'83)*, Karlsruhe, Germany. San Mateo, CA: Morgan Kaufmann, Vol. 2, pp. 616–620. http://ijcai.org/search.php

Jamieson, A. (2004). A rational approach to the principles and practice of crime scene investigation: I, principles. *Science & Justice, 44*(1), 3–7.

Janner, G. (1984). *Janner on presentation.* London: Business Books.

Jedrzejek, C., Falkowski, M., & Smolenski, M. (2009). Link analysis of fuel laundering scams and implications of results for scheme understanding and prosecutor strategy. In G. Governatori (Ed.), *Proceedings of legal knowledge and information systems: JURIX 2009, The twenty-second annual conference*, 25 July 2009 (pp. 79–88). Amsterdam: IOS Press.

Jefferson, M. (1992). *Criminal law* (1st ed.). London: Pitman.

Jenkins, R. V. (1987). Words, images, artifacts and sound: Documents for the history of technology. *The British Journal for the History of Science*, Part I,[61] *20*(64), 39–56.

Jennings, N., Parsons, S., Sierra, C., & Faratin, P. (2000). Automated negotiation. In *Proceedings of the fifth international conference on the practical application of intelligent agents and multi-agent technology.* The Practical Application Company, pp. 23–30.

Jerdon, T. C. (1847). *Illustrations of Indian Ornithology. Containing fifty figures of new, unfigured and interesting species of birds, chiefly from the south of India.* Madras [now Chennai], India: Printed by P. R. Hunt, American Mission Press.

Jerdon, T. C. (1862–1864). *The Birds of India. Being a natural history of all the birds known to inhabit continental India, with descriptions of the species, genera, families, tribes, and orders, and a brief notice of such families as are not found in India, making it a manual of ornithology specially adapted for India.* (2 vols., vol. 2 being in 2 parts.) Printed for the Author by the Military Orphan Press, Calcutta, 1862–1864. (Vol. 2, Pt. 2 imprint is G. Wyman in Calcutta, 1864; it is also known as Vol. 3 of the three-parts work. The publisher of all parts is sometimes given as P. S. d'Rozario in Calcutta; this actually is the imprint of the 1877 edition. Another edition of the three volumes was published by C. M. Mission P. in Cherrapoonje, in 1870.)

Jha, S. K., & Yadava, R. D. S. (2010). Development of surface acoustic wave electronic nose using pattern recognition system. *Defence Science Journal, 60*(4), 364–376.

---

[61] *The British Journal for the History of Science* is published in Oxford by Blackwell.

Jiang, X., Yau, W., & Ser, W. (2001). Detecting the fingerprint minutiae by adaptively tracing the gray-level ridge. *Pattern Recognition, 34*, 999–1013.

Jin, F., Fieguth, P., & Winger, L. (2005). Image denoising using complex wavelets and Markov prior models. In M. Kamel & A. Campilho (Eds.), *Image analysis and recognition: Proceedings of the second International Conference (ICIAR 2005)*, Toronto, Canada, September 28–30, 2005 (pp. 73–80). (Lecture Notes in Computer Science, 3656). Berlin: Springer.

Jin, F., Fieguth, P., & Winger, L. (2006). Wavelet video denoising with regularized multiresolution motion estimation. *EURASIP Journal on Applied Signal Processing* (2006), Article 72705.

Joachims, T. (1998). Text categorization with support vector machines: Learning with many relevant features. In *Proceedings of the European Conference on Machine Learning (ECML)*. Berlin: Springer.

Joachims, T., Hofmann, T., Yue, Y., & Yu, C.-N. (2009). Predicting structured objects with support vector machines. *Communications of the ACM, 52*(11), 97–104.

Johnson, M. K. (2007). *Lighting and optical tools for image forensics*. Ph.D. dissertation, Dartmouth College, September 2007. Posted at www.cs.dartmouth.edu/farid/publications/mkjthesis07.html

Johnson, S. L. (1985). Two actions equals no response: Misinterpretations of motorcycle collision causes. In I. D. Brown, R. Goldsmith, K. Coombes, & M. A. Sinclair (Eds.), *Ergonomics international 85: Proceedings of the ninth congress of the international ergonomics association*, Bournemouth, England, September. Basingstoke, Hamsphire: Taylor & Francis.

Johnson, G. W., Ehrlich, R., & Full, W. (2002). Principal components analysis and receptor models in environmental forensics. Chapter 12 In B. L. Murphy & R. D. Morrison (Eds.), *Introduction to environmental forensics* (pp. 461–515). San Diego, CA & London, U.K.: Academic.

Johnson, M. K., & Farid, H. (2005). Exposing digital forgeries by detecting inconsistencies in lighting. At the *ACM Multimedia and Security Workshop*, 2005.

Johnson, M. K., & Farid, H. (2006a). Exposing digital forgeries through chromatic aberration. At the *ACM Multimedia and security Workshop*, Geneva, Switzerland, 2006.

Johnson, M. K., & Farid, H. (2006b). *Metric measurements on a plane from a single image*. Technical Report TR2006-579. Hanover, New Hampshire: Department of Computer Science, Dartmouth College.

Johnson, M. K., & Farid, H. (2007a). Exposing digital forgeries in complex lighting environments. *IEEE Transactions on Information Forensics and Security, 2*(3), 450–461.

Johnson, M. K., & Farid, H. (2007b). Exposing digital forgeries through specular highlights on the eye. At the *Ninth International Workshop on Information Hiding*, Saint Malo, France, 2007.

Johnson, M. K., Hashtroudi, S., & Lindsay, D. S. (1993). Source monitoring. *Psychological Bulletin, 114*, 3–28.

Johnson, P. E., Zualkernan, I. A., & Tukey, D. (1993). Types of expertise: An invariant of problem solving. *International Journal of Man Machine Studies, 39*, 641.

Johnston, V. S., & Caldwell, C. (1997). Tracking a criminal suspect through face space with a genetic algorithm. In T. Bäck, D. B. Fogel, & Z. Michalewics (Eds.), *Handbook of evolutionary computation*. Bristol, England: Institute of Physics Publishing, & New York & Oxford: Oxford University Press.

Jones, A. J. I., & Sergot, M. (1992). Deontic logic in the representation of law: Towards a methodology. *Artificial Intelligence and Law, 1*(1), 45–64.

Jones, C. A. G. (1994). *Expert witnesses: Science, medicine, and the practice of law*. Oxford Socio-Legal Studies. Oxford: Clarendon Press.

Jones, S. S. (1979). The pitfalls of snow white scholarship. *Journal of American Folklore, 90*, 69–73.

Jøsang, A., & Bondi, V. A. (2000). Legal reasoning with subjective logic. *Artificial Intelligence and Law, 8*, 289–315.

Jøsang, A., Ismail, R., & Boyd, C. (2007). A survey of trust and reputation systems for online service provision. *Decision Support Systems, 43*(2), 618–644. doi://10.1016/j.dss.2005.05.019. http://persons.unik.no/josang/papers/JIB2007-DSS.pdf

Josephson, J. R., & Josephson, S. G. (Eds.). (1994). *Abductive inference: Computation, philosophy, technology*. Cambridge: Cambridge University Press.

Joshi, A., & Krishnapuram, R. (1998). Robust fuzzy clustering methods to support web mining. In *Proceedings of the 15th workshop on data mining and knowledge discovery (SIGMOD '98)*, Seattle, WA, June 2–4 1998. Seattle, WA and New York: ACM, 1998, pp. 1–8.

Josselson, R., & Lieblich, A. (Eds.) (1993). *The narrative study of lives*. Newsbury Park, CA, and London: Sage.

Joyce, C. (1984). The detective from the laboratory. *New Scientist*, 15 November 1984, pp. 12–16.

Juan, L., Kreibich, C., Lin, C. H., & Paxson, V. (2008). A tool for offline and live testing of evasion resilience in network intrusion detection systems. In *Detection of Intrusions and Malware, and Vulnerability Assessment: Proceedings of the fifth international conference (DIMVA 2008)*. Berlin: Springer, pp. 267–278.

Judson, G. (1995). Mother guilty in the killings of 5 babies. *The New York Times*, April 22 (Late Edn., Final): Sec. 1, p. 25, col. 5, Metropolitan Desk, Second Front.

Julius, A. (2010). *Trials of the diaspora: A history of anti-semitism in England*. Oxford: Oxford University Press.

Jung, C., Han, I., & Suh, B. (1999). Risk analysis for electronic commerce using case-based reasoning. *International Journal of Intelligent Systems in Accounting, Finance & Management, 8*, 61–73.

Junger, E. P. (1996). Assessing the unique characteristics of close-proximity soil samples: Just how useful is soil evidence? *Journal of Forensic Science, 41*(1), 27–34.

Junkin, T. (2004). *Bloodsworth: The true story of the first death row inmate exonerated by DNA*. Chapel Hill, NC: Algonquin.

Kadane, J., & Schum, D. (1996). *A probabilistic analysis of the Sacco and Vanzetti evidence*. New York: Wiley.

Kahan, D. M., & Braman, D. (2006). Cultural cognition and public policy. *Yale Law & Policy Review, 24*, 147–170.

Kahn, D. (1967). *The codebreakers: The story of secret writing*. New York: Scribner. 2nd edn., 1996.

Kakas, T., Kowalski, K., & Toni, F. (1992). Abductive logic programming. *Journal of Logic and Computation, 2*(6), 719–770.

Kakas, T., Kowalski, R., & Toni, F. (1998). The role of logic programming in abduction. In D. Gabbay, C. J. Hogger, & J. A. Robinson (Eds.), *Handbook of logic in artificial intelligence and programming* (Vol. 5, pp. 235–324). Oxford: Oxford University Press.

Kalender, W. A., Seissler W., Klotz, E., & Vock, P. (1990). Spiral volumetric CT with single-breathhold technique, continuous transport, and continuous scanner rotation. *Radiology, 176*, 181–183.

Kalera, M. K., Srihari, S. N., & Xu, A. (2004). Offline signature verification and identification using distance statistics. *International Journal of Pattern Recognition and Artificial Intelligence, 18*(7), 1339–1360.

Kamisar, Y., LaFave, W. R., Israel, J. H., & King, N. J. (2003). *Modern criminal procedure* (10th ed.). St. Paul, MN: West Publishing.

Kanellis, P., Kiountouzis, E., Kolokotronis, N., & Martakos, D. (2006). *Digital crime and forensic science in cyberspace*. Hershey, PA: Idea Press.

Kangas, L. J., Terrones, K. M., Keppel, R. D., & La Moria, R. D. (2003). Computer aided tracking and characterization of homicides and sexual assaults (CATCH). Sec. 12.6 In J. Mena (Ed.), *Investigative data mining for security and criminal detection* (pp. 364–375). Amsterdam & Boston: Butterworth-Heinemann (of Elsevier).

Kannai, R., Schild, U. J., & Zeleznikow, J. (2007). Modeling the evolution of legal discretion: An artificial intelligence approach. *Ratio Juris, 20*(4), 530–558.

Kantrowitz, M. (1990, July). *GLINDA: Natural language generation in the Oz interactive fiction project*. Technical report CMU-CS-90-158. Pittsburgh, PA: School of Computer Science, Carnegie Mellon University.

Kaptein, H., Prakken, H., & Verheij, B. (Eds.). (2009). *Legal evidence and proof: Statistics, stories, logic.* (Applied Legal Philosophy Series). Farnham, England: Ashgate Publishing.

Karttunen, L. (1976). Discourse referents. *Syntax and Semantics, 7,* 363–385.

Karunatillake, N. (2006). *Argumentation-based negotiation in a social context.* Ph.D. thesis in Computer Science. Southampton, England: University of Southampton, School of Electronics and Computer Science.

Karunatillake, N., & Jennings, N. (2004). Is it worth arguing? In I. Rahwan, P. Moraïs, & C. Reed (Eds.), *Argumentation in multi-agent systems (Proc. of ArgMAS'04)* (pp. 234–250). Berlin: Springer.

Kass, A. M. (1990). *Developing creative hypotheses by adapting explanations.* Doctoral dissertation. New Haven, CT: Computer Science Department, Yale University. Also: Technical Report #6, Institute for the Learning Sciences. Chicago: Northwestern University.

Kass, A. M. (1994). Tweaker: Adapting old explanations to new situations. In R. C. Schank, A. Kass, & C. K. Riesbeck (Eds.), *Inside case-based explanation* (pp. 263–295). Hillsdale, NJ: Erlbaum.

Kass, A. M., Leake, D. B., & Owens, C. (1986). SWALE: A program that explains. In R. C. Schank (Ed.), *Explanation patterns: Understanding mechanically and creatively.* Hillsdale, NJ: Lawrence Erlbaum Associates.

Kassin, S. (1997). The psychology of confession evidence. *American Psychologist, 52,* 221–233.

Kassin, S. (2004). The detection of false confessions. Chapter 8 In P. A. Granhag & L. A. Strömwall (Eds.), *Detection deception in forensic contexts.* Cambridge: Cambridge University Press.

Kassin, S. (2005). On the psychology of confessions: Does *innocence* put the *innocents* at risk? *American Psychologist, 60,* 215–228.

Kassin, S. (2006). A critical appraisal of modern police interrogations. In T. Williamson (Ed.), *Investigative interviewing: Rights, research, regulation* (pp. 207–228). Cullompton: Willan Publishing.

Kassin, S., & Dunn, M. A. (1997). Computer-animated displays and the jury: Facilitative and prejudicial effects. *Law and Human Behavior, 21,* 269–281.

Kassin, S., & Fong, C. T. (1999). "I'm innocent!" Effects of training on judgments of truth and deception in the interrogation room. *Law and Human Behavior, 23,* 499–516.

Kassin, S. M., & Gudjonsson, G. H. (2004). The psychology of confession evidence: A review of the literature and issues. *Psychological Science in the Public Interest, 5,* 35–69.

Kassin, S. M., & Kiechel, K. L. (1996). The social psychology of false confessions: Compliance, internalization, and confabulation. *Psychological Science, 7,* 125–128.

Kassin, S. M., & McNall, K. (1991). Police interrogations and confessions: Communicating promises and threats by pragmatic implication. *Law and Human Behavior, 15,* 233–251.

Kassin, S. M., & Neumann, K. (1997). On the power of confession evidence: An experimental test of the "fundamental difference" hypothesis. *Law and Human Behavior, 21,* 469–484.

Kassin, S., & Norwick, R. (2004). Why people waive their Miranda rights: The power of innocence. *Law and Human Behavior, 28,* 211–221.

Kassin, S. M., & Wrightsman, L. S. (1985). Confession evidence. In S. Kassin & L. Wrightsman (Eds.), *The psychology of evidence and trial procedure* (pp. 67–94). Beverly Hills, CA, & London: Sage.

Kassin, S. M., Goldstein, C. J., & Savitsky, K. (2003). Behavioral confirmation in the interrogation room: On the dangers of presuming guilt. *Law and Human Behavior, 27,* 187–203.

Katai, O., Kawakami, H., Shiose, T., & Notsu, A. (2010). Formalizing coexistential communication as co-creation of Leibnizian spatio-temporal fields. *AI & Society, 25,* 145–153.

Kassin, S. M., Leo, R. A., Meissner, C. A., Richman, K. D., Colwell, L. H., Leach, A.-M., et al. (2007). Police interviewing and interrogation: A self-report survey of police practices and beliefs, *Law and Human Behavior, 31,* 381–400.

Kassin, S. M., Meissner, C. A., & Norwick, R. J. (2005). I'd know a false confession if I saw one, a comparative study of police officers and college students. *Law and Human Behaviour, 29,* 211–227.

Kato, Z., & Pong, T.-C. (2001). A Markov random field image segmentation model using combined color and texture features. In W. Skarbek (Ed.), *Computer Analysis of Images and Patterns: Proceedings of the 9th international conference (CAIP 2001)*, Warsaw, Poland, September 5–7, 2001 (pp. 547–554). (Lecture Notes in Computer Science, 2124). Berlin: Springer.

Katz, L. (1953). A new status index derived from sociometric analysis. *Psychometrika, 18*(1), 39–43.

Kaufman, L., & Rousseeuw, P. J. (2005). *Finding groups in data: An introduction to cluster analysis* (2nd ed.). New York: Wiley. The 1st edn. was of 1990.

Kaufmann, M., & Wagner, D. (Eds.). (2001). *Drawing graphs: Methods and models*. (Lecture Notes in Computer Science, Vol. 2025). Berlin: Springer.

Kaye, B. H. (1995). *Science and the detective: Selected readings in forensic science*. Weinheim, Baden-Württemberg: VCH Verlag.[62]

Kaye, D. (1982). Statistical evidence of discrimination. *Journal of the American Statistical Association, 77*(380), 773–783.

Kaye, D. H. (2003). Questioning a courtroom proof of the uniqueness of fingerprints. *International Statistical Review, 71*, 521–533.

Kaye, D. H., & Koehler, J. (2003). The misquantification of probative value. *Law and Human Behavior, 27*, 645–659.

Kearey, P., & Brooks, M. (1984). *An introduction to geophysical exploration* (1st ed.). Oxford: Blackwell Science (as cited); 2nd edn.: 1991. 3rd edn.: Kearey, P., Brooks, M., & Hill, I., ibid., 2002.

Keh, B. (1984). Scope and applications of forensic entomology. *Annual Review of Entomology, 30*, 137–154. Palo Alto, CA: Annual Reviews.

Keila, P. S., & Skillicorn, D. B. (2005). Structure in the Enron email dataset. In *Proceedings of the SIAM international conference on data mining, SIAM workshop on link analysis, counterterrorism and security*. Philadelphia, PA: SIAM.

Kelly, J., & Davis, L. (1991). Hybridizing the genetic algorithm and the K-nearest neighbour. In *Proceedings of the fourth international conference on genetic algorithms and their applications*. San Mateo, CA: Morgan Kaufman, pp. 377–383.

Kelsen, H. (1967). *Pure theory of law* (M. Knight, Trans., 2nd ed.). Berkeley, CA: University of California Press.

Kempe, D., Kleinberg, J., & Tardos, E. (2003). Maximizing the spread of influence through a social network. In *Proceedings of the ninth ACM SIG KDD interantional conference on knowledge discovery and data mining*, pp. 137–146.

Kempe, D., Kleinberg, J. M., & Tardos, E. (2005). Influential nodes in a diffusion model for social networks. In *Proceedings of ICALP*, pp. 1127–1138.

Kenji, T., Aoki, T., Sasaki, Y., Higuchi, T., & Kobayashi, K. (2003). High-accuracy subpixel image registration based on phase-only correlation. *IEICE Transactions on Fundamentals of Electronics, Communications and Computer Sciences,*[63] *E86-A*(8), 1925–2934.

Kennedy, D. (2001). Legal formalism. In *International encyclopedia of the social and behavioral sciences* (Vol. 13, 8634–8646). Amsterdam: Elsevier.

Kennedy, I. (2007). Public inquiries: Experience from the Bristol public inquiry. In J. Carrier, G. Freilich, V. Hoffbrand, & S. Parbhoo (Eds.), *Law, medicine and ethics: Essays in honour of Lord Jakobovits* (pp. 13–48). London: The Cancerkin Centre, The Royal Free Hospital.

Kephart, J., & Arnold, W. (1994). Automatic extraction of computer virus signatures. At the *4th Virus Bulletin International Conference*, pp. 178–184.

---

[62] http://www.wiley-vch.de The city of Weinheim is approximately 15 km north of Heidelberg and 10 km northeast of Mannheim. Together with these cities, it makes up the Rhine-Neckar triangle.

[63] This is a journal of the Institute of Electronics, Information and Communication Engineers (IEICE).

Keppel, R. D. (1995a). Signature murders: A report of several related cases. *Journal of Forensic Sciences, 40*(4), 658–662.

Keppel, R. D. (1995b). *The riverman: Ted Bundy and I Hunt the Green Rover Killer.* New York: Pocket Books.

Keppel, R. D. (1997). *Signature killers.* New York: Pocket Books.

Keppel, R. D. (2005). Serial offenders: Linking cases by modus operandi and signature. Chapter 30 In S. H. James & J. J. Nordby (Eds.), *Forensic science: An introduction to scientific and investigative techniques* (2nd ed.). Boca Raton, FL: CRC Press. Also in 3rd edition, 2009.

Keppel, R. D., & Weis, J. P. (1997). Time and distance as solvability factors in murder cases. *Journal of Forensic Sciences, 39*(2), 386–401.

Keppens, J. (2007). Towards qualitative approaches to bayesian evidential reasoning. In *Proceedings of the 11th international conference on artificial intelligence and law*, pp. 17–25.

Keppens, J. (2009). Conceptions of vagueness in subjective probability for evidential reasoning. In *Proceedings of the 22nd annual conference on legal knowledge and information systems*, pp. 89–99.

Keppens, J., & Schafer, B. (2003a). Using the box to think outside it: Creative skepticism and computer decision support in criminal investigations. In *Proceedings of the IVR 21st world congress special workshop on artificial intelligence in the law: Creativity in legal problem solving.* http://www.meijigakuin.ac.jp/~yoshino/documents/ivr2003/keppens-schafer.pdf

Keppens, J., & Schafer, B. (2003b). Assumption based peg unification for crime scenario modelling. In *Proceeding of the 2003 conference on legal knowledge and information systems; JURIX 2003: The eighteenth annual conference.* Amsterdam: IOS Press. http://www.jurix.nl/pdf/j05-07.pdf

Keppens, J., & Schafer, B. (2004). "Murdered by persons unknown" – Speculative reasoning in law and logic. In T. Gordon (Ed.), *Legal knowledge and information systems. Jurix 2004: The seventeenth annual conference* (pp. 109–118). Amsterdam: IOS Press.

Keppens, J., & Schafer, B. (2005). Assumption based peg unification for crime scenario modelling. In *Proceeding of the 2005 conference on legal knowledge and information systems; JURIX 2005: The eighteenth annual conference.* (Frontiers in Artificial Intelligence and Applications, 134). Amsterdam: IOS Press, pp. 49–58.

Keppens, J., & Schafer, B. (2006). Knowledge based crime scenario modelling. *Expert Systems with Applications, 30*(2), 203–222.

Keppens, J., & Shen, Q. (2001). On compositional modelling. *Knowledge Engineering Review, 16*(2), 157–200.

Keppens, J., & Shen, Q. (2004). Compositional model repositories via dynamic constraint satisfaction with order-of-magnitude preferences. *Journal of Artificial Intelligence Research, 21,* 499–550.

Keppens, J., Shen, Q., & Lee, M. (2005). Compositional Bayesian modelling and its application to decision support in crime investigation. In *Proceedings of the 19th international workshop on qualitative reasoning*, pp. 138–148.

Keppens, J., Shen, Q., & Price, C. (2010). Compositional Bayesian modelling for computation of evidence collection strategies. *Applied Intelligence.* In press. doi://10.1007/s10489-009-0208-5

Keppens, J., Shen, Q., & Shafer, B. (2005). Probabilistic abductive computation of evidence collection strategies in crime investigation. In *Proceedings of the 10th international conference on artificial intelligence and law*, pp. 215–224.

Keppens, J., & Zeleznikow, J. (2002). On the role of model-based reasoning in decision support in crime investigation. In *Proceedings of the IASTED third international conference on Law and Technology (LawTech2002).* Anaheim, CA: ACTA Press, pp. 77–83.

Keppens, J., & Zeleznikow, J. (2003). A model based reasoning approach for generating plausible crime scene scenarios from evidence In G. Sartor (Ed.), *Proceedings of the ninth International Conference on Artificial Intelligence and Law (ICAIL 2003)*, Edinburgh, Scotland, 24–28 June 2003. New York: ACM Press, pp. 51–59.

Kerr, N. L., Boster, F. J., Callen, C. R., Braz, M. E., O'Brien, B., & Horowitz, I. (2008). Jury nullification instructions as amplifiers of bias. *International Commentary on Evidence, 6*(1), Article 2. http://www.bepress.com/ice/vol6/iss1/art2

Khuwaja, G. A. (2004). Best parameter-based compression of fingerprints with wavelet packets. *International Journal of Computer Applications in Technology, 19,* 51–62.

Khuwaja, G. A. (2006). A multimodal biometric identification system using compressed finger images. *Cybernetics and Systems, 37*(1), 23–46.

Kibble, R. (2004). Elements of social semantics for argumentative dialogue. In F. Grasso, C. Reed, & G. Carenini (Eds.), *Proceedings of the fourth workshop on Computational Models of Natural Argument (CMNA IV) at ECAI 2004,* Valencia, Spain, pp. 25–28.

Kieras, D. (2001). *Using the keystroke-level model to estimate execution times.* University of Michigan. http://www.cs.loyola.edu/~lawrie/CS774/S06/homework/klm.pdf

Kim, B. M., & Henry, R. C. (1999). Extension of self-modeling curve resolution to mixtures of more than 3 components. Part 2: Finding the complete solution. *Chemometrics and Intelligent Laboratory Systems, 49,* 67–77.

Kim, D. S., & Park, J. S. (2003). Network-based intrusion detection with support vector machines. In H.-K. Kahng (Ed.), *Information networking, networking technologies for enhanced internet services international conference (ICOIN 2003),* Cheju Island, Korea, February 12–14, 2003 (pp. 747–756). (Lecture Notes in Computer Science, Vol. 2662.) Heidelberg & Berlin: Springer.

Kim, P., Gargi, U., & Jain, R. (2005). Event-based multimedia chronicling system. In *Proceedings of the 2nd ACM workshop on Continuous Archival and Retrieval of Personal Experiences (CARPE'05),* Singapore, November 2005.

Kim, S.-M., & Hovy, E. (2006). Identifying and analyzing judgment opinions. In *Proceedings of HLT/NAACL-2006,* New York City, NY, pp. 200–207.

Kinder, J., Katzenbeisser, S., Schallhart, C., & Veith, H. (2005). Detecting malicious code by model checking. In K. Julisch & C. Krügel (Eds.), *Detection of intrusions and malware, and vulnerability assessment: Proceedings of the second international conference (DIMVA 2005),* Vienna, Austria, July 7–8, 2005 (pp. 174–187). (Lecture Notes in Computer Science, Vol. 3548.) Berlin: Springer.

Kindermann, R., & Snell, J. R. (1980). *Markov random fields and their applications.* (Contemporary Mathematics, 1.) Providence, RI: American Mathematical Society.

Kingsnorth, R., MacIntosh, R., & Sutherland, S. (2002). Criminal charge or probation violation? Prosecutorial discretion and implications for research in criminal court processing. *Criminology: An Interdisciplinary Journal, 40,* 553–578. doi://10.1111/j.1745-9125.2002.tb00966.x

Kingston, J., Schafer, B., & Vandenberghe, W. (2003). No model behaviour: Ontologies for fraud detection. In *Proceedings of law and the semantic web,* pp. 233–247.

Kingston, J., Schafer, B., & Vandenberghe, W. (2004). Towards a financial fraud ontology: A legal modelling approach. *Artificial Intelligence and Law, 12*(4), 419–446.

Kingston, J., & Vandenberghe, W. (2003). A comparison of a regulatory ontology with existing legal ontology frameworks. In *OTM Workshops 2003 =* R. Meersman & Z. Tari (Eds.), *On The Move to Meaningful Internet Systems 2003: [Proceedings of the] OTM 2003 Workshops, OTM Confederated International Workshops, HCI-SWWA, IPW, JTRES, WORM, WMS, and WRSM 2003,* Catania, Sicily, Italy, 3–7 November 2003 (pp. 648–661). (Lecture Notes in Computer Science, Vol. 2889). Berlin: Springer.

Kingston, J., Schafer, B., & Vandenberghe, W. (2004). Towards a financial fraud ontology: A legal modelling approach. *Artificial Intelligence and Law, 12,* 419–446.

Kinton, R., Ceserani, V., & Foskett, D. (1992). *The theory of catering* (7th ed.). London: Hodder & Stoughton.

Kintsch, W., & van Dijk, T. (1978). Recalling and summarizing stories. In W. Dressier (Ed.), *Current trends in textlinguistics.* Berlin: de Gruyter.

Kirkpatrick, S., Gellatt, D., & Vecchi, M. (1983). Optimization by simulated annealing. *Science, 220,* 671–680.

Kirschenbaum, A. (1970). *Self-incrimination in Jewish law.* New York: Burning Bush Press.

Kirschner, P. A., Buckingham Shum, S. J., & Carr, C. S. (Eds.). (2003). *Visualizing argumentation.* London & Berlin: Springer.

Kitayama, Sh., & Markus, H. R. (Eds.). (1994). *Emotion and culture: Empirical studies of mutual influence.* Washington, DC: American Psychological Association.

Klein, S. (1973). Automatic novel writer: A status report. In J. S. Petöfi (Ed.), *Papers in text analysis and text description.* (Research in Text Theory, 3). Berlin: de Gruyter.

Klein, S. (2002). The analogical foundations of creativity in language, culture & the arts: The upper paleolithic to 2100CE. In P. McKevitt, C. Mulvihill, & S. O'Nuallin (Eds.), *Language, vision & music* (pp. 347–371). Amsterdam: John Benjamin.

Klein, S., Aeschlimann, J. F., Appelbaum, M. A., Blasiger, D. F., Curtis, E. J., Foster, M., et al. (1974). Modeling propp and lévi-strauss in a metasymbolic simulation system. In H. Jason & D. Segal (Eds.), *Patterns in oral literature* (pp. 141–171). Chicago, IL: Aldine. World Anthropology Series. The Hague: Mouton.

Klein, S., Aeschliman, J. F., Applebaum, M. A., Blasiger, D. F., Curtis, E. J., Foster, M., et al. (1976, March). Simulation d'hypothèses émisés par Propp et Lévi-Strauss en utilisant un système de simulation meta-symbolique. *Informatique et Sciences Humaines, 28,* 63–133. A revised and expanded French translation of Klein et al. (1974).

Klein, S., & Simmons, R. F. (1963a). A computational approach to grammatical coding of English words. *Journal of the Association for Computing Machinery, 10,* 334–347.

Klein, S., & Simmons, R. F. (1963b). Syntactic dependence and the computer generation of coherent discourse. *Mechanical Translation and Computational Linguistics, 7,* 50–61.

Kleinberg, J. (1998). Authoritative sources in a hyperlinked environment. In *Proceedings of the ninth ACM-SIAM symposium on discrete algorithms.* New York: ACM, & Philadelphia, PA: SIAM. Extended version in *Journal of the ACM,* 46 (1999). Also appears as IBM Research Report RJ 10076, May 1997. http://www.cs.cornell.edu/home/kleinber/auth.pdf

Kleinberg, J. (2000a). Navigation in a small world. *Nature, 406,* 845. http://www.cs.cornell.edu/home/kleiber/nat00.pdf

Kleinberg, J. (2000b). The small-world phenomenon: An algorithmic perspective. In *Proceedings of the 32nd ACM symposium on theory of computing.* Also appears as Cornell Computer Science Technical Report 99-1776 (October 1999). http://www.cs.cornell.edu/home/kleiber/swn.pdf

Kleinberg, J. (2001). Small-world phenomena and the dynamics of information. *Advances in Neural Information Processing Systems (NIPS), 14.* http://www.cs.cornell.edu/home/kleiber/nips14.pdf

Kleinberg, J. (2004). The small-world phenomenon and decentralized search. A short essay as part of *Math Awareness Month 2004,* appearing in *SIAM News, 37*(3), April 2004. http://www.mathaware.org/mam/04/essays/smallworld/html

Kleinberg, J. (2006). Complex networks and decentralized search algorithms. In *Proceedings of the International Congress of Mathematicians (ICM),* 2006. http://www.cs.cornell.edu/home/kleiber/icm06-swn.pdf

Klimt, B., & Yang, Y. (2004a). The Enron corpus: A new dataset for email classification research. In *Proceedings of the European Conference on Machine Learning (ECML),* 2004, pp. 217–226.

Klimt, B., & Yang, Y. (2004b). Introducing the Enron corpus. At the *First Conference on Email and Anti-Spam. CEAS 2004.* Mountain View, CA.

Klock, B. A. (2001, April). *Project plan for the evaluation of X-ray threat detection of explosives at different subcertification weights.* DOT/FAA/AR-01/81, Washington, DC: Office of Aviation Research. http://www.tc.faa.gov/its/worldpac/techrpt/ar01-81.pdf

Klovdahl, A. S. (1981). A note on images of networks. *Social Networks, 3,* 197–214.

Klusch, M., & Sycara, K. (2001). Brokering and matchmaking for coordination of agent societies: A survey. Chapter 8 In A. Omicini, F. Zambonell, M. Klusch, & R. Tolksdorf (Eds.), *Coordination of internet agents: Models, technologies, and applications* (pp. 197–224). Berlin: Springer.

Kneller, W., Memon, A., & Stevenage, S. (2001). Simultaneous and sequential lineups: Decision processes of accurate and inaccurate witnesses. *Applied Cognitive Psychology, 15,* 659–671.

Knight, B., Ma, J., & Nissan, E. (1998). Representing temporal knowledge in legal discourse. In A. A. Martino & E. Nissan (Eds.), *Formal models of legal time.*, Special issue, *Information and Communications Technology Law, 7*(3), 199–211.

Knight, B., Nissan, E., & Ma, J. (Eds.). (1999). Temporal logic in engineering. Special issue, *Artificial Intelligence for Engineering Design, Analysis and Manufacturing (AIEDAM)*, 13(2).

Knott, A. W. (1987). Are you an expert? *Forensic Engineering, 1*(1), 7–16.

Knox, A. G. (1993). Richard Meinertzhagen – a case of fraud examined. *Ibis, 135*(3), July 1993, 320–325.

Kobayashi, M., & Ito, T. (2008). A transactional relationship visualization system in Internet auctions. *Studies in Computational Intelligence, 110*, 87–99.

Koehler, J. J. (2008). A welcome exchange on the scientific status of fingerprinting (Editorial). *Law, Probability and Risk, 7*, 85–86.

Kohonen, T. (1982). Self-organised formation of topologically correct feature maps. *Biological Cybernetics, 43*, 59–69.

Kohonen, T. (1990). The self-organizing map. *Proceedings of the IEEE, 78*(9), 1464–1480.

Köller, N., Nissen, K., Reiß, M., & Sadorf, E. (2004). *Probabilistische Schlussfolgerungen in Schriftgutachten./Probability conclusions in expert opinions on handwriting.* Munich, Germany: Luchterhand. This document, available in German & English, can be downloaded from: www.bka.de/vorbeugung/pub/probabilistische_schlussfolgerungen_in_schriftgutachten. pdf

Kolmogorov, V., & Zabih, R. (2004). What energy functions can be minimized via graph cuts? *IEEE Transactions on Pattern Analysis and Machine Intelligence (IEEE PAMI), 26*, 147–159.

Kolodner, J. L. (1984). *Retrieval and organizational strategies in conceptual memory: A computer model.* Hillsdale, NJ: Erlbaum.

Kong, A., Zhang, D., & Kamel, M. (2006). Palmprint identification using feature-level fusion. *Pattern Recognition, 29*(3), 478–487.

Kompatsiaris, Y., & Hobson, P. (Eds.). (2008). *Semantic multimedia and ontologies: Theory and applications.* Berlin: Springer.

Koppenhaver, K. (2007). *Forensic document examination, principles and practice.* Totowa, NJ: Humana Press.

Kort, F. (1964). Simultaneous equations and Boolean Algebra. In G. Schubert (Ed.), *Judicial behaviour:*
A reader in theory and research (pp. 477–491). Chicago, IL: Rand McNally and Company.

Kosala, R., & Blockeel, H. (2000). Web mining research: A survey. *ACM SIGKDD Explorations, 2*(1), 1–15.

Kothari, R., & Dong, M. (2002). Decision trees for classification: A review and some new results. In S. K. Pal & A. Pla (Eds.), *Pattern Recognition from classical to modern approaches* (pp. 169–186). Singapore: World Scientific.

Kou, Y., Lu, C. T., Sirwongwattana, S., & Huang Y. P. (2004). Survey of fraud detection techniques. In *Proceedings of the 2004 International Conference on Networking, Sensing, and Control*, Taipei, Taiwan, 2004, pp. 749–754.

Kovacs, D. (1992). *Family property proceedings in Australia.* Sydney: Butterworths.

Kovács-Vajna, Z. M. (2000). A fingerprint verification system based on triangular matching and dynamic time warping. *IEEE Transactions on Pattern Analysis and Machine Intelligence (IEEE PAMI), 22*(11), 1266–1276.

Kovács-Vajna, Z. M., Rovatti, R., & Frazzoni, M. (2000). Fingerprint ridge distance computation methodologies. *Pattern Recognition, 33*(1), 69–80.

Kowalski, R. (1979). *Logic for problem solving.* New York: Elsevier North-Holland.

Kowalski, R. A., & Toni, F. (1996). Abstract argumentation. *Artificial Intelligence and Law, 4*(3/4), 275–296. Also In H. Prakken & G. Sartor (Eds.), *Logical models of legal argumentation.* Dordrecht, The Netherlands: Kluwer, 1997.

Krackhardt, D. (1996). Social networks and the liability of newness for managers. In C. L. Cooper & D. M. Rousseau (Eds.), *Trends in organizational behavior* (Vol. 3, pp. 159–173). New York & Chichester, West Sussex, England: John Wiley & Sons.

Krackhardt, D., Blythe, J., & McGrath, C. (1994). KrackPlot 3.0: An improved network drawing program. *Connections, 17*(2), 53–55.

Krane, D., Ford, S., Gilder, J., Inman, K., Jamieson, A., Koppl, R., et al. (2008). Sequential unmasking: A means of minimizing observer effects in forensic DNA interpretation. *Journal of Forensic Sciences, 53*(4),1006–1007. http://www.bioforensics.com/sequential_unmasking/ http://www.bioforensics.com/sequential_unmasking/Sequential_Unmasking_2008.pdf

Kraus, S. (1996). An overview of incentive contracting. *Artificial Intelligence, 83*(2), 297–346.

Kraus, S. (2001). *Strategic negotiation in multiagent environments.* Cambridge, MA: The MIT Press.

Kraus, S., Sycara, K., & Evenchik, A. (1998). Reaching agreements through argumentation: A logical model and implementation. *Artificial Intelligence, 104*, 1–69.

Krause, P., Ambler, S., Elvang-Goransson, M., & Fox, J. (1995). A logic of argumentation for reasoning under uncertainty. *Computational Intelligence, 11*(1), 113–131.

Krawczak, M., & Schmidtke, J. (1994). *DNA fingerprinting.* Medical Perspectives Series. Oxford: BIOS Scientific.

Kreibich, C., & Crowcroft, J. (2004). Honeycomb: Creating intrusion detection signatures using honeypots. *Computer Communication Review, 34*(1), 51–56.

Kreibich, C., & Jahnke, M. (Eds.). (2010). *Detection of Intrusions and Malware, and Vulnerability Assessment: Proceedings of the seventh international conference (DIMVA 2010)*, Bonn, Germany, July 8–9, 2010. (Lecture Notes in Computer Science, Vol. 6201). Berlin: Springer.

Kristensen, T. (2010). Fingerprint identification: A support vector machine approach. In *Proceedings of the second International Conference on Agents and Artificial Intelligence, ICAART 2010*, Valencia, Spain, 22–24 January 2010, pp. 451–458.

Krogman, W. M., & İşcan, M. Y. (1986). *The human Skeleton in forensic medicine.* Springfield, IL: Charles C. Thomas.

Kronman, A. T. (1988). Jurisprudential responses to legal realism. *Cornell Law Review, 73*, 335–340. Also, New Haven, CT: Yale Law School, Faculty Scholarship Series, Paper 1061. http://digitalcommons.law.yale.edu/fss_papers/1061 or: http://digitalcommons. law.yale.edu/cgi/viewcontent.cgi?article=2060&context=fss_papers&sei-redir=1# search="Kronman+"Jurisprudential+responses+to+legal+realism""

Kruse, W., & Heiser, J. (2002). *Computer forensics: Incident response essentials.* Reading, MA: Addison-Wesley.

Kruskal, J. B., & Wish, M. (1978). *Multidimensional scaling.* Beverly Hills, CA & London: Sage.

Ku, Y., Chen, Y.-C., & Chiu, C. (2007a). A proposed data mining approach for internet auction fraud detection. In C. C. Yang, D. Zeng, M. Chau, K. Chang, Q. Yang, X. Cheng, et al. (Eds.), *Intelligence and security informatics: Proceedings of the Pacific Asia Workshop, PAISI 2007*, Chengdu, China, April 11–12, 2007 (pp. 238–243). (Lecture Notes in Computer Science, 4430). Berlin: Springer.

Ku, Y., Chen, Y.-C., Wu, K.-C., & Chiu, C. (2007b). An empirical analysis of online gaming crime characteristics from 2002 to 2004. In C. C. Yang, D. Zeng, M. Chau, K. Chang, Q. Yang, X. Cheng, et al. (Eds.), *Intelligence and security informatics: Proceedings of the Pacific Asia Workshop, PAISI 2007*, Chengdu, China, April 11–12, 2007 (pp. 34–45). (Lecture Notes in Computer Science, 4430). Berlin: Springer.

Kuflik, T., Nissan, E., & Puni, G. (1989). Finding excuses with ALIBI: Alternative plans that are deontically more defensible. In *Proceedings of the International Symposium on Communication, Meaning and Knowledge vs. Information Technology*, Lisbon, September. Then again in *Computers and Artificial Intelligence, 10*(4), 297–325, 1991. Then in a selection from the Lisbon conference: Lopes Alves, J. (Ed.). (1992). *Information technology & society: Theory, uses, impacts* (pp. 484–510). Lisbon: Associação Portuguesa para o Desenvolvimento das Comunicações (APDC), & Sociedade Portuguesa de Filosofia (SPF).

Kuglin, C. D., & Hines, D. C. (1975). The phase correlation image alignment method. In *Proceedings of the international conference on cybernetics and society*, pp. 163–165.

Kumar, A., Wong, D. C. M., Shen, H. C., & Jain, A. K. (2003). Personal verification using palmprint and hand geometry biometric. In *Proceedings of the fourth international conference on Audio and Video-Based Biometric Person Authentication (AVBPA)*, Guildford, UK, pp. 668–678.

Kurosawa, A. (director) 1950. *Rashomon* (a film). Producer: Daiei (Japan). Script: T. Matsuama. Based on the short story *In the Forest* (1921), by R. Akutagawa.

Kurzon, D. (1985). How lawyers tell their tales. *Poetics, 14*, 467–481.

Kvart, I. (1994). Overall positive causal impact. *Canadian Journal of Philosophy, 24*(2), 205–227.

Kwan, M., Chow, K. P., Law, F., & Lai, P. (2008). Reasoning about evidence using Bayesian networks. In I. Ray & S. Shenoy (Eds.), *Advances in Digital Forensics IV*, International Federation for Information Processing (IFIP), Tokyo, January 2008 (pp. 142–155). Berlin: Springer.

Kwan, M. Y. K., Overill, R. E., Chow, K. P., Silomon, J. A. M., Tse, H., Law, F. Y. W., et al. (2010). Internet auction fraud investigations. Chapter 7 in *Advances in Digital Forensics VI: Proceedings of the 6th annual IFIP WG 11.9 international conference on digital forensics*, Hong Kong, 3–6 January 2010. Berlin: Springer, on behalf of the International Federation for Information Processing (IFIP), pp. 95–106. http://www.kcl.ac.uk/staff/richard/IFIP_2010

Labor, E. (1994). Review of: J. Watson, *Forensic Fictions: The Lawyer Figure in Faulkner* (Athens, Georgia, U.S.A.: University of Georgia Press, 1993). *American Literature,*[64] 66(4), 858–859.

LaFond, T., & Neville, J. (2010). Randomization tests for distinguishing social influence and homophily effects. In *Proceedings of the International World Wide Web Conference (WWW)*. http://www.cs.purdue.edu/homes/neville/papers/lafond-neville-www2010.pdf

Lagerwerf, L. (1998). *Causal connectives have presuppositions: Effects on coherence and discourse structure*. Doctoral dissertation, Netherlands Graduate School of Linguistics, Vol. 10. The Hague, The Nertherlands: Holland Academic.

Lakoff, G. P. (1972). Structural complexity in fairy tales. *The Study of Man, 1*, 128–150.

Lam, S. C. J. (2007). *Methods for resolving inconsistencies in ontologies*. Ph.D. thesis. Department of Computing Science, University of Aberdeen, Aberdeen, Scotland.

Lamarque, P. V., & Olsen, S. H. (1994). *Truth, fiction, and literature: A philosophical perspective*. Oxford: Clarendon Press.

Landman, F. (1986). *Towards a theory of information: The status of partial objects in semantics*. Dordrecht, The Netherlands: Foris.

Lane, B., Tingey, M., & Tingey, R. (Eds.). (1993). *The encyclopedia of forensic science*. London: Headline.

Lane, S. M., & Zaragoza, M. S. (2007). A little elaboration goes a long way: The role of generation in eyewitness suggestibility. *Memory & Cognition, 35*(6), 125–126.

Lang, R. R. (2003). Story grammars: Return of a theory. Chapter 12 In M. Mateas & P. Sengers (Eds.), *Narrative intelligence* (pp. 199–212). Amsterdam: Benjamins.

Langbein, J. H. (1977). *Torture and the law of proof: Europe and England in the Ancien Régime*. Chicago: University of Chicago Press.

Lange, T. E., & Dyer, M. G. (1989). High-level inferencing in a connectionist network. *Connection Science, 1*, 181–217. ftp://ftp.cs.ucla.edu/tech-report/198_-reports/890063.pdf

Lange, T. E., & Wharton, C. M. (1992). *Remind: Retrieval from episodic memory by inferencing and disambiguation*. Technical Teport 920047. Los Angeles, CA: Computer Science Department, University of California, Los Angeles. ftp://ftp.cs.ucla.edu/tech-report/1992-reports/920047.pdf

Langenburg, G. M. (2004). Pilot study: A statistical snalysis of the ACE-V methodology – Analysis stage. *Journal of Forensic Identification, 54*, 64–79.

Langston, M.C., Trabasso, T., & Magliano, J.P. (1999). A connectionist model of narrative comprehension. In A. Ram & K. Moorman (Eds.), *Understanding language understanding* (pp. 181–226). Cambridge, MA: MIT Press.

---

[64] The journal *American Literature* is published in Durham, NC, by Duke University Press.

Lara-Rosano, F., & del Socorro Téllez-Silva, M. (2003). Fuzzy support systems for discretionary judicial decision making. In V. Palade, R. J. Howlett, & L. C. Jain (Eds.), *Knowledge-based intelligent information and engineering systems: 7th international conference, KES 2003,* Oxford, UK, September 3–5, 2003, *Proceedings,* Part II (pp. 94–100). (Lecture Notes in Computer Science, LNAI, Vol. 2774.) Berlin: Springer.

Lassiter, D. (Ed.). (2004). *Interrogations, confessions and entrapment.* Dordrecht, The Netherlands: Kluwer.

Latendresse, M. (2005). Masquerade detection via customized grammars. In K. Julisch & C. Krügel (Eds.), *Detection of intrusions and malware, and vulnerability assessment: Proceedings of the second international conference (DIMVA 2005),* Vienna, Austria, July 7–8, 2005 (pp. 141–159). Lecture Notes in Computer Science, Vol. 3548. Berlin: Springer.

Latour, B. (1986). Editorial. *Technologos, 3* (Paris: Laboratoire d'Informatique pour les Sciences de l'Homme), 3–5.

Latourette, K. S. (1936). *Biographical Memoir of Berthold Laufer, 1874–1934.* Biographical Memoirs, 18(3). National Academy of Sciences of the United States of America. http://books.nap.edu/html/biomems/blaufer.pdf

Laufer, B. (1913). History of the fingerprint system. In *Smithsonian Report for 1912* (pp. 631–652) (with 7 plates). Washington, DC: Smithsonian Institution.

Laufer, B. (1917, May 25). Concerning the history of finger-prints. *Science,* 504, 505.

Laughery, K. R., & Fowler, R. H. (1980). Sketch artist and Identi-kit procedures for recalling faces. *Journal of Applied Psychology, 65*(3), 307–316.

Laurel, B. (1986). *Towards the design of a computer-based interactive fantasy system.* Ph.D. Dissertation. Cleveland, OH: The Ohio State University.

Lauritsen, J. L. (2005). Social and scientific influences on the measurement of criminal victimization. *Journal of Quantitative Criminology, 21*(3), 245–266.

Lauritsen, J. L. (2010). Advances and challenges in empirical studies of victimization. *Journal of Quantitative Criminology, 26*(4), 501–508.

Lauritzen, S. L., & Mortera, J. (2002). Bounding the number of contributors to mixed DNA stains. *Forensic Science International, 130,* 125–126.

Laxman, S., & Sastry, P. S. (2006). A survey of temporal data mining. *SADHANA, Academy Proceedings in Engineering Sciences, 31*(2), 173–198.

Leach, A.-M., Talwar, V., Lee, K., Bala, N., & Lindsay, R. C. L. (2004). "Intuitive" lie detection of children's deception by law enforcement officials and university students. *Law and Human Behavior, 28,* 661–685.

Leake, D. B. (1992). *Evaluating explanations: A content theory.* Hillsdale, NJ: Erlbaum.

Leake, D. B. (1994). Accepter: Evaluating explanations. In R. C. Schank, A. Kass, & C. K. Riesbeck (Eds.), *Inside case-based explanation* (pp. 167–206). Hillsdale, NJ: Erlbaum.

Leake, D. B. (1996). CBR in context: The present and the future. Chapter 1 In D. B. Leake (Ed.), *Case-based reasoning: Experiences, lessons, and future directions.* Menlo Park, CA: AAAI Press, and Cambridge, MA: MIT Press.

Leary, R. M. (2001). *Evaluation of the impact of the FLINTS software system in West Midlands and Elsewhere.* London: Home Office Policing & Reducing Crime Unit, The Home Office.

Leary, R. M. (2002). *The role of the National Intelligence Model and FLINTS in improving police performance.* London: Home Office Policing & Reducing Crime Unit, The Home Office. http://www.homeoffice.gov.uk/docs2/

Leary, R. M. (2004). *Evidential reasoning and analytical techniques in criminal pre-trial fact investigation.* Ph.D. thesis, University College, London.

Leary, R. M., VanDenBerghe, W., & Zeleznikow, J. (2003a). User requirements for financial fraud modeling. In *Proceedings of BILETA 2003: British & Irish Law, Education & Technology Association 18th annual conference.*

Leary, R. M., Vandenberghe, W., & Zeleznikow, J. (2003b). Towards a financial fraud ontology: A legal modelling approach. Presentation at the *ICAIL Workshop on Legal Ontologies and Web Based Legal Information Management.* Originally a technical report; Edinburgh, Scotland:

Joseph Bell Centre for Forensic Statistics and Legal Reasoning, School of Law, University of Edinburgh. http://www.forensic-pathways.com/PDFs/Leary-Ontology.pdf

Lebbah, M., Bennani, Y., & Rogovschi, N. (2009). Learning self-organizing maps as a mixture Markov models. In *Proceedings of the third International Conference on Complex Systems and Applications (ICCSA'09)*, Le Havre, Normandy, France, June 29–July 02, 2009. pp. 54–59.

Lebowitz, M. (1983). Creating a story-telling universe. In *Proceedings of the 8th international joint conference on artificial intelligence*, pp. 63–65.

Lee, C.-J., & Wang, S.-D. (1999). A Gabor filter-base approach to fingerprint recognition. In *Proceedings of the IEEE workshop on Signal Processing Systems (SiPS 99)*, pp. 371–378.

Lee, G., Flowers, M., & Dyer, M. G. (1992). Learning distributed representations for conceptual knowledge and their application to script-based story processing. Chapter 11 In N. Sharkey (Ed.), *Connectionist natural language processing: Readings from connection science* (pp. 215–247). Norwell, MA: Kluwer. Reprinted from *Connection Science*, 2(4).

Lee, H. C., & Gaensslen, R. E. (Eds.). (1991). *Advances in fingerprint technology*. Elsevier Series in Forensic and Police Science. New York & Amsterdam: Elsevier. 2nd edition published in the CRC Series in Forensic and Police Science, Boca Raton, Florida: CRC Press, 2001.

Lee, H. C., Palmbach, T., & Miller, M. T. (2001). *Henry Lee's crime scene handbook*. London: Academic.

Lee, J.-M., & Hwang, B.-Y. (2005). Two-phase path retrieval method for similar XML document retrieval. In R. Khosla, R. J. Howlett, & L. C. Jain (Eds.), *Knowledge-based intelligent information and engineering systems: 9th international conference, KES 2005*, Melbourne, Australia, September 14–16, 2005, *Proceedings, Part I* (pp. 967–971). (Lecture Notes in Computer Science, Vol. 3684.) Berlin: Springer.

Lee, R. (1995). An NLToolset-based system for MUC-6. In *Proceedings of the sixth Message Understanding Conference (MUC-6)*. Columbia, MD: DARPA, and San Mateo, CA: Morgan Kaufmann Publishers, pp. 249–261.

Lee, R. (1998). Automatic information extraction from documents: A tool for intelligence and law enforcement analysts. In D. Jensen & H. Goldberg (Eds.), *Artificial intelligence and link analysis: Papers from the 1998 fall symposium* (pp. 63–65). Menlo Park, CA: AAAI Press.

Leff, L. (2001). Automated reasoning with legal XML documents. In *Proceedings of the eighth international conference on artificial intelligence and law*, St. Louis, MO. New York: ACM Press, pp. 215–216.

Legrand, J. (1999). Some guidelines for fuzzy sets application in legal reasoning. *Artificial Intelligence and Law, 7*(2/3), 235–257.

Lehmann, F. (Ed.). (1992). *Semantic networks in artificial intelligence*. Oxford: Pergamon Press. Also published as a special issue of *Computers and Mathematics with Applications, 23*(6–9).

Lehnert, W., & Loiselle, C. (1985). Plot unit recognition for narratives. In G. Tonfoni (Ed.), *Artificial intelligence and text-understanding: Plot units and summarization procedures* (pp. 9–47). Quaderni di Ricerca Linguistica, Vol. 6. Parma, Italy: Edizioni Zara.

Lehnert, W. G. (1977). Question answering in a story understanding system. *Cognitive Science, 1*, 47–73.

Lehnert, W. G. (1978). *The process of question answering*. Hillsdale, NJ: Erlbaum.

Lehnert, W. G. (1981). Plot units and narrative summarization. *Cognitive Science, 4*, 293–331.

Lehnert, W. G. (1982). Plot units: A narrative summarization strategy. In W. G. Lehnert & M. H. Ringle (Eds.), *Strategies for natural language processing* (pp. 375–412). Hillsdale, NJ: Erlbaum.

Lehnert, W. G., Alker, H., & Schneider, D. (1983). The heroic Jesus: The affective plot structure for Toynbee's Christus Patiens. In S. K. Burton & D. D. Short (Eds.), *Proceedings of the sixth international conference on computers and the humanities* (pp. 358–367). Rockville, MD: Computer Science Press.

Lehnert, W. G., Dyer, M. G., Johnson, P. N., Yang, C. J., & Harley, S. (1983). BORIS: An experiment in in-depth understanding of narratives. *Artificial Intelligence, 20*(2), 15–62.

Leippe, M. R. (1985). The influence of eyewitness nonidentifications on mock jurors' judgments of a court case. *Journal of Applied Social Psychology, 15*, 656–672.

Leith, P. (1998). The judge and the computer: How best 'decision support'? *Artificial Intelligence and Law, 6*, 289–309.

Lemar, C., & Chilvers, D. R. (1995). *Litigation support* (3rd ed.). (The Coopers & Lybrand Guide to the Financial Assessment of Damages and Forensic Accounting.) London: Butterworths.

Lemons, J., Shrader-Frechette, K., & Cranor, C. (1997). The precautionary principle: Scientific uncertainty and Type I and Type II errors. In M. Kaiser (Ed.), *The precautionary principle and its implications for science.* Special issue of *Foundations of Science, 2*(2), 207–236.

Lempert, R. (1977). Modeling relevance. *Michigan Law Review, 75*, 1021–1057.

Lenat, D., & Guha, R. V. (1990). *Building large knowledge-based systems: Representation and inference in the CYC project.* Reading, MA: Addison Wesley.

Lenci, A., Bel, N., Busa, F., Calzolari, N., Gola, E., Monachini, M., et al. (2000). SIMPLE: A general framework for the development of multilingual lexicons. *International Journal of Lexicography, 13*(4), 249–263.

Lengers, R. J. C. (1995). *Evolving artificial neural networks: A design approach.* Masters Thesis. Tilburg, The Netherlands: Tilburg University.

Lenzi, V. B., Biagioli, C., Cappelli, A., Sprugnoli, R., & Turchi, F. (2009). The LME project: Legislative metadata based on semantic formal models. *International Journal of Metadata, Semantics and Ontologies, 4*(3), 154–164.

Leo, R. A. (2005). Re-thinking the study of miscarriages of justice: Developing a criminology of wrongful conviction. *Journal of Contemporary Criminal Justice, 21*, 201–223.

Leo, R. A. (2008). *Police interrogation and American justice.* Cambridge, MA: Harvard University Press.

Leo, R. A., Drizin, S., Neufeld, P., Hall, B., & Vatner, A. (2006). Bringing reliability back in: False confessions and legal safeguards in the twenty-first century. *Wisconsin Law Review, 2006*, 479–539.

Leo, R. A., & Ofshe, R. J. (1998). The consequences of false confessions: Deprivations of liberty and miscarriages of justice in the age of psychological interrogation. *Journal of Criminal Law and Criminology, 88*, 429–496.

Leon, C., Peinado, F., Navarro, A., & Cortiguera, H. (2008). An intelligent plot-centric interface for mastering computer role-playing games. In U. Spierling & N. Szilas (Eds.), *Proceedings of the first international conference on interactive digital storytelling*, Erfurt, Germany, 26–29 November 2008 (pp. 321–324). (Lecture Notes in Computer Science, Vol. 5334). Berlin: Springer.

Lerti (2006). *Note d'information 4, version 0.94, dated 23 September 2006, produced in France by Lerti: La preuve informatique.* Accessible on the Web.

Leskovec, J., Chakrabarti, D., Kleinberg, J., & Faloutsos, C. (2005). Realistic, mathematically tractable graph generation and evolution, using Kronecker multiplication. In *Proceedings of ECML/PKDD 2005*, Porto, Portugal, 2005. http://www.cs.cmu.edu/~jure/pubs/kronecker-pkdd05.pdf http://ecmlpkdd05.liacc.up.pt

Leskovec, J., & Faloutsos, C. (2007). Scalable modeling of real graphs using Kronecker multiplication. In *Proceedings of ICML 2007*, Corvallis, OR.

Leskovec, J., Kleinberg, J., & Faloutsos, C. (2005). Graphs over time: Densification laws, shrinking diameters and possible explanations. In *Proceedings of the 2005 international conference on Knowledge Discovery and Data mining (KDD 2005)*, Chicago, IL, August 2005. http://www.cs.cmu.edu/~christos/PUBLICATIONS/icdm05-power.pdf

Leskovec, J., Singh, A., & Kleinberg, J. (2006). Patterns of influence in a recommendation network. In *Proceedings of the Pacific-Asia Conference on Knowledge Discovery and Data Mining (PAKDD)*, 2006. http://www.cs.cornell.edu/home/kleiber/pakdd06-cascade.pdf

Lester, J. C., & Stone, B. A. (1997). Increasing believability in animated pedagogical agents. In W. L. Johnson (Ed.), *Autonomous Agents '97*, Marina del Rey, California (pp. 16–21). New York: ACM Press.

Leung, W. F., Leung, S. H., Lau, W. H., & Luk, A. (1991). Fingerprint recognition using neural networks. In *Proceedings of the IEEE workshop on neural networks for signal processing*, pp. 226–235.

Levene, M. (1992). *The nested universal relation database model.* (Lecture Notes in Computer Science, Vol. 595.) Berlin: Springer.

Levene, M., & Loizou, G. (1990). The nested relation type model: An application of domain theory to databases. *The Computer Journal, 33*(1), 19–30.

Levene, M., & Loizou, G. (1993). Semantics of null extended nested relations. *ACM Transactions on Database Systems, 18*, 414–459.

Levene, M., & Loizou, G. (1994). The nested universal relation data model. *Journal of Computer and System Sciences, 49*, 683–717.

Levi, J. N. (1994). Language as evidence: The linguist as expert witness in North American courts. *Forensic Linguistics, 1*(1), 1–26.

Levi, M. (1998). Perspectives on 'organized crime': An overview. *Howard Journal of Criminal Justice, 37*, 1–11.

Levine, F. J., & Tapp, J. L. (1982). Eyewitness identification: Problems and pitfalls. In V. J. Konečni & E. E. Ebbesen (Eds.), *The criminal justice system: A social psychological analysis* (pp. 99–127). San Francisco, CA: Freeman.

Levine, T. R., Kim, R. K., & Blair, J. P. (2010). (In_accuracy at detecting true and false confessions and denials: An initial test of a projected motive model of veracity judgments. *Human Communication Research, 36*, 82–102.

Levinson, J. (2000). *Questioned documents: A lawyer's handbook.* London & San Diego, CA: Academic.

Levinson, J. (2001). *Questioned documents: A lawyer's handbook.* San Diego, CA: Academic Press.

Levitt, T. S., & Laskey, K. B. (2002). Computational inference for evidential reasoning in support of judicial proof. In M. MacCrimmon & P. Tillers, P. (Eds.), *The dynamics of judicial proof: Computation, logic, and common sense* (pp. 345–383). (Studies in Fuzziness and Soft Computing, Vol. 94). Heidelberg, Germany: Physical-Verlag.

Lewis, D. (1973). *Counterfactuals.* Oxford: Blackwell.

Lewis, D. (1997). Finkish dispositions. *The Philosophical Quarterly, 47*(187), 143–158.

Lewis, C. M., & Sycara, K. (1993). Reaching informed agreement in multispecialist cooperation. *Group Decision and Negotiation, 2*(3), 279–300.

Lewis, P. R., Gagg, C., & Reynolds, K. (2004). *Forensic materials engineering: Case studies.* Boca Raton, FL: CRC Press.

Lewis, P. R., & Hainsworth, S. (2006). Fuel line failure from stress corrosion cracking. *Engineering Failure Analysis, 13*, 946–962.

Li, Ch.-Ts. (2008). *Multimedia forensics and security.* Hershey, PA: IGI Global.

Li, J., Zheng, R., & Chen, H. (2006). From fingerprint to writeprint. *Communications of the ACM, 49*(4), 76–82.

Li, M., Yunhong, W., & Tan, T. (2002). Iris recognition using circular symmetric filters. *IEEE International Conference on Pattern Recognition (ICPR 2002), 2*, 414–417.

Li, S. Z. (2009). Mathematical MRF models. In S. Z. Li (Ed.), *Markov random field modeling in image analysis* (3rd ed.) (Advances in Computer Vision and Pattern Recognition series; originally published in the series: Computer Science Workbench). Both softcover and hardcover editions, 2009, pp. 1–28. Previous edition (also cited), Tokyo: Springer, 2001.

Li, Q., Niu, X., Wang, Zh., Jiao, Y., & Sun, Sh. H. (2005). A verifiable fingerprint vault scheme. In R. Khosla, R. J. Howlett, & L. C. Jain (Eds.), *Knowledge-based intelligent information and engineering systems: 9th international conference, KES 2005, Melbourne, Australia, September 14–16, 2005, Proceedings, Part III* (pp. 1072–1078). (Lecture Notes in Computer Science, Vol. 3684.) Berlin: Springer.

Li, S. Z., & Jain, A. K. (Eds.). (2009). *Encyclopedia of biometrics.* New York: Springer.

Li, Z., Yang, M. C., & Ramani, K. (2009). A methodology for engineering ontology acquisition and validation. *Artificial Intelligence for Engineering Design, Analysis and Manufacturing, 23*(1), 37–51.

Liang, T., & Moskowitz, H. (1992). Integrating neural networks and semi markov processes for automated knowledge acquisition: An application to real-time scheduling. *Decision Sciences, 23*(6), 1298–1314.

Light, R. (1997). *Presenting XML.* Indianapolis, IN: Sams.net

Linde, C. (1993). *Life stories: The creation of coherence.* New York: Oxford University Press.

Lindsay, R. C. L., Lim, R., Marando, L., & Cully, D. (1986). Mock-juror evaluations of eyewitness testimony: A test of metamemory hypotheses. *Journal of Applied Social Psychology, 15*, 447–459.

Lindsay, R. C. L., & Malpass, R. S. (1999). Measuring lineup fairness. Special issue of *Applied Cognitive Psychology, 13*, S1–S7.

Lindsay, R. C. L., Ross, D. F., Read, J. D., & Toglia, M. P. (Eds.). (2006). *Handbook of eyewitness psychology: Memory for people.* Mahwah, NJ: Lawrence Erlbaum Associates.

Lindsay, R. C. L., & Wells, G. L. (1980). What price justice? Exploring the relationship between lineup fairness and identification accuracy. *Law and Human Behavior, 4*, 303–314.

Linford, N. (2002). The English heritage geophysical survey database. http://www.eng-h.gov.uk/SDB/

Lingras, P., & Peters, G. (2011). Rough clustering. *Wiley Interdisciplinary Reviews (WIREs): Data Mining and Knowledge Discovery, 1*(1), 64–72. doi://10.1002/widm.16

Lipske, M. (1999). Forest owlet thought to be extinct is spotted anew. *Smithsonian Institution Research Reports*, No. 96, Spring 1999. http://www.si.edu/opa/researchreports/9996/owlet.htm

Lipton, P. (2004). *Inference to the best expanation* (2nd ed.) (revised, augmented). London & New York: Routledge.

Lipton, L. (2007). Alien abduction: Inference to the best explanation and the management of testimony. *Episteme, 4*(3), 238–251.

Lisetti, C. L., & Schiano, D. J. (2000). Automatic facial expression interpretation: Where human-computer interaction, artificial intelligence and cognitive science intersect. In I. E. Dror & S. V. Stevenage (Eds.), *Facial information processing: A multidisciplinary perspective.* Special issue of *Pragmatics & Cognition, 8*(1): 185–235.

Liu, H., & Motoda, H. (1998). *Feature selection for knowledge discovery and data mining.* Dordrecht, The Netherlands: Kluwer.

Liu, H., & Singh, P. (2002). MAKEBELIEVE: Using commonsense knowledge to generate stories. In *Proceedings of the eighteenth national conference on artificial intelligence and fourteenth conference on innovative applications of artificial intelligence*, pp. 957–958. http://web/media.mit.edu/~hugo/publications/papers/AAAI2002-makebelieve.pdf

Liu, D., Yue, J., Wang, X., Raja, A., & Ribarsky, W. (2008). The role of blackboard-based reasoning and visual analytics in RESIN's predictive analysis. In *Proceedings of 2008 IEEE/WIC/ACM international conference on Intelligent Agent Technology (IAT 2008)*, Sydney, December 9–12, 2008, pp 508–511. An extended version is: CVC Technical Report CVC-UNCC-08-29, Charlotte: University of North Carolina, July 2008. http://www.sis.uncc.edu/~anraja/PAPERS/IAT08-Final.pdf

Llewellyn, K. N. (1962). *Jurisprudence: Realism in theory and practice.* Chicago, IL: University of Chicago Press. Published again, with a new introduction by J. J. Chriss, in Somerset, NJ: Transaction; distrib. London: Eurospan, 2008. [Compilation of writings from the 1930s through the 1950s.]

Lloyd, C. (1995). *Forensic psychiatry for health professionals.* London: Chapman & Hall.

Locard, E. (1930). Analysis of dust traces. *American Journal of Police Science, 1*(276), 401–496.

Locard, E. (1937). *La Criminalistique à l'usage des gens du monde et des auteurs de romans policiers.* Lyon: Desvignes et Cie.

Lodder, A. R. (2004). Law, logic, rhetoric: A procedural model of legal argumentation. In S. Rahman & J. Symons (Eds.), *Logic, epistemology and the unity of science* (pp. 569–588). Dordrecht: Kluwer.

Lodder, A. R., & Zeleznikow, J. (2005). Developing an online dispute resolution environment: Dialogue tools and negotiation systems in a three step model. *Harvard Negotiation Law Review, 10*, 287–338.

Lodder, A. R., & Zeleznikow, J. (2010). *Enhanced dispute resolution through the use of information technology*. Cambridge: Cambridge University Press.

Loftus, E. F. (1974). Reconstructing memory: The incredible witness. *Psychology Today, 8*, 116–119.

Loftus, E. F. (1975). Leading questions and the eye witness report. *Cognitive Psychology, 7*, 560–572.

Loftus, E. F. (1976). Unconscious transference in eyewitness identification. *Law and Psychology Review, 2*, 93–98.

Loftus, E. F. (1979). *Eyewitness testimony*. Cambridge, MA: Harvard University Press. (Revised edn.: 1996).

Loftus, E. F. (1980). Impact of expert psychological testimony on the unreliability of eye- witness identification. *Journal of Applied Psychology, 65*, 915.

Loftus, E. F. (1981a). Eyewitness testimony: Psychological research and legal thought. In N. Morris & M. Tonry (Eds.), *Crime and justice 3*. Chicago: University of Chicago Press.

Loftus, E. F. (1981b). Mentalmorphosis: Alteration in memory produced by the bonding of new information to old. In J. Long & A. Baddeley (Eds.), *Attention and performance IX* (pp. 417–434). Hillsdale, NJ: Lawrence Erlbaum Associates.

Loftus, E. F. (1983). Silence is not golden. *American Psychologist, 38*, 9–15.

Loftus, E. F. (1986a). Experimental psychologist as advocate or impartial educator. *Law and Human Behavior, 10*, 63–78.

Loftus, E. F. (1986b). Ten years in the life of an expert witness. *Law and Human Behavior, 10*, 241–263.

Loftus, E. F. (1987). Trials of an expert witness. In the My Turn column, in *Newsweek, 109*, 29 June 1987, pp. 10–11.

Loftus, E. F. (1991). Resolving legal questions with psychological data. *American Psychologist, 46*, 1046–1048.

Loftus, E. F. (1993a). The reality of repressed memories. *American Psychologist, 48*, 518–537. http://faculty.washington.edu/eloftus/Articles/lof93.htm

Loftus, E. F. (1993b). Psychologists in the eyewitness world. *American Psychologist, 48*, 550–552.

Loftus, E. F. (Sept. 1997). Creating false memories. *Scientific American, 277*, 70–75. http://faculty.washington.edu/eloftus/Articles/sciam.htm

Loftus, E. F. (1998). The price of bad memories. *Skeptical Inquirer, 22*, 23–24.

Loftus, E. F. (2002). Memory faults and fixes. *Issues in Science and Technology, 18*(4), National Academies of Science, 2002, pp. 41–50. http://faculty.washington.edu/eloftus/Articles/IssuesInScienceTechnology02%20vol%2018.pdf

Loftus, E. F. (2003a). Our changeable memories: Legal and practical implications. *Nature Reviews: Neuroscience, 4*, 231–234. http://faculty.washington.edu/eloftus/Articles/2003Nature.pdf

Loftus, E. F. (2003b). Make-believe memories. *American Psychologist, 58*(11), 867–873. Posted at: http://faculty.washington.edu/eloftus/Articles/AmerPsychAward+ArticlePDF03%20(2).pdf

Loftus, E. F. (2005). Planting misinformation in the human mind: A 30-year investigation of the malleability of memory. *Learning and Memory, 12*, 361–366.

Loftus, E. F., Donders, K., Hoffman, H. G., & Schooler, J. W. (1989). Creating new memories that are quickly accessed and confidently held. *Memory and Cognition, 17*, 607–616.

Loftus, E. F., & Doyle, J. M. (1997). *Eyewitness testimony: Civil and criminal*. Charlottesville, VA: Lexis Law Publishing.

Loftus, E. F., & Greene, E. (1980). Warning: Even memory for faces may be contagious. *Law and Human Behavior, 4*, 323–334.

Loftus, E. F., & Hoffman, H. G. (1989). Misinformation and memory: The creation of new memories. *Journal of Experimental Psychology: General, 118*, 100–104. http://faculty.washington.edu/eloftus/Articles/hoff.htm

Loftus, E. F., & Ketcham, K. (1991). *Witness for the defense: The accused, the eyewitness and the expert who puts memory on trial*. New York: St. Martin's Press.

Loftus, E. F., & Ketcham, K. (1994). *The Myth of repressed memory: False memories and allegations of sexual abuse*. New York: St. Martin's Press.

Loftus, E. F., & Loftus, G. R. (1980). On the permanence of stored information in the brain. *American Psychologist, 35*, 409–420.

Loftus, E. F., Loftus, G. R., & Messo, J. (1987). Some facts about 'weapon focus'. *Law and Human Behavior, 11*, 55–62.

Loftus, E. F., Miller, D. G., & Burns, H. J. (1978). Semantic integration of verbal information into a visual memory. *Journal of Experimenal Psychology: Human Learning and Memory, 4*, 19–31.

Loftus, E. F., & Palmer, J. C. (1974). Reconstruction of automobile destruction: An example of the interaction between language and memory. *Journal of Verbal Learning and Verbal Behaviour, 13*, 585–589.

Loftus, E. F., & Pickrell, J. E. (1995). The formation of false memories. *Psychiatric Annals, 25*(12), 720–725.

Loftus, E. F., & Rosenwald, L. A. (1993) Buried memories, shattered lives. *American Bar Association Journal, 79*, 70–73.

Loftus, E. F., Weingardt, J. W., & Wagenaar, W. A. (1985). The fate of memory: Comment on McCloskey and Zaragoza. *Journal of Experimental Psychology: General, 114*, 375–380.

Loftus, E. F., & Zanni, G. (1975). Eyewitness testimony: The influence of the wording of a question. *Bulletin of the Psychonomic Society, 5*, 86–88.

Loh, W.-Y. (2011). Classification and regression trees. *Wiley Interdisciplinary Reviews (WIREs): Data Mining and Knowledge Discovery, 1*(1), 14–23. doi://10.1002/widm.8

Lonergan, M. C., Severin, E. J., Doleman, B. J., Beaber, S. A., Grubbs, R. H., & Lewis, N. S. (1996). Array-based vapor sensing using chemically sensitive, carbon black-polymer resistors. *Chemistry of Materials, 8*, 2298–2312.

Longley, P. A., Goodchild, M. F., Maguire, D. J., & Rhind, D. W. (2001). *Geographic information systems and science*. New York: Wiley.

Lönneker, B. (2005). Narratological knowledge for natural language generation. In *Proceedings of the 10th European workshop on natural language generation*, Aberdeen, Scotland, August 2005, pp. 91–100.

Lönneker, B., & Meister, J. C. (2005). "Dream on": Designing the ideal story generator algorithms. Short communication at the session on story generators: Approaches for the generation of literary artefacts. At the *ACH/ALLC 2005 Conference*, of the Association for Computing and the Humanities and the Association for Linguistic and Literary Computing.

Lönneker, B., Meister, J. C., Gervás, P., Peinado, F., & Mateas, G. (2005). Story generators: Approaches for the generation of literary artefacts. Session at the *ACH/ALLC 2005 Conference*, of the Association for Computing and the Humanities and the Association for Linguistic and Literary Computing. In *Proceedings of the 17th joint international conference of the Association for Computers and the Humanities and the Association for Literary and Linguistic Computing (ACH/ALLC 2005 Conference Abstracts)*, Victoria, BC, Canada, June 15–18, 2005, pp. 126–133.

Lonsdorf, R. G. (1995). Review of H. Bluestone, S. Travin, & D. Marlowe, Psychiatric-legal decision making by the mental health practitioner: The clinician as de facto magistrate. (New York: Wiley, 1994). *The Journal of Legal Medicine, 16*(2), 319–324.

Lord, J. (1971). *Duty, honour, empire*. London: Hutchinson.

Louchart, S., & Aylett, R. (2003). Towards a narrative theory of virtual reality. *Virtual Reality, 7*(1), 2–9.

Loui, R. P., & Norman, J. (1995). Rationales and argument moves. *Artificial Intelligence and Law, 2*(3), 159–190.

Loui, R. P., Norman, J., Alpeter, J., Pinkard, D., Craven, D., Lindsay, J., et al. (1997). Progress on Room 5: A testbed for public interactive semi-formal legal argumentation. In *Proceedings of the sixth International Conference on Artificial Intelligence and Law (ICAIL 1997)*. New York: ACM Press, pp. 207–214.

Louis, J.-H. (1987). *L'engrenage de la violence. La guerre psychologique aux États-Unis pendant la Seconde Guerre Mondiale*. Paris: Payot.

Löwe, B., & Pacuit, E. (2008). An abstract approach to reasoning about games with mistaken and changing beliefs. *Australasian Journal of Logic, 6*, 162–181. http://www.philosophy.unimelb. edu.au/ajl/2008

Löwe, B., Pacuit, E., & Saraf, S. (2008). *Analyzing stories as games with changing and mistaken beliefs*. Technical report. ILLC Publications PP-2008-31. Amsterdam: Institute for Logic, Language and Computation of the University of Amsterdam. [This is the version we referred to.] Later published as: Identifying the structure of a narrative via an agent-based logic of preferences and beliefs: Formalizations of episodes from *CSI: Crime Scene Investigation*™, In M. Duvigneau & D. Moldt (Eds.), *Proceedings of the fifth international workshop on Modelling of Objects Components and Agents, MOCA'09*, Hamburg, 2009 [FBI-HH-B-290/09], pp. 45–63.

Loyall, A. B. (1997). *Believable agents: Building interactive personalities* (Technical Report CMU-CS-97-123). Pittsburgh, PA: School of Computer Science, Carnegie Mellon University. Retrieved from http://www-2.cs.cmu.edu/afs/cs.cmu.edu/project/oz/web/papers/CMU-CS-97-123.ps

Loyka, S. A., Faggiani, D. A., & Karchmer, C. (2005). *The production and sharing of intelligence. Vol. 4: Protecting your community from terrorism*. Washington, DC: Office of Community Oriented Policing Services and the Police Executive Research Forum. http://www.cops.usdoj. gov/mime/open.pdf?Item=1438

Lu, Q., Korniss, G., & Szymanski, B. K. (2009). The naming game on social networks: Community formation and consensus engineering. *Journal of Economic Interaction and Coordination, 4*(2), 221–235.

Lucas, R. (1986). An expert system to detect burglars using a logic language and a relational database. *Fifth British National Conference on Databases*, Canterbury, Kent, England.

Lucy, D. (2005). *Introduction to statistics for forensic scientists*. Chichester: Wiley.

Luger, G. F., & Stubblefield, W. A. (1998). *Artificial intelligence: Structures and strategies for complex problem solving* (3rd ed.). Reading, MA: Addison Wesley Longman.

Luhmann, T., Robson, S., Kyle, S., & Harley, I. (2006). *Close range photogrammetry: Principles, techniques and applications*. (Translated from the German.) Scotland: Whittles Publishing.

Luhn, H. P. (1958). The automatic creation of literature abstracts. *IBM Journal of Research and Development, 2*, 159–165.

Lukáš, J., Fridrich, J.,[65] & Goljan, M. (2006). Detecting digital image forgeries using sensor pattern noise. In *Proceedings of the SPIE*, Vol. 6072.

Lutomski, L. S. (1989). The design of an attorney's statistical consultant. In *Proceedings of the second international conference of artificial intelligence and law*. New York: ACM Press, pp. 224–233.

Luus, C. A. E., & Wells, G. L. (1994). The malleability of eyewitness confidence: Co witness and perseverance effects. *Journal of Applied Psychology, 79*, 714–723.

Lykken, D. T. (1998). *A tremor in the blood: Uses and abuses of the lie detector*. Reading, MA: Perseus Books.

Maas, A., & Köhnken, G. (1989). Eye-witness identification: Simulating the 'weapon effect'. *Law and Human behavior, 13*, 397–409.

MacCormick, D. N. (1981). *H. L. A. Hart*. Stanford, CA: Stanford University Press.

MacCormick, N. (1980). The coherence of a case and the reasonableness of doubt. *The Liverpool Law Review, 2*, 45–50.

MacCormick, N. (1995). Argumentation and interpretation in law. *Argumentation, 9*, 467–480.

---

[65] This is Jessica Fridrich. Also Juri Fridrich is at the Computer Science Department of Dartmouth College in Hanover, New Hampshire. They both work in the given domain of research.

MacCrimmon, M. (1989). Facts, stories and the hearsay rule. In A. A. Martino (Ed.), *Pre-proceedings of the third international conference on "Logica, Informatica, Diritto: Legal Expert Systems"*, Florence, 1989 (2 vols. + Appendix) (Vol. 1, pp. 461–475). Florence: Istituto per la Documentazione Giuridica, Consiglio Nazionale delle Ricerche.

MacCrimmon, M., & Tillers, P. (Eds.). (2002). *The dynamics of judicial proof: Computation, logic, and common sense*. (Studies in Fuzziness and Soft Computing, Vol. 94). Heidelberg: Physical-Verlag.

MacDonell, H. L. (1993). *Bloodstain patterns*. Corning, NY: Laboratory of Forensic Science.

MacDonell, H. L., & Bialousz, L. F. (1979). *Laboratory manual for the geometric interpretation of human bloodstain evidence* (2nd ed.). Corning, NY: Laboratory of Forensic Science.

MacDougall, K. A., Fenning, P. J., Cooke, D. A., Preston, H., Brown, A., Hazzard, J., et al. (2002). *Non intrusive investigation techniques for groundwater pollution studies*. Research & Development Technical Report P2-178/TR/10. Bristol, England: Environment Agency.

MacLane, S., & Birkhoff, G. (1979). *Algebra*. London: Macmillan.

Macneil, I. (1980). *The new social contract: An inquiry into modern contractual relations*. New Haven, CT: Yale University Press.

Macrae, C. N., Stangor, C., & Hewstone, M. (Eds.). (1996). *Stereotypes and stereotyping*. New York: Guilford Press.

Maedche, A., & Staab, S. (2001). Ontology learning for the Semantic Web. *IEEE Intelligent Systems, 16*(2), 72–79.

Magerko, B., & Laifo, J. (2003). Building an interactive drama architecture with a high degree of interactivity. At the *First International Conference on Technologies for Interactive Digital Storytelling and Entertainment (= TIDSE '03)*, Darmstadt, Germany, March 2003.

Magnenat-Thalmann, N., & Gilles, B. (2007). Towards an individualised physiological model of the musculoskeletal system. In *The Digital Patient*, special issue of *ERCIM News*, 69 (April), 25–26. Accessible at the webpage http://ercim-news.ercim.org/ of the European Research Consortium for Informatics and Mathematics.

Magnenat Thalmann, N., & Thalmann, D. (1991a). Complex models for visualizing synthetic actors. *IEEE Computer Graphics and Applications, 11*(5), 32–44.

Magnenat Thalmann, N., & Thalmann, D. (1991b). *Animation of synthetic actors and 3D interaction*. Laboratoire d'Infographie, École Polytechnique Fédérale, Lausanne, and Groupe MIRALab, Université de Génève, Geneva, Switzerland, pp. 27–49.

Magnenat Thalmann, N., & Thalmann, D. (Eds.). (1996). *Interactive computer animation*. London: Prentice Hall.

Magnenat Thalmann, N., & Thalmann, D. (Eds.). (2001). *Deformable avatars*. Dordrecht, The Netherlands: Kluwer.

Magnenat Thalmann, N., & Thalmann, D. (Eds.). (2005). Virtual humans: Thirty years of research, what next? *The Visual Computer, 21*(12), 997–1015.

Magnussen, S., Melinder, A., Stridbeck, U., & Raja, A. (2010). Eliefs about factors affecting the reliability of eyewitness testimony: A comparison of judges, jurors and the general public. *Applied Cognitive Psychology, 24*, 122–133. doi://10.1002/acp.1550

Maguire, M. (2000). Policing by risks and targets: Some dimensions and implications of intelligence-led crime control. In J. Sheptycki (Ed.), special issue on Surveillance and Intelligence-Leg Policing, *Policing and Society, 9*, 315–336.

Maguire, M., & John, T. (1995). *Intelligence, surveillance and informants: Integrated approaches*. Crime Detection and Prevention Series Paper 64. London: Home Office.

Mahendra, B. (2007). Expert witness update. In an *Expert Witness Supplement* to *The New Law Journal, 157*(7294) (London, 26 October 2007), 1490–1491.

Mahesh, K. (1996). *Ontology development for machine translation: Ideology and methodology*. Memoranda in Computer and Cognitive Science, MCCS-96-292. Las Cruces, NM: New Mexico State University, Computing Research Laboratory.

Maida, A. S. (1991). Maintaining mental models of agents who have existential misconceptions. *Artificial Intelligence, 50*, 331–383.

Maida, A. S. (1995). Review of Ballim & Wilks (1991). *Minds and Machines, 5*(2), 277–280.

Maida, A. S., & Shapiro, S. C. (1982). Intensional concepts in propositional semantic networks. *Cognitive Science, 6*(4), 291–330.

Maji, P., & Pal, S. K. (2007). RFCM: A hybrid clustering algorithm using rough and fuzzy sets. *Fundamenta Informaticae, 80*, 477–498.

Maley, Y., & Fahey, R. (1991). Presenting the evidence: Constructions of reality in court. *International Journal for the Semiotics of Law, 4*(10), 3–17.

Malinowski, E. R. (1991). *Factor analysis in chemistry.* New York: Wiley.

Maloney, K., Carter, A. L., Jory, S., & Yamashita, B. (2005). Three-dimensional representation of bloodstain pattern analysis. *Journal of Forensic Identification, 55*(6), 711–725.

Maloney, K., Killeen, J., & Maloney, A. (2009). The use of HemoSpat to include bloodstains located on nonorthogonal surfaces in area-of-origin calculations. *Journal of Forensic Identification, 59*(5), 513–524. http://hemospat.com/papers/pdf/JFI%20-%20HemoSpat%20Using%20Nonorthogonal%20Surfaces.pdf

Maloney, A., Nicloux, C., Maloney, K., & Heron, F. (2001). One-sided impact spatter and area-of-origin calculations. *Journal of Forensic Identification, 61*(2), 123–135. http://hemospat.com/papers/pdf/JFI%20-%20One-Sided%20Impact%20Spatter%20and%20Area-of-Origin%20Calculations.pdf

Malpass, R. S., & Devine, P. G. (1981). Eye-witness identification: Lineup instructions and the absence of the offender. *Journal of Applied Psychology, 66*, 482–489.

Malsch, M., & Nijboer, J. F. (Eds.). (1999). *Complex cases: Perspectives on the Netherlands criminal justice system.* (Series Criminal Sciences). Amsterdam: THELA THESIS.

Maltoni, D., Maio, D., Jain, A. K., & Prabhakar, S. (2009). *Handbook of fingerprint recognition* (2nd ed.). New York: Springer. The 1st edition was of 2003.

Mandler, J. M., & Johnson, N. S. (1977). Remembrance of things parsed: Story structure and recall. *Cognitive Psyhology, 9*, 111–191.

Mani, I. (2001). *Automatic summarization.* (Natural Language Processing, 3). Amsterdam: Benjamins.

Mann, S., Vrij, A., & Bull, R. (2004). Detecting true lies: Police officers' ability to detect suspect' lies. *Journal of Applied Psychology, 89*, 137–149.

Mannila, H., Toivonen, H., & Verkamo, A. I. (1997). Discovery of frequent episodes in event sequences. *Data Mining and Knowledge Discovery, 1*(3), 259–289.

Manning, C., & Schutze, H. (1999). *Foundations of statistical natural language processing.* Cambridge, MA: The MIT Press.

Manning, K., & Srihari, S. N. (2009). Computer-assisted handwriting analysis: interaction with legal issues in U. S. courts. In *Proceedings of the third international workshop on computational forensics*, The Hague, Netherlands. Berlin: Springer.

Manouselis, N., Salokhe, G., & Johannes Keizer, J. (2009). Agricultural metadata and semantics. Special issue of the *International Journal of Metadata, Semantics and Ontologies, 4*(1–2).

Manschreck, T. C. (1983). Modeling a paranoid mind: A narrower interpretation of the results. [A critique of Colby (1981).] *The Behavioral and Brain Sciences, 6*(2), 340–341. [Answered by Colby (1983).]

Marafioti, L. (2000). *Scelte autodifensive dell'indagato e alternative al silenzio.* Turin, Italy: Giappichelli.

Marcus, P. (2000). The process of interrogating criminal suspects in the United States. In *Proceedings of the second world conference on new trends in criminal investigation and evidence*, Amsterdam, 10–15 December 1999; = C. M. Breur, M. M. Kommer, J. F. Nijboer, & J. M. Reijntjes. (Eds.). (2000). *New trends in criminal investigation and evidence* (Vol. 2, pp. 447–456). Antwerp, Belgium: Intersentia.

Mares, E. (2006). Relevance logic. *Stanford Encyclopedia of Philosophy* (entry revised from an original version of 1998). http://plato.stanford.edu/entries/logic-relevance/

Mares, E., & Meyer, R. K. (2001). Relevant logics. In L. Goble (Ed.), *The Blackwell guide to philosophical logic* (pp. 280–308). Oxford: Blackwell.

Mares, E. D. (1992). Andersonian deontic logic. *Theoria, 58*, 3–20.

Mares, E. D. (1997). Relevant logic and the theory of information. *Synthese, 109*, 345–360.

Mares, E. D. (2004). *Relevant logic: A philosophical interpretation*. Cambridge: Cambridge University Press.

Marinai, S., & Fujisawa, H. (Eds.). (2008). *Machine learning in document analysis and recognition*. (Studies on Computational Intelligence, 90). Berlin: Springer.

Marineau, R. F. (1989). *Jacob Levy Moreno, 1889–1974: Father of psychodrama, sociometry, and group psychotherapy*. London: Routledge.

Marshall, C. C. (1989). Representing the structure of legal argument. In *Proceedings of the second international conference on artificial intelligence and law*. New York: ACM Press, pp. 121–127.

Martino, A. A. (1997). Quale logica per la politica. In A. A. Martino (Ed.), *Logica delle norme* (pp. 5–21). Pisa, Italy: SEU: Servizio Editoriale Universitario di Pisa, on behalf of Università degli Studi di Pisa, Facoltà di Scienze Politiche. English translation: A logic for politics. Accessible online at a site of his publications: http://www.antonioanselmomartino.it/index.php? option=com_content&task=view&id=26&Itemid=64

Martino, A. A., & Nissan, E. (Eds.). (1998). Formal models of legal time. Special issue, *Information and Communications Technology Law, 7*(3).

Martino, A. A., & Nissan, E. (Eds.). (2001). Formal approaches to legal evidence. Special issue, *Artificial Intelligence and Law, 9*(2/3), 85–224.

Martins, J. P. (1990). The truth, the whole truth, and nothing but the truth: An indexed bibliography to the literature of truth maintenance systems. *AI Magazine, 11*(5), 7–25.

Martins, J. P., & Shapiro, S. C. (1983). Reasoning in multiple belief spaces. In *Proceedings of the eighth International Joint Conference on Artificial Intelligence (IJCAI'83)*, Karlsruhe, Germany. San Mateo, CA: Morgan Kaufmann, pp. 370–373. http://ijcai.org/search.php

Martins, J. P., & Shapiro, S. C. (1988). A model for belief revision. *Artificial Intelligence, 35*, 25–79.

Maslow, A. H. (1943). A theory of human motivation. *Psychological Review*, 50, 370–396.

Mateas, M. (2001). A preliminary poetics for interactive drama and games. *Digital Creativity, 12*(3), 140–152. Also in *Proceedings of SIGGRAPH 2001: Art Gallery, art and culture papers*, New York: Association for Computing Machinery, pp. 51–58.

Mateas, M. (2004). A preliminary poetics for interactive drama and games [a longer version]. In N. Wardrip-Fruin & P. Harrigan (Eds.), *First person: New media as story, performance, and game*, Cambridge, MA: MIT Press.

Mateas, M. (2005). Beyond story graphs: Story management in game worlds. Short communication at the Session on Story generators: Approaches for the generation of literary artefacts. At the *ACH/ALLC 2005 Conference*, of the Association for Computing and the Humanities and the Association for Linguistic and Literary Computing.

Mateas, M., & Sengers, P. (Eds.). 2003. *Narrative intelligence*. Amsterdam: Benjamins.

Mateas, M., Domike, S., & Vanouse, P. (1999). Terminal Time: An ideologically biased history machine. In a special issue on *Creativity in the Arts and Sciences* of the *AISB Quarterly, 102*, 36–43.

Mateas, M., & Stern, A. (2003). Integrating plot, character and natural language processing in the interactive drama Façade. At the *First International Conference on Technologies for Interactive Digital Storytelling and Entertainment (= TIDSE '03)*, Darmstadt, Germany, March 2003.

Mateas, M., & Stern, A. (2005). Build it to understand it: Ludology meets narratology in game design space. In *Proceedings of the Digital Interactive Games Research Association conference (DiGRA 2005)*, Vancouver, BC, Canada, June 2005; included in the *Selected Papers* volume.

Matthijssen, L. J. (1999). *Interfacing between lawyers and computers: An Architecture for knowledge based interfaces to legal databases*. Dordrecht, The Netherlands: Kluwer Law International.

Maxion, R. A., & Townsend, T. N. (2002). Masquerade detection using truncated command lines. In *Proceeedings of the International Conference on Dependable Systems and Networks (DSN-02)*, Washington, DC, June 2002. Los Alamitos, CA: IEEE Computer Society Press, pp. 219–228.

Mazzoni, G. A. L., Loftus, E. F., & Kirsch, I. (2001). Changing beliefs about implausible autobiographical events: A little plausibility goes a long way. *Journal of Experimental Psychology: Applied, 7*, 51–59. Posted at: http://faculty.washington.edu/eloftus/Articles/mazzloft.htm

McAllister, H. A., & Bregman, N. J. (1989). Juror underutilization of eyewitness nonidentifications: A test of the disconfirmed expectancy explanation. *Journal of Applied Social Psychology, 19*, 20–29.

McBurney, P., & Parsons, S. (2001). Intelligent systems to support deliberative democracy in environmental regulation. In D. M. Peterson, J. A. Barnden, & E. Nissan (Eds.), *Artificial Intelligence and Law*, special issue, *Information and Communications Technology Law, 10*(1), 79–89.

McBurney, P., & Prakken, H. (2004). Argumentation in dialogues. In J. Fox (Ed.), *Theoretical framework for argumentation* (pp. 57–84). ASPIC Consortium.

McCabe, S. (1988). Is jury research dead? In M. Findlay & P. Duff (Eds.), *The Jury under attack* (pp. 27–39). London: Butterworths.

McCallum, A., Corrada-Emmanuel, A., & Wang, X. (2005). The author-recipient-topic model for topic and role discovery in social networks, with application to Enron and academic email. In *Proceedings of the SIAM international conference on data mining, SIAM workshop on link analysis, counterterrorism and security*. Philadelphia, PA: SIAM.

McCann, D., Culshaw, M. G., & Fenning, P. J. (1997). Setting the standard for geophysical surveys in site investigations. In D. M. McCann, M. Eddleston, P. J. Fenning, & G. M. Reeves (Eds.), *Modern geophysics in engineering geology* (pp. 3–34). (Engineering Geology Special Publications, 12.) London: Geological Society.

McClelland, J. L., & Rumelhart, D. E. (1989). *Explorations in parallel distributed processing*. Cambridge, MA: The MIT Press.

McConville, M., Saunders, A., & Leng, R. (1991). *The case for the prosecution*. London: Routledge.

McCormick, E. J. (1964). *Human factors engineering*. New York: McGraw-Hill.

McCornack, S. A. (1992). Information manipulation theory. *Communication Monographs, 59*(1), 1–16.

McCornack, S. A., Levine, T. R., Solowczuk, K. A., & Torres, H. I. (1992). When the alteration of information is viewed as deception: An empirical test of information manipulation theory. *Communication Monographs, 59*(1), 17–29.

McCulloch, W. S., & Pitts, W. (1943). A logical calculus of the ideas imminent in nervous activity. *Bulletin of Mathematical Biophysics*,[66] *5*(4), 115–133. doi://10.1007/BF02478259

McCulloch, M., Jezierski, T., Broffman, M., Hubbard, A., Turner, K., & Janecki, T. (2006). Diagnostic accuracy of canine scent detection in early- and late-stage lung and breast cancers. *Integrative Cancer Therapies, 5*, 1–10.

McGrath, C., Blythe, J., & Krackhardt, D. (1997). The effect of spatial arrangement on judgments and errors in interpreting graphs. *Social Networks, 19*(3), 223–242.

McGuire, P. G. (2000). The New York Police Department COMPSTAT process. In V. Goldsmith, P. G. McGuire, J. H. Mollenkopf, & T. A. Ross (Eds.), *Analyzing crime patterns: Frontiers of practice* (pp. 11–22). Thousand Oaks, CA: Sage.

McHugh, J. (2001). Intrusion and intrusion detection. *International Journal of Information Security, 1*(1), 14–35. Berlin: Springer.

McLeod, J. A. (2011). *Daughter of the empire state: The life of Judge Jane Bolin*. Champaign, IL: University of Illinois Press.

McLeod, M. (1991). Death on the doorstep (As the police searched for clues, they began to ask, Is some killer playing a game with us?). *Reader's Digest* (U.S. edition), September 1991, pp. 135–140. Condensed from *Florida Magazine* (the Sunday supplement of *Orlando Sentinel*) of 12 May 1991.

---

[66] The current name of the journal is *Bulletin of Mathematical Biology*.

McMenamin, G. R. (Ed.). (1993). *Forensic stylistics*. Amsterdam: Elsevier. Also: special issue, *Forensic Science International*, 58(1/2), 1993.

McNally, R. J. (2003). *Remembering Trauma*. Cambridge, MA: Harvard University Press.

McNeal, G. S. (2007). Unfortunate legacies: Hearsay, ex parte affidavits and anonymous witnesses at the IHT [i.e., Iraqi High Tribunal]. In G. Robertson (Ed.), *Fairness and evidence in war crimes trials*. Special issue of *International Commentary on Evidence, 4*(1). The Berkeley Electronic Press (article accessible on the Web at this address: http://www.bepress.com/ice/vol4/iss1/art5)

McQuiston-Surret, D., Topp, L. D. & Malpass, R. S. (2006). Use of facial composite systems in US law enforcement agencies, *Psychology, Crime & Law, 12*, 505–517.

Me, G. (2008). Investigation strategy for the small pedophiles world. In M. Quigley (Ed.), *Encyclopedia of information ethics and security* (pp. 418–425). Hershey, PA: IGI Global (formerly Idea Group).

Meade, M. L., & Roediger, H. L., III. (2002). Explorations in the social contagion of memory. *Memory & Cognition, 30*, 995–1009.

Meester, R. W. J., & Sjerps, M. (2004). Why the effect of prior odds should accompany the likelihood ratio when reporting DNA evidence (with discussion between A. P. Dawid, D. J. Balding, J. S. Buckleton and C. M. Triggs). *Law, Probability and Risk, 3*, 51–86.

Mégret, M. (1956). *La guerre psychologique*. (Collection "Que sais-je?", 713.) Paris: Presses Universitaires de France (PUF).

Meehan, J. (1976). *The metanovel: Writing stories by computer*. Ph.D. Dissertation, Research Report #74 (now YALE/DCS/tr074). New Haven, CT: Computer Science Department, Yale University.

Meehan, J. R. (1977). TALE-SPIN, an interactive program that writes stories. In *Proceedings of the fifth International Joint Conference on Artificial Intelligence (IJCAI'77)*, Cambridge, MA, August 1977. San Mateo, CA: Morgan Kaufmann, Vol. 1, pp. 91–98. http://ijcai.org/search.php

Meehan, J. (1981a). TALE-SPIN. Chapter 9 In R. C. Schank & C. K. Riesbeck (Eds.), *Inside computer understanding: Five programs plus miniatures* (pp. 197–226). Hillsdale, NJ: Lawrence Erlbaum Associates; cf. J. Meehan's "Micro TALE-SPIN", ch. 10, ibid., 227–258. (There is a consolidated bibliography at the end of the volume: pp. 373–377.)

Meehan, J. (1981b). Micro TALE-SPIN. Chapter 10 In R. C. Schank & C. K. Riesbeck (Eds.), *Inside computer understanding: Five programs plus miniatures* (pp. 227–258). Hillsdale, NJ: Lawrence Erlbaum Associates. (There is a consolidated bibliography at the end of the volume: pp. 373–377.)

Meikle, T., & Yearwood, J. (2000). A framework for designing a decision support system to support discretion. At *Intelligent Decision Support for Legal Practice (IDS 2000)*. In *Proceedings of the International ICSC Congress "Intelligent Systems & Applications" (ISA 2000)*, Wollongong, NSW, Australia, December 2000. Wetaskiwin, AB, Canada: ICSC Academic Press, Vol. 1, pp. 101–108.

Meissner, C., & Kassin, S. (2002). He's guilty: Investigator bias in judgements of truth and deception. *Law and Human Behavior, 26*, 469–480.

Meissner, C. A., & Brigham, J. C. (2001). Thirty years of investigating the own-race bias in memory for faces: A meta-analytic review. *Psychology, Public Policy, and Law, 7*(1), 3–35. doi://10.1037/1076-8971.7.1.3

Meister, J. C. (2003). *Computing action*. Berlin: de Gruyter.

Meldman, J. A. (1975). *A preliminary study in computer-aided legal analysis*. Dissertation. Technical Report MAC-TR-157. Cambridge, MA: Massachusetts Institute of Technology.

Mellett, J. S. (1996). GPR in forensic and archaeological work: Hits and misses. In *Symposium on the Application of Geophysics to Environmental Engineering Problems (SAGEEP)*, 1991. Environmental & Engineering Geophysical Society Co., USA, pp. 487–491.

Melnik, M., & Alm, J. (2002). Does a seller's ecommerce reputation matter? Evidence from eBay auctions. *Journal of Industrial Economics, 50*, 337–349.

Menard, V. S. (1993). Admission of computer generated visual evidence: Should there be clear standards? *Software Law Journal, 6*, 325.

Memon, A. (2008). *A field evaluation of the VIPER system in Scotland.* http://www.sipr.ac.uk/downloads/Memon_%20VIPER%20Field%20study.pdf

Memon, A., Bartlett, J. C., Rose, R., & Gray, C. (2003). The aging eyewitness: The effects of face-age and delay upon younger and older observers. *Journal of Gerontology, 58*, 338–345.

Memon, A., & Bull, R. (Eds.). (1999). *Handbook of the psychology of interviewing.* Chichester: Wiley. Published in paperback, 2001.

Memon, A., & Gabbert, F. (2003a). Unravelling the effects of a sequential lineup. *Applied Cognitive Psychology, 6*, 703–714.

Memon, A., & Gabbert, F. (2003b). Improving the identification accuracy of senior witnesses: Do pre-lineup questions and sequential testing help? *Journal of Applied Psychology, 88*(2), 341–347.

Memon, A., Hope, L., Bartlett, J., & Bull, R. (2002). Eyewitness recognition errors: The effects of mugshot viewing and choosing in young and old adults. *Memory and Cognition, 30*, 1219–1227.

Memon, A., Hope, L., & Bull, R. H. C. (2003). Exposure duration: Effects on eyewitness accuracy and confidence. *British Journal of Psychology, 94*, 339–354.

Memon, A., & Wright, D. (1999). The search for John Doe 2: Eyewitness testimony and the Oklahoma bombing. *The Psychologist, 12*, 292–295.

Memon, A., Vrij, A., & Bull, R. (1998). *Psychology and law: Truthfulness, accuracy and credibility.* London: McGraw-Hill. Second edition: *Psychology and law. Truthfulness, accuracy and credibility of victims, witnesses and suspects.* Chichester: Wiley, 2003.

Mena, J. (2003). *Investigative data mining for security and criminal detection.* Amsterdam & Boston (Newton, MA): Butterworth-Heinemann (of Elsevier).

Mendelsohn, S. (1891). *The criminal jurisprudence of the jews.* Baltimore, MD: M. Curlander; 2nd edn., New York: Sepher-Hermon Press, 1968.

Merkl, D., & Schweighofer, D. (1997). The exploration of legal text corpora with hierarchical neural networks: A guided tour in public international law. In *Proceedings of sixth International Conference on Artificial Intelligence and Law (ICAIL'97),* Melbourne, Australia. New York: ACM Press, pp. 98–105.

Merkl, D., Schweighofer, E., & Winiwarter, W. (1999). Exploratory analysis of concept and document spaces with connectionist networks. *Artificial Intelligence and Law, 7*(2/3), 185–209.

Merlino, A., Morey, D., & Maybury, M. T. (1997). Broadcast news navigation using story segments. In *Proceedings of ACM Multimedia '97,* pp. 381–391.

Merricks, T. (1995). Warrant entails truth. *Philosophy and Phenomenological Research, 55*(4), 841–855.

Merrill, T. W., & Smith, H. E. (2000). Optimal standardization in the law of property: The numerus clausus principle. *Yale Law Journal, 110*, 1–70.

Merton, R. K. (1948) The self-fulfilling prophecy. *The Antioch Review, 8*, 193–210.

Mertz, E., & Yovel, J. (2005). Courtroom narrative. In D. Herman, M. Jahn, & M.-L. Ryan (Eds.), *Routledge encyclopedia of narrative theory* (pp. 86–88). London: Routledge, 2005 (hardcover), 2008 (paperback).

Meudell, P. R., Hitch, G. J., & Boyle, M. M. (1995). Collaboration in recall: Do pairs of people cross-cue each other to produce new memories? *The Quarterly Journal of Experimental Psychology, 48*a, 141–152.

Meyer, R. K., & Friedman, H. (1992). Whither relevant arithmetic? *The Journal of Symbolic Logic, 57*, 824–831.

Michie, D., Spiegelhalter, D. J., & Taylor, C. C. (Eds.). (1994). *Machine learning, neural and statistical classification.* West Sussex. England: Ellis Horwood.

Michon, J. A., & Pakes, F. J. (1995). Judicial decision-making: A theoretical perspective. Chapter 6.2 In R. Bull & D. Carson (Ed.), *Handbook of psychology in legal contexts* (pp. 509–525). Chichester: Wiley.

Miikkulainen, R. (1993). *Subsymbolic natural language processing*. Cambridge, MA: MIT Press. The book is based on a dissertation posted at: ftp://ftp.cs.utexas.edu/pub/neural-nets/papers/miikkulainen.diss.tar

Miikkulainen, R., & Dyer, M. G. (1991). Natural language processing with modular PDP networks and distributed lexicon. *Cognitive Science, 15*, 343–400.

Miller, F. (1969). *Prosecution: The decision to charge a suspect with a crime*. Boston: Little, Brown.

Miller, L. S. (1984). Bias among forensic document examiners: A need for procedural changes. *Journal of Police Science and Administration, 12*(4), 407–411.

Miller, L. S. (1987). Procedural bias in forensic science examinations of human hair. *Law and Human Behavior, 11*(2), 157–163.

Miller, M. T. (2003). Crime scene investigation. Chapter 8 In S. H. James & J. J. Nordby (Eds.), *Forensic science: An introduction to scientific and investigative techniques* (1st ed.). Boca Raton, FL: CRC Press. Also as Chapter 10 in 2nd edition, 2005. Also published in the 3rd edition, 2009.

Miller, R. E. (1973). A comparison of some theoretical models of parallel computation. *IEEE Transactions on Computers, C 22*, 710–717.

Milne, R., & Bull, R. (1999). *Investigative interviewing: Psychology and practice*. Chichester: Wiley.

Minh, T. T. H. (2007). *Approaches to XML schema matching*. Ph.D. Thesis. Norwich, England: University of East Anglia.

Minkov, E., & Cohen, W. W. (2006). An email and meeting assistant using graph walks. In *Third Conference on Email and Anti-Spam CEAS 2006*, Palo Alto, CA. New York: ACM, pp. 14–20.

Minsky, M. (1975). A framework for representing knowledge. In P. Winston (Ed.), *The psychology of computer vision*. New York: McGraw-Hill.

Minsky, M. (2002). *The emotion machine* (Part 6). New York: Pantheon. http://web.media.mit.edu/~minsky/E6/eb6.html

Minsky, M., & Papert, S. (1969). *Perceptrons: An introduction to computational geometry*. Cambridge, MA: MIT Press.

Mishler, E. G. (1995). Models of narrative analysis: A typology. *Journal of Narrative and Life History, 5*(2), 87–123. Mahwa, NJ: Lawrence Erlbaum Associates.

Misra, S., Abraham, K. I., Obaidat, M. S., & Krishna, P. V. (2009). LAID: A learning automata-based scheme for intrusion detection in wireless sensor networks. *Security in Wireless Sensor Networks*,[67] *2*(2), 105–115.

Mitchell, H. B. (2010). Markov random fields. Chapter 17 In H. B. Mitchell, *Image fusion: Theories, techniques and applications* (pp. 205–209). Berlin: Springer. doi://10.1007/978-3-642-11216-4_17

Mitchell, T. M. (1997). *Machine learning*. New York: McGraw-Hill.

Mitra, S., Banka, H., & Pedrycz, W. (2006). Rough-fuzzy collaborative clustering. *IEEE Transactions on Systems, Man & Cybernetics, B, 36*, 795–805.

MITRE. (2001). S*topping traffic: Anti drug network (ADNET). MITRE digest archives*. http://www.mitre.org/news/digest/archives/2001/adnet.html

Mitschick, A., & Meissner, K. (2008). Metadata generation and consolidation within an ontology-based document management system. *International Journal of Metadata, Semantics and Ontologies, 3*(4), 249–259.

Mittag, D. (2004). Evidentialism. *Internet Encyclopedia of Philosophy*. www.iep.utm.edu

Mizanur Rahman, S. M., Nasser, N., Inomata, A., Okamoto, T., Mambo, M., & Okamoto, E. (2008). Anonymous authentication and secure communication protocol for wireless mobile ad hoc networks. *Security and Communication Networks, 1*(2), 179–189.

Moens, M.-F. (2000). *Automatic indexing and abstracting of document texts*. Dordrecht, The Netherlands: Kluwer.

---

[67] The journal *Security in Wireless Sensor Networks* is published by Wiley.

Moens, M.-F. (2001). Legal text retrieval. *Artificial Intelligence and Law, 9*(1), 29–57.

Moens, M.-F., Uyttendaele, C., & Dumortier, J. (1997). Abstracting of legal cases: The SALOMON experience. In *Proceedings of the sixth international conference on artificial intelligence and law*. Melbourne, Australia. New York: ACM Press, pp. 114–122.

Moens, M.-F., Uyttendaele, C., & Dumortier, J. (1999). Abstracting of legal cases: The potential of clustering based on the selection of representative objects. *Journal of the American Society for Information Science, 50*(2), 151–161.

Moenssens, A. (1999). Is fingerprint identification a "science"? *Forensic-Evidence.com.* http://www.forensicevidence.com/site/ID00042.html

Moenssens, A. (2003). Fingerprint identification: A valid reliable "forensic science"? *Criminal Justice, 18*, 31–37.

Moh, S.-K. (1950). The deduction theorems and two new logical systems. *Methodos, 2*, 56–75.

Mokherjee, D., & Sopher, B. (1994). Learning behavior in an experimental matching pennies game. *Games and Economic Behavior, 7*(1), 62–91. Orlando, FL: Academic.

Molina, D. K. (2009). *Handbook of forensic toxicology for medical examiners*. Boca Raton, FL: CRC Press.

Mommers, L. (2003). Application of a knowledge-based ontology of the legal domain in collaborative workspaces. In G. Sartor (Ed.), *Proceedings of the ninth International Conference on Artificial Intelligence and Law (ICAIL 2003)*, Edinburgh, Scotland, 24–28 June 2003 (pp. 70–76). New York: ACM Press.

Monahan, J., & Loftus, E. F. (1982). The psychology of law. *Annual Review of Psychology, 33*, 441–475.

Monmonier, M. S. (1996). *How to lie with maps*. Chicago: University of Chicago Press.

Moore, D. S. (2007). Recent advances in trace explosives detection instrumentation. *Sense Imaging, 8*, 9–38. doi://10.1007/s11220-007-0029-8

Moorman, K. (1997). *A functional theory of creative reading: Process, knowledge, and evaluation*. Doctoral dissertation. Atlanta, GA: College of Computing, Georgia Institute of Technology.

Moorman, K., & Ram, A. (1994). Integrating creativity and reading: A functional approach. At the *Sixteenth annual conference of the cognitive science society*.

Moreno, J. L. (1953). *Who shall survive: Foundations of sociometry, group psychotherapy, and sociodrama*. Boston, MA: Beacon House. (Originally published in 1934 and later in 1953 and 1978)

Morgan, J. E. (2008). Noncredible competence: How to handle "newbies", "wannabes", and forensic "experts" who know better or should know better. In R. L. Heilbronner (Ed.), *Neuropsychology in the courtroom: Expert analysis of reports and testimony*. New York: Guilford Press.

Morris, R. N. (2000). *Forensic handwriting identification: Fundamental concepts and principles*. London & San Diego, CA: Academic.

Morrison, R. D. (2002). Subsurface models used in environmental forensics. Chapter 8 In B. L. Murphy & R. D. Morrison (Eds.), *Introduction to environmental forensics* (pp. 311–367). San Diego, CA & London: Academic pp. 311–367.

Mortera, J., & Dawid, A. P. (2006). *Probability and evidence*. Research Report 264, March. Department of Statistical Science, University College London.

Mortera, J., Dawid, A. P., & Lauritzen, S. L. (2003). Probabilistic expert systems for DNA mixture profiling. *Theoretical Population Biology, 63*, 191–205.

Morton, A. (2003). *A guide through the theory of knowledge* (3rd ed.). Oxford: Blackwell.

Mørup, M. (2011). Applications of tensor (multiway array) factorizations and decompositions in data mining. *Wiley Interdisciplinary Reviews (WIREs): Data Mining and Knowledge Discovery, 1*(1), 24–40. doi://10.1002/widm.1

Morzy, M. (2008). New algorithms for mining the reputation of participants of online auctions. *Algorithmica, 52*, 95–112.

Moulin, B. (1992). A conceptual graph approach for representing temporal information in discourse. *Knowledge-Based Systems, 5*(3), 183–192.

Moulin, B., & Rousseau, D. (1994). A multi-agent approach for modelling conversations. In *Proceedings of the international avignon conference AI 94, Natural language processing sub-conference*, Paris, France, June 1994, pp. 35–50.

Mueller, E. T. (1987). *Daydreaming and computation: A computer model of everyday creativity, learning, and emotions in the human stream of thought*. Doctoral dissertation. Technical Report CSD-870017, UCLA-AI-87-8 Computer Science Department, University of California, Los Angeles. On microfilm, Ann Arbor, MI: UMI.

Mueller, E. T. (1990). *Daydreaming in humans and machines: A computer model of the stream of thought*. Norwood, NJ: Ablex.

Mueller, E. T. (1998). *Natural language processing with ThoughtTreasure*. New York: Signiform.

Mueller, E. T. (1999a). *A database and lexicon of scripts for ThoughtTreasure*. CogPrints cog00000555.

Mueller, E. T. (1999b). *Prospects for in-depth story understanding by computer*. CogPrints cog00000554. http://web.media.mit.edu/~mueller/papers/storyund.html

Mueller, E. T. (2002). Story understanding. In *Nature encyclopedia of cognitive science*. London: Nature Publishing Group.

Mueller, E. T. (2003). Story understanding through multi-representation model construction. In G. Hirst & S. Nirenburg (Eds.), *Text meaning: Proceedings of the HLT-NAACL 2003 workshop* (pp. 46–53). East Stroudsburg, PA: Association for Computational Linguistics.

Mueller, E. T. (2004). Understanding script-based stories using commonsense reasoning. *Cognitive Systems Research, 5*(4), 307–340.

Mueller, E. T. (2004). Event calculus reasoning through satisfiability. *Journal of Logic and Computation, 14*(5), 703–730.

Mueller, E. T. (2006). *Commonsense reasoning*. San Francisco: Morgan Kaufmann.

Mueller, E. T. (2007). Modelling space and time in narratives about restaurants. *Literary and Linguistic Computing, 22*(1), 67–84.

Mueller, E. T., & Dyer, M. G. (1985a). Towards a computational theory of human daydreaming. In *Proceedings of the seventh annual conference of the cognitive science society*. Hillsdale, NJ: Lawrence Erlbaum, pp. 120–129.

Mueller, E. T., & Dyer, M. G. (1985b). Daydreaming in humans and computers. In *Proceedings of the ninth International Joint Conference on Artificial Intelligence (IJCAI'85)*, Los Angeles, CA, 18–24 August 1985. San Mateo, CA: Morgan Kaufmann. http://ijcai.org/search.php

Mukherjee, I., & Schapire, R. E. (2011). A theory of multiclass boosting. *Advances in Neural Information Processing Systems, 23*. http://www.cs.princeton.edu/~schapire/papers/multiboost.pdf

Munn, K., & Smith, B. (Eds.). (2008). *Applied ontology: An introduction*. Lancaster, (Metaphysical Research, 9.) Frankfurt/M, Germany: Ontos Verlag, & England: Gazelle.

Murbach, R., & Nonn, E. (1991). Sentencing by artificial intelligence tools: Some possibilities and limitations. Paper presented at *The Joint Meeting of the Law and Society Association and the Research Committee of the Sociology of Law of the International Sociological Association*, Amsterdam, 1991.

Murphy, B. L., & Morrison, R. D. (Eds.). (2002). *Introduction to environmental forensics*. San Diego, CA & London: Academic.

Murray, R. C., & Tedrow, J. C. F. (1975). *Forensic geology: Earth sciences and criminal investigations*. New Brunswick, NJ: Rutgers University Press.

Musatti, C. L. (1931). *Elementi di psicologia della testimonianza* (1st ed.). Padova, Italy: CEDAM, 1931. Second edition, with comments added by the author, Padova: Liviana Editrice, 1989.

Na, H.-J., Yoon, D.-H., Kim, Ch.-S., & Hwang, H. S. (2005). Vulnerability evaluation tools of matching algorithm and integrity verification in fingerprint recognition. In R. Khosla, R. J. Howlett, & L. C. Jain (Eds.), *Knowledge-based intelligent information and engineering systems: 9th international conference, KES 2005, Melbourne, Australia, September 14–16, 2005, Proceedings, Part IV* (pp. 993–999). (Lecture Notes in Computer Science, Vol. 3684). Berlin: Springer.

Naess, E., Frincke, D. A., McKinnon, A. D., &. Bakken, D. E. (2005). Configurable middleware-level intrusion detection for embedded systems. At the *Second International Workshop on Security in Distributed Computing Systems (SDCS)*, In: *Proceedings of the 25th International Conference on Distributed Computing Systems Workshops (ICDCS 2005 Workshops)*, 6–10 June 2005, Columbus, OH, USA. IEEE Computer Society 2005, pp. 144–151.

Nagel, I. H., & Hagan, J. (1983). Gender and crime: Offense patterns and criminal court sanctions. In M. Tonry & N. Morris (Eds.), *Crime and justice: An annual review of research* (Vol. 4, pp. 91–144). Chicago, IL: University of Chicago Press.

Nagel, S. (1962). Judicial backgrounds and criminal cases. *Journal of Criminal Law, Criminology and Police Science, 53*, 333–339.

Nagel, S. (1964). Testing empirical generalisations. In G. Schubert (Ed.), *Judicial behaviour: A reader in theory and research* (pp. 518–529). Chicago, IL: Rand McNally & Company.

Nakhimovsky, A., & Myers, T. (2002). *XML programming: Web applications and web services with JSP and ASP.* (The Expert's Voice Series.) Berkeley, CA: Apress.

Nambiar, P., Bridges, T. E., & Brown, K. A. (1995). Quantitative forensic evaluation of bite marks with the aid of a shape analysis computer program. I: The development of SCIP and the similarity index. *Journal of Forensic Odontostomatology, 13*(2), 18–25.

Nance, D. A., & Morris, S. B. (2002). An empirical assessment of presentation formats for trace evidence with a relatively large and quantifiable random match probability. *Jurimetrics Journal, 42*, 403–445.

Nance, D. A., & Morris, S. B. (2005). Juror understanding of DNA evidence: An empirical assessmeng of presentation formats for trace evidence with a relatively small random-match probability. *Journal of Legal Studies, 34*, 395–443.

Nanto, H., Sokooshi, H., & Kawai, T. (1993). Aluminum-doped ZnO thin film gas sensor capable of detecting freshness of sea foods. *Sensors & Actuators, 14*, 715–717.

Napier, M. R., & Baker, K. P. (2005). Criminal personality profiling. Chapter 31 In S. H. James & J. J. Nordby (Eds.), *Forensic science: An introduction to scientific and investigative techniques* (2nd ed.). Boca Raton, FL: CRC Press. Also in 3rd edition, 2009.

National Criminal Intelligence Service. (2000). *The national criminal intelligence model.* London: NCIS.

National Research Council. (1996). *The evaluation of forensic DNA evidence.* Washington, DC: National Academy Press.

Nebel, B. (1994). Base revision operations and schemes: semantics, representation, and complexity. In A. G. Cohn (Ed.), *Proceedings of the 11th European conference on artificial intelligence.* New York: Wiley.

Neill, A. (1991). Fear, fiction and make-believe. *The Journal of Aesthetics and Art Criticism, 49*, 47–56.

Neill, A. (1993). Fiction and the emotions. *American Philosophical Quarterly, 30*, 1–13.

Neill, A. (1995). Emotional responses to fiction: Reply to Radford. *The Journal of Aesthetics and Art Criticism, 53*(1), 75–78.

Neimark, J. (1996). The diva of disclosure, memory researcher Elizabeth Loftus. *Psychology Today, 29*(1). Article downloadable from: http://faculty.washington.edu/eloftus/Articles/psytoday.htm

Nenov, V. I., & Dyer, M. G. (1993). Perceptually grounded language learning: Part 1: A neural network architecture for robust sequential association. *Connection Science, 5*(2), 115–138.

Nenov, V. I., & Dyer, M. G. (1994). Perceptually grounded language learning: Part 2: DETE: A neural/procedural model. *Connection Science, 6*(1), 3–41.

Neville, J., Adler, M., & Jensen, D. (2003). Clustering relational data using attribute and link information. In *Proceedings of the Text Mining and Link Analysis Workshop, 18th International Joint Conference on Artificial Intelligence.*

Neville, J., & Jensen, D. (2003). Collective classification with relational dependency networks. In S. Džeroski, L. De Raedt, & S. Wrobel (Eds.), *Proceedings of the second Multi-Relational Data Mining workshop (MRDM-2003)*, Washington, DC, 27 August 2003, at the *Ninth ACM*

SIGKDD International Conference on Knowledge Discovery and Data Mining (KDD'03), pp. 77–91. http://www.cs.purdue.edu/homes/neville/papers/neville-jensen-mrdm2003.pdf

Neville, J., Jensen, D., Friedland, L., & Hay, M. (2003). Learning relational probability trees. In *Proceedings of the 9th ACM SIGKDD International Conference on Knowledge Discovery and Data Mining*, pp. 625–630. http://www.cs.purdue.edu/homes/neville/papers/neville-et-al-kdd2003.pdf

Neville, J., Rattigan, M., & Jensen, D. (2003). Statistical relational learning: Four claims and a survey. In *Proceedings of the Workshop on Learning Statistical Models from Relational Data, 18th International Joint Conference on Artificial Intelligence.*

Neville, J., Simsek, O., Jensen, D., Komoroske, J., Palmer, K., & Goldberg, H. (2005). Using relational knowledge discovery to prevent securities fraud. In *Proceedings of the 11th ACM SIGKDD international conference on Knowledge Discovery and Data Mining (KDD'05)*, Chicago, IL, 21–24 August 2005. New York: ACM Press, pp. 449–458. http://www.cs.purdue.edu/homes/neville/papers/neville-et-al-kdd2005.pdf

Newburn, T., Williamson, T., & Wright, A. (Eds.). (2007). *Handbook of criminal investigation.* Cullompton: Willan Publishing.

Newell, A. (1962). Some problems of the basic organisation in problem solving programs. In M. C. Yovits, G. T. Jacobi & G. D. Goldstein (Eds.), *Proceedings of the second conference on self-organizing systems* (pp. 393–423). Washington, DC: Spartan Books.

Newman, M. E. (2003). The structure and function of complex networks. *SIAM Review, 45*(2), 167–256.

Newman, M. E. (2010). *Networks: An introduction.* Oxford: Oxford University Press.

Ng, H. T., Teo, L. H., & Kwan, J. L. P. (2000). A machine learning approach to answering questions for reading comprehension tests. In *Proceedings of the 2000 joint SIGDAT conference on Empirical Methods in Natural Language Processing and Very Large Corpora* (EMNLP/VLC-2000), pp. 124–132. http://www.comp.nus.edu.sg/~nght/pubs/emnlp_vlc00.pdf.gz

Ng, T.-T., & Chang, S.-F. (2004). A model for image splicing. At the *IEEE International Conference on Image Processing (ICIP)*, Singapore, October 2004.

Ng-Thow-Hing, V. (1994). *A biomechanical musculotendon model for animating articulated objects.* MSc Thesis (supervised by E. Fiume). Toronto, Canada: University of Toronto, Department of Computer Science.

Ng-Thow-Hing, V. (2001). *Anatomically based models for physical and geometric reconstruction of animals.* PhD Thesis (supervised by E. Fiume). Toronto, Canada: University of Toronto, Department of Computer Science.

Nicolle, D. (1990). *The Mongol Warlords: Genghis Khan, Kublai Khan, Hülegü, Tamerlane*, with plates by R. Hook. Poole, Dorset, England: Firebird Books.

Nicoloff, F. (1989). Threats and illocutions. *Journal of Pragmatics, 13*(4), 501–522.

Nicolson, D. (1994). Truth, reason and justice: Epistemology and politics in evidence discourse. *The Modern Law Review, 57*(5), 726–744.

Nielsen, L., & Nespor, S. (1993). *Genetic test, screening, and use of genetic data by public authorities: In criminal justice, social security, and alien and foreigners acts.* Copenhagen: Danish Centre for Human Rights.

Niesz, A. J., & Holland, N. (1984). Interactive fiction. *Critical Inquiry, 11*, 110–129.

Nigro, H. O., González Císaro, S. E., & Xodo, D. H. (Eds.). (2008). *Data mining with ontologies: implementations, findings and frameworks.* Hershey, PA: Information Science Reference.

Nijboer, J. F. (2000). Challenges for the law of evidence. In C. M. Breur, M. M. Kommer, J. F. Nijboer, & J. M. Reijntjes (Eds.), *New trends in criminal investigation and evidence, Vol. 2 = Proceedings of the second world conference on new trends in criminal investigation and evidence*, Amsterdam, 10–15 December 1999. Antwerp, Belgium: Intersentia, 2000, pp. 1–9.

Nijboer, J. F. (2008). Current issues in evidence and procedure: Comparative comments from a Continental perspective. *International Commentary on Evidence*,[68] 6(2), Article 7. http://www.bepress.com/ice/vol6/iss2/art7

---

[68] The e-journal *International Commentary on Evidence* is published in Berkeley, California.

Nijboer, H., & Sennef, A. (1999). Justification. Chapter 2 In M. Malsch & J. F. Nijboer (Eds.), *Complex cases: Perspectives on the Netherlands criminal justice system* (pp. 11–26). Amsterdam: THELA THESIS.

Nijholt, A. (2002). Embodied agents: A new impetus for humor research. In O. Stock, C. Strapparava, & A. Nijholt (Eds.), *The April Fools' Day workshop on computational humour*, April 2002 (*Proceedings of the 20th Twente Workshop on Language Technology, TWLT 20*) (pp. 101–112). Enschede, The Netherlands: University of Twente.

Nirenburg, S., & Raskin, V. (1987). The subworld concept lexicon and the lexicon management system. *Computational Linguistics, 13*(3/4), 276–289.

Nirenburg, S., & Raskin, V. (1996). *Ten choices for lexical semantics.* Memoranda in Computer and Cognitive Science, MCCS-96-304. Las Cruces, NM: New Mexico State University, Computing Research Laboratory.

Nirenburg, S., & Raskin, V. (2004). *Principles of ontological semantics.* Cambridge, MA: MIT Press.

Nissan, E. (1982). *Proprietà formali nel progetto logico-concettuale di basi di dati.* (Italian: *Formal properties in the logical and conceptual design of databases.*) 2 vols., 400+200 pages. Tesi di Laurea in Ingegneria Elettronica, Dipartimento di Elettronica. Milan: Politecnico di Milano (= Technical University of Milan). Awarded the Burroughs Italiana Prize.

Nissan, E. (1983). The info-spatial derivative: A new formal tool for database design. In *Proceedings of the AICA'83 conference*, Naples, Vol. 2, pp. 177–182.

Nissan, E. (1986). The frame-definition language for customizing the RAFFAELLO structure-editor in host expert systems. In Z. Raś & M. Zemankova (Eds.), *Proceedings of the first International Symposium on Methodologies for Intelligent Systems (ISMIS'86)*, Knoxville, TN. New York: ACM SIGART Press, pp. 8–18.

Nissan, E. (1987a). Nested-relation based frames in RAFFAELLO. Representation & meta-representation structure & semantics for knowledge engineering. In H. J. Schek & M. Scholl (Eds.), *International workshop on theory and applications of nested relations and complex objects*, Darmstadt, Germany, 1987. Report. Rocquencourt, France: INRIA, 1987, pp. 95–99.

Nissan, E. (1987b). The *wining and dining* project. Part II: An expert system for gastronomy and terminal food-processing. In a special issue on information technology, *International Journal of Hospitality Management, 6*(4), 207–215.

Nissan, E. (1987c). Data analysis using a geometrical representation of predicate calculus. *Information Sciences, 41*(3), 187–258.

Nissan, E. (1987d). ONOMATURGE: An expert system for word-formation and morpho-semantic clarity evaluation (in two parts). In H. Czap & C. Galinski (Eds.), *Terminology and knowledge engineering [Proceedings of the First International Conference]*, Trier, West Germany (pp. 167–176 and 177–189). Frankfurt/M, West Germany: Indeks Verlag.

Nissan, E. (1988). *ONOMATURGE: An expert system in word-formation.* Ph.D. Dissertation (Computer Science). 3 vols., ca. 600 pages (in English). Beer-Sheva, Israel: Ben-Gurion University of the Negev. Project awarded the 1988 IPA Award in Computer Science.

Nissan, E. (1991). Artificial intelligence as a dialectic of science and technology, and other aspects. Chapter 5 In M. Negrotti (Ed.), *Understanding the artificial: On the future shape of artificial intelligence* (pp. 77–90). Heidelberg: Springer. Italian version: L'intelligenza artificiale come dialettica fra scienza e tecnologia. Chapter 5 In M. Negrotti (Ed.), *Capire l'artificiale* (pp. 119–140). Turin: Bollati-Boringhieri (1990); also in the 2nd edition of the Italian book, of 1993.

Nissan, E. (1992). Deviation models of regulation: A knowledge-based approach. *Informatica e Diritto*, year 18 (= 2nd series, vol. 1), (1/2), 181–212.

Nissan, E. (1995a). Meanings, expression, and prototypes. *Pragmatics & Cognition, 3*(2), 317–364.

Nissan, E. (1995b). SEPPHORIS: An augmented hypergraph-grammar representation for events, stipulations, and legal prescriptions. *Law, Computers, and Artificial Intelligence, 4*(1), 33–77.

Nissan, E. (1996). From ALIBI to COLUMBUS. In J. Hulstijn & A. Nijholt (Eds.), *Automatic interpretation and generation of verbal humor: Proceedings of the 12th Twente workshop on language technology*, Twente (pp. 69–85). Enschede, The Netherlands: University of Twente.

Nissan, E. (1997a). Notions of place: A few considerations. In A. A. Martino (Ed.), *Logica delle norme* (pp. 256–302). Pisa, Italy: SEU.

Nissan, E. (1997b). Notions of place, II. In A. A. Martino (Ed.), *Logica delle norme* (pp. 303–361). Pisa, Italy: SEU.

Nissan, E. (1997c). Emotion, culture, communication. *Pragmatics & Cognition, 5*(2), 355–369.

Nissan, E. (1997d). Review of: N. Sharkey (Ed.), *Connectionist natural language processing*, Kluwer, Dordrecht & Intellect, Oxford, 1992. *Pragmatics and Cognition, 5*(2), 383–384.

Nissan, E. (1998a). Advances in deontic logic (review). *Computers and Artificial Intelligence, 17*(4), 392–400.

Nissan, E. (1998b). Review of: A. G. B. ter Meulen, Representing time in natural language: The dynamic interpretation of tense and aspect (Cambridge, MA: The MIT Press, 1997). *Computers and Artificial Intelligence, 17*(1), 98–100.

Nissan, E. (1999). Using the CuProS metarepresentation language for defining flexible nested-relation structures for monolingual and multilingual terminological databases. [*Proceedings of the EAFT*] *Conference on co-operation in the field of terminology in Europe*, Paris, 17–19 May 1999. Paris: Union Latine, 2000, pp. 337–343.

Nissan, E. (2000a). Artificial intelligence and criminal evidence: A few topics. In C. M. Breur, M. M. Kommer, J. F. Nijboer, & J. M. Reijntjes (Eds.), *New trends in criminal investigation and evidence, Vol. 2 = Proceedings of the second world conference on new trends in criminal investigation and evidence*, Amsterdam, 10–15 December 1999 (pp. 495–521). Antwerp, Belgium: Intersentia.

Nissan, E. (2000b). Computer-generated alternative coinages: An automated ranking model for their psychosemantic transparency. In *Proceedings of the EAFT conference on co-operation in the field of terminology in Europe*, Paris, May 17–19, 1999 (Union Latine, Paris, 2000), pp. 321–336.

Nissan, E. (2000c). Registers of use, and ergolectal versus literary niches for neologizing creativity: What do the makers of technical terminology stand to learn from such contrastive analysis? In *Proceedings of the EAFT conference on co-operation in the field of terminology in Europe*, Paris, May 1999, pp. 227–239.

Nissan, E. (2001a). The Bayesianism debate in legal scholarship. [Review article on Allen & Redmayne (1997).] *Artificial Intelligence and Law, 9*(2/3), 199–214.

Nissan, E. (2001b). Can you measure circumstantial evidence? The background of probative formalisms for law. [A review essay on I. Rosoni, *Quae singula non prosunt collecta iuvant: la teoria della prova indiziaria nell'età medievale e moderna*. Milan, Italy: Giuffrè, 1995.]. *Information and Communications Technology Law, 10*(2), 231–245.

Nissan, E. (2001c). The Jama legal narrative. Part II: A foray into concepts of improbability. *Information & Communications Technology Law, 10*(1), 39–52. Part I is Geiger et al. (2001).

Nissan, E. (2001d). An AI formalism for competing claims of identification: Capturing the "Smemorato di Collegno" amnesia case. *Computing and Informatics, 20*(6), 625–656.

Nissan, E. (2001e). Review of: E. Harnon & A. Stein (Eds.), *Rights of the Accused, Crime Control and Protection of Victims* [special volume of the *Israel Law Review*, 31(1–3), 1997]. *Information and Communications Technology Law, 10*(2), 247–254.

Nissan, E. (2001f). Review of: R. Bull and D. Carson (Eds.), *Handbook of Psychology in Legal Contexts* (Chichester, West Sussex, England: Wiley, 1995). *Artificial Intelligence and Law, 9*(2/3), pp. 219–224.

Nissan, E. (2001g). Modelling spatial relations in the traveller's conditional divorce problem. In M. Koppel & E. Merzbach (Eds.), *Higgaion: Studies in rabbinic logic* (Vol. 5, pp. 8–21). Jerusalem: Aluma.

Nissan, E. (2002a). The COLUMBUS Model (2 parts). *International Journal of Computing Anticipatory Systems, 12*, 105–120 and 121–136.

Nissan, E. (2002b). A formalism for misapprehended identities: Taking a leaf out of Pirandello. In O. Stock, C. Strapparava, & A. Nijholt (Eds.), *The April Fools' Day Workshop on Computational Humour, Proceedings of the Twentieth Twente Workshop on Language Technology (TWLT20)*, Trento, Italy, April 15–16, 2002 (pp. 113–123). Enschede, The Netherlands: University of Twente.

Nissan, E. (2003a). Identification and doing without it, I: A situational classification of misapplied personal identity, with a formalism for a case of multiple usurped identity in Marivaux. *Cybernetics and Systems, 34*(4/5), 317–358.

Nissan, E. (2003b). Identification and doing without it, II: Visual evidence for pinpointing identity. How Alexander was found out: Purposeful action, enlisting support, assumed identity, and recognition. A goal-driven formal analysis. *Cybernetics and Systems, 34*(4/5), 359–380.

Nissan, E. (2003c). Identification and doing without it, III: Authoritative opinions, purposeful action, relabelled goods, and forensic examinations. The case of the stuffed birds: Its narrative dynamics set in formulae. *Cybernetics and Systems, 34*(6/7), 467–500.

Nissan, E. (2003d). Identification and doing without it, IV: A formal mathematical analysis for the feveroles case, of mixup of kinds and ensuing litigation; and a formalism for the "Cardiff Giant" double hoax. *Cybernetics and Systems, 34*(6/7), 501–530.

Nissan, E. (2003e). Facets of abductive reasoning. [Review essay on: Magnani, L. (2001). *Abduction, reason, and science: Processes of discovery and explanation.* New York: Kluwer/Plenum; Josephson, J. R., & Josephson, S. G. (Eds.). (1994). *Abductive inference: Computation, philosophy, technology.* Cambridge: Cambridge University Press; Bunt, H., & Black, W. (Eds.). (2000). *Abduction, belief and context in dialogue: Studies in computational pragmatics.* Amsterdam: Benjamins.] *Cybernetics and Systems, 34*(4/5), 381–399.

Nissan, E. (2003f). Review of Hastie (1993). *Cybernetics and Systems, 34*(6/7), 551–558.

Nissan, E. (2003g). Review of Murphy & Morrison (2002). *Cybernetics & Systems, 34*(6/7), 571–579.

Nissan, E. (2003h). Review of Mani (2001). *Cybernetics & Systems, 34*(4/5), 559–569.

Nissan, E. (2003i). Recollecting from abroad: Marco Somalvico (1941–2002). In the special section (pp. 36–81) "In memoria di Marco Somalvico", *AI*IA Notizie: Periodico dell'Associazione Italiana per l'Intelligenza Artificiale, 16*(3), 38–39.

Nissan, E. (2004). Legal evidence scholarship meets artificial intelligence. [Reviewing MacCrimmon & Tillers (2002).] *Applied Artificial Intelligence, 18*(3/4), 367–389.

Nissan, E. (2007a). Tools for representing and processing narratives. In M. Quigley (Ed.), *Encyclopedia of information ethics and security* (pp. 638–644). Hershey, PA: IGI Global (formerly Idea Group), 2008 (but available from June 2007).

Nissan, E. (2007b). Goals, arguments, and deception: A formal representation from the AURANGZEB project. I: An Episode from the Succession War. II: A Formalism for the Capture of Murad. *Journal of Intelligent & Fuzzy Systems, 18*(3), 281–305 and 307–327.

Nissan, E. (2007c). Three perspectives on pretexts: Seeking self-exoneration by hierarchical decomposition; making an archetype-evoking claim; and rhetorical cover-up. In M. T. Turell, J. Cicres, & M. Spassova (Eds.), *Proceedings of the second IAFL European conference on forensic linguistics/language and the law (IAFL'06)*, Barcelona, Spain, 14–16 September 2006 (pp. 293–303). Barcelona: Documenta Universitaria, 2008.

Nissan, E. (2007d). Guest editorial of "Marco Somalvico Memorial Issue". Issue edited by M. Colombetti, G. Gini & E. Nissan. *Journal of Intelligent & Fuzzy Systems, 18*(3), 211–215.

Nissan, E. (2008a). Select topics in legal evidence and assistance by artificial intelligence techniques. *Cybernetics and Systems, 39*(4), 333–394.

Nissan, E. (2008b). Tools from artificial intelligence for handling legal evidence. In M. Quigley (Ed.), *Encyclopedia of information ethics and security* (pp. 42–48). Hershey, PA: IGI Global.

Nissan, E. (2008c). Argument structure models and visualization. In M. Pagani (Ed.), *Encyclopedia of multimedia technology and networking* (Vol. 1, pp. 75–82). Hershey, PA: IGI Global., 2nd Edition (3 vols.).

Nissan, E. (2008d). Argumentation and computing. In M. Quigley (Ed.), *Encyclopedia of information ethics and security* (pp. 30–35). Hershey, PA: IGI Global.

Nissan, E. (2008e). Argumentation with Wigmore Charts and computing. In M. Quigley (Ed.), *Encyclopedia of information ethics and security* (pp. 36–41). Hershey, PA: IGI Global.

Nissan, E. (2008f). Tools for representing and processing narratives. In M. Quigley (Ed.), *Encyclopedia of information ethics and security* (pp. 638–644). Hershey, PA.

Nissan, E. (2008g). Nested beliefs, goals, duties, and agents reasoning about their own or each other's body in the TIMUR model: A formalism for the narrative of tamerlane and the three painters. *Journal of Robotic and Intelligent and Robotic Systems, 52*(3–4), 515–582 (68 pages) + this paper's contents on pp. 340–341.

Nissan, E. (2008h). From embodied agents or their environments reasoning about the body, to virtual models of the human body: A quick overview. *Journal of Robotic and Intelligent and Robotic Systems, 52*(3–4), 489–513 + contents of this paper (on p. 340).

Nissan, E. (2008i). Medieval (and later) compulsory signs of group identity disclosure. Part I: The general pattern at the core of the social dynamics of the Jewish badge, set in episodic formulae and in systems & control block schemata. *Journal of Sociocybernetics, 6*(1), Summer 2008, 11–30. At www.unizar.es/sociocybernetics/

Nissan, E. (2008j). Epistemic formulae, argument structures, and a narrative on identity and deception: A formal representation from the AJIT subproject within AURANGZEB. *Annals of Mathematics and Artificial Intelligence, 54*(4), 2008 [2009], 293–362.

Nissan, E. (2008k). Chance vs. causality, and a taxonomy of explanations. In M. Negrotti (Ed.), *Natural chance, artificial chance,* thematic volume of *Yearbook of the Artificial: Nature, Culture & Technology,* 5. Basel, Switzerland: Peter Lang, 2008, pp. 195–258. Also an Italian translation: Il caso in relazione alla causalità, ed una tassonomia delle eziologie. In: Lanzavecchia, G., & Negrotti, M. (Eds.). (2008). *L'enigma del caso: Fatti, ipotesi e immagini* (pp. 93–149). Milan: Edizioni Goliardiche.

Nissan, E. (2008) [2010]. Un mistero risolto? Riflessioni in margine a *Il serpente biblico* di Valerio Marchi. *Rassegna Mensile di Israel* (Rome), *74*(1/2), 95–124. A different version, shorter but with an additional final section, is: La storia regionale come chiave per comprendere un para-dosso della storia d'Italia: Considerazioni su *Il serpente biblico* di Valerio Marchi. *Stradalta: Rivista dell'Associazione Storica Gonarese, 2* (Gonars, Friuli, 2009), 73–80.

Nissan, E. (2009a). Legal evidence, police intelligence, crime analysis or detection, forensic testing, and argumentation: An overview of computer tools or techniques. *Journal of Law and Information Technology, 17*(1), 1–82.

Nissan, E. (2009b). Eude and Eglon, Eleazar the Maccabee, and two early modern Indian narratives: Factors explaining the convergence of phylogenetically unconnected tales. *Journal of Indo-Judaic Studies, 10,* 81–92.

Nissan, E. (2009c). Computational models of the emotions: from models of the emotions of the individual, to modelling the emerging irrational behaviour of crowds. *AI & Society: Knowledge, Culture and Communication, 24*(4), 403–414.

Nissan, E. (2009d). Review of: A. Adamatzky, *Dynamics of Crowd-Minds: Patterns of Irrationality in Emotions, Beliefs and Actions* (World Scientific Series on Nonlinear Science, Series A, Vol. 54), Singapore, London, and River Edge, NJ: World Scientific, 2005. *Pragmatics & Cognition, 17*(2), 472–481.

Nissan, E. (2009) [2010]. Medieval (and later) compulsory signs of group identity disclosure. Part II: The intervention of Joseph Cazès in Teheran in 1898, set in episodic formulae. *Journal of Sociocybernetics, 7*(1), 54–96. At www.unizar.es/sociocybernetics/

Nissan, E. (2010a). Wearing the badge of the Alliance, vs. having to wear a badge to be told apart: Joseph Cazès in Teheran in 1898. Cognitive analysis, and cultural aspects. In a special issue on "Knowledge and Cognitive Science" of the *International Journal on Humanistic Ideology: Studies into the Nature and Origin of Humanistic Ideas, 3*(1), 59–108.

Nissan, E. (2010b). Revisiting Olender's *The Languages of Paradise,* placed in a broader context. *Quaderni di Studi Indo-Mediterranei,* 3. Alessandria, Piedmont, Italy: Edizioni dell'Orso, pp. 330–360.

Nissan, E. (2010c). Multilingual lexis, semantics, and onomasiology. Terminological database modelling, by using the CuProS metarepresentation language: An XML-compatible XML-precursor enabling flexible nested-relation structures. In N. Dershowitz & E. Nissan (Eds.), *Language, culture, computation: Essays in honour of Yaacov Choueka*. Vol. 2: *Tools for text and language, and the cultural dimension* (in press). Berlin: Springer.

Nissan, E. (2010d). Narratives, formalism, computational tools, and nonlinearity. In N. Dershowitz & E. Nissan (Eds.), *Language, culture, computation: Essays in Honour of Yaacov Choueka* (2 vols.), *Vol. 1: Theory, techniques, and applications to e-science, law, narratives, information retrieval, and the cultural heritage* (in press). Berlin: Springer.

Nissan, E. (2010e). Ethnocultural barriers medicalized: A critique of Jacobsen. *Journal of Indo-Judaic Studies, 11*, 75–119.

Nissan, E. (2010) [2011]. Ancient Jewish ideas about the Ocean and about how the Mediterranean Sea originated. Part III (§§ 12–15) in: E. Nissan, Going west vs. going east: Ancient Greek, Roman, Carthaginian, Mauretanian, and Celtic conceptions about or involvement with the Ocean, what early rabbinic texts say about the Ocean and the formation of the Mediterranean, and beliefs about reaching the Antipodes. (Review article.) *MHNH* [μηνη]: *revista internacional de investigación sobre magia y astrología antiguas* (Málaga), *10*, 279–310.

Nissan, E. (2011a). The rod and the crocodile: Temporal relations in textual hermeneutics: An application of Petri nets to semantics. *Semiotica, 184*(1/4), 187–227.

Nissan, E. (2011b). Aspects of Italy's Jewish experience, as shaped by local and global factors. In C. Gelbin & S. L. Gilman (Eds.), *Jewish culture in the age of globalisation*. Special issue in the *European Review of History/Revue européenne d'histoire, 18*(1), 131–142.

Nissan, E. (2011c). The Paradox of the Italian Jewish Experience in 1990–2010. *Changing Jewish Communities*, no. 66, 15 March 2011 (online, refereed monthly of the Institute for Global Jewish Affairs/Jerusalem Center for Public Affairs). http://jcpa.org/JCPA/Templates/ShowPage.asp?DRIT=4&DBID=1&LNGID=1&TMID=111&FID=623&FID=0&IID=6194&TTL=The_Paradox_of_the_Italian_Jewish_Experience_in_1990-2010

Nissan, E. (2011d). Reflections on a New Edition of Martial's *Liber spectaculorum:* Supplementary information from Jewish sources about the arena games. *Ludica: annali di storia e civiltà del gioco*, nos. 13/14 (pp. 224–240). Rome: Viella, for Treviso: Fondazione Benetton, 2007–2008 [March 2011].

Nissan, E. (2011e). Risks of ingestion: On eating tomatoes in Agnon, and on the water of Shittim. *Revue européenne des études hébraïques (REEH)*, Paris, 14, 2009 [2011], 46–79.

Nissan, E. (2011f). The dog ate it: The fate of homework as a situational archetype for a pretext. Social context, medium, and formalism. *The American Journal of Semiotics, 27*(1–4), 115–162.

Nissan, E. (forthcoming a). *All the* appearance of a pr*etext – In Courtroom examples, and in Gag cartoons*. Submitted book.
    Contains four fairly autonomous essays:
        Cognitive states, arguments, and representing legal narratives: The pragmatics of a claim with little credibility, Part **I:** "The dog ate it, m'lud" – The Newcastle case. An analysis with Wigmore charts.
        Cognitive states, arguments, and representing legal narratives: The pragmatics of a claim with little credibility, Part **II:** Mice ate the evidence – The Sofri case: An analysis with episodic formulae.
        The pragmatics of a claim with little credibility. Part **III:** A typology for "My dog ate my homework": (1) An analysis with decision tables of a topos in humour.
        The pragmatics of a claim with little credibility. Part **IV:** A typology for "My dog ate my homework": (2) Taxonomy enrichment by devising further situations and analysing their cognitive features.

Nissan, E. (forthcoming b). An Analysis with Wigmore Charts of Gulotta's last speech in defence to the bench in defence at the Bolzano trial. To appear in: G. Gulotta, M. Liberatore, & E. Nissan. *Memories Under Trial*.

Nissan, E., Cassinis, R., & Morelli, L. M. (2008). Have computation, animatronics, and robotic art anything to say about emotion, compassion, and how to model them? The *survivor* project. *Pragmatics & Cognition, 16*(1), 3–37 (2008). As a continuation of 15(3) (2007), special issue on "Mechanicism and autonomy: What can robotics teach us about human cognition and action?", third in the series Cognition and Technology.

Nissan, E., & Dragoni, A. F. (2000). Exoneration, and reasoning about it: A quick overview of three perspectives. Session on *Intelligent Decision Support for Legal Practice (IDS 2000)*, In *Proceedings of the international ICSC congress "Intelligent Systems & Applications" (ISA'2000)*, Wollongong, Australia, December 2000, Vol. 1, pp. 94–100.

Nissan, E., & El-Sana, J. (2012). A retrospective of a pioneering project. Earlier than XML, other than SGML, still going: CuProS metadata for deeply nested relations, and navigating for retrieval in RAFFAELLO. In N. Dershowitz & E. Nissan (Eds.), *Language, culture, computation: Essays in honour of Yaacov Choueka. Vol. 2: Tools for text and language, and the cultural dimension* (in press). Berlin: Springer.

Nissan, E., Galperin, A., Soper, A., Knight, B., & Zhao, J. (2001). Future states for a present-state estimate, in the contextual perspective of in-core nuclear fuel management. *International Journal of Computing Anticipatory Systems, 9*, 256–271.

Nissan, E., Gini, G., & Colombetti, M. (2008) [2009]. Guest editorial: Marco Somalvico Memorial Issue. *Annals of Mathematics and Artificial Intelligence, 54*(4), 257–264. doi:10.1007/s10472-008-9102-9

Nissan, E., Gini, G., & Colombetti, M. (2009a). Guest editorial: An artificial intelligence miscellanea, remembering Marco Somalvico. In: Marco Somalvico Memorial Issue. *Applied Artificial Intelligence, 23*(3), 197–185.

Nissan, E., Gini, G., & Colombetti, M. (2009b). Guest editorial: Marco Somalvico Memorial Issue. In: Marco Somalvico Memorial Issue (Part I of II). *Computational Intelligence, 25*(2), 109–113.

Nissan, E., Hall, D., Lobina, E., & de la Motte, R. (2004). A formalism for a case study in the WaterTime project: The city water system in Grenoble, from privatization to remunicipalization. *Applied Artificial Intelligence, 18*(3/4), 367–389.

Nissan, E., & Martino, A. A. (Eds.). (2001). *Software, Formal Models, and Artificial Intelligence for Legal Evidence*, special issue of *Computing and Informatics, 20*(6), 509–656.

Nissan, E., & Martino, A. A. (Eds.). (2003a). *Building blocks for an artificial intelligence framework in the field of legal evidence*, special issue (two parts), *Cybernetics and Systems, 34*(4/5), 233–411, 34(6/7), 413–583.

Nissan, E., & Martino, A. A. (2003b). Guest editorial. Building blocks for an artificial intelligence framework in the field of legal evidence, Part I. In Nissan & Martino (2003a), Part I. *Cybernetics and Systems, 34*(4/5), 233–244.

Nissan, E., & Martino, A. A. (Eds.). (2004a). *The construction of judicial proof: A challenge for artificial intelligence modelling*, special issue, *Applied Artificial Intelligence, 18*(3/4), 183–393.

Nissan, E., & Martino, A. A. (2004b). Artificial intelligence and formalisms for legal evidence: An introduction. *Applied Artificial Intelligence, 18*(3/4), 185–229.

Nissan, E., & Rousseau, D. (1997). Towards AI formalisms for legal evidence. In Z. W. Ras & A. Skowron (Eds.), *Foundations of intelligent systems: Proceedings of the 10th international symposium, ISMIS'97* (pp. 328–337). Berlin: Springer.

Nissan, E., & Shemesh, A. O. (2010). Saturnine traits, melancholia, and related conditions as ascribed to Jews and Jewish culture (and Jewish responses) from Imperial Rome to high modernity. In A. Grossato (Ed.), *Umana, divina malinconia*, special issue on melancholia, *Quaderni di Studi Indo-Mediterranei*, 3 (pp. 97–128). Alessandria, Piedmont, Italy: Edizioni dell'Orso.

Nissan, E., & Shimony, S. E. (1996). TAMBALACOQUE: For a formal account of the gist of a scholarly argument. *Knowledge Organization, 23*(3), 135–146.

Nissan, E., & Shimony, S. E. (1997). VEGEDOG: Formalism, vegetarian dogs, and partonomies in transition. *Computers and Artificial Intelligence, 16*(1), 79–104.

Nitta, K., Hasegawa, O., & Akiba, T. (1997). An experimental multimodal disputation dystem. In the *Proceedings of the IJCAI workshop on intelligent multimodal systems, IJCAI'97*, pp. 23–28. [The web page of ETL, with which the authors were affiliated, is http://www.etl.go.jp/welcome.html]

Noon, R. K. (1992). *Introduction to forensic engineering*. (The Forensic Library). Boca Raton, FL: CRC Press.

Noon, R. K. (2002). *Forensic engineering investigation*. Boca Raton, FL: CRC Press.

Noon, R. K. (2005a). Structural failures. Chapter 23 In S. H. James & J. J. Nordby (Eds.), *Forensic science: An introduction to scientific and investigative techniques* (2nd ed.). Boca Raton, FL: CRC Press. Also in 3rd edition, 2009.

Noon, R. K. (2005b). Vehicular accident reconstruction. Chapter 25 In S. H. James & J. J. Nordby (Eds.), *Forensic science: An introduction to scientific and investigative techniques* (2nd ed.). Boca Raton, FL: CRC Press. Also in 3rd edition, 2009.

Norman, D. A., & Rumelhart, D. E. (1975). *Explorations in cognition*. San Francisco: W. H. Freeman and Company.

Norvig, P. (1987). *A unified theory of inference for text understanding*. Technical Report CSD-87-339. Berkeley, CA: Computer Science Division, University of California. ftp://sunsite.berkeley.edu/pub/techreps/CSD-87-339.html

Norvig, P. (1989). Marker passing as a weak method for text inferencing. *Cognitive Science, 13*, 569–620.

Nourkova, V. V., Bernstein D. M., & Loftus, E. F. (2004). Altering traumatic memories. *Cognition and Emotion, 18*, 575–585.

Novitz, D. (1980). Fiction, imagination and emotion. *The Journal of Aesthetics and Art Criticism, 38*, 279–288.

Nowakowska, M. (1973a). A formal theory of actions. *Behavioral Science, 18*, 393–416.

Nowakowska, M. (1973b). *Language of motivation and language of actions*. The Hague: Mouton.

Nowakowska, M. (1976a). Action theory: Algebra of goals and algebra of means. *Design Methods and Theories, 10*(2), 97–102.

Nowakowska, M. (1976b). Towards a formal theory of dialogues. *Semiotica, 17*(4), 291–313.

Nowakowska, M. (1978). Formal theory of group actions and its applications. *Philosophica, 21*, 3–32.

Nowakowska, M. (1984). *Theories of research* (2 Vols.). Seaside, CA: Intersystems Publications.

Nowakowska, M. (1986). *Cognitive sciences: Basic problems, new perspectives, and implications for artificial intelligence*. Orlando, FL: Acedemic.

Nowakowski [sic], M. (1980). Possibility distributions in the linguistic theory of actions. *International Journal of Man-Machine Studies, 12*, 229–239.

NRC. (1995). *National Review Council (U.S.) Committee on Declassification of Information for the Department of Energy Environmental Remediation and Related Programs 1995. A Review of the Department of Energy Classification Policy and Practice*. Washington, DC: National Academic Press.

NYT. (1995). Woman guilty of murdering husband no. 9. *The New York Times*, March 19 (Late Edn., Final): Sec. 1, p. 31, col. 1, National Desk.

Oatley, G., & Ewart, B. (2003). Crimes analysis software: 'Pins in Maps', clustering and Bayes net prediction. *Expert Systems with Applications, 25*(4), 569–588.

Oatley, G., & Ewart, B. (2011). Data mining and crime analysis. *Wiley Interdisciplinary Reviews (WIREs): Data Mining and Knowledge Discovery, 1*(2), 147–153. doi://10.1002/widm.6

Oatley, G., Ewart, B., & Zeleznikow, J. (2006). Decision support systems for police: Lessons from the application of data mining techniques to 'soft' forensic evidence. *Journal of Artificial Intelligence and Law, 14*(1/2), 35–100.

Oatley, G., Zeleznikow, J., & Ewart, B. (2004). Matching and predicting crimes. In A. Macintosh, R. Ellis, & T. Allen (Eds.), *Applications and innovations in intelligent systems XII. Proceedings of AI2004, the 24th SGAI international conference on knowledge based systems and applications of artificial intelligence* (pp. 19–32). Berlin: Springer.

Oatley, G., Zeleznikow, J., Leary, R., & Ewart, B. (2005). From links to meaning: A burglary data case study. In R. Khosla, R. J. Howlett, & L. C. Jain (Eds.), *Knowledge-based intelligent information and engineering systems: 9th international conference, KES 2005*, Melbourne, Australia, September 14–16, 2005, *Proceedings, Part IV* (pp. 813–822). (Lecture Notes in Computer Science, Vol. 3684). Berlin: Springer.

Oatley, G. C., MacIntyre, J., Ewart, B. W., & Mugambi, E. (2002). SMART software for decision Makers KDD experience. *Knowledge Based Systems, 15*, 323–333.

O'Barr, W. M. (1982). *Linguistic evidence: Language, power and strategy in the courtroom*. New York: Academic.

Ochaeta, K. E. (2008). *Fraud detection for internet auctions: A data mining approach*. PhD thesis. Hsinchu, Taiwan: National Tsing-Hua University.

ODBASE. (2005). *Ontologies, databases and applications of semantics (ODBASE) 2005 international conference*. Berlin: Springer.

Oehler, D. (2009). Rediscovered: Forest owlet. *Bird Watcher's Digest*, November/December.

Ofshe, R. J., & Leo, R. A. (1997a). The social psychology of police interrogation: The theory and classification of true and false confessions. *Studies in Law, Politics, and Society, 16*, 189–251.

Ofshe, R. J., & Leo, R. A. (1997b). The decision to confess falsely: Rational choice and irrational action. *Denver University Law Review, 74*, 979–1122.

Ogata, T. (2004). A computational approach to literary and narrative production: Toward computational narratology. In *Art and Science: Proceedings of the 18th congress of the international association of empirical aesthetics*, Lisbon, September 2004, pp. 509–516.

Ogden, J. (1992). Restoration jocularity at Othello's expense. *Notes and Queries, 39*(4), 464. (Vol. 237, new series, Oxford: Oxford University Press.)

Ogston, E., & Vassiliadis, S. (2002). Unstructured agent matchmaking: Experiments in timing and fuzzy matching. In *Proceedings of the special track on coordination models, languages and applications of the 17th ACM symposium on applied computing*, Madrid, Spain, pp. 300–305.

Oinonen, K., Theune, M., Nijholt, A., & Heylen, D. (2005). Getting the story right: Making computer-generated stories more entertaining. In M. Maybury, O. Stock, & W. Wahlster (Eds.), *Proceedings of intelligent technologies for interactive entertainment (INTETAIN'05)* (pp. 264–268). (Lecture Notes in Artificial Intelligence, 3814). Berlin: Springer. http://dx.doi.org/10.1007/11590323_32

Oinonen, K., Theune, M., Nijholt, A., & Uijlings, J. (2006). Designing a story database for use in automatic story generation. In R. Harper, M. Rauterberg, & M. Combetto (Eds.), *Proceedings of the fifth International Conference on Entertainment Computing (ICEC 2006)*, Cambridge, UK (pp. 298–301). (Lecture Notes in Computer Science, 4161). Berlin: Springer. http://dx.doi.org/10.1007/11872320_36

Okada, N., & Endo, Ts. (1992). Story generation based on dynamics of the mind. *Computational Intelligence, 8*(1), 123–160.

Olderog, E.-R. (1991). *Nets, terms and formulas: Three views of concurrent processes and their relationship*. (Cambridge Tracts in Theoretical Computer Science, 23.) Cambridge: Cambridge University Press.

O'Looney, J. (2000). *Beyond maps: GIS and decision making in local government*. Redlands, CA: ESRI Press.

Olson, E. A., & Wells, G. L., (2002). *What makes a good alibi? A proposed taxonomy*. Ames, IA: Iowa State University, n.d. (but 2002). Portions of the data in this report were presented at the 2001 Biennial Meeting of the Society for Applied Research in Memory and Cognition. http://www.psychology.iastate.edu/~glwells/alibi_taxonomy.pdf

Olson, S. L. (2008). The Meinertzhagen mystery: The life and legend of a colossal fraud. *The Wilson Journal of Ornithology, 120*(4), 917–926. Reviewing Garfield (2007).

Onega, S., & Garcia Landa, J. A. (1996). *Narratology*. London: Longman.

Onyshkevych, B., & Nirenburg, S. (1995). A lexicon for knowledge-based MT. *Machine Translation, 10*(1/2), 5–57.

Orgun, M. A., & Meyer, T. (Eds.). (2008). *Advances in ontologies*. Oxford: Blackwell.

Ormerod, T. C., Barrett, E. C., & Taylor, P. J. (2008). Investigating sensemaking in criminal contexts. In J. M. Schraagen, L. G. Militello, T. C. Ormerod, & R. Lipshitz (Eds.), *Naturalistic decision making and macrocognition* (pp. 81–102). Farnham, England: Ashgate.

O'Rorke, P., & Ortony, A. (1994). Explaining emotions. *Cognitive Science, 18*, 283–323.

Osborn, A. S. (1929). *Questioned documents* (2nd ed.). Albany, NY: Boyd Printing Company. Reprinted, Chicago: Nelson-Hall Co.

Osborne, C. (1997). *Criminal litigation* (5th ed.). London: Blackstone.

O'Shea, C. (2005). Intrusion detection with honeypots. Course presentation [a student project, supervised by K. Jeffay], COMP 290, Spring 2005. Department of Computer Science. Chapel

Hill: The University of North Carolina. [A slideshow turned into .pdf] http://www.cs.unc. edu/~jeffay/courses/nidsS05/slides/12-Honeypots.pdf http://www.cs.unc.edu/~jeffay/courses/ nidsS05/slides/Student-Project-Summaries.pdf

Oskamp, A., Walker, R. F., Schrickx, J. A., & van den Berg, P. H. (1989). PROLEXS divide and rule: A legal application. In J. C. Smith & R. T. Franson (Eds.), *Proceedings of the second International Conference on Artificial Intelligence and Law (ICAIL'89)* (pp. 54–62). New York: ACM Press. doi://10.1145/74014.74022

O'Sullivan, M., Ekman, P., & Friesen, W. V. (1988). The effect of comparisons on detecting deceit. *Journal of Nonverbal Behavior, 12,* 203–215.

Osuna, R. G., & Nagle, H. T. (1999). A method for evaluating data preprocessing techniques for odour classification with an array of gas sensors. *IEEE Transactions on Systems, Man and Cybernetics, B, 29*(5), 626–632.

Otgaar, H. (2009). Not all false memory paradigms are appropriate in court. In L. Strömwall & P.A. Granhag (Eds.), *Memory: Reliability and personality* (pp. 37–46). Göteborg, Sweden: Göteborg University.

Otgaar, H., Candel, I., Memon, A., & Almerigogna, J. (2010a). Differentiating between children's true and false memories using reality monitoring criteria. *Psychology, Crime & Law, 16,* 555–566. http://www.personeel.unimaas.nl/henry.otgaar/Otgaar_ChildrenFalseMemoriesRM_ inpress_PCL.pdf

Otgaar, H., Candel, I., Scoboria, A., & Merckelbach, H. (2010c). Script knowledge enhances the development of children's false memories. *Acta Psychologica, 133,* 57–63. http://www. personeel.unimaas.nl/henry.otgaar/Otgaar_Scriptfalsememories_2010_AP.pdf

Otgaar, H., Candel, I., Smeets, T., & Merckelbach, H. (2010d). "You didn't take Lucy's skirt off": The effect of misleading information on omissions and commissions in children's memory reports. *Legal & Criminological Psychology, 15,* 229–241. http://www.personeel.unimaas.nl/ henry.otgaar/Otgaar_ChildrenOmissionsCommissionMisleading_2010_LCP.pdf

Otgaar, H., Meijer, E. H., Giesbrecht, G., Smeets, T., Candel, I., & Merckelbach, H. (2010b). Children's suggestion-induced omission errors are not caused by memory erasure. *Consciousness and Cognition, 19,* 265–269. http://www.personeel.unimaas.nl/henry.otgaar/ Otgaar_OmissionErrorserasure_2010_C&C.pdf

Otgaar, H., & Smeets, T. (2010). Adaptive memory: Survival processing increases both true and false memory in adults and children. *Journal of Experimental Psychology: Learning, Memory, and Cognition, 36,* 1010–1016. http://www.personeel.unimaas.nl/henry. otgaar/Otgaar_AdaptiveMemoryFalseMemory_2010_JEPLMC.pdf

Otgaar, H. P., Candel, I., & Merckelbach, H. (2008). Children's false memories: Easier to elicit for a negative than a neutral event. *Acta Psychologica, 128,* 350–354. http://www.personeel. unimaas.nl/henry.otgaar/Otgaar_Children'sFalseMemoriesNegativeNeutral3_2008_AP.pdf

Otgaar, H. P., Candel, I., Merckelbach, H., & Wade, K. A. (2009). Abducted by a UFO: Prevalence information affects young children's false memories for an implausible event. *Applied Cognitive Psychology, 23,* 115–125. http://www.personeel.unimaas.nl/henry.otgaar/ Otgaar_PrevalenceUFOChildren'sfalsememories3_2009_ACP.pdf

Oudot, L. (2003). *Fighting spammers with honeypots: Part 1.* http://www.securityfocus.com/

Oudot, L., & Holz, T. (2004). *Defeating honeypots: Network issues, Part 1.* http://www. securityfocus.com/

Ouellette, J. (1999). Electronic noses sniff our new markets. *Industrial Physics, 5,* 26–29.

Overill, R. E. (2009). Development of Masters modules in computer forensics and cybercrime for computer science and forensic science students. *International Journal of Electronic Security & Digital Forensics, 2*(2), 132–140. http://www.dcs.kcl.ac.uk/staff/richard/IJESDF_2009.pdf

Overill, R. E., Silomon, J. A. M., Kwan, Y. K., Chow, K.-P., Law, Y. W., & Lai, K. Y. (2009). A cost-effective digital forensics investigation model. In *Proceedings of the Fifth Annual IFIP WG 11.9 International Conference on Digital Forensics,* Orlando, FL, 25–28 January 2009, *Advances in Digital Forensics V.* Berlin: Springer, pp. 193–202.

Overill, R. E., & Silomon, J. A. M. (2010a). Digital meta-forensics: Quantifying the investigation. In *Proceedings of the Fourth International Conference on Cybercrime Forensics Education &*

Training (CFET 2010), Canterbury, Kent, England, 2–3 September 2010. http://www.dcs.kcl. ac.uk/staff/richard/CFET_2010.pdf

Overill, R. E, Silomon, J. A. M., & Chow, K.-P. (2010b). A complexity based model for quantifying forensic evidential probabilities. In *Proceedings of the Third International Workshop on Digital Forensics (WSDF 2010)*, Krakow, Poland, 15–18 February 2010, pp. 671–676. http://www.dcs. kcl.ac.uk/staff/richard/F2GC_2010.pdf

Overill, R. E, Silomon, J. A. M., Kwan, Y. K., Chow, K.-P., Law, Y. W., & Lai, K. Y. (2010). Sensitivity analysis of a Bayesian network for reasoning about digital forensic evidence. In *Proceedings of the Fourth International Workshop on Forensics for Future Generation Communication environments (F2GC-2010)*, Cebu, Philippines, 11–13 August 2010. http:// www.dcs.kcl.ac.uk/staff/richard/F2GC_2010.pdf

Owen, G. (1995). *Game theory* (3rd ed.). San Diego, CA: Academic.

Owens, C. C. (1990). *Indexing and retrieving abstract planning knowledge*. Doctoral dissertation. New Haven, CT: Computer Science Department, Yale University.

Owens, C. C. (1994). Retriever and Anon: Retrieving structures from memory. In R. C. Schank, A. Kass, & C. K. Riesbeck (Eds.), *Inside case-based explanation* (pp. 89–126). Hillsdale, NJ: Erlbaum.

Özsoyoğlu, Z. M. (Ed.). (1988). *Nested relations*. Special issue of *The IEEE Data Engineering Bulletin, 11*(3), September. New York: IEEE.

Özsoyoğlu, Z. M., & Yuan, L. Y. (1987). A new normal form for nested relations. *ACM Transactions on Database Systems, 12*, 111–136.

Pacuit, E. (2005). *Topics in social software: Information in strategic situations*. Doctoral dissertation. New York: City University of New York.

Pacuit, E., & Parikh, R. (2007). Social interaction, knowledge, and social software. In D. Goldin, S. Smolka, & P. Wegner (Eds.), *Interactive computation: The new paradigm* (pp. 441–461). New York: Springer.

Pacuit, P., Parikh, R., & Cogan, E. (2006). The logic of knowledge based obligation. *Knowledge, Rationality and Action*, a subjournal of *Synthese, 149*(2), 311–341.

Paglieri, F. (2009). Ruinous arguments: Escalation of disagreement and the dangers of arguing. In H. Hansen, C. Tindale, R. Johnson, & A. Blair (Eds.), *Argument cultures: Proceedings of OSSA 2009*. CD-ROM. Windsor, ON: OSSA.

Paglieri, F., & Castelfranchi, C. (2005). Revising beliefs through arguments: Bridging the gap between argumentation and belief revision in MAS. In I. Rahwan, P. Moraitis, & C. Reed (Eds.), *Argumentation in multi-agent systems* (pp. 78–94). Berlin: Springer.

Paglieri, F., & Castelfranchi, C. (2010). Why argue? Towards a cost–benefit analysis of argumentation. *Argument & Computation, 1*(1), 71–91.

Paley, B., & Geiselman, R. E. (1989). The effects of alternative photospread instructions on suspect identification performance. *American Journal of Forensic Psychology, 7*, 3–13.

Pallotta, G. (1977). *Dizionario storico della mafia*. (Paperbacks società d'oggi, 8.) Rome: Newton Compton Editori.

Palmer, M. S., Passonneau, R. J., Weir, C., & Finin, T. W. (1993). The KERNEL text understanding system. *Artificial Intelligence, 63*(1/2), 17–68.

Pamplin, C. (2007a). Cross-examining the experts. In *Expert Witness Supplement* to *The New Law Journal, 157*(7294) (London, 26 October 2007), 1480–1481.

Pamplin, C. (2007b). Limiting the evidence. In *Expert Witness Supplement* to *The New Law Journal, 157*(7294) (London, 26 October 2007), 1488–1489.

Pamula, V. K. (2003). Detection of explosives. Chapter 23 In T. C. Pearce, S. S. Schiffman, H. T. Nagle, & J. W. Gardner (Eds.), *Handbook of machine olfaction: Electronic nose technology* (pp. 547–560). Weinheim, Baden-Württemberg: Wiley VCH Verlag. Published online: 2004. doi://10.1002/3527601597.ch23

Panangadan, A., Ho, Sh.-Sh., & Talukder, A. (2009). Cyclone tracking using multiple satellite image sources. In *Proceedings of the 17th ACM SIGSPATIAL International Conference on Advances in Geographic Information Systems*, Seattle, WA, 4–6 November 2009.

Pandit, S., Chau, D. H., Wang, S., & Faloutsos, C. (2007). NetProbe: A fast and scalable system for fraud detection in online auction networks. In *WWW 2007: Proceedings of the 16th International Conference on World Wide Web*, Banff, AB, Track: Data Mining, Session: Mining in Social Networks. New York: ACM, pp. 201–210.

Pang, B., Lee, L., & Vaithyanathan, S. (2002). Thumbs up? Sentiment classification using machine learning techniques. In *Proceedings of EMNLP 02, 7th Conference on Empirical Methods in Natural Language Processing*, Association for Computational Linguistics, Morristown, US, pp. 79–86. http://www.cs.cornell.edu/home/llee/papers/sentiment.pdf

Pankanti, S., Prabhakar, S., & Jain, A. K. (2002). On the individuality of fingerprints. *IEEE Transactions on Pattern Analysis & Machine Intelligence (IEEE PAMI), 24*, 1010–1025.

Pannu, A. S. (1995). Using genetic algorithms to inductively reason with cases in the legal domain. In *Proceedings of Fifth International Conference on Artificial Intelligence and Law*. New York: ACM Press, pp. 175–184.

Papadimitriou, C. H. (1994). *Computational complexity*. Reading, MA: Addison-Wesley.

Papageorgis, D., & McGuire, W. J. (1961). The generality of immunity to persuasion produced by pre-exposure to weakened counterarguments. *Journal of Abnormal and Social Psychology, 62*, 475–481.

Papineau, D. (1991). Correlations and causes. *British Journal for the Philosophy of Science, 42*, 397–412.

Pardo, M. S. (2005). The field of evidence and the field of knowledge. *Law and Philosophy, 24*, 321–391.

Pardue, H. L. (Ed.). (1994). *Analytical aspects of forensic science*. Special issue, *Analytica Chimica Acta, 288*(1/2). Amsterdam: Elsevier.

Parent, X. (2003). Remedial interchange, contrary-to-duty obligation and commutation. *Journal of Applied Non-Classical Logics, 13*(3/4), 345–375.

Parikh, R. (2001). Language as social software. In J. Floyd & S. Shieh (Eds.), *Future pasts: The analytic tradition in twentieth century philosophy* (pp. 339–350). Oxford: Oxford University Press.

Parikh, R. (2002). Social software. *Synthese, 132*, 187–211.

Parkinson, B. (1995). *Ideas and realities of emotion*. London: Routledge.

Parry, A. (1991). A universe of stories. *Family Process, 30*(1), 37–54.

Parsons, S., & McBurney, P. (2003). Argumentation-based communication between agents. In M.-P. Huget (Ed.), *Communication in multiagent systems: Agent communication languages and conversation policies*. (Lecture Notes in Computer Science, 2650). Berlin: Springer.

Parton, D. A., Hansel, M., & Stratton, J. R. (1991). Measuring crime seriousness: Lessons from the National Survey of Crime Severity. *The British Journal of Criminology, 31*, 72–85.

Partridge, R. E. (1991). Battle scarred. [A two-paragraph item.] *Reader's Digest* (U.S. edition), April 1991, p. 120.

Parunak, H., Ward, A., Fleischer, M., & Sauter, J. (1997). A marketplace of design agents for distributed concurrent set-based design. In *Proceedings of the Fourth ISPE International Conference on Concurrent Engineering: Research and Applications (ISPE/CE97)*, Troy, MI.

Pattenden, R. (1993). Conceptual versus pragmatic approaches to hearsay. *Modern Law Review*,[69] *56*(2), 138–156.

Pawlak, Z. (1991). *Rough sets: Theoretical aspects of reasoning about data*. (Theory and Decision Library, 9. System Theory, Knowledge Engineering, and Problem Solving, Series D). Dorrdrecht, The Netherlands: Kluwer.

PCMLP. (n.d.). *Geographical links*. Inside the website of the Programme in Comparative Media Law & Policy (PCMLP), Centre for Socio-Legal Studies, Wolfson College, University of Oxford. Retrieved ca. 2000; http://pcmlp.socleg.ox.ac.uk/regional.html

---

[69] The journal *Modern Law Review* is published in Oxford by Blackwell.

Pearce, T. C., Schiffman, S. S., Nagle, H. T., & Gardner, J. W. (Eds.). (2002). *Handbook of machine olfaction: Electronic nose technology.* Weinheim, Baden-Württemberg: Wiley-VCH. doi://10.1002/3527601597

Pearl, J. (1988). *Probabilistic reasoning in intelligent systems: Networks of plausible inference.* San Mateo, CA: Morgan-Kaufmann.

Pearl, J. (1993). From conditional oughts to qualitative decision theory. In *Uncertainty in AI: Proceedings of the Ninth Conference*,[70] Washington, DC, July 1993, pp. 12–20.

Pearl, J. (2001). Bayesianism and causality, and why I am only a half-Bayesian. In D. Corfield & J. Williamson (Eds.), *Foundations of Bayesianism* (pp. 19–36). (Kluwer Applied Logic Series, 24). Dordrecht, The Netherlands: Kluwer. http://ftp.cs.ucla.edu/pub/stat_ser/r284-reprint.pdf

Pearman, D. A., & Walker, K. J. (2004). An examination of J. W. Heslop Harrison's unconfirmed plant records from Rum. *Watsonia, 25,* 45–63.

Pease, K., Ireson, J., Billingham, S., & Thorpe, J. (1977). The development of a scale of offence seriousness. *International Journal of Criminology and Penology, 5,* 17–29.

Pei, J., Jiang, D., & Zhang, A. (2005). On mining cross-graph quasi-cliques. In *Proceedings of the 2005 International Conference on Knowledge Discovery and Data Mining (KDD 2005),* Chicago, IL, August 2005, pp. 228–238.

Peinado, F., Cavazza, M., & Pizzi, D. (2008). Revisiting character-based affective storytelling under a narrative BDI framework. In U. Spierling & N. Szilas (Eds.), *Proceedings of the first international conference on interactive digital storytelling,* Erfurt, Germany, 26–29 November 2008 (pp. 83–88). (Lecture Notes in Computer Science, Vol. 5334.), Berlin: Springer.

Peinado, F., & Gervás, P. (2004). Transferring game mastering laws to interactive digital story-telling. In S. Göbel, U. Spierling, A. Hoffmann, I. Iurgel, O. Schneider, J. Dechau, et al. (Eds.), *Technologies for interactive digital storytelling and entertainment: Proceedings of the 2nd international conference on technologies for interactive digital storytelling and entertainment, TIDSE'04,* Darmstadt, Germany, 24–26 June 2004 (pp. 48–54). (Lecture Notes in Computer Science, 3105). Berlin: Springer.

Peinado, F., & Gervás, P. (2005a). Creativity issues in plot generation. In P. Gervás, T. Veale, & A. Pease (Eds.), *Workshop on computational creativity, working notes. 19th international joint conference on artificial intelligence,* Edinburgh, Scotland, 30 July–5 August 2005 (pp. 45–52). Also: Technical Report 5-05. Departamento de Sistemas Informáticos y Programación, Universidad Complutense de Madrid.

Peinado, F., & Gervás, P. (2005b). A Generative and Case-based Implementation of Proppian Morphology. In B. Lönneker, J. C. Meister, P. Gervás, F. Peinado, & M. Mateas (Eds.), *Story generators: Models and approaches for the generation of literary artifacts.* At the *17th Joint International Conference of the Association for Computers and the Humanities and the Association for Literary and Linguistic Computing (ACH/ALLC),* Victoria, BC, 15–18 June 2005 (pp. 129–133). Humanities Computing and Media Centre, University of Victoria.

Peinado, F., & Gervás, P. (2006a). Minstrel reloaded: From the magic of Lisp to the formal semantics of OWL. In S. Göbel, R. Malkewitz, & I. Iurgel (Eds.), *Proceedings of the third international conference on Technologies for Interactive Digital Storytelling and Entertainment (TIDSE),* Darmstadt, Germany, 4–6 December 2006 (pp. 93–97). (Lecture Notes in Computer Science, 4326.) Berlin: Springer.

Peinado, F., & Gervás, P. (2006b). Evaluation of automatic generation of basic stories. In a special issue on Computational Creativity, *New Generation Computing, 24*(3), 289–302.

Peinado, F., & Gervás, P. (2007) Automatic direction of interactive storytelling: Formalizing the game master paradigm. In M. Cavazza & S. Donikian (Eds.), *Proceedings of the fourth*

---

[70] The UAI conference has been held every year since 1985. Proceedings of some past conferences (most of those from the 2000s) can be viewed online at http://uai.sis.pitt.edu/ Hardcopy versions of the proceedings can be purchased through Brightdoc, at https://store.brightdoc.com/store/default.asp?clientid=212

International Conference on Virtual Storytelling: Using virtual reality technologies for storytelling (ICVS), Saint-Malo, France, 5–7 December 2007 (pp. 196–201). (Lecture Notes in Computer Science, 4871.) Berlin: Springer.

Peinado, F., & Navarro, A. (2007). RCEI: An API for remote control of narrative environments. In M. Cavazza & S. Donikian (Eds.), *Proceedings of the fourth International Conference on Virtual Storytelling: Using virtual reality technologies for storytelling (ICVS)*, Saint-Malo, France, 5–7 December 2007 (pp. 181–186). (Lecture Notes in Computer Science, 4871). Berlin: Springer.

Peinado, F., Gervás, P., & Díaz-Agudo, B. (2004). A Description Logic Ontology for Fairy Tale Generation. In T. Veale, A. Cardoso, F. Camara Pereira, & P. Gervás (Eds.), *4th international conference on Language Resources and Evaluation, Proceedings of the workshop on language resources for linguistic creativity, LREC'04*, Lisbon, 29 May 2004 (pp. 56–61). ELRA.

Peirce, C. S. (1903). Harvard lectures on pragmatism. In C. Hartshorne & P. Weiss (Eds.), *Collected papers of Charles Sanders Peirce* (Vol. 5). Cambridge, MA: Harvard University Press. (8 vols. published in 1931–1958 (vols. 7 and 8, ed. A. W. Burks).[71] Volumes reissued as 8 vols. in 4 by the Belknap Press of Harvard University Press, ca. 1965–1967. The 1931–1958 edn. was reprinted as 8 vols. in Bristol, England: Thoemmes Press, 1998.)

Peirce, C. S. [1901] (1955). Abduction and induction. In J. Buchler (Ed.), *Philosophical writings of peirce* (pp. 150–156). New York: Dover.

Pelosi, P., & Persaud, K. C. (1988). Gas sensors: towards an artificial nose. In P. Dario (Ed.), *Sensors and sensory systems for advanced robotics* (pp. 361–381). Berlin: Springer.

Pemberton, L. (1989). A modular approach to story generation. In *Proceedings of the Fourth European Meeting of the Association for Computational Linguistics* (EACL-89), Manchester, England, 10–12 April 1989, pp. 217–224.

Pennec, X. (2007). From Riemannian geometry to computational anatomy of the brain. In *The Digital Patient*, special issue of *ERCIM News*, 69 (April), pp. 15–16. Article downloadable from the webpage http://ercim-news.ercim.org/content/view/166/314/ of the European Research Consortium for Informatics and Mathematics.

Pennington, N., & Hastie, R. (1981). Juror decision-making models: The generalization gap. *Psychological Bulletin, 89*, 146–287.

Pennington, N., & Hastie, R. (1986). Evidence evaluation in complex decision making. *Journal of Personality and Social Psychology, 51*, 242–258.

Pennington, N., & Hastie, R. (1988). Explanation-based decision making: Effects of memory structure on judgment. *Journal of Experimental Psychology: Learning, Memory and Cognition, 14*, 521–533.

Pennington, N., & Hastie, R. (1992). Explaining the evidence: Tests of the story model for juror decision making. *Journal of Personality and Social Psychology, 62*, 189–206.

Pennington, N., & Hastie, R. (1993). The story model for juror decision making. In R. Hastie (Ed.), *Inside the Juror: The psychology of juror decision making* (pp. 192–221). Cambridge, England: Cambridge University Press.

Pennington, D. C., & Lloyd-Bostock, S. (Eds.). (1987). *The psychology of sentencing: Approaches to consistency and disparity*. Oxford: Centre for Socio-Legal Studies.

Penrod, S. (2005). Eyewitness identification evidence: How well are witnesses and police performing? *Criminal Justice Magazine, 54*, 36–47.

Penrod, S., Loftus, E., & Winkler, J. (1982). The reliability of witness testimony: A psychological perspective. In N. L. Kerr & R. M. Bray (Eds.), *The criminal justice system* (pp. 119–168). New York: Academic.

Penry, J. (1974). Photo-Fit. *Forensic Photography, 3*(7), 4–10.

---

[71] Vol. 1: *Principles of Philosophy*. Vol. 2: *Elements of Logic*. Vol. 3: *Exact Logic*. Vol. 4: *The Simplest Mathematics*. Vol. 5: *Pragmatism and Pragmaticism*. Vol. 6: *Scientific Metaphysics*. Vol. 7: *Science and Philosophy*. Vol. 8: *Reviews, Correspondence, and Bibliography*.

Perdisci, R., Ariu, D., Fogla, P., Giacinto, G., & Lee, W. (2009). McPAD: A multiple classier system for accurate payload-based anomaly detection. In a special issue on *Traffic Classification and Its Applications to Modern Networks* of *Computer Networks, 5*(6), 864–881. http://3407859467364186361-a-1802744773732722657-s-sites.googlegroups.com/site/robertoperdisci/publications/publication-files/McPAD-revision1.pdf

Pérez y Pérez, R., & Sharples, M. (2001). MEXICA: A computer model of a cognitive account of creative writing. *Journal of Experimental and Theoretical Artificial Intelligence, 13*(2), 119–139. http://www.eee.bham.ac.uk/sharplem/Papers/mexica_jetai.pdf

Perloff, M. (2003). Taking agents seriously. *Cybernetics and Systems, 34*(4/5), 253–281.

Peron C. S. J, & Legary, M. (2005). *Digital anti-forensics: Emerging trends data transformation techniques.* http://www.seccuris.com/documents/papers/Seccuris-Antiforensics.pdf

Perrins, C. (1988). Obituary: Salim Moizuddin Abdul Ali (1896–1987). *Ibis: Journal of the British Ornithologists' Union, 130*(2), 305–306. Oxford: Blackwell.

Persaud, K. C. (1992). Electronic gas and odor detectors that mimic chemoreception in animals. *TRAC Trends in Analytical Chemistry, 11*, 61–67.

Persaud, K. C. (2005). Medical applications of odor-sensing devices. *International Journal of Lower Extremities Wounds, 4*, 50–56.

Persaud, K. C., Bartlett, J., & Pelosi, P. (1993). Design strategies for gas and odour sensors which mimic the olfactory system. In P. Dario, G. Sandini, & P. Aebisher (Eds.), *Robots and biological systems: Towards a new bionics?* (pp. 579–602). Berlin: Springer.

Persaud, K. C., & Dodd, G. (1982). Analysis of discrimination mechanisms in the mammalian olfactory system using a model nose. *Nature, 299*, 352–355.

Persaud, K. C., Qutob, A. A., Travers, P., Pisanelli, A. M., & Szyszko, S. (1994). Odor evaluation of foods using conducting polymer arrays and neural net pattern recognition. In K. Kurihara, N. Suzuki, & H. Ogawa (Eds.), *Olfaction and taste XI* (pp. 708–710). Tokyo & Berlin: Springer.

Petacco, A. (1972). *Joe Petrosino.* (In Italian.) Milan: Arnoldo Mondadori Editore.

Peter, R. (1999). *Bird taxidermy.* (Norman Cottage Pocket Book.) Oakham, Rutland, East Midlands, England: R. Merchant.

Peters, G. A., & Peters, B. J. (1994). *Automotive engineering and litigation.* (Wiley Law Publications.) New York: Wiley.

Peterson, D. M., Barnden, J. A., & Nissan, E. (Eds.) (2001). Artificial Intelligence and Law, special issue of *Information & Communications Technology Law, 10*(1).

Peterson, J. L. (1981). *Petri net theory and the modelling of systems.* Englewood Cliffs, NJ: Prentice-Hall.

Peterson, M. (2005). *Intelligence-led policing: The new intelligence architecture.* Washington, DC: Bureau of Justice Assistance. http://www.ojp.usdoj.gov/BJA/pdf/IntelLedPolicing.pdf

Petri, C. A. (1966). *Communication with automata.* Supplement 1 to Technical Report RADC-TR-65-377, Vol. 1. Rome, NY: Rome Air Development Center, Griffiths Air Force Base, January 1966. Translated by C. F. Greene, Jr., from: Kommunikation mit Automaten, University of Bonn, Bonn, West Germany, 1962.

Petty, R. E., & Cacioppo, J. T. (1986). *Communication and persuasion: Central and peripheral routes to attitude change.* New York: Springer.

Petty R. E., Wegener, D. T., & White, P. H. (1998). Flexible correction processes in social judgment: implications for persuasion. *Social Cognition, 16*, 93–113.

Peuquet, D. J., & Duan, N. (1995). An event-based spatiotemporal data model (ESTDM) for temporal analysis of geographical data. *International Journal of Geographical Information Science, 9*(1), 7–24.

Pfeiffer III, J., & Neville, J. (2011). Methods to determine node centrality and clustering in graphs with uncertain structure. In *Proceedings of the Fifth International AAAI Conference on Weblogs and Social Media.* http://www.cs.purdue.edu/homes/neville/papers/pfeiffer-icwsm2011.pdf

Pharr, M., & Humphreys, G. (2004). *Physically based rendering: From theory to implementation.* San Francisco: Morgan Kaufmann.

Philipps, L. (1989). Are legal decisions based on the application of rules or prototype recognition? Legal science on the way to neural networks. In *Pre-Proceedings of the 3rd International Conference on Logica, Informatica, Diritto*. Florence: Istituto per la Documentazione Giudiziaria, pp. 673–680.

Philipps, L. (1991). Distribution of damages in car accidents through the use of neural networks. *Cardozo Law Review, 13*(2/3), 987–1001.

Phillips, L. (1993). Vague legal concepts and fuzzy logic: An attempt to determine the required period of waiting after traffic accidents. In *Proceedings of the Computer and Vagueness: Fuzzy Logic and Neural Nets*, Munich. In *Informatica e diritto* (Florence), 2, 37–51.

Philipps, L. (1999). Approximate syllogisms: On the logic of everyday life. *Artificial Intelligence and Law, 7*(2/3), 227–234.

Phillips, M., & Huntley, C. (1993). *Dramatica: A new theory of story*. http://www.dramatica.com/theory/theory_book/dtb.html

Phillips, L., & Sartor, G. (1999). From legal theories to neural networks and fuzzy reasoning. *Artificial Intelligence and Law, 7*(2/3), 115–128.

Philp, R. P. (2002). Application of stable isotopes and radioisotopes in environmental forensics. Chapter 5 In B. L. Murphy & R. D. Morrison (Eds.), *Introduction to environmental forensics* (pp. 99–136). San Diego, CA & London: Academic.

Phua, C., Lee, V., Smith-Miles, K., & Gayler, R. (2005). *A comprehensive survey of data-mining-based fraud detection research*. Clayton, VIC: Clayton School of Information Technology, Monash University; 2005. In 2010, it was accessible at: http://clifton.phua.googlepages.com/

Phuoc, N. Q., Kim, S.-R., Lee, H.-K., & Kim, H. S. (2009). PageRank vs. Katz Status Index, a theoretical approach. In *Proceedings of the Fourth International Conference on Computer Sciences and Convergence Information Technology (ICCIT'09)*, Seoul, South Korea, 24–26 November 2009, pp. 1276–1279.

Pickel, D., Manucy, G., Walker, D., Hall, S., & Walker, J. (2004). Evidence for canine olfactory detection of melanoma. *Applied Animal Behaviour Science, 89*, 107–116.

Pietroski, P. M. (1994). A "should" too many. *Behavioral and Brain Sciences, 17*(1), 26–27.

Pildes, R. H. (1999). Forms of formalism. *Chicago Law Review, 66*, 607–621.

Pisanelli, A. M., Qutob, A. A., Travers, P., Szyszko, S., & Persaud, K. C. (1994). Applications of multi-array polymer sensors to food industries. *Life Chemistry Reports, 11*, 303–308.

Plamper, J. (2010). The history of emotions: An interview with William Reddy, Barbara Rosenwein, and Peter Stearns. *History and Theory,*[72] 49, 237–265.

Plantinga, A. (1993a). *Warrant: The current debate*. Oxford: Oxford University Press.

Plantinga, A. (1993b). *Warrant and proper function*. Oxford: Oxford University Press.

Planty, M., & Strom, K. J. (2007). Understanding the role of repeat victims in the production of annual US victimization rates. *Journal of Quantitative Criminology, 23*(3), 179–200.

Plewe, B. (1997). *GIS online: Information retrieval, mapping, and the internet*. Santa Fe, NM: Onword Press.

Poesio, M. (2005). Domain modelling and NLP: Formal ontologies? Lexica? Or a bit of both? *Applied Ontology, 1*(1), Amsterdam: IOS Press, pp. 27–33.

Politis, D., Donos, G., Christou, G., Giannakopoulos, P., & Papapanagiotou-Leza, A. (2008). Implementing e-justice on a national scale: Coping with Balkanization and socio-economical divergence. *Journal of Cases on Information Technology, 10*(2), 41–59. http://www.igi-global.com/articles/details.asp?ID=7910 http://www.igi-global.com/journals/details.asp?id=202

Pollard, D. E. B. (1997). Logic of fiction. In P. V. Lamarque & R. E. Asher (Eds.), *Concise encyclopedia of philosophy of language* (pp. 264–265). Oxford: Pergamon.

Pollock, J. (1989). *How to build a person: A prolegomenon*. Cambridge, MA: Bradford (MIT Press).

Pollock, J. L. (2010). Defeasible reasoning and degrees of justification. *Argument & Computation, 1*(1), 7–22.

---

[72] See fn. 141 in Chapter 8.

Poole, D. (1989). Explanation and prediction: An architecture for default and abductive reasoning. *Computational Intelligence, 5*(2), 97–110.

Poole, D. L. (1988). A Logical framework for default reasoning. *Artificial Intelligence, 36*, 27–47.

Poole, D. (2002) Logical argumentation, abduction and Bayesian decision theory: A Bayesian approach to logical arguments and its application to legal evidential reasoning. In M. MacCrimmon & P. Tillers (Eds.), *The dynamics of judicial proof: Computation, logic, and common sense* (pp. 385–396). (Studies in Fuzziness and Soft Computing, Vol. 94). Heidelberg: Physical-Verlag.

Pound, R. (1908). Mechanical jurisprudence. *Columbia Law Review, 8*, 605–623.

Popescu, A.-M., & Etzioni, O. (2005). Extracting product features and opinions from reviews. In *Proceedings of HLT-EMNLP*, 2005, pp. 339–346.

Popescu, A. C., & Farid, H. (2004). *Exposing digital forgeries by detecting duplicated image regions*. Technical Report TR2004-515. Hanover, NH: Department of Computer Science, Dartmouth College.

Popescu, A. C., & Farid, H. (2005a). Exposing digital forgeries by detecting traces of re-sampling. *IEEE Transactions on Signal Processing, 53*(2), 758–767.

Popescu, A. C., & Farid, H. (2005b). Exposing digital forgeries in color filter array interpolated images. *IEEE Transactions on Signal Processing, 53*(10), 3948–3959. www.cs.dartmouth.edu/farid/publications/sp05a.html

Popov, V. (2003). *Social network analysis in decision making: A literature review*. WaterTime Background Paper, PSIRU. London: University of Greenwich, January.

Porat, A., & Stein, A. (2001). *Tort liability under uncertainty*. Oxford: Oxford University Press.

Porter, S., Woodworth, M., Earle, J., Drugge, J., & Boaer, D. (2003). Characteristics of violent behaviour exhibited during sexual homicides by psychopathic and non-psychopathic murderers. *Law & Human Behavior, 27*, 459–470.

Porter, S., & Yuille, J. C. (1995). Credibility assessment of criminal suspects through statement analysis. *Psychology, Crime, and Law, 1*, 319–331.

Porter, S., & Yuille, J. C. (1996). The language of deceit: An investigation of the verbal clues to deception in the interrogation context. *Law and Human Behavior, 20*, 443–459.

Porter, A., & Prince, R. (2010). Lie detector tests on your taxes in Clegg's 'War on middle class'. London: *The Daily Telegraph*, 20 September, p. 1, bottom left.

Porter, S., & Yuille, J. C. (1995). Credibility assessment of criminal suspects through statement analysis. *Psychology, Crime, and Law, 1*, 319–331.

Posner, R. A. (1999). An economic approach to the law of evidence. *Stanford Law Review, 51*, 1477–1546.

Pouget, F., & Holz, T. (2005). A pointillist approach for comparing honeypots. In K. Julisch & C. Krügel (Eds.), *Detection of Intrusions and Malware, and Vulnerability Assessment: Proceedings of the Second International Conference (DIMVA 2005)*, Vienna, Austria, July 7–8, 2005 (pp. 51–68). Lecture Notes in Computer Science, Vol. 3548. Berlin: Springer.

Poulin, D., Mackaay [sic], E., Bratley, P., & Frémont, J. (1989). Time server: A legal time specialist. In A. A. Martino (Ed.), *Pre-proceedings of the third international conference on "logica, Informatica, Diritto: Legal Expert Systems"*, Florence, 1989 (2 vols. + Appendix) (Vol. 2, pp. 733–760). Florence: Istituto per la Documentazione Giuridica, Consiglio Nazionale delle Ricerche.

Poulin, D., Mackaay [sic], E., Bratley, P., & Frémont, J. (1992). Time server: A legal time specialist. In A. Martino (Ed.), *Expert systems in law* (pp. 295–312). Amsterdam: North-Holland.

Poulovassilis, A., & Levene, M. (1994). A nested-graph model for the representation and manipulation of complex objects. *ACM Transactions on Information Systems, 12*, 35–68.

Pour Ebrahimi, B., Bertels, K., Vassiliadis, S., & Sigdel, K. (2004). Matchmaking within multiagent systems. In *Proceedings of ProRisc2004*, Veldhoven, The Netherlands, pp. 118–124.

Prada, R., Machado, I., & Paiva, A. (2000). TEATRIX: Virtual environment for story creation. In *Proceedings of the Fifth International Conference in Intelligent Tutoring Systems*, pp. 464–473.

Prag, J., & Neave, R. (1997) *Making faces: Using forensic and archaeological evidence*. London: Published for the Trustees of the British Museum by British Museum Press.

Prakken, H. (1993a). *Logical tools for modelling legal argument*. Ph.D. thesis. Amsterdam: Vrije University.

Prakken, H. (1993b). A logical framework for modelling legal argument. In *Proceedings of the Fourth International Conference on Artificial Intelligence and Law*. New York: ACM Press, pp. 1–9.

Prakken, H. (1997). *Logical tools for modelling legal argument: A study of defeasible reasoning in law*. Dordrecht, The Netherlands: Kluwer.

Prakken, H. (2000). On dialogue systems with speech acts, arguments, and counterarguments. In M. Ojeda-Aciego, I. P. de Guzman, G. Brewka, & L. Moniz Pereira (Eds.), *Proceedings of JELIA'2000: The seventh European workshop on logic for artificial intelligence* (pp. 239–253). (Springer Lecture Notes in Artificial Intelligence, 1919). Berlin: Springer.

Prakken, H. (2001). Modelling reasoning about evidence in legal procedure. In *Proceedings of the Eighth International Conference on Artificial Intelligence and Law (ICAIL 2001)*, St. Louis, MO. New York: ACM Press, pp. 119–128.

Prakken, H. (2002). Incomplete arguments in legal discourse: A case study. In T. J. M. Bench-Capon, A. Daskalopulu, & R. Winkels (Eds.), *Legal knowledge and information systems. JURIX 2002: The fifteenth annual conference* (pp. 93–102). Amsterdam: IOS Press.

Prakken, H. (2004). Analysing reasoning about evidence with formal models of argumentation. *Law, Probability & Risk, 3*, 33–50.

Prakken, H. (2005). Coherence and flexibility in dialogue games for argumentation. *Journal of Logic and Computation, 15*, 1009–1040.

Prakken, H. (2006). Formal systems for persuasion dialogue. *The Knowledge Engineering Review, 21*, 163–188.

Prakken, H. (2008a). A formal model of adjudication dialogues. *Artificial Intelligence and Law, 16*, 305–328.

Prakken, H. (2008b). Formalising ordinary legal disputes: A case study. *Artificial Intelligence and Law, 16*, 333–359.

Prakken, H., & Renooij, S. (2001). Reconstructing causal reasoning about evidence: A case study. In B. Verheij, A. R. Lodder, R. P. Loui, & A. J. Muntjwerff (Eds.), *Legal knowledge and information systems. Jurix 2001: The 14th annual conference* (pp. 131–137). Amsterdam: IOS Press.

Prakken, H., & Sartor, G. (1995a). On the relation between legal language and legal argument: Assumptions, applicability and dynamic priorities. In *Proceedings of the Fifth International Conference on Artificial Intelligence and Law*. New York: ACM Press, pp. 1–10.

Prakken, H., & Sartor, G. (1995b). Argumentation framework: The missing link between arguments and procedures. *European Journal of Law, Philosophy and Computer Science, 1/2*, 379–396. Bologna, Italy: CLUEB.

Prakken, H., & Sartor, G. (1996a). A dialectical model of assessing conflicting arguments in legal reasoning. *Artificial Intelligence and Law, 4*(3/4), 331–368. Alternative title: Rules about rules: Assessing conflicting arguments in legal reasoning; reprinted in H. Prakken & G. Sartor (Eds.), *Logical models of legal argumentation* (pp. 175–212). Dordrecht, The Netherlands: Kluwer, 1997.

Prakken, H., & Sartor, G. (Eds.). (1996b). *Logical* models of legal argumentation, special issue of *Artificial Intelligence and Law, 5* (1996), 157–372. Reprinted as *Logical Models of Legal Argumentation*, Dordrecht, The Netherlands: Kluwer, 1997.

Prakken, H., & Sartor, G. (1998). Argumentation frameworks: The missing link between arguments and procedure. *European Journal of Law, Philosophy and Computer Science, 1/2*, 379–396.

Prakken, H., & Sartor, G. (2002). The role of logic in computational models of logic argument: A critical survey. In A. Kakas & F. Sadri (Eds.), *Computational logic: Logic programming and beyond. Essays in Honour of Robert A. Kowalski, Part II* (pp. 342–380). (Lecture Notes in Computer Science, 2048). Berlin: Springer.

Prakken, H., & Sergot, M. J. (1996). Contrary-to-duty obligations. *Studia Logica, 57*, 91–115.

Prakken, H., & Sergot, M. J. (1997). Dyadic deontic logic and contrary-to-duty obligations. In D. N. Nute (Ed.), *Defeasible deontic logic: Essays in nonmonotonic normative reasoning* (pp. 223–262). (Synthese Library, 263.) Dordrecht: Kluwer.

Prakken, H., Reed, C., & Walton, D. N. (2003). Argumentation schemes and generalisations in reasoning about evidence. In G. Sartor (Ed.), *Proceedings of the ninth International Conference on Artificial Intelligence and Law (ICAIL 2003)*, Edinburgh, Scotland, 24–28 June 2003 (pp. 32–41). New York: ACM Press.

Prakken, H., Reed, C., & Walton, D. N. (2004). Argumentation schemes and burden of proof. In F. Grasso, C. Reed, & G. Carenini (Eds.), *Proceedings of the fourth workshop on Computational Models of Natural Argument (CMNA IV)* at *ECAI 2004*, Valencia, Spain, pp. 81–86.

Prakken, H., & Vreeswijk, G. A. W. (2002). Encoding schemes for a discourse support system for legal argument. In G. Carenini, F. Grasso, & C. Reed (Eds.), *Proceedings of the ECAI-2002 workshop on computational models of natural argument*, at *ECAI 2002*, Lyon, France, pp. 31–39.

Prendinger, H., & Ishizuka, M. (Eds.). (2004). *Life-like characters: Tools, affective functions and applications.* Berlin: Springer.

Priebe, C. E., Conroy, J. M., Marchette, D. J., & Park, Y. (2005). Scan statistics on Enron graphs. In *Proceedings of the SIAM International Conference on Data Mining, SIAM Workshop on Link Analysis, Counterterrorism and Security.* Philadelphia, PA: SIAM.

Principe, G., & Ceci, S. (2002). I saw it with my own ears: The effect of peer conversations on children's reports of non-experienced events. *Journal of Experimental Child Psychology, 83,* 1–25.

Principe, J. C., Euliano, N. R., & Lefebvre, W. C. (2000). *Neural and adaptive systems: Fundamentals through simulations.* New York: Wiley.

Propp, V. (1928). Morfologija skazki. In *Voprosy poetiki* (Vol. 12). Leningrad: Gosudarstvennyi Institut Istorii Iskusstva. English editions: *Morphology of the Folktale*, edited by S. Pirkova-Jakobson, translated by L. Scott (Indiana University Research Center in Anthropology, Folklore and Linguistics, publication series, 10; Indiana University, Bloomington, IN, 1958). Reprinted in: *International Journal of American Linguistics*, Vol. 24, No. 4, Part 3 (Bibliographical and Special Series of the American Folklore Society, 9). New English translation: *Morphology of the Folktale*, 2nd edn., ed. by L.A. Wagner (Austin, TX: University of Texas Press, 1968.)[73] Revised Russian edn., Leningrad: Nauka, 1969; whence French edn., *Morphologie du conte* (collection Poétique; Paris: Éditions du Seuil, 1970).

Proth, J.-M., & Xie, X. (1996). *Petri nets: A tool for design and management of manufacturing systems.* Chichester: Wiley.

Provos, N., & Holz, T. (2007). *Virtual honeypots: From Botnet tracking to intrusion detection.* Reading, MA: Addison-Wesley.

Pu, D., & Srihari, S. N. (2010). A probabilistic measure for signature verification based on Bayesian learning. In *Proceedings of the 20th International Conference on Pattern Recognition*, Istanbul, Turkey, August 23–26, 1010.

Pühretmair, F., & Wöβ, W. (2001). XML-based integration of GIS and heterogeneous tourism information. In K. Dittrich, A. Geppert, & M. Norrie (Eds.), *Advanced information systems engineering* (pp. 346–358). Berlin: Springer.

Purchase, H. C., Cohen, R. F., & James, M. (1997). An experimental study of the basis for graph drawing algorithms. *ACM Journal of Experimental Algorithmics, 2*(4), 4-es.

Pye, K. (2006). Evaluation of the significance of geological and soil trace evidence (abstract). In A. Ruffell (Ed.), *Abstract book* of *geoscientists at crime scenes: First, inaugural meeting of the Geological Society of London*, 20 December 2006 (pp. 24–15). *Forensic Geoscience Group.* http://www.geolsoc.org.uk/pdfs/FGtalks&abs_pro.pdf

---

[73] American authors are used to refer to the Austin, Texas editions of Propp's book.

Pye, K. (2007). *Geological and soil evidence: Forensic applications*. Boca Raton, FL: CRC Press.

Pye, K., & Croft, D. J. (Eds.). (2004). *Forensic geoscience: Principles, techniques and applications*. (Special Publications, 232.) London: Geological Society.

Pyle, D. (1999). *Data preparation for data mining*. San Francisco: Morgan Kaufmann.

Quinlan, J. R. (1986). Induction of decision trees. *Machine Learning, 1*, 81–106.

Quinlan, J. R. (1993). *C4.5: Programs for machine learning*. San Mateo, CA: Morgan Kaufmann.

Quinlan, J. R. (1996). Bagging Boosting and C4.5. In *Proceedings of the Thirteenth National Conference on Artificial Intelligence (AAAI 96)*, Portland, OR. American Association for Artificial Intelligence, pp. 725–730.

Rabinovich, A. (1997). A birdwatcher with an attitude. *Jerusalem Post Internet Edition*, June 9, 1997. http://www.jpost.com/com/Archive/09.Jun.1997/Features/Article-22.html

Racter (1984). *The policeman's beard is half constructed*. New York: Warner.

Radev, D. R., Jing, H., & Budzikowska, M. (2000). Summarization of multiple documents: Clustering, sentence extraction, and evaluation. In *Proceedings of the Workshop of Automatic Text Summarization*, New Brunswick, NJ: Association for Computational Linguistics, pp. 21–30.

Radford, C. (1975). How can we be moved by the fate of Anna Karenina? In *Proceedings of the Aristotelian Society*, Supplementary volume 49.

Radford, C. (1995). Fiction, pity, fear, and jealousy. *The Journal of Aesthetics and Art Criticism, 53*(1), 71–75.

Rahman, H. (2009). Prospects and scopes of data mining applications in society development activities. Chapter 9 In H. Rahman (Ed.), *Data mining applications for empowering knowledge societies* (pp. 162–213). Hershey, PA: Information Science Reference (IGI Press).

Rahwan, I. (2005). Guest editorial: Argumentation in multi-agent systems. (Special issue.) *Journal of Autonomous Agents and Multi-Agent Systems, 11*, 115–125.

Rahwan, I., & McBurney, P. (2007). Guest editors' introduction: Argumentation technology. (Special issue.) *IEEE Intelligent Systems, 22*, 21–23.

Rahwan, I., & Simari, G. R. (Eds.). (2009). *Argumentation in artificial intelligence*. Berlin: Springer.

Raja, A., & Goel, A. (2007). Introspective self-explanation in analytical agents. In *Proceedings of AAMAS 2007 Workshop on Metareasoning in Agent-based Systems*, Hawaii, May 2007, pp. 76–91. http://www.viscenter.uncc.edu/TechnicalReports/CVC

Rakover, S. S., & Cahlon, B. (1989). To catch a thief with a recognition test: The model and some empirical results. *Cognitive Psychology, 21*, 423–468.

Rakover, S. S., & Cahlon, B. (2001). *Face recognition: Cognitive and computational processes*. (Advances in Consciousness Research, Series B, Vol. 31.) Amsterdam: Benjamins.

Ram, A. (1989). *Question-driven understanding: An integrated theory of story understanding, memory, and learning*. Technical Report YALE/DCS/tr710. New Haven, CT: Computer Science Department, Yale University.

Ram, A. (1994). AQUA: Questions that drive the explanation process. In R. C. Schank, A. Kass, & C. K. Riesbeck (Eds.), *Inside case-based explanation* (pp. 207–261). Hillsdale, NJ: Erlbaum.

Ramakrishnan, V., Malgireddy, M., & Srihari, S. N. (2008). Shoe-print extraction from latent images using CRFs. In *Computational Forensics: Proceedings of the International Workshop*, Washington D.C., 2008. (Lecture Notes in Computer Science, 5158.) Berlin: Springer, pp. 105–112.

Ramakrishnan, V., & Srihari, S. N. (2008). Extraction of shoeprint patterns from impression evidence using conditional random fields. In *Proceedings of the International Conference on Pattern Recognition*, Tampa, FL, 2008.

Ramamoorthi, R., & Hanrahan, P. (2001) An efficient representation for irradiance environment maps. In *SIGGRAPH '01: Proceedings of the 28th Annual Conference on Computer Graphics and Interactive Techniques*. New York: ACM Press, 2001, pp. 497–500.

Randell, D. A., & Cohn, A. G. (1992). Exploiting lattices in a theory of space and time. *Computers and Mathematics with Applications, 23*(6/9), 459–476. Also in: Lehmann, F. (Ed.). *Semantic networks*. Oxford: Pergamon Press. The book was also published as a special issue of *Computers and Mathematics with Applications, 23*(6–9).

Raskin, V. (1987). Semantics of lying. In R. Crespo, B. Dotson-Smith, & H. Schultink (Eds.), *Aspects of language: Studies in honour of Mario Alinei, Vol. 2: Theoretical and applied semantics* (pp. 443–469). Amsterdam: Rodopi.

Raskin, V. (1993). *Semantics of lying*. Dordrecht, The Netherlands: Kluwer.

Raskin, J.-F., Tan, Y.-H., & van der Torre, L. W. N. (1996). *Modeling deontic states in Petri nets*. Discussion Paper 111. Rotterdam, The Netherlands: Erasmus University Research Institute for Decision and Information Systems (EURIDIS).

Raskin, V., Atallah, M. J., Hempelmann, C. F., & Mohamed, D. H. (2001). *Hybrid data and text system for downgrading sensitive documents*. Technical Report, Center for Education and Research in Information Assurance and Security. West Lafayette, IN: Purdue University. https://www.cerias.purdue.edu/assets/pdf/bibtex_archive/2001-154.pdf

Rasmussen, P. C. (1998). Rediscovery of an Indian enigma: The Forest Owlet. *Bulletin of the Oriental Bird Club, 27*. http://www.orientalbirdclub.org/publications/bullfeats/forowlet.html

Rasmussen, P. C., & Ishtiaq, F. (1999). Vocalizations and behaviour of Forest Spotted Owlet *Athene blewitti. Forktail, 15*, 61–66. http://orientalbirdclub.org/publications/forktail/15pdfs/Rasmussen-ForestOwlet.pdf

Rasmussen, P. C., & King, B. F. (1998). The rediscovery of the Forest Owlet *Athene (Heteroglaux) blewitti. Forktail, 14*, 53–55. http://www.orientalbirdclub.org/publications/forktail/14pdfs/King-Owlet.pdf

Rasmussen, P. C., & Prŷs-Jones, R. P. (2003). History vs mystery: The reliability of museum specimen data. *Bulletin of the British Ornithologists' Club, 123A*, 66–94.

Ratcliffe, J. H. (2002). Intelligence-led policing and the problems of turning rhetoric into practice. *Policing and Society, 12*(1), 53–66.

Ratcliffe, J. H. (2003). Intelligence-led policing. *Trends and Issues in Crime and Criminal Justice, 248*, 6.

Ratcliffe, J. H. (2004). Geocoding crime and a first estimate of an acceptable minimum hit rate. *International Journal of Geographical Information Science, 18*(1), 61–73.

Ratcliffe, J. H. (2005). The effectiveness of police intelligence management: A New Zealand case study. *Police Practice and Research, 6*(5), 435–451.

Ratcliffe, J. H. (2007). *Integrated intelligence and crime analysis: Enhanced information management for law enforcement leaders* (2nd ed.). Washington, DC: Police Foundation. COPS: Community Oriented Policing Services, U.S. Department of Justice. http://www.policefoundation.org/pdf/integratedanalysis.pdf

Ratcliffe, J. H. (2008). *Intelligence-led policing*. Cullompton: Willan Publishing.

Rattani, A., Mehrotra, H., & Gupta, P. (2008). Multimodal biometric systems. In M. Quigley (Ed.), *Encyclopedia of information ethics and security* (pp. 478–485). Hershey, PA: IGI Global (formerly Idea Group), 2008 (but available from June 2007).

Rattner, K. (1988). Convicted but innocent: Wrongful conviction and the criminal justice system. *Law and Human Behavior, 12*, 283–293.

Read, S. (1988). *Relevant logic: A philosophical examination of inference*. Oxford: Blackwell. Revised edition published online and freely accessible, 2010, at http://www.st-andrews.ac.uk/~slr/Relevant_Logic.pdf

Reddy, W. M. (1997). Against constructionism: The historical ethnography of emotions. *Current Anthropology, 38*(2), 327–351.

Reddy, W. M. (2001). *The navigation of feeling: A framework for the history of emotions*. Cambridge: Cambridge University Press.

Redlich, A., & Goodman, G. (2003). Taking responsibility for an act not committed: The effects of age and suggestibility. *Law and Human Behavior, 27*, 141–156.

Redmayne, M. (1999). A likely story! [A review of W.A. Dembsky, *The Design Inference: Eliminating Chance Through Small Probabilities*. Cambridge, England: Cambridge University Press, 1998.] *Oxford Journal of Legal Studies, 19*, 659–672.

Redmayne, M. (2002). Appeals to reason. *The Modern Law Review, 65*(1), 19–35. Oxford: Blackwell.

Redmond, M. A., & Blackburn, C. (2003). Empirical analysis of case-based reasoning and other prediction methods in a social science domain: Repeat criminal victimization. In

K. D. Ashley & D. G. Bridge (Eds.), *Case-based reasoning research and development: Proceedings of the 5th International Conference on Case-Based Reasoning (ICCBR 2003),* Trondheim, Norway, June 23–26, 2003. (Lecture Notes in Computer Science, 2689.) Berlin: Springer.

Redsicker, D. R. (2005). Basic fire and explosion ivestigation. Chapter 24 In S. H. James & J. J. Nordby (Eds.), *Forensic science: An introduction to scientific and investigative techniques* (2nd ed.). Boca Raton, FL: CRC Press, 2005. Also in 3rd edition, 2009.

Reed, C., & Grasso, F. (Eds.). (2007). *Recent advances in computational models of natural argument.* Special issue in the *International Journal of Intelligent Systems, 22.*

Reed, C., & Norman, T. J. (Eds.). (2003). *Argumentation machines: New frontiers in argument and computation.* Dordrecht, The Netherlands: Kluwer.

Reed, C., & Norman, T. J. (Eds.). (2004). *Argumentation machines: New frontiers in argument and computation.* (Argumentation Library, 9.) Dordrecht, Netherlands: Kluwer.

Reed, C. A., & Rowe, G. W. A. (2001). *Araucaria: Software for puzzles in argument diagramming and XML.* Technical report, Department of Applied Computing, University of Dundee. (The Araucaria software is in the public domain, and can be downloaded free of charge from the website http://www.computing.dundee.ac.uk/staff/creed/araucaria/).

Reed, C. A., & Rowe, G. W. A. (2004). Araucaria: Software for argument analysis, diagramming and representation. *International Journal on Artificial Intelligence Tools, 14*(3/4), 961–980.

Reeves, J. (1991). *Computational morality: A process model of belief conflict and resolution for story understanding.* Technical Report 910017, Computer Science Department. Los Angeles, CA: University of California, Los Angeles. ftp://ftp.cs.ucla.edu/tech-report/1991-reports/910017.pdf

Reichenbach, H. (1949). *The theory of probability.* Berkeley, CA: University of California Press.

Reilly, W. S. N. (1996). *Believable social and emotional agents.* Technical Report CMU-CS-96-138. Pittsburgh, PA: School of Computer Science, Carnegie Mellon University. http://www-2.cs.cmu.edu/afs/cs.cmu.edu/project/oz/web/papers/CMU-CS-96-138-1sided.ps

Reiner, R. (2000). *The politics of the police.* Oxford: Oxford University Press.

Reis, D., Melo, A., Coelho, A. L., & Furtado, V. (2006). GAPatrol: An evolutionary multiagent approach for the automatic definition of hotsports and patrol routes. In J. S. Sichman, H. Coelho, & S. O. Rezende (Eds.), *Advances in artificial intelligence – IBERAMIA-SBIA 2006, 2nd International Joint Conference, 10th Ibero-American Conference on AI, 18th Brazilian AI Symposium* (pp. 118–127). (Lecture Notes in Computer Science, 4140). Berlin: Springer.

Ren, A., Stakhanova, N., & Ghorbani, A. A. (2010). An online adaptive approach to alert correlation. In C. Kreibich & M. Jahnke (Eds.), *Detection of Intrusions and Malware, and Vulnerability Assessment: Proceedings of the seventh international conference (DIMVA 2010),* Bonn, Germany, July 8–9, 2010 (pp. 153–172). (Lecture Notes in Computer Science, Vol. 6201.) Berlin: Springer.

Rendell, K. W. (1994). *Forging history: The detection of fake letters & manuscripts.* Norman, OK: University of Oklahoma Press.

Resnick, P., Zeckhauser, R., Friedman, E., & Kuwabara. K. (2000). Reputation systems. *Communications of the ACM, 43*(12), 45–48. http://www.si.umich.edu/~presnick/papers/cacm00/reputations.pdf

Resnick, P., Zeckhauser, R., Swanson, J., & Lockwood, K. (2003). *The value of reputation on eBay: A controlled experiment.* Technical report.

Restall, G. (1996). Information flow and relevant logics. In J. Seligman & D. Westerstahl (Eds.), *Logic, language and computation* (Vol. 1, pp. 463–478). Stanford, CA: Center for the Study of Language and Information (CSLI).

Reutenauer, C. (1990). *The mathematics of petri nets.* London: Prentice-Hall International.

Ribaux, O., & Margot, P. (1999). Inference structures for crime analysis and intelligence: The example of burglary using forensic science data. *Forensic Science International, 100,* 193–210.

Richards, W. D. (1999). MultiNet. [Software tool.] At http://www.sfu.ca/~richards/Multinet/

Richards, W. D., & Rice, R. E. (1981). The NEGOPY network analysis program. *Social Networks, 3*(3), 215–223.

Rickman, B. (2003). The Dr. K– project. In M. Mateas & P. Sengers (Eds.), *Narrative intelligence* (pp. 131–142). Amsterdam: Benjamins.

Ricordel, P., & Demazeau, Y. (2000). From analysis to deployment: A multi-agent platform survey. In A. Omicini, R. Tolksdorf, & F. Zambonelli (Eds.), *Proceedings of the first international workshop on Engineering Societies in the Agents World (ESAW), ECAI2000* (pp. 93–105). Lectures Notes in Artificial Intelligence, Vol. 1972. Berlin: Springer.

Riedl, M., Saretto, C. J., & Young, R. M. (2003). Managing interaction between users and agents in a multi-agent storytelling environment. In *AAMAS '03: Proceedings of the Second International Joint Conference on Autonomous Agents and Multiagent Systems*. New York: ACM.

Riedl, M., & Young, R. M. (2004). An intent-driven planner for multi-agent story generation. In *Proceedings of the Third International Conference on Autonomous Agents and Multi-Agent Systems*, July 2004. http://liquidnarrative.csc.ncsu.edu/papers.html

Riedl, M. O. (2003). *Actor conference: Character-focused narrative planning.* Liquid Narrative Technical Report TR03-000. Raleigh, NC: North Carolina State University. http://liquidnarrative.csc.ncsu.edu/pubs/tr03-000.pdf

Riedl, M. O. (2004). *Narrative generation: Balancing plot and character.* PhD Dissertation. Raleigh, NC: Department of Computer Science, North Carolina State University. http://people.ict.usc.edu/~riedl/pubs/dissertation.pdf

Riedl, M. O., Rowe, J. P., & Elson, D. K. (2008). Toward intelligent support of authoring *Machinima* media content: Story and visualization. In *INTETAIN '08: Proceedings of the 2nd International Conference on INtelligent TEchnologies for Interactive EnterTAINment*. Institute for Computer Sciences, Social-Informatics and Telecommunications Engineering (ICST), Brussels, Belgium. New York: ACM.

Riepert, T., Drechsler, T., Schild, H., Nafe, B., & Mattern, R. (1996). Estimation of sex on the basis of radiographs of the calcaneus. *Forensic Science International, 77*(3), 133–140.

Riloff, E., & Thelen, M. (2000). A rule-based question answering system for reading comprehension tests. In *Proceedings of the ANLP/NAA CL 2000 Workshop on Reading Comprehension Tests as Evaluation for Computer-Based Language Understanding Systems*.

Ringle, M. (1979). Philosophy and artificial intelligence. In M. Ringle (Ed.), *Philosophical perspectives in artificial intelligence*. Atlantic Highlands, NJ: Humanities Press.

Ringle, M. (1983). Psychological studies and artificial intelligence. *The AI Magazine, 4*(1), 37–43.

Ripley, S. D. (1976). Reconsideration of *Athene blewitti* (Hume). *Journal of the Bombay Natural History Society, 73*, 1–4.

Ripley, B. D. (1996). *Pattern recognition and neural networks*. Cambridge: Cambridge University Press.

Risinger, D. M. (2007a). Goodbye to all that, or a fool's errand, by one of the fools: How I stopped worrying about court responses to handwriting identification (and "forensic science" in general) and learned to love misinterpretations of *Kumho Tire v. Carmichael. Tulsa Law Review, 43*(2), 447–475. With an Appendix, being Risinger (2007b).

Risinger, D. M. (2007b). Appendix: Cases involving the reliability of handwriting identification expertise since the decision in *Daubert. Tulsa Law Review, 43*(2), 477–596. http://www.bioforensics.com/sequential_unmasking/Risinger-Appendix.pdf

Risinger, D. M., Saks, M. J., Thompson, W. C., & Rosenthal, R. (2002). The Daubert/Kumho implications of observer effects in forensic science: Hidden problems of expectation and suggestion. *California Law Review, 90*(1), 1–56. http://www.bioforensics.com/sequential_unmasking/observer_effects.pdf

Rissland, E. L., & Friedman, M. T. (1995). Detecting change in legal concepts. In *Proceedings of the Fifth International Conference on Artificial Intelligence and Law (ICAIL'95)*. New York: ACM Press, pp. 127–136.

Rissland, E. L., & Skalak, D. B. (1991). CABARET: Statutory interpretation in a hybrid architecture. *International Journal of Man-Machine Studies, 34*, 839–887.

Rissland, E. L., Skalak, D. B., & Friedman, M. T. (1996). BankXX: Supporting legal arguments through heuristic retrieval. *Artificial Intelligence and Law, 4*(1), 1–71.

Ritchie, G. (2004). *The linguistic analysis of jokes*. London: Routledge.

Ritterband, P., & Wechsler, H. S. (1994). *Jewish learning in American universities: The first century*. Bloomington, IN: Indiana University Press.

Roberts, A. (2008). Eyewitness identification evidence: Procedural developments and the ends of adjudicative accuracy. *International Commentary on Evidence, 6*(2), Article 3. http://www.bepress.com/ice/vol6/iss2/art3

Roberts, D. L., Elphick, C. S., & Reed, J. M. (2009). Identifying anomalous reports of putatively extinct species and why it matters. *Conservation Biology*, online publication at doi://10.1111/j.1523-1739.2009.01292.x The paper was then published in print, in *Conservation Biology, 24*(1), 189–196, in Feb. 2010.

Roberts, L. (1991). Fight erupts over DNA fingerprinting. *Science, 254*, 1721–1723.

Robertson, B., & Vignaux, G. A. [T.] (1995). *Interpreting evidence: Evaluating forensic science in the courtroom*. Chichester: Wiley.

Rogers, M. (2005). *Anti-forensics*. http://www.cyberforensics.purdue.edu/docs/Lockheed.ppt

Rokach, L., & Maimon, O. Z. (2008). *Data mining with decision trees: Theory and applications*. (Series in Machine Perception and Artificial Intelligence, Vol. 69.) Singapore: World Scientific.

Roscoe, A. W. (1998). *The theory and practice of concurrency*. (Prentice Hall Series in Computer Science.) Hemel Hempstead, Hertfordshire: Prentice Hall.

Roscoe, B. A., & Hopke, P. K. (1981). Comparison of weighted and unweighted target transformation rotations in factor analysis. *Computers and Chemistry, 5*, 1–7.

Rosenberg, N. (1994). Hollywood on trials: Courts and films, 1930–1960. *Law and History Review, 12*(2), 342–367.

Rosenberg, S. T. (1977). *Frame-based text processing*. Technical Report AIM-431. Cambridge, MA: Artificial Intelligence Laboratory, Massachusetts Institute of Technology. ftp://publications.ai.mit.edu/ai-publications/pdf/AIM-431.pdf

Rosenblatt, F. (1958). The perceptron: A probabilistic model for information storage and organization in the brain. *Psychological Review, 65*, 386–408.

Rosoni, I. (1995). *Quae singula non prosunt collecta iuvant: la teoria della prova indiziaria nell'età medievale e moderna*. Milan, Italy: Giuffrè. [Reviewed in Nissan (2001b).]

Ross, A., & Jain, A. K. (2003). Information fusion in biometrics. *Pattern Recognition Letters, 24*(13), 2115–2125.

Ross, A. A. (2003). *Information fusion in fingerprint authentication*. Ph.D. Dissertation. Department of Computer Science & Engineering, Michigan State University. http://www.csee.wvu.edu/~ross/pubs/RossPhDThesis_03.pdf

Ross, D. F., Read, J. D., & Toglia, M. P. (Eds.). (1994). *Adult eyewitness testimony: Current trends and developments*. Cambridge: Cambridge University Press.

Ross, S., Spendlove, D., Bolliger, S., Christe, A., Oesterhelweg, L., Grabherr, S., et al. (2008). Postmortem whole-body CT angiography: Evaluation of two contrast media solutions. *AJR: American Journal of Roentgenology, 190*(5), 1380–1389.

Ross, T. (1995). *Fuzzy logic with engineering applications*. New York: McGraw-Hill.

Rossiter, B. N., Sillitoe, T. J., & Heather, M. A. (1993). *Models for legal documentation: Using formal methods for quality assurance in hypertext systems*. (Technical Report Series, 464.) Newcastle upon Tyne, England: University of Newcastle upon Tyne, Computing Science.

Rousseau, D. (1995). *Modelisation et simulation de conversations dans un univers multi-agent*. Ph.D. Dissertation. Technical Report #993, Montreal, Canada: Department of Computer Science and Operational Research, University of Montreal.

Rousseau, D. (1996). *Personality in synthetic agents*. Technical Report KSL-96-21, Knowledge Systems Laboratory, Stanford University.

Rousseau, D., Moulin, B., & Lapalme, G. (1996). Interpreting communicative acts and building a conversational model. *Journal of Natural Language Engineering, 2*(3), 253–276.

Rousseeuw, P. J., & Hubert, M. (2011). Robust statistics for outlier detection. *Wiley Interdisciplinary Reviews (WIREs): Data Mining and Knowledge Discovery, 1*(1), 73–79. doi://10.1002/widm.2

Routley, R., Meyer, R. K., Plumwood, V., & Brady, R. (Eds.). (1983). *Relevant logic and its rivals, I*. Atascadero, CA: Ridgeview. Vol. 2 is Brady (2003).

Rubinstein, A. (1998). *Modelling bounded rationality*. Cambridge, MA: MIT Press.

Rubinstein, R. (1997). Optimization of computer simulation models with rare events. *European Journal of Operations Research, 99*, 89–112.

Rudman, J. (1997). The state of authorship attribution studies: Some problems and solutions. *Computers and the Humanities, 31*(4), 351–365. Dordrecht: Kluwer.

Ruffell, A. (Ed.). (2006) *Abstract book* of *geoscientists at crime scenes: First, inaugural meeting of the Geological Society of London, Forensic Geoscience Group*, London, 20 December 2006. http://www.geolsoc.org.uk/pdfs/FGtalks&abs_pro.pdf

Rumble, W. E., Jr. (1965). Legal realism, sociological jurisprudence and Mr. Justice Holmes. *Journal of the History of Ideas, 26*(4), 547–566.

Rumelhart, D. E. (1975). Notes on a schema for stories. In D. G. Bobrow & A. Collins (Eds.), *Representation and understanding: studies in cognitive science* (pp. 185–210). New York: Academic.

Rumelhart, D. E. (1977a). Toward an interactive model of reading. In S. Domic (Ed.), *Attention and performance VI*. Hillsdale NJ: Lawrence Erlbaum Associates.

Rumelhart, D. E. (1977b). Understanding and summarizing brief stories. In D. La Berge & S. J. Samuels (Eds.), *Basic processes in reading: Perception and comprehension*. Hillsdale, NJ: Lawrence Erlbaum Associates.

Rumelhart, D. E. (1980a). Schemata: The building blocks of cognition. In R. J. Spiro, B. C. Bruce, & W. F. Brewer (Eds.), *Theoretical issues in reading comprehension* (pp. 38–58). Hillsdale, NJ: Erlbaum.

Rumelhart, D. E. (1980b). On evaluating story grammars. *Cognitive Science, 4*, 313–316.

Rumelhart, D. E., Hinton, G. E., & Williams, R. (1986a). Learning internal representations by error propagation. In D. E. Rumelhart & J. L. McClelland (Eds.), *Parallel distributed processing: Explorations in the microstructure of cognition*. Cambridge, MA: MIT Press.

Rumelhart, D. E., Hinton, G. E., & Williams, R. (1986b, October 9). Learning representations by back-propagating errors. *Letters to Nature (Nature), 323*, 533–536.

Rumelhart, D. E., & Ortony, A. (1977). The representation of knowledge in memory. In R. C. Anderson, R. J. Spiro, & W. E. Montague (Eds.), *Schooling and the acquisition of knowledge*. Hillsdale, NJ: Lawrence Erlbaum Associates.

Rumelhart, D. E., Smolensky, P., McClelland, J. L., & Hinton, G. E. (1986c). Schemata and sequential thought processes in PDP models. In D. E. Rumelhart & J. L. McClelland (Eds.), *Parallel distributed processing: Explorations in the microstructure of cognition* (Vol. 2, pp. 7–57). Cambridge, MA: MIT Press.

Russano, M. B., Meissner, C. A., Narchet, F. M., & Kassin, S. M. (2005). Investigating true and false confessions within a novel experimental paradigm. *Psychological Science, 16*, 481–486.

Ryan, M.-L. (2005). Narrative. In D. Herman, M. Jahn, & M.-L. Ryan (Eds.), *Routledge encyclopedia of narrative theory* (pp. 344–348). London: Routledge, 2005 (hbk), 2008 (pbk).

Ryan, P. Y. A, Schneider, S. A., Goldsmith, M., Lowe, G., & Roscoe, A. W. (2000). *Modelling and analysis of security protocols*. Harlow: Pearson Education.

Sabater, J., & Sierra, C. (2005). Review on computational trust and reputation models. *Artificial Intelligence Review, 24*, 33–60.

Saferstein, R. E. (1995). *Criminalistics: An introduction to forensic science* (5th ed.). Englewood Cliffs, NJ: Prentice-Hall. 6th edn., 1998.

Sainsbury, R. M. (1990). *Concepts without boundaries*. Inaugural Lecture, King's College London. Reprinted in: R. Keefe & P. Smith (Eds.), *Vagueness: A reader*. Cambridge, MA: MIT Press, 1996.

Saks, M. J., & Koehler, J. J. (2008). The individualization fallacy in forensic science evidence. *Vanderbilt Law Review, 61*, 199–219.

Sakurai, Y., & Yokoo, M. (2003). A false-name-proof double auction protocol for arbitrary evaluation values. In *AAMAS 2003: Proceedings of the Second International Joint Conference on Autonomous Agents and Multiagent Systems*.

Salmon, W. C. (1967). *The foundations of scientific inference*. Pittsburgh, PA: Universitgy of Pittsburgh Press.

Salton, G. (1989). *Automatic text processing: The transformation, analysis, and retrieval of information by computer*. Reading, MA: Addison-Wesley Publishing Company.

Salton, G., & Buckley, C. (1988). Term-weighting approaches in automatic text retrieval. *Information Processing and Management, 24*(5), 513–523.

Sammes, T., & Jenkinson, B. (2000). *Forensic computing: A practitioner's guide*. London & Heidelberg: Springer.

Sanders, W. B. (1977). *Detective work: A study of criminal investigation*. New York: Free Press.

Santos, E., Jr., & Shimony, S. E. (1994). Belief updating by enumerating high-probability independence-based assignments. In R. Lopez de Mántaras & D. Poole (Eds.), *Uncertainty in artificial intelligence: Proceedings of the tenth conference* (pp. 506–513). San Mateo, CA: Morgan Kaufmann.

Santtila, P., Alkiora, P., Ekholm, M., & Niemi, P. (1999). False confessions to robbery: The role of suggestibility, anxiety, memory disturbance and withdrawal symptoms. *The Journal of Forensic Psychiatry, 10*, 399–415.

Sappington, D. (1984). Incentive contracting with asymmetric and imperfect precontractual knowledge. *Journal of Economic Theory, 34*, 52–70.

Saretto, C. J. (2001). *Mediating user interaction in narrative-structured virtual environments*. M.Sc. thesis (advisor: R. M. Young). Raleigh, NC: Computer Science, North Carolina State University. http://liquidnarrative.csc.ncsu.edu/papers.html

Sartor, G. (1994). A formal logic for legal argumentation. *Ratio Juris, 7*, 212–226.

Sartwell, C. (1992). Why knowledge is merely true belief. *Journal of Philosophy, 89*, 167–180.

Sartwell, C. (1995). Radical externalism concerning experience. *Philosophical Studies, 78*, 55–70.

Sattler, U. (2003). Description logics for ontologies. In *Proceedings of the International Conference on Conceptual Structures (ICCS 2003)*. (Lecture Notes in AI, Vol. 2746.) Berlin: Springer.

Savage, L. J. (1962). *The foundations of statistical inference*. London: Methuen and Co. Ltd.

Sawday, J. (1996). *The body emblazoned: Dissection and the human body in renaissance culture*. London: Routledge.

Sawyer, A. G. (1981). Repetition, cognitive responses and persuasion. In R. E. Petty, T. M. Ostrom, & T. C. Brock (Eds.), *Cognitive responses in persuasion* (pp. 237–261). Hillsdale, NJ: Erlbaum.

Sbriccoli, M. (1991). "Tormentum id est torquere mentem". Processo inquisitorio e interrogatorio per tortura nell'Italia comunale. In J.-C. Maire Vigeur & A. Paravicini Bagliani (Eds.), *La parola all'accusato* (Prisma, 139.) (pp. 17–33). Palermo: Sellerio.

Scampicchio, M., Ballabio, D., Arecchi, A., Cosio, S. M., & Mannino, S. (2008). Amperometric electronic tongue for food analysis. *Microchimica Acta, 163*, 11–21.

Schafer, B., & Keppens, J. (2007). Legal LEGO: Model based computer assisted teaching in evidence courses. *Journal of Information, Law & Technology*, Special Issue on Law, Education and Technology, http://www2.warwick.ac.uk/fac/soc/law/elj/jilt/2007_1/schafer_keppens/schafer_keppens.pdf

Schank, P., & Ranney, M. (1995). Improved reasoning with Convince Me. In *CHI '95: Conference Companion on Human Factors in Computing Systems*. New York: ACM Press, pp. 276–277.

Schank, R., & Abelson, R. (1977). *Scripts, plans, goals and understanding*. Hillsdale, NJ: Lawrence Erlbaum.

Schank, R. C., Goldman, N., Rieger, C., & Riesbeck, C. K. (1973). MARGIE: Memory, analysis, response generation and inference in English. In *Proceedings of the Third International Joint Conference on Artificial Intelligence*, pp. 255–261.

Schank, R. C., Goldman, N., Rieger, C., & Riesbeck, C. K. (1975). Inference and paraphrase by computer. *Journal of the ACM, 22*(3), 309–328.

Schank, R. C., Kass, A., & Riesbeck, C. K. (Eds.). (1994). *Inside case-based explanation*. Hillsdale, NJ: Erlbaum.

Schank, R. G. (1972). Conceptual dependency: A theory of natural language understanding. *Cognitive Psychology, 3*, 552–631.

Schank, R. G. (1986). *Explanation patterns: Understanding mechanically and creatively.* Hillsdale, NJ: Lawrence Erlbaum Associates.

Schank, R. G., & Riesbeck, C. K. (Eds.). (1981). *Inside computer understanding: Five programs plus miniatures.* Hillsdale, NJ: Lawrence Erlbaum Associates.

Shannon, C. E., & Weaver, W. (1949). *The mathematical theory of communication.* Urbana, IL: University of Illinois Press.

Schartum, D. W. (1994). Dirt in the machinery of government? Legal challenges connected to computerized case processing in public administration. *International Journal of Law and Information Technology, 2,* 327–354.

Schild, U. J. (1995). Intelligent computer systems for criminal sentencing. In *The Fifth International Conference on Artificial Intelligence and Law: Proceedings of the Conference,* Washington, DC. New York: ACM Press, pp. 229–239.

Schild, U. J. (1998). Criminal sentencing and intelligent decision support. *Artificial Intelligence and Law, 6*(2–4), 151–202.

Schild, U. J., & Kerner, Y. (1994). Multiple explanation patterns. In S. Wess, K.-D. Althoff, & M. Richter (Eds.), *Topics in case-based reasoning, Proceedings of the First European Workshop, EWCBR 93* (pp. 353–364). (Lecture Notes in Artificial Intelligence, 837.) Berlin: Springer.

Shirley, S. G., & Persaud, K. C. (1990). The biochemistry of vertebrate olfaction and taste. *Seminars Neuroscience, 2,* 59–68.

Schlesinger, P., & Tumber, H. (1994). *Reporting crime: The media politics of criminal justice.* Oxford: Clarendon Press.

Schmid, N (2009). *Handbuch des Schweizerischen Strafprozessrechts.* Zürich & St. Gallen, Switzerland: Dike Verlag.

Schneider, S. A. (1999). *Concurrent and real time systems: The CSP approach.* Chichester: Wiley.

Schneider, S. A. (2001). *The B-method: An introduction.* Palgrave Cornerstones in Computer Science. London: Palgrave Macmillan.

Schneider, V., Nagano, T., & Geserick, G. (Eds). (1994). *Advances in legal medicine.* Special issue, *Forensic Science International, 69*(3). Amsterdam: Elsevier.

Schoenlein, R. W., Chattopadhyay, S., Chong, H. H. W., Glover, T. E., Heimann, P. A., Shank, C. V., et al. (2000). Generation of femtosecond pulses of synchrotron radiation. *Science, 287,* 2237.

Schonlau, M., DuMouchel, W., Ju, W., Karr, A. F., Theus, M., & Vardi, Y. (2001). Computer intrusion: Detecting masquerades. *Statistical Science, 16*(1), 58–74.

Schooler, J. W., Gerhard, D., & Loftus, E. F. (1986). Qualities of the unreal. *Journal of Experimental Psychology: Learning, Memory and Cognition, 12,* 171–181.

Schraagen, J. M., & Leijenhorst, H. (2001). Searching for evidence: Knowledge and search strategies used by forensic scientists. In E. Salas & G. Klein (Eds.), *Linking expertise and naturalistic decision making* (pp. 263–274). Mahwah, NJ: LEA.

Schreiber, F. A. (1991). State and time granularity in systems description: An example. *IEEE Real-Time Systems Newsletter, 7*(3), 12–17. http://home.dei.polimi.it/schreibe/papers/states2.ps (*sic:/schreibe/not/schreiber/*)

Schreiber, F. A. (1994). Is time a real time? An overview of time ontology in informatics. In W. A. Halang & A. D. Stoyenko (Eds.), *Real time computing* (pp. 283–307). (NATO ASI, Vol. F 127.) Berlin: Springer.

Schreiber, T. J., Akkermanis, A. M., Anjewierden, A. A., de Hoog, R., Shadbolt, A., Van de Velde, W., et al. (1999). *Knowledge engineering and management: The common Kads methodology.* Cambridge, MA: MIT Press.

Schreiber, F. A., Belussi, A., De Antonellis, V., Fugini, M. G., Pozzi, G., Tanca, L., et al. (2003). The design of the DEAFIN web-geographical information system: An experience in the integration of territorial reclamation support services. In A. Dahanayake & W. Gerhardt (Eds.), *Web-enabled systems integration: Practice and challenges* (pp. 142–168). Hershey, PA: Idea Group Publishing.

Schroeder, J., Xu, J., Chen, H., & Chau, M. (2007). Automated criminal link analysis based on domain knowledge. *Journal of the American Society for Information Science and Technology, 58*(6), 842–855. doi://10.1002/asi.v58:6

Schubert, L. K., & Hwang, C. H. (1989). An episodic knowledge representation for narrative texts. In *Proceedings of the First International Conference on Principles of Knowledge Representation and Reasoning*. San Mateo, CA: Morgan Kaufmann, pp. 444–458.

Schubert, L. K., & Hwang, C. H. (2000). Episodic logic meets Little Red Riding Hood: A comprehensive natural representation for language understanding. In L. M. Iwanska & S. C. Shapiro (Eds.), *Natural language processing and knowledge representation* (pp. 111–174). Cambridge, MA: MIT Press. http://www.cs.rochester.edu/~schubert/papers/el-meets-lrrh.ps

Schultz, M., Eskin, E., Zadok, E., & Stolfo, S. (2001). Data mining methods for detection of new malicious executables. At the *2001 IEEE Symposium on Security and Privacy*, pp. 38–49.

Schum, D. A. (1986). Probability and the processes of discovery, proof, and choice. *Boston University Law Review, 66*, 825–876.

Schum, D. A. (1987). *Evidence and inference for the intelligence analyst* (2 Vols.). Lanham, MD: University Press of America.

Schum, D. A. (1989). Knowledge, credibility, and probability. *Journal of Behavioural Decision Making, 2*, 39–62.

Schum, D. A. (1993). Argument structuring and evidence evaluation. In R. Hastie (Ed.), *Inside the Juror: The psychology of Juror decision making* (pp. 175–191). Cambridge, England: Cambridge University Press.

Schum, D. A. (1994). *The evidential foundations of probabilistic reasoning*. (Wiley Series in Systems Engineering.) New York: Wiley. Reprinted, Evanston, IL: Northwestern University Press, 2001.

Schum, D. (2001). Evidence marshaling for imaginative fact investigation. *Artificial Intelligence and Law, 9*(2/3), 165–188.

Schum, D. A., & Martin, A. W. (1982). Formal and empirical research on cascaded inference in jurisprudence. *Law and Society Review, 17*, 105–151.

Schum, D., & Tillers, P. (1989). *Marshalling evidence throughout the process of fact investigation: A simulation*. Report Nos. 89-01 through 89-04, supported by NSF Grant No. SES 8704377. New York: Cardozo School of Law.

Schum, D., & Tillers, P. (1990a). *A technical note on computer-assisted Wigmorean argument structuring*. Report No. 90-01 (Jan. 15, 1990), supported by NSF Grant No. SES 8704377. New York: Cardozo School of Law.

Schum, D., & Tillers, P. (1990b). *Marshalling thought and evidence about witness credibility (March 15, 1990), supported by NSF Grants Nos. SES 8704377 and 9007693*. New York: Cardozo School of Law.

Schum, D., & Tillers, P. (1991). Marshalling evidence for choice and inference in litigation. *Cardozo Law Review, 13*, 657–704. Also Report 91–03 (March 18, 1991), supported by NSF Grant Nos. SES 8704377 and 9007693. New York: Cardozo School of Law.

Schunn, C. D., Okada, T., & Crowley, K. (1995). Is cognitive science truly interdisciplinary? The case of interdisciplinary collaborations. In J. D. Moore & J. F. Lehman (Eds.), *Proceedings of the 17th annual conference of the cognitive science society* (pp. 100–105). Mahwa, NJ: Elbaum.

Schwartz, A., & Scott, R. E. (2003). Contract theory and the limits of contract law. *Yale Law Journal, 113*, 541–619.

Schweighofer, E., & Merkl, D. (1999). A learning technique for legal document analysis. In *Proceedings of the Seventh International Conference on Artificial Intelligence and Law (ICAIL'99)*, Oslo, Norway, 14–17 June 1999. New York: ACM Press, pp. 156–163.

Schwikkard, P. J. (2008). The muddle of silence. *International Commentary on Evidence, 6*(2), Article 4. http://www.bepress.com/ice/vol6/iss2/art4

Scientific Working Group on Friction Ridge Analysis Study and Technology. (2002). *Friction ridge examination methodology for latent print examiners*. http://www.swgfast.org/

Scientific Working Group on Friction Ridge Analysis Study and Technology. (2003). *Standards for conclusions*. http://www.swgfast.org/

Scott, J. (2003). *How to write for animation*. Woodstock, NY and New York: The Overlook Press.

Scott, J. (2006). *Social network analysis: A handbook*. London: Sage. [Previously: 2nd edition, 2000 (also cited).]

Scott, M. S. (2000). *Problem-oriented policing: Reflections on the first 20 years*. Washington, DC: Office of Community Oriented Policing Services [COPS Office], U.S. Department of Justice. http://www.popcenter.org/Library/RecommendedReadings/Reflections.pdf

Seabrook, J. (2006). *The Meinertzhagen Ruse*. New York: The New Yorker.

Searle, J. (1969). *Speech acts: An essay in the philosophy of language*. Cambridge: Cambridge University Press.

Sebastiani, F. (2002). Machine learning in automated text categorization. *ACM Computing Surveys, 34*(1), 1–47.

Sebeok, T. A., & Umiker-Sebeok, J. (1979). "You know my method": A juxtaposition of Sherlock Holmes and C. S. Peirce. In N. Baron & N. Bhattacharya (Eds.), *Methodology in semiotics*, special issue of *Semiotica, 26*(3/4), 203–250.

Sebeok, T. A., & Umiker-Sebeok, J. (1980). *"You know my method": A juxtaposition of Sherlock Holmes and C. S. Peirce*. Bloomington, IN: Gaslight Publications.

Sebeok, T. A., & Umiker-Sebeok, J. (1981). *Sherlock Holmes no Kogoron: C. S. Peirce to Holmes no Hikakukenkyn*, translated into Japanese by T. Tomiyama. Tokyo: Iwanami Shoten.

Sebeok, T. A., & Umiker-Sebeok, J. (1982a). *"Du kennst meine Methode": Charles S. Peirce und Sherlock Holmes*. Frankfurt am Main, Germany: Suhrkamp.

Sebeok, T. A., & Umiker-Sebeok, J. (1982b, March). Sherlock Holmes e le abduzioni. *Alfabeta, 34*, 15–17.

Sebeok, T. A., & Umiker-Sebeok, J. (1983). "Voi conoscete il mio metodo": un confronto fra Charles S. Peirce e Sherlock Holmes. In T. A. Sebeok & U. Eco (Eds.), *The sign of three: Holmes, Dupin, Peirce* (pp. 11–54). Bloomington, IN: Indiana University Press.

Sebeok, T. A., & Umiker-Sebeok, J. (1989). *Peirce and Holmes* [In Chinese]. Beijin: Chinese Academy of Social Sciences.

Sebeok, T. A., & Umiker-Sebeok, J. (1994). *Din Nou Pe Urmele Lui Sherlock Holmes*. Cluj: Editura Echinox. [Romanian translation of *"You Know My Method": A Juxtaposition of Sherlock Holmes and C.S. Peirce*.]

Sebok, A. (1998). *Legal positivism in American jurisprudence*. Cambridge: Cambridge University Press.

Segal, U., & Stein, A. (2006). Ambiguity aversion and the criminal process. *Notre Dame Law Review, 81*(4), 1495–1551.

Segal, M., & Xiao, Y. (2011). Multivariate random forests. *Wiley Interdisciplinary Reviews (WIREs): Data Mining and Knowledge Discovery, 1*(1), 80–87. doi://10.1002/widm.12

Seidmann, D. J., & Stein, A. (2000). The right to silence helps the innocent: A game-theoretic analysis of the Fifth Amendment privilege. *Harvard Law Review, 114*, 430–510.

Selbak, J. (1994). Digital litigation: The prejudicial effects of computer-generated animation in the courtroom. *High Technology Law Journal, 9*, 337.

Sellier, K. G., & Kneubuehl, B. P. (1994). *Wound ballistics and the scientific background*. Amsterdam: Elsevier.

Seltzer, M. (2006). *True crime: Observations on violence and modernity*. London: Routledge.

Sergot, M. (2005). Modelling unreliable and untrustworthy agent behaviour. In B. Dunin Keplicz, A. Jankowski, A. Skowron, & M. Szczuka (Eds.), *International workshop on monitoring, security, and rescue techniques in multiagent systems*, Plock, Poland, 7–9 June 2004 (pp. 161–177). Berlin: Springer.

Seto, Y. (2002). Development of personal authentication systems using fingerprint with smart cards and digital signature technologies. In *Proceedings of the Seventh International Conference on Control, Automation, Robotics and Vision (ICARCV 2002)*, Singapore, 2–5 December 2002. IEEE, Vol. 2, pp. 996–1001.

Seto, Y. (2009). Retina recognition. In S. Z. Li & A. K. Jain (Eds.), *Encyclopedia of biometrics* (pp. 1128–1130). New York: Springer.

Sgouros, N. M. (1999). Dynamic generation, management and resolution of interactive plots. *Artificial Intelligence, 107*(1), 29–62.

Shafer, G. (1976). *A mathematical theory of evidence*. Princeton, NJ: Princeton University Press.

Shannon, C. E., & Weaver, W. (1949). *The mathematical theory of communication*. Urbana, IL: University of Illinois Press.

Shapira, R. (1999). Fuzzy measurements in the Mishnah and Talmud. *Artificial Intelligence and Law, 7*(2/3), 273–288.

Shapira, R. A. (2002). Saving Desdemona. In M. MacCrimmon & P. Tillers (Eds.), *The dynamics of judicial proof: Computation, logic, and common sense* (pp. 419–435). Studies in Fuzziness and Soft Computing, Vol. 94. Heidelberg: Physical-Verlag.

Shapiro, S. C., & Rapaport, W. J. (1995). An introduction to a computational reader of narratives. In J. F. Duchan, G. A. Bruder, & L. E. Hewitt (Eds.), *Deixis in narrative* (pp. 79–105). Hillsdale, NJ: Erlbaum.

Sharkey, N. (Ed.). (1992). *Connectionist natural language processing*. Dordrecht, The Netherlands: Kluwer, & Oxford: Intellect.

Shebelsky, R. C. (1991). [Joke under the rubric 'Laughter, the Best Medicine'.] *Reader's Digest* (U.S. edition), November 1991, p. 103.

Sheptycki, J. (2003). *Review of the influence of strategic intelligence on organised crime policy and practice*. London: Home Office, Police and Reducing Crime Unit.

Sheptycki, J. (2004). Organizational pathologies in police intelligence systems: Some contributions to the lexicon of intelligence-led policing. *European Journal of Criminology, 1*(3), 307–332.

Shereshevsky, B.-Z. (1960/61). *Hoda'ah (Hoda'at beit-din). A. Lefi din-Torah*. [in Hebrew: 'Confession: In Jewish law']. S.v. *Hoda'ah* ['Confession'], by B. Z. Shereshevsky & M. Ben-Porat. *Encyclopaedia Hebraica*, 13, cols. 665–668.

Shetty, J., & Adibi, J. (2004). *The Enron email dataset database schema and brief statistical report*. Los Angeles, CA: University of Southern California, Information Sciences Institute. http://www.isi.edu/adibi/Enron/Enron_Dataset_Report.pdf

Shim, C.-B., & Shin, Y.-W. (2005). Spatio-temporal modeling of moving objects for content- and semantic-based retrieval in video data. In R. Khosla, R. J. Howlett, & L. C. Jain (Eds.), *Knowledge-based intelligent information and engineering systems: 9th international conference, KES 2005, Melbourne, Australia, September 14–16, 2005, Proceedings, Part IV* (pp. 343–351). (Lecture Notes in Computer Science, Vol. 3684.) Berlin: Springer.

Shimony, S. E. (1993). The role of relevance in explanation. I: Irrelevance as statistical independence. *International Journal of Approximate Reasoning, 8*(4), 281–324.

Shimony, S. E., & Charniak, E. (1990). A new algorithm for finding MAP assignments to belief networks. In P. P. Bonissone, M. Henrion, L. N. Kanal, & J. F. Lemmer (Eds.), *Uncertainty in artificial intelligence: Proceedings of the sixth conference* (pp. 185–193). Amsterdam: North-Holland.

Shimony, S. E., & Domshlak, C. (2003). Complexity of probabilistic reasoning in directed-path singly connected Bayes networks. *Artificial Intelligence, 151*, 213–225.

Shimony, S. E., & Nissan, E. (2001). Kappa calculus and evidential strength: A note on Åqvist's logical theory of legal evidence. *Artificial Intelligence and Law, 9*(2/3), 153–163.

Shiraev, E., & Levy, D. (2007). *Cross-cultural psychology: Critical thinking and contemporary applications* (3rd ed.). Boston: Allyn and Bacon.

Shirani, B. (2002). *Anti-forensics. High Technology Crime Investigation Association*. http://www.aversion.net/presentations/HTCIA-02/anti-forensics.ppt

Shoham, Y., & Leyton-Brown, K. (2009). *Multiagent systems: Algorithmic, game-theoretic, and logical foundations*. Cambridge: Cambridge University Press.

Shoham, Y., & McDermott, D. (1988). Problems in formal temporal reasoning. *Artificial Intelligence, 36*(1), 49–90.

Shortliffe, E. H. (1976). *Computer based medical consultations: MYCIN*. New York: Elsevier.

Shortliffe, E. H., & Buchanan, B. G. (1975). A method of inexact reasoning, *Mathematical Biosciences, 23*, 351–379.

Shuirman, G., & Slosson, J. E. (1992). *Forensic engineering: Environmental case histories for civil engineers and geologists*. San Diego, CA: Academic.

Shurmer, H. V. (1990). An electronic nose: A sensitive and discrimination substitute for a mammalian olfactory system. *International Electrical Engineering Proceedings, 137*, 197–204.

Shurmer, H. V., Gardner, J. W., & Chan, H. T. (1989). The application of discrimination techniques to alcohols and tobacco using tin oxide sensors. *Sensors & Actuators, 18*, 359–369.

Shuy, R. W. (1993). *Language crimes: The use and abuse of language evidence in the courtroom*. Oxford: Blackwell.

Shyu, C. H., Fu, C.-M., Cheng, T., & Lee, C. H. (1989). A heuristic evidential reasoning model. In A. A. Martino (Ed.), *Pre-proceedings of the third international conference on "Logica, Informatica, Diritto: Legal Expert Systems"*, Florence, 1989 (2 vols. + Appendix) (Vol. 1, pp. 661–670). Florence: Istituto per la Documentazione Giuridica, Consiglio Nazionale delle Ricerche.

Siddiqui, M. A. (2008). *Data mining methods for malware detection*. Ph.D. dissertation in Modeling and Simulation (supervised by M.C. Wang). Orlando, FL: College of Sciences, University of Central Florida. http://etd.fcla.edu/CF/CFE0002303/Siddiqui_Muazzam_A_200808_PhD.pdf

Siegel, J. A., Knupfer, G. C., & Saukko, P. J. (Ed.). (2000). *Encyclopedia of forensic sciences* (3 Vols.). London: Academic.

Sigmund, W. (Ed.). (1995). *Environmental poisoning and the law: Proceedings of the conference*, 17 September 1994, Kings College, London. London: South West Environmental Protection Agency & Environmental Law Foundation, 1995.

Sigurdsson, J. F., & Gudjonsson, G. H. (1996). The psychological characteristics of false confessors: A study among Icelandic prison inmates and juvenile offenders. *Personality and Individual Differences, 20*, 321–329.

Sigurdsson, J. F., & Gudjonsson, G. H. (2001). False confessions: The relative importance of psychological, criminological and substance abuse variables. *Psychology, Crime and Law, 7*, 275–289.

Silberman, C. E. (1978). *Criminal violence, criminal justice*. New York: Random House.

Simhon, D., Nissan, E., & Zigdon, N. (1992). Resource evaluation and counterplanning with multiple-layer rulesets, in the BASKETBALL expert system. In G. Tenenbaum, Ts. Raz-Liebermann, & Tz. Artzi (Eds.), *Proceedings of the international conference on computer applications in sport and physical education*, Natania, Israel (pp. 60–80). Natania: The Wingate Institute.

Simon, E., & Gaes, G. (1989). ASSYST: Computer support for guideline sentencing. In *The Second International Conference on Artifical Intelligence and Law: Proceedings of the Conference*, Vancouver, 1989, pp. 195–200.

Simon, E., Gaes, G., & Rhodes, W. (1991). ASSYST: The design and implementation of computer assisted sentencing. *Federal Probation, 55*, 46–55.

Sinai, J. (2006). Combating terrorism insurgency resolution software. In *Proceedings of the IEEE International Conference on Intelligence and Security Informatics (ISI 2006)*, pp. 401–406.

Singh, M. (1999). A social semantics for agent communication languages. In *Proceedings of the IJCAI'99 Workshop on Agent Communication Languages*, Stockholm, Sweden, pp. 75–88. http://ijcai.org/search.php

Singh, M., & Huhns, M. (2005). *Service-oriented computing: Semantics, processes, agents*. New York: Wiley.

Siroky, D. S. (2009). Navigating random forests and related advances in algorithmic modeling. *Statistics Surveys, 3*,147–163. Accessible online by searching the journal's site at http://www.i-journals.org/ss/search.php

Skabar, A., Stranieri, A., & Zeleznikow, J. (1997). Using argumentation for the decomposition and classification of tasks for hybrid system development. In N. Kasabov, R. Kozma, K. Ko, R. O'Shea, G. Coghill, & T. Gedeon (Eds.), *Progress in connectionist based information systems* (pp. 814–818). *Proceedings of the 1997 international conference on neural information processing and intelligent information systems*, Singapore. Berlin: Springer.

Skagerberg, E. M. (2007). Co-witness feedback in line-ups. *Applied Cognitive Psychology, 21*, 489–497.

Skalak, D. B., & Rissland, E. L. (1992). Arguments and cases: An inevitable intertwining. *Artificial Intelligence and Law, 1*(1), 3–44.

Skulsky, H. (1980). On being moved by fiction. *The Journal of Aesthetics and Art Criticism, 39*, 5–14.

Smith, A. S. (2006). Geomaterials from civil to criminal law; One small step for the geoscientist (abstract). In A. Ruffell, (Ed.), *Abstract book* of *geoscientists at crime scenes: First, inaugural meeting of the Geological Society of London*, 20 December 2006 (p.12). London: *Forensic Geoscience Group*. http://www.geolsoc.org.uk/pdfs/FGtalks&abs_pro.pdf

Smith, H. F. (2003). The language of property: Form, context, and audience. *Stanford Law Review, 55*, 1105–1191.

Smith, J. C., Gelbart, D., MacCrimmon, K., Atherton, B., McClean, J., Shinehoft, M., et al. (1995). Artificial intelligence and legal discourse: The Flexlaw legal text management system. *Artificial Intelligence and Law, 3*, 55–95.

Smith, J. M. (1992). *SGML and related standards: Document description and processing languages*. Ellis Horwood Series in Computers and Their Applications. New York & London: Ellis Horwood.

Smith, P. A., Baber, C., Hunter, J., & Butler, M. (2008). Measuring team skills in crime scene examination: Exploring ad hoc teams. *Ergonomics, 51*, 1463–1488.

Smith, R. G. (1977). The CONTRACT NET: A formalism for the control of distributed problem solving. In *Proceedings of the Fifth International Joint Conference on Artificial Intelligence (IJCAI-77)*, Cambridge, MA. http://ijcai.org/search.php

Smith, R. G. (1980a). The contract net protocol: High-level communication and control in a distributed problem solver. *IEEE Transactions on Computers, C-29*(12), 1104–1113.

Smith, R. G. (1980b). *A framework for distributed problem solving*. Ph.D. Dissertation, University of Stanford. Available from UMI Research Press.

Smith, S., & Bates, J. (1989). *Towards a theory of narrative for interactive fiction*. Technical Report CMU-CS-89-121. Pittsburgh, PA: School of Computer Science, Carnegie Mellon University. http://www-2.cs.cmu.edu/afs/cs.cmu.edu/project/oz/web/papers/CMU-CS-89-121.ps

Smith, T. C., & Witten, I. H. (1991). A planning mechanism for generating story text. *Literary and Linguistic Computing, 6*(2), 119–126. Also: Technical Report 1991-431-15). Calgary, Canada: Department of Computer Science, University of Calgary. http://pharos.cpsc.ucalgary.ca/Dienst/Repository/2.0/Body/ncstrl.ucalgary_cs/1991-431-15/pdf

Smith, T. F., & Waterman, M. S. (1981). Identification of common molecular subsequences. *Journal of Molecular Biology, 147*, 195–197.

Smullyan, R. M. (1986). Logicians who reason about themselves. In *Proceedings of the 1986 Conference on Theoretical Aspects of Reasoning about Knowledge*, Monterey, CA. San Francisco, CA: Morgan Kaufmann Publ., pp. 341–352.

Snook, B., Taylor, P. J., & Bennell C. (2005). False confidence in computerised geographical profiling [a reply to Rossmo]. *Applied Cognitive Psychology, 19*, 655–661.

Snow, P., & Belis, M. (2002) Structured deliberation for dynamic uncertain inference. In M. MacCrimmon & P. Tillers (Eds.), *The dynamics of judicial proof: Computation, logic, and common sense* (pp. 397–416). (Studies in Fuzziness and Soft Computing, Vol. 94.) Heidelberg: Physical-Verlag.

Söderström, C., Borén, H., Winquist, F., & Krantz-Rülcker, C. (2003). Use of an electronic tongue to analyze mold growth in liquid media. *International Journal of Food Microbiology, 83*, 253–261.

Solan, Z., Horn, D., Ruppin, E., & Edelman, S. (2005). Unsupervised learning of natural languages. *Proceedings of the National Academy of Sciences, USA, 102*(33), 11629–11634.

Solka, J. L. (2008). Text data mining: Theory and methods. *Statistics Surveys, 2,* 94–112. Accessible online by searching the journal's site at http://www.i-journals.org/ss/search.php

Solow, A. R., Kitchener, A. C., Roberts, D. L., & Birks, J. D. S. (2006). Rediscovery of the Scottish polecat, *Mustela putorius:* Survival or reintroduction? *Biological Conservation, 128,* 574–575.

Song, C. H., Koo, Y. H., Yoo, S. J., & Choi, B. H. (2005). An ontology for integrating multimedia databases. In R. Khosla, R. J. Howlett, & L. C. Jain (Eds.), *Knowledge-based intelligent information and engineering systems: 9th international conference, KES 2005, Melbourne, Australia, September 14–16, 2005, Proceedings, Part III* (pp. 157–162). (Lecture Notes in Computer Science, Vol. 3684.) Berlin: Springer.

Song, Q., Hu, W., & Xie, W. (2002). Robust support vector machine for bullet hole image classification. *IEEE Transaction on Systems, Man and Cybernetics, Part C, 32*(4), 440–448.

Sorg, M. H. (2005). Forensic anthropology. Chapter 7 In S. H. James & J. J. Nordby (Eds.), *Forensic science: An introduction to scientific and investigative techniques* (2nd ed.). Boca Raton, FL: CRC Press. Also in 3rd edition, 2009.

Sosa, E. (1991). *Knowledge in perspective.* Cambridge: Cambridge University Press.

Sotomayor, S. (2002). A Latina judge's voice. Judge Mario G. Olmos Memorial Lecture, University of California Berkeley Law School, 2001. Published in the Spring 2002 issue of *Berkeley La Raza Law Journal* as part of a Symposium entitled *Raising the Bar: Latino and Latina Presence in the Judiciary and the Struggle for Representation.* The full text of the speech is available at http://www.nytimes.com/2009/05/15/us/politics/15judge.text.html

Sowa, J. F. (1984). *Conceptual structures: Information processing in mind and machine.* Reading, MA: Addison Wesley.

Sowa, J. F. (Ed.). (1991). *Principles of semantic networks: Explorations in the representation of knowledge.* San Mateo, CA: Morgan Kaufmann Publishers.

Sowa, J. (1994). *Conceptual structures: Information processing in mind and machine.* Reading, MA: Addison Wesley.

Sowa, J. (1995). Top-level ontological categories. *International Journal of Human-Computer Studies, 43*(5–6), 669–686.

Sowa, J. F. (2006). *Semantic networks.* Last revised in 2006 (posted at http://www.jfsowa.com/pubs/semnet.htm). Revised and extended version of an article In: Shapiro, S. C. (Ed.). (1987). *Encyclopedia of artificial intelligence.* New York: Wiley; 2nd edn., 1992.

Sparck Jones, K. (1993). What might be in a summary? In *Proceedings of Information Retrieval '93,* Konstanz, Germany, Konstanz: Universitätsverlag, pp. 9–26.

Sparrow, M. K. (1991). The application of network analysis to criminal intelligence: An assessment of the prospects. *Social Networks, 13,* 251–274.

Spears, D. (1993). *Providing computerised sentencing information to judicial officers: The New South Wales experience.* Sydney, NSW: Judicial Commission of New South Wales.

Specter, M. M. (1987). The national academy of forensic engineers. *Forensic Engineering, 1*(1), 61–63.

Sperber, D., & Wilson, D. (1986). Loose talk. *Proceedings of the Aristotelian Society, New Series, 86,* 153–171. Reprinted in Davis, S. (Ed.). (1991). *Pragmatics: A reader.* Oxford: Oxford University Press.

Sperber, D., & Wilson, D. (1990). Literalness looseness, metaphor. A section in their: Rhetoric and relevance. In D. Wellbery & J. Bender (Eds.), *The ends of rhetoric: History, theory, practice* (pp. 140–155). Stanford, CA: Stanford University Press.

Spitzner, L. (2002). *Honeypots tracking hackers.* Reading, MA: Addison-Wesley Professional.

Spitzner, L. (2003a). The honeynet project: Trapping the hackers. IEEE *Security and Privacy, 1*(2), 15–23.

Spitzner, L. (2003b). *Honeypots: Definitions and value of honeypots.* http://www.tracking-hackers.com

Spitzner, L. (2004). *Problems and challenges with honeypots.* http://www.securityfocus.com/

Spivak, J. (1996). *The SGML primer.* Cambridge, MA: CTI.

Spohn, W. (1988). A dynamic theory of epistemic states. In W. L. Harper & B. Skyrms (Eds.), *Causation in decision, belief change, and statistics* (pp. 105–134). Dordrecht, The Netherlands: Reidel (Kluwer).

Spooren, W. (2001). Review of Lagerwerf (1998). *Journal of Pragmatics, 33*, 137–141.

Srihari, R. K. (2009). Unapparent information revelation: Text mining for counter-terrorism. In S. Argamon & N. Howard (Eds.), *Computational methods for counterterrorism*. Berlin: Springer.

Srihari, S. N., & Ball, G. R. (2008). Writer verification of handwritten Arabic. In *Proceedings of the IEEE Eighth International Workshop on Document Analysis Systems (DAS 2008)*, Nara, Japan, pp. 28–34.

Srihari, S. N., Ball, G. R., & Ramakrishnan, V. (2009). Identification of forgeries in handwritten petitions for ballot propositions. In *Proceeedings of the SPIE 16th Conference on Document Recognition and Retrieval*, San José, CA, January 2009, pp. 7247OS 1–8.

Srihari, S. N., Ball, G. R., & Srinivasan, H. (2008). Versatile search of scanned arabic handwriting. In D. Doermann & S. Jaeger (Eds.), *Arabic and chinese handwriting recognition. SACH 2006 Summit, College Park, MD, USA, September 27–28, 2006: Selected Papers* (pp. 57–69). Lecture Notes in Computer Science, Vol. 4768. Berlin: Springer.

Srihari, S. N., Collins, J., Srihari, R. K., Srinivasan, H., & Shetty, S. (2008). Automatic scoring of short handwritten essays in reading comprehension tests. *Artificial Intelligence, 172*(2/3), 300–324.

Srihari, S. N., & Leedham, G. (2003). A survey of computer methods in forensic document examination. In *Proceedings of the International Graphonomics Society Conference*, Phoenix, AZ, November 2003, pp. 278–282.

Srihari, S. N., Srinivasan, H., & Beal, M. (2008). Machine learning for signature verification. In S. Marinai & H. Fujisawa (Eds.), *Machine learning in document analysis and recognition* (pp. 387–408). (Studies on Computational Intelligence, Vol. 90). Berlin: Springer.

Srihari, S. N., Srinivasan, H., & Desai, K. (2007). Questioned document examination using CEDAR-FOX. *Journal of Forensic Document Examination, 18*(2), 1–20.

Srihari, S. N., Srinivasan, H., & Fang, G. (2008). Discriminability of the fingerprints of twins. *Journal of Forensic Identification, 58*(1), 109–127.

Srihari, S. N., & Su, C. (2008). Computational methods for determining individuality. In *Computational Forensics: Proceedings of the International Workshop*, Washington, DC. (Lecture Notes in Computer Science, Vol. 5158). Berlin: Springer, pp. 11–21.

Srinivasan, H., & Srihari, S. N. (2009). Use of conditional random fields for signature-based retrieval of scanned documents. In S. Argamon & N. Howard (Eds.), *Computational methods for counterterrorism*. Berlin: Springer.

Staab, S., & Studer, R. (Eds.). (2009). *Handbook on ontologies*. (International Handbooks on Information Systems.) Berlin: Springer, 2004; 2nd edn., 2009.

Stærkeby, M. (2002). Forensic Entomology Pages, International (website). Division of Zoology, Department of Biology, University of Oslo, Oslo, Norway. http://www.uio.no/~mostarke/forens_ent/forensic_entomology.html

Staples, E. J. (1999). Electronic nose simulation of olfactory response containing 500 orthogonal sensors in 10 seconds. In *Proceedings of the 1999 IEEE Ultrasonics Frequency Control and Ferroelectrics Symposium*, Lake Tahoe, CA, 2000, pp. 307–313.

Staples, E. J. (2000). Electronic nose simulation of olfactory response containing 500 orthogonal sensors in 10 seconds. In *Proceedings of the 1999 IEEE Ultrasonics Frequency Control and Ferroelectrics Symposium*, Lake Tahoe, CA, 2000, pp. 307–313.

Stearns, C. Z., & Stearns, P. N. (1986). *Anger: The struggle for emotional control in America's history*. Chicago: University of Chicago Press.

Stearns, C. Z., & Stearns, P. N. (1988). *Emotion and social change: Toward a new psychohistory*. New York: Holmes & Meier.

Stearns, P. N. (1989). *Jealousy: The evolution of an emotion in American history*. New York: New York University Press.

Stearns, P. N. (1994). *American cool: Constructing a twentieth-century emotional style*. (The History of Emotions, 3). New York: New York University Press.

Stearns, P. N. (1995). Emotion. Chapter 2 In R. Harré & P. Stearns (Eds.), *Discursive psychology in practice*. London: Sage.

Stearns, P. N. & Haggerty, T. (1991). The role of fear: Transitions in American emotional standards for children, 1850–1950. *American Historical Review, 96*, 63–94.

Stearns, P. N., & Stearns, C. Z. (1985). Emotionality: Clarifying the history of emotions and emotional standards. *American History Review, 90*, 813–836.

Stein, A. (1996). The refoundation of evidence law. *Canadian Journal of Law & Jurisprudence, 9*, 279–284 & 289–322.

Stein, A. (2000). Evidential rules for criminal trials: Who should be in charge? In S. Doran & J. Jackson (Eds.), *The judicial role in criminal proceedings* (pp. 127–143). Oxford: Hart Publishing.

Stein, A. (2001). Of two wrongs that make a right: Two paradoxes of the Evidence Law and their combined economic justification. *Texas Law Review, 79*, 1199–1234.

Stein, A. (2005). *Foundations of evidence law*. Oxford:Oxford University Press.

Stein, N. L., & Glenn, C. G. (1979). An analysis of story comprehension in elementary school children. In R. Freedle (Ed.), *New directions in discourse processing II*. Norwood, NJ: Ablex.

Steingrimsdottir, G., Hreinsdottir, H., Gudjonsson, G. H., Sigurdsson, J. F, &. Nielsen, T. (2007). False confessions and the relationship with offending behaviour and personality among Danish adolescents. *Legal and Criminological Psychology, 12*, 287–296.

Steinwart, I., & Christmann, A. (2008). *Support vector machines*. New York: Springer.

Stenross, B., & Kleinman, S. (1989). The highs and lows of emotional labor: Detectives' encounters with criminals and victims. *Journal of Contemporary Ethnography, 17*, 435–452.

Stephen, J. F. (1863). *General view of the criminal law* (1st ed.). London: McMillan; 2nd cdn., 1890. Reprint, 2nd edn., Littleton, Colorado: F. B. Rothman, 1985.

Stephen, J. F. (1948). *A digest of the law of evidence* (12th ed.). Revision by H. L. Stephen & L. F. Sturge. London: McMillan and Co. Ltd. Reprint, with additions, of the 1936 edition.

Stephenson, K., & Zelen, M. (1989). Rethinking centrality: Methods and examples. *Social Networks, 11*(1), 1–38.

Sterling, L., & Shapiro, E. (1986). *The art of Prolog: Advanced programming techniques*. Cambridge, MA: The MIT Press.

Stern, D. N. (1985). *The interpersonal world of the infant: A view from psychoanalysis and developmental psychology*. New York: Basic Books.

Stevens, R., Wroe, C., Lord, P. W., & Goble, C. A. (2004). Ontologies in bioinformatics. In S. Staab & R. Studer (Eds.), *Handbook on ontologies* (pp. 635–658). (International Handbooks on Information Systems.) Berlin: Springer.

Steyvers, M., & Tenenbaum, J. B. (2005). The large-scale structure of semantic networks: Statistical analyses and a model of semantic growth. *Cognitive Science, 29*(1), 41–78.

Stiegler, B. (1986). La faute d'Epiméthée. *Technologos*,[74] *3*, 7–16.

Stiff, J. B. (1994). *Persuasive communication*. New York: Guilford.

St. John, M. F. (1992). The story gestalt: A model of knowledge-intensive processes in text comprehension. *Cognitive Science, 16*, 271–306.

Stock, O., Strapparava, C., & Nijholt, A. (Eds.). (2002). *The April Fools' Day workshop on computational humour: Proceedings of the twentieth Twente Workshop on Language Technology (TWLT20)*, Trento, Italy, April 15–16, 2002. Enschede, The Netherlands: University of Twente.

Stockmarr, A. (1999). Likelihood ratios for evaluating DNA evidence when the suspect is found through a database search. *Biometrics, 55*, 671–677.

Stolfo, S. J., Creamer, G., & Hershkop, S. (2006). A temporal based forensic analysis of electronic communication. At the *2006 National Conference on Digital Government Research*.

---

[74] The French-language journal Technologos used to be published in Paris by the Laboratoire d'Informatique pour les Sciences de l'Homme.

Stone, M. (2009, August 22). Criminal trials: The reliability of evidence – Part I. *CL&J: Criminal law & Justice Weekly, 173*(34), 532–533.

Stoney, D. A. (1997). Fingerprint identification: Scientific status. In D. L. Faigman, D. H. Kaye, M. J. Saks, & J. Sanders (Eds.), *Modern scientific evidence: The law and science of expert testimony* (Vol. 2). St. Paul, MN: West Publishing.

Stoney, D. A. (2001). Measurement of fingerprint individuality. In H. C. Lee & R. E. Gaensslen (Eds.), *Advances in fingerprint technology* (pp. 327–387). Boca Raton, FL: CRC Press.

Strange, D., Sutherland, R., & Garry, M. (2006). Event plausibility does not determine children's false memories. *Memory, 14*, 937–951.

Stranieri, A. (1999). *Automating legal reasoning in discretionary domains.* Ph.D. Thesis. Melbourne, Australia: La Trobe University.

Stranieri, A., Yearwood, J., & Meikl, T. (2000). The dependency of discretion and consistency on knowledge representation. *International Review of Law, Computers and Technology, 14*(3), 325–340.

Stranieri, A., & Zeleznikow, J. (2001a). WebShell: The development of web based expert system shells. At *SGES British Expert Systems Conference ES'01.* Cambridge: SGES.

Stranieri, A., & Zeleznikow, J. (2001b). Copyright regulation with argumentation agents. In D. M. Peterson, J. A. Barnden, & E. Nissan (Eds.), *Artificial intelligence and law*, special issue of *Information & Communications Technology Law, 10*(1), 109–123.

Stranieri, A., & Zeleznikow, J. (2005a). *Knowledge discovery from legal databases.* (Springer Law and Philosophy Library, 69.) Dordrecht, The Netherlands: Springer.

Stranieri, A., & Zeleznikow, J. (2005b). Knowledge discovery from legal databases. Tutorial given at *Tenth International Conference on Artificial Intelligence and Law (ICAIL 2005)*, in Bologna, Italy.

Stranieri, A., Zeleznikow, J., Gawler, M., & Lewis, B. (1999). A hybrid rule–neural approach for the automation of legal reasoning in the discretionary domain of family law in Australia. *Artificial Intelligence and Law, 7*(2/3), 153–183.

Stranieri, A., Zeleznikow, J., & Yearwood, J. (2001). Argumentation structures that integrate dialectical and non-dialectical reasoning. *The Knowledge Engineering Review, 16*(4), 331–348.

Strömwall, L. A., & Granhag, P. A. (2003a). Affecting the perception of verbal cues to deception. *Applied Cognitive Psychology, 17*, 35–49.

Strömwall, L. A., & Granhag, P. A. (2003b). How to detect deception? Asessing the beliefs of police officers, prosecutors and judges. *Psychology, Crime and Law, 9*(1), 19–36.

Strömwall, L. A., & Granhag, P. A. (2007). Detecting deceit in pairs of children. *Journal of Applied Social Psychology, 37*, 1285–1304.

Strömwall, L. A., Hartwig, M., & Granhag, P. A. (2006). To act truthfully: Nonverbal behavior and strategies during a police interrogation. *Psychology, Crime & Law, 12*, 207–219.

Su, X., & Tsai, Ch.-L. (2011). Outlier detection. *Wiley Interdisciplinary Reviews (WIREs): Data Mining and Knowledge Discovery, 1*(3), 261–268. doi://10.1002/widm.19

Summers, R. S. (1978). Two types of substantive reasons: The core of a theory of common-law justification. *Cornell Law Review, 63*, 707–788.

Sun, J., Tao, D., & Faloutsos, C. (2006). Beyond streams and graphs: Dynamic tensor analysis. In *Proceedings of KDD 2006*, Philadelphia, PA. http://www.cs.cmu.edu/~christos/PUBLICATIONS/kdd06DTA.pdf

Sun, J., Xie, Y., Zhang, H., & Faloutsos, C. (2007). Less is more: Compact matrix decomposition for large sparse graphs. In *Proceedings of SDM*, Minneapolis, MN, April 2007. http://www.cs.cmu.edu/~jimeng/papers/SunSDM07.pdf

Suprenant, B. A. (1988). *Introduction to forensic engineering.* Oxford: Pergamon.

Sutton, P. T. (1998). *Bloodstain pattern interpretation.* Short Course Manual. Memphis, TN: University of Tennessee.

Swartjes, I. (2009). *Whose story is it anyway? How improve informs agency and authorship of emergent narrative.* PhD thesis. Enschede, The Netherlands: University of Twente. http://wwwhome.cs.utwente.nl/~swartjes/dissertation/

Swartjes, I., & Theune, M. (2006). A fabula model for emergent narrative. In S. Göbel, R. Malkewitz, & I. Iurgel (Eds.), *Technologies for interactive digital storytelling and entertainment: Proceedings of the third international conference, Tidse 2006*. (Lecture Notes in Computer Science, Vol. 4326.) Berlin: Springer.

Sweetser, E. (1987). The definition of *lie*: An examination of the folk theories underlying a semantic prototype. In D. Holland & N. Quinn (Eds.), *Cultural models in language and thought* (pp. 43–66). Chicago: University of Chicago Press.

Sycara, K. (1989a). Argumentation: Planning other agents' plans. In *Proceedings of the eleventh International Joint Conference on Artificial Intelligence (IJCAI'89)*, Detroit, MI, pp. 517–523. http://ijcai.org/search.php

Sycara, K. (1989b). Multiagent compromise via negotiation. In L. Gasser & M. Huhns (Eds.), *Distributed artificial intelligence, 2* (pp. 119–138). San Mateo, CA: Morgan Kaufmann, and London: Pitman.

Sycara, K. (1990). Persuasive argumentation in negotiation. *Theory and Decision, 28*, 203–242.

Sycara, K. (1992). The PERSUADER. In D. Shapiro (Ed.), *The encyclopedia of artificial intelligence*. Chichester: Wiley.

Sycara, K. P. (1998). Multiagent systems. *AI Magazine*, Summer 1998, pp. 79–92.

Szilas, N. (1999). Interactive Drama on Computer: Beyond Linear Narrative. In *AAAI Fall Symposium on Narrative Intelligence*, Falmouth, MA: AAAI Press, pp. 150–156.

Szilas, N., & Rety, J.-H. (2004). Minimal structure for stories. In *Proceedings of the First ACM Workshop on Story Representation, Mechanism, and Context, 12th ACM International Conference on Multimedia*. New York: ACM, pp. 25–32.

Szymanski, B. K., & Chung, M.-S. (2001). A method for indexing Web pages using Web bots. In *Proceedings of the International Conference on Info-Tech & Info-Net, ICII'2001*, Beijing, China, November 2001, IEEE Computer Society Press, pp. 1–6.

Szymanski, B., & Zhang, Y. (2004). Recursive data mining for masquerade detection and author identification. In *Proceedings of the Fifth IEEE System, Man and Cybernetics Information Assurance (SMC IA) Workshop*, West Point, NY, June 2004, pp. 424–431.

Taddei Elmi, G. (1992). Cultura informatica e cultura giuridica. *Informatica e diritto* (Florence), Year 18, 2nd Series, 1(1/2), 111–124.

Talukder, A. (2010). Event-centric multisource stream processing and multimedia assimilation for geospatiotemporal phenomena. In *Proceedings of the 2nd ACM international workshop on Events in multimedia (EiMM'10)*. New York: ACM.

Tan, X., & Bhanu, B. (2006). Fingerprint matching by genetic algorithms. *Pattern Recognition, 29*(3), 465–477.

Tang, Y., & Daniels, T. E. (2005). A simple framework for distributed forensics. At the *Second International Workshop on Security in Distributed Computing Systems (SDCS)*, in: *Proceedings of the 25th International Conference on Distributed Computing Systems Workshops (ICDCS 2005 Workshops)*, 6–10 June 2005, Columbus, OH. IEEE Computer Society, pp. 163–169.

Tapiero, I., den Broek, P. V., & Quintana, M.-P. (2002). The mental representation of narrative texts as networks: The role of necessity and sufficiency in the detection of different types of causal relations. *Discourse Processes, 34*(3), 237–258.

Taroni, F., Aitken, C., Garbolino, P., & Biedermann, A. (2006). *Bayesian networks and probabilistic inference in forensic science*. (Statistics in Practice Series.) Chichester: Wiley.

Taruffo, M. (1998). Judicial decisions and artificial intelligence. *Artificial Intelligence and Law, 6*, 311–324.

Tata, C., Wilson, J. N., & Hutton, N. (1996). Representations of knowledge and discretionary decision-making by decision-support systems: The case of judicial sentencing. *Journal of Information Law & Technology, 2* (http://elj.warwick.ac.uk/jilt/artifint/2tata/pr2tata.htm and in Ascii format: 2tata.TXT).

Tatti, N. (2009). Significance of episodes based on minimal windows. In *Proceedings of the Ninth IEEE International Conference on Data Mining (ICDM-2009)*, 2009, pp. 513–522.

Tatti, N., & Cule, B. (2010). Mining closed strict episodes. In *Proceedings of the Tenth IEEE International Conference on Data Mining (ICDM-2010)*, pp. 501–510.

Taubes, G. (2002). *An interview with Dr. Michael I. Miller. In-Cytes,* ISI accessible at http://www. incites.com/scientists/DrMichaelIMiller.html

Tavris, C. (2002). The high cost of skepticism. *Skeptical Inquirer, 26*(4), 41–44 (July/August 2002).

Taylor, J. (1994a). *A multi-agent planner for modelling dialogue.* Ph.D. thesis, School of Cognitive and Computing Sciences, University of Edinburgh, Edinburgh, Scotland.

Taylor, J. A. (1994b). Using hierarchical autoepistemic logic to model beliefs in dialogue. In J. R. Koza (Ed.), *Artificial life at Stanford 1994.* Stanford, CA: Stanford Bookstore. Also: Technical report HCRC/RP-60 (November), Human Communication Research Centre, University of Edinburgh, Edinburgh, Scotland.

Tebbett, I. (1992). *Gas chromatography in forensic science.* (Ellis Horwood Series in Forensic Science.) London: Ellis Horwood.

Templeman, Lord, & Reay, R. (1999). *Evidence* (2nd ed.). London: Old Bailey Press. The 1st edn. (1997) was by Lord Templeman & C. Bell.

Terluin, D. (2008). *From fabula to fabulous: Using discourse structure to separate paragraphs in automatically generated stories.* Master's thesis, supervised by R. Verbrugge, Institute of Artificial Intelligence, University of Groningen, Groningen, Netherlands. See at http://www.rinekeverbrugge.nl/PDF/Supervisor%20for%20Masters% 20Students/thesisDouweTerluin2008.pdf

ter Meulen, A. G. B. (1995). *Representing time in natural language: The dynamic interpretation of tense and aspect.* Cambridge, MA: The MIT Press. Paperback, 1997. The paperback edition is augmented with an appendix.

Tesauro, G., Kephart, J., & Sorkin, G. (1996). Neural networks for computer virus recognition. *IEEE Expert, 11*(4), 5–6.

Thagard, P. (1989). Explanatory coherence. *Behavioural and Brain Sciences, 12*(3), 435–467. Commentaries and riposte up to p. 502.

Thagard, P. (2000a). *Coherence in thought and action.* Cambridge, MA: The MIT Press.

Thagard, P. (2000b). Probabilistic networks and explanatory coherence. *Cognitive Science Quarterly, 1*, 91–114.

Thagard, P. (2004). Causal inference in legal decision making: Explanatory coherence vs. Bayesian networks. *Applied Artificial Intelligence, 18*(3/4), 231–249.

Thagard, P. (2005). Testimony, credibility and explanatory coherence. *Erkenntnis, 63*, 295–316.

Thali, M. J., Braun, M., & Dirnhofer, R. (2003). Optical 3D surface digitizing in forensic medicine. *Forensic Science International, 137*, 203–208.

Thali, M. J., Braun, M., Wirth, J., Vock, P., & Dirnhofer, R. (2003). 3D surface and body documentation in forensic medicine: 3D/CAD photogrammetry merged with 3D radiological scanning. *Journal of Forensic Science, 48*(6), 1356–1365.

Teran, J., Sifakis, E., Blemker, S., Ng-Thow-Hing, V., Lau, C., & Fedkiw, R. (2005). Creating and simulating skeletal muscle from the visible human data set. *IEEE Transactions on Visualization and Computer Graphics, 11*(3), 317–328.

Teufel, S., & Moens, M. (2002). Summarising scientific articles: Experiments with relevance and rhetorical status. *Computational Linguistics, 28*(4), 409–445.

Theune, M., Faas, S., Nijholt, A., & Heylen, D. (2003). The virtual storyteller: Story creation by intelligent agents. In S. Gömbel, N. Braun, U. Spierling, J. Dechau, & H. Diener (Eds.), *Proceedings of TIDSE 2003: Technologies for interactive digital storytelling and entertainment* (pp. 204–215). Fraunhofer IRB Verlag.

Thomas, E. A. C., & Hogue, A. (1976). Apparent weight of evidence, decision criteria, and confidence ratings in juror decision-making. *Psychological Review, 83*, 442–465.

Thomas, M. [but Anon.] (2004). Plot, story, screen: An introduction to narrativity. Deliverable (from the University of Cambridge) of *NM2: New Media for a New Millennium* (IST-004124), Version 1, 26 October 2004.

Thompson, P. (2001). Automatic categorization of case law. In *Proceedings of the Eighth International Conference on Artificial Intelligence and Law* (ICAIL 2001), May 21–25, 2001, St. Louis, Missouri. New York: ACM Press, pp. 70–77.

Thorndyke, P. W. (1977). Cognitive structures in comprehension and memory of narrative discourse. *Cognitive Psychology, 9,* 111–191.

Tidmarsh, J. (1992). Unattainable justice: The form of complex litigation and the limits of judicial power. *George Washington University Law Review, 60,* 1683.

Tillers, P. (1983). *Modern theories of relevancy.* Boston: Little, Brown & Co.

Tillers, P. (2005). If wishes were horses: Discursive comments on attempts to prevent individuals from being unfairly burdened by their reference classes. *Law, Probability, and Risk, 4,* 33–49.

Tillers, P. (Ed.). (2007). *Graphic and visual representations of evidence and inference in legal settings.* Special issue. *Law, Probability and Risk, 6*(1–4). Oxford: Oxford University Press.

Tillers, P., & Green, E. (Eds.). (1988). *Probability and inference in the law of evidence: The uses and limits of bayesianism.* (Boston Studies in the Philosophy of Science, 109). Boston & Dordrecht (Netherlands): Kluwer.

Tillers, P., & Schum, D. (1992). Hearsay logic. *Minnesota Law Review, 76,* 813–858.

Tillers, P., & Schum, D. (1998). A theory of preliminary fact investigation. In S. Brewer & R. Nozick (Eds.), *The philosophy of legal reasoning: Scientific models of legal reasoning.* New York: Garland.

Tillers, P., & Schum, D. A. (1988). Charting new territory in judicial proof: Beyond Wigmore. *Cardozo Law Review, 9*(3), 907–966.

Tilley, N. (2003). Community policing, problem-oriented policing and intelligence-led policing. In T. Newburn (Ed.), *Handbook of policing* (pp. 311–339). Cullompton: Willan Publishing.

Tinsley, Y. (2001). Even better than the real thing? The case for reform of identification procedures. *The International Journal of Evidence & Proof, 5*(2), 99–110. Sark, Channel Islands: Vathek Publishing (vatheksubs@cassis.co.uk).

Toland, J., & Rees, B. (2005). Applying case-based reasoning to law enforcement. *International Association of Law Enforcement Intelligence Analysts Journal, 15.*

Tomberlin, J. E. (1981). Contrary-to-duty imperatives and conditional obligation. *Noûs, 16,* 357–375.

Tonfoni, G. (Ed.). 1985. *Artificial intelligence and text-understanding: Plot units and summarization procedures.* (Quaderni di Ricerca Linguistica, Vol. 6.) Parma, Italy: Edizioni Zara.

Tong, H., & Faloutsos, F. (2006). Center-piece subgraphs: Problem definition and fast solutions. *Proceedings of KDD 2006,* Philadelphia, PA. http://www.cs.cmu.edu/~christos/PUBLICATIONS/kdd06CePS.pdf

Tong, H., Faloutsos, C., & Jia-Yu Pan, J.-Y. (2006). Fast random walk with restart and its applications. In *Proceedings of ICDM 2006,* Hong Kong. http://www.cs.cmu.edu/~christos/PUBLICATIONS/icdm06-rwr.pdf

Toni, F., & Kowalski, R. (1995). Reduction of abductive logic programs to normal logic programs. In L. Sterling (Ed.), *Proceedings of the 12th international conference on logic programming* (pp. 367–381). Cambridge, MA: MIT Press.

Toni, F., & Kowalski, R. (1996). An argumentation-theoretic approach to transformation of logic programs. In *Proceedings of LOPSTR.* (Lecture Notes in Computer Science, 1048.) Heidelberg, Germany: Springer, pp. 61–75.

Tonini, P. (1997). *La Prova Penale.* Padua, Italy: CEDAM.

Topolnicki, D. M., & MacDonald, E. M. (1991). How the IRS abuses taxpayers. *Reader's Digest* (U.S. edn.), March 1991, pp. 83–86. Longer version in *Money,* October 1990.

Toppano, E., Roberto, V., Giuffrida, R., & Buora, G. B. (2008). Ontology engineering: Reuse and integration. *International Journal of Metadata, Semantics and Ontologies, 3*(3), 233–247.

Toulmin, S. E. (1958). *The uses of argument.* Cambridge, England: Cambridge University Press (reprints: 1974, 1999).

Trankell, A. (1972). *The reliability of evidence: Methods for analyzing and assessing witness statements.* Stockholm: Beckmans.

Travis, C. (2004). The silence of the senses. *Mind, 113,* 57–94.

Tredoux, C. G., Nunez, D. T., Oxtoby, O., & Prag, B. (2006). An evaluation of ID: An eigenface based construction system. *South African Computer Journal, 37,* 1–9.

Tribe, L. H. (1971). Trial by mathematics: Precision and ritual in the legal process. *Harvard Law Review, 84*, 1329–1393.

Tribondeau, N. (accessed in 2006). *Glossaire de la police Technique et Scientifique*. Salon du Polar (accessible on the Web at: http://www.salondupolar.com/pages/texte/glossaire.htm).

Trithemius, J. (1500s). Latin treatise *Steganographia, hoc est, ars per occultam scripturam animi sui voluntatem absentibus aperiendi certa*. [Partly completed in 1503.] Frankfurt/Main: "ex officina typographica Matthiae Beckeri, sumptibus Joannis Berneri", 1605, 1608, and 1621. Partial English edition, A. McLean (Ed.), F. Tait, C. Upton, & J. W. H. Walden (trans.), *The Steganographia of Johannes Trithemius*, Edinburgh, Scotland: Magnum Opus Hermetic Sourceworks, 1982.

Tsai, F. S., & Chan, K. L. (2007). Detecting cyber security threats in weblogs using probabilistic models. In C. C. Yang, D. Zeng, M. Chau, K. Chang, Q. Yang, X. Cheng, et al. (Eds.), *Intelligence and security informatics: Proceedings of the Pacific Asia workshop, PAISI 2007*, Chengdu, China, April 11–12, 2007 (pp. 46–57). Lecture Notes in Computer Science, Vol. 4430. Berlin: Springer.

Tschudy, R. H. (1961). Palynomorphs as indicators of facies environments in Upper Cretaceous and Lower Tertiary strata, Colorado and Wyoming. Wyoming Geological Association Guidebook 16. In *Annual Field Conference*, pp. 53–59.

Tsiamyrtzis, P., Dowdall, J., Shastri, D., Pavlidis, I. T., Frank, M. G., & Ekman, P. (2005). Imaging facial physiology for the detection of deceit. *International Journal of Computer Vision, 71(2)*, 197–214.

Tulving, E. (1972). Episodic and semantic memory. In E. Tulving & W. Donaldson (Eds.), *Organization of memory* (pp. 381–403). New York: Academic.

Tupman, W. A. (1995). Cross-national criminal databases: The ongoing search for safeguards. *Law, Computers and Artificial Intelligence, 4*, 261–275.

Turner, B. (1987). Forensic entomology: Insects against crime. *Science Progress, 71(1)* = #281, pp. 133–144. Abingdon, Oxfordshire: Carfax (Taylor & Francis).

Turner, S. R. (1992). *MINSTREL: A computer model of creativity and storytelling*. Ph.D. dissertation, Computer Science, University of California, Los Angeles, December 1992, technical report CSD-920057/UCLA-AI-92-04. ftp://ftp.cs.ucla.edu/tech-report/1992-reports/920057.pdf

Turner, S. R. (1994). *The creative process: A computer model of storytelling and creativity.*, Mahwah, NJ: Erlbaum.

Turney, P. D. (2002). Thumbs up or thumbs down? Semantic orientation applied to unsupervised classification of reviews. In *Proceedings of ACL-2002*.

Turvey, B. (1999). *Criminal profiling: An introduction to behavioral evidence analysis*. San Diego, CA: Academic.

Twining, W. (1997). Freedom of proof and the reform of criminal evidence. In E. Harnon & A. Stein (Eds.), *Rights of the accused, crime control and protection of victims*, special volume of the *Israel Law Review, 31(1–3)*, 439–463.

Twining, W., & Miers, D. (1976). *How to do things with rules: A primer of interpretation*. (Law in Context Series). London: Weidenfeld & Nicolson.

Twining, W. L. (1984). Taking facts seriously. *Journal of Legal Education, 34*, 22–42.

Twining, W. L. (1985). *Theories of evidence: Bentham and Wigmore*. London: Weidenfeld & Nicolson.

Twining, W. L. (1989). Rationality and scepticism in judicial proof: Some signposts. *International Journal for the Semiotics of Law, 2(4)*, 69–83.

Twining, W. L. (1990). *Rethinking evidence: Exploratory essays*. Oxford: Blackwell; also, Evanston, IL: Northeastern University Press, 1994.

Twining, W. L. (1999). Necessary but dangerous? Generalizations and narrative in argumentation about 'facts' in criminal process. Chapter 5 in M. Malsch & J. F. Nijboer (Eds.), *Complex cases: Perspectives on the Netherlands criminal justice system* (pp. 69–98). (Series Criminal Sciences). Amsterdam: THELA THESIS.

Ukpabi, P., & Peltron, W. (1995). Using the scanning electron microscope to identify the cause of fibre damage. Part I: A review of related literature. *Journal of the Canadian Society of Forensic Science, 28*(3), 181–187.

Ulmer, S. (1969). The discriminant function and a theoretical context for the use in estimating the votes of judges. In J. N. Grossman & J. Tanenhaus (Eds.), *Frontiers of judicial research: Shambaugh conference on judicial research*, University of Iowa, October 1967 (pp. 335–369). New York: Wiley.

Umaschi, M. (1996). SAGE storytellers: Learning about identity, language and technology. In *Proceedings of the Second International Conference on the Learning Sciences (ICLS 96)*. Association for the Advancement of Computing in Education (AACE), 1996, pp. 526–531.

Umaschi Bers, U. (2003). We are what we tell: Designing narrative environments for children. In M. Mateas & P. Sengers (Eds.), *Narrative intelligence* (pp. 113–128). Amsterdam: Benjamins.

Undeutsch, U. (1982). Statement reality analysis. In A. Trankell (Ed.), *Reconstructing the past: The role of psychologists in criminal trials* (pp. 27–56). Deventer, The Netherlands: Kluwer (now Dordrecht & Berlin: Springer).

Ursu, M. F., & Zimmer, R. (2002). On the notion of compliance in critiquing intelligent design assistants: Representing duty and contrary-to-duty statements. In *Proceedings of the Sixth International Conference on Information Visualisation; Symposium on Computer Aided Design*, London, 10–12 July 2002. IEEE Computer Society, pp. 644–649.

Uschold, M. (2003). Where are the semantics in the Semantic Web? *AI Magazine, 24*(3), 25–36.

Uschold, M. (2005). An ontology research pipeline. *Applied Ontology, 1*(1), 13–16. Amsterdam: IOS Press.

Uschold, M., & Grüninger, M. (1996). Ontologies: Principles, methods and applications. *Knowledge Engineering Review, 11*(2), 93–136. We quoted from the previous version (accessed on the Web in 2009): Technical Report AIAI-TR-191. Edinburgh, Scotland: Artificial Intelligence Applications Institute (AIAI), University of Edinburgh, February 1996.

Uschold, M., & Grüninger, M. (2004). Ontologies and semantics for seamless connectivity. In the special section on Semantic Integration. *ACM SIGMOD Record, 33*(4), 58–64.

Uther, H.-J. (2004). *The types of international folktales: A classification and bibliography. Based on the system of Antti Aarne and Stith Thompson*. Part I: *Animal Tales, Tales of Magic, Religious Tales, and Realistic Tales, with an Introduction*. Part II: *Tales of the Stupid Ogre, Anecdotes and Jokes, and Formula Tales*. Part III: *Appendices*. (Folklore Fellows Communications, Vols. 284–286.) Helsinki, Finland: Suomalainen Tiedeakatemia = Academia Scientiarum Fennica.

Uyttendaele, C., Moens, M.-F., & Dumortier, J. (1998). SALOMON: Automatic abstracting of legal cases for effective access to court decisions. *Artificial Intelligence and Law, 6*(1), 59–79.

Vafaie, H., Abbott, D. W., Hutchins, M., & Matkovskly, I. P. (2000). Combining multiple models across algorithms and samples for improved results. At *The Twelfth International Conference on Tools with Artificial Intelligence*, Vancouver, BC, Canada, 13–15 November 2000.

Valcour, L. (1997). *Investigate B & E: Break & enter expert system*. Technical Report TR-11-97, Canadian Police Research Centre.

Valente, A. (1995). *Legal knowledge engineering: A modeling approach*. Amsterdam: IOS Press.

Valente, A. (2005). Types and roles of legal ontologies. In V. R. Benajmins, P. Casanovas, J. Breuker, & A. Gangemi (Eds.), *Proceedings of law and the semantic web [2005]: Legal ontologies, methodologies, legal information retrieval, and applications* (pp. 65–76). (Lecture Notes in Computer Science, Vol. 3369.) Berlin: Springer. http://lib.dnu.dp. ua:8001/l/%D0%9A%D0%BE%D0%BF%D1%8C%D1%8E%D1%82%D0%B5%D1% 80%D1%8B%D0%98%D1%81%D0%B5%D1%82%D0%B8/_Lecture%20Notes%20in% 20Computer%20Science/semantic/Law%20and%20the%20Semantic%20Web..%20Legal% 20Ontologies,%20Methodologies,%20Legal%20Information%20Retrieval,%20and% 20Applications(LNCS3369,%20Springer,%202005)(ISBN%203540250638)(258s)_CsLn_. pdf#page=75

Valentine, T., Darling, S., & Memon, A. (2006). How can psychological science enhance the effectiveness of identification procedures? An international comparison. *Public Interest Law Reporter, 11*, 21–39.

Valentine, T., Darling, S., & Memon, A. (2007). Do strict rules and moving images increase the reliability of sequential identification procedures? *Applied Cognitive Psychology, 21*, 933–949.

Valentine, T., Pickering, A., & Darling, S. (2003). Characteristics of eyewitness identification that predict the outcome of real lineups. *Applied Cognitive Psychology, 17*, 969–993. http://www.valentinemoore.fsnet.co.uk/trv/

Valette, R., & Pradin-Chézalviel, B. (1998). Time Petri nets for modelling civil litigation. In A. A. Martino & E. Nissan (Eds.), *Formal models of legal time*, special issue, *Information and Communications Technology Law, 7*(3), 269–280.

Valeur, F., Mutz, D., & Vigna, G. (2005). A learning-based approach to the detection of SQL attacks. In K. Julisch & C. Krügel (Eds.), *Detection of Intrusions and Malware, and Vulnerability Assessment: Proceedings of the second international conference (DIMVA 2005)*, Vienna, Austria, July 7–8, 2005 (pp. 123–140). (Lecture Notes in Computer Science, Vol. 3548.) Berlin: Springer.

Valitutti, A., Strapparava, C., & Stock, O. (2005). Developing affective lexical resources. *Psychnology Journal, 2*(1), 61–83. http://www.psychnology.org/File/PSYCHNOLOGY_JOURNAL_2_1_VALITUTTI.pdf

van Andel, P. (1994). Anatomy of the unsought finding. Serendipity: Origin, history, domains, traditions, appearances, patterns and programmability. *British Journal of the Philosophy of Science, 45*(2), 631–647.

van Benthem, J. (1983). *The logic of time* (1st ed.). Dordrecht, The Netherlands: Kluwer. 2nd edition, 1991.

van Benthem, J. (1995). Temporal logic. In D. M. Gabbay, C. J. Hogger, & J. A. Robinson (Eds.), *Handbook of logic in artificial intelligence and logic programming* (Vol. 4, pp. 241–350). Oxford: Clarendon Press.

Van Cott, H. P., & Kinkade, R. G. (Eds.). (1972). *Human engineering guide to equipment design*. New York: McGraw-Hill.

Vandenberghe, W., Schafer, B., & Kingston, J. (2003). Ontology modelling in the legal domain: Realism without revisionism. In P. Grenon, C. Menzel, & B. Smith (Eds.), *Proceedings of the KI2003 Workshop on Reference Ontologies and Application Ontologies*, Hamburg, Germany, September 16, 2003. (CEUR Workshop Proceedings, Vol. 94.) CEUR-WS.org. http://www.informatik.uni-trier.de/~ley/db/indices/a-tree/s/Schafer:Burkhard.html

van den Braak, S. W., van Oostendorp, H., Prakken, H., & Vreeswijk, G. A. W. (2006). A critical review of argument visualization tools: Do users become better reasoners? At the *Sixth International Workshop on Computational Models of Natural Argument*, held with *ECAI'06*, Riva del Garda, Italy, August 2006.

van den Braak, S. W., & Vreeswijk, G. A. W. (2006). A knowledge representation architecture for the construction of stories based on interpretation and evidence. At the *Sixth International Workshop on Computational Models of Natural Argument*, held with *ECAI'06*, Riva del Garda, Italy, August 2006.

van der Schoor, J. (2004). Brains voor de recherche. (In Dutch.) *Justitiële Verkenningen, 30*, 96–99.

van der Torre, L. W. N., & Tan, Y.-H. (1999). Contrary-to-duty reasoning with preference-based dyadic obligations. *Annals of Mathematics and Artificial Intelligence, 27*(1–4), 49–78.

van der Vet, P. E., & Mars, N. J. I. (1995). Ontologies for very large knowledge bases in materials science: A case study. In N. J. I. Mars (Eds.), *Towards very large knowledge bases: Knowledge building and knowledge sharing 1995* (pp. 73–83). Amsterdam: IOS Press.

van Dijk, T. A. (1979). Relevance assignment in discourse comprehension. *Discourse Processes, 2*, 113–126.

van Dijk, T. A. (1989). Relevance in logic and grammar. Chapter 2 In J. Norman & R. Sylvan (Eds.), *Directions in relevant logic* (pp. 25–57). Boston: Kluwer. http://www.discourses.org/OldArticles/Relevance%20in%20logic%20and%20grammar.pdf

van Eemeren, E. H., & Grootendorst, R. (1995). Argumentation theory. In J. Verschueren, J.-O. Östman, & J. Blommaert (Eds.), *Handbook of pragmatics* (pp. 55–61). Amsterdam: John Benjamins.

van Eemeren, E. H., Grootendorst, R., & Snoek Henkemans, F. (1996). *Fundamentals of argumentation theory*. Mahwah, NJ: Lawrence Erlbaum Associates.

van Eemeren, E. H., Grootendorst, R., & Kruiger, T. (1987a). *Handbook of argumentation theory: Pragmatics and discourse analysis*. Amsterdam: Foris.

van Engers, T. M., & Glasee, E. (2001). Facilitating the legislation process using a shared conceptual model. *IEEE Intelligent Systems, 16*, 50–57.

van Gelder, T. J. (2002). Argument mapping with Reason!Able [sic]. *The American Philosophical Association Newsletter on Philosophy and Computers, 2002*, 85–90.

van Gelder, T. J., & Rizzo, A. (2001). Reason!Able across the curriculum. In *Is IT an Odyssey in Learning? Proceedings of the 2001 Conference of the Computing in Education Group of Victoria*. Victoria, Australia.

Van Koppen, P. J. (1995). Judges' decision-making. Chapter 6.7 In R. Bull & D. Carson (Ed.), *Handbook of psychology in legal contexts* (pp. 581–610). Chichester: Wiley.

van Kralingen, R. W. (1995). *Frame based conceptual models of statute law*. Dordrecht, The Nertherlands: Kluwer Law International (now Springer).

Van Reenen, P. Th., & van Mulken, M. J. P. (Eds.). (1996). *Studies in stemmatology*. Amsterdam: Benjamins.

Vapnik, V. N. (1995). *The nature of statistical learning theory*. New York & Berlin: Springer.

Vapnik, V. N. (1998). *Statistical learning theory: Adaptive and learning systems for signal processing, communications, and control*. New York: Wiley.

Vellani, K., & Nahoun, J. (2001). *Applied criminal analysis*. Boston: Butterworth-Heinemann.

Veloso, M. (1994). *Planning and learning by analogical reasoning*. Berlin: Springer.

Veloso, M., & Aamodt, A. (Eds.). (1995). *Case-based reasoning research and development: Proceedings of the first international conference on case-based reasoning*. Berlin: Springer.

Vendler, Z. (1975a). On what we know. In K. Gunderson (Ed.), *Language, mind, and knowledge* (pp. 370–390). (Minnesota Studies in the Philosophy of Science, 7). Minneapolis, MN: University of Minnesota Press.

Vendler, Z. (1975b). Reply to Professor Aune. In K. Gunderson (Ed.), *Language, mind, and knowledge* (pp. 400–402). (Minnesota Studies in the Philosophy of Science, 7). Minneapolis, MN: University of Minnesota Press.

Verheij, B. (1999). Automated argument assistance for lawyers. In *Proceedings of the Seventh International Conference on Artificial Intelligence and Law (ICAIL 1999)*. New York: ACM Press, pp. 43–52.

Verheij, B. (2000). Dialectical argumentation as a heuristic for courtroom decision-making. In P. J. van Koppen & N. H. M. Roos (Eds.), *Rationality, information and progress in law and psychology: Liber Amicorum Hans F. Crombag* (pp. 203–226). Maastricht, The Netherlands: Metajuridica Publications.

Verheij, B. (2002). Dialectical argumentation with argumentation schemes: Towards a methodology for the investigation of argumentation schemes. In *Proceedings of the Fifth International Conference on Argumentation, ISSA 2002*. Amsterdam.

Verheij, B. (2003). Dialectical argumentation with argumentation schemes: An approach to legal logic. *Artificial Intelligence and Law, 11*, 167–195.

Verheij, B. (2005). *Virtual arguments: On the design of argument assistants for lawyers and other arguers*. The Hague, The Netherlands: T. M. C. Asser Press.

Vicard, P., & Dawid, A. P. (2004). A statistical treatment of biases affecting the estimation of mutation rates. *Mutation Research, 547*, 19–33.

Vicard, P., & Dawid, A. P. (2006). Remarks on: 'Paternity analysis in special fatherless cases without direct testing of alleged father' [Forensic Science International 146S (2004) S159–S161]. *Forensic Science International, 163*(1–2), 158–160. http://tinyurl.com/pur8q

Vicard, P., Dawid, A. P., Mortera, J., & Lauritzen S. L. (2008). Estimating mutation rates from paternity casework. *Forensic Science International: Genetics, 2*, 9–18. doi:10.1016/j.fsigen.2007.07.002

Viegas, E., & Raskin, V. (1998). *Computational semantic lexicon acquisition: Methodology and guidelines.* Memoranda in Computer and Cognitive Science, MCCS-98-315. Las Cruces, NM: New Mexico State University, Computing Research Laboratory.

Vila, L., & Yoshino, H. (1995). Temporal representation for legal reasoning. In: *Proceedings of the Third International Workshop on Legal Expert Systems for the CISG,* May 1995.

Vila, L., & Yoshino, H. (1998). Time in automated legal reasoning. In A. A Martino & E. Nissan (Eds.), *Law, computers and artificial intelligence: Special issue on Formal Models of Legal Time.* In *Information and Communications Technology Law, 7*(3), 173–197.

Vila, L., & Yoshino, H. (2005). Time in automated legal reasoning. In M. Fisher, D. Gabbay, & L. Vila (Eds.), *Handbook of temporal reasoning in artificial intelligence* (electronic resource; Foundations of Artificial Intelligence, 1). Amsterdam: Elsevier.

Visser, P. R. S. (1995). *Knowledge specification for multiple legal tasks: A case study of the interaction problem in the legal domain.* Kluwer Computer/Law Series, Vol. 17. Dordrecht, The Netherlands: Kluwer (now Springer).

Vossos, G., Zeleznikow, J., & Hunter, D. (1993). Building intelligent litigation support tools through the integration of rule based and case based reasoning. *Law, Computers and Artificial Intelligence, 2*(1), 77–93.

Vreeswijk, G. (1993). Defeasible dialectics: A controversy-oriented approach towards defeasible argumentation. *The Journal of Logic and Computation, 3*(3), 3–27.

Vreeswijk, G. A. W., Brewka, G., & Prakken, H. (2003). Special issue on computational dialectics: An introduction. *Journal of Logic and Computation, 13*(3).

Vreeswijk, G. A. W., & Prakken, H. (2000). Credulous and sceptical argument games for preferred semantics. In M. Ojeda-Aciego, I. P. de Guzman, G. Brewka, & L. Moniz Pereira (Eds.), *Proceedings of JELIA'2000: The seventh European workshop on logic for artificial intelligence* (pp. 239–253). Springer Lecture Notes in Artificial Intelligence, Vol. 1919. Berlin: Springer.

Vrij, A. (1998a). Physiological parameters and credibility: The polygraph. Chapter 4 in Memon et al.

Vrij, A. (1998b). Interviewing suspects. Chapter 6 in Memon et al.

Vrij, A. (2000). *Detecting lies and deceit: The psychology of lying and implications for professional practice.* Wiley Series on the Psychology of Crime, Policing and Law. Chichester, West Sussex, England: Wiley. Second edition: 2008.

Vrij, A. (2001). Detecting the liars. *Psychologist, 14,* 596–598.

Vrij, A. (2005). Co-operation of liars and truth-tellers. *Applied Cognitive Psychology, 19,* 39–50.

Vrij, A., Akehurst, L., Soukara, S., & Bull, R. (2004). Let me inform you how to tell a convincing story: CBCA and reality monitoring scores as a function of age, coaching, and deception. *Canadian Journal of Behavioral Science, 36*(2), 113–126.

Vrij, A., Mann, S., Fisher, R., Leal, S., Milne, R., & Bull, R. (2008). Increasing cognitive load to facilitate lie detection: The benefit of recalling an event in reverse order. *Law and Human Behavior, 32,* 253–265.

Vrij, A., & Semin, G. (1996). Lie experts' beliefs about nonverbal indicators of deception. *Journal of nonverbal behavior, 20*(1), 65–80.

Vrochidis, S., Doulaverakis, C., Gounaris, A., Nidelkou, E., Makris, L., & Kompatsiaris, I. (2008). A hybrid ontology and visual-based retrieval model for cultural heritage multimedia collections. *International Journal of Metadata, Semantics and Ontologies, 3*(3), 167–182.

Wache, H., Voegele, T., Visser, U., Stuckenschmidt, H., Schuster, G., Neumann, H., et al. (2001). Ontology-based integration of information: A survey of existing approaches. In *Proceedings of the IJCAI-01 Workshop on Ontologies and Information Sharing,* Seattle, WA, August 4–5, 2001, pp. 108–118.

Wade, K. A., Garry, M., Read, J. D., & Lindsay, D. S. (2002). A picture is worth a thousand lies: Using false photographs to create false childhood memories. *Psychonomic Bulletin & Review, 9,* 597–603.

Wade, K. A., Sharman, S. J., Garry, M., Memon, A., Merckelbach, H., & Loftus, E. (2007). False claims about false memories. *Consciousness and Cognition, 16,* 18–28.

Waegel, W. B. (1981). Case routinization in investigative police work. *Social Problems, 28,* 263–275.

Wagenaar, W. A. (1996). Anchored narratives: A theory of judicial reasoning and its consequences. In G. Davies, S. Lloyd-Bostock, M. McMurran, & C. Wilson (Eds.), *Psychology, law, and criminal justice* (pp. 267–285). Berlin: Walter de Gruyter.

Wagenaar, W. A., van Koppen, P. J., & Crombag, H. F. M. (1993). *Anchored narratives: The psychology of criminal evidence.* Hemel Hempstead, Hertfordshire: Harvester Wheatsheaf, & New York: St. Martin's Press.

Wagenaar, W. A., & Veefkind, N. (1992). Comparison of one-person and many-person line ups: A warning against unsafe practices. In F. Lösel, D. Bender, & P. T. Bliesener (Eds.), *Psychology and law: International perspectives.* Berlin: De Gruyter.

Wahab, M. S. (2004). E-commerce and internet auction fraud: The E-Bay community model. Computer Crime Research Center, 29 April 2004. http://www.crime-research.org/

Waismann, F. (1951). Verifiability. In A. Flew (Ed.), *Logic and language.* Oxford: Blackwell.

Walker, C., & Starmer, K. (Eds.). (1999). *Miscarriage of justice: A Review of justice in error* (2nd ed.). London: Blackstone Press. Previously, C. Walker & K. Starmer (Eds.), *Justice in error.* London: Blackstone Press, 1993.

Walker, D. P. (1958). *Spiritual and demonic magic from Ficino to Campanella.* London: Warburg Institute.

Walker, R. F., Oskamp, A, Schrickx, J. A., Opdorp, G. J., & van den Berg P. H. (1991). PROLEXS: Creating law and order in a heterogeneous domain. *International Journal of Man–Machine Studies, 35*(1), 35–68.

Wallsten, T. S., Budescu, D. V., Rapoport, A., Zwick, R. and Forsyth, B. (1986). Measuring the vague meanings of probability terms. *Journal of Experimental Psychology: General, 115*(4), 348–365.

Walsh, W. F. (2001). Compstat: An analysis of an emerging police managerial paradigm. *Policing: An International Journal of Police Strategies & Management, 24*(3), 347–362.

Walton, D. (1989). *Informal logic.* Cambridge: Cambridge University Press.

Walton, D. (1996a). The witch hunt as a structure of argumentation. *Argumentation, 10,* 389–407.

Walton, D. (2007). *Character evidence: An abductive theory.* Berlin: Springer.

Walton, D. (2010). A dialogue model of belief. *Argument & Computation, 1*(1), 23–46.

Walton, D. N. (1996b). *Argumentation schemes for presumptive reasoning.* Mahwah, NJ: Lawrence Erlbaum Associates.

Walton, D. N. (1996c). *Argument structure: A pragmatic theory.* Toronto Studies in Philosophy. Toronto, ON: University of Toronto Press.

Walton, D. N. (1997). *Appeal to expert opinion.* University Park, PA: Pennsylvania State University Press.

Walton, D. N. (1998a). *The new dialectic: Conversational contexts of argument.* Toronto, ON: University of Toronto Press.

Walton, D. N. (1998b). *Ad Hominem arguments.* Tuscaloosa: University of Alabama Press.

Walton, D. N. (2002). *Legal argumentation and evidence.* University Park, PA: Pennsylvania State University Press.

Walton, D. N. (2004). *Abductive reasoning.* Tuscaloosa, AL: University of Alabama Press.

Walton, D. N. (2006a). Examination dialogue: An argumentation framework for critically questioning an expert opinion. *Journal of Pragmatics, 38,* 745–777.

Walton, D. N. (2006b). *Character evidence: An abductive theory.* Dordrecht, The Netherlands: Springer.

Walton, D. N., & Krabbe, E. C. W. (1995). *Commitment in dialogue: Basic concepts of interpersonal reasoning.* Albany, NY: State University of New York Press.

Walton, D., & Macagno, F. (2005). Common knowledge in legal reasoning about evidence. *International Commentary on Evidence, 3*(1), Article 1. http://www.bepress.com/ice/vol3/iss1/art1

Walton, D., Reed, C., & Macagno, F. (2008). *Argumentation schemes.* Cambridge: Cambridge University Press.

Walton, D., & Schafer, B. (2006). Arthur, George and the mystery of the missing motive: Towards a theory of evidentiary reasoning about motives. *International Commentary on Evidence, 4*(2), 1–47.

Walton, K. (1978). Fearing fictions. *The Journal of Philosophy, 75*, 5–27.

Walton, K. (1990). *Mimesis as make-believe*. Cambridge, MA: Harvard University Press.

Wang, J. (2004). Microchip devices for detecting terrorist weapons. *Analytical Chimica Acta, 507*, 3–10.

Wang, P., & Gedeon, T. D. (1995). A new method to detect and remove the outliers in noisy data using neural networks: Error sign testing. *Systems Research and Information Science, 7*(1), 55–67.

Wang, W., Guo, W., Luo, Y., Wang, X., & Xu, Z. (2005). The study and application of crime emergency ontology event model. In R. Khosla, R. J. Howlett, & L. C. Jain (Eds.), *Knowledge-based intelligent information and engineering systems: 9th international conference, KES 2005, Melbourne, Australia, September 14–16, 2005, Proceedings, Part IV* (pp. 806–812). Lecture Notes in Computer Science, Vol. 3684. Berlin: Springer.

Wang, W., Wang, C., Zhu, Y., Shi, B., Pei, J., Yan, X., et al. (2005). GraphMiner: a structural pattern-mining system for large disk-based graph databases and its applications. In *Proceedings of the SIGMOD 2005 Conference: 24th ACM SIGMOD International Conference on Management of Data/Principles of Database Systems*, Baltimore, MD, June 13–16, 2005. New York: ACM Press, pp. 879–881.

Wansing, H. (2002). Diamonds are a philosopher's best friends. *Journal of Philosophical Logic, 31*, 591–612.

Ward, K. M., & Duffield, J. W. (1992). *Natural resource damages: Law and economics*. (Environmental Law Library, Wiley Law Publications.) New York: Wiley (with pocket supplements).

Warner, D. (1994). A neural network-based law machine: The problem of legitimacy. *Law, Computers & Artificial Intelligence, 2*(2), 135–147.

Wasserman, S., & Faust, K. (1994). *Social network analysis: Methods and applications*. Cambridge: Cambridge University Press.

Watson, J. A. F. (1975). *Nothing but the truth: Expert evidence in principle and practice for surveyors, valuers and others* (2nd ed.). London: Estates Gazette.

Watson, J. G., & Chow, J. C. (2002). Particulate pattern recognition. Chapter 11 In B. L. Murphy & R. D. Morrison (Eds.), *Introduction to environmental forensics* (pp. 429–460). San Diego, CA & London: Academic.

Wavish, P., & Connah, D. (1997). Virtual actors that can perform scripts and improvise roles. In W. L. Johnson (Ed.), *Autonomous agents '97*, Marina del Rey, CA. New York: ACM Press, pp. 317–322.

Weatherford, M. (2002). Mining for fraud. *IEEE Intelligent Systems, 17*, 4–6.

Webb, G. I. (2000). MultiBoosting: A technique for combining boosting and wagging. *Machine Learning, 40*(2), 159–196.

Weidensaul, S. (2002). *The ghost with trembling wings. Science, wishful thinking, and the search for lost species*. New York: North Point Press.

Weiss, G. (1999). *Multiagent systems: A modern approach to distributed artificial intelligence*. Cambridge, MA: The MIT Press.

Weiss, S., & Kulikowski, C. (1992). *Computer systems that learn: Classification and prediction methods from statistics, neural nets, machine learning and expert systems*. San Mateo, CA: Morgan Kaufmann Publishers Inc.

Wells, G. L. (1978). Applied eyewitness testimony research: System variables and estimator variables. *Journal of Personality and Social Psychology, 36*, 1546–1557.

Wells, G. L. (1984). The psychology of lineup identifications. *Journal of Applied Social Psychology, 14*, 89–103.

Wells, G. L. (1985). Verbal descriptions of faces from memory: Are they diagnostic of identification accuracy? *Journal of Applied Psychology, 70*, 619–626.

Wells, G. L. (1988). *Eyewitness identification: A system handbook*. Toronto, ON: Carswell Legal Publications.

Wells, G. L. (1993). What do we know about eyewitness identification? *American Psychologist, 48*, 553–571.

Wells, G. L. (2000). From the lab to the police station: A successful application of eyewitness research. *American Psychologist, 55*, 581–598.

Wells, G. L. (2006). Eyewitness identification: Systemic reforms. *Wisconsin Law Review, 2006*, 615–643.

Wells, G. L., & Bradfield, A. L. (1998). "Good, you identified the suspect": Feedback to eyewitnesses distorts their reports of the witnessing experience. *Journal of Applied Psychology, 83*, 360–376.

Wells, G. L., & Bradfield, A. L. (1999). Distortions in eyewitnesses' recollections: Can the postidentification feedback effect be moderated? *Psychological Science, 10*, 138–144.

Wells, G. L., & Charman, S. D. (2005). Building composites can harm lineup identification performance. *Journal of Experimental Psychology: Applied, 11*, 147–156.

Wells, G. L., Ferguson, T. J., & Lindsay, R. C. L. (1981). The tractability of eyewitness confidence and its implication for triers of fact. *Journal of Applied Psychology, 66*, 688–696.

Wells, G. L., & Hryciw, B. (1984). Memory for faces: Encoding and retrieval operations. *Memory and Cognition, 12*, 338–344.

Wells, G. L., & Leippe, M. R. (1981). How do triers of fact infer the accuracy of eyewitness identifications? Memory for peripheral detail can be misleading. *Journal of Applied Psychology, 66*, 682–687.

Wells, G. L., Leippe, M. R., & Ostrom, T. M. (1979a). Guidelines for empirically assessing the fairness of a lineup. *Law and Human Behavior, 3*, 285–293.

Wells, G. L., Lindsay, R. C. L., & Ferguson, T. J. (1979b). Accuracy, confidence, and juror perceptions in eyewitness identification. *Journal of Applied Psychology, 64*, 440–448.

Wells, G. L., & Loftus, E. F. (1991). Commentary: Is this child fabricating? Reactions to a new assessment technique. In J. Doris (Ed.), *The suggestibility of children's recollections* (pp. 168–171). Washington, DC: American Psychological Association.

Wells, G. L., Malpass, R. S., Lindsay, R. C. L., Fisher, R. P., Turtle, J. W., & Fulero, S. (2000). From the lab to the police station: A successful application of eyewitness research. *American Psychologist, 55*, 581–598.

Wells, G. L., Memon, A., & Penrod, S. (2006) Eyewitness evidence: Improving its probative value. *Psychological Science in the Public Interest, 7*, 45–75.

Wells, G. L., & Murray, D. M. (1983). What can psychology say about the *Neil vs. Biggers* criteria for judging eyewitness identification accuracy? *Journal of Applied Psychology, 68*, 347–362.

Wells, G. L., & Olson, E. A. (2001). *The psychology of alibis or Why we are interested in the concept of alibi evidence*. Ames, IA: Iowa State University, January 2001. http://www.psychology.iastate.edu/~glwells/alibiwebhtml.htm

Wells, G. L., & Olson, E. A. (2003). Eyewitness testimony. *Annual Review of Psychology, 54*, 277–295.

Wells, G. L., Olson, E. A., & Charman, S. (2003). Distorted retrospective eyewitness reports as functions of feedback and delay. *Journal of Experimental Psychology: Applied, 9*, 42–52.

Wells, G. L., & Quinlivan, D. S. (2009). Suggestive eyewitness identification procedures and the Supreme Court's reliability test in light of eyewitness science: 30 years later. *Law and Human Behavior, 33*, 1–24. http://www.psychology.iastate.edu/~glwells/Wells_articles_pdf/Manson_article_in_LHB_Wells.pdf

Wells, G. L., Rydell, S. M., & Seelau, E. P. (1993). On the selection of distractors for eyewitness lineups. *Journal of Applied Psychology, 78*, 835–844.

Wells, G. L., Small, M., Penrod, S., Malpass, R. S., Fulero, S. M., & Brimacombe, C. A. E. (1998). Eyewitness identification procedures: Recommendations for lineups and photospreads. *Law and Human Behavior, 22*, 603–647.

Werbos, P. (1974). *Beyond regression: New tools for prediction and analysis in the behavioural sciences*. Ph.D. dissertation. Cambridge, MA: Harvard University.

Wertheim, K., Langenburg, G., & Moenssens, A. (2006). A report of latent print examiner accuracy during comparison training exercises. *Journal of forensic identification, 56*, 55–93.

Wertheim, K., & Maceo, A. (2002). The critical stage of friction ridge pattern formation. *Journal of Forensic Identification, 52*, 35–85.

Westermann, G. U., & Jain, R. (2006a). Events in multimedia electronic chronicles (E Chronicles). *International Journal of Semantic Web and Information Systems, 2*(2), 1–27.

Westermann, G. U., & Jain, R. (2006b). A generic event model for event-centric multimedia data management in eChronicle applications. In *Proceedings of the 2006 IEEE International Workshop on Electronic Chronicles (eChronicle 2006), at the 22nd International Conference on Data Engineering Workshops (ICDEW'06)*, Atlanta, GA, April 2006. Los Alamitos, California: IEEE Computer Society Press, 2006.

Westermann, G. U., & Jain, R. (2007, January). Toward a common event model for multimedia applications. *IEEE MultiMedia*, 19–29.

Weyhrauch, P. (1997). *Guiding interactive drama*. Ph.D. Dissertation, Technical report CMU-CS-97-109. Pittsburgh, PA: Carnegie Mellon University.

White, J., Kauer, J. S., Dickinson, T. A., & Walt, D. R. (1996). Rapid analyte recognition in a device based on optical sensors and the olfactory system. *Analytical Chemistry, 68*, 2191–2202.

White, M. (1957). *Social thought in America: The revolt against formalism*. Edition cited, 1957. First published, New York: Viking Press, 1949. Extended edn., (Beacon paperback, 41), Boston, MA: Beacon Press, 1957; 4th printing, 1963. With a new foreword, (A Galaxy Book), Oxford: Oxford University Press, 1976.

White, W. S. (1989). Police trickery in inducing confessions. *University of Pennsylvania Law Review, 127*, 581–629.

White, W. S. (1997). False confessions and the constitution: Safeguards against untrustworthy confessions. *Harvard Civil Rights-Civil Liberties Law Review, 32*, 105–157.

Whitely, R. (1993). [A joke. Last item under the rubric] Laughter, the best medicine. *Reader's Digest*, U.S. edition, 143(859), November 1993, p. 86. Previously in *Executive Speechwriter Newsletter*.

Wierzbicka, A. (2000). The semantics of human facial expressions. In I. E. Dror & S. V. Stevenage (Eds.), *Facial information processing: A multidisciplinary perspective*. Special issue of *Pragmatics & Cognition, 8*(1), 147–183.

Wigmore, J. H. (1913). The problem of proof. *Illinois Law Review, 8*(2), 77–103.

Wigmore, J. H. (1937). *The science of judicial proof as given by logic, psychology, and general experience, and illustrated judicial trials* (3rd ed.). Boston: Little, Brown & Co. Previously: *The Principles of Judicial Proof; or, the Process of Proof as Given by Logic, Psychology, and General Experience, and Illustrated Judicial Trials*, Boston, 1931, 1934, 2nd edn.; *The Principles of Judicial Proof: As Given by Logic* (etc.), Boston, 1913, 1st edn.

Wilder, H. H., & Wentworth, B. (1918). *Personal identification: methods for the identification of individuals, living or dead*. Boston: Gorham.

Wilensky, R. (1978). *Understanding goal-based stories*. Technical Report YALE/DCS/tr140. New Haven, CT: Computer Science Department, Yale University.

Wilensky, R. (1981). PAM; Micro PAM. Chapters 7 and 8 In R. C. Schank & C. K. Riesbeck (Eds.), *Inside computer understanding* (pp. 136–179 & 180–196). Hillsdale, NJ: Erlbaum.

Wilensky, R. (1982). Points: A theory of the structure of stories in memory. In W. G. Lehnert & M. H. Ringle (Eds.), *Strategies for natural language processing* (pp. 345–374). Hillsdale, NJ: Erlbaum.

Wilensky, R. (1980). *Understanding goal-based stories*. New York: Garland.

Wilensky, R. (1983a). *Planning and understanding: A computational approach to human reasoning*. Reading, MA: Addison-Wesley.

Wilensky, R. (1983b). Story grammar versus story points. *The Behavioural and Brain Sciences, 6*, 579–623.

Wilkins, D., & Pillaipakkamnatt, K. (1997). The effectiveness of machine learning techniques for predicting time to case disposition. In *Proceedings of Sixth International Conference on Artificial Intelligence and Law*, Melbourne, Australia. New York: ACM Press, pp. 39–46.

Wilkinson, C. (2004). *Forensic facial reconstruction.* Cambridge: Cambridge University Press.

Wilks, Y. (1975). A preferential, pattern-matching semantics for natural language understanding. *Artificial Intelligence, 6,* 53–74.

Williams, D. R. (1996). Goodbye, my little ones (book review). *New York Law Journal,* April 30, Section "The Lawyer's Bookshelf", p. 2.

Williams, K. D., & Dolnik, L. (2001). Revealing the worst first. In J. P. Forgas & K. D. Williams (Eds.), *Social influence: Direct and indirect processes* (pp. 213–231). Lillington, NC: Psychology Press.

Williams, P., & Savona, E. (Eds.). (1995). Special issue on the united nations and transnational organized crime. *Transnational Organized Crime, 1.*

Williams, S. (1992). Putting case-based learning into context: Examples from legal, business, and medical education. *The Journal of the Learning Sciences, 2*(4), 367–427.

Williamson, T. (2007). Psychology and criminal investigations. In T. Newburn, T. Williamson, & A. Wright (Eds.), *Handbook of criminal investigation* (pp. 68–91). Cullompton: Willan Publishing.

Willis, C. M., Church, S. M., Guest, C. M., Cook, W. A., McCarthy, N., Bransbury, A. J., et al. (2004). Olfactory detection of human bladder cancer by dogs: proof of principle study. *British Medical Journal, 329,* 712–715.

Willmer, M. A. P. (1970). *Crime and information theory.* Edinburgh: Edinburgh University Press.

Wilson, A. D., & Baietto, M. (2009). Applications and advances in electronic-nose technologies. *Sensors, 9*(7), 5099–5148. Open access. doi://10.3390/s90705099 http://www.mdpi.com/1424-8220/9/7/5099/pdf

Wilson, G., & Banzhaf, W. (2009). Discovery of email communication networks from the Enron corpus with a genetic algorithm using social network analysis. In *Proceedings of the Eleventh Conference on Evolutionary Computation,* May 18–21, 2009, Trondheim, Norway, pp. 3256–3263.

Winer, D. (in press). Review of ontology based storytelling devices. In N. Dershowitz & E. Nissan (Eds.), *Language, culture, computation: Essays in honour of Yaacov Choueka, Vol. 1: Theory, techniques, and applications to E-science, law, narratives, information retrieval, and the cultural heritage.* Berlin: Springer.

Winograd, T. (1972). *Understanding natural language.* New York: Academic.

Winquist, F. (2008). Voltammetric electronic tongues: Basic principles and applications. *Mikrochimica Acta, 163,* 3–10.

Winquist, F., Holmin, S., Krantz-Rülcker, C., Wide, P., & Lundström, I. (2000). A hybrid electronic tongue. *Analytica Chimica Acta, 406,* 147–157.

Winston, P. H. (1984). *Artificial intelligence* (2nd ed.). Reading, MA: Addison-Wesley.

Witten, I. H., & Frank, E. (2000). *Data mining: Practical machine learning tools and techniques with java implementations.* San Francisco: Morgan Kaufmann Publishers.

Wogalter, M. S., & Marwitz, D. B. (1991). Face composite construction: In-view and from-memory quality and improvement with practice. *Ergonomics, 34*(4), 459–468.

Wojtas, O. (1996). Forensics unmask dead poet. *The Times Higher Education Supplement,* London, August 23, p. 4.

Woods, J. H. (1974). *The logic of fiction.* The Hague, The Netherlands: Mouton.

Woods, W. A. (1975). What's in a link: Foundations for semantic networks. In D. G. Bobrow & A. Collins (Eds.), *Representation and understanding* (pp. 35–82). New York: Academic.

Wooldridge, M. (2000). Semantic issues in the verification of agent communication languages. *Journal of Autonomous Agents and Multi-Agent Systems, 3*(1), 9–31.

Wooldridge, M. (2002). *An introduction to multiagent systems.* Chichester: Wiley 2nd edition, 2009. [Page numbers as referred to in this book are to the 1st edition.]

Wooldridge, M., & Jennings, N. R. (1995). Intelligent agents: Theory and practice. *The Knowledge Engineering Review, 10*(2), 115–152.

Wooldridge, M., & van der Hoek, W. (2005). On obligations and normative ability: Towards a logical analysis of the social contract. *Journal of Applied Logic, 3,* 396–420.

Worboys, M. F., & Duckham, M. (2004). *GIS: A computing perspective* (2nd ed.). Boca Raton, FL: CRC Press.

Wright, D. B., & Skagerberg, E. M. (2007). Post-identification feedback affects real eyewitnesses. *Psychological Science, 18*, 172–178.

Wright, R. K. (2005). Investigation of traumatic deaths. In S. H. James & J. J. Nordby (Eds.), *Forensic science: An introduction to scientific and investigative techniques* (2nd ed.). Boca Raton, FL: CRC Press. Also in 3rd edition, 2009.

Wu, D. (1992). *Automatic inference: A probabilistic basis for natural language interpretation.* Technical Report CSD-92-692, Computer Science Division. Berkeley, CA: University of California. ftp://sunsite.berkeley.edu/pub/techreps/CSD-92-692.html

Wu, J., & Chung, A. C. S. (2005a). Cross entropy: A new solver for markov random field modeling and applications to medical image segmentation. In J. S. Duncan & G. Gerig (Eds.), *Medical image computing and computer-assisted intervention: MICCAI 2005, 8th international conference*, Palm Springs, CA, USA, October 26–29, 2005, *Proceedings, Part I* (pp. 229–237). Lecture Notes in Computer Science, Vol. 3749. Berlin: Springer.

Wu, J., & Chung, A. C. S. (2005b). A segmentation method using compound Markov random fields based on a general boundary model. In *Proceedings of the 2005 International Conference on Image Processing (ICIP 2005)*, Genoa, Italy, September 11–14, 2005. Vol. 2: *Display Algorithms: Image Processing for New Flat Panel Displays*. New York: IEEE, pp. 1182–1185.

Wu, F., Ng-Thow-Hing, V., Singh, K., Agur, A., & McKee, N. H. (2007). Computational representation of the aponeuroses as NURBS surfaces in 3-D musculoskeletal models. *Computer Methods and Programs in Biomedicine, 88*(2), 112–122.

Würzbach, N. (2005). Motif. In D. Herman, M. Jahn, & M.-L. Ryan (Eds.), *Routledge encyclopedia of narrative theory* (pp. 322–323). London: Routledge, 2005 (hbk), 2008 (pbk).

Xiang, Y., Chau, M., Atabakhsh, H., & Chen, H. (2005). Visualizing criminal relationships: Comparisons of a hyperbolic tree and a hierachical list. *Decision Support System, 41*, 69–83. doi://10.1016/j.dss.2004.02.006

XML. (2002). *XML and information retrieval: Proceedings of the 2nd workshop*, Tampere, Finland, August 2002. ACM Special Interest Group on Information Retrieval. New York: ACM, 2002.

Xu, J. J., & Chen, H. (2004). Fighting organized crimes: using shortest-path algorithms to identify associations in criminal networks. *Decision Support Systems, 38*, 473–487. doi://10.1016/S0167-9236(03)00117-9

Xu, M., Kaoru, H., & Yoshino, H. (1999). A fuzzy theoretical approach to case-based representation and inference in CISG. *Artificial Intelligence and Law, 7*(2/3), 115–128.

Yager, R. R., & Zadeh, L. A. (1994). *Fuzzy sets, neural networks and soft computing.* New York: Van Nostrand Reinhold.

Yan, X., & Han, J. (2002). gSpan: Graph-based substructure pattern mining. In *Proceedings of the 2002 International Conference on Data Mining (ICDM 2002)*, pp. 721–724. Expanded Version, UIUC Technical Report, UIUCDCS-R-2002-2296. Department of Computer Science, University of Illinois at Urbana-Champaign.

Yan, X., Zhou, X. J., & Han, J. (2005). Mining closed relational graphs with connectivity constraints. In *Proceedings of the 2005 International Conference on Knowledge Discovery and Data Mining (KDD 2005)*, Chicago, IL, August 2005, pp. 324–333.

Yan, X., Zhu, F., Yu, P. S., & Jan, J. (2006). Feature-based substructure similarity search. *ACM Transactions on Database Systems, 31*(4), 1418–1453. Pre-final version posted at: http://www.cs.ucsb.edu/~xyan/papers/tods06_similarity.pdf

Yang, C. C. (2008). Knowledge discovery and information visualization for terrorist social networks. In H. Chen & C. C. Yang (Eds.), *Intelligence and security informatics* (pp. 45–64). Studies in Computational Intelligence, Vol. 135. Berlin: Springer. doi://10.1007/978-3-540-69209-6

Yang, C. C., & Wang, F. L. (2008). Hierarchical summarization of large documents. *Journal of the American Society for Information Science and Technology (JASIST), 59*(6), 887–902.

Yarmey, A. D. (1995). Eyewitness and evidence obtained by other senses. Chapter 3.7 In R. Bull & D. Carson (Eds.), *Handbook of psychology in legal contexts* (pp. 216–273). Chichester: Wiley.

Yazdani, M. (1983). *Generating events in a fictional world of stories.* Research Report R-113. Exeter: Department of Computer Science, University of Exeter.

Ybarra, L. M. R., & Lohr, S. L. (2002). Estimates of repeat victimization using the national crime victimization survey. *Journal of Quantitative Criminology, 18*(1), 1–21.

Yea, B., Konishi, R., Osaki, T., & Sugahara, K. (1994). The discrimination of many kinds of odor species using fuzzy reasoning and neural networks. *Sensors & Actuators, 45,* 159–165.

Yearwood, J. (1997). Case-based retrieval of refugee review tribunal text cases. In *Legal knowledge and information systems* (pp. 67–83). *JURIX 1997: The Tenth Annual Conference.* Amsterdam: IOS Press.

Yearwood, J., & Stranieri, A. (1999). The integration of retrieval, reasoning and drafting for refugee law: A third generation legal knowledge based system. In *Proceedings of* the *Seventh International Conference on Artificial Intelligence and Law (ICAIL'99).* New York: ACM Press, pp. 117–137.

Yearwood, J., & Stranieri, A. (2000). An argumentation shell for knowledge based systems. In *Proceedings of the IASTED International Conference on Law and Technology (LawTech 2000),* 30 October – 1 November 2000. Anaheim: ACTA Press, pp. 105–111.

Yearwood, J., & Stranieri, A. (2006). The generic/actual argument model of practical reasoning. *Decision Support Systems, 41*(2), 358–379.

Yearwood, J., & Stranieri, A. (2009). Deliberative discourse and reasoning from generic argument structures. *AI & Society, 23*(3), 353–377.

Yearwood, J., Stranieri, A., & Anjaria, C. (1999). The use of argumentation to assist in the generation of legal documents. At the *Fourth Australasian Document Computing Symposium (ADCS'99).* New South Wales: Southern Cross University Press.

Yearwood, J., & Wilkinson, R. (1997). Retrieving cases for treatment advice in nursing using text representation and structured text retrieval. *Artificial Intelligence in Medicine, 9*(1), 79–99.

Yedidia, J. S., Freeman, W. T., & Weiss, Y. (2003). Understanding belief propagation and its generalizations. In G. Lakemeyer & B. Nebel (Eds.), *Exploring artificial intelligence in the new millennium* (pp. 239–269). San Francisco: Morgan Kaufmann Publishers. Previously, Technical Report TR 2001 22, Mitsubishi Electric Research, 2001.

Yim, H. S., Kibbey, C. E., Ma, S. C., Kliza, D. M., Liu, D., Park, S. B., et al. (1993). Polymer membrane-based ion-, gas-, and bio-selective potentiometric sensors. *Biosensors and Bioelectronics, 8,* 1–38.

Yinon, J. (2003). Detection of explosives by electronic noses. *Analytical Chemistry, 75*(5), 99A–105A.

Young, A. W., & Ellis, H. D. (Eds.). (1989). *Handbook of research on face processing.* Amsterdam: Elsevier.

Young, P., & Holmes, R. (1974). *The English civil war: A military history of the three civil wars 1642–1651.* London: Eyre Methuen; Ware, Hertfordshire: Wordsworth Editions, 2000.

Young, R. M. (2007). Story and discourse: A bipartite model of narrative generation in virtual worlds. *Interaction Studies, 8*(2), 177–208. Amsterdam: Benjamins. http://liquidnarrative.csc.ncsu.edu/papers.html

Yovel, J. (2003). Two conceptions of relevance. In A. A. Martino & E. Nissan (Eds.), *Formal approaches to legal evidence.* Special issue, *Cybernetics and Systems, 34*(4/5), 283–315.

Yovel, J. (2007). Quasi-checks: An apology for a mutation of negotiable instruments. *DePaul Journal of Business and Commercial Law, 5,* 579–603. http://works.bepress.com/cgi/viewcontent.cgi?article=1004&context=jonathan_yovel

Yovel, J. (2010). Relational formalism, linguistic theory and legal construction. *Yale Law School Faculty Scholarship Series.* Paper 33. http://digitalcommons.law.yale.edu/fss_papers/33

Yu, F.-R., Tang, T., Leung, V.-C.-M., Liu, J., & Lung, C-H. (2008). Biometric-based user authentication in mobile ad hoc networks. *Security in Wireless Sensor Networks,*[75] *1*(1), 5–16.

---

[75] The journal *Security in Wireless Sensor Networks* is published by Wiley.

Yue, J., Raja, A., Liu, D., Wang, X., & Ribarsky, W. (2009). A blackboard-based approach towards predictive analytics. In *Proceedings of AAAI Spring Symposium on Technosocial Predictive Analytics*, Stanford University, CA, March 23–25, 2009, pp. 154–161. http://www.sis.uncc.edu/~anraja/PAPERS/TPA_JYue.pdf

Yue, J., Raja, A., & Ribarsky, B. (2010). Predictive analytics using a blackboard-based reasoning agent. Short Paper in *Proceedings of 2010 IEEE/ WIC/ ACM International Conference on Intelligent Agent Technology (IAT-2010)*, Toronto, Canada, pp. 97–100. http://www.sis.uncc.edu/~anraja/PAPERS/IAT10Visual.pdf

Yuille, J. C. (1993). We must study forensic eye-witnesses to know about them. *American Psychologist, 48*, 572–573.

Yunhong, W., Tan, T., & Jain, A. K. (2003). Combining face and iris biometrics for identity verification. In *Proceedings of the Fourth International Conference on Audio and Video-Based Biometric Person Authentication (AVBPA)*, Guildford, UK, pp. 805–813.

Zabell, S. L. (1988). The probabilistic analysis of testimony. *Journal of Statistical Planning and Inference, 20*, 327–354.

Zadeh, L. A. (1965). Fuzzy sets. *Information and Control, 8*, 338–353.

Zahedi, F. (1993). *Intelligent systems for business*. Belmont, CA: Wadsworth.

Zander, M. (1979). The investigation of crime: A study of cases tried at the Old Bailey. *Criminal Law Review, 1979*, 203–219.

Zarri, G. P. (1996). NKRL, a knowledge representation language for narrative natural language processing. In *Proceedings of COLING 1996*, pp. 1032–1035. http://acl.ldc.upenn.edu/C/C96/C96-2181.pdf

Zarri, G. P. (1998). Representation of temporal knowledge in events: The formalism, and its potential for legal narratives. In A. A. Martino & E. Nissan (Eds.), *Formal models of legal time*, special issue, *Information and Communications Technology Law, 7*(3), 213–241.

Zarri, G. P. (2009). *Representation and management of narrative information: Theoretical principles and implementation*. (Series: Advanced Information and Knowledge Processing). Berlin: Springer.

Zarri, G. P. (2011). Representation and management of complex 'narrative' information. In N. Dershowitz & E. Nissan (Eds.), *Language, culture, computation: Studies in honour of Yaacov Choueka, Vol. 1: Theory, techniques, and applications to E-science, law, narratives, information retrieval, and the cultural heritage* (in press). Berlin: Springer.

Zeide, J. S., & Liebowitz, J. (1987). Using expert systems: The legal perspective. *IEEE Expert*, Spring issue, pp. 19–20.

Zeleznikow, J. (2002a). Risk, negotiation and argumentation: A decision support system based approach. *Law, Probability and Risk: A Journal for Reasoning Under Uncertainty, 1*(1), 37–48. Oxford: Oxford University Press.

Zeleznikow, J. (2002b). Using web-based legal decision support systems to improve access to justice. *Information and Communications Technology Law, 11*(1), 15–33.

Zeleznikow, J. (2004). Building intelligent legal decision support systems: Past practice and future challenges. Chapter 7 In J. A. Fulcher & L. C. Jain (Eds.), *Applied intelligent systems: New directions* (pp. 201–254). Berlin: Springer.

Zeleznikow, J., & Hunter, D. (1994). *Building intelligent legal information systems: Knowledge representation and reasoning in law*. Computer/Law Series, Vol. 13. Dordrecht: Kluwer.

Zeleznikow, J., & Stranieri, A. (1995). The Split Up system: Integrating neural networks and rule based reasoning in the legal domain. In *Proceedings of the Fifth International Conference on Artificial Intelligence & Law (ICAIL'95)*. New York: ACM Press, pp. 185–194.

Zeleznikow, J., & Stranieri, A. (1998). Split Up: The use of an argument based knowledge representation to meet expectations of different users for discretionary decision making. In *Proceedings of IAAI'98: Tenth Annual Conference on Innovative Applications of Artificial Intelligence*. Cambridge, MA: AAAI/MIT Press, pp. 1146–1151.

Zeleznikow, J., Vossos, G., & Hunter, D. (1994). The IKBALS project: Multimodal reasoning in legal knowledge based systems. *Artificial Intelligence and Law, 2*(3), 169–203.

Zeng, Y., Wang, R., Zeleznikow, J., & Kemp, E. (2005). Knowledge representation for the intelligent legal case retrieval. In R. Khosla, R. J. Howlett, & L. C. Jain (Eds.), *Knowledge-based intelligent information and engineering systems: 9th international conference, KES 2005*, Melbourne, Australia, September 14–16, 2005, *Proceedings, Part I* (pp. 339–345). Lecture Notes in Computer Science, Vol. 3684. Berlin: Springer.

Zeng, Z., Wang, J., Zhou, L., & Karypis, G. (2006). Coherent closed quasi-clique discovery from large dense graph databases. In *Proceedings of the 12th ACM Conference on Knowledge Discovery and Data Mining (SIG KDD 2006)*, Philadelphia, PA, August 20–23, 2006, pp. 797–802.

Zhang, B., & Srihari, S.N. (2004). Handwriting identification using multiscale features. *Journal of Forensic Document Examination, 16*, 1–20.

Zhang, L., Zhu, Z., Jeffay, K., Marron, S., & Smith, F. D. (2008). Multi-resolution anomaly detection for the internet. In *Proceedings of the IEEE Workshop on Network Management*, Phoenix, AZ, 13–18 April 2008. IEEE INFOCOM Workshops, 2008, pp. 1–6. doi://10.1109/INFOCOM.2008.4544618

Zhang, X., & Hexmoor, H. (2002). Algorithms for utility-based role exchange. In M. Gini, W. Shen, C. Torras, & H. Yuasa (Eds.), *Intelligent autonomous systems 7* (pp. 396–403). Amsterdam: IOS Press.

Zhang, Z., & Shen, H. (2004). Online training of SVMs for real-time intrusion detection. In *Proceedings of the 18th International Conference on Advanced Information Networking and Applications*, March 29–31, 2004, p. 568.

Zhao, J., Knight, B., Nissan, E., Petridis, M., & Soper, A. J. (1998). The FUELGEN alternative: An evolutionary approach. The architecture. In E. Nissan (Ed.), *Forum on refuelling techniques for nuclear power plants*, in New Review of Applied Expert Systems, 4, 177–183.

Zhong Ren, P., & Ming Hsiang, T. (2003). *Internet GIS*. New York: Wiley.

Zhou, W., Liu, H., & Cheng, H. (2010). Mining closed episodes from event sequences efficiently. In *Proceedings of the 14th Pacific-Asia Conference on Knowledge Discovery and Data Mining*, Vol. 1, pp. 310–318.

Zhu, S. C., Wu, Y., & Mumford, D. (1996). FRAME: Filters, random fields, and minimax entropy towards a unified theory for texture modeling. In *Proceedings of the IEEE Conference on Computer Vision and Pattern Recognition (CVPR)*, Vol. 6, pp. 686–693.

Zhu, S. C., Wu, Y., & Mumford, D. (1998). Filters, random fields and maximum entropy (FRAME): Towards a unified theory for texture modeling. *International Journal of Computer Vision, 27*(2), 107–126.

Zier, J. (1993). *The expert accountant in civil litigation*. Toronto, ON: Butterworths.

Zimmer, A. C. (1984). A Model for the interpretation of verbal predictions. *International Journal of Man-Machine Studies, 20*, 121–134.

Ziv, A. & Zajdman, A. (Eds.). (1993). *Semites and stereotypes*. New York: Greenwood Press.

Zuckerman, M., & Driver, R. E. (1985). Telling lies: Verbal and nonverbal correlates of deception. In A. W. Siegman & S. Feldstein (Eds.), *Multi-channel integrations of non-verbal behavior* (pp. 129–147). Hillsdale, NJ: Erlbaum.

Zuckerman, M., DePaulo, B. M., & Rosenthal, R. (1981). Verbal and non-verbal communication of deception. In L. Berkowitz (Ed.), *Advances in experimental and social psychology* (Vol. 14, pp. 1–59). New York: Academic.

Zukerman, I., McConachy, R., & Korb, K. (1998). Bayesian reasoning in an abductive mechanism for argument generation and analysis. In *Proceedings of the AAAI-98 Conference*, Madison, WI, July 1998, pp. 833–838.

Zuckermann, G. (2000). *Camouflaged borrowing: Folk-etymological nativization in the service of puristic language engineering*. D.Phil. Dissertation in Modern and Medieval Languages. Oxford, England: University of Oxford.

Zuckermann, G. (2003). *Language contact and lexical enrichment in Israeli Hebrew*. (Palgrave Studies in Language History and Language Change.) London: Palgrave Macmillan.

Zuckermann, G. (2006). "Ety*myth*ological othering" and the power of "lexical engineering" in Judaism, Islam and Christianity. A socio-philo(sopho)logical perspective. Chapter 16 In

T. Omoniyi & J. A. Fishman (Eds.), *Explorations in the sociology of language and religion* (pp. 237–258). (Discourse Approaches to Politics, Society and Culture series.) Amsterdam: Benjamins.

Zulueta Cebrián, C. (1996). Los Procuradores y su proyección informática en la justicia: presente y futuro. *Actas (Volumen I), II Congreso Internacional de Informática y Derecho*, Mérida, Spain, April 1995 (Mérida: UNED, Centro Regional de Extremadura). Published as: *Informática y Derecho*, Vol. 9/10/11, Part 1, 1996, pp. 621–628.

Zurada, J. M. (1992). *Introduction to artificial neural networks*. New York: West Publishing.

Author Index

Subject Index

Printed by Publishers' Graphics LLC